Economic Analysi
for
Lawyers

Economic Analysis
for
Lawyers

Henry N. Butler

CAROLINA ACADEMIC PRESS
Durham, North Carolina

Library of Congress Cataloging-in-Publication Data
Butler, Henry N.
   Economic Analysis for Lawyers / Henry N. Butler.
      p.   cm.
   Includes index.
   ISBN 0-89089-698-4
      1. Practice of law—Economic aspects—United States.
2. Law—United States—Methodology.   I. Title.
KF315.B88   1997
340'.11—dc21   97-35249
                                                                          CIP

CAROLINA ACADEMIC PRESS
700 Kent Street
Durham, North Carolina 27701
Telephone (919) 489-7486
Fax (919) 493-5668
www.cap-press.com

Printed in the United States of America

To Mary, Sarah, Andy and Hank!

Contents

Table of Cases

Preface

This casebook is designed to help law students and lawyers learn the principles of microeconomics. A quick review of the table of contents reveals that economics concepts provide the organizational structure of the book. Instead of organizing around substantive areas of the law, it follows the building block approach used in most successful principles of economics textbooks. This proven approach to teaching economics differs from other law-and-economics casebooks that tend to focus on applications of economics to legal issues rather than teaching economics. After fifteen years of teaching economics—often to law students, law school professors, lawyers, and judges—I am convinced of the pedagogical advantages of this approach. For the many law professors who share this view and have been forced to supplement principles of economics textbooks with cases, I believe that this casebook offers a more convenient and coherent alternative.

My involvement with this casebook started as an effort to revise the first edition of *Quantitative Methods for Lawyers* by Professor Steven M. Crafton and Margaret F. Brinig of George Mason University School of Law. Their ambitious effort to create a casebook introduction to economics, finance, accounting, statistics, and econometrics has met with considerable success as judged by adoptions at numerous leading law schools. Nevertheless, my interest in these materials quickly turned to concentrating on a more traditional approach to teaching economics. The result is a very different type of casebook than Crafton and Brinig's initial effort. Keith Sipe, the publisher of Carolina Academic Press, has encouraged me to incorporate some materials from the first edition of *Quantitative Methods for Lawyers* and I have done so in numerous areas of this casebook. It is our hope that many of the materials presented here will be incorporated in the second edition of *Quantitative Methods for Lawyers* by Crafton and Butler. The materials remain a "work in progress." I encourage you to send your comments, criticisms, and suggestions for improvements of subsequent editions.

This casebook is not intended to be an encyclopedic treatise on either the principles of economics or the economic analysis of law. Some topics typically covered in a principles textbook are not found here; similarly, numerous legal issues susceptible to economic analysis are not covered. Nevertheless, there is plenty of material for a typical one-semester course. I encourage you to work through the first five chapters and then choose chapters according to your interests. Figures are available in PowerPoint. Many of the edited cases presented here are longer than one would expect if they were excerpted in a specialized casebook on their particular area of the law. The pedagogical reason for this is that I was concerned that first or second year law students needed to have more information about the particular substantive law (especially in some regulatory cases) in order to understand the economic issues. I have attempted to ease this pain by minimizing and shortening many case citations in the cases presented.

Numerous individuals have helped me complete this book. I am especially grateful to two individuals. Geoffrey Lysaught, a J.D./Ph.D. in finance student at the University of Kansas, has been involved in every aspect of the project. He was especially helpful on the finance and risk issues covered in Chapters IV, IX, and XI. Christopher Drahozal, a colleague in the School of Law, provided detailed comments and suggestions on the entire manuscript. Geoff and Chris, thank you! I also acknowledge the valuable contributions of research assistants Gary Eastman, Matt Hoy, and Alok Srivastava. The Smith Richardson Foundation provided essential financial support at the start of this project.

I have used earlier drafts of these materials in my Law and Economics classes as well as in the *Economics Institutes for State Judges* offered by the University of Kansas Law and Organizational Economics Center (LOEC). Comments from law students, professors in the *Economics Institutes for State Judges* (Barry Baysinger, Keith Chauvin, and Maurice Joy of Kansas; Terry L. Anderson of PERC and the Hoover Institution; and W. Kip Viscusi of Harvard Law School), and judges have improved the final product. I would like to offer my thanks to three judges—Victor T. Barrera of California, Richard T. Jessen of Minnesota, and Donald S. Owens of Michigan—who took great pride in their ability to spot typos. Accordingly, any remaining typos are their responsibility.

Finally, I wish to express my sincerest gratitude and appreciation to Cathy Lysaught and Missy Amlong at the LOEC for their loyal and tireless assistance. They "hung in there" during the long and tedious process of compiling these materials.

Henry N. Butler
Lawrence, Kansas

Economic Analysis
for
Lawyers

Chapter I

The Economics Perspective: Incentives Matter

Economics is an analytical discipline and a practical science — its aim is to provide a set of tools to understand, analyze, and sometimes, solve problems. Just as a physicist must take into account the effects of gravity, so too must a lawyer understand the effects of economic forces. In a very real sense, economic forces are the gravity of the social world — often invisible, but omnipresent. As imposing as this view of economics may sound, this casebook presupposes no prior exposure to economics — it concentrates on the few foundational concepts and analytical tools necessary for the lawyer to take advantage of the economics perspective.

Economics is the study of the rational behavior of individuals when choices are limited or constrained in relation to human desires. This broad definition should serve to dispel two common myths about economics. First, economics is not simply about money — it is about how incentives influence behavior. In fact, the crucial point of economics is simply that **incentives matter**. Second, economics is concerned with more than just economy-wide, macroeconomic phenomena such as inflation, unemployment, trade deficits, and business cycles. In contrast, microeconomics uses individual decision-makers and individual markets as the basic units of analysis. In this casebook, the principles of microeconomics are introduced by analyzing the impact of changes in various legal rules on the behavior of economic actors.[1] Changes in laws and regulations affect incentives, and incentives matter!

This chapter introduces the economics perspective by describing several fundamental concepts and assumptions. In Section A, the economists' assumptions about human behavior and firm behavior as well as the important concepts of scarcity, opportunity costs, and marginal analysis are developed. In Section B, the importance of private property rights to the functioning of a market economy is explored. In Section C, the basic supply and demand model of how market prices are determined is introduced.

---

1. Microeconomics is also referred to as price theory. It is important to note that there is much more agreement among economists about certain principles of microeconomic theory than there is about macroeconomic theory and policy. The principles of price theory presented in this chapter have been supported by numerous empirical studies.

A. Economic Behavior

The concept of scarcity is fundamental to the study of economics. **Scarcity** means that our behavior is constrained because we live in a world of limited resources and unlimited desires. Scarcity is thus a relative concept in that it means that we cannot satisfy every desire. The fact that there is an "abundance" of a certain resource does not mean that there is not scarcity, it simply means that at current prices everyone who wants to control a certain amount of that resource can do so by paying the market price. Scarcity implies that individuals, families, governments, businesses, and other economic actors must make choices or trade-offs among competing uses of limited resources.

Economic actors are assumed to maximize their well-being subject to constraints. In this section, assumptions about what guides decision-making by individuals and firms are developed.

1. Opportunity Costs, Economic Choices, and the Margin

There are only twenty-four hours in a day and any decision to engage in one activity entails a decision to forego some other activity. People must choose how to spend their time, and choice requires a sacrifice. This sacrifice illustrates the fundamental economic concept of **opportunity cost**. In general, the opportunity cost of using a resource in a particular manner is defined as the value of the next best alternative use of that resource. For example, your time—a valuable resource—can be used in several different ways: sleeping, studying, partying, vacationing, exercising, working, eating, watching television, and so forth. The opportunity cost to you of reading this material is the next best alternative use of your time.

The classic phrase that illustrates the concept of opportunity cost is "There ain't no such thing as a free lunch," or "TANSTAAFL." Someone else may pay for your lunch, but someone paid and you also gave up some other activity in order to go to lunch. Another way to think of the concept of opportunity cost is to recognize that "whenever you have a choice, there is a cost."

Choices or trade-offs, however, are rarely between extremes. For example, individuals are rarely faced with the choice between a twelve-course feast or going hungry; more often, individuals confront choices of a smaller magnitude—say, between steak and hamburger. Economists say that economic actors make choices "at the margin," where the **margin** refers to the impact of a small change in one variable on another variable. For example, if the price (cost) of a product increases relative to the prices of other products, then people "at the margin" will substitute the now lower cost products for the higher cost product. Raise the price of Toyotas and some people will buy fewer Toyotas and more (say) Nissans. Raise the price of heating oil, and even people who "need" it will substitute other products (e.g., sweaters and blankets) to keep warm. In general, when one speaks of the margin, one means the difference in cost, benefit, or some other measure (e.g., profit, revenue, etc.) between the existing situation and a proposed change.

Suppose, for example, that you attempt to purchase a bag of pretzels by inserting fifty cents into a vending machine and pushing the appropriate buttons.

Your actions demonstrate that your expected marginal benefit from the bag of pretzels is greater than fifty cents. Unfortunately, you failed to notice (prior to selecting the pretzels) that the next slot for a pretzel bag was empty and you did not receive anything for your fifty cents. You are very confident that a bag of pretzels will be dispensed if you pay another fifty cents. Your friend says you are crazy to pay $1.00 for a bag of pretzels, but you reply that on the margin the next bag costs fifty cents and that the marginal benefit to you of a bag of pretzels is still more than fifty cents. You buy the pretzels, but your friend gives you a hard time for paying so much. You then explain to him that the first fifty cents was in the past, and there was nothing that could be done about it. The first fifty cents was a sunk cost, and sunk costs do not affect your future decisions because you make decisions on the margin.

The basic marginal analysis decision-making rule is that *if the marginal benefit of an activity is greater than the marginal cost of an activity, then do it!* It is important to appreciate the individual basis of decision making because many costs and benefits are subjective in the sense that they differ from individual to individual. Thus, an observer is often left to infer relative costs and benefits from observed behavior. All economic analysis is concerned with consequences "at the margin." Thus, one would expect that a change in a legal rule that affects a cost or benefit—that is, affects incentives—will have measurable (at least in principle) effects at the margin.

2. Assumptions About Human Behavior

Economists have employed certain abstractions and assumptions to help predict the behavioral consequences of changes in the constraints faced by individuals, businesses, and other economic actors. One of the most important assumptions is that individuals are assumed to behave rationally—that is, they seek to maximize their "self-interest." The self-interest assumption does not mean that individuals are cold, harsh calculators, rather it means that their behavior is consistent with a model of rational choice. Self-interest also does not mean that individuals are necessarily selfish; rational decision makers may benefit—that is, receive satisfaction—from making others happy. The significance of the self-interest assumption is that it allows economists to predict changes in individual behavior in response to changes in economic variables. The rational maximizer responds to changes in incentives in a predictable manner.

The Nature of Man*

Michael C. Jensen and William H. Meckling
7 Journal of Applied Corporate Finance 4–19 (Summer 1994)

* * *

The usefulness of any model of human nature depends on its ability to explain a wide range of social phenomena; the test of such a model is the degree to which it is consistent with observed human behavior. A model that explains behavior only in one small geographical area, or only for a short period in history, or only for people engaged in certain pursuits is not very useful. For this reason we must use a limited number of general traits to characterize human behavior. Greater detail limits the explanatory ability of a model because individual people differ so greatly. We want a set of characteristics that captures the essence of human nature, but no more.

While this may sound abstract and complex, it is neither. Each of us has in mind and uses models of human nature every day. We all understand, for example, that people are willing to make trade-offs among things that they want. Our spouses, partners, children, friends, business associates, or perfect strangers can be induced to make substitutions of all kinds. We offer to go out to dinner Saturday night instead of the concert tonight. We offer to substitute a bicycle for a stereo as a birthday gift. We allow an employee to go home early today if the time is made up next week.

If our model specified that individuals were never willing to substitute some amount of a good for some amounts of other goods, it would quickly run aground on inconsistent evidence. It could not explain much of the human behavior we observe. While it may sound silly to characterize individuals as unwilling to make substitutions, that view of human behavior is not far from models that are widely accepted and used by many social scientists (for example, Maslow's hierarchy of human needs and sociologists' models portraying individuals as cultural role players or social victims).

* * *

RESOURCEFUL, EVALUATIVE, MAXIMIZING MODEL: REMM

...While the term is new, the concept is not. REMM is the product of over 200 years of research and debate in economics, the other social sciences, and philosophy. As a result, REMM is now defined in very precise terms, but we offer here only a bare-bones summary of the concept. Many specifics can be added to enrich its descriptive content without sacrificing the basic foundation provided here.

Postulate I. Every individual cares; he or she is an evaluator.

(a) The individual cares about almost everything: knowledge, independence, the plight of others, the environment, honor, interpersonal relationships, status, peer approval, group norms, culture, wealth, rules of conduct, the weather, music, art, and so on.

---

* We use the word "man" here in its use as a non-gender-specific reference to human beings. We have attempted to make the language less gender-specific because the models being discussed describe the behavior of both sexes. We have been unable to find a genderless term for use in the title which has the same desired impact.

(b) REMM is always willing to make trade-offs and substitutions. Each individual is always willing to give up some sufficiently small amount of any particular good (oranges, water, air, housing, honesty, or safety) for some sufficiently large quantity of other goods. Furthermore, valuation is relative in the sense that the value of a unit of any particular good decreases as the individual enjoys more of it relative to other goods.

(c) Individual preferences are transitive—that is, if A is preferred to B, and B is preferred to C, then A is preferred to C.

*   *   *

Postulate II. Each individual's wants are unlimited.

(a) If we designate those things that REMM values positively as "goods," then he or she prefers more goods to less. Goods can be anything from art objects to ethical norms.

(b) REMM cannot be satiated. He or she always wants more of some things, be they material goods such as art, sculpture, castles, and pyramids; or intangible goods such as solitude, companionship, honesty, respect, love, fame, and immortality.

Postulate III. Each individual is a maximizer.

He or she acts so as to enjoy the highest level of value possible. Individuals are always constrained in satisfying their wants. Wealth, time, and the laws of nature are all important constraints that affect the opportunities available to any individual. Individuals are also constrained by the limits of their own knowledge about various goods and opportunities; and their choices of goods or courses of action will reflect the costs of acquiring the knowledge or information necessary to evaluate those choices.

The notion of an opportunity set provides the limit on the level of value attainable by any individual. The opportunity set is usually regarded as something that is given and external to the individual. Economists tend to represent it as a wealth or income constraint and a set of prices at which the individual can buy goods. But the notion of an individual's opportunity set can be generalized to include the set of activities he or she can perform during a 24-hour day or in a lifetime.

Postulate IV. The individual is resourceful.

Individuals are creative. They are able to conceive of changes in their environment, foresee the consequences thereof, and respond by creating new opportunities.

Although an individual's opportunity set is limited at any instant in time by his or her knowledge and the state of the world, that limitation is not immutable. Human beings are not only capable of learning about new opportunities, they also engage in resourceful, creative activities that expand their opportunities in various ways.

The kind of highly mechanical behavior posited by economists—that is, assigning probabilities and expected values to various actions and choosing the action with the highest expected value—is formally consistent with the evaluating, maximizing model defined in Postulates I through III. But such behavior falls short of the human capabilities posited by REMM; it says nothing about the individual's ingenuity and creativity.

REMMs AT WORK

One way of capturing the notion of resourcefulness is to think about the effects of newly imposed constraints on human behavior. These constraints might be new operating policies in a corporation or new laws imposed by governments. No matter how much experience we have with the response of people to changes in their environment, we tend to overestimate the impact of a new law or policy intended to constrain human behavior. Moreover, the constraint or law will almost always generate behavior which was never imagined by its sponsors. Why? Because of the sponsors' failure to recognize the creativity of REMMs. REMMs' response to a new constraint is to begin searching for substitutes for what is now constrained, a search that is not restricted to existing alternatives. REMMs will invent alternatives that did not previously exist.

An excellent illustration of how humans function as REMMs is the popular response to the 1974 federal imposition of a 55-mile-per-hour speed limit in all states under penalty of loss of federal transportation and highway moneys. The primary reason offered for this law was the conservation of gasoline and diesel fuel (for simplicity, we ignore the benefits associated with the smaller number of accidents that occur at slower speeds).[2]

The major cost associated with slower driving is lost time. At a maximum speed of 55 mph instead of 70 mph, trips take longer. Those who argue that lost time is not important must recognize that an hour of time consumed is just as irreplaceable as—and generally more valuable than—the gallon of gasoline consumed. On these grounds, the law created inefficiencies, and the behavior of drivers is consistent with that conclusion.[3] Let's calculate the dollar benefits of fuel saved by the 55 mph speed limit and the value of these savings per additional hour of driving time. These dollar savings can then be compared to the value of the driver's time. Suppose driving at 55 mph instead of 70 saves 10% on gasoline consumption, so that, for example, if gasoline mileage is 14 mpg at 70 mph, it will be 15.4 mpg at 55 mph. To travel 70 miles at 55 mph will take 1.273 hours instead of one hour at 70 mph. The gasoline consumed is 4.545 gallons at 55 mph instead of 5 gallons at 70 mph. This means that for every additional hour of travel time required by the slower speed, a driver saves 1.665 gallons of gasoline = (5.0 – 4.545) divided by (1.273 – 1–0). At a price of $1.20 per gallon for gasoline, the driver saves $2.00 per hour of additional travel time—a sum significantly less than the minimum wage. If there are two occupants in the car, they each save $1.00 per hour; and the rate sinks to 66¢ per hour per person if there are three occupants. Therefore, the law requires that drivers and their passengers spend time in an activity that earns them about $2.00 per hour or less, depending on the particular car, the driver's habits, and the number of passengers. Judging

---

2. The original temporary law was made permanent in 1975 with safety being cited as a primary reason.

3. Moreover, in 1987 the law was changed to allow states the option of raising the speed limit to 65 mph on interstate highways outside highly populated areas, and later extended to certain non-interstate highways. [Authors' note: In 1995, it was changed to give the states complete discretion.]

from the widespread difficulties state authorities have had in enforcing the law, drivers understand the value of their time quite well. People responded in REMM-like fashion to this newly imposed constraint in a number of ways. One was to reduce their automobile, bus, and truck travel, and, in some cases, to shift to travel by other means such as airplanes and trains. Another response was to defy the law by driving at speeds exceeding the 55 mph maximum. Violating the speed limit, of course, exposes offenders to potential costs in the form of fines, higher insurance rates, and possible loss of driver's licenses. This, in turn, provides incentives for REMMs to search out ways to reduce such costs. The result has been an entire new industry, and the rapid growth of an already existing one. Citizen's Band radios (CBs), which had been used primarily by truckers, suddenly became widely used by passenger car drivers and almost all truckers. There were about 800,000 FCC CB radio licenses outstanding throughout the period 1966–1973. By the end of 1977, there were 12.25 million licensed CBs in use.[4] These two-way radios with relatively short ranges (less than 15 miles) allowed drivers to inform each other about the location of police cars, radar traps, unmarked cars, and so on. They significantly reduced the likelihood of arrest for speeding. REMMs by the millions were willing to pay from $50 to $300 for radios in order to save time and avoid speeding tickets. CB radios have been largely replaced by radar detectors that warn drivers of the presence of police radar. These devices have become so common that police have taken countermeasures, such as investing in more expensive and sophisticated radar units that are less susceptible to detection. Manufacturers of radar detectors retaliated by manufacturing increasingly sophisticated units.

The message is clear: people who drive value their time at more than $2 per hour. When the 55 mph maximum speed limit was imposed, few would have predicted the ensuing chain of events. One seemingly modest constraint on REMMs has created a new electronic industry designed to avoid the constraint. And such behavior shows itself again and again in a variety of contexts—for example, in taxpayers' continuous search for, and discovery of, "loopholes" in income tax laws; the development of so-called clubs with private liquor stock in areas where serving liquor at public bars is prohibited; the ability of General Dynamics' CEO George Anders and his management team, when put under a lucrative incentive compensation plan tied to shareholder value, to quadruple the market value of the company even as the defense industry was facing sharp cutbacks; and the growth in the number of hotel courtesy cars and gypsy cabs in cities where taxicab licensing results in monopoly fares.

These examples are typical of behavior consistent with the REMM model, but not, as we shall see, with other models that prevail in the social sciences. The failure of the other models is important because the individual stands in relation to organizations as the atom is to mass. From small groups to entire societies, organizations are composed of individuals. If we are to have a science of such organizations, it will have to be founded on building blocks that capture as simply as possible the most important traits of humans. Although clearly not a complete description of human behavior, REMM is the model of human behavior that best meets this criterion.[5]

---

4. Obtained in private communication with the Federal Communications Commission.

5. REMM is not meant to describe the behavior of any particular individual. To do so requires more complete specification of the preferences, values, emotions, and talents of each

REMM MEANS THERE ARE NO "NEEDS"

REMM implies that there is no such thing as a need, a proposition that arouses considerable resistance. The fallacy of the notion of needs follows from the proposition that the individual is always willing to make trade-offs. That proposition means individuals are always willing to substitute—that is, they are always willing to give up a sufficiently small amount of any good for a sufficiently large amount of other goods.[6] Failure to take account of substitution is one of the most frequent mistakes in the analysis of human behavior.

George Bernard Shaw, the famous playwright and social thinker, reportedly once claimed that while on an ocean voyage he met a celebrated actress on deck and asked her whether she would be willing to sleep with him for a million dollars. She was agreeable. He followed with a counterproposal: "What about ten dollars?" "What do you think I am?," she responded indignantly. He replied, "We've already established that—now we're just haggling over price."

Like it or not, individuals are willing to sacrifice a little of almost anything we care to name, even reputation or morality, for a sufficiently large quantity of other desired things, and these things do not have to be money or even material goods. Moreover, the fact that all individuals make trade-offs (or substitute in virtually every dimension imaginable) means that there are no such things as human "needs" in the sense that word is often used. There are only human wants, desires, or, in the economist's language, demands. If something is more costly, less will be wanted, desired, demanded than if it were cheaper.

Using the word need as an imperative is semantic trickery. The media and press are filled with talk about housing needs, education needs, food needs, energy needs, and so on. Politicians and others who use that language understand that the word need carries emotional impact. It implies a requirement at any cost; if the need is not met, some unspecified disaster will take place. Such assertions have a far different impact if restated to reflect the facts. The proposition that "people want more housing if they can get it cheaply enough" does not ring out from the podium or over the airwaves with the same emotional appeal as "people need more housing."

If individuals are required to specify what they mean by need, the emotional specter of the unexamined catastrophe that lies behind the need simply becomes another cost. Needs would be exposed for what they are—desires or wants—and discussion would focus on alternatives, substitutes, and costs in a productive manner.

---

person. Moreover, individuals respond very differently to factors such as stress, tension, and fear, and, in so doing, often violate the predictions of the REMM model. For purposes of organizational and public policy, many of these violations of REMM "cancel out" in the aggregate across large groups of people and over time—but by no means all. For a discussion of a Pain Avoidance Model (PAM) that complements REMM by accommodating systematically non-rational behavior, see Michael C. Jensen, "Economics, Organizations, and Non-Rational Behavior," *Economic Inquiry* (1995).

6. The word need has meaning only when used in the conditional sense. For example: An individual needs X cubic liters of air per hour in order to live. This statement, or others like it, do not imply, however, that individuals are willing to pay an infinite price for that air.

*   *   *

Notes and Questions

1. Self-Interest Assumption and the Critics' "Straw Man": Economics is often criticized based on the mistaken impression that economists assume that economic decision-makers are interested in money only. Jensen and Meckling make it clear that this "straw man" is not an accurate reflection of the economists' view of human behavior and human interaction:

> The economic model is a reductive version of REMM. This individual is an evaluator and maximizer who has only one want: money income. He or she is a short-run money maximizer who does not care for others, art, morality, love, respect, or honesty. In its simplest form, the economic model characterizes people as unwilling to trade current money income for future money income, no matter what rate of return they could earn.
>
> The economic model is, of course, not very interesting as a model of human behavior. People do not behave this way. In most cases, use of this model reflects economists' desire for simplicity in modeling; the exclusive pursuit of wealth or money income is easier to model than the complexity of the actual preferences of individuals. As a consequence, however, noneconomists often use this model as a foil to discredit economics, that is, to argue that economics is of limited use because economists focus only on a single characteristic of behavior—and one of the least attractive at that, the selfish desire for money.

Clearly, properly understood, the self-interest assumption does not mean that individuals are cold, "Dickensian" Scrooges, totally selfish and uncaring in their choices.

2. Transitive Preferences: An important assumption about economic behavior is that economic actors' preferences are transitive (that is, if A is preferred to B, and B is preferred to C, then A is preferred to C), at least over short periods of time. Suppose a lady goes into a restaurant and is informed that the only three entrees are chicken, lobster and steak. She orders chicken, but the waiter returns and tells her that they are out of chicken. She replies, "I'll settle for the lobster." However, the waiter returns again and says, "I made a mistake, it turns out that we do have chicken after all. Would you prefer chicken instead of lobster?" To which she replies: "No, I'd like the steak." Such behavior violates the transitive preferences assumption.

3. Uncertainty and Risk Aversion: Individuals often make decisions when they are not certain of the outcome. Such uncertainty introduces risk into the decision making process. Economists assume that most individuals are risk averse. When given a choice between a certain value, say $1,000, and an uncertain outcome of a coin toss—heads you win $2,000, and tails you get $0—a risk averse individual will prefer the certain amount even if the expected payoff from the coin toss is $1,000. [Expected value of the coin toss is the weighted average of the possible payoffs. So, in this example, the expected value is $(.5 \times \$2,000) + (.5 \times \$0) = \$1,000.00$.] The concept of risk aversion is the basis for many important weights in economics, finance, and law. Chapter IX, "Risk," explores this important assumption about economic decision making in great detail.

3. Assumptions About Firm Behavior

A corollary of the self-interest assumption for individual behavior is the assumption that business firms attempt to maximize economic profit. Economic profit is defined as the total revenues received from selling a product or service *minus* the total costs of producing the product or service, including the opportunity costs.

Matsushita Elec. Indus. Co. v. Zenith Radio Corp.
Supreme Court of the United States
475 U.S. 574; 106 S. Ct. 1348 (1986)

POWELL, J.

*   *   *

Petitioners, defendants below, are 21 corporations that manufacture or sell "consumer electronic products" (CEPs)—for the most part, television sets. Petitioners include both Japanese manufacturers of CEPs and American firms, controlled by Japanese parents, that sell the Japanese-manufactured products. Respondents, plaintiffs below, are Zenith Radio Corporation (Zenith) and National Union Electric Corporation (NUE). Zenith is an American firm that manufactures and sells television sets. NUE is the corporate successor to Emerson Radio Company, an American firm that manufactured and sold television sets until 1970, when it withdrew from the market after sustaining substantial losses. Zenith and NUE began this lawsuit in 1974,[1] claiming that petitioners had illegally conspired to drive American firms from the American CEP market. According to respondents, the gist of this conspiracy was a " 'scheme to raise, fix and maintain artificially *high* prices for television receivers sold by [petitioners] in Japan and, at the same time, to fix and maintain *low* prices for television receivers exported to and sold in the United States.' " 723 F.2d, at 251 (quoting respondents' preliminary pretrial memorandum). These "low prices" were allegedly at levels that produced substantial losses for petitioners. 513 F.Supp., at 1125. The conspiracy allegedly began as early as 1953, and according to respondents was in full operation by sometime in the late 1960's. Respondents claimed that various portions of this scheme violated §§ 1 and 2 of the Sherman Act, § 2(a) of the Robinson-Patman Act, § 73 of the Wilson Tariff Act, and the Antidumping Act of 1916.

*   *   *

...The thrust of respondents' argument is that petitioners used their monopoly profits from the Japanese market to fund a concerted campaign to price predatorily and thereby drive respondents and other American manufacturers of CEPs out of business. Once successful, according to respondents, petitioners would cartelize the American CEP market, restricting output and raising prices above the level that fair competition would produce. The resulting monopoly profits, respondents contend, would more than compensate petitioners for the losses they incurred through years of pricing below market level.

---

1. NUE had filed its complaint four years earlier, in the District Court for the District of New Jersey. Zenith's complaint was filed separately in 1974, in the Eastern District of Pennsylvania. The two cases were consolidated in the Eastern District of Pennsylvania in 1974.

*   *   *

...According to petitioners, the alleged conspiracy is one that is economically irrational and practically infeasible. Consequently, petitioners contend, they had no motive to engage in the alleged predatory pricing conspiracy; indeed, they had a strong motive not to conspire in the manner respondents allege. Petitioners argue that, in light of the absence of any apparent motive and the ambiguous nature of the evidence of conspiracy, no trier of fact reasonably could find that the conspiracy with which petitioners are charged actually existed. This argument requires us to consider the nature of the alleged conspiracy and the practical obstacles to its implementation.

IV

A

A predatory pricing conspiracy is by nature speculative. Any agreement to price below the competitive level requires the conspirators to forgo profits that free competition would offer them. The forgone profits may be considered an investment in the future. For the investment to be rational, the conspirators must have a reasonable expectation of recovering, in the form of later monopoly profits, more than the losses suffered. As then-Professor Bork, discussing predatory pricing by a single firm, explained:

> "Any realistic theory of predation recognizes that the predator as well as his victims will incur losses during the fighting, but such a theory supposes it may be a rational calculation for the predator to view the losses as an investment in future monopoly profits (where rivals are to be killed) or in future undisturbed profits (where rivals are to be disciplined). The future flow of profits, appropriately discounted, must then exceed the present size of the losses." R. Bork, The Antitrust Paradox 145 (1978).

See also McGee, *Predatory Pricing Revisited*, 23 J. Law & Econ. 289, 295–297 (1980). As this explanation shows, the success of such schemes is inherently uncertain: the short-run loss is definite, but the long-run gain depends on successfully neutralizing the competition. Moreover, it is not enough simply to achieve monopoly power, as monopoly pricing may breed quick entry by new competitors eager to share in the excess profits. The success of any predatory scheme depends on *maintaining* monopoly power for long enough both to recoup the predator's losses and to harvest some additional gain. Absent some assurance that the hoped-for monopoly will materialize, *and* that it can be sustained for a significant period of time, "[the] predator must make a substantial investment with no assurance that it will pay off." Easterbrook, Predatory Strategies and Counter strategies, 48 U. Chi. L. Rev. 263, 268 (1981). For this reason, there is a consensus among commentators that predatory pricing schemes are rarely tried, and even more rarely successful. See, e. g., Bork, *supra*, at 149–155; Areeda & Turner, Predatory Pricing and Related Practices Under Section 2 of the Sherman Act, 88 Harv. L. Rev. 697, 699 (1975); Easterbrook, *supra*; Koller, The Myth of Predatory Pricing—An Empirical Study, 4 Antitrust Law & Econ. Rev. 105 (1971); McGee, Predatory Price Cutting: The Standard Oil (N. J.) Case, 1 J. Law & Econ. 137 (1958); McGee, Predatory Pricing Revisited, 23 J. Law & Econ., at 292–294. See also *Northeastern Telephone Co. v. American Telephone & Telegraph Co.*, 651 F.2d 76, 88 (CA2 1981) ("[Nowhere] in the recent outpouring of literature on the subject do commentators suggest that [predatory] pricing is either common or likely to increase"), cert. denied, 455 U.S. 943 (1982).

These observations apply even to predatory pricing by a *single firm* seeking monopoly power. In this case, respondents allege that a large number of firms have conspired over a period of many years to charge below-market prices in order to stifle competition. Such a conspiracy is incalculably more difficult to execute than an analogous plan undertaken by a single predator. The conspirators must allocate the losses to be sustained during the conspiracy's operation, and must also allocate any gains to be realized from its success. Precisely because success is speculative and depends on a willingness to endure losses for an indefinite period, each conspirator has a strong incentive to cheat, letting its partners suffer the losses necessary to destroy the competition while sharing in any gains if the conspiracy succeeds. The necessary allocation is therefore difficult to accomplish. Yet if conspirators cheat to any substantial extent, the conspiracy must fail, because its success depends on depressing the market price for *all* buyers of CEPs. If there are too few goods at the artificially low price to satisfy demand, the would-be victims of the conspiracy can continue to sell at the "real" market price, and the conspirators suffer losses to little purpose.

Finally, if predatory pricing conspiracies are generally unlikely to occur, they are especially so where, as here, the prospects of attaining monopoly power seem slight. In order to recoup their losses, petitioners must obtain enough market power to set higher than competitive prices, and then must sustain those prices long enough to earn in excess profits what they earlier gave up in below-cost prices. See *Northeastern Telephone Co.* v. *American Telephone & Telegraph Co., supra*, at 89; Areeda & Turner, 88 Harv. L. Rev., at 698. Two decades after their conspiracy is alleged to have commenced,[13] petitioners appear to be far from achieving this goal: the two largest shares of the retail market in television sets are held by RCA and respondent Zenith, not by any of petitioners. 6 App. to Brief for Appellant in No. 81-2331 (CA3), pp. 2575a–2576a. Moreover, those shares, which together approximate 40% of sales, did not decline appreciably during the 1970's. *Ibid.* Petitioners' collective share rose rapidly during this period, from one-fifth or less of the relevant markets to close to 50%. 723 F.2d, at 316.[14] Neither the District Court nor the Court of Appeals found, however, that petitioners' share presently allows them to charge monopoly prices; to the contrary, respondents contend that the conspiracy is ongoing—that petitioners are still artificially *depressing* the market price in order to drive Zenith out of the market. The data in the record strongly suggest that goal is yet far distant.[15]

---

13. NUE's complaint alleges that petitioners' conspiracy began as early as 1960; the starting date used in Zenith's complaint is 1953. NUE Complaint para. 52; Zenith Complaint para. 39.

14. During the same period, the number of American firms manufacturing television sets declined from 19 to 13. 5 App. to Brief for Appellant in No. 81-2331 (CA3), p. 1961a. This decline continued a trend that began at least by 1960, when petitioners' sales in the United States market were negligible. Ibid. See Zenith Complaint paras. 35, 37.

15. Respondents offer no reason to suppose that entry into the relevant market is especially difficult, yet without barriers to entry it would presumably be impossible to maintain supra competitive prices for an extended time. Judge Easterbrook, commenting on this case in a law review article, offers the following sensible assessment:

The plaintiffs [in this case] maintain that for the last fifteen years or more at least ten Japanese manufacturers have sold TV sets at less than cost in order to

The alleged conspiracy's failure to achieve its ends in the two decades of its asserted operation is strong evidence that the conspiracy does not in fact exist. Since the losses in such a conspiracy accrue before the gains, they must be "repaid" with interest. And because the alleged losses have accrued over the course of two decades, the conspirators could well require a correspondingly long time to recoup. Maintaining supra competitive prices in turn depends on the continued cooperation of the conspirators, on the inability of other would-be competitors to enter the market, and (not incidentally) on the conspirators' ability to escape antitrust liability for their *minimum* price-fixing cartel.[16] Each of these factors weighs more heavily as the time needed to recoup losses grows. If the losses have been substantial—as would likely be necessary in order to drive out the competition[17]—petitioners would most likely have to sustain their cartel for years simply to break even.

Nor does the possibility that petitioners have obtained supra competitive profits in the Japanese market change this calculation. Whether or not petitioners have the means to sustain substantial losses in this country over a long period of time, they have no motive to sustain such losses absent some strong likelihood that the alleged conspiracy in this country will eventually pay off. The courts below found no evidence of any such success, and—as indicated above—the facts actually are to the contrary: RCA and Zenith, not any of the petitioners, continue to hold the largest share of the American retail market in color television sets. More important, there is nothing to suggest any relationship between petitioners' profits in Japan and the amount petitioners could expect to gain from a conspiracy to monopolize the American market. In the absence of any such ev-

---

drive United States firms out of business. Such conduct cannot possibly produce profits by harming competition, however. If the Japanese firms drive some United States firms out of business, they could not recoup. Fifteen years of losses could be made up only by very high prices for the indefinite future. (The losses are like investments, which must be recovered with compound interest.) If the defendants should try to raise prices to such a level, they would attract new competition. There are no barriers to entry into electronics, as the proliferation of computer and audio firms shows. The competition would come from resurgent United States firms, from other foreign firms (Korea and many other nations make TV sets), and from defendants themselves. In order to recoup, the Japanese firms would need to suppress competition among themselves. On plaintiffs' theory, the cartel would need to last at least thirty years, far longer than any in history, even when cartels were not illegal. None should be sanguine about the prospects of such a cartel, given each firm's incentive to shave price and expand its share of sales. The predation recoupment story therefore does not make sense, and we are left with the more plausible inference that the Japanese firms did not sell below cost in the first place. They were just engaged in hard competition.

Easterbrook, The Limits of Antitrust, 63 Texas L. Rev. 1, 26–27 (1984) (footnotes omitted).

16. The alleged predatory scheme makes sense only if petitioners can recoup their losses. In light of the large number of firms involved here, petitioners can achieve this only by engaging in some form of price fixing after they have succeeded in driving competitors from the market. Such price fixing would, of course, be an independent violation of § 1 of the Sherman Act. United 475 U.S. 574, 106 S. Ct. 1348, 89 L. Ed. 2d 538 States v. Socony-Vacuum Oil Co., 310 U.S. 150 (1940).

17. The predators' losses must actually increase as the conspiracy nears its objective: the greater the predators' market share, the more products the predators sell; but since every sale brings with it a loss, an increase in market share also means an increase in predatory losses.

idence, the possible existence of supra competitive profits in Japan simply cannot overcome the economic obstacles to the ultimate success of this alleged predatory conspiracy.[18]

*   *   *

...petitioners had no motive to enter into the alleged conspiracy. To the contrary, as presumably rational businesses, petitioners had every incentive not to engage in the conduct with which they are charged, for its likely effect would be to generate losses for petitioners with no corresponding gains....

*   *   *

...the absence of any plausible motive to engage in the conduct charged is highly relevant to whether a "genuine issue for trial" exists within the meaning of Rule 56(e). Lack of motive bears on the range of permissible conclusions that might be drawn from ambiguous evidence: if petitioners had no rational economic motive to conspire, and if their conduct is consistent with other, equally plausible explanations, the conduct does not give rise to an inference of conspiracy.... Here, the conduct in question consists largely of (i) pricing at levels that succeeded in taking business away from respondents, and (ii) arrangements that may have limited petitioners' ability to compete with each other (and thus kept prices from going even lower). This conduct suggests either that petitioners behaved competitively, or that petitioners conspired to *raise* prices. Neither possibility is consistent with an agreement among 21 companies to price below market levels. Moreover, the predatory pricing scheme that this conduct is said to prove is one that makes no practical sense: it calls for petitioners to destroy companies larger and better established than themselves, a goal that remains far distant more than two decades after the conspiracy's birth. Even had they succeeded in obtaining their monopoly, there is nothing in the record to suggest that they could recover the losses they would need to sustain along the way. In sum, in light of the absence of any rational motive to conspire, neither petitioners' pricing practices, nor their conduct in the Japanese market, nor their agreements respecting prices and distribution in the American market, suffice to create a "genuine issue for trial." Fed. Rule Civ. Proc. 56(e).[21]

*   *   *

The decision of the Court of Appeals is reversed, and the case is remanded for further proceedings consistent with this opinion.

It is so ordered.

---

18. The same is true of any supposed excess production capacity that petitioners may have possessed. The existence of plant capacity that exceeds domestic demand does tend to establish the ability to sell products abroad. It does not, however, provide a motive for selling at prices lower than necessary to obtain sales; nor does it explain why petitioners would be willing to lose money in the United States market without some reasonable prospect of recouping their investment.

21. We do not imply that, if petitioners had had a plausible reason to conspire, ambiguous conduct could suffice to create a triable issue of conspiracy. Our decision in Monsanto Co. v. Spray-Rite Service Corp., 465 U.S. 752 (1984), establishes that conduct that is as consistent with permissible competition as with illegal conspiracy does not, without more, support even an inference of conspiracy. Id., at 763–764. See supra, at 588.

Notes and Questions

1. Rationality and Profit Maximization: The Court assumes the Japanese firms behaved rationally by selecting strategies through which they could maximize profits. The plaintiffs' theory required irrational behavior by the Japanese manufacturers. Thus, the plaintiffs' theory was rejected as being inconsistent with standard assumptions about economic behavior.

2. Managerial Incentives: The Court implicitly assumes that profit maximization is the goal of the firm. In fact, firms are managed by individuals whose incentives may not always be aligned with the firm's goal of profit maximization. Managers may be more interested in increasing their salary or increasing the size of the firm than in maximizing profits. This divergence between managers' incentives and the profit maximization goal is an example of the principal-agent problem. Managers, who are agents of the firm's owners (the principals), do not always act in their principals' best interest. For corporations with publicly traded shares and dispersed shareholders, the principal-agent problem is often characterized as the result of a "separation of ownership and control." Principal-agent problems are addressed in more detail in Chapter VII on the Economics of Information and Chapter X on Organizational Economics.

3. Profits and Cartel Agreements: The court recognizes that each Japanese firm, as a profit maximizer, would have incentives to cheat on the cartel agreement both before and after any success in dominating the market. Again, the assumption of profit maximizing behavior strained the credibility of the plaintiffs' theory.

4. Opportunity Cost of Profits Earned in Japan: The plaintiffs argue that the profits earned in Japan and then, allegedly, used to subsidize losses in the United States are somehow not as valuable as other profits—herein lies the incentive to accept the present lost profits in hope of greater future profits from exploiting American consumers. As demonstrated in the following analysis of cross-subsidization across product lines, the opportunity cost of the profits is not determined by the source of the profits:

> ...If a nonbanking subsidiary of a bank holding company is losing money, a decision must be made whether to support that business, in the hope that its fortunes will improve, or to abandon it. This calculus, which is recurrently required of many businesses, is unaffected by the presence of an affiliated bank. No incentive exists for the bank to "subsidize" its financially troubled affiliate by extending credit at below the market rate of interest. It is important to recognize that the profits of banks are not constrained by regulation to any particular level—banks are not subject to rate-of-return regulation. Consequently there is no incentive for a bank to shift profits to an unregulated affiliate.[16] An example illustrates the lack of incentive for a bank to cross-subsidize an affiliate.

---

16. Obviously, if loans between affiliates are made at the market rate of interest (i.e., at the same rate an independent third-party bank would charge the troubled affiliate), no cross-subsidy or conflict of interest occurs. Indeed, such loans may illustrate efficiencies wherein transaction costs are less for an intrafirm transfer than an arm's-length transaction.

If the "troubled" affiliate can obtain debt financing at arm's length from an independent bank at an annual interest rate of, say, fifteen percent, that cost of credit reflects an independent and realistic assessment of the risks attendant to the loan. A related bank has no incentive to lend at less than fifteen percent. The bank could have made a loan to a third party of identical risk at fifteen percent. The difference between fifteen percent and the lower rate charged the affiliate (say, ten percent) is the opportunity cost of transferring credit at less than the market rate. The forgone interest (five percent in this case) represents an income stream the bank could have realized and, consequently, is a cost of the below-market loan to the affiliate. The total cost of credit to the holding company is the cost the affiliate pays (ten percent) plus the lost earnings of the bank (five percent), which is equal to the cost of borrowing in the market (fifteen percent). Put simply, although a troubled business might appear to pay less than market rate for its loan, the related bank suffers a corresponding loss in income. The firm as a whole cannot reduce the cost of borrowing by charging an uneconomical transfer price. Thus, the fear of cross-subsidization is groundless because nothing can be gained by causing a below-market transfer of credit from the bank to a troubled affiliate.

The concept of opportunity cost likewise demonstrates the fallacy of the argument that banks would make loans at below-market rates to purchasers of securities from a related underwriter or would purchase the securities themselves at prices in excess of the market price. Such decisions would simply transfer a loss from the underwriter to the bank but would do nothing to reduce the size of the loss itself. The bank would therefore have no incentive to engage in these practices.

Fischel, Rosenfield, & Stillman, The Regulation of Banks and Bank Holding Companies, *73 Va. L. Rev. 301, 326–327 (1987).*

5. Costs of Production and Economic Profit: Profit is defined as total revenue minus total costs. Economists use the phrase **costs of production** in a way that reflects the concept of opportunity cost. In order for a firm to undertake a productive activity, it must attract inputs (resources or factors of production) from other alternative uses. The firm attracts inputs by paying the owners of the inputs at least the value of their services in their next best alternative use — opportunity cost. Costs of production (firm outlays) are the payments made to the owners of resources to assure the availability of those resources for use in the firm's production process. In discussing the costs of production, economists and many courts are careful to recognize both the **explicit costs** recorded in the firm's books and the **implicit costs** that reflect the value of resources used in production by the firm for which no explicit payments are made. When a firm does not make an explicit payment for the use of resources it owns, then the implicit cost is the income that those resources could have commanded in some alternative use. A consideration of explicit and implicit costs reveals the total opportunity cost of the production process.

Consider, for example, a small "Mom & Pop" corner tavern organized as a sole proprietorship and located on a busy corner of an area undergoing a commercial "boom." "Mom & Pop" own the building in which the tavern is located. Their explicit costs of operation include the payments for inventory, advertising, legal and accounting services, and labor. Each of these payments involves an explicit contractual outlay that is recorded as a cost in the firm's books. On the other hand, "Mom & Pop" may leave out some important implicit costs of production. For example, "Mom & Pop" may not record on the firm books a salary for their own services. Or, they may enter a salary below what they could earn while working for another firm. The opportunity cost of working for themselves is an implicit cost—a real economic cost—that should be relevant in their decision making process. Another implicit cost that may be left out of "Mom & Pop's" accounting records is the opportunity cost of using their building. If "Mom & Pop" did not occupy the building, it could be rented to another business or sold (with the proceeds invested in another income earning asset). The failure to include the implicit cost of using the building means that the firm is ignoring an important opportunity cost: the **opportunity cost of capital**—the value of the payments that they could receive from the next best alternative investment of the capital tied up in the firm. The opportunity cost of capital is typically assumed to be the market rate of return on an asset of similar risk, and is an implicit cost of production.

Including implicit costs as well as explicit costs in the cost calculation lets one determine **economic profit**—the difference between total revenue and total cost of production. In contrast, the **accounting profit** found on a firm's income statement is the amount by which total revenue exceeds total **explicit** costs. Obviously, if accounting costs do not account for implicit costs, then accounting profit may overstate actual (economic) profit. In other words, positive accounting profit does not imply that positive economic profit is being earned. To the contrary, a positive accounting profit can be consistent with an economic loss.

A final, related point about a firm's cost of production concerns the accounting convention of relying on **historical costs**, i.e., payments that were incurred in the past. Historical cost means that the accounting value of an asset—such as inventory or a building—is determined by the price that the firm paid for the asset. This is the exact opposite of the perspective inherent in the concept of opportunity cost. Opportunity cost is a forward-looking concept. It involves a decision today to commit resources to one use as opposed to another use. Thus, in a real sense, opportunity cost is the value of "the road not taken." Decisions by economic actors rely on predictions about the future—not on past events. Past outlays (unless they affect prospective costs) are not costs because they exert no influence on current decisions.

Consider, for example, the market value today of a commercial building in California purchased in 1987 for $1,000,000 at the height of the real estate boom. If the market price of the building has fallen to $150,000, should the owner refuse to sell at that price simply because its current **book value** (historical cost minus accumulated depreciation) is $500,000? Alternatively, if the owner of the building tried to use it as collateral for a bank loan, would the banker use historical value or current market value as an indicator of its value as collateral? The prudent banker will look at the market value.

B. Property Rights and Exchange in a Free Market Economy

The fundamental problem faced by any economic system is the allocation of society's scarce resources among the unlimited desires of the individuals who make up the society. A **capitalistic market economy**, which is the basis of the American economic system, attempts to solve this social problem by tapping the individual's self-interest in a manner that encourages him or her to put resources to their most highly valued use. Scarce resources—i.e., resources that have an opportunity cost—are combined by individuals or firms to produce economic goods and services which are desired by other economic actors. In the American economic system, economic goods and services are allocated primarily through the market system. The willingness and ability of individuals to trade-off the alternative uses of the resources at their command determines who receives the goods and services.

1. Private Property Rights

A property right is a socially enforced right to determine and control the use of an economic good. A property right is private when it is assigned to a specific person. Property rights are alienable in that they can be transferred (sold or given) to other individuals. The ownership of private property rights is the foundation of a free market economy. Owners of land and other resources have the legal rights to decide how to use these resources and frequently trade these rights to other individuals. They are free to start new businesses and to close existing businesses. In contrast, in centrally planned economies, property tends to be owned by the state; government officials decide how to use these resources. In a system of private property, the individual (as opposed to the government) holds the right to control property. The individual receives the benefit and must pay the costs associated with the use of the property. In a capitalist society, the law protects property rights. Without some guarantee that property rights will be protected, there would be little incentive to accumulate capital stock and, therefore, to grow economically. Without state guarantees of rights to property, individuals would have to protect their own property at a high personal cost.

Enforcement of property rights is important because if the fruits of one's labor are not protected, individuals will have little incentive to be productive. The government of the Soviet Union experimented years ago trying to discover why agricultural production was falling. The government allowed farmers to keep the production from a small portion of their land for their own use. Not only did production on this land increase tenfold, but black markets came into existence for farmers to barter the goods that they now owned.

Certain types of property are difficult to protect because they are intangible. An idea, although it cannot be touched or felt, is no less important than tangible property. In fact, an idea may be the result of years of work and millions of dollars of expenditures. In order to protect the profits of research, the government issues patents and copyrights that represent ideas and create protectable property rights.

Other types of property are tangible but difficult to keep in one's possession. Real estate cannot be placed in a bank to be protected, but state governments keep the records of ownership so owners can enforce their property rights. States also proscribe procedures for the transfer of ownership so there will be less conflict over the ownership of property rights.

Other property, because of its character, cannot be divided and, therefore, ownership cannot be established. Resources such as air, water, and wildlife are owned in common by many. Since it would be difficult for all owners to agree on the appropriate use of these resources, the government is often designated as the agent for all owners and must determine how these resources are used and protected.

2. Dimensions of Property Rights

Ownership of property rights involves two general dimensions: use rights and alienability rights. These aspects of ownership are not always held by the same individual. You own your body in the sense that you decide what activities to pursue, but there are significant legal restrictions on alienability. For example, you cannot enter a legally enforceable contract to sell one of your kidneys, despite the fact that you have two, can live comfortably with one, and might value your second kidney much less than a wealthy individual who is dying of kidney failure. Due to this restriction, there is no free market in kidneys. In some transactions, it is possible to sell use rights while retaining ownership. In a rental contract, the renter obtains the right to use an office, but does not have the right to sell the property. Conversely, the landlord has the right to sell the apartment, but does not have the right to use it while the lease is in force.

3. Gains from Trade

A key point in understanding the operation of markets is to appreciate the significance of the observation that market exchanges are voluntary. Individuals engage in transactions because they expect to receive more than they give up. An exchange results in reciprocal net benefits. In very real terms, mutually beneficial exchange increases the wealth of both parties. For example, assume that Sarah is willing to sell her car for $10,000 and Andy is willing to pay $12,000 for it. If Sarah sells the car to Andy for $11,000, then both Sarah and Andy are $1,000 better off than before the transaction. The $2,000 in gains from trade represents the increase in wealth created by the transaction. This simple mutually-beneficial exchange illustrates how wealth is created simply by transferring the same physical good from one individual to another. Mutually beneficial exchanges not only create wealth (and, for many individuals, happiness), they also allocate resources to their most highly valued use—e.g., the car is worth more to Andy than to Sarah. Moreover, when all possible mutually-beneficial exchanges are realized, then resources are allocated to their most highly valued uses and society's wealth is maximized. In sum, voluntary exchange means that wealth is created.

In the preceding example, the gains from trade arose from differences in preferences. The buyer and seller simply place different values on the item of trade.

Another important source of gains from trade is that the seller may be able to produce the item at a lower cost than the buyer and thus may have a **comparative advantage** in its production. Although a lawyer may be able to type faster than her secretary (that is, the lawyer has an absolute advantage over her secretary), it still makes sense for the secretary to handle the typing because the opportunity cost of the lawyer's time is probably much higher than the secretary's foregone opportunity. Thus, the secretary has a comparative advantage over the lawyer in the sense that she can produce typed pages more cheaply than the lawyer.

In advanced economies, individuals specialize in producing goods and services where they have a comparative advantage and make trades to acquire other goods. Specialization greatly enhances the standard of living in a society. It also enhances the productivity of economic organizations, such as law firms. Moreover, specialization often lowers the opportunity cost of production. The concept of comparative advantage also teaches us that the saying "if you want it done right, do it yourself" can be very expensive.

Despite the simplicity of the comparative advantage argument, we often see laws and regulations that ignore this principle. Consider, for example, the many tariffs and quotas placed on goods traded internationally. The law of comparative advantage is often used to explain the benefits of international trade. Resources are used most effectively when they are moved to their most highly valued use. By definition, this means putting resources in their lowest marginal opportunity cost use relative to other resources available for production. Countries that ignore this logic by enacting tariffs and quotas will become overly self sufficient and therefore waste resources. The more mutually beneficial transactions that a society undertakes, the more wealth it creates. International trade is based on mutually beneficial exchange. Tariffs and quotas increase the costs of international trade and, thus, decrease the quantity of mutually beneficial transactions. Tariffs and quotas deter wealth creating transactions.

4. Individual Self-Interest, Free Markets, and Social Welfare: The Invisible Hand

An important economic principle about market allocation of resources is that resources tend to flow towards their most highly valued uses if voluntary exchange is permitted. For example, producers of stereos and video cassette recorders compete with each other for skilled labor and materials to produce their final products. The reason some entrepreneurs are willing to pay more for particular resources is that they think that the final output produced by the combination of resources will be worth more to consumers than any other product that could be produced from those same resources. This activity causes the value of resources ("costs") to be determined by the prices consumers are willing to pay for final products.

The process of voluntary exchange facilitates the allocation of resources to those uses in which the value to consumers, as measured by their willingness and ability to pay, is highest. This allocation of resources has traditionally been considered to be efficient. This point was best made in 1776 by Adam Smith, the father of economic analysis of the free-market system.

An Inquiry Into the Nature and Causes of The Wealth of Nations

Adam Smith

(1776; reprint, Edwin Cannan, ed., New York: Modern Library, 1937) at p. 423

[E]very individual necessarily labours to render the annual revenue of the society as great as he can. He generally, indeed, neither intends to promote the public interest, nor knows how much he is promoting it. By preferring the support of domestic to that of foreign industry, he intends only his own security; and by directing that industry in such a manner as its produce may be of the greatest value, he intends only his own gain, and he is in this, as in many other cases, led by an invisible hand to promote an end which was in no part of his intention. Nor is it always the worse for the society that it was no part of it. By pursuing his own interest he frequently promotes that of the society more effectually than when he really intends to promote it. I have never known much good done by those who affected to trade for the public good. It is an affectation, indeed, not very common among merchants, and very few words need to be employed in dissuading them from it.

What is the species of domestic industry which his capital can employ, and of which the produce is likely to be of the greatest value, every individual, it is evident, can, in his local situation, judge much better than any statesman or lawgiver can do for him. The statesman, who should attempt to direct private people in what manner they ought to employ their capitals, would not only load himself with a most unnecessary attention, but assume an authority which could safely be trusted, not only to no single person, but to no council or senate whatever, and which would nowhere be so dangerous as in the hands of a man who had folly and presumption enough to fancy himself fit to exercise it.

Notes and Questions

1. Individual Wealth Maximization and Social Welfare: According to Smith, a baker does not bake bread because he or she is benevolent or has the interests of society at heart. The baker bakes bread to earn a profit, and it is this self-interest, or "invisible hand," that causes the baker to do something for others. As a result, consumers are freed from the task of baking their own bread and can use their time in a more efficient manner. Although Smith's reasoning (as well as his insightful critique of government intervention) has been refined considerably by economists over the years, his basic logic is still the cornerstone for the free market. Whether or not one agrees with the proposition that "wealth maximization" should be the goal of public policy, it has been demonstrated empirically that in an entrepreneurial competitive economy, the constant reallocation of resources by entrepreneurs to higher valued uses does maximize the "size of the economic pie."

2. Individual Judgment: One advantage of the market system is that individuals decide for themselves what is best for them and can pursue those activities that increase their own well-being. They are motivated by self-interest to get the highest price for their resources. These resources will be purchased by those (of the many competing users) who have the highest valued use, because it is those users who are willing to pay the highest price. The well-being of society is enhanced by each individual acting in this way, because each of society's resources is used in the most efficient manner possible to produce goods and services for which individuals are willing to pay. Society is protected against an inefficient use of resources because it costs users, in terms of lost profits, to use resources inefficiently.

3. Dynamic Market Adjustment Process: Another advantage of the market system is that it constantly adjusts to changes in consumers' tastes and desires because producers have a profit incentive to seek out information concerning what consumers want. The profit incentive also leads producers to develop and implement new technology which allows them to produce at a lower cost, which saves society's limited resources.

4. Spontaneous Order and Market Coordination: Another advantage of the market system is the low cost manner through which it coordinates economic activity. No one individual in the world knows everything about how to make an automobile, yet, millions of them are produced every year. More specifically, no individual knows how to mine the ore that makes the steel or refine the rubber that makes up the tires or manufacture the plastics used in production. The market system provides incentives and rewards for individuals to engage in all these activities in order to produce the automobiles consumers want in the most efficient manner possible, and it also punishes those who fail.

5. Decentralized Decision-Making: Another advantage of the market system is that decision-making is decentralized. If a large number of people wanted the government to change one of its policies, it could take years for Congress to do so after much debate and consumption of resources. However, if a large number of people wanted a new product produced or even a different color of a current product, you can be sure that the self-interest of some producer would guide the producer to do so. Resources in the market system are allocated according to decisions made by millions of individuals and producers. Millions of households decide how their budgets will be spent according to their preferences, and thousands of businesses compete not only to give consumers what they desire, but to do so by the most efficient means possible, so they can offer such goods and services at lower prices than their competitors. While mistakes are often made by decision makers, their impact is overwhelmed by correct decisions made by the vast majority of others. This decentralized system should be strongly contrasted with the economic systems that existed in formerly Communist countries that relied on a centralized authority to allocate resources. When those with concentrated economic decision-making power made mistakes, their impact was felt throughout the entire economy and there was no self-correcting mechanism to eliminate mistakes. In a market economy, mistakes are eliminated through the demise of unprofitable enterprises.

5. Externalities, Property Rights, and the Coase Theorem

The operation of the Invisible Hand mechanism described by Adam Smith was based in part on the assumption that producing firms incur all of the costs associated with the production of their product. However, in many instances, some of the costs of producing a product "spill over" and injure third parties that are not part of the production process. The total cost to society in terms of resources consumed is the sum of the private costs paid by the producer and the external costs that must be borne by third parties. If the legal system does not require the producer to compensate third parties, then the producer will be able to operate at a cost of production that does not fully reflect the cost in terms of society's resources. Thus, the consequences of self-interested behavior may not always be in the best interest of society.

Externalities exist when the actions of one party affect the utility or production possibilities of another party outside the exchange relationship. Externalities can prevent a free market from being efficient. If a firm emits pollution into the air, it can adversely affect the welfare of the firm's surrounding neighbors. If the firm does not bear these costs, it is likely to select an inefficient level of pollution (that is, to overpollute). In choosing how much to invest in pollution control equipment, the firm will consider only its own private costs and benefits. A socially-efficient investment would also consider the costs and benefits imposed on the neighbors. Externalities are covered in detail in Chapter VI.

Prior to 1960, most economists thought that externalities would surely prevent a free market from producing an efficient allocation of resources. Government intervention seemed to be needed to enhance efficiency. For example, the traditional recommendation would have been to tax firms based on their levels of pollution. Given this tax, firms would have incentives to reduce pollution in order to reduce their taxes.

In 1960, Nobel Laureate Ronald Coase presented a convincing argument that free-market exchange is much more powerful in producing efficient results than many economists had thought. As long as property rights can be traded, there is an incentive to rearrange these rights to enhance economic efficiency. The often-recommended government intervention might be unnecessary and, in many cases, undesirable. Suppose that a firm has the legal right to pollute as much as it wants. The neighbors can always offer to pay the firm to reduce its pollution level. Thus, the firm faces a cost for polluting (if the firm pollutes, there is an opportunity cost of not receiving compensation from its neighbors). The firm will pollute only if the pollution generating activity is more valuable to the firm than the costs it imposes on its neighbors.

Consider a factory belching smoke over a nearby community. Figure I-1 illustrates the analysis. Firm output per unit of time is given along the horizontal axis. The marginal benefits to the firm of producing this output are given in dollar terms on the vertical axis. For the sake of this analysis, marginal benefits (MB) can be thought of as the net profits of producing additional units of output. The MB schedule, therefore, declines with increases in output because the rate of return on additional production generally declines. The marginal costs (MC) curve represents the externality caused by the firm's production. It is also given in dollar terms along the vertical axis. The MC measures the additional costs created at each output level by additional smoke. (Assuming that the amount of smoke the firm produces is directly related to its rate of output, more production will cause more smoke.) The MC curve rises as output increases.

If the homeowners in the surrounding neighborhood own the right to clean air, and assuming that the bargaining costs nothing, the factory will be able to purchase the right to pollute up to output Q, where MB = MC. For rates of output up to Q, the MB > MC—the firm's profits on those units are greater than the additional pollution costs borne by the neighborhood. This means that the firm

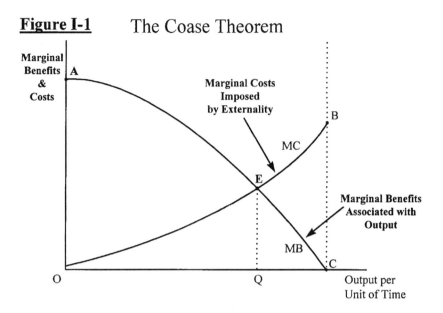

Figure I-1   The Coase Theorem

would be willing to buy and the neighborhood willing to sell the right of using the air to produce those units. The total benefit of producing output Q is indicated by AEQO. Since the total cost of the externality caused by this output is represented by the area under the MC curve, OEQ, a bargain can be struck between the firm and the neighborhood to produce Q by agreeing on how to divide the surplus benefit, AEO. Beyond Q, MC > MB. A bargain to produce these units cannot be reached between the firm and the neighborhood because the firm would not be willing to bid enough to obtain the right to produce those units. So Q, where MB = MC, is the equilibrium outcome when the neighborhood is given the transferable right to use the air.

Suppose that a judge decided to award the firm the right to use the air as it chooses. The same analysis indicates that the neighborhood would pay the firm to produce less output. For up to Q units of output, MB > MC, which means that the neighborhood will not offer a large enough sum of money to induce the firm to reduce its output and its smoke. Beyond Q, the situation has changed. The firm would be willing to accept an offer of money to reduce its output. Beyond Q, the smoke causes EBCQ in damage to the neighborhood and the benefits to the firm for this output are only ECQ. The neighborhood is therefore willing to make it worthwhile to the firm to reduce pollution to the point where MB = MC at Q.

This is a powerful result. No matter who has the legal right to use the air, the amount of pollution is the same. When the firm must pay to pollute, it produces Q. When the firm has the unfettered right to pollute, it produces Q. In a world where bargaining costs nothing, the assignment of legal liability does not matter. A certain equilibrium level of output and its resulting level of pollution will exist regardless of whether firms or consumers own the air. The insight that the same property rights assignment will emerge regardless of the initial assignment of ownership rights, when the costs of negotiation are nonexistent or trivial, is referred to as the **Coase Theorem.**

Fontainebleau Hotel Corp. v. Forty-Five Twenty-Five, Inc.

District Court of Appeal of Florida, Third District
114 So. 2d 357 (1959)

OPINION: PER CURIAM.

This is an interlocutory appeal from an order temporarily enjoining the appellants from continuing with the construction of a fourteen-story addition to the Fontainebleau Hotel, owned and operated by the appellants. Appellee, plaintiff below, owns the Eden Roc Hotel, which was constructed in 1955, about a year after the Fontainebleau, and adjoins the Fontainebleau on the north. Both are luxury hotels, facing the Atlantic Ocean. The proposed addition to the Fontainebleau is being constructed twenty feet from its north property line, 130 feet from the mean high water mark of the Atlantic Ocean, and 76 feet 8 inches from the ocean bulkhead line. The 14-story tower will extend 160 feet above grade in height and is 416 feet long from east to west. During the winter months, from around two o'clock in the afternoon for the remainder of the day, the shadow of the addition will extend over the cabana, swimming pool, and sunbathing areas of the Eden Roc, which are located in the southern portion of its property.

In this action, plaintiff-appellee sought to enjoin the defendants-appellants from proceeding with the construction of the addition to the Fontainebleau (it appears to have been roughly eight stories high at the time suit was filed), alleging that the construction would interfere with the light and air on the beach in front of the Eden Roc and cast a shadow of such size as to render the beach wholly unfitted for the use and enjoyment of its guests, to the irreparable injury of the plaintiff; further, that the construction of such addition on the north side of defendants' property, rather than the south side, was actuated by malice and ill will on the part of the defendants' president toward the plaintiff's president; and that the construction was in violation of a building ordinance requiring a 100-foot setback from the ocean. It was also alleged that the construction would interfere with the easements of light and air enjoyed by plaintiff and its predecessors in title for more than twenty years and "impliedly granted by virtue of the acts of the plaintiff's predecessors in title, as well as under the common law and the express recognition of such rights by virtue of Chapter 9837, Laws of Florida 1923 * * * ." Some attempt was also made to allege an easement by implication in favor of the plaintiff's property, as the dominant, and against the defendants' property, as the servient, tenement.

The defendants' answer denied the material allegations of the complaint, pleaded laches and estoppel by judgment.

The chancellor heard considerable testimony on the issues made by the complaint and the answer and, as noted, entered a temporary injunction restraining the defendants from continuing with the construction of the addition. His reason for so doing was stated by him, in a memorandum opinion, as follows:

> "In granting the temporary injunction in this case the Court wishes to make several things very clear. The ruling is not based on any alleged presumptive title nor prescriptive right of the plaintiff to light and air nor is it based on any deed restrictions nor recorded plats in the title of the plaintiff nor of the defendant nor of any plat of record. It is not based on

any zoning ordinance nor on any provision of the building code of the City of Miami Beach nor on the decision of any court, nisi prius or appellate. It is based solely on the proposition that no one has a right to use his property to the injury of another. In this case it is clear from the evidence that the proposed use by the Fontainebleau will materially damage the Eden Roc. There is evidence indicating that the construction of the proposed annex by the Fontainebleau is malicious or deliberate for the purpose of injuring the Eden Roc, but it is scarcely sufficient, standing alone, to afford a basis for equitable relief."

This is indeed a novel application of the maxim *sic utere tuo ut alienum non laedas*. This maxim does not mean that one must never use his own property in such a way as to do any injury to his neighbor. Beckman v. Marshall, Fla.1956, 85 So.2d 552. It means only that one must use his property so as not to injure the lawful *rights* of another. Cason v. Florida Power Co., 74 Fla. 1, 76 So. 535, L.R.A. 1918A, 1034. In Reaver v. Martin Theatres, Fla.1951, 52 So.2d 682, 683, 25 A.L.R.2d 1451, under this maxim, it was stated that "it is well settled that a property owner may put his own property to any reasonable and lawful use, so long as he does not thereby deprive the adjoining landowner of any right of enjoyment of his property which is recognized and protected by law, and so long as his use is not such a one as the law will pronounce a nuisance."

No American decision has been cited, and independent research has revealed none, in which it has been held that—in the absence of some contractual or statutory obligation—a landowner has a legal right to the free flow of light and air across the adjoining land of his neighbor. Even at common law, the landowner had no legal right, in the absence of an easement or uninterrupted use and enjoyment for a period of 20 years, to unobstructed light and air from the adjoining land. Blumberg v. Weiss, 1941, 129 N.J.Eq. 34, 17 A.2d 823; 1 Am.Jur., Adjoining Landowners, § 51. And the English doctrine of ancient lights" has been unanimously repudiated in this country. 1 Am.Jur., Adjoining Landowners, § 49, p. 533; Lynch v. Hill, 1939, 24 Del.Ch. 86, 6 A.2d 614, overruling Clawson v. Primrose, 4 Del.Ch. 643.

There being, then, no legal right to the free flow of light and air from the adjoining land, it is universally held that where a structure serves a useful and beneficial purpose, it does not give rise to a cause of action, either for damages or for an injunction under the maxim *sic utere tuo ut alienum non laedas*, even though it causes injury to another by cutting off the light and air and interfering with the view that would otherwise be available over adjoining land in its natural state, regardless of the fact that the structure may have been erected partly for spite....

We see no reason for departing from this universal rule. If, as contended on behalf of plaintiff, public policy demands that a landowner in the Miami Beach area refrain from constructing buildings on his premises that will cast a shadow on the adjoining premises, an amendment of its comprehensive planning and zoning ordinance, applicable to the public as a whole, is the means by which such purpose should be achieved. (No opinion is expressed here as to the validity of such an ordinance, if one should be enacted pursuant to the requirements of law. Cf. City of Miami Beach v. State ex rel. Fontainebleau Hotel Corp., Fla.App.1959, 108 So.2d 614, 619; certiorari denied, Fla.1959, 111 So.2d 437.) But to change the universal rule—and the custom followed in this state since its inception—that adjoining landowners have an equal right under the law to build to the line of their respective tracts and to such a height as is desired by them (in absence, of course, of building restrictions or regulations) amounts, in our opinion, to judicial legislation. As stated in Musumeci v. Leonardo, supra [77 R.I. 255, 75 A.2d 177], "So use your own as not to injure another's property is, indeed, a sound and salutary principle for the promotion of justice, but it may not and should not be applied so as gratuitously to confer upon an adjacent property owner incorporeal rights incidental to his ownership of land which the law does not sanction."

We have also considered whether the order here reviewed may be sustained upon any other reasoning, conformable to and consistent with the pleadings, regardless of the erroneous reasoning upon which the order was actually based. See McGregor v. Provident Trust Co. of Philadelphia, 119 Fla. 718, 162 So. 323. We have concluded that it cannot.

The record affirmatively shows that no statutory basis for the right sought to be enforced by plaintiff exists. The so-called Shadow Ordinance enacted by the City of Miami Beach at plaintiff's behest was held invalid in City of Miami Beach v. State ex rel. Fontainebleau Hotel Corp., supra. It also affirmatively appears that there is no possible basis for holding that plaintiff has an easement for light and air, either express or implied, across defendants' property, nor any prescriptive right thereto—even if it be assumed, arguendo, that the common-law right of prescription as to "ancient lights" is in effect in this state. And from what we have said heretofore in this opinion, it is perhaps superfluous to add that we have no desire to dissent from the unanimous holding in this country repudiating the English doctrine of ancient lights.

The only other possible basis—and, in fact, the only one insisted upon by plaintiff in its brief filed here, other than its reliance upon the law of private nuisance as expressed in the maxim *sic utere tuo ut alienum non laedas*—for the order here reviewed is the alleged violation by defendants of the setback line prescribed by ordinance. The plaintiff argues that the ordinance applicable to the Use District in which plaintiff's and defendants' properties are located, prescribing "a front yard having a depth of not less than one hundred (100) feet, measured from the ocean, * * * ," should be and has been interpreted by the City's zoning inspector as requiring a setback of 100 feet from an established ocean bulkhead line. As noted above, the addition to the Fontainebleau is set back only 76 feet 8 inches from the ocean bulkhead line, although it is 130 feet from the ocean measured from the mean high water mark.

While the chancellor did not decide the question of whether the setback ordinance had been violated, it is our view that, even if there was such a violation, the plaintiff would have no cause of action against the defendants based on such violation. The application of simple mathematics to the sun studies filed in evidence by plaintiff in support of its claim demonstrates conclusively that to move the existing structure back some 23 feet from the ocean would make no appreciable difference in the problem which is the subject of this controversy. Cf. Taliaferro v. Salyer, supra. The construction of the 14-story addition is proceeding under a permit issued by the city pursuant to the mandate of this court in City of Miami Beach v. State ex rel. Fontainebleau Hotel Corp., supra, which permit authorizes completion of the 14-story addition according to a plan showing a 76-foot setback from the ocean bulkhead line. Moreover, the plaintiff's objection to the distance of the structure from the ocean appears to have been made for the first time in the instant suit, which was filed almost a year after the beginning of the construction of the addition, at a time when it was roughly eight stories in height, representing the expenditure by defendants of several million dollars. In these circumstances, it is our view that the plaintiff has stated no cause of action for equitable relief based on the violation of the ordinance—assuming, arguendo, that there has been a violation.

Since it affirmatively appears that the plaintiff has not established a cause of action against the defendants by reason of the structure here in question, the order granting a temporary injunction should be and it is hereby reversed with directions to dismiss the complaint.

Reversed with directions.

Notes and Questions

1. The Coase Theorem: Coase's analysis suggests that free-market economies will tend to produce an efficient resource allocation whenever property rights are clearly assigned and the transaction costs of exchanging them are sufficiently low. When these conditions are met, efficiency will occur regardless of the initial distribution of property rights. Moreover, under the stated conditions of the Coase Theorem, government intervention in the form of pollution guidelines, tax penalties and the like cannot improve upon a settlement negotiated by those parties who are directly involved in the externality problem. The Coase Theorem, which is discussed in more detail in Chapter VI on Externalities, was first published in 1960. Ronald H. Coase, The Problem of Social Cost, 3 Journal of Law & Economics 1–44 (1960), is the most cited economics article for the period since its publication. Other economists, not Coase himself, named his insight The Coase Theorem.

2. Let the Bargaining Begin: In order for the Coasian bargaining to begin, property rights must be clearly assigned and alienable. Suppose that there was no legal system to enforce property rights and contracts dealing with property rights. Neighbors would be reluctant to pay a firm not to pollute because, after accepting the payment, the firm could renege on its promise to reduce pollution and the neighbors would have no legal recourse. Obviously, one would be surprised to see market solutions to externality problems under such conditions. In one sense, the *Fontainebleau* case is merely about clarifying the initial assignment of rights. Once it is clear that the Fontainebleau has the right to build, there is opportunity for the Eden Roc to purchase that right from the Fontainebleau. On the other hand, suppose the plaintiff had won the lawsuit and the court issued a permanent injunction against building the addition. Does the initial assignment of property rights affect the ultimate allocation?

3. Caveat: Transaction Costs: Coase recognized that, in order for the free market to solve the problem of externalities, transaction costs—which include search and information costs, bargaining and decision costs, and policing and enforcement costs—must be low. High transaction costs can prevent a preferred, wealth enhancing exchange from occurring. In our pollution example, the firm might be willing to limit its pollution for a payment that is far less than the collective damage imposed on the neighbors, but the costs of bargaining with the firm combined with the costs of reaching agreement on how the neighbors split the payment can prevent the mutually beneficial agreement from being reached. Generally, the costs of reaching an agreement increase with the number of bargainers. In our example, the likelihood of reaching an efficient agreement is highest if the firm only has to bargain with one neighbor who owns all the surrounding property. Were the transaction costs low in *Fontainebleau*?

4. *Caveat: Wealth Effects:* The Coase Theorem concerns the allocation of resources; it also has important implications for the distribution of resources (wealth). For example, the initial allocation of legal rights means that the initial holder of the rights will be able to continue a given activity without having to pay or will have to be paid to stop engaging in the activity, instead of vice versa. The opportunity cost of refusing to sell one's initial allocation of property rights is determined by how much others are willing to pay. If the others do not have the wealth to purchase the rights, then transactions will not occur. Moreover, some parties might find it easier to refuse to accept offers to buy their rights than to garner the resources to buy the rights if they are initially allocated to the other party.

5. *Politics and the Assignment of Property Rights:* The Coase Theorem demonstrates how voluntary exchange can solve conflicts over the use of property. The plaintiff in *Fontainebleau* attempted to avoid the bargaining process by using the political process to engineer the passage of the Shadow Ordinance. Evidently, the plaintiff believed that it was cheaper to use the power of the state to coerce the defendant into not building the addition than to pay for the right. Plaintiff then attempted a novel legal theory to avoid having to pay the Fontainbleau not to expand.

C. The Market Price Mechanism: Basics of Supply and Demand

A fundamental tool of economic analysis is the supply-and-demand model of price and quantity determination. The supply-and-demand model can be used to analyze many real-world events. In a free market, consumers' demands for products and producers' ability to supply the products interact to determine a market price and quantity. Consumers and businesses make numerous decisions on the basis of the information contained within the market price. This interaction between buyers and sellers in the market has been formalized by economists in the Laws of Supply and Demand.

Both "Laws" state empirically-verified relationships between the price and quantity of a good. The law of demand states that there is an inverse relationship between price and the quantity of goods that consumers are willing and able to purchase. As price rises, quantity demanded decreases; as price falls, quantity demanded increases. The law of supply states that there is a positive relationship between price and the quantity that producers are willing and able to supply. As price rises, the quantity supplied increases; as price falls, the quantity supplied decreases. When market prices change, producers and consumers simultaneously adjust their production and consumption decisions until the quantity supplied equals the quantity demanded. Many powerful insights into the effects of various changes in market conditions can be made by applying this abstract analysis to complicated situations.

1. The Law of Demand

The **law of demand** states that, other things being equal, an inverse relationship exists between price and quantity demanded. Thus, the **quantity demanded** of a good or service increases as the price of the good or service declines. In general, this holds for individuals (as explained by the theory of consumer choice) and markets (where market demand is an aggregation of individual demand).

a. Consumer Choice

The assumptions regarding individual behavior introduced in the beginning of this Chapter—consumers are resourceful, evaluative maximizers—are consistent with the law of demand. Why is it that an individual is willing to purchase more of a particular good or service as price decreases? One answer to this question can be found in the theory of consumer choice and the law of diminishing marginal utility.

Individuals desire to consume goods and services because they perceive a benefit in doing so. Economists define the benefit that individuals derive from consumption activities as **utility**. In relation to our understanding of human behavior developed earlier in this Chapter, we can say that REMMs seek to maximize their utility. However, the ability of individuals to consume those goods and services that provide them with the greatest amount of utility faces an important constraint—individuals must choose those items that provide the highest level of utility attainable within their given **income constraint**. How does the consumer decide to allocate scarce income resources among the goods and services that provide utility? An economic proposition that helps guide this analysis is the law of diminishing marginal utility.

The **law of diminishing marginal utility** states that as greater quantities of any good or service are consumed, the utility derived from each additional (or marginal) unit consumed will decrease—holding all else constant. For example, consider your desire for pizza when you first go to lunch. At first, you are very hungry and the satisfaction derived from the first piece of pizza consumed is very high. As additional pieces are consumed, however, the utility derived from each additional piece declines. In other words, the second piece does not provide as much satisfaction as the first, and the thought of eating a tenth piece may make you sick. In trying to maximize **total utility**, an individual consumer will consider the **marginal utility** of purchasing each additional unit of any good or service. To the extent that an individual consumer has more than one item that can be consumed next, a rational individual will choose to spend their next dollar on the item which offers the highest marginal utility per dollar spent. A consumer's total utility is maximized when the utility derived from the last dollar spent on each item is equal. Intuitively, this makes sense. If the utility derived from the last dollar spent on each item is equal, then the consumer would have no rational reason to adjust his or her consumption pattern. When no alterations to the consumption pattern can make the consumer better off within given income constraints, then total utility has been maximized. This utility maximizing situation is known as a **consumer equilibrium**.

Consider the relationship between the law of diminishing marginal utility and the law of demand. What happens to an individual in consumer equilibrium if the price of good x changes? If the price of good x decreases, then the per dollar cost of a marginal unit of utility derived from x becomes relatively less expensive, thus upsetting the consumer equilibrium. In other words, the marginal utility per dollar spent on x increases as the price of x falls relative to other goods or services. Thus, as the price of a good decreases relative to the prices of other goods, consumers tend to buy more of the lower priced good. This tendency is known as the **substitution effect**. A decrease in the price of good x, holding income and the prices of other goods constant, will also increase the real purchasing power of the consumer. This **income effect** allows the consumer to purchase more goods and services overall. In sum, a change in the quantity demanded is composed of a substitution and income effect that are rational responses formulated under the law of diminishing marginal utility.

b. Market Demand

In addition to the individual consumer choice and law of diminishing marginal utility explanations of individual demand, economists are interested in understanding the consumption behavior of a large set of individuals—**market demand**. Market demand is simply the aggregation of each individual consumer's demand. Regardless of the level of analysis, both individual and market demand reflect the same basic properties—an inverse relationship between price and quantity demanded.

In discussing the law of demand, only the price and the quantity demanded are variable. All other things that might have an effect on the price or quantity demanded—such as income, tastes and preferences, laws and regulations, and the prices of other goods—are held constant. This "holding constant" assumption is what economists mean when they say *ceteris paribus*. The assumption *ce-*

Figure I-2

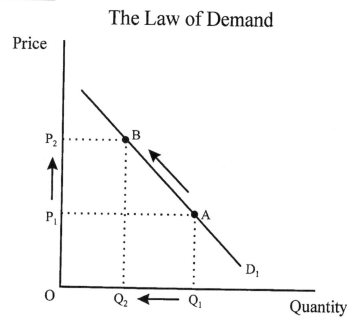

The Law of Demand

teris paribus is used in order to clarify and isolate the relationship between price and quantity demanded in the determination of market price.

For most analytical purposes, demand curves can be drawn to illustrate the inverse relationship between price and quantity demanded. A **market demand curve** represents the quantities of a good or service that consumers are willing and able to purchase at different prices. Figure I-2 demonstrates how the demand curve D_1 reflects the law of demand. It is important to understand that a change in price causes a movement along a stationary demand curve—that is, a change in price causes a change in quantity demanded. For example, an increase in price from P_1 to P_2 causes a decrease in quantity demanded from Q_1 to Q_2 —a movement from point A to point B along the demand curve. A change in price does not cause a change in the position of the curve.

2. The Law of Supply

The supply side of any market represents the willingness of individuals controlling certain resources to transfer those resources to other parties for a price. Obviously, a supplier will not be willing to part with its goods unless the compensation received is greater than the good's value in the supplier's control. In other words, in order for a good to be supplied, the good's value in exchange (price) must exceed its value in use (opportunity cost).

The **law of supply** states that, other things being equal, there is a positive relationship between price and the quantity supplied. Thus, owners of resources are willing and able to sell greater quantities of a good or service as the price of that good or service rises. The law of supply can be explained in two related ways—one is based on demand theory and opportunity cost; the other is based on the technical characteristics of the costs of production. As with the law of demand, our analysis of the incentives to supply goods and services begins with the *individual's* supply curve. Then, we will consider the *market* supply curve, which is simply the aggregation of all individual supply curves in the market.

a. The Opportunity Costs of Supply

The positive relationship underlying the law of supply is merely a reflection of the law of demand, as illustrated by the following almost true story. Imagine a beautiful, deserted, Caribbean island. John Marshall is dropped off by a dinghy from a cruise ship. He is by himself, looking forward to a day of relaxation on the beach. Fortunately, John has lugged along a cooler containing twenty-four cans of ice cold beer. John asserts that beer and salt water are complementary goods— their use together increases their value. After a short swim, John is ready to drink and the perceived marginal benefit from that first can of beer is extremely high. We can imagine that the marginal benefit John derives from consuming the beer would look something like Figure I-3. For convenience, we use price as a proxy for utility and John's marginal benefit curve becomes a demand curve.

The marginal benefit from the first beer is extremely high as John has been planning this day on the island for years. But as he continues to drink the per-

Figure I-3

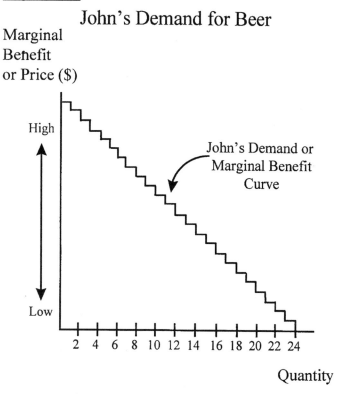

John's Demand for Beer

Marginal
Benefit
or Price ($)

High

John's Demand or
Marginal Benefit
Curve

Low

Quantity

2 4 6 8 10 12 14 16 18 20 22 24

ceived marginal benefit from each additional beer consumed decreases—remember the law of diminishing marginal utility.

Now imagine that a clone of John is dropped off by a dinghy from another cruise ship. It's Mohn Jarshall! John says, "Hey Mohn!" These two are the same in every way, including their preference for beer consumption. However, there is one difference between the John and Mohn—the only thing that Mohn has with him is cash (remember that all John has is beer). Mohn is incredibly thirsty and he is very disappointed when he realizes that there are no thatched hut bars on the island. Normally, John would have just given Mohn a beer, but John really wanted to be alone. However, John might be willing to sell some beer to Mohn. Consider the process of exchange that might develop.

The threshold question is which of his twenty-four beers will John sell first? Obviously, he will part with the one worth the least to him. The twenty-fourth beer that John could consume will be the one that he chooses to sell first, because it has the lowest perceived benefit. Mohn wants to buy this twenty-fourth beer because he really wants a beer. Mohn's marginal utility from his first beer is sure to be very high—in fact, as we know, it is the same as John's marginal utility from his first beer. Moreover, Mohn's marginal utility of his first beer is greater than John's marginal utility of his twenty-fourth beer. Obviously, Mohn and John can make each other better off by exchanging dollars for beer. We cannot determine the exact price at which the exchange would take place. Nonetheless, a large amount of gains from trade exist at the twenty-fourth beer and an exchange will occur.

Figure I-4

Which Beer Would John Sell First?

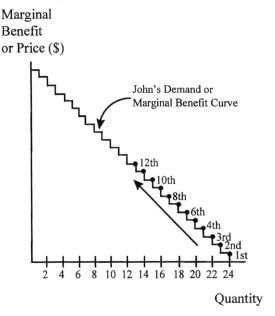

What if Mohn wants to buy a second beer? Or a third? Figure I-4 demonstrates that the process of exchange will continue in the same manner as above. John will be willing to sell the unit that represents the lowest perceived benefit—opportunity cost—to him at that point in time. Thus, John will supply his 23rd and 22nd beers, respectively. Every additional unit sold will follow this same pattern—as Mohn buys more beer from John he will move up John's demand curve. Thus, John's supply curve is the mirror image of his demand curve. Equilibrium will occur at 12 units under the assumption that their preferences are the same.

How many beers will John sell? The answer to this supply question is found in a surprising place—John's demand curve. To see this graphically, simply consider the mirror image of Figure I-4. By taking the mirror image of the demand curve, as in Figure I-5, it should become clear that John's supply curve is simply a reflection of his demand curve. Thus, the law of supply is merely a reflection of the law of demand.

It is important to observe that both John and Mohn were made better off by the process of exchange that developed on the island. John was better off because he valued cash more highly than beers 13–24 and Mohn was better off because he valued those same 12 beers more highly than the cash he paid to John. The physical property of the beer was the same in Mohn's possession as in John's. Likewise, the absolute dollar value of the cash Mohn paid is the same in both Mohn and John's possession. However, a process of exchange arose because of a difference in the subjective value that each of these individuals placed upon the

Figure I-5

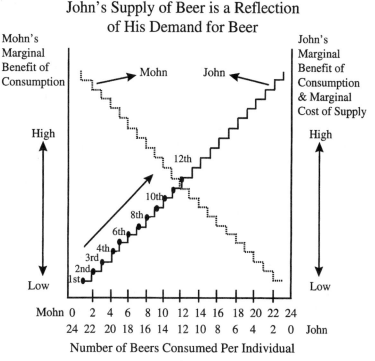

John's Supply of Beer is a Reflection
of His Demand for Beer

twenty fourth beer and the first dollar paid. In other words, John and Mohn *disagreed* about the value of those 12 beers — the beer that John values the least, Mohn values the most; and the dollar that Mohn values the least, John values the most. Moreover, note that no coercive force compelled John to exchange with Mohn; no overriding humanitarian goal drove John to share his beer. Instead, because of a difference in the subjective value that each of these individuals placed upon a particular set of beers, a process of mutually beneficial exchange arose in which both parties were made better off by following their own self interest.

b. Supply and Costs of Production

The Mohn Jarshall example deals with the exchange of goods already in existence. The law of supply also deals with the incentives to produce goods and services. Remember that the law of supply states that firms are *willing* and *able* to supply more of any good or service as price increases. When relative price increases, it is a signal that more of a particular good or service is desired in the market place. If the market price of any good or service increases relative to the rest of the market, firms have an incentive to shift factors of production into the relatively higher priced good or service because they can capture some of that price increase in the form of increased profits. In this way, price acts as a signal to existing and potential suppliers about the relative rewards for producing various goods. This process helps to explain why producers are *willing* to move factors of production to their highest valued use.

Higher prices also increase the *ability* of firms to supply more of any good or service. Because of scarcity, as the output of any particular good or service increases, resources are drawn away from the production of other goods and services. The increased demand for these various factors of production causes the price of these inputs to rise. Thus, for each additional unit of output, the marginal costs rise. In order for firms to increase output, price must increase so that the firm can afford to purchase additional factors of production away from alternative uses. **Factors of production** may be placed into several different classifications. **Natural resources** include land, air, and water. **Human resources** are labor and entrepreneurship. **Capital resources** are machinery and buildings. Remember that economics deals with the allocation of resources within the face of varying levels of scarcity. Because of scarcity, our choices regarding resource usage involves opportunity costs. The factors of production mentioned above are scarce resources and thus, determining their appropriate allocation is important. As noted above, the law of supply plays both a signaling and incentive role in the allocation process. A more detailed analysis of the costs of production is presented in Chapter V.

Like the law of demand, the law of supply can also be depicted in a graph. A **supply curve** shows the quantities of any good or service that a firm is willing and able to supply at any given price at a particular point in time, *ceteris paribus*. As was the case with the law of demand, the *ceteris paribus* qualification is invoked in order to clarify and isolate the relationship between price and quantity supplied. In Figure I-6, the positively-sloped supply curve S_1 represents the direct relationship between price and quantity supplied. For example, as price increases from P_1 to P_2, the quantity supplied increases from Q_1 to Q_2—a movement from point A to point B.

An important element in combining factors of production and supplying finished goods to the market is the entrepreneur. An appreciation of entrepreneurship provides many valuable insights into economic behavior. An **entrepreneur** is an individual who believes that they see profit opportunities that others do not. These profit opportunities come from combining scarce resources in a new way. In other words, the entrepreneur believes he can obtain a profit because the mar-

Figure I-6

The Law of Supply

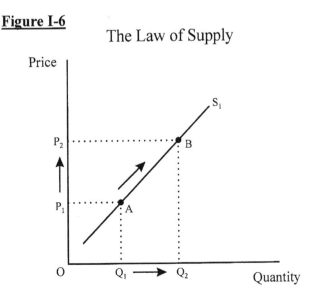

ket has not fully reflected the price of resources in a new, unanticipated, higher valued use. By taking the initiative to combine scarce resources in a new way, the entrepreneur assumes a risk. The primary risk borne by the entrepreneur is that the market will not value this new combination of scarce resources higher than their cost of acquiring them. Beyond identifying new ways to combine scarce resources and organizing the production of this new combination, entrepreneurs also inform other market participants of the availability of the new good or service. A successful entrepreneur is rewarded by earning an economic profit.

3. Equilibrium: Market Price and Quantity

A market exists when the continuous interactions of buyers and sellers force price toward the level where quantity demanded equals quantity supplied. When the quantity demanded is equal to the quantity supplied, the market is said to be in **equilibrium**. The price that prevails at equilibrium is called the **market price**. Thus, the market process forces prices to adjust until the plans of buyers and sellers coincide. This spontaneous coordination occurs because of the voluntary interaction of resourceful, evaluative, maximizing individuals.

The interaction of supply and demand can be illustrated by combining supply and demand curves on a single graph, as in Figure I-7. If the price is P_2, then the quantity supplied, Q_2, is greater than the quantity demanded, Q_0. This excess supply is called a **surplus** and is indicated by the quantity Q_0 to Q_2. The excess of quantity supplied over quantity demanded means that suppliers will have to lower their prices in order to sell their goods. The lower price will encourage additional consumption—that is, cause the quantity demanded to increase—and discourages production—that is, causes the quantity supplied to decrease. As a

Figure I-7
Equilibrium: Market Price & Quantity

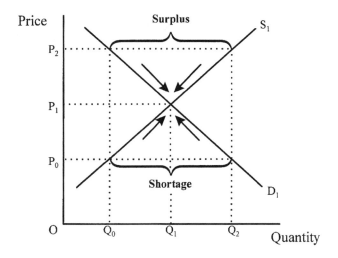

result of the change in price, the quantity demanded converges towards the quantity supplied. When quantity demanded equals quantity supplied, the market clears. The equilibrium or market clearing price in Figure I-7 is P_1, where quantity demanded equals the quantity supplied at Q_1.

If the price is below P_1, then the quantity demanded is greater than the quantity supplied. This excess demand is known as a **shortage**. Through a similar adjustment process, the excess demand will cause the market price to rise, which in turn discourages consumption and encourages additional production. The price adjusts to correct a temporary disequilibrium in the market.

4. Gains From Trade: Consumer Surplus and Producer Surplus

Individuals and firms engage in exchange when the benefits of doing so are greater than the costs. This would mean that for any one particular transaction, both the buyer and the seller perceive the exchange as being in their best interest. In other words, voluntary transactions are mutually-beneficial exchanges—observed market transactions are win-win situations. Economists call the buyer's winnings a consumer surplus and the seller's winnings a producer surplus. **Consumer surplus** is the difference between the maximum amount a buyer would have been willing to pay for a good or service and the actual purchase price that she paid. **Producer surplus** is the difference between the minimum amount a supplier would actually be willing to sell a particular quantity of some good or service for and its selling price. Together, consumer and producer surplus represent the total **gains from trade**.

The idea of consumer and producer surplus can best be illustrated graphically. Figure I-8 represents a market for cheeseburgers that is in equilibrium at $P^*=\$3.00$ and $Q^*=5$. The demand curve represents the quantity of cheeseburgers that individuals are willing and able to purchase at a particular price. In our example, some individuals are willing to pay \$4.00 for one cheeseburger—indicated by point A. Despite the fact that some individuals are willing to consume one cheeseburger for four dollars, the equilibrium market price is \$3.00. This means that some consumers are willing to pay \$4.00, but only have to pay \$3.00. The difference between their individual valuation and the purchase price (\$4.00 – \$3.00 = \$1.00) represents consumer surplus. In fact, the entire area under the demand curve and to the left of Q^* represents the consumer utility derived from the cheeseburgers actually purchased. The area under the demand curve, to the left of Q^* and above the market price P^* (\$3.00), represents the total consumer surplus in this market.

A similar reasoning process applies for producer surplus. The supply curve represents the quantity of a particular good or service that suppliers are willing and able to supply at a particular price. Thus, in our cheeseburger market, some suppliers are apparently willing and able to sell one cheeseburger for \$2.00—indicated by point B. Despite this, all cheeseburgers sell at the market price of \$3.00. The difference between the minimum amount the seller is willing to accept and the market price represents producer surplus. Graphically, producer surplus is equal to the area above the supply curve, to the left of the equilibrium quantity Q^* and below the market price P^* (\$3.00).

Figure I-8

Gains From Trade: Consumer Surplus
& Producer Surplus

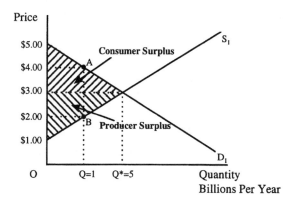

The sum of consumer surplus and producer surplus represents the gains available from trade. Allocative efficiency—all resources moved to their highest valued use—occurs when the market is in equilibrium because, at this point, the sum of consumer and producer surplus is maximized. In other words, all gains from trade are realized.

5.   Changes in Demand and Supply

The discussion of the supply-and-demand model has focused on the manner in which price and quantity interact when everything else is held constant. The supply-and-demand model can also be used to investigate the impact of changes in non-price variables on market price and quantity. Those variables are the items which were held constant in the previous analysis. Understanding the dynamics of price change in response to market conditions enables one to think about the determination of market prices as a spontaneous and dynamic process. This section examines the impact on market price and quantity of changes in demand and supply.

a. Changes in Demand

Changes in non-price determinants of market demand—the other things that are normally held constant—can cause shifts in the entire demand curve. Only variables other than price can shift the position of the demand curve, and the shift can go left or right depending on the nature of the change. A shift to the left is called a **decrease in demand,** which indicates that consumers are no longer willing to purchase the same quantity at the initial price. The shift from D_1 to D_2 in Figure I-9 represents a decrease in demand. Note that the decrease in demand means that quantity demanded at P_1 has declined from Q_1 to Q_2—indicated by points A and B. As a result of the decrease in demand, the market is in disequilibrium—the quantity supplied, Q_1, is greater than quantity demanded, Q_2. Equilibrium is restored when the market clearing price declines from P_1 to P_2 and the equilibrium quantity declines from Q_1 to Q_3—indicated by point C.

An **increase in demand** is indicated by a shift to the right—for example, from D_1 to D_3 in Figure I-9. The increase in demand tells us that consumers are willing to purchase more at the same price than they were willing to purchase before the shift. Note that the increase in demand means that the quantity demanded at P_1 has increased from Q_1 to Q_4—indicated by points A and D. As a result, the equilibrium price moves from P_1 to P_3 and the equilibrium quantity increases from Q_1 to Q_5—indicated by point E.

The types of non-price developments that can cause shifts in demand include changes in (1) income, (2) prices of related goods, (3) expectations about the future prices or availability of the good, (4) tastes and preferences, (5) population, and (6) laws and regulations.

A change in income can affect both individual and firm demand for a particular good or service. Economists have categorized the effects of changes in income on demand for goods and services into two categories. **Normal goods** are those goods and services for which demand increases (decreases) as income increases (decreases). Consider for example, the demand for medical services. As income increase, most individuals will consult their doctors more often. In contrast, **inferior goods** are those goods and services for which an increase (decrease) in income causes a decrease (increase) in demand. An example of an inferior good is public transportation. As their income increases, most individuals stop riding the city bus.

Figure I-9

Changes in Demand

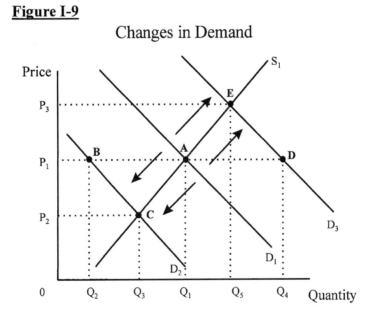

The demand for a particular good or service is affected by the prices of related goods. This relationship can take one of two forms—substitutes or complements. **Substitute goods** are goods that can replace the utility provided by another good. Butter and margarine are straightforward examples of substitutes.
Complementary goods are goods used in conjunction with one another. Examples include bread and butter, tennis rackets and tennis balls, airplanes and
airports, or, in the case of Mohn Jarshall, beer and salt water. Substitute and
complementary goods are identified and distinguished in terms of how the
change in the price of one commodity affects the demand for the other commodity. If there is a positive relationship between the changes, the goods are substitutes. If the relationship is negative, they are complements. For example, if an increase in the price of butter causes an increase in the demand for margarine (a
shift to the right for the demand of margarine), the goods are said to be substitutes. The same increase in the price of butter could also decrease the demand for
bread (shift to the left), which would indicate that bread and butter are complementary products.

Changes in expectations about future prices or the availability of goods in
the future often cause immediate changes in the demand for goods. For example, if the price of personal computers is expected to decline substantially
within a few months, then some potential customers may alter their plans and
decide to wait for the price decrease. Of course, if enough customers decide to
wait, then the decline in market demand may cause the price to fall sooner than
expected. Similarly, expectations of an impending "shortage" often create a real
shortage in the short run as demand increases before merchants have a chance
to raise prices.

It is clear that the demand for products is determined by the tastes and preferences of consumers. However, economists do not have a quantitative method for
determining or predicting consumers tastes and preferences. For example, the demand for hula hoops has virtually disappeared—that is, the demand shifted to the
left as consumers lost interest in the product. Why consumers lose interest in any
particular good has not yet been systematically quantified. Economists do study the
economics of advertising and information. Advertising does have an impact on
tastes and preferences of consumers, but the effect is often very difficult to quantify.

b. Changes in Supply

The supply curve shifts positions in response to changes in non-price variables in much the same manner as the demand curve. An increase in supply is
represented by a shift to the right. An **increase in supply** indicates that suppliers
are willing to sell a greater quantity at the initial price than they were previously. For example, in Figure I-10, a shift from S_1 to S_2 demonstrates an increase in supply. Note that the increase in supply means that the quantity supplied at P_1 has increased from Q_1 to Q_2—indicated by points A and B. The
interaction of the increased supply with the demand curve indicates that the
equilibrium price declines to P_2 while the equilibrium quantity increases to
Q_3—indicated by point C. Thus, an increase in supply with no corresponding
change in demand results in a decrease in market price and an increase in quantity. A **decrease in supply** means that the supply curve shifts to the left—for example, from S_1 to S_3. Such a shift indicates that suppliers are now only willing

Figure I-10

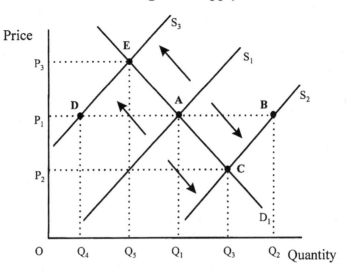

Changes in Supply

to supply Q_4 at P_1—indicated by point D. Hence, the market is in disequilibrium—the quantity demanded, Q_1 is greater than the quantity supplied, Q_4. Assuming no change in demand, a decrease in supply causes the new equilibrium quantity to decrease from Q_1 to Q_5, while the market price increases from P_1 to P_3—indicated by point E.

Changes in the supply curve can be caused by changes in the prices of inputs, improvements in technology, or certain international trade restrictions. For example, an increase in the costs of inputs causes the supply curve to shift to the left. However, improvements in technology lower the costs of production, thereby causing the supply curve to shift to the right. International trade restrictions—such as tariffs or quotas—reduce the number of suppliers to domestic markets. Such a reduction is a shift to the left of the supply curve—causing an increase in the market price and a decrease in quantity available.

Competitive Enterprise Institute v. National Highway Traffic Safety Admin.

United States Court of Appeals, District of Columbia Circuit
956 F.2d 321 (1992)

Williams, J.

Choice means giving something up. In deciding whether to relax the previously established "corporate average fuel economy" ("CAFE") standard for model year 1990, the National Highway Traffic Safety Administration ("NHTSA") confronted a record suggesting that refusal to do so would exact some penalty in auto safety. Rather than affirmatively choosing extra energy savings over extra safety, however, NHTSA obscured the safety problem, and thus its need to choose. Because NHTSA failed to reason through to its decision...we remand the case for further consideration.

*   *   *

The Energy Policy and Conservation Act, Pub.L. No. 94-163, 89 Stat. 871, codified at 15 U.S.C. § 2001 *et seq.* (1988), requires every major car maker to keep the average fuel economy of its fleet, in each model year, at or above a prescribed level. The Act holds manufacturers to a standard of 27.5 miles per gallon for model year 1985 and each model year thereafter, but authorizes NHTSA to modify the standard, up or down. Where the agency chooses to modify, it must set the replacement standard at the "maximum feasible average fuel economy level." 15 U.S.C. § 2002(a)(4). In determining "feasibility," NHTSA has always taken passenger safety into account, see *Competitive Enterprise Inst. v. NHTSA,* 901 F.2d 107, 120 n. 11 (D.C.Cir. 1990) ("*CEI I*"), and the agency maintains that safety concerns are relevant to whether the agency should adopt one CAFE standard over another.

In August 1988, at the behest of various parties, including several major car makers and petitioner Competitive Enterprise Institute ("CEI"), NHTSA initiated a rulemaking proceeding on whether to reduce the CAFE standards for model years 1989 and 1990. See 53 Fed.Reg. 33080. The agency quickly lowered the standard for model year 1989 to 26.5 mpg, but it continued to hear public comment on whether to reduce the 1990 standard as well. Then, in May 1989, NHTSA terminated its proceedings on that issue and left the statutory standard in place.

While the agency rejected a variety of attacks on that standard, we are concerned with only one of the defeated arguments: the contention that the standard will force car makers to produce smaller, less safe cars, thus making it more difficult and expensive for consumers to buy larger, safer cars. We find that the agency has not coherently addressed this concern.

*   *   *

We must remand this case to NHTSA if the agency has not adequately explained why one of the following is false: (1) adopting a 27.5 standard (as opposed to a lower standard) will have some constraining effect on car makers; (2) car makers will, as one consequence of the standard, decrease the average size of their cars below what it would have been absent the standard; (3) this decrease will make it more difficult for consumers to drive large cars; and (4) all other things being equal, a large car is safer than a small car. The agency actually admits the truth of the fourth proposition, and we can find no passage in the record where the agency has coherently explained the falsehood of any of the others.

Constraining Automakers.

As the agency conceded at oral argument, the 27.5 mpg standard obviously affects car makers' behavior—if not in model year 1990, at least in subsequent years. Under the statute, if a car maker exceeds the applicable CAFE standard in one year, it earns credits that it may use to offset CAFE deficiencies over the next three years. See 15 U.S.C. § 2002(l). At the very least, keeping the 1990 standard at 27.5 mpg reduces the number of carry over credits that GM can use to blunt the effect of the CAFE standards for model years 1991–93. Accordingly, NHTSA expressed its quite reasonable belief that "the potential actual [sic] impacts on energy and conservation [from retention of the 27.5 mpg standard for model year 1990] are largely related to multi-year considerations." NHTSA, *Passenger Automobile Average Fuel Economy Standards for Model Year 1990, Termination of Rulemaking*, 54 Fed.Reg. 21985, 21994/3 (1989). In fact, NHTSA recently declared that it would be unlawful for it to set "CAFE standards deliberately low enough to be 'nonconstraining.'" NHTSA, *Passenger Automobile Average Fuel Economy Standards for Model Years 1989 and 1990, Notice of Proposed Rulemaking*, 53 Fed.Reg. 33080, 33094/3 (1988). It seems obvious, then, that the 27.5 mpg standard is constraining in one way or another.

Automakers' Likely Choice to Downsize.

Second, the agency insisted at oral argument that even if the 27.5 standard constrains the behavior of car makers, it will not lead to smaller cars. Yet nowhere has the agency actually justified this claim or even purported to make such a finding. It came closest in the following passage:

> [T]here are still a number of fuel-efficiency enhancing methods that [GM and Ford have] not fully utilized throughout their fleets....NHTSA believes that the domestic manufacturers *should be able* to improve their fuel economy in the future by these and/or other technological means, without outsourcing their larger cars, without further downsizing or mix shifts toward smaller cars, and without sacrificing acceleration or performance.

54 Fed.Reg. at 21996/2–3....At any rate, it has never claimed that domestic manufacturers *will* in fact meet the standard without downsizing their fleets, or even that there is a substantial probability that they will do so, or even that there is a substantial likelihood that they will use methods other than downsizing for the lion's share of the work. Presumably NHTSA does not assert such facts because it could not ground them in the record.

Moreover, to the extent that car makers choose technological innovation over downsizing (and further assuming that such innovation would not itself compromise aspects of auto safety), that choice would involve significant costs in implementation, even if we assume that research and development are complete. That cost would translate into higher prices for large cars (as well as small), thereby pressuring consumers to retain their old cars and make the associated sacrifice in safety. The result would be effectively the same harm that concerns petitioners and that the agency fails to negate or justify.

The historical fact is, however, that car makers respond to CAFE standards by reducing the size of their fleets. NHTSA itself has explicitly acknowledged as much in the past, see, e.g., NHTSA, *Passenger Automobile Average Fuel Economy Standards for Model Year 1989: Final Rule*, 53 Fed.Reg. 39278/1 (Oct. 6, 1988); MY 1987–88 Environmental Assessment 19–20, and we ourselves have insisted that "the evidence shows that manufacturers are likely to respond to lower CAFE standards by continuing or expanding production of larger, heavier vehicles," CEI I, 901 F.2d at 117. Even in the decision below the agency acknowledged this link, explaining that "Chrysler's CAFE has been higher than that of GM or Ford in recent years primarily because it does not compete, or compete as heavily, in all the market segments in which GM and Ford sell cars, particularly the large car market." 54 Fed.Reg. at 21991/2–3.

The agency now tries to obscure this reality by pointing out that "the average fuel economy of the new car fleet has improved steadily from 26.6 mpg in model year 1982 to 28.2 mpg in model year 1987, while the average weight of a new car increased two pounds during the same period." NHTSA Br. at 13, citing 54 Fed.Reg. at 21993/1. This argument misses the point. The appropriate comparison, which NHTSA must but did not address, is between the world with more stringent CAFE standards and the world with less stringent standards. The fact that weight has remained constant over time despite mileage improvements shows the effect of technological improvements, to be sure, but in no way undermines the natural inference that weight is lower than it would be absent CAFE regulation. Here we can be quite sure that it is lower, since, as NHTSA observed in this decision, economic recovery and declining gasoline prices sharply raised consumer demand for large cars over the relevant period. 54 Fed.Reg. at 21987/1; see also CEI I, 901 F.2d at 117 ("consumer demand has shifted back toward larger vehicles"). If consumers demanded substantially bigger cars, car makers—absent regulation—would have produced substantially bigger cars, not cars that remained, on average, within two pounds of the cars made when consumers favored smaller cars. Moreover, NHTSA has given us no reason to think that whatever technological innovations permitted automakers to meet CAFE requirements while keeping weight constant did not also cost consumers more, again pricing some consumers out of the market for new large cars.[1]

Effect on Consumer Access to Large Cars.

NHTSA also argues that even if the 27.5 mpg standard will deplete the supply of large GM or Ford cars, a consumer looking for a big car "will buy a large car from another manufacturer, or will buy a minivan, or will keep his or her older, large car.... [A]ny one of those alternative consumer outcomes is far more likely than the possibility that the consumer will buy a smaller car than he or she wanted to buy." 54 Fed.Reg. at 21993/2. Nothing in the record suggests that any of these will give consumers large-car safety at the prices that would have prevailed if NHTSA had made a less stringent choice.

The reference to buying large cars from "another manufacturer" is somewhat in the spirit of Marie Antoinette's suggestion to "let them eat cake." By NHTSA's own hypothesis, the "other manufacturers" are Chrysler, which has essentially removed itself from the large car market, id. at 21991/2–3, and foreign manufacturers, which are subject to CAFE standards on their U.S. sales, see 15 U.S.C. § 2002(a)(1). To the limited extent that foreign firms produce truly large cars at all, they are expensive ones....

In suggesting minivans (which are exempt from the 27.5 standard), the agency disingenuously obscures their dangers by citing safety figures only for vans in general. 54 Fed.Reg. at 21993/2–3. As NHTSA itself has amply documented, however, minivans are considerably less safe than vans generally, with a

---

1. It is significant that even NHTSA makes no more than the lame claim that "[t]his example illustrates the point that not all CAFE gains come by reducing weight." 54 Fed.Reg. at 21993/1. The issue is whether a material portion of the "CAFE gains" are likely to entail downsizing. NHTSA never even purports to deny this.

fatality rate per registered vehicle about 25–33% higher than that of large cars. NHTSA, *Safety Programs for Light Trucks and Multipurpose Passenger Vehicles* (April 1988), at 4, reprinted at J.A. 94. Finally, NHTSA's notion that the consumer should "keep his or her older, large car" ignores both its own finding that new cars "appear to experience fewer accidents per mile traveled," NHTSA, Final Rule: Federal Motor Vehicle Safety Standards, 42 Fed.Reg. 34289, 34292/3 (1977), and the plight of consumers seeking to buy a large car for the first time.

Impact on Safety.

By making it harder for consumers to buy large cars, the 27.5 mpg standard will increase traffic fatalities if, as a general matter, small cars are less safe than big ones. They are, as NHTSA itself acknowledges. See 54 Fed.Reg. at 21993/3–21994/1. The agency explains:

> Occupants of the smaller cars generally are at greater risk because: (a) the occupant's survival space is generally less in small cars (survival space, in simple terms, means enough room for the occupant to be held by the vehicle's occupant restraint system without being smashed into injurious surfaces, and enough room to prevent being crushed or hit by a collapsing surface); (b) smaller and lighter vehicles generally have less physical structure available to absorb and manage crash energy and forces; and (c) in most collisions between vehicles of different weight, the forces imposed on occupants of lighter cars are proportionately greater than the forces felt by occupants of heavier vehicles.

NHTSA, *Small Car Safety in the 1980's* at 64 (1980), reprinted at J.A. 85.[2]

The agency tries to skirt the obvious conclusion with two specious arguments. First, it essentially argues that the 27.5 mpg standard will have no effect on the availability of large cars (i.e., will accomplish nothing at all). This, we have seen, is simply untrue. Second, the agency observes that new cars now come with a variety of mandatory and optional safety features (airbags, anti-lock brakes, etc.) that will presumably compensate for a decline in size. *Id.* at 21994/1–2.

There are two things wrong with this latter argument. First, so far as we can tell, the agency nowhere claims that these safety innovations fully or even mostly compensate for the safety dangers associated with downsizing. More critically, as in the relation between fuel economy and downsizing, the relevant inquiry is whether stringent CAFE standards reduce auto safety below what it would be

---

2. One might argue that the third factor indicates that if all cars were small, there would be fewer traffic fatalities. Any such inference appears quite doubtful. Cars can hit a variety of objects, including trucks, trees, and other cars; fatalities in car-to-car crashes do not account for even a majority of passenger-car occupant fatalities. See Failure Analysis Associates, The Impact of "Downsizing" the American Automobile Fleet on Overall Motor Vehicle Safety (August 1986), at 38, reprinted at J.A. 180. Unless NHTSA outlaws trucks and trees, smaller cars will probably always mean higher fatality rates, as NHTSA recognizes. See Small Car Safety in the 1980's at 59, reprinted in J.A. at 80 ("in single vehicle crashes, there is increased risk of serious injury or death"); see also The Impact of "Downsizing" at 6, reprinted at J.A. 176; Insurance Institute for Highway Safety, Status Report, Dec. 30, 1982, at 5, reprinted at J.A. 223. Moreover, while the record is not clear on the matter, it appears that the chance of fatality in crashes involving two big cars is substantially lower than the chance of fatality in crashes involving two small ones. See NHTSA, Traffic Safety Trends and Forecasts (October 1981), at 58, reprinted at J.A. 79.

absent such standards. That new safety devices may be coming on the market is all well and good, but it is immaterial to our inquiry unless the implementation of those devices somehow depends on or is caused by more stringent CAFE standards; no one even hints at such a link. Whatever extra safety devices may contribute to either type, small cars remain more dangerous than large ones, *all other things being equal.*[3]

    *   *   *

Nothing in the record or in NHTSA's analysis appears to undermine the inference that the 27.5 mpg standard kills people, although, as we observed before, we cannot rule out the possibility that NHTSA might support a contrary finding. Assuming it cannot, the number of people sacrificed is uncertain. Forced to confront the issue, the agency might arrive at an estimate lower than that of two independent analysts who came up with an annual death rate running into the thousands (for the cars produced in any *one* model year). See Robert W. Crandall & John D. Graham, *The Effect of Fuel Economy Standards on Automobile Safety,* 32 J.L. & Econ. 97 (April 1989). Yet the actual number is irrelevant for our purposes. Even if the 27.5 mpg standard for model year 1990 kills "only" several dozen people a year, NHTSA must exercise its discretion; that means conducting a serious analysis of the data and deciding whether the associated fuel savings are worth the lives lost.

When the government regulates in a way that prices many of its citizens out of access to large-car safety, it owes them reasonable candor. If it provides that, the affected citizens at least know that the government has faced up to the meaning of its choice. The requirement of reasoned decision making ensures this result and prevents officials from cowering behind bureaucratic mumbo-jumbo. Accordingly, we order NHTSA to reconsider the matter and provide a genuine explanation for whatever choice it ultimately makes.

    So ordered.

    *   *   *

Notes and Questions

1. Gasoline Prices and the Demand for Big Cars: The court, citing the NHTSA ruling, observes that "economic recovery and declining gasoline prices sharply raised consumer demand for large cars over the relevant period." The negative relationship between gasoline prices and consumer demand for large cars indicates that these two goods are complements.

2. First Order Effects: Impacts on Supply and Demand: Economics can be used to predict the effects of changes in constraints such as price, income, and regulations. CAFE requirements constrain manufacturers choices regarding the possible combinations of fuel efficiency and safety in new cars. Thus, when the CAFE standard is changed, manufacturers must attempt to maximize profits sub-

---

3. The point is widely recognized. See, e.g., NHTSA, *Small Car Safety in the 1980s* at 77 ("In the event of a crash, the likelihood of injury is increased as the car's size decreases."); cf. Center for Auto Safety, *Small on Safety* 87 (Clarence Ditlow ed. 1972) ("Small size and light weight impose inherent limitations on the degree of safety that can be built into a vehicle. All known studies relating car size to crash injury conclude that occupants of smaller cars run a higher risk of serious or fatal injury than occupants of larger cars.").

Figure I-11

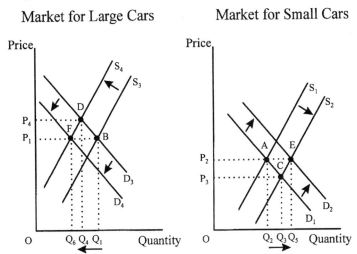

ject to the new constraint. Let us assume that automobile manufacturers respond to the new constraint by shifting the productive capacity of their factories from large cars to small cars, because new technology is either too expensive or not currently available. Remember, however, that this substitution is at the margin. In other words, the manufacturers do not stop making large cars. The impact of these marginal changes on the markets for large and small cars can be seen by using supply and demand diagrams. Consider Figure I-11, which provides a diagrammatic representation of the large and small car markets prior to the imposition of higher CAFE standards. Note that before the standard is increased, the large car market is in equilibrium at price P_1 and quantity Q_1 and the small car market is in equilibrium at price P_2 and quantity Q_2. In order to increase the average fuel efficiency of its fleet, economic theory predicts that car manufacturers will respond by changing their production mix. That is, they shift their productive capacity from large cars to small, more fuel efficient, cars. This action is represented by an increase in supply for the small car market—a shift from S_1 to S_2—and a decrease in supply for large cars—a shift from S_3 to S_4. The effect of this action is to increase the quantity of small cars available—a move from Q_2 to Q_3—while simultaneously decreasing the number of large cars available—a move from Q_1 to Q_4. Moreover, as the supply of small cars increases, the equilibrium price for small cars will fall to P_3 at Q_3. In the large car market, the decrease in supply leads to an increase in market price to P_4 at Q_4.

3. Manufacturers Substitute at the Margin: Economics can be used to predict the consequences of changes in constraints such as prices, income, and regulations. The higher CAFE requirement constrains manufacturers' possible combinations of MPG and safety (weight), and manufacturers must then attempt to maximize profits subject to the new constraint. Economic theory suggests that they will adapt to the new constraint by substituting smaller (higher MPG) cars for larger cars. This substitution is at the margin—the manufacturers do not stop making large cars.

4. Second Order Effects: Impacts on Supply and Demand: The increase in the price of large cars and the decrease in the price of small cars, described as first order effects in note 2, will have an additional (or second order) effect on the market for cars. Among the other things that are usually held constant, the price of substitutes impacts the demand for products. The first order effects increase the price of large cars relative to small cars and decrease the price of small cars relative to large cars. These changes in relative prices should impact the demand for large and small cars. Specifically, we would expect a decrease in the demand for large cars and an increase in demand for small cars. In Figure I-11, this can be seen as an increase in demand from D_1 to D_2 in the small car market and a decrease in demand from D_3 to D_4 in the large car market. Both the first and second order effects cause the quantity of small cars to increase and the quantity of large cars to decrease. What is the ultimate impact on price?

5. Supply, Demand, and Changes in Technology: Assume that in order to meet the demand for large cars and also conform with more stringent CAFE standards, automakers could add a new fuel efficient technology to each new large car. This new technology can be added at a marginal cost of $5000. With this added marginal cost, what would happen to the supply of large cars? An increase in the marginal cost of production causes the supply curve to shift to the left, indicating a decrease in supply. The effect of this change in supply is to decrease the quantity of large cars available and to increase the price of large cars. The end result is that fewer large cars are purchased and more small cars are purchased. Thus, regardless of whether manufacturers respond by changing the mix of small and large cars they produce (as in notes 2 and 3) or by adding new fuel efficient technology to new large cars, the effect in the new car market is an increase in the quantity of small cars and a decrease in the quantity of large cars. In other words, no matter how you want to look at it, the net effect of an increase in the CAFE standards is reduced automobile safety as small cars are substituted for large cars.

6. The Market for Used Cars: In general, older cars are less fuel efficient and emit more pollution than newer cars. Studies indicate that about 80% of automobile emission pollution is caused by about 20% of cars. An alternative to forgoing the purchase of a new large car would be to hold on to your old large car or purchase a large used car. This seems to circumvent the intent of The Energy Policy and Conservation Act. Given that people are rational maximizers, it seems that the likely effects of more stringent CAFE standards are an increase in sales of small cars—resulting in a loss in safety—and a longer life for large old cars—resulting in higher gas consumption and pollution. A common source of error in economic policy analysis is to ignore the secondary effects of any action.

7. Judge Williams and the Margin: "The appropriate comparison, which NHTSA must but did not address, is between the world with more stringent CAFE standards and the world with less stringent standards." Marginal analysis concerns the costs and benefits caused by a change in the law, regulation or some other constraint.

8. Manufacturers' Opportunity Costs: If manufacturers could comply with a 27.5 standard, why should they be concerned about the increase from 26.5 to 27.5? Remember, whenever there is a choice, there is a cost.

9. Consumers Substitute at the Margin: The increase in the price of large cars and the decrease in the price of small cars would lead some consumers to purchase small cars instead of large cars. Some consumers will shift to smaller cars and, in doing so, knowingly increase their risk of being killed in an auto-mobile accident. For these marginal consumers, their "marginal cost" of the ad-ditional risk is less than the marginal benefit due to savings from buying a cheaper, smaller, more fuel efficient, and riskier car. People often claim that life is priceless, but consumers' behavior often indicates that they are willing to trade-off the increased risk of being killed in order save money on the purchase of an automobile.

10. Infra-marginal consumers: Some consumers are not at the margin. For example, an increase in the relative price of a bigger car may not affect an indi-vidual's decision to purchase a big car. Such consumers are said to be **infra-mar-ginal**; that is, the higher price for bigger cars does not affect their decision. This could be a reflection of their attitude toward the risk associated with getting killed in an automobile accident or it could be a reflection of their strong prefer-ence for bigger cars. Can you think of products where a price change would not affect your behavior?

6. The Role of Prices

An important attribute of the market allocation is that it reduces the amount of information consumers need to know in order to make rational decisions—that is, consumers do not need to know why relative prices change in order for the price system to work. In this regard, the allocation role of the decentralized price system may be viewed as a huge informational network through which the relative scarcity of different goods and services is transmitted by price changes. For example, a prolonged drought in the Midwest will decrease the supply of wheat available for making bread. However, this will not result in a shortage of bread. The decreased supply of wheat will result in the price of wheat being bid up, and part of that price increase will be passed on to consumers in the form of higher prices for bread and other bakery products. As a result of the higher price, some farms will not purchase grain for their livestock and some consumers will not purchase as much bread. There will not be a shortage of bread. The market clears, but more importantly, it allocates the scarce resources to their highest val-ued uses in a very low cost manner.

The Use of Knowledge in Society
Friedreich Von Hayek
American Economic Review, XXXV, No. 4. pp: 519–30, September, 1945.

The peculiar character of the problem of a rational economic order is deter-mined precisely by the fact that the knowledge of the circumstances of which we must make use never exists in concentrated or integrated form but solely as the dispersed bits of incomplete and frequently contradictory knowledge which all the separate individuals possess. The economic problem of society is thus not merely a problem of how to allocate "given resources. . . . It is rather a problem of how to secure the best use of resources known to any of the members of society, for ends whose relative importance only these individuals know . . . it is a problem of the utilization of knowledge which is not given to anyone in its totality.

*   *   *

But a little reflection will show that there is beyond question a body of knowledge of the particular circumstances of time and place. It is with respect to this that practically every individual has some advantage over all others because he possesses unique information of which beneficial use might be made, but of which use can be made only if the decisions depending on it are left to him or are made with his active co-operation.

*   *   *

This view disregards the fact that the method by which such knowledge can be made as widely available as possible is precisely the problem to which we have to find an answer.

*   *   *

It is, perhaps, worth stressing that economic problems arise always and only in consequence of change. As long as things continue as before, or at least as they were expected to, there arise no new problems requiring a decision, no need to form a new plan. The belief that changes, or at least day-to-day adjustments, have become less important in modern times implies the contention that economic problems also have become less important....

*   *   *

Is it true that, with the elaborate apparatus of modern production, economic decisions are required only at long intervals, as when a new factory is to be erected or a new process to be introduced? Is it true that, once a plant has been built, the rest is all more or less mechanical, determined by the character of the plant, and leaving little to be changed in adapting to the ever changing circumstances of the moment?

The fairly widespread belief in the affirmative is not, as far as I can ascertain, borne out by the practical experience of the businessman....

*   *   *

...It follows from this that central planning based on statistical information by its nature cannot take direct account of these circumstances of time and place and that the central planner will have to find some way or other in which the decisions depending on them can be left to the "man on the spot."

V.

If we can agree that the economic problem of society is mainly one of rapid adaptation to changes in the particular circumstances of time and place, it would seem to follow that the ultimate decisions must be left to the people who are familiar with these circumstances, who know directly of the relevant changes and of the resources immediately available to meet them.... We must solve it by some form of decentralization. But this answers only part of our problem. We need decentralization because only thus can we insure that the knowledge of the particular circumstances of time and place will be promptly used. But the "man on the spot" cannot decide solely on the basis of his limited but intimate knowledge of the facts of his immediate surroundings. There still remains the problem of communicating to him such further information as he needs to fit his decisions into the whole pattern of changes of the larger economic system.

*   *   *

There is hardly anything that happens anywhere in the world that *might* not have an effect on the decision he ought to make. But he need not know of these events as such, nor of *all* their effects.... All that is significant for him is how *much more or less* difficult to procure they have become compared with other things with which he is also concerned, or how much more or less urgently wanted are the alternative things he produces or uses. It is always a question of the relative importance of the particular things with which he is concerned, and the cases which alter their relative importance are of no interest to him beyond the effect on those concrete things of his own environment.

It is in this connection that what have called the "economic calculus" (or the Pure Logic of Choice) helps us, at least by analogy, to see how this problem can be solved, and in fact is being solved, by the price system....

    *   *   *

The whole acts as one market, not because any of its members surveys the whole field, but because their limited individual fields of vision sufficiently overlap so that through many intermediaries the relevant information is communicated to all....

...The most significant fact about this system is the economy of knowledge with which it operates, or how little the individual participants need to know in order to be able to take the right action. In abbreviated form, by a kind of symbol, only the most essential information is passed on and passed on only to those concerned.

    *   *   *

But those who clamor for "conscious direction" — and who cannot believe that anything which has evolved without design (and even without our understanding it) should solve problems which we should not be able to solve consciously should remember this: The problem is precisely how to extend the span of our utilization of resources beyond the span of the control of any one mind; and, therefore, how to dispense with the need of conscious control and how to provide inducements which will make the individuals do the desirable things without anyone having to tell them what to do.

    *   *   *

As Alfred Whitehead has said in another connection... "...Civilizations advance by extending the number of important operations which we can perform without thinking about them."

Notes and Questions

1. Who Can Do Better Than the Market? The discussion of the laws of supply and demand suggests several important societal roles for prices and the market process. The market price simultaneously fulfills at least two roles in solving the economic problem of limited resources and unlimited desires. First, price rations the supply of goods among consumers. Second, price provides an incentive to suppliers to produce the goods and services that society desires most. The efficiency of the market system as a means of allocating resources to their most highly valued uses is unparalleled. Interference with the functioning of the market, through policies such as price controls, carries a substantial cost in terms of reduced allocative efficiency.

2. Competition and Market Coordination: The American economic system is characterized by free competitive markets. Competition tends to keep prices of goods and services at a reasonable level, usually the costs of production plus a reasonable profit for the sellers. When the number of buyers and sellers is large, no individual buyer can affect the market price of a product or service. No single buyer purchases enough to affect market price, and no single seller can acquire enough power to alter the market for his or her gain. Crucial to the effects of large numbers is the condition that firms be free to enter and leave markets in response to profit opportunities or actual losses. New firms entering particular lines of business, bankruptcies, and business failures are expected consequences of a competitive system. Competition requires that entry and exit into business be free and unregulated. Businesses must be free to fail. Coordinating the billions of individual decisions involved in competition is an interconnected system of prices for inputs and outputs that is so complex that no individual or computer can fully comprehend it. Thus, an economy driven by central planning can *never* match the results of competitive economic markets. In other words, the wealth maximizing results of mutually beneficial exchange will not occur under central planning.

3. Experimental Data: In reviewing the results of a wide array of economic experiments on asset markets, Professor Shyam Sunder wrote the following:

> The Hayekian hypothesis about the importance of the informational role of prices in markets has received consistent support. Dissemination of information, from informed to the uninformed, and aggregation of individual traders' diverse bits of information through the market process alone have been shown to be concrete, verifiable phenomena, bringing abstract theory into empirical domain.

Kagel, J.H. and Roth, A.E. *Handbook of Experimental Economics.* Princeton: Princeton University Press (1995).

Chapter II

The Methodology of Law
and Economics

The use of economics to analyze legal issues is a natural extension of economics. Economists argue that persons at the margin will respond to changes in incentives in a predictable manner. The application of economic analysis to law studies the impact of changes in legal rules and institutions by using these assumptions to determine how incentives are altered by such changes. In this view, laws are just like prices and income—they are constraints on individual's decisions and thus we expect rational individuals to respond in predictable ways to changes in laws. For example, in *Competitive Enterprise Institute*, the court and the NHTSA both agreed that automobile manufacturers would respond to the higher CAFE requirements by reducing their production of large cars.

This chapter provides an overview of the distinctive characteristics of economic analysis of law. Section A demonstrates the natural interface of law and economics. Section B explains the positive scientific methodology of economics and how it is applicable to legal disputes. Section C explores the significance of alternative meanings of the concept of efficiency. Section D identifies the limited economic circumstances where government intervention is justified to correct market failures, discusses why economists tend to be agnostic about issues involving the distribution of wealth, and suggests a framework for evaluating the effectiveness of govenment policies. Section E presents a theory of government failure which suggests that it would be inappropriate to assume that market imperfections will be corrected by perfect government policies.

A. Legal Analysis and the Art of Economics

An important distinction between traditional legal analysis of cases and the economic analysis of law is found in the overall perspectives of legal versus economic analysis. Legal analysis tends to adopt an *ex post* perspective while economic analysis adopts an *ex ante* perspective. An **ex post perspective** means that one makes a decision today on the basis of yesterday's activity. By the time a case reaches a courtroom, the events that have precipitated the litigation have occurred. In other words, the court is faced with apportioning gains (or loss) among the parties to the suit, with the total gain (or loss) having been fixed by the prior events. Traditional legal analysis tends to focus on the distribution of wealth in a static setting. Yet, any decision by the court which modifies or creates a legal rule will affect the decisions of future parties. In contrast, an *ex ante* **perspective** means that one considers the consequences of today's decisions on tomorrow's activity. Instead of static analysis of the distributional consequences of a ruling, the *ex ante* perspective considers the dynamic consequences of today's decision on future economic actors who are not parties to the present dispute.

The *ex ante* perspective is merely a reflection of economic principles:

> *"The art of economics consists in looking not merely at the immediate but also at the longer effects of any act or policy; it consists in tracing the consequences of that policy not merely for one group but for all groups."*[1]

Economics is forward looking. For example, the concept of opportunity cost tells us that the cost of engaging in any activity is the value of the next best alternative activity that could have been undertaken. That is, opportunity cost is determined by making the decision to do one activity in the future at the expense of some alternative future activity. Also, economics says that incentives matter — alternative legal rules will have an impact on future behavior.

Haugan v. Haugan
Supreme Court of Wisconsin
117 Wis. 2d 200; 343 N.W.2d 796 (1984)

Abrahamson, J.

This is a review of an unpublished decision of the court of appeals filed April 26, 1983, . . . affirming a division of property in a judgment of divorce of the circuit court for Brown County, Charles E. Kuehn, Circuit Judge. The issue on review is whether the circuit court abused its discretion by failing to compensate the wife adequately for her contribution to her husband's medical education and training when the circuit court divided the marital property and denied an award for maintenance upon dissolution of the marriage. Because we conclude that the circuit court abused its discretion, we reverse the decision of the court of appeals; we vacate that part of the circuit court's judgment relating to the division of the property and denial of an award for maintenance; and we remand the matter to the circuit court.

The couple, Patricia and Gordon Haugan, were married on August 4, 1973. About a month later the husband entered medical school and the wife began gainful employment. Each already had a bachelor's degree. For the first four years of their marriage the wife taught elementary school while the husband attended medical school in South Dakota and then in Minnesota. The wife's total earnings of between $26,187 and $28,974 supported the couple during these four years. The husband received a stipend of $2,200 and borrowed money to pay education expenses.

The wife continued to teach school for the next three years of their marriage while the husband, having graduated from medical school, was in a medical residency in Chicago. The husband's aggregate earnings for that three-year period

---

1. Henry Hazlitt, *Economics in One Lesson* (1947).

were between $49,254 and $49,548, and the wife's were between $43,339 and $45,056. In addition to working full time outside the home, the wife performed virtually all of the household duties over the seven years.

In 1980, in anticipation of the husband's completing his medical training and beginning his practice of medicine, the couple bought a house in Green Bay, Wisconsin, and the wife resigned from her teaching job. On May 13, 1980, however, about two months before the husband completed his medical residency, the couple separated. In August 1980 the husband began practicing pediatric medicine in Green Bay at an annual salary of $48,000 ($4,000 a month) plus bonuses, for a total annual compensation of $55,498. The wife was unemployed until February 1981, when she began a job with IBM in Green Bay at an annual salary of $19,680 ($1,640 a month). Between August 1980 and August 1981 the husband voluntarily paid the wife a total of $10,150 ($817 a month in temporary maintenance plus half of a joint income tax refund of $693).

The wife testified that at the time of the marriage she and her husband shared the expectation that she would support him while he obtained his medical education and that he would support her after he began his medical practice, allowing her to pursue the career of a homemaker, wife, and mother. The husband argued that the record did not establish a "mutual agreement" since it contained no evidence of a written or formalized agreement. The trial court concluded that "no mutuality of such 'contract' had been established" and that the wife's expectation was "not an express or implied contractual arrangement." Nonetheless, cognizance must be taken of the fact that the husband had a general idea of the wife's expectations. Roberto v. Brown, 107 Wis.2d 17, 20, 318 N.W.2d 358 (1982).

At the time of the divorce the couple had acquired few assets and substantial liabilities.

The couple's assets included cars (valued at $4,650), furniture (valued at $10,675), an interest in a teacher's retirement fund (valued at $2,808), shares of stock in the clinic where the husband worked (valued at $4,000), and the house in Green Bay (valued at $102,000). The couple's total assets were valued at $124,133.

The couple's liabilities included debts the husband incurred before marriage ($1,365), debts incurred during marriage for living expenses and acquisition of property ($28,529), debts incurred for the husband's medical education ($13,457), the land contract on the Green Bay home ($80,013), and the 1981 real estate taxes ($2,812). The couple's total liabilities at the time of the divorce amounted to approximately $126,176, thus exceeding the value of the assets.

The trial court divided the parties' assets as follows: It treated the $20,000 equity in the house as an asset subject to property division and awarded the wife $10,000, payable by the husband in four equal annual installments, with interest at 10 percent. The husband was awarded the other $10,000 equity by being awarded the house subject to the land contract liability.

The trial court divided the tangible personal property as follows: It awarded the wife one car (valued at $1,800) and furniture (valued at $7,300); it awarded the husband two cars (valued at $2,850) and furniture (valued at $3,375). The wife received the interest in the teacher's retirement funds (valued at $2,808 before taxes); the husband received the clinic stock (valued at $4,000). Thus she received assets valued at $11,908 plus the $10,000 payable in installments that represented one half of the equity in the house; he received assets valued at $10,225, plus one half of the equity in the house valued at $10,000.

All of the debts of the parties—the debts the husband incurred before marriage, the debts the parties incurred during marriage, and the debts the husband incurred for medical education—were assigned to the husband.

The trial court's explanation of its division of the marital property—assets and liabilities—was limited. The trial court stated that although it was not enumerating all the factors set forth in sec.s 767.255 and 767.26, Stats. 1981–82, it had considered all the statutory factors and it intended to award the wife more than 50 percent of the marital property.

The trial court denied the wife's request for maintenance payments on the grounds that her post-divorce income would exceed her pre-divorce income and she would not be in financial need after the divorce.

On appeal from the portion of the judgment denying maintenance and awarding property division, the court of appeals affirmed the judgment of the circuit court. It concluded that the circuit court had not abused its discretion in denying maintenance since the wife was employed and in good health. It concluded that the property division was equitable because the marital estate had a negative value; the husband's net property award was a negative figure because he had to pay the debts; and the wife's share of the assets valued at $21,908 was greatly in excess of the 50–50 marital property division set forth in the statutes.

The problem this case poses is not uncommon. University degree—divorce decree cases are frequent. In many marriages, while one spouse pursues an undergraduate, graduate, or professional degree or license, the other works to support the couple and foregoes his or her own education or career and the immediate benefits of a second income which the student spouse might have provided. The couple typically expects that the degree will afford them a higher shared standard of living in the future. That standard of living is never realized by the supporting spouse when the marriage breaks up just as the newly educated spouse is beginning the long-awaited career. In addition, little marital property has accumulated, because the couple's income was used for education and living expenses.

In a marriage of significant duration, the marital partners in sharing life together—with all its joys, sorrows, debts, and assets—share the return on their investment in the marriage. When the marriage ends in divorce the accumulated property is divided according to law and maintenance may be awarded.

But in a marital partnership where both parties work toward the education of one of the partners and the marriage ends before the economic benefit is realized and property is accumulated, it is unfair under these circumstances to deny the supporting spouse a share in the anticipated enhanced earnings while the student spouse keeps the degree and all the financial rewards it promises. As this court has recognized, "in a sense," the degree "is the most significant asset of the marriage" and "it is only fair" that the supporting spouse be compensated for costs and opportunities foregone while the student spouse was in school. *Lundberg v. Lundberg*, 107 Wis.2d 1, 14, 318 N.W.2d 918 (1982). A compensatory award to the supporting spouse can ensure that both marital partners, and not only the one who has received the education, participate in the financial rewards attributable to the enhanced earnings of the student spouse.

*   *   *

In exercising its broad discretion in rendering a fundamentally fair and equitable decision in each case, the trial court has the difficult task of quantifying the value of the supporting spouse's and student spouse's contributions to the marriage and determining the rights and responsibilities of the parties on divorce. Because circumstances vary so much from case to case, this court cannot set down a formula for the trial court to apply in assigning a dollar value to each partner's contribution. We can, however, suggest several approaches for the trial court to consider in reaching its decision as to a maintenance award, property division, or both for the supporting spouse. These approaches are illustrative only; there are other approaches.

One approach the trial court may consider is the cost value approach whereby it calculates the value of the supporting spouse's contributions, not only in terms of money for education and living expenses but also in terms of services rendered during the marriage. In this case, for example, the wife worked full-time outside the home and also performed the household duties, and the fair market value of those homemaking services might be considered along with her financial input. Furthermore, the trial court should consider adjusting the value of the supporting spouse's contributions by a fair rate of return or for inflation. Such an award is restitutionary in nature; it does not account for a return on the supporting spouse's investment in terms of a share in the future enhanced earnings of the student spouse.

On review the wife in this case urges that the trial court should have calculated the contributions she made to the support of her student husband by using the cost value approach set forth in DeLa Rosa v. DeLa Rosa, 309 N.W.2d 755 (Minn. 1981).

Although this court in Lundberg did not directly address the question of calculating the costs of support to determine compensation to the supporting spouse, we did refer to DeLa Rosa v. DeLa Rosa, 309 N.W.2d 755 (Minn. 1981), as an example of a case where a court compensated the working wife by awarding reimbursement for her contributions to the student husband's support and education. *Lundberg v. Lundberg*, supra, 107 Wis.2d at 9, 318 N.W.2d 918. In DeLa Rosa, supra, 309 N.W.2d at 759, the Minnesota court developed the following formula for awarding such compensation to the working wife:

> "We subtract from...[the working spouse's]...earnings her own living expenses. This has the effect of imputing one-half of the living expenses and all the educational expenses to the student spouse. The formula subtracts from...[the working spouse's]...contributions one-half of the couple's living expenses, that amount being the contributions of the two parties which were not used for direct educational costs; working spouse's financial contributions to joint living expenses and educational costs of student spouse less 1/2 (working spouse's financial contributions plus student spouse's financial contributions less cost of education) equals equitable award to working spouse."

DeLa Rosa, supra, 309 N.W.2d at 759.

Using this formula, the wife in this case asserts that she contributed $69,526 to $74,030 in earnings to the marriage; that her husband contributed earnings and stipends of $51,454 to $51,748; that the direct costs of his medical education were $18,220; and that he contributed medical school loans of $13,457 (valued as of the trial date). Applying these figures to the DeLa Rosa formula, the wife calculates her contribution as $13,000, without including interest, adjustments for inflation, or her non-financial contributions. The wife introduced evidence at trial that the value of the $13,000 contribution indexed for inflation is $28,560. See also Lundberg, supra, 107 Wis.2d at 5, 318 N.W.2d 918.

A second approach is looking at opportunity costs. The trial court may in determining the award to the supporting spouse consider the income the family sacrificed because the student spouse attended school rather than accepting employment. In this case the wife introduced evidence that the husband's increased earnings during the seven-year marriage had he not pursued medical education and training would have been $45,700 after taxes, or $69,800 indexed for inflation. See also Lundberg, supra, 107 Wis.2d at 5, 318 N.W.12d 918.

A third approach enables the trial court to consider compensating the supporting spouse according to the present value of the student spouse's enhanced earning capacity. This approach recognizes the spouse's lost expectation of sharing in the enhanced earning capacity; it gives the supporting spouse a return on his or her "investment" in the student spouse measured by the student spouse's enhanced earning capacity. In this case an economist, called as a witness by the wife, estimated the value of the husband's enhanced earning capacity to be $266,000. The economist's figure was the product of multiplying the husband's after-tax annual enhanced earnings were $13,000 (the difference between the husband's annual salary as a physician and the 1979 mean salary for white college-educated males in his age group) by 32.3 (estimated years remaining in the husband's expected working life) discounted to its present value. See also Lundberg, supra, 107 Wis.2d at 5. Using this calculation the wife asserts she would be entitled to one half of the present value of the husband's enhanced earning capacity, or $133,000.

Because many unforeseen events may affect future earnings, this third approach has been subject to criticism. Calculations of the expected stream of income may not take into account such variables as market opportunities, individual career choices and abilities, and premature death. Other approaches are, however, subject to criticism for giving the student spouse a windfall and for failing to recognize the supporting spouse's lost expectations.

Another approach is a variation of the labor theory of value suggested by wife's counsel at oral argument. Under this approach the trial court considers the value of the supporting spouse's contribution to the marriage at one half of the student spouse's enhanced yearly earning power for as many years as the supporting spouse worked to support the student. Under this theory the wife's contribution might be valued at $45,500 (one half of $13,000 [times] 7), which perhaps should be discounted to present value.

As stated before, no mathematical formula or theory of valuation settles the case. Each case must be decided on its own facts. The guiding principles for the trial court are fairness and justice. Our legislature has created a progressive and flexible scheme for trial courts to compensate a supporting spouse; flexibility will maximize the fairness achieved in each case. Leaving the ultimate determination of the award and the manner of arriving at it to the trial court's discretion comports with the notion of flexibility inherent in secs. 767.255 and 767.26, Stats. 1981–82, and recognized by this court in Lundberg and Roberto. Accordingly the trial court may in each case use one or more of the above described approaches, as well as any other approach suitable for that case.

The trial court's discretion must, of course, be exercised within the guidelines set forth in the statutes and cases. And whatever factors the trial court takes into account in determining the award to the supporting spouse, it must also take into account the student spouse's contributions and efforts in supporting the family and attaining the degree and the efforts that will be expended in earning the enhanced income. The student spouse has worked hard to obtain the degree, will have to work hard to earn the future stream of income, and should not be penalized. Granting equity to the supporting spouse should not result in inequity to the student spouse.

*   *   *

In the trial court's division of property the wife received approximately 50 percent of the assets and was held responsible for none of the debts. Thus the wife might be viewed as having received more than the statutory 50 percent presumptive share of property through her release from debts. To calculate the amount of benefit she may have received from her release from debt, we must analyze the debts the husband assumed upon the divorce. We do not view the wife as benefiting from the husband's assumption of the education expenses, the land contract liability, or the real estate taxes. Since the husband received both the enhanced earning capacity and the home (in which he had lived during the separation), he should rightfully pay the education expenses, the land contract balance, and the real estate taxes. These debts go along with the assets.

The wife did, however, benefit when the trial court required the husband to pay the joint marital debt of approximately $28,000 incurred for acquisition of property and living expenses. The wife's share of this debt would apparently be $14,000. Indeed on review the wife acknowledges that she received an approximate $14,000 benefit from the trial court's assignment of debts, but she asserts that the release from debts is inadequate to compensate her for contributing total financial and homemaking support of the family unit for four years, contributing almost one half of the financial support of the unit for three years, and foregoing the husband's earnings during this period and his enhanced earnings in the future.

The husband argues, in effect, that the $14,000 the wife received in excess of the 50–50 marital property division is adequate compensation for her contribution since her total financial contribution during the marriage was $18,000 to $22,000 more than the husband's and that one half of this sum is attributable to his support and one half to hers.[6] The husband therefore argues that the wife was

---

6. The court of appeals calculated this sum as follows: "Gordon earned $1,000 for the years 1973 through 1976, and $50,454.50 to $50,748 for the years 1977 through 1980, and therefore contributed $51,454.50 to $51,748 to the marriage. Patricia earned $26,187 to $28,974.15 for the years 1973 through 1976, including a $546.47 withdrawal from her retirement fund. During the years 1977 through 1980, Patricia earned $43,339 to $45,056.31, including an $808.57 withdrawal from her retirement fund. Patricia's total contribution to

compensated $14,000 for her financial contribution to her husband of $9,000 to $12,000.

We are not persuaded by the husband's reasoning. His calculation ignores the wife's non-financial contribution to the marriage and does not include a rate of return on the wife's contribution or adjustment for inflation or consideration of her lost expectation of sharing in his enhanced earning capacity to which she contributed. Using only a factor for inflation, the wife estimates her $13,000 contribution to the marriage as being worth $28,000 at the time of divorce. Thus the wife asserts on review that in addition to the release from liability of $14,000, she is entitled to an additional award of at least $14,000.

The husband further argues that the award puts the wife in the same position after divorce as she was in before marriage. She leaves the marriage with some property and a job. She did not want further education and was not thwarted in the enjoyment of a career. We are not persuaded by this reasoning because it fails to address the issue which this court has recognized in the university degree-divorce decree cases, namely, that concepts of fairness and equity require that the supporting spouse be compensated when the student spouse leaves the marriage with an earning capacity substantially increased through the other spouse's efforts and sacrifices and the supporting spouse leaves the marriage with little property and a lower earning capacity than the student spouse. Although the trial court may not be able to compensate the wife in this case by giving her the opportunity to pursue the career she wanted as a homemaker and parent,...the court can compensate her for the contribution she made in supporting the couple while the husband pursued his professional education.[7] According to the record the wife's contribution was valued between $13,000 (without adjustment for interest and inflation) and $133,000.

Where the marriage terminates before the parties benefited economically from the university degree or license acquired during the marriage and before substantial assets are accumulated, an award of 50 percent or even more of the marital assets is unlikely to compensate the supporting spouse fully. The wife would have received 50 percent of the assets even if she had not supported her husband while he was in school. In Roberto v. Brown, supra, 107 Wis.2d at 23, 318 N.W.2d 358, we held that a property award of 70 percent of the property was insufficient to compensate the wife for her contributions and foregone opportunities. The award in this case which denied maintenance, divided the assets equally, and relieved the wife of approximately $14,000 in debts seems insuffi-

---

the marriage was $69,526 to $74,030.46. Subtracting Gordon's total contribution from Patricia's, a figure of $18,071.50 to $22.282.46 results. (Footnote 2 of court of appeals decision) This calculation of the supporting spouse's contribution results in a slightly different figure than the DeLa Rosa formula. The wife claims the court of appeals calculation does not take into account the education expenses paid by the couple during the residency period which should be viewed as additional support for the husband.

7. The husband suggests that the voluntary maintenance payments he made to the wife during the separation should be considered as additional compensation for her previous support. The trial court did not consider the temporary maintenance payments in this manner and neither do we. Temporary maintenance payments made during the pendency of a divorce action generally are not considered in making the final award. Cf. Van Wyk v. Van Wyk, 86 Wis.2d 100,115, 271 N.W.2d 860 (1978); Leighton v. Leighton, 81 Wis.2d 620, 632, 261 N.W.2d 457 (1978) (court-ordered temporary alimony).

cient compensation for her significant financial and non-financial contributions to this marriage over a seven-year period, her lost expectation of sharing in his enhanced earning capacity, and the valuations of her contribution.

Because the trial court did not articulate its reasoning and did not specifically address the guidelines set forth in the statutes and the cases and because the award on its face appears inadequate, we conclude that the trial court abused its discretion. We therefore vacate the award and remand the cause to the trial court to reconsider all the evidence and provide for fair and equitable compensation to the wife for her contribution to the enhanced earning capacity of the husband, whether it be by further award of property or award of maintenance or both.

We reverse the decision of the court of appeals. We vacate that part of the judgment of the circuit court relating to the property division and denial of maintenance payments and remand the matter to the circuit court for further proceedings consistent with this opinion. * * *

Notes and Questions

1. Ex Ante Analysis: Marriages on the Margin?: Ex ante analysis focuses on the impact of the decision on future behavior. Would you expect the court's decision to impact some couples' decision to get married? Would the court's decision impact one spouse's decision to "invest" in the other spouse's career?

2. Present Value: As we will see throughout these materials, present value is a fundamental concept underlying value. The present value of an asset (or anything) is a single number which captures the future stream of benefits or costs of an activity, adjusted for the fact that a benefit received later is worth less than the same benefit received sooner. This adjustment is calculated by discounting the stream by the appropriate interest rate. This process is explained in Chapter IV.

3. Ex Post Analysis: Dividing Up the Pie?: The *Haugan* Court proposes three methods to value the medical degree/marital asset: the cost-value approach, the opportunity cost approach, and the present value approach. All three of these methods focus on valuing the size of the pie before it is divided amongst the parties. This is *ex post* analysis. It is primarily concerned with the past. It is not concerned with the future activities of other parties. The present value calculation in *Haugan* does attempt to take the future into account, but it is only the future income of the Haugans. Note that the court does not consider the impact of its decision on Dr. Haugan's incentive to work.

4. Ex Ante Analysis of Patent Rights: Patent infringement cases illustrate the differences between the ex ante and ex post perspectives. The defendant's case will probably contain a policy argument that the information embodied in the patent has already been created and "efficiency" requires widespread use. The marginal cost of additional use is low or possibly zero. From an ex post perspective that argument makes some sense. However, restricting the ability of the patent holder to prevent infringement and collect royalties will reduce the gains that can be expected from any patent and thus reduce, at the margin, the ex ante incentive for persons to invest in patentable activities. Thus, the court's decision will affect the trade-off between optimal use and optimal creation. In other words, the perspective the court adopts, either ex ante or ex post or some combination, will change incentives and behavior at the margin.

5. Beware of Unintended Consequences: Many laws and regulations are intended to correct perceived problems with the market allocation of goods and services. It is important in designing laws and regulations to consider how rational economic actors are likely to respond to new constraints on their behavior. Consider, for example, the Superfund requirement that contaminated soil at toxic waste sites be sterilized. This requirement means that companies looking for new industrial sites steer away from Superfund sites for fear of being held liable for cleaning up some else's pollution (the Superfund law calls for joint and several liability of anyone who has ever owned the site). The result is that companies tend to locate in areas where the soil is not contaminated, and we end up with two dirty lots instead of one. "Brownsfield" is the name that has been given to this totally predictable result.

B. Positive Economic Analysis and Scientific Methodology

Economists have traditionally distinguished between positive and normative analysis. **Positive economic analysis** seeks to describe the world as it is, not as one thinks it should be, and thus is (theoretically) "value free." It seeks to explore the "natural" economic forces that constrain economic behavior. For example, positive economics look to the consequences of a change in a legal rule. Thus, positive economic analysis looks to the future in an effort to compare the consequences of alternative incentive structures. In some instances, the positive economist will identify one arrangement as more **efficient** (within the context of the model) than another, but the positive economist will not say that efficiency is necessarily the best outcome.

Normative analysis, in contrast, makes value judgments when it describes the world as it "ought to be." There is nothing inherently wrong with making normative statements about alternative economic arrangements; much of our Western philosophical tradition from Plato and Aristotle to the present Pope (see, e.g., *Centissimus Annis*) is concerned with such issues. However, according to the dominant epistemology, there is no scientific way to show whether or not so-called normative statements are correct. Normative statements cannot be empirically tested. They cannot be falsified.

Positive economic analysis employs the scientific method—it uses logic to develop **hypotheses**, and tests these hypotheses against empirical evidence. The major advantage of engaging in positive analysis is that you will be able, at least theoretically, to identify the testable implications—in terms of benefits and costs—of implementing alternative institutional arrangements. That is, positive economic analysis provides a method to identify the trade-offs inherent in many policy decisions.

Because of the complexity of markets, economists use numerous abstract models, such as supply and demand, to develop social science theories about real world behavior. Theory may help us to **understand** and to explain **why**; it helps to develop a broad framework that can be applied to a large number of phenomena. A theory can not be merely descriptive and dependent upon personalities, like history, but must develop a framework that survives over time. In the jargon of logic, theory deals in **universals.**

Additionally, a theory does not have to be realistic in order to be useful. Obviously, in order to have broad applicability, a theory must simplify and abstract from reality. In one important sense, a theory can be viewed as an instrument, whose value is not how well it conforms with complex reality, but rather in how well it predicts the results of events whose consequences it was designed to predict. The supply and demand model, for example, has proven to be very useful in predicting the price and quantity consequences of various shocks on almost every conceivable type of market, even when the market does not exhibit all the characteristics (assumptions) of the model. Thus, it is clear that in one important sense — **prediction** — a theory does not have to be realistic in order to be useful.

Economists employ a rigorous **scientific methodology** in investigating economic phenomenon. Standard data collection and testing procedures must be followed in order for conclusions to be accepted as valid. Economists are often called upon to testify in lawsuits. In order for an economist's testimony to be admitted as evidence, the testifying economist must adhere to scientific standards. As illustrated by the following case, the question of appropriate scientific methodology has taken on added significance in recent years.

In Re Aluminum Phosphide Antitrust Litigation
United States District Court for the District of Kansas
893 F. Supp. 1497 (1995)

Kathryn H. Vratil, United States District Judge

This price-fixing case comes before the Court on *Defendants' Joint Motion in Limine to Exclude Dr. Richard C. Hoyt's Testimony and Expert Report From this Case* (Doc. # 443), filed May 5, 1995. Class action plaintiffs claim that defendants engaged in an illegal price-fixing conspiracy under the Sherman Act, 15 U.S.C. § 1, and — more specifically — that defendants conspired to fix the case price of aluminum phosphide pellets and tablets in the United States from January 1, 1988, through December 31, 1992. Plaintiffs seek damages on behalf of all entities (except those owned by defendants) which purchased such products during that period. Movants seek to preclude certain portions of the testimony and report of plaintiffs' economic expert, Dr. Richard C. Hoyt, under Federal Rules of Evidence 104(a), 403, 702, and 703.

On May 16, 1995, the Court held an evidentiary hearing on defendants' motion and heard the testimony of both Dr. Hoyt and defendants' economic expert, Dr. John J. Siegfried. Having considered the evidence adduced at that hearing, along with the expert reports of both Dr. Hoyt and Dr. Siegfried, the Court finds that defendants' motion should be and hereby is sustained in the respects and for the reasons set forth below.

A. Factual Background[1]

Aluminum phosphide is a fumigant used to control insects in the storage of raw agricultural commodities and other food and non-food products. Aluminum phosphide reacts with moisture in the air and releases phosphine gas, which is toxic to insects. In the United States, aluminum phosphide is primarily sold in pellets and tablets. Until the early 1980's, the aluminum phosphide industry was dominated by a legal patent on a product called Phostoxin, sold by Degesch America. Around 1980, the patent expired and new manufacturers began to enter the market. Aluminum phosphide prices began to fall steadily over time as the advantage of the original patent monopoly eroded and new entrants into the market gained market share.

Aluminum phosphide products may be imported and sold in the United States, but only by those companies which are registered with the Environmental Protection Agency. Between 1988 and 1993, those companies were Degesch America, Inc., Inventa Corporation, McShares, Inc., Pestcon Systems, Inc., Bernardo Chemicals, and Midland Fumigant[2]. During the relevant time period, these defendants—along with co-defendants United Phosphorus Ltd., Casa Bernardo, Detia Degesch GmbH, and Detia Freyberg GmbH—manufactured or distributed aluminum phosphide products for sale in the United States.[3]

In the late summer and early fall of 1991, the United States Department of Justice issued subpoenas with respect to an ongoing investigation of criminal price-fixing in the aluminum phosphide industry. On November 1, 1993, that investigation resulted in criminal indictments against Detia Degesch, Detia Freyberg, Degesch America, Pestcon, Casa Bernardo, Inventa, and United Phosphorus.[4] In those indictments, the United States alleged that defendants had conspired to raise the price of aluminum phosphide pellets and tablets from January, 1990, to November, 1990. Detia Degesch and Pestcon pleaded guilty to these charges, admitting that they had conspired to fix prices at a meeting in Rio de Janeiro in January, 1990. Casa Bernardo entered a plea of *nolo contendere*. The United States dismissed the charges against Detia Freyberg and Degesch America. Inventa and United Phosphorus proceeded to trial, but the United States District Court for the District of Kansas ultimately dismissed the charges against them.

B. Findings of Fact

The Court makes the following findings of fact by a preponderance of the evidence based on the evidence and testimony presented at the hearing on May 16, 1995:

*   *   *

---

1. Though the factual record remains to be fully developed through trial of these matters, the Court believes that the facts stated herein are generally undisputed, based on the proceedings to date.
2. Midland Fumigant is not a defendant in this case.
3. Non-defendants Sinochem (China), Lian Yun Gang (China), and Excel Industries (India) also manufactured aluminum phosphide products for sale and distribution in the United States.
4. Of the defendants in this case, McShares and Bernardo Chemicals (a wholly-owned subsidiary of Casa Bernardo) were not charged in the criminal case.

Once causation of damages has been established, the amount of damages may be determined by a just and reasonable estimate, as long as the jury verdict is not the product of speculation or guesswork. *MCI Communications v. American Tel. & Tel. Co.*, 708 F.2d 1081, 1161 (7th Cir.), *cert. denied*, 464 U.S. 891, 104 S.Ct. 234, 78 L.Ed.2d 226 (1983).

Plaintiffs propose to supply this evidence through the expert testimony of Richard C. Hoyt, Ph.D., president of Analytics, Inc., an economics and statistical consulting firm in Excelsior, Minnesota. Dr. Hoyt has a doctorate in Agriculture and Applied Economics. He held teaching positions at the William Mitchell College of Law in St. Paul, Minnesota from 1977 to 1978, and the College of St. Thomas in St. Paul, Minnesota from 1978 to 1979. Since that time, Dr. Hoyt has devoted his full-time attention to forensic ends: a "partial list" of his experience as an expert witness includes 121 cases (42 antitrust cases, 15 contract cases, 21 discrimination cases, 29 injury/death cases, two patent cases, 10 stockholder suits, and two toxic waste cases). In addition, in the last 25 years, Dr. Hoyt has published eight articles. Two articles, published in the Minnesota Law Review and the Hamline Law Review in 1976 and 1988, respectively, deal with comprehensive models for calculating future damage awards. Four articles on similar topics appear in the *Journal of Legal Economics* (1991 and 1993) and *Issues & Methods in Litigation Economics* (1991). Dr. Hoyt is an expert for hire[5].

Before and After Model

Dr. Hoyt proposes to testify to the fact and amount of damages caused by defendants' alleged conspiracy. Dr. Hoyt's opinion, according to his report dated March 27, 1995, is as follows: (1) from January 1, 1988 through October 31, 1993, defendants had the ability and the economic incentive to maintain prices for aluminum phosphide pellets and tablets at "higher than competitive levels" throughout the United States;[7] (2) the market structure of the aluminum phosphide industry, "in conjunction with an agreement to fix prices...had the effect of raising, stabilizing and maintaining prices of aluminum phosphide products at

---

5. Because he has devoted his career to partisan adjudicatory purposes, it is perhaps no surprise that Dr. Hoyt's professional stature is unequal to that of defendants' expert, Dr. John J. Siegfried. Dr. Siegfried is a professor of economics at Vanderbilt University, where he has served with distinction for 22 years. His professional credentials include numerous visiting professorships throughout the world, service as a Fulbright Senior Scholar (1991–92), selection as current president-elect of the Southern Economic Association (the largest regional association of economists in the United States), and service on the senior staff of President Gerald Ford's Council of Economic Advisors. In 1990, the National Association of Economic Educators honored Dr. Siegfried for lifetime contributions to research on economics education. In addition, Dr. Siegfried has authored more than 100 books and articles in prestigious economic journals throughout the United States, and currently serves on the editorial boards of three such journals. In noteworthy contrast with Dr. Hoyt, Dr. Siegfried has testified as an expert in six to nine cases. Dr. Siegfried does not advertise his availability as an expert witness and he devotes only five to eight percent of his time to consulting.

7. According to Dr. Hoyt, the following factors provided defendants the ability and economic incentive to maintain prices at higher than competitive levels: four firms (Degesch America, Pestcon, Research and Bernardo) controlled 90% of the market; demand was inelastic and declining during the time period; market entry was limited by relatively high barriers in the form of licensing and/or registration requirements by the United States government; and aluminum phosphide products are fungible. *Expert Report of Richard C. Hoyt,* at p. 7, ¶6.

supra-competitive levels over an extended period of time"; and (3) the fact and
the extent of defendants' supra competitive pricing can be measured by a "before
and after" model which "generally compares defendants' prices in two distinct
time periods (conspiratorial and normative) and calculates the degree to which
prices were raised and/or maintained at artificially high levels." *Expert Report of
Richard C. Hoyt*, p. 8, ¶ 8. All parties agree that the "before and after" model is
well accepted within the field of economics, and that it may be properly applied
to determine the fact and the amount of damages in this case. The dispute is
whether Dr. Hoyt indeed applied the "before and after" model, or whether his
purported application is so fundamentally flawed as to render his conclusions inadmissible under *Daubert v. Merrell Dow Pharmaceuticals, Inc.*, U.S., 113 S. Ct.
2786, 125 L. Ed. 2d 469, (1993).

The theoretical basis for the "before and after" model, in Dr. Hoyt's words,
is as follows:

> [T]his model is based upon the premise that the normative period is a
> measure of what the competitive price would have been absent illegal
> conduct. Under this well accepted approach, the monetary impact to the
> class is the difference between the actual price and the estimated competi-
> tive price, multiplied times the quantities purchased by all class members.
> Expert Report of Richard C. Hoyt, p. 8, ¶ 8. As noted, the "before and
> after" model requires that actual prices during the conspiracy period be
> compared to estimated competitive prices that would have prevailed dur-
> ing that period, absent the conspiracy. The model therefore required Dr.
> Hoyt to determine estimated prices that would have prevailed during the
> conspiracy period, based on prices that prevailed during the normative or
> non-conspiratorial period. By definition, "estimated competitive prices"
> are just that: they cannot be ascertained as historical facts but must be
> calculated through the exercise of expert judgment and opinion. Through
> application of established scientific procedures within the field of econom-
> ics, economists are qualified to make such judgments and calculations.

In this case, Dr. Hoyt made the following findings and opinions concerning
the estimated competitive prices that would have prevailed in the absence of a
conspiracy:

> (1) Estimated competitive prices for the conspiracy period (January 1,
> 1988 through December 31, 1992) are the prices which prevailed during
> the normative period (the ten consecutive months from January 1
> through October 31, 1993); and (2) The sole cause of the actual price
> differences between the conspiracy period and the normative period was
> the conspiracy itself.

The two prongs of Dr. Hoyt's analysis are critical to plaintiffs' case and they are
discussed, in detail, below.

Selection of January 1 to October 31, 1993 as the Normative Period

Plaintiffs' price-fixing claim is set against a stage of generally declining prices
after 1980. As noted above, prior to 1980, the aluminum phosphide industry
was dominated by a legal patent. After the patent expired, new competitors entered the market. Prices fell steadily as the advantage of the original patent monopoly eroded and four new competitors (Pestcon, Bernardo, Inventa and Mid-

land) gained market share. The overall decline in the selling price of aluminum phosphide progressed steadily and continuously from 1980 through October, 1993—except for a noticeable spike during roughly two quarters of 1990, coinciding with the admitted price-fixing episode by Detia Degesch, Pestcon, and Casa Bernardo.

The price decline is evidenced by the following figures: In 1988, at the beginning of the alleged conspiracy, the Degesch companies,[8] Pestcon, and Casa Bernardo almost exclusively dominated the market for aluminum phosphide pellets and tablets. In 1988, prices for those products ranged from approximately $350 to $500 per case. Over the next five years, Inventa and Midland gained increased market shares at the expense of the three formerly dominant companies. By 1993, market shares were somewhat evenly distributed among the five manufacturers, with Inventa having the largest market share and Casa Bernardo the smallest. By late 1993, prices per case had dropped by about $150, to approximately $200 to $350 per case.[9]

Dr. Hoyt's opinion is that absent a conspiracy, the prices which prevailed during the first ten months of 1993—the normative period—would have prevailed throughout each of the five preceding years, from January 1, 1988 through December 31, 1992.

* * *

Upon analysis, Dr. Hoyt's opinion is flawed in several obvious respects which render his conclusions irrelevant and inadmissible in this case:

First, Dr. Hoyt's opinion ignores the before component of the "before and after" model. Dr. Hoyt concedes that if pre-conspiracy data is available, the preferred scientific approach is to consult the data both before and after the conspiracy period. *Transcript* (Vol. II) at 108, 111. Under that approach, the economist has statistical bookends and may *interpolate* an estimated price line for any given conspiracy period instead of extrapolating an estimated price line from a single point in time. Although Dr. Hoyt had price information for all defendants for 1986 and 1987, his opinion does not address in any way the pre-conspiracy period. Therefore, Dr. Hoyt cannot account for the fact that prices before the alleged conspiracy are so substantially higher than the purportedly normal prices after the conspiracy.[11]

* * *

In the end, Dr. Hoyt's selection of January 1 through October 31, 1993 as the normative period comes to rest on his belief that 1993 prices are normative

---

8. For purposes of this motion, the Court refers to Degesch Weyers, Degesch Divisions, and Detia Export as the "Degesch companies."

9. According to Dr. Hoyt, when differences between the actual prices and the 1993 normative prices are multiplied times the quantities actually purchased, the total overcharge to plaintiffs is $6,263,428.24.

11. Dr. Hoyt offers no scientific rationale for his refusal to consider data from the pre-conspiracy period. Whether we accept his premise that a "before or after" model is just as valid as a "before *and* after" model, we must hold Dr. Hoyt to those conclusions and opinions which are grounded in the methods and procedures of science and not based on subjective belief or unsupported speculation. Dr. Hoyt's method fails to address (let alone account for) an obvious sign of error in his analytical approach—the elevated pre-conspiracy price structure—and to this extent it is not grounded in the methods and procedures of the science of economics.

because prices were falling during 1992 but leveled off in 1993. Dr. Hoyt does not purport to explain why—in an industry characterized by declining demand from January 1, 1988 through October 31, 1993,[12] and generally declining prices from 1980 to date—stable prices are "normal" prices for purposes of this analysis. Nor does he purport to account for factors other than "normalization" that may have brought post-conspiracy prices to what Dr. Hoyt views as their 1993 resting place. Indeed, other post-indictment time periods demonstrate the same pattern of falling prices, followed by a leveling off. They equally comply with Dr. Hoyt's criteria for what evidences a normative period. Dr. Hoyt's analysis yields no scientific basis for adopting one period as opposed to any other.

*   *   *

Dr. Hoyt's methodology in selecting a normative period is not sound. Scientific learning in the field of economics offers no defensible reason why a prudent economist would select January 1 through October 31, 1993 as the normative period in this case. Recognized methodology for distinguishing the alleged violation period from the alleged non-violation period requires analysis of price patterns and statistical tests, including a "dummy variable approach," to determine whether for any proposed violation period the price was systematically higher than it would otherwise have been.[14] Because Dr. Hoyt failed to perform this and other relevant analysis, his choice of a normative period is not consistent with accepted economic practice. To use Dr. Siegfried words, "the way he selected the benchmark is [not] consistent with the way an economist would do it."

Cause of Price Differences between the Conspiracy Period and the Normative Period

The goal of a prudent economist in performing the "before and after" analysis is to determine the hypothetical or "counter-factual" prices that would have prevailed during the conspiracy period, but for the conspiracy.[15] In applying the "before and after" model of damages, it is fundamentally necessary to explain the pattern of forces outside the violation period using factors that might have changed (*i.e.*, supply, demand, and differences in competition) to predict the prices during the conspiratorial period. In this context, as in most economic problems, failure to keep "other things equal" is one of the known "pitfalls...in the path of the serious economist." Samuelson, P. and Nordhaus, W.D., *Economics* (13th ed.) at p. 7. This case presents two potential normative periods, a "be-

---

12. See *Expert Report of Richard C. Hoyt* (March 27, 1995) at 6–7, paragraphs 5–6.

14. Dr. Siegfried applied the dummy variable approach to Dr. Hoyt's purported normative period, with surprising results. For two of the four companies on which Dr. Siegfried performed the dummy variable analysis, the statistical indicator method revealed that defendants' prices were actually *lower* than what would have been expected during the conspiracy period, January, 1988 through December, 1992. As a result, Dr. Siegfried concluded that Dr. Hoyt's benchmark period had "no basis."

15. The before and after model cannot be properly applied unless an appropriate normative period, however selected, has been identified. In view of the Court's finding with respect to Dr. Hoyt's selection of the normative period in this case, the proposed before and after model cannot be properly applied. Therefore, it is arguably unnecessary to discuss Dr. Hoyt's conclusion that the difference in prices between the conspiracy period and the post-conspiracy period results solely from the alleged conspiracy. In order that the record is complete, however, the Court finds in the alternative that defendants' motion should be sustained for additional reasons as well.

fore" period and an "after" period that have distinctly different price levels. One therefore must identify the reasons for the disparate price levels.[16] According to Dr. Siegfried, the field of economics supplies a statistical methodology for making this determination on a scientific basis, and the generally accepted means of predicting the prices that would have prevailed absent the conspiracy is regression analysis. At a minimum, regression analysis addresses supply and demand factors by looking at price trends over time. A prudent economist must account for these differences and would perform a minimum regression analysis if utilizing the "before and after" model.[17]

Dr. Hoyt did not perform a regression analysis to address such obvious points as (1) why normative prices before the alleged conspiracy so greatly exceeded allegedly normative prices after the alleged conspiracy; or (2) the effect of supply, demand, competition or other factors that might impact price levels during both normative periods. Instead, Dr. Hoyt opined that any price increase between 1993 and the conspiracy period was caused solely by the alleged conspiracy. He took a simple weighted average of the actual prices for ten months during 1993 and assumed that price should have prevailed at all prior points in history. In doing so, Dr. Hoyt ignored price trends inside and outside the 1993 period, violating a fundamental rule of application for the "before and after" model. According to Dr. Siegfried, Dr. Hoyt's calculations did not take into account the effect of four factors: (1) a precipitous decline in demand for aluminum phosphide pellets and tablets, with downward pressure on prices, after 1988; (2) increased competition, with downward pressure on prices, because of new entrants into the market; (3) marked realignment in position between 1990 and 1993, as newcomers to the market Midland and Inventa captured the majority of the pellets and tablets market, leaving the existing sellers to defend on the residual market by reducing prices; and (4) the fact that the aluminum phosphide market is an oligopolistic market, characterized by interdependent pricing, in which no independent seller believes that its actions will be ignored by the other sellers....

Dr. Hoyt claims that the "before and after" model "traditionally assumes" that "the conspiracy was the sole cause of the price difference between the conspiracy period and normative period." *Expert Report of Richard C. Hoyt*, p. 8, n. 8. This is not a scientifically valid assumption, and the economic literature on the "before and after" model conclusively refutes. One of the basic principles of economics, as applied to the "before and after" model, is that changes in supply, demand, and competition affect prices, and one cannot properly assume that the sole cause of any price difference between the conspiracy period and the normative period is the conspiracy itself. All of the literature on the "before and after" model (including that cited by Dr. Hoyt) includes the essential elements of modeling how changes in supply, demand, and competition affect prices—so that an estimated non-conspiracy price can be predicted for the period of violation.

---

16. It is improper to assume that all prices compared to 1993 are non-normative, because if one looks to the period before January, 1988, one sees much higher prices than occur in 1993.

17. An economist could go farther, by identifying specific demand and supply factors such as the cost of aluminum and phosphorus ingredients, stocks of grains, numbers of competitors, and so forth. Dr. Siegfried explained, however, that under the minimalistic analysis use of time as a variable "folds those into a single variable that's capturing all of those things put together."

*   *   *

C. Conclusions of Law

Rule 702 of the Federal Rules of Evidence governs the admissibility of expert testimony. That rule provides that

> [i]f scientific, technical, or other specialized knowledge will assist the trier of fact to understand the evidence or to determine a fact in issue, a witness qualified as an expert by knowledge, skill, experience, training, or education, may testify thereto in the form of an opinion or otherwise.

In Daubert v. Merrell Dow Pharmaceuticals, Inc., 125 L. Ed. 2d 469, U.S. , 113 S. Ct. 2786, 2795 (1993), the United States Supreme Court held that Rule 702, in conjunction with Rule 104(a), requires the trial judge to act as gatekeeper to ensure that scientific expert testimony is both reliable and relevant. The court found that the term "scientific knowledge" establishes a standard of evidentiary reliability. *Id.* at 2795. The court noted that the adjective "scientific" implies a "grounding in the methods and procedures of science," and the word "knowledge" means more than subjective belief or unsupported speculation and applies to any body of known facts or ideas inferred from such facts or accepted as truths on good grounds. *Id.* at 2794. The court concluded that in order to qualify as scientific knowledge, proposed expert testimony must be supported by appropriate validation, *i.e.*, good grounds based on what is known. Id. at 2795.

At issue in *Daubert* was the admissibility of expert testimony on the causal connection between plaintiffs' birth defects and a prescription drug, Bendectin. The *Daubert* court specifically limited its discussion to expert testimony based on scientific knowledge, but noted that Rule 702 also applies to expert testimony on technical or other specialized knowledge. See *Daubert*, U.S., 113 S. Ct. at 2795 n.8. Plaintiffs argue that Daubert applies only to "hard" physical sciences which may be tested by scientific method, not social sciences such as economics. *Daubert* indeed enumerates four non-exclusive non-dispositive factors which the Court may consider: (1) whether the scientific theory or technique can be (and has been) tested; (2) whether the theory or technique has been subjected to peer review and publication; (3) known or potential rate of error; and (4) general acceptance in the scientific community. While each of these factors may not be relevant in determining the reliability of expert testimony on non-scientific or social science subjects, the Court has no doubt that *Daubert* requires it to act as a gatekeeper, to determine whether Dr. Hoyt's testimony and report are reliable and relevant under Rule 702. To the extent that *Daubert* factors are relevant to its determination, the Court considers them along with any other relevant factors.

*   *   *

Here...plaintiffs call upon Dr. Hoyt not to supply specialized knowledge, but to plug evidentiary holes in plaintiffs' case, to speculate, and to surmise. One does not need an expert economist to do what Dr. Hoyt proposes to do. A non-expert, using Dr. Hoyt's criteria, could pick as an equally valid normative period any arbitrary time period, of any length, occurring at any time after the date of the admitted conspiracy. Dr. Hoyt's analysis is driven by a desire to enhance the measure of plaintiffs' damages, even at the expense of well-accepted scientific principles and methodology. Nothing in Dr. Hoyt's analysis makes the data for his so-called "normative" period more relevant than the data for any other pre-

or post-conspiracy period, and the record yields no factual basis for any hypothesis that will support his calculations and opinion. Similarly, a non-expert could *assume* that price-fixing accounts for all differences in price between the conspiratorial period and the normative period. To the extent that Dr. Hoyt purports to cast that assumption as an affirmative declaration based upon scientific reason and analysis, however, the Court must reject it. Dr. Hoyt's conclusions are scientifically unsound and irrelevant under *Daubert*.

* * *

Because Dr. Hoyt's opinion is based on unjustified assumptions and does not account for changes in other relevant market conditions, it would not assist a trier of fact to determine the fact or amount of plaintiffs' damages. *See, e.g., Farley Transp.*, 786 F.2d at 1351 (economist's assumption that lost profits were caused solely by defendant's illegal activities did not provide reasonable basis for calculation of damages); *MCI Communications*, 708 F.2d at 1162 (plaintiff's improper attribution of all losses to defendant's illegal acts, despite presence of significant other factors, not sufficient to permit jury to make reasonable and principled estimate of amount of damage); *Southern Pac. Communications Co. v. American Tel. & Tel.*,556 F. Supp. 825, 1075–76 (D.D.C. 1982)....

...Dr. Hoyt's opinion is economically unreliable and therefore inadmissible under Rule 702....

In evaluating the consequences of this ruling, the Court recognizes the apparent anomaly of its holding: that without Dr. Hoyt's opinion, plaintiffs may be stripped of their ability to recover substantial actual damages from admitted conspirators. In the final analysis, however, the problem is one of plaintiffs' making. Plaintiffs are well represented by competent, knowledgeable, experienced trial counsel. Class counsel and their expert have charted an aggressive course with respect to their damage calculations, one which under Daubert was not without foreseeable risk....

Notes and Questions

1. The Hired Gun: Dr. Hoyt's application of the "before and after" model was a poorly disguised attempt to increase the damages owed to the plaintiffs. Damages are supposed to be the difference between the actual price paid by the plaintiffs and the hypothetical price they would have paid "but for" the conspiracy. Obviously, plaintiffs want to show that prices would have been much lower "but for" the conspiracy. In fact, the actual "before" prices were higher than the actual "after" prices. Not surprisingly, Dr. Hoyt opted for the lower "after" price. Obviously, Judge Vratil was not favorably impressed by the rigor of his analysis.

2. Ceteris paribus: Dr. Siegfried explained that Dr. Hoyt's approach was overly simplistic and did not take advantage of the standard economic techniques for investigating explanations for price changes. Market prices are determined by the interaction of supply and demand. The basic supply and demand model assumes that all forces that could impact market prices are held constant. This *ceteris paribus* assumption—*ceteris paribus* is the Latin phrase for "all other things held constant"—allows for the isolation and analysis of important variables. Unfortunately for Dr. Hoyt, the real world is more complicated—with numerous events impacting market prices at any given time. Fortunately, economists have developed and applied statistical techniques to study the simultaneous impact of numerous changes on market prices. Judge Vratil simply held Dr. Hoyt to the professional standards of economists, as articulated by Dr. Siegfried.

3. Econometrics and Multiple Regression Analysis: Econometrics is the use of statistics to study and test economic phenomena. Multiple regression analysis is a statistical process for making precise and quantitative estimates of the effects of different factors on some variable of interest. For example, the variable of interest in the present case is the market price of aluminum phosphide. Data about factors that would be expected to impact on market price—that is, the factors affecting market demand and supply—could be collected for the periods before, during, and after the conspiracy. For example, demand could be affected by the crop size at a particular time of the year; supply could be affected by a change in the cost of a major input into the aluminum phosphide production process or by an increase in the number of competitors supplying aluminum phosphide to the market. In effect, multiple regression analysis attempts to isolate the impact of one variable on the price of aluminum phosphide by holding everything else constant (the *ceteris paribus* assumption). In other words, multiple regression analysis is a statistically controlled experiment designed to estimate the impact of the conspiracy on market prices.

4. New Entrants: The entrance of new competitors (after the expiration of the patent) is one possible explanation for the decline in prices. Dr. Hoyt made no effort to isolate the impact of the new entrants. This type of incomplete economic analysis has been attacked in other cases. For example, Judge Posner has lamented the failure of an expert to segregate the effect of the entrance of a new competitor in the market from the effect of unlawful acts:

> For years we have been saying, without much visible effect, that people who want damages have to prove them, using methodologies that need not be intellectually sophisticated but must not insult the intelligence. [citations ommitted]. *Post hoc ergo propter hoc* will not do; nor the enduing of simplistic extrapolation and childish arithmetic with the appearance of authority by hiring a professor to mouth damages theories that make a joke of the concept of expert knowledge. The expert should have tried to separate the damages that resulted from the lawful entry of a powerful competitor... from the damages that resulted from particular forms of misconduct allegedly committed by that competitor.... No such effort was made.

Schiller & Schmidt, Inc. v. Nordisco Corp., 969 F.2d 410, 415–16 (7th Cir. 1992).

5. Scientific Methodology: "Scientific methodology today is based on generating hypotheses and testing them to see if they can be falsified; indeed, this methodology is what distinguishes science from other fields of human inquiry." *Daubert v. Merrell Dow Pharmaceuticals,* 509 U.S. 579, 593 (1993). Economic theory could have been used to generate hypotheses about the impact of the conspiracy on market prices, and econometric techniques could have been used to reject or accept the hypotheses. Dr. Hoyt failed to produce a report that took declining demand and new entrants in the market into account. Thus, Judge Vratil held that Dr. Hoyt's testimony was "economically unreliable" and therefore inadmissible at trial. The court concluded that Dr. Hoyt's testing procedures were not sufficient for his conclusions to be valid. Should experts be allowed to testify at trial to explain their testing procedures and assumptions or should they prove beforehand that their procedures are valid?

C. Efficiency and Other Normative Goals

Appreciation of the distinction between positive and normative analysis can help to clarify disputes about tradeoffs between efficiency and other goals, such as the relation between efficiency and equity.

1. Definitions of Efficiency

Efficiency has many different meanings. Most non-economists are concerned with what economists call **productive efficiency**—are goods and services being produced at the lowest cost of production? If the answer is no, then we are wasting resources. Although productive efficiency is an important concept, most economists' discussions of efficiency are concerned with **allocative efficiency**—are resources being allocated to their highest value use?

The traditional definition of efficiency is that a change in some relevant economic variable creates more benefits than it does costs. If no possible changes in economic arrangements which result in greater benefits than costs can be identified, then it can be said that the wealth of society is maximized. However, the crucial question is whose costs and benefits are to be compared. (And, maybe more critical for public policy considerations, how does one measure "costs" and "benefits.") Of the two most commonly-used formulations of the traditional definition, one takes a very individualistic approach, while the other takes a broader, more collective view.

The **Pareto Efficiency** criterion is based on the belief that the individual is the best judge of his own welfare: a Pareto efficient allocation of resources (a particular state of the world) is one in which the welfare of any one member of society cannot be improved without reducing the welfare of any other member of society. If a change in the allocation of resources would result in greater benefit to one party than cost to another party, then one would expect to see a voluntary transaction take place to capture the gain—assuming the gain is greater than the costs of engaging in the transaction. Such an alternative is considered to be **Pareto superior.** Thus, the criterion of Pareto efficiency prevents external observers from assessing a change in policy by comparing the gain in welfare of one individual to the loss in welfare of another. The Pareto criterion would require the losing party to be compensated so that he is at least as well off as before the change occurred. Thus, in order to satisfy the Pareto criterion, there must be unanimity among the parties affected by any transaction. Any trade between consenting parties is considered Pareto superior, ex ante, since both parties believe they will be better off. An allocation in which all voluntary exchanges have taken place is Pareto Efficient.

Another definition of efficiency is based on the **Kaldor-Hicks efficiency** criterion. A change is Kaldor-Hicks superior if those who gain from the change—for example, parties who gain from a tax change or from a change in a liability or property rule—could compensate theoretically those that have been harmed by the change and still have a net gain. The Kaldor-Hicks rule, which is often referred to as **cost-benefit** analysis, can be viewed as a quasi-Pareto rule—the gainers could compensate the losers, but they are **not** required to do so. Thus, in order to satisfy this cost-benefit efficiency standard, the harmed party does not actually have to be compensated for the harm that resulted from the policy change. The result is that changes in legal rules that meet the cost-benefit standard may involve non-compensated harms to some individuals. For example, the building of a new irrigation project may bring about benefits to farmers of $100 million at the cost to taxpayers of $75 million. This would be considered a Kaldor-Hicks superior move even though those who receive the benefits are not required to compensate the taxpayers.

The Kaldor-Hicks criterion is thought by planners to be a more practical basis for evaluating alternative public policies than the Pareto rule for the simple reason that the Pareto standard has severe informational requirements. Since it is virtually impossible to identify or measure all of the impacts of a change in legal rules, much of the impact being subjective and thus immeasurable, when most public policy analysts speak of efficiency, they mean Kaldor-Hicks efficiency. In general, when all potential changes that satisfy the criteria of Kaldor-Hicks efficiency are realized, then it is argued that resources are being allocated to their most highly valued uses. No one change can increase net benefits. Often, economic analyses of public policies are concerned with identifying the conditions under which changes that have net benefits can be achieved.

2. Equity v. Efficiency

The term **equity** refers to the distribution of income or wealth among individuals. Both equity and efficiency are accepted as goals of public policies on various issues. In contrast to the allocative concerns of efficiency, equity is concerned with the "division of the pie," rather than "maximizing the size of the pie." Another way of stating the relationship between equity and efficiency is that equity addresses distributional issues and efficiency addresses allocation issues. The discussion of Kaldor-Hicks efficiency illustrates some distributional considerations that may be involved in the analysis of changes in legal rules.

In many instances, equity and efficiency goals appear to be incompatible. The pursuit of either goal often involves costs in terms of reduced ability to pursue the other goal. The most straightforward example concerns a policy designed to impose an equitable distribution of income, where equitable is defined as equal. If everyone is entitled to the same income, the overall wealth of society will surely decline because there is no monetary reward for superior performance. The potential conflict between equity and efficiency arises in many areas of law and economics.

3. Efficiency and Public Policies

Positive economic analysis allows for the presentation of economic costs and benefits of alternative public policies; it does not require the analyst to impose their own value judgments. Understanding what is optimal from the perspective of allocative efficiency does not necessarily make it the best policy. In many areas, our political process has exhibited a willingness to sacrifice efficiency in order to achieve the furtherance of other social policies. The use of economic analysis can identify the magnitude of the allocative costs of a given policy before the trade-off is made.

United States v. Atlantic Richfield Company
United States District Court
429 F.Supp. 830 (E.D. Penn. 1977)

BECKER, J.

These cases raise issues concerning the proper construction and the constitutionality of the "civil penalty" provision of the oil and hazardous substance sections of the Federal Water Pollution Control Act Amendments of 1972 (FWPCA), § 1321 (b)(6) of 33 U.S.C. §§ 1251 *et seq.* (Supp. 1976).[1] The constructional issues boil down to whether Congress intended to impose the civil penalty on persons who spill oil accidentally, report such spill to the appropriate authorities, and clean it up at their own expense (hereinafter "accidental, reporting self-cleaners"). The constitutional issues of importance are: (1) whether a penalty imposed in such circumstances is irrational and, hence, a denial of due process; and (2) whether the penalty is in actuality criminal in nature so as to trigger various Sixth Amendment rights....

* * *

...In each case either Arco or Gulf owned or operated a vessel or facility from which oil was discharged in harmful quantity into the navigable waters of the United States. The discharges were "accidental" or "unintentional," but, perforce, they violated the prohibition on discharge of (b)(3); hence, without more, they subjected the owners (defendants) to liability for the civil penalty under (b)(6). However, the appropriate defendant (or its agent) promptly reported each spill and cleaned it up within the limits of technological feasibility and to the satisfaction of the Coast Guard. Despite defendants' compliance with their reporting and clean up duties, the Coast Guard, following the prescribed administrative procedure, assessed a civil penalty in each case. Upon defendants' refusal to pay, the government sued.

* * *

Defendants contend that where a discharge is accidental, either the reporting, or the cleaning up, or the combination of both, insulates them from (b)(6) liabil-

---

1. The FWPCA fundamentally revised the existing structure of federal water pollution control law. The changes in the "oil" section, § 1321, are either minor or irrelevant to these cases. The basic provisions at issue were reenacted from the Water Quality Improvement Act of 1970, 84 Stat. 91, formerly codified at 33 U.S.C. § 1161.

We have jurisdiction over these actions under 33 U.S.C. § 1321 (n). Because FWPCA contains this jurisdictional grant, we need not resolve the parties' dispute as to which other jurisdictional basis would be appropriate. The government claims that 28 U.S.C. § 1345, which provides for district court jurisdiction over any "civil action...commenced by the United States," is the proper basis. The defendants disagree and argue that 28 U.S.C. § 1355, providing jurisdiction over actions for fines or penalties, is the relevant grant. We note this disagreement because it is symptomatic of the parties' fundamental disagreement about the character of these cases.

ity. They characterize an accidental, reporting, self-cleaner as absolutely without fault. As a matter of statutory construction they argue: (1) that the scope of the (b)(5) immunity in "criminal [cases]" should be construed to reach (b)(6) penalties against accidental, reporting, self-cleaners; and (2) that the determination of whether (b)(3) was violated by a harmful discharge should measure harmfulness in light of the clean up results. Defendants' due process contention is that to impose the clean up costs attributable to those who do not report their spills and do not get caught upon accidental, reporting, self-cleaners is shocking to the conscience or, at least, irrational. Their claim to a Sixth Amendment jury trial and its incidents relies on the converse of their "statutory" claim; namely, that the statutory scheme and its legislative history demonstrates punitive intent and must be treated as creating a criminal penalty.

* * *

Most of defendants' statutory argument is designed to convince us that we should construe the phrase "criminal case" in (b)(5) as including the instant (b)(6) actions.... defendants claim that, as applied to accidental, reporting, self-cleaners, (b)(6) is really criminal rather than civil because, where defendants are not at fault, the penalty serves none of the ends of civil regulation, but acts only as a punishment....

* * *

The...defendants' argument goes as follows: The stipulated facts would not survive a motion to dismiss for failure to state a claim under the common law of negligence; *i.e.*, although the facts reveal "accidental" spills, they do not reveal a basis for inferring that defendants caused the spills through a lack of due care; but "negligence" is the lowest level of "fault" recognized by our law; *i.e.*, non-negligent conduct is reasonable conduct; therefore, if the spills were not negligent, we can infer that there was no reasonable means for defendants to prevent the spills.

We find that defendants' argument makes most sense when translated into simple economic terms. A rational owner of an oil facility, recognizing his potential liabilities for clean ups under § 1321 (and for damages under common law damage remedies which § 1321 leaves untouched), will attempt to minimize the costs of spills. To accomplish this he will calculate the marginal costs of preventing spills and of potential liabilities. He will thereupon engage in prevention to the point where the marginal cost of prevention equals his marginal liability for spills. Because that point defines *reasonable* spill prevention, a reasonable person will spend money for just that much prevention and no more. To spend less would be negligent. *See United States v. Carroll Towing Co.*, 159 F.2d 169 (2d Cir. 1947); Posner, *Economic Analysis of Law* (1972). To spend more would be wasteful or inefficient. See Ackerman, *Economic Foundations of Property Law*, at xi–xiv (1975) (brief definition and analysis of efficiency).

On this basis we can make some sense of defendants' argument that (b)(6) serves no regulatory purpose when applied to "faultless" spillers. But defendants move from the claim that they were "faultless" to the claim that no regulatory purpose would be served by imposing a (b)(6) penalty, an argument we reject because it proceeds from a faulty premise. While it is true that the stipulated facts about the spills themselves would not be sufficient to support an action in negligence, this is not such an action, but rather an action to enforce a penalty.

The elements of this statutory action are only that defendant violated (b)(3) and that the Coast Guard following the appropriate procedure assessed the (b)(6) penalty. The statute does not make "fault" an element of the cause of action, but rather a factor in the administrative penalty setting procedure. This is proper because there is no principle of law which requires that civil regulability through imposition of penalty be predicated upon a finding of fault. Moreover, a number of factors support civil regulability here in the absence of fault. First, as we explain more fully in our discussion of the Constitutional issues, *infra*, the principal goal of (b)(6) is to deter spills. Second, the Congressional purpose here was to impose a standard of conduct higher than that related just to economic efficiency. Additionally, the Congress obviously believed: (a) that no clean up effort could be complete because, after discharge, it is impossible to guarantee against residual harm from quantities of oil too small or too well dispersed to be detectable; and (b) that even the transitory pollution of waters was deleterious to the environment....

We concluded earlier that we have no power to conduct a *de novo* trial to establish the correct penalty; but we do, of course, have the power of judicial review under the Administrative Procedure Act of 1966, 5 U.S.C. § 551 et seq. That Act provides that adjudications, § 554, made at agency hearings, § 556, shall be subject to "judicial review in civil...proceedings for judicial enforcement," § 703, under the "substantial evidence" test, § 706 (2)(E). Actions to enforce (b)(6) penalties are appropriate occasions for such judicial review; however, despite our invitation, defendants have not brought the administrative record before us. Our task, at this juncture, is but to construe the statute.[11]

In view of the foregoing analysis we must reject defendant's contention that, as applied to accidental, reporting, self-cleaners, (b)(6) is really criminal rather than civil because, (1) the statutory language is not ambiguous; and (2) even where defendants are not at fault, the penalty does not act only as a punishment but serves the ends of civil regulation.

*   *   *

The constitutional guarantee of "due process" has been applied by the courts in myriad situations. Defendants argue that the application of the (b)(6) penalty to persons who have spilled oil, irrespective of whether the spill was accidental or not, of whether the spiller reported or not, and of whether the spiller cleaned up or not, is unfair and "shocking to the conscience."

The Supreme Court has, of course, held that "conduct that shocks the conscience" can reach the level of a due process violation. *Rochin v. California*, 342 U.S. 165, 172, 72 S. Ct. 205, 96 L. Ed. 183 (1952). However, for forty years that Court has consistently applied only a rationality test to economic regulation of business. Justice Roberts, in an early formulation of that test, stated: ["]If the laws passed are seen to have a reasonable relation to a proper, legislative purpose and are neither arbitrary nor discriminatory, the requirements of due process are satisfied.... ["]

*   *   *

---

11. Defendants' contention that (b)(6) as applied to accidental, reporting, self-cleaners serves no regulatory purpose is not solely constructional. Because it also sounds in due process, we have reserved our more theoretical response to the argument until the due process discussion. *See infra*, § III, B.

Defendants contend that it is irrational to charge a penalty against those who report and clean up their discharges in order to build a fund to pay for cleaning up the spills of those who do not report and do not get caught. The government responds that the (b)(6) penalties go into the revolving fund, whose use includes surveillance of the waters and supervision of clean ups. Therefore, the government claims there is a sufficient rational nexus between the behavior being penalized and the purpose of the revolving fund.

It may, of course, be argued that the rational nexus is broken or nonexistent because Congress did not authorize the assessment of (b)(6) penalties according to the demands on the revolving fund, or that the penalty setting procedure does not lead to assessments that fairly correspond to the costs attributable to the activities of a given defendant.

We believe, however, that there is a rational nexus between the behavior being penalized and the purpose of the revolving fund, in part because of the use of the fund to supervise clean up, but mainly because of the magnitude of the Coast Guard's surveillance task, given the length and breadth of our coastline and navigable waterways, and the need for a fund to support that effort. We note too that an accidental, reporting, self-cleaner might not always be so. However, the principal rational basis for (b)(6) as we see it lies not in the creation and use of the fund but in its deterrent purpose and the goal of preventing spills.

Earlier in the opinion we discussed briefly the notion of economic efficiency and its relationship to the legal notions of fault and deterrence. At that point we posited that the defendants' claim that they were faultless meant, in economic terms, that the marginal cost of prevention exceeded the marginal cost of clean up and damages. That posit rested on the "more is better" value concept which is central to classical economics. *See* Ackerman, *supra*. In that discussion we were trying to explain defendants' contention about fault, though we rejected them as being repugnant to the statutory intent. Now, however, we are not considering rationality as an economic notion but as a requirement of due process. We do not believe that the two are identical; *i.e.*, we believe that Congress has the power to elevate other values over economic efficiency and that it can properly design statutes to promote such values. Moreover, while the test of whether the statute is rationally designed will often take the form of an economic efficiency analysis, that analysis may itself be subordinated to the ultimate non-efficiency goal.

It is widely recognized that the FWPCA policy subordinates economic efficiency to the goals of clean water. The general declaration of "goals and policy" includes the elimination of all polluting discharges by 1985. 33 U.S.C. § 1251. And § 1321 announces an immediate no discharge policy for oil and hazardous substances. On the level of abstract policy neither section yields to simple claims of economic efficiency or accepts pollution on the ground that its prevention would be unreasonably expensive. *See* Wildavsky, *Economy and Environment/ Rationality and Ritual*, 29 Stan.L.Rev. 183, 191 (1976). Indeed, Dean Wildavsky has presciently analyzed the clash of values that has led to the frustration which the defendants in our case express:

> The exasperation with which [they] regard the behavior of the environmentalists and their political allies would be justified if everyone agreed the goals could be expressed in terms of economic rationality. Then the

means to this end would indeed be perverse—spending much to gain little....But it is precisely this mode of thinking in terms of opportunity costs to which environmentalists object.

       *   *   *

If purification is what you are after, more is better than less and you would expect to pay more for each increment. Confusion enters because the transactions occur between two worlds, so that homage must still be paid to the old economic costs and benefits while choices are predicated on quite different environmental values.

It is clear that Congress has rejected the economic efficiency or rationality test as the ultimate test of value under the FWPCA. Nonetheless, it has chosen to use economic means—the (b)(6) penalty in order to deter spills. It is only in evaluating whether the economic sanctions are reasonably calculated to deter, hence to achieve the non-economic values that Congress has selected, that the test of economic rationality is appropriate. It is our judgment that the economic sanction of the (b)(6) penalty is reasonably calculated to deter and to achieve those values. Defendants' due process claim must therefore be denied.

       *   *   *

Notes and Questions

1. Incentives Matter: In simple terms, the defendants argue that they are being forced to pay twice—first when they clean up the spill at their own expense, and again when they are hit with the civil penalty. Consider how the double payment affects their incentives to self-report and "voluntarily" clean up their spills. Is their least cost response to an accidental spill to clean-up the spill, but then not report it? Do the incentives created by the imposition of the civil penalty on accidental, self-reported, self-cleaned up spills require that they be backed up by criminal sanctions for non-reporters (whether the spill was accidental or cleaned-up)? What do you think the court means when it says "[W]e note too that an accidental, reporting, self-cleaner might not always be so?"

2. Overdeterrence: Accidents happen. The frequency with which they occur is often a function of the penalties associated with the accident. Thus, many accidents can be avoided, at a cost. Many accidents that harm the environment involve activities that are socially beneficial. For example, fuel oil pipelines move heating oil to areas that need to heat homes. One of the costs of moving the heating oil is the environmental damage caused by occasional pipeline leaks. Holding pipeline companies liable for the damage caused by the leaks forces the pipelines to exercise care up to the point where the marginal cost of exercising additional care is equal to the expected marginal reduction in clean-up costs associated with a spill. Adding fines and other penalties to the clean-up encourage the pipelines to exercise additional care. Additional care reduces the number of spills and increases the costs of operating the pipeline. This results in reduced production by the pipelines. Obviously, there is some rational limit to the imposition of fines—otherwise, we might as well ban the operation of fuel oil pipelines. At some point, the costs of deterring the social beneficial activity are greater than the benefits from reduced spills. Just as there can be underdeterrence, there can also be overdeterrence. Thus, deterrence of spills is a balancing act. Where the balance is struck often depends upon different subjective valuations of the costs of the environmental harms that result from spills. Could you argue that Congress did not reject an economic efficiency test of the value of FWPCA, but instead required that more than objectively determined costs should be included in evaluating the Act's requirements?

3. Waste: The court says that "FWPCA policy subordinates economic efficiency to the goals of clean water." Should this statement be read to condone economic waste? What criteria should policy makers use to determine when economic efficiency is "trumped" for other values? If we can achieve a given level of clean water at a lower cost, should we care? If the goals are not achieved at their lowest possible cost, who wins and who loses?

D. Government Intervention

Free enterprise, the freedom to pursue one's economic self-interest, is an intrinsic part of the capitalist system. Men and women are free to choose their own line of work with few or no governmental restraints or subsidies, and businesses and entrepreneurs are free to combine any resources at their command to produce products and services for profit. Workers and consumers are free to produce, purchase, and exchange any good or service, provided that their activity does not infringe on others' rights. Of course, individuals are not free of the constraints of limited resources and unlimited wants. Moreover, some actions are also constrained by the rule of law.

American capitalism as an economic system is based on the principle of *laissez-faire* (from the French, meaning, roughly, "to let do"). Laissez-faire has come to mean minimum government interference and regulation in private and economic lives. In a pure laissez-faire economy, government has a role limited to setting the rules—a system of law establishing and defining contract and property rights, ensuring national defense, and providing certain public goods that the private sector cannot and would not provide. Public goods are goods and services, such as roads, canals, and national defense, that are not always generated by market transactions.

In reality, the role of government in modern American capitalism is greatly expanded from merely setting the rules and providing public goods. No society has ever conformed to the laissez-faire ideal. In particular, in addition to government efforts to provide public assistance and to attempt to stabilize the economy, government intervention is often in response to widely recognized failures of the free market system.

Under some fairly well-defined circumstances, the market fails to produce the allocative efficiencies predicted by economic theory. A **market failure** is a situation where the private market fails to produce the optimal level of a particular good. Widely recognized market failures are information problems (market prices cannot reflect risk unless those risks are known), externalities (positive or negative third-party effects that are not considered in private decision making), monopoly (dominance of a product market by a single firm), and public goods (goods for which it is very costly to exclude consumption by individuals who are not willing to pay for the good). These market failures are discussed in greater detail later in this section.

Market failures are often viewed as justifications for government intervention in a market. The government can respond to market failures in a number of ways. One approach is for the government to not do anything at all. Such an approach could be a reflection of an ideological position that absolute freedom in the market place is more important than government intervention in the name of efficiency. This approach may also reflect a belief that the cost of the cure is often greater than the disease. A second approach, and one that occupies the opposite end of the continuum of possible responses, is for the government to takeover the market or industry and try to do a more efficient job. An intermediate approach calls for the government to intervene in the market as a regulator of certain limited activities of otherwise competitive firms. Regulation can range from requiring certain types of warnings on package labels, to tax incentives, to total control over prices.

This section begins with a more detailed consideration of market failures as a justification for government regulation. This is followed by an introduction to the principles of public policy analysis—the methodology for evaluating whether the government intervention is achieving its goals. A final subsection provides an introduction to public choice economics—a theory of why government regulation often fails to achieve its putative goals.

1. Market Failures

The four most widely accepted economic justifications for government intervention in the free market are information problems, externalities, monopoly, and public goods.

a. Information Problems

In the economist's purely competitive market, all economic actors are assumed to have perfect knowledge of all information relevant to making a decision. Under those conditions, the consumer's decision to purchase an "unsafe" product—for example, a product for which normal use results in a serious injury to 5 percent of the users over the useful life of the product—is simply a decision on the part of the consumer to bear the risk. Of course, the producer bears part of the risk in the form of a lower price. Thus, the market makes adjustments to properly account for risk. Similar examples of market adjustment under perfect information about relevant risks can be developed for the sale of risky securities and employment at unsafe workplaces. The fact that the market takes the risk into account means that the market is functioning properly—that is, according to theory.

In the real world, however, the market often fails to make adjustments because one of the parties to a transaction—typically the worker or consumer— does not have the information that is necessary to make an informed choice about the risk bearing that the individual is about to undertake. The failure of the market to assimilate all relevant information is referred to as an **information problem**. This is not to say that informed choices regarding risk are not commonly made in the real world. For example, a worker's decision to go to work for a company is based on many considerations, including hours, wages, retirement benefits, health insurance, job security, and working conditions (including safety and the overall environment). It is conceivable that a worker would accept a very risky job if the wages were high enough to compensate for the risk of getting killed. (The workers who hang girders in skyscrapers willingly accept the risk because either they prefer the risk, or they are compensated for it, or both). On the other hand, in many industrial workplaces there is a possibility of coming into contact with dangerous chemicals that may appear harmless, but may nevertheless have serious long-term effects. In some instances, even the employer will not know that the chemical is dangerous. Accordingly, the risk is not known. Obviously, the market cannot adjust to unknown risks. Thus, under some circumstances, government intervention in the form of safety inspections, research, and worker's compensation may be justified on efficiency grounds.

Several major federal regulatory schemes, including securities, consumer protection, and worker safety, are designed to correct the information problems in the market. The primary philosophy of the federal securities laws, which govern the issuance and trading of corporate stock and bonds, is the disclosure of information about the soundness of financial instruments. Even if the information disclosed reveals that the instrument is very risky, the company is allowed to sell the instrument because the investor is assumed to have based his or her decision to incur the risk on the information made available under the regulation. Product-safety and worker-safety legislation addresses some of the information issues raised in the preceding paragraphs. Consumer-protection legislation regarding deceptive trade practices and debtor-creditor relations may be viewed as government solutions to problems that can arise when one party to a transaction has an informational advantage. Here, the primary regulatory response is to require the disclosure of information in an understandable manner.

b. Externalities

The operation of the invisible-hand mechanism envisioned by Adam Smith was based in part on the assumption that producing firms incur all of the costs associated with the production of their product. The industrialization and urbanization of society have made individuals' actions much more interdependent than in Smith's time. In many instances, some of the costs of producing a product "spill over" and injure third parties that are not part of the production process. The total cost to society in terms of resources consumed is the sum of the private costs paid by the producer and the external costs—externalities—that must be borne by the third party. If the legal system does not provide for compensation to the third parties, then the producer will be able to operate at a cost of production that does not fully reflect the cost in terms of society's resources. Thus, the presence of externalities suggests that the social consequences of self-interested behavior may not always be in the interest of "society."

Pollution is the most obvious example of an externality. The traditional manner in which the law has dealt with externalities is through tort law. **Tort law** enables property owners to bring lawsuits whenever their private-property rights are infringed upon in a manner inconsistent with their use of the property. However, tort law is generally inadequate to handle the problems associated with externalities such as industrial pollution, because of the inability to define enforceable property rights in clean air and clean water. Moreover, a large number of individuals who may claim a right to clean air are not able to negotiate with the polluter because of the enormous transaction costs. Affected third parties often do not have the incentive or the legal right to bring suit. As a result, in some instances, tort law may be inadequate to force polluters to bear the full cost of their activities. In the absence of regulation, polluters will generally produce a greater output (of both goods and pollution) than would have been forthcoming in a competitive market with zero transaction costs and well-defined property rights. This overallocation of resources to the production of the product is considered a misallocation from society's perspective.

The misallocation of resources that results from the inability of the market to define or enforce property rights in "free" goods like air and water provides a theoretical justification for government intervention in the market. The federal government's response to externalities is reflected in a number of environmental protection statutes, which are the basis of several cases in this casebook.

c. Monopoly

The competitive market system is the primary regulator of the behavior of business companies. Rivalry generated in the pursuit of profits forces firms to produce at maximum efficiency. Competition among firms prevents the realization of excessive private economic power. As with any general rule, however, there are exceptions. For several different reasons, an individual firm (or group of competing firms acting as one firm) may occasionally dominate a particular market—that is, become a **monopoly**. For example, DeBeers dominates the world diamond trade because it controls the primary source of new diamonds.

Monopoly power may lead to a misallocation of resources that justifies government intervention in the market. A monopoly restricts the production of its product, resulting in buyers bidding up the product's price until the price becomes so high that some buyers decide to stop bidding (that is, they drop out of the market). The consumers who end up purchasing the product at the higher price have done so voluntarily and thus have indicated that the exchange is mutually beneficial. The economic problem with monopoly is that the potential gains from the mutually beneficial exchanges that would have occurred at the competitive market price, but which do not occur at the monopoly price, are not realized. Those potential gains from trade are lost forever. The consumers who dropped out of the market for the monopolized product will be able to spend their money elsewhere, but, since they would have preferred to purchase the monopolized good at the competitive price, they are worse off then they would have been in a competitive market. In summary, the misallocation of resources that results from a monopoly is related to the restriction of output, which suggests that resources are underallocated to the monopolized market. This market failure is developed in more detail in Chapter V.

The misallocation of resources attributed to monopoly is another theoretical justification for government intervention into the market. The federal antitrust laws are the government's response to this market failure. It is important to realize, however, that the antitrust laws present business with a perplexing paradox. On the one hand, becoming the biggest and the best at the particular business is

the goal of almost all firms; on the other hand, the antitrust laws do not look favorably upon firms that have grown to dominate their industry. Thus, it has been
suggested that the antitrust laws inhibit firms from maximizing their economic
potential. However, this inherent conflict is not generally much of a problem. Antitrust cases are presented and analyzed throughout this book.

d. Public Goods and Free Rider Problems

A public good is a good where consumption by one individual does not prevent its consumption by other individuals. This means that when a supplier supplies a public good to one person, he or she supplies the good to all. In contrast, a
private good is one that, when consumed by one individual, cannot be consumed
by other individuals. An example of a private good is a cheeseburger; once I eat
that cheeseburger, no one else can consume it. Individuals have an incentive to
hide their preferences or demands for public goods because they cannot be excluded from consuming public goods produced by others, so why should they volunteer to pay for such goods? For individuals, such **free riding** behavior is rational.

The classic example of a public good is national defense. National defense
must protect all individuals in the country; it is physically impossible to protect
some people and leave others unprotected. Everyone agrees that national defense
is needed. But will everyone, as individuals, supply it, or will everyone rely on
someone else to do it? Rational, self-interested people would like to enjoy the benefits of national defense, while letting everyone else pay for it. Because national
defense is a public good, if someone else defends the country, you are defended for
free. You can be a free rider. The problem is that everyone has an incentive to be a
free rider, but if everyone is a free rider, then there won't be any national defense.
In such cases, the government can step in to require that everyone pay part of the
cost of national defense to make sure that no one is a free rider.

2. Distributional Issues

Some individuals do not fare very well under the market system, while others
prosper. Lawyers, law professors, the federal government, the president, and
Congress devote much time, rhetoric, and effort to the issue of the equity of income distribution (or, as the case may be, income redistribution). Whether the
proposal is imposing new gasoline taxes, extending dairy price supports, or decreasing corporate income taxes, the matter of the equity of such an action is
sure to be debated. In following these debates, it becomes clear that there is
much genuine disagreement over what constitutes a fair distribution of income.
Opponents of higher gasoline taxes will argue that higher taxes on gasoline are
unfair to poor Americans who must use their cars to commute to work; in turn,
advocates of higher gasoline taxes will argue that it is only fair for car users to be
taxed, since they cause many of the pollution problems in urban areas. Members
of the farm lobby will argue for price supports on milk to increase the incomes of
poor dairy farmers; consumer groups will oppose the measure on the grounds
that it unfairly transfers income away from milk consumers.

Some economists also may have strong personal views concerning the equity
of various income distributions. However, economists recognize that their views

are subjective value judgments. In spite of his or her personal subjective views, most economists recognize that positive economic analysis cannot generate testable hypotheses concerning the optimal distribution of income in society. Because of their training in scientific methodology, most economists (as economists) are agnostic with regards to such questions.

Instead of evaluating the fairness of various income distributions, economists tend to focus on other aspects of redistribution proposals. In particular, they pay much attention to the efficiency consequences of various proposals to redistribute income. Although it is tempting to imagine that programs such as tax reform simply transfer income from those who need it less to those who need it more without any adverse side effects, redistribution never works so simply. Inevitably, some individuals will incur costs to avoid paying higher taxes, while others will adjust their circumstances to qualify for new subsidies. Due to such activity, it almost always ends up costing some groups in society more than a dollar for each dollar that is transferred to other groups. Economists, therefore, are aware that any program to redistribute income involves a trade-off between equity and efficiency. And, as discussed above, economists are ill-equipped to evaluate the correctness of such a trade-off.

Finally, as discussed in Chapter VIII, an individual's position in the income distribution depends on luck (health, genetic and financial inheritance, socioeconomic position), choice (incentives, investments in human capital and skills), and political decisions—taxes and public benefits—about the justice of market created distribution of income.

3. Principles of Public Policy Analysis

Public policy analysis uses all of the tools and perspectives of economics and the economic analysis of law. Several questions should be asked to determine whether a particular public policy should be implemented or modified. First, consider the justification for the government regulation—what is the market failure that is supposed to be corrected by the regulation? Second, are the regulatory policies achieving their goals? If yes, can they be achieved in a less restrictive or less costly manner? If no, can the goals be attained through other forms of regulation or should the market be left alone as the best, albeit imperfect, alternative?

A major tool of public policy analysis is cost-benefit analysis. Many public policy questions revolve around determining the proper degree of government intervention—that is, often the question is not whether intervention is desirable, but rather whether the coverage or extent of the intervention is optimal. Cost-benefit analysis attempts to address this issue by comparing the marginal costs and marginal benefits of different levels of regulation. The net benefit of engaging in any activity is maximized at the level of activity where the marginal benefit is equal to the marginal cost. Marginal analysis can identify situations where regulations have gone "too far."

A policy analyst who compares total costs and total benefits can reach the wrong conclusion. For example, the National Highway Traffic Safety Administration is charged with promoting safety on U.S. highways. An assumption justifying the existence of this federal agency is the need for government regulation of

Table II-1
Cost per Life Saved for Arsenic Regulation

Stringency	Standard Level (mg/m^3)	Average Cost Per Life Saved	Marginal Cost Per Life Saved
Loose	0.10	$1.25 Million	$1.25 Million
Medium	0.05	$2.92 Million	$11.5 Million
Tight	0.004	$5.63 Million	$68.1 Million

Source: W. Kip Viscusi, *Risk by Choice: Regulating Health and Safety in the Workplace* (Cambridge: Harvard University Press, 1983), p. 124.

automobile safety. The battles between the automobile industry and government regulators have been over marginal adjustments in mandated safety measures. Once the installation of safety glass and seatbeats was required, the marginal benefit of mandating airbags could be fairly small. Assume, for illustrative purposes, that the marginal benefit of requiring airbags is less than the marginal cost. The net benefit of adding airbags would be negative. However, if the benefits of installation of seatbelts and safety glass are large compared to the costs so that the *net* benefit (that is, benefits minus costs) of those measures is positive, then it is conceivable that the *total net* benefits of all mandated safety measures—seatbelts, safety glass, and airbags—would still be positive even though the marginal benefit of adding airbags was negative. Thus, a policy analyst who uses total analysis instead of marginal analysis would reach a different (and incorrect) decision.

Similarly, reliance on average costs and average benefits can lead to mistakes. Consider, for example, the Environmental Protection Agency's regulation of acceptable levels of exposure to arsenic.[2] Table II-1 shows that the average and marginal costs per life saved by moving from relatively loose to strict standards. Assume the regulators are using $7.5 million per life saved as the marginal benefit (Note that average benefit is equal to marginal benefit because the marginal benefit is constant.). Comparison of average cost per life saved to the value of the life saved indicates that the strict standard should be adopted. However, the comparison of marginal cost per life saved indicates that it would be very wasteful to require the strict standard. The loose standard would be optimal.

In analyzing a particular public policy, it is important to understand and maintain the distinction between positive and normative analysis; recognize that the concept of opportunity cost means that policies involve costly trade-offs; analyze trade-offs on the margin; and appreciate the fact that efficiency is a normative concept that is often sacrificed by policy makers to achieve other goals. Recall that the first step in policy analysis must be to examine critically the asserted link between the law or regulation and alleged market failure that it is supposed to be correcting.

---

2. This example is from W. Kip Viscusi, John M. Vernon, and Joseph E. Harrington, Economics of Regulation and Antitrust (Cambridge: The MIT Press, Second Edition, 1995), pp. 667–68.

American Financial Services Association v. FTC
United States Court of Appeals, District of Columbia Circuit
767 F.2d 957 (1985)

WALD, J.

* * *

The Credit Practices Rule as finally promulgated contains provisions relating to the following creditor remedies: confessions of judgment; wage assignments; security interests in household goods; waivers of exemption; pyramiding of late charges; and cosigner liability. Petitioners, as a whole, specifically challenge the provisions relating to wage assignments and security interests in household goods. The challenged provisions read in pertinent part:

(a) In connection with the extension of credit to consumers in or affecting commerce, as commerce is defined in the Federal Trade Commission Act, it is an unfair act or practice within the meaning of Section 5 of that Act for a lender or retail installment seller directly or indirectly to take or receive from a consumer an obligation that:

* * *

(3) Constitutes or contains an assignment of wages or other earnings unless:

(i) The assignment by its terms is revocable at the will of the debtor, or

(ii) The assignment is a payroll deduction plan or preauthorized payment plan, commencing at the time of the transaction, in which the consumer authorizes a series of wage deductions as a method of making each payment, or

(iii) The assignment applies only to wages or other earnings already earned at the time of the assignment.

(4) Constitutes or contains a nonpossessory security interest in household goods other than a purchase money security interest.

...Household goods are defined as:

(i)...Clothing, furniture, appliances, one radio and one television, linens, china, crockery, kitchenware, and personal effects (including wedding rings) of the consumer and his or her dependents, provided that the following are not included within the scope of the term "household goods":

(1) Works of art;

(2) Electronic entertainment equipment (except one television and one radio);

(3) Items acquired as antiques; and

(4) Jewelry (except wedding rings).

(j) *Antique.* Any item over one hundred years of age, including such items that have been repaired or renovated without changing their original form or character.

A non-purchase, non-possessory security interest in household goods ("HHG security interest") allows the creditor to seize and sell the debtor's household goods upon default without a judgment or court order. Similarly, a wage assignment allows the creditor to file the assignment with the debtor's employer and receive all or part of the debtor's wages until the debt is satisfied without first obtaining a court judgment. The Commission found that both these creditor remedies were "unfair" because they cause substantial and unavoidable injury to consumers which is not outweighed by countervailing benefits to consumers or competition. Petitioners argue that the Rule is beyond the Commission's section 5 authority to proscribe unfair practices because in the absence of seller overreaching in the form of deceit, coercion or nondisclosure of material information, the FTC may not intercede in the market as an "invisible hand" to obtain "better bargains" for consumers.

The petitioners' challenges to the household goods and wage assignment provisions of the Credit Practices Rule raise the following issues:...

> *   *   *

C. *The FTC's Exercise of Unfairness Authority Under Section 5(a)*

Applying the three-part consumer unfairness standard, the Commission found that HHG security interests and wage assignments were unfair creditor remedies because they caused substantial, unjustified consumer injury. Our analysis begins with a review of the Commission's reasoning with respect to each of the three criteria set out in the consumer unfairness standard.

1. *Substantial Injury*

In elaborating the term "substantial injury" in its Policy Statement, the Commission stated that in most cases substantial injury would involve monetary harm and that "ordinarily" "emotional impact and other more subjective types of harm" would not make a practice unfair. *See* Policy Statement at 36. The Commission further clarified that it "is not concerned with trivial or merely speculative harms." *Id.* "An injury may be sufficiently substantial, however, if it does a small harm to a large number of people, or if it raises a significant risk of concrete harm." *Id.* at n. 12. With these guidelines in mind, we turn to the specific injuries found to result from HHG security interests and wage assignments.

(a) Security interests in household goods. In return for credit, consumers may be required to give a non-possessory security interest in their household goods and personal effects. These goods may be seized by the creditor in the event of a default. *See* Credit Practices Rule, 49 Fed. Reg. at 7761. Such non-possessory security interests were not recognized at common law and are of comparatively recent origin. *Id.* Based on the rulemaking record, the Commission found the practice of securing loans with non-purchase, non-possessory security interests in household goods to be widespread, with finance companies being the preeminent users. *Id.* at 7762. HHG security interests may be created by simply checking a box labeled "chattel mortgage" or by other general provisions in the text of standard form contracts, thus, giving consumers little notice of the nature and extent of the collateral they are pledging. *Id.*

Based on evidence in the record, including the testimony of a large majority of industry witnesses, the Commission found that HHG security interests have little, if any, economic value to creditors. The creditors cannot ordinarily recover their loss on default by seizing and selling the goods. Consequently actual seizure of household goods by creditors is rare. The Commission summarized its findings as follows:

> The record reflects the fact that creditors rarely engage in actual repossession of household goods. When it does occur, the furniture and other items seized frequently have little or no economic value; occasionally, the act of seizure appears to be undertaken for punitive or psychological deterrent effect.

Id. at 7763 (footnotes omitted).

Although the household goods are of little value to creditors and are rarely seized, when seizure does occur the Commission found that it can have severe economic consequences for the consumer. The consumer, most likely already enmeshed in a financial crisis, loses the possession and use of household necessities such as furniture, appliances, linens and kitchenware. While the monetary gain realized by the creditor upon seizure and sale of goods is minimal to nonexistent, the replacement cost to the consumer is substantial, not to mention the sentimental value of the possessions and psychological impact of the loss on the consumer. "Thus seizure often imposes a cost on the consumer which is seriously disproportionate to any benefit the creditor obtains." *Id.*

The Commission further found that even in the absence of actual seizure, HHG security interests still resulted in injury to consumers. Creditors rely on HHG security interests primarily as a "psychological lever to seek payment and to persuade consumers to take other actions the creditors may deem appropriate...." *Id.* The Commission recognized that not all creditors use threats of seizure to coerce consumer response but concluded that "the preponderance of evidence supports a conclusion that such threats are commonplace." *Id.* at 7764. Because the loss occasioned by the seizure of household goods is so profound, threats of seizure in themselves are uniquely harmful and disruptive to the consumer and the family. *Id.* The injury resulting from "threats" or "suggestions" of seizure is not limited to psychological harm. Consumers threatened with the loss of their most basic possessions become desperate and peculiarly vulnerable to any suggested "ways out." As a result, "creditors are in a prime position to urge debtors to take steps which may worsen their financial circumstances." *Id.* The consumer may default on other debts or agree to enter refinancing agreements which may reduce or defer monthly payments on a short-term basis but at the cost of increasing the consumer's total long-term debt obligation. Consumers may also forego assertion of valid defenses, set-offs or counterclaims in their haste to reach acceptable repayment agreements so as to avoid the perceived imminent seizure of their property. *Id.* at 7764–65. In sum, consumers at risk of losing their household necessities will take steps which substantially worsen their overall financial condition.

(b) *Wage assignments.* A wage assignment allows the creditor, upon filing with the debtor's employer, to receive all or a portion of the debtor's wages directly from the employer. Wage assignments, unlike wage garnishments, do not require a judgment and can be filed without any judicial review of the creditor's claim. The Commission found that wage assignments were used primarily by small loan and finance companies in California, Illinois, Michigan and New York. *Id.* at 7757. Although estimates varied, the Commission concluded that wage assignments are prevalent in states where they are permitted and are used in a significant number of consumer transactions. *Id.*

The Commission found wage assignments particularly harmful to consumers because they can be invoked without the due process safeguards of a hearing and opportunity to present defenses. *Id.* Although some states provide debtors some statutory procedural protections allowing them to prevent effectuation of a wage assignment by serving a notice of defense on the employer and creditor, the Commission found such protective schemes generally ineffective, due to lack of awareness and understanding on the part of the debtor. "[D]espite the existence of state statutes, many wage assignments result in collection by creditors even when there have [sic] been a breach of warranty, fraud, or other violation of law that may constitute a defense to payment." *Id.* at 7758.

The rulemaking record further established that wage assignments injure consumers by detrimentally injecting the creditor into the employment relationship. Employers are hostile to wage assignments due to added administrative costs and burdens and the fear that the employee's job motivation and performance will suffer as a result of the reduction in wages. *Id.* Moreover, employers tend to view the consumer's failure to repay the debt as a sign of irresponsibility. As a consequence many lose their jobs after wage assignments are filed. Even if the consumer retains the job, promotions, raises, and job assignments may be adversely affected. *Id.*

Wage assignments are usually invoked at a time when the debtor is already experiencing severe financial hardship. Loss of a substantial portion of wages tends to cause further disruption of family finances and may even put at risk the wage earner's ability to provide necessities for the family. *Id.* at 7758–59. Even when wage assignments are not actually invoked, consumer injury may still result. As with HHG security interests, the Commission found that creditors use wage assignments as *in terrorem* devices to coerce consumers to pay. The invocation of a wage assignment or just simply the threat of invocation may lead a debtor to enter into costly refinancing, to improvidently default on other obligations, or to forego valid defenses. Thus consumers will act against their own best economic interests to avoid the greater potential injury of having creditors contact their employers and risk losing their jobs. "[C]reditors exploit that fear despite the fact that job loss would be economically counterproductive to the creditor." *Id.* at 7758.

The Commission, thus, concluded:

> In the absence of procedural safeguards, the potential for severe, substantial disruption of employment, the pressure that results from threats to file wage assignments, and the disruption of family finances constitute significant consumer injury. State law is inconsistent and does not offer sufficient protection to prevent this consumer injury.

Id. at 7759.

The harms to consumers resulting from the use of HHG security interests and wage assignments identified by the Commission on the basis of the rulemaking record are neither trivial or speculative nor based merely on notions of subjective distress or offenses to taste. The use of HHG security interests and wage assignments result in or create a significant risk of substantial economic and monetary harm to the consumer as well as potential deprivations of their legal rights. Hence the Commission clearly met its first criterion of establishing substantial consumer injury.

2. Countervailing Benefits

The Commission recognizes that most business practices entail a balancing of costs and benefits to the consumer. Therefore the Commission "will not find that a practice unfairly injures consumers unless it is injurious in its net effects." Policy Statement at 37. To make this cost-benefit determination, the Commission examines the potential costs that the proposed remedy would impose on the parties and society in general. In the present case, the Commission made the following assessment:

> The potential costs of most significance in this proceeding include increased collection costs, increased screening costs, larger legal costs and increases in bad debt losses or reserves. Increased creditor costs generally would be reflected in higher interests to borrowers, reduced credit availability, or other restrictions such as increased collateral or down payment requirements.

49 Fed.Reg. at 7744 (footnotes omitted).

In weighing the costs and benefits of the Credit Practices Rule to consumers and the credit industry, the Commission first noted that the potential cost of eliminating HHG security interests and wage assignments is diminished by the presence of other remedies retained by creditors under the Rule. Creditor remedies unaffected by the Rule include the right to take purchase-money security interests which allow for repossession of the particular item purchased, to obtain a deficiency judgment or bring a suit directly on the debt, and to garnish the debtor's wages. Thus, "[t]he remedies subject to the rule must be evaluated in light of their more *incremental* contribution to deterring default or reducing other creditor costs given remedies that remain available." *Id.* at 7744–45 (emphasis added).

Of course, to the extent HHG security interests and wage assignments actually reduce creditor costs, consumers will theoretically benefit by the greater availability of credit at a lower cost. In short, the crucial issue before the Commission was whether prohibiting HHG security interests and wage assignments would decrease availability and increase the cost of credit to consumers and, if so, whether this cost was outweighed by the benefits of the Rule to the same consumers (the benefits being the avoidance of the harms incurred by consumers as a result of the use of HHG security interests and wage assignments). Based on record evidence, the Commission concluded that the Rule would have only a marginal impact on the cost or availability of credit, and that this marginal cost was clearly overshadowed by the much greater risks to consumers resulting from the use of HHG security interests and wage assignments. *See infra* pp. 985–88. Thus we find that the Commission satisfied the second prong of the three-part consumer injury test set out in its Policy Statement.

3. Injury is Not Reasonably Avoidable

The requirement that the injury cannot be reasonably avoided by the consumers stems from the Commission's general reliance on free and informed consumer choice as the best regulator of the market. "Normally we expect the marketplace to be self-correcting, and we rely on consumer choice—the ability of individual consumers to make their own private purchasing decisions without regulatory intervention—to govern the market." Policy Statement at 37. As long recognized, however, certain types of seller conduct or market imperfections may unjustifiably hinder consumers' free market decisions and prevent the forces of supply and demand from maximizing benefits and minimizing costs. In such instances of market failure, the Commission may be required to take corrective action. Such corrective action is taken "not to second-guess the wisdom of particular consumer decisions, but rather to halt some form of seller behavior that unreasonably creates or takes advantage of an obstacle to the free exercise of consumer decisionmaking." *Id.* at 37.

The Commission found that the injuries occasioned by the use of HHG security interests and wage assignments are not reasonably avoidable by consumers for two interrelated reasons: (1) consumers are not, as a practical matter, able to shop and bargain over alternative remedial provisions; and (2) default is ordinarily the product of forces beyond a debtor's control. 49 Fed. Reg. at 7744. The Commission identified a confluence of factors which create "an obstacle to the free exercise of consumer decisionmaking" and which creditors are able to use to their advantage.

First, the Commission found that most creditors rely on standardized form contracts with boilerplate provisions defining the rights and duties of the parties. *Id.* at 7745–47. The Presiding Officer's Report concludes:

> Creditors universally make use of standardized forms in extending credit to consumers. These forms are prepared for creditors or obtained by them, and the completed contract is presented to the prospective borrower on a "take it or leave it" basis. The primary reason for this is simply that it is not feasible to conduct the transaction in any other way.

P.O. Report, J.A. at 395. The Commission acknowledges that standard form contracts are a business necessity for small-loan creditors. 49 Fed. Reg. at 7744. The Commission further found, however, that due to certain characteristics of the consumer credit market, it could not reasonably conclude that the mix of remedies included in the contracts reflects consumer preferences. *Id.* at 7744, 7746. Whereas consumers may bargain over terms such as interest rates, and the amount or number of payments, their ability and incentive to bargain over the boilerplate remedial provisions is substantially limited. *Id.* at 7746–47.

Several aspects of the credit transaction combine to prevent consumers from making meaningful efforts to search, compare, and bargain over remedial provisions. As noted, standard form contracts are presented on a take it or leave it basis. While there are differences in the kinds of contracts offered by different creditors, certain creditors, namely finance companies serving higher-risk borrowers, are most likely to include HHG security interests and wage assignments. Furthermore while the incidence of use of these provisions may differ across different regions of the country, contracts offered by creditors of a given class in local areas are often substantially identical. *Id.* at 7746. Given the substantial similarity of contracts, consumers have little ability or incentive to shop for a better contract.

Consumers' ability to shop and bargain is further constricted by the fine print and technical language used in the contracts. *Id.* at 7747. Moreover, consumers are limited in their ability to seek explanations from lenders since inquiries about remedies are likely to make creditors wary and hesitant to grant a loan. Finally, "[i]n some cases, comparison is impossible because the creditor re-

fuses to give out the loan contract until the borrower seems ready to sign it."
Id.[24]

Consumers' limited ability and incentive to search out better contracts is compounded by creditors' lack of incentive to advertise or compete on the basis of remedies. *Id.* Consumers' lack of understanding of contractual terms is the first obstacle. Before competing on the basis of exclusion or inclusion of particular contract terms, creditors would have to educate the consumer as to the ramifications of the inclusion of a particular clause and why a contract excluding the clause is preferable. Such an educational effort would entail substantial costs and would tend to create a free-rider problem with competing creditors reaping benefits from the advertising creditor's educational efforts. The second disincentive to creditors is the problem of adverse selection. If a creditor advertised less onerous remedies, the creditor is likely to attract a disproportionately greater share of those debtors who intend to or who are most likely to default.

The Commission also relied upon the fact that default is a relatively infrequent occurrence and generally not within consumers' control. *Id.* at 7747–48. Consumers could avoid the injuries attendant on the use of HHG security interests and wage assignments if they avoided defaulting on their payments. Relying principally on two large complementary survey studies of the causes of default, the Commission concluded that default is ordinarily the product of forces beyond the debtor's control. Default is usually precipitated by unforeseeable and unavoidable events that reduce income (*e.g.,* job loss or pay reduction) or increase demands (*e.g.,* incapacitation, relocation, unplanned emergency expenses, marital separation or divorce). When these events, outside the debtor's immediate control, occur default is generally an involuntary response. *Id.* at 7747. The unforeseeable and unavoidable nature of default not only make the implementation of the creditor remedies unavoidable but also limit consumers' incentive to search for contracts which do not include particular remedies. Since consumers do not expect to default, the invocation of particular creditor remedies seems remote and speculative at the time of contracting and thus is not a material element in the consumer's decision. Instead consumers quite reasonably focus their attention on the more immediate terms such as interest rates and payments. *Id.* at 7746.

On the basis of the foregoing analysis, the Commission concluded that consumers cannot reasonably avoid the inclusion of HHG security interests and wage assignments in credit contracts or their implementation. We conclude that the Commission's finding of unavoidable injury comports with the criteria set out in the Commission's Policy Statement.

---

24. Contrary to the dissent's assertion, discussion of the use of standard form contracts and fine print is *not* "empty rhetoric" simply because no deception is involved or because the Commission found that additional information would not alter the consumer's choice. See Dissent at 993; *see also infra* pp. 978, 989. As the discussion in the text illustrates, the Commission *relies* on these attributes of the contracts as contributing factors in its overall analysis of the characteristics of the consumer credit market which limit consumers' incentive and ability to bargain over remedial provisions and creditors' ability to compete on the basis of such terms.

D. *Challenge to the FTC's Exercise of Unfairness Authority Under Section 5(a)*

Although the Commission has identified a substantial consumer injury, which is not offset by countervailing benefits, and which cannot be reasonably avoided by consumers, petitioners nonetheless challenge the ban on HHG security interests and wage assignments as outside the scope of the Commission's unfairness authority...

In essence, petitioners ask the court to limit the FTC's exercise of its unfairness authority to situations involving deception, coercion, or withholding of material information. As noted earlier, despite considerable controversy over the bounds of the FTC's authority, neither Congress nor the FTC has seen fit to delineate the specific "kinds" of practices which will be deemed unfair within the meaning of section 5. Instead the FTC has adhered to its established convention, envisioned by Congress, of developing and refining its unfair practice criteria on a progressive, incremental basis....

      *   *   *

While we agree with petitioners that the Commission cannot be allowed to intervene at will whenever it believes the market is not producing the "best deal" for consumers, we nonetheless believe that this court would be overstepping its authority if we were to mandate, as petitioners urge, that the Commission's unfairness authority is limited solely to the regulation of conduct involving deception, coercion or the withholding of material information. As previously discussed, the Commission's consumer injury test, set forth in its Policy Statement, while not specifically defining the "kinds" of practices or injuries encompassed, is the most precise definition of unfairness articulated to date by either the Commission or Congress. Upon reviewing it, Congress has not seen fit to enact any more particularized definition of unfairness to limit the Commission's discretion. Indeed, the most significant congressional response to the Policy Statement has not been criticisms or rejection, but proposals to enact the Commission's three-part consumer injury standard into law. *See supra* pp. 970–71, n. 14. Thus, the Commission has, for all practical purposes, been left to develop its unfairness doctrine on an incremental, evolutionary basis. *See supra* p. 967. At this juncture, it is not for this court to step in and confine, by judicial fiat, the Commission's unfairness authority to acts or practices found to be deceptive or coercive. Our role is simply to review the Commission's exercise of its unfairness authority in this case. *See supra* pp. 968–69. We find that the Commission's articulated rationale for its determination that the taking of HHG security interests and wage assignments constitute unfair practices fully comports with the criteria set out in the FTC's Policy Statement. The Commission has sufficiently identified and documented the factors resulting in an obstacle to free consumer decisionmaking which is being exploited by creditors to the detriment of consumers.[59] We cannot

---

59. The dissent claims that the Commission cannot intervene "when it does not know the 'obstacle to free choice.'" See Dissent at 994. As the foregoing discussion illustrates, however, this is not a case where the Commission failed to articulate and document the factors resulting in an obstacle to free consumer choice. The dissent simply chooses to disregard the Commission's comprehensive analysis of the confluence of factors which create an obstacle to free consumer choice and a self-correcting market. Instead, the dissent places principal reliance on the fact that HHG security interests and wage assignments are used primarily by finance companies dealing with lower-income, higher risk borrowers, whereas higher-income, creditworthy consumers may obtain credit without these onerous provisions. Thus while the dissent acknowledges that an obstacle to the free exercise of consumer decision-

therefore say that the Commission has exceeded the boundaries of its statutory authority to define unfair practices in this case.

The Commission's economic rationale for finding the taking of HHG security interests and wage assignments to be unfair practices is additionally bolstered by considerations of equity and public policy. It is well established that certain types of contracts or contractual provisions may be prohibited simply because they violate accepted principles of fair play and equity, e.g., contracts of adhesion. *Cf.* U.C.C. § 2-302 (1978) (unconscionable contracts or clauses). And courts have recognized that the Commission was never intended to disregard principles of equity in reaching its decisions. *See Sperry & Hutchinson,* 405 U.S. at 244, 92 S. Ct. At 905 (FTC may "like a court of equity" consider "public values beyond those enshrined in the letter or...spirit of the antitrust laws"); *FTC v. Standard Educ. Soc'y,* 86 F.2d 692, 696 (2d Cir. 1936) (Hand, J.) (FTC's "duty in part at any rate, is to discover and make explicit those unexpressed standards of fair dealing which the conscience of the community may progressively develop"), *rev'd on other grounds,* 302 U.S. 112, 58 S.Ct. 113, 82 L. Ed. 141 (1937) (reversing that part of Second Circuit's holding which modified and weakened FTC's cease and desist order); *see also Spiegel, Inc. v. FTC,* 540 F.2d 287, 292 (7th Cir. 1976) (invoking a public policy rationale and stating that FTC has "authority to prohibit conduct that, although legally proper, [is] unfair to the public"). In its Policy Statement, the Commission states that considerations of public policy are frequently used as confirmatory evidence of the unfairness of a particular practice but that "[s]ometimes public policy will independently support a Commission action." Policy Statement at 38–39. *See generally* Averitt, *supra* note 15, at 275–78 (discussing FTC's reliance on public policy considerations); Craswell, *supra* note 15, at 135–39 (discussing FTC's reliance on considerations of equity).

In the present case, the Commission found that wage assignments are prohibited in Uniform Credit Code states, several other states, and the District of Columbia. 49 Fed.Reg. at 7756. The substantial majority of states permitting wage assignments impose restrictions on their use. *Id.* Similarly, several states prohibit the taking of non-possessory, non-purchase security interests in household goods, and others place limitations on their use. *Id.* at 7781–82 & n.10. Both the NCCF study and the Creditor Remedies Project, which provided the impetus for the Commission's rulemaking, *see supra* pp. 961–62, delineated the creditor abuses and concomitant consumer injuries entailed in the use of HHG security interests and wage assignments, and recommended that the use of these creditor remedies be substantially restricted or eliminated. In addition, the Commission stated its opinion that:

> [T]he use of blanket security interests to exhort an overextended or unemployed consumer to make a decision which may lead to increased fi-

---

making does exist for the lower-income, higher-risk consumer, it finds this justified by the higher risk level of these borrowers and consequently not evidence of a market failure. But the fact that the Commission's analysis applies predominantly to certain creditors dealing with a certain class of consumers (lower-income, higher-risk borrowers) does not, as the dissent suggests, undercut its validity. The Commission has identified a market failure with respect to a particular category of credit transactions which is being exploited by the creditors involved to the detriment of the consumers involved, and thus the dissent's argument that higher-income, more creditworthy consumers can obtain credit on better terms from banks is unavailing.

nancial difficulties has many of the attributes of economic duress. Threats to seize the personal possessions of a consumer and his or her family clearly meet many of the criteria for economic duress, especially given the dire financial circumstances in which the consumer finds himself. Although the Commission has premised its findings regarding the unfairness of threats to seize household goods on the resulting psychological and economic injury to consumers, as demonstrated by information contained in the rulemaking record, these common law doctrines provide evidence of public policy supporting the Commission's findings.

49 Fed.Reg. at 7765 (footnotes omitted). Thus the Commission's exercise of its unfairness authority in proscribing the use of HHG security interests and wage assignments can be fairly viewed as falling within the Commission's authority to take into consideration principles of equity and public policy and to proscribe acts or practices found to violate those principles.

*   *   *

V. CONCLUSION

After carefully considering each of petitioners' challenges, we conclude that the FTC has not exceeded its authority to promulgate rules proscribing unfair practices under sections 5(a) and 18(a) of the FTC Act. Accordingly, AFSA's and SCDCA's petitions for review are *Denied*.

TAMM, J. dissenting

The Commission's decision to ban security interests in household goods and future earnings is in excess of its statutory authority to regulate unfair trade practices. Although rationalized in terms of "market imperfection" and "consumer choice," the Commission's action reflects nothing more than its paternalistic judgment that lenders should not extend credit to low-income consumers. Such a judgment not only violates the approach to consumer protection outlined in the Policy Statement but also will have the practical effect of forcing needy consumers out of the credit market. I therefore dissent.

*   *   *

Because no market responds perfectly to consumer choice, any market could conceivably be subject to wholesale Commission regulation. The reviewing court's first task, therefore, is to ensure that the Commission's intervention is a genuine response to a market failure "which prevents free consumer choice from effectuating a self-correcting market," Maj. op. at 981, and not a disguised attempt to impose a paternalistic purchasing decision upon consumers. To perform this task adequately, the court must insist that the Commission sufficiently understand and explain the dynamics of the marketplace. Furthermore, unless the Commission manifests an understanding of how the market responds to consumer choice, it cannot measure the costs and benefits of Commission intervention.

If the Commission has identified with sufficient clarity the impediment that blocks the market's natural allocation, it *may* be appropriate for the Commission to intervene. Whether intervention is appropriate, and if so, what form it should take, can only be answered by weighing the costs and benefits of the Commission's action.

III. APPLICATION OF THE UNFAIRNESS TEST

A. *Market Failure or "Reasonably Avoidable Injury"*

The Commission discusses market failure in terms of what the consumer can "reasonably avoid"; if the consumer can "reasonably avoid" the practice, there is no market imperfection and, hence, no justification for intervention. The most common example of an injury consumers cannot "reasonably avoid" occurs when a seller has failed to disclose a risk involved in the exchange. Although the Commission states that the consumer's ability to shop and bargain for credit remedies is constricted by fine print and technical language, it found not only that consumers generally understand the consequences of default, but that more information would not lead to different consumer decisions. 49 Fed.Reg. at 7746–47. Moreover, while it is true that creditors present standard form credit contracts on a take-it-or-leave-it basis, everyone in this proceeding recognizes that such contracts are the only efficient method of conducting loan transactions. *Id.* Presiding Officer's Report at 76, J.A. at 410 ("It is, beyond doubt, absolutely necessary to use form contracts in the interests of both creditors and consumers. Without such aids the consumer credit marketplace could not function in a reasonably efficient manner."). Creditors, therefore, do not unfairly take advantage of a market imperfection by imposing upon consumers hidden risks. Discussion by the Commission and the majority about standard form contract and fine print is thus empty rhetoric, completely irrelevant to the market analysis.

Lacking any evidence of inadequate or undisclosed information that would distort consumer choice, the Commission alternatively concludes that consumer choice is restricted because consumers do not have access to standard form contracts that do not contain the provisions in question. This conclusion rests on one of two premises — one factually incorrect, the other theoretically bankrupt.

First, the Commission could mean that consumers generally do not have access to loan contracts without these provisions. This is wrong as a matter of fact. Millions of consumers acquire credit each year without pledging any collateral. Millions more, forced to do business with pawnbrokers or loan sharks, do not even have access to loan contracts *with* these provisions. It is not simply common sense and everyday experience, however, that refutes the Commission's finding. The Presiding Officer found that "[i]t was generally agreed that consumers shopping among different classes of creditors *would find differences in terms* offered by banks as opposed to finance companies." J.A. at 404 (emphasis added).

Second, the Commission could mean that *high-risk* consumers do not have access to loan contracts that do not contain these provisions. Some consumers, to be sure, cannot avoid these provisions in loan contracts, so the provisions may constitute, for those consumers, an "obstacle to the free exercise of consumer decisionmaking." *Policy Statement* at 7. This phenomenon reflects a market failure, however, only if one is willing to accept the proposition that the high-risk consumer should be free to choose the same credit as the credit-worthy consumer. Under the Commission's reasoning, since not every driver can choose the lowest insurance premium, by selling more expensive automobile insurance to the high-risk driver, the insurer takes advantage of an "obstacle to free choice." The only obstacle to free choice identified by the Commission is the level of risk the borrower, like the insured, brings to the transaction.

The Commission's analysis of the credit marketplace mocks the approach to consumer protection outlined in the Policy Statement. In the Policy Statement, the Commission asserts that the *status quo* is presumed to be the product of a well-functioning market. In the Credit Practices Rule, the Commission turns this presumption on its head: it proceeds from an *a priori* vision of the mix of options that would be available in a "well-functioning market," and, with little difficulty, concludes that the existing market, which does not provide that mix, is "imperfect." As the majority recognizes, the Statement prevents the Commission from intervening whenever "it believes the market is not producing the 'best deal' for consumers." Maj. op. at 982. Yet this is precisely what the Commission has done in this case. It simply identifies a particular class of consumers (those who cannot avoid loan contracts without security interests in household goods and future earnings) and concludes that those consumers ought to have access to credit without pledging household goods—that is, those consumers ought to have credit at a *better price.*

This is not to suggest that the credit marketplace responds perfectly to consumer choice. To justify its intervention, however, the Commission must at least rationally explain *how* the market fails to respond to consumer choice. Allowing the Commission to intervene when it does not know the "obstacle to free choice" essentially reverses the presumption that each person is the best judge of his or her own needs. Such a paternalistic approach to consumer protection is fundamentally incompatible with the limits imposed upon the Commission's authority in the Policy Statement.

B. *The Cost-Benefit Analysis*

The Policy Statement's definition of "unfairness" provides that for an unavoidable consumer injury to be unfair, "the injury must not be outweighed by any offsetting consumer or competitive benefits that the sales practice also produces." *Policy Statement* at 6. Business practices entail a mixture of costs and benefits for consumers. Purchase money security agreements in automobiles, for example, can be a great cost to consumers because, upon default, consumers must forfeit the automobile, in many circumstances a vital necessity, or face costly refinancing agreements. The security agreements cannot be deemed unfair, however, because the benefits of the trade practice—making credit available to those who wish to purchase automobiles—clearly outweigh the costs.

The Commission makes two fatal errors in its cost-benefit analysis of security interests in household goods. First, in measuring the costs of these security interests, the Commission fails to separate the injury *caused by* these creditor practices from the financial and emotional hardships that inevitably accompany default. Second, in evaluating the offsetting benefits of these provisions, the Commission never squarely addresses the single critical question: the extent to which the intended beneficiaries of the Rule depend upon the ability to pledge household goods and future earnings to acquire credit.

*   *   *

The economic hardships that inevitably accompany indebtedness and default will remain despite the prohibition of these creditor remedies. The Commission, therefore, grossly exaggerates the beneficial impact of the Rule. The Rule does not eliminate the need for credit, does not provide debtors with any more cash with which to discharge obligations, does not make default a less likely occurrence, does not relieve the financial and emotional hardships that accompany default, does not insulate household necessities from forfeit, does not protect consumers from unscrupulous lenders intent in any event upon breaking the law, and does not lessen the compounding burden unpaid debts place upon debtors.

2. Offsetting Benefits

Security interests in household goods benefit consumers to the extent that they enable consumers to acquire credit without resorting to the pawnbroker or the loan shark. The Commission, however, never squarely addresses whether any consumers' access to credit depends upon their ability to pledge household goods as collateral.[7] Instead, it evaluates the impact of the Rule—not upon the high-risk consumer it purports to protect—but upon the credit-worthy consumer who needs no protection from these "abusive" credit practices in the first instance.

The Presiding Officer considered this question and came to the following conclusion:

> However, this record does support the conclusion that the ability to take household goods as security is of very great importance to finance company creditors and that loss of this right would *undoubtedly have a very considerable impact on their operations and upon the availability of credit to consumers.*

Presiding Officer's Report at 162, J.A. at 494 (emphasis added). In a feeble attempt to weaken the force of the Presiding Officer's conclusions, the Commission states that the definition of "household goods," narrowed since the Officer's report, would address the problems of availability. Thus, the Commission notes, under the new definition of "household goods," consumers may still pledge works of art, antiques, jewelry, video tape recorders, home computers, and the like. Similarly, the Commission puts great stock in the finding that forty percent of finance company clients are homeowners and therefore have other assets to pledge. Furthermore, the Commission states, banks, which seldom take security interests in household goods or future earnings, remain available to the consumer.

What happened to the high-risk consumer the Commission so vividly describes when assessing the hardships caused by the creditor remedies? That consumer owned household goods of "little or no value." He had no cash with which

---

7. The majority seems to place great weight on the econometric analysis conducted by various participants in the rulemakings, evidence which "by all accounts, contains deficiencies which prevent definitive answers." Maj. op. at 987. In spite of these deficiencies, however, the majority insists that the evidence reveals that the Credit Practices Rule "would have only a marginal impact on the cost or availability of credit." Id. at 33. What is "marginal" apparently is in the eyes of the beholder. The econometric studies revealed that the Credit Practices Rule would cost in 1979 between $623 million and $10.6 billion in increased interest rates. J.A. at 1528. I would agree, however, that the Rule has a *"marginal"* impact on credit availability: that is, those consumers currently at the *margin* will be forced out of the credit marketplace.

to pay back the loan, no assets to liquidate to prevent the forfeiture of household necessities or the imposition of "costly refinancing arrangements." In assessing the impact of the Rule upon the availability of credit, the Commission converts the distraught debtor into a homeowner, able to acquire credit without pledging his household goods because he can always visit his suburban bank or pledge his handy Matisse. The problem with the Commission's analysis is that the Rule unfortunately does not make the poor rich, or the high-risk consumer credit worthy. The Commission proves only that security interests in household goods cost the high-risk consumer more than they benefit the credit-worthy consumer.

Rather than address the Presiding Officer's conclusions, the Commission wishfully insists that creditors *should* extend credit to low-income, high-risk consumers without requiring from them security interests in household goods. 49 Fed. Reg. at 7766. Such security interests are of no real value to the creditor, the Commission reasons, because they do not deter default. Default cannot be deterred by security interests because it flows from circumstances beyond the debtor's control. This is nonsense on stilts. First, according to the record, twenty-five to thirty percent of defaulting debtors do so because of circumstances *within* their control. Five percent default because of "debtor irresponsibility"; twenty-five percent because of "voluntary overextension." *Id.* at 7748. The Commission never considers, however, whether eliminating these security interests would increase the number of debtors who default because of "voluntary overextension" or "debtor irresponsibility."

Second, even if every default occurred for reasons beyond the debtor's control, the Commission's conclusion that security interests do not deter default is a mammoth *non sequitur*. The Commission's reasoning is this: household goods security interests do not deter those who default; therefore, by eliminating the security interest the rate of default will not increase. By the Commission's logic, the existence of criminal laws does not deter those who violate the law. Can we therefore repeal the criminal laws and expect no impact upon crime? Of course not; just as we evaluate the impact of criminal laws upon those who do not violate the law, so must we evaluate the impact of security interests upon those who do not default. As the Commission found, a majority of consumers face financial trauma that could result in a default. 49 Fed. Reg. at 7748. Yet only a small number of consumers actually default. *Id.* This disparity is explained to some extent by the varying degrees of financial trauma that individual consumers undergo. Unrebutted evidence in the record and a healthy dose of common sense also suggest, however, that the more equity a debtor has in collateral the less likely he is to default. *See* Bureau of Social Science Research, *Federal Trade Commission Proposals for Credit Contract Regulations and the Availability of Consumer Credit* 129, J.A. at 1518 (the ratio of the value of collateral to the size of the loan "is the principle determinant of the probability of default"). If, as common sense and record evidence suggest, security interests in household goods do deter default, lenders will rationally refuse to extend credit to at least some consumers who have no other assets to pledge. See Presiding Officer's Report 162, J.A. at 494 (elimination of household goods security interests "would undoubtedly have a very considerable impact...upon the availability of credit"). Derailed by its faulty logic, the Commission never makes the critical finding of how many low-income consumers, the intended beneficiaries of the Rule, will be unable, because of the Credit Practices Rule, to obtain credit.

IV. CONCLUSION

The flaws in the Commission's analysis form an intriguing pattern, a pattern resulting from the imperfect superimposition of the "market failure" and "consumer choice" rationale upon a simple, paternalistic judgment: those whose access to credit depends upon the pledge of meager household goods and future earnings would be better off if creditors were unable and unwilling to extend to them credit. If this is the rationale underlying the Rule, most, if not all, inconsistencies in logic and shortcomings in evidence disappear. The imperfections of the marketplace need not be understood because it is not the obstacle to free choice that the Commission wishes to prevent but the free exercise thereof. Similarly, the harms caused by these practices need not be separated from the harms that inevitably accompany default because, if excluded from the credit marketplace altogether, these consumers will avoid not only these security interests but also all the other attendant hardships of default. Consumers who do not seek credit will, of course, avoid "costly refinance agreements" and never default "improvidently" on other loans. The Commission need not evaluate the impact of the Rule upon the intended beneficiary because the intended beneficiary, in its benevolent judgment, should not be seeking credit in the first instance.

The consumer law specialists involved in this case have at least been forthright in their support of the Credit Practices Rule. People who must pledge household goods or future earnings to acquire credit, they testified, would be better off without credit. Presiding Officer's Report at 162, J.A. at 484. Although held with genuine compassion, this belief cannot form the basis for the decision. First, it assumes that government intervention will eliminate the need for credit and that these people will not find credit elsewhere. Credit will be made available to them, however, by the pawnbroker or, worse, the loan shark, whose "creditor remedies" are infinitely more severe than those banned by the decision. Second, *"these people" are not children.* To suggest that "they" are incapable of making such decisions for themselves replaces healthy respect for the choice of the individual with unwarranted confidence in the wisdom of those who happen to be in power. Aware that such an approach to consumer protection is antagonistic to the basic principles outlined in the Policy Statement submitted to Congress, the Commission has couched its purely paternalistic judgment in terms of the market failure and cost-benefit analysis with enough skill to sneak past a court anesthetized by a misplaced deference to agency authority. If judicial review is to have any meaning, however, agency action must be tested by the basis upon which it purports to rest and not by an agenda hidden from the court. *See* SEC *v. Chenery Corp.*, 318 U.S. 80, 95, 63 S. Ct. 454, 87 L.Ed. 626 (1943). Tested against the approach to consumer protection outlined in the Policy Statement, the Commission's decisionmaking must fail. I therefore respectfully dissent.

Notes and Questions

1. Public Policy Analysis: Consider the justification for the Credit Practices Rule — what is the market failure that is supposed to be corrected by the regulation? Is the market failure corrected by the Rule? At what cost? Can the regulatory goals be achieved in a less restrictive or less costly manner? If no, can the goals be attained through other forms of regulation or should the market be left alone as the best, albeit imperfect, alternative?

2. Debtors on the Margin: Is the Rule likely to help the debtors it was intended to help?

3. Cost-Benefit Analysis of Regulations: Most federal agencies are required to perform a cost-benefit analysis of proposed regulations. Several cases in these materials involve review of the governments analysis. For example, the CAFE standards case *(Competitive Enterprise Institute v. NHTSA)* in Chapter I was a challenge to NHTSA's cost-benefit analysis which failed to take into account the possibility that additional people would die in automobile accidents as the regulations forced people into smaller cars.

E. Public Choice Economics: A Theory of Government Failure

Most of economics is concerned with private choices. Numerous analytical tools, such as the supply-and-demand model and marginal analysis, have been developed to help economists understand how markets work. Public choice economics applies the methodology of economics to political decision making. In other words, it applies generally accepted principles of rational economic behavior to decisions made by politicians, bureaucrats, and interest groups.

The basic assumption of public choice economics is that political decision makers behave just like consumers and businesses—they attempt to maximize their own self interest. For example, the politician is viewed as responding to incentives in the same utility maximizing manner when making legislative and executive decisions as he or she does when shopping for groceries, housing, or an automobile. This is hardly a startling revelation for long-time observers and participants in the Washington public policy arena, but it is important to take these incentives into consideration when analyzing laws, regulations and other new political institutions. In this view, interest groups, lobbyists, politicians, bureaucrats, and even public policy analysts, have one thing in common—they all are entrepreneurs. They are constantly looking to exploit opportunities for gain within the political system. As a consequence, much government regulation fails to achieve its putative goals.

This section illustrates the public choice perspective by considering the incentives of two groups involved in the development of public policies—politicians and bureaucrats. Government policy making is far removed from the anonymous decision making that characterizes market transactions. Although markets appear to be chaotic, they guide resources to their highest value uses when allowed to work. In contrast, government is personal and political, and it is a serious mistake to talk about "the government" or "the federal and state governments" as if they are benevolent despots. When "the government" guides the allocation of resources, every decision becomes a political decision. Moreover, it is naive to view government decision makers as merely benign agents of the people, carrying out the people's will.

1. Interest Groups, Rent Seeking, and Rent Extraction

The public choice perspective on legislation suggests that interest groups compete against one another for the passage of favorable legislation. In this view, legislation is the result of a rent-seeking process in which legislation is "sold" by legislators and "bought" by the highest bidders. Special-interest legislation provides relatively large benefits (rents) to a relatively small, but well-organized group, at the expense of a much larger number of unorganized voters—taxpayers and consumers. A large amount of empirical research provides support for interest-group explanations for the emergence of economic regulations that apply to specific industries. Interest groups demand—and all levels of government supply—protective regulation, monopoly, and other special privileges. The political activity of interest groups seeking special favors from legislators and other government decision makers is referred to as **rent seeking**, where the excessive (monopoly) profits earned by interest groups as a result of their political activity are referred to as rents. Recently, this approach to legislative activity has incorporated a more entrepreneurial role for legislators.

Money for Nothing: Politicians, Rent Extraction, and Political Extortion
Fred S. McChesney
(1997) pp. 20–23, 41–42

* * *

Extraction of Politically Created Rents

...the basic economic model of regulation...remains one of rent creation. Rent creation is the standard perspective undoubtedly because...the economic model of regulation...[is]...one of *exchange*....Politicians and their beneficiaries conclude a bargain that, like the typical contract, makes them both better off. Newly created rents are exchanged for votes and money; the multiparty auction allocates rents across groups. To the understandable confusion of lawyers, economists frequently use the word "bribe" to describe the "consideration" (the lawyers' term) paid over—quite legally—to politicians in return for regulatory favors.

It is not surprising that, perhaps instinctively, economists would turn to models of contract (exchange) to model regulation. Economics is often described as the study of the allocation of scarce resources among competing ends....The principal mechanism by which scarce goods and services are allocated in market-based economies is exchange. Thus, economists have been interested in exchange since the development of economic science as a distinct discipline. Adam Smith began *The Wealth of Nations* (1776) with a description of people's "propensity to truck, barter and exchange one thing for another."

But analysis of regulation via a contract-based model entails three conceptual problems. First, the essence of contract is Pareto superiority: contracting parties are better off, and no one is worse off. That is obviously not true in the regulatory setting, where the benefits to producers (to some extent shared with politicians) come at the expense of consumers.[8] ... But there remains the problem of how to fit these losses into an overall notion of regulatory exchange or contract.

Second, consider that the "contract" between regulator-supplier and regulated beneficiary is not an ordinary legal contract. Payment is made in order to make the private party better off, and in the process the politician gains as well. But were the politician to take the money and then refuse to create the rents, the aggrieved private party would have no legal recourse. The law effectively does not prohibit an agreement involving money in exchange for political favors (although ... it does regulate it). But the law does not enforce it, either.

The rent-creation contract is not illegal, but extralegal. The parties to the regulatory contract therefore must find their own, self-help ways to ensure that the promised performance is rendered on both sides. In this sense, rent creation is no different from any number of private exchanges made every day, in which individuals rely on one another's good faith and the desirability of continued relations, not the courts, for enforcement of the agreement.

Describing regulation as essentially a contract between politicians and regulated beneficiaries entails a third conceptual question: might other sorts of relationships also exist between the two groups? In the real world, voluntary contracts do not make up the complete set of human interactions. ... People are thrown together involuntarily — on one side at least, if not both — in settings involving torts, even crimes, such as theft.

Obviously, these interactions do not leave both sides better off. But to the criminal (thief), the fact that his victims suffer while he gains is of scant importance. His only concern is whether he gains more through the involuntary exchange (theft) than he could by any voluntary exchange.[9]

In short, bribery (contract) is not the only form of interaction observed in the world. "In the general case, the individual will observe two ways to persuade: by a threat and by a bribe." In the course of the ordinary day, an individual will typically combine bribes to some people (for example, his spouse) with threats to others (for example, his children) in order to induce the behavior that is desired or expected. Other people do the same with him: his boss probably relies on a combination of carrots and sticks.

Why would politicians not use the same dual strategy in their dealings with people? Certainly, private beneficiaries may pay bribes (legal or illegal) to politicians for regulatory largesse. But instead of or in addition to accepting bribes, might not politicians also take, or extort, from private parties?

---

8. Indeed, since the losses to consumers must be greater than the gains to producers, the regulatory contract is not even Kaldor-Hicks superior, which is the same as saying that regulation, unlike private contracts, is on net wealth-reducing.

9. ... Of course, an agreement to make payments to avoid imposition of harm could be called a contract, in the same sense that responding to the choice "Your money or your life," offered by one wielding a gun, could be deemed a gift. Both popularly and legally, however, such a transaction — whatever option is chosen — "is still regarded as a robbery even though the participation of the victim was necessary to its completion, for the victim is compelled to choose between two alternatives, both of which are his as of right" (Epstein 1983, p.556).

A politician has alternative ways to interact with private parties. He may seek votes or money from producers and offer rents from consumers in exchange, as in the orthodox economic theory of regulation-as-bribery. But a politician may also make his demands on private parties, not by promising benefits, but by threatening to impose costs—a form of political extortion or blackmail. If the expected cost of the act threatened exceeds the value of what private parties must give up to avoid legislative action, they rationally will surrender the tribute demanded of them. With constant marginal utility of wealth, a private citizen will be just as willing to pay legislators to have rents of $1 million created as she will to avoid imposition of $1 million in losses. With declining marginal utility of income, the citizen will pay more to avoid the losses than she will to obtain the gains.

Once the politician is seen as an independent actor in the regulatory process, his objective function cannot be treated as single-valued. He will maximize total returns to himself by equating at the margin the returns from votes, contributions, bribes, power, and other sources of personal gain or utility. All these, in turn, are positive functions not only of private benefits he confers but also of private costs he agrees not to impose.

The political strategy of cost forbearance can assume several forms. Perhaps most obvious is the threat to deregulate an industry previously cartelized. Expected political rents created by earlier regulation are quickly capitalized into firm share prices. If politicians later breach their contract and vote unexpectedly to deregulate, the shareholders suffer a wealth loss. Rather than suffer the costs of deregulation, shareholders will pay politicians a sum, up to the amount of wealth loss threatened, to have them refrain from deregulating. And in fact one routinely observes payments to politicians to protect previously enacted cartel measures. Dairy interests pay handsomely for continuation of congressional milk-price supports; physician and dentist political action committees (PACs) contribute large sums for continuation of self-regulation....

Subsequent payments to avoid postcontractual opportunism by politicians are to be distinguished from contractual payments to enhance rent longevity *ex ante*. Both politicians and rent recipients gain when the durability of regulation can be increased, that is, when legislators are held to longer contracts. But new arrivals on both sides succeed to the interests of the original contracting parties. A legislator not party to the original bargain has less incentive to abide by the political rent-creation deal struck by his predecessors unless he too is compensated. Guaranteed rent durability is thus impossible. Among owners of firms, subsequent purchasers of shares with expected rents capitalized into their prices are vulnerable to extraction of previously created rents on the part of opportunistic politicians. Payments to political newcomers to secure performance of previously negotiated contracts earn no rents. Rather, they protect against windfall losses that new legislators could impose otherwise.

*   *   *

Conclusion

The rent-extraction model...is essentially a model of extortion by politicians. They are paid not to legislate—money for nothing. The model extends the economic theory of regulation to include the gains available to politician-maximizers from alleviating costs threatened or actually imposed on private actors by legislators themselves and by specialized bureaucratic agencies. Status as a legislator confers a property right not only to create political rents but also to impose costs that would destroy private rents. In order to protect these returns, private owners have an incentive to strike bargains with legislators, as long as the side payments to politicians are lower than the losses expected from the law threatened.

Their ability to impose costs enables politicians to demand payments not to do so. As with rent creation, the process of rent extraction in the short run might seem to involve only transfers—from capital owners to politicians, rather than from consumers to producers. But the long-run implications are the more important ones. The transfers required to protect returns to private investments create disincentives to invest in valuable specific capital in the first place. Even when politicians eventually eschew intervention, the mere threat and the payments required to remove it must distort private investment decisions.

The model of rent extraction set out here in no way undermines the orthodox model of rent-creating regulation; rather, it supplements the rent-creation model by recognizing alternative sources of political gains.[27] Indeed, [Nobel Laureate George] Stigler's original article foreshadowed a complementary rent-extraction model: "The state—the machinery and power of the state—is a potential resource or threat to every industry in the society. With its power to prohibit or compel, to take or give money, the state can and does selectively help or hurt a vast number of industries... Regulation may be actively sought by an industry, or it may be thrust upon it." Conditions that make political rent creation relatively unattractive to politicians make private rent extraction more attractive. The relative attraction of rent extraction has also increased as constitutional protection of private rights has diminished.

True, credibility issues, problems of political opportunism, and perhaps other imperfections in private-capital protection may create disincentives for capital owners to buy off legislators—just as opportunism and political-rent protection may discourage payments for rent creation. Yet rent creation is an ongoing, frequently observed phenomenon of modern politics. The complementary question thus is posed: do private actors in fact pay significant sums to induce government *not* to act?

That is the question addressed in Part II, where much evidence of actual rent extraction is presented. Despite the political impediments to contract, then, the demonstrated willingness of capital owners to purchase protection indicates that appreciable capital stocks are credibly imperiled by regulations that are never actually enacted.

If so, one cost of government regulation has been missed. Heretofore, the economic model has identified several different costs of government regulation: deadweight consumer loss, resources expended as private parties seek rents, costs of compliance with regulation.... To these should be added the costs of protect-

---

27. To return to the bribery/extortion analogy, one who solicits bribes from some people to increase their welfare is hardly precluded thereby from demanding payment from other people not to decrease theirs.

ing private capital, even when politicians ultimately are persuaded not to regulate. As Part II demonstrates, there is no such thing as a free market.

Notes and Questions

1. The Welfare Costs of Rent Seeking and Rent Extraction: Rent seeking is harmful to society because it results in two types of social costs. First, the political creation of monopoly harms society in the same way as any other monopoly — through the restriction of output and misallocation of resources. Second, the potential for government-conferred rents leads interest groups to use resources to capture those rents through the political process. Such rent seeking expenditures attempt to transfer wealth from one group to another. This use of scarce resources represents a social loss, because the resources could have been used for productive purposes instead of merely dividing up the economic pie. See, for example, Gordon Tullock, *The Welfare Costs of Tariffs, Monopoly, and Theft*, Western Economic Journal (June 1967); Richard A. Posner, *The Social Costs of Monopoly and Regulation*, 83 Journal of Politican Economy 807 (1975).

2. Public Policy Analysts and the Search for Market Failures: Many economists, public policy analysts, and legal commentators scrutinize markets looking for market imperfections which provide the justification for some form of government intervention. It is generally and implicitly assumed by such investigators that the government policy that emerges will be faithfully executed by legislators and bureaucrats. Public choice economists, in contrast, are specialists at identifying government failures — instances where the incentive structures facing legislators and regulators make it almost impossible for a government policy to meet its stated objectives. Moreover, Professors Jensen and Meckling, who introduced the REMM model in Chapter I, argue that there are strong reasons to suspect that economists, legislators and bureaucrats are not unbiased in their search for problems in need of their solutions:

*   *   *

ECONOMISTS, POLITICIANS, AND BUREAUCRATS
AS REMMs

National Planning and Needs

While economists generally profess fidelity to REMM, their loyalty is neither universal nor constant. Their economic models of human behavior often fall short of REMM — such as, for example, when they characterize the individual as a pure money-income maximizer. Moreover, in matters of public policy, there is a systematic relationship between the policies espoused and the degree of infidelity to REMM. One of the better-known members of the economics profession and a recipient of the Nobel Prize, Professor Wassily Leontieff, was featured as a proponent of "national economic planning" in a New York Times advertisement that said:

> No reliable mechanism in the modern economy relates needs to available manpower, plant and material....The most striking fact about the way we organize our economic life is that we leave so much to chance. We give little thought to the direction in which we would like to go. (March 16, 1975)

Notice that the emotional content and force of the statement is considerably strengthened by the authors' use of the word "needs" rather than "desires" or "wants."

But let's examine this statement more closely. If by "needs" the authors mean individual preferences, wants, or desires, the first sentence is simply false. There is a mechanism that relates such needs or wants to "manpower, plant, and materials" and it is central to the study of economics: namely, the price system. What the authors are saying is that no one organization or group of individuals directs (not plans) production in such a way that what is actually produced is what the advertisement's authors would define as needs. When they go on to say, "We give little thought to the direction we would like to go," the antecedent of we is meant to be "we the general public." But, of course, we as individuals (and REMMs) give a great deal of thought to where we want to study and work, how much we will save, where we will invest our savings, what we will buy, what we will produce, and so on.

Professor Leontieff's reputation rests largely on his work on input-output models. It is not surprising that he is a planning buff, for input-output models generally ignore most of the adjustment processes (that is, price changes and substitutions) that serve to balance supply and demand in a market economy. His input-output models specify fixed relations between inputs like labor, materials, and capital and outputs like tons of steel. More or less steel can be produced only by adding or subtracting inputs in fixed proportions. There are no resourceful, evaluative maximizers in Leontieff's models. Like ants in an ant colony, his individuals possess productive capacities but very limited adaptability. In a society of such dolts, planning (or, more accurately, directing) appears unavoidable. In the words of another Nobel Prize winner, Professor Friedrich von Hayek, the real planning issue is not whether individuals should plan their affairs, but rather who should plan their affairs.[61]

The implication of input-output models, then, is that people are incapable of planning and thus require the direction and leadership of "planners." This import has not escaped the notice of bureaucrats, politicians, and managers, who themselves behave as REMMs when they recognize the value of models and theories that imply an increased demand for their services. By their very framing of the issue, Leontieff and politicians assume the answer to Hayek's question: planning does not exist unless the government does it.

For example, politicians are likely to see the value of an energy industry input-output model which, given projections of future energy "needs" (no prices and no substitutions here), tells how many nuclear energy plants must be built, how many strip mines should be opened, and how many new coal cars must be produced in order to become independent of foreign oil sources. The model suggests that, without extensive govern-

---

61. See Friedrich von Hayek, "The Use of Knowledge in Society,: *American Economic Review*, Vol. 35, No. 4 (September, 1945); and "Planning Our Way to Serfdom," *Reason* (March, 1977).

ment intervention, the country cannot achieve energy independence. Such intervention, of course, implies an increase in politicians' power.

It is worth noting that the "we" in the Leontieff endorsed planning statement is a common but generally unrecognized debating trick. It is standard practice in the political arena to label one's own preferences as the "people's preferences" or as the " public's preferences," and to label the policies one supports as "in the public interest." But organizations or groups of individuals cannot have preferences; only individuals can have preferences. One could supply content to terms like the people's preferences or the public interest by making them synonymous with other concepts-for example, with what a majority would support or what every voter would approve in a referendum. But the typical user would then find the terms far less persuasive, therefore less attractive, and, in the case of a complete consensus, never relevant.

Self-interest and the Demand for Disequilibrium

Bureaucrats and politicians, like many economists, are also predisposed to embrace the concept of market "failure" or "disequilibrium" with the same enthusiasm they have shown for input-output models, and for the same reasons. If something is in disequilibrium, government action is required to bring about equilibrium.

Generally, economists tend to identify, equilibrium with stable prices and quantities: a market is in equilibrium when there are no forces causing changes in the price or the quantity exchanged. Yet it is reasonable to argue that all markets are always in equilibrium, and all forces must always be in balance at all times—just as there is an equilibrium rate of heat transfer when heat is applied to one end of a steel bar. This is simply another way of saying that sophisticated, rational individuals always adapt to their opportunity set, where the opportunity set is defined to take account of the cost of adapting. That is, all voluntary exchanges will take place that will make both parties better off (taking all costs into account).

The view that markets are always in equilibrium does not depend on the stability of prices; prices and quantities can change dramatically. Their rate of change, however, is controlled by individual behavior—a balance is struck between the cost of change and the benefits. For example, if the dollar price of a good is prevented by law from changing, the opposing forces are balanced by the introduction of other costs such as queues and waiting time, or by the introduction of other goods as a consideration in the exchange.[62]

Although it is a tautology, the view that markets are always in equilibrium has important advantages. It focuses attention on interesting adjustment phenomena, on information and search costs and how they affect behavior, and on qualitative characteristics of the exchanges that

---

62. For example, it is common practice in rent controlled areas for new tenants to make higher-than-market-price payments to old tenants and/or landlords for furniture or minor improvements they have no use for to get the right to rent the apartment for a below-market rate.

arise to balance the opposing forces. If markets are always in equilibrium, the task of the scientist is to explain how the equilibrium is brought about.

In contrast, the word disequilibrium has strong emotional content. It denotes something unnatural, unsightly, and undesirable that requires "corrective action." A market—whether for labor, energy, sugar, health care, or derivative securities—described as being "in disequilibrium" is generally regarded as bad, and we are immediately led to think of the desirability of some form of government intervention (e.g., price controls, embargoes, subsidies, or output restrictions) to eliminate the assumed problem.

One popular pursuit of bureaucrats—making projections of supply and demand—is the outgrowth of their preoccupation with disequilibrium. Such projections usually consist of estimates of numbers of physicists, doctors, mining engineers, barrels of oil, or tons of steel "required and/or available" at some future date, again without reference to prices. Not surprisingly, the projections invariably imply a disequilibrium (a shortage or surplus) that requires government action.

But if these supply and demand projections are interpreted as forecasts of the quantities and prices that will prevail in a future economy in equilibrium, they lose all interest for policy makers. None of the usual policy implications follow—no subsidies, taxes, or constraints on individual behavior are called for, nor can any governmental enterprise be justified. Yet the practice of making projections goes on because politicians and bureaucrats, as REMMs, find them useful tools for expanding the role of government and the market for their services.

Michael C. Jensen & William H. Meckling, The Nature of Man, 7 *Journal of Applied Corporate Finance* 4–19 (Summer 1994).

3. Rationally-Ignorant Voters: Politicians are able to cater to special interests because they are not closely monitored by voters. Interestingly, the self-interest that is so important in the market system leads to ignorance in the political system. Recall that every activity involves an opportunity cost. The time a voter spends becoming knowledgeable about the candidates requires that the voter forego some other valuable use of that time. Hence, rational voters would require that they gain some benefit from the use of such time. Clearly, there is some benefit to each voter if the best candidate wins an election. However, the only time a single vote has any value is when it is the tie breaking vote. With millions of voters, the chance of any one voter casting the tie breaking vote is minuscule. Hence, the expected benefit of casting an informed vote is virtually zero. Faced with a comparison of the cost of informing oneself about the candidates and the benefit of doing so, it is little wonder that voters are simply advancing their self-interest by spending their time where it will have the greatest impact on their well-being. Many voters, therefore, are **rationally ignorant** of politicians and public policies. They take a free ride and legislators are able to pass legislation that does not come close to anyone's understanding of the public interest. Moreover, by cloaking interest-group legislation in public-interest rhetoric, politicians make it even more costly to monitor their behavior.

City of Columbia v. Omni Outdoor Advertising, Inc.
Supreme Court of the United States
499 U.S. 365 (1991)

Justice SCALIA delivered the opinion of the Court.

This case requires us to clarify the application of the Sherman Act to municipal governments and to the citizens who seek action from them.

I

Petitioner Columbia Outdoor Advertising, Inc. (COA), a South Carolina corporation, entered the billboard business in the city of Columbia, South Carolina (also a petitioner here), in the 1940's. By 1981 it controlled more than 95% of what has been conceded to be the relevant market. COA was a local business owned by a family with deep roots in the community, and enjoyed close relations with the city's political leaders. The mayor and other members of the city council were personal friends of COA's majority owner, and the company and its officers occasionally contributed funds and free billboard space to their campaigns. According to respondent Omni Outdoor Advertising, Inc., these beneficences were part of a "longstanding" "secret anticompetitive agreement" whereby "the City and COA would each use their [sic] respective power and resources to protect... COA's monopoly position," in return for which "City Council members received advantages made possible by COA's monopoly."

In 1981, Omni, a Georgia corporation, began erecting billboards in and around the city. COA responded to this competition in several ways. First, it redoubled its own billboard construction efforts and modernized its existing stock. Second — according to Omni — it took a number of anticompetitive private actions, such as offering artificially low rates, spreading untrue and malicious rumors about Omni, and attempting to induce Omni's customers to break their contracts. Finally (and this is what gives rise to the issue we address today), COA executives met with city officials to seek the enactment of zoning ordinances that would restrict billboard construction. COA was not alone in urging this course concerned about the city's recent explosion of billboards, a number of citizens including writers of articles and editorials in local newspapers advocated restrictions.

In the spring of 1982, the city council passed an ordinance requiring the council's approval for every billboard constructed in downtown Columbia. This was later amended to impose a 180-day moratorium on the construction of billboards throughout the city, except as specifically authorized by the council. A state court invalidated this ordinance on the ground that its conferral of unconstrained discretion upon the city council violated both the South Carolina and Federal Constitutions. The city then requested the State's regional planning authority to conduct a comprehensive analysis of the local billboard situation as a basis for developing a final, constitutionally valid, ordinance. In September 1982, after a series of public hearings and numerous meetings involving city officials, Omni, and COA (in all of which, according to Omni, positions contrary to COA's were not genuinely considered), the city council passed a new ordinance restricting the size, location, and spacing of billboards. These restrictions, particularly those on spacing, obviously benefited COA, which already had its bill-boards in place; they severely hindered Omni's ability to compete.

In November 1982, Omni filed suit against COA and the city in Federal District Court, charging that they had violated §§ 1 and 2 of the Sherman Act[1], 26 Stat. 209, as amended, 15 U.S.C. §§ 1, 2,... as well as South Carolina's Unfair Trade Practices Act, S.C. Code Ann. § 39-5-140 (1976). Omni contended, in particular, that the city's billboard ordinances were the result of an anticompetitive conspiracy between city officials and COA that stripped both parties of any immunity they might otherwise enjoy from the federal antitrust laws. In January 1986, after more than two weeks of trial, a jury returned general verdicts against the city and COA on both the federal and state claims. It awarded damages, before trebling, of $600,000 on the § 1 Sherman Act claim, and $400,000 on the § 2 claim. The jury also answered two special interrogatories, finding specifically that the city and COA had conspired both to restrain trade and to monopolize the market. Petitioners moved for judgment notwithstanding the verdict, contending among other things that their activities were outside the scope of the federal antitrust laws. In November 1988, the District Court granted the motion.

A divided panel of the United States Court of Appeals for the Fourth Circuit reversed the judgment of the District Court and reinstated the jury verdict on all counts, 891 F.2d 1127 (1989). We granted certiorari, 496 U.S. 955 (1990).

II

In the landmark case of *Parker v. Brown,* 317 U.S. 341 (1943), we rejected the contention that a program restricting the marketing of privately produced raisins, adopted pursuant to California's Agricultural Prorate Act, violated the Sherman Act. Relying on principles of federalism and state sovereignty, we held that the Sherman Act did not apply to anticompetitive restraints imposed by the States "as an act of government." *Id.* at 352.

Since *Parker* emphasized the role of sovereign *States* in a federal system, it was initially unclear whether the governmental actions of political subdivisions enjoyed similar protection. In recent years, we have held that *Parker* immunity does not apply directly to local governments.... We have recognized, however, that a municipality's restriction of competition may sometimes be an authorized implementation of state policy, and have accorded *Parker* immunity where that is the case.

The South Carolina statutes under which the city acted in the present case authorize municipalities to regulate the use of land and the construction of buildings and other structures within their boundaries. It is undisputed that, as a matter of state law, these statutes authorize the city to regulate the size, location, and spacing of billboards. It could be argued, however, that a municipality acts beyond its delegated authority, for *Parker* purposes, whenever the nature of its regulation is substantively or even procedurally defective. On such an analysis it could be con-

---

1. Section 1 provides in pertinent part: "Every contract, combination in the form of trust or otherwise, or conspiracy, in restraint of trade or commerce among the several States, or with foreign nations, is declared to be illegal." Section 2 provides in pertinent part: "Every person who shall monopolize, or attempt to monopolize, or combine or conspire with any other person or persons, to monopolize any part of the trade or commerce among the several States, or with foreign nations, shall be deemed guilty of a felony."

tended, for example, that the city's regulation in the present case was not "authorized"..., if it was not, as that statute requires, adopted "for the purpose of promoting health, safety, morals or the general welfare of the community." As scholarly commentary has noted, such an expansive interpretation of the *Parker*-defense authorization requirement would have unacceptable consequences.

> "To be sure, state law 'authorizes' only agency decisions that are substantively and procedurally correct. Errors of fact, law, or judgment by the agency are not 'authorized.' Erroneous acts or decisions are subject to reversal by superior tribunals because unauthorized. If the antitrust court demands unqualified 'authority' in this sense, it inevitably becomes the standard reviewer not only of federal agency activity but also of state and local activity whenever it is alleged that the governmental body, though possessing the power to engage in the challenged conduct, has actually exercised its power in a manner not authorized by state law...."

We agree with that assessment, and believe that in order to prevent *Parker* from undermining the very interests of federalism it is designed to protect, it is necessary to adopt a concept of authority broader than what is applied to determine the legality of the municipality's action under state law.... It suffices for the present to conclude that here no more is needed to establish, for *Parker* purposes, the city's authority to regulate than its unquestioned zoning power over the size, location, and spacing of billboards.

Besides authority to regulate, however, the *Parker* defense also requires authority to suppress competition—more specifically, "clear articulation of a state policy to authorize anticompetitive conduct" by the municipality in connection with its regulation. *Hallie*, 471 U.S. 34, 40. We have rejected the contention that this requirement can be met only if the delegating statute explicitly permits the displacement of competition.... It is enough, we have held, if suppression of competition is the "foreseeable result" of what the statute authorizes.... That condition is amply met here. The very purpose of zoning regulation is to displace unfettered business freedom in a manner that regularly has the effect of preventing normal acts of competition, particularly on the part of new entrants. A municipal ordinance restricting the size, location, and spacing of billboards (surely a common form of zoning) necessarily protects existing billboards against some competition from newcomers.[4]

---

4. The dissent contends that, in order successfully to delegate its Parker immunity to a municipality, a State must expressly authorize the municipality to engage (1) in specifically "economic regulation," (2) of a specific industry. These dual specificities are without support in our precedents, for the good reason that they defy rational implementation. If, by authority to engage in specifically "economic" regulation, the dissent means authority specifically to regulate competition, we squarely rejected that in Hallie v. Eau Claire. Seemingly, however, the dissent means only that the state authorization must specify that sort of regulation whereunder "decisions about prices and output are not made by individual firms, but rather by a public body." But why is not the restriction of billboards in a city a restriction on the "output" of the local billboard industry? It assuredly is—and that is indeed the very gravamen of Omni's complaint. It seems to us that the dissent's concession that "it is often difficult to differentiate economic regulation from municipal regulation of health, safety, and welfare," is a gross understatement. Loose talk about a "regulated industry" may suffice for what the dissent calls "antitrust parlance," but it is not a definition upon which the criminal liability of public officials ought to depend. Under the dissent's second requirement for a valid delegation of Parker immunity—that the authorization to regulate pertain to a specific

The Court of Appeals was therefore correct in its conclusion that the city's restriction of billboard construction was prima facie entitled to *Parker* immunity. The Court of Appeals upheld the jury verdict, however, by invoking a "conspiracy" exception to *Parker* that has been recognized by several Courts of Appeals. See, *e.g., Whitworth v. Perkins, 559* F.2d 378 (1979).... That exception is thought to be supported by two of our statements in *Parker:* "[W]e have no question of the state or its municipality becoming a *participant in a private agreement* or combination by others for restraint of trade... [and] [T]he state in adopting and enforcing the prorate program made no contract or agreement *and entered into no conspiracy in restraint of trade or to establish monopoly* but, as sovereign, imposed the restraint as an act of government which the Sherman Act did not undertake to prohibit." *Parker* does not apply, according to the Fourth Circuit, "where politicians or political entities are involved as conspirators" with private actors in the restraint of trade. 891 F.2d, at 1134.

There is no such conspiracy exception. The rationale of *Parker* was that, in light of our national commitment to federalism, the general language of the Sherman Act should not be interpreted to prohibit anticompetitive actions by the States in their governmental capacities as sovereign regulators. The sentences from the opinion quoted above simply clarify that this immunity does not necessarily obtain where the State acts not in a regulatory capacity but as a commercial participant in a given market. These sentences should not be read to suggest the general proposition that even governmental *regulatory* action may be deemed private—and therefore subject to antitrust liability—when it is taken pursuant to a conspiracy with private parties. The impracticality of such a principle is evident if, for purposes of the exception, "conspiracy" means nothing more than an agreement to impose the regulation in question. Since it is both inevitable and desirable that public officials often agree to do what one or another group of private citizens urges upon them, such an exception would virtually swallow up the *Parker* rule....

Omni suggests, however, that "conspiracy" might be limited to instances of governmental "corruption," defined variously as "abandonment of public responsibilities to private interests," ... "corrupt or bad faith decisions," and "self-ish or corrupt motives," *ibid*. Ultimately, Omni asks us not to define "corruption" at all, but simply to leave that task to the jury: "[a]t bottom, however, it was within the jury's province to determine what constituted corruption of the governmental process in their community." *Id.,* at 43. Omni's *amicus* eschews this emphasis on "corruption," instead urging us to define the conspiracy exception as encompassing any governmental act "not in the public interest."

A conspiracy exception narrowed along such vague lines is similarly impractical. Few governmental actions are immune from the charge that they are "not

---

industry—the problem with the South Carolina statute is that it used the generic term "structures," instead of conferring its regulatory authority industry-by-industry (presumably "billboards," "movie houses," "mobile homes," "TV antennas," and every other conceivable object of zoning regulation that can be the subject of a relevant "market" for purposes of antitrust analysis). To describe this is to refute it. Our precedents not only fail to suggest, but positively reject, such an approach. "[T]he municipality need not 'be able to point to a specific, detailed legislative authorization' in order to assert a successful Parker defense to an antitrust suit." Hallie v Eau Claire(quoting Lafayette v. Louisiana Power & Light Co., 435 U.S. 389, 415, 98 S.Ct. 1123, 1138, 55 L.Ed.2d 364 (1978)).

in the public interest" or in some sense "corrupt." ... The fact is that virtually all regulation benefits some segments of the society and harms others; and that it is not universally considered contrary to the public good if the net economic loss to the losers exceeds the net economic gain to the winners. *Parker* was not written in ignorance of the reality that determination of "the public interest" in the manifold areas of government regulation entails not merely economic and mathematical analysis but value judgment, and it was not meant to shift that judgment from elected officials to judges and juries. If the city of Columbia's decision to regulate what one local newspaper called "billboard jungles," Columbia Record, May 21, 1982, p. 14-A, col. 1 is made subject to *ex post facto* judicial assessment of "the public interest," with personal liability of city officials a possible consequence, we will have gone far to "compromise the States' ability to regulate their domestic commerce," *Southern Motor Carriers Rate Conference, Inc.* v. *United States*, 471 U.S. 48, 56 (1985). The situation would not be better, but arguably even worse, if the courts were to apply a subjective test: not whether the action was in the public interest, but whether the officials involved thought it to be so. This would require the sort of deconstruction of the governmental process and probing of the official "intent" that we have consistently sought to avoid. "[W]here the action complained of ... was that of the State itself, the action is exempt from antitrust liability regardless of the State's motives in taking the action." *Hoover* v. *Ronwin,* 466 U.S. 558, 579–580 (1984). See also *Llewellyn v. Crothers,* 765 F.2d 769, 774 (CA9 1985) (Kennedy, J.).

*   *   *

For these reasons, we reaffirm our rejection of any interpretation of the Sherman Act that would allow plaintiffs to look behind the actions of state sovereigns to base their claims on "perceived conspiracies to restrain trade." *Hoover,* 466 U.S., at 580. We reiterate that, with the possible market participant exception, *any* action that qualifies as state action is "*ipso facto* ... exempt from the operation of the antitrust laws," *id.,* at 568. This does not mean, of course, that the States may exempt *private* action from the scope of the Sherman Act; we in no way qualify the well-established principle that "a state does not give immunity to those who violate the Sherman Act by authorizing them to violate it, or by declaring that their action is lawful." *Parker,* 317 U.S., at 351 (citing Northern Securities Co. v. United States, 193 U.S. 197)....

III

While *Parker* recognized the States' freedom to engage in anticompetitive regulation, it did not purport to immunize from antitrust liability the private parties who urge them to engage in anticompetitive regulation. However, it is obviously peculiar in a democracy, and perhaps in derogation of the constitutional right ... to establish a category of lawful state action that citizens are not permitted to urge. Thus, beginning with *Eastern Railroad Presidents Conference* v. *Noerr Motor Freight, Inc., supra,* we have developed a corollary to *Parker*: The federal antitrust laws also do not regulate the conduct of private individuals in seeking anticompetitive action from the government. This doctrine, like *Parker,* rests ultimately upon a recognition that the antitrust laws, "tailored as they are for the business world, are not at all appropriate for application in the political arena." *Noerr, supra,* at 141. That a private party's political motives are selfish is irrelevant: "*Noerr* shields from the Sherman Act a concerted effort to influence public officials regardless of intent or purpose." *Mine Workers v. Pennington*, 381 U.S. 657, 670 (1965).

Noerr recognized, however, what has come to be known as the "sham" exception to its rule: "There may be situations in which a publicity campaign, ostensibly directed toward influencing governmental action, is a mere sham to cover what is actually nothing more than an attempt to interfere directly with the business relationships of a competitor and the application of the Sherman Act would be justified." 365 U.S., at 144. The Court of Appeals concluded that the jury in this case could have found that COA's activities on behalf of the restrictive billboard ordinances fell within this exception. In our view that was error.

The "sham" exception to *Noerr* encompasses situations in which persons use the governmental process—as opposed to the *outcome* of that process—as an anticompetitive weapon. A classic example is the filing of frivolous objections to the license application of a competitor, with no expectation of achieving denial of the license but simply in order to impose expense and delay....

Neither of the Court of Appeals' theories for application of the "sham" exception to the facts of the present case is sound. The court reasoned, first, that the jury could have concluded that COA's interaction with city officials " 'was actually nothing more than an attempt to interfere directly with the business relations [sic] of a competitor,' " 891 F.2d at 1139 (quoting *Noerr, supra*, at 144). This analysis relies upon language from *Noerr*, but ignores the import of the critical word "directly." Although COA indisputably set out to disrupt Omni's business relationships, it sought to do so not through the very process of lobbying, or of causing the city council to consider zoning measures, but rather through the ultimate *product* of that lobbying and consideration, viz., the zoning ordinances. The Court of Appeals' second theory was that the jury could have found "that COA's purposes were to delay Omni's entry into the market and even to deny it a meaningful access to the appropriate city administrative and legislative fora." 891 F.2d, at 1139. But the purpose of delaying a competitor's entry into the market does not render lobbying activity a "sham," unless (as no evidence suggested was true here) the delay is sought to be achieved only by the lobbying process itself, and not by the governmental action that the lobbying seeks. "If *Noerr* teaches anything it is that an intent to restrain trade as a *result* of the government action sought...does not foreclose protection." Sullivan, Developments in the Noerr Doctrine, 56 Antitrust L.J. 361, 362 (1987). As for "deny[ing]...meaningful access to the appropriate city administrative and legislative fora," that may render the manner of lobbying improper or even unlawful, but does not necessarily render it a "sham." We did hold in *California Motor Transport, supra*, that a conspiracy among private parties to monopolize trade by excluding a competitor from participation in the regulatory process did not enjoy *Noerr* protection. But *California Motor Transport* involved a context in which the conspirators' participation in the governmental process was itself claimed to be a "sham," employed as a means of imposing cost and delay. The holding of the case is limited to that situation. To extend it to a context in which the regulatory process is being invoked genuinely, and not in a "sham" fashion, would produce precisely that conversion of antitrust law into regulation of the political process that we have sought to avoid. Any lobbyist or applicant, in addition to getting himself heard, seeks by procedural and other means to get his opponent ignored. Policing the legitimate boundaries of such defensive strategies, when they are conducted in the context of a genuine attempt to influence governmental action, is not the role of the Sherman Act. In the present case, of course, any denial to Omni of "meaningful access to the appropriate city administrative and legislative fora" was achieved by COA in the course of an attempt to influence governmental action that, far from being a "sham," was if anything more in earnest than it should have been. If the denial was wrongful there may be other remedies, but as for the Sherman Act, the *Noerr* exemption applies.

Omni urges that if, as we have concluded, the "sham" exception is inapplicable, we should use this case to recognize another exception to *Noerr* immunity—a "conspiracy" exception, which would apply when government officials conspire with a private party to employ government action as a means of stifling competition. We have left open the possibility of such an exception.... At least one Court of Appeals has affirmed the existence of such an exception in dicta, see *Duke & Co. v. Foerster,* 521 F.2d 1277, 1282 (CA3 1975), and the Fifth Circuit has adopted it as holding, see *Affiliated Capital Corp. v. Houston,* 735 F.2d 1555, 1566–1568 (1984) (en banc).

Giving full consideration to this matter for the first time, we conclude that a "conspiracy" exception to *Noerr* must be rejected. We need not describe our reasons at length, since they are largely the same as those set forth in Part II above for rejecting a "conspiracy" exception to *Parker.* As we have described, *Parker* and *Noerr* are complementary expressions of the principle that the antitrust laws regulate business, not politics; the former decision protects the States' acts of governing, and the latter the citizens' participation in government. Insofar as the identification of an immunity-destroying "conspiracy" is concerned, *Parker* and *Noerr* generally present two faces of the same coin. The *Noerr*-invalidating conspiracy alleged here is just the *Parker*-invalidating conspiracy viewed from the standpoint of the private-sector participants rather than the governmental participants. The same factors which, as we have described above, make it impracticable or beyond the purpose of the antitrust laws to identify and invalidate lawmaking that has been infected by selfishly motivated agreement with private interests likewise make it impracticable or beyond that scope to identify and invalidate lobbying that has produced selfishly motivated agreement with public officials. "It would be unlikely that any effort to influence legislative action could succeed unless one or more members of the legislative body became...'co-conspirators' " in *some* sense with the private party urging such action, *Metro Cable Co. v. CATV of Rockford, Inc.* In *Noerr* itself, where the private party "deliberately deceived the public and public officials" in its successful lobbying campaign, we said that "deception, reprehensible as it is, can be of no consequence so far as the Sherman Act is concerned." 365 U.S., at 145.

IV

Under *Parker* and *Noerr*, therefore, both the city and COA are entitled to immunity from the federal antitrust laws for their activities relating to enactment of the ordinances. This determination does not entirely resolve the dispute before us, since other activities are at issue in the case with respect to COA. Omni asserts that COA engaged in private anticompetitive actions such as trade libel, the setting of artificially low rates, and inducement to breach of contract. Thus, although the jury's general verdict against COA cannot be permitted to stand (since it was based on instructions that erroneously permitted liability for seeking the ordinances..., if the evidence was sufficient to sustain a verdict on the basis of these other actions alone, and if this theory of liability has been properly preserved, Omni would be entitled to a new trial.

*   *   *

...The judgment of the Court of Appeals is reversed, and the case is remanded for further proceedings consistent with this opinion.

Justice STEVENS, with whom Justice WHITE and Justice MARSHALL join, dissenting.

...Although we have previously recognized that a completely literal interpretation of the word "every" [in section 1 of the Sherman Act] cannot have been intended by Congress,[1] the Court today carries this recognition to an extreme by deciding that agreements between municipalities, or their officials, and private parties to use the zoning power to confer exclusive privileges in a particular line of commerce are beyond the reach of § 1. History, tradition, and the facts of this case all demonstrate that the Court's attempt to create a "better" and less inclusive Sherman Act... is ill advised.

I

As a preface to a consideration of the "state action" and so-called "*Noerr-Pennington*" exemptions to the Sherman Act, it is appropriate to remind the Court that one of the classic common-law examples of a prohibited contract in restraint of trade involved an agreement between a public official and a private party. The public official—the Queen of England—had granted one of her subjects a monopoly in the making, importation, and sale of playing cards in order to generate revenues for the crown. A competitor challenged the grant in *The Case of Monopolies*, 11 Co. Rep. 84, 77 Eng.Rep. 1260 (Q.B.1602), and prevailed...

In the case before us today, respondent alleges that the city of Columbia, S.C., has entered into a comparable agreement to give the private petitioner a monopoly in the sale of billboard advertising. After a 3-week trial, a jury composed of citizens of the vicinage found that, despite the city fathers' denials,

---

1. Construing the statute in the light of the common law concerning contracts in restraint of trade, we have concluded that only unreasonable restraints are prohibited.

"One problem presented by the language of § 1 of the Sherman Act is that it cannot mean what it says. The statute says that 'every' contract that restrains trade is unlawful. But, as Mr. Justice Brandeis perceptively noted, restraint is the very essence of every contract; read literally, § 1 would outlaw the entire body of private contract law. Yet it is that body of law that establishes the enforceability of commercial agreements and enables competitive markets—indeed, a competitive economy—to function effectively.

"Congress, however, did not intend the text of the Sherman Act to delineate the full meaning of the statute or its application in concrete situations. The legislative history makes it perfectly clear that it expected the courts to give shape to the statute's broad mandate by drawing on common-law tradition. The Rule of Reason, with its origins in common-law precedents long antedating the Sherman Act, has served that purpose.... [The Rule of Reason] focuses directly on the challenged restraint's impact on competitive conditions." *National Society of Professional Engineers v. United States* (footnotes omitted).

We have also confined the Sherman Act's mandate by holding that the independent actions of the sovereign States and their officials are not covered by the language of the Act. *Parker v. Brown*, 317 U.S. 314 (1943).

there was indeed such an agreement, presumably motivated in part by past favors in the form of political advertising, in part by friendship, and in part by the expectation of a beneficial future relationship—and in any case, not exclusively by a concern for the general public interest.[2] Today the Court acknowledges the anticompetitive consequences of this and similar agreements but decides that they should be exempted from the coverage of the Sherman Act because it fears that enunciating a rule that allows the motivations of public officials to be probed may mean that innocent municipal officials may be harassed with baseless charges. The holding evidences an unfortunate lack of confidence in our judicial system and will foster the evils the Sherman Act was designed to eradicate.

II

There is a distinction between economic regulation, on the one hand, and regulation designed to protect the public health, safety, and environment. In antitrust parlance a "regulated industry" is one in which decisions about prices and output are made not by individual firms, but rather by a public body or a collective process subject to governmental approval. Economic regulation of the motor carrier and airline industries was imposed by the Federal Government in the 1930's; the "deregulation" of those industries did not eliminate all the other types of regulation that continue to protect our safety and environmental concerns.

The antitrust laws reflect a basic national policy favoring free markets over regulated markets[3]. In essence, the Sherman Act prohibits private unsupervised regulation of the prices and output of goods in the marketplace. That prohibition is inapplicable to specific industries which Congress has exempted from the antitrust laws and subjected to regulatory supervision over price and output decisions. Moreover, the so-called "state-action" exemption from the Sherman Act reflects the Court's understanding that Congress did not intend the statute to preempt a State's economic regulation of commerce within its own borders.

---

2. The jury returned its verdict pursuant to the following instructions given by the District Court:

"So if by the evidence you find that person involved in this case procured and brought about the passage of ordinances solely for the purpose of hindering, delaying or otherwise interfering with the access of the Plaintiff to the marketing area involved in this case...and thereby conspired, then, of course, their conduct would not be excused under the antitrust laws.

"So once again an entity may engage in...legitimate lobbying...to procure legislati[on] even if the motive behind the lobbying is anti-competitive.

"If you find Defendants conspired together with the intent to foreclose the Plaintiff from meaningful access to a legitimate decision making process with regard to the ordinances in question, then your verdict would be for the Plaintiff on that issue." App. 81.

3. "The Sherman Act reflects a legislative judgment that ultimately competition will produce not only lower prices, but also better goods and services. 'The heart of our national economic policy long has been faith in the value of competition.' *Standard Oil Co. v. FTC*, 340 U.S. 231, 248 [(1951)]. The assumption that competition is the best method of allocating resources in a free market recognizes that all elements of a bargain—quality, service, safety, and durability—and not just the immediate cost, are favorably affected by the free opportunity to select among alternative offers. Even assuming occasional exceptions to the presumed consequences of competition, the statutory policy precludes inquiry into the question whether competition is good or bad." *National Society of Professional Engineers*, 435 U.S., at 695.

The contours of the state-action exemption are relatively well defined in our cases. Ever since our decision in *Olsen* v. *Smith*, 195 U.S. 332 (1904), which upheld a Texas statute fixing the rates charged by pilots operating in the Port of Galveston, it has been clear that a State's decision to displace competition with economic regulation is not prohibited by the Sherman Act. *Parker* v. *Brown*, 317 U.S. 341 (1943), the case most frequently identified with the state-action exemption, involved a decision by California to substitute sales quotas and price control—the purest form of economic regulation—for competition in the market for California raisins.

In *Olsen*, the State itself had made the relevant pricing decision. In Parker, the regulation of the marketing of California's 1940 crop of raisins was administered by state officials. Thus, when a state agency, or the State itself, engages in economic regulation, the Sherman Act is inapplicable....

Underlying the Court's recognition of this state-action exemption has been respect for the fundamental principle of federalism. As we stated in *Parker*, 317 U.S., at 351. "In a dual system of government in which, under the Constitution, the states are sovereign, save only as Congress may constitutionally subtract from their authority, an unexpressed purpose to nullify a state's control over its officers and agents is not lightly to be attributed to Congress."

However, this Court recognized long ago that the deference due States within our federal system does not extend fully to conduct undertaken by municipalities. Rather, all sovereign authority "within the geographical limits of the United States" resides with "the Government of the United States, or [with] the States of the Union. There exist within the broad domain of sovereignty but these two. There may be cities, counties, and other organized bodies with limited legislative functions, but they are all derived from, or exist in, subordination to one or the other of these." *United States* v. *Kagama*, 118 U.S. 375, 379 (1886).

Unlike States, municipalities do not constitute bedrocks within our system of federalism. And also unlike States, municipalities are more apt to promote their narrow parochial interests "without regard to extraterritorial impact and regional efficiency." *Lafayette* v. *Louisiana Power & Light Co.*, 435 U.S. 389, 404 (1978); see also The Federalist No. 10 (J. Madison) (describing the greater tendency of smaller societies to promote oppressive and narrow interests above the common good). "If municipalities were free to make economic choices counseled solely by their own parochial interests and without regard to their anticompetitive effects, a serious chink in the armor of antitrust protection would be introduced at odds with the comprehensive national policy Congress established." *Lafayette* v. *Louisiana Power & Light Co*, 435 U.S., at 408. Indeed, "[i]n light of the serious economic dislocation which could result if cities were free to place their own parochial interests above the Nation's economic goals reflected in the antitrust laws,...we are especially unwilling to presume that Congress intended to exclude anticompetitive municipal action from their reach." *Id.*, at 412–13.

Nevertheless, insofar as municipalities may serve to implement state policies, we have held that economic regulation administered by a municipality may also be exempt from Sherman Act coverage if it is enacted pursuant to a clearly articulated and affirmatively expressed state directive "to replace competition with regulation."...However, the mere fact that a municipality acts within its delegated authority is not sufficient to exclude its anticompetitive behavior from the reach of the Sherman Act. "Acceptance of such a proposition—that the general grant of power to enact ordinances necessarily implies state authorization to enact specific anticompetitive ordinances—would wholly eviscerate the concepts of 'clear articulation and affirmative expression' that our precedents require." *Community Communications Co. v. Boulder*, 455 U.S. 40, 45 (1982).

Accordingly, we have held that the critical decision to substitute economic regulation for competition is one that must be made by the State. That decision must be articulated with sufficient clarity to identify the industry in which the State intends that economic regulation shall replace competition. The terse statement of the reason why the municipality's actions in *Hallie* v. *Eau Claire*, 471 U.S. 34 (1985), was exempt from the Sherman Act illustrates the point: "They were taken pursuant to a clearly articulated state policy to replace competition in the provision of sewage services with regulation." *Id.*, at 47.

III

Today the Court adopts a significant enlargement of the state-action exemption. The South Carolina statutes that confer zoning authority on municipalities in the State do not articulate any state policy to displace competition with economic regulation in any line of commerce or in any specific industry. As the Court notes, the state statutes were expressly adopted to promote the " 'health, safety, morals or the general welfare of the community,' "...Like Colorado's grant of "home rule" powers to the city of Boulder, they are simply neutral on the question whether the municipality should displace competition with economic regulation in any industry. There is not even an arguable basis for concluding that the State authorized the city of Columbia to enter into exclusive agreements with any person, or to use the zoning power to protect favored citizens from competition[6]. Nevertheless, under the guise of acting pursuant to a state legislative grant to regulate health, safety, and welfare, the city of Columbia in this case enacted an ordinance that amounted to economic regulation of the billboard market; as the Court recognizes, the ordinance "obviously benefited COA, which already had its billboards in place...[and] severely hindered Omni's ability to compete." *Ante*, at 368.

Concededly, it is often difficult to differentiate economic regulation from municipal regulation of health, safety, and welfare. "Social and safety regulation have economic impacts, and economic regulation has social and safety effects." D. Hjelmfelt, Antitrust and Regulated Industries 3 (1985). It is nevertheless important to determine when purported general welfare regulation in fact constitutes economic regulation by its purpose and effect of displacing competition. "An example of economic regulation which is disguised by another stated purpose is the limitation of advertising by lawyers for the stated purpose of protect-

---

6. The authority to regulate the " 'location, height, bulk, number of stories and size of buildings and other structures,' " may of course have an indirect effect on the total output in the billboard industry,...as well as on a number of other industries, but the Court surely misreads our cases when it implies that a general grant of zoning power represents a clearly articulated decision to authorize municipalities to enter into agreements to displace competition in every industry that is affected by zoning regulation.

ing the public from incompetent lawyers. Also, economic regulation posing as safety regulation is often encountered in the health care industry." *Id.*, at 3–4.

In this case, the jury found that the city's ordinance—ostensibly one promoting health, safety, and welfare—was in fact enacted pursuant to an agreement between city officials and a private party to restrict competition. In my opinion such a finding necessarily leads to the conclusion that the city's ordinance was fundamentally a form of economic regulation of the billboard market rather than a general welfare regulation having incidental anticompetitive effects. Because I believe our cases have wisely held that the decision to embark upon economic regulation is a nondelegable one that must expressly be made by the State in the context of a specific industry in order to qualify for state-action immunity,...I would hold that the city of Columbia's economic regulation of the billboard market pursuant to a general state grant of zoning power is not exempt from antitrust scrutiny.

Underlying the Court's reluctance to find the city of Columbia's enactment of the billboard ordinance pursuant to a private agreement to constitute unauthorized economic regulation is the Court's fear that subjecting the motivations and effects of municipal action to antitrust scrutiny will result in public decisions being "made subject to ex post facto judicial assessment of 'the public interest.'" *Ante*, at 377. That fear, in turn, rests on the assumption that "it is both inevitable and desirable that public officials often agree to do what one or another group of private citizens urges upon them." *Ante*, at 375.

The Court's assumption that an agreement between private parties and public officials is an "inevitable" precondition for official action, however, is simply wrong. Indeed, I am persuaded that such agreements are the exception rather than the rule, and that they are, and should be, disfavored. The mere fact that an official body adopts a position that is advocated by a private lobbyist is plainly not sufficient to establish an agreement to do so....Nevertheless, in many circumstances, it would seem reasonable to infer—as the jury did in this case—that the official action is the product of an agreement intended to elevate particular private interests over the general good.

In this case, the city took two separate actions that protected the local monopolist from threatened competition. It first declared a moratorium on any new billboard construction, despite the city attorney's advice that the city had no power to do so. When the moratorium was invalidated in state court litigation, it was replaced with an apparently valid ordinance that clearly had the effect of creating formidable barriers to entry in the billboard market. Throughout the city's decisionmaking process in enacting the various ordinances, undisputed evidence demonstrated that Columbia Outdoor Advertising, Inc., had met with city officials privately as well as publicly. As the Court of Appeals noted: "Implicit in the jury verdict was a finding that the city was not acting pursuant to the direction or purposes of the South Carolina statutes but conspired solely to further COA's commercial purposes to the detriment of competition in the billboard industry." 891 F.2d 1127, 1133 (CA4 1989).

Judges who are closer to the trial process than we are do not share the Court's fear that juries are not capable of recognizing the difference between independent municipal action and action taken for the sole purpose of carrying out an anticompetitive agreement for the private party. See, *e.g.*, In re *Japanese Elec-*

tronic Products Antitrust Litigation, 631 F.2d 1069, 1079 (CA3 1980) ("The law presumes that a jury will find facts and reach a verdict by rational means. It does not contemplate scientific precision but does contemplate a resolution of each issue on the basis of a fair and reasonable assessment of the evidence and a fair and reasonable application of the relevant legal rules"). Indeed, the problems inherent in determining whether the actions of municipal officials are the product of an illegal agreement are substantially the same as those arising in cases in which the actions of business executives are subjected to antitrust scrutiny.[10]

The difficulty of proving whether an agreement motivated a course of conduct should not in itself intimidate this Court into exempting those illegal agreements that are proved by convincing evidence. Rather, the Court should, if it must, attempt to deal with these problems of proof as it has in the past—through heightened evidentiary standards rather than through judicial expansion of exemptions from the Sherman Act. See, *e.g., Matsushita Electric Industrial Co.* v. *Zenith Radio Corp.,* 475 U.S. 574 (1986) (allowing summary judgment where a predatory pricing conspiracy in violation of the Sherman Act was founded largely upon circumstantial evidence); *Monsanto Co.* v. *Spray-Rite Service Corp.,* 465 U.S. 752, 768 (1984) (holding that a plaintiff in a vertical price-fixing case must produce evidence which "tends to exclude the possibility of independent action").

Unfortunately, the Court's decision today converts what should be nothing more than an anticompetitive agreement undertaken by a municipality that enjoys no special status in our federalist system into a lawful exercise of public decisionmaking. Although the Court correctly applies principles of federalism in refusing to find a "conspiracy exception" to the *Parker* state-action doctrine when a State acts in a nonproprietary capacity, it errs in extending the state-action exemption to municipalities that enter into private anticompetitive agreements under the guise of acting pursuant to a general state grant of authority to regulate health, safety, and welfare. Unlike the previous limitations this Court has imposed on Congress' sweeping mandate in § 1, which found support in our common-law traditions or our system of federalism, see n.1, *supra,* the Court's wholesale exemption of municipal action from antitrust scrutiny amounts to little more than a bold and disturbing act of judicial legislation which dramatically curtails the statutory prohibition against "every" contract in restraint of trade.[11]

---

10. "There are many obstacles to discovering conspiracies, but the most frequent difficulties are three. First, price-fixers and similar miscreants seldom admit their conspiracy or agree in the open. Often, we can infer the agreement only from their behavior. Second, behavior can sometimes be coordinated without any communication or other observable and reprehensible behavior. Third, the causal connection between an observable, controllable act—such as a solicitation or meeting—and subsequent parallel action may be obscure." 6 P. Areeda, Antitrust Law ¶ 1400, at 3–4 (1986). See also Turner, The Definition of Agreement under the Sherman Act: Conscious Parallelism and Refusals to Deal, 75 Harv.L.Rev. 655 (1962) (discussing difficulties of condemning parallel anticompetitive action absent explicit agreement among the parties).

11. As the Court previously has noted:

"In 1972, there were 62,437 different units of local government in this country. Of this number 23,885 were special districts which had a defined goal or goals for the provision of one or several services, while the remaining 38,552 represented the number of counties, municipalities, and townships, most of which have broad authority for general governance subject to limitations in one way or another imposed by the State. These units may, and do, participate in and affect the economic life of this Nation in a great number and variety of ways. When these bodies act as owners and providers of services, they are fully capable of aggran-

IV

Just as I am convinced that municipal "lawmaking that has been infected by selfishly motivated agreement with private interests," *ante*, at 383, is not authorized by a grant of zoning authority, and therefore not within the state-action exemption, so am I persuaded that a private party's agreement with selfishly motivated public officials is sufficient to remove the antitrust immunity that protects private lobbying under *Eastern Railroad Presidents Conference* v. *Noerr Motor Freight, Inc.,* ... and *Mine Workers* v. *Pennington* ... Although I agree that the "sham" exception to the *Noerr-Pennington* rule exempting lobbying activities from the antitrust laws does not apply to the private petitioner's conduct in this case for the reasons stated by the Court in Part III of its opinion, I am satisfied that the evidence in the record is sufficient to support the jury's finding that a conspiracy existed between the private party and the municipal officials in this case so as to remove the private petitioner's conduct from the scope of *Noerr-Pennington* antitrust immunity. Accordingly, I would affirm the judgment of the Court of Appeals as to both the city of Columbia and Columbia Outdoor Advertising, Inc.

I respectfully dissent.

Notes and Questions

1. Paying for Special Interest Legislation: The interest group perspective suggests that legislation is "sold" to the highest bidder. COA is clearly the beneficiary of the billboard ordinances imposed by the City of Columbia. What did COA use to outbid Omni? Who bears the expense of COA's favorable legislation? Besides COA, who else benefits from the billboard ordinances?

2. Federalism v. Rent Seeking: The Court uses both *Parker* and *Noerr* to draw a line between the actions of COA and the City of Columbia, and actions that fall within the scope of the Sherman Act. *Parker* is based upon the notion that the federal government shall not interfere with those decisions which belong to the state — federalism. Thus, states can enact policy that limits intrastate competition. *Noerr* allows citizens to encourage the state to use the powers that it has been granted under the state action exemption of *Parker*. Thus, citizens can ask the state to make policy that limits intrastate competition. Does the combination of these two decisions clear the way for rent seeking behavior regarding state policy? It appears that the Court is willing to allow some amount of rent seeking behavior at the state level in order to protect federalism and self-determination. Is this trade-off wise? How about in the long-run?

3. Rationally-Ignorant Voters: Why don't the voters of Columbia seem to care about the dominant position granted to COA in the billboard market? How does the fact that COA gives free space to political candidates figure into this analysis? Does the fact that voters are rationally ignorant detract from the

---

dizing other economic units with which they interrelate, with the potential of serious distortion of the rational and efficient allocation of resources, and the efficiency of free markets which the regime of competition embodied in the antitrust laws is thought to engender." *Lafayette v. Louisiana Power & Light Co.*, 435 U.S. 389, 407–408 (1978) (footnotes omitted).

Court's reliance on federalism in deciding this case? It would certainly seem like companies who advertised via billboard would have an incentive to organize and fight legislation limiting their choices. Why doesn't this happen? What incentives exist for two different special interest groups seeking two separate pieces of favorable legislation from the same government?

4. Bootleggers and Baptists: Can you think of an example where two different special interest groups would favor the same piece of legislation for different reasons? In the times of prohibition, two unusual groups became partners in the fight for anti-drinking legislation. The Baptists found such legislation to be favorable for religious reasons; and the bootleggers found their covert trade to be much more profitable when liquor was illegal. Thus, the bootleggers and Baptists joined forces in the fight for prohibition laws.

2. Bureaucratic Incentives and Regulatory Capture

The history of economic regulation shows that industry-specific regulatory agencies tend to lose sight of their public interest mission over time. That is, although an agency may be created to control a particular industry, experience reveals that most regulatory agencies eventually adopt the perspective of the regulated industry. This is referred to as **regulatory capture**. Thus, eventually, the regulated industry frequently benefits from the regulation.

This observation has led some students of the regulatory process to suggest that one should look to the beneficiaries of the regulation in attempting to identify the parties that demanded and procured the regulation. For example, the Interstate Commerce Commission was created to control price discrimination by railroads. Some customers complained that price cuts were helping large shippers at the expense of small shippers. However, the primary effect of price discrimination was the destruction of the railroads' cartel which tried to raise prices above competitive levels. The railroads were competing for the large customers through price cuts and rebates, and the cartel was crumbling as a result. This socially beneficial competition was eliminated by the government's imposition of fixed rates which effectively enforced the cartel. Consumers, who presumably represented the "public interest," did not benefit from the regulation. Instead the benefits flowed to the railroads through the higher prices that resulted from the elimination of competition. In fact, some scholars have argued that the railroads engineered (pun intended) the creation of the ICC.

It is not unusual for administrative agencies to act in the interest of the regulated industry rather than in the so-called public interest. One explanation that has often been given is that the selection of board or commission members is biased toward choosing individuals from the industry. This is likened to hiring the fox to guard the henhouse. On the other hand, the hiring of industry insiders may be necessary because they may be the only available individuals with the special knowledge of the industry that is required to make a meaningful contribution to the agency. Such knowledge is rarely found in "outsiders." Further, it is not clear that selecting board and commission members from outside the industry would change the result. As outsiders become aware of the special problems facing an industry, they are likely to become sympathetic and supportive of the industry.

There are other reasons why the regulated industries will tend to have relatively more impact on the regulations than representatives of the public interest. The regulated industry has the greatest interest in the rules and regulations to be promulgated by the agency. Thus, in administrative hearings on proposed rule-makings, their perspective is likely to be better articulated than the public interest. This bias is not surprising, because individual citizens do not have the incentive to voice their positions on public policy issues because of free-rider problems. Thus, there is an underrepresentation of dispersed citizens' interests in the political process in general and the administrative process in particular.

The economics of regulation has revealed numerous instances when public-interest sounding regulations in the name of public safety and health have turned out to be well-disguised restrictions on competition. This is especially true in fields where licenses and board certifications are required.

Economists and legal commentators often treat the adoption and implementation of public policies as if the individuals who make up "the government" selflessly act in the public interest. However, experience teaches us that it is often the case that the self-interest of government decision makers does not guide them to make decisions that are in the public interest.

Chapter III

Markets, Prices, and Voluntary Exchange

The basic supply-and-demand model was introduced in Chapter I. This chapter provides a more in-depth presentation of salient aspects of this important tool of economic analysis. Section A examines the meaning of market price and quantity in a dynamic market setting. Section B explores the idea of individual preferences relative to market prices and considers the ways in which the subjective valuations of individuals may be protected. In Section C, the supply-and-demand model is used to analyze the responsiveness of both consumers and suppliers to price changes. In Section D, the effects of artificial controls on market prices are demonstrated. Finally, the role of prices in coordinating economic activity in a market system is examined in Section E.

A. Market Price and Quantity

In the theoretical supply-and-demand model, market price and quantity are determined by the intersection of supply and demand. In reality, dynamic markets often make it difficult to determine market prices because different sellers might be selling the same product at different prices because they have different opinions about where the market price is headed. The competitive process rewards the sellers and buyers who are best at interpreting market conditions. The following case illustrates that manufacturers and their retailers sometimes underestimate demand and are surprised by the market price for their products.

Sedmak v. Charlie's Chevrolet, Inc.
Missouri Court of Appeals
622 S.W. 2d 694 (1981)

Satz, J.

In their petition, plaintiffs, Dr. and Mrs. Sedmak (Sedmaks), alleged they entered into a contract with defendant, Charlie's Chevrolet, Inc. (Charlie's), to purchase a Corvette automobile for approximately $15,000. The Corvette was one of a limited number manufactured to commemorate the selection of the Corvette as the Pace Car for the Indianapolis 500. Charlie's breached the contract, the Sedmaks alleged, when, after the automobile was delivered, an agent for Char-

131

lie's told the Sedmaks they could not purchase the automobile for $15,000 but would have to bid on it.

The trial court found the parties entered into an oral contract and also found the contract was excepted from the Statute of Frauds. The court then ordered Charlie's to make the automobile "available for delivery" to the Sedmaks.

Charlie's raises three points on appeal: (1) the existence of an oral contract is not supported by the credible evidence; (2) if an oral contract exists, it is unenforceable because of the Statute of Frauds; and (3) specific performance is an improper remedy because the Sedmaks did not show their legal remedies were inadequate.

...[T]he record reflects the Sedmaks to be automobile enthusiasts, who, at the time of trial, owned six Corvettes. In July, 1977, "Vette Vues," a Corvette fancier's magazine to which Dr. Sedmak subscribed, published an article announcing Chevrolet's tentative plans to manufacture a limited edition of the Corvette. The limited edition of approximately 6,000 automobiles was to commemorate the selection of the Corvette as the Indianapolis 500 Pace Car. The Sedmaks were interested in acquiring one of these Pace Cars to add to their Corvette collection. In November, 1977, the Sedmaks asked Tom Kells, sales manager at Charlie's Chevrolet, about the availability of the Pace Car. Mr. Kells said he did not have any information on the car but would find out about it. Kells also said if Charlie's were to receive a Pace Car, the Sedmaks could purchase it.

On January 9, 1978, Dr. Sedmak telephoned Kells to ask him if a Pace Car could be ordered. Kells indicated that he would require a deposit on the car, so Mrs. Sedmak went to Charlie's and gave Kells a check for $500. She was given a receipt for that amount bearing the names of Kells and Charlie's Chevrolet, Inc. At that time, Kells had a pre-order form listing both standard equipment and options available on the Pace Car. Prior to tendering the deposit, Mrs. Sedmak asked Kells if she and Dr. Sedmak were "definitely going to be the owners." Kells replied, "yes." After the deposit had been paid, Mrs. Sedmak stated if the car was going to be theirs, her husband wanted some changes made to the stock model. She asked Kells to order the car equipped with an L82 engine, four speed standard transmission and AM/FM radio with tape deck. Kells said that he would try to arrange with the manufacturer for these changes. Kells was able to make the changes, and, when the car arrived, it was equipped as the Sedmaks had requested.

Kells informed Mrs. Sedmak that the price of the Pace Car would be the manufacturer's retail price, approximately $15,000. The dollar figure could not be quoted more precisely because Kells was not sure what the ordered changes would cost, nor was he sure what the "appearance package"—decals, a special paint job—would cost. Kells also told Mrs. Sedmak that, after the changes had been made, a "contract"—a retail dealer's order form—would be mailed to them. However, no form or written contract was mailed to the Sedmaks by Charlie's.

On January 25, 1978, the Sedmaks visited Charlie's to take delivery on another Corvette. At that time, the Sedmaks asked Kells whether he knew anything further about the arrival date of the Pace Car. Kells replied he had no further information but he would let the Sedmaks know when the car arrived. Kells also requested that Charlie's be allowed to keep the car in their showroom for promotional purposes until after the Indianapolis 500 Race. The Sedmaks agreed to this arrangement.

On April 3, 1978, the Sedmaks were notified by Kells that the Pace Car had arrived. Kells told the Sedmaks they could not purchase the car for the manufacturer's retail price because demand for the car had inflated its value beyond the suggested price. Kells also told the Sedmaks they could bid on the car. The Sedmaks did not submit a bid. They filed this suit for specific performance.

> [The court held that the contract was valid, and then turned to the specific performance issue.]

*   *   *

Finally, Charlie's contends the Sedmaks failed to show they were entitled to specific performance of the contract. We disagree. Although it has been stated that the determination whether to order specific performance lies within the discretion of the trial court, *Landau v. St. Louis Public Service Co.* , 273 S.W.2d 255, 259 (Mo. 1954), this discretion is, in fact, quite narrow. When the relevant equitable principles have been met and the contract is fair and plain, "specific performance goes as a matter of right." *Miller v. Coffeen*, 280 S.W.2d 100, 102 (Mo. 1955). Here, the trial court ordered specific performance because it concluded the Sedmaks "have no adequate remedy at law for the reason that they cannot go upon the open market and purchase an automobile of this kind with the same mileage, condition, ownership and appearance as the automobile involved in this case, except, if at all, with considerable expense, trouble, loss, great delay and inconvenience." Contrary to defendant's complaint, this is a correct expression of the relevant law and it is supported by the evidence.

Under the Code, the court may decree specific performance as a buyer's remedy for breach of contract to sell goods "where the goods are unique or in other proper circumstances." § 400.2-716(1) RSMo 1978. The general term "in other proper circumstances" expresses the drafters' intent to "further a more liberal attitude than some courts have shown in connection with the specific performance of contracts of sale." § 400.2-716, U.C.C., Comment 1. This Comment was not directed to the courts of this state, for long before the Code, we, in Missouri, took a practical approach in determining whether specific performance would lie for the breach of contract for the sale of goods and did not limit this relief only to the sale of "unique" goods. *Boeving v. Vandover*, 218 S.W.2d 175 (Mo. App. 1945). In *Boeving*, plaintiff contracted to buy a car from defendant. When the car arrived, defendant refused to sell. The car was not unique in the traditional legal sense but, at that time, all cars were difficult to obtain because of war-time shortages. The court held specific performance was the proper remedy for plaintiff because a new car "could not be obtained elsewhere except at considerable expense, trouble or loss, which cannot be estimated in advance and under such circumstances [plaintiff] did not have an adequate remedy at law." *Id.* at 177–178. Thus, *Boeving* presaged the broad and liberalized language of § 400.2-716(1) and exemplifies one of the "other proper circumstances" contemplated by this subsection for ordering specific performance. § 400.2-716, Missouri Code Comment 1. The present facts track those in *Boeving*.

The Pace Car, like the car in *Boeving* , was not unique in the traditional legal sense. It was not an heirloom or, arguably, not one of a kind. However, its "mileage, condition, ownership and appearance" did make it difficult, if not impossible, to obtain its replication without considerable expense, delay and inconvenience. Admittedly, 6,000 Pace Cars were produced by Chevrolet. However, as the record reflects, this is limited production. In addition, only one of these cars was available to each dealer, and only a limited number of these were equipped with the specific options ordered by plaintiffs. Charlie's had not received a car like the Pace Car in the previous two years. The sticker price for the car was $14,284.21. Yet Charlie's received offers from individuals in Hawaii and Florida to buy the Pace Car for $24,000 and $28,000 respectively. As sensibly inferred by the trial court, the location and size of these offers demonstrated this limited edition was in short supply and great demand. We agree with the trial court. This case was a "proper circumstance" for ordering specific performance.

Judgment affirmed.

Notes and Questions

1. Knowledge of Market Conditions: The dealership refused to sell the car at the manufacturer's suggested retail price because "demand for the car had inflated its value beyond the suggested price." In other words, because quantity demanded exceeded quantity supplied a market shortage existed at the manufacturer's suggested price. A market shortage places upward pressure on price, discourages consumption and encourages additional production. In this case, however, the Corvette Pace car was to be a special edition and therefore its supply was fixed. Because supply was fixed, the market price ended up higher than the manufacturer's suggested retail price. If the Chevrolet manufacturer had known the strength of demand for Corvette Pace cars, they might have responded by increasing the suggested retail price or increasing the quantity supplied.

2. Who Draws These Graphs Anyway?: How did Charlie's Chevrolet know that the market price was significantly higher than the manufacturer's suggested retail price? Did Mr. Kells think through the supply and demand model? Did he draw a supply and demand graph? In practice, most consumers and businesses do not draw graphs to illustrate what is happening in the market. Consumers and businesses, at the margin, respond to changes in their individual circumstances. If a business notices that its inventory of a particular good has fallen below its usual level, then the business may rationally respond by raising the price of the good while at the same time ordering more of the good from the producer. Such spontaneous price adjustments bring order to the market.

3. Assumptions about the Supply and Demand Model: Relative Prices, Constant Quality, and Flows: Price theory is concerned with how prices are determined and how they affect peoples' behavior. Microeconomic theory suggests that individuals respond to changes in relative prices. Responding to **relative prices** means that an individual's behavior is guided by the price of a product stated in terms of what other goods could be purchased for the same amount of money—the opportunity cost of a product. Consumers respond to changes in the prices of goods relative to one another, rather than the absolute dollar price of something. Consider, for example, a period of inflation during which the price of all goods and services increases by 10%. In other words, the absolute dollar price of all goods and services increases by the same percentage amount. Therefore, the ratio of the price of one good in terms of another would not change. What effect would this have on an individual's purchasing decisions? Under the assumption that personal income also increases by 10%, individuals are not expected to alter their purchasing decisions. This result stems from the fact that there has been no change in the relative price of goods and services. Thus, individuals are not expected to alter their purchasing decisions if the opportunity cost of purchasing a product has not changed.

In addition to focusing on relative prices, a distinction must be drawn between the money price and full price of a product or service. Notwithstanding the obvious, the **money price** is the actual dollar amount required by the seller to consummate the exchange. The **full price** includes the money price and the opportunity costs of a particular purchase. For example, consider the cost of getting the oil changed in your car. Suppose that the auto mechanic charges $30 for an oil change. Does $30 adequately represent the cost of having your oil changed? What about the time you spend driving to the auto garage, sitting in the waiting room, waiting in line to pay and driving home? You could have done something else with your time—your next best alternative or opportunity cost. These are real costs and must always be considered in any economic analysis. Thus, the supply and demand model is concerned with the full price of any good or service. Any time that the term price is used in economic analysis, it is assumed to be the full price.

Microeconomic analysis typically relies on the simplifying assumption that the quality of a particular economic good or service is held constant. For example, in a discussion involving the market price and quantity for shoes, it is assumed that there is no difference in the quality of any particular pair of shoes relative to others, regardless of its source. "Price" should be understood to mean the relative price of a quantity without regard to the quality of any particular unit. Unless otherwise indicated, economic analysis is conducted as if all units are identical and, therefore, of **constant quality**.

Finally, microeconomic theory is interested in the flow of goods and services. A **flow** is a quantity received, used, or spent at a particular rate over a specified time period. In contrast, a **stock** is a quantity of something that exists at a moment in time. Price theory is concerned with the relative price of constant quality units received, used, or spent over a given time period. For example, microeconomists might analyze the quantity of shoes sold per year at a given relative price. They are not particularly concerned with the total quantity of shoes in existence on a given date.

4. Why Specific Performance?: The Market for Substitutes: Specific performance is valuable when there is not a well-developed market for substitute goods. If there is a well developed market for substitutes, then either the buyer or seller could purchase a replacement product for roughly the same price and there is no need to require the seller to do anything other than pay compensatory damages for the breach. Was there a well-developed market for substitute Corvette Pace Cars? Could the Sedmaks have gone out and purchased a different Corvette Pace Car for the manufacturer's suggested retail price?

5. Michael Jordan, Barry Bonds, Troy Aikman, and many professional athletes: Why do professional athletes get paid so much when their "value" to society is not as great as, say, an elementary school teacher? Is this simply supply and demand? How is value reflected in the market?

6. Cost-Price Illusion: It is often difficult to determine why market prices have changed. In many instances, the retailer of a particular product will blame price increases on the higher prices charged by the retailer's suppliers (which represent the retailer's costs). However, the important issue in determining why the retailer's prices changed is to identify why the supplier's prices were raised. For example, an increase in the demand for computer processing chips would, other things equal, cause the price of such chips to increase. Consumers might notice this price increase when they go to purchase a new computer. In other words, the increased cost of processing chips would be reflected in higher prices for computers. When consumers ask the computer maker about the higher prices for computers, the computer maker may simply respond by noting that the cost of computer processing chips has gone up. This answer focuses on the cost of production—the supply side of the market—and ignores the fact that the price increase was a result of increased demand. In general, one should be skeptical of explanations for price increases that concentrate on only one side of the market—the cost-price illusion.

B. Market Prices and Subjective Value

Market prices represent an objective measure of the value of the products or services exchanged in a particular market. Market prices often do not reveal much information about individuals' personal subjective valuations of the products or services. Recall that mutually beneficial exchange occurs so long as the buyer values the product more than the seller. A market price can be viewed as determining the division of the gains from trade. The subjective valuations of the marginal buyers and sellers—that is, the last transaction to occur—are close to each other and determine the market price. At the margin, the gains from trade are small. The inframarginal subjective valuations are not revealed by market prices. All that is learned from the market price is that the buyers valued the product more than market price and the sellers valued it less than the market price.

Families often value their home substantially more than the market price—that is, their subjective value is greater than the market's objective valuation. Their subjective value is revealed by their decision to not sell their home at the market price. Figure III-1 represents a market for existing, constant-quality, single-family homes sold in a year. The supply curve reflects the number of homeowners who are willing to sell their homes at the different prices. The homes are already built, thus, the supply curve reflects different valuations by individuals, not the cost of building a new home. The number of transactions that actually occur in this market is represented by Q*. Actual buyers of homes, represented by the transactions that actually occur—those to the left of Q*—value their homes more than the market price, as indicated by the shaded area to the left of Q*. Thus, transactions move the homes from a lower to a higher valued use. Potential suppliers of homes to the right of the market clearing quantity, Q*, value their homes more than the market price as indicated by the shaded area to the right of Q*. Thus, we can conclude that subjective value is revealed by market behavior.

In many instances, our legal system has great difficulty in dealing with subjective value because, well, it is subjective. Consider two examples. First, although the Takings Clause of the Fifth Amendment requires "just compensation" for governmental takings of private property for public use, the Supreme Court has interpreted "just compensation" to mean market value. *See, e.g.,* United States v. Miller, 317 U.S. 369, 374 (1943). Some homeowners who have their

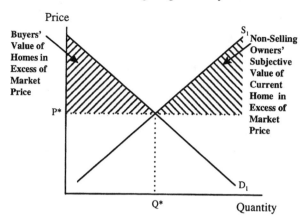

Figure III-1

Market for Existing Single-Family Homes

homes taken for a public purpose are not compensated for their lost subjective value. In Figure III-1, this is represented by homeowners to the right of Q^* on supply curve S_1. Second, most property insurance contracts do not cover lost subjective value because of concerns that compensation for such losses would encourage the insured party to overstate their subjective value and then not exercise appropriate care in protecting the property because loss of the property would result in a windfall for the insured. The latter behavior is referred to as a moral hazard.

In other instances, however, a contract could provide for the recognition of subjective value. Freedom of contract is a fundamental principle of the common law. As long as the parties to the contract have legal capacity and the performance of the contract does not violate public policy, the general rule is that parties may structure their contractual relations in any manner they desire, and the courts will enforce the terms of their contract. One advantage of this principle is that it allows individuals to protect assets that are more valuable to them personally than they are valued in the market. In general, freedom of contract allows the idiosyncratic, subjective preferences of individuals to be protected—but not always.

Peevyhouse v. Garland Coal & Mining Co.

Supreme Court of Oklahoma
382 P.2d 109 (1962)

JACKSON, J.

In the trial court, plaintiffs Willie and Lucille Peevyhouse sued the defendant, Garland Coal and Mining Company, for damages for breach of contract. Judgment was for plaintiffs in an amount considerably less than was sued for. Plaintiffs appeal and defendant cross-appeals.

In the briefs on appeal, the parties present their argument and contentions under several propositions; however, they all stem from the basic question of whether the trial court properly instructed the jury on the measure of damages.

Briefly stated, the facts are as follows: plaintiffs owned a farm containing coal deposits, and in November, 1954, leased the premises to defendant for a period of five years for coal mining purposes. A "strip-mining" operation was contemplated in which the coal would be taken from pits on the surface of the ground, instead of from underground mine shafts. In addition to the usual covenants found in a coal mining lease, defendant specifically agreed to perform certain restorative and remedial work at the end of the lease period. It is unnecessary to set out the details of the work to be done, other than to say that it would involve the moving of many thousands of cubic yards of dirt, at a cost estimated by expert witnesses at about $29,000. However, plaintiffs sued for only $25,000.

During the trial, it was stipulated that all covenants and agreements in the lease contract had been fully carried out by both parties, except the remedial work mentioned above; defendant conceded that this work had not been done.

Plaintiffs introduced expert testimony as to the amount and nature of the work to be done, and its estimated cost. Over plaintiffs' objections, defendant thereafter introduced expert testimony as to the "diminution in value" of plaintiffs' farm resulting from the failure of defendant to render performance as agreed in the contract—that is, the difference between the present value of the farm, and what its value would have been if defendant had done what it agreed to do.

At the conclusion of the trial, the court instructed the jury that it must return a verdict for plaintiffs, and left the amount of damages for jury determination. On the measure of damages, the court instructed the jury that it might consider the cost of performance of the work defendant agreed to do, "together with all of the evidence offered on behalf of either party."

It thus appears that the jury was at liberty to consider the "diminution in value" of plaintiffs' farm as well as the cost of "repair work" in determining the amount of damages.

It returned a verdict for plaintiffs for $ 5000—only a fraction of the "cost of performance," *but more than the total value of the farm even after the remedial work is done.*

On appeal, the issue is sharply drawn. Plaintiffs contend that the true measure of damages in this case is what it will cost plaintiffs to obtain performance of the work that was not done because of defendant's default. Defendant argues that the measure of damages is the cost of performance "limited, however, to the total difference in the market value before and after the work was performed."

It appears that this precise question has not heretofore been presented to this court. In Ardizonne v. Archer, 72 Okl. 70, 178 P. 263, this court held that the measure of damages for breach of a contract to drill an oil well was the reasonable cost of drilling the well, but here a slightly different factual situation exists. The drilling of an oil well will yield valuable geological information, even if no oil or gas is found, and of course if the well is a producer, the value of the premises increases. In the case before us, it is argued by defendant with some force that the performance of the remedial work defendant agreed to do will add at the most only a few hundred dollars to the value of plaintiffs' farm, and that the damages should be limited to that amount because that is all plaintiffs have lost.

Plaintiffs rely on Groves v. John Wunder Co., 205 Minn. 163, 286 N.W. 235, 123 A.L.R. 502. In that case, the Minnesota court, in a substantially similar situation, adopted the "cost of performance" rule as-opposed to the "value" rule. The result was to authorize a jury to give plaintiff damages in the amount of $60,000, where the real estate concerned would have been worth only $12,160, even if the work contracted for had been done.

It may be observed that Groves v. John Wunder Co., supra, is the only case which has come to our attention in which the cost of performance rule has been followed under circumstances where the cost of performance greatly exceeded the diminution in value resulting from the breach of contract. Incidentally, it appears that this case was decided by a plurality rather than a majority of the members of the court.

Defendant relies principally upon Sandy Valley & E.R. Co., v. Hughes, 175 Ky. 320, 194 S.W. 344; Bigham v. Wabash-Pittsburg Terminal Ry. Co., 223 Pa. 106, 72 A. 318; and Sweeney v. Lewis Const. Co., 66 Wash. 490, 119 P. 1108. These were all cases in which, under similar circumstances, the appellate courts followed the "value" rule instead of the "cost of performance" rule. Plaintiff points out that in the earliest of these cases (Bigham) the court cites as authority on the measure of damages an earlier Pennsylvania *tort* case, and that the other two cases follow the first, with no explanation as to why a measure of damages ordinarily followed in cases sounding in tort should be used in contract cases. Nevertheless, it is of some significance that three out of four appellate courts have followed the diminution in value rule under circumstances where, as here, the cost of performance greatly exceeds the diminution in value.

The explanation may be found in the fact that the situations presented are artificial ones. It is highly unlikely that the ordinary property owner would agree to pay $29,000 (or its equivalent) for the construction of "improvements" upon his property that would increase its value only about ($300) three hundred dollars. The result is that we are called upon to apply principles of law theoretically based upon reason and reality to a situation which is basically unreasonable and unrealistic.

In Groves v. John Wunder Co., supra, in arriving at its conclusions, the Minnesota court apparently considered the contract involved to be analogous to a building and construction contract, and cited authority for the proposition that the cost of performance or completion of the building as contracted is ordinarily the measure of damages in actions for damages for the breach of such a contract.

In an annotation following the Minnesota case beginning at 123 A.L.R. 515, the annotator places the three cases relied on by defendant (Sandy Valley, Bigham and Sweeney) under the classification of cases involving "grading and excavation contracts."

We do not think either analogy is strictly applicable to the case now before us. The primary purpose of the lease contract between plaintiffs and defendant was neither "building and construction" nor "grading and excavation". It was merely to accomplish the economical recovery and marketing of coal from the premises, to the profit of all parties. The special provisions of the lease contract pertaining to remedial work were incidental to the main object involved.

Even in the case of contracts that are unquestionably building and construction contracts, the authorities are not in agreement as to the factors to be considered in determining whether the cost of performance rule or the value rule should be applied. The American Law Institute's Restatement of the Law, Contracts, Volume 1, Sections 346(1)(a)(i) and (ii) submits the proposition that the cost of performance is the proper measure of damages "if this is possible and does not involve *unreasonable economic waste*"; and that the diminution in value caused by the breach is the proper measure "if construction and completion in accordance with the contract would involve *unreasonable economic waste*". (Emphasis supplied). In an explanatory comment immediately following the text, the Restatement makes it clear that the "economic waste" referred to consists of the destruction of a substantially completed building or other structure. Of course no such destruction is involved in the case now before us.

On the other hand, in McCormick, Damages, Section 168, it is said with regard to building and construction contracts that " * * * in cases where the defect is one that can be repaired or cured without *undue expense*" the cost of performance is the proper measure of damages, but where " * * * the defect in material or construction is one that cannot be remedied without *an expenditure for reconstruction disproportionate to the end to be attained*" (emphasis supplied) the value rule should be followed. The same idea was expressed in Jacob & Youngs, Inc. v. Kent, 230 N.Y. 239, 129 N.E. 889, 23 A.L.R. 1429, as follows:

> "The owner is entitled to the money which will permit him to complete, unless the cost of completion is grossly and unfairly out of proportion to the good to be attained. When that is true, the measure is the difference in value."

It thus appears that the prime consideration in the Restatement was "economic waste"; and that the prime consideration in McCormick, Damages, and in Jacob & Youngs, Inc. v. Kent, supra, was the relationship between the expense involved and the "end to be attained" — in other words, the "relative economic benefit".

In view of the unrealistic fact situation in the instant case, and certain Oklahoma statutes to be hereinafter noted, we are of the opinion that the "relative economic benefit" is a proper consideration here. This is in accord with the recent case of Mann v. Clowser, 190 Va. 887, 59 S.E.2d 78, where, in applying the cost rule, the Virginia court specifically noted that " * * * the defects are remediable from a practical standpoint and the costs *are not grossly disproportionate to the results to be obtained*". (Emphasis supplied)

23 O.S. 1961 §§ 96 and 97 provide as follows:

> "§ 96. * * * Notwithstanding the provisions of this chapter, no person can recover a greater amount in damages for the breach of an obligation, than he would have gained by the full performance thereof on both sides * * *."

> "§ 97. * * * Damages must, in all cases, be reasonable, and where an obligation of any kind appears to create a right to unconscionable and grossly oppressive damages, contrary to substantial justice no more than reasonable damages can be recovered."

Although it is true that the above sections of the statute are applied most often in tort cases, they are by their own terms, and the decisions of this court, also applicable in actions for damages for breach of contract. It would seem that they are peculiarly applicable here where, under the "cost of performance" rule, plaintiffs might recover an amount about nine times the total value of their farm. Such would seem to be "unconscionable and grossly oppressive damages, contrary to substantial justice" within the meaning of the statute. Also, it can hardly be denied that if plaintiffs here are permitted to recover under the "cost of performance" rule, they will receive a greater benefit from the breach than could be gained from full performance, contrary to the provisions of Sec. 96.

An analogy may be drawn between the cited sections, and the provisions of 15 O.S. 1961 §§ 214 and 215. These sections tend to render void any provisions of a contract which attempt to fix the amount of stipulated damages to be paid in case of a breach, except where it is impracticable or extremely difficult to determine the actual damages. This results in spite of the agreement of the parties, and the obvious and well known rationale is that insofar as they exceed the actual damages suffered, the stipulated damages amount to a penalty or forfeiture which the law does not favor.

23 O.S. 1961 §§ 96 and 97 have the same effect in the case now before us. *In spite of the agreement of the parties*, these sections limit the damages recoverable to a reasonable amount not "contrary to substantial justice"; they prevent plaintiffs from recovering a "greater amount in damages for the breach of an obligation" than they would have "gained by the full performance thereof".

We therefore hold that where, in a coal mining lease, lessee agrees to perform certain remedial work on the premises concerned at the end of the lease period, and thereafter the contract is fully performed by both parties except that the remedial work is not done, the measure of damages in an action by lessor against lessee for damages for breach of contract is ordinarily the reasonable cost of performance of the work; however, where the contract provision breached was merely incidental to the main purpose in view, and where the economic benefit which would result to lessor by full performance of the work is grossly disproportionate to the cost of performance, the damages which lessor may recover are limited to the diminution in value resulting to the premises because of the non-performance.

We believe the above holding is in conformity with the intention of the Legislature as expressed in the statutes mentioned, and in harmony with the better-reasoned cases from the other jurisdictions where analogous fact situations have been considered. It should be noted that the rule as stated does not interfere with the property owner's right to "do what he will with his own" (Chamberlain v. Parker, 45 N.Y. 569), or his right, if he chooses, to contract for "improvements" which will actually have the effect of reducing his property's value. Where such result is in fact contemplated by the parties, and is a main or principal purpose of those contracting, it would seem that the measure of damages for breach would ordinarily be the cost of performance.

The above holding disposes of all of the arguments raised by the parties on appeal.

Under the most liberal view of the evidence herein, the diminution in value resulting to the premises because of non-performance of the remedial work was $300.00. After a careful search of the record, we have found no evidence of a higher figure, and plaintiffs do not argue in their briefs that a greater diminution in value was sustained. It thus appears that the judgment was clearly excessive, and that the amount for which judgment should have been rendered is definitely and satisfactorily shown by the record....

We are of the opinion that the judgment of the trial court for plaintiffs should be, and it is hereby, modified and reduced to the sum of $ 300.00, and as so modified it is affirmed.

IRWIN, J. (dissenting).

By the specific provisions in the coal mining lease under consideration, the defendant agreed as follows:

> 7b Lessee agrees to make fills in the pits dug on said premises on the property line in such manner that fences can be placed thereon and access had to opposite sides of the pits.
>
> 7c Lessee agrees to smooth off the top of the spoil banks on the above premises.
>
> 7d Lessee agrees to leave the creek crossing the above premises in such a condition that it will not interfere with the crossings to be made in pits as set out in 7b.
>
> *   *   *
>
> 7f Lessee further agrees to leave no shale or dirt on the high wall of said pits....

Following the expiration of the lease, plaintiffs made demand upon defendant that it carry out the provisions of the contract and to perform those covenants contained therein.

Defendant admits that it failed to perform its obligations that it agreed and contracted to perform under the lease contract and there is nothing in the record which indicates that defendant could not perform its obligations. Therefore, in my opinion defendant's breach of the contract was willful and not in good faith.

Although the contract speaks for itself, there were several negotiations between the plaintiffs and defendant before the contract was executed. Defendant admitted in the trial of the action, that plaintiffs insisted that the above provisions be included in the contract and that they would not agree to the coal mining lease unless the above provisions were included.

In consideration for the lease contract, plaintiffs were to receive a certain amount as royalty for the coal produced and marketed and in addition thereto their land was to be restored as provided in the contract.

Defendant received as consideration for the contract, its proportionate share of the coal produced and marketed and in addition thereto, the *right to use* plaintiffs' land in the furtherance of its mining operations.

The cost for performing the contract in question could have been reasonably approximated when the contract was negotiated and executed and there are no conditions now existing which could not have been reasonably anticipated by the parties. Therefore, defendant had knowledge, when it prevailed upon the plaintiffs to execute the lease, that the cost of performance might be disproportionate to the value or benefits received by plaintiff for the performance.

Defendant has received its benefits under the contract and now urges, in substance, that plaintiffs' measure of damages for its failure to perform should be the economic value of performance to the plaintiffs and not the cost of performance.

If a peculiar set of facts should exist where the above rule should be applied as the proper measure of damages, (and in my judgment those facts do not exist in the instant case) before such rule should be applied, consideration should be given to the benefits received or contracted for by the party who asserts the application of the rule.

Defendant did not have the right to mine plaintiffs' coal or to use plaintiffs' property for its mining operations without the consent of plaintiffs. Defendant had knowledge of the benefits that it would receive under the contract and the approximate cost of performing the contract. With this knowledge, it must be presumed that defendant thought that it would be to its economic advantage to enter into the contract with plaintiffs and that it would reap benefits from the contract, or it would have not entered into the contract.

Therefore, if the value of the performance of a contract should be considered in determining the measure of damages for breach of a contract, the value of the benefits received under the contract by a party who breaches a contract should also be considered. However, in my judgment, to give consideration to either in the instant action, completely rescinds and holds for naught the solemnity of the contract before us and makes an entirely new contract for the parties. * * *

I therefore respectfully dissent to the opinion promulgated by a majority of my associates.

*   *   *

Notes and Questions

1. Bargaining for Subjective Value: The court seems to treat the plaintiffs' demand for specific performance as unreasonable in light of the very large expenditure necessary to restore the property relative to the very small increase in market value. For example, the court accepts the defendant's contention that "... damages should be limited to [diminution in value] because that is all that plaintiffs have lost." An alternative interpretation is that the plaintiffs accepted a lower royalty rate in order to get the defendant to agree to restore the land. Under this view, the plaintiffs have already paid for the restoration. Why would the plaintiff be willing to pay so much for work that has an objective market value of only $300? Perhaps the plaintiffs' actions have revealed that the plaintiffs' subjective valuation of the restoration is at least $29,000. In this case, should the remedy be cost of completion ($29,000) or specific performance ($29,000) or diminution in value ($300)? What happened to freedom of contract?

2. Efficient Breach: If contingencies occur that make it unprofitable for a promisor to perform as promised, the promisor may refuse to perform the contract and pay damages to the non-breaching party. If damages are measured properly, then the non-breaching party is as well-off as he would have been if the contract had been performed and the breaching party is better off because he bought his way out of an unprofitable situation by paying damages. This scenario would seem to satisfy the criteria for Pareto Efficiency: one party is made better off without harming another party. For this reason, this situation is often referred to as one of "efficient breach." Is the preceding case an example of an efficient breach? What contingencies occurred to make performance unprofitable? Were damages measured properly?

3. Bargaining During Performance: Assume that the plaintiff initially valued restoration at $29,000 and that the terms of the contract reflected the cost to the defendant of restoration. Also, assume that there is no doubt that the court will order specific performance or cost of completion. Now, assume that the plaintiff has a change of heart and no longer values the restoration more than its impact on market value ($300). Because the plaintiff still has the right to a remedy that will cost the defendant $29,000, there is a clear opportunity for gain through settlement at an amount somewhere between $300 and $29,000. Obviously, the plaintiff would prefer to collect $29,000 in cash from the defendant, but the defendant can thwart that opportunity by spending (or threatening to spend) the $29,000 on specific performance thereby providing the plaintiff with only the $300 increase in market value. Does the potential for this type of strategic bargaining provide an argument for the doctrine of economic waste?

4. There is More Than One Way to Skin a Cat: The plaintiff's desire for restoration can be realized through a clause requiring specific performance or a clause requiring cost of completion. However, uncertainty over judicial enforcement of a cost-of-completion clause—that is, the court ordering diminution in value damages instead of cost of completion—means that contracting parties will often prefer a clause with specific performance as a remedy. The particular legal rule governing these types of transactions does not affect the ultimate allocation of resources because the parties can contract around the rules, provided transaction costs are low. If the remedies of specific performance and cost of completion are not available (because of judicial concerns about "economic waste"), the landowner can still receive the desired result by charging a higher royalty rate to reflect the cost of restoration and then using the additional funds to hire an additional contractor to do the restoration. Is it "efficient" to require the landowner to go through this two-step process?

C. Elasticity: The Responsiveness of Supply and Demand to a Price Change

The supply and demand framework is helpful in analyzing many real-world problems. Thus far, we have established the simple proposition that the quantity supplied or demanded will be responsive to changes in the market price. This proposition leads us to a second line of analysis—*how responsive* are quantity demanded and supplied to changes in price. Will a small change in price lead to a large change in the quantity demanded or only a relatively small change? Economists use the concept of elasticity to measure the relative responsiveness of the quantity demanded or supplied to changes in price. In general, **elasticity** is a measure of the relative responsiveness of a dependent variable to a change in an independent variable. As such, many different types of elasticity can be measured. In this section, we are only concerned with price elasticity. **Price elasticity** is a measure of the relative responsiveness of the quantity demanded or supplied to changes in price.

1. Elasticity of Demand

Elasticity of demand is a measure of consumer responsiveness to price changes. Specifically, the elasticity of demand is the percent change in quantity demanded divided by the percent change in price.[1] The elasticity of demand is often indicated by the demand elasticity coefficient E_d—a numerical representation of the ratio of the percent change in quantity over the percent change in price.

Elasticity of Demand = % Change in Quantity Demanded ÷ % Change in Price

$$E_d = \frac{\%\Delta Q^D}{\%\Delta P}$$

Elastic demand describes a situation in which the percent change in quantity demanded is greater than the percent change in price—thus, the demand elasticity coefficient is greater than 1. Elastic demand means buyers are very responsive to price changes. As the demand elasticity coefficient increases above 1, demand becomes more elastic. In contrast, **inelastic demand** describes a situation in which buyers are not very responsive to changes in price—the percent change in quantity demanded is less than the percentage change in price. In this situation, the demand elasticity coefficient is less than 1. As the coefficient moves away from 1 and becomes infinitely closer to 0, demand is said to be more inelastic. **Unit elasticity of demand** is a situation in which the percent change in quantity demanded is the same as the percent change in price. Thus, the demand elasticity coefficient is equal to one.

Figure III-2 illustrates the relationship between price and quantity demanded for the different categories of elasticity. Each panel shows the effect of a 25% price increase on the quantity demanded. Thus, the shifting of price along the vertical axis is the same in all three panels. In terms of impact on the quantity demanded, each of the panels shows a different horizontal shift. The varying results for quantity demanded are a result of differently sloped demand curves. In panel (a), quantity demanded falls by 10% which is less than the 25% change in price. Thus, panel (a) provides an example of an inelastic demand curve. Notice that inelastic demand curves have a relatively steeper slope—a slope with an absolute value greater than one. Price and quantity both change by 25% in panel (b) indi-

---

1. In actual calculation, the demand elasticity coefficient will always be negative, because of the law of demand. If price goes up, quantity demanded for a good or service goes down, and vice versa. For purposes of our exposition, this point is irrelevant to the interpretation of elasticity. We will accordingly eliminate the use of a negative sign before the demand elasticity coefficient.

Figure III-2

Elasticities of Demand

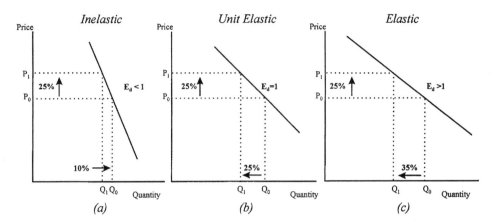

(a)   (b)   (c)

cating the presence of unit elasticity. Demand curves exhibiting unit elasticity have a slope with an absolute value equal to one. Quantity demanded falls by 35% in panel (c) which exceeds the 25% change in price. The demand curve in panel (c) is therefore elastic as demonstrated by is relatively flat slope—a slope less with an absolute value less than one.

Two extreme forms of the demand curve are especially helpful in analyzing many economic problems. Figure III-3(a) shows a demand curve that is totally elastic. When the demand curve is **totally elastic**, the quantity demanded is completely responsive to price changes—a small increase in price will cause the quantity demanded to disappear. Thus, the demand elasticity coefficient equals infinity. A totally elastic demand curve would occur in a perfectly competitive market. However, perfectly competitive markets are rare. Figure III-3(b) shows a

Figure III-3

Totally Elastic & Inelastic Demand Curves

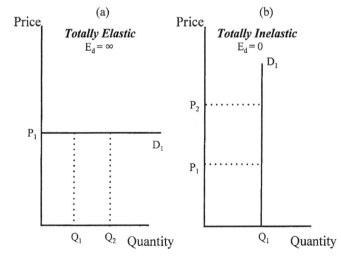

demand curve that is **totally inelastic**—quantity demanded is unresponsive to changes in price. A totally inelastic demand curve has a demand elasticity coefficient of zero. It is often suggested that a heroin addict's demand for heroin is totally inelastic.

For ease of exposition, demand curves are usually drawn as straight lines. The elasticity of demand for such linear demand curves contain portions that are elastic, unit elastic, and inelastic. Thus, the elasticity coefficient will vary along demand curves. For example, consider the market demand for pizza graphed in Figure III-4. The slope of the curve is constant throughout, as indicated by the fact that the increase in quantity demanded in response to a price decrease of $1 is the same for every $1 price interval. Another way of stating this is to observe that a decline in price from $7 to $6 results in the same increase in the quantity demanded as does a decline from $4 to $3. Despite this, the elasticity of demand is greater at the higher prices. The move from A to B represents a 50% increase in quantity demanded and a 14.29% decrease in price—and this translates into an elasticity of demand of 3.49. Note that the move from B to A indicates elasticity of 1.9. The difference between the calculations illustrates that the relevant percentages change depending on the direction of the change in price. A $1 decline resulting in a move from C to D yields a relatively inelastic demand of 0.61—a 20% increase in quantity and a 33% decrease in price.

Two conclusions can be drawn from the analysis in Figure III-4. First, it does not make sense to refer to the demand for a particular good or service as being

<u>Figure III-4</u>

Differing Elasticities Along a Market Demand Curve

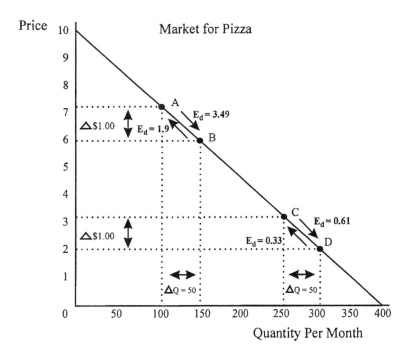

elastic or inelastic unless that reference is qualified by a price range. This is due to the fact that the elasticity of goods and services can change as prices change. Second, consumers are generally more responsive to price changes at higher prices than lower prices. Notice that the portion of the demand curve associated with higher prices is elastic and the portion associated with lower prices is inelastic. In Figure III-5, the point at which the curve goes from being elastic to inelastic is where there is unitary elasticity of demand.

The demand elasticity concept can also be utilized to analyze the effect of price changes on total revenue or total expenditures. First, it is necessary to point out that the terms total revenue and total expenditures describe two perspectives for the same money. **Total revenue** is the product of price times quantity. Total revenue represents the total amount of money that the supplier receives from the buyer. It is intuitive that a dollar spent by the consumer is the same dollar that the seller considers to be revenue. Thus, **total expenditures** can also be defined as the product of price and quantity. Total expenditures represent the total amount of money that the buyer gives to the supplier.

What happens to total revenue (total expenditures) when price decreases? According to the law of demand, if the price falls, the quantity demanded increases. The lower price means that revenue (expenditures) per unit decreases, which tends to decrease total revenue (total expenditures). However, the greater quantity demanded means that the number of units sold increases, and this tends to increase total revenue (total expenditures). The overall change in total revenue (total expenditures) resulting from a lower price is the net result of these opposite effects. When demand is elastic, the percentage increase in quantity demanded

<u>Figure III-5</u>
Elasticity & Higher Prices

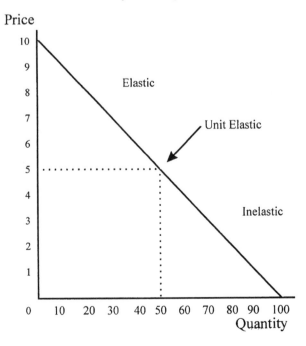

Figure III-6

Total Expenditures/Total Revenues &
Demand Elasticity

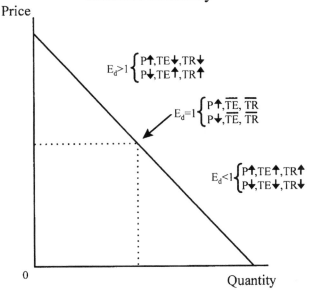

Price

$E_d > 1$ { P↑,TE↓,TR↓
           P↓,TE↑,TR↑

$E_d = 1$ { P↑,$\overline{TE}$, $\overline{TR}$
           P↓,$\overline{TE}$, $\overline{TR}$

$E_d < 1$ { P↑,TE↑,TR↑
           P↓,TE↓,TR↓

0   Quantity

exceeds the percentage decrease in price, so a price decrease will increase total revenue (total expenditures). When demand is unit elastic, the percentage increase in quantity demanded is just equal to the percentage decrease in price, so a price decrease will not change total revenue (total expenditures). Finally, when demand is inelastic, the percentage increase in quantity demanded is less than the percentage decrease in price, so a price decrease will decrease total revenue (total expenditures). These relationships are illustrated in Figure III-6. Thus, the general rule is that if price and total revenue (total expenditures) move in the same direction, then demand is inelastic; if price and total revenue (total expenditures) move in opposite directions, then demand is elastic.

There are three major determinants of the elasticity of demand. First, and most important, the number, availability, and price of substitutes indicates the ability of buyers to purchase other products in response to a price increase. Second, in general, the size and importance of the product in the consumer's budget determines whether or to what extent the consumer will respond to a price change—the larger and more important the product to the budget, the more likely consumers will respond to a change in price. Third, the time period involved in the adjustment to a price change will affect the elasticity of demand. The effect of time will be discussed in more detail in a later section.

The law of demand states that, other things being equal, an inverse relationship exists between price and quantity demanded. The law of demand is an undefeated proposition in economics. Nonetheless, in analyzing individuals' demand curves for a product, we may occasionally be presented with a situation that appears not to support the law of demand. Consider the impact of a $0.25 increase in the price of a Big Mac. It is undoubtedly true that some individuals will not reduce their consumption of Big Macs in the face of the price increase, but that does not refute or even contradict the law of demand. Although some individuals do not react to the price increase, others will reduce their consumption. The individuals who reduce their consumption are referred to as the **marginal consumers**—the economic actors who are the first to respond to a change in relative prices. Another way to describe the marginal consumers is to say that their elasticity of demand for Big Macs is greater than the elasticity of the consumers who did not change their quantity demanded in the face of a price increase.

2.   Elasticity of Supply

Elasticity of supply is a measure of producer responsiveness to changes in the market price for goods or services. Specifically, the elasticity of supply is the percent change in quantity supplied divided by the percent change in price. Thus, an elasticity of supply coefficient can be calculated for any type of supply curve.

Elasticity of Supply = % Change in Quantity Supplied ÷ % Change in Price

$$E = \frac{\%\Delta Q^S}{\%\Delta P}$$

Elastic supply describes a situation in which the percent change in quantity supplied is greater than the percent change in price—the supply elasticity coefficient is greater than 1. Elastic supply means that suppliers are very responsive to price changes. The larger the supply elasticity coefficient is above 1, the more elastic supply is said to be. In contrast, **inelastic supply** describes a situation in which suppliers are not very responsive to changes in price—the percent change in quantity supplied is less then the percentage change in price. In this situation, the supply elasticity coefficient is less than 1. As the coefficient moves away from 1 and becomes closer to 0, supply is said to be more inelastic.

As was the case with demand elasticity, study of the totally elastic and totally inelastic supply curves is helpful in analyzing many types of economic problems. **Totally elastic supply** is represented graphically by a horizontal supply curve—as in Figure III-7. At any price below P producers will supply a quantity of zero. As the price moves from just below P to P producers will supply an unlimited amount to the market—a totally elastic supply curve has an elasticity coefficient of infinity. In this case, the quantity actually supplied to the market depends upon the demand curve. At the other extreme is the case of the totally inelastic supply curve. **Totally inelastic supply** curves are vertical and represent a zero percentage change in the quantity supplied regardless of the percentage change in price. Figure III-7 shows the relationship between price and quantity supplied for the totally inelastic supply curve. Total inelasticity reflects a market with completely unresponsive suppliers and results in a supply elasticity coefficient of zero.

The responsiveness of the quantity supplied to an increase in price will depend on the suppliers willingness and ability to transfer resources to the production of that good. If it is perceived to be economically costly to transfer resources from other uses then it will take a large price increase to obtain a given quantity increase and supply will be relatively inelastic. On the other hand, if resources can be trans-

Figure III-7

Totally Elastic & Inelastic Supply Curves

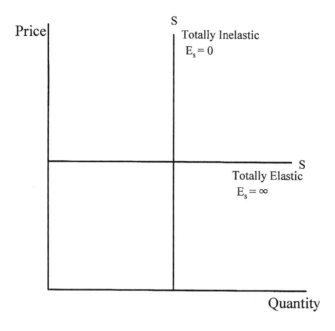

ferred at a relatively low economic cost, a smaller price increase will suffice to bring about a given increase in quantity and supply will be relatively elastic.

3. Time and Elasticity

Both demand and supply elasticity are affected by the time period allowed for adjustment. The more time that suppliers have to adjust to the price change, the more elastic supply will be. Likewise, elasticity of demand increases the longer consumers have to react to any given price change. To analyze the responsiveness of supply and demand over a period of time, economists have divided the time of adjustment into three periods: the market period, the short run, and the long run. The following example, in the supply elasticity context, demonstrates the effect of time.

Assume that Congress passes, and the President signs, legislation that imposes sweeping new regulatory requirements on business. In order to comply with the regulations, businesses demand additional legal services. In Figure III-8, we show this as an increase in demand from D_1 to D_2. However, in the market period, the supply curve for legal services is perfectly inelastic—represented by S_1. Because resources cannot be shifted to new uses instantaneously, the supply of legal services is fixed. Thus, in the market period, supply is fixed in the face of increasing demand resulting in an increase in price from P_1 to P_2—indicated by movement from point A to point B. Individuals providing legal services will notice that the price that can be charged has increased. The new higher price creates

Figure III-8

Time & Elasticity of Supply

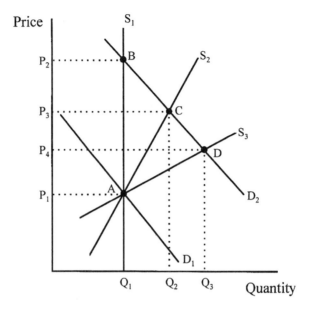

the incentive to shift resources into the provision of legal services. In the short run, lawyers will shift currently available resources into the provision of legal services. This may include spending more time at work and less time in leisure activities or more time on regulatory law than divorce law. The effect of this short run supply response is illustrated by S_2 and P_3—indicated by movement from point B to point C.

If an economic profit is still being earned after all currently available resources have been moved into the provision of regulatory legal services, then an incentive exists to make further changes. In the long run, all possible adjustments can be made and resources that were not available in the short run can now be shifted into the provision of regulatory legal services. For example, law firms that were previously unsure of the permanency of the change will now begin to provide regulatory legal services, persons with law degrees who are not practicing will take the bar, and college graduates seeking the higher incomes of lawyers relative to other professions will apply and graduate from law schools. The effect of these long run adjustments will be to shift the long run supply curve to S_3 and increase the quantity supplied to Q_3—indicated by movement from point C to point D. Note that the effect of all of these responses is to increase the number of lawyers and reduce price towards the old level. Will price fall back to P_1? This depends upon factors specific to the industry. The main point to remember is that the elasticity of supply will tend to increase over time.

The same type of analysis applies to demand elasticity. As a general rule, the more time that both producers and consumers have to respond to a change in market price, the more elastic will be supply and demand.

4. Tax Incidence

A major source of revenue for governments is the excise tax. An **excise tax** is a per unit tax on the sale of a particular item. Well known examples of excise taxes are those levied on the sale of cigarettes, tires, and gasoline. Confusion often arises as to who pays an excise tax. Because the seller sends a check to the government, many people believe that the seller bears the burden of an excise tax. However, sellers might be capable of passing the burden of an excise tax on to consumers through increased prices. A study of **tax incidence** reveals whether consumers or sellers bear the burden of a particular tax. Analyzing tax incidence uses the supply and demand elasticity concepts introduced in the previous sections. A simple example will help explain the tax incidence concept.

Consider a $2.00 tax levied on every automobile tire sold. The tire tax is paid to the government by the tire manufacturer. Figure III-9 shows the supply and demand for tires prior to the $2.00 excise tax—represented by D_1 and S_1. Prior to the tax, the market was in equilibrium at 50 million tires produced for a price of $50.00 per tire—indicated by point A. What is the effect on market price and quantity of imposing a $2.00 per tire tax? Remember that the supply curve represents the amount that sellers are willing and able to supply at each price. Once the tax is imposed, suppliers per unit costs will be $2.00 higher at each quantity level. The result of the excise tax is to shift the supply curve to the left—to S_2. The vertical distance between S_1 and S_2 is equal to the excise tax amount of $2.00. From Figure III-9 it is easy to see that one effect of the tax is to reduce the total quantity of tires sold. This is because the demand for tires is not totally inelastic. Despite the fact that the supply curve shifts to reflect the excise tax, the demand curve does not move because nothing has happened to change the demand for tires—only the quantity demanded will be affected.

As a result of the tax, sellers would be willing to supply the old equilibrium quantity of 50 million tires at a price of $52.00—indicated by point B. However,

Figure III-9

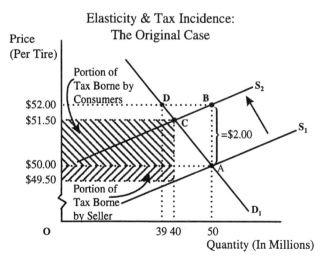

Elasticity & Tax Incidence: The Original Case

because the demand for tires is not totally inelastic, consumers are not willing to purchase 50 million tires at $52.00. At $52.00, consumers are only willing to purchase 39 million tires—indicated by point D. Thus, at the old equilibrium quantity level a market surplus would develop putting downward pressure on price and quantity supplied. After the imposition of the tax we can see that the market moves to a new equilibrium price of $51.50 and quantity of 40 million—indicated by point C. The shaded area represents the tax revenue collected, which is equal to the quantity of tires sold multiplied by the $2.00 tax rate. In our example, the total tax revenue equals 40,000,000 × $2.00 = $80,000,000. Note that the old equilibrium price line indicates how both the seller and purchaser are effected by the excise tax. Prior to the tax, the equilibrium price was $50.00. The new equilibrium price is $51.50 and consumers must now pay $1.50 more for a tire. Thus, consumers bear 75% of the new $2.00 tax as indicated by the shaded area above the original equilibrium price. Although the price increases $1.50, sellers must send $2.00 to the government for every tire sold. The remaining $.50 must come from the seller. Thus, at a market price of $51.50, the sellers' price net of taxes is $49.50. This is $.50 below the old equilibrium price of $50.00. The sellers' burden is reflected diagrammatically as the shaded portion below the old equilibrium price—the seller bears 25% of the tax burden.

Tax incidence changes with changes in the elasticity of demand. If demand is highly elastic, sellers tend to bear more of the burden. Figure III-10 shows the original tire market in equilibrium at 50 million tires for $50.00 per tire—indicated by point A. The only difference between this and the previous example is that the slope of the demand curve is flatter, representing more elastic demand. As in the previous example, a $2.00 tax is levied per tire causing the supply curve to shift to the left by an amount equal to $2.00 for each possible quantity. In this example, the new equilibrium price is only $50.50—indicated by point B. This is $.50 above the old equilibrium price and thus consumers bear 25% of the $2.00 tax burden. The seller must still send $2.00 to the government and can only force the consumer to pay for $.50 of the tax. Thus, the seller must deduct $1.50 from

<u>Figure III-10</u>

Elasticity & Tax Incidence:
The Case of Greater Demand Elasticity

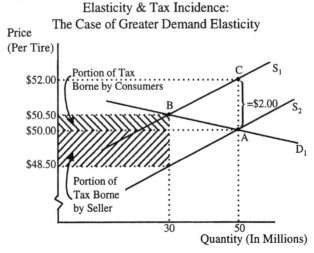

the old $50.00 selling price, meaning that the sales price net of taxes is $48.50. This means the seller now bears 75% of the tax.

A comparison of the examples in Figures III-9 and III-10 indicates that relatively elastic demand means that consumers bear less of the burden of an excise tax. Sellers cannot pass on much of the tax when demand is relatively elastic. However, when demand is relatively inelastic, consumers bear more of the tax in the form of higher prices. In addition, note that when demand was more elastic, the total quantity demanded by the market fell by a greater amount than when demand was relatively inelastic. As a result, an excise tax is a more effective revenue source when the demand for the taxed good is relatively inelastic.

The elasticity of supply plays a similar role in the tax incidence question. In all instances, the supply curve shifts to the left by an amount equal to the per unit tax. However, the slope of the supply curve—its relative elasticity—will play a role in whether consumers or suppliers bear the tax burden. In general, the more elastic supply, the more a tax is passed on to consumers in the form of higher prices. The flip side of this is that the more inelastic supply, the more the tax burden is borne by the supplier.

In general, an excise tax increases the price that consumers must pay and decreases the price that sellers receive. Obviously, this is a cost to the particular individuals who engage in buying and selling the taxed good or service. It is a cost for these individuals because it represents a loss in their respective consumer or producer surpluses. This loss is demonstrated in Figure III-11, which shows the effect of an excise tax on tires. The area above the equilibrium market price and

Figure III-11

Deadweight Loss or Excess Burden Due to a Government Excise Tax

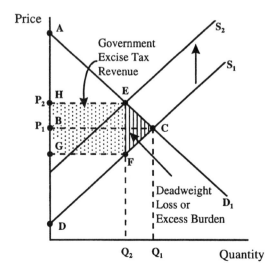

below the demand curve represents consumer surplus, and the area under the equilibrium market price and above the supply curve is producer surplus. Prior to the tax, consumer surplus was equal to the area ABC and producer surplus was equal to the area BCD. After the imposition of the tax, the supply curve shifts to the left—indicated by movement from S_1 to S_2—and market price moves from P_1 to P_2. The vertical distance between S_1 and S_2 is equal to the amount of the excise tax. Notice that as a result of the tax, consumer and producer surplus has been reduced by the area HECFG.

The entire reduction in consumer and producer surplus due to the excise tax should not be viewed as a loss borne by society. Remember that the government gains tax revenue in an amount equal to the area HEFG. The government revenue is spent either by purchasing goods and services directly or by giving the money to other citizens (e.g., welfare payments) for them to spend on goods and services. If the benefit to consumers and producers of government spending is equal to the area HEFG, then the remaining area of lost consumer and producer surplus is equal to ECF. This is the real cost of the tax. This area represents a reduction in the total output of the economy due to the tax that can *never* be regained. This loss, represented by the area ECF, is known as the **deadweight loss** of the tax or the **excess burden** of the tax.

D. Price Controls

In general, the interaction of supply and demand results in a market clearing price where the quantity demanded equals the quantity supplied. Occasionally, however, artificial (non-market) restraints on the ability of the market price to adjust to disequilibria between the quantity demanded and quantity supplied are imposed. The most common types of **price controls** are price ceilings and price floors.

1. Price Ceilings

A **price ceiling** is a restraint on the maximum price that may be charged for a particular good or service. In order to have an impact on market behavior, the price ceiling must be set below the market clearing price. The impact of a price ceiling is demonstrated in Figure III-12, where P* and Q* represent the market clearing price and quantity. P_C represents the price ceiling. At P_C, the quantity demanded, Q_D, is greater than the quantity supplied, Q_S. When the quantity demanded is greater than the quantity supplied, a **shortage** or **excess demand** exists. However, the price control prevents the market from adjusting to correct this disequilibrium.

In general, as illustrated by the next two cases, the existence of a shortage usually results in the allocation of supply through less efficient means such as waiting in line, bribes, or the requirement that the buyer also purchase other goods from the seller.

Figure III-12

Price Controls: A Price Ceiling

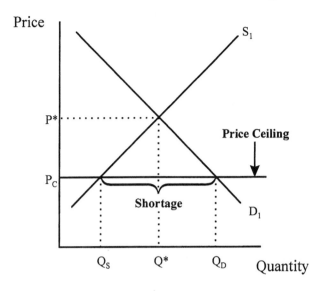

M. Kraus & Bros., Inc. v. United States

Supreme Court of the United States
327 U.S. 614 (1945)

Justice Murphy announced the conclusion and judgment of the Court.

The problem here is whether the petitioner corporation was properly convicted of a crime under the Emergency Price Control Act of 1942.

The petitioner is engaged in the wholesale meat and poultry business in New York City. Poultry is a commodity subject to the provisions of Revised Maximum Price Regulation No. 269, promulgated by the Price Administrator pursuant to § 2(a) of the Emergency Price Control Act of 1942....

The theory of the Government is that [during Thanksgiving in November, 1943] the petitioner was guilty of an evasion of the price limitations set forth in this particular regulation if it required the purchase of chicken feet and skin as a necessary condition to obtaining the primary commodity, the poultry. This practice is commonly known as a "combination sale" or a "tying agreement." It is argued that the petitioner thereby received for the poultry the ceiling price plus the price of the secondary commodities, the chicken parts.

*   *   *

The jury acquitted petitioner's president but convicted the petitioner on nine counts. Petitioner was fined $2,500 on each count, a total of $22,500. The conviction was affirmed by the court below,... In our opinion, however, the conviction must be set aside.

Section 205(b) of the Emergency Price Control Act of 1942 imposes criminal sanctions on "Any person who willfully violates any provisions of section 4 of this Act..." Section 4(a) of the Act in turn provides that "It shall be unlawful... for any person to sell or deliver any commodity,... in violation of... section 2..." Section 2(a) authorizes the Price Administrator under prescribed conditions to establish by regulation or order such maximum prices "as in his judgment will be generally fair and equitable and will effectuate the purposes of this Act." Section 2(g) further states that "Regulations... may contain such provisions... as the Administrator deems necessary to prevent the circumvention or evasion thereof."

The Price Administrator, pursuant to § 2(a), issued Revised Maximum Price Regulation No. 269 on December 18, 1942, which regulation was in effect at the time the poultry sales in question were made. § 1429.5 of this regulation, referred to in the information, stems from § 2(g) of the Act. It is entitled "Evasion" and reads as follows: "Price limitations set forth in this Revised Maximum Price Regulation No. 269 shall not be evaded whether by direct or indirect methods, in connection with any offer, solicitation, agreement, sale, delivery, purchase of receipt of, or relating to, the commodities prices of which are herein regulated, alone or in conjunction with any other commodity, or by way of commission, service, transportation, or other charge, or discount, premium, or other privilege or other trade understanding or otherwise."

*   *   *

This delegation to the Price Administrator of the power to provide in detail against circumvention and evasion, as to which Congress has imposed criminal sanctions, creates a grave responsibility. In a very literal sense the liberties and fortunes of others may depend upon his definitions and specifications regarding evasion. Hence to these provisions must be applied the same strict rule of construction that is applied to statutes defining criminal action. In other words, the Administrator's provisions must be explicit and unambiguous in order to sustain a criminal prosecution; they must adequately inform those who are subject to their terms what conduct will be considered evasive so as to bring the criminal penalties of the Act into operation.

*   *   *

In light of these principles we are unable to sustain this conviction of the petitioner based upon § 1429.5 of Revised Maximum Price Regulation No. 269. For purposes of this case we must assume that the Administrator legally could include tying agreements and combination sales involving the sale of valuable secondary commodities at their market value among the prohibited evasion devices.... The only issue bearing upon the regulation which is open in this criminal proceeding is whether the Administrator did in fact clearly and unmistakably prohibit tying agreements of this nature by virtue of the language he used in § 1429.5. That issue we answer in the negative.

Section 1429.5, so far as here pertinent, provides that price limitations shall not be evaded by any method, direct or indirect, whether in connection with any offer or sale of a price-regulated commodity alone "or in conjunction with any other commodity," or by way of any trade understanding "or otherwise." No specific mention is made of tying agreements or combination sales.

*   *   *

The language of § 1429.5 is appropriate to and consistent with a desire on the Administrator's part to prohibit only those tying agreements involving tied-in commodities that are worthless or that are sold at artificial prices. The Administrator may have thought that other tied-in sales did not constitute a sufficient threat to the price economy of the nation to warrant their outlawry, or that they were such an established trade custom that they should be recognized. But we are told that he had no such thought, that prohibition of all tying agreements is essential to prevent profiteering, and that this blanket prohibition is the only policy consistent with the purposes of the Act. All of this may well be true. But these are administrative judgments with which the courts have no concern in a criminal proceeding. We must look solely to the language actually used in § 1429.5. And when we do we are unable to say that the Administrator has made his position in this respect self-evident from the language used.

The Administrator's failure to express adequately his intentions in § 1429.5 is emphasized by the complete and unmistakable language he has used in other price regulations to prohibit tying agreements, including those involving the sale of valuable secondary products....

The case must therefore be remanded for a new trial, allowing full opportunity for the introduction of evidence as to the value of the chicken parts and charging the jury in accordance with the proper interpretation of § 1429.5.

It is so ordered.

*   *   *

Black, J. dissenting.

We were at war in 1943. Scarcity of food had become an acute problem throughout the nation. To keep the public from being gouged the government had set ceiling prices.... When Thanksgiving Day approached there were not enough turkeys to supply the demand of the many American families who wanted to celebrate in customary style.

...This meat shortage was felt acutely during the Thanksgiving season, when petitioner instead of his usual 100 to 150 cars of turkeys received only one car. When the retail butchers and poultry market proprietors came clamoring for their share of the small supply (which the defendant rationed among them) they found that along with the turkeys which they wanted so badly petitioner gave and charged them for large amounts of chicken feet, skins and gizzards which they had not asked for at all and which for the most part they had never before sold as separate items. While the butchers paid in addition to the ceiling price charged for the turkeys the price charged for the chicken skins and feet, they do so only because they understood that unless they bought these unwanted items they could get no turkeys. Only one of the butchers sold all the chicken skins to his customers. He explained that he operated his store in a poor neighborhood where the food shortage had become so acute that people were willing to buy anything they could get. As to the rest of the butchers, some simply dumped the chicken skins and feet while other, after diligent efforts, sold a few pounds then gave the rest away either to their customers, or to charitable institutions. Certainly these particular butchers forced to buy these unwanted items for the first time were not the regular retail outlet for disjointed chicken feet and peeled chicken skins, if there ever was such an outlet on a voluntary basis. It is clear therefore that as a result of petitioner's forcing his customers to buy the feet and skins along with the turkeys, the retailers' cost price of the turkeys was in effect increased beyond the ceiling.

In my opinion petitioner's practice in forcing the butchers to buy unwanted chicken feet in order to get wanted turkeys amounted to a direct violation of the Price Control Act. It certainly was no less a violation of the Administrator's regulation against evasion. In promulgating this regulation the Administrator could not possibly foresee every ingenious scheme or artifice the business mind might contrive to shroud violations of the Price Control Act. The regulation does not specifically describe all manner of evasive device. The term "tying agreement" nowhere appears in it and a discussion of such agreements is irrelevant. We need not decide whether what a petitioner did would have violated every possible hypothetical regulation the Administrator might have promulgated. The regulation here involved prohibits every evasion of the Price Control Act....

*   *   *

When food is scarce and people are hungry it is a violation, both of the letter and spirit of the Price Control Laws, to require consumers or retail stores where they make their purchases, to buy things that they neither need nor want as a condition to obtaining articles which they must have. I dissent from the Court's disposition in this case.

Notes and Questions

1. The Value of Chicken Feet and Skin: In this case, the Court does not say anything regarding the merits of price control laws. Rather, the Court finds the section regarding evasion of the price control law to be defective. The defect identified by the Court is that the section lacks clarity regarding the types of behavior that would be regarded as evasive. Specifically, the statutory language was consistent with a prohibition against tie-in sales involving only worthless commodities—it is possible that the chickens' feet and skin has a market value equal to the difference between the total price paid to petitioner and the market value of the turkey. Whether the chickens' feet and skin is a worthless commodity is a decision left to the finder of fact upon remand.

2. Punishing the Nature of Man?: The Court applies a "strict rule of construction" in defining the evasion provision. This is done because the price fixing regulation was enforced with criminal penalties. Why does the Court use a higher standard of interpretation when criminal penalties are involved? What implicit assumption regarding human behavior is the Court using to justify this standard?

3. Price Gouging or a Change in Demand?: We often hear political and social commentators accuse the business world of engaging in price gouging. It is supposed that price gouging occurs when the seller recognizes that supply will be short in the future and raises present prices in order capture a windfall. Does this allegation make any sense? What do you think happened to the demand for plywood after Hurricane Andrew hit Florida? Based on the tremendous amount of damage to housing in Florida, it is likely that the demand for plywood increased. As suppliers of plywood in Florida recognized that they did not have enough plywood in stock, we would expect profit maximizing individuals in the rest of the country to begin sending plywood to Florida. Thus, the price of plywood would be expected to increase in both Florida and the remainder of the country due to the increase in demand for this commodity. In general, one should be very skeptical of accusations of price gouging.

4. Using the Market to Solve the Hurricane Problem: From the previous note, we know that as a result of the hurricane, the demand for plywood in Florida increased causing the price of plywood across the country to rise. Consider the effect that a price increase would have on consumer behavior? Suppose Walt Williams, who lives in Virginia, is thinking about building his dog a house. As the price of plywood increases, Walt decides that it is getting too expensive to build a dog house and that his dog can just sleep in the rain. However, the people who have lost their homes in Florida value this same plywood very highly—they are pleased with Walt's decision. In fact, social welfare is maximized by having the people in Florida use the plywood to rebuild their homes, as opposed to Walt building a dog house. Was any law passed by Congress to get this result? Did President Bush need to issue an executive order commanding that plywood not be used to build dog houses? Was the fact that the hardware store in Walt's neighborhood raised its price for plywood—because people were willing to pay more in Florida—generally helpful or harmful to society? Did Walt forgo the use of wood because he is a humanitarian and felt sorry for the homeless people in Florida? The answer to all of these questions is that the market works—it quickly and anonymously allocates resources to those who desire them the most.

5. Using Price Controls to Solve the Hurricane Problem: What would have happened in the hurricane Andrew example if Congress had enacted an Emergency Plywood Price Control Act? Assume that the price control imposes a market price equal to the historical price level for plywood. What effect does this have on consumer behavior? What does Walt now think about building his dog a house? Because the price of plywood is now at its historical level, Walt decides to build a dog house. Thus, less plywood is available to rebuild homes in Florida—quantity demanded exceeds quantity supplied. In other words, we have a shortage in the plywood market. Is the result achieved using the market or price controls more beneficial to society in general?

6. Laws Against Scarcity?: Justice Black observes that scarcity of food had become a nationwide problem and that "[t]o keep the public from being gouged"—that is, facing higher prices—"the government had set ceiling prices." Moreover, "[w]hen Thanksgiving Day approached there were not enough turkeys to supply the demand of many American families who wanted to celebrate in the customary style." It should be obvious by this point that Justice Black is misguided in his assessment that the public is being gouged—see note 3. However, what do you think about his statement regarding the supply of turkey? Justice Black observes that there will not be enough turkeys for many Americans to celebrate Thanksgiving in the "customary style." What is the point of this observation? The facts of the case seem to indicate that the same quantity of turkey will be available no matter what the method of distribution. That is, even if a price control were imposed and there was no evasion, people would still have to stand in a line in hopes of getting one of the few available turkeys. In fact, the same number of people who got a turkey with the evasion present will get one without it. The flip side of this is that, no matter what, the same number of Americans will be able to celebrate Thanksgiving in the "customary way."

Perhaps Justice Black is concerned with the "fairness" of the distribution method. The likely alternative if all evasion could be stopped would be a long line forming in front of the store. Is this the best use of our time and resources? Consider two possible results of full enforcement of price control laws. First, everyone takes off work to get in line, days ahead of time, in order to get a turkey. Would this have been a good result? Remember that during this time period, labor was in great demand—the opportunity cost of not working was high. Second, a more likely story is that people would not have taken off work, because they could not afford to sacrifice that income for a turkey. Thus, only those families generating enough income to allow some family members to not work outside of the home, would be able to stand in the line to buy turkey. Was this the desired result? Even here we have an efficiency loss, because these individuals are no longer working at home if they are standing in line. If the market had been allowed to work (i.e., no price controls), families with greater incomes probably would have purchased the turkeys. The fact that turkeys would have sold for a higher price and would have been allocated to those who valued turkey the highest, is further supported by a third possibility. Even if turkeys were some how allocated in a random manner at the price controlled level, an incentive exists for a black market to develop. That is, individuals who get a turkey for the controlled price will turn around and sell it to someone else for a higher price—presumably, the market price. This analysis seems to indicate that through some way or another, turkeys will be allocated to those individuals willing to pay the *market* price. Then why opt for the less efficient distribution method?

7. The Chicken Skin Entrepreneur?: It is a fact of the case that not only is turkey scarce, but food in general is scarce. According to the testimony of one of the butchers, he was able to sell the chicken skin to his customers. That is, people who were not able to afford turkey or find other food now had food available to purchase. Thus, we can assume that to many consumers these skin and feet were worth something. In fact, those butchers who threw the skin away wasted a resource that some consumers value. Moreover, for Justice Black to assume that these commodities have a zero value adopts a static view of the market process. In other words, perhaps when turkey is widely available, chicken skin has zero value, but when turkey and food in general are more difficult to obtain, chicken skin is valuable to those who are hungry. When an individual sees a new use for a resource that is valued more highly than its opportunity cost, that individual is called an entrepreneur and is rewarded with economic profits. Why is the petitioner not seen in this light? Why is the petitioner not rewarded for his entrepreneurial behavior?

The next case, *Jones v. Star Credit Corp.*, involves the sale of a freezer for four times its retail value to a welfare recipient. At the time of sale, the state of New York had imposed usury laws which put a limit on the maximum interest rate that creditors could charge—a limit on the maximum price that can be charged for a loan. How would you expect the market to allocate credit under a usury, price ceiling, scenario. While reading the case, consider how Star Credit Corp. attempts to circumvent the usury law. Furthermore, is this an efficient way to allocate credit?

Jones v. Star Credit Corp.

Supreme Court of New York, Special Term, Nassau County
298 N.Y.S.2d 264 (1969)

Sol Wachtler, J.

On August 31, 1965 the plaintiffs, who are welfare recipients, agreed to purchase a home freezer unit for $900 as the result of a visit from a salesman representing Your Shop At Home Service, Inc. With the addition of the time credit charges, credit life insurance, credit property insurance, and sales tax, the purchase price totaled $1,234.80. Thus far the plaintiffs have paid $619.88 toward their purchase. The defendant claims that with various added credit charges paid for an extension of time there is a balance of $819.81 still due from the plaintiffs. The uncontroverted proof at the trial established that the freezer unit, when purchased, had a maximum retail value of approximately $300. The question is whether this transaction and the resulting contract could be considered unconscionable within the meaning of Section 2-302 of the Uniform Commercial Code which provides in part:

> (1) If the court as a matter of law finds the contract or any clause of the contract to have been unconscionable at the time it was made the court may refuse to enforce the contract, or it may enforce the remainder of the contract without the unconscionable clause, or it may so limit the application of any unconscionable clause as to avoid any unconscionable result.

> (2) When it is claimed or appears to the court that the contract or any clause thereof may be unconscionable the parties shall be afforded a reasonable opportunity to present evidence as to its commercial setting, purpose and effect to aid the court in making the determination. (L. 1962, ch. 553, eff. Sept. 27, 1964.

There was a time when the shield of "caveat emptor" would protect the most unscrupulous in the marketplace — a time when the law, in granting parties unbridled latitude to make their own contracts, allowed exploitive and callous practices which shocked the conscience of both legislative bodies and the courts.

The effort to eliminate these practices has continued to pose a difficult problem. On the one hand it is necessary to recognize the importance of preserving the integrity of agreements and the fundamental right of parties to deal, trade, bargain, and contract. On the other hand there is the concern for the uneducated and often illiterate individual who is the victim of gross inequality of bargaining power, usually the poorest members of the community.

Concern for the protection of these consumers against overreaching by the small but hardy breed of merchants who would prey on them is not novel. The dangers of inequality of bargaining power were vaguely recognized in the early English common law when Lord Hardwicke wrote of a fraud, which "may be apparent from the intrinsic nature and subject of the bargain itself; such as no man in his senses and not under delusion would make". The English authorities on this subject were discussed in Hume v. United States 132 U.S. 406, 411, 10 S. Ct. 134, 136, 33 L.Ed. 343 (1889) where the United States Supreme Court characterized (p. 413, 10 S.Ct. p. 137) these as "cases in which one party took advantage of the other's ignorance of arithmetic to impose upon him, and the fraud was apparent from the face of the contracts."

The law is beginning to fight back against those who once took advantage of the poor and illiterate without risk of either exposure or interference. From the common law doctrine of intrinsic fraud we have, over the years, developed common and statutory law which tells not only the buyer but also the seller to beware. This body of laws recognizes the importance of a free enterprise system but at the same time will provide the legal armor to protect and safeguard the prospective victim from the harshness of an unconscionable contract.

Section 2-302 of the Uniform Commercial Code enacts the moral sense of the community into the law of commercial transactions. It authorizes the court to find, as a matter of law, that a contract or a clause of a contract was "unconscionable at the time it was made", and upon so finding the court may refuse to enforce the contract, excise the objectionable clause or limit the application of the clause to avoid an unconscionable result. "The principle", states the Official Comment to this section, "is one of the prevention of oppression and unfair surprise." It permits a court to accomplish directly what heretofore was often accomplished by construction of language, manipulations of fluid rules of contract law and determinations based upon a presumed public policy.

There is no reason to doubt, moreover, that this section is intended to encompass the price term of an agreement. In addition to the fact that it has already been so applied...the statutory language itself makes it clear that not only a clause of the contract, but the contract *in toto*, may be found unconscionable as a matter of law. Indeed, no other provision of an agreement more intimately touches upon the question of unconscionability than does the term regarding price.

Fraud, in the instant case, is not present; nor is it necessary under the statute. The question which presents itself is whether or not, under the circumstances of this case, the sale of a freezer unit having a retail value of $300 for $900 ($1,439.69 including credit charges and $18 sales tax) is unconscionable as a matter of law. The court believes it is.

Concededly, deciding the issue is substantially easier than explaining it. No doubt, the mathematical disparity between $300, which presumably includes a reasonable profit margin, and $900, which is exorbitant on its face, carries the greatest weight. Credit charges alone exceed by more than $100 the retail value of the freezer. These alone, may be sufficient to sustain the decision. Yet, a caveat is warranted lest we reduce the import of Section 2-302 solely to a mathematical ratio formula. It may, at times, be that; yet it may also be much more. The very limited financial resources of the purchaser, known to the sellers at the time of the sale, is entitled to weight in the balance. Indeed, the value disparity itself leads inevitably to the felt conclusion that knowing advantage was taken of the plaintiffs. In addition, the meaningfulness of choice essential to the making of a contract can be negated by a gross inequality of bargaining power. (Williams v. Walker-Thomas Furniture Co., 121 U.S. App. D.C. 315, 350 F. 2d 445.)

There is no question about the necessity and even the desirability of installment sales and the extension of credit. Indeed, there are many, including welfare recipients, who would be deprived of even the most basic conveniences without the use of these devices. Similarly, the retail merchant selling on installment or extending credit is expected to establish a pricing factor which will afford a degree of protection commensurate with the risk of selling to those who might be default prone. However, neither of these accepted premises can clothe the sale of this freezer with respectability.

Support for the court's conclusion will be found in a number of other cases already decided. In American Home Improvement v. MacIver, supra, the Supreme Court of New Hampshire held that a contract to install windows, a door and paint, for the price of $2,568.60, of which $809.60 constituted interest and carrying charges and $800 was a salesman's commission was unconscionable as a matter of law. In State by Lefkowitz v. ITM, Inc., supra a deceptive and fraudulent scheme was involved, but standing alone, the court held that the sale of a vacuum cleaner, among other things, costing the defendant $140 and sold by it for $749 cash or $920.52 on time purchase was unconscionable as a matter of law. Finally, in Frostifresh Corp. v. Reynoso, supra the sale of a refrigerator costing the seller $ 348 for $ 900 plus credit charges of $245.88 was unconscionable as a matter of law.

* * *

Having already paid more than $600 toward the purchase of this $300 freezer unit, it is apparent that the defendant has already been amply compensated. In accordance with the statute, the application of the payment provision should be limited to amounts already paid by the plaintiffs and the contract be reformed and amended by changing the payments called for therein to equal the amount of payment actually so paid by the plaintiffs.

Notes and Questions

1. Usury Laws: A Form of Price Control: A limit on the maximum interest rate that a lender can charge is called a usury law. To be effective, the maximum interest rate must be set at a level below the current market interest rate. A usury law is simply a form of price ceiling—an interest rate is simply the price paid for financing. When the maximum legal rate is below the market rate, the quantity of credit demanded will exceed the quantity of credit supplied. However, because of the legal constraint, interest rates will not be allowed to adjust upward in order to eliminate the shortage. Thus, it appears as if a shortage will continue to exist. However, this is not the end of the story. Creditors and borrowers have an incentive to get around usury laws. In other words, loans will be allocated by a non-interest rate mechanism.

2. Interest Rates: In general, an interest rate has three components contributing to its sum. First, a portion of the interest rate reflects the opportunity cost of the principal in some other use. Second, an addition is made to reflect the expectation of inflation. Third, a premium is added to any interest rate based upon the risk of default. The riskier the investment, the higher the rate. This formulation of the interest rate suggests that a systematic bias will develop under usury laws. Namely, high risk individuals will not be able to obtain loans. The question then becomes: are these high risk individuals better off paying high interest rates for credit or not having the option of credit at all?

3. Circumventing Usury Laws: Some firms who extend credit to high risk individuals as a regular part of their business have found ways to circumvent usury laws. Consider the local appliance store who wishes to make a sale on credit to a high risk individual but cannot charge the market interest rate. Instead of forgoing the sale, store owners have developed resourceful methods for maximizing profits. For example, assume that the market price for the new appliance is $500. The customer, however, is considered to be a high risk for default. Thus, an interest rate in excess of the legal limit would be required to consummate the sale. One way around this is for the seller to charge the buyer a price in excess of the market price for the appliance. For example, the appliance store may charge $750 for the appliance despite its market price of $500. The seller has parted with a $500 appliance, but is charging interest on the principal of $750. Monthly payments to the store owner will include an amount based on the principal and interest of this fictional credit extension. The payments on the fictional credit of $250, paid back over the course of the loan at the legal interest rate, will be sufficient to compensate the store owner as if he had charged the high risk interest rate on the true market price of $500. By raising the price, and therefore the original principal above the market price, the seller is compensated for its below market interest rate. The calculation of numbers is covered in Chapter IV, Principles of Valuation.

2. Price Floors

A **price floor** is a price control that prevents the sale of a product below a certain minimum level. A price floor must be set greater than the market clearing price in order to have an impact on market behavior. In Figure III-13, the equilibrium price and quantity are indicated by P^* and Q^*, respectively. The price floor, P_F, causes quantity supplied, Q_S, to be greater than quantity demanded, Q_D. This disequilibrium condition is referred to as a **surplus** or **excess supply**. In

Figure III-13

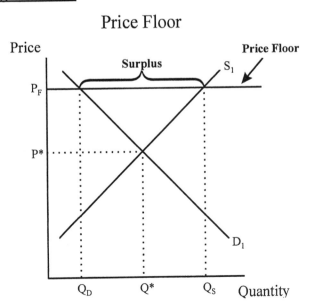

Price Floor

order to sell their goods and services when the market is constrained by a price floor, the sellers must offer non-price incentives, such as better services, "free" gifts, and rebates.

A familiar example of a price floor is the minimum wage law enacted by the federal government. The intent of the minimum wage law is to provide workers with a "fair wage" for their work and to reduce the incidence of poverty. Using the supply and demand model, we can quickly determine whether minimum wage laws work and whether they have unintended consequences.

In order for the minimum wage to have an impact, it must be set at a rate above the market wage for those employees who are the intended beneficiaries of the law. In Figure III-14, the market wage is represented by W^* and the mandated minimum wage is denoted by W_{MIN}. As we observed above, the result of mandating a price floor is to cause quantity supplied to exceed quantity demanded. At the higher wage, the quantity demanded decreases to Q_1 and the quantity supplied increases to Q_2. The excess supply, equal to $Q_2 - Q_1$, is a surplus of labor. However, because of the minimum wage law, price and quantity cannot adjust back to the market equilibrium. Under an effective minimum wage—that is, a minimum wage above the market clearing wage—some individuals keep their jobs and increase their earnings, some individuals lose their jobs, and some individuals enter the job market.

Think about the result of minimum wage laws: the quantity of available jobs has decreased but those who do have jobs are paid a higher "fair wage." Moreover, the remaining jobs are allocated in a highly competitive process to those with the best potential or skill. Those who cannot find jobs in the labor market are those with lower education or little work experience. Such laws seem to perpetuate the poverty of some while increasing the wages of others. Was this the intended consequence?

<u>Figure III-14</u>
Minimum Wage Law's Effect on the Labor Market

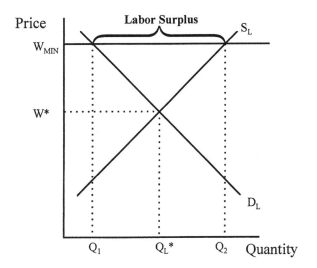

3.   The Quality of Products and Services in a Price Controlled Market

An additional implication of price controls is interesting and relevant to understanding the competitive market process. We have assumed in the foregoing discussion, that the quality of goods and services produced remains the same after price controls are established. However, this is generally not the case. Consider a price control example from the area of property law.

Rent controls are a form of price ceiling. Often the justification for such laws is the protection of low income individuals. Nonetheless, the long run effect of rent control seems to harm low income individuals the most. For example, one effect of rent control is the decay of the buildings. This is understandable because landlords' maintenance costs often exceed their rental income. Furthermore, what incentive for improvements exist when rental income is fixed? A second negative effect is the disincentive rent controls create for building new rental property. As populations grow, the demand for rental space begins to exceed supply. However, because of rent control there is little incentive to build new rental property. Thus, it is not unusual to find several families living in very cramped quarters. Rent controls also create the incentive for a black market to develop. Those who were lucky enough to be renting property at the controlled rate, make a profit by subletting at very high prices. The market clears, but only with the help of illegal transactions.

E. Unequal Bargaining Power and the Limits of Mutually Beneficial Exchange

Economic analysis focuses on the voluntary, consensual, and reciprocal aspects of exchange. *Ex ante*, individuals would not agree to a contract unless it were in their interest. In some instances, individuals agree to contracts that do not appear to be reasonable deals from the perspective of a reasonable external observer. It is often alleged that such *ex ante* unfair contracts are the result of unequal bargaining power and that the courts should reform the contracts or specific terms of the contract. In this section, two categories of contracts that are often attacked as alleged manifestations of unequal bargaining power are examined: unconscionable contracts for consumer goods and opportunistic modification during performance.

1.   Unconscionability

Section 2-302 of the U.C.C. allows the courts to choose not to enforce "unconscionable" contracts. In general, an unconscionable contract may be said to be one that is so grossly unfair that it shocks the conscience of the court. This principle is one designed to prevent oppression and unfair surprise. Thus, it is a form of consumer protection legislation. The principle is most frequently applied in retail sales to individuals who cannot read or do not understand the provisions of a contract. The following case illustrates the type of situation where courts will refuse to enforce a contract because it is unconscionable.

Williams v. Walker Thomas Furniture Company
District of Columbia Court of Appeals
198 A.2d 914 (1964)

QUINN, J.

Appellant, a person of limited education separated from her husband, is maintaining herself and her seven children by means of public assistance. During the period 1957–1962 she had a continuous course of dealings with appellee from which she purchased many household articles on the installment plan. These included sheets, curtains, rugs, chairs, a chest of drawers, beds, mattresses, a washing machine, and a stereo set. In 1963 appellee filed a complaint in replevin for possession of all the items purchased by appellant, alleging that her payments were in default and that it retained title to the goods according to the sales contracts. By the writ of replevin appellee obtained a bed, chest of drawers, washing machine, and the stereo set. After hearing testimony and examining the contracts, the trial court entered judgment for appellee.

Appellant's principal contentions on appeal are (1) there was a lack of meeting of the minds, and (2) the contracts were against public policy.

Appellant signed fourteen contracts in all. They were approximately six inches in length and each contained a long paragraph in extremely fine print. One of the sentences in this paragraph provided that payments, after the first purchase, were to be prorated on all purchases then outstanding. Mathematically, this had the effect of keeping a balance due on all items until the time balance was completely eliminated. It meant that title to the first purchase, remained in appellee until the fourteenth purchase, made some five years later, was fully paid.

At trial appellant testified that she understood the agreements to mean that when payments on the running account were sufficient to balance the amount due on an individual item, the item became hers. She testified that most of the purchases were made at her home; that the contracts were signed in blank; that she did not read the instruments; and that she was not provided with a copy. She admitted, however, that she did not ask anyone to read or explain the contracts to her.

We have stated that "one who refrains from reading a contract and in conscious ignorance of its terms voluntarily assents thereto will not be relieved from his bad bargain." Bob Wilson, Inc. v. Swann, D.C.Mun.App., 168 A.2d 198, 199 (1961). "One who signs a contract has a duty to read it and is obligated according to its terms." Hollywood Credit Clothing Co. v. Gibson, D.C.App., 188 A.2d 348, 349 (1963). "It is as much the duty of a person who cannot read the language in which a contract is written to have someone read it to him before he signs it, as it is the duty of one who can read to peruse it himself before signing it." Stern v. Moneyweight Scale Co., 42 App.D.C. 162, 165 (1914).

A careful review of the record shows that appellant's assent was not obtained "by fraud or even misrepresentation falling short of fraud." Hollywood Credit Clothing Co. v. Gibson, supra. This is not a case of mutual misunderstanding but a unilateral mistake. Under these circumstances, appellant's first contention is without merit.

Appellant's second argument presents a more serious question. The record reveals that prior to the last purchase appellant had reduced the balance in her account to $164. The last purchase, a stereo set, raised the balance due to $678. Significantly, at the time of this and the preceding purchases, appellee was aware of appellant's financial position. The reverse side of the stereo contract listed the name of appellant's social worker and her $218 monthly stipend from the government. Nevertheless, with full knowledge that appellant had to feed, clothe and support both herself and seven children on this amount, appellee sold her a $514 stereo set.

We cannot condemn too strongly appellee's conduct. It raises serious questions of sharp practice and irresponsible business dealings. A review of the legislation in the District of Columbia affecting retail sales and the pertinent decisions of the highest court in this jurisdiction disclose, however, no ground upon which this court can declare the contracts in question contrary to public policy. We note that were the Maryland Retail Installment Sales Act, Art. 83 §§ 128–153, or its equivalent, in force in the District of Columbia, we could grant appellant appropriate relief. We think Congress should consider corrective legislation to protect the public from such exploitive contracts as were utilized in the case at bar.

Affirmed.

Williams v. Walker Thomas Furniture Company II
United States Court of Appeals District of Columbia Circuit
350 F.2d 445 (1965)

J. SKELLY WRIGHT, J.

*   *   *

Appellants' principal contention, rejected by both the trial and the appellate courts below, is that these contracts, or at least some of them, are unconscionable and, hence, not enforceable....

*   *   *

We do not agree that the court lacked the power to refuse enforcement to contracts found to be unconscionable. In other jurisdictions, it has been held as a matter of common law that unconscionable contracts are not enforceable. While no decision of this court so holding has been found, the notion that an unconscionable bargain should not be given full enforcement is by no means novel. In Scott v. United States, 79 U.S. (12 Wall.) 443, 445, 20 L. Ed. 438 (1870), the Supreme Court stated:

> " * * * If a contract be unreasonable and unconscionable, but not void for fraud, a court of law will give to the party who sues for its breach damages, not according to its letter, but only such as he is equitably entitled to. * * * * "

Since we have never adopted or rejected such a rule, the question here presented is actually one of first impression.

Congress has recently enacted the Uniform Commercial Code, which specifically provides that the court may refuse to enforce a contract which it finds to be unconscionable at the time it was made. 28 D.C. CODE § 2-302 (Supp. IV 1965). The enactment of this section, which occurred subsequent to the contracts here in suit, does not mean that the common law of the District of Columbia was otherwise at the time of enactment, nor does it preclude the court from adopting a similar rule in the exercise of its powers to develop the common law for the District of Columbia. In fact, in view of the absence of prior authority on the point, we consider the congressional adoption of § 2-302 persuasive authority for following the rationale of the cases from which the section is explicitly derived. Accordingly, we hold that where the element of unconscionability is present at the time a contract is made, the contract should not be enforced.

Unconscionability has generally been recognized to include an absence of meaningful choice on the part of one of the parties together with contract terms which are unreasonably favorable to the other party. Whether a meaningful choice is present in a particular case can only be determined by consideration of all the circumstances surrounding the transaction. In many cases the meaningfulness of the choice is negated by a gross inequality of bargaining power. The manner in which the contract was entered is also relevant to this consideration. Did each party to the contract, considering his obvious education or lack of it, have a reasonable opportunity to understand the terms of the contract, or were the important terms hidden in a maze of fine print and minimized by deceptive sales practices? Ordinarily, one who signs an agreement without full knowledge of its terms might be held to assume the risk that he has entered a one-sided bargain. But when a party of little bargaining power, and hence little real choice, signs a commercially unreasonable contract with little or no knowledge of its terms, it is hardly likely that his consent, or even an objective manifestation of his consent, was ever given to all the terms. In such a case the usual rule that the terms of the agreement are not to be questioned should be abandoned and the court should consider whether the terms of the contract are so unfair that enforcement should be withheld.

In determining reasonableness or fairness, the primary concern must be with the terms of the contract considered in light of the circumstances existing when the contract was made. The test is not simple, nor can it be mechanically applied. The terms are to be considered "in the light of the general commercial background and the commercial needs of the particular trade or case." Corbin suggests the test as being whether the terms are "so extreme as to appear unconscionable according to the mores and business practices of the time and place." 1 Corbin, *Contracts*. We think this formulation correctly states the test to be applied in those cases where no meaningful choice was exercised upon entering the contract.

Because the trial court and the appellate court did not feel that enforcement could be refused, no findings were made on the possible unconscionability of the contracts in these cases. Since the record is not sufficient for our deciding the issue as a matter of law, the cases must be remanded to the trial court for further proceedings.

So ordered.

DANAHER, J. (dissenting):

The District of Columbia Court of Appeals obviously was as unhappy about the situation here presented as any of us can possibly be. Its opinion in the

Williams case, quoted in the majority text, concludes: "We think Congress should consider corrective legislation to protect the public from such exploitive contracts as were utilized in the case at bar."

My view is thus summed up by an able court which made no finding that there had actually been sharp practice. Rather the appellant seems to have known precisely where she stood.

There are many aspects of public policy here involved. What is a luxury to some may seem an outright necessity to others. Is public oversight to be required of the expenditures of relief funds? A washing machine, e.g., in the hands of a relief client might become a fruitful source of income. Many relief clients may well need credit, and certain business establishments will take long chances on the sale of items, expecting their pricing policies will afford a degree of protection commensurate with the risk. Perhaps a remedy when necessary will be found within the provisions of the "Loan Shark" law, D.C. CODE §§ 26-601 *et seq.* (1961).

I mention such matters only to emphasize the desirability of a cautious approach to any such problem, particularly since the law for so long has allowed parties such great latitude in making their own contracts. I dare say there must annually be thousands upon thousands of installment credit transaction in this jurisdiction, and one can only speculate as to the effect the decision in these cases will have.

I join the District of Columbia Court of Appeals in its disposition of the issues.

Notes and Questions

1. Bargaining Power and Freedom of Choice: No one forced Williams to purchase the household goods. Indeed, some of the goods do not appear to be necessities. The court says Williams had "no meaningful choice." Williams had the freedom to choose not to purchase the products, but it is not clear that she had the opportunity to purchase the same items from a different seller. What does the court mean? Can you think of a plausible economic justification for the court's position?

2. Ex ante versus ex post analysis of terms: Assume the terms were fully and clearly explained to Williams and that she still accepted the contract. Would it still be unconscionable? Does the doctrine of unconscionability have any economic meaning?

3. Effect of Unconscionability on Availability of Credit: Williams is just one of many cases in which low-income households have used the doctrine of unconscionability to get the courts to rewrite their contracts. In many of the cases, the prices are very high because state usury laws — price ceilings on interest rates — prevent the sellers from charging an interest rate that reflects the true risk of lending to very low income households. That is, the higher prices are really a way to get around the interest rate ceilings. For example, in *Jones v. Star Credit Corp., supra* at page 164, the plaintiffs were welfare recipients. They purchased a freezer which had a fair market value of approximately $300. They signed a sales contract agreeing to pay $1439.69 for the freezer which included $900 for the purchase price with additional amount for credit charges, credit life insurance, and so forth. The plaintiffs sued to reform the contract after paying $619.88 on the grounds that it was unconscionable under § 2-302 of the U.C.C. The court held that the contract was unconscionable as a matter of law. With respect to the interest rate charged on the installment sales contract, the court said:

> There is no question about the necessity and even the desirability of installment sales and the extension of credit. Indeed, there are many, including welfare recipients, who would be deprived of even the most basic conveniences without the use of these devices. Similarly, the retail merchant selling on installment or extending credit is expected to establish a pricing factor which will afford a degree of protection commensurate with the risk of selling to those who might be default prone. However, neither of these accepted premises can clothe the sale of the freezer with respectability.

> Having already paid more than $600 toward the purchase of this $300 freezer unit, it is apparent that the defendant had already been amply compensated. In accordance with the statute, the application of the payment provision should be limited to amounts already paid by the plaintiffs and the contract be reformed and amended by changing the payments called for therein to equal the amount of payment actually so paid by the plaintiffs.

If the courts do not allow merchants to "establish a pricing factor which will afford a degree of protection commensurate with the risk of selling to those who might be default prone," what do you think will happen to the availability of credit for the "default prone?" In the second paragraph, the court suggests that this "default prone" plaintiff had paid her fair share, but this analysis ignores the possibility that other "default prone" debtors may have defaulted before they paid even $100. In effect, the "default prone" debtors who pay off their debts are bearing the cost of the merchant's granting credit to similarly-situated debtors. Of course, ex ante, the merchant can't tell who is going to pay and who is going to default. If the merchant could tell, then some would get credit and some would not, and those who got it would get it at a lower interest rate. So, the bottom line is, will the availability of credit to welfare recipients increase or decrease as a result of decisions like *Jones* and *Williams*? Given the choice between being able to purchase freezers on credit or having to go without a freezer, what choice do you think the Jones would have taken?

4. Adhesion Contracts: Consider the facts of *Henningsen v. Bloomfield Motors*, 32 N.J. 358, 161 A.2d 69 (N.J. Sup. Ct., 1960). Plaintiffs Claus and Helen Henningsen purchased a Plymouth from the defendant, Bloomfield Motors. Mr. Henningsen signed a preprinted purchase order which contained various provisions setting out the rights and liabilities of each party to the contract. One of the provisions limited the liability of the manufacturer, Chrysler, and the dealer, defendant Bloomfield Motors, to a 90-day warranty on "each new motor vehicle... chassis or parts manufactured by it to be free from defects in material or workmanship under normal use and service." Any other warranties, express or implied, made by any party, were expressly disavowed. Ten days and 468 miles after the purchase, the steering mechanism failed, causing Mrs. Henningsen to crash into a brick wall, totaling the car and seriously injuring herself. Plaintiffs sued for breach of express and implied warranties, and negligence. Defendants relied on the signed purchase order as a defense to the allegations.

> What influence should these circumstances have on the restrictive effect of Chrysler's express warranty in the framework of the purchase contract? As we have said, warranties originated in the law to safeguard the

buyer and not to limit the liability of the seller or manufacturer. It seems obvious in this instance that the motive was to avoid the warranty obligations which are normally incidental to such sales. The language gave little and withdrew much. In return for the delusive remedy of replacement of defective parts at the factory, the buyer is said to have accepted the exclusion of the maker's liability for personal injuries arising from the breach of the warranty, and to have agreed to the elimination of any other express or implied warranty. An instinctively felt sense of justice cries out against such a sharp bargain. But does the doctrine that a person is bound by his signed agreement, in the absence of fraud, stand in the way of any relief?

In the modern construction of problems such as this, Corbin suggests that practically all judges are "chancellors" and cannot fail to be influenced by any equitable doctrines that are available. And he opines that "there is sufficient flexibility in the concepts of fraud, duress, misrepresentation and undue influence, not to mention differences in economic bargaining power" to enable the courts to avoid enforcement of unconscionable provisions in long printed standardized contracts. 1 Corbin on Contracts (1950) § 128, p. 188. Freedom of contract is not such an immutable doctrine as to admit of no qualification in the area in which we are concerned....

The warranty before us is a standardized form designed for mass use. It is imposed upon the automobile consumer. He takes it or leaves it, and he must take it to buy an automobile. No bargaining is engaged in with respect to it. In fact, the dealer through whom it comes to the buyer is without authority to alter it; his function is ministerial—simply to deliver it. The form warranty is not only standard with Chrysler but, as mentioned above, it is the uniform warranty of the American Automobile Manufacturers Association. Members of the Association are: General Motors, Inc., Ford, Chrysler, Studebaker-Packard, American Motors, (Rambler), Willys Motors, Checker Motors Corp., and International Harvester Company. Automobile Facts and Figures (1958 Ed., Automobile Manufacturers Association) 69. Of these companies, the "Big Three" (General Motors, Ford, and Chrysler) represent 93.5% of the passenger-car production for 1958 and the independents 6.5%. Standard & Poor (Industrial Surveys, Autos, Basic Analysis, June 25, 1959) 4109. And for the same year the "Big Three" had 86.72% of the total passenger vehicle registrations. Automotive News, 1959 Almanac (Slocum Pub. Co., Inc.) p. 25.

The gross inequality of bargaining position occupied by the consumer in the automobile industry is thus apparent. There is no competition among the car makers in the area of the express warranty. Where can the buyer go to negotiate for better protection? Such control and limitation of his remedies are inimical to the public welfare and, at the very least, call for great care by the courts to avoid injustice through application of strict common-law principles of freedom of contract. Because there is no competition among the motor vehicle manufacturers with respect to the scope of protection guaranteed to the buyer, there is no incentive on their part to stimulate good will in that field of public relations. Thus, there is lacking a factor existing in more competitive fields, one which tends to guarantee the safe construction of the article sold.

Since all competitors operate in the same way, the urge to be careful is not so pressing. . . .

. . . The status of the automobile industry is unique. Manufacturers are few in number and strong in bargaining position. In the matter of warranties on the sale of their products, the Automotive Manufactures Association has enabled them to present a united front. From the standpoint of the purchaser, there can be no arms length negotiating on the subject. Because his capacity for bargaining is so grossly unequal, the inexorable conclusion which follows is that he is not permitted to bargain at all. He must take or leave the automobile on the warranty terms dictated by the maker. He cannot turn to a competitor for better security.

How does the doctrine of adhesion contracts affect the relative bargaining positions of the parties to a contract? Is the doctrine only applicable when parties have grossly disparate bargaining power? Isn't the court doing exactly what the free market would do anyway? In the oligopoly-type situation, as described here, wouldn't it be profitable for a car manufacturer to have a contract which states that the manufacturers are liable for everything (at a price premium, of course)? Here, the court imposes the same type entrepreneurial spirit onto all manufacturers by allowing consumers to sue and recover. In sum, everyone pays for the ability to recover when their car fails instead of just those who would be willing to pay the premium. Is freedom of contract the solution? Modern warranties generally run for three years or 36,000 miles. Domestic automobile manufacturers no longer enjoy the dominant position they held in 1958. How would a modern court analyze a situation similar to that in *Henningsen* with these additional facts? What cost do modern consumers face as a result of increased warranty coverage and length? Should consumers be allowed to waive liability claims against manufacturers in exchange for a lower price?

2. Modification and the Pre-Existing Duty Rule

Occasionally contingencies occur that make performance by one party a losing proposition. Assume D is the party disadvantaged by the contingency, and A is the other party. After the contingency occurs, D is faced with three possible choices: (1) D can perform as promised and lose money; (2) D can breach the contract and pay damages (so-called efficient breach); or (3) D and A can renegotiate the terms of the contract in a way that makes them both better off than they would be under option (2). In general, each contracting party has incentives to engage in good faith modification if the total cost of performance can be minimized through cooperation. The courts will enforce modifications if they are supported by consideration.

Alaska Packers' Association v. Domenico
United States Court of Appeals, Ninth Circuit
117 F. 99 (1902)

ROSS, J.

The libel in this case was based upon a contract alleged to have been entered into between the libelants and the appellant corporation on the 22d day of May, 1900, at Pyramid Harbor, Alaska, by which it is claimed the appellant promised to pay each of the libelants, among other things, the sum of $100 for services rendered and to be rendered. In its answer the respondent denied the execution, on its part, of the contract sued upon, averred that it was without consideration, and for a third defense alleged that the work performed by the libelants for it was performed under other and different contracts than that sued on, and that, prior to the filing of the libel, each of the libelants was paid by the respondent the full amount due him thereunder, in consideration of which each of them executed a full release of all his claims and demands against the respondent.

The evidence shows without conflict that on March 26, 1900, at the city and county of San Francisco, the libelants entered into a written contract with the appellant, whereby they agreed to go from San Francisco to Pyramid Harbor, Alaska, and return, on board such vessel as might be designated by the appellant, and to work for the appellant during the fishing season of 1900, at Pyramid Harbor, as sailors and fishermen, agreeing to do "regular ship's duty, both up and down, discharging and loading; and to do any other work whatsoever when requested to do so by the captain or agent of the Alaska Packers' Association." By the terms of this agreement, the appellant was to pay each of the libelants $50 for the season, and two cents for each red salmon in the catching of which he took part.

On the 15th day of April, 1900, 21 of the libelants signed shipping articles by which they shipped as seamen on the Two Brothers, a vessel chartered by the appellant for the voyage between San Francisco and Pyramid Harbor, and also bound themselves to perform the same work for the appellant provided for by the previous contract of March 26th; the appellant agreeing to pay them therefor the sum of $60 for the season, and two cents each for each red salmon in the catching of which they should respectively take part. Under these contracts, the libelants sailed on board the Two Brothers for Pyramid Harbor, where the appellant had about $150,000 invested in a salmon cannery. The libelants arrived there early in April of the year mentioned, and began to unload the vessel and fit up the cannery. A few days thereafter, to wit, May 19th, they stopped work in a body, and demanded of the company's superintendent there in charge $100 for services in operating the vessel to and from Pyramid Harbor, instead of the sums stipulated for in and by the contracts; stating that unless they were paid this additional wage they would stop work entirely, and return to San Francisco. The evidence showed, and the court below found, that it was impossible for the appellant to get other men to take the places of the libelants, the place being remote, the season short and just opening; so that, after endeavoring for several days without success to induce the libelants to proceed with their work in accordance with their contracts, the company's superintendent, on the 22d day of May, so far yielded to their demands as to instruct his clerk to copy the contracts executed in San Francisco, including the words "Alaska Packers' Association" at the end, substituting, for the $50 and $60 payments, respectively, of those contracts, the sum of $100, which document, so prepared, was signed by the libelants before a shipping commissioner whom they had requested to be brought from Northeast Point; the superintendent, however, testifying that he at the time told the libelants that he was without authority to enter into any such contract, or to in any way alter the contracts made between them and the company in San Francisco. Upon the return of the libelants to San Francisco at the close of the fishing season, they demanded pay in accordance with the terms of the alleged contract of May 22d, when the company denied its validity, and refused to pay other than as provided for by the contracts of March 26th and April 5th, respectively. Some of the libelants, at least, consulted counsel, and, after receiving his advice, those of them who had signed the shipping articles before the shipping commissioner at San Francisco went before that officer, and received the amount due them thereunder, executing in consideration thereof a release in full, and the others being paid at the office of the company, also receipting in full for their demands.

* * *

The real questions in the case as brought here are questions of law, and, in the view that we take of the case, it will be necessary to consider but one of those. Assuming that the appellant's superintendent at Pyramid Harbor was authorized to make the alleged contract of May 22d, and that he executed it on behalf of the appellant, was it supported by a sufficient consideration? From the foregoing statement of the case, it will have been seen that the libelants agreed in writing, for certain stated compensation, to render their services to the appellant in remote waters where the season for conducting fishing operations is extremely short, and in which enterprise the appellant had a large amount of money invested; and, after having entered upon the discharge of their contract, and at a time when it was impossible for the appellant to secure other men in their places, the libelants, without any valid cause, absolutely refused to continue the services they were under contract to perform unless the appellant would consent to pay them more money. Consent to such a demand, under such circumstances, if given, was, in our opinion, without consideration, for the reason that it was based solely upon the libelants' agreement to render the exact services, and none other, that they were already under contract to render. The case shows that they willfully and arbitrarily broke that obligation. As a matter of course, they were liable to the appellant in damages, and it is quite probable, as suggested by the court below in its opinion, that they may have been unable to respond in damages. But we are unable to agree with the conclusions there drawn, from these facts, in these words:

> "Under such circumstances, it would be strange, indeed, if the law would not permit the defendant to waive the damages caused by the libelants' breach, and enter into the contract sued upon, — a contract mutually beneficial to all the parties thereto, in that it gave to the libelants reasonable compensation for their labor, and enabled the defendant to employ to advantage the large capital it had invested in its canning and fishing plant."

Certainly, it cannot be justly held, upon the record in this case, that there was any voluntary waiver on the part of the appellant of the breach of the original contract. The company itself knew nothing of such breach until the expedition returned to San Francisco, and the testimony is uncontradicted that its superintendent at Pyramid Harbor, who, it is claimed, made on its behalf the contract sued on, distinctly informed the libelants that he had no power to alter the original or to make a new contract; and it would, of course, follow that, if he had no power to change the original, he would have no authority to waive any rights thereunder. The circumstances of the present case bring it, we think, directly within the sound and just observations of the supreme court of Minnesota in the case of King v. Railway Co., 61 Minn. 482, 63 N.W. 1105:

> "No astute reasoning can change the plain fact that the party who refuses to perform, and thereby coerces a promise from the other party to the contract to pay him an increased compensation for doing that which he is legally bound to do, takes an unjustifiable advantage of the necessities of the other party. Surely it would be a travesty on justice to hold that the party so making the promise for extra pay was estopped from asserting that the promise was without consideration. A party cannot lay the foundation of an estoppel by his own wrong, where the promise is simply a repetition of a subsisting legal promise. There can be no consideration for the promise of the other party, and there is no warrant for inferring that the parties have voluntarily rescinded or modified their contract. The promise cannot be legally enforced, although the other party has completed his contract in reliance upon it."

In Lingenfelder v. Brewing Co., 103 Mo. 578, 15 S.W. 844, the court, in holding void a contract by which the owner of a building agreed to pay its architect an additional sum because of his refusal to otherwise proceed with the contract, said:

> "It is urged upon us by respondents that this was a new contract. New in what? Jungenfeld was bound by his contract to design and supervise this building. Under the new promise, he was not to do anything more or anything different. What benefit was to accrue to Wainwright? He was to receive the same service from Jungenfeld under the new, that Jungenfeld was bound to tender under the original, contract. What loss, trouble, or inconvenience could result to Jungenfeld that he had not already assumed? No amount of metaphysical reasoning can change the plain fact that Jungenfeld took advantage of Wainwright's necessities, and extorted the promise of five percent on the refrigerator plant as the condition of his complying with his contract already entered into. Nor had he even the flimsy pretext that Wainwright had violated any of the conditions of the contract on his part. Jungenfeld himself put it upon the simple proposition that 'if he, as an architect, put up the brewery, and another company put up the refrigerating machinery, it would be a detriment to the Empire Refrigerating Company,' of which Jungenfeld was president. To permit plaintiff to recover under such circumstances would be to offer a premium upon bad faith, and invite men to violate their most sacred contracts that they may profit by their own wrong. That a promise to pay a man for doing that which he is already under contract to do is without consideration is conceded by respondents. The rule has

been so long imbedded in the common law and decisions of the highest courts of the various states that nothing but the most cogent reasons ought to shake it. [Citing a long list of authorities.] But it is "carrying coals to Newcastle" to add authorities on a proposition so universally accepted, and so inherently just and right in itself. The learned counsel for respondents do not controvert the general proposition. Their contention is, and the circuit court agreed with them, that, when Jungenfeld declined to go further on his contract, the defendant then had the right to sue for damages, and not having elected to sue Jungenfeld, but having acceded to his demand for the additional compensation, defendant cannot now be heard to say his promise is without consideration. While it is true Jungenfeld became liable in damages for the obvious breach of his contract, we do not think it follows that defendant is estopped from showing its promise was made without consideration....

＊   ＊   ＊

It results from the views above expressed that the judgment must be reversed, and the cause remanded, with directions to the court below to enter judgment for the respondent, with costs. It is so ordered.

Notes and Questions

1. Cost Minimization or Opportunism? A cost-minimization modification would take place after a contingency made it uneconomical for one party to perform, and this modification of the terms could make both parties better off. The key in *Alaska Packers* is that there was no triggering contingency. The workers merely noticed that the cannery owners were in a very vulnerable position—the workers could appropriate all of the cannery's expected net cash flow for that summer because it was too late for the cannery to hire replacement workers for the season—and engaged in an opportunistic modification of the contract. In other words, nothing had changed since the signing of the original contract, there was no incentive for joint cost minimization, and, the workers gave nothing to the cannery which would contribute to cost minimization—in fact, all the workers did was increase the cannery's cost.

2. Modification as Extortion: Richard Posner has addressed opportunistic contract modification in the following terms:

> ...In economic terms, the making of a contract may confer on the seller a monopoly vis-à-vis the buyer which the seller can exploit by threatening to terminate the contract unless the buyer agrees to pay a higher price than originally agreed upon.... This raises the question...whether extortion can be given a meaningful definition in the modification setting. To answer this question, it is helpful to distinguish three situations in which modification might be sought:
>
> 1. Nothing has changed since the contract was made, but the promisor, realizing that the remedies for breach of contract would not fully compensate the promisee, gives the promisee the unhappy choice of either paying the promisor more to complete the contract or pursuing his legal remedies.
>
> 2. Something has changed since the contract signing: the promisee has given up alternative sources of supply or otherwise increased his de-

pendence on the promisor. If modification is permitted the promisor can extract a monopoly rent from the promisee.

3. Something has changed since the contract signing: an unexpected event which...prevents the (willing) promisor from completing the promised performance without a modification of the contract.

The third case is the clearest for allowing modification. The inability of a willing promisor to complete performance removes the factor of strategic behavior that is present is cases one and two....The first case might also seem one where modification should be allowed,...the legal obligation is to perform or pay damages. If the promisee wants more—wants in effect specific performance—he must pay extra for it. That is all that *seems* to be involved in the first case but if we pause to ask why the promisee in the first case would ever agree to pay extra, we shall see that the first case is in reality a version of the second, the monopoly case. If the promisee in the first case has equally good alternative sources of supply, or at least no worse than he had when he made the original contract, he will have no incentive to pay a premium above the contract price for the promisor to perform as agreed; he will allow the promisor to breach and turn elsewhere. He will pay the premium only if his dependence on the promisor has increased since the signing of the contract, i.e., only if the contract gave the promisor a monopoly position vis-à-vis the promisee.

Posner, *Gratuitous Promises in Economics and Law*, 6 J. Legal Studies 411 (1977). How does *Alaska Packers* fit into this analysis?

3. U.C.C. §2-209: The Uniform Commercial Code modifies the common law pre-existing duty rule to provide for contract enforcement so long as the modification is made in good faith. Charles J. Goetz and Robert E. Scott offer the following insights on the relative merits of the common law and U.C.C. rules:

Contract rules policing contractual modification are another response to the heightened risk of extortion in specialized environments. For example, the common-law preexisting duty rule can be usefully contrasted with the more permissive regulation of contractual modification under the Uniform Commercial Code. The preexisting duty rule denies enforcement of a renegotiation or contractual modification where an obligor agrees merely to do that which he is already contractually obligated to do. The rule is primarily designed to reduce the incidence of extortionate modification in construction, employment, and other specialized contractual relationships.

The preexisting duty rule, however, often fails accurately to mirror the underlying bad faith behavior. First, the rule discourages cost-reducing negotiations in addition to threats. Moreover, the obligor satisfies the rule by assuming *any* additional obligations whether or not the "additional" duties are themselves part of the strategic maneuver. The Code abandoned this ill-fitting rule of thumb and instead applies a general good faith standard.... Because this standard is substantially more difficult to enforce, however, the Code may not deter extortionate renegotiation as effectively as did the common law. Nonetheless, if parties generally execute contracts for the sale of goods in the context of a well-developed market for substitutes, the costs saved through legitimate renegotiations will exceed the increased enforcement costs of policing bad faith modification....

Courts also express concern with bad faith extortion through the rules restraining economic duress. Such cases arise when the obligor has *performed* the modified contract, but the "injured party" seeks restitution of the value of his performance because economic duress forced his agreement to modified terms. The market for substitutes is the key variable in economic duress cases. Because a market for substitutes will effectively control a defendant's behavior with no need for legal rules, a prima facie claim of economic duress thus requires a plaintiff to show a specialized environment.

It is difficult to police such bad faith behavior, however, because the distinction between legitimate requests for renegotiation and bad faith threats lies entirely in the honesty of a party's assertion that a readjustment contingency made *performance* less attractive than quasi-performance (breach with damages).

Goetz & Scott, *The Mitigation Principle: Toward a General Theory of Contractual Obligation*, 69 VA. L. REV. 967, at note 106 (1983).

Chapter IV

Principles of Valuation

Market prices are often viewed as the best measure of the value of a good or service. Market prices can be determined objectively, and generally cannot be manipulated. Thus, market prices are often relied upon to generate unbiased, independent measures of value. Obviously, market prices are important in many legal contexts, whether they are used for filling gaps in contracts or determining the appropriate compensation for governmental takings of property. However, in many important legal situations, adequate market indicators are not available and surrogates for market value must be calculated. This chapter focuses on present value calculations, the basic methodology for determining the value today of future payments.

Section A considers some general principles of valuation in terms of interest rates and discounting of future payments into present values. Section B demonstrates how those general principles are applied in lawsuits by focusing on the determination of the relevant future stream of dollars and the selection of the proper discount rate. Section C considers two methodologies that courts apply in determining the value of life. Section D demonstrates how to value close corporations using two different methodologies.

A. Discounted Present Value

Discounting is a method of translating a flow of future dollars into its current worth. For example, suppose a smooth-talking, high-pressure defense attorney has offered your client a settlement in a personal injury case of $20,000 a year for the rest of your client's life and the rest of her children's lives. The defense attorney claims that the payments could easily last 50 years. Your client is 45, but she has two children in their twenties. The defense attorney exclaims that the settlement could result in "payments totaling more than $1 million!" Prior to this offer, you advised your client that she should accept any settlement worth more than $250,000. In fact, on your advice, she has already rejected a $200,000 settlement. Is the new offer acceptable? What do you advise your client to do?

To decide how much the offered annuity is worth, you need some way of valuing the $20,000 per year. You can't simply add up the $20,000 fifty times. To do so would be wrong, and could result in a terrible injustice for your client. (That is, to do so could be considered malpractice!) Instead, you must discount all future dollars by the appropriate interest rate. Discounting is required because a dollar in the future is not worth a dollar now.

Present value calculations are used to determine the difference in future value versus present value. Several reasons explain the difference in value. The reasons are best explained by considering your personal preferences when given the choice between receiving a dollar today or a dollar exactly one year from today. First, a dollar is worth less in the future than today because during the interim period you are not able to enjoy the consumption benefits of whatever the dollar could have purchased today. Even if you do not spend the dollar in the interim period, you had the choice to spend or save, and generally, more choices, or opportunities, are preferred to fewer. Second, inflation may erode the value of money in that the dollar today has greater purchasing power. Third, a dollar today may earn interest in a savings account and thus total more than one dollar a year from now, and alternatively, if you wish to borrow money today in exchange for a promise to pay one dollar a year from now, the amount lenders would be willing to lend is less than one dollar. Finally, there may be some risk that some unforeseen contingency will occur and prevent the payment of a dollar a year from now ("A bird in the hand is worth two in the bush.").

If you have $1 now, you can take that dollar, put it in the bank, and in a year you will have that dollar plus interest. If the interest rate you can get from the bank is 5 percent, then the dollar will grow to $1.05 a year from now. That also means that if the interest rate in the economy is 5 percent, if you have 95 cents now, in a year it will be worth $.9975 (5% × $.95 = $.0475). Reversing the reasoning, $1 one year in the future is worth approximately 95 cents today. So the present value of $1 one year in the future at 5 percent interest is approximately 95 cents.

A dollar two years from now is worth even less today. Carry out that same reasoning and you'll find that if the interest rate is 5 percent, $1 two years from now is worth approximately 90 cents today. You could put 90 cents in the bank now at 5 percent interest, and in two years have $1.

1. The Present Value Formula

Carrying out such reasoning for every case would be very tedious. Fortunately, there is a simple formula that can be used to determine the present value (PV) of future income. The formula is:

$$PV = A_1/(1+I) + A_2/(1+I)^2 + A_3/(1+I)^3 + \ldots + A_n/(1+I)^n$$

where

A_n = the amount of money received in n periods in the future

I = the interest rate in the economy (assumed constant)

Solving this formula for any time period longer than two or three years can be very tedious. The easiest way to solve the formula is to use a spreadsheet, a multifunction calculator, or a present-value table like that in Table IV-1.

Table IV-1 gives the present value of a single dollar at some time in the future at various interest rates. The table reveals two important relationships that should become an intuitive part of your understanding of present value. First, the further into the future one goes, the lower the present value. Second, the higher the interest rate, the lower the present value.

Table IV-1
Present Value of a Future $1: What a Dollar at End of Future Year
Is Worth Today

Year	3%	4%	5%	6%	7%	8%	10%	12%	15%	20%	Year
1	.971	.962	.962	.943	.935	.926	.909	.883	.870	.833	1
2	.943	.925	.907	.880	.873	.857	.826	.787	.758	.804	2
3	.915	.880	.864	.839	.816	.794	.751	.711	.658	.578	3
4	.886	.855	.823	.782	.763	.735	.683	.636	.572	.482	4
5	.863	.823	.784	.747	.713	.681	.620	.587	.487	.402	5
6	.838	.790	.748	.705	.666	.630	.564	.507	.432	.335	6
7	.813	.780	.711	.685	.623	.583	.513	.452	.376	.279	7
8	.790	.731	.677	.627	.582	.540	.486	.404	.326	.233	8
9	.756	.703	.645	.581	.855	.500	.424	.380	.284	.194	9
10	.744	.676	.614	.558	.508	.463	.385	.322	.247	.182	10
11	.722	.650	.585	.526	.475	.429	.350	.287	.215	.134	11
12	.701	.626	.557	.497	.444	.397	.318	.257	.187	.112	12
13	.681	.601	.530	.468	.415	.368	.298	.229	.182	.0835	13
14	.661	.577	.505	.442	.388	.340	.263	.204	.141	.0779	14
15	.642	.555	.481	.417	.382	.315	.230	.183	.122	.0649	15
16	.623	.534	.458	.383	.338	.282	.217	.183	.107	.0541	18
17	.605	.513	.436	.371	.317	.270	.187	.146	.083	.0541	17
18	.587	.494	.416	.350	.296	.250	.179	.130	.0808	.0376	18
19	.570	.475	.396	.330	.277	.332	.163	.116	.0703	.0313	19
20	.554	.456	.377	.311	.258	.215	.148	.104	.0611	.0261	20
25	.478	.375	.295	.232	.184	.148	.0823	.0588	.0304	.0105	25
30	.412	.308	.231	.174	.131	.0984	.0573	.0334	.0151	.00421	30
40	.307	.208	.142	.0972	.067	.0450	.0221	.0107	.00373	.000630	40
50	.228	.141	.087	.0543	.034	.0213	.00852	.00345	.000922	.000108	50

Table IV-2 shows the impact of compound interest over time. Compound interest accrues when interest is earned on the prior interest earned. For example, at a 10 percent interest rate, $1 earns $.10 per year. If the $.10 is compounded at the end of the first year, interest for the second year is earned on $1.10. So, the interest earned for the second year is $.11. As indicated in Table IV-2, the value of $1 after earning 10 percent interest for 2 years is $1.21.

Table IV-3 is an annuity table; it tells us how much a constant stream of payments for a specific number of years is worth. Notice that as the interest rate rises, the value of an annuity falls. At a 10 percent interest rate, $1 per year for 50 years has a present value of $9.91; while at a 15 percent interest rate, $1 per year for 50 years has a present value of $6.60. To get the value of amounts other than $1, you simply multiply the entry in the table by the amount of the annuity. For example, using the information from the settlement offer discussed at the start of this section, and assuming a 15 percent interest rate, $20,000 per year for 50 years has a present value of $132,000. If you told your client to accept the offer, you might be guilty of malpractice. The interest rate would have to be below eight percent in order for the present value to rise to $250,000.

Table IV-2
Impact of Compound Interest Over Time

Year	3%	4%	5%	6%	7%	8%	10%	12%	15%	20%	Year
1	1.03	1.04	1.05	1.06	1.07	1.08	1.10	1.12	1.15	1.20	1
2	1.06	1.08	1.10	1.12	1.14	1.17	1.21	1.25	1.32	1.44	2
3	1.09	1.12	1.16	1.19	1.23	1.26	1.33	1.40	1.52	1.73	3
4	1.13	1.17	1.22	1.26	1.31	1.36	1.46	1.57	1.75	2.07	4
5	1.16	1.22	1.28	1.34	1.40	1.47	1.61	1.76	2.01	2.49	5
6	1.19	1.27	1.34	1.42	1.50	1.59	1.77	1.97	2.31	2.99	6
7	1.23	1.32	1.41	1.50	1.61	1.71	1.95	2.21	2.66	3.58	7
8	1.27	1.37	1.48	1.59	1.72	1.85	2.14	2.48	3.06	4.30	8
9	1.30	1.42	1.55	1.69	1.84	2.00	2.36	2.77	3.52	5.16	9
10	1.34	1.48	1.63	1.79	1.97	2.16	2.59	3.11	4.05	6.19	10
11	1.38	1.54	1.71	1.90	2.10	2.33	2.85	3.48	4.65	7.43	11
12	1.43	1.60	1.80	2.01	2.25	2.52	3.14	3.90	5.35	8.92	12
13	1.47	1.67	1.89	2.13	2.41	2.72	3.45	4.36	6.15	10.70	13
14	1.51	1.73	1.98	2.26	2.58	2.94	3.80	4.89	7.08	12.84	14
15	1.56	1.80	2.08	2.40	2.76	3.17	4.18	5.47	8.14	15.41	15
16	1.60	1.87	2.18	2.54	2.95	3.43	4.59	6.13	9.36	18.49	16
17	1.65	1.95	2.29	2.69	3.16	3.70	5.05	6.87	10.76	22.19	17
18	1.70	2.03	2.41	2.85	3.38	4.00	5.56	7.69	12.38	26.62	18
19	1.75	2.11	2.53	3.03	3.62	4.32	6.12	8.61	14.23	31.95	19
20	1.81	2.19	2.65	3.21	3.87	4.66	6.73	9.65	16.37	38.34	20
25	1.86	2.28	2.79	3.40	4.14	5.03	7.40	10.80	18.82	46.01	25
30	1.92	2.37	2.93	3.60	4.43	5.44	8.14	12.10	21.64	55.21	30
40	1.97	2.46	3.07	3.82	4.74	5.87	8.95	13.55	24.89	66.25	40
50	2.03	2.56	3.23	4.05	5.07	6.34	9.85	15.18	28.63	79.50	50

2. Rules of Thumb for Determining Present Value

Most lawyers don't carry computers or present value tables with them. Fortunately, a few simple rules of thumb can serve as initial guides to present value calculations. The two most useful rules are the Perpetuity Rule and the Rule of 72.

a. The Perpetuity Rule

A perpetuity is an annuity that pays the same amount every year forever. To find the present value of an annuity that will pay $1 per year for an infinite number of years in the future when the interest rate is 5 percent, simply divide $1 by 5 percent (.05), which yields a present value of $20. The general perpetuity rule for an annuity of any amount is:

$$PV = X/I$$

That is, the present value of an infinite flow of income, X, is that income divided by the interest rate, I.

Most of the time, people don't offer to sell annuities for the infinite future. A typical annuity runs for 30, 40, or 50 years. However, the perpetuity rule is still useful because it serves as a reality check on other present value calculations. We can use the perpetuity rule as an approximation of long-lasting, but less than infinite, flows of future income because the longer the time period, the closer the

Table IV-3
Present Value of Annuity of $1, Received at End of Each Year

Year	3%	4%	5%	6%	7%	8%	10%	12%	15%	20%	Year
1	0.971	0.96	0.952	0.943	0.935	0.926	0.909	0.89	0.087	0.833	1
2	1.91	1.89	1.86	1.83	1.81	1.78	1.73	1.69	1.63	1.53	2
3	2.83	2.78	2.72	2.67	2.62	2.58	2.48	2.4	2.28	2.11	3
4	3.72	3.63	3.55	3.46	3.39	3.31	3.16	3.04	2.86	2.58	4
5	4.58	4.45	4.33	4.21	4.1	3.89	3.79	3.6	3.35	2.99	5
6	5.42	5.24	5.08	4.91	4.77	4.62	4.35	4.11	3.78	3.33	6
7	6.23	6	5.79	5.58	5.39	5.21	4.86	4.56	4.16	3.6	7
8	7.02	6.73	6.48	6.2	5.97	5.75	5.33	4.97	4.49	3.84	8
9	7.79	7.44	7.11	6.8	6.52	6.25	5.75	5.33	4.78	4.03	9
10	8.53	8.11	7.72	7.36	7.02	6.71	6.14	5.65	5.02	4.19	10
11	9.25	8.76	8.31	7.88	7.5	7.14	6.49	5.94	5.23	4.33	11
12	9.95	9.39	8.86	8.38	7.94	7.54	6.81	6.19	5.41	4.64	12
13	10.6	9.99	9.39	8.85	8.36	7.9	7.1	6.42	5.65	4.53	13
14	11.3	10.6	9.9	9.29	8.75	8.24	7.36	6.63	5.76	4.61	14
15	11.9	11.1	10.4	9.71	9.11	8.56	7.5	6.81	5.87	4.68	15
16	12.6	11.6	10.8	10.1	9.45	8.85	7.82	6.97	5.95	4.73	18
17	13.2	12.2	11.3	10.4	9.76	9.12	8.02	7.12	6.03	4.77	17
18	13.8	12.7	11.7	10.8	10.1	9.37	8.2	7.25	6.1	4.81	18
19	14.3	13.1	12.1	11.1	10.3	9.6	8.36	7.37	6.17	8.84	19
20	14.9	13.6	12.5	11.4	10.6	9.82	8.51	7.47	3.23	4.87	20
25	17.4	15.6	14.1	12.8	11.7	10.7	9.08	7.84	6.46	4.95	25
30	19.6	17.3	15.4	13.8	12.4	11.3	9.43	8.06	6.57	4.98	30
40	23.1	19.8	17.2	15	13.3	11.9	9.78	8.24	6.64	5	40
50	25.7	21.5	18.3	15.8	13.8	12.2	9.91	8.25	6.6	5	50

perpetuity rule is to the actual present value. Dollars way off in the future are not worth much—as you can see from Table IV-1, in 30 years at a 10 percent interest rate, the present value of $1 is only 5.73 cents. Returning to the example at the start of this section, and assuming that the interest rate is 10 percent, then the present value of the $20,000 per year for fifty years must be less than $200,000 (= $20,000/.10), the present value of $20,000 in perpetuity. In fact, according to Table IV-3 the present value is $198,200 (= $20,000 × 9.91).

b. The Rule of 72

A rule of thumb for determining present value across shorter time periods is the rule of 72, which states:

> The number of years it takes for a certain amount to double in value is equal to 72 divided by the rate of interest.

If the interest rate is 4 percent, how long will it take for your $100 to become worth $200? Dividing 72 by 4 yields 18. So, the present value of $200 at a 4 percent interest rate 18 years in the future is about $100. Actually, according to Table IV-I, it's $98.80 (.494 × $200). Thus, the Rule of 72 gets you pretty close to the correct answer.

Alternatively, say that you will receive $1000 in 10 years. Would you accept $500 for that amount now if the interest rate is 8 percent? Using the rule of 72, we know that at a 8 percent interest rate it will take about nine years (72/8 = 9) for $500 to double. Thus, the future value of $500 today is more than the $1,000 in ten years. In fact, using Table IV-2, we know that the $500 dollars today will be worth $1,080 (2.16 × $500) in ten years. You should accept the $500.

B. Discounting and Litigation

There are two major components to present value calculations, the future dollars and the interest rate. Both of these are extremely important to lawyers. Much litigation focuses on determining the present value of lost earnings, future profits, and structured settlements. This section focuses on how courts determine the relevant future stream of income or damages as well as which interest rate should be used in the present value calculation of some identified stream of dollars.

1. Determining the Relevant Future Stream

Haugan v. Haugan
Supreme Court of Wisconsin
343 N.W.2d 796 (1984)

Read excerpt in Chapter II.

Notes and Questions

1. Wealth v. Income: Income is a flow received in specified period of time, usually a calendar year. Wealth is the capitalized value of future income. Students often experience low incomes while their wealth is increasing.

2. Investments in Human Capital: Some occupations, such as medicine and law, require many years of training. The fact that the wages in these skilled professions are higher than the wages of unskilled labor is not coincidental. Before people are willing to endure the years of training to become highly skilled professionals, they must be reasonably sure that their investment of time and other resources will pay off in the long run. People frequently choose to invest in some form of training to make themselves more productive and to enhance their income earning potential. While a person is going to college, attending trade school, or gaining on-the-job training, he or she is building human capital. Gaining human capital requires an investment, such as three years of law school. This investment involves a large opportunity cost. A law student loses the next-best alternative when attending law school. For most law students, the lost opportunity is the income that they would have earned if working. The expected return on the investment is higher wages. For more on human capital, see the discussion in Chapter VII, "Labor Markets."

3. The Haugans' Human Capital Investment: The court stated: "In a marriage of significant duration, the marital partners in sharing life together—with all its joys, sorrows, debts, and assets—share the return on their investment in the marriage." It could be argued that both spouses made a substantial investment in Dr. Haugan's education: they both endured periods of significantly lower income because of their devotion to their common goal. Clearly the supporting spouse expected to reap some of the benefits of the investment. The question for the court to determine, of course, was what is the proper compensation? See *O'Brien v. O'Brien*, 66 N.Y.2d 576 (1985), excerpted in Chapter VII, for a determination that a human capital investment is marital property.

4. Opportunity Cost is the Next-Best Alternative to the Human Capital Investment: It is reasonable to assume that the supporting spouse chose to invest in her husband's education because she expected to be better off than if they did not invest. Thus, compensation for past opportunities foregone would be less than the return expected from the investment. Instead of looking to the past, the proper approach is to consider the future—the enhanced earning capacity of Dr. Haugan.

Diocese of Buffalo v. State of New York
Court of Appeals of New York
248 N.E.2d 155 (1969)

FULD, C. J.

In each of these three condemnation proceedings, we are primarily called upon to decide the method to be employed in computing a claimant's damages where there has been a partial taking of cemetery lands. Since this question of law is applicable to all three appeals, it may be helpful to discuss it before undertaking a more detailed consideration of each of the several appeals themselves.

It is settled that, as a general proposition, the measure of damages in partial taking cases is the difference between the value of the whole *before* the taking and the value of the remainder *after* the taking....Consequently, the decision on each of these appeals turns on whether that rule should have been applied in these cemetery cases.

Our decision in St. Agnes Cemetery v. State of New York, 3 N.Y. 2d 37... pointed the method of valuing cemetery lands in condemnation proceedings.... After first observing that these lands were to be appraised on the basis of their value for their highest and best use—in that case, for continued cemetery use— the court went on to hold that such value is to be ascertained by first arriving at a probable sale price of the land as cemetery plots or graves, based on the "average" price which the cemetery obtained for the sale of burial plots located in adjoining sections....After the cost of making such future sales is deducted, an estimate is made of the number of years it would take to sell off all the plots in the cemetery as it existed prior to the condemnation. The amount of net income expected annually over the projected number of years is treated as if it were an annuity whose present value, determined by reference to annuity tables, is regarded as the fair market value of the cemetery's undeveloped grave sites. In other words, the value of the land is equivalent to the present worth of future net income to be derived from the steady sale of a continuously diminishing inventory of cemetery plots, year by year, until the supply of land is depleted.

On the appeals before us, the claimants as well as the State accept the formula adopted in *St. Agnes* as the method to be followed in determining the valuation of a cemetery. More, the State acknowledges that the courts below correctly applied that formula to find the value of the entire area of unsold plots or graves *before* the taking. However, contends the State, the courts below erred in failing to use the formula in order to ascertain the value of the property retained by the claimants *after* such taking; indeed, they made no attempt whatsoever to find that vitally significant figure, the value of the land retained *after* the taking. Instead of employing the "before and after" measure of damages rule, the trial court averaged the value of all the unsold graves before the taking—according to the *St. Agnes* formula—and, then, simply multiplied the average unit plot value by the number of unsold plots which had been taken in condemnation.

The departure from the "before and after" rule resulted in error. The court's decision in the *St. Agnes* case was premised on the dual assumption that cemetery land is valuable as an inventory of individual grave sites which may properly be treated as fungible and that sales will continue at a constant rate until they are all sold. On this premise, any particular undeveloped cemetery plot could be substituted for any other, and the only direct effect of a partial taking is to reduce the economic life of a cemetery. In other words, since the sales will presumably continue at the same rate, the condemnation taking will merely decrease the period of time during which the supply will be available. This economic assumption—that the only effect of a partial taking is to reduce the economic life of the cemetery—underlies the "before and after" approach urged by the State, a contention which relates to the measure of damages in these cases. This particular question, critical to decision herein, was not raised by the parties nor considered by the court in *St. Agnes*. In that case and in the others which followed it, we were concerned only with the method of valuation, not with the measure of damages.

No reason exists for not applying the "before and after" rule in cases involving a partial taking of cemetery lands. What the owner has lost is, after all, the ultimate measure of damages.... In the main, uncomplicated by any claim or issue of consequential damages or benefits to the retained property...the only effect of the taking has been to reduce the size of each cemetery, just as would a street widening, if the cemeteries had fronted on city streets. The remaining property still retains its essential characteristics *after* the taking, is still just as useful for cemetery purposes, as it was *before* the taking.

This being so, there is no reason why the *St. Agnes* method of valuation should not be used to determine the value of the retained land *after* the taking in precisely the same way as it was used by the courts below to determine the value of the entire cemetery *before* the taking. Indeed, our decision in Matter of City of New York (Fourth Ave.) 255 N. Y. 25, *supra*, furnishes strong authority for this conclusion. In that case, the claimant owned an entire square block (then undeveloped) in Manhattan, from Park (Fourth) to Lexington Avenue and from 32nd to 33rd Streets. The city took a 20-foot strip along the entire Park Avenue frontage for a widening of that thoroughfare. The court rejected the claimant's contention—very similar to that made by the cemeteries on these appeals—that it should look solely to the land taken (the Park Avenue frontage), viewed as an independent parcel, as the measure of the award to be made. Instead, it recognized that, in reality, the claimant still had a square block fronting on Park Avenue and that it was damaged only to the extent that the block was 20 feet shorter from east to west.

Just as in the *Fourth Avenue* case, so in the cases before us, we can only make our determination on the basis of a realistic view of what the claimant lost, and that was to be measured by valuing the property retained by the claimant after the taking. In the *Diocese of Buffalo* case, for example, the only effect of the taking was to reduce that claimant's supply of unsold graves from 65,450 to 61,950. So visualized and regarded, the measure of damages should be, to quote from our opinion in the *Fourth Avenue* case (255 N.Y. 25, 29, *supra*), "the difference between the fair market value of the whole before the taking and the fair market value of what remains."

There is, of course, a difference between the methods of valuation in a cemetery case and a case such as *Fourth Avenue*. Cemetery land is to be valued—*St. Agnes* teaches—by reference to a projected annual net income from sales over a period of years while in the other case the land is to be appraised by using the more common method of estimating square foot or unit lot values by reference to sales of neighboring and similar property. The distinction should not, however, affect the conclusion that the damages are to be measured by considering the impact of the appropriation on the property retained by the claimant. Since, as already indicated, the only effect of a partial taking of a cemetery is to shorten its economic life, a claimant—to borrow the figures from the *Diocese of Buffalo* case—who sells 1,190 graves a year and who has lost 3,500 grave sites is in the same economic situation as a person left with an annuity smaller by three years.

A leading manual, dealing with partial taking cases, describes the "before and after" method as "decidedly the best one in all cases". (McMichael's Appraising Manual [4th ed.], pp. 442–443.) The author emphasizes—what is, indeed, self-evident where the highest and best use of the property has not been affected by the taking—that the "before and after" method "involves two calculations" and that both calculations (i.e., appraisals) must be made by identical methods. The courts below, having used the *St. Agnes* formula to determine the "before" values, should likewise have made "after" value determinations and, of course, in doing so, would have been required to employ the same method. Their failure to do so resulted in error, the extent of which will become evident when we approximate the findings which would result from application of the correct rule in each of the cases to which we now turn and compare them with the findings actually made.

*   *   *

In this case, the Court of Claims found that it would have taken 55 years to sell off the grave sites as the cemetery stood before the taking. The claimant owned 65,450 grave sites which would have been sold at the rate of 1,190 a year. And, since the parcel taken involved 3,500 graves, the effect of the appropriation was simply to reduce the life of the annuity by three years, the length of time during which they would have been sold. The court found the "before" value—i.e., the value of the income from the sale of 1,190 plots a year over a 55-year period—to be $1,870,462.33 but made no finding as to the "after" value—i.e., the value of the income from the annual sale of those 1,190 plots over a period of 52 years—and there must, therefore, be a new trial.[1]

---

1. According to the State, reliance on the same actuarial tables used to obtain the "before" value would have yielded an "after" value of $1,855,354.77. The State argues that the

The court made an award of $100,030; it arrived at this figure by (1) taking the "before" value of the entire property—$1,870,462 for the 65,450 graves—(2) finding the average value of each grave to be $28.58 and, then, (3) multiplying that figure by the total number of graves appropriated, 3,500. Quite obviously, if, as the State maintains, the value of the property retained after the appropriation is $1,855,354.77, an award of $100,030 for the land taken would leave the claimant with property worth their combined sum—$1,955,384—an amount far in excess of $1,870,462 which the trial court found to be the value of its property before the taking. Simply put, the "averaging" procedure adopted below resulted in a windfall to the claimant.

There was a flaw in the reasoning of the courts below which led to such a result. The present value of a grave site depends, to a great extent, on the time when it will be sold. Thus, in this particular case, plots which were to be sold immediately were found to be worth over $130 each, while those which would not yield any income for 55 years were only worth about $5. The figure used by the Court of Claims—$28.58 per grave—represented an "average value" which would apply only to those graves sold toward the middle of the cemetery's life. However, as we have already stated, the claimant's sales will presumably continue at an undiminished rate of 1,190 a year throughout its life, in consequence of which the claimant will experience no loss until 52 years have elapsed and it is forced to terminate its sales three years earlier than had there been no condemnation. It is only the value of the sales lost during the period at the very end of the cemetery's existence, rather than an "average" figure, which properly reflects the damage resulting from the taking.

Before bringing our discussion of the *Diocese of Buffalo* case to a conclusion, it is necessary to treat another issue, one raised by the claimant as cross appellant—namely, that the 6% discount rate employed in arriving at the present value of the annuity calculations was too high. We need but observe that, since this determination is based upon factual considerations, relating to "prudent" investments, which have support in the evidence, it is conclusive upon us, beyond the scope of our review.

     *   *   *

In sum, then, there must be a reversal and a new trial in each of these cases. The Court of Claims failed to consider the value of the land which remained in the ownership of the claimant after the taking and, in so doing, rendered awards which were far in excess of the claimants' actual loss. Upon the new trials, it will be incumbent on the court to make awards solely on the basis of the difference between the value of the claimants' property before and after the taking plus such special damages as may be shown to be appropriate in the individual case.

The order appealed from...should be reversed, and the matter remanded to the Court of Claims for further proceedings in accordance with this opinion.

---

difference between those figures—$15,107.56—would represent the damages to the claimant. It will be for the trial court to take evidence on this issue and determine the exact amount of the claimant's damages.

BURKE, J. (dissenting).

In this case, here by permission of this court, the claimants...have been denied just compensation.

When the State takes land for a public purpose, the owner of the taken land is indeed entitled to be compensated for what he has actually lost in economic terms. The majority today concludes that an established cemetery which, as has been found by the trial court and the Appellate Division, is currently selling burial plots for over $130 each is entitled to be paid only about $5 each for those plots which it loses by reason of the taking. By applying the approach which this court has followed since our decision in the *St. Agnes* case...the claimant would be entitled to be paid approximately $28 for each burial plot lost due to the taking....This obvious disparity results from the majority's incongruous application of inconsistent approaches to the question of valuation for a partial taking. The incongruity lies in the fact that the *St. Agnes* approach, as heretofore applied in this court in each case in which it was presented, attempted to take into account the unique fact that cemetery real property is sold, over the course of time, in fungible units and, therefore, the award should reflect a discount, designed to approximate the effects of deferred realization of income, based upon past annual sales and sales prices. The *Fourth Avenue* approach relied upon by the majority is of course the traditional approach employed in the *ordinary* case of a partial taking. What the majority does is wed the usual with the unusual and produce by that union what can only be termed a bizarre offspring. The *St. Agnes* approach, in an attempt to arrive at a method of valuation which is fair to both condemnor and condemnee, seeks to approximate the economic effects of the taking by use of averages of past sales and sale prices but it does not in any way purport to produce a mathematically precise award for the very good reason that the very process of projecting the past into the future is itself imprecise (will the population served by the particular cemetery increase or decrease? will the death rate increase, decrease or remain fairly constant? will competition increase? will cremation replace burial? and, most importantly, will prices continue to increase at an annual rate of close to 4% as is shown by the evidence of one of the claimants?). In the face of this uncertainty, the approach adopted sought to balance the competing facets of these uncertainties by use of averages and a discount which would closely approximate the loss to the condemnee. That approach is now discarded without any discussion of the uncertainties which the discarded approach at least attempted to meet and deal with, and it does so by use of a method which, if used as the case relied upon by the majority used it, would result in an award in excess of $100,000 instead of the award of some $15,000 which results from the majority's approach. For instance, the majority states that, because the burial plot units are fungible, there is no way of telling when any particular area would be used and that, therefore, the average discounted price used below would reflect the expected earnings from sales in the middle years of the cemetery's life. The implication is that this results in an excessive award to the claimant. What the majority does not recognize is that, by its approach, it decides that the taken plots would *necessarily be the last ones to be sold* and, therefore, awards only the discounted value of the expected income flow for the last years of the cemetery's life lost due to the taking. The approach heretofore followed recognized that it could not be determined whether the taken plots would have been sold first, last or somewhere in between and, therefore, in fairness both to the State and to the claimant, chose the *via media* which, in effect, "split the difference" between the two extremes. Thus, at the same time that the majority deplores the idea of a "windfall" to the claimant by use of this average, it summarily and incongruously endorses a "windfall" for the State by use of its arbitrary determination that the taken plots should be considered as those which would necessarily be sold last.

* * *

Notes and Questions

1. Reasonable Expectations About the Future: An old adage from the real estate business — "Location, location, location!" — could be applicable here. If every plot has the same price, and if some plots are in more desirable locations than others (a reasonable assumption), the condemned plots would have to be in the least desirable locations in order to be the last ones sold. Did the court need more information before making its assumptions about the order of sale? What information could lead to a more accurate estimate of the timing of the sales revenue?

2. Expected Value: People (and courts) often guess at numbers they don't know, such as the score of tomorrow's ball game, their income after ten years, their salary upon graduation from law school, or the order in which condemned burial plots would have been sold. Under certain conditions, a rational guess is the expected value — an average of the sum of every possible number, weighted by the probabilities (chances) that they will occur. An expected value is calculated in three steps:

(1) List the number (e.g., the score or the income) in each possible situation.

(2) Multiply each number by its probability or chance of occurring.

(3) Add the results from Step 2.

For example, suppose that you have a 9/10 chance of earning $50,000 per year ten years from now and a 1/10 chance of earning $300,000. Then your expected salary is:

$$(9/10) (\$50,000) + (1/10) (\$300,000) = \$75,000$$

3. Expectations about the Timing of the Sale of the Burial Plots: Suppose that plots sold immediately were worth $130 and plots sold in 55 years had a present value of $5. Assume there was a 50 percent chance that all of the lots would be sold immediately and a 50 percent chance that all of them would be sold in 55 years. The expected value of each condemned burial plot, if it had not been condemned, would be:

$$EV = .5 (\$130) + .5 (\$5) = \$65 + \$2.50 = \$67.50$$

2. Determining the Proper Interest Rate

An important determinant in evaluating the value of money across time is the interest rate. The higher the current (and assumed constant) interest rate, the more a given amount of money invested today will be worth in the future. Alternatively, the higher the current interest rate, the less a given amount of money in the future will be worth in the present. Thus, after the future flow of dollars has been determined, the key issue is to determine the proper interest rate for discounting.

The earlier discussion of present value calculations did not distinguish between what economists call the **nominal** or **market rate** of interest and the **real** or **pure rate**. The nominal rate differs from the pure rate because the market includes a premium reflecting the fact that the promised dollar payments will be affected by changes in the purchasing power of those payments (as well as the risk of the asset). The following case illustrates how inflation affects the selection of a discount rate and the calculation of damages.

Trevino v. United States of America
United States Court of Appeals for the Ninth Circuit
804 F.2d 1512 (1986)

SNEED, J.

Sophia Trevino and her parents sued the United States for medical malpractice, pursuant to the Federal Torts Claims Act (FTCA), 28 U.S.C. §§ 1346(b), 2674, arising from the negligent treatment given to Sophia's mother during Sophia's birth. The government concedes liability but appeals the award of over $6.3 million in damages. We modify in part, reverse in part, and remand.

I. FACTS AND PROCEEDINGS BELOW

On November 3, 1981, Rachael Trevino gave birth to Sophia at Madigan Army Medical Center in Tacoma, Washington (Madigan). During labor, Rachael suffered from a condition known as abruptio placentae, meaning that her placenta was partially detached from the uterine wall. The medical care that she received during labor did not take this condition into account. As a result, Sophia was born severely disabled. She has permanent brain damage, a form of cerebral palsy that involves all four extremities, and a seizure disorder. Evaluations by the University of Kansas Children's Rehabilitation Unit (the Kansas team) and by the government's expert witnesses suggest that Sophia will be mildly mentally retarded, but that she will be able to attend school and attain a fourth-grade level of reading and writing. Her emotional development should be normal. It is her set of physical disabilities, rather than her mental or emotional disabilities, that affect her the most. Experts assessed her gross motor skills as being at the level of a twelve-month-old child and her fine motor skills as being at the level of a twenty-four-month-old child. Although she probably will be able to walk unassisted at home, she will need crutches or a wheelchair outside the home. The Kansas team predicted that, with proper training and encouragement, Sophia will be able to function in a fairly independent manner. They contend that she probably will be able to work in a sheltered workshop setting and that she might even be able to work in the competitive market. The Trevinos contend that she will never be able to work in the competitive market. Her life expectancy is normal.

Sophia and her parents filed a FTCA action against the United States, alleging that Sophia's injuries had been caused by the negligent treatment provided by Madigan. After a five-day bench trial, the district court entered a judgment for the plaintiffs. It awarded Sophia $2,000,000 in nonpecuniary damages and $3,932,504 in pecuniary damages, and it awarded her parents as a unit $200,000 for loss of love and companionship and $200,000 for injury to the parent-child relationship. The United States moved for a new trial or, in the alternative, for an amended judgment. The court denied the motion, and the United States appeals.

II. DISCUSSION

A. *Standard of Review*

We review damage awards in FTCA cases for clear error. *Shaw v. United States*, 741 F.2d 1202, 1205 (9th Cir. 1984). The award is clearly erroneous if, after a review of the record, we are " 'left with the definite and firm conviction that a mistake has been committed.' " *Id.* (quoting *United States v. United State Gypsum Co.*, 333 U.S. 364, 395 (1948)). To determine whether a given award is excessive, we look to the relevant state's case law on excessive awards. *Id.* The state of Washington considers awards excessive "only if the amount shocks the court's sense of justice or sound judgment" and if it "appears that the trial judge was swayed by passion or prejudice." *Id.* at 1209. To make that determination, we compare the challenged award to awards in similar cases in the same jurisdiction. The choice of a discount rate, used to adjust to present value an award based on an income stream spread over time and, at the same time, to adjust for the effects of inflation, should be reviewed for an abuse of discretion. *Cf. Jones & Laughlin Steel Corp. v. Pfeifer*, 462 U.S. 523, 546–47 (1983) (suggesting caution be used in determining a discount rate, given the uncertainties of future economic events).

*   *   *

E. The Pecuniary Award to Sophia

1. *Choice of a Discount Rate*

The district court applied a –2% discount rate to the pecuniary component of the damage award. It explained its reason for this choice as follows:

> The –2% discount rate was determined by the application of a set formula which assumes as [sic] constant relationship between inflation and discount rates. The differential between the growth rates and the tax-free rate of return has been stable and has averaged more than two percentage points during the 30-year period 1954–1984. To obtain the present value of economic loss using tax-free short-term interest as the appropriate discount rate, a net discount rate of –2% was applied (wage and cost increases exceed tax-free interest rates by 2%) and calculated [with] the amounts testified to by the economic expert, Dr. Lowell Bassett.

R.E. at 14. We hold that the district court abused its discretion in applying a negative discount rate to the estimated pecuniary losses. Such a rate relies on assumptions not generally accepted by the courts or economists.

The Supreme Court addressed the discount rate issue in its opinion in *Jones & Laughlin Steel Corp. v. Pfeifer*, 462 U.S. 523 (1983). Its analysis of the methods of computing damage awards, including the choice of the proper discount rate, need not be repeated except to the extent necessary to reveal our thinking. We quickly point out, however, that the Supreme Court did not approve the use of a negative discount rate even though its survey of the economic and legal literature touched on material that might have suggested it. *See* 462 U.S. at 548 n.30.

We begin by recognizing that awards based on income streams spread over time are usually discounted to present value to account for the fact that a plaintiff, by receiving the money in a lump sum, "up front," will invest the sum and earn additional income from the investment. *See Pfeifer*, 462 U.S. at 536–37; Fitzgerald, *Economic Loss in Wrongful Death: Principles of Evaluation*, 44 Ins.Couns.J. 427, 431 (1977). The discount rate should be based on " 'the best and safest investments.' " *Pfeifer*, 462 U.S. at 537 (quoting *Chesapeake & Ohio Ry. v. Kelly*, 241 U.S. 485, 491 (1916)).[1] Were it not for inflation, that simple calculation would end the matter. With inflation, however, dollars received in the future will buy less than would those same dollars if received today. A net positive discount rate implies that the gains from safe investments exceed the losses induced by inflation—in other words, that the rate chosen to reflect the interest rate on the safest investments over a fixed period of time will be a larger number than the rate chosen to reflect the rate of inflation over the same period of time. Professor Jerome Sherman's analysis of the relationship between government bond yields (the investment factor) and inflation illustrates the point:

> [Yields on treasury bonds have stayed slightly ahead of the rate of inflation during the past 32 years [1947–78] (4.4 percent vs. 3.6 percent). This means that the real return on treasury bonds was 0.8 percent.] Sherman, Projection of Economic Loss: Inflation v. Present Value, 14 Creighton L. Rev. 723, 732 (1981).

Obviously it is possible for the true rate of inflation to outstrip the return on the safest investments for some period of time. This would justify for that period of time a negative discount rate. The district court's use of a negative discount rate is based on this possibility.

The district court's choice is flawed, however. First, it relied on an unrepresentative timespan. That period was from 1954 to 1984. R.E. at 14. This span includes the aberrational years 1974–82: years in which oil prices tripled from 1974 to 1979, inflation reached double-digit proportions, and "[r]ecessions in 1974, 1975, 1980, and 1982 mark[ed] the 1974–82 period as the most recession-plagued nine years since the Great Depression." Formuzis & Pickersgill, *Present Value of Economic Loss*, Trial, Feb. 1985, at 22, 23. As one article summarized the state of the economy for the past thirty-five years or so,

> In addition to the upward trend in inflation and interest rates evident in most of the post-1947 period, there has been an increase in the variability about the trend. Between 1947 and 1967, the average yearly inflation rate was 2 percent, and the range between the high and low values

---

1. The reason that risk-free investments are preferred to more remunerative but riskier investments is that the plaintiff should not be faced with the burden of becoming a full-time broker merely to safeguard his award.

was 4.6 percent. For interest rates on long-term government securities, the corresponding figures were 3.37 average and a range of 2.6 percent. In the following sixteen-year period, however, the average figures for inflation and interest rates were 7.27 percent and 7.93 percent while the ranges were 10.5 percent and 7.62 percent respectively. In fact, the interest rate on ten-year government bonds fluctuated nearly as much in 1981 alone as it did for the entire period 1947 to 1967. This volatility indicates that forecasters have had a more difficult assignment in recent years and that forecast errors, which have been large in recent years, can be expected to remain that way.

Mead, *Calculating Present Value*, Trial, July 1984, at 16, 18. The truth of this observation is borne out when one examines the period 1926–1981, in which the average annual inflation rate was around 3 percent. R. Ibbotson & R. Sinquefield, *Stocks, Bonds, Bills, and Inflation* 15 (1982 ed.).

We cannot deny history, nor can history provide an always reliable basis for predicting the future. However, we can base our estimates on long time periods that will diminish the effect of shorter aberrational periods. Fluctuations that are great for a short time span are less dramatic, and skew results less, when they are seen as part of a longer period. We have no confidence in the ability of experts, the district court, or this court, to predict inflation or interest rates over the period of Sophia's life other than by extrapolating from the past.

The district court must also select an accurate measure of historical inflation as the basis for its prediction of future inflation. Here, the district court used the historical increase in wages and medical costs. Supplemental Record Excerpts at 48. But this gives the illusion of greater inflation, because some portion of wage increases is not due to inflation:

> Because the growth rate of wages includes a component attributable to pay increases due to increased education, age and maturity, and increases in productivity, as well as a component attributable to inflation, the difference between the interest rate on a secure investment and the rate of growth of wages *understates* the real interest rate by whatever proportion of the growth rate of wages is not attributable to inflation.

Sauers v. Alaska Barge & Transp., Inc., 600 F.2d 238, 246 n.15 (9th Cir. 1979). The district court might have supposed that the historical rise in wage rates was a proper measure of inflation for the purpose of calculating a discount rate to be applied to the wage portion only of Sophia's award, because Sophia deserved to be compensated for future increases in her wages due to her projected increased productivity, as well as for increases in her wages due to projected inflation. But *Pfeifer* denies that supposition. A plaintiff may be compensated for projected future increases in his wages due to increases in his productivity if he proves that he would have been likely to receive wage increases by reason of his increased productivity. 462 U.S. at 534–36. Because Sophia made no such showing, the district court erred when it used the historical rise in wages as a measure of inflation for the purpose of calculating the discount rate for the lost wage portion of Sophia's award. Furthermore, the rate of increase in wages may not be the same as the rate of increase in medical costs over the same period. For this reason, the measure of inflation for the purpose of calculating the discount rate to be applied to the medical expense portion of Sophia's award may be different than that employed in fixing the discount rate applicable to the lost wage portion of her award.

Pfeifer's discussion of discount rates technically is only an interpretation of section 5(b) of the Longshoremen's and Harbor Workers' Compensation Act (LHWCA). *See* 462 U.S. at 547. But the general discussion of alternative methods of calculating discount rates is extensive. The Court mentions several options:

> 1. Calculate the lost income stream by excluding the effects of inflation and the "real" interest rate by fixing the difference between the market rate of interest and the anticipated rate of inflation, *id.* at 541–42, 548;
>
> 2. Calculate the size of the lost income stream by including the effects of inflation and discounting by the market interest rate, *id.* at 543, 547–48; and,
>
> 3. Calculate the value of pecuniary damages by employing a zero discount rate (the total offset approach), *id.* at 544–46, 549–50.

The last option (the total offset approach) was considered unacceptable as a uniform method to calculate damages, although it could be stipulated to by the parties, or applied by the trial court in an appropriate case. *See id.* at 550–51. After examining a plethora of economic studies, the Court concluded as to the "real" interest rate option that: "Although we find the economic evidence distinctly inconclusive regarding an essential premise of those approaches, we do not believe a trial court...should be reversed if it adopts a rate between 1 and 3% and explains its choice." *Id.* at 548–49 (footnote omitted). Obviously a decision interpreting section 5(b) of the LHWCA is not binding in an FTCA case; however, the Court's guidance on the issue of economic predictions and discount rates cannot be disregarded. We accept this guidance and choose to regard it as controlling in this case. In reliance on *Pfeifer*, and in the absence of Washington state law to the contrary, we decline to embrace a negative discount rate on the basis of this record.

We do not hold, however, that any discount rate above 3% or below 1% is impermissible. Supported by credible expert testimony, a court could certainly adopt a different rate. *Cf. Culver v. Slater Boat Co.* (Culver II) 722 F.2d 114, 121–22 (5th Cir. 1983) (en banc) (requiring courts to use a below-market rate calculation and permitting courts to use a −1.5% discount rate if supported by expert opinion). We do hold, however, that it is impermissible to select a time period over which to compare inflation and interest rates that provides a decidedly aberrational result. We also point out that it is impermissible either (1) *to exclude* the effects of inflation in determining the size of the lost income stream and employ a discount rate equal to the market rate of interest, or (2) *to include* the effects of inflation in determining the size of the lost income stream and employ a discount rate measured by the difference between the market rate of interest and the rate of inflation. The former denies the injured party any adjustment for inflation while making available such adjustment to the party deemed responsible for the injury. The latter, on the other hand, provides to the injured party an adjustment for inflation in determining the size of the lost income stream and denies to the party deemed responsible for the injury any benefit of that adjustment in determining the proper discount rate. *See Pfeifer*, 462 U.S. at 538–52 *passim*. Put more succinctly, the former accords the party deemed responsible for the injury a "double benefit," while in the latter the "double benefit" passes to the injured party. Neither party is entitled to a "double benefit."

Finally, we point out that the choice of an interest rate yield on Sophia's lump sum award, or for other purposes in fixing the final amount of the award for the loss of earning capacity, is not dictated by the manner in which taxes are treated. The yield of tax-free securities enjoys no special status. That yield merely indicates what a yield would be to an investor who is strongly averse to both risk and taxes. No sensible investment counselor would advise Sophia to invest the entire lump sum in tax-free securities. Nor is it probable that she will do so. For these reasons the use of the yield of tax-free securities to arrive at the "real rate" of interest is suspect. The tax-free rate of interest is substantially below that yielded by securities not enjoying that privilege. Its use, when coupled with a period of unrepresentative high inflation, as was done in this case, yields an unnaturally low discount rate. This should be avoided on remand.

     *   *   *

We remand for the recalculation of Sophia's pecuniary loss in accordance with the Part II.E. of this opinion.

MODIFIED IN PART, REVERSED IN PART, AND REMANDED.

Notes and Questions

1. The Real Rate of Return: The real rate of return on an investment, r, is defined as the nominal rate of return (that return stated on the face of the bond or the total percent change from stock), R, minus the rate of inflation, π, over the same time period. Alternatively,

$$R = r + \pi,$$

which is adjusted to

$$r = R - \pi.$$

Thus, the nominal rate must be greater than inflation for money to grow in real terms. As the court points out, it is doubtful that the plaintiffs will put all of Sophia's money into a tax-free bond which typically grows at a slower rate than inflation. Thus, since the nominal rate of return should be above inflation (usually 2–3%), the lower court erred in its negative discount value. The court is correct in assuming that Sophia's family will invest in instruments with a positive expected real rate of return.

2. Inflation Expectations and Interest Rates: The court states that the inflationary period that the lower court used is unrealistic because it included the oil embargo and a period of stagflation. Predicting the future is perilous, but it must be done in order to make present value calculations. The bond market reflects inflation because it must provide an interest rate greater than inflation to attract investors. Thus, the long term and short term bond market gives interest rates that are greater than projected long term and short term inflation.

3. Risk Aversion and Discounting: In each of these cases, the court had to address the question of the appropriate discount rate to be applied in the present value calculation. However, in considering this issue, courts appear to ignore an important assumption about economic behavior—the concept of **risk aversion**. Risk aversion implies the existence of a positive relationship between risk and return. An example should make this clear. Suppose a rich relative sends you a check for $1,000. Your roommate offers you a bet consisting of the flipping of a fair coin with the result that if you flip a head you double your money, but if you flip a tail you lose the entire $1,000. The expected value of the bet is zero [i.e., (.5)($1,000) + (.5)(–$1,000) = 0]. However, most people would refuse this gamble because the value placed on the one thousand dollars lost is greater than the additional value that would be obtained if you won an additional thousand dollars. In other words, because of risk aversion, one would demand additional compensation for taking such a bet. For example, you might refuse to play unless the payoff is increased to compensate you for taking the risk—e.g., you could demand that the payoff be $1,500 instead of $1,000 if you win. Then the expected value would be positive—[i.e. (.5)($1,500) + (.5)(–$1,000) = ($750 – $500) = $250].

That most people are risk averse is seen by: (1) the widespread purchase of insurance, which is nothing more than a substitution of a certain small loss—the insurance premium—for the probability of a large loss; (2) and the observation of security markets where riskier investments have higher returns than less risky investments.

How does this insight affect the choice of a discount rate? As we saw in *Trevino*, the rule appears to be that the court should apply a riskless interest rate in discounting lost future earnings to present value. In other words, the use of a riskless discount rate will result in the award of a present value sum that can be invested at a riskless rate of return to yield a guaranteed stream of earnings equal to what was lost. Note, however, what a plaintiff loses in a wrongful injury case is not a **riskless stream**, i.e., a guaranteed amount in each particular year, but a risky stream of future income. Moreover, if the plaintiff is risk averse, he or she will *prefer* the sum certain to its expected value equivalent, i.e., its actuarial value, since he could not have diversified away all of the risk in his earnings stream.

4. Risk, Diversification, and Human Capital: Assuming (for now) this positive relationship between risk and return, the next insight ignored by courts is that not every risk will be compensated. Modern portfolio theory teaches that risks that can be diversified away command no increased return. In other words, the market will pay no premium to bear fully diversifiable risk. The primary source of income to an individual is what economists refer to as **human capital**. Human capital is the acquired skills and knowledge from which an individual generates an earning stream. (Recall that this was the asset being valued in *Haugan*. Was it riskless?) It is asserted that the risk implicit in human capital cannot be diversified away since an individual cannot hold a portfolio of occupations. (Is this literally true?) Thus, if a court uses a riskless discount rate to calculate the present value of lost earnings, the plaintiff will be overcompensated in the sense that the plaintiff will value the sum certain received by a lump sum payment more than the stream of income he or she would have earned absent the tort.[3]

---

3. It is important here to note that the risk we speak about in the text is not physical risk of a profession, but economic risk. Economists have long recognized that the market compensates workers in jobs that require a greater risk of physical injury or death, e.g., a

3. Pulling It All Together

There are two fundamental components to any present value calculation. First, the relevant future stream of cash flows must be identified. Second, an appropriate interest rate needs to be selected. The cases in the preceding subsections dealt with each of these components independently. As the following case demonstrates, however, the correct method for calculating either one of these components depends upon how the other component is calculated.

O'Shea v. Riverway Towing Co.
U.S. Court of Appeals, Seventh Circuit
677 F.2d 1194 (1982)

POSNER, Circuit Judge

This is a tort case under the federal admiralty jurisdiction. We are called upon to decide questions of contributory negligence and damage assessment, in particular the question—one of first impression in this circuit—whether, and if so how, to account for inflation in computing lost future wages.

On the day of the accident, Margaret O'Shea was coming off duty as a cook on a towboat plying the Mississippi River. A harbor boat operated by the defendant, Riverway Towing Company, carried Mrs. O'Shea to shore and while getting off the boat she fell and sustained the injury complained of. The district judge found Riverway negligent and Mrs. O'Shea free from contributory negligence, and assessed damages in excess of $150,000. Riverway appeals only from the finding that there was no contributory negligence and from the part of the damage award that was intended to compensate Mrs. O'Shea for her lost future wages.

The accident happened in the following way. When the harbor boat reached shore it tied up to a seawall the top of which was several feet above the boat's deck. There was no ladder. The other passengers, who were seamen, clambered up the seawall without difficulty, but Mrs. O'Shea, a 57 year-old woman who weighs 200 pounds (she is five foot seven), balked. According to Mrs. O'Shea's testimony, which the district court believed, a deckhand instructed her to climb the stairs to a catwalk above the deck and disembark from there. But the catwalk was three feet above the top of the seawall, and again there was no ladder. The deckhand told her that she should jump and that the men who had already disembarked would help her land safely. She did as told, but fell in the landing, carrying the assisting seaman down with her, and broke her leg.

[The district judge's finding that Mrs. O'Shea was not contributorily negligent is not clearly erroneous on these facts....]

The more substantial issues in this appeal relate to the computation of lost wages. Mrs. O'Shea's job as a cook paid her $40 a day, and since the custom was

---

roughneck in the North Sea oil fields. This market risk premium will be included in wage estimates used to calculate the lost earnings.

to work 30 days consecutively and then have the next 30 days off, this comes to $7200 a year although, as we shall see, she never had earned that much in a single year. She testified that when the accident occurred she had been about to get another cook's job on a Mississippi towboat that would have paid her $60 a day ($10,800 a year). She also testified that she had been intending to work as a boat's cook until she was 70—longer if she was able. An economist who testified on Mrs. O'Shea's behalf used the foregoing testimony as the basis for estimating the wages that she lost because of the accident. He first subtracted federal income tax from yearly wage estimates based on alternative assumptions about her wage rate (that it would be either $40 or $60 a day); assumed that this wage would have grown by between six and eight percent a year; assumed that she would have worked either to age 65 or to age 70; and then discounted the resulting lost-wage estimates to present value, using a discount rate of 8.5 percent a year. These calculations, being based on alternative assumptions concerning starting wage rate, annual wage increases, and length of employment, yielded a range of values rather than a single value. The bottom of the range was $50,000. This is the present value, computed at an 8.5 percent discount rate, of Mrs. O'Shea's lost future wages on the assumption that her starting wage is $40 a day and that it would have grown by six percent a year until she retired at the age of 65. The top of the range was $114,000, which is the present value (again discounted at 8.5 percent) of her lost future wages assuming she would have worked till she was 70 at a wage that would have started at $60 a day and increased by eight percent a year. The judge awarded a figure—$86,033—near the midpoint of this range. He did not explain in his written opinion how he had arrived at this figure, but in a preceding oral opinion he stated that he was "not certain that she would work until age 70 at this type of work," "although she certainly was entitled to" do so and "could have earned something"; and that he had not "felt bound by (the economist's) figure of eight percent increase in wages" and had "not found the wages based on necessarily a 60 dollar a day job." If this can be taken to mean that he thought Mrs. O'Shea would probably have worked till she was 70, starting at $40 a day but moving up from there at six rather than eight percent a year, the economist's estimate of the present value of her lost future wages would be $75,000.

There is no doubt that the accident disabled Mrs. O'Shea from working as a cook on a boat. The break in her leg was very serious: it reduced the stability of the leg and caused her to fall frequently. It is impossible to see how she could have continued working as a cook, a job performed mostly while standing up, especially on a boat, with its unsteady motion. But Riverway argues that Mrs. O'Shea (who has not worked at all since the accident, which occurred two years before the trial) could have gotten some sort of job and that the wages in that job should be deducted from the admittedly higher wages that she could have earned as a cook on a boat.

* * * We cannot say that [to find that Mrs. O'Shea could not by reasonable diligence have found gainful employment, given the physical condition in which the accident left her]... was clearly erroneous.

Riverway argues next that it was wrong for the judge to award damages on the basis of a wage not validated, as it were, by at least a year's employment at that wage. Mrs. O'Shea had never worked full time, had never in fact earned more than $3600 in a full year, and in the year preceding the accident had earned only $900. But previous wages do not put a cap on an award of lost future wages. If a man who had never worked in his life graduated from law school, began working at a law firm at an annual salary of $35,000, and was killed the second day on the job, his lack of a past wage history would be irrelevant to computing his lost future wages. The present case is similar if less dramatic. Mrs. O'Shea did not work at all until 1974, when her husband died. She then lived on her inheritance and worked at a variety of part-time jobs till January 1979, when she started working as a cook on the towboat. According to her testimony, which the trial judge believed, she was then working full time. It is immaterial that this was her first full-time job and that the accident occurred before she had held it for a full year. Her job history was typical of women who return to the labor force after their children are grown or, as in Mrs. O'Shea's case, after their husband dies, and these women are, like any tort victims, entitled to damages based on what they would have earned in the future rather than on what they may or may not have earned in the past.

If we are correct so far, Mrs. O'Shea was entitled to have her lost wages determined on the assumption that she would have earned at least $7200 in the first year after the accident and that the accident caused her to lose that entire amount by disabling her from any gainful employment. And since Riverway neither challenges the district judge's (apparent) finding that Mrs. O'Shea would have worked till she was 70 nor contends that the lost wages for each year until then should be discounted by the probability that she would in fact have been alive and working as a boat's cook throughout the damage period, we may also assume that her wages would have been at least $7200 a year for the 12 years between the date of the accident and her seventieth birthday. But Riverway does argue that we cannot assume she might have earned $10,800 a year rather than $7200, despite her testimony that at the time of the accident she was about to take another job as a boat's cook where she would have been paid at the rate of $60 rather than $40 a day. The point is not terribly important since the trial judge gave little weight to this testimony, but we shall discuss it briefly. Mrs. O'Shea was asked on direct examination what "pay you would have worked" for in the new job. Riverway's counsel objected on the ground of hearsay, the judge overruled his objection, and she answered $60 a day. The objection was not well taken. Riverway argues that only her prospective employer knew what her wage was, and hence when she said it was $60 she was testifying to what he had told her. But an employee's wage is as much in the personal knowledge of the employee as of the employer. If Mrs. O'Shea's prospective employer had testified that he would have paid her $60, Riverway's counsel could have made the converse hearsay objection that the employer was really testifying to what Mrs. O'Shea had told him she was willing to work for. Riverway's counsel could on cross-examination have probed the basis for Mrs. O'Shea's belief that she was going to get $60 a day in a new job, but he did not do so and cannot complain now that the judge may have given her testimony some (though little) weight.

We come at last to the most important issue in the case, which is the proper treatment of inflation in calculating lost future wages. Mrs. O'Shea's economist based the six to eight percent range which he used to estimate future increases in the wages of a boat's cook on the general pattern of wage increases in service occupations over the past 25 years. During the second half of this period the rate of inflation has been substantial and has accounted for much of the increase in nominal wages in this period; and to use that increase to project future wage increases is therefore to assume that inflation will continue, and continue to push up wages. Riverway argues that it is improper as a matter of law to take inflation into account in projecting lost future wages. Yet Riverway itself wants to take inflation into account-one-sidedly, to reduce the amount of the damages computed. For Riverway does not object to the economist's choice of an 8.5 percent discount rate for reducing Mrs. O'Shea's lost future wages to present value, although the rate includes an allowance—a very large allowance—for inflation.

To explain, the object of discounting lost future wages to present value is to give the plaintiff an amount of money which, invested safely, will grow to a sum equal to those wages. So if we thought that but for the accident Mrs. O'Shea would have earned $7200 in 1990, and we were computing in 1980 (when this case was tried) her damages based on those lost earnings, we would need to determine the sum of money that, invested safely for a period of ten years, would grow to $7200. Suppose that in 1980 the rate of interest on ultra-safe (i.e., federal government) bonds or notes maturing in 10 years was 12 percent. Then we would consult a table of present values to see what sum of money invested at 12 percent for 10 years would at the end of that time have grown to $7200. The answer is $2318. But a moment's reflection will show that to give Mrs. O'Shea $2318 to compensate her for lost wages in 1990 would grossly undercompensate her. People demand 12 percent to lend money risklessly for 10 years because they expect their principal to have much less purchasing power when they get it back at the end of the time. In other words, when long-term interest rates are high, they are high in order to compensate lenders for the fact that they will be repaid in cheaper dollars. In periods when no inflation is anticipated, the risk-free interest rate is between one and three percent.... Additional percentage points above that level reflect inflation anticipated over the life of the loan. But if there is inflation it will affect wages as well as prices. Therefore to give Mrs. O'Shea $2318 today because that is the present value of $7200 10 years hence, computed at a discount rate—12 percent—that consists mainly of an allowance for anticipated inflation, is in fact to give her less than she would have been earning then if she was earning $7200 on the date of the accident, even if the only wage increases she would have received would have been those necessary to keep pace with inflation.

There are (at least) two ways to deal with inflation in computing the present value of lost future wages. One is to take it out of both the wages and the discount rate—to say to Mrs. O'Shea, "we are going to calculate your probable wage in 1990 on the assumption, unrealistic as it is, that there will be zero inflation between now and then; and, to be consistent, we are going to discount the amount thus calculated by the interest rate that would be charged under the same assumption of zero inflation." Thus, if we thought Mrs. O'Shea's real (i.e., inflation-free) wage rate would not rise in the future, we would fix her lost earnings in 1990 as $7200 and, to be consistent, we would discount that to the present (1980) value using an estimate of the real interest rate. At two percent, this procedure would yield a present value of $5906. Of course, she would not invest this money at a mere two percent. She would invest it at the much higher prevailing interest rate. But that would not give her a windfall; it would just enable her to replace her lost 1990 earnings with an amount equal to what she would in fact have earned in that year if inflation continues, as most people expect it to do. (If people did not expect continued inflation, long-term interest rates would be much lower; those rates impound investor's inflationary expectations.)

An alternative approach, which yields the same result, is to use a (higher) discount rate based on the current risk-free 10-year interest rate, but apply that rate to an estimate of lost future wages that includes expected inflation. Contrary to Riverway's argument, this projection would not require gazing into a crystal ball. The expected rate of inflation can, as just suggested, be read off from the current long-term interest rate. If that rate is 12 percent, and if as suggested earlier the real or inflation-free interest rate is only one to three percent, this implies that the market is anticipating 9–11 percent inflation over the next 10 years, for a long-term interest rate is simply the sum of the real interest rate and the anticipated rate of inflation during the term.

*   *   *

Applying our analysis to the present case, we cannot pronounce the approach taken by the plaintiff's economist unreasonable. He chose a discount rate—8.5 percent—well above the real rate of interest, and therefore containing an allowance for inflation. Consistency required him to inflate Mrs. O'Shea's starting wage as a boat's cook in calculating her lost future wages, and he did so at a rate of six to eight percent a year. If this rate had been intended as a forecast of purely inflationary wage changes, his approach would be open to question, especially at the upper end of his range. For if the estimated rate of inflation were eight percent, the use of a discount rate of 8.5 percent would imply that the real rate of interest was only .5 percent, which is lower than most economists believe it to be for any substantial period of time. But wages do not rise just because of inflation. Mrs. O'Shea could expect her real wages as a boat's cook to rise as she became more experienced and as average real wage rates throughout the economy rose, as they usually do over a decade or more. It would not be outlandish to assume that even if there were no inflation, Mrs. O'Shea's wages would have risen by three percent a year. If we subtract that from the economist's six to eight percent range, the inflation allowance built into his estimated future wage increases is only three to five percent; and when we subtract these figures from 8.5 percent we see that his implicit estimate of the real rate of interest was very high (3.5–5.5 percent). This means he was conservative, because the higher the discount rate used the lower the damages calculated.

If conservative in one sense, the economist was most liberal in another. He made no allowance for the fact that Mrs. O'Shea, whose health history quite apart from the accident is not outstanding, might very well not have survived and been working as a boat's cook full time or in an equivalent job—until the age of 70. The damage award is a sum certain, but the lost future wages to which that award is equated by means of the discount rate are mere probabilities. If the probability of her being employed as a boat's cook full time in 1990 was only 75 percent, for example, then her estimated wages in that year should have been multiplied by .75 to determine the value of the expectation that she lost as a result of the accident; and so with each of the other future years.... The economist did not do this, and by failing to do this he overstated the loss due to the accident.

But Riverway does not make an issue of this aspect of the economist's analysis. Nor of another: the economist selected the 8.5 percent figure for the discount rate because that was the current interest rate on Triple A 10-year state and municipal bonds, but it would not make sense in Mrs. O'Shea's federal income tax bracket to invest in tax-free bonds. If he wanted to use nominal rather than real interest rates and wage increases (as we said was proper), the economist should have used a higher discount rate and a higher expected rate of inflation. But as these adjustments would have been largely or entirely offsetting, the failure to make them was not a critical error.

Although we are not entirely satisfied with the economic analysis on which the judge, in the absence of any other evidence of the present value of Mrs. O'Shea's lost future wages, must have relied heavily, we recognize that the exactness which economic analysis rigorously pursued appears to offer is, at least in the litigation setting, somewhat delusive. Therefore, we will not reverse an award of damages for lost wages because of questionable assumptions unless it yields an unreasonable result—especially when, as in the present case, the defendant does not offer any economic evidence himself and does not object to the questionable steps in the plaintiff's economic analysis. We cannot say the result here was unreasonable. If the economist's method of estimating damages was too generous to Mrs. O'Shea in one important respect it was, as we have seen, niggardly in another. Another error against Mrs. O'Shea should be noted: the economist should not have deducted her *entire* income tax liability in estimating her future lost wages.... While it is true that the damage award is not taxable, the interest she earns on it will be (a point the economist may have ignored because of his erroneous assumption that she would invest the award in tax-exempt bonds), so that his method involved an element of double taxation.

If we assume that Mrs. O'Shea could have expected a three percent annual increase in her real wages from a base of $7200, that the real risk-free rate of interest (and therefore the appropriate discount rate if we are considering only real wage increases) is two percent, and that she would have worked till she was 70, the present value of her lost future wages would be $91,310. This figure ignores the fact that she did not have a 100 percent probability of actually working till age 70 as a boat's cook, and fails to make the appropriate (though probably, in her bracket, very small) net income tax adjustment; but it also ignores the possibility, small but not totally negligible, that the proper base is really $10,800 rather than $7200.

So we cannot say that the figure arrived at by the judge, $86,033, was unreasonably high. But we are distressed that he made no attempt to explain how he had arrived at that figure, since it was not one contained in the economist's testimony though it must in some way have been derived from that testimony. Unlike many other damage items in a personal injury case, notably pain and suffering, the calculation of damages for lost earnings can and should be an analytical rather than an intuitive undertaking. Therefore, compliance with Rule 52(a) of the Federal Rules of Civil Procedure requires that in a bench trial the district judge set out the steps by which he arrived at his award for lost future earnings, in order to assist the appellate court in reviewing the award.... The district judge failed to do that here. We do not consider this reversible error, because our own analysis convinces us that the award of damages for lost future wages was reasonable. But for the future we ask the district judges in this circuit to indicate the steps by which they arrive at damage awards for lost future earnings.

JUDGMENT AFFIRMED.

Notes and Questions

1. Consistency in Accounting for Inflation: The defendant in *Riverway* argues "that it is improper as a matter of law to take inflation into account in projecting lost future wages." However, Judge Posner is quick to draw attention to a very important conceptual error made by the defendant. Specifically, the defendant objected to incorporating inflation into the future cash flow component, but continued to utilize an interest rate component which accounted for inflation. As Judge Posner noted, the defendant's method would result in the plaintiff being under compensated. Can you make an intuitive explanation for why this is so? The defendant's conceptual error clearly demonstrates that the correct method for estimating one of the present value components depends upon the manner in which the other was estimated. In other words, consistency is an important element of sound present value calculations.

2. The Probability of Future Income: Judge Posner questions the validity of the assumption that Mrs. O'Shea would continue to work until the age of 70. In Posner's opinion the failure to account for the chance that Mrs. O'Shea would not work that long results in an overstatement of the loss. To account for this uncertainty, Posner suggests that estimates of future income should be multiplied by the probability that she would actually be working in that year. For example, assume that the expert projects that Mrs. O'Shea would have earned $12,000 in the tenth year. However, there is only a 75% chance that Mrs. O'Shea will be working in 10 years. Thus, Posner suggests that Mrs O'Shea's expected future income for the tenth year be calculated as .75 × $12,000 = $9,000. What do you think of this suggestion? Can you think of an alternative way to account for this uncertainty?

3. Tax Considerations: Section 104(a)(2) of the Internal Revenue Code excludes from income any damages received, whether by suit or agreement, lump-sum or periodic payment, on account of personal injury or sickness. Thus, Mrs. O'Shea's award for the present value of lost future wages will not be taxed. However, any interest or other income that Mrs. O'Shea receives as a result of investing her award will be taxed. As a result, Judge Posner observes that by accounting for taxes in the estimate of future income the plaintiff has been subjected to double taxation. Do you agree with Posner's assessment? Are there alternative methods for avoiding double taxation? How would a structured settlement fit into this analysis?

C. The Value of Life

People often claim that life is priceless—that there is no amount of money that they would accept for their own life or the life of a family member or a close friend. Yet, as illustrated by the CAFE case in Chapter I, it is common for people knowingly to accept life-threatening risks. Moreover, when a court has to determine the value of a deceased person's life, it must put a dollar figure on that life. In this section, we explore two methodologies for determining the value of life.

1. Economic Value of Life

Traditionally, most courts have focused on the economic value of life—that is, the amount of money a person would have made over his lifetime discounted to a present value. This includes a valuation of all wages and other sources of income minus living expenses, such as food and rent. Figuring the exact amount of economic value that a person has been deprived of can be an emotional and somewhat speculative process.

Cappello v. Duncan Aircraft Sales of Florida
U.S. Ct. Of Appeals, Sixth Circuit
79 F.3d 1465 (1996)

MERRITT, C.J.

This diversity case for wrongful death arises from an airplane crash. The parties agreed that the substantive questions in the case are governed by Tennessee law.

At 1:42 in the early morning of March 16, 1991, in fair weather, the pilot of a small "Hawker" jet chartered from the defendant flew into the side of a 3,500 [foot high] mountain two minutes after taking off from a closed airport in San Diego. All nine people on board were killed. The pilot, Donald Holmes, had chosen to take off at night in a mountainous area under the visual flight rules ("VFR") of the Federal Aviation Administration, rather than the instrument flight rules ("IFR")....He was therefore not under the direction or control of an FAA controller, and consequently, he had received no radio instructions or clearances before the crash. Under these circumstances of VFR flight, as explained in more detail below, the pilot in command had the sole responsibility to maintain eye contact with the ground and to avoid obstructions.... The defendant corporation, Duncan Aviation, had chartered the plane and provided the pilot in order to carry a band for country music singer, Reba McEntire, to her next concert engagement. The plaintiffs' decedent in this wrongful death action was the band leader, Kirk Cappello. Able counsel for the defendant declined to admit that pilot negligence was the cause of the accident and sought successfully at the jury trial below to shift responsibility to two nonparty FAA employees on the basis of comparative negligence. The plaintiffs, the parents of the deceased band leader, assign as error on appeal the decision of the trial judge to allow this comparative negligence defense to go to the jury. The jury found the pilot who flew into the mountain only 45% responsible, attributing 55% of the responsibility for the crash to the FAA employees. After the deduction for FAA negligence, the jury awarded plaintiffs $329,773 in damages against defendant for their son's death.

*   *   *

V.

This leaves as the last question a serious issue concerning the propriety of the jury's award of total damages of $732,829 prior to making its 55% deduction for comparative fault.

The parties concede that the jury accepted in its entirety the view of defendant's expert, John Sartain, that the economic value of the deceased band leader was $732,829. The jury accepted this testimony instead of the testimony of four other experts, including another for the defendant who testified that the decedent's income would have been substantially higher than Sartain assumed. In addition, the jury made obvious errors by refusing to include in the award the decedent's substantial funeral expenses and by refusing to bring forward to the date of trial the discounted economic value of the life in question.

The worst mistake made by Sartain, and hence by the jury, however, was in relying upon an assumption that the economic value of decedent's life should be based on an average income for the last five years before his death of $59,920. The unreasonableness of this assumption is demonstrated by the fact that decedent was only 28 years old when he died and had earned as a musician an average of $98,171 for the last two years. He earned over $100,000 in income during the last year before his death. Sartain could only reach his rock bottom figures by averaging the decedent's very low earnings for the preceding five years when he was in music school and then when he was just getting started in his profession. Those early low income years reduced by almost a half the income used in the calculation of a portion of the stream of income, the discounted present value of which represents the economic evaluation of the decedent's projected earnings. If Sartain had based his evaluation on the $98,171 figure the result would have exceeded $1.2 million. Sartain assumed that the decedent's income would have been much less for each of the next seven years than it had been for the last two years of his life. We believe that there is no justification for such an approach in the evaluation of this decedent's life. As pointed out in detail in plaintiff's briefs, Sartain's assumption is entirely inconsistent with his own chart based on empirical studies projecting the average lifetime earnings profile of college educated males.[18]

Unfortunately, the jury in this case went far astray on both liability and damages. Thus, in accordance with this opinion, the judgment of the court below must be vacated and the case remanded to the district court with instructions that (1) the liability of the defendant has been established, and (2) the damages issue must be retried.

Accordingly, it is so ordered.

---

18. Plaintiff's reply brief at page 24 accurately explains the situation: He [Sartain] introduced as Exhibit 101 a chart showing the average age earnings profile of male full-time workers with four years of college. The curve on this chart shows that the average worker had 40% higher earnings at age 28 than at 23 and that for every year after age 28, the income increases until age 54 and the income at age 36 is 30% higher than the income at 28. Although Sartain testified that he relied on that age earnings profile "to show how earnings change at different ages for men with college education, like with Cappello's," his conclusion that Kirk P. Cappello's 1991 income at age 28 would have been only $59,920, the average of his previous five years is in direct conflict with the earnings profile. (Ex. 101). If Sartain had relied on the earnings curve on the profile, he could not have concluded that Kirk P. Cappello's 1991 income would have reduced to his average income for the previous five years or that he would not again have equaled his 1990 income until he reached the age of 36. If he had relied on the profile, he would have concluded that Kirk P. Cappello's 1991 income would have been more than his 1990 income of $100,000 and would have increased every year until he reached 54. This would have resulted in a pecuniary value of far more than $732,829. Sartain's own testimony established that there was absolutely no justification for using $59,920 as the 1991 income of Kirk P. Cappello.

Notes and Questions

1. The Earnings Projection: The judge says that the damages were understated because Cappello's earnings had begun an upward trend in the two years before his death. Does a straight line extrapolation of his earnings along the more recent trend make sense? Does it overestimate or underestimate his worth?

2. Economic Loss: Why should Cappello's family be allowed to sue for an economic loss to an adult son? Is there any economic rationalization for allowing the family of the deceased to sue the airline for the actions of the deceased pilot?

3. Regulations, Cost-Benefit Analysis, and the Value of Life: Government health and safety regulations are intended to reduce injuries and save lives. Compliance with those regulations is costly. In attempting to determine whether a certain regulation should be adopted, regulators often need to compare the costs of the regulation with the benefits of the lives that the regulation is intended to save. Choices, preferably informed choices, must be made. Judge Williams of the District of Columbia Circuit has observed:

> ...Cost-benefit analysis requires identifying values for lost years of human life and for suffering and other losses from non-fatal injuries. Nothing we say here should be taken as confining the discretion of OSHA to choose among reasonable evaluation methods. While critics of cost-benefit analysis argue that any such valuation is impossible, that is so only in the sense that pin-point figures are necessarily arbitrary, so that the decisionmaker is effectively limited to considering some range of values. In fact, we make implicit life and safety valuations each day when we decide, for example, whether to travel by train or car, the former being more costly (at least if several family member are traveling together) but safer per passenger-mile. Where government makes decisions for others, it may reasonably be expected to make the trade-offs somewhat more explicitly than individuals choosing for themselves. The difficulty of securing agreement even on a range of values hardly justifies making decisions on the basis of a pretense that resources are not scarce. In any event, OSHA has an existing obligation under Executive Order No. 12,291, 46 Fed. Reg. 13, 193 (1981), to complete a cost-benefit analysis for each major rulemaking, so use of such a standard not only is doable in the qualified sense of which we have spoken but can be done without additional regulatory resources. Thus, cost-benefit analysis entails only a systematic weighing of pros and cons...

United Automobile Workers v. Occupational Safety and Health Administration, U.S. Department of Labor, 938 F.2d. 1310, 1320–21 (1991).

4. A Rational Upper Limit on the Value of Life?: Health and safety regulations are intended to reduce injuries and save lives. The costs of complying with regulations, however, may result in lost lives. Judge Stephen Williams of the U.S. Court of Appeals for the District of Columbia has explained this trade-off:

> ...even where the application of cost-benefit analysis would result in less stringent regulation, the reduced stringency is not necessarily adverse to health or safety. More regulation means some combination of reduced value of firms, higher product prices, fewer jobs in the regulated industry, and lower cash wages. All the latter three stretch workers' budgets

tighter (as does the first to the extent that the firms' stock is held in worker's pension trusts). And larger incomes enable people to lead safer lives. One study finds a 1 percent increase in income associated with a mortality reduction of about 0.05 percent. Jack Hadley & Anthony Osei, "Does Income Affect Mortality?", 20 Medical Care 901, 913 (September 1982). Another suggests that each $7.5 million of costs generated by regulation may, under certain assumptions, induce one fatality. Ralph L. Keeney, "Mortality Risks Induced by Economic Expenditures", 10 Risk Analysis 147, 155 (1990) (relying on E.M. Kitagawa & P.M. Hauser, Differential Mortality in the United States of America: A Study of Socioeconomic Epidemiology (1973)). Larger incomes can produce health by enlarging a person's access to better diet, preventative medical care, safer cars, greater leisure, etc. See Aaron Wildavsky, Searching for Safety 59–71 (1988).

Of course, other causal relations may be at work too. Healthier people may be able to earn higher income, and characteristics and advantages that facilitate high earnings (e.g., work ethic, education) may also lead to better health. Compare C.P. Wen, et al., "Anatomy of the Healthy Worker Effect: A Critical Review", 25 J. of Occupation Medicine 283 (1983). Nonetheless, higher income can secure better health, and there is no basis for a casual assumption that more stringent regulation will always save lives.

It follows that while officials involved in health or safety regulation may naturally be hesitant to set any kind of numerical value on human life, [19] undue squeamishness may be deadly. Incremental safety regulation reduces incomes and thus may exact a cost in human lives. For example, if analysis showed that "an individual life was lost for every $12 million taken from individuals [as a result of regulation], this would be a guide to a reasonable value trade-off for many programs designed to save lives." Keeney, "Mortality Risks Induced by Economic Expenditures", 10 Risk Analysis at 158. Such a figure could serve as a ceiling for value-of-life calculated by other means, since regulation causing greater expenditures per life expected to be saved would, everything else being equal, result in a net loss of life.

United Automobile Workers v. OSHA, U.S. Department of Labor, 938 F.2d. 1310, 1326–27 (concurring opinion).

2. The Hedonic Value of Life

In addition to damages for lost earnings, plaintiffs in personal injury or wrongful death actions will assert claims to a variety of other losses. One of the

---

19. Preference-based techniques are a commonly used approach, but are subject to such pitfalls as wealth bias, age bias and inconsistency. See, e.g., Lewis A. Kornhauser, "The Value of Life," 38 Clev. St. L. Rev. 209 (1990). For example, if estimates of the benefit of reducing risks are based on the affected workers' willingness to pay for risk reduction, low-paid workers will receive less protection than better paid ones. See id. at 221. There are, however, solutions. The wealth bias problem, for example, could be avoided by estimating the willingness to pay by persons of median or mean wealth. See id. at 221–22.

most controversial types of loss claimed by plaintiffs in such actions are hedonic damages. **Hedonic damages** compensate parties who are condemned to watch life's amenities pass them by and, therefore, suffer from an inability to enjoy life's pleasures. For example, a party who suffers from complete paralysis due to defendant's negligence and no longer has the ability to engage in a pickup game of basketball has suffered a hedonic loss. However, for a variety of reasons, courts have denied or constrained plaintiff's access to awards for hedonic damages.

Claims for hedonic damages in wrongful death actions have met with little success. Almost all of the courts who have considered the issue have decided that hedonic damages are not available to plaintiffs in such actions. There are three reasons for this almost universal denial. First, wrongful death actions are brought for the benefit of surviving relatives for *the damages that they have suffered*. Hedonic damages contemplate a loss suffered by the decedent. Thus, such an award would be an inappropriate element of damages to a surviving relative. Second, hedonic damages are supposed to compensate a party for the suffering they must endure while standing on the sideline and watching life's pleasures pass them by. A decedent, however, does not stand on the sideline and watch life's pleasures pass them by. In short, a dead person can not suffer the type of harm which hedonic damages are intended to cover. Third, most wrongful death statutes do not provide for the recovery of hedonic damages. In this regard, it is important to remember that actions for wrongful death did not exist at common law. Because wrongful death is a purely statutory creation, damages available under such provisions are limited to those clearly provided for in the statute.

Claims for hedonic damages in personal injury cases have also met resistance. There are two fundamental reasons for resistance in such cases. First, awards for pain and suffering have traditionally included compensation for the types of harms claimed as hedonic damages. In a sense, pain and suffering is simply the "flip side" of hedonic damages. For example, consider a person who suffers brain damage as a result of defendant's negligence and no longer has the ability to participate fully in advising and raising his children. Watching his children develop without his advice causes the plaintiff a great deal of mental anguish, commonly the ground for an award of pain and suffering. These same facts can be reinterpreted, however, as a restriction on the plaintiff's ability to enjoy participation in raising his children with all of the pleasures and heart breaks that such a pursuit can provide. By instructing a jury to make an award for pain and suffering and hedonic damages, courts have felt that they run the risk of providing plaintiffs with a double recovery. A second source of resistance to hedonic damage awards stems from limitations on the type of expert testimony which courts will entertain. The following case illustrates the difficulties courts have in allowing expert testimony as to the hedonic value of life.

Mercado v. Ahmed

United States Court of Appeals for the Seventh Circuit
974 F.2d 863 (1992)

COFFEY, Circuit Judge.

In this diversity suit, plaintiff Lucy Mercado ("Mercado"), individually and as next friend of her minor son, Brian, filed a complaint in the district court against defendants Salim Ahmed ("Ahmed") and his former employer, the Checker Taxi Company, Inc. ("Checker"), alleging that due to Ahmed's negligence his taxi struck and injured Brian. The plaintiff further alleged that Checker was negligent in employing Ahmed because he was not qualified to operate the taxi. Mercado sought damages for Brian's personal injuries, pain and suffering, mental anguish, and medical expenses, and for her own mental anguish. The jury found for the plaintiff and awarded $50,000 for Brian's pain and suffering and $29,000 for his medical expenses. The district court judge denied Mercado's motion for a new trial and motion to amend the judgment. On appeal, the plaintiff argues that the jury's verdict was inconsistent and that the judge made several evidentiary errors, and requests a new trial on the issue of damages only. In the alternative, plaintiff asks that we amend the judgment and add to the damages award $2,995,933 for Brian's future medical care and $1,116,836 for Brian's future lost wages. We affirm the verdict of the jury.

I.

On October 13, 1985, Lucy Mercado traveled to Chicago, Illinois, from her home in Hammond, Indiana, with her four sons—including six-year-old Brian—to visit the Museum of Science and Industry. While walking in the museum parking lot, Brian slipped away from his mother, stepped out onto a crosswalk between two aisles of parked cars, and was struck on the crosswalk by a taxi driven by defendant Ahmed. The impact of the blow threw Brian four or five feet into the air and a distance of about one and one half car lengths.

Brian was taken by ambulance to the University of Chicago, Wyler's Children's Hospital. The boy was examined for an extended period of time, about three to four hours, by a team of doctors and other hospital personnel and then released that same day. According to the information in the hospital records testified to at trial, Brian never lost consciousness, reported no feeling of any pain, and was alert, stable and able to answer the emergency room doctors' questions. An examination of Brian's skull, eyes and ears revealed no signs of head injury. The boy's reflexes, blood pressure, heart rate, and pulse were all normal.

Trial testimony established that Brian, 11 years old, suffered from a wide range of problems prior to the accident. His ability to process visual and auditory information is substantially impaired, making reading, writing, and arithmetic very difficult for him. The boy has been diagnosed as suffering from severe emotional problems and as suicidal. He is unable to perform such rudimentary tasks as dressing properly or managing his personal hygiene. Both the plaintiff's and defendants' witnesses testified that Brian will require some form of institutionalization or structured environment for the remainder of his life. At the time of trial, Brian was a patient in the children's unit of Hartgrove Hospital. His employment prospects are limited to those positions which require the performance of only the most menial tasks.

Mercado argued at trial that Brian's many problems were caused by a closed head injury he suffered when he was struck by the taxi in the museum parking lot, an injury which she claims went undetected the day of the accident. The defendants countered that Brian's myriad problems stem from a condition which predated the taxi accident and are not related to the injuries he suffered when he was struck by Ahmed's taxi. The jury found against both Ahmed and Checker on the plaintiff's complaint, and awarded $29,000 for medical expenses and $50,000 for pain and suffering. The jury awarded no damages for disability from the injury, or for future medical expenses, much less anything for future lost earnings.

*   *   *

III.

The plaintiff also argues that the trial judge committed four evidentiary errors, each of which require a reversal of the damages verdict and a new trial on damages. We will address the claimed errors seriatim.

A.

The first alleged evidentiary error centers on the district court's refusal to allow the receipt in evidence of the testimony of Stanley Smith. Smith was offered by the plaintiff as an expert on the disability damages owed Brian Mercado because of the "pleasure of living" the boy will be denied as a result of the injuries he received in the taxi accident. Smith, a professional economist who holds a Masters degree in Business Administration from the University of Chicago, would have testified as to the monetary value of "the reduction of Brian's ability to engage in and experience the ordinary value of life that he was experiencing prior to the injury." Appellant's brief at 14. These damages are sometimes referred to as "hedonic damages."[3]

The district court conducted an extensive voir dire to determine the method Smith employs in calculating the monetary value of the "lost pleasure of living" an individual such as Brian suffers due to an injury. Smith testified that in his computation he first assumes a "percentage range" representing the degree an injured individual's capacity to experience life has been diminished. This method measures an individual's impairment in four areas: occupational, practical functioning, emotional, and social functioning. Smith does not compute this figure himself, but instead consults with a medical expert to arrive at the appropriate range. In this case the expert was Dr. Kathleen Pueschel, a clinical neuropsychologist. According to the plaintiff, Dr. Pueschel concluded that Brian's disabilities were "severe", and that the boy's capacity to experience life was diminished 66% to 83%.

Smith then applies his own analysis to the diminished capacity figure. As the district court noted, the method attempts to get at the value of life by indirection; no one is ever asked "what is the monetary value of living?", because most people would probably respond that life is priceless, scuttling the endeavor. Instead, Smith focuses on how much Americans are willing to pay for reductions in health and safety risks, and how much they are compensated for assuming extra risk. This method, according to Smith's economic theory, reveals the value we actually place on living, and avoids the astronomical answers people would give in response to a hypothetical question. He relies on three types of willingness-to-pay studies: studies of how much consumers, through the purchase of devices

---

3. Defendants do not argue that damages for the lost pleasure of living are unavailable under Illinois law. Thus, we, like the district court, will assume their availability in our consideration of the admissibility of Smith's testimony. Mercado v. Ahmed, 756 F. Supp. 1097, 1102 (N.D. Ill. 1991).

such as smoke detectors and seat belts, pay for increased personal safety; studies of how much more people who assume extra risk (e.g., policemen) are paid because their jobs are dangerous; and studies of cost-benefit analyses conducted in the evaluation of government safety regulation. Smith testified that he relied on some 75 such studies in his valuation.

Through this analysis, Smith concluded that the value of the enjoyment of a statistically average person's life was $2.3 million in 1988 dollars. (The statistically average person is 31 years old with a 45 year additional life expectancy.) This averages out to approximately a $60,000-per-year value on the enjoyment of life. Smith took this figure and multiplied it by the percentage range of Brian's loss of the full experience of life, 66% to 83% (drawn from Dr. Pueschel's calculations). Adjusting for Brian's young age, the plaintiff informs us that Smith concluded the value of Brian's lost pleasure of living due to the injuries he suffered in the taxi accident was $2,207,827 to $2,762,227. Appellant's Brief at 15.

The district judge, after listening to Smith out of the presence of the jury, ruled, pursuant to Fed. R. Evid. 702,[4] that Smith's proposed testimony on the value of Brian Mercado's lost pleasure of living would not be allowed. The district court provided a thorough and scholarly explanation of the reasoning supporting this decision. Mercado v. Ahmed, 756 F. Supp. 1097 (N.D. Ill. 1991). The opinion sets out two basic doubts about Smith's testimony. First, the court was troubled by the lack of any "basic agreement among economists as to what elements ought to go into" or "which studies ought to be considered" in life valuation. Id. at 1103. In order to allow a witness to testify as an expert, the court must be convinced that the witness will rely only upon evidence a reasonable expert in the field would rely. United States v. Lundy, 809 F.2d 392, 395 (7th Cir. 1987). The court determined that no consensus existed among economists as to what was proper evidence of the value of living.

The district court's second and more significant concern centered on Smith's methodology. The court reasoned that Smith's valuation, based as it was on studies meant to determine how much Americans pay to reduce risks or charge for assuming them, did not qualify as the sort of "scientific, technical or other specialized" knowledge contemplated in Fed. R. Evid. 702. Referring to Smith's method of valuing life, the district court observed:

> "Survey of attitudes and views of others as a basis for concluding something is true is not necessarily wrong. Some science as it comes into court is the result of consensus by practitioners of some area of expertise that a certain law of nature is correct. What is wrong here is not that the evidence is founded on consensus or agreement, it is that the consensus is that of persons who are no more expert than are jurors on the value of life. Even if reliable and valid, the evidence may fail to 'assist the trier of fact to understand the evidence or determine a fact in issue' [quoting Fed. R. Evid. 702] in a way more meaningful than would occur if the jury asked a group of wise courtroom bystanders for their opinions." Mercado, 756 F. Supp at 1103.

---

4. Fed. R. Evid. 702 provides that "if scientific, technical, or other specialized knowledge will assist the trier of fact to understand the evidence or to determine a fact in issue, a witness qualified as an expert by knowledge, skill, experience, training or education, may testify thereto in the form of an opinion or otherwise."

A witness who knows no more than the average person is not an expert. The "theory upon which expert testimony is...[admitted] is that such testimony serves to inform the court about affairs not within the full understanding of the average man." United States v. West, 670 F.2d 675, 682 (7th Cir.), cert. denied sub. nom., King v. United States, 457 U.S. 1124, 73 L. Ed. 2d 1340, 102 S. Ct. 2944 (1982) (quoting United States v. Webb, 625 F.2d 709, 711 (5th Cir. 1980)). As the Supreme Court has noted, "expert testimony not only is unnecessary but indeed may properly be excluded in the discretion of the trial judge 'if all the primary facts can be accurately and intelligibly described to the jury, and if they, as men of common understanding, are as capable of comprehending the primary facts and of drawing correct conclusions from them as are witnesses possessed of special or peculiar training, experience, or observation in respect of the subject under investigation.'" Salem v. United States Lines Co., 370 U.S. 31, 35, 8 L. Ed. 2d 313, 82 S. Ct. 1119 (1962) (citation omitted).

The district court, confronting this novel legal problem,[5] was not persuaded that Smith's technique for valuing the lost pleasure of living provided expert assistance to the jury. On appeal, the plaintiff attacks the reasoning of the trial judge directly, asserting that Smith should have been given the "opportunity to supplant the jurors' own knowledge as to the value of life...." Appellant's reply brief at 11. This frames the issue precisely: does Stanley Smith, supported by his extensive willingness-to-pay research, know better than the average juror how much life is worth?

As we noted above, the district judge did not believe that Smith offered the jury any "expertise" because (1) no consensus among experts supported Smith's method of valuing life and (2) Smith's research was no more than a compilation of the opinions, expressed through spending decisions, of a large number of Americans as to the value of life. The first criticism is irrefutable: the plaintiff could point to no expert consensus supporting Smith's methodology. The second criticism is also on the mark, since Smith concedes that his method relies on arriving at a valuation of life based on analyzing the behavior of non-experts.

However, even accepting Smith's premise that his method of determining the value of life is different in an important way from submitting the question to a jury because it focuses on observable behavior and not opinion, we have serious doubts about his assertion that the studies he relies upon actually measure how much Americans value life. For example, spending on items like air bags and smoke detectors is probably influenced as much by advertising and marketing decisions made by profit-seeking manufacturers and by government-mandated safety requirements as it is by any consideration by consumers of how much life

---

5. One district court in this circuit allowed Smith to testify as to the value of the lost pleasure of living in a 42 U.S.C. § 1983 wrongful death suit, Sherrod v. Berry, 629 F. Supp 159 (N.D. Ill. 1985). That decision was initially affirmed by a panel of this court, 827 F.2d 195 (7th Cir. 1987), but then vacated, 835 F.2d 1222 (7th Cir. 1988), and eventually reversed en banc on other grounds, 856 F.2d 802 (7th Cir. 1988), although our en banc opinion stated that the district court should consider the issues left undecided "in light of this court's prior discussion of those matters, specifically those found in our earlier vacated opinion." 856 F.2d at 807–808. One Illinois appellate court, in a wrongful death case, affirmed a ruling barring testimony by Stanley Smith on the economic value of the deceased's loss of enjoyment of life because it concluded that the damages were not "amenable to such analytic precision" and Smith's testimony would be "overly speculative" and "invade the province of the jury." Fetzer v. Wood, 211 Ill. App. 3d 70, 569 N.E.2d 1237, 1246, 155 Ill. Dec. 626 (Ill. App. 1991).

is worth. Also, many people may be interested in a whole range of safety devices and believe they are worth-while, but are unable to afford them. More fundamentally, spending on safety items reflects a consumer's willingness to pay to reduce risk, perhaps more a measure of how cautious a person is than how much he or she values life. Few of us, when confronted with the threat, "Your money or your life!" would, like Jack Benny, pause and respond, "I'm thinking, I'm thinking." Most of us would empty our wallets. Why that decision reflects less the value we place on life than whether we buy an airbag is not immediately obvious.

The two other kinds of studies Smith relies upon are open to valid and logical criticism as well. To say that the salary paid to those who hold risky jobs tells us something significant about how much we value life ignores the fact that humans are moved by more than monetary incentives. For example, someone who believes police officers working in an extremely dangerous city are grossly under-compensated for the risks they assume might nevertheless take up the badge out of a sense of civic duty to their hometown. Finally, government calculations about how much to spend (or force others to spend) on health and safety regulations are motivated by a host of considerations other than the value of life: is it an election year? how large is the budget deficit? on which constituents will the burden of the regulations fall? what influence and pressure have lobbyists brought to bear? what is the view of interested constituents? And so on.

All this is not to imply that we can state conclusively that Smith's approach is devoid of any merit. But given that "we review a district court's decision to exclude expert testimony under an abuse of discretion standard," United States v. Welch, 945 F.2d 1378, 1381 (7th Cir. 1991), cert. denied, 117 L. Ed. 2d 469, 112 S. Ct. 1235 (1992), and that the trial court's "determination will be affirmed unless it is 'manifestly erroneous,'" Carroll v. Otis Elevator Company, 896 F.2d 210, 212 (7th Cir. 1990) (quoting Bob Willow Motors Inc. v. General Motors, 872 F.2d 788, 797 (7th Cir. 1989)), we can say with confidence that the district court's decision to bar Smith's testimony was not reversible error. Smith has taken up a daunting task: to develop a methodology capable of producing specialized knowledge to assist jurors in determining the monetary value of being alive. The district court ruled that, despite Smith's training, extensive research and countless calculations, his testimony would not aid the jury in evaluating the evidence and arriving at its verdict (the true test of expert testimony under Fed.R.Evid. 702) because Smith was no more expert in valuing life than the average person. This conclusion may be less a reflection of the flaws in Smith's methodology than on the impossibility of any person achieving unique knowledge of the value of life.

*   *   *

IV.

The verdict of the jury is AFFIRMED.

Notes and Questions

1. Mutually Beneficial Exchange and the Value of Life: The methodology used by the plaintiff's expert attempts to develop a value for life based upon society's revealed preferences. For example, by using the prices paid for air bags or smoke detectors, plaintiff's expert portends to have developed a value of life calculation based on objectively determined market values. However, as the court properly observes, to the extent that market participants are required by regulation to make such purchases, the prices paid are not determined by a voluntary mutually beneficial exchange. Thus, the expert's value of life calculations are not based on objectively determined market prices. Due to this fact, can we rely on the expert's numbers as revealing the value that society places on life? In which way would the expert's value of life number be biased as a result of this error? How does the economic reasoning developed thus far in the casebook square with the court's analysis of the expert's wage differential analysis?

2. Evidentiary Hurdles to Hedonic Damage Awards: Federal Rule of Evidence 702 contemplates that courts will play a "gate keeping" function with respect to the types of testimony which will be allowed into evidence as that of an expert. In *Mercado*, the court felt that jurors were in as good a position to place a value on life as plaintiff's expert. In other words, there is no need for expert testimony as to the value of life. The fear is that, by allowing plaintiff's expert to testify, jurors will develop the impression that they do not have the requisite knowledge or skill to determine the value of life. The result of allowing such testimony would be to prejudice the jury's factual determination of value. In a sense, Rule 702 is an attempt to prevent "junk science" from misleading the fact finder. In *Daubert v. Merrill Dow Chemical Co.*, the Supreme Court provided a non-exclusive list of four considerations to assist courts in their gate keeping function. The considerations introduced by the *Daubert* court are: 1) Is the evidence capable of being tested; 2) Has the evidence been subject to peer review; 3) What is the potential rate of error for the evidence; and 4) What is the acceptance level of the methodology in the relevant scientific community. How would plaintiff's expert in *Mercado* fare under the considerations introduced in *Daubert*? If the court is in a position where it must determine a subjective value for purposes of a damages award, who should make the calculation?

3. The Break-Up-Value of Human Life: In discussing the value of a business, investors often refer to a firm's break-up-value. That is, the value of the firm if all of its components were divided up and sold separately. Would it make sense to value a human life in the same manner? Why not place the value of life at the amount of money that can be received for each of the parts that make up a human body? For example, hearts sell at $500, blood at $350, kidneys at $610, etc. How much would a person with terminable heart disease pay for the heart of a recently deceased donor? Wouldn't this be a voluntary mutually beneficial exchange—that is, an objective measure for the value of life. This is obviously an extreme example, but when compared to the method used by the plaintiff's expert, is it any less reasonable?

4. Property Law—The Case of Takings: The Fifth Amendment of the Constitution of the United States provides that individuals are entitled to just compensation for property taken by the government. Courts have interpreted just compensation to be the objectively determined market value for the property in question. Why not allow someone to testify as to the subjective enjoyment they receive as a result of owning the property in question? Would it be reasonable to allow expert testimony as to the loss of enjoyment due to a taking? Couldn't one formulate a methodology similar to that used by the plaintiff's expert to make such estimates?

5. Pain and Suffering v. Hedonic Damages: Pain and suffering describes the physical discomfort and emotional trauma which are recoverable as an element of damages in a tort claim. Do the type of losses contemplated by hedonic damages differ from those for pain and suffering?

D. Valuation of Close Corporations

A **close corporation**, or **closely held corporation**, is characterized by a concentrated group of shareholders who are often involved in setting corporate policy and whose shares are infrequently traded. Legal questions regarding the value of such shares arise in a variety of circumstances, ranging from bankruptcy reorganizations to estate and gift taxes. Difficulties in the valuation of close corporations stem from the fact that there is no organized market on which such shares are actively traded. Thus, the determination of value is not simply a matter of looking to an efficiently determined market price.

In general, the valuation of close corporations is no different than the valuation questions that have been discussed in previous sections of this chapter. Namely, the value of a closely held share depends on the present value of future benefits attributable to ownership of the share. The value of such shares is calculated by projecting some stream of future benefits and choosing an appropriate discount rate. The fundamental difficulty behind a discounted future returns methodology is the estimation of future benefits and the selection of an appropriate discount rate. This difficulty is compounded in the courtroom because of evidentiary requirements. Unlike the entrepreneurial business person, judges and juries are often not willing to rely on a "hunch" or "best guess" regarding projected financial performance. They are often reluctant to rely on data that is "too speculative." Despite these potential difficulties, the discounted future benefits method and its reliance on projected financial data remains the generally accepted theoretical model for valuing close corporations.

Because of the "proof problems" that often arise when using projected financial data, historical data often becomes a significant factor in calculating the value of shares in a closely held corporation. However, regardless of whether one is using projected or historical financial data, the goal is still to develop a present value for future economic benefits attributable to the shares. Thus, in theory, present value calculations using projected financial data and methodologies should equal such calculations based on historical data and methodologies. In practice, it is wise to use these alternative sources of data and methods as a means for checking the accuracy and strength of one's results. Moreover, it is important to recognize that although the use of historical and projected financial data are being discussed as alternatives here, they are not mutually exclusive. For example, in making earnings projections, a financial analyst will surely consider the corporation's historic earnings trend. Alternatively, when using historic earnings numbers, the financial analyst will consider whether or not historic performance is likely to be representative of future performance.

An important lesson regarding the valuation of closely held shares is that the decision as to whether to place emphasis on projected data and methodologies or historical data and methodologies depends on the particular purpose for the valuation. Different areas of the law have developed different legal standards based upon varying statutory and decisional backgrounds. For example, gift and estate tax questions tend to be resolved by an analysis which uses historical data to project the present value of closely held shares. On the other hand, it would be quite contradictory for courts to rely on historical data for projecting the future benefits stream of firms involved in bankruptcy reorganizations. Thus, valuation analysis in the bankruptcy reorganization context tends to rely much more on projected data. Thus, prudence lies in checking statutory and decisional authority when choosing the specific method and standards for purposes of business valuation.

A critical factor behind the derivation of value for closely held shares is the assumption regarding the future status of the business. In general, an appraiser makes one of two assumptions regarding the future status of the business—either it will continue to operate or it will shut down. This assumption will have a specific effect on the manner in which a business is valued. **Going-concern value** assumes that the business will continue to operate for an indefinite period of time and represents the present value of the future economic benefits to be derived from the operation of the business. On the other hand, **liquidation value** assumes that business operations will be terminated and represents the net amount that can be realized by breaking up the company and selling the individual assets.

Another factor that has a significant impact on the valuation of a business is the perspective from which value will be determined. Because of the perceived benefits of using a market price, the goal in many legal contexts is to attempt to replicate a market determination of price. Thus, the most common standard of value invoked in legal proceedings is fair market value. **Fair market value** is the price at which property would change hands between a hypothetical willing buyer and a hypothetical willing seller, neither of whom are under any compulsion to buy or sell and both of whom have reasonable knowledge of the relevant facts. Thus, fair market value attempts to establish an objective measure of value. In opposition to the objective nature of fair market value, the concept of investment value represents a very subjective notion of value. **Investment value** represents the value of a business in a particular investor's hands. Investment value helps to explain why some individuals are willing to pay a premium in order to acquire a business. For example, XYZ manufacturing may be willing to pay a higher price than any other bidder to acquire ABC distributors because of specific synergies between the operations of XYZ and ABC. In most instances, courts attempt to eliminate the idiosyncratic value that particular parties attach to closely held shares.

1. Discounted Future Returns Approach

An important tool in determining the value of close corporation stock is the discounted future returns approach to present value. Much of the discussion throughout this chapter has focused on the two primary hurdles in the use of such present value analysis—determination of the relevant stream of benefits and selection of the appropriate discount rate. Estimating the stream of benefits and the relevant discount rate continue to be the challenging factors in valuing close corporations using discounted future returns. In fact, much of the litigation that arises in the valuation of closely held shares involves disputes among expert witnesses as to the appropriate stream of future benefits and the discount rate.

Of primary importance in selecting the appropriate benefits stream is to choose a measure of benefits that accurately reflects the economic value of holding the shares. In this regard, five important proxies for economic value are widely used in the valuation of close corporations—earnings, cash flow, dividends, revenue, and assets. Despite the common usage of these measures, a great deal of litigation revolves around two important issues. First, how does one define earnings, cash flow, dividend capacity, revenue, or assets? Variations in the manner in which each of these financial variables is defined can explain to a large degree differences in the present value numbers generated by different experts valuing the same business. Second, if different measures lead to different present value calculations, which calculation should be relied on by the judge or jury? The following case demonstrates both of these issues and the manner in which such differences are often resolved.

Kleinwort Benson, Ltd. v. Silgan Corporation
Court of Chancery of Delaware, New Castle
(1995 Del. Ch. LEXIS 75)

CHANDLER, Vice Chancellor

Petitioners, holders of 400,000 shares of Class B common stock of Silgan Corporation ("Silgan" or "Respondent"), seek an appraisal...to assess the fair value of their shares. Petitioners seek an appraisal as a result of a June 30, 1989 merger, by which Silgan merged into a wholly owned subsidiary of Silgan Holdings, Inc. ("Silgan Holdings"). In the merger, Silgan's Class B shareholders received $6.50 per share for their stock. During the trial of this action, the Court heard testimony from expert witnesses whose opinions of the value of Silgan stock ranged from $4.88 per share to $12.65 per share. For the reasons set forth below, I find the fair value of Silgan on the date of the merger to be $5.94 per share...

I. BACKGROUND

Silgan, a Delaware corporation, was organized in August 1987 under the name MS/S&H Holdings, Inc. Silgan had three classes of common stock, Classes A, B and C. Classes A and B are identical, except that each class votes separately to elect two directors. Class C stock is non-voting. R. Philip Silver ("Silver") and D. Greg Horrigan ("Horrigan") beneficially owned all of the Class A stock. The Morgan Stanley Group, and the Morgan Stanley Leveraged Equity Fund, L.P. (MSLEF I), owned more than two thirds of the Class B stock. Morgan Stanley Leveraged Capital Fund, Inc., an affiliate of Morgan Stanley, and CIGNA Leveraged Capital Fund, Inc., an affiliate of CIGNA Corporation, are the general partners of MSLEF I.

*   *   *

On April 28, 1989, Silgan entered into a merger agreement with Silgan Holdings, whereby Silgan was to combine with Silgan Holdings' wholly owned subsidiary, Silgan Acquisition Inc. Under the terms of the merger agreement, Class B stockholders were to receive $6.50 per share, and Class A stockholders were to receive $12.2 million in cash and shares of Class A common stock of Silgan Holdings equal to 50% of Silgan Holdings's voting stock. Silgan retained William Blair & Co. to render a fairness opinion on the price offered to Silgan stockholders. Silgan distributed the fairness opinion, as well as management's financial projections for Silgan, along with its Solicitation of Stockholders Consents. The merger was approved by a majority of Silgan stockholders, with Morgan Stanley and MSLEF I consenting to the merger. The merger was completed on June 30, 1989, making Silgan a wholly owned subsidiary of Silgan Holdings.

Petitioners dissented to the merger and validly exercised their appraisal rights...During the trial, Petitioners and Respondent presented expert testimony as to the value of Silgan. Petitioners' expert, Louis Paone ("Paone"),...valued Silgan at $12.65 per share. Respondent's expert, James Kovacs ("Kovacs"),...valued Silgan at $4.88 per share. In addition to the parties' experts, the Court appointed a neutral expert, Joel Lawson ("Lawson")...Lawson critiqued the opinions of the parties' expert witnesses, but the Court instructed him not to provide an independent valuation of Silgan.

II. THE EXPERTS' VALUATION METHODS

Paone and Kovacs used fairly similar methods to appraise Silgan. Paone conducted a reconstructed market analysis, which looked at market prices of comparable publicly traded corporations and at the price paid in comparable mergers. He also conducted a discounted cash flow ("DCF") analysis to establish a present value for Silgan's projected returns. Like Paone, Kovacs conducted a market analysis and a DCF analysis. However, he did not look at comparable mergers in his market analysis. I will weigh the reliability of each method employed by the experts, then adopt the methods that most reliably measure Silgan's fair value as of June 30, 1989.

In addition to Paone's opinion testimony and report, Petitioners contend that the amount of money Silgan Holdings borrowed to finance the acquisition of Silgan represents Silgan's value. Respondent's expert, Kovacs, testified that the money market's willingness to lend money to Silgan Holdings relates to the lenders' confidence in being repaid, but does not provide a credible value for Silgan. I agree that the amount of money loaned to Silgan Holdings does not reliably correlate to the value of Silgan. I consider this method of valuing Silgan untrustworthy, and assign it no weight.

III. MARKET ANALYSIS

Both experts used a comparative market analysis as part of their evaluations. Kovacs analyzed five similar publicly traded companies in order to estimate the market value of Silgan's stock. Paone considered the same five companies plus Kerr Glass in his analysis. The most dramatic difference in the approaches taken by the experts is Paone's inclusion of an 86% premium over market price to adjust for an inherent minority discount in the price of publicly traded shares. In addition to a study of similar publicly traded companies, Paone reviewed eight merger transactions that involved companies he believed were similar to Silgan.

Respondent contends that Paone's market analysis is improper as a matter of law, citing several decisions of this Court for the proposition that the appraisal value of a corporation does not include a "control premium." Petitioners respond that Paone did not include a "control premium," but merely adjusted the price for minority interests available in publicly traded markets to reflect the enterprise value of the entire corporation.

Section 262 provides two fundamental guideposts for an expert witness opining on the value of a corporation for the purposes of... appraisal. The expert should value the entire corporation as a going concern, then allocate that value pro rata among the shareholders.... In determining the enterprise value of the corporation, the expert cannot consider "any element of value arising from the accomplishment or expectation of the merger."... Both Petitioners and Respondent recognize that these principles provide the framework for conducting an appraisal. Yet the parties disagree over whether these legal rules require or exclude a premium over the price available in a market for publicly traded shares. Petitioners believe a control premium must be applied to the market price to reflect the enterprise value of a corporation, while Respondent believes a control premium includes forbidden post-merger value.

Paone premised his use of a control premium on the theory that the market price for publicly traded shares contains an inherent minority discount. Paone's decision to remove a minority discount imbedded in the market price does not violate Delaware law.... However, Petitioners cannot add a premium to the market price unless they prove that publicly traded shares include a minority discount.

Paone testified that the market price reflects the value of a minority interest in a corporation because only small lots of stock are available at the market price. Kovacs, the Respondent's expert, and Lawson, the Court's neutral expert, also expressed a belief that publicly traded shares trade below the proportionate enterprise value of the stock. Respondent's expert stated at trial that "the preponderance of opinion is that there is some minority interest that's implicit in a publicly traded company's price." Upon the record presented, I conclude that both experts should have adjusted market value to compensate for an inherent minority discount.

*   *   *

Although Kovacs erred in not attempting to account for an implicit minority discount in the market data, I find his market analysis much more reliable than Paone's market analysis. Paone purportedly adjusted the available market data to remove the imbedded minority discount, but his methods do not discriminate between a minority discount and a premium that includes post-merger value. In prior appraisal actions, this Court has rejected the use of a control premium derived from merger and acquisition data because the control premium incorporates post-merger value.... Kovacs and Lawson testified that the premium over market price paid by an acquiror includes more than an adjustment for a minority discount. The acquiror may value the target corporation above its going concern value because of potential synergies or because the acquiror believes it will manage the target better. This portion of a control premium cannot be included in the appraisal value of a corporation because it reflects value arising from the accomplishment or expectation of the merger.... Paone applied a premium in his market analysis that explicitly includes value arising from the expectation of a merger.

Paone looked at control premiums paid in merger transactions in the years just prior to 1989. In the studies he reviewed, the median control premiums ranged from 34% to 48%. Paone believed that Silgan would have fetched an even higher premium because it was highly leveraged. Paone testified that he found a strong positive relationship between the amount of leverage employed by a company and the control premium paid for that company's common equity. Because of the purported effect leverage has on control premiums, Paone believed that Silgan would receive an 86% premium over market price.

For reasons based in law and in fact, I do not give Paone's control premium study any weight. First, Paone has failed to demonstrate a strong correlation between leverage and a control premium that justifies an 86% premium for Silgan. Kovacs persuasively demonstrated at trial that leverage has only a slight relationship to the size of a control premium. Lawson also found only a slight correlation between these factors. Paone has not demonstrated a factual foundation for enhancing the control premium above the 34–48% range. Paone's study also strays from the clear directive of Delaware law to exclude value arising from the merger. Had Paone used a 34–48% premium, he would have included some value arising from synergies or new management plans. Instead of increasing the premium to 86%, Paone should have discounted the control premium data so that it reflected just the minority discount. Lawson explained that the premium necessary to remove the minority discount inherent in publicly traded stock is somewhere between zero and the control premium which Paone's study places between 34–48%.

Kovacs did not attempt to account for a minority discount in the price of publicly traded stock because Respondent's counsel instructed him that it was improper as a matter of law. Had Kovacs attempted to present such evidence, he probably would have been stymied anyway. Lawson states in his report that setting an exact figure for the minority discount comes down to an arbitrary determination. Respondent asserts that the Court should not adjust the market data to remove the minority discount because no reliable proof has been presented on the issue. It seems to me that acknowledging the existence of the minority discount, but setting it at zero, is more arbitrary than endeavoring to find its true value. At trial, Kovacs stated that a reasonable estimate of the minority discount is around 10–15%. Based on that testimony, I will adjust Kovacs' market analysis by 12.5% to account for the minority discount inherent in publicly traded shares.

In addition to an analysis of similar publicly traded corporations, Paone conducted an analysis of eight mergers involving companies similar to Silgan. For the same reasons that I give Paone's control premium data no weight, I consider his merger and acquisition analysis unhelpful for appraising the going concern value of Silgan. The merger and acquisition data undoubtedly contains post-merger value, such as synergies with the acquiror, that must be excluded from appraisal value....

IV. DISCOUNTED CASH FLOW ANALYSIS

Kovacs and Paone each valued Silgan by using a DCF analysis. Kovacs labels his study an Income Approach, while Paone refers to his study as a Discounted Future Returns Analysis, but they used nearly identical methods. They estimated Silgan's revenues from 1989–1995 on a debt free basis, set a terminal value for the company at the end of the period, and then discounted those future values to reach a present value for Silgan's market value of invested capital ("MVIC"). Because they valued Silgan's revenues on a debt free basis, they subtracted the market value of Silgan's debt from its MVIC to reach a value for Silgan's common equity....

*   *   *

A. Managements' Projections

As this Court has noted before, the outcome of a DCF analysis depends heavily on the projections used in the model....Prior to the merger, Silgan's management projected Silgan's costs and revenues for the period from 1989–1995 for use by Silgan's lenders. Silgan distributed these projections with its Solicitation of Stockholder Consents. Both experts relied heavily on these projections in their DCF analyses, but Kovacs revised some of the estimates. Kovacs testified that he needed to revise some of management's original projections because they were not generated for use in an appraisal proceeding. He altered some of the projections based on Silgan's books and records, discussions with Silgan's management, and general trends in the industry. Petitioners criticize Kovacs for revising management's contemporaneous projections to reach a lower value for Silgan's stock. Paone worked exclusively from the original projections, adjusting them only for the purposes of a debt free analysis. Petitioners contend that by conducting interviews with Silgan's managers Kovacs improperly considered evidence that was unavailable as of the merger date. Petitioners request that I prevent Respondent from revising its optimistic pre-merger forecast to suit its purposes in this lawsuit.

The Court will not bar Respondent from presenting evidence relevant to the fair value of Silgan,...but Respondent's revisions of its original projections merit close inspection. The revisions may impeach the credibility of Respondent's expert witness. Therefore, I will carefully consider the justification for each revision.

B. June 30, 1989–1995 Cash Flows

In both DCF models, the experts used management's projections to estimate Silgan's cash flows from June 30, 1989 through the end of 1995. In his estimates of cash flows, Kovacs revised management's original projections in several respects...

Kovacs revised management's 1989 forecast concerning Silgan's 1994 investment in working capital. Kovacs testified that management's forecast of investment in working capital for 1994 struck him as unusual. The projections show an increase in additional working capital every year except for 1994, which has a dramatic drop in investment in working capital. Silver, the co-executive officer of Silgan, testified that Silgan was to begin paying cash interest on merger related debt in 1994, and those payments had a negative effect on investment in working capital. Kovacs believes that interest on merger related long-term debt should not be considered in working capital, so he ignored the figure projected for 1994. He constructed his own estimate of investment in working capital from the averages of 1993 and 1995.

Petitioners contend that Kovacs should not have adjusted management's projection for 1994, despite unrebutted evidence of a problem with the projection. I find that Kovacs properly adjusted investment in working capital for 1994.

Petitioners also complain that Kovacs' improperly reduced management's projected deferred taxes. In management's projections, deferred taxes rise throughout the 1989–1995 period. Kovacs considered the projected steady rise in deferred taxes impossible, so he adjusted the figure. Kovacs explained that deferred taxes must correspond to purchases of capital assets because they result from the tax code's accelerated recognition of depreciation. In the projections, Silgan does not make the large investments in capital assets necessary to justify the yearly increases in deferred taxes. Lawson concurs with Kovacs' adjustment. I find that Kovacs properly adjusted management's projection of deferred taxes.

Petitioners also challenge Kovacs' estimate of cash flows for the remainder of 1989. On this issue, Petitioners do not assert that Respondent improperly altered Silgan's original projections. Rather, they claim that Respondent's expert erred as a matter of law in relying on the June 30, 1989, balance sheet, a document that was unavailable on the date of the merger.

In estimating the cash flows for the 1989 stub, Kovacs subtracted the actual figures in the June 30, 1989 balance sheet from management's projection for the entire year. Instead of using the actual figures from the first half of 1989, Paone divided the projected earnings for 1989 in half. Petitioners contend that Respondent cannot use the June 30, 1989, balance sheet for this appraisal because it was not available until a few months after the merger date. Respondent replies that the balance sheet was not yet available, but the information reflected on the balance sheet relates to Silgan's pre-merger financial position.

In assessing fair value…the Court considers all elements of value that are "known or susceptible of proof as of the date of the merger and not the product of speculation…." The June 30, 1989, balance sheet contains information about events that occurred prior to June 30, 1989. Silgan may not have described this information in the form of a balance sheet as of June 30, but the data was "susceptible of proof as of the date of the merger." *See id.* Subtracting the real figures for the first half of 1989 provides a more credible estimate of the earnings for the remainder of 1989 than dividing the annual estimate in half. I accept Kovacs' treatment of the 1989 stub.

The last material disagreement in the experts' estimation of cash flows for the projection period is their treatment of working capital interest. Kovacs treated some of Silgan's working capital interest as an expense to be deducted from cash flow. Because Silgan's working capital interest fluctuates, Kovacs treated most of it as an expense, excepting a "fixed working capital interest" figure, which Silgan's working capital interest historically never dipped below. Paone categorized all working capital interest as debt, subtracting it from the debt free value of Silgan. Petitioners assert that Paone's approach is preferable. However, Kovacs' treatment of working capital interest actually increases the fair value of Silgan in Kovacs' DCF model. Lawson describes Kovacs' approach to working capital interest as non-traditional, but he advocates adopting it. I find that treating working capital interest as an expense provides a more reliable indication of Silgan's fair value.

C. Terminal Value

In addition to estimating cash flows for the projection period, the DCF model requires the experts to set a value for Silgan at the end of the period, which is labeled a terminal value. The two experts' extremely divergent estimates of Silgan's terminal value account for much of the difference in the outcomes of the two experts' DCF analyses. Kovacs estimated Silgan's terminal value with a "growth in perpetuity model," which sets a flat growth rate for Silgan and projects it into perpetuity. Paone applied a growth in perpetuity model as one factor in setting Silgan's terminal value, but he also considered a hypothetical sale of Silgan at the end of the projection period. Paone estimates Silgan's terminal value at $685,530, while Kovacs places it at $415,336.

Kovacs' terminal value differs drastically from Paone's because he did not use management's projections for 1989–1995 to create a terminal value. Paone extrapolated a value in perpetuity from Silgan's expected performance from 1989 through 1995. Kovacs believes that management's projections for the specific time period, 1989 through 1995, cannot be used to value Silgan in perpetuity. During the projection period, Silgan's depreciation exceeds its investment, which Kovacs believes cannot be sustained in the long run. Kovacs believes Paone's extrapolation of the current data ignores Silgan's need to make new capital investments to sustain its growth...I find that Kovacs' has presented the more reliable terminal value calculation. Paone's model unrealistically extrapolates Silgan's short run circumstances into perpetuity. Kovacs correctly recognized the need for an adjustment in the data so that capital investment relates to growth and depreciation in a sustainable manner. Kovacs projected Silgan's future capital expenditures from the historical trends of the company and comparable industry data. Kovacs testified that capital investment should slightly exceed depreciation to sustain perpetual growth....I will not alter Kovacs' terminal value calculation.

I do not give Paone's "hypothetical sale" approach any weight. Paone's hypothetical sale approach incorporates the problems associated with comparable market data into the DCF analysis, which undercuts the greatest advantage of the DCF model. A DCF model actually values Silgan as a going concern, rather than looking at the comparable merger and acquisition data. Using a hypothetical sale at the end of the projection period brings the uncertainties inherent in the acquisition data, such as discounting for a "control premium," into the DCF model. In some circumstances a hypothetical sale may have advantages over the growth in perpetuity approach, but in this case it has no such advantage....

D. Respondent Has Presented The More Reliable DCF Analysis

In every respect, Respondent has provided more reliable valuations of Silgan's cash flows and terminal value. I carefully scrutinized Respondent's revision of the original projections, but each revision is supported by well-reasoned analysis. In contrast, Petitioners' steadfast refusal to reassess any of the original figures damages their expert witness' credibility. I conclude that Kovacs' DCF analysis is a better indicator of Silgan's fair value than Paone's DCF analysis. Yet, many aspects of Kovacs analysis reflect an overly adversarial approach. I have accepted Kovacs' conclusion as to Silgan's MVIC, but, as discussed below, I cannot accept his discounting methods and deductions from MVIC without adjustment. By contrasting the methods used by Kovacs and Paone, and employing Lawson's very helpful critique of both experts' opinions, I will make those adjustments.

E. Discounting Future Returns To Present Value

In a DCF analysis, the future returns must be discounted to their present value. The parties' experts used similar discount rates: Kovacs, 12.8%, Paone, 12.5%. Kovacs rounded the 12.8% rate to 13% for his calculations. Kovacs offered no justification for rounding the figure, and I believe it was done to create as low a final result as possible. I will remove the effect of this rounding from Kovacs' DCF analysis.

Kovacs also timed Silgan's cash flows in a manner that unreasonably lowers Silgan's value. Kovacs assumed that Silgan receives all of its cash at the end of the year. Paone assumed a mid-year receipt of cash flows as a surrogate for receipts occurring over the course of the year. Respondent submitted some evidence that Silgan, a company with a seasonal business, receives most of its cash at the end of the year. Other evidence in the record indicates that Silgan received cash throughout the year. I find the mid-year point to be the better estimate for receipt of Silgan's cash flows....

   *   *   *

V. FAIR VALUE

I have decided that Kovacs' market study and DCF analysis, with some adjustments, provide reliable methods for valuing Silgan. In reaching a final conclusion as to fair value, I do not give the two approaches equal weight. I give greater weight to the DCF model because it actually values Silgan as a going concern, rather than comparing Silgan to other businesses. I apply ⅔ weight to the DCF analysis and ⅓ weight to the market study to reach a value of Silgan's common equity of $79,429, unadjusted for stock options. For the purposes of this appraisal, all of the experts agree that the stock options should be treated as fully outstanding and the proceeds from the exercise of these options included in the equity value. Kovacs subtracted a market value for the options in his original report, so I add back that $9,100. Finally, I add $1,646 to reflect the exercise price of the options to reach a fair value of Silgan's common equity of $90,177. Dividing $90,177 by 15,179,000 shares, I find the fair value for Silgan's stock as of the merger date to be $5.94 per share.

   *   *   *

Notes and Questions

1. Controlling Versus Minority Interests: One of the primary issues that arose in *Kleinwort Benson v. Silgan* was whether a premium for control should be applied to the estimated share values. Control can take on a variety of forms. For example, one might have the ability to control the board of directors, the selection of management, the direction of the business in general, compensation policy, capital expenditures and liquidations, dividend policy, capital structure, or the decision to go public. Moreover, the extent to which any individual shareholder has control over particular decisions is a matter of varying degrees. For the shareholders of a widely traded public corporation, an individual shareholder may have very little control over the decisions of the corporation. At the other extreme, a corporation wholly owned by a single individual places these control rights with that one individual. In between these two extremes are innumerable levels of control.

It makes sense to assume that purchases of widely traded public shares do not carry any sort of a premium for control rights. However, does the absence of public trading necessarily imply that shareholders have control? The best approach is to consider the various control rights that might exist and the extent to which the shareholders actually possess such power—a willing buyer would certainly conduct such analysis. Reconsider the share classifications in *Kleinwort Benson v. Silgan*. Does it appear clear that the holders of Class B shares had any control rights? Moreover, an important source of constraint on control rights would be restrictive covenants included in the debt contracts. The facts of the case indicate that Silgan was highly leveraged. In short, does the chancery court sufficiently consider the issue of control?

2. Capital Base Must Support Projected Growth: Capital base refers to those assets which are expected to create future returns more than a year into the future. Capital base usually includes such items as manufacturing plants and equipment. As a business continues to grow it eventually reaches a point where it is constrained by the existing capital base. Thus, if such a firm intends to continue to grow, it must spend money to expand its capital base. Funding for such investments can come from two different sources—the earnings retained from profitable operations or outside financing. Where an assumption of earnings growth is made in present value calculations, it may be necessary to investigate whether such growth can be achieved with the current capital base. If expenditures for an expanded capital base—capital expenditures—are necessary to achieve the projected growth rates, then present value would be overestimated by not deducting such expenditures from the flow of future benefits.

3. Appraisal Rights and the Delaware Block Rule: The issue in *Kleinwort Benson v. Silgan* revolved around the legal concept of appraisal rights. **Appraisal rights** are essentially a statutory remedy for shareholders who object to certain extraordinary actions taken by a corporation. The effect of appraisal rights is to allow dissenting shareholders to exit the corporate form by requiring the corporation to purchase the dissenter's shares for a price equal to the share value immediately prior to the objectionable action. For years, the primary method of appraisal valuation was the Delaware Block Rule. Under the Delaware Block Rule, share values were determined by the weighted average of four "measures of value"—earnings, dividends, assets, and market price. Earnings, dividends, and asset values were determined primarily through the use of historical data under the Delaware Block Rule. Market values under the Delaware Block Rule were determined by studying the trading prices for stocks of comparable public corporations. In general, projected financial data were not utilized under the Delaware Block Rule and, thus, discounted future returns methodologies did not factor heavily in appraisal rights litigation.

However, in *Weinberger v. UOP, Inc.* (1983), the Delaware Supreme Court held that the four factors considered under the Delaware Block Rule were not exclusive in the determination of appraised values. Rather, the Delaware Supreme Court indicated that all relevant factors should be considered in determining share values including methods which utilized projections of future earnings. In *Kleinwort Benson v. Silgan*, a Delaware Chancery Court placed primary emphasis on values determined through the use of projected financial data. Given the historical preeminence of Delaware corporate law, it would appear that present value and discounted future returns methodologies may come to play a greater role in valuations for appraisal rights.

4. Investment Value Versus Fair Value: On two occasions, the Chancery Court rejects the use of data from mergers which involved companies similar to Silgan. In the context of the control premium, the Chancery Court notes that the premiums paid in mergers usually include more than just a premium for control:

"The acquiror may value the target corporation above its going concern value because of potential synergies or because the acquiror believes it will manage the target better." It is important in estimating the value of close corporations to determine and follow the relevant standard of value. Here, the petitioners' expert used comparison values that were characteristic of idiosyncratic transactions (investment value) not hypothetical bargainers (fair market value). The use of such data by the petitioners' expert harmed the expert's credibility in the eyes of the Chancery Court. Not only did this error result in the share value being miscalculated, but the loss of credibility suffered by petitioners' expert probably affected the Chancery Court's decisions regarding other aspects of the expert's analysis.

5. The Timing of Future Returns: In working with discounted future benefits problems, the timing of future returns is critical. This fact should be intuitively obvious from our general discussion of the time value of money. Specifically, the longer one has to wait for a future return, the more such a return will be discounted, all else being equal. Thus, a party who has to wait until the end of the year to receive cash will have a lower present value than some other individual who receives cash at mid-year, all else being equal. Even small differences in the timing of future benefits can matter greatly, especially when such values are extrapolated over several years.

6. Use of a Terminal Value: In general, the discounted future returns model contemplates that all future benefits will be estimated. The assumption behind the corporate form of organization is that the life of the firm is perpetual. Combining these two factors suggests that the future benefits from owning closely held shares must be calculated for each year in perpetuity. Obviously, this is an impossible task. A common method for resolving this difficulty is to divide the future into two periods. During the first period, called the near-term, a financial analyst will attempt to estimate the future benefits attributable to each specific year. In *Kleinwort Benson v. Silgan*, both expert witnesses estimated specific values for future benefits six years into the future. The period beyond which the analyst feels comfortable estimating future benefits for specific years can be called the distant-period. For the distant period, the financial analyst will estimate a terminal value to represent an infinite stream of future benefits. The most common method for calculating a terminal value is to make some assumption regarding the future growth of benefits and then utilize the perpetuity or a growth perpetuity model of present value.

2. Approaches Using Current or Historical Data

Due to the difficulty of estimating the stream of future benefits attributable to closely held shares and courts' general reluctance to rely on financial data that is "too speculative," a number of valuation approaches based on current or historical data have become widely used. As is the case with projected financial data, historical data is used to make projections regarding the future economic benefits from share ownership. In this sense, the use of historical data is simply another means from which the present value of future benefits can be estimated. There are a variety of methods from which current or historical data can be used to calculate the value of closely held shares. The choice of methods in any given case will depend upon the facts of the situation and legal precedent.

The most common way in which current or historical data can be used in the estimation of share value is through the process of capitalization. **Capitalization** refers to the simple mathematical process of taking some measure of historical or current benefits known as the **base value** and either dividing by a capitalization rate or multiplying by a capitalization multiple. Such calculations result in a measure for the share value. For example, the general form for valuations using a capitalization rate is:

$$\text{Share Value} = \text{Base Value} \div \text{Capitalization Rate}$$

The general form for the capitalization multiple method of valuation is:

$$\text{Share Value} = \text{Base Value} \times \text{Capitalization Multiple}$$

However, as is the case with the discounted future benefits method, despite the relative simplicity of the formulas, a great deal of controversy can arise regarding the proper application of capitalization methods. Three primary difficulties encountered when using such valuation methods are: choosing an appropriate proxy for current or historical economic benefit (choosing the base value); the measurement of the selected proxy (measuring the base value); and the estimation of the capitalization rate or multiple. In general, the process of capitalization for the valuation of closely held shares using current or historical data can be characterized by the following steps:

1. Selection of the relevant base value.

2. Selecting the appropriate historical time frame from which to estimate the base value.

3. Accounting for historical trends in the estimation of the base value.

4. Adjusting base values across firms for comparison purposes.

5. Estimating the appropriate capitalization rate or multiple.

6. Calculating share values.

The first step in the process of using a capitalization method for the valuation of closely held shares is to select an appropriate economic variable to serve as the base value. A wide variety of proxies for historical or current economic benefits have been used as base values when determining the value of closely held corporations. Such proxies include earnings, revenue, dividends, asset value, and output or capacity. Selection of the best base value for a particular valuation will depend on a number of factors. First, the goal is to value the economic benefits of share ownership, and the best measure of economic benefits will often vary as a result of the line of business in which the corporation is involved. For example, the primary economic benefit to the shareholders of an ongoing manufacturing concern comes from the firm's ability to generate net income and cash flow. Thus, some measure of earnings will be the relevant measure of economic benefit to those shareholders and should be used as the base value. On the other hand, the economic benefit from owning shares in a holding company is derived from the financial value of the assets. Capitalization on the basis of asset values would then be appropriate. Second, capitalization rates and multiples are calculated by studying such rates and multiples for comparable publicly traded corporations. Thus, the measure of economic benefit selected as a base value must be one that is measurable for both the closely held corporation and the comparable publicly traded corporations.

The second step in the capitalization method of valuation is to select the appropriate historical time frame from which to estimate the base value. Selection of the appropriate historical time frame involves a balancing between two confounding considerations. First, data used in calculating the base value must go back far enough to develop a range of performance possibilities that are likely to reflect probable future outcomes. Second, the collection of data must not go so far back as to include information that will no longer have relevance in predicting future financial performance. For example, it would be highly unlikely if the cash flows generated from the preceding years alone were the best estimate of future performance. In fact, the most recent year may represent either a high or a low for the cash flow performance variable. Moreover, any particular variable such as cash flow is likely to vary to some degree simply as a matter of general fluctuations in the economy. Thus, it is probably best to include more than one year of data when estimating the base value. On the other hand, the level of cash flow generated by a firm ten years ago may have no relevance to the firm's ability to generate cash in the future. For instance, a firm may have doubled its production capacity in the past four years and, thus, measures of cash flow before this period are likely to severely understate cash flow potential.

The third step in the process of valuing closely held shares using a capitalization method is to account for historical trends in the estimation of the base value. This is basically a question of how much weight should be assigned to the data from each of the past years used in the calculation of the base value. Consider, for example, an estimation of cash flows based on the last three years of data. If these cash flow numbers demonstrate an identifiable trend, then it might be appropriate to assign greater weights to the cash flow numbers generated in the most recent years. However, if the cash flow number displays a high degree of variability, then it is perhaps best to assign equal weight to each of the past three years. Alternatively, it may be the case that the most recent years' cash flows were highly unusual and not likely to occur again. Under such circumstances, the financial analyst may choose to give a great deal of weight to the cash flow numbers generated several years ago and give very little weight to the most recent years' cash flow.

The fourth step in the capitalization process is to adjust the financial statements of the relevant comparison firms so that the base values can be fairly compared. It is unlikely that the financial statements for the closely held corporation and publicly traded comparison corporations as they currently exist will be ready for accurate comparison. Accounting terms such as earnings or cash flows are not universally defined. In fact, firms often have wide latitude in terms of how such financial variables are calculated. Thus, for example, one would expect to find that the exact components of the term "cash flow" will vary across firms. In order to fairly compare the performance of the closely held corporation with that of publicly traded corporations, the financial analyst must adjust such numbers so that they approximate the same economic benefit (base value) across comparison firms. A failure to do so would result in distorted estimations of share value.

The fifth step in the capitalization process is to determine the appropriate capitalization rate or multiple. Two important considerations dominate litigation issues involving capitalization rates or multiples. First, these variables are estimated by looking at the financial data of publicly traded corporations that are sufficiently comparable to the closely held firm for which we are estimating a value. The issue of sufficient comparability is highly contested among the experts in such litigation. Second, as a general matter, these capitalization variables are an attempt to establish a relationship between the base value and price in terms of an amount buyers would be willing to pay per unit of the base variable. For example, the price to earnings ratio is a measure of the market price of a share in terms of a particular firm's earnings. After determining that earnings is the relevant base value, a financial analyst would identify a set of publicly traded corporations comparable to the close corporation which is being appraised. After identifying a good set of comparison firms, the analyst would calculate the average price to earnings ratio for the group of comparison firms. Dividing this average market price by the average of comparable firms' earnings establishes the appropriate earnings multiple to apply to the earnings base of our close corporation. In this regard, questions may arise concerning the correct variable for capitalizing a particular base value.

The variety of potential capitalization rates or multiples that exist are as varying as the number of different base values that might be calculated. Unfortunately, the actual calculation of capitalization rates or multiples is not sufficiently generic to lend itself to easy exposition in this book. The following case demonstrates a great variety in the methodologies used to construct a value for a closely held corporation. Moreover, all of the analysis in this case is based on current or historic data, not on a projection of future benefits.

Central Trust Company v. United States
United States Court of Claims
305 F.2d 393 (1962)

*   *   *

OPINION OF THE COMMISSIONER

These suits are for the refund of federal gift taxes. They involve the common question of the value of shares of stock of the same company. A joint trial was therefore conducted.

On August 3, 1954, Albert E. Heekin made gifts totaling 30,000 shares of stock of The Heekin Can Company. The donor had formerly, for 20 years, been president of the Company and at the time of the gifts was a member of its board of directors. The gifts were composed of 5,000 shares to each of six trusts created for the benefit of his three sons, each son being the beneficiary under two trusts. Following his death on March 10, 1955, the executors of his estate filed a gift tax return in which the value of the stock was fixed at $10 a share. On October 28, 1957, however, they filed an amended gift tax return and a claim for refund, contending that the correct value of the Heekin Company stock on August 3, 1954 was $7.50 a share.

On October 25, 1954, James J. Heekin made gifts totaling 40,002 shares of Heekin Can Company stock. This donor, a brother of Albert E., had also formerly been, for 23 years, the president of the Company and at the time of the gifts was chairman of the board. The gifts were composed of 13,334 shares to each of three trusts created for the benefit of his three children and their families. Separate gift tax returns with respect to these (and other) gifts were filed by both

James J. Heekin and his wife, Alma (who joined in the stock gifts), in which the value of the stock was similarly declared to be $10 a share. However, on January 21, 1958, James filed an amended gift tax return and a claim for refund, also contending that the correct value of the stock on October 25, 1954, was $7.50 a share, and on the same day, the executor of Alma's estate (she having died on November 9, 1955) filed a similar amended return and claim for refund.

On February 5, 1958, the District Director of Internal Revenue sent to James J. Heekin and the executors of the estates of Alma and Albert E. Heekin notices of deficiency of the 1954 gift taxes. Each of the three deficiencies was based on a determination by the Commissioner of Internal Revenue that the value of the Heekin Company stock on the gift dates was $24 a share.

Consistent with his deficiency notices, the District Director, on May 15, 1958, disallowed the three refund claims that had been filed, and in July 1958 payment was made of the amounts assessed pursuant to the deficiency notices. After the filing in August and September 1958 of claims for refund concerning these payments, the claims again being based on a valuation of $7.50, and the rejection thereof by the District Director, these three refund suits were instituted in the amounts of $169,876.19, $95,927.08, and $94,753.70 with respect to the Albert E. Heekin, James J. Heekin and Alma Heekin gifts, respectively, plus interest.

The Heekin Can Company is a well-established metal container manufacturer in Cincinnati, Ohio. In 1954, the year involved in these proceedings, its principal business consisted of manufacturing two kinds of containers, its total production being equally divided between them. One is known as packer's cans, which are generally the type seen on the shelves of food markets in which canned food products are contained. The other is referred to as general line cans, which consist of large institutional size frozen fruit cans, lard pails, dairy cans, chemical cans, and drums. This line also includes such housewares as canisters, bread boxes, lunch boxes, waste baskets, and a type of picnic container familiarly known by the trade names of Skotch Kooler and Skotch Grill. On the gift dates its annual sales, the production of five plants, were approximately $17,000,000.

The Company was founded in 1901 in Cincinnati by James Heekin, the father of the donors Albert and James. In 1908, it built a six-story 250,000 square foot factory in Cincinnati, which is still its headquarters and one of its main operating plants, producing general line cans. In 1917 it acquired a plant in Norwood, a suburb of Cincinnati, which has since become entirely surrounded by the city, and entered the packer's can business. By 1954, it was a multistory plant with about 275,000 square feet, having grown irregularly throughout the years, one section having four floors, another three, and another only one.

*   *   *

On the gift dates, the Company had 254,125 shares of common stock outstanding, there being no restrictions on their transferability or sale. There was no other class of stock. Including the 70,002 shares involved in these cases, a total of 180,510 shares were owned by 79 persons who were related to James Heekin, the founder. Thus, the Heekin family owned approximately 71 percent of all of the outstanding stock. The remaining 73,615 shares were owned by 54 unrelated persons, most of whom were employees of the Company and friends of the family.

Six major customers accounted for almost one-half of Heekin's 1954 business. Relations with these important customers were long-standing and excellent.

One of these customers, the Hamilton Metal Products Company, which placed over $2,000,000 worth of business with Heekin in 1954, and for whom Heekin manufactured the Skotch Kooler and Grill, had, prior to the gift dates, advised Heekin of its need for certain new products, and on August 3, 1954 (one of the gift dates), Heekin's board of directors authorized the expenditure of approximately $90,000 for new tooling and equipment at its Cincinnati plant for the manufacture of such products. Another major customer was the Reynolds Tobacco Company, which placed almost $1,500,000 of business with Heekin in 1954 and with whom Heekin had dealt since 1908.

As indicated, freight costs play an important part in Heekin's business. These costs are significant in two aspects. One is the cost of transporting raw material to Heekin's plants. In this respect Heekin was quite favorably located. It has a dock on the Ohio River in Cincinnati, permitting it to take advantage of inexpensive water transportation of steel shipped from Pittsburgh, with a consequent advantage over some of its competitors in the same area who receive their raw materials by rail. The other important freight aspect is, as above noted, the cost of shipping the final product to the customer, and which factor motivated the establishment of its Springdale, Arkansas, plant. The Hamilton Metal Products Company was located only 25 miles from Cincinnati, giving Heekin an important freight advantage. And also, on August 3, 1954, Heekin's board of directors authorized the expenditure of about $650,000 for new tooling, machinery and equipment for its Norwood plant so that Heekin could enter the new field of manufacturing beer cans. At that time no other company in the Cincinnati area was engaged in the production of such cans, and Heekin concluded that, with the freight advantage it would have over its competitors in serving the brewers of the Cincinnati area, a profitable new source of business would be developed.

In 1954, favorable economic conditions generally prevailed in the can-manufacturing industry, and demand was at a record level. Indeed, this was the condition throughout the container and packaging industry, and optimism generally prevailed about the continuation of the then current high demand.

But Heekin had its problems too. It is a relatively tiny factor in a highly competitive industry dominated by two giants, the American Can Company and the Continental Can Company. In 1954, these two companies, each with over $600,000,000 of annual sales produced from 76 and 40 plants respectively, together accounted for about 75 percent of the country's total can sales. Three other can manufacturing companies, the National Can Corporation, the Pacific Can Company, and Crown Cork & Seal Co., Inc., together made about 8 percent of the sales. Heekin, with its five plants, did a little less than 1 percent of the total business. Prices in the can-making industry are for practical purposes established by American and Continental. When they announce prices, Heekin goes up or down with them. Unable to compete on a price basis, Heekin strives to give its customers better personal service, which, because it is smaller and closer knit, it can frequently do.

*　*　*

Similarly, Heekin's Cincinnati and Norwood multistory plants, which accounted for about 75 percent of Heekin's total 1954 production, were less efficient than modern, single-story buildings. The can-making business is primarily a material-handling one, requiring a rapid and efficient flow of large amounts of material through the plant, from the receipt of the raw materials to the shipment of finished products. In a single-story building, materials can freely be moved horizontally with fork-lift trucks and conveyors, whereas in its six-story Cincinnati and four-story Norwood plants, elevators are used for the vertical movement of materials, resulting in excessive labor and handling costs and more difficult production controls. The proceeds of a $3,000,000 long-term loan which Heekin secured in 1950 were for the most part not available for such a plant and equipment modernization program.

However, the competitive disadvantage of lack of modern equipment was reflected more on the packer's can phase of its business than on the general line cans, which are produced both by Heekin and its competitors on only semiautomatic equipment. Such equipment does not lend itself as readily to the speed and automation required with respect to packer's cans. Heekin's semiautomatic lines were capable of producing around 300 cans a minute.

The Heekin stock was not listed on any stock exchange, and trading in it was infrequent. There was some such activity in 1951 and 1952 resulting from the desire of certain minority stockholders (the descendants of a partner of James Heekin, the founder) to liquidate their holdings, consisting of 13,359 shares. One individual alone had 10,709 shares. Arrangements were privately made in early 1951 by these stockholders with Albert E. Heekin and his son, Albert E. Heekin, Jr., to sell these holdings at the prearranged price of $7.50 a share. These shares were all sold, commencing March 22, 1951, and ending April 16, 1952, in 44 separate transactions, 35 of which took place in 1951 and 9 in 1952. No attempt was made to sell the shares to the general public on the open market. All sales were made to Heekin employees and friends of the Heekin family at such $7.50 price. Other than these 1951 and 1952 sales, the only sales of stock made prior to the gift dates consisted of one sale of 100 shares in 1953 by one Heekin employee to another, and one sale in 1954 of 200 shares, again by one Heekin employee to another, both sales also being made for $7.50 a share.

Against these background facts, the valuation question in dispute may be approached. Section 1000 of the Internal Revenue Code of 1939, ... the applicable statute, imposed a tax upon transfers of property by gift, whether in trust or otherwise. Section 1005 provided that "If the gift is made in property, the value thereof at the date of the gift shall be considered the amount of the gift."

Section 86.19(a) of the Regulations issued with respect thereto ... defines such property value as the price at which the property "would change hands between a willing buyer and a willing seller, neither being under any compulsion to buy or to sell. * * * Such value is to be determined by ascertaining as a basis the fair market value at the time of the gift of each unit of the property. For example, in the case of shares of stock * * *, such unit of property is a share * * *. All relevant facts and elements of value as of the time of the gift should be considered." With respect to determining the fair market value per share at the date of the gift, subsection (c)(6) stated that, if actual sales or bona fide bid and asked prices are not available, the value should be arrived at "on the basis of the company's net worth, earning power, dividend-paying capacity, and all other relevant factors having a bearing upon the value of the stock."

Further, a lengthy Revenue Ruling ... entitled "Valuation of stock of closely held corporations in estate tax and gift tax returns," was in effect at the time of these gifts which outlined "the approach, methods and factors to be considered in valuing shares of the capital stock of closely held corporations for estate tax and gift tax purposes." After warning in section 3 that fair market value, "being a question of fact," depends on the "circumstances in each case," and that "No formula can be devised that will be generally applicable to the multitude of different valuation issues arising in estate and gift tax cases," and that there is ordinarily "wide differences of opinion as to the fair market value of a particular" closely held stock, section 4 goes on to enumerate the following factors which "are fundamental and require careful analysis in each case": (1) the nature of the business and its history, (2) the general economic outlook of business in general and the specific industry in particular, (3) the book value of the stock and the company's financial condition, (4) the company's earning capacity, (5) its dividend-paying capacity, (6) its goodwill, (7) such sales of the stock as have been made as well as the size of the block to be valued and (8) "the market price of stocks of corporations engaged in the same or similar line of business which are listed on an exchange." After discussing each factor in detail, the Ruling goes on to consider such matters as (a) the weight to be accorded the various factors, concluding that, in a product selling company, primary consideration should normally be given to the earnings factor, and (b) the necessity of capitalizing the earnings and dividends at appropriate rates.

     *   *   *

One of plaintiffs' experts was the senior partner of a firm of investment bankers and brokers. He felt that the limited prior sales of the stock at $7.50 warranted the consideration of the other factors listed in the Revenue Ruling applicable to closely held corporations. There were four major factors which he considered in arriving at his conclusion. The first was book value. Utilizing the Company's balance sheet as of December 31, 1954 (a date subsequent to the gift dates), the book value came to about $33 a share. In this connection he noted that the Company's financial position at that time was sound, with a ratio of current assets to current liabilities of about 4.3 to 1. However, principally because of the age and multistoried inefficiency of the Company's two main plants at Cincinnati and Norwood, he reduced the book value factor by 50 percent. The second factor was earnings. The Company's audited annual statements for 1952, 1953 and 1954, which he accepted without adjustment, showed that the average of its earnings for these 3 years was $1.77 a share. He felt that, in the case of this Company, a price earnings ratio of 6 to 1 would be appropriate, but, recognizing that this was the most important factor, he weighted it to give it double value. The third factor was dividend yield. In said 3 years, the Company paid an annual dividend of 50 cents. Accepting this figure as the dividend the Company would be likely to pay in the future, he concluded that an investor would look for a 7 percent yield on this stock, and capitalized it on that basis. The fourth factor was the prior sales at $7.50. Adding and weighting these figures, he derived a value of $10.50 a share. However, because the stock was not listed on any exchange, and was closely held, with sales being infrequent, he discounted that value by 25 percent to reflect the stock's lack of marketability, and came out with an ultimate valuation of $7.88 a share.[1] This is the value plaintiffs now rely on in these cases.

---

    1. Book value = $ 33.20, less 50%   16.60
       Earnings = Average 3 years = 1.77;

This value was applied to the entire block of 70,002 shares and to both dates, a block which, he noted, would give a purchaser only a minority position. Considering the Revenue Ruling's suggestion to investigate "the market price of stocks of corporations engaged in the same or similar line of business which are listed on an exchange," this witness felt that there were no listed companies that could properly be compared with Heekin.

Plaintiffs' second expert, a certified public accountant who had experience in and was familiar with the principles involved in valuing stocks of closely held corporations, arrived at the somewhat higher valuations of $9.50 per share for the 30,000 shares given on August 3, 1954, and $9.65 for the 40,002 given on October 25, 1954. He recognized that the previous sales of the stock in 1951, 1952, 1953 and 1954 at $7.50 could not be determinative because, being all at the same selling price, they could not have reflected the month-to-month or year-to-year fluctuations of actual value, which was the problem herein involved. He concluded that that price was predicated primarily to give a yield of 6⅔ percent based on an annual dividend rate of 50 cents, which the Company had paid each year from 1946 through 1954, except for a 1½-year period in 1950 and 1951. In 1950, the Company suffered extraordinary losses and dividends were suspended, and in 1951, only 25 cents was paid. Accordingly, he considered the situation appropriate for the application of the principles enunciated in the Revenue Ruling.

In so doing, he too concluded that the four major factors to be considered were earnings, dividend yield, book value, and the price of the prior sales. As to earnings, he computed, from the Company's audited statements for the years 1950–54, without adjustment, average annual earnings of $1.68. Using the comparative method of calculating price-earnings ratios of listed companies in the same or similar business and then correlating such results to Heekin, he selected 11 leading corporations in the container industry (only two of which, American Can and Continental Can, were can companies), and computed their average price-earnings ratio over the similar 5-year period at 10 to 1, with 1954 alone producing a ratio of 11.6 to 1 because of the rise in prices of container industry stocks in that year.[2] However, he capitalized Heekin's 5-year average earnings of $1.68 at an earnings multiple of only eight times which he considered appropriate for a "marginal" company like Heekin. Since this produced a value of $13.44 based only on earnings, as of December 31, 1954, due to his using the figures for the full year 1954, he adjusted the figure to August 3, 1954, the first gift date, by reducing the figure by 14.1 percent, a figure derived by calculating the general rise in a relatively large group of certain other industry stocks between August 3

---

price to earnings ratio = 6:1 = $10.62.	
Weighted to two factors	21.24
Dividends = To give yield of 7% at rate of 50 cents per annum, would have to sell at	7.14
Prior Sales =	7.50
Total all factors	52.48
Divided by 5 to obtain weighted average 52.48/5 =	10.50
Less 25% for lack of marketability	2.62
[Estimated Value]	7.88

2. He noted that this 10-to-1 ratio was higher than the Dow-Jones average of 9.9 for 30 industrials, the Standard & Poor average of 9.3 for 50 industrials, and the Moody average of 9.7 for 125 industrials for the same 5-year period.

and December 31. Thus, on the basis of earnings alone, he calculated a value of $11.55 as of August 3.

As to dividends, this witness then calculated Heekin's average for the 5 years ended December 31, 1954, at 35 cents per share and capitalized that figure at 6 percent, which he considered to be appropriate in Heekin's case in view of the 5-year average dividend yield of 5.1 percent for the 11 leading companies in the container industry which he used as comparatives, and the even higher returns, on a 5-year average basis, afforded by general groups of leading industrials during that period. Thus, on the basis of a 6 percent dividend yield alone, he calculated a value of $5.83.

Using as factors the value figures derived as described on the bases of price earnings ($11.55) and dividend yield ($5.83) ratios, together with a book value figure of $33.23 as of December 31, 1954, and a $7.50 figure as the price of the prior sales, the witness then weighted these four factor figures, giving the earnings and dividend factors 40 percent each (i.e. each figure multiplied by 4), and the book value and prior sales figure 10 percent each (i.e. each figure multiplied by 1). This total figure was then reduced by 15 percent to reflect the stock's lack of marketability (which was equated to the underwriting cost of floating 30,000 shares) which, after dividing by the weight factor (10), gave the market price as of August 3 as $9.37,[3] which he rounded out to $9.50.

Using the same criteria and method, the witness valued the 40,002 shares given on October 25, 1954, at the slightly higher price of $9.65, the price of listed stocks having generally risen between the two dates.

The taxpayers' third expert, a senior officer in a firm specializing in valuing the stocks of closely held corporations, came out with the still higher valuation of $11.41 per share on August 3, in blocks of 10,000 ($11.76 in a block of 30,000 shares). For the shares given on October 25, however, his value was only $9.40 per share in blocks of 13,334 shares ($9.47 in a block of 40,002 shares).

This witness also used the technique of selecting comparable companies traded on a national exchange, ascertaining, by a very comprehensive study, the relationship between their market prices and their earnings, "earnings paid out," and return on invested capital (to which he added long-term debt), and then correlating the data to Heekin. Unlike the other two experts, he did not accept the exact figures of the audited statements of annual earnings, but studied them with a view to detecting and eliminating abnormal and nonrecurring items of loss or profit in order to obtain a better picture of the Company's normal operation and of what an investor, therefore, might reasonably conclude the Company's future performance would be. With such adjustments and eliminations, he thus recast the Company's earnings for the years 1949–1953. He

---

3.

	Weight	Total
Price earning ratio 11.55	4	46.20
Dividend — 35 cents capitalized at 6% 5.83	4	23.32
Stock sales 7.50	1	7.50
Book value 33.23	1	33.23
[Total]		110.25
Less 15% amount for nonmarketability		16.51
Divided by factor 10		9.37

selected eight companies in both the can and glass container fields to use as comparatives.

In calculating Heekin's earnings, the witness used a 5-year average, as adjusted. One of the adjustments was to the Company's abnormal profits in 1951 as a result of the Korean war, which he eliminated and reduced to more normal levels. Another was to eliminate, as abnormal and nonrecurring, rather large losses the Company suffered in 1950, 1951 and 1952 as a result of the operations of a subsidiary which was liquidated. By applying a price-earnings ratio of 11.82, as derived from the comparative companies, he determined a value of the Heekin stock on August 3, based only on earnings, of $13.78 per share; a value based on earnings paid out (in which he included not only dividends but also interest on long-term debt) on the capital invested in the business of $9.59 per share; and a value based on invested capital of $31.34 per share. To these three determinants of value, he added the fourth factor of $7.50 derived from the prior sales price. He too then weighted these figures, assigning a weight of 33 ⅓ percent each to the values based on earnings and earnings-paid-out, and 16 ⅔ percent each to the values based on invested capital and the prior stock sales. This gave a total weighted value of $14.26. He then too applied a 20-percent reduction for lack of marketability, which he also equated with flotation costs for blocks of 10,000 shares, resulting in the net figure of $11.41 as of August 3.[4]

The same technique produced a figure of $9.40 per share as of October 25, 1954, in blocks of 13,334 shares. This lower valuation is attributable to the drop in the market prices of the comparative companies between August 3 and October 25, 1954. One of the comparatives (Pacific Can Company) which had been used for the August 3 valuation was dropped since it enjoyed a rather atypical sharp rise after such date due to a proposed merger.

Various major criticisms can fairly be made of these three appraisals offered by plaintiffs. First, they all give undue weight as a factor to the $7.50 price of the prior stock sales. Almost all of these sales occurred in the relatively remote period of 1951 and early 1952. Only one small transaction occurred in each of the more recent years of 1953 and 1954. Such isolated sales of closely held corporations in a restricted market offer little guide to true value.... In an evaluation issue, this court recently even gave little weight to the sale of shares on a stock exchange when the amount sold was "relatively insignificant".... To the same effect is Heiner v. Crosby, 24 F.2d 191 (C.C.A.3d) in which the court rejected stock exchange sales as being determinative and upheld the resort to "evidence of intrinsic value" (p. 194). Furthermore, the $7.50 price of the 1951 and 1952 sales evolved in early 1951 during a period when the Company was experiencing rather severe financial difficulties due to an unfortunate experience with a subsidiary which caused a loss of around $1,000,000, and when, consequently, the

---

4. Value based on earnings — 13.78 at 33 ⅓%   4.59
Value based on earnings paid out — 9.59 at 33 ⅓%   3.20
Value based on invested capital — 31.34 at 16 ⅔%   5.22
Value based on stock sales — 7.50 at 16 ⅔%   1.25
100%   14.26
Less 20% for lack of marketability
   (flotation cost in blocks of 10,000 shares)   2.85
Net value   11.41
Less 17.5% reduction if in a block of 30,000 shares   11.76

Company found itself in a depleted working capital position and was paying no dividends. Further, there is no indication that the $7.50 sales price evolved as a result of the usual factors taken into consideration by informed sellers and buyers dealing at arm's length. Fair market value presupposes not only hypothetical willing buyers and sellers, but buyers and sellers who are informed and have "adequate knowledge of the material facts affecting the value...." The sales were all made at a prearranged price to Heekin employees and family friends. The artificiality of the price is indicated by its being the same in 1951, 1952, 1953 and 1954, despite the varying fortunes of the Company during these years and with the price failing to reflect, as would normally be expected, such differences in any way.

Secondly, in using the Company's full 1954 financial data, and then working back from December 31, 1954, to the respective gift dates, data were being used which would not have been available to a prospective purchaser as of the gift dates. "The valuation of the stock must be made as of the relevant dates without regard to events occurring subsequent to the crucial dates." Furthermore, in the working-back procedure, general market data were used although it is evident that the stocks of a particular industry may at times run counter to the general trend. This was actually the situation here. Although the market generally advanced after August 3, 1954, container industry stocks did not.

Thirdly, the converse situation applies with respect to the data used by the third expert. His financial data only went to December 31, 1953, since the Company's last annual report prior to the gift dates was issued for the year 1953. But the Company also issued quarterly interim financial statements, and by the second gift date, the results of three-quarters of 1954 operations were available. In evaluating a stock, it is essential to obtain as recent data as is possible, as section 4 of the Revenue Ruling makes plain. Naturally, an investor would be more interested in how a corporation is currently performing than what it did last year or in even more remote periods. Although the use of interim reports reflecting only a part of a year's performance may not be satisfactory in a seasonal operation such as canning, it is possible here to obtain a full year's operation ending on either June 30 or September 30, 1954, which would bring the financial data up closer to the valuation dates.

Fourth, it is accepted valuation practice, in ascertaining a company's past earnings, to attempt to detect abnormal or nonrecurring items and to make appropriate eliminations or adjustments. As shown, only the plaintiffs' expert who came out with the highest August 3 valuation attempted to do this by adjusting the excessive Korean war earnings and by eliminating the unusual losses suffered in 1950, 1951 and 1952 arising from the operations of a financing subsidiary (Canners Exchange, Inc.) that had been liquidated in 1952. The reason this is important is that past earnings are significant only insofar as they reasonably forecast future earnings. The only sound basis upon which to ground such a forecast is the company's normal operation, which requires the elimination or adjustment of abnormal items which will not recur.... In American Steel Foundries v. United States, supra, the court similarly viewed the "earning prospects" of the company whose stock was being evaluated in light of its past earnings "as constructed by the accountants, eliminating or adjusting losses due to strikes or other nonrecurring events." And the court in White & Wells Co. v. Commissioner, also held that: " * * * past earnings * * * should be such as fairly reflect the probable future earnings" and that to this end "abnormal years" may even be entirely disregarded. The Revenue Ruling (sec. 4.02(d)) specifically points out the necessity of separating "recurrent from nonrecurrent items of income and expense."

Fifth, in deriving a past earnings figure which could be used as a reasonable basis of forecasting future earnings, none of plaintiffs' experts gave any consideration to the trend of such past earnings. They simply used the earnings of prior years and averaged them. But such averages may be deceiving. Two corporations with 5-year earnings going from the past to the present represented by the figures in one case of 5, 4, 3, 2, and 1, and in the other by the same figures of 1, 2, 3, 4, and 5, will have the same 5-year averages, but investors will quite naturally prefer the stock of the latter whose earnings are consistently moving upward. The Revenue Ruling specifically recognizes this in providing that: "Prior earnings records usually are the most reliable guide as to the future expectancy, but resort to arbitrary five-or-ten-year averages without regard to current trends or future prospects will not produce a realistic valuation. If, for instance, a record of progressively increasing or decreasing net income is found, then greater weight may be accorded the most recent years' profits in estimating earning power."

And further, since the most recent years' earnings are to be accorded the greatest weight, care must be taken to make certain that the earnings figures for such years are realistically set forth. For instance, in Heekin's case, profits for 1952–54 were understated because a noncontributory retirement plan for hourly employees was established in 1951 for which the costs attributable to 1950 and 1951 were borne in the later years of 1952–54. Similarly, 1954 profits were further understated because they reflected (1) a renegotiation refund arising out of excess profits made in 1951, and (2) they were subjected to a charge of $174,203.54 ($83,617.70 after taxes) as a result of a deduction from 1954 profits only of certain expenses attributable to both 1954 and 1955. This abnormal doubling up of 2 years' expenses in one year was permitted by a change in the tax laws which became effective in 1954 (and which was later revoked retroactively) which allowed taxpayers such as Heekin to change their methods of accounting so as to effect the accrual in 1954 of these 1955 expenses. If proper adjustments are made in Heekin's 1954 statements for these items, the earnings for the 1954 period prior to the gift dates would be realistically increased and given due weight insofar as earning trends are concerned.

None of plaintiffs' experts made any of these adjustments in connection with a trend study or otherwise.

Sixth, it is generally conceded that, as stated by the Revenue Ruling, in evaluating stocks of manufacturing corporations such as Heekin, earnings are the most important factor to be considered.... Yet only one of plaintiffs' experts, who assigned double value to this factor, gave it such weight. As shown, the other two assigned the dividend factor equal weight. Some investors may indeed depend upon dividends. In their own investment programs, they may therefore stress yield and even compare common stocks with bonds or other forms of investment to obtain the greatest yields. However others, for various reasons, may care little about dividends and may invest in common stocks for the primary purpose of seeking capital appreciation. All investors, however, are primarily concerned with earnings, which are normally a prerequisite to dividends. In addition, the declaration of dividends is sometimes simply a matter of the policy of a particular company. It may bear no relationship to dividend-paying capacity. Many investors actually prefer companies paying little or no dividends and which reinvest their earnings, for that may be the key to future growth and capital appreciation.

And further, in capitalizing the dividend at 6 and 7 percent, as did two of the experts, rates of return were used which well exceeded those being paid at the time by comparable container company stocks. And still further, one of the experts used a 35-cent dividend rate as the basis for his capitalization because that was the average paid for the 5 years ended December 31, 1954. However, it seems clear that an annual dividend rate of 50 cents a share would be the proper rate to capitalize since that was the dividend paid by Heekin every year since 1945 except for the year 1950 and the first half of 1951 when, as shown, dividends were temporarily suspended. By the end of 1951 the Company had recovered from the situation causing the suspension and the normal dividend (quarterly payments of 12 ½ cents per share) was then resumed. By August and October 1954, Heekin's demonstrated earning capability and financial position were such that there was little doubt it would at least continue its 50-cent annual dividend, which represented only about 25 percent of its current earnings per share. To dip back into this 1950–51 a typical period to compute an "average" of dividends paid for the past 5 years is unrealistic.

Finally, the record indicates that all three experts took too great a discount for lack of marketability. Defendant disputes the propriety of taking this factor into consideration at all. It seems clear, however, that an unlisted closely held stock of a corporation such as Heekin, in which trading is infrequent and which therefore lacks marketability, is less attractive than a similar stock which is listed on an exchange and has ready access to the investing public. This factor would naturally affect the market value of the stock. This is not to say that the market value of any unlisted stock in which trading is infrequent would automatically be reduced by a lack of marketability factor. The stock of a well-known leader in its field with a preeminent reputation might not be at all affected by such a consideration, as was the situation with Ford Motor Company stock before it was listed.... But the stock of a less well-known company like Heekin which is a comparatively small factor in its industry is obviously in a different position. In such a situation, a consideration of this factor is appropriate, especially where, as here, only a minority interest is involved. ...

Defendant concedes that if such a factor is appropriate in these cases, a reasonable method of determining the diminution in value attributable to lack of marketability is to determine how much it would cost to create marketability for the block of stock in question. This was the method used by the court in First Trust Co. v. United States, supra. The record shows that for a company of Heekin's size, and for blocks of 30,000 and 40,000 shares, which would appear to be the appropriate considerations, flotation costs would amount to about 12.17 percent of the gross sales prices. However, as shown, the discounts taken by plaintiffs' experts for this factor ranged from 15 to 25 percent

For all the above reasons, the opinions of plaintiffs' experts are not wholly acceptable.

Defendant produced one expert, an employee of a recognized appraisal company. His primary work over many years was the valuation of intangibles, including closely held stock. His opinion was that the value of the Heekin stock in question on August 3 and October 25, 1954, was $16 and $15.25 per share, respectively. This witness also used the comparative appraisal method, considering a group of stocks in the can and glass container industries. As part of a very comprehensive study, he selected eight container companies, six engaged in can production and two in glass container production, glass container enterprises being similar to those engaged in can production. He considered net assets as a key factor in the determination of a stock price, and one which keeps a stock price from declining to zero when earnings become zero or even when losses are suffered and when a price-to-earnings ratio would therefore become meaningless. He therefore developed for the comparative companies percentage ratios of profits and dividends to net worth as well as market value to net worth. In developing figures for the profits and dividends of the comparative companies for the past 5 years, he gave weight to the trends thereof. He then developed Heekin's profits over the period 1950 through September 1954, making adjustments for the retirement plan costs, the losses from subsidiaries, the renegotiation refund, and the abnormal 1951 profits, in order to reflect the more nearly normal operations over the period. Adjusted profits were developed for the 12-month periods ending June 30 and September 30, 1954. Before correlating the percentages developed for the comparative companies to Heekin, however, he concluded that only two of such companies, United Can and Glass Company and Crown Cork & Seal Company, Inc., could be considered conformable to Heekin. The others, including the giants of their industries, such as American Can, Continental Can, and Owens Illinois Glass Company which, because of acquisitions, diversification, premium investment quality position, and mere size, were not considered fairly comparable, were eliminated. Correlating the data developed with respect to such two companies, he concluded that, as of August 3, Heekin would be worth 59.5 percent of net worth, or $19.72 per share, a stock exchange equivalent of 19¾ per share. The similar method produced $18.78 per share as the value as of October 25, 1954, or a trading equivalent of 18¾.

This witness too felt that the correlation process resulted in comparing Heekin with seasoned listed stocks enjoying marketability, and that an adjustment should be made for the closely held nature of the Heekin stock with its resultant lack of marketability, especially where only a minority interest was involved. Similarly equating this adjustment to deductions a seller would experience through floating the shares through an underwriter, which he calculated to be almost 20 percent, resulted in net valuations of 16 and 15¼ as of August 3 and October 25, 1954, respectively. Since these values approximate Heekin's current assets (including inventories) less all of its liabilities, without giving any value at all to any of its plants, equipment, or other noncurrent assets, he concluded they were extremely conservative. Employing the common tests of price-to-earnings ratio and yield on the basis of the current 50-cent dividend, these values would result in a price-to-earnings ratio of 7.24:1 as of August 3, based on $2.21 adjusted net profit per share for the 12 months ending June 30, as well as a 3.13 percent dividend yield, and a ratio of 8.29:1 as of October 25, based on $1.84 adjusted net profit per share for the 12 months ending September 30, as well as a 3.28 percent dividend yield.

This witness' study has certain meritorious features. It is based on justifiable adjustments in Heekin's earnings records to eliminate abnormal and nonrecurring items (although he made no adjustment for the 1954 doubling up of certain expenses). It considers earnings trend. It disregards the prior $7.50 sales prices as a major factor. And in employing the Company's financial data going up to June

30 and September 30, 1954, it is based on its most recent performance. However, it has certain weaknesses too, the principal one being the limitation of the comparative companies to two, one of which, Crown Cork & Seal, leaves much to be desired as a comparative because its principal business is the manufacture of bottle caps and bottling machinery, an entirely different business. Only 40 percent of its business is in can production. On the basis of size too there are great differences. At that time, Crown, including its foreign subsidiaries, was doing about $115,000,000 worth of business as against Heekin's $17,000,000. And the other comparative, United Can and Glass, presents the complication that it declared periodic stock dividends to which the witness gave no consideration, although it seems that some element of value should fairly be attributed to them. Although no two companies are ever exactly alike, it being rare to have such almost ideal comparatives as were present in Cochran v. Commissioner, supra, so that absolute comparative perfection can seldom be achieved, nevertheless the comparative appraisal method is a sound and well-accepted technique. In employing it, however, every effort should be made to select as broad a base of comparative companies as is reasonably possible, as well as to give full consideration to every possible factor in order to make the comparison more meaningful.

Further, in compiling Heekin's financial data for correlation purposes, this witness used Heekin's average dividends for the 4½ years preceding the valuation dates, thus including the atypical period when no dividends were paid.

Defendant, considering its own expert's valuations to be unduly conservative, and disagreeing as a matter of law with any deduction for lack of marketability (and in any event with the amount deducted by its expert for such factor), now offers valuations on what it claims to be a more realistic basis. It also adjusts and redistributes Heekin's profits, including the "doubling up" expenses in 1954, the renegotiation refund, and the retirement plan. As comparatives, it uses for the purpose of developing a price-earnings ratio 11 can and glass container manufacturing companies, including American Can and Continental Can (although it concedes that with respect to the stock of such companies in this field, the investing public affords "some extra value coincident with size"), as well as Crown Cork & Seal and United Can. The dividend yield of seven comparative companies, based on their 1954 dividend payments, was 3.77 percent. Defendant too gives no cognizance to United Can's stock dividends, although it concedes that "stock dividends have some effect on market value." On Heekin's 50-cent dividend, the market price of Heekin stock would be $13.33, based solely on a 3.75 (the figure used by defendant) percent dividend yield.

Defendant then computes representative earnings for Heekin as $1.89 per share, based on 1953 and 1954 adjusted earnings. The average price to current earnings ratio of the 11 comparative companies in 1954 was 13 to 1. On this formula, Heekin's stock would sell for $24.57 per share if earnings were the sole factor. However, defendant reduces this figure to $22.50 for the purpose in question.

On the basis of the book value of Heekin stock being $33.15 as of June 30, 1954, and comparing the market prices of various alleged comparable companies to their book value (i.e., the stocks of 11 unidentified comparatives used by the Commissioner of Internal Revenue in making his valuation sold for 1.4 times book value), defendant concludes that Heekin stock would not sell for less than $33 per share.

The three factors of earnings, dividend yield, and book value are then weighted, earnings, considering their recognized importance for valuation purposes and the upward trend thereof, being assigned 50 percent weight, and dividend yield and book value receiving 30 percent and 20 percent respectively. On this basis, defendant arrives at a fair market value figure of $21.85 as of August 3, 1954.[7]

Since there was a slight drop in the market price of can manufacturing stocks between August 3 and October 25, 1954, defendant concludes the fair market value on the latter date would be about 50 cents less per share, or $21.35.

Thus, defendant now seeks a fair market value determination as of the gift dates of $21.85 and $21.35 respectively, in lieu of the $24 value fixed by the Commissioner of Internal Revenue.[8]

In its selection of the three basic factors to be considered in determining fair market value, the weights to be assigned to these factors, the earnings adjustments, and the use of 50 cents per annum as the proper dividend basis, this estimate has merit. However, the selection of such companies as American Can and Continental Can as comparatives—companies held in esteem in the investment world—will obviously give an unduly high result. It simply is not fair to compare Heekin with such companies and to adopt their market ratios for application to Heekin's stock. Furthermore, defendant's use of the comparatives is confusing. The employment of different comparatives for different purposes is unorthodox. When the comparative appraisal method is employed the comparatives should be clearly identified and consistently used for all purposes. And the refusal to make any allowance for lack of marketability contributes further to the unrealistic nature of defendant's fair market value estimate.

To summarize, Heekin's stock has been valued as of August 3 and October 25, 1954, in blocks of 30,000 and 40,002 shares respectively, as follows: $10, originally, by two donors and the executor of the third; $7.50, in amended returns; $7.88 by one expert of plaintiffs (upon which valuation plaintiffs now stand); $9.50 and $9.65 respectively by plaintiffs' second expert; $11.76 and $9.47 respectively by plaintiffs' third expert; $16 and $15.25 respectively by defendant's expert; $21.85 and $21.35 respectively by defendant in these proceedings; and $24 by the Commissioner of Internal Revenue.

---

7. Earnings $ 22.50 × .5 =   11.25
   Dividend yield 13.33 × .3 =   4.00
   Book value 33.00 × .2 =   6.6
                                                                                  21.85

8. This $24 value resulted from a study by the Commissioner of 11 comparatives. Their price to book value ratio was 1.4; price to average earnings, 14.3; price to current earnings, 13; and price to current dividends, 31.1.

Applying these ratios to Heekin, 1.4 times book value of $33.23 as of December 31, 1954, equals $46.52 per share. Average earnings for a 5-year period of $1.68 per share times 14.3 equals $24.02 per share. Current earnings times 13 equals $17.16 a share. Price to current dividend equals $15.55 per share.

In addition, in 1954 National Can purchased Pacific Can and the Commissioner analyzed the sale price for comparative purposes. The sales price came to 12.5 times Pacific's earnings. Application of that ratio to Heekin's 1953 earnings would price Heekin's stock at $24.38 per share. Pacific's price also represented 17 times its average 1949–1953 earnings. Application of such ratio to Heekin would price its stock at $28.39 per share. Further, Pacific's price bore a ratio of 1.6 to book value. Application of such ratio to Heekin's stock would price it at $53.17 per share.

The proper use of the comparative appraisal method, applying the principles already indicated, should provide a reasonably satisfactory valuation guide in these cases. In its application, it would under all the circumstances herein involved appear appropriate to select the three factors of (1) earnings, (2) dividends and dividend-paying capacity, and (3) book value, as being the important and significant ones to apply....

As to earnings, an examination of them for the periods from 1950 to June 30 and September 30, 1954, which are the most recent periods in relation to the gift dates, would be most representative. For this purpose, the annual profit and loss statements, plus the Company's interim balance sheets, from which can be derived with reasonable accuracy the Company's earnings for the 12-month periods ending June 30 and September 30, 1954 (thus eliminating distortions due to seasonal factors), are the starting points. As stated, it would then be proper to make such adjustments therein as would be necessary to eliminate abnormal and nonrecurring items and to redistribute items of expense to their proper periods. In these cases, this normalizing process would require (a) the elimination from the years 1950 to 1952 of the abnormal, nonrecurring losses incident to its financing subsidiary, which had been completely liquidated by 1952; (b) the elimination of the abnormally large 1951 profits due to the Korean war; (c) the redistribution of the expenses attributable to the establishment subsequent to 1951 of a retirement plan, which expenses, although borne in later years, were also applicable to 1950 and 1951, thereby overstating 1950 and 1951 profits and similarly depressing 1953 and 1954 profits; (d) the shift from 1954 to 1951 of a renegotiation refund paid with respect to excessive 1951 profits; (e) the elimination from 1954 of the abnormally large charge relating to the accrual in 1954 of certain expenses actually attributable to 1955, as hereinabove explained, and which resulted in the doubling up of 2 years of such expenses in 1954, as permitted by a then recent change in the tax laws. The method adopted in making these adjustments, and the adjusted profit figures resulting therefrom, are set forth in detail in finding 47.

As indicated, it would then be appropriate to give due consideration and weight to the trend of such earnings. Greater weight should fairly be given to the most recent years and periods. The method adopted in finding 48 of assigning greater weight to the later periods is a reasonably accurate one, and indicates that as of June 30 and September 30, 1954, Heekin's reasonably expected annual earnings per share would be $1.93 and $1.79, based on average annual earnings of $491,460.86 and $454,492.82, respectively.

As to dividends and dividend-paying capacity, it has already been indicated that as of the gift dates, it could reasonably be expected that Heekin would continue to pay in the foreseeable future its usual 50-cent annual dividend. Indeed, on its aforesaid earnings basis, this would appear to be a conservative distribution. However, while the declaration by the board of directors of a small increase might have been considered a possibility—a 10-cent increase would, for instance, result in a corporate outlay of only $25,412 on the 254,125 shares outstanding—it seems clear, nevertheless, that no substantially larger payment, at least for some time to come, could reasonably have been anticipated. Heekin's equipment was, as shown, not modern and the Company was in need of relatively large sums for equipment and plant modernization if it hoped to continue to be a competitive factor in the industry. For such a program, the Company would have to depend almost entirely on retained earnings. A further limitation on the Company's dividend-paying capacity was its repayment obligations on its long-term debt. Annual installments on principal of $150,000 had to be made through 1965, plus 20 percent of the net income (less $150,000) for the preceding year.

As to book value, the Company's balance sheets showed the book value per share to be, conservatively, $33.15 and $33.54 as of June 30 and September 30, 1954, respectively (findings 51–53). These statements also showed the Company to be in a current sound financial condition. As of June 30, 1954, current assets alone, amounting to almost $8,700,000, far exceeded its total liabilities of approximately $4,700,000, including its long-term debt. Its ratio of current assets to current liabilities was 3.17 to 1.

With the above basic data applicable to Heekin, it is then appropriate to select as closely comparable companies as is possible whose stocks are actively traded on an exchange, and to ascertain what ratios their market prices bear to their earnings, dividends, and book values. The application of such ratios to Heekin would then give a reasonable approximation of what Heekin's stock would sell for if it too were actively traded on an exchange.

A study of all the numerous companies considered by the experts as proper comparatives indicates that five of them, i.e., Pacific Can Company, United Can and Glass Company, National Can Corporation, Brockway Glass Co., Inc., and Thatcher Glass Manufacturing Co., Inc., are, while by no means perfect comparables, certainly at least reasonably satisfactory for the purpose in question. The detailed reasons for their selection are set forth in finding 57. In size they all fall generally into Heekin's class, and the nature of their operations is also comparable. In addition, five companies give a sufficiently broad base. Such companies as American Can, Continental Can, and Crown Cork & Seal, for the reasons already indicated, are eliminated (finding 56).

After similarly computing the earnings, as adjusted, of the comparatives for the same periods as for Heekin, and similarly weighting them to give effect to the trend factor, the average ratio of their market prices to their adjusted earnings as of August 3 and October 25, 1954 (the "price-earnings" ratio), was 9.45 and 9.84 to 1, respectively. Thus, on the basis only of earnings, Heekin's stock would similarly sell for $18.24 and $17.61 per share on such dates.

Similarly, the comparatives' dividend payments for the 12 months ending June 30 and September 30, 1954, after making some allowance for United's stock dividend, show an average percent yield of 3.50 and 3.56 respectively. Thus, on the basis only of dividend yield, Heekin's stock would similarly sell for $14.29 and $14.05 per share on August 3 and October 25, 1954, respectively (finding 65).

As to book value, the average market prices of the comparatives were 83.96 and 86.39 percent, respectively, of the book values of their common stocks on said dates. Thus, on the sole basis of the average relationship between such book values and market prices, Heekin's comparable market prices on said dates would be $27.83 and $28.98 (finding 67).

However, since the three factors of earnings, dividends, and book value are not entitled to equal weight, it becomes necessary to consider their relative importance in the case of a company such as Heekin. In this connection, plaintiffs' contention that in these cases no factor is to be considered of greater importance than dividend yield and that no investor would reasonably be expected to buy Heekin stock at a price which would afford a yield of less than 7 percent, cannot be accepted, not only for the reasons set forth above concerning the general relative importance of this factor but also because it is not supported by the specific data relating to the container industry as shown by the comparatives' yields. Investors were purchasing the stocks of comparable container companies which were yielding much less return than 7 percent. As shown, the average dividend yield of the five comparative companies was only around 3½ percent. Investors were purchasing Pacific Can at a price which afforded a yield of less than 3 percent. Indeed, they were purchasing National Can at more than $13 a share although it was paying no dividend at all.

Considering all the circumstances, it would appear appropriate to accept defendant's proposals in this respect and to consider earnings as entitled to 50 percent of the contribution to total value, and to give dividend yield (which in this case would appear to be substantially equivalent to dividend-paying capacity) 30 percent, and book value 20 percent, thereof. Cf. Bader v. United States, supra, in which the court gave 50 percent weight to earnings, and dividend the remaining 50 percent equally between the dividend yield and book value factors. Book value indicates how much of a company's net assets valued as a going concern stands behind each share of its stock and is therefore an important factor in valuing the shares. As defendant's expert pointed out, this is the factor that plays such a large part in giving a stock value during periods when earnings may vanish and dividends may be suspended. However, principally because book value is based upon valuing the assets as a going concern, which would not be realistic in the event of a liquidation of the corporation, a situation which a minority stockholder would be powerless to bring about in any event, and for the additional reasons set forth in finding 50, this factor is, in the case of a manufacturing company with a consistent earnings and dividend record, normally not given greater weight than the other two factors.

On the above percentage bases, the fair market value of Heekin's stock on August 3 and October 25, 1954, would be $18.98 and $18.83 respectively (finding 69).

These prices, however, assume active trading for Heekin's stock on an exchange, as was the situation with the comparatives. As shown, the closely held nature of, and the infrequent trading in, Heekin's stock resulted in a lack of marketability which would affect its market value. Equating the proper discount to be taken for this factor with the costs that would be involved in creating a market for the stock, a method which defendant concedes is reasonable, results in a deduction of approximately 12.17 percent for a company of Heekin's size and for blocks of 30,000 and 40,000 shares. On this basis, the fair market values of the Heekin stock as of August 3 and October 25, 1954, would be $16.67 and $16.54 respectively.

These are the values resulting largely from strictly formula and statistical applications. While such use of figures and formulas produces, of course, results which are of important significance, and may in certain instances be given conclusive weight, it is nevertheless recognized that determinations of fair market value can not be reduced to formula alone, but depend "upon all the relevant facts," including "the elements of common sense, informed judgment and reasonableness." The question of fair market value of a stock "is ever one of fact and not of formula" and evidence which gives "life to [the] figures" is essential.... The selection of comparatives has been a particularly troublesome problem in these cases. National Can's erratic earnings record, even though adjustments are attempted to normalize its situation, and its nonpayment of dividends, certainly weaken its position as a comparative, and suggest the desirability of an adjustment in the final market value figures set forth above. Pacific Can's sharp rise in price after August 3, 1954, justifies a similar adjustment for the October 25, 1954, valuation. While the inclusion of the glass container manufacturers with their higher dividend yields tends to neutralize somewhat the National Can situation, an adjustment downward would, in fairness to plaintiffs, nevertheless guard against their being prejudiced by the aforementioned selections of comparatives. Furthermore, while the sales of Heekin stock at $7.50 warrant, as hereinabove pointed out, only minimal consideration, the figures derived from the above formula give them no cognizance whatsoever.

Giving important weight to the figure of $16.67 produced by the application of the comparative appraisal method as applied herein, but viewing it in light of all the facts and circumstances involved in these cases, it is concluded that the fair market value of the 30,000 shares given on August 3, 1954, was $15.50 per share.

The market for stocks of the can and glass container manufacturing companies fell somewhat between August 3 and October 25, 1954, so that ordinarily on that basis as well as on the basis of Heekin's own financial and operating positions on October 25 as compared with August 3, a slightly lower value would be justified as of October 25 (although one of plaintiffs' experts felt that, insofar as Heekin stock is concerned, the same value should be applied to both dates, and another came out with a higher value for the second date). It seems clear, however, that the brightened prospects for increased business and profits resulting from the Company's decision in August 1954 to embark upon the beer can business and to satisfy further the demands of its largest customer for new products would, in Heekin's instance, tend to neutralize the market decline and to make its stock at least as valuable on October 25 as it had been on August 3. Accordingly, it is concluded that the fair market value of the 40,002 shares given on October 25, 1954, was also $15.50 per share.

A $15.50 valuation represents a price to adjusted earnings ratio on the gift dates of between 8 and 9 percent (somewhat less than the 9–10 percent average of the comparatives), a dividend yield of 3.23 percent (slightly less than the 3.5 percent average of the comparatives), and only 46 percent of book value (considerably less than the approximately 85 percent of the comparatives). On these bases, it is a figure that is fair to both sides.

Plaintiffs should consider that such a valuation prices the stock only at an amount representing the difference between current assets and total liabilities, including its long-term debt, as shown by its June 30, 1954, balance sheet. Thus, at such price, the value of the stock would be represented in whole by current assets, with no consideration whatsoever given to plant, equipment, or any other assets. As such, it would appear to be a conservative price indeed. Despite the difficulties under which it is laboring in a highly competitive industry, Heekin was, as of the valuation dates, a profitable, dividend-paying company, in sound financial condition, in an industry in which demand was at record levels, and in which it was forging ahead with relatively large investments in new fields holding bright prospects. Only a disregard of these favorable factors would warrant any lower valuation.

On the other hand, defendant should consider that such a valuation would give an investor a dividend yield of less than 3.5 percent on his investment, with little prospect of any significant increase in the foreseeable future. The fact that the Company was, on the gift dates, a relatively small one competing, with a comparatively old plant, against the giants of the industry operating at high efficiency with the most modern equipment, makes unwarranted a valuation of this closely held stock representing only a minority interest on any significantly higher basis. For these reasons also the $15.50 valuation is considered to be fair and just to both plaintiffs and defendant.

On this valuation basis, plaintiffs are entitled to recover, the amount of the recovery to be determined in accordance with Rule 38(c).

*   *   *

Notes and Questions

1. Prior Market Transactions and the Fair Market Value Standard: In *Central Trust*, several transactions involving the shares of Heekin Can Co. were executed. The court suggests that the plaintiff's experts relied too much on the share price established in these transactions. Why was the price established in these transactions not acceptable to the court? Were these not market prices? Consider how the fair market value standard relates to the court's decision regarding these transactions.

2. Calculating the Base Value: Several different financial variables were introduced as potential base values by the experts in *Central Trust*. The court criticized several aspects of these base values including their estimation and relative merits as proxies for future economic benefits. Return to the steps for estimating a capitalized value given in the section preceding the *Central Trust* case. In what ways did the experts fail to follow this procedure? What things did the experts do right? Which of the court's criticisms are valid?

3. Discounts for the Lack of Marketability: Marketability relates to the relative ease by which one can conduct transactions in the shares of a particular corporation. If shares of a particular corporation are traded on a widely recognized stock exchange, then it is probably fairly easy to buy and sell such shares. The ability to find a willing buyer with ease can be of great value to the holder of a company's shares because it makes his investments relatively more liquid. Individuals who purchase the shares of closely held corporations, on the other hand, tend to be relatively locked-in to their purchase decision. In general, it is safe to assume that most shareholders value liquidity and are willing to pay a premium for liquidity. Why? Alternatively, purchasers of closely held shares desire to be compensated for sacrificing liquidity by paying a lower purchase price relative to a comparable publicly traded share, all else being equal. Thus, it seems relatively clear that some discount for the lack of marketability is valid. How should the court measure marketability? Does marketability exist at varying degrees? Does the court's analysis contemplate such a continuum?

4. Qualitative Factors Affecting Value: What was the value to Heekin Can Co. of the human capital possessed by the Heekin Family? If this trial were about the Heekin family selling the company to the Smith family, would it be correct to arrive at the same value for share prices? What other qualitative factors might factor into the value of a company? In general, there are many potential factors affecting the value of a close corporation which are very difficult to quantify in any meaningful sense. Nonetheless, these factors clearly affect future economic benefit and, accordingly, some discount should be made.

Chapter V

Competition and Monopoly

This chapter provides an introduction to Industrial Organization Economics—the study of firm behavior under various market conditions ranging from perfect competition to monopoly. Earlier chapters have provided the foundation for materials covered here. Chapters I and III demonstrated that the basic supply-and-demand model can provide valuable insights regarding market reactions to changes in legal rules and regulations. A more in-depth appreciation of market reactions to legal constraints is found in understanding the rational behavior of market participants. Obviously, this can be of great importance in analyzing or crafting legal rules and regulations. In Chapter I, standard assumptions regarding individual utility maximization and firm profit maximization were introduced. In particular, the underlying assumptions of consumer choice were examined. In this chapter, some of the factors that determine an individual firm's response to changes in market conditions as well as changes in legal rules and regulations are examined in detail.

In Section A, the neoclassical theory of firm production, with its emphasis on the underlying relationships that determine costs of production, is developed. The firm's costs of production are central to the economic analysis of competition and monopoly presented in Sections B and D, respectively. In Sections B and C, two alternative conceptions of competition are developed. In Section B, the static and abstract model of perfect competition is presented as a useful analytical tool that provides a benchmark for the evaluation of markets exhibiting less-than-perfect competition. Unfortunately, the extremely abstract and restrictive assumptions of the model of perfect competition often times lead to inaccurate characterizations of real world competition. Thus, in Section C, a market process perspective is used to examine the dynamic competitive process that results from rivalrous behavior and entrepreneurship. Section D, which focuses on monopoly and monopolistic behavior, first explains the monopolist's profit maximizing price and quantity combination. This is followed by an examination of the social costs of monopoly in terms of the misallocation of resources that result from monopoly restrictions on quantity and the wasteful use of resources in the pursuit of monopoly power through government action. Section D then explores monopoly power as the ability to restrict the entry of potential competitors into the industry. This is followed by an introduction to cartel theory and the difficult problems faced by firms that attempt to increase their market power through collusive agreements to reduce output. Finally, section D concludes with an examination of a number of business practices—price fixing, price discrimination, and predatory pricing—that have been attacked as violations of the antitrust laws.

A. Costs of Production

Producers of any good or service are faced with the constant task of adjusting their output in response to changes in market demand. The effectiveness of a firm in responding to changes in market demand is in part determined by its ability to alter the quantity and mix of inputs used in its production process. In analyzing the ability of firms to alter input use, economists distinguish between the short-run and the long-run.

In the **short-run**, at least one input used in the production process cannot be altered. Inputs that can be altered within the short-run are called **variable resources**. Inputs that cannot be altered within the short-run are called **fixed resources**. Thus, in the short-run, firm output can be adjusted by changing the variable resources used, but some of the necessary resources are fixed and cannot be altered in response to changes in the desired output level. Traditionally, this distinction has led to a separation of the costs of production into two components: fixed and variable costs. **Fixed costs** are those that do not vary with the amount of output produced and must be paid even if output is zero. **Variable costs** are those that change based upon the amount of output produced and are equal to zero if output is zero.

In the **long-run**, all inputs used in the production process can be varied. Thus, in the long-run, there are no fixed resources—all inputs can be varied in response to a change in the desired level of output. Accordingly, all of the firm's costs of production are variable in the long-run.

1. Short-Run Production

The firms analyzed in this section have both fixed and variable costs. In the short-run, firms can respond to changes in demand by altering the level of variable resources employed, but not by changing the quantity of fixed resources. This fact leads to the most important concept in the analysis of short-run production decisions and costs—the law of diminishing marginal returns.

a. The Law of Diminishing Marginal Returns

Consider a hypothetical home construction company—Sam's Shacks. In its production of new homes, Sam's Shacks uses several different fixed inputs. Examples of Sam's fixed inputs include trucks, an office, and heavy equipment. For Sam's the most important variable input in the production of homes is labor. In the short run, as the market demand for new homes changes, Sam is able to alter his firm's output by increasing or decreasing the number of workers he employs. The most important decision that Sam must make is how many workers he should hire with his given level of fixed inputs.

When the construction season starts, Sam approaches the hiring of workers conservatively—Sam always starts by hiring one worker. As demand for new homes picks up, Sam realizes that this one worker can not complete all of the necessary work. As a result, Sam hires a second worker. After Sam hires the second worker, he always notices something unusual about the company's total level of output. When only one worker was employed, Sam's output was twenty square feet per day. However, by hiring a second worker, the total output of the company jumps to fifty square feet per day. In other words, the addition of a second worker more than doubles the total output of his company. Yet, Sam knows this increase in production has nothing to do with the inherent abilities of the second worker. Having taken an economics course in college, Sam wisely attributes this result to the division of labor and specialization. No longer does the single worker have to perform all of the tasks necessary to build a new home. Now, one worker spends her day doing carpentry while the other does electrical work. With each worker focused only on a single task, they become better at what they do—they become specialists.

As the building season progresses, Sam continues to notice unusual output results as he hires additional workers. For the first few workers employed, each additional worker adds more to total output than the one hired previously. Again, Sam wisely attributes this to the division of labor and specialization. However, Sam always seems to hit a point where each additional worker hired adds less and less to his company's total output. Sam is very confused by this. It seems as if he hits a point where the division of labor and specialization just doesn't add as much to the company's output.

The phenomenon that Sam witnesses as he hires additional workers is known as the law of diminishing marginal returns. The **law of diminishing marginal returns** states that, as additional quantities of a variable resource are added to a given amount of fixed resources, a point is eventually reached where each additional variable resource will add smaller and smaller amounts to total output. This law states an empirical fact. If it were not true, then Sam's Shacks would be able to produce an unlimited number of new homes by simply adding more and more labor (and other variable factors of production) to its fixed amount of equipment. When total output increases by greater amounts for each additional variable input added to the firm's fixed resources, the firm is said to be experiencing **increasing marginal returns**. Increasing marginal returns are, as Sam noted, caused by the division of labor and specialization.

The law of diminishing marginal returns can be demonstrated diagrammatically by studying the total and marginal product curves. **Total product** (TP) is the total output of goods or services produced by a firm. For Sam's, total product is measured in square feet of construction. **Marginal product** (MP) is the change in total product that results from a one unit change in variable resources—in this case each additional worker hired. Figure V-1 displays these two curves for Sam's Shacks Construction Company. The MP curve is graphed in panel (b). Each of the first four workers that Sam hires, adds more to TP than the worker hired previously. Thus, Sam's MP of labor increases for the first four units hired. This is reflected in panel (b) with a MP curve that increases over the first four units of labor. For each of the next five workers that Sam hires, marginal product becomes progressively smaller because of the law of diminishing marginal returns—each additional worker hired adds a smaller amount to total product. As a result, the MP curve declines over this range. If Sam hired so much labor that his total product actually decreased when he hired an additional worker, then the MP curve would drop below zero indicating that marginal product is negative.

The TP curve is graphed in panel (a). Note that when MP is increasing, TP grows at an increasing rate. However, as MP begins to decline because of the law

Figure V-1

The Law of Diminishing Marginal Returns
Product Curves for Sam's Shacks

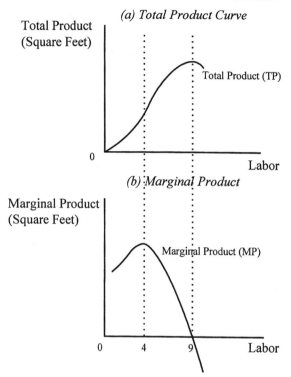

(a) Total Product Curve

Total Product
(Square Feet)

Total Product (TP)

0   Labor

(b) Marginal Product

Marginal Product
(Square Feet)

Marginal Product (MP)

0   4   9   Labor

of diminishing marginal returns, the TP curve begins to grow at a decreasing rate. Finally, as MP becomes negative, the TP curve begins to decline.

The law of diminishing marginal returns also suggests something about the economic reasoning that firms use in their determination of how much of any given variable resource to employ. As long as it is profitable to do so, firms employ variable inputs that have increasing marginal productivity. Such units add to a firm's total product at an increasing rate. Moreover, as marginal productivity begins to decline, firms may still continue to employ additional variable inputs because they still add to the total product of the firm—the increase is just occurring at a decreasing rate. However, when marginal productivity of additional variable inputs becomes negative, the firm stops employing variable inputs because these inputs actually decrease the total product of the company. Thus, even if variable inputs with negative marginal product were free, the firm would never employ them. It is economically rational for Sam to hire labor up to some point in the range of diminishing marginal returns. Exactly how many units of labor Sam will hire depends upon the cost of each additional unit and the market price for new homes.

b. Short-Run Costs

In order for a firm to know how much output to produce, it needs to know the marginal cost of producing more output as well as the price at which that output can be sold. It makes sense to produce an additional unit as long as the revenue generated from its sale exceeds its cost of production (MC). Marginal cost of production depends on the price of the variable resource *and its marginal product*.

Let us return to the example of Sam's Shacks in order to examine the relationship between costs and marginal productivity. For Sam's, MC first decreases and then increases. This pattern is a function of the law of diminishing marginal returns. Remember that for each of the first four workers employed, MP increases. Thus, fewer and fewer units of labor are required to produce an additional unit of output. This greater productivity causes MC to decrease as these four workers are employed. Furthermore, remember that marginal product decreases as Sam hires workers 5 through 9. In this range, more and more workers are required to produce an additional unit of output. This drop in marginal productivity causes the MC of production to start increasing. In other words, when diminishing marginal returns set in, the MC of production begins to increase. The relationship between marginal productivity and MC can be seen in Figure V-2(b). Notice that the MC curve is U-shaped. MC decreases because of increasing marginal returns and then increases because of diminishing marginal returns.

Figure V-2

Total and Marginal Cost Curves

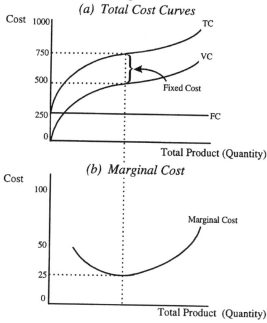

(a) Total Cost Curves

(b) Marginal Cost

Short-run cost curves describe the relationship between costs and output when there is at least one fixed input. The critical point in this analysis is that short-run costs are a function of the law of diminishing marginal returns. Seven different measures of short-run costs are of interest. First, **marginal cost (MC)** is the cost of producing each additional unit of output. Second, **fixed cost (FC)** is the price paid for inputs that cannot be varied in the short-run. This cost will be the same regardless of the level of output produced and will be incurred even if nothing is produced. Third, **variable cost (VC)** is equal to the price of the variable input multiplied by the quantity of the variable input used. Fourth, **total cost (TC)** is equal to the sum of fixed and variable costs — TC = FC + VC. Fifth, **average fixed cost (AFC)** is fixed cost divided by the firm's total output — AFC = FC ÷ Q. Sixth, **average variable cost (AVC)** is equal to variable costs divided by the firm's total output (Q) — AVC = VC ÷ Q. Seventh, **average total cost (ATC)** is the total cost of production divided by the firm's total output — ATC = TC ÷ Q. ATC is the per unit cost at a particular output level.

It is important to recognize that the cost curves reflect the explicit and implicit costs of production. Thus, fixed costs, such as the cost of a building or factory, include the rent or return that the building could earn in its next best alternative use. When all costs are covered, the firm is receiving a normal return on the fixed assets. Of course, the goal of most firms is to achieve more than a normal return.

Figure V-2 (a) also shows the FC curve for Sam's Shacks. Note that FC is represented by a horizontal line at the $250 level, demonstrating that FC does not vary with changes in output. VC is also graphed in Figure V-2 (a). This curve indicates that VC equals zero when output is zero. VC initially increases at a decreasing rate as the firm realizes increasing marginal returns, and then begins to increase at an increasing rate at the point where diminishing marginal returns sets in. The TC curve for Sam's is also shown in Figure V-2 (a). The TC curve is simply the vertical summation of the fixed and variable cost curves. Thus, the TC curve is the VC curve shifted upwards by the amount of FC.

Average cost data for Sam's Shacks graphed in Figure V-3 also reflect the law of diminishing marginal returns. The shape of the AVC curve is determined by

Figure V-3

Average and Marginal Cost Curves

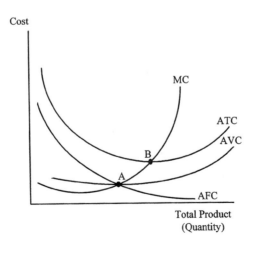

Total Product
(Quantity)

the shape of the MC curve. When MC is below AVC, AVC declines. When MC is above AVC, AVC begins to rise. The MC curve intersects the AVC curve at its minimum point—indicated by point A. This basic relationship is known as the **average-marginal rule.** The MC curve has the same relationship with the ATC curve as it did with the AVC curve—the MC curve will intersect the ATC curve at its minimum point—indicated by point B. AFC declines over the entire range of output. This reflects the fact that FC is spread over a larger total output as production expands.

2.   Long-Run Production

For many firms, the most important fixed input is their plant. The short-run shows the relationship between output and costs for a particular plant size. In the long-run, all inputs are variable, including plant size. Thus, one of the most important long-run decisions that the firm must make is the selection of the optimal plant size—the plant size that will minimize the long-run costs of producing the profit maximizing output.

a. Long-Run Costs

Assume that a particular manufacturer has five choices regarding plant size, and that the ATC curve for each of these plants is depicted in Figure V-4. The plant size that is best for a particular manufacturer depends on the level of output to be produced. For example, if output less than Q_1 needs to be produced, then the plant size that corresponds to ATC_1 is the optimal choice. For output choices between Q_1 and Q_2, ATC_2 is optimal. Likewise, for output between Q_2 and Q_3, ATC_3 is optimal. Thus, the optimal plant size for any given output can be found along the continuous portion of the five ATC curves in Figure V-4. The continuous portion of the five ATC curves in Figure V-4 are the basis for a new curve—the long-run average cost curve.

Figure V-4

Adjusting Plant Size to Minimize Cost

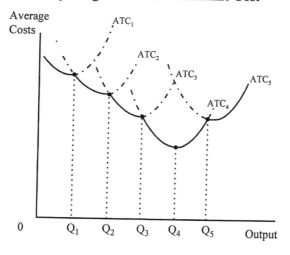

Long-run average cost (LRAC) is the lowest per unit cost of producing any level of output when the firm can choose from all possible plant sizes. For the firm in Figure V-4, the continuous portion of the ATC curves represent the LRAC curve where only five possible plant sizes are available. Figure V-5 shows a smooth LRAC curve. This curve represents the lowest per unit cost of producing any level of output when a firm can choose from an infinite number of possible plant sizes. Notice that this smooth LRAC curve is tangent to an infinite number of short-run ATC curves. As the LRAC curve slopes downward, it is tangent to the short-run ATC curves before the point of minimum cost for each plant size; as the LRAC curve slopes upward, it is tangent to the short-run ATC curves past the point of minimum cost. At the lowest point on the LRAC curve, the LRAC curve is tangent to the minimum point on a short-run ATC curve. Figure V-5, also depicts the long run marginal cost curve. **Long-run marginal cost** (LRMC) is the change in *total cost* that results from a one unit increase in production. This reflects the fact that, in the long-run, all resources are variable. Thus, everything from labor to plant size is incorporated into the LRMC number. As is the case with short-run average costs curves, LRMC intersects long-run average curves at their minimum point. Thus, as long as LRMC is below LRAC, LRAC will decrease. When LRMC is greater than LRAC, LRAC will increase.

b. Economies, Diseconomies, and Minimum Efficient Scale

The LRAC curve is U-shaped over the full range of possible levels of output. This shape is the result of two opposing production relationships—economies of scale and diseconomies of scale. **Economies of scale** cause LRAC to decrease as the firm's output increases. There are several potential sources of economies of scale. First, as output expands, the opportunities for specialization and division of labor increase. Second, firms often learn how to reduce the costs of production after gaining some experience in actually producing the product. In other words,

Figure V-5

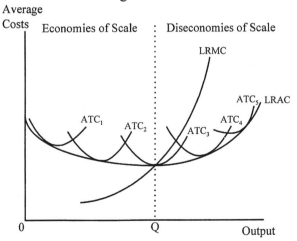

Long-Run Average Total Cost
& Marginal Cost Curves

as the firm's output grows, managers and employees gain more and more experience with the production process and hence learn more efficient production techniques. Third, as output expands, firms can begin to take advantage of mass production technology. The combination of these factors helps to explain why
LRAC decreases as output approaches Q from the left in Figure V-5.

Diseconomies of scale begin to set in as the firm's output grows larger. Diseconomies of scale arise primarily as a result of the fact that, at some point, the
firm grows too large for its managers to control. As firm output expands, more
employees and managers are hired, which increases the firm's bureaucracy. As
this bureaucracy grows, communication becomes difficult and decision making
can grind to a halt. Eventually, the diseconomies outweigh the economies of
scale. Thus, in Figure V-5, LRAC increases as output expands to the right of Q.

Economies of scope exist when the joint production of multiple outputs is
more cost efficient than producing each output separately. For example, the provision of both savings and checking accounts by the same bank is more cost efficient
than having bank A provide checking and bank B provide savings. Imagine the
amount of duplication that is avoided by having one bank provide both savings
and checking accounts. When such economies arise, one firm would produce both
outputs rather than two firms each producing only one. Moreover, it would be a
better use of resources for a single firm to produce both outputs, because to do so
would minimize the total opportunity cost of the resources used in production.

In Figure V-5, LRAC came to a unique minimum point at Q. This implies
that there is one specific plant size — output level — that minimizes the costs of
production in the long-run. The LRAC curve does not have to decrease to a
unique minimum point however. Two other types of LRAC curves can be observed. First, Figure V-6(a) depicts a LRAC curve that is exhibiting constant returns to scale. **Constant returns to scale** occur when long-run average cost does
not change as output expands over some range. In Figure V-6(a), economies of

Figure V-6

Alternative LRAC Curves

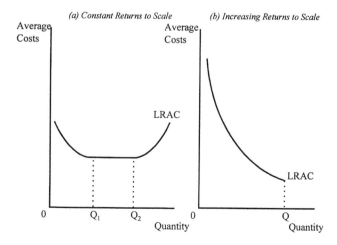

scale exist to the left of Q_1, constant returns to scale exist between Q_1 and Q_2, and diseconomies of scale exist to the right of Q_2. Constant returns to scale indicate that firms can produce at output levels between Q_1 and Q_2 without a difference in per unit costs.

Another LRAC cost curve of interest is one that exhibits increasing returns to scale, as depicted in Figure V-6(b). **Increasing returns to scale** occur when LRAC decreases continually as output expands, indicating that economies of scale persist over all levels of output. This LRAC curve would indicate that the larger the firm, the better. In fact, such a curve suggests that a single firm would supply the entire industry output at the lowest average cost in the long-run. Industries such as electricity, gas, and water are often assumed to exhibit LRAC curves with increasing returns to scale.

Much of our discussion thus far has been concerned with identifying the minimum point on the LRAC curve. The output level which minimizes LRAC is called the **minimum efficient scale**. Minimum efficient scale can have a large impact on the number of firms that compete in a particular industry. When minimum efficient scale can be achieved at low levels of output, relative to industry demand, many firms will be able to enter the industry. On the other hand, if minimum efficient scale can be reached only at levels of output that constitute a large portion of the entire market demand, then only a few firms will compete in the industry. In the case of a LRAC curve that exhibits decreasing returns to scale over the entire range of industry output, minimum efficient scale occurs at the right end of the curve — thus, only one firm will supply the industry output. When it is most efficient for one firm to supply the entire industry output, the firm is said to be a **natural monopoly**.

In addition to considering the level of output at which LRAC reaches minimum efficient scale, insight into the nature of an industry can be gained by studying the slope of the LRAC curve to the left of minimum efficient scale. When the slope of the LRAC curve is rather flat, it indicates that the cost advantages of producing at minimum efficient scale are not all that great. Thus, in industries with relatively flat LRAC curves, firms may be able to compete at all levels of output. On the other hand, when the slope of the LRAC curve is very steep, it indicates that the cost advantages of producing at minimum efficient scale are more significant.

3. Changes in Costs of Production

Changes in the cost of producing any good or service cause the cost curves to shift by an amount reflective of the change in cost. In general, there are four important sources of change in the costs of production: (1) changes in the cost of inputs; (2) changes in excise taxes; (3) changes in government regulation; and (4) changes in production technology. When the costs of production increase, the MC curve shifts to the left; when the costs of production decrease, the MC curve shifts to the right. Similarly, when the costs of production increase, the ATC curve shifts up; when the costs of production decrease, the ATC curve shifts down.

Consider Figure V-7, which shows two sets of MC and ATC curves for some firm — MC_1, MC_2, ATC_1, and ATC_2. If the cost of an input used in the production of this firm's goods or services increases, the MC curve shifts to the left. This

Figure V-7

The Effect of a Decrease in Resource Prices on Costs

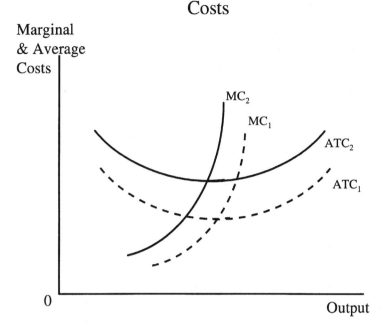

can be seen in Figure V-7 as a shift from MC_1 to MC_2. Furthermore, increased input costs force the ATC curve to shift up from ATC_1 to ATC_2. An increase in the excise tax shifts the MC and ATC curves in the same way. Changes in regulation that increase the costs of compliance, impact the costs of production in a similar manner. Technology, on the other hand, rarely moves backwards and therefore it is unlikely to see an increase in the cost of production due to a loss of technology. Improvements in technology cause the MC curve to shift to the right, indicating a decrease in the costs of production—movement from MC_2 to MC_1 in Figure V-7. Likewise, the ATC curve shifts down from ATC_2 to ATC_1.

4. Profits and the Costs of Production

Costs of production information is very important to the individual firm because it plays a critical role in determining the profit maximizing level of output. To fully understand firm behavior, the cost of production analysis must be combined with the conception of economic profit introduced in Chapter I. Economic profits are important because they play both a signaling and incentivizing role in the allocation of scarce resources. Chapter I defined economic profit as being equal to total revenue minus total costs, where total costs include both the explicit and implicit (opportunity) costs of production.

When total revenue is equal to total costs of production, economic profit is zero because the revenue is just covering the opportunity cost of the resources used. Another way to state this concept is that the firm is earning a normal profit or normal return—that is, the same return that the resources would earn if they were employed in their next best alternative use—when economic profit is zero. Often firms earning an accounting profit are actually suffering an economic loss because their accounting costs do not include payments for some resources used in the production process. For example, if a business firm owns the building that houses its offices and does not pay rent or recognize that it could receive rent by leasing the building to another business, then the firm's accounting profits will be greater than its economic profits. Economic profits (or above-normal profits) attract new competitors to an industry. Economic losses (or below-normal profits) encourage firms to look for better opportunities in other industries.

Because firms in all industry structures are assumed to be profit maximizers, they are expected to behave in a way that maximizes the difference between total revenue and total costs. The general profit maximizing rule is that firms should produce at the output level where MR=MC.

B. The Competitive Market

Competition occupies a central role in the economic analysis of firm activity. In general, the effects of competition are seen as highly desirous and beneficial to our overall welfare. In this section, the structural characteristics of competitive markets are examined. These structural characteristics are enumerated in the model of perfect competition. The perfectly competitive market is a theoretical model demonstrating the price and output decisions that should occur when there is no resistance to mutually beneficial exchange. In other words, in a perfectly competitive market, all possible mutually beneficial exchanges are realized. In this sense, the model represents a static ending point in which no individual or firm has any reason to buy or sell. This model is often used as a benchmark for analyzing real world markets.

A perfectly competitive industry structure is defined by the following four characteristics. First, there are a large number of anonymous buyers and sellers in the market, each of whom buys or sells only a very small portion of the total amount exchanged in the market. Second, the goods or services produced are completely homogenous—the product of firm A is identical to the product of firm B. Third, firms and resources can enter or exit the market with zero resistance. Fourth, both buyers and sellers have full information regarding prices, availability, location and production technology. Thus, no firm has an incentive to invest in improving technology because such innovations can be immediately imitated. Furthermore, no firm has an incentive to advertise because all products and prices are alike.

When all of these conditions exist, no individual firm will have meaningful control over the price it can charge. Intuitively, this makes sense. The firm's output is so small relative to the market that its individual transactions do not affect the market price. Furthermore, because all products are identical and market participants have complete information, no individual firm can raise its price

Figure V-8

The Firm's Demand Curve &
Market Equilibrium in Perfect Competition

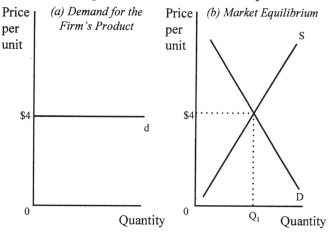

without losing all of its sales. If firm A tries to raise its price, consumers already know about firm B that sells an identical product at the lower price. Because individual firms in a perfectly competitive market have no control over price, they are said to be **price takers**. Firms in a perfectly competitive market must offer their goods and services for sale at whatever price is established by the interaction of market demand and supply.

1. Short-Run Individual Firm Behavior: Profit Maximization

The perfectly competitive firm as a price taker is illustrated graphically in Figure V-8. Market demand and supply appear in panel (b) and the demand curve for the output of a single firm is shown in panel (a). In panel (b), market demand and supply intersect at a price of $4.00 per unit. This market price is the price that the perfectly competitive firm must accept. Thus, the demand curve for a single competitive firm is a horizontal line drawn at the level of the market price—$4.00. Recall from the discussion of demand elasticity in Chapter III that a horizontal demand curve signifies totally elastic demand. If the firm were to try to raise its price above $4.00, its output would drop to zero. At the market price, the firm can sell as much as it can produce. A profit maximizing firm would never sell below the market price because it can already sell as much as it wants at the market price. Firms that face totally elastic demand have no power over price—no market power.

Firms in a perfectly competitive market attempt to maximize economic profit. Although a firm in a perfectly competitive industry has no control over price, it does control its level of output. Thus, the perfectly competitive firm must find that level of output that maximizes profits. **Profit maximization** occurs at the level of output where the difference between total revenue (TR) and total costs

Figure V-9   Profit-Maximizing Output for a Purely Competitive Firm

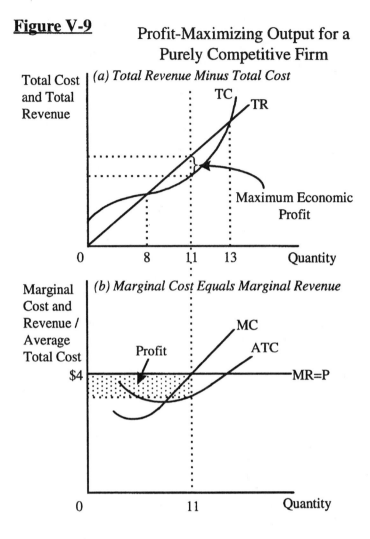

(TC) is maximized. **Total revenue** is equal to the market price multiplied by the quantity of output sold. Figure V-9(a) can be used to illustrate the profit maximizing decision making process. As each additional unit is sold, the firm earns additional revenue equal to $4.00. Thus, the TR curve is a straight line which increases $4.00 for every additional unit of output sold. The TC curve first increases at a decreasing rate—increasing marginal returns—and then increases at an increasing rate—diminishing marginal returns. Figure V-9(a) shows that TC exceeds TR at output levels below 8 and above 13. Thus, if the firm were to produce less than 8 or more than 13 units of output, it would incur an economic loss. Figure V-9(a) also shows that TR exceeds TC at output levels between 8 and 13. It follows then that an economic profit can be earned by the firm when it produces at any level between 8 and 13 units of output. However, economic profits are maximized when the vertical distance between the TR curve and the

TC curve is maximized. This profit maximizing result occurs at an output of 11 units in Figure V-9(a).

In addition to comparing the TR and TC of a firm, the profit maximizing output can also be determined by comparing a firm's MC and marginal revenue (MR) at various output levels. **Marginal revenue** is the change in total revenue for a one unit change in output. In a perfectly competitive market, the firm can sell as many additional units as it likes at the market price (P) because the firm is a price taker. Therefore, the market price represents the marginal revenue gained by the firm when it sells an additional unit of output. Thus, for firms in a perfectly competitive industry, marginal revenue equals price—MR = P.

Common sense tells us that the firm should continue to produce additional units of output as long as the gain in TR exceeds the gain in TC. In other words, a firm will continue to produce additional units as long as the MR from producing an additional unit exceeds its MC. This method for determining the profit maximizing level of output is illustrated in Figure V-9(b), which shows the MR and MC curves for a firm in a perfectly competitive market. The MR curve is a horizontal line at $4.00 reflecting the fact that the firm is a price taker and will earn $4.00 in MR for each additional unit sold. The MC curve is U-shaped reflecting the law of diminishing marginal returns. ATC is U-shaped, which illustrates its relationship with MC—the average-marginal rule.

Consider the output decisions available to the profit maximizing firm faced with these MR and MC curves. At output levels from 0 to 10 MR > MC. Thus, the firm can increase profits by producing additional units. At any output level greater than 11, MC > MR and profits are increased by cutting back output. When the firm produces 11 units of output, MR = MC. At this level of output, the firm would incur an economic loss if it expanded production and would sacrifice profits if output was reduced—the firm can do no better than produce 11 units. More generally, the profit maximizing level of output for all firms occurs where MR = MC. The amount of profit that the firm will earn at this level of production can be determined by multiplying the vertical difference between P and ATC by total output. Profit is shown by the shaded area in Figure V-9(b).

2. Loss Minimization: The Shut-Down Decision

Whenever market price falls below a firm's ATC, the firm will incur an economic loss. This loss will be equal to the difference between ATC and price multiplied by output—(P − ATC)Q. In the short-run, the firm has two options: First, it can continue to operate and attempt to minimize losses; second, it can shut down and suffer losses equal to its FC.

Because the firm has both fixed and variable costs in the short run, it is possible to incur smaller losses by operating than by shutting down. When a firm shuts down, it will suffer an economic loss equal to its FC. The shut down solution may not always be the best, however. The profit maximizing firm will make its decision on whether to operate in the face of economic losses based upon the relationship between market price and AVC. If price exceeds AVC, then the revenue generated by the firm will cover all VC and some revenue will be left over.

Figure V-10

Loss Minimization: The Shutdown Decision

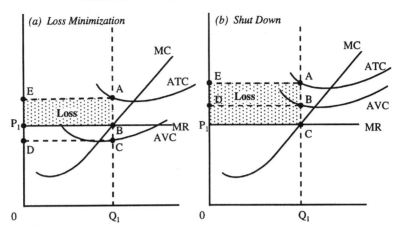

This residual revenue is applied to FC. By continuing to operate, the firm's economic loss is less than its FC.

Figure V-10(a) demonstrates how to derive the loss minimizing result via marginal analysis. The figure shows the MC, ATC, AVC, and MR curves for a perfectly competitive firm. The loss minimizing level of output is found by increasing production as long as MR > MC. This MR = MC rule is subject to one limitation. Namely, the MR and MC curves must intersect—be equal—at a point above the AVC curve. Recall that the vertical distance between the ATC and AVC curves is equal to AFC: recall that FC = AFC(Q). Thus, when price moves above AVC, revenue cuts into some portion of the AFC that lies between ATC and AVC. In Figure V-10(a), the loss minimizing strategy is indeed met where MR = MC at Q_1 units of output. Total revenue generated at this level of output is equal to the area P_1BQ_10. Because the firm is able to cover all of its VC and a portion of its FC it is better off not shutting down. The economic loss is equal to (ATC-P)Q.

The case for shutting down is considered in Figure V-10(b). Notice that at Q_1, P_1 < AVC, AFC > ATC – AVC, total revenue ($0P_1CQ_1$) earned by the firm does not cover variable costs ($0DBQ_1$), and losses (P_1EAC) are greater than fixed costs (ABDE). The rational firm will minimize losses by shutting down and incurring losses only equal to FC.

3. The Short-Run Supply Curve

The perfectly competitive firm considers three factors in determining its profit maximizing level of output: (1) price (where P = MR); (2) marginal cost (MC); and (3) average variable cost (AVC). As P changes, the firm will produce the quantity where P = MC as long as P is above AVC. This relationship can be seen in Figure

<u>Figure V-11</u>

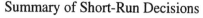

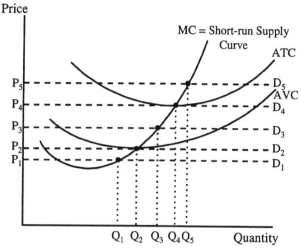

Summary of Short-Run Decisions

V-11. At P_5, P > ATC and the firm earns positive economic profits. At P_4, P = ATC of production and the firm earns a normal economic profit. At P_3, AVC < P < ATC, the firm seeks to minimize its economic loss by continuing to operate. At P_2, P = AVC, the firm is indifferent between shutting down with a loss equal to its FC or producing an output just sufficient to cover VC. Regardless of whether the firm produces or shuts down at this price level, the economic loss is equal to FC. Finally, P_1 < AVC and, thus, the firm will produce zero output in order to minimize economic losses. The above analysis leads us to an important conclusion regarding the perfectly competitive firm's MC curve in the short-run. For the perfectly competitive firm, the portion of the MC curve that lies above the AVC curve is the firm's short-run supply curve. Thus, in the short-run, firms minimize losses or maximize profits by adjusting their output subject to their MC curve.

4. Long-Run Firm Behavior: Industry Supply

In the long-run, all resources can be varied—there are no fixed inputs or fixed costs—and firms are capable of expanding or contracting their plant size as well as entering or exiting an industry. In the short-run, firms are capable of earning economic profits because new firms cannot construct plants and enter the market and existing firms cannot expand production beyond the capacity of current plants. In the long-run, economic profits attract new firms to the market and encourage existing firms to expand their plant and output. As firms move into industries earning positive economic profits, industry supply expands. The result of this increase in supply is to force the market price down. As the market price drops, so do economic profits. In the long-run, the entry of firms into industries earning positive economic profits eliminates those profits.

A short-run economic loss will have a similar impact on the industry in the long-run. Firms suffering from an economic loss will observe other industries that are either making a normal return or a positive economic return. The rational response for these firms is to transfer their resources to a more profitable use. In the long-run, profit maximizing firms exit industries with short-run economic losses. As firms leave the industry, industry supply decreases. This decrease in supply causes the price for the good or service in that industry to increase. This process continues until supply contracts to the point that a normal profit is earned by the remaining firms.

The tendency for perfectly competitive firms to earn only a normal profit in the long-run, is at the core of understanding long-run production decisions. As firms enter or exit a market, they impact industry supply and market price. The process of entry or exit will continue, in the long-run, until the market supply curve intersects the market demand curve at a price that is equal to the lowest point on each firm's LRAC curve. At any price that does not meet this condition, further adjustments to market supply will occur. A price above the minimum point on the LRAC curve will result in economic profits, attracting more firms or expanded output to the industry. On the other hand, a price below the minimum point on the LRAC curve would indicate that economic losses were being incurred. This would encourage additional firms to exit or cut back on production.

In this quest to maximize economic profits in the long-run, firms vary their scale of production until their average costs of production are minimized. Figure V-12 demonstrates the equilibrium position at which the firm will earn a normal

Figure V-12
Long-Run Equilibrium for the Firm
& the Industry

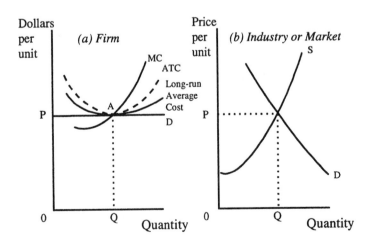

profit. At point A, the firm's MC, short-run average total cost (SRATC), and LRAC are all equal. At this point, no firm in the industry has a reason to alter its output, and no firm outside of the industry has an incentive to enter the market.

Further insight into the long-run adjustment process can be gained by considering a specific example. For purposes of this example, assume that the costs of production do not change based on the number of firms in the industry. Figure V-13(b) shows a perfectly competitive market in equilibrium at point A. Here, S_1 intersects D_1 and equilibrium price and quantity are P_1 and Q_1 respectively. Consider what occurs as a result of an increase in demand for the industry product in the short-run. In Figure V-13(b) this is represented by movement to point B as demand shifts from D_1 to D_2. In the short-run, equilibrium price is P_2. Figure V-13(a) demonstrates the reaction of individual firms to this increase in demand. At P_2, MR > MC at the original level of production, q_1. Thus, the profit maximizing firms will increase output along their short-run supply curve, up to the point where MR = MC. For this particular firm, MR = MC after the demand shift at an output of q_2. As all firms in the industry respond in this way to the price increase, industry supply will increase to Q_2 in panel (b). Note that in the short-run, each firm is earning an economic profit equal to the area P_2EFG.

In the long-run, the firms' economic profits disappear because of the entry of new firms into the industry. Firms who are in industries earning a normal profit or an economic loss have an incentive to switch their productive resources to industries in which positive economic profits are being earned. The entry of these new firms causes the supply of the industry product to increase. New firms will continue to enter and industry supply will increase as long as individual firms in the industry are capable of earning economic profits. Thus, in the long-run, equilibrium moves from point B to point C as supply shifts from S_1 to S_2. At this

Figure V-13

Long-Run Adjustment to an Increase in Demand

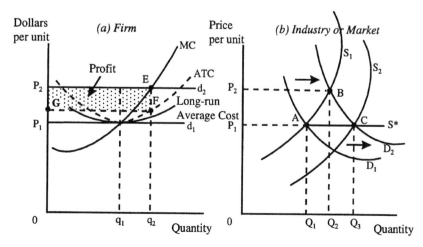

point, equilibrium quantity has increased to Q_3 and equilibrium price is once again P_1.

The effect on the individual firm of the decrease in price that results from new firms entering the industry can be seen in Figure V-13(a). The fall in the market price causes the demand curve faced by the individual firm to decline from d_2 to d_1. As a result, the firm reduces output from q_2 to q_1. At this equilibrium price and quantity combination, the firm earns only a normal profit. In other words, the individual firm's marginal cost, price (marginal revenue), and long-run average cost are equal and the long-run average cost curve is at a minimum—MC = MR = P = LRAC. In the long-run, the price of a good or service is determined by the minimum point on the firm's long-run average cost curve. Despite the fact that industry output increases from Q_1 to Q_3, individual firm output remains at q_1 in the long-run. Thus, the increase in industry output is supplied by the entry of new firms.

A decrease in demand has an opposite effect on both the industry and the individual firm. Figure V-14(b), shows the industry in equilibrium at point A, with demand curve, D_1, supply curve, S_1, market price, P_1, and quantity, Q_1. Point A represents the current long-run equilibrium, where MC = MR = SRATC = LRAC. The equilibrium condition for the firm is shown in Figure V-14(a).

Let us suppose that demand in this industry suddenly decreases. This decrease is seen as a shift in demand from D_1 to D_2. This decline in demand causes the market price to decrease to P_2—the market is now in equilibrium at point B in the short-run. Because of the decrease in market price, the demand curve facing the individual firm declines. This event can be seen in Figure V-14(a) as movement from d_1 to d_2. Again, the firm will determine the level of output to produce by identifying the point at which MR = P = MC. This causes individual firms to cut production from q_1 to q_2. As a result of each individual firm cutting

Figure V-14
Long-Run Adjustment to a Decrease in Demand

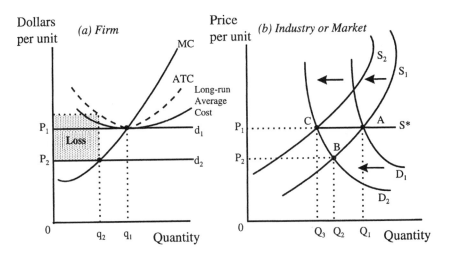

back output in the short-run, industry-wide output declines from Q_1 to Q_2. This is a change in the quantity supplied which is indicated by movement along the supply curve from point A to point B. Thus, the market is now in equilibrium at point B, with an output of Q_2 and a price P_2.

At this lower price, the firm is selling q_2 units at a price below the average total cost of production. In other words, the firm operates at a loss equal to the vertical difference between the ATC curve and the demand curve at q_2 multiplied by total output, q_2. This is the shaded portion of Figure V-14(a). In the long-run, these losses force some firms to exit the industry. As these firms leave, market supply decreases. Firms will continue to exit the market until the supply curve has shifted from S_1 to S_2. In the long-run, the market will be in equilibrium at point C, where S_2 and D_2 intersect. As a result of these changes, industry output has declined to Q_3 and market price has returned to P_1. At this new equilibrium position, marginal cost, price (marginal revenue), short-run average total cost, and long-run average cost are equal—P = MC = SRATC = LRAC. In other words, individual firms in the industry are once again earning a normal profit. As was the case with an increase in demand, after long-run adjustments, individual firms again produce an output of q_1—the same output as before the change in demand. However, market output has declined from Q_1 to Q_3. The decline in industry output came as the result of firms exiting the market and not as a result of cuts in the remaining firms' production.

The above analysis considered the response of an industry and its individual firms to a change in demand. In the short-run, firms responded by changing the quantity supplied to the market—movement along their marginal cost curve. In the long-run, however, firms entered or exited the industry until a new short-run supply curve was established that returned individual firms to a normal profit. The long-run supply curve for any particular industry can be identified by connecting the points of long-run equilibrium. This can be seen in Figure V-13(b) and V-14(b) as the horizontal line marked S*. This long-run supply curve is horizontal and, thus, totally elastic. This implies that as output expands, the costs of production do not increase because in the long-run, firms do not need a price increase to supply the additional output. This type of industry is known as a **constant cost industry** because it can expand without affecting the prices of the resources it employs.

A constant cost industry is usually one in which the industry consumes only a small portion the total amount of a particular productive resource available in the market. The producers of golf tees are an example of a constant cost industry. A large increase in the demand for golf tees is not likely to cause the market price of timber to increase. The production of golf tees utilizes only a small portion of all wood that is available as a productive input.

Increasing cost industries are industries where increasing output in the long-run leads to an increase in the costs of production. Because the costs of some resources increase as output expands in these industries, individual firms' cost curves shift upward. Thus, long-run supply curves for increasing cost industries have a positive slope. **Decreasing cost industries** experience lower production costs as output increases in the long-run. This decrease in the cost of production causes a downward shift in the individual firms' cost curves. Thus, such firms experience downward sloping supply curves in the long-run. Regardless of the effect of expanding output on the costs of production, the long-run conclusion is always the same. Individual firms in perfectly competitive markets can earn economic profits in the short-run, but the entry or exit of firms in the long-run results in a normal economic profit.

5. The Economic Benefits of Competition

When firms produce exactly the goods that consumers desire most at the lowest possible price, they are said to be achieving **allocative efficiency**. Perfect competition results in allocative efficiency. The market demand curve reflects the consumers' value for each additional unit of consumption, and the value attached to the last unit of output purchased by consumers is equal to the market price. In the perfectly competitive model, market price equals the marginal cost of the last unit producers are willing to supply. Furthermore, marginal cost is defined as a measure of the opportunity cost of the resources used in the production of each additional unit. By putting together the fact that the marginal benefit consumers attach to the last unit consumed is equal to the marginal opportunity cost of the resources used to produce that same unit, the last unit produced is valued as much or more than any other good or service that could have been produced using those same resources. In other words, resources could not be reallocated, in any way, in order to increase the value of output to society. That is, allocative efficiency is achieved—and social welfare is maximized—in perfectly competitive industries

The perfect competition model provides a **competitive benchmark** for the economic analysis of other industry structures. In general, industry production at the quantity where P = MC provides a benchmark for comparing an industry's performance with the allocative efficiency of the ideal perfectly competitive market.

The model for competition causes market price to reflect the value of the resources that are used in the production of a product. This is important because prices are the most important signal in guiding the allocation of resources. If prices are distorted by a lack of competition, then the allocation of resources that results is less than efficient. In order to make sure that the role of competition in determining accurate prices is absolutely clear, consider the following example.

Suppose, in the beginning, everyone in a small town bakes his or her own bread. One day a baker moves into town and decides that there is a profit to be made by baking bread for others. The baker adds all the expenses for a loaf of bread, including labor time, plus a premium for risk bearing, and determines that this cost should be the price to charge customers. Many people in town decide that it is cheaper to buy bread than to bake it themselves, and use their increased time to produce other products. Those people who do not produce other products or services with their time continue to bake their own bread. After a while, the baker determines that she could make more profit by exerting her market power and raising her price. Although some customers would return to baking their own bread, the additional revenue gained from the loaves sold would more than make up for the lost sales volume.

Although it may appear that the increase in profits to the baker is simply a transfer of wealth from her customers and that there is no net effect on society, there is a hidden efficiency loss that makes society worse off. The customers who return to baking their own bread because of the artificially higher price must now reduce the time they spend producing other products in order to bake bread for themselves. Hence, society has less of other products because the price of bread has increased.

If baking bread were a relatively easy industry to enter, new competitors would enter the market and charge a lower price. The original baker, finding that she is losing her customers, would have to match her new competitor's price or perhaps charge less in order to get all of her customers back. The price war would continue until neither baker could lower prices any more without losing money. At this point, the price of bread accurately reflects the value of the resources it embodies. That is, competition has generated a market price that equals the marginal cost of production. Customers who returned to baking their own bread can buy their bread again and return to producing other products.

C. The Dynamic Competitive Process

The perfect competition model is an interesting and important tool in economic analysis. However, its sometimes overly restrictive assumptions limit its applicability to the real world. Allocative efficiency, as reflected in the competitive benchmark, is a measure of economic activity that is limited to a description of the world at a point in time. That is, allocative efficiency is a static measure of the economy. In contrast, real world competition is a dynamic process where change is a constant. This fact limits the usefulness of the model of perfect competition in describing actual competitive behavior. It should be clear that, in reality, there is no specific point on "the graph" that firms strive to reach. Rather, the economy is a dynamic, evolving process.

Competition in the real world is characterized by a wide variety of rivalrous behavior. Competitors engage in advertising, price-cutting, and quality improvement programs. Some economists argue that the presence of such dynamic competitive behavior indicates that welfare maximizing competition is at work. Consider the following observation by Professor McNulty regarding the dangers of confusing the model of perfect competition with the meaning of competition:

> [T]he most general tendency concerning the meaning of competition in economic theory is to regard it as the opposite of monopoly. An unfortunate result of this way of thinking has been no little confusion concerning the relationship between economic efficiency and business behavior. There is a striking contrast in economic literature between the analytical rigor and precision of competition when it is described as a market structure, and the ambiguity surrounding the ideas of competition whenever it is discussed in behavioral terms. Since, as Hayek has rightly noted, "the law cannot effectively prohibit states of affairs but only kinds of action," a concept of economic competition, if it is to be significant for economic policy, ought to relate to patterns of business behavior such as might reasonably be associated with the verb "to compete." That was the case with the competition which Adam Smith made the central organizing principle of economic society in the *Wealth of Nations*...Whether it was seen as price undercutting by sellers, the bidding up of prices by buyers,

or the entry of new firms into profitable industries, the fact is that competition entered economics as a concept which had empirical relevance and operational meaning in terms of contemporary business behavior. Yet on the question of whether such common current practices as advertising, product variation, price undercutting, or other forms of business activity do or do not constitute competition, modern economic theory offers the clarification that they are "monopolistically" competitive. While this is a useful way of illustrating the truth that most markets are in some degree both controlled and controlling, it is less useful as a guide in implementing a policy, such as our antitrust policy, which seeks at once to restrain monopoly and promote competition.

McNulty, *Economic Theory and the Meaning of Competition*, 82 Quarterly Journal of Economics 639, 639–40 (1968).

Most people think of competition as a type of behavior exhibited by rivals. For example, sports teams prepare for games against each other by watching videos, developing new plays, and practicing. On game day, the strategic maneuvering continues until time runs out and one team is declared the winner. This example describes competition as a process. The process approach to competition is very important in explaining the progression of society. For example, competition among business firms for profit drives them to supply the goods and services that consumers want at the lowest possible cost. Recall the quote from Adam Smith in Chapter I observing that the competitive process channels the pursuit of individual self-interest into socially beneficial outcomes. This is why the process of competition is so important.

The perfect competition model assumes perfect information is available at zero cost. But, in reality, information is scarce and costly to obtain (see Chapter VII on The Economics of Information). The market process approach stresses that economic decision making in the real world is a "discovery process." The discovery process takes place under conditions of ignorance far removed from the perfect knowledge assumption in the model of perfect competition. Most relevant for our purposes here, the process approach serves as a constant reminder that the model of perfect competition means the absence of all competitive activities—for example, the absence of advertising, customer service, and product improvement. In the following subsections, two types of behavior normally associated with the process of competition—advertising and point-of-sale services—are examined.

1. Advertising

Differentiated products have distinguishing features relative to the goods or services they are in competition with. For example, product quality can be an important source of product differentiation. Another common source of product differentiation is customer service. In the model of perfect competition, it was assumed that all firms produced an identical product. Thus, perfectly competitive firms face a totally-elastic demand curve. A firm with a differentiated product faces a less than totally-elastic demand curve. That is, the firm with a differentiated product has some degree of price control. In general, the more (less) elastic the demand curve, the more (less) similar are competitor's products, and the less (more) control competitors have over price.

One characteristic of firms that produce differentiated products is the use of advertising. Advertising is a means of communicating both the existence of alternate sellers as well as the distinguishing features of a product. Advertising is a critical and necessary condition for dynamic competitive markets. For example, new firms need to make consumers aware of their product's existence, location, and characteristics. Without advertising, it would be very difficult for a new entrant to challenge an established firm. The greater consumer awareness of product alternatives, availability, prices, and other characteristics, the less the consumer is bound to any one seller. Economists have argued that the provision of product information contained in advertising lowers the total search costs to consumers. Moreover, empirical studies have shown that continued advertising does improve product quality and maximize firm profitability. Thus, it seems clear that consumers are a prime beneficiary of advertising.

Bates v. State Bar of Arizona
Supreme Court of the United States
433 U.S. 350 (1977)

BLACKMUN, J.

As part of its regulation of the Arizona Bar, the Supreme Court of that State has imposed and enforces a disciplinary rule that restricts advertising by attorneys. This case presents two issues: whether §§ 1 and 2 of the Sherman Act, 15 U.S.C. §§ 1 and 2 forbid such state regulation, and whether the operation of the rule violates the First Amendment, made applicable to the States through the Fourteenth. (Internal cites omitted)

I.

Appellants John R. Bates and Van O'Steen are attorneys licensed to practice law in the State of Arizona. As such, they are members of the appellee, the State Bar of Arizona. * * *

In March 1974, appellants...opened a law office, which they call a "legal clinic," in Phoenix. Their aim was to provide legal services at modest fees to persons of moderate income who did not qualify for governmental legal aid. In order to achieve this end, they would accept only routine matters, such as uncontested divorces, uncontested adoptions, simple personal bankruptcies, and changes of name, for which costs could be kept down by extensive use of paralegals, automatic typewriting equipment, and standardized forms and office procedures. More complicated cases, such as contested divorces, would not be accepted. Because appellants set their prices so as to have a relatively low return on each case they handled, they depended on substantial volume.

After conducting their practice in this manner for two years, appellants concluded that their practice and clinical concept could not survive unless the availability of legal services at low cost was advertised and, in particular, fees were advertised. Consequently, in order to generate the necessary flow of business, that is, "to attract clients," appellants on February 22, 1976, placed an advertisement... in the Arizona Republic, a daily newspaper of general circulation in the Phoenix metropolitan area.... the advertisement stated that appellants were offering "legal services at very reasonable fees," and listed their fees for certain services.[4]

Appellants concede that the advertisement constituted a clear violation of Disciplinary Rule 2-101(B), incorporated in Rule 29(a) of the Supreme Court of Arizona, 17A Ariz. Rev. Stat., p. 26 (Supp. 1976). The disciplinary rule provides in part:

> "(B) A lawyer shall not publicize himself, or his partner, or associate, or any other lawyer affiliated with him or his firm, as a lawyer through newspaper or magazine advertisements, radio or television announcements, display advertisements in the city or telephone directories or other means of commercial publicity, nor shall he authorize or permit others to do so in his behalf."

Upon the filing of a complaint initiated by the president of the State Bar, a hearing was held... [where] the committee took the position that it could not consider an attack on the validity of the rule, it allowed the parties to develop a record on which such a challenge could be based. The committee recommended that each of the appellants be suspended from the practice of law for not less than six months. Upon further review... the Board recommended only a one-week suspension for each appellant, the weeks to run consecutively.

Appellants,... then sought review in the Supreme Court of Arizona, arguing, among other things, that the disciplinary rule violated §§ 1 and 2 of the Sherman Act because of its tendency to limit competition, and that the rule infringed their First Amendment rights. The court rejected both claims. The plurality may have viewed with some skepticism the claim that a restraint on advertising might have an adverse effect on competition. But, even if the rule might otherwise violate the Act, the plurality concluded that the regulation was exempt from Sherman Act attack because the rule "is an activity of the State of Arizona acting as sovereign." The regulation thus was held to be shielded from the Sherman Act by the state-action exemption of *Parker v. Brown*, 317 U.S. 341 (1943).

Turning to the First Amendment issue, the plurality noted that restrictions on professional advertising have survived constitutional challenge in the past...

*   *   *

Of particular interest here is the opinion of Mr. Justice Holohan in dissent. In his view, the case should have been framed in terms of "the right of the public as consumers and citizens to know about the activities of the legal profession," rather than as one involving merely the regulation of a profession. Observed in this light, he felt that the rule performed a substantial disservice to the public:

---

4. The office benefited from an increase in business after the appearance of the advertisement. App. 235–236, 479–480. It is doubtful, however, whether the increase was due solely to the advertisement, for the advertising itself prompted several news stories. *Id.*, at 229. It might be expected, nonetheless, that advertising will increase business. See Hobbs, Lawyer Advertising: A Good Beginning but Not Enough, 62 A. B. A. J. 735, 736 (1976) (lawyer referral service that advertised referred more than 11 times as many clients as one that did not advertise in another city of comparable size).

"Obviously the information of what lawyers charge is important for private economic decisions by those in need of legal services. Such information is also helpful, perhaps indispensable, to the formation of an intelligent opinion by the public on how well the legal system is working and whether it should be regulated or even altered.... The rule at issue prevents access to such information by the public."

Although the dissenter acknowledged that some types of advertising might cause confusion and deception, he felt that the remedy was to ban that form, rather than all advertising. Thus, despite his "personal dislike of the concept of advertising by attorneys," he found the ban unconstitutional.

II
The Sherman Act

*　*　*

We conclude that the Arizona Supreme Court's determination that appellants' Sherman Act claim is barred by the *Parker v. Brown* exemption must be affirmed.

III
The First Amendment

A

Last Term, in *Virginia Pharmacy Board v. Virginia Consumer Council*, 425 U.S. 748 (1976), the Court considered the validity under the First Amendment of a Virginia statute declaring that a pharmacist was guilty of "unprofessional conduct" if he advertised prescription drug prices.... The statute thus effectively prevented the advertising of prescription drug price information. We recognized that the pharmacist who desired to advertise did not wish to report any particularly newsworthy fact or to comment on any cultural, philosophical, or political subject; his desired communication was characterized simply: " 'I will sell you the X prescription drug at the Y price.' " Nonetheless, we held that commercial speech of that kind was entitled to the protection of the First Amendment.

Our analysis began, with the observation that our cases long have protected speech even though it is in the form of a paid advertisement, *Buckley v. Valeo*, 424 U.S. 1 (1976); in a form that is sold for profit, *Smith v. California*, 361 U.S. 147 (1959); or in the form of a solicitation to pay or contribute money, *New York Times Co. v. Sullivan, supra*. If commercial speech is to be distinguished, it "must be distinguished by its content." 425 U.S., at 761. But a consideration of competing interests reinforced our view that such speech should not be withdrawn from protection merely because it proposed a mundane commercial transaction. Even though the speaker's interest is largely economic, the Court has protected such speech in certain contexts. The listener's interest is substantial: the consumer's concern for the free flow of commercial speech often may be far keener than his concern for urgent political dialogue. Moreover, significant societal interests are served by such speech. Advertising, though entirely commercial, may often carry information of import to significant issues of the day. See *Bigelow v. Virginia*, 421 U.S. 809 (1975). And commercial speech serves to inform the public of the availability, nature, and prices of products and services, and thus performs an indispensable role in the allocation of resources in a free enterprise system. In short, such speech serves individual and societal interests in assuring informed and reliable decisionmaking. 425 U.S., at 761–765.

Arrayed against these substantial interests in the free flow of commercial speech were a number of proffered justifications for the advertising ban. Central among them were claims that the ban was essential to the maintenance of professionalism among licensed pharmacists. It was asserted that advertising would create price competition that might cause the pharmacist to economize at the customer's expense. He might reduce or eliminate the truly professional portions of his services: the maintenance and packaging of drugs so as to assure their effectiveness, and the supplementation on occasion of the prescribing physician's advice as to use. Moreover, it was said, advertising would cause consumers to price-shop, thereby undermining the pharmacist's effort to monitor the drug use of a regular customer so as to ensure that the prescribed drug would not provoke an allergic reaction or be incompatible with another substance the customer was consuming. Finally, it was argued that advertising would reduce the image of the pharmacist as a skilled and specialized craftsman—an image that was said to attract talent to the profession and to reinforce the good habits of those in it—to that of a mere shopkeeper.

Although acknowledging that the State had a strong interest in maintaining professionalism among pharmacists, this Court concluded that the proffered justifications were inadequate to support the advertising ban. High professional standards were assured in large part by the close regulation to which pharmacists in Virginia were subject.... But we noted the presence of a potent alternative to this "highly paternalistic" approach: "That alternative is to assume that this information is not in itself harmful, that people will perceive their own best interests if only they are well enough informed, and that the best means to that end is to open the channels of communication rather than to close them." The choice between the dangers of suppressing information and the dangers arising from its free flow was seen as precisely the choice "that the First Amendment makes for us."

We have set out this detailed summary of the *Pharmacy* opinion because the conclusion that Arizona's disciplinary rule is violative of the First Amendment might be said to flow *a fortiori* from it. Like the Virginia statutes, the disciplinary rule serves to inhibit the free flow of commercial information and to keep the public in ignorance. * * *

In the instant case we are confronted with the arguments directed explicitly toward the regulation of advertising by licensed attorneys.

B

* * *

The heart of the dispute before us today is whether lawyers also may constitutionally advertise the *prices* at which certain routine services will be performed. Numerous justifications are proffered for the restriction of such price advertising. We consider each in turn:

1. The Adverse Effect on Professionalism. Appellee places particular emphasis on the adverse effects that it feels price advertising will have on the legal profession. The key to professionalism, it is argued, is the sense of pride that involvement in the discipline generates. It is claimed that price advertising will bring about commercialization, which will undermine the attorney's sense of dignity and self-worth. The hustle of the marketplace will adversely affect the profession's service orientation, and irreparably damage the delicate balance between the lawyer's need to earn and his obligation selflessly to serve. Advertising is also said to erode the client's trust in his attorney: Once the client perceives that the lawyer is motivated by profit, his confidence that the attorney is acting out of a commitment to the client's welfare is jeopardized. And advertising is said to tarnish the dignified public image of the profession.

* * * [W]e find the postulated connection between advertising and the erosion of true professionalism to be severely strained. At its core, the argument presumes that attorneys must conceal from themselves and from their clients the real-life fact that lawyers earn their livelihood at the bar. We suspect that few attorneys engage in such self-deception.[19] And rare is the client...who enlists the aid of an attorney with the expectation that his services will be rendered free of charge....If the commercial basis of the relationship is to be promptly disclosed on ethical grounds, once the client is in the office, it seems inconsistent to condemn the candid revelation of the same information before he arrives at that office.

Moreover, the assertion that advertising will diminish the attorney's reputation in the community is open to question. Bankers and engineers advertise, and yet these professions are not regarded as undignified. In fact, it has been suggested that the failure of lawyers to advertise creates public disillusionment with the profession. The absence of advertising may be seen to reflect the profession's failure to reach out and serve the community: Studies reveal that many persons do not obtain counsel even when they perceive a need because of the feared price of services or because of an inability to locate a competent attorney. * * *

          * * *

2. *The Inherently Misleading Nature of Attorney Advertising.* It is argued that advertising of legal services inevitably will be misleading (a) because such services are so individualized with regard to content and quality as to prevent informed comparison on the basis of an advertisement, (b) because the consumer of legal services is unable to determine in advance just what services he needs, and (c) because advertising by attorneys will highlight irrelevant factors and fail to show the relevant factor of skill.

We are not persuaded that restrained professional advertising by lawyers inevitably will be misleading.... The only services that lend themselves to advertising are the routine ones: the uncontested divorce, the simple adoption, the uncontested personal bankruptcy, the change of name, and the like—the very services advertised by appellants. Although the precise service demanded in each task may vary slightly, and although legal services are not fungible, these facts do not make advertising misleading so long as the attorney does the necessary work at the advertised price.[27] The argument that legal services are so unique that fixed

---

19. Counsel for the appellee at oral argument readily stated: "We all know that law offices are big businesses, that they may have billion-dollar or million-dollar clients, they're run with computers, and all the rest. And so the argument may be made that to term them noncommercial is sanctimonious humbug." Tr. of Oral Arg. 64.

27. One commentator has observed: "[A] moment's reflection reveals that the same argument can be made for barbers; rarely are two haircuts identical, but that does not mean that barbers cannot quote a standard price. Lawyers perform countless relatively standard-

rates cannot meaningfully be established is refuted by the record in this case: The appellee State Bar itself sponsors a Legal Services Program in which the participating attorneys agree to perform services like those advertised by the appellants at standardized rates. Indeed, until the decision of this Court in *Goldfarb v. Virginia State Bar*, 421 U.S. 773 (1975), the Maricopa County Bar Association apparently had a schedule of suggested minimum fees for standard legal tasks. We thus find of little force the assertion that advertising is misleading because of an inherent lack of standardization in legal services.[28]

The second component of the argument—that advertising ignores the diagnostic role—fares little better. It is unlikely that many people go to an attorney merely to ascertain if they have a clean bill of legal health. Rather, attorneys are likely to be employed to perform specific tasks. Although the client may not know the detail involved in performing the task, he no doubt is able to identify the service he desires at the level of generality to which advertising lends itself.

The third component is not without merit: Advertising does not provide a complete foundation on which to select an attorney. But it seems peculiar to deny the consumer, on the ground that the information is incomplete, at least some of the relevant information needed to reach an informed decision. The alternative— the prohibition of advertising—serves only to restrict the information that flows to consumers.[30] Moreover, the argument assumes that the public is not sophisticated enough to realize the limitations of advertising, and . . . we view as dubious any justification that is based on the benefits of public ignorance. Although, of

---

ized services which vary somewhat in complexity but not so much as to make each job utterly unique." Morgan, *supra*, n. 25, at 714.

28. THE CHIEF JUSTICE and MR. JUSTICE POWELL argue in dissent that advertising will be misleading because the exact services that are included in an advertised package may not be clearly specified or understood by the prospective client. *Post*, at 386–387 and 392–394. The bar, however, retains the power to define the services that must be included in an advertised package, such as an uncontested divorce, thereby standardizing the "product." We recognize that an occasional client might fail to appreciate the complexity of his legal problem and will visit an attorney in the mistaken belief that his difficulty can be handled at the advertised price. The misunderstanding, however, usually will be exposed at the initial consultation, and an ethical attorney would impose, at the most, a minimal consultation charge or no charge at all for the discussion. If the client decides to have work performed, a fee could be negotiated in the normal manner. The client is thus in largely the same position as he would be if there were no advertising. In light of the benefits of advertising to those whose problem can be resolved at the advertised price, suppression is not warranted on account of the occasional client who misperceives his legal difficulties.

30. It might be argued that advertising is undesirable because it allows the potential client to substitute advertising for reputational information in selecting an appropriate attorney. See, *e.g.*, Note, Sherman Act Scrutiny of Bar Restraints on Advertising and Solicitation by Attorneys, 62 Va. L. Rev. 1135, 1152–1157 (1976). Since in a referral system relying on reputation an attorney's future business is partially dependent on current performance, such a system has the benefit both of providing a mechanism for disciplining misconduct and of creating an incentive for an attorney to do a better job for his present clients. Although the system may have worked when the typical lawyer practiced in a small, homogeneous community in which ascertaining reputational information was easy for a consumer, commentators have seriously questioned its current efficacy. See, *e.g.*, B. Christensen, Lawyers for People of Moderate Means 128–135 (1970). The trends of urbanization and specialization long since have moved the typical practice of law from its small-town setting. See R. Pound, The Lawyer from Antiquity to Modern Times 242 (1953). Information as to the qualifications of lawyers is not available to many. And, if available, it may be inaccurate or biased.

course, the bar retains the power to correct omissions that have the effect of presenting an inaccurate picture, the preferred remedy is more disclosure, rather than less. * * *

3. The Adverse Effect on the Administration of Justice. Advertising is said to have the undesirable effect of stirring up litigation. * * *

Although advertising might increase the use of the judicial machinery, we cannot accept the notion that it is always better for a person to suffer a wrong silently than to redress it by legal action. As the bar acknowledges, "the middle 70% of our population is not being reached or served adequately by the legal profession." ABA, Revised Handbook on Prepaid Legal Services 2 (1972). Among the reasons for this underutilization is fear of the cost, and an inability to locate a suitable lawyer. Advertising can help to solve this acknowledged problem: Advertising is the traditional mechanism in a free-market economy for a supplier to inform a potential purchaser of the availability and terms of exchange. The disciplinary rule at issue likely has served to burden access to legal services, particularly for the not-quite-poor and the unknowledgeable. A rule allowing restrained advertising would be in accord with the bar's obligation to "facilitate the process of intelligent selection of lawyers, and to assist in making legal services fully available."

4. The Undesirable Economic Effects of Advertising. It is claimed that advertising will increase the overhead costs of the profession, and that these costs then will be passed along to consumers in the form of increased fees. Moreover, it is claimed that the additional cost of practice will create a substantial entry barrier, deterring or preventing young attorneys from penetrating the market and entrenching the position of the bar's established members.

These two arguments seem dubious at best.... The ban on advertising serves to increase the difficulty of discovering the lowest cost seller of acceptable ability. As a result, to this extent attorneys are isolated from competition, and the incentive to price competitively is reduced. Although it is true that the effect of advertising on the price of services has not been demonstrated, there is revealing evidence with regard to products; where consumers have the benefit of price advertising, retail prices often are dramatically lower than they would be without advertising.[34] It is entirely possible that advertising will serve to reduce, not advance, the cost of legal services to the consumer.[35]

---

34. See Benham, The Effect of Advertising on the Price of Eyeglasses, 15 J. Law & Econ. 337 (1972)....

35. On the one hand, advertising does increase an attorney's overhead costs, and, in light of the underutilization of legal services by the public, see FN33, supra, it may increase substantially the demand for services. Both these factors will tend to increase the price of legal services. On the other hand, the tendency of advertising to enhance competition might be expected to produce pressures on attorneys to reduce fees. The net effect of these competing influences is hard to estimate. We deem it significant, however, that consumer organizations have filed briefs as amici urging that the restriction on advertising be lifted. And we note as well that, despite the fact that advertising on occasion might increase the price the consumer must pay, competition through advertising is ordinarily the desired norm.

Even if advertising causes fees to drop, it is by no means clear that a loss of income to lawyers will result. The increased volume of business generated by advertising might more than compensate for the reduced profit per case. See Frierson, Legal Advertising, Barrister 6, 8 (Winter 1975).

...In the absence of advertising, an attorney must rely on his contacts with the community to generate a flow of business. In view of the time necessary to develop such contacts, the ban in fact serves to perpetuate the market position of established attorneys. Consideration of entry-barrier problems would urge that advertising be allowed so as to aid the new competitor in penetrating the market.

5. The Adverse Effect of Advertising on the Quality of Service. It is argued that the attorney may advertise a given "package" of service at a set price, and will be inclined to provide, by indiscriminate use, the standard package regardless of whether it fits the client's needs.

Restraints on advertising, however, are an ineffective way of deterring shoddy work.... And the advertisement of a standardized fee does not necessarily mean that the services offered are undesirably standardized. Indeed, the assertion that an attorney who advertises a standard fee will cut quality is substantially undermined by the fixed-fee schedule of appellee's own prepaid Legal Services Program. Even if advertising leads to the creation of "legal clinics" like that of appellants' — clinics that emphasize standardized procedures for routine problems — it is possible that such clinics will improve service by reducing the likelihood of error.

6. The Difficulties of Enforcement. Finally, it is argued that the wholesale restriction is justified by the problems of enforcement if any other course is taken. Because the public lacks sophistication in legal matters, it may be particularly susceptible to misleading or deceptive advertising by lawyers.... Thus, the vigilance of a regulatory agency will be required. But because of the numerous purveyors of services, the overseeing of advertising will be burdensome.

It is at least somewhat incongruous for the opponents of advertising to extol the virtues and altruism of the legal profession at one point, and, at another, to assert that its members will seize the opportunity to mislead and distort. We suspect that, with advertising, most lawyers will behave as they always have: They will abide by their solemn oaths to uphold the integrity and honor of their profession and of the legal system.... It will be in the [honest lawyers'] interest, as in other cases of misconduct at the bar, to assist in weeding out those few who abuse their trust.

In sum, we are not persuaded that any of the preferred justifications rise to the level of an acceptable reason for the suppression of all advertising by attorneys.

*   *   *

We conclude that it has not been demonstrated that the advertisement at issue could be suppressed.

IV

*   *   *

The constitutional issue in this case is only whether the State may prevent publication in a newspaper of appellants' truthful advertisement concerning the availability and terms of routine legal services. We rule simply that the flow of such information may not be restrained, and we therefore hold the present application of the disciplinary rule against appellants to be violative of the First Amendment.

The judgment of the Supreme Court of Arizona is therefore affirmed in part and reversed in part.

It is so ordered.

MR. CHIEF JUSTICE BURGER, concurring in part and dissenting in part.

I am in general agreement with MR. JUSTICE POWELL's analysis and with Part II of the Court's opinion. I particularly agree with MR. JUSTICE POWELL's statement that "today's decision will effect profound changes in the practice of law." Although the exact effect of those changes cannot now be known, I fear that they will be injurious to those whom the ban on legal advertising was designed to protect—the members of the general public in need of legal services.

*   *   *

MR. JUSTICE POWELL, with whom MR. JUSTICE STEWART joins, concurring in part and dissenting in part.

...I cannot join the Court's holding that under the First Amendment "truthful" newspaper advertising of a lawyer's prices for "routine legal services" may not be restrained. Although the Court appears to note some reservations (mentioned below), it is clear that within undefined limits today's decision will effect profound changes in the practice of law, viewed for centuries as a learned profession. The supervisory power of the courts over members of the bar, as officers of the courts, and the authority of the respective States to oversee the regulation of the profession have been weakened...

I

*   *   *

...[T]he question before us is whether the application of the disciplinary rule to appellants' advertisement violates the First Amendment.

The Court finds the resolution of that question in our recent decision in *Virginia Pharmacy Board v. Virginia Consumer Council*, 425 U.S. 748 (1976). In that case, we held unconstitutional under the First and Fourteenth Amendments a Virginia statute declaring it unprofessional conduct for a licensed pharmacist to advertise the prices of prescription drugs....But we were careful to note that we were dealing in that case with price advertising of a *standardized product*. The Court specifically reserved judgment as to the constitutionality of state regulation of price advertising with respect to *professional services*:

> "We stress that we have considered in this case the regulation of commercial advertising by pharmacists. Although we express no opinion as to other professions, the distinctions, historical and functional, between professions, may require consideration of quite different factors. Physicians and lawyers, for example, do not dispense standardized products; they render professional services of almost infinite variety and nature, with the consequent enhanced possibility for confusion and deception if they were to undertake certain kinds of advertising." *Id.*, at 773 n. 25.

This case presents the issue so reserved, and the Court resolves it on the assumption that what it calls "routine" legal services are essentially no different for purposes of First Amendment analysis from prepackaged prescription drugs. In so holding, the Court fails to give appropriate weight to the two fundamental ways in which the advertising of professional services presents a different issue from that before the Court with respect to tangible products: the vastly increased potential for deception and the enhanced difficulty of effective regulation in the public interest.

A

It has long been thought that price advertising of legal services inevitably will be misleading because such services are individualized with respect to content and quality and because the lay consumer of legal services usually does not know in advance the precise nature and scope of the services he requires....[t]he Court's basic response in view of the acknowledged potential for deceptive advertising of "unique" services is to divide the immense range of the professional product of lawyers into two categories: "unique" and "routine." The only insight afforded by the opinion as to how one draws this line is the finding that services similar to those in appellants' advertisement are routine: "the uncontested divorce, the simple adoption, the uncontested personal bankruptcy, the change of name, and the like."...But the advertising of such services must, in the Court's words, flow "both freely and cleanly."

*   *   *

This definitional problem is well illustrated by appellants' advertised willingness to obtain uncontested divorces for $195 each. A potential client can be grievously misled if he reads the advertised service as embracing all of his possible needs....More important from the viewpoint of the client is the diagnostic and advisory function: the pursuit of relevant inquiries of which the client would otherwise be unaware, and advice with respect to alternative arrangements that might prevent irreparable dissolution of the marriage or otherwise resolve the client's problem. Although those professional functions are not included within appellants' packaged routine divorce, they frequently fall within the concept of "advice" with which the lay person properly is concerned when he or she seeks legal counsel. The average lay person simply has no feeling for which services are included in the packaged divorce, and thus no capacity to judge the nature of the advertised product.[6] As a result, the type of advertisement before us inescapably will mislead many who respond to it. In the end, it will promote distrust of lawyers and disrespect for our own system of justice.

*   *   *

B

Even if one were to accept the view that some legal services are sufficiently routine to minimize the possibility of deception, there nonetheless remains a serious enforcement problem. The Court does recognize some problems....After recognizing that problems remain in defining the boundary between deceptive and nondeceptive advertising, the Court then observes that the bar may be expected to have "a special role to play in assuring that advertising by attorneys flows both freely and cleanly."

The Court seriously understates the difficulties, and overestimates the capabilities of the bar—or indeed of any agency public or private—to assure with a

---

6. Similar complications surround the uncontested adoption and the simple bankruptcy.

reasonable degree of effectiveness that price advertising can at the same time be both unrestrained and truthful. There are some 400,000 lawyers in this country. They have been licensed by the States, and the organized bars within the States—operating under codes approved by the highest courts acting pursuant to statutory authority—have had the primary responsibility for assuring compliance with professional ethics and standards....the problem of disciplinary enforcement in this country has proved to be extremely difficult. See generally ABA, Special Committee on Evaluation of Disciplinary Enforcement, Problems and Recommendations in Disciplinary Enforcement (1970).

...The very reasons that tend to make price advertising of services inherently deceptive make its policing wholly impractical. With respect to commercial advertising, MR. JUSTICE STEWART, concurring in *Virginia Pharmacy*, noted that since "the factual claims contained in commercial price or product advertisements relate to tangible goods or services, they may be tested empirically and corrected to reflect the truth." 425 U.S., at 780. But there simply is no way to test "empirically" the claims made in appellants' advertisement of legal services....These are not factual questions for which there are "truthful" answers; in most instances, the answers would turn on relatively subjective judgments as to which there could be wide differences of opinion. These difficulties with appellants' advertisement will inhere in any comparable price advertisement of specific legal services. Even if public agencies were established to oversee professional price advertising, adequate protection of the public from deception, and of ethical lawyers from unfair competition, could prove to be a wholly intractable problem.

II

The Court emphasizes the need for information that will assist persons desiring legal services to choose lawyers. Under our economic system, advertising is the most commonly used and useful means of providing information as to goods and other services, but it generally has not been used with respect to legal and certain other professional services. Until today, controlling weight has been given to the danger that general advertising of such services too often would tend to mislead rather than inform. Moreover, there has been the further concern that the characteristics of the legal profession thought beneficial to society—a code of professional ethics, an imbued sense of professional and public responsibility, a tradition of self-discipline, and duties as officers of the courts—would suffer if the restraints on advertising were significantly diluted.

Pressures toward some relaxation of the proscription against general advertising have gained force in recent years with the increased recognition of the difficulty that low- and middle-income citizens experience in finding counsel willing to serve at reasonable prices....

Study and experimentation continue. Following a series of hearings in 1975, the American Bar Association amended its Code of Professional Responsibility to broaden the information, when allowed by state law, that a lawyer may provide in approved means of advertising. DR 2-102 (1976). In addition to the customary data published in legal directories, the amended regulation authorizes publication of the lawyer's fee for an initial consultation, the fact that other fee information is available on specific request, and the willingness of the attorney to accept credit cards or other credit arrangements. The regulation approves placement of such advertisements in the classified section of telephone directories, in the customary law lists and legal directories, and also in directories of lawyers prepared by consumer and other groups.

The Court observes, and I agree, that there is nothing inherently misleading in the advertisement of the cost of an initial consultation.... [Advertising of fee] rates, in an appropriate medium, duly designated, would not necessarily be misleading if this fee information also made clear that the total charge for the representation would depend on the number of hours devoted to the client's problem—a variable difficult to predict. Where the price content of the advertisement is limited to the finite item of rate per hour devoted to the client's problem, the likelihood of deceiving or misleading is considerably less than when specific services are advertised at a fixed price.

*   *   *

IV

The area into which the Court now ventures has, until today, largely been left to self-regulation....

In this context, the Court's imposition of hard and fast constitutional rules as to price advertising is neither required by precedent nor likely to serve the public interest. One of the great virtues of federalism is the opportunity it affords for experimentation and innovation, with freedom to discard or amend that which proves unsuccessful or detrimental to the public good. The constitutionalizing—indeed the affirmative encouraging—of competitive price advertising of specified legal services will substantially inhibit the experimentation that has been underway and also will limit the control heretofore exercised over lawyers by the respective States.

I am apprehensive, despite the Court's expressed intent to proceed cautiously, that today's holding will be viewed by tens of thousands of lawyers as an invitation—by the public-spirited and the selfish lawyers alike—to engage in competitive advertising on an escalating basis. Some lawyers may gain temporary advantages; others will suffer from the economic power of stronger lawyers, or by the subtle deceit of less scrupulous lawyers.[13] Some members of the public may benefit marginally, but the risk is that many others will be victimized by simplistic price advertising of professional services "almost infinite [in] variety and nature...."

---

13. It has been suggested that price advertising will benefit younger lawyers and smaller firms, as well as the public, by enabling them to compete more favorably with the larger, established firms. The overtones of this suggestion are antitrust rather than First Amendment in principle. But whatever the origin, there is reason seriously to doubt the validity of the premise. With the increasing complexity of legal practice, perhaps the strongest trend in the profession today is toward specialization. Many small firms will limit their practice to intensely specialized areas; the larger, institutionalized firms are likely to have a variety of departments, each devoted to a special area of the law. The established specialist and the large law firm have advantages that are not inconsiderable if price competition becomes commonplace. They can advertise truthfully the areas in which they practice; they enjoy economies of scale that may justify lower prices; and they often possess the economic power to disadvantage the weaker or more inexperienced firms in any advertising competition. Whether the potential for increased concentration of law practice in a smaller number of larger firms would be detrimental to the public is not addressed by the Court.

Virginia Pharmacy Board, 425 U.S., at 773 n. 25. Until today, in the long history of the legal profession, it was not thought that this risk of public deception was required by the marginal First Amendment interests asserted by the Court.

MR. JUSTICE REHNQUIST, dissenting in part.

...Largely for the reasons set forth in my dissent in *Virginia Pharmacy Board v. Virginia Consumer Council*, 425 U.S. 748, 781 (1976), however, I dissent from Part III because I cannot agree that the First Amendment is infringed by Arizona's regulation of the essentially commercial activity of advertising legal services. *Valentine v. Chrestensen*, 316 U.S. 52 (1942).

I continue to believe that the First Amendment speech provision, long regarded by this Court as a sanctuary for expressions of public importance or intellectual interest, is demeaned by invocation to protect advertisements of goods and services. I would hold quite simply that the appellants' advertisement, however truthful or reasonable it may be, is not the sort of expression that the Amendment was adopted to protect.

I think my Brother POWELL persuasively demonstrates in his opinion that the Court's opinion offers very little guidance as to the extent or nature of permissible state regulation of professions such as law and medicine. I would join his opinion except for my belief that once the Court took the first step down the "slippery slope" in *Virginia Pharmacy Board, supra*, the possibility of understandable and workable differentiations between protected speech and unprotected speech in the field of advertising largely evaporated. Once the exception of commercial speech from the protection of the First Amendment which had been established by *Valentine v. Chrestensen, supra*, was abandoned, the shift to case-by-case adjudication of First Amendment claims of advertisers was a predictable consequence.

While I agree with my Brother POWELL that the effect of today's opinion on the professions is both unfortunate and not required by the First and Fourteenth Amendments, I cannot join the implication in his opinion that some forms of legal advertising may be constitutionally protected. The *Valentine* distinction was constitutionally sound and practically workable, and I am still unwilling to take even one step down the "slippery slope" away from it.

I therefore join Parts I and II of the Court's opinion, but dissent from Part III and from the judgement.

Notes and Questions

1. Beyond the Reach of the First Amendment?: The Court makes the following observation: "The choice between the dangers of suppressing information and the dangers arising from its free flow was seen as precisely the choice 'that the First Amendment makes for us.'" Does this observation seem to be dispositive of the issue before the Court in *Bates?* Why does the State Bar of Arizona and the dissent believe that the legal profession should be exempt from this standard? Are they persuasive?

2. The Free Flow of Information: Desirous or Disastrous?: The economic model places a high value on information. In fact, perfect information is an assumption underlying the model of perfect competition. It is possible to imagine a continuum of market information, ranging from perfectly uninformed to perfectly informed. The Court appears to believe that advertising will push information in the legal services market closer to the perfect information end of the continuum. Why does the Court see this increase in information as desirous? Does the fact that this added information is not perfect, or may be misleading, indicate that no efficiency gains will be realized? What do you think about the Court's accusation that to withhold such information from the public under the assumption that individuals would not be able to understand and therefore benefit from it is "highly paternalistic?"

3. *Efficiency: Gains v. Losses Due to Advertising:* The Court appears to be arguing that because of the fact that legal services are not fungible and that information regarding the quality, price, and availability of legal services is not perfect, some benefits could be gained by encouraging more rigorous competition through advertising. However, the dissent appears to focus more on the fact that the lack of homogeneity among legal services can cause difficulty in advertising. Does the fact that a market does not meet the underlying assumptions of perfect competition cast doubt on its ability to allocate resources efficiently? How far can the homogeneity assumption break down before the efficiency gains from competition are lost? How far can the perfect information assumption break down before the efficiency gains from competition are lost?

4. *Optimization:* In general, economics is about maximizing the value of resource uses in the face of scarcity. This definition requires making the most effective use of resources—that is, optimization. When alternative courses of action are available, the decision that adds the most net value is the optimal decision. Historically, the Court has allowed some restrictions to be placed on the First Amendment. Thus, in some cases, the benefits from restricting certain types of speech outweigh the costs. This indicates that rather than free speech being an absolute right, there is some optimal amount of free speech. What then can you say about the Court's perception regarding the optimal amount of attorney advertising? What about the dissent? Does the Court support unconstrained attorney advertising? The dissent seems willing to hold the legal field to a very stringent standard by supporting a blanket ban on attorney advertising and, by doing so, sacrificing all of the potential gains from advertising. Is a blanket ban consistent with the idea of optimization? Can this optimization concept be applied to the supposed defects of attorney advertising? In other words, is it rational to make decisions in terms of the optimal amount of deception by unethical attorneys?

2.   Point of Sale Services

The production and sale of goods and services is a complicated and competitive process. Specialization creates certain economic efficiencies to be gained by dividing the manufacturing, distribution, and retail sales functions among separate firms. **Vertical relationships** are arrangements down the chain of distribution—from input suppliers to manufacturers to wholesale distributors to retailers.

A typical vertical relationship may be organized in the following way. A manufacturer of bicycles recognizes that certain efficiencies can be gained by selling its product to wholesale distributors who, in turn, sell the bikes to local retailers rather than performing all of these functions itself. For the manufacturer, there is a fundamental danger in this type of vertical relationship. Specifically, the bicycle manufacturer wants to sell the profit maximizing quantity of bikes; however, it does not control the retail sales function. The manufacturer wants its retailers to engage in aggressive competitive behavior geared (no pun intended) toward selling its bikes. The cases that follow, however, demonstrate that retailers do not necessarily have the same incentive—a desire to maximize the sale of manufacturer's bikes—and manufacturers have resorted to numerous contractual devices in order to encourage their retailers to promote their products.

Continental T.V., Inc. v. GTE Sylvania, Inc.
Supreme Court of the United States
433 U.S. 36 (1977)

MR. JUSTICE POWELL delivered the opinion of the Court.

Franchise agreements between manufacturers and retailers frequently include provisions barring the retailers from selling franchised products from locations other than those specified in the agreements. This case presents important questions concerning the appropriate antitrust analysis of these restrictions under § 1 of the Sherman Act...(cites omitted, with exceptions)

I

Respondent GTE Sylvania Inc. (Sylvania) manufactures and sells television sets through its Home Entertainment Products Division. Prior to 1962, like most other television manufacturers, Sylvania sold its televisions to independent or company-owned distributors who in turn resold to a large and diverse group of retailers. Prompted by a decline in its market share to a relatively insignificant 1% to 2% of national television sales, Sylvania conducted an intensive reassessment of its marketing strategy, and in 1962 adopted the franchise plan challenged here. Sylvania phased out its wholesale distributors and began to sell its televisions directly to a smaller and more select group of franchised retailers. An acknowledged purpose of the change was to decrease the number of competing Sylvania retailers in the hope of attracting the more aggressive and competent retailers thought necessary to the improvement of the company's market position.[2] To this end, Sylvania limited the number of franchises granted for any given area and required each franchisee to sell his Sylvania products only from the location or locations at which he was franchised.[3] A franchise did not constitute an exclusive territory, and Sylvania retained sole discretion to increase the number of retailers in an area in light of the success or failure of existing retailers in developing their market. The revised marketing strategy appears to have been successful during the period at issue here, for by 1965 Sylvania's share of national television

---

2. The number of retailers selling Sylvania products declined significantly as a result of the change, but in 1965 there were at least two franchised Sylvania retailers in each metropolitan center of more than 100,000 population.

3. Sylvania imposed no restrictions on the right of the franchisee to sell the products of competing manufacturers.

sales had increased to approximately 5%, and the company ranked as the Nation's eighth largest manufacturer of color television sets.

This suit is the result of the rupture of a franchiser-franchisee relationship that had previously prospered under the revised Sylvania plan. Dissatisfied with its sales in the city of San Francisco,[4] Sylvania decided in the spring of 1965 to franchise Young Brothers, an established San Francisco retailer of televisions, as an additional San Francisco retailer. The proposed location of the new franchise was approximately a mile from a retail outlet operated by petitioner Continental T.V., Inc. (Continental), one of the most successful Sylvania franchisees. Continental protested that the location of the new franchise violated Sylvania's marketing policy, but Sylvania persisted in its plans. Continental then canceled a large Sylvania order and placed a large order with Phillips, one of Sylvania's competitors.

During this same period, Continental expressed a desire to open a store in Sacramento, Cal., a desire Sylvania attributed at least in part to Continental's displeasure over the Young Brothers decision. Sylvania believed that the Sacramento market was adequately served by the existing Sylvania retailers and denied the request.[6] In the face of this denial, Continental advised Sylvania in early September 1965, that it was in the process of moving Sylvania merchandise from its San Jose, Cal., warehouse to a new retail location that it had leased in Sacramento. Two weeks later, allegedly for unrelated reasons, Sylvania's credit department reduced Continental's credit line from $300,000 to $50,000. In response to the reduction in credit and the generally deteriorating relations with Sylvania, Continental withheld all payments owed to John P. Maguire & Co., Inc. (Maguire), the finance company that handled the credit arrangements between Sylvania and its retailers. Shortly thereafter, Sylvania terminated Continental's franchises, and Maguire filed this diversity action in the United States District Court for the Northern District of California seeking recovery of money owed and of secured merchandise held by Continental.

The antitrust issues before us originated in cross-claims brought by Continental against Sylvania and Maguire. Most important for our purposes was the claim that Sylvania had violated § 1 of the Sherman Act by entering into and enforcing franchise agreements that prohibited the sale of Sylvania products other than from specified locations. At the close of evidence in the jury trial of Continental's claims, Sylvania requested the District Court to instruct the jury that its location restriction was illegal only if it unreasonably restrained or suppressed competition. Relying on this Court's decision in *United States v. Arnold, Schwinn & Co.*, the District Court rejected the proffered instruction in favor of the following one:

> "Therefore, if you find by a preponderance of the evidence that Sylvania entered into a contract, combination or conspiracy with one or more of its dealers pursuant to which Sylvania exercised dominion or control over the products sold to the dealer, after having parted with title and risk to the products, you must find any effort thereafter to restrict outlets

---

4. Sylvania's market share in San Francisco was approximately 2.5% — half its national and northern California average.

6. Sylvania had achieved exceptional results in Sacramento, where its market share exceeded 15% in 1965.

or store locations from which its dealers resold the merchandise which they had purchased from Sylvania to be a violation of Section 1 of the Sherman Act, regardless of the reasonableness of the location restrictions."

In answers to special interrogatories, the jury found that Sylvania had engaged "in a contract, combination or conspiracy in restraint of trade in violation of the antitrust laws with respect to location restrictions alone," and assessed Continental's damages at $591,505, which was trebled * * * to produce an award of $1,774,515.

On appeal, the Court of Appeals for the Ninth Circuit, sitting en banc, reversed by a divided vote.... [I]t concluded that *Schwinn* was distinguishable on several grounds. Contrasting the nature of the restrictions, their competitive impact, and the market shares of the franchisers in the two cases, the court concluded that Sylvania's location restriction had less potential for competitive harm than the restrictions invalidated in *Schwinn* and thus should be judged under the "rule of reason" rather than the *per se* rule stated in *Schwinn*....

We granted Continental's petition for certiorari....

II

A

...[In *Schwinn*]...[e]ach distributor had a defined geographic area in which it had the exclusive right to supply franchised retailers. Sales to the public were made only through franchised retailers, who were authorized to sell Schwinn bicycles only from specified locations. In support of this limitation, Schwinn prohibited both distributors and retailers from selling Schwinn bicycles to nonfranchised retailers. At the retail level, therefore, Schwinn was able to control the number of retailers of its bicycles in any given area according to its view of the needs of that market.

* * *

...[In *Schwinn*] the Court proceeded to articulate the following "bright line" *per se* rule of illegality for vertical restrictions: "Under the Sherman Act, it is unreasonable without more for a manufacturer to seek to restrict and confine areas or persons with whom an article may be traded after the manufacturer has parted with dominion over it." But the Court expressly stated that the rule of reason governs when "the manufacturer retains title, dominion, and risk with respect to the product and the position and function of the dealer in question are, in fact, indistinguishable from those of an agent or salesman of the manufacturer."

Application of these principles to the facts of Schwinn produced sharply contrasting results depending upon the role played by the distributor in the distribution system. With respect to that portion of Schwinn's sales for which the distributors acted as ordinary wholesalers, buying and reselling Schwinn bicycles, the Court held that the territorial and customer restrictions challenged by the Government were *per se* illegal.... Applying the rule of reason to the restrictions that were not imposed in conjunction with the sale of bicycles, the Court had little difficulty finding them all reasonable in light of the competitive situation in "the product market as a whole."

B

In the present case, it is undisputed that title to the television sets passed from Sylvania to Continental. Thus, the *Schwinn per se* rule applies unless Sylvania's restriction on locations falls outside *Schwinn's* prohibition against a manufacturer's attempting to restrict a "retailer's freedom as to where and to whom it will resell the products." As the Court of Appeals conceded, the language of *Schwinn* is clearly broad enough to apply to the present case. Unlike the Court of Appeals, however, we are unable to find a principled basis for distinguishing Schwinn from the case now before us.

...In intent and competitive impact, the retail-customer restriction in Schwinn is indistinguishable from the location restriction in the present case. In both cases the restrictions limited the freedom of the retailer to dispose of the purchased products as he desired. The fact that one restriction was addressed to territory and the other to customers is irrelevant to functional antitrust analysis and, indeed, to the language and broad thrust of the opinion in *Schwinn*....

III

Sylvania argues that if *Schwinn* cannot be distinguished, it should be reconsidered. Although *Schwinn* is supported by the principle of *stare decisis*, we are convinced that the need for clarification of the law in this area justifies reconsideration. *Schwinn* itself was an abrupt and largely unexplained departure from *White Motor Co. v. United States*, 327 U.S. 253 (1963), where only four years earlier the Court had refused to endorse a *per se* rule for vertical restrictions. Since its announcement, *Schwinn* has been the subject of continuing controversy and confusion, both in the scholarly journals and in the federal courts. The great weight of scholarly opinion has been critical of the decision,[13] and a number of the federal courts confronted with analogous vertical restrictions have sought to limit its reach. In our view, the experience of the past 10 years should be brought to bear on this subject of considerable commercial importance.

---

13. A former Assistant Attorney General in charge of the Antitrust Division has described *Schwinn* as "an exercise in barren formalism" that is "artificial and unresponsive to the competitive needs of the real world." Baker, Vertical Restraints in Times of Change: From *White* to *Schwinn* to Where?, 44 Antitrust L.J. 537 (1975). See, *e.g.*, Handler, The Twentieth Annual Antitrust Review—1967, 53 Va. L. Rev. 1667 (1967); McLaren, Territorial and Customer Restrictions, Consignments, Suggested Retail Prices and Refusals to Deal, 37 Antitrust L. J. 137 (1968); Pollock, Alternative Distribution Methods After *Schwinn*, 63 Nw. U. L. Rev. 595 (1968); Posner, Antitrust Policy and the Supreme Court: An Analysis of the Restricted Distribution, Horizontal Merger and Potential Competition Decisions, 75 Colum. L. Rev. 282 (1975); Robinson, Recent Antitrust Developments: 1974, 75 Colum. L. Rev. 243 (1975); Note, Vertical Territorial and Customer Restrictions in the Franchising Industry, 10 Colum. J. L. & Soc. Prob. 497 (1974); Note, Territorial and Customer Restrictions: A Trend Toward a Broader Rule of Reason?, 40 Geo. Wash. L. Rev. 123 (1971); Note, Territorial Restrictions and Per Se Rules—A Re-evaluation of the *Schwinn* and *Sealy* Doctrines, 70 Mich. L. Rev. 616 (1972). But see Louis, Vertical Distributional Restraints Under *Schwinn* and *Sylvania*: An Argument for the Continuing Use of a Partial Per Se Approach, 75 Mich. L. Rev. 275 (1976); Zimmerman, Distribution Restrictions After *Sealy* and *Schwinn*, 12 Antitrust Bull. 1181 (1967). For a more inclusive list of articles and comments, see 537 F.2d, at 988 n. 13.

The traditional framework of analysis under § 1 of the Sherman Act is familiar and does not require extended discussion. Section 1 prohibits "[e]very contract, combination..., or conspiracy, in restraint of trade or commerce." Since the early years of this century a judicial gloss on this statutory language has established the "rule of reason" as the prevailing standard of analysis. *Standard Oil Co. v. United States*, 221 U.S. 1 (1911). Under this rule, the fact-finder weighs all of the circumstances of a case in deciding whether a restrictive practice should be prohibited as imposing an unreasonable restraint on competition. Per se rules of illegality are appropriate only when they relate to conduct that is manifestly anticompetitive. As the Court explained in Northern Pac. R. Co. v. United States, "there are certain agreements or practices which because of their pernicious effect on competition and lack of any redeeming virtue are conclusively presumed to be unreasonable and therefore illegal without elaborate inquiry as to the precise harm they have caused or the business excuse for their use." [16]

In essence, the issue before us is whether Schwinn's per se rule can be justified under the demanding standards of Northern Pac. R. Co. The Court's refusal to endorse a per se rule in White Motor Co. was based on its uncertainty as to whether vertical restrictions satisfied those standards.

*   *   *

Only four years later the Court in *Schwinn* announced its sweeping *per se* rule without even a reference to *Northern Pac. R. Co.* and with no explanation of its sudden change in position. We turn now to consider *Schwinn* in light of *Northern Pac. R. Co.*

The market impact of vertical restrictions[18] is complex because of their potential for a simultaneous reduction of intrabrand competition and stimulation of

---

16. *Per se* rules thus require the Court to make broad generalizations about the social utility of particular commercial practices. The probability that anticompetitive consequences will result from a practice and the severity of those consequences must be balanced against its procompetitive consequences. Cases that do not fit the generalization may arise, but a *per se* rule reflects the judgment that such cases are not sufficiently common or important to justify the time and expense necessary to identify them. Once established, *per se* rules tend to provide guidance to the business community and to minimize the burdens on litigants and the judicial system of the more complex rule-of-reason trials, see *Northern Pac. R. Co. v. United States, supra; United States v. Topco Associates, Inc.*, 40 U.S. 596, 609–10 (1972), but those advantages are not sufficient in themselves to justify the creation of *per se* rules. If it were otherwise, all of antitrust law would be reduced to *per se* rules, thus introducing an unintended and undesirable rigidity in the law.

18. As in *Schwinn*, we are concerned here only with nonprice vertical restrictions. The *per se* illegality of price restrictions has been established firmly for many years and involves significantly different questions of analysis and policy. As MR. JUSTICE WHITE notes, *post*, at 69–70, some commentators have argued that the manufacturer's motivation for imposing vertical price restrictions may be the same as for nonprice restrictions. There are, however, significant differences that could easily justify different treatment. In his concurring opinion in *White Motor Co. v. United States*, MR. JUSTICE BRENNAN noted that, unlike nonprice restrictions, "[r]esale price maintenance is not only designed to, but almost invariably does in fact, reduce price competition not only *among* sellers of the affected product, but quite as much *between* that product and competing brands." Professor Posner also recognized that "industrywide resale price maintenance might facilitate cartelizing." [S]ee R.Posner, Antitrust: Cases, Economic Notes and Other Materials 134 (1974); E. Gellhorn, Antitrust Law and Economics 252 (1976). Furthermore, Congress recently has expressed its

interbrand competition.[19] Significantly, the Court in *Schwinn* did not distinguish among the challenged restrictions on the basis of their individual potential for intrabrand harm or interbrand benefit....The pivotal factor was the passage of title: All restrictions were held to be per se illegal where title had passed, and all were evaluated and sustained under the rule of reason where it had not....

It appears that this distinction between sale and nonsale transactions resulted from the Court's effort to accommodate the perceived intrabrand harm and interbrand benefit of vertical restrictions. The *per se* rule for sale transactions reflected the view that vertical restrictions are "so obviously destructive" of intrabrand competition that their use would "open the door to exclusivity of outlets and limitation of territory further than prudence permits."[21] Conversely, the continued adherence to the traditional rule of reason for nonsale transactions reflected the view that the restrictions have too great a potential for the promotion of interbrand competition to justify complete prohibition.[22] The Court's opinion

---

approval of a *per se* analysis of vertical price restrictions by repealing those provisions of the Miller-Tydings and McGuire Acts allowing fair trade pricing at the option of the individual States. Consumer Goods Pricing Act of 1975....No similar expression of congressional intent exists for nonprice restrictions.

19. Interbrand competition is the competition among the manufacturers of the same generic product—television sets in this case—and is the primary concern of antitrust law. The extreme example of a deficiency of interbrand competition is monopoly, where there is only one manufacturer. In contrast, intrabrand competition is the competition between the distributors—wholesale or retail—of the product of a particular manufacturer.

The degree of intrabrand competition is wholly independent of the level of interbrand competition confronting the manufacturer. Thus, there may be fierce intrabrand competition among the distributors of a product produced by a monopolist and no intrabrand competition among the distributors of a product produced by a firm in a highly competitive industry. But when interbrand competition exists, as it does among television manufacturers, it provides a significant check on the exploitation of intrabrand market power because of the ability of consumers to substitute a different brand of the same product.

21. The Court also stated that to impose vertical restrictions in sale transactions would "violate the ancient rule against restraints on alienation." This isolated reference has provoked sharp criticism from virtually all of the commentators on the decision, most of whom have regarded the Court's apparent reliance on the "ancient rule" as both a misreading of legal history and a perversion of antitrust analysis. We quite agree with MR. JUSTICE STEWART's dissenting comment in *Schwinn* that "the state of the common law 400 or even 100 years ago is irrelevant to the issue before us: the effect of the antitrust laws upon vertical distributional restraints in the American economy today."

We are similarly unable to accept Judge Browning's interpretation of *Schwinn*. In his dissent below he argued that the decision reflects the view that the Sherman Act was intended to prohibit restrictions on the autonomy of independent businessmen even though they have no impact on "price, quality, and quantity of goods and services." This view is certainly not explicit in *Schwinn*, which purports to be based on an examination of the "impact [of the restrictions] upon the marketplace." Competitive economies have social and political as well as economic advantages, see e.g., *Northern Pac. R. Co. v. United States*, but an antitrust policy divorced from market considerations would lack any objective benchmarks. * * * Although MR. JUSTICE WHITE's opinion endorses Judge Browning's interpretation, it purports to distinguish Schwinn on grounds inconsistent with that interpretation.

22. In that regard, the Court specifically stated that a more complete prohibition "might severely hamper smaller enterprises resorting to reasonable methods of meeting the competition of giants and of merchandising through independent dealers." The Court also broadly hinted that it would recognize additional exceptions to the per se rule for new entrants in an industry and for failing firms, both of which were mentioned in *White Motor* as candidates for such exceptions. The Court might have limited the exceptions to the *per se* rule to these situations, which present the strongest arguments for the sacrifice of intrabrand

provides no analytical support for these contrasting positions. Nor is there even an assertion in the opinion that the competitive impact of vertical restrictions is significantly affected by the form of the transaction.…

Vertical restrictions reduce intrabrand competition by limiting the number of sellers of a particular product competing for the business of a given group of buyers.… Although intrabrand competition may be reduced, the ability of retailers to exploit the resulting market may be limited both by the ability of consumers to travel to other franchised locations and, perhaps more importantly, to purchase the competing products of other manufacturers. None of these key variables, however, is affected by the form of the transaction by which a manufacturer conveys his products to the retailers.

Vertical restrictions promote interbrand competition by allowing the manufacturer to achieve certain efficiencies in the distribution of his products. These "redeeming virtues" are implicit in every decision sustaining vertical restrictions under the rule of reason. Economists have identified a number of ways in which manufacturers can use such restrictions to compete more effectively against other manufacturers.[23] For example, new manufacturers and manufacturers entering new markets can use the restrictions in order to induce competent and aggressive retailers to make the kind of investment of capital and labor that is often required in the distribution of products unknown to the consumer. Established manufacturers can use them to induce retailers to engage in promotional activities or to provide service and repair facilities necessary to the efficient marketing of their products. Service and repair are vital for many products, such as automobiles and major household appliances. The availability and quality of such services affect a manufacturer's goodwill and the competitiveness of his product. Because of market imperfections such as the so-called "free rider" effect, these services might not be provided by retailers in a purely competitive situation, despite the fact that each retailer's benefit would be greater if all provided the services than if none did.

Economists also have argued that manufacturers have an economic interest in maintaining as much intrabrand competition as is consistent with the efficient distribution of their products. Bork, The Rule of Reason and the Per Se Concept: Price Fixing and Market Division [II], 75 Yale L. J. 373, 403 (1966).[24] Although

---

competition for interbrand competition. Significantly, it chose instead to create the more extensive exception for nonsale transactions which is available to all businesses, regardless of their size, financial health, or market share. This broader exception demonstrates even more clearly the Court's awareness of the "redeeming virtues" of vertical restrictions.

23. Marketing efficiency is not the only legitimate reason for a manufacturer's desire to exert control over the manner in which his products are sold and serviced. As a result of statutory and common-law developments, society increasingly demands that manufacturers assume direct responsibility for the safety and quality of their products. For example, at the federal level, apart from more specialized requirements, manufacturers of consumer products have safety responsibilities under the Consumer Product Safety Act, and obligations for warranties under the Consumer Product Warranties Act. Similar obligations are imposed by state law. The legitimacy of these concerns has been recognized in cases involving vertical restrictions.

24. "Generally a manufacturer would prefer the lowest retail price possible, once its price to dealers has been set, because a lower retail price means increased sales and higher manufacturer revenues." Note, 88 Harv. L. Rev. 636, 641 (1975). In this context, a manufacturer is likely to view the difference between the price at which it sells to its retailers and

the view that the manufacturer's interest necessarily corresponds with that of the public is not universally shared, even the leading critic of vertical restrictions concedes that *Schwinn's* distinction between sale and nonsale transactions is essentially unrelated to any relevant economic impact. Comanor, Vertical Territorial and Customer Restrictions: White Motor and Its Aftermath, 81 Harv. L. Rev. 1419, 1422 (1968).[25] Indeed, to the extent that the form of the transaction is related to interbrand benefits, the Court's distinction is inconsistent with its articulated concern for the ability of smaller firms to compete effectively with larger ones. Capital requirements and administrative expenses may prevent smaller firms from using the exception for nonsale transactions.

We conclude that the distinction drawn in *Schwinn* between sale and nonsale transactions is not sufficient to justify the application of a *per se* rule in one situation and a rule of reason in the other. The question remains whether the per se rule stated in Schwinn should be expanded to include nonsale transactions or abandoned in favor of a return to the rule of reason. We have found no persuasive support for expanding the per se rule. As noted above, the *Schwinn* Court recognized the undesirability of "prohibit[ing] all vertical restrictions of territory and all franchising...." And even Continental does not urge us to hold that all such restrictions are *per se* illegal.

We revert to the standard articulated in *Northern Pac. R. Co.*, and reiterated in *White Motor*, for determining whether vertical restrictions must be "conclusively presumed to be unreasonable and therefore illegal without elaborate inquiry as to the precise harm they have caused or the business excuse for their use." Such restrictions, in varying forms, are widely used in our free market economy. As indicated above, there is substantial scholarly and judicial authority supporting their economic utility. There is relatively little authority to the contrary.[28] Certainly, there has been no showing in this case, either generally or with respect to Sylvania's agreements, that vertical restrictions have or are likely to have a "pernicious effect on competition" or that they "lack...any redeeming virtue."[29] Accordingly, we

---

their price to the consumer as its "cost of distribution," which it would prefer to minimize. Posner, *supra*, n. 13, at 283.

25. Professor Comanor argues that the promotional activities encouraged by vertical restrictions result in product differentiation and, therefore, a decrease in interbrand competition. This argument is flawed by its necessary assumption that a large part of the promotional efforts resulting from vertical restrictions will not convey socially desirable information about product availability, price, quality, and services. Nor is it clear that a *per se* rule would result in anything more than a shift to less efficient methods of obtaining the same promotional effects.

28. There may be occasional problems in differentiating vertical restrictions from horizontal restrictions originating in agreements among the retailers. There is no doubt that restrictions in the latter category would be illegal *per se*, see, *e.g.*, *United States v. General Motors Corp* (1966); *United States v. Topco Associates, Inc.*, but we do not regard the problems of proof as sufficiently great to justify a *per se* rule.

29. The location restriction used by Sylvania was neither the least nor the most restrictive provision that it could have used. But we agree with the implicit judgment in *Schwinn* that a *per se* rule based on the nature of the restriction is, in general, undesirable. Although distinctions can be drawn among the frequently used restrictions, we are inclined to view them as differences of degree and form. We are unable to perceive significant social gain from channeling transactions into one form or another. Finally, we agree with the Court in *Schwinn* that the advantages of vertical restrictions should not be limited to the categories of

conclude that the *per se* rule stated in *Schwinn* must be overruled. In so holding we do not foreclose the possibility that particular applications of vertical restrictions might justify *per se* prohibition under *Northern Pac. R. Co.* But we do make clear that departure from the rule-of-reason standard must be based upon demonstrable economic effect rather than—as in *Schwinn*—upon formalistic line drawing.

In sum, we conclude that the appropriate decision is to return to the rule of reason that governed vertical restrictions prior to *Schwinn*. When anticompetitive effects are shown to result from particular vertical restrictions they can be adequately policed under the rule of reason, the standard traditionally applied for the majority of anticompetitive practices challenged under § 1 of the Act. Accordingly, the decision of the Court of Appeals is

Affirmed.

MR. JUSTICE WHITE, concurring in the judgment.

Although I agree with the majority that the location clause at issue in this case is not a *per se* violation of the Sherman Act and should be judged under the rule of reason, I cannot agree that this result requires the overruling of *United States v. Arnold, Schwinn & Co.* In my view this case is distinguishable from *Schwinn* because there is less potential for restraint of intrabrand competition and more potential for stimulating interbrand competition. As to intrabrand competition, Sylvania, unlike *Schwinn*, did not restrict the customers to whom or the territories where its purchasers could sell. As to interbrand competition, Sylvania, unlike *Schwinn*, had an insignificant market share at the time it adopted its challenged distribution practice and enjoyed no consumer preference that would allow its retailers to charge a premium over other brands. In two short paragraphs, the majority disposes of the view, adopted after careful analysis by the Ninth Circuit en banc below, that these differences provide a "principled basis for distinguishing *Schwinn*," ... [and] that the per se rule established in that case does not apply to location clauses such as Sylvania's. To reach out to overrule one of this Court's recent interpretations of the Sherman Act, after such a cursory examination of the necessity for doing so, is surely an affront to the principle that considerations of *stare decisis* are to be given particularly strong weight in the area of statutory construction.

One element of the system of interrelated vertical restraints invalidated in *Schwinn* was a retail-customer restriction prohibiting franchised retailers from selling *Schwinn* products to nonfranchised retailers. The Court rests its inability to distinguish *Schwinn* entirely on this retail-customer restriction.... The customer restriction may well have, however, a very different "intent and competitive impact" than the location restriction: It prevents discount stores from getting the manufacturer's product and thus prevents intrabrand price competition. Suppose, for example, that interbrand competition is sufficiently weak that the franchised retailers are able to charge a price substantially above wholesale. Under a location restriction, these franchisers are free to sell to discount stores seeking to exploit the potential for sales at prices below the prevailing retail level. One of the franchised retailers may be

---

new entrants and failing firms. Sylvania was faltering, if not failing, and we think it would be unduly artificial to deny it the use of valuable competitive tools.

tempted to lower its price and act in effect as a wholesaler for the discount house in order to share in the profits to be had from lowering prices and expanding volume.

Under a retail customer restriction, on the other hand, the franchised dealers cannot sell to discounters, who are cut off altogether from the manufacturer's product and the opportunity for intrabrand price competition. This was precisely the theory on which the Government successfully challenged *Schwinn's* customer restrictions in this Court. The District Court in that case found that "[e]ach one of [*Schwinn's* franchised retailers] knows also that he is not a wholesaler and that he cannot sell as a wholesaler or act as an agent for some other enfranchised dealer, such as a discount house retailer who has not been franchised as a dealer by *Schwinn*." The Government argued on appeal, with extensive citations to the record, that the effect of this restriction was "to keep *Schwinn* products out of the hands of discount houses and other price cutters so as to discourage price competition in retailing. . . ."[2]

It is true that, as the majority states, Sylvania's location restriction inhibited to some degree "the freedom of the retailer to dispose of the purchased products" by requiring the retailer to sell from one particular place of business. But the retailer is still free to sell to any type of customerincluding discounters and other unfranchised dealers—from any area. I think this freedom implies a significant difference for the effect of a location clause on intrabrand competition. The District Court on remand in *Schwinn* evidently thought so as well, for after enjoining *Schwinn's* customer restrictions as directed by this Court it expressly sanctioned location clauses, permitting *Schwinn* to "designat[e] in its retailer franchise agreements the location of the place or places of business for which the franchise is issued."

        *   *   *

Just as there are significant differences between *Schwinn* and this case with respect to intrabrand competition, there are also significant differences with respect to interbrand competition. Unlike *Schwinn*, Sylvania clearly had no economic power in the generic product market. At the time they instituted their respective distribution policies, *Schwinn* was "the leading bicycle producer in the Nation," with a national market share of 22.5%, whereas Sylvania was a "faltering, if not failing" producer of television sets, with "a relatively insignificant 1% to 2%" share of the national market in which the dominant manufacturer had a 60% to 70% share. Moreover, the *Schwinn* brand name enjoyed superior consumer acceptance and commanded a premium price as, in the District Court's words, "the Cadillac of the bicycle industry." This premium gave *Schwinn* dealers a margin of protection from interbrand competition and created the possibilities for price cutting by discounters that the Government argued were forestalled by *Schwinn's* customer restrictions. Thus, judged by the criteria economists use to measure market power—product

---

2. Given the Government's emphasis on the inhibiting effect of the *Schwinn* restrictions on discounting activities, the Court may well have been referring to this effect when it condemned the restrictions as "obviously destructive of competition." But the Court was also heavily influenced by its concern for the freedom of dealers to control the disposition of products they purchased from Schwinn. See *infra*, at 66–69. In any event, the record in *Schwinn* illustrates the potentially greater threat to intrabrand competition posed by customer as opposed to location restrictions.

differentiation and market share—*Schwinn* enjoyed a substantially stronger position in the bicycle market than did Sylvania in the television market....

In my view there are at least two considerations, both relied upon by the majority to justify overruling *Schwinn*, that would provide a "principled basis" for instead refusing to extend *Schwinn* to a vertical restraint that is imposed by a "faltering" manufacturer with a "precarious" position in a generic product market dominated by another firm. The first is that, as the majority puts it, "when interbrand competition exists, as it does among television manufacturers, it provides a significant check on the exploitation of intrabrand market power because of the ability of consumers to substitute a different brand of the same product." Second is the view, argued forcefully in the economic literature cited by the majority, that the potential benefits of vertical restraints in promoting interbrand competition are particularly strong where the manufacturer imposing the restraints is seeking to enter a new market or to expand a small market share. The majority even recognizes that *Schwinn* "hinted" at an exception for new entrants and failing firms from its *per se* rule.

In other areas of antitrust law, this Court has not hesitated to base its rules of *per se* illegality in part on the defendant's market power. Indeed, in the very case from which the majority draws its standard for *per se* rules, *Northern Pac. R. Co. v. United States*, the Court stated the reach of the *per se* rule against tie-ins under § 1 of the Sherman Act as extending to all defendants with "sufficient economic power with respect to the tying product to appreciably restrain free competition in the market for the tied product...." And the Court subsequently approved an exception to this per se rule for "infant industries" marketing a new product. *United States v. Jerrold Electronics Corp.* See also United States v. Philadelphia Nat. Bank * * * . I see no doctrinal obstacle to excluding firms with such minimal market power as Sylvania's from the reach of the *Schwinn* rule.

I have, moreover, substantial misgivings about the approach the majority takes to overruling *Schwinn*. The reason for the distinction in *Schwinn* between sale and nonsale transactions was not, as the majority would have it, "the Court's effort to accommodate the perceived intrabrand harm and interbrand benefit of vertical restrictions," the reason was rather, as Judge Browning argued in dissent below, the notion in many of our cases involving vertical restraints that independent businessmen should have the freedom to dispose of the goods they own as they see fit....

After summarily rejecting this concern...for "the autonomy of independent businessmen," the majority not surprisingly finds "no justification" for *Schwinn's* distinction between sale and nonsale transactions because the distinction is "essentially unrelated to any relevant economic impact." But while according some weight to the businessman's interest in controlling the terms on which he trades in his own goods may be anathema to those who view the Sherman Act as directed solely to economic efficiency, this principle is without question more deeply embedded in our cases than the notions of "free rider" effects and distributional efficiencies borrowed by the majority from the "new economics of vertical relationships." Perhaps the Court is right in partially abandoning this principle and in judging the instant non-price vertical restraints solely by their "relevant economic impact"; but the precedents which reflect this principle should not be so lightly rejected by the Court....

I have a further reservation about the majority's reliance on "relevant economic impact" as the test for retaining per se rules regarding vertical restraints. It is common ground among the leading advocates of a purely economic approach to the question of distribution restraints that the economic arguments in favor of allowing vertical nonprice restraints generally apply to vertical price restraints as well. Although the majority asserts that "the *per se* illegality of price restrictions...involves significantly different questions of analysis and policy," I suspect this purported distinction may be as difficult to justify as that of *Schwinn* under the terms of the majority's analysis. Thus Professor Posner, in an article cited five times by the majority, concludes: "I believe that the law should treat price and nonprice restrictions the same and that it should make no distinction between the imposition of restrictions in a sale contract and their imposition in an agency contract." Indeed, the Court has already recognized that resale price maintenance may increase output by inducing "demand creating activity" by dealers (such as additional retail outlets, advertising and promotion, and product servicing) that outweighs the additional sales that would result from lower prices brought about by dealer price competition. *Albrecht v. Herald Co.* These same output-enhancing possibilities of nonprice vertical restraints are relied upon by the majority as evidence of their social utility and economic soundness, and as a justification for judging them under the rule of reason. The effect, if not the intention, of the Court's opinion is necessarily to call into question the firmly established per se rule against price restraints.

Although the case law in the area of distributional restraints has perhaps been less than satisfactory, the Court would do well to proceed more deliberately in attempting to improve it....In order to decide this case, the Court need only hold that a location clause imposed by a manufacturer with negligible economic power in the product market has a competitive impact sufficiently less restrictive than the *Schwinn* restraints to justify a rule-of-reason standard, even if the same weight is given here as in *Schwinn* to dealer autonomy. I therefore concur in the judgment.

Notes and Questions

1. Intrabrand v. Interbrand Rivalry: The Court recognizes a distinction between intrabrand and interbrand competition. Should these two different types of competition be analyzed in the same manner for purposes of antitrust regulation? The Court observes that some vertical nonprice restraints on intrabrand competition may actually improve interbrand competition. How does this work? Does this also mean that the losses in efficiency resulting from restraints in intrabrand competition are made-up-for by improved interbrand competition?

2. Territorial v. Location Restraints: Manufacturers and franchisors frequently impose nonprice restraints on their distributors, retailers, or franchisees. The two types of nonprice restraints discussed in *Continental T.V.* are territorial and location restraints. **Territorial restraints** are a nonprice restraint that may take the form of exclusive territories to which the designated distributor's sales are limited and where only the designated distributor is allowed to sell the product. **Location restraints** limit the location from which a distributor, dealer, or franchisee may sell the product. In *Schwinn*, the nonprice restraint at issue was a territorial restraint while in *Continental T.V.* a location restraint was called into question. Is this distinction important as a legal matter? How about as an economic matter? The Court found that there was no reason to distinguish between the two forms of nonprice restraints because both restrictions effectively fore-close significant intrabrand competition. Does the concurring opinion agree with this conclusion?

3. The Rule of Reason and Perfect Competition: In *Schwinn*, the Court considered whether vertical non-price restrictions on distributors are lawful and whether such restrictions should be subject to a per se or rule of reason test for purposes of liability. The *Schwinn* Court developed an unusual rule based upon antiquated notions of alienability. Specifically, if the manufacturer had passed title and risk for the goods in question on to the distributor or retailer, then nonprice vertical restraints were a per se violation of antitrust law. However, if the manufacturer by way of consignments retained title and risk to goods in the possession of distributors or retailers, the nonprice restraint was subject to rule of reason analysis. The Court in *Sylvania* overruled *Schwinn*. First, the Court found the line drawn between holding title and not holding title to be formalistic and not related to any economic justification for per se illegality. Moreover, the Court observed that it is possible for nonprice restraints in intrabrand markets to cause efficiency gains in interbrand markets. The *Sylvania* Court demonstrates a good appreciation for the competitive market as a dynamic process. Specifically, the Court recognizes that rivalrous behavior can lead to unique contractual solutions that improve efficiency.

4. Perverse Incentives to Integrate Vertically: Vertical integration is the ownership of vertically related parts of a distribution network. For example, owning both the production and distribution parts of a business would constitute vertical integration. To the extent that vertical contractual restraints are not allowed, vertical integration becomes a method for controlling the free-rider problems. As part of its justification for not holding vertical non-price constraints to the *per se* standard, the Court notes that such a rule "would create a perverse incentive for manufacturers to integrate vertically into distribution, an outcome hardly conducive to fostering the creation and maintenance of small businesses." Why doesn't the same perverse incentive arise from holding vertical price restraints to the *per se* standard? In deciding on its distribution method, the manufacturer will choose that method with the lowest cost for the benefit desired. If vertical price restraints are more cost effective than vertical integration and vertical integration is more cost effective than non-price vertical restraints, would there be a perverse effect? What happens if vertical price restraints are more efficient than non-price restraints and both vertical price restraints and non-price restraints are more efficient than vertical integration? Does it make sense to have a perverse incentive encouraging the use of vertical non-price restraints as opposed to price restraints?

5. Ancillary v. Naked Restraints: The dissent argues that vertical non-price restraints can be considered ancillary contractual terms. That is, a retailer must agree to the restraints in order to get his franchise, but that the contractual term is subordinate to the franchise agreement itself. Moreover, the dissent argues that such ancillary agreements are legal unless they fail a rule of reason analysis. Thus, a retailer can be terminated for violation of such a restraint. Can the same argument be made for vertical price restraints?

Figure V-15

The Dual Effects of a Price Reduction on Total Revenues

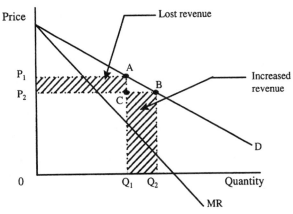

D. Monopoly

A monopoly exists when there is only one producer of a particular good or service for which there are no close substitutes and the producer is protected from competition by impenetrable barriers to entry. Barriers to entry allow monopolies to earn above normal profits by reducing their output below competitive levels and raising their prices above competitive levels. Monopolies are a form of market failure—they result in a misallocation of resources. Yet, the very existence of monopolies poses a difficult question for policy makers—in a market economy, it is the striving to earn monopoly profits that encourages innovation and efficiency. Public policies designed to restrain monopolistic practices must be carefully designed to avoid dampening competitive incentives.

1. Profit Maximizing Price and Quantity

A monopolist is the only producer of a particular good or service and, therefore, by its actions alone, determines the market price. The monopolist is referred to as a **price searcher** because it searches for the price and output combination that maximizes profits. In contrast to the perfectly competitive model where the demand curve faced by price taking firms is horizontal and equal to a market price established by the interaction of industry supply and demand, the monopolist is the only firm in the industry and its demand curve is the same as the industry demand curve. Thus, the monopolist faces a downward sloping demand curve—the monopolist must lower price in order to sell additional units. This has important implications for the monopolist's production decisions because, unlike the price taker, the monopolist's marginal revenue does not equal price.

For the monopolist, marginal revenue is less than price except for the very first unit sold. The divergence of marginal revenue and price occurs because the demand curve faced by the monopolist is downward sloping. When demand is downward sloping, and a uniform price is charged for all units sold, marginal revenue will always be less than market price. This result is illustrated in Figure V-15. A price cut from P_1 to P_2 increases the quantity sold from Q_1 to Q_2. So, total revenue at point A on the demand curve is equal to P_1AQ_10; at point B, it is equal to P_2BQ_20. The change in total revenue in moving from A to B is the result of two offsetting influences. First, revenue is increased as a result of the sale of additional units of output from Q_1 to Q_2. This increase in revenue is the area CBQ_2Q_1. Second, revenue is lost due to a lower price on units 0 to Q_1 that could have been sold at the higher price P_1 instead of P_2. This reduction is represented by the area P_1ACP_2. The marginal revenue derived from the sale of an additional unit is the difference between these two offsetting effects. That is, marginal revenue is the difference between the total revenue at A and the total revenue at B. Because the marginal revenue for any output charged is less than the corresponding price for that level of output, the marginal revenue (MR) curve will always lie below the demand curve (with the one exception being the first unit sold). For the first unit sold, marginal revenue is equal to market price. Beyond that the general rule always holds—P > MR.

Figure V-16, which shows a standard demand curve with MR below price at every level of output, demonstrates the relationship between total revenue, marginal revenue, demand, and elasticity. Recall from Chapter III that when price reductions cause total revenue to rise, demand is elastic. If MR > 0, then TR in-

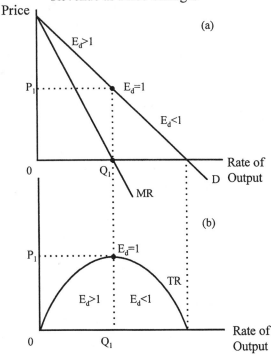

<u>Figure V-16</u>

Changes in Elasticity of Demand and Total
Revenue as Price Changes

Figure V-17

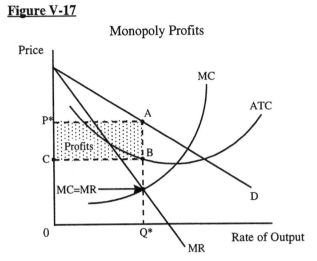

Monopoly Profits

creases with increases in output. The only way to sell the increased output is to lower price. Thus, if MR > 0, then demand is elastic. In Figure V-16, E_d > 1 to the left of Q_1 and E_d < 1 to the right of Q_1. A minute change in price around P_1 will not change total revenue, so E_d = 1 at output Q_1.

The relationship between total revenue, marginal revenue, and demand elasticity is the starting point for analyzing the profit maximizing output and pricing decisions of a monopolist. Common sense tells us that no rational profit maximizer will produce output in the range where marginal revenue is negative. Thus, the profit maximizing monopolist will always operate along the elastic or unit elastic portion of the demand curve. If a firm were to find itself at an output level in the inelastic range, it could increase profits by simply reducing output (and costs) while increasing revenue.

Of course, in determining the profit maximizing level of output for the monopolist, the costs of production must be considered. Generally speaking, the monopolist has no special power in the resource or input market. In other words, when it comes to buying factors of production, the monopolist is just like any perfectly competitive firm. Thus, the cost curves for the monopolist have the same characteristics as those of the perfectly competitive firm. Moreover, profit maximizing monopolists follow the same general rule as firms in a perfectly competitive industry—expand production until marginal revenue (MR) equals marginal cost (MC). The monopolist follows this rule for exactly the same reasons as the perfect competitor. For example, if marginal revenue for the next unit of production is greater than its marginal cost, then profits will grow by producing that unit.

The profit maximizing decision of the monopolist is demonstrated in Figure V-17. The profit maximizing output is Q^*, where MR = MC. To the left of Q^*, MR > MC and the firm can increase profits by expanding production. To the right of Q^*, MC > MR and the firm can increase profits by reducing production.

At Q*, the firm cannot increase profits by changing the level of production—
profits are maximized at Q*. The demand curve shows that Q* units can be sold
at P*. In Figure V-17, this corresponds with point A on the demand curve. Thus,
P* is the profit maximizing price.

The level of monopoly profits is calculated in the same manner as profits for
the perfectly competitive firm. Specifically, profit is equal to Q*(P* − ATC), for
ATC at the output level where MR = MC. In Figure V-17, monopoly profits are
equal to the area P*ABC.

When the monopolist earns a profit, it means that the firm has earned a return in excess of the opportunity cost of the resources used to produce its output.
In a perfectly competitive industry, such above normal profits attract the entry of
new firms. However, entry is not possible for a pure monopoly industry because,
by definition, new entry is precluded. Thus, unlike the competitive industry,
which is restored to a normal return in the long-run, economic profits can continue to exist in the long-run for the monopolist.

An important note of caution is in order here. Not all monopolies are profitable. Consider the cost and revenue information for the monopolist graphed in
Figure V-18. MR = MC at Q* which yields a profit maximizing price of P*. Q*
corresponds to point A on the demand curve and point B on the ATC curve.
Thus, at Q*, ATC > P*, and losses equal to Q*(P* − ATC) are shown by the rectangle ABCP*. When a monopolist suffers a loss, the firm is earning a return on
the resources it uses that is less than their opportunity cost. As under perfect
competition, in the face of a short-run economic loss, the monopolist has a
choice between continuing production or shutting down. The same loss mini-

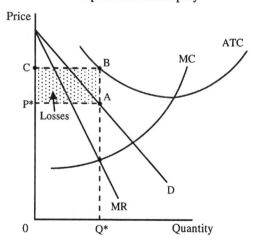

Figure V-18

An Unprofitable Monopoly

mization decision rule applies here as well. That is, as long as revenue exceeds variable cost, the monopolist firm will continue to produce in the short-run. If these loss conditions persist in the long-run, however, the firm will transfer its resources to an industry in which it can earn a normal return.

One final point must be made regarding the profit maximizing price and quantity decision of a monopolist. A supply curve is evidence of a unique relationship between market price and the quantity that the firm is willing and able to supply. In a perfectly competitive market, the price taking firm's marginal cost curve is its supply curve. The monopolist, however, does not set price equal to marginal cost. In order to determine the profit maximizing output, the monopolist needs to know a marginal revenue curve and the marginal cost curve. After determining the profit maximizing quantity, the monopolist finds the corresponding price on the demand curve. Thus, for the monopolist, there is no unique relation between quantity supplied and price. In other words, the monopolist does not have a supply curve.

2. The Social Costs of Monopoly

Recall that perfect competition provides a benchmark, P = MC, for evaluating the allocative efficiency of a market. A monopolist operates at a quantity where P > MC and, thus, the monopolist falls short of the competitive benchmark for allocative efficiency. Monopoly is a form of market failure. This section explores the social costs of this market failure.

a. Deadweight Costs

The most widely accepted criticism of monopolies is that monopolists distort the allocation of resources by restricting output when buyers are willing to pay a price greater than the marginal costs of producing additional output. Consider the cost and demand curves for a hypothetical industry presented in Figure V-19. For simplicity, assume that the average total cost of production is the same at all levels of production—that is, this is a constant cost industry and MC = ATC at all levels of output.

If this were a perfectly competitive industry, the firms would produce Q_C where P_C = MC. At Q_C, the sum of producer and consumer surplus (ABP_C) is maximized. All potential gains from trade are realized, and the last unit produced is valued by customers at an amount equal to the opportunity cost of the resources used in its production.

The monopolist's profit maximizing quantity occurs at Q_M where MR = MC. Q_M is less than the competitive level, Q_C. As a consequence of the restriction of output, consumer surplus is reduced to the area ADP_M, which is considerably less than the consumer surplus (ABP_C) in the competitive industry. Some of the consumer surplus goes to the monopolist in the form of monopoly profits, P_MDEP_C. Although consumers are harmed by having to pay the higher price that results from the monopoly restriction of output, the monopolist is made better off by the increased profits. Economists claim no particular expertise at determining whether society is better off with those profits going to consumers or the monopolist. Such distributional issues (i.e., how the economic pie is di-

Figure V-19

Social Costs of Monopoly

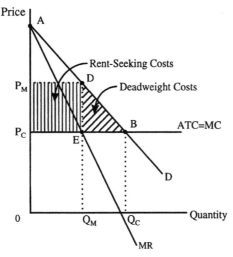

vided) are usually not addressed by economists because it is difficult to develop and test hypotheses that deal with interpersonal comparisons of utility from wealth.

Economists are concerned, however, with another portion of consumer surplus that disappears when monopolists restrict output—the triangle DBE in Figure V-19. The monopolist's decision to not produce beyond Q_M means that buyers located between points D and B on the demand curve are unable to purchase the product even though they are willing to pay a price greater than the marginal costs of producing those additional units. The triangle DBE represents unrealized potential gains from trade. Those opportunities are lost. The triangle DBE represents a reduction in social welfare which is referred to as the **deadweight costs of monopoly.**

The impact of this deadweight cost on society can be illustrated by returning to the example of the baker, which was developed earlier in this chapter. Suppose that the total cost of making a loaf of bread (assuming constant marginal cost) is $1.00, including a normal return to the baker for labor time and entrepreneurship. Suppose, further, that it takes a particular individual, who paints houses competitively for $1.50 an hour, a total of one hour to bake a loaf of bread. When the baker opens the bakery selling bread for $1.00, the painter begins buying bread rather than baking his own. Instead of using an hour to bake bread, the painter spends the time painting houses. Not only is the painter better off by $.50, but society is also better off because it has gained $1.50 in output at a cost of only $1.00. Since the baker has no competition (that is, she is a monopolist), she discovers that she can increase profits by increasing the price of her bread to $2.00. As a result, the painter must return to baking his own bread and society loses $1.50 of output and gains only $1.00 (not $2.00, because the true value of baking bread is only $1.00—this is the point where P > MC). The deadweight cost equals $.50. This lost production can never be regained—bygones are bygones.

The size of the deadweight costs has been estimated in several empirical studies by economists.[3] Although the results of the studies are controversial because of their methodology and assumptions, it is worth noting that the studies indicate that the deadweight costs of monopoly are less than one percent of gross national product. Those low estimates sent industrial organization economists scurrying to come up with explanations for why the estimates were low. After all, it is difficult to justify any government antitrust policy if the potential gains from an effective policy are less than one percent of GNP; and the repeal of the antitrust laws would eliminate a major source of consulting income for economists. Of course, one explanation for the low estimates of deadweight costs is that they prove that antitrust policy was effectively preventing monopolistic practices.

One general criticism of the deadweight cost estimates is that they use above-normal profits as one of the proxies for the presence of monopoly power. Thus, the explanations for the relatively low estimates are, at least in part, really concerned with explaining why monopoly profits are not very high. In that regard, one of the most persuasive explanations for the low deadweight cost estimates is that political competition for the right to earn monopoly profits (economists refer to monopoly profits as **rents**) may have increased the monopolist's costs to the point that the monopoly return was simply a normal profit. This explanation is investigated in the following subsection.

b. Rent-Seeking Costs

The potential of earning monopoly profits (rents) leads firms to use resources to capture those rents. Such rent-seeking expenditures represent an additional social cost of monopoly. Rent-seeking expenditures attempt to use the power of the state to transfer wealth from one group to another. See subsection E.1. "Interest Groups, Rent Seeking, and Rent Extraction," in Chapter II. This use of scarce resources represents a social loss, because the resources could have been used for more productive purposes. That is, rent-seeking expenditures are concerned with merely dividing up the economic pie, rather than increasing the size of the pie.

Firms invest resources in the pursuit of monopoly profits up to the point where the marginal opportunity cost of the last dollar invested is equal to its expected return in increased profits. For example, if the sole domestic producer of a certain product expects a proposed import restriction or tariff (designed to solidify its monopoly) to increase the value of the firm by $1 million (the present value of future monopoly profits), then the domestic producer would be willing to spend up to $1 million on lobbying and campaign contributions in order to get the transfer. Moreover, those who expect to be injured by the change in the law would be willing to make similar investments to prevent the adoption of the

---

3. The most famous of the studies is Arnold C. Harberger, "Monopoly and Resource Allocation," 54 *American Economic Review* 77 (1954).

import restriction or tariff. The total effect, therefore, is that rent-seeking expenditures will come close to equaling the total amount transferred from consumers to the monopoly. That is, the rectangle representing monopoly profits, $P_M DEP_C$, will be consumed by rent-seeking expenditures. Thus, in Figure V-19, the social costs of monopoly include the deadweight costs, DBE, plus the rent seeking costs, $P_M DEP_C$.

c. Other Criticisms of Monopoly

Some economists have argued that monopolies should be attacked because the lack of product market competition makes the managers lazy and allows them to deviate from technically efficient decisions concerning cost minimization and innovation. As Sir John Hicks, a famous English economist, once put it: "[T]he best of all monopoly profits is a quiet life." See J.R. Hicks, "Annual Survey of Economic Theory: The Theory of Monopoly," 3 Econometrica 1, 8 (1935). This view, however, has never been supported by empirical studies. Moreover, there are strong theoretical reasons for doubting the validity of the hypothesis.

Competition in the product market is not the only constraint on managerial behavior. Managers are forced to attempt to maximize profits by a number of competitive mechanisms other than product market competition. For example, from the typical shareholder's perspective, profits that are sacrificed due to managerial laziness are an opportunity cost that is reflected in lower stock price. Competition in the stock market will lead to the identification of the poorly performing firm as an attractive takeover target, and managers may lose their jobs in the event of a takeover. Thus, even in monopoly firms, managers have the incentive to maximize profits through cost minimization.

In summary, the absence of product market competition does not appear to allow monopoly managers to be slack in controlling costs. Nevertheless, the social costs of monopoly provide a strong theoretical justification for attempting to correct the market failure through government intervention.

In addition to the economic criticisms of monopoly, there are several sociopolitical arguments against monopoly. The following excerpt from Professor (now Judge) Richard Posner's *Antitrust Law: An Economic Perspective* summarizes many of these criticisms and their validity.

> Having considered the economic objections to monopoly, I want to discuss now three broadly political arguments against it. The first is that monopoly transfers wealth from consumers to the stockholders of monopolistic firms, a redistribution that goes from the less to the more wealthy. This appealing argument is undermined by the point made earlier that competition to become a monopolist will tend to transform the expected gains from monopoly into social costs. To the extent that this occurs, consumers' wealth will not be transferred to the shareholders of monopoly firms but will instead be dissipated in the purchase of inputs into the activity of becoming a monopolist.

> A second argument is that monopoly, or more broadly any condition (such as concentration) that fosters cooperation among competing firms,

will facilitate an industry's manipulation of the political process to obtain protective legislation aimed at increasing the industry's profits. Often such protection takes the form of controls over entry and price competition, coupled with exemption from the antitrust laws, that result in cartelizing the industry much more effectively than could be done by private agreement. This is not the place to pursue the intricacies of the nascent economic analysis of the determinants of political power. It is enough to note that, while concentration may reduce the costs of organizing effectively to manipulate the political process, it may also reduce the demand for public assistance in suppressing competition, since, as we shall see . . . , a concentrated industry, other things being equal, is in a better position to suppress competition through private agreement, express or tacit, than an unconcentrated industry. It is therefore unclear whether on balance concentrated, or monopolistic, industries will obtain greater help from the political process than unconcentrated, or competitive, industries. This theoretical indeterminacy is mirrored in the empirical world, where we observe many unconcentrated industries—agriculture, trucking, local broadcasting, banking, medicine, to name a few—enjoying governmental protection against competition.

In any event, however, this political objection to monopoly and concentration is not sharply different from the economic objection. The legislation sought by an industry—a tariff, a tax on substitute products, control of entry—will usually have economic effects similar or even identical to those of a private cartel agreement. The political argument—which is simply that concentration facilitates monopoly pricing indirectly through the legislative process, as well as directly through cartelization—thus implies no change in the character of an antitrust policy deduced from economic considerations. (This is also true, incidentally, of the wealth-redistribution argument: the implications for public policy are not sharply different whether one objects to monopoly pricing because it wastes resources or because it brings about undesirable changes in the redistribution of wealth.)

The last political argument that I shall discuss has, in contrast, implications for antitrust policy that diverge sharply from those of economic analysis. The popular (or Populist) alternative to an antitrust policy designed to promote economic efficiency by limiting monopoly is a policy of restricting the freedom of action of large business firms in order to promote small business. (It may be possible to conceive of a different alternative to an efficiency-based antitrust policy, but this is the only one suggested with any frequency.) The idea that there is some special virtue in small business compared to large is a persistent one. I am not prepared to argue that it has no merit whatever. I am, however, confident that antitrust enforcement is an inappropriate method of trying to promote the interests of small business as a whole. The best overall antitrust policy from the standpoint of small business is no antitrust policy, since monopoly, by driving a wedge between the prices and the costs of the larger firms in the market (it is presumably they who take the lead in forming cartels), enable the smaller firms in the market to survive even if their costs are higher than those of the large firms. The only kind of antitrust policy that would benefit small business would be one whose principal objective was to limit the attempts of large firms to underprice less efficient small firms by sharing their lower costs with consumers in the form of lower prices. Apart from raising in acute form the question of whether it is socially desirable to promote small business at the expense of the consumer, such a policy would be unworkable because it would require comprehensive and continuing supervision of the prices of large firms. There are no effective shortcuts. For example, if mergers between large firms are forbidden because of concern that they will enable the firms to take advantage of economies of scale and thereby underprice smaller firms operating at less efficient scale, one (or more) of the larger firms will simply expand until it has achieved the most efficient scale of operation. If franchise termination is made difficult in order to protect small dealers, the costs of franchising will be higher, and there will be less franchising, which will hurt the very class of small businessmen intended to be benefitted. The tools of antitrust enforcement are poorly designed for effective discrimination in favor of small firms, compared, for example, to the effectiveness of taxing larger firms at higher rates. We shall have frequent occasion in this book to remark how difficult it is to press the antitrust laws into the service of small business. The realistic choice is between shaping antitrust policy in accordance with the economic (and congruent political) objections to monopoly and—if we think that limiting big business and promoting small is more important than efficiency—abandoning it.

Richard A. Posner, *Antitrust Law: An Economic Perspective* (1976), pages 18–20.

3. Barriers to Entry

"But for" barriers to entry, long-run profits would not exist in a pure monopoly. Monopoly profits would dissipate as a result of competition from new entrants. Thus, the fundamental source of monopoly power is the fact that barriers to entry persist even in the long-run.

a. Economic Barriers: Natural Monopoly

Economic barriers to entry can result from very large economies of scale or the total control of an essential resource. Previously, the notion of a long-run average cost curve that decreases continually as output expands was introduced. This suggests that one firm could supply the entire industry output at the lowest possible cost. When such conditions arise, the process of competition guarantees that only one firm will survive. Firms that gain monopoly power because of these pronounced economies of scale are called **natural monopolies**. Another economic barrier to entry is the control of the entire supply of an essential resource. In this case, entry by new firms is blocked because they cannot gain access to the particular resource. However, absolute control over a resource will be reflected in the value of the firm. Thus, individuals who purchase a firm that controls an essential resource will not earn a monopoly profit.

b. Legal Barriers

Legal barriers to entry are restrictions placed upon the entry of new firms into an industry by the government. A familiar example of a government granted monopoly is the right to be the sole provider of basic public utilities. Other examples include patents and licenses. **Patents** give the inventor of a product or process a monopoly over the use of that invention for 17 years. **Licenses** are required to participate in many professions—e.g., medical and legal—and to operate many types of businesses—e.g., radio stations, cable, and airlines.

c. State Regulation and Federal Antitrust Law

Rent seekers—as rational, evaluative, maximizers—are often able to evade the reach of federal antitrust laws. The next case deals with the scope of federal antitrust laws. The Court relies on the concept of federalism to defend its position that the Sherman Act does not impede a state's decision to impose laws that restrict competition. In effect, the Court must balance the benefits of economic efficiency against the benefits of federalism. While reading the following case, consider whether or not you agree with the Court's balancing.

City of Columbia v. Omni Outdoor Advertising, Inc.

Supreme Court of the United States
499 U.S. 365, 111 S. Ct. 1344 (1991)

Read case excerpt in Chapter II

Notes and Questions

1. American Federalism: The United States Constitution is based on the principle of federalism. Federalism conceives of governmental power that is split between a central governing body and state governments. This is accomplished by having state governments recognize the sovereignty of a central government and surrendering certain powers to it. All powers not surrendered to the central government are retained by the states. In the United States, the federal government's scope of activity is limited by the powers granted in the Constitution. All other powers are reserved to the states. In *City of Columbia v. Omni Outdoor Advertising*, the Court clarifies the limits of the Sherman Act. The justification for these limits is federalism.

2. Parker State Action Immunity v. Perfect Competition: In the 1943 Supreme Court case of *Parker v. Brown*, the Court held that state officials and private economic entities who act pursuant to "state action" are provided antitrust immunity. Thus, states could adopt laws that stifled local competition. The *Parker* decision was based on the notion of federalism. In effect, the *Parker* state action immunity represents a willingness to sacrifice some of the benefits of competition in the name of federalism. How significant is this trade-off? From an economic perspective, was *Parker* the correct decision?

3. The Right to Seek Rents?: The Court observes that "with *Eastern Railroad Presidents Conference v. Noerr Motor Freight, Inc.* we have developed a corollary to *Parker*: the federal antitrust laws also do not regulate the conduct of private individuals in seeking anticompetitive action from the government." The right to seek anticompetitive action seems to be a prima facie example of rent-seeking. Is the Court condoning rent-seeking by its decision in *Noerr* and the application of *Noerr* to the facts in *Omni*? Alternatively, is the Court merely deferring to other laws in the protection of the policy making process? Clearly, some rent-seeking behavior like bribing public officials will be disciplined by other laws. However, conduct such as lobbying appears to be an acceptable form of rent-seeking. Is there an optimal level of rent-seeking? Is rent-seeking ever good?

4. More-Rent Seeking Behavior: Clearly, the billboard ordinances benefited COA. In fact, these ordinances helped to solidify COA's monopoly position. As a monopolist, COA will be able to set output and price at a level that creates monopoly profits, but will COA actually see any of these profits? A careful reading of the facts reveals how important these monopoly profits are to COA. The Court's summary of the facts indicates that COA contributed money to the campaign funds of local officials and donated billboard space. When Omni attempted to enter the market in 1981, one of COA's counter measures was to develop and support billboard ordinances. After a year of meeting with city officials, ordinances were finally enacted to protect COA's monopoly. In addition, the Supreme Court opinion came in 1992, ten years after Omni's attempted entry. At any time during the past ten years, COA could have settled or come to some other agreement with Omni. Instead, it obviously saw the benefits of a victory in the Supreme Court after ten years of litigation expense to be worth the cost. In sum, this case is a clear example of rent-seeking behavior by a monopolist. It is likely that much of the monopolist's profits were devoured by its attempt to protect those profits. The resources used in rent-seeking could have been consumed in productive industries.

5. Federalism v. Rent Seeking: The Court uses both *Parker* and *Noerr* to draw a line between the actions of COA and the City of Columbia, and actions that fall within the scope of the Sherman Act. *Parker* is based upon the notion that the federal government shall not interfere with those decisions which belong to the states—federalism. Thus, states can enact policies that limit intrastate competition. *Noerr* allows citizens to encourage the states to use the powers that they have been granted under the state action exemption of *Parker*. Thus, citizens can ask the states to make policy that limit intrastate competition. Does the combination of these two decisions clear the way for rent-seeking behavior regarding state policy? It appears as if the Court is willing to allow some amount of rent-seeking behavior at the state level in order to protect federalism and self-determination. Is this trade-off wise? How about in the long-run?

4. Collusion and Cartel Theory

A **cartel** is a combination of independent producers attempting to limit competition amongst themselves by acting together to fix prices, divide markets, or restrict entry into a market. A cartel exists when individual firms collude to act as one firm—as a monopoly—and make price and output decisions that maximize the profits to the industry. Such **collusive behavior** is a major focus of antitrust law because, if successful, it can result in a misallocation of resources similar to that generated by single-firm monopoly behavior.

The typical cartel is faced with three major problems: (1) agreeing on a common price; (2) dividing the market share between members; and (3) monitoring the agreement. When a pure monopolist sets price, it only needs to compare its own cost and revenue data. When a cartel attempts to set price, it must aggregate all of the members' cost curves in order to select the profit-maximizing price and output combination. In order for the cartel to be profitable, it requires a restriction in output relative to the quantity the firms were producing when they were competing with one another. The restricted output will lead to a higher price, and the price will be greater than the marginal cost of producing the last unit sold by each firm.

The second problem facing the cartel is the division of the market, because each firm desires to increase its output at the cartel price and thus maximize its own profits. For example, suppose the cartel has agreed to restrict total output by 20 percent. The most straightforward solution to this would be for every firm to agree to restrict its output by exactly 20 percent. However, the firms with the lowest costs of production may argue that they shouldn't have to reduce their output as much because they are more profitable. In other words, it would cost them more to reduce output by 20%. Alternatively, the firms with the highest costs of production might argue that the other firms should absorb most of the restrictions in output because the higher-cost firms need to sell more in order to earn as much from the cartel as do the other firms. There is no way to predict how this conflict will be resolved, but it seems clear that haggling over the division of the market can threaten the formation of a cartel.

The third problem faced by the cartel involves the enforcement of the cartel agreement. Assume that the cartel is formed and that its members have agreed upon a price and the division of the restricted output. The cartel must now deal with the incentive that each member has to cheat on the cartel. In Figure V-20, the cartel and each firm has agreed to restrict output by 20% — from Q_C to Q_M for the industry and from q_* to q_M for each firm. Restricting output causes price to increase from P_C to P_M. If the cartel agreement works as planned, then each firm earns monopoly profits of abP_CP_M. However, each cartel member is aware that the sale of a few additional units at the cartel price, which is well above the marginal cost of producing those additional units, will yield a substantial profit in addition to their cartel (monopoly) profits. That is, on the margin, each individual firm observes that P_M is greater than their marginal cost of producing each unit of output from q_M to q_X. Each firm has the incentive to increase its output to q_X and earn additional profits equal to the area axy. Because the cartelized industry has numerous competitors, each cartel member thinks that its increased output is so small that it will not have an adverse impact on the cartel price and thus will not be detected. For example, suppose that 100 firms form a cartel; a firm with 1 percent of the cartel's market share would not expect to have a significant impact on the total output of the cartel, so the firm has the impression that it can cheat — and earn even higher profits — by increasing its output and still have little chance of detection. The problem arises because every firm feels that it can get away with the cheating, so everyone cheats and the cartel dies.

Figure V-20

Individual Firm's Incentive to Cheat Under a Cartel

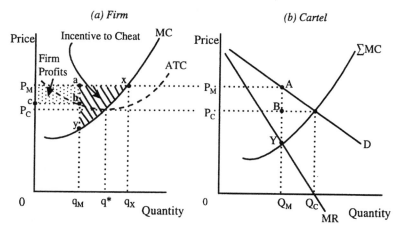

Because of these incentives, economists argue that all cartels are unstable in the long-run. This, however, is not a justification for an antitrust policy that ignores the existence of cartels, because the cartels may impose considerable costs on society before they collapse.

An understanding of the incentives to cheat on a cartel can also provide some guidance to antitrust authorities about conditions conducive to cartelization and, thus, where to look for collusion and cartelization. For example, as the number of firms in an industry increase, then successful cartelization is less likely; it is more difficult to reach agreement, it is more difficult to detect cheating should an agreement be reached, and also there is more incentive to cheat because each firm feels that it will have an inconsequential impact on total output. Alternatively, firms in highly concentrated industries are more prone to cartelization.

Another factor conducive to cartelization is the presence of highly standardized products across firms. Standardized products permit easier monitoring of the cartel agreement. Price differences between firms are not due to differences in quality because of the standardized product, but instead most likely reflect cheating on the cartel arrangement. Firms are not able to raise prices above the cartel price, because consumers will switch to other producers. However, if a firm lowers its price, consumers will switch to that producer. The other producers will observe shifts by consumers and, in all likelihood, learn of the lower price and the cheating. Because all producers know they will be detected if they cheat, cheating is less likely. It is interesting to note that the most famous attempt to form a cartel in recent decades, the Organization of Petroleum Exporting Countries (OPEC), was not successful in setting a uniform price. Saudi Arabia, in particular, consistently undercut the cartel price.

Finally, it must be understood that the existence of a uniform price in an industry is not definitive evidence of the presence of a cartel. The perfectly competitive model of economic theory—the model that is often used as the example of the optimum allocation of resources—also predicts that all firms in an industry will sell at the same price. A major challenge in the application of the antitrust laws is determining whether a certain observed practice is indicative of competition or collusion.

5. The Quest for Monopoly Profits

Because firms are profit maximizers and the individuals who run these firms are rational maximizers as well, it is not surprising that all sorts of methods for capturing above normal profits have been devised. In an attempt to stifle the quest for monopoly profits, the government has held some specific methods for achieving monopoly power to be illegal. In this section, three of these outlawed behaviors—price fixing, price discrimination, and predatory pricing—are investigated.

a. Price Fixing

Price fixing is an agreement between individual firms that are competitors for the purpose of setting a specific price, a range of prices, or otherwise raising, depressing or stabilizing the market price. One of the greatest difficulties that cartels face in earning monopoly profits is enforcing the cartel price. Given the difficulty of enforcing the cartel agreement, it is not surprising that many cartels seek government assistance in policing the agreement. In lobbying for public policy to enforce the cartel agreement, cartels often attempt to invoke a public interest rationale.

Goldfarb v. Virginia State Bar
Supreme Court of the United States
421 U.S. 773 (1975)

Mr. Chief Justice BURGER delivered the opinion of the Court (Internal cites omitted).

We granted certiorari to decide whether a minimum-fee schedule for lawyers published by the Fairfax County Bar Association and enforced by the Virginia State Bar violates § 1 of the Sherman Act. The Court of Appeals held that, although the fee schedule and enforcement mechanism substantially restrained competition among lawyers, publication of the schedule by the County Bar was outside the scope of the Act because the practice of law is not "trade or commerce," and enforcement of the schedule by the State Bar was exempt from the Sherman Act as state action as defined in *Parker v. Brown.*

I

In 1971 petitioners, husband and wife, contracted to buy a home in Fairfax County, Va. The financing agency required them to secure title insurance; this required a title examination, and only a member of the Virginia State Bar could legally perform that service. Petitioners therefore contacted a lawyer who quoted them the precise fee suggested in a minimum-fee schedule published by respondent Fairfax County Bar Association; the lawyer told them that it was his policy to keep his charges in line with the minimum-fee schedule which provided for a fee of 1% of the value of the property involved. Petitioners then tried to find a lawyer who would examine the title for less than the fee fixed by the schedule. They sent letters to 36 other Fairfax County lawyers requesting their fees. Nineteen replied, and none indicated that he would charge less than the rate fixed by the schedule; several stated that they knew of no attorney who would do so.

The fee schedule the lawyers referred to is a list of recommended minimum prices for common legal services. Respondent Fairfax County Bar Association published the fee schedule although, as a purely voluntary association of attorneys, the County Bar has no formal power to enforce it. Enforcement has been provided by respondent Virginia State Bar which is the administrative agency through which the Virginia Supreme Court regulates the practice of law in that State; membership in the State Bar is required in order to practice in Virginia. Although the State Bar has never taken formal disciplinary action to compel adherence to any fee schedule, it has published reports[5] condoning fee schedules, and has issued two ethical opinions indicating that fee schedules cannot be ignored. The most recent opinion states that 'evidence that an attorney *habitually* charges less than the suggested minimum fee schedule adopted by his local bar Association, raises a presumption that such lawyer is guilty of misconduct....'[6]

---

5. In 1962 the State Bar published a minimum-fee-schedule-report that listed a series of fees and stated that they 'represent the considered judgment of the Committee (on Economics of Law Practice) as to (a) fair minimum fee in each instance.' The report stated, however, that the fees were not mandatory, and it recommended only that the State Bar consider adopting such a schedule. Nevertheless, shortly thereafter the County Bar adopted its own minimum-fee schedule that purported to be 'a conscientious effort to show lawyers in their true perspective of dignity, training and integrity.' The suggested fees for title examination were virtually identical to those in the State Bar report. In accord with Opinion 98 of the State Bar Committee on Legal Ethics the schedule stated that, although there is an ethical duty to charge a lower fee in a deserving case, if a lawyer "purely for his own advancement, intentionally and regularly bills less than the customary charges of the bar for similar services...(in order to) increase his business with resulting personal gain, it becomes a form of solicitation contrary to Canon 27 and also a violation of Canon 7, which forbids the efforts of one lawyer to encroach upon the employment of another." App. 30. In 1969 the State Bar published a second fee-schedule report that, as it candidly stated, 'reflect(ed) a general scaling up of fees for legal services.' The report again stated that no local bar association was bound by its recommendations; however, respondent County Bar again quickly moved to publish an updated minimum-fee schedule, and generally to raise fees. The new schedule stated that the fees were not mandatory, but tempered that by referring again to Opinion 98. This time the schedule also stated that lawyers should feel free to charge more than the recommended fees; and to avoid condemnation of higher fees charged by some lawyers, it cautioned County Bar members that 'to...publicly criticize lawyers who charge more than the suggested fees herein might in itself be evidence of solicitation....'

6. *Ibid.* The parties stipulated that these opinions are a substantial influencing factor in lawyers' adherence to the fee schedules. One reason for this may be because the State Bar is required by statute to "investigat(e) and report...the violation of...rules and regulations as are adopted by the (Virginia Supreme Court) to a court of competent jurisdiction for such proceedings as may be necessary...." Therefore any lawyer who contemplated ignoring the fee schedule must have been aware that professional sanctions were possible, and that an enforcement mechanism existed to administer them.

Because petitioners could not find a lawyer willing to charge a fee lower than the schedule dictated, they had their title examined by the lawyer they had first contacted. They then brought this class action against the State Bar and the County Bar alleging that the operation of the minimum-fee schedule, as applied to fees for legal services relating to residential real estate transactions, constitutes price fixing in violation of § 1 of the Sherman Act. Petitioners sought both injunctive relief and damages.

After a trial solely on the issue of liability the District Court held that the minimum-fee schedule violated the Sherman Act. The court viewed the fee-schedule system as a significant reason for petitioners' failure to obtain legal services for less than the minimum fee, and it rejected the County Bar's contention that as a "learned profession" the practice of law is exempt from the Sherman Act.

Both respondents argued that their actions were also exempt from the Sherman Act as state action. *Parker v. Brown, supra.* The District Court agreed that the Virginia State Bar was exempt under that doctrine because it is an administrative agency of the Virginia Supreme Court, and more important, because its 'minor role in this matter...derived from the judicial and 'legislative command of the State and was not intended to operate or become effective without that command.' The County Bar, on the other hand, is a private organization and was under no compulsion to adopt the fee schedule recommended by the State Bar. Since the County Bar chose its own course of conduct the District Court held that the antitrust laws "remain in full force and effect as to it." The court enjoined the fee schedule, and set the case down for trial to ascertain damages.

The Court of Appeals reversed as to liability. Despite its conclusion that it is abundantly clear from the record before us that the fee schedule and the enforcement mechanism supporting it act as a substantial restraint upon competition among attorneys practicing in Fairfax County, the Court of Appeals held the State Bar immune under *Parker v. Brown* and held the County Bar immune because the practice of law is not "trade or commerce" under the Sherman Act. There has long been judicial recognition of a limited exclusion of "learned professions" from the scope of the antitrust laws, the court said; that exclusion is based upon the special form of regulation imposed upon the professions by the States, and the incompatibility of certain competitive practices with such professional regulation. It concluded that the promulgation of a minimum-fee schedule is one of "those matters with respect to which an accord must be reached between the necessities of professional regulation and the dictates of the antitrust laws." The accord reached by that court was to hold the practice of law exempt from the antitrust laws.

Alternatively, the Court of Appeals held that respondents' activities did not have sufficient effect on interstate commerce to support Sherman Act jurisdiction. Petitioners had argued that the fee schedule restrained the business of financing and insuring home mortgages by inflating a component part of the total cost of housing, but the court concluded that a title examination is generally a local service, and even where it is part of a transaction which crosses state lines its effect on commerce is only "incidental," and does not justify federal regulation.

We granted certiorari, and are thus confronted for the first time with the question of whether the Sherman Act applies to services performed by attorneys in examining titles in connection with financing the purchase of real estate.

II

Our inquiry can be divided into four steps: did respondents engage in price fixing? If so, are their activities in interstate commerce or do they affect interstate commerce? If so, are the activities exempt from the Sherman Act because they involve a "learned profession?" If not, are the activities "state action" within the meaning of *Parker v. Brown*, and therefore exempt from the Sherman Act?

A

The County Bar argues that because the fee schedule is merely advisory, the schedule and its enforcement mechanism do not constitute price fixing. Its purpose, the argument continues, is only to provide legitimate information to aid member lawyers in complying with Virginia professional regulations. Moreover, the County Bar contends that in practice the schedule has not had the effect of producing fixed fees. The facts found by the trier belie these contentions, and nothing in the record suggests these findings lack support.

A purely advisory fee schedule issued to provide guidelines, or an exchange of price information without a showing of an actual restraint on trade, would present us with a different question. The record here, however, reveals a situation quite different from what would occur under a purely advisory fee schedule. Here a fixed, rigid price floor arose from respondents' activities: every lawyer who responded to petitioners' inquiries adhered to the fee schedule, and no lawyer asked for additional information in order to set an individualized fee. The price information disseminated did not concern past standards, but rather minimum fees to be charged in future transactions, and those minimum rates were increased over time. The fee schedule was enforced through the prospective professional discipline from the State Bar, and the desire of attorneys to comply with announced professional norms, the motivation to conform was reinforced by the assurance that other lawyers would not compete by underbidding. This is not merely a case of an agreement that may be inferred from an exchange of price information, for here a naked agreement was clearly shown, and the effect on prices is plain.

Moreover, in terms of restraining competition and harming consumers like petitioners the price-fixing activities found here are unusually damaging. A title examination is indispensable in the process of financing a real estate purchase, and since only an attorney licensed to practice in Virginia may legally examine a title, consumers could not turn to alternative sources for the necessary service. All attorneys of course, were practicing under the constraint of the fee schedule. The County Bar makes much of the fact that it is a voluntary organization; however, the ethical opinions issued by the State Bar provide that any lawyer, whether or not a member of his county bar association, may be disciplined for "habitually charg(ing) less than the suggested minimum fee schedule adopted by his local bar Association...." These factors coalesced to create a pricing system that consumers could not realistically escape. On this record respondents' activities constitute a classic illustration of price fixing.

*   *   *

C

The County Bar argues that Congress never intended to include the learned professions within the terms "trade or commerce" in § 1 of the Sherman Act, and therefore the sale of professional services is exempt from the Act. No explicit exemption or legislative history is provided to support this contention; rather, the existence of state regulation seems to be its primary basis. Also, the County Bar maintains that competition is inconsistent with the practice of a profession because enhancing profit is not the goal of professional activities; the goal is to provide services necessary to the community.[16] That, indeed, is the classic basis traditionally advanced to distinguish professions from trades, businesses, and other occupations, but it loses some of its force when used to support the fee control activities involved here.

In arguing that learned professions are not "trade or commerce" the County Bar seeks a total exclusion from antitrust regulation. Whether state regulation is active or dormant, real or theoretical, lawyers would be able to adopt anticompetitive practices with impunity. We cannot find support for the proposition that Congress intended any such sweeping exclusion. The nature of an occupation, standing alone, does not provide sanctuary from the Sherman Act nor is the public-service aspect of professional practice controlling in determining whether § 1 includes professions. Congress intended to strike as broadly as it could in § 1 of the Sherman Act, and to read into it so wide an exemption as that urged on us would be at odds with that purpose.

The language of § 1 of the Sherman Act, of course, contains no exception. "Language more comprehensive is difficult to conceive." And our cases have repeatedly established that there is a heavy presumption against implicit exemptions. Indeed, our cases have specifically included the sale of services within § 1. Whatever else it may be, the examination of a land title is a service; the exchange of such a service for money is "commerce" in the most common usage of that word. It is no disparagement of the practice of law as a profession to acknowledge that it has this business aspect,[17] and § 1 of the Sherman Act

> "(o)n its face . . . shows a carefully studied attempt to bring within the Act every person engaged in business whose activities might restrain or monopolize commercial intercourse among the states."

In the modern world it cannot be denied that the activities of lawyers play an important part in commercial intercourse, and that anticompetitive activities by lawyers may exert a restraint on commerce.

D

In *Parker v. Brown*, the Court held that an anticompetitive marketing program which 'derived its authority and its efficacy from the legislative command

---

16. The reason for adopting the fee schedule does not appear to have been wholly altruistic. The first sentence in respondent State Bar's 1962 Minimum Fee Schedule Report states: "The lawyers have slowly, but surely, been committing economic suicide as a profession."

17. The fact that a restraint operates upon a profession as distinguished from a business is, of course, relevant in determining whether that particular restraint violates the Sherman Act. It would be unrealistic to view the practice of professions as interchangeable with other business activities, and automatically to apply to the professions antitrust concepts which originated in other areas. The public service aspect, and other features of the professions, may require that a particular practice, which could properly be viewed as a violation of the Sherman Act in another context, be treated differently. We intimate no view on any other situation than the one with which we are confronted today.

of the state' was not a violation of the Sherman Act because the Act was intended to regulate private practices and not to prohibit a State from imposing a restraint as an act of government. Respondent State Bar and respondent County Bar both seek to avail themselves of this so-called state-action exemption.

Through its legislature Virginia has authorized its highest court to regulate the practice of law. That court has adopted ethical codes which deal in part with fees, and far from exercising state power to authorize binding price fixing, explicitly directed lawyers not "to be controlled" by fee schedules. The State Bar, a state agency by law, argues that in issuing fee schedule reports and ethical opinions dealing with fee schedules it was merely implementing the fee provisions of the ethical codes. The County Bar, although it is a voluntary association and not a state agency, claims that the ethical codes and the activities of the State Bar 'prompted' it to issue fee schedules and thus its actions, too, are state action for Sherman Act purposes.

The threshold inquiry in determining if an anticompetitive activity is state action of the type the Sherman Act was not meant to proscribe is whether the activity is required by the State acting as sovereign. Here we need not inquire further into the state-action question because it cannot fairly be said that the State of Virginia through its Supreme Court Rules required the anticompetitive activities of either respondent. Respondents have pointed to no Virginia statute requiring their activities; state law simply does not refer to fees, leaving regulation of the profession to the Virginia Supreme Court; although the Supreme Court's ethical codes mention advisory fee schedules they do not direct either respondent to supply them, or require the type of price floor which arose from respondents' activities. Although the State Bar apparently has been granted the power to issue ethical opinions, there is no indication in this record that the Virginia Supreme Court approves the opinions. Respondents' arguments, at most, constitute the contention that their activities complemented the objective of the ethical codes. In our view that is not state action for Sherman Act purposes. It is not enough that, as the County Bar puts it, anticompetitive conduct is "prompted" by state action; rather, anticompetitive activities must be compelled by direction of the State acting as a sovereign.

The fact that the State Bar is a state agency for some limited purposes does not create an antitrust shield that allows it to foster anticompetitive practices for the benefit of its members. The State Bar, by providing that deviation from County Bar minimum fees may lead to disciplinary action, has voluntarily joined in what is essentially a private anticompetitive activity, and in that posture cannot claim it is beyond the reach of the Sherman Act. Its activities resulted in a rigid price floor from which petitioners, as consumers, could not escape if they wished to borrow money to buy a home.

III

We recognize that the States have a compelling interest in the practice of professions within their boundaries, and that as part of their power to protect the public health, safety, and other valid interests they have broad power to establish standards for licensing practitioners and regulating the practice of professions. We also recognize that in some instances the State may decide that "forms of competition usual in the business world may be demoralizing to the ethical standards of a profession." The interest of the States in regulating lawyers is especially great since lawyers are essential to the primary governmental function of administering justice, and have historically been "officers of the courts." In holding that certain anticompetitive conduct by lawyers is within the reach of the Sherman Act we intend no diminution of the authority of the State to regulate its professions.

The judgment of the Court of Appeals is reversed and the case is remanded to that court with orders to remand to the District Court for further proceedings consistent with this opinion.

Reversed and remanded...

Notes and Questions

1. Price Fixing Under the Sherman Act: Price fixing is a violation of the antitrust laws under the Sherman Act. For purposes of the Sherman Act, price fixing is divided into two forms. **Horizontal price fixing** addresses anticompetitive price agreements that are formed between competing firms. For example, an agreement between Ford Motor Company and Chrysler Corporation regarding the selling price of sport utility vehicles would constitute horizontal price fixing. **Vertical price fixing** deals with price agreements that try to control the resale price of a commodity. An example of vertical price fixing would be an agreement between Ford Motor Company and its dealers not to sell sport utility vehicles below some minimum price.

2. Ethics and Economic Suicide?: Why does the State Bar Association publish a schedule of suggested minimum fees? In light of the costs imposed upon society by these fees — note 1 — the answer to this question is very important. The State Bar's Committee on Legal Ethics seems to play a large role in the justification for the minimum fee schedule. What is the ethical justification for the minimum fee schedule? Consider what the Court observes in footnote 16: "The reason for adopting the fee schedule does not appear to have been wholly altruistic. The first sentence in respondent State Bar's 1962 Minimum Fee Schedule Report states: 'The lawyers have slowly, but surely, been committing economic suicide as a profession.'"

3. Ethics or Monopoly Profits? That is the Question: How would you characterize the industry structure in *Goldfarb?* The market for legal services is limited to those who have gone to law school and passed a state bar examination. Thus, the number of sellers in the market is limited. Moreover, the State Bar Association could be used as a tool by which attorneys could engage in collusion. For example, the State Bar could help the legal profession act in concert for restriction of output and increased prices.

4. Policing the Cartel: A cartel for legal services would face the same fundamental problem that all cartels face. Each individual attorney has an incentive to cheat by setting his price just below the minimum imposed by the cartel. In this way he can increase the quantity of his services provided and earn a greater portion of the monopoly profits. If enough cheating were to occur, the cartel would fall apart and the attorneys would earn only a normal profit for their services. The challenge to the Bar Association is how to stop individual attorneys from cheating on the cartel. Footnote 4 of the Court's opinion contains a quote from the State Bar Committee on Legal Ethics suggesting that any attorney who lowers his price below the "customary charges" risks violation of ethical canons forbidding solicitation and encroachment. In addition, professional sanctions were available to enforce these "ethical" considerations against those who would cut prices. Moreover, the State Bar's second fee schedule stated that "lawyers should feel free to charge more than the recommended fees; and to avoid condemnation of higher fees charged by some lawyers...."

5. Rent Seeking by the Learned Professions: An **economic rent** is a return earned for an activity in excess of the opportunity cost of attracting resources to the activity. Monopoly profits are also called economic rents. When individuals spend resources to capture economic rents, they are said to be **rent seeking**. See the discussion in Section E.1 of Chapter II and Section D.2 of this chapter. Rent seeking is an added social cost to society because the resources used to capture the rent could have been used in the production of some other good or service. Firms and individuals engage in rent seeking by using the power of government to limit the supply of their particular good or service into the market. The (so called) learned professions are notoriously successful at such rent seeking. For example, by requiring state licensing, the number of new entrants to an occupation can be limited. In general, the more restrictions on entry, the greater the rents to the existing market players. These learned professions often cite the public interest as their rationale for licensing requirements. Consider, for example, the market for attorneys. Attorneys claim that the public interest is served by requiring that they be licensed. Specifically, it ensures that they have had rigorous legal training, have stayed abreast of current developments in their field, and have good standing in their communities. However, couldn't all of these "public interest" factors be provide through a free market? For example, the reputation of your law school provides information about the quality of your legal training. Moreover, the reputation and, hence, profitability of your firm would depend upon its reputation for well educated attorneys with strong ethics. Why is it that despite the fact individuals desiring to be attorneys must graduate from law school, pass a bar exam in each state that they wish to practice, and maintain continuing legal education hours, the number of individuals going to law school continues to increase?

6. What is the Opportunity Cost of Going to Law School?: Consider the validity of the following justification for the barriers to entry for the legal profession. When Randal Rents graduated from high school, he considered the set of opportunities then available to him. The two most obvious choices were work or college. Randal decided that the best use of his resources was to invest in a college education. The opportunity cost of this action is the forgone income over the four years that he will be in college. His expected benefits from a college degree exceed the opportunity cost of other uses of his time, money, and skill. Upon graduation from college, Randal was again faced with the same question: work or school? Randal decided that of all the possible options available to him, the best use of his time, money, and skill was to attend law school. Randal has now sacrificed seven years of income, studied for countless hours, and given up the chance to work in other professions (i.e., he could have gone to medical school). Upon graduation from law school, Randal begins a job at a large, prestigious firm, and begins to pay back his school loans. In fact, he has even been heard to comment that "all of the years of sacrifice are starting to pay off." Years later, economists gain control of Congress and outlaw all barriers to entry into the learned professions. Randal is very upset because he believes that this will drive the price of his services down substantially. Randal argues that he has incurred great costs in becoming a lawyer. Moreover, he incurred those costs based on the expected potential payoff of a life long career as an attorney. Randal is very upset because he relied on the information regarding attorneys' salaries available to him when he was choosing between potential careers. In fact, he has commented that to "force attorneys' salaries down after he has incurred such great costs is entirely unfair." Because of the cost that he has endured in expectation of this particular payoff, he does not believe he is earning any rents. In other words, he invested resources in becoming an attorney up to the point that his initial expected return was merely a normal return. Any lowering of rates below his expected return would be an economic loss to him. What do you think?

b. Price Fixing and Intellectual Property Rights

The creation of new information is an important part in improving our societal standard of living. New medicines lead to healthier and more productive lives. New technologies improve efficiency, reducing the amount of resources consumed in production and, therefore, increasing the scope of activities that can be pursued. A problem with information is that it is not tangible. This leaves information open to easy duplication. The rewards for discovering new information then may be short lived. In other words, despite the costs that one may incur in order to develop new information, the rewards may be easily confiscated by competitors. This fact may serve as a disincentive towards investment in discovering new information. In response to this disincentive, Congress has created statutory patent and copyright laws.

Patents and copyrights provide their holder with a time-constrained monopoly. This time constraint is just as economically important as the original monopoly grant. The monopoly grant creates an incentive to invest time and other resources in the production of new information. Limiting the time that the monopoly is "good for" ensures that at some point this information will be handed over to a competitive market. This presents a delicate balancing act. On the one hand, it is desirable to encourage the innovation of new information; on the other hand, enormous benefits emerge from competitive markets.

Broadcast Music, Inc. v. Columbia Broadcasting System, Inc.
Supreme Court of the United States
441 U.S. 1 (1979)

Mr. Justice WHITE delivered the opinion of the Court.

This case involves an action under the antitrust and copyright laws brought by respondent Columbia Broadcasting System, Inc. (CBS), against petitioners, American Society of Composers, Authors and Publishers (ASCAP) and Broadcast Music, Inc. (BMI), and their members and affiliates. The basic question presented is whether the issuance by ASCAP and BMI to CBS of blanket licenses to copyrighted musical compositions at fees negotiated by them is price fixing *per se* unlawful under the antitrust laws.

I

CBS operates one of three national commercial television networks, supplying programs to approximately 200 affiliated stations and telecasting approximately 7,500 network programs per year. Many, but not all, of these programs make use of copyrighted music recorded on the soundtrack. CBS also owns television and radio stations in various cities....

Since 1897, the copyright laws have vested in the owner of a copyrighted musical composition the exclusive right to perform the work publicly for profit, but the legal right is not self-enforcing. In 1914, Victor Herbert and a handful of other composers organized ASCAP because those who performed copyrighted music for profit were so numerous and widespread, and most performances so fleeting, that as a practical matter it was impossible for the many individual copyright owners to negotiate with and license the users and to detect unauthorized uses. "ASCAP was organized as a 'clearing-house' for copyright owners and users to solve these problems" associated with the licensing of music. As ASCAP operates today, its 22,000 members grant it nonexclusive rights to license nondramatic performances of their works, and ASCAP issues licenses and distributes royalties to copyright owners in accordance with a schedule reflecting the nature and amount of the use of their music and other factors.

BMI, a nonprofit corporation owned by members of the broadcasting industry, was organized in 1939, is affiliated with or represents some 10,000 publishing companies and 20,000 authors and composers, and operates in much the same manner as ASCAP. Almost every domestic copyrighted composition is in the repertory either of ASCAP, with a total of three million compositions, or of BMI, with one million.

Both organizations operate primarily through blanket licenses, which give the licensees the right to perform any and all of the compositions owned by the members or affiliates as often as the licensees desire for a stated term. Fees for blanket licenses are ordinarily a percentage of total revenues or a flat dollar amount, and do not directly depend on the amount or type of music used. Radio and television broadcasters are the largest users of music, and almost all of them hold blanket licenses from both ASCAP and BMI. Until this litigation, CBS held blanket licenses from both organizations for its television network on a continuous basis since the late 1940's and had never attempted to secure any other form of license from either ASCAP[5] or any of its members.

The complaint filed by CBS charged various violations of the Sherman Act and the copyright laws.[7] CBS argued that ASCAP and BMI are unlawful monopolies and that the blanket license is illegal price fixing, an unlawful tying arrangement, a concerted refusal to deal, and a misuse of copyrights. The District Court, though denying summary judgment to certain defendants, ruled that the practice did not fall within the *per se* rule. After an 8-week trial, limited to the issue of liability, the court dismissed the complaint, rejecting again the claim that the blanket license was price fixing and a *per se* violation of § 1 of the Sherman Act, and

---

5. Unless the context indicates otherwise, references to ASCAP alone in this opinion usually apply to BMI as well.

7. CBS Seeks injunctive relief for the antitrust violations and a declaration of copyright misuse.

holding that since direct negotiation with individual copyright owners is available and feasible there is no undue restraint of trade, illegal tying, misuse of copyrights, or monopolization.

Though agreeing with the District Court's factfinding and not disturbing its legal conclusions on the other antitrust theories of liability,[8] the Court of Appeals held that the blanket license issued to television networks was a form of price fixing illegal *per se* under the Sherman Act. This conclusion, without more, settled the issue of liability under the Sherman Act, established copyright misuse,[9] and required reversal of the District Court's judgment, as well as a remand to consider the appropriate remedy. [10]

ASCAP and BMI petitioned for certiorari, presenting the questions of the applicability of the *per se* rule and of whether this constitutes misuse of copyrights. CBS did not cross petition to challenge the failure to sustain its other antitrust claims. We granted certiorari because of the importance of the issues to the antitrust and copyright laws. Because we disagree with the Court of Appeals' conclusions with respect to the *per se* illegality of the blanket license, we reverse its judgment and remand the cause for further appropriate proceedings.

II

In construing and applying the Sherman Act's ban against contracts, conspiracies, and combinations in restraint of trade, the Court has held that certain agreements or practices are so "plainly anticompetitive," and so often "lack... any redeeming virtue," that they are conclusively presumed illegal without further examination under the rule of reason generally applied in Sherman Act cases. This *per se* rule is a valid and useful tool of antitrust policy and enforcement. And agreements among competitors to fix prices on their individual goods or services are among those concerted activities that the Court has held to be within the *per se* category. But easy labels do not always supply ready answers.

---

8. The Court of Appeals affirmed the District Court's rejection of CBS's monopolization and tying contentions but did not rule on the District Court's conclusion that the blanket license was not an unreasonable restraint of trade.

9. At CBS's suggestion, the Court of Appeals held that the challenged conduct constituted misuse of copyrights solely on the basis of its finding of unlawful price fixing.

10. The Court of Appeals went on to suggest some guidelines as to remedy, indicating that despite its conclusion on liability the blanket license was not totally forbidden. The Court of Appeals said: "Normally, after a finding of price-fixing, the remedy is an injunction against the price-fixing—in this case, the blanket license. We think, however, that if on remand a remedy can be fashioned which will ensure that the blanket license will not affect the price or negotiations for direct licenses, the blanket license need not be prohibited in all circumstances. The blanket license is not simply a 'naked restraint' ineluctably doomed to extinction. There is not enough evidence in the present record to compel a finding that the blanket license does not serve a market need for those who wish full protection against infringement suits or who, for some other business reason, deem the blanket license desirable. The blanket license includes a practical covenant not to sue for infringement of any ASCAP copyright as well as an indemnification against suits by others. "Our objection to the blanket license is that it reduces price competition among the members and provides a disinclination to compete. We think that these objections may be removed if ASCAP itself is required to provide some form of per use licensing which will ensure competition among the individual members with respect to those networks which wish to engage in per use licensing."

A

To the Court of Appeals and CBS, the blanket license involves "price fixing" in the literal sense: the composers and publishing houses have joined together into an organization that sets its price for the blanket license it sells.[13] But this is not a question simply of determining whether two or more potential competitors have literally "fixed" a "price." As generally used in the antitrust field, "price fixing" is a shorthand way of describing certain categories of business behavior to which the *per se* rule has been held applicable. The Court of Appeals' literal approach does not alone establish that this particular practice is one of those types or that it is "plainly anticompetitive" and very likely without "redeeming virtue." Literalness is overly simplistic and often overbroad. When two partners set the price of their goods or services they are literally "price fixing," but they are not *per se* in violation of the Sherman Act. Thus, it is necessary to characterize the challenged conduct as falling within or without that category of behavior to which we apply the label "*per se* price fixing." That will often, but not always, be a simple matter.

Consequently, as we recognized in United States v. Topco Associates, Inc., "[i]t is only after considerable experience with certain business relationships that courts classify them as *per se* violations...." We have never examined a practice like this one before; indeed, the Court of Appeals recognized that "[i]n dealing with performing rights in the music industry we confront conditions both in copyright law and in antitrust law which are *sui generis*." And though there has been rather intensive antitrust scrutiny of ASCAP and its blanket licenses, that experience hardly counsels that we should outlaw the blanket license as a *per se* restraint of trade.

B

*   *   *

The Department of Justice first investigated allegations of anticompetitive conduct by ASCAP over 50 years ago. A criminal complaint was filed in 1934, but the Government was granted a midtrial continuance and never returned to the courtroom. In separate complaints in 1941, the United States charged that the blanket license, which was then the only license offered by ASCAP and BMI, was an illegal restraint of trade and that arbitrary prices were being charged as the result of an illegal copyright pool. The Government sought to enjoin ASCAP's exclusive licensing powers and to require a different form of licensing by that organization. The case was settled by a consent decree that imposed tight restrictions on ASCAP's operations. Following complaints relating to the television industry, successful private litigation against ASCAP by movie theaters, and a Government challenge to ASCAP's arrangements with similar foreign organizations, the 1941 decree was reopened and extensively amended in 1950.

---

13. CBS also complains that it pays a flat fee regardless of the amount of use it makes of ASCAP compositions and even though many of its programs contain little or no music. We are unable to see how that alone could make out an antitrust violation or misuse of copyrights: "Sound business judgment could indicate that such payment represents the most convenient method of fixing the business value of the privileges granted by the licensing agreement....Petitioner cannot complain because it must pay royalties whether it uses Hazeltine patents or not. What it acquired by the agreement into which it entered was the privilege to use any or all of the patents and developments as it desired to use them." *Automatic Radio Mfg. Co. v. Hazeltine Research, Inc.*

Under the amended decree, which still substantially controls the activities of ASCAP, members may grant ASCAP only nonexclusive rights to license their works for public performance. Members, therefore, retain the rights individually to license public performances, along with the rights to license the use of their compositions for other purposes. ASCAP itself is forbidden to grant any license to perform one or more specified compositions in the ASCAP repertory unless both the user and the owner have requested it in writing to do so. ASCAP is required to grant to any user making written application a nonexclusive license to perform all ASCAP compositions either for a period of time or on a per-program basis. ASCAP may not insist on the blanket license, and the fee for the per-program license, which is to be based on the revenues for the program on which ASCAP music is played, must offer the applicant a genuine economic choice between the per-program license and the more common blanket license. If ASCAP and a putative licensee are unable to agree on a fee within 60 days, the applicant may apply to the District Court for a determination of a reasonable fee, with ASCAP having the burden of proving reasonableness.

The 1950 decree, as amended from time to time, continues in effect, and the blanket license continues to be the primary instrument through which ASCAP conducts its business under the decree. The courts have twice construed the decree not to require ASCAP to issue licenses for selected portions of its repertory. It also remains true that the decree guarantees the legal availability of direct licensing of performance rights by ASCAP members; and the District Court found, and in this respect the Court of Appeals agreed, that there are no practical impediments preventing direct dealing by the television networks if they so desire. Historically, they have not done so. Since 1946, CBS and other television networks have taken blanket licenses from ASCAP and BMI. It was not until this suit arose that the CBS network demanded any other kind of license.

Of course, a consent judgment, even one entered at the behest of the Antitrust Division, does not immunize the defendant from liability for actions, including those contemplated by the decree, that violate the rights of nonparties. But it cannot be ignored that the Federal Executive and Judiciary have carefully scrutinized ASCAP and the challenged conduct, have imposed restrictions on various of ASCAP's practices, and, by the terms of the decree, stand ready to provide further consideration, supervision, and perhaps invalidation of asserted anticompetitive practices. In these circumstances, we have a unique indicator that the challenged practice may have redeeming competitive virtues and that the search for those values is not almost sure to be in vain. Thus, although CBS is not bound by the Antitrust Division's actions, the decree is a fact of economic and legal life in this industry, and the Court of Appeals should not have ignored it completely in analyzing the practice. That fact alone might not remove a naked price-fixing scheme from the ambit of the *per se* rule, but, as discussed *infra*, Part III, here we are uncertain whether the practice on its face has the effect, or could have been spurred by the purpose, of restraining competition among the individual composers.

After the consent decrees, the legality of the blanket license was challenged in suits brought by certain ASCAP members against individual radio stations for copyright infringement. The stations raised as a defense that the blanket license was a form of price fixing illegal under the Sherman Act. The parties stipulated that it would be nearly impossible for each radio station to negotiate with each copyright holder separate licenses for the performance of his works on radio.

Against this background, and relying heavily on the 1950 consent judgment, the Court of Appeals for the Ninth Circuit rejected claims that ASCAP was a combination in restraint of trade and that the blanket license constituted illegal price fixing.

The Department of Justice, with the principal responsibility for enforcing the Sherman Act and administering the consent decrees relevant to this case, agreed with the result reached by the Ninth Circuit. In a submission *amicus curiae* opposing one station's petition for certiorari in this Court, the Department stated that there must be "some kind of central licensing agency by which copyright holders may offer their works in a common pool to all who wish to use them." And the Department elaborated on what it thought that fact meant for the proper application of the antitrust laws in this area:

> "The Sherman Act has always been discriminatingly applied in the light of economic realities. There are situations in which competitors have been permitted to form joint selling agencies or other pooled activities, subject to strict limitations under the antitrust laws to guarantee against abuse of the collective power thus created. This case appears to us to involve such a situation. The extraordinary number of users spread across the land, the ease with which a performance may be broadcast, the sheer volume of copyrighted compositions, the enormous quantity of separate performances each year, the impracticability of negotiating individual licenses for each composition, and the ephemeral nature of each performance all combine to create unique market conditions for performance rights to recorded music."

The Department concluded that, in the circumstances of that case, the blanket licenses issued by ASCAP to individual radio stations were neither a *per se* violation of the Sherman Act nor an unreasonable restraint of trade.

*   *   *

Finally, we note that Congress itself, in the new Copyright Act, has chosen to employ the blanket license and similar practices.... Though these provisions are not directly controlling, they do reflect an opinion that the blanket license, and ASCAP, are economically beneficial in at least some circumstances.

There have been District Court cases holding various ASCAP practices, including its licensing practices, to be violative of the Sherman Act, but even so, there is no nearly universal view that either the blanket or the per-program licenses issued by ASCAP at prices negotiated by it are a form of price fixing subject to automatic condemnation under the Sherman Act, rather than to a careful assessment under the rule of reason.

III

Of course, we are no more bound than is CBS by the views of the Department of Justice, the results in the prior lower court cases, or the opinions of various experts about the merits of the blanket license. But while we must independently examine this practice, all those factors should caution us against too easily finding blanket licensing subject to *per se* invalidation.

A

As a preliminary matter, we are mindful that the Court of Appeals' holding would appear to be quite difficult to contain. If, as the court held, there is a *per se* antitrust violation whenever ASCAP issues a blanket license to a television network for a single fee, why would it not also be automatically illegal for ASCAP to negotiate and issue blanket licenses to individual radio or television stations or to other users who perform copyrighted music for profit? Likewise, if the present network licenses issued through ASCAP on behalf of its members are *per se* violations, why would it not be equally illegal for the members to authorize ASCAP to issue licenses establishing various categories of uses that a network might have for copyrighted music and setting a standard fee for each described use?

Although the Court of Appeals apparently thought the blanket license could be saved in some or even many applications, it seems to us that the *per se* rule does not accommodate itself to such flexibility and that the observations of the Court of Appeals with respect to remedy tend to impeach the *per se* basis for the holding of liability.

CBS would prefer that ASCAP be authorized, indeed directed, to make all its compositions available at standard per-use rates within negotiated categories of use. But if this in itself or in conjunction with blanket licensing constitutes illegal price fixing by copyright owners, CBS urges that an injunction issue forbidding ASCAP to issue any blanket license or to negotiate any fee except on behalf of an individual member for the use of his own copyrighted work or works. Thus, we are called upon to determine that blanket licensing is unlawful across the board. We are quite sure, however, that the *per se* rule does not require any such holding.

B

In the first place, the line of commerce allegedly being restrained, the performing rights to copyrighted music, exists at all only because of the copyright laws. Those who would use copyrighted music in public performances must secure consent from the copyright owner or be liable at least for the statutory damages for each infringement and, if the conduct is willful and for the purpose of financial gain, to criminal penalties. Furthermore, nothing in the Copyright Act of 1976 indicates in the slightest that Congress intended to weaken the rights of copyright owners to control the public performance of musical compositions. Quite the contrary is true. Although the copyright laws confer no rights on copyright owners to fix prices among themselves or otherwise to violate the antitrust laws, we would not expect that any market arrangements reasonably necessary to effectuate the rights that are granted would be deemed a *per se* violation of the Sherman Act. Otherwise, the commerce anticipated by the Copyright Act and protected against restraint by the Sherman Act would not exist at all or would exist only as a pale reminder of what Congress envisioned.[32]

---

32. Cf. *Silver v. New York Stock Exchange*, 373 U.S. 341, 83 S. Ct. 1246, 10 L.Ed.2d 389 (1963). Because a musical composition can be "consumed" by many different people at the same time and without the creator's knowledge, the "owner" has no real way to demand reimbursement for the use of his property except through the copyright laws and an effective way to enforce those legal rights. See *Twentieth Century Music Corp. v. Aiken*, 422 U.S. 151, 162 95 S.Ct. 2040, 2047, 45 L.Ed.2d 84 (1975). It takes an organization of rather large size to monitor most or all uses and to deal with users on behalf of the composers. Moreover, it is inefficient to have too many such organizations duplicating each other's monitoring of use.

C

More generally, in characterizing this conduct under the *per se* rule, our inquiry must focus on whether the effect and, here because it tends to show effect, the purpose of the practice are to threaten the proper operation of our predominantly free-market economy—that is, whether the practice facially appears to be one that would always or almost always tend to restrict competition and decrease output, and in what portion of the market, or instead one designed to "increase economic efficiency and render markets more, rather than less, competitive."

The blanket license, as we see it, is not a "naked restrain[t] of trade with no purpose except stifling of competition," *White Motor Co. v. United States*, but rather accompanies the integration of sales, monitoring, and enforcement against unauthorized copyright use. As we have already indicated, ASCAP and the blanket license developed together out of the practical situation in the marketplace: thousands of users, thousands of copyright owners, and millions of compositions. Most users want unplanned, rapid, and indemnified access to any and all of the repertory of compositions, and the owners want a reliable method of collecting for the use of their copyrights. Individual sales transactions in this industry are quite expensive, as would be individual monitoring and enforcement, especially in light of the resources of single composers. Indeed, as both the Court of Appeals and CBS recognize, the costs are prohibitive for licenses with individual radio stations, nightclubs, and restaurants, and it was in that milieu that the blanket license arose.

A middleman with a blanket license was an obvious necessity if the thousands of individual negotiations, a virtual impossibility, were to be avoided. Also, individual fees for the use of individual compositions would presuppose an intricate schedule of fees and uses, as well as a difficult and expensive reporting problem for the user and policing task for the copyright owner. Historically, the market for public-performance rights organized itself largely around the single-fee blanket license, which gave unlimited access to the repertory and reliable protection against infringement. When ASCAP's major and user-created competitor, BMI, came on the scene, it also turned to the blanket license.

With the advent of radio and television networks, market conditions changed, and the necessity for and advantages of a blanket license for those users may be far less obvious than is the case when the potential users are individual television or radio stations, or the thousands of other individuals and organizations performing copyrighted compositions in public. But even for television network licenses, ASCAP reduces costs absolutely by creating a blanket license that is sold only a few, instead of thousands, of times, and that obviates the need for closely monitoring the networks to see that they do not use more than they pay for. ASCAP also provides the necessary resources for blanket sales and enforcement, resources unavailable to the vast majority of composers and publishing houses. Moreover, a bulk license of some type is a necessary consequence of the integration necessary to achieve these efficiencies, and a necessary consequence of an aggregate license is that its price must be established.

D

This substantial lowering of costs, which is of course potentially beneficial to both sellers and buyers, differentiates the blanket license from individual use licenses. The blanket license is composed of the individual compositions plus the aggregating service. Here, the whole is truly greater than the sum of its parts; it is, to some extent, a different product. The blanket license has certain unique characteristics: It allows the licensee immediate use of covered compositions, without the delay of prior individual negotiations and great flexibility in the choice of musical material. Many consumers clearly prefer the characteristics and cost advantages of this marketable package, and even small-performing rights societies that have occasionally arisen to compete with ASCAP and BMI have offered blanket licenses. Thus, to the extent the blanket license is a different product, ASCAP is not really a joint sales agency offering the individual goods of many sellers, but is a separate seller offering its blanket license, of which the individual compositions are raw material.[33] ASCAP, in short, made a market in which individual composers are inherently unable to compete fully effectively.

E

Finally, we have some doubt—enough to counsel against application of the *per se* rule—about the extent to which this practice threatens the "central nervous system of the economy," *United States v. Socony-Vacuum Oil Co.*, that is, competitive pricing as the free market's means of allocating resources. Not all arrangements among actual or potential competitors that have an impact on price are *per se* violations of the Sherman Act or even unreasonable restraints. Mergers among competitors eliminate competition, including price competition, but they are not *per se* illegal, and many of them withstand attack under any existing antitrust standard. Joint ventures and other cooperative arrangements are also not usually unlawful, at least not as price-fixing schemes, where the agreement on price is necessary to market the product at all.

Here, the blanket-license fee is not set by competition among individual copyright owners, and it is a fee for the use of any of the compositions covered by the license. But the blanket license cannot be wholly equated with a simple horizontal arrangement among competitors. ASCAP does set the price for its blanket license, but that license is quite different from anything any individual owner could issue. The individual composers and authors have neither agreed not to sell individually in any other market nor use the blanket license to mask price fixing in such other markets. Moreover, the substantial restraints placed on ASCAP and its members by the consent decree must not be ignored. The District Court found that there was no legal, practical, or conspiratorial impediment to CBS's obtaining individual licenses; CBS, in short, had a real choice.

With this background in mind, which plainly enough indicates that over the years, and in the face of available alternatives, the blanket license has provided an acceptable mechanism for at least a large part of the market for the performing rights to copyrighted musical compositions, we cannot agree that it should automatically be declared illegal in all of its many manifestations. Rather, when

---

33. Moreover, because of the nature of the product—a composition can be simultaneously "consumed" by many users—composers have numerous markets and numerous incentives to produce, so the blanket license is unlikely to cause a decreased output, one of the normal undesirable effects of a cartel. And since popular songs get an increased share of ASCAP's revenue distributions, composers compete even within the blanket license in terms of productivity and consumer satisfaction.

attacked, it should be subjected to a more discriminating examination under the rule of reason. It may not ultimately survive that attack, but that is not the issue before us today.

IV

As we have noted, the enigmatic remarks of the Court of Appeals with respect to remedy appear to have departed from the court's strict, *per se* approach and to have invited a more careful analysis. But this left the general import of its judgment that the licensing practices of ASCAP and BMI under the consent decree are *per se* violations of the Sherman Act. We reverse that judgment, and the copyright misuse judgment dependent upon it, see n. 9, *supra*, and remand for further proceedings to consider any unresolved issues that CBS may have properly brought to the Court of Appeals. Of course, this will include an assessment under the rule of reason of the blanket license as employed in the television industry, if that issue was preserved by CBS in the Court of Appeals.

The judgment of the Court of Appeals is reversed, and the cases are remanded to that court for further proceedings consistent with this opinion.

It is so ordered.

Mr. Justice STEVENS, dissenting.

The Court holds that ASCAP's blanket license is not a species of price fixing categorically forbidden by the Sherman Act. I agree with that holding. The Court remands the cases to the Court of Appeals, leaving open the question whether the blanket license as employed by ASCAP and BMI is unlawful under a rule-of-reason inquiry. I think that question is properly before us now and should be answered affirmatively.

There is ample precedent for affirmance of the judgment of the Court of Appeals on a ground that differs from its rationale, provided of course that we do not modify its judgment. In this litigation, the judgment of the Court of Appeals was not that blanket licenses may never be offered by ASCAP and BMI. Rather, its judgment directed the District Court to fashion relief requiring them to offer additional forms of license as well. Even though that judgment may not be consistent with its stated conclusion that the blanket license is "illegal *per se*" as a kind of price fixing, it is entirely consistent with a conclusion that petitioners' exclusive all-or-nothing blanket-license policy violates the rule of reason.

The Court of Appeals may well so decide on remand. In my judgment, however, a remand is not necessary. The record before this Court is a full one, reflecting extensive discovery and eight weeks of trial. The District Court's findings of fact are thorough and well supported. They clearly reveal that the challenged policy does have a significant adverse impact on competition. I would therefore affirm the judgment of the Court of Appeals.

I

In December 1969, the president of the CBS television network wrote to ASCAP and BMI requesting that each "promptly...grant a new performance rights license which will provide, effective January 1, 1970, for payments measured by the actual use of your music." ASCAP and BMI each responded by stating that it considered CBS's request to be an application for a license in accordance with the provisions of its consent decree and would treat it as such,[6] even though neither decree provides for licensing on a per-composition or per-use basis. Rather than pursuing further discussion, CBS instituted this suit.

Whether or not the CBS letter is considered a proper demand for per-use licensing is relevant, if at all, only on the question of relief. For the fact is, and it cannot seriously be questioned, that ASCAP and BMI have steadfastly adhered to the policy of only offering overall blanket or per-program licenses,[8] notwithstanding requests for more limited authorizations. Thus, ASCAP rejected a 1971 request by NBC for licenses for 2,217 specific compositions, as well as an earlier request by a group of television stations for more limited authority than the blanket licenses which they were then purchasing. Neither ASCAP nor BMI has ever offered to license anything less than its entire portfolio, even on an experimental basis. Moreover, if the response to the CBS letter were not sufficient to characterize their consistent policy, the defense of this lawsuit surely is. It is the refusal to license anything less than the entire repertoire—rather than the decision to offer blanket licenses themselves—that raises the serious antitrust questions in this case.

II

Under our prior cases, there would be no question about the illegality of the blanket-only licensing policy if ASCAP and BMI were the exclusive sources of all licenses. A copyright, like a patent, is a statutory grant of monopoly privileges. The rules which prohibit a patentee from enlarging his statutory monopoly by conditioning a license on the purchase of unpatented goods, or by refusing to grant a license under one patent unless the licensee also takes a license under another, are equally applicable to copyrights.

It is clear, however, that the mere fact that the holder of several patents has granted a single package license covering them all does not establish any illegality. This point was settled by *Automatic Radio Mfg. Co. v. Hazeltine Research, Inc.*, and reconfirmed in *Zenith Radio Corp. v. Hazeltine Research, Inc.*. The Court is therefore unquestionably correct in its conclusion that ASCAP's issuance of blanket licenses covering its entire inventory is not, standing alone, automatically unlawful. But both of those cases identify an important limitation on this rule. In the former, the Court was careful to point out that the record did not present the question whether the package license would have been unlawful if Hazeltine had refused to license on any other basis. And in the latter case, the Court held that the package license was illegal because of such a refusal.

---

6. ASCAP responded in a letter from its general counsel, stating that it would consider the request at its next board of directors meeting, and that it regarded it as an application for a license consistent with the decree. The letter from BMI's president stated: "The BMI Consent Decree provides for several alternative licenses and we are ready to explore any of these with you." *Id.*, at 753–754.

8. The 1941 decree requires ASCAP to offer per-program licenses as an alternative to the blanket license. *United States v. ASCAP*, 1940–1043 Trade Cases P 56,104, p. 404 (S.D.N.Y.). Analytically, however, there is little difference between the two. A per-program license also covers the entire ASCAP repertoire; it is therefore simply a miniblanket license. As is true of a long-term blanket license, the fees are set in no way dependent on the quantity or quality of the music used. See *infra*, at 30–33.

Since ASCAP offers only blanket licenses, its licensing practices fall on the illegal side of the line drawn by the two *Hazeltine* cases. But there is a significant distinction: unlike Hazeltine, ASCAP does not have exclusive control of the copyrights in its portfolio, and it is perfectly possible—at least as a legal matter—for a user of music to negotiate directly with composers and publishers for whatever rights he may desire. The availability of a practical alternative alters the competitive effect of a blockbooking or blanket-licensing policy. ASCAP is therefore quite correct in its insistence that its blanket license cannot be categorically condemned on the authority of the blockbooking and package-licensing cases. While these cases are instructive, they do not directly answer the question whether the ASCAP practice is unlawful.

The answer to that question depends on an evaluation of the effect of the practice on competition in the relevant market. And, of course, it is well settled that a sales practice that is permissible for a small vendor, at least when no coercion is present, may be unreasonable when employed by a company that dominates the market.[13] We therefore must consider what the record tells us about the competitive character of this market.

III

The market for music at issue here is wholly dominated by ASCAP-issued blanket licenses.[14] Virtually every domestic copyrighted composition is in the repertoire of either ASCAP or BMI. And again, virtually without exception, the only means that has been used to secure authority to perform such compositions is the blanket license.

The blanket all-or-nothing license is patently discriminatory.[15] The user purchases full access to ASCAP's entire repertoire, even though his needs could be satisfied by a far more limited selection. The price he pays for this access is unrelated either to the quantity or the quality of the music he actually uses, or, indeed, to what he would probably use in a competitive system. Rather, in this unique all-or-nothing system, the price is based on a percentage of the user's advertising revenues, a measure that reflects the customer's ability to pay[17] but is totally unrelated to factors—such as the cost, quality, or quantity of the product—that normally affect price in a competitive market. The ASCAP system requires users to buy more music than they want at a price which, while not beyond their ability

---

13.... While our cases make clear that a violation of the Sherman Act requires both that the volume of commerce affected be substantial and that the seller enjoy a dominant position, proof of actual compulsion has not been required. The critical question is one of the likely practical effect of the arrangement: whether the "court believes it probable that performance of the contract will foreclose competition in a substantial share of the line of commerce affected." *Tampa Electric Co. v. Nashville Coal Co.*

14. As in the majority opinion, my references to ASCAP generally encompass BMI as well.

15. See Cirace, *CBS v. ASCAP*: An Economic Analysis of A Political Problem, 47 Ford.L.Rev. 277, 286 (1978) ("the all-or-nothing bargain allows the monopolist to reap the benefits of perfect price discrimination without confronting the problems posed by dealing with different buyers on different terms").

17. See Cirace, *supra*, at 288: "This history indicates that, from its inception, ASCAP exhibited a tendency to discriminate in price. A license fee based upon a percentage of gross revenue is discriminatory in that it grants the same number of rights to different licensees for different total dollar amounts, depending upon their ability to pay. The effectiveness of price discrimination is significantly enhanced by the all-or-nothing blanket license."

to pay and perhaps not even beyond what is "reasonable" for the access they are getting, [18] may well be far higher than what they would choose to spend for music in a competitive system. It is a classic example of economic discrimination.

The record plainly establishes that there is no price competition between separate musical compositions. Under a blanket license, it is no more expensive for a network to play the most popular current hit in prime time than it is to use an unknown composition as background music in a soap opera. Because the cost to the user is unaffected by the amount used on any program or on all programs, the user has no incentive to economize by, for example, substituting what would otherwise be less expensive songs for established favorites or by reducing the quantity of music used on a program. The blanket license thereby tends to encourage the use of more music, and also of a larger share of what is really more valuable music, than would be expected in a competitive system characterized by separate licenses. And since revenues are passed on to composers on a basis reflecting the character and frequency of the use of their music, the tendency is to increase the rewards of the established composers at the expense of those less well known. Perhaps the prospect is in any event unlikely, but the blanket license does not present a new songwriter with any opportunity to try to break into the market by offering his product for sale at an unusually low price. The absence of that opportunity, however unlikely it may be, is characteristic of a cartelized rather than a competitive market.

The current state of the market cannot be explained on the ground that it could not operate competitively, or that issuance of more limited—and thus less restrictive—licenses by ASCAP is not feasible. The District Court's findings disclose no reason why music-performing rights could not be negotiated on a per-composition or per-use basis, either with the composer or publisher directly or with an agent such as ASCAP. In fact, ASCAP now compensates composers and publishers on precisely those bases. If distributions of royalties can be calculated on a per-use and per-composition basis, it is difficult to see why royalties could not also be collected in the same way. Moreover, the record also shows that where ASCAP's blanket-license scheme does not govern, competitive markets do. A competitive market for "synch" rights exists,[23] and after the use of blanket licenses in the motion picture industry was discontinued, such a market promptly developed in that industry. In sum, the record demonstrates that the market at issue here is one that could be highly competitive, but is not competitive at all.

IV

Since the record describes a market that could be competitive and is not, and since that market is dominated by two firms engaged in a single, blanket method

---

18. Under the ASCAP consent decree, on receipt of an application, ASCAP is required to "advise the applicant in writing of the fee which it deems reasonable for the license requested." If the parties are unable to agree on the fee within 60 days of the application, the applicant may apply to the United States District Court for the Southern District of New York for the determination of a "reasonable fee." *United States v. ASCAP*, 1950–1951 Trade Cases P 62,595, p. 63,754 (S.D.N.Y.1950). The BMI decree contains no similar provision for judicial determination of a reasonable fee.

23. The "synch" right is the right to record a copyrighted song in synchronization with the film or videotape, and is obtained separately from the right to perform the music. It is the latter which is controlled by ASCAP and BMI. See *CBS, Inc. v. ASCAP*, 400 F.Supp., at 743.

of dealing, it surely seems logical to conclude that trade has been restrained unreasonably. ASCAP argues, however, that at least as to CBS, there has been no restraint at all since the network is free to deal directly with copyright holders.

The District Court found that CBS had failed to establish that it was compelled to take a blanket license from ASCAP. While CBS introduced evidence suggesting that a significant number of composers and publishers, satisfied as they are with the ASCAP system, would be "disinclined" to deal directly with the network, the court found such evidence unpersuasive in light of CBS's substantial market power in the music industry and the importance to copyright holders of network television exposure. Moreover, it is arguable that CBS could go further and, along with the other television networks, use its economic resources to exploit destructive competition among purveyors of music by driving the price of performance rights down to a far lower level. But none of this demonstrates that ASCAP's practices are lawful, or that ASCAP cannot be held liable for injunctive relief at CBS's request.

The fact that CBS has substantial market power does not deprive it of the right to complain when trade is restrained. Large buyers, as well as small, are protected by the antitrust laws. Indeed, even if the victim of a conspiracy is himself a wrongdoer, he has not forfeited the protection of the law. Moreover, a conclusion that excessive competition would cause one side of the market more harm than good may justify a legislative exemption from the antitrust laws, but does not constitute a defense to a violation of the Sherman Act. Even though characterizing CBS as an oligopolist may be relevant to the question of remedy, and even though free competition might adversely affect the income of a good many composers and publishers, these considerations do not affect the legality of ASCAP's conduct.

More basically, ASCAP's underlying argument that CBS must be viewed as having acted with complete freedom in choosing the blanket license is not supported by the District Court's findings. The District Court did not find that CBS could cancel its blanket license "tomorrow" and continue to use music in its programming and compete with the other networks. Nor did the District Court find that such a course was without any risk or expense. Rather, the District Court's finding was that within a year, during which it would continue to pay some millions of dollars for its annual blanket license, CBS would be able to develop the needed machinery and enter into the necessary contracts. In other words, although the barriers to direct dealing by CBS as an alternative to paying for a blanket license are real and significant, they are not insurmountable.

Far from establishing ASCAP's immunity from liability, these District Court findings, in my judgment, confirm the illegality of its conduct. Neither CBS nor any other user has been willing to assume the costs and risks associated with an attempt to purchase music on a competitive basis. The fact that an attempt by CBS to break down the ASCAP monopoly might well succeed does not preclude the conclusion that smaller and less powerful buyers are totally foreclosed from a competitive market.[30] Despite its size, CBS itself may not obtain music on a com-

---

30. For an individual user, the transaction costs involved in direct dealing with the individual copyright holders may well e prohibitively high, at least in the absence of any broker or agency routinely handling such requests. Moreover, the District Court found that writers and publishers support and prefer the ASCAP system to direct dealing. *Id.*, at 767. While their apprehension at direct dealing with CBS could be overcome, the District Court found,

petitive basis without incurring unprecedented costs and risks. The fear of unpredictable consequences, coupled with the certain and predictable costs and delays associated with a change in its method of purchasing music, unquestionably inhibits any CBS management decision to embark on a competitive crusade. Even if ASCAP offered CBS a special bargain to forestall any such crusade, that special arrangement would not cure the marketwide restraint.

Whatever management decision CBS should or might have made, it is perfectly clear that the question whether competition in the market has been unduly restrained is not one that any single company's management is authorized to answer. It is often the case that an arrangement among competitors will not serve to eliminate competition forever, but only to delay its appearance or to increase the costs of new entry. That may well be the state of this market. Even without judicial intervention, the ASCAP monopoly might eventually be broken by CBS, if the benefits of doing so outweigh the significant costs and risks involved in commencing direct dealing. But that hardly means that the blanket-licensing policy at issue here is lawful. An arrangement that produces marketwide price discrimination and significant barriers to entry unreasonably restrains trade even if the discrimination and the barriers have only a limited life expectancy. History suggests, however, that these restraints have an enduring character.

Antitrust policy requires that great aggregations of economic power be closely scrutinized. That duty is especially important when the aggregation is composed of statutory monopoly privileges. Our cases have repeatedly stressed the need to limit the privileges conferred by patent and copyright strictly to the scope of the statutory grant. The record in this case plainly discloses that the limits have been exceeded and that ASCAP and BMI exercise monopoly powers that far exceed the sum of the privileges of the individual copyright holders. Indeed, ASCAP itself argues that its blanket license constitutes a product that is significantly different from the sum of its component parts. I agree with that premise, but I conclude that the aggregate is a monopolistic restraint of trade proscribed by the Sherman Act.

Notes and Questions

1. The Competitive Virtues of Blanket Licensing: Section 1 of the Sherman Act prohibits contracts, conspiracies, and combinations in restraint of trade. Moreover, the Court has established a *per se* rule for practices that "lack...any redeeming virtue" and are "plainly anticompetitive." As a decision rule for when to utilize this *per se* standard, the Court takes note of the following quote from *United States v. Topco Associates Inc*: "[i]t is only after considerable experience with certain business relationships that courts classify them as *per se* violations." The Court concludes that it has never dealt with practices like those of ASCAP and BMI. However, the Court observes that the fact that the Antitrust Division of the Department of Justice has issued a consent decree governing the now challenged practices "[is] a unique indicator that the challenged practice may have some redeeming competitive virtues..." What are the redeeming virtues of ASCAP and BMI's challenged practices? The free market is suppressed in favor

by CBS's market power and the importance of television exposure, a similar conclusion is far less likely with respect to other users.

of some other structural method for making price and output decisions. The blanket licensing agreement in BMI provided an alternative to free market transactions between each individual copyright holder and each firm that wanted to use the copyrighted material. It is possible and in fact likely that ASCAP and BMI were developed and are maintainable because their method for making price and output decisions for copyright material is superior to a free market. How can this be?

2. Transaction Costs Economics: The field of **transaction costs economics** studies the costs of carrying out certain transactions based upon the type of transaction and the way such transactions are organized. **Transaction costs** are the costs of time, information, contracting and monitoring that are required to execute an exchange. If the goal is to maximize the efficiency by which transactions are made, then it makes sense to utilize the structure that minimizes transaction costs. In this light, when transaction costs are minimized by allocation through a free market, then that structure will be used. However, when transaction costs are minimized by using some other formal structure, then a free market may no longer be superior. What are the transaction costs involved in buying the right to use copyrighted material? Would market exchange or ASCAP's current method minimize these transaction costs? Can you think of an even more efficient method for the copyright use market?

3. Developing the Rights of Copyright Holders: The benefits of intellectual property rights were discussed just prior to the *BMI* case. As a result of these benefits, Congress has enacted patent and copyright laws. These laws are supposed to encourage the development of new creations and information by granting a time constrained monopoly. Moreover, these laws also protect the rights of the creators to their monopoly. Part of the Court's decision in *BMI* relied on the fact that, absent ASCAP and BMI's blanket licensing agreement, copyright holders would have a difficult time marketing their products and enforcing their rights against infringement. That is, individual negotiation and enforcement would be very costly both to the copyright holders and users. Thus, the blanket licensing agreement seems to encourage the sale and use of copyrighted material in conjunction with a cost effective method for enforcing the copyrights. Moreover, those copyright holders or potential users who found individual negotiation to be more cost efficient were not foreclosed from using market mechanisms. In other words, the Court found the blanket licensing price restraint to be a necessary component in further developing the goals of copyright laws. Can you think of an alternative for marketing individual copyrights that is more in line with the model of pure competition? Will technology have an effect on the necessity of the blanket licensing agreement in supporting trade? Is there any other way for individual copyright holders to enforce their monopoly rights?

c. Price Discrimination

The practice of selling the same product to different customers at different prices is known as price discrimination. Under certain conditions, firms can increase their economic profits by engaging in price discrimination. Three conditions must be met in order for a firm to engage in successful price discrimination. First, the firm must face a downward sloping demand curve—the firm must be a price searcher. Recall that perfectly competitive firms are price takers. These firms have no control over price and therefore, cannot charge different customers different prices. On the other hand, a pure monopolist has a great deal of control over market price. Second, the firm must have some way of identifying separate groups of customers with differing demands for its product. In general, the price discriminating seller will charge a higher price to those customers with a relatively inelastic demand. Third, the firm must be able to prevent **arbitrage**—resale by low-price purchasers to the higher price purchasers.

Commonly observed forms of price discrimination satisfy these criteria. Senior citizens typically have more elastic demand curves, they are easily identified, and the goods and services sold to them at a discount are difficult to resell. Judge Frank Easterbrook recently described an innovative manner that software developers can price discriminate between consumer and commercial users of software:

* * *

I

ProCD, the plaintiff, has compiled information from more than 3,000 telephone directories into a computer database.... ProCD sells a version of the database, called SelectPhone (trademark), on CD-ROM discs. (CD-ROM means "compact disc—read only memory." The "shrinkwrap license" gets its name from the fact that retail software packages are covered in plastic or cellophane "shrinkwrap," and some vendors, though not ProCD, have written licenses that become effective as soon as the customer tears the wrapping from the package. Vendors prefer "end user license," but we use the more common term.)...

The database in SelectPhone (trademark) cost more than $10 million to compile and is expensive to keep current. It is much more valuable to some users than to others. The combination of names, addresses, and SIC codes enables manufacturers to compile lists of potential customers. Manufacturers and retailers pay high prices to specialized information intermediaries for such mailing lists; ProCD offers a potentially cheaper alternative. People with nothing to sell could use the database as a substitute for calling long distance information, or as a way to look up old friends who have moved to unknown towns, or just as an electronic substitute for the local phone book. ProCD decided to engage in price discrimination, selling its database to the general public for personal use at a low price (approximately $150 for the set of five discs) while selling information to the trade for a higher price. It has adopted some intermediate strategies too: access to the SelectPhone (trademark) database is available via the America Online service for the price America Online charges to its clients (approximately $3 per hour), but this service has been tailored to be useful only to the general public.

If ProCD had to recover all of its costs and make a profit by charging a single price—that is, if it could not charge more to commercial users than to the general public—it would have to raise the price substantially over $150. The ensuing reduction in sales would harm consumers who value the information at, say, $200. They get consumer surplus of $50 under the current arrangement but would cease to buy if the price rose substantially. If because of high elasticity of demand in the consumer segment of the market the only way to make a profit turned out to be a price attractive to commercial users alone, then all consumers would lose out—and so would the commercial clients, who would have to pay more for the listings because ProCD could not obtain any contribution toward costs from the consumer market.

To make price discrimination work, however, the seller must be able to control arbitrage. An air carrier sells tickets for less to vacationers than to business travelers, using advance purchase and Saturday-night-stay requirements to distinguish the categories. A producer of movies segments the market by time, releasing first to theaters, then to pay-per-view services, next to the videotape and laserdisc market, and finally to cable and commercial tv. Vendors of computer software have a harder task. Anyone can walk into a retail store and buy a box. Customers do not wear tags saying "commercial user" or "consumer user." Anyway, even a commercial-user-detector at the door would not work, because a consumer could buy the software and resell to a commercial user. That arbitrage would break down the price discrimination and drive up the minimum price at which ProCD would sell to anyone.

Instead of tinkering with the product and letting users sort themselves—for example, furnishing current data at a high price that would be attractive only to commercial customers, and two-year-old data at a low price—ProCD turned to the institution of contract. Every box containing its consumer product declares that the software comes with restrictions stated in an enclosed license. This license, which is encoded on the CD-ROM disks as well as printed in the manual, and which appears on a user's screen every time the software runs, limits use of the application program and listings to non-commercial purposes.

ProCD, Inc. V. Zeidenberg, 86 F.3d 1447, 1449–1450 (1996)(ruling that shrinkwrap licenses are enforceable contracts).

A diagrammatic example demonstrates the advantages of price discrimination to a monopolist. The monopolist is able to divide the market into two segments of buyers. The demand for each of these segments is depicted in the two panels of Figure V-21. The demand for the monopolist's product is relatively more elastic in panel (a) than in panel (b). Because one firm supplies both of these "markets," the marginal cost of supplying the product is the same in both markets.

The monopolist desires to maximize profit in each of these "markets." To maximize profits, the monopolist will set $MR_1 = MC$ in panel (a) and $MR_2 = MC$ in panel (b). In panel (a), the market with the more elastic demand, the monopolist charges P_1. However, in panel (b), the market with the relatively inelastic demand, the monopolist charges a higher price of P_2. In this case, individuals with relatively inelastic demand are charged a high price and those with a relative elastic demand are charged a low price.

Two warnings are in order regarding the analysis of price discrimination. First, selling the same product to different customers at different prices is not price discrimination if there is a cost justification for the price differential. Sec-

Figure V-21

Price Discrimination

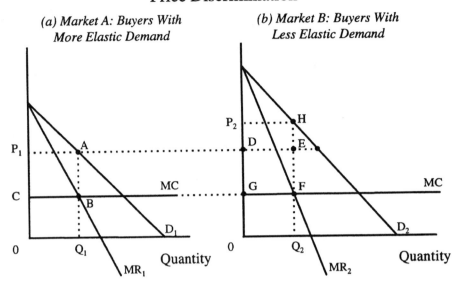

(a) Market A: Buyers With More Elastic Demand

(b) Market B: Buyers With Less Elastic Demand

ond, the fact that the same dollar price has been charged to all customers does not mean that price discrimination is absent. Each customer's opportunity cost of completing the transaction must also be taken into account in determining if prices are equal.

Texaco, Inc. v. Hasbrouck, et al.

Supreme Court of the United States
496 U.S. 543 (1990)

STEVENS, J., delivered the opinion of the Court.

Petitioner (Texaco) sold gasoline directly to respondents and several other retailers in Spokane, Washington, at its retail tank wagon prices (RTW) while it granted substantial discounts to two distributors. During the period between 1972 and 1981, the stations supplied by the two distributors increased their sales volume dramatically, while respondents' sales suffered a corresponding decline. Respondents filed an action against Texaco under the Robinson-Patman amendment to the Clayton Act. Respondents recovered treble damages, and the Court of Appeals for the Ninth Circuit affirmed the judgment. We...consider Texaco's contention that legitimate functional discounts do not violate the Act because a seller is not responsible for its customers' independent resale pricing decisions. While we agree with the basic thrust of Texaco's argument, we conclude that in this case it is foreclosed by the facts of record.

I

Given the jury's general verdict in favor of respondents, disputed questions of fact have been resolved in their favor. There seems, moreover, to be no serious doubt about the character of the market, Texaco's pricing practices, or the relative importance of Texaco's direct sales to retailers ("throughput" business) and its sales to distributors.

Respondents are 12 independent Texaco retailers. They displayed the Texaco trademark, accepted Texaco credit cards, and bought their gasoline products directly from Texaco....

The retail gasoline market in Spokane was highly competitive throughout the damages period, which ran from 1972 to 1981. Stations marketing the nationally advertised Texaco gasoline competed with other major brands as well as with stations featuring independent brands. Moreover, although discounted prices at a nearby Texaco station would have the most obvious impact on a respondent's trade, the cross-city traffic patterns and relatively small size of Spokane produced a city-wide competitive market. Texaco's throughput sales in the Spokane market declined from a monthly volume of 569,269 gallons in 1970 to 389,557 gallons in 1975. Texaco's independent retailers' share of the market for Texaco gas declined from 76% to 49%. Seven of the respondents' stations were out of business by the end of 1978.

Respondents tried unsuccessfully to increase their ability to compete with lower priced stations. Some tried converting from full service to self-service stations. Two of the respondents sought to buy their own tank trucks and haul their gasoline from Texaco's supply point, but Texaco vetoed that proposal.

While the independent retailers struggled, two Spokane gasoline distributors supplied by Texaco prospered. Gull Oil Company (Gull) had its headquarters in Seattle and distributed petroleum products in four western States under its own name. In Spokane it purchased its gas from Texaco at prices that ranged from 6¢ to 4¢ below Texaco's RTW price. Gull resold that product under its own name; the fact that it was being supplied by Texaco was not known by either the public or the respondents.... Its policy was to price its gasoline at a penny less than the prevailing price for major brands. Gull employed two truck drivers in Spokane who picked up product at Texaco's bulk plant and delivered it to the Gull stations.... Apart from its trucks and investment in retail facilities, Gull apparently owned no assets in that market. At least with respect to the commission stations, Gull is fairly characterized as a retailer of gasoline throughout the relevant period.

The Dompier Oil Company (Dompier) started business in 1954 selling Quaker State Motor Oil. In 1960 it became a full line distributor of Texaco products, and by the mid-1970's its sales of gasoline represented over three-quarters of its business. App. 114–115. Dompier purchased Texaco gasoline at prices of 3.95¢ to 3.65¢ below the RTW price. Dompier thus paid a higher price than Gull, but Dompier, unlike Gull, resold its gas under the Texaco brand names. It supplied about eight to ten Spokane retail stations. Dompier's president estimated at trial that the share of its total gasoline sales made at retail during the middle 1970's was "[p]robably 84 to 90 percent."

Like Gull, Dompier picked up Texaco's product at the Texaco bulk plant and delivered directly to retail outlets. Unlike Gull, Dompier owned a bulk storage facility, but it was seldom used because its capacity was less than that of many retail stations. Again unlike Gull, Dompier received from Texaco the equivalent of the common carrier rate for delivering the gasoline product to the retail outlets. Thus, in addition to its discount from the RTW price, Dompier made a profit on its hauling function.

The stations supplied by Dompier regularly sold at retail at lower prices than respondents'. Even before Dompier directly entered the retail business in 1974, its customers were selling to consumers at prices barely above the RTW price. Dompier's sales volume increased continuously and substantially throughout the relevant period. Between 1970 and 1975 its monthly sales volume increased from 155,152 gallons to 462,956 gallons; this represented an increase from 20.7% to almost 50% of Texaco's sales in Spokane.

There was ample evidence that Texaco executives were well aware of Dompier's dramatic growth and believed that it was attributable to "the magnitude of the distributor discount and the hauling allowance." In response to complaints from individual respondents about Dompier's aggressive pricing, however, Texaco representatives professed that they "couldn't understand it."

II

*   *   *

... Texaco contended that the special prices to Gull and Dompier were justified by cost savings, were the product of a good faith attempt to meet competition, and were lawful "functional discounts." The District Court withheld the cost justification defense from the jury because it was not supported by the evidence and the jury rejected the other defenses. It awarded respondents actual damages of $449,900. The jury apparently credited the testimony of respondents' expert witness who had estimated what the respondents' profits would have been if they had paid the same prices as the four stations owned by Dompier.

In Texaco's motion for judgment notwithstanding the verdict, it claimed as a matter of law that its functional discounts did not adversely affect competition within the meaning of the Act because any injury to respondents was attributable to decisions made independently by Dompier. The District Court denied the motion.... [T]he Court assumed, *arguendo*, that Dompier was entitled to a functional discount, even on the gas that was sold at retail, but nevertheless concluded that the "presumed legality of functional discounts" had been rebutted by evidence that the amount of the discounts to Gull and Dompier was not reasonably related to the cost of any function that they performed.

The Court of Appeals affirmed. It reasoned:

> "As the Supreme Court long ago made clear, and recently reaffirmed, there may be a Robinson-Patman violation even if the favored and disfavored buyers do not compete, so long as the customers of the favored buyer compete with the disfavored buyer or its customers. Despite the fact that Dompier and Gull, at least in their capacities as wholesalers, did not compete directly with Hasbrouck, a section 2(a) violation may occur if (1) the discount they received was not cost-based and (2) all or a portion of it was passed on by them to customers of theirs who competed with Hasbrouck. *Morton Salt*, 384 U.S. at 43–44.

> Hasbrouck presented ample evidence to demonstrate that....the services performed by Gull and Dompier were insubstantial and did not justify the functional discount."

*　　*　　*

III

It is appropriate to begin our consideration of the legal status of functional discounts by examining the language of the Act. Section 2(a) provides in part:

> "It shall be unlawful for any person engaged in commerce, in the course of such commerce, either directly or indirectly, to discriminate in price between different purchasers of commodities of like grade and quality, where either or any of the purchases involved in such discrimination are in commerce, where such commodities are sold for use, consumption, or resale within the United States or any Territory thereof or the District of Columbia or any insular possession or other place under the jurisdiction of the United States, and where the effect of such discrimination may be substantially to lessen competition or tend to create a monopoly in any line of commerce, or to injure, destroy, or prevent competition with any person who either grants or knowingly receives the benefit of such discrimination, or with customers of either of them...."

*　　*　　*

In order to establish a violation of the Act, respondents had the burden of proving four facts: (1) that Texaco's sales to Gull and Dompier were made in interstate commerce; (2) that the gasoline sold to them was of the same grade and quality as that sold to respondents; (3) that Texaco discriminated in price as between Gull and Dompier on the one hand and respondents on the other; and (4) that the discrimination had a prohibited effect on competition. Moreover, for each respondent to recover damages, he had the burden of proving the extent of his actual injuries.

The first two elements of respondents' case are not disputed in this Court, and we do not understand Texaco to be challenging the sufficiency of respondents' proof of damages. Texaco does argue, however, that although it charged different prices, it did not "discriminate in price" within the meaning of the Act, and that, at least to the extent that Gull and Dompier acted as wholesalers, the price differentials did not injure competition. We consider the two arguments separately.

IV

Texaco's first argument would create a blanket exemption for all functional discounts. Indeed, carried to its logical conclusion, it would exempt all price differentials except those given to competing purchasers....

*　　*　　*

Since we have already decided that a price discrimination within the meaning of § 2(a) "is merely a price difference," we must reject Texaco's first argument.

V

In *FTC v. Morton Salt Co.*, 334 U.S. 37, 46–47 (1948), we held that a injury to competition may be inferred from evidence that some purchasers had to pay their supplier "substantially more for their goods than their competitors had to pay." Texaco, supported by the United States and the Federal Trade Commission as *amici curiae*, (the Government), argues that this presumption should not apply to differences between prices charged to wholesalers and these charged to retailers. Moreover, they argue that it would be inconsistent with fundamental antitrust policies to construe the Act as requiring a seller to control his customers' resale prices. The seller should not be held liable for the independent pricing decisions of his customers. As the Government correctly notes, this argument endorses the position advocated 35 years ago in the Report of the Attorney General's National Committee to Study the Antitrust Laws (1955).

After observing that suppliers ought not to be held liable for the independent pricing decisions of their buyers, and that without functional discounts distributors might go uncompensated for services they performed,[17] the Committee wrote:

> "...Price cutting at the resale level is not in fact, and should not be held in law, 'the effect of' a differential that merely accords due recognition and reimbursement for actual marketing functions. The price cutting of a customer who receives this type of differential results from his own independent decision to lower price and operate at a lower profit margin per unit. The legality or illegality of this price cutting must be judged by the usual legal tests. In any event, consequent injury or lack of injury should not be the supplier's legal concern.

> "On the other hand, the law should tolerate no subterfuge. For instance, where a wholesaler-retailer buys only part of his goods as a wholesaler, he must not claim a functional discount on all. Only to the extent that a buyer *actually* performs certain functions, assuming all the risk, investment, and costs involved, should he legally qualify for a functional discount. Hence a distributor should be eligible for a discount corresponding to any part of the function he actually performs on that part of the goods for which he performs it."

We generally agree with this description of the legal status of functional discounts. A supplier need not satisfy the rigorous requirements of the cost justification defense in order to prove that a particular functional discount is reasonable and accordingly did not cause any substantial lessening of competition between a wholesaler's customers and the supplier's direct customers. The record in this case, however, adequately supports the finding that Texaco violated the Act.

The hypothetical predicate for the Committee's entire discussion of functional discounts is a price differential "that merely accords due recognition and reimbursement for actual marketing functions." Such a discount is not illegal. In this case, however, both the District Court and the Court of Appeals concluded that even without viewing the evidence in the light most favorable to the respondents, there was no substantial evidence indicating that the discounts to Gull and Dompier constituted a reasonable reimbursement for the value to Texaco of their

---

17. "In our view, to relate discounts or prices solely to the purchaser's resale activities without recognition of his buying functions thwarts competition and efficiency in marketing. It compels affirmative discrimination against a substantial class of distributors, and hence serves as a penalty on integration. If a businessman actually fulfills the wholesale function by relieving his suppliers of risk, storage, transportation, administration, etc., his performance, his capital investment, and the saving to his suppliers, are unaffected by whether he also performs the retailing function, or any number of other functions. A legal rule disqualifying him from discounts recognizing wholesaling functions actually performed compels him to render these functions free of charge."

actual marketing functions. Indeed, Dompier was separately compensated for its hauling function, and neither Gull and Dompier maintained any significant storage facilities.

*   *   *

[A] functional discount that constitutes a reasonable reimbursement for the purchasers' actual marketing functions will not violate the Act. When a functional discount is legitimate, the inference of injury to competition recognized in the Morton Salt case will simply not arise. Yet it is also true that not every functional discount is entitled to a judgment of legitimacy, and that it will sometimes be possible to produce evidence showing that a particular functional discount caused a price discrimination of the sort the Act prohibits. When such anti-competitive effects are proved—as we believe they were in this case—they are covered by the Act.[30]

*   *   *

The judgment is affirmed.

It is so ordered.

JUSTICE WHITE, concurring in the result.

Texaco's first submission urging a blanket exemption for all functional discounts is rejected by the Court on the ground stated in *FTC v. Anheuser Busch, Inc.*, 363 U.S. 536, 550 (1960), that the "statute itself spells out the conditions which make a price difference illegal or legal, and we would derange this integrated statutory scheme" by providing a defense not contained in the statute. In the next section of its opinion, however, the Court not only declares that a price differential that merely accords due recognition and reimbursement for actual marketing functions not only does not trigger the presumption of an injury to competition, but also announces that "such a discount is not illegal." There is nothing in the Act to suggest such a defense to a charge of price discrimination that "may... substantially... lessen competition... in any line of commerce, or to injure, destroy, or prevent competition with any person who either grants or knowingly receives the benefit of such discrimination, or with customers of either of them." Nor is there any indication in prior cases that the Act should be so construed....

Thus, a Texaco retailer charged a higher price than a distributor who is given what the Court would call a legitimate discount is entirely foreclosed, even though he offers to prove, and could prove, that the distributor sells to his customers at a price lower than the plaintiff retailer pays Texaco and that those customers of the distributor undersell the plaintiff and have caused plaintiff's business to fail. This kind of injury to the Texaco retailer's ability to compete is squarely covered by the language of § 13(a), which reaches not only injury to competition but injury to Texaco retail customers' ability to compete with the distributor's customers. The Court neither explains why this is not the case nor justifies its departure from the provisions of the Act other than by suggesting that when there is a legitimate discount, it is the distributor's decision, not the discount given by Texaco, that causes

---

30. The parties do not raise, and we therefore need not address, the question whether the inference of injury to competition might also be negated by evidence that disfavored buyers could make purchases at a reasonable discount from favored buyers.

the injury, even though the latter makes possible the distributor's discount. Perhaps this is the case if the concept of a legitimate price discrimination other than those legitimated by the Act's provisions is to be implied. But that poses the question whether the Act is open to such a construction.

*   *   *

In the absence of Congressional attention to this long-standing issue involving antitrust policy, I doubt that at this late date we should attempt to set the matter right, at least not in a case that does not require us to define what a legitimate functional discount is. If the FTC now recognizes that functional discounts given by a producer who sells both to distributors and retailers are legitimate if they reflect only proper factors and are not subterfuges, I would await a case challenging such a ruling by the FTC. We would then be reviewing a construction of the Act by the FTC and its explanation of legitimate functional discount pricing.

*   *   *

JUSTICE SCALIA, with whom JUSTICE KENNEDY joins, concurring in the judgment.

I agree with the Court that none of the arguments pressed by petitioner for removing its conduct from the coverage of the Robinson-Patman Act is persuasive. I cannot, however, adopt the Court's reasoning, which seems to create an exemption for functional discounts that are "reasonable" even though prohibited by the text of the Act.

*   *   *

. . . [J]oined by the United States as *amicus curiae*, petitioner argues at length that even if petitioner's discounts to Gull and Dompier cannot be shown to be cost-based they should be exempted, because the "functional discount" is an efficient and legitimate commercial practice that is ordinarily cost-based, though it is all but impossible to establish cost justification in a particular case. The short answer to this argument is that it should be addressed to Congress.

*   *   *

I suppose a functional discount can be "reasonable" (in the relevant sense of being unlikely to subvert the purposes of the Act) if it is not commensurate with the supplier's costs *saved* (as the cost-justification defense requires), but is commensurate with the wholesaler's costs *incurred* in performing services for the supplier. Such a discount would not produce the proscribed effect upon competition, since if it constitutes only reimbursement for the wholesaler one would not expect him to pass it on. The relevant measure of the discount in order to determine "reasonableness" on that basis, however, is not the measure the Court applies to Texaco ("value to [the supplier] of [the distributor's] actual marketing functions," *ante*, at 562), but rather "cost to the distributor of the distributor's actual marketing functions"—which is of course not necessarily the same thing. I am therefore quite unable to understand what the Court has in mind by its "reasonable" functional discount that is not cost justified.

To my mind, there is one plausible argument for the proposition that a functional basis for differential pricing *ipso facto*—cost justification or not—negates the probability of competitive injury, thus destroying an element of the plaintiff's prima facie case: In a market that is really functionally divided, retailers are in

competition with one another, not with wholesalers. That competition among retailers cannot be injured by the supplier's giving lower prices to wholesalers—
because if the price differential is passed on, all retailers will simply purchase
from wholesalers instead of from the supplier. Or, to put it differently, when the
market is functionally divided all competing retailers have the opportunity of obtaining the same price from wholesalers, and the supplier's functional price discrimination alone does not cause any injury to competition. Therefore (the argument goes), if functional division of the market is established, it should be up to
the complaining retailer to show that some special factor (e. g., an agreement between the supplier and the wholesaler that the latter will not sell to the former's
retailer-customers) prevents this normal market mechanism from operating. As
the Court notes, this argument was not raised by the parties here or below, and it
calls forth a number of issues that would benefit from briefing and factual development. I agree that we should not decide the merit of this argument in the first
instance.

For the foregoing reasons, I concur in the judgment.

Notes and Questions

1. The Nature of Competition: The Court characterized the retail gasoline market in Spokane as "highly competitive." Moreover, gasoline is a highly fungible
good—especially when it all comes from the same manufacturer. This suggests that
the main focus of competition in the retail gas market was price. Thus, any difference in cost to the retailer could have a huge impact on the nature of competition.

2. Why Did Texaco Do That?: During the period in question, Texaco's independent retailer's share of sales declined from 76% to 49%. Moreover, seven
Texaco retailers went out of business during this time frame. Texaco claims that
it was able to offer Gull and Dompier a discount based on the valuable function
they performed in the distribution process. However, the record shows that Gull
and Dompier did little more than ship gasoline by tanker from the Texaco bulk
plant to their retailers. Further, two of Texaco's independent retailers sought to
purchase their own tankers—thus, providing themselves with the same service
that Gull and Dompier provided their retailers. Why wouldn't Texaco go for
this? In addition, Texaco executives ignored the requests of its retailers for relief
from this pricing scheme. Why did Texaco let the retailers flounder? Based on
our assumption that firms are profit maximizers and that the individuals running
firms are also rational maximizers, does Texaco's behavior seem unusual?

3. Functional Discounts: The Court holds that functional discounts are a defense to charges of price discrimination where the "discount constitutes a reasonable
reimbursement for the purchasers' actual marketing functions...." Why doesn't the
Court buy Texaco's argument that its discounts to Gull and Dompier were related to
function? What level of proof should be required to show an actual functional discount? Is recognition of functional discounts just a looser standard for proving a
justified cost difference? In concurring, Justice White seems to believe that functional
discounts should not be a recognized defense. Do you agree? Is his argument based
on economic reasoning or evidentiary standards? Are these necessarily different?

4. The Claim not Raised: The Court recognizes a potentially important argument that was not raised by Texaco. Specifically, that "the inference of injury to

competition might...be negated by evidence that a disfavored buyer could make purchases at a reasonable discount from favored buyers." Based on the facts in this case, should this argument exculpate Texaco?

d. Predatory Pricing

Predatory pricing is a strategy by which a firm reduces its price below its costs of production in order to drive its rivals out of the market in and then to capture monopoly profits once it has the market to itself. In practice it is difficult to distinguish predatory behavior from normal rivalrous competition. Because it is rational for a profit maximizing firm to continue to operate in the short-run even if P<ATC, as long as P>AVC, setting price below ATC is not considered evidence of predatory pricing — price must be less than AVC in order to establish something other than normal competitive behavior. By setting price below its average variable cost, the predator firm operates in a range where most firms shut down in the short-run. Thus, the theory of predatory pricing states that the predator attempts to earn monopoly profits in the long run by incurring economic losses in the short-run. It's alleged that such behavior can increase the value of the firm. For this to occur, the present value of the long-run monopoly profits must be greater than the short-run losses.

A major difficulty for predatory pricing theory is explaining why new firms do not attempt to enter the market once the successful predator begins charging monopoly prices. Remember that the key to reaping monopoly profits in the long-run is barriers to entry. It is not at all clear where the predator gains such a barrier. A common response to this criticism is to trust that the predator's past price reductions discourage potential entrants from entering the market.

Predatory pricing may be attacked under Section 2 of the Sherman Act as an attempt to monopolize. However, the following case raises doubts about the future of predatory pricing as an antitrust violation.

Matsushita Elec. Indus. Co., Ltd. v. Zenith Radio Corp.

Supreme Court of the United States
475 U.S. 574, 106 S. Ct. 1348 (1986)

Read *supra,* Chapter I

Notes and Questions

1. Predatory Pricing: The Probability of Success: The Court observes that the success of any predatory pricing scheme depends on the ability of the predator to charge monopoly profits after its rivals have exited the market. Moreover, to be economically rational, the present value of the monopoly profits must exceed the losses incurred in driving rivals out of the market. Zenith and NUE allege that the Japanese firms have been pricing below cost for over twenty years—thereby incurring substantial losses in a not yet successful effort to drive the American firms out of the CEP industry. How long will it take to recoup these losses? Does it seem likely that Japanese firms will be able to charge monopoly profits for a period long enough to break even? How about making an economic profit?

2. Predatory Pricing by a Cartel: The Probability of Success?: For any single firm, predatory pricing is a risky strategy. The risk arises because of the need to maintain barriers of entry after the extinction of rivals for a period long enough to recapture losses and make an economic profit. Zenith and NUE do not accuse a single firm of predatory pricing. Rather, they claim that over twenty-one Japanese firms engaged in this predatory pricing scheme. In other words, Zenith and NUE have accused a cartel of predatory pricing. What are the inherent difficulties of organizing and maintaining a cartel? If the probability of a single firm engaging in predatory pricing are remote, what would happen to that probability if the accusation were against a cartel? The payoff for a successful predatory pricing scheme is the monopoly profits earned after all rivals have been eliminated. Thus, post elimination, a monopoly price and output must be set. For a cartel to engage in predatory pricing, all firms in the cartel must agree on price and output. Not only would coming to such an agreement be difficult, but there is a huge incentive to cheat. After sustaining losses in order to drive rivals out of the market, each individual firm in the cartel will be eager to earn monopoly profits. Each individual firm will believe that by increasing its output by only a small amount over the agreed upon level, no other firm in the cartel will notice and the cheating firm will be able to earn even greater monopoly profits. The greater the number of firms in the cartel, the greater the incentive to cheat. What does this say about the alleged Japanese cartel's chance for success? Moreover, the longer the time period involved, the less likely the cartel will succeed. What does this say about the alleged Japanese cartel's chance for success? If all of these factors are combined, what can be said about the probability that a predatory pricing scheme was in fact under way in the CEP market?

3. An Alternative Story: Price Discrimination: Recall the prerequisites for a firm to engage in price discrimination. First, the seller must have some way of identifying separate groups of customers with differing demands for the seller's product. Second, the seller must be able to prevent the resale of its good or service from the low-price purchasers to the high-price purchasers. For the Japanese firms, there are clearly two markets for CEPs — one in the United States and one in Japan. Japanese consumers are faced with a well organized cartel that is protected by government restrictions on foreign competition. Therefore, Japanese consumers face monopoly prices and output. On the other hand, the American CEP market is much more competitive and prices are lower. Thus, Japanese firms face two markets with differing elasticities of demand for the seller's product, and resale between these two markets is prohibited by the Japanese government. What is the effect on American consumers of Japanese price discrimination?

Chapter VI

Externalities

In many instances, some of the costs of producing a product "spill over" and injure third parties that are not part of the production process. The total cost to society in terms of resources consumed is the sum of the private costs paid by the producer and the external costs that must be borne by third parties. If the legal system does not provide for the producer to compensate third parties, then the producer will be able to operate at a cost of production that does not fully reflect the social costs of the resources consumed. Some of the producer's costs are then *external* to his production decisions. The existence of such externalities means that self-interested behavior may not always be in the best interest of society. Externalities are a form of market failure, and thus are an often stated justification for government intervention in the market system.

Externalities exist because of poorly defined property rights. If no one owns the air, then no property owner can use the legal system to force the polluter to stop polluting. It seems logical, then, for the examination of externalities to start with a consideration of the economics of property rights in Section A. Section B provides a more technical definition of externalities and their welfare effects. Section C considers a variety of ways in which externalities can be addressed—ranging from establishing property rights to corrective taxes to government regulation. Section D uses the tools of public choice economics to critique the (often implicit) assumption that imperfect markets can be corrected by perfect governments.

A. The Economics of Property Rights

The ownership of private property is a fundamental concept to most Americans. It is often suggested that private property is the feature most important to the operation of a market-oriented economic system. Property represents an aggregate of rights in some object, parcel of land, or intangible thing where those rights can be enforced. The owner of property is anyone who can enforce and control the bundle of rights associated with property. The rights associated with ownership of property include the right to possess, enjoy, sell, destroy, or otherwise control the use of the property. In free market economies, the rights of ownership are typically enforced by the government. This is perhaps the most productive role that government plays. Imagine the amount of resources that would be wasted if owners had to spend significant amounts of their time protecting their private property rights—through physical force, for example. The system of property rights creates a set of expectations upon which individuals may rely in dealing with one another.

357

The economics of property rights has received a great deal of attention with the development of law and economics. The basic points of the analysis can be summarized quite briefly. For purposes of the present discussion, a property right is a legally enforceable power to exclude others from using a resource, without the need to contract with them. A simple example of ownership of a pasture is used to illustrate some of the important insights. If Sarah owns a pasture, she can forbid others from grazing their cattle on it—and, importantly, there is no need for her to negotiate an agreement for exclusive use.

1. An Overview of the Efficient Property Rights System

Legal protection of property rights is important because it creates incentives to use resources efficiently. A truly efficient system of property rights requires three attributes: (1) universality—every resource is owned; (2) exclusivity—the owner of property may exclude all others from using it; and (3) transferability—it is costless for possessors of property rights to exchange their rights. A property rights system with these attributes, when combined with a free market economy, will generate the efficient allocation of resources. The legal system and property law, however, do not always fulfill these criteria.

In general, the granting of property rights confers two types of economic benefits, static and dynamic. Static refers to the impact of the property right on behavior during one particular time period—for example, one year or one growing season. The static benefit is illustrated by considering alternative assignments of property rights to a natural, uncultivated pasture. If the property rights are attenuated—that is, not exclusive or fully enforceable—so that Sarah can't exclude others from using her pasture (or cannot secure compensation when others use the pasture without her permission), then the property will not be used in a value maximizing manner because some (or, perhaps, all) users of the pasture will ignore the costs they impose on other users in deciding how much to let their cattle graze in the pasture. The use of the pasture by the trespassers imposes an externality on Sarah, and also biases the use of the pasture towards overgrazing. The overgrazing results in reduced total weight for cattle because the owners of the cattle allow their cattle to expend more energy in finding enough to eat than they would expend if each cattle owner had to pay the full cost of the grass, which is the case when the cattle owner has exclusive use of his own pasture. The attenuated property rights—even in the static situation—results in an outcome that is clearly not optimal. Granting enforceable property rights to Sarah will result in the static benefit of preventing overgrazing.

The dynamic benefit of a property right is the incentive to invest in the creation or improvement of some resource over time. For example, if Sarah is guaranteed exclusive rights to the pasture in both period 1 and period 2, then she has the incentive to invest resources (for example, through fertilization and careful management to avoid overgrazing) in period 1. She can then reap the benefits of the investment in period 2. Sarah would be unwilling to make such an investment if she were not able to exclude other potential users of the pasture in period 2. Similarly, a business firm is less likely to invest resources on the research and development of a new product if competing firms that have not borne that expense can duplicate it without having to compensate the original firm. As a result, when property rights are not enforceable, the initial investment is less likely to occur or, if it is forthcoming, it is likely to be smaller than with enforceable property rights. Thus, attenuated (poorly-defined) property rights prevent the achievement of the optimal outcome in the dynamic setting as well as the static setting.

The transferability of property rights facilitates the maximization of the static and dynamic benefits of well-defined property rights. In the preceding example, one would expect the cattle owners to attempt to capture the static and dynamic benefits of private property by negotiating a set of exclusive use property rights among themselves, provided their numbers are small enough for negotiation to occur (that is, provided that transaction costs are less than the gains from the transaction).

Costless transfer of property rights assures that the property rights are allocated to the highest valued uses. For example, if Sarah (the owner of the pasture) is a relatively unproductive rancher, then she should be able to increase her wealth by selling the pasture to a more productive rancher at a price that reflects some portion of the increased value of the pasture in the hands of the more productive rancher.

The allocation and use of property rights is affected by transaction costs — the costs of acquiring information about alternative uses and in negotiating and enforcing contracts. In general, if the potential benefits of a transaction are greater than the costs of reaching and enforcing a bargain, then a voluntary, mutually-beneficial exchange will result in the property rights being controlled by the parties that value them the most. Private property rights tend to be more carefully defined, more fully allocated, and better enforced when transaction costs are relatively low or benefits of defining rights are relatively high, other things being equal.

2. Enforcement of Property Rights

An important distinction in the economic analysis of property rights concerns the type of legal rule that protects the rights. A **property rule** is a legal rule that protects a property right through the absolute right to exclude others, with an injunction, for example. In the preceding example, Sarah's property right is protected by a property rule — she has the absolute right to exclude others from her property. Of course, she is allowed to reach voluntary agreements which allow others to use the property in return for some type of compensation.

Another way to protect Sarah's property right is with a **liability rule** under which Sarah has the right to collect damages from anyone who uses the pasture without her permission. A property rule requires that bargaining occur before others use the property; a liability rule allows the other party to use the property and then pay damages. Property rules require voluntary exchanges, while liability rules result in forced exchanges. Thus, liability rules are the domain of tort law, since it is impossible to negotiate a tort prior to its occurrence. Much of the economic analysis of law has been concerned with identifying situations where one rule is more appropriate than the other.

Property Rules, Liability Rules, and Inalienability: One View of the Cathedral

Guido Calabresi & A. Douglas Melamed
85 Harv. L. Rev. 1089, 1092–93, 1105–06 (1972)

Only rarely are Property and Torts approached from a unified perspective. Recent writings by lawyers concerned with economics and by economists concerned with law suggest, however, that an attempt at integrating the various legal relationships treated by these subjects would be useful both for the beginning student and the sophisticated scholar. By articulating a concept of "entitlements" which are protected by property, liability, or inalienability rules, we present one framework for such an approach....

*   *   *

An entitlement is protected by a property rule to the extent that someone who wishes to remove the entitlement from its holder must buy it from him in a voluntary transaction in which the value of the entitlement is agreed upon by the seller....

Whenever someone may destroy the entitlement if he is willing to pay an objectively determined value for it, the entitlement is protected by a liability rule. This value may be what it is thought the original holder of the entitlement would have sold it for. But the holder's complaint that he would have demanded more will not avail him once the objectively determined value is set.

*   *   *

An entitlement is inalienable to the extent that its transfer is not permitted between a willing buyer and a willing seller....

It should be clear that most entitlements to most goods are mixed. Taney's house may be protected by a property rule in situations in which Marshall wishes to purchase it, by a liability rule where the government decides to take it by eminent domain, and by a rule of inalienability in situations where Taney is drunk or incompetent....

*   *   *

Whenever society chooses an initial entitlement it must also determine whether to protect the entitlement by property rules, by liability rules, or by rules of inalienability. In our framework, much of what is generally called private property can be viewed as an entitlement protected by a property rule. No one can take the entitlement to private property from the holder unless the holder sells it willingly and at the price at which he subjectively values the property. Yet a nuisance with sufficient public utility to avoid an injunction has, in effect, the right to take property with compensation. In such a circumstance the entitlement to the property is protected only by what we call a liability rule: an external, objective standard of value used to facilitate the transfer of the entitlement from the holder to the nuisance. Finally, in some instances we will not allow the sale of the property at all, that is, we will occasionally make the entitlement inalienable.

*   *   *

Notes and Questions

1. Entitlements: Property and Liability Rules: Property rules are premised on the hypothetical exchange between a willing seller and a buyer. Yet, it appears that all property taken subject to a property or liability rule is undervalued because there is no willing seller. See Section B, "Market Prices and Subjective Value" in Chapter III. That is, the person with the property before the taking values it higher than a voluntary transaction price. What public policy justifications or questions can you think of to create such a rule?

2. Entitlements and Inalienability: What incentive does inalienability have on creating wealth? Is alienability only paternalistic in scope or is there another purpose behind the doctrine?

3. Why the Distinction?: Why is there this distinction between property and liability rules and inalienability? Is it merely semantics? Or are there different policy reasons that affect the implementation and enforcement of these doctrines?

3. Poorly Defined Property Rights

Some resources, like air and water, are not privately-owned. Because of the common ownership of these resources, no one has adequate legal rights to protect against their use. Thus, economic actors are able to use them without paying for them. For example, pollution occurs because manufacturers are able to avoid paying the cost of the damage to the air because no one owns the air. Such externalities would not occur, or at least people would have to pay for them (that is, internalize them), if the three attributes of an efficient property rights system were satisfied.

Common ownership means that the property rights to a resource are nonexistent or poorly defined. As a result, anyone may use or consume the resource. The fundamental economic disadvantage of common ownership is the absence of any incentive to invest in the productivity of the common property. Rather each person with access to the resource has an incentive to exploit it and neglect the effects of his or her actions on the resource's productivity.

The Tragedy of the Commons
Garrett Hardin
162 Science 1243,1244–45 (1968)

The tragedy of the commons develops this way. Picture a pasture open to all. It is to be expected that each herdsman will try to keep as many cattle as possible on the commons... At this point, the inherent logic of the commons remorselessly generate tragedy.

As a rational being, each herdsman seeks to maximize his gains. Explicitly or implicitly, more or less consciously, he asks, "What is the utility to me of adding one more animal to my herd?" This utility has one negative and one positive component.

1. The positive component is a function of the increment of one animal. Since the herdsman receives all the proceeds from the sale of the additional animal, the positive utility is nearly +1.

2. The negative component is a function of the additional overgrazing created by one animal. Since, however, the effects of overgrazing are shared by all the herdsmen, the negative utility for any particular decision-making herdsman is only a fraction of −1.

Adding together the component partial utilities, the rational herdsman concludes that the only sensible course for him is to add another animal to his herd. And another; and another.... But this is the conclusion reached by each and every rational herdsman sharing a commons. Therein is the tragedy. Each man is locked into a system that compels him to increase his herd without limit—in a world that is limited. Ruin is the destination toward which all men rush, each pursuing his own best interest in a society that believes in the freedom of the commons. Freedom in a commons brings ruin to all.

       *   *   *

In an approximate way, the logic of the commons has been understood for a long time, perhaps since the discovery of agriculture or the invention of private property....

Notes and Questions

1. Tragedy Everywhere: The tragedy of the commons has been used for hundreds of years (at least since Reverend C.L. Dodgson—a.k.a. Lewis Carroll—first introduced collective action analysis) to explain why mankind cannot achieve total economic prosperity. That is, rational self-interested people have limits as to how far they can progress without controls and laws to shape the overall economy. What laws and reforms are centered around this argument?

2. Congress, Businesses, and Law Schools: The U.S. Congress is probably the most expensive example of a tragedy of the commons. Because of the pressure to get reelected, each Senator and each member of Congress tries to pass legislation to benefit their constituents, without regard to the whole country. Vote trading and logrolling results in numerous pork barrel projects that would not pass if evaluated on an individual basis. Other economic organizations—such as businesses and law schools—are not exempt, either. Can you think of examples where one person has rationally pursued their self-interest only to hurt, directly or otherwise, the common interests?

The following case illustrates how the Tragedy of the Commons impacts oil and gas extraction.

Wronski v. Sun Oil Co.
Michigan Ct. of Appeals
89 Mich.App. 11, 279 N.W.2d 564 (1979)

HOLBROOK, J.

[Plaintiffs own several tracts of land comprising 200 acres within the Columbus 3 oil pool. Defendant, Sun Oil has drilled several wells on nearby property. The Supervisor of Wells, Michigan Department of Natural Resources, issued an order, under the authority of the Michigan oil and gas conservation act, establishing 20-acre well drilling units for the Columbus 3 pool; this order limits the number of wells that may be drilled to one well for each designated 20-acre tract within the boundaries of this oil field. The Supervisor also issued an order which limited production from each well within the field to a maximum of 75 barrels of oil per day. Plaintiffs contend the Sun Oil illegally overproduced oil from three wells and that such oil was drained from beneath the plaintiffs' tracts. The trial court found the Sun Oil had intentionally and unlawfully produced 150,000 barrels of oil, and that 50,000 barrels had been drained from beneath plaintiffs' property. The court awarded compensatory and exemplary damages to the plaintiffs. Sun Oil appealed.]

*   *   *

* * * Review of the record discloses sufficient facts upon which the trial court could find that Sun Oil systematically, intentionally and illegally produced...150,000 barrels over that allowed by the proration order. The record also supports the finding that one-third of this illegally produced oil was drained from the property of the plaintiffs. We are not convinced that had this Court been the trier of fact that we would have come to a different result, and do not reverse or modify these findings.

The trial court found that...

> Sun Oil Company has violated the common law rights of Plaintiffs Wronski and Koziara by illegally, unlawfully and secretly draining valuable oil from beneath their properties.

The nature of Sun Oil's violation, while not clearly stated by the trial court, was a claim for the conversion of oil.

*   *   *

Oil and gas, unlike other minerals, do not remain constantly in place in the ground, but may migrate across property lines. Because of this migratory tendency the rule of capture evolved. This rule provides:

> The owner of a tract of land acquires title to the oil and gas which he produces from wells drilled thereon, though it may be proved that part of such oil or gas migrated from adjoining lands. Under this rule, *absent some state regulation of drilling practices*, a landowner...is not liable to adjacent landowners whose lands are drained as a result of such operations....The remedy of the injured landowner under such circumstances has generally been said to be that of self-help "go and do likewise."
> William and Meyers, Supra, § 204.4, pp. 55–57 (Emphasis supplied.)

This rule of capture was a harsh rule that could work to deprive an owner of oil and gas underneath his land. To mitigate the harshness of this rule and to protect the landowners' property rights in the oil and gas beneath his land, the "fair share" principle emerged.

> As early as 1931, the Board of Directors of the American Petroleum Institute expressed this principle by declaring a policy:

> that it endorses, and believes the petroleum industry endorses the principle that each owner of the surface is entitled only to his equitable and ratable share of the recoverable oil and gas energy in the common pool in the proportion which the recoverable reserves underlying his land bears to the recoverable reserves in the pool. Graham, *Fair Share or*

Fair Game? Great Principle, Good Technology—But Pitfalls in Practice,
8 Nat.Res.Law. 61, 64–65 (1975).

The API clarified the principle in 1942 by saying:

> Within reasonable limits, each operator should have an opportunity
> equal to that afforded other operators to recover the equivalent of the
> amount of recoverable oil (and gas) underlying his property. The aim
> should be to prevent reasonably avoidable drainage of oil and gas across
> property lines that is not offset by counter drainage. Id. at 65.

This fair-share rule does not do away with the rule of capture, but rather acts to
place limits on its proper application.

Texas has adopted both the ownership-in-place doctrine and the fair-share
principle. Its courts have addressed the interrelationship between these two principles and the rule of capture.

> It must be conceded that under the law of capture there is no liability
> for reasonable and legitimate drainage from the common pool. The
> landowner is privileged to sink as many wells as he desires upon his tract
> of land and extract therefrom and appropriate all the oil and gas that he
> may produce, *so long as he operates within the spirit and purpose of
> conservation statutes and orders of the Railroad Commission.* These
> laws and regulations are designed to afford each owner a reasonable op-
> portunity to produce his proportionate part of the oil and gas from the
> entire pool and to prevent operating practices injurious to the common
> reservoir. In this manner, if all operators exercise the same degree of skill
> and diligence, each owner will recover in most instances his fair share of
> the oil and gas. *This reasonable opportunity to produce his fair share of
> the oil and gas is the landowner's common law right* under our theory of
> absolute ownership of the minerals in place. But from the very nature of
> this theory the right of each land holder is qualified, and is limited to le-
> gitimate operations. Elliff v. Texon Drilling Co., 146 Tex. 575, 582, 210
> S.W.2d 558, 562 (1948). (Emphasis supplied.)

The rule of capture is thus modified to exclude operations that are in violation of
valid conservation orders.

Michigan recognizes the fair-share principle and its subsequent modifications
of the rule of capture. When an adjacent landowner drilled an oil well too close
to a property line the Supreme Court said that this:

> [D]eprived plaintiff of the opportunity of claiming and taking the oil
> that was rightfully hers; and defendants must respond in damages for
> such conversion. Ross v. Damm, 278 Mich. 388, 396, 270 N.W. 722,
> 725 (1936).

The Supervisor of Wells Act also incorporated the fair share principle into Section 13. This section concerns proration orders and states in part that:

> The rules, regulations, or orders of the supervisor shall, so far as it is
> practicable to do so, afford the owner of each property in a pool *the op-
> portunity to produce his just and equitable share of the oil and gas in the
> pool,* being an amount, so far as can be practicably determined and ob-
> tained without waste, and without reducing the bottom hole pressure

materially below the average for the pool, substantially in the proportion that the quantity of the recoverable oil and gas under such property bears to the total recoverable oil and gas in the pool, and for this purpose to use his just and equitable share of the reservoir energy. M.C.L. § 319.13; M.S.A. § 13.139(13). (Emphasis supplied.)

This right to have a reasonable opportunity to produce one's just and equitable share of oil in a pool is the common-law right that the trial court found Sun Oil violated. Under the authority of Ross v. Damm, *supra*, if it can be said that Sun Oil's overproduction deprived plaintiffs of the opportunity to claim and take the oil under their respective properties, then Sun Oil will be liable for a conversion.

Production in the Columbus 3 field was restricted to 75 barrels of oil per well per day. Compulsory pooling was also in effect, limiting the number of oil wells to one per twenty acres, and specifying their location. The purpose behind proration is that the order itself, if obeyed, will protect landowners from drainage and allow each to produce their fair share. A violation of the proration order, especially a secret violation, allows the violator to take more than his fair share and leaves the other landowners unable to protect their rights unless they also violate the proration order. We therefore hold that any violation of a proration order constitutes conversion of oil from the pool, and subjects the violator to liability to all the owners of interests in the pool for conversion of the illegally-obtained oil. *See* Bolton v. Coates, 533 S.W.2d 914 (Tex., 1975), Ortiz Oil Co. v. Geyer, 138 Tex. 373, 159 S.W.2d 494 (1942). The trial court found that Sun Oil produced 150,000 barrels of oil from the Columbus 3 pool in contravention of the order of the Supervisor of Wells, and that 50,000 barrels of this oil had been drained from the lands of plaintiffs, which the trial court identified as a violation of the plaintiffs' common-law rights. The finding that Sun Oil is liable to plaintiffs for the conversion of 50,000 barrels of oil is affirmed.

*   *   *

Notes and Questions

1. Fishing: The **Tragedy of the Commons** argument applies to both renewable resources, such as fish, and nonrenewable resources, such as oil. Consider the example of fishing in international waters. In international waters, anyone may acquire exclusive ownership of fish by catching them, and no one has rights to the fish until they are caught. This system causes each fisherman to ignore the effect of the well-known biological law that the current stock of species of fish determines its reproductive life. Thus, the fish harvested today reduce today's stock and thereby affect the size of tomorrow's stock and tomorrow's harvesting costs and revenues. However, overfishing results because no single fisherman has an incentive to act on this bioeconomic relationship. If all fisherman would cooperate to restrain themselves today, tomorrow's stock would be larger and future harvesting cheaper and more profitable. However, under competitive conditions, each individual knows that if he or she abstains now, rivals will not abstain and much of the effect of one individual's abstention is lost. Further, the reduction in future costs would accrue to everyone not just to the abstainer. Hence, each person has little reason to abstain since the major effect is to lower others' future costs at the immediate present cost to the abstainer.

2. Three Solutions to Overfishing. *(1) A Single Owner:* Individual ownership removes this dilemma. If only one person is fishing, he or she need not worry that rivals will not abstain. (Of course, groups such as tribes of indigenous people can also be sole owners, but the group must be able to control the behavior of its members with respect to the resource.) *(2) Contracting Among Multiple Owners:* When there is more than one owner, all parties involved could negotiate an agreement to abstain and all would benefit. The fact that such agreements are not usually successful in negotiations is due to the cost of dealing with all current and potential people who will fish and the difficulty in ensuring that all abstain as agreed. *(3) Government Regulation:* A third method of dealing with the Tragedy of the Commons in international fishing is government regulation. Such regulation usually sets an annual catch quota. To allocate the quota, regulators rely on restrictions on fishing technology or simply close the season when the quota is taken. Both means create difficult enforcement problems and potential economic waste. If the season is closed when the quota is taken, for example, excess profits are dissipated in competition among fishermen to buy bigger, faster boats and thus get a larger share of the quota. The season progressively shrinks, and resources stand idle for much of the year or are devoted to inferior employment.

3. Environmental Protection and Federalism. A leading rationale for federal domination of environmental regulation is to prevent states from competing for economic growth opportunities by lowering their environmental standards in a so-called "race for the bottom." The notion is that all states compete for economic growth by lowering environmental standards below the level they would select if they acted collectively at the national level. What is individually rational for individual states is collectively irrational at the national level. Professor Richard Stewart describes the implication of this dynamic in concise terms:

> ...Given the mobility of industry and commerce, any individual state or community may rationally decline unilaterally to adopt high environment standards that entail substantial costs for industry and obstacles to economic development for fear that the resulting environmental gains will be more than offset by movement of capital to other areas with lower standards. If each locality reasons in the same way, all will adopt lower standards of environmental quality than they would prefer if there were some binding mechanism that enabled them simultaneously to enact higher standards, thus eliminating the threatened loss of industry or development.

Richard B. Stewart, Pyramids of Sacrifice? Problems of Federalism in Mandating State Implementation of National Environmental Policy, 86 Yale L. J. 1196, 1212 (1977). Thus, according to this logic, federal regulation is necessary to correct a political market failure at the state level. For thorough documentation of the influence of this argument, as well as a devastating critique of this argument, see Richard L. Revesz, Rehabilitating Interstate Competition: Rethinking the "Race-to-the-Bottom" Rationale for Federal Environmental Regulation, 67 N.Y.U.L.Rev. 1210, 1233–44 (1992).

4. Public Goods

A **public good** is a good where one individual's consumption of the good does not reduce or exclude the ability of other individuals to consume the good.

A pure public good is both nonrival and nonexcludable. A good is nonrival when the quantity available for other people does not diminish when one consumes it. A good is nonexcludable if it is prohibitively costly to provide the good only to people who pay for it while preventing or exclude other people from obtaining it. The classic example of a public good is national defense. Once provided to one person, national defense is available to all on a noncompeting or nonrivalrous basis. It is difficult or impossible to exclude anyone from the use of national defense public good and its enjoyment by one person does not prevent its use by another.

In contrast, a private good is consumed exclusively by the person who owns it. If you eat an apple, one less apple remains for other people. If you watch a television show, however, you do not reduce the number of viewers who can watch the show on their own televisions.

Public goods present a unique economic problem because firms have little incentive to produce them. Few buyers willingly pay for nonexcludable goods because they can get them free. The problem facing producers of public goods is that **free riding** behavior makes it difficult to discover the true preferences of consumers of a public good. Individuals will not reveal their true preferences for public goods because it is not in their self interest to do so. For example, your neighborhood might try to organize a crime watch group. Many neighbors might not contribute but would still appreciate any protection provided, thus, concealing group preferences for the service. On the other hand, some who do contribute voluntarily might be totally disinterested in the service. Free riding makes it difficult to determine the true level of demand for the public good. The free rider problem holds the equilibrium quantity of public goods below the economically efficient quantity.

If everyone free rides and no one contributes to the production of public goods, then everyone will be worse off as a result. No public goods will be produced even though each individual would like some provision of public goods. Herein lies the rationale for government provision of public goods. Government has the power of coercion and taxation and it can force consumers to contribute to the production of public goods. Citizens cannot refuse to pay taxes; they are forced to contribute to the cost of the public sector output.

Government provision of public goods has two main drawbacks. First, the government lacks information about the amount of money that various people are willing to pay for any particular public good. This creates two more problems. The government cannot calculate the economically efficient level of a public good and it may tax some people more (and others less) than they are willing to pay for the public good. The counterargument to this objection is that the government may get closer to the economically efficient level of the public good than would emerge in the free market. The second main drawback of government provision of public goods is that actual government program will reflect political pressures to benefit special interests rather than the provision of true public goods. That is, the political determination of what is a "public good" may stray from the economic definition of a public good.

B. Externalities

Economics addresses the incentives to pollute the air and water, incentives to conserve or destroy natural resources, and incentives to conduct economic activities that affect ecological systems and could eradicate entire species. Pollution and similar problems occur when people do not bear all of the costs of their actions. They force polluted air or water on the rest of society. They overuse or destroy natural resources. Analysis of these problems must begin by making a careful distinction between the private costs and social costs, as well as private benefits and social benefits, of human actions.

The **private cost** of producing a good is the cost paid by the firm that produces and sells it. Sometimes producing a good creates costs for other people as well, such as when a factory causes air pollution that harms people who live nearby. Therefore, the cost of producing a good should include the value of the harm that the pollution creates for those people, measured by the amount of money they would be willing to pay to eliminate the harm. Consumption of some products may also impose costs on other people, such as when driving a car pollutes the air. The **social cost** of producing a good is the total private cost plus the total cost to other people from producing various quantities of the good.

Private costs and social costs differ whenever production or use of a good directly affects people who do not buy or sell it. When a factory pollutes the air, the social costs of the good produced includes the harm to other people from that pollution. Similarly, the social cost of driving a car includes the pollution harm imposed on third parties.

Economists distinguish between private benefits and social benefits in the same way. The **private benefit** of consuming a good is its benefit to the people who buy and consume it. The **social benefit** of consuming a good is its total benefit to everyone in society. For example, the private benefit from planting a tree may be its beauty or its shade. The social benefit includes enrichment of the atmosphere from the oxygen the tree produces. If a scientist discovers a better medicine to treat a disease, her gains (and her firm's profits) from selling the medicine are private benefits. The gains to people who use the medicine are also private benefits. The social benefits include these private benefits plus gains to other people, perhaps because the scientist's discovery provides new ideas that help other scientists working on other problems and saved health care costs.

An externality occurs when the private costs or benefits of a good differs from its social costs or benefits. A **negative externality** occurs when the social cost of a good exceeds its private cost. A **positive externality** occurs when the social benefit exceeds the private benefit.

1. Negative Externalities

A common example of a negative externality is a factory's emission of smoke as a byproduct of production. If the factory is able to avoid responsibility for the consequences of its smoke, such as the expenses for painting soot covered buildings nearby or laundering dirty clothes, the output of the factory will be excessive in that the value of additional output is less than the additional costs of the additional output plus the damage. If the factory were held responsible for the

Figure VI-1

Equilibrium with a Negative Externality

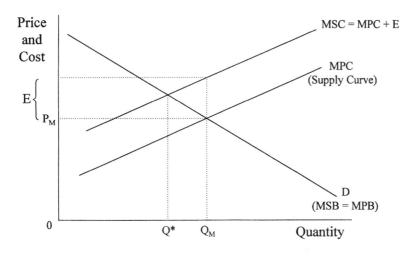

damage done by its smoke, it costs would rise, its product would become more expensive, and it would produce less.

Any economic entity, including firms, government agencies, and individuals, can create a negative externality. Examples of negative externalities include exhaust emissions of automobiles, a neighbor's excessively loud stereo, low flying jet airplanes landing at an airport, drunk drivers, the contamination of underground water by toxic chemical dumps, and poor health practices that raise others people's chances of contracting contagious diseases.

Figure VI-1 shows a basic demand and supply graph with a negative externality. The graph shows the demand for a product, its marginal private cost (MPC), and its marginal social cost (MSC). The marginal private cost of producing a good is the increase in total private cost from producing one more unit. The negative externality is the marginal cost to third parties from producing that same additional unit. The marginal social cost of producing a good, MSC, is the increase in the total social cost from producing one more unit.

The marginal social cost (MSC) curve lies above the marginal private cost (MPC) curve. The negative externality (E) is the vertical difference between MSC and MPC, so that E = MSC − MPC. Note that marginal social benefit (MSB) equals marginal private benefit (MPB) because it is assumed that there are no positive externalities associated with consumption or production. The private, market-determined level of production is Q_M, where MPC = MPB. The socially optimal level of production is Q*, where MSC = MSB. Any quantity produced above Q* is economically inefficient because the MSC of production is greater than the MSB. In Figure VI-1, there is an overproduction of the product as indicated by the difference between the market equilibrium at Q_M and the social optimum at Q*.

The market failure associated with negative externalities is that individuals' decisions are based on private rather than social benefit. Production decisions are based on private costs and benefits, and production will be above the opti-

Figure VI-2

Equilibrium and Economic Inefficiency with a Negative Externality

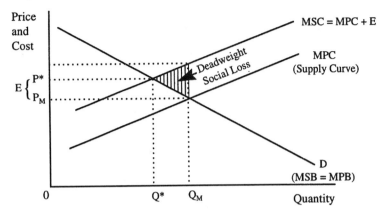

mum level. The market failure caused by a negative externality is shown as a **deadweight social loss** in Figure VI-2. The shaded area indicates that the marginal social cost of producing units Q^* to Q_M is greater than the marginal social benefits. Notice that the consumers would buy the economically efficient quantity of the product if its price were P^*; but the equilibrium price, P_M, is less than P^*, so firms produce and people buy more than the economically efficient quantity. This divergence between the market outcome and the optimal outcome is often used as justification for government intervention in the form of taxation or regulation.

Also, notice in Figure VI-2 that the economically efficient quantity (Q^*) of the good is positive, not zero. Applying this analysis to pollution, we find that it would not be economically efficient to eliminate pollution entirely. This would require doing without the product entirely. Some pollution would result even if firms were to produce the economically efficient quantity of the product. Thus, the economically efficient level of the pollution is not zero. The economically efficient level of pollution occurs when the marginal benefit of producing it equals the marginal cost of producing it.

Orchard View Farms, Inc. v. Martin Marietta Aluminum, Inc.

United States District Court, District of Oregon
500 F. Supp. 984 (1980)

Barns, Chief Judge:

HISTORY OF THIS CASE

This diversity case is before the court on remand from the Ninth Circuit Court of Appeals for a retrial on the issue of punitive damages.

On March 31, 1971, Orchard View Farms, Inc. (Orchard View) filed this trespass action, seeking compensatory and punitive damages for injuries to its orchards between March 31, 1965 and the filing date. These injuries were alleged to have been caused by fluoride emitted from the aluminum reduction plant operated by Martin Marietta Aluminum, Inc. (the company or Martin Marietta). In April and May, 1973, the case was tried to a jury, which awarded Orchard View $103,655 compensatory damages and $250,000 punitive damages. The company appealed this judgment on numerous grounds.

The Ninth Circuit affirmed the award of compensatory damages but reversed and remanded the punitive damages award because in various rulings at the trial I erroneously admitted evidence of certain events that had occurred before the 1965–71 claim period, events which had been insufficiently linked by the evidence to the company's conduct and policies during the claim period.

*   *   *

FACTUAL BACKGROUND

Martin Marietta Aluminum, Inc., is a California corporation that owns and operates aluminum reduction plants, including plants located in The Dalles, Oregon, and Goldendale, Washington. Harvey Aluminum, Inc. (Harvey) constructed the plant located at The Dalles, and owned and operated it when production began in 1958. In 1968 Martin Marietta Corporation purchased a controlling share of Harvey common stock. It voted its representatives into a majority of the Harvey directorship in 1969. In 1972, the name of Harvey Aluminum, Inc., was changed to Martin Marietta Aluminum, Inc. In 1974 Martin Marietta Aluminum, Inc., became a wholly-owned subsidiary of Martin Marietta Corporation.

Orchard View Farms, Inc., is an Oregon corporation. It operates three orchards with a combined total acreage of approximately five hundred acres. The orchards are located between 2.5 and 5 miles from the aluminum plant. Donald Bailey is the president and treasurer of Orchard View; he, his wife, and five of their children are the sole stockholders. Orchard View owns part of the land; the Baileys own the rest and lease it to Orchard View. The Bailey family operates the orchards.

This case is one of an ever-increasing number filed against Harvey, and later Martin Marietta, by orchardists who charged that fluorides emitted from the plant have damaged their crops. The first such suit, *Renken v. Harvey Aluminum, Inc.*, 226 F. Supp. 169 (D.Or.1963), was filed in May, 1961. It was finally closed in 1966 when the court approved a consent decree providing for arbitration of the growers' claims and dismissal of the related actions filed in state court during the interim. Since February, 1977, thirteen actions have been filed in the United States District Court. These suits seek compensatory and punitive damages for injury allegedly inflicted by emissions from the plant during the years 1971 through 1977.

OPINION

*   *   *

I. OREGON LAW OF PUNITIVE DAMAGES.

The Oregon Supreme Court has provided specific guidance on punitive damage liability in the context of industrial air pollution. In *McElwain v.*

Georgia-Pacific Corporation, 245 Or. 247, 421 P.2d 957 (1966), the court stated:

> Although this court has on occasion indulged in the dictum that punitive damages are not "favored in the law," it has, nevertheless, uniformly sanctioned the recovery of punitive damages whenever there was evidence of a wrongful act done intentionally, with knowledge that it would cause harm to a particular person or persons.... The intentional disregard of the interest of another is the equivalent of legal malice, and justifies punitive damages for trespass. Where there is proof of an intentional, unjustifiable infliction of harm with deliberate disregard of the social consequences, the question of award of punitive damages is for the jury. 245 Or. at 249, 421 P.2d at 958.

The court reversed the trial judge's withdrawal of the issue of punitive damage liability from the jury because the "defendant knew when it decided to construct its kraft mill in Toledo, that there was danger, if not a probability, that the mill would cause damage to adjoining property," 245 Or. at 250, 421 P.2d at 958, and because of "the substantial evidence from which the jury could have found that during the period involved in this action the defendant had not done everything reasonably possible to eliminate or minimize the damage to adjoining properties by its mill." 245 Or. at 252, 421 P.2d at 959.

In *Davis v. Georgia-Pacific Corporation,* 251 Or. 239, 445 P.2d 481 (1968), the court remanded a jury's award of punitive damages because the trial judge had refused to admit evidence pertaining to "the utility of defendant's operations and its efforts, as compared with others similarly engaged, to prevent damage to surrounding properties." 251 Or. at 245, 445 P.2d at 484.

In a more recent review of punitive damages liability in Oregon, the court in *Harrell v. Travelers Indemnity Company,* 279 Or. 199, 567 P.2d 1013 (1977), noted:

> One whose business involves the operation of a plant which emits smoke, fumes or "particulates" may also have...liability for punitive damages, even in the absence of any "wanton" or "fraudulent" conduct, upon the ground that he has "intentionally" permitted fumes, smoke or particles to be released and blown by the wind upon another's property, for the reason that "[t]he intentional disregard of the interest of another is the legal equivalent of legal malice and justifies punitive damages for trespass." 279 Or. at 210–11, 567 P.2d at 1018, quoting *McElwain,* 245 Or. at 249, 421 P.2d at 958 (and adding an additional "legal" to the quotation).

*   *   *

> Where there is evidence that the injury was done maliciously or wilfully and wantonly or committed with bad motive or recklessly so as to imply a disregard of social obligations, punitive damages are justified. *Fisher v. Carlin,* 219 Or. 159, 346 P.2d 641.

> Here the record discloses that appellants had known for several years that fluorides from their plant were settling on appellees' land, with resultant damage to appellees' crops. It thus could have been found that

their trespass was done knowingly and wilfully, that it was intentional and in wanton disregard of appellants' social obligations.

> To justify an award of punitive damages, it is not necessary that the act have been done maliciously or with bad motive. Where it has become apparent, as it has here, that compensatory damages alone, while they might compensate the injured party, will not deter the actor from committing similar trespasses in the future, there is ample justification for an award of punitive damages.... Accordingly, the issue of punitive damages should have been submitted to the jury. 316 F.2d at 275.

Upon remand a second jury denied any award of punitive damages, and the plaintiff appealed. In *Lampert v. Reynolds Metals Company*, 372 F.2d 245 (9th Cir. 1967), the court noted that its earlier view of punitive damages had been confirmed in the interim by the Oregon Supreme Court's *McElwain* opinion. During the retrial, the District of Oregon judge hearing the case instructed the jury that, "with regard to punitive damages, it should weigh the apparent value to society of plaintiffs' farming activities." 372 F.2d at 247. The Ninth Circuit rejected this view, stating:

> Without doubt, the operation of the Reynolds Metals Company at Troutdale has social value in that community. But in legal contemplation, the company has no obligation to provide that social value, and certainly no right to do so in disregard of its legal obligation not to cause trespass injuries upon the property of plaintiffs. We find no Oregon decision nor, indeed, any decision from any jurisdiction, which supports the weighing process sanctioned by the trial court. 372 F.2d at 248.

The decision was reversed and the cause remanded for a new trial.

This guidance provided by the Oregon Supreme Court and the Ninth Circuit Court of Appeals, though specific to the context of industrial air pollution, does not define with precision the circumstances justifying the imposition of punitive damage liability. A broad synthesis of these opinions provides the conclusion that punitive damage awards may be imposed for business activities, harmful to others, carried out in disregard of the corporation's societal obligations. In brief, the issue is whether the defendant has damaged the property of plaintiff by conduct evidencing an "I don't give a damn" attitude. For a case as complex as this, however, it is important to describe in some greater detail the societal obligations of business enterprises.

II. SOCIETAL OBLIGATIONS OF BUSINESS ENTERPRISES.

In essence, any business is socially obliged to carry on an enterprise that is a net benefit, or at least not a net loss, to society. The company's management recognized this obligation in a 1960 letter to the Wasco County Fruit and Produce League.

> In closing I (Lawrence Harvey) would like to reemphasize our desire to foster the prosperity of the entire community.... We are doing, and will continue to do so, the best scientific job of control that is possible under the circumstances. These are obligations which we consider part of our community responsibility. Ex. 305a at 2.

In a world where all costs of production were borne by the enterprise, determining whether a firm produced a net benefit, or at least not a net detriment, to society would be as simple as examining the company's balance sheet of income and expenses. In the real world the task is more complex, because enterprises can sometimes shift a portion of their costs of production onto others. In the case of an industrial plant emitting pollution, those harmed by the emissions are, in effect, involuntarily bearing some of the firm's production costs.

Our society has not demanded that such externalized costs of production be completely eliminated. Instead, we tolerate externalities such as pollution as long as the enterprise remains productive: that is, producing greater value than the total of its internalized and externalized costs of production. A business that does not achieve net productivity is harmful to society, detracting from the standard of living it is designed to enhance. Because firms can sometimes impose a portion of their production costs upon others, the mere fact that a company continues to operate at a profit is not in itself conclusive evidence that it produces a net benefit to society.

Our system of law attempts to ensure that businesses are, on balance, socially beneficial by requiring that each enterprise bear its total production costs, as accurately as those costs can be ascertained. A fundamental means to this end is the institution of tort liability, which requires that persons harmed by business or other activity be compensated by the perpetrator of the damage. In the context of pollution, however, the tort system does not always operate smoothly to impose liability for compensatory damages. Among the difficulties encountered are: (1) that the harm may be gradual or otherwise difficult to perceive; (2) that the cause of the harm may be difficult to trace to the pollution and from the pollution to its source; and (3) that the harm may be inflicted in small amounts upon a large number of people, none of whom individually suffer sufficient damage to warrant the time and expense of legal action and whose organization into a plaintiff class is hindered by what has come to be known as the tragedy of the commons.[1]

Because of these impediments to smooth operation of the tort system and to ensuring that each enterprise bears its own costs of production, the law imposes upon businesses a societal obligation not to obstruct legal procedures designed to provide compensation to persons harmed by externalized costs of production. Enterprises must cooperate with their neighbors in ascertaining the nature, severity and scope of the harm and in arranging to prevent the damage or to neutralize it through some form of compensation.

A breach of societal obligations justifies the imposition of punitive damages to deter uncooperative behavior that impedes the legal system from ensuring that enterprises produce a net benefit to society.

---

1. Organizing a plaintiff class is hindered by the fact that the benefit of a successful lawsuit against the polluter for compensation is not limited to the plaintiffs. Persons damaged by the pollution but not contributing to the legal action also benefit due to the collateral estoppel effects of the initial lawsuit in subsequent actions and because the first plaintiff or group of plaintiffs has already done the work of organizing some relevant evidence and locating experts willing to testify. Thus, each person damaged by the pollution has an economic incentive to let someone else bring the first lawsuit and then to take a "free ride" or at least a discount excursion to obtaining his own compensation.

III. EVALUATION OF THE DEFENDANT'S CONDUCT IN LIGHT OF ITS SOCIETAL OBLIGATIONS.

Although the company did not fail to carry out its societal obligations in every respect, I have concluded that the overall conduct of the business with respect to ascertaining the harm from the plant's emissions, efficiently controlling the harmful emissions and arranging to compensate for the remaining harm constitutes breach of societal responsibility sufficient to justify the imposition of punitive damages.

A. Ascertaining the Harm from Plant Emissions.

A business enterprise has a societal obligation to determine whether its emissions will result in harm to others. Because the damage from pollution can be difficult to perceive due to its subtle or incremental nature, and because it can be difficult to trace to its cause, the obligation of the enterprise extends not only to observation of property in the surrounding region but also to initiation and completion of unbiased scientific studies designed to detect the potential adverse effects of the substances emitted. I find that the company failed to fulfill this obligation before or during the 1965–71 claim period by taking less than full cognizance of the damage inflicted upon the orchards and by generally shirking its responsibility to undertake competent scientific inquiry into the adverse effects of its emissions.

*   *   *

In sum, I find that the company's failure to exercise sufficient diligence in obtaining information pertinent to damage to crops and trees that might have been caused by the plant's emissions and to evaluate objectively the relevant information compiled by others constitutes evidence that the company was not fulfilling its societal obligations during the 1965–71 claim period.

B. Efficiently Controlling the Harmful Emissions.

During the claim period the company had a societal obligation to adopt and maintain reasonable pollution control measures, at least those capable of reducing the harm at a cost less than the damage caused by the emissions. Failure to adhere to such a course would result in a net detriment to society. An efficient program of pollution control also requires at least occasional monitoring of emissions as a check on the effectiveness of the control strategy.

The plaintiffs contend that the company did not implement reasonably efficient and economical pollution control measures that could have reduced the fluoride emissions from the plant during the 1965–71 claim period. The company's response is that its control system during that period was among the best in any aluminum plant in the world. Simply being "among the best" does not necessarily discharge the company's societal obligations, because the performance of other plants might also evidence social disregard. Moreover, a company's obligation to restrict its emissions depends upon the damage they might cause; a greater degree of control is called for in a populated agricultural area than in more sparsely inhabited and cultivated surroundings. Because calculating the precise costs and benefits of various pollution control strategies is impossible, however, descriptions of the feasibility and effectiveness of systems employed in other plants are useful to indicate the degree of emission control the company might have reasonably been expected to achieve during the claim period.

Although the company's social obligation extends to the implementation of only those pollution control measures that efficiently reduce the damage to others, an award of punitive damages does not require the plaintiff to provide detailed analyses of alternative emission control strategies and their costs. Instead, the plaintiff need only show, by a preponderance of the evidence, the existence of pollution reduction measures that could have been adopted and reasonably might have been expected to efficiently decrease the plant's emissions. It then becomes the burden of the company, with its superior access to scientific, technological, engineering, economic and management expertise, to show, by a preponderance of the evidence, that the measures proposed by the plaintiff were not available before or during the claim period or would not have resulted in efficient emission control.

My examination of the evidence leads me to conclude that the company failed to implement reasonably efficient and economical pollution control measures that could have reduced the fluoride emissions from the plant during the 1965–71 claim period.

    *   *   *

The preponderance of the technical and evaluative testimony supports the conclusion that the company did not implement reasonably efficient and economical pollution control measures that could have substantially reduced the fluoride emissions from the plant during the 1965–71 period.

4. Mitigation Measures.

It is possible that the adverse effects of emissions from the plant might have been reduced by a strategy of mitigation, including the installation of tall stacks to propel the fluorides through the occasional atmospheric inversion layer and the spraying of susceptible fruit with a calcium chloride solution.

a. Tall Stacks.

The Stanford Research Institute 1955 proposal to the company "for an investigation of potential air pollution conditions in the vicinity of your future aluminum reduction plant at The Dalles" noted among the methods for minimizing the effects of pollutants "discharge from a tall stack." In fact, the proposal stated:

> ...If particulate fluorides and tar fog are present in (pot room) air to an excessive degree, the most feasible method of reducing their influence in the vicinity may be the installation of a tall or high-velocity stack for the discharge of ventilating air. Ex. 220d at 2.

    *   *   *

5. Conclusion.

The company did not fulfill its societal obligation to adopt and maintain reasonable, efficient pollution control measures. Having located the plant in a rich agricultural district, the company did not diligently monitor the plant's emissions nor the ambient concentrations of fluoride in the surrounding orchards. Nor did the company implement before or during the 1965–71 claim period efficient available methods for reducing the emissions. In particular, the company did not adopt cell operating procedures to minimize the escape of fumes from the primary collection system until several years after the end of the claim period, did not install wet electrostatic precipitators in the primary treatment system until 1972, and did not utilize a forced-draft secondary collection system until 1971. All of these measures could have been taken prior to the start of the claim period and would have substantially reduced the plant's emissions of fluoride, perhaps by as much as 80% and at least by 40%. In addition, use of tall or high-velocity stacks might have prevented the occasional concentration of emissions beneath the atmospheric inversion layer. The company's sponsorship of calcium chloride spraying of peach trees was laudable but not sufficient to overcome the preponderance of evidence showing that the company faltered in carrying out its social responsibility to control its harmful emissions.

C. Arranging to Compensate for the Remaining Harm.

As the court in determining the propriety of a punitive damage award may consider evidence of harm by the defendant's conduct to persons other than the plaintiff, see *Orchard View Farms, Inc. v. Martin Marietta Aluminum, Inc.*, No. 73-3080, slip op. at 1–2 (9th Cir. June 23, 1975), so should the court take note of the defendant's efforts to neutralize that harm by voluntary payment of compensation, even though this compensation did not extend to the damage for which the jury in this case made a compensatory award.

In 1961 the company agreed to compensate peach and apricot growers in the vicinity of the plant for soft suture damage to their peaches and for apricot leaf necrosis believed to inhibit tree growth. TR 795–800. According to Byrne, the company paid out about $100,000 in settlements during the 1961–66 period. TR 887, 889–90.

On November 3, 1966, the United States District Court entered a consent decree settling the claims of 15 orchardists filed against the company in federal court and providing for the dismissal of 17 other cases then pending in the Oregon state courts. The company agreed to

> ...pay each of the plaintiff peach orchard owners the then prevailing market price of his peach fruit which has been or is made unmarketable by soft suture caused by fluorides emitted from defendant's plant; provided, however, that the defendant will have no such obligation for any soft suture occurring in the future unless the orchard owner involved sprays his peach orchards with a calcium chloride or lime spray or other spray, as designated from time to time by defendant, in accordance with methods prescribed by defendant, for which spraying defendant agrees to pay the reasonable cost. Consent Decree ¶2.

For damage other than soft suture the company agreed to

> ...pay to the respective plaintiffs such amounts as may be necessary to compensate them for past or future economic damage (other than soft suture in peaches) in their respective orchards, caused by fluorides emitted from defendant's plant; subject, however, to the terms and conditions herein stated, including arbitration pursuant to paragraph 10. Consent Decree ¶3.

Paragraph 10 of the decree provided for a three-member claim arbitration panel, one member selected by the company, one by the orchardists and the third member by the other two, to settle claims according to Oregon statutory provisions governing arbitration.

On February 11, 1971, the claim arbitration panel awarded the 15 orchardist plaintiffs a total of $942,305 for damage to their crops and trees during the 1960–69 period. On February 19, 1972, the panel awarded $120,900 to five orchardists for damage during 1970 and 1971. The orchardists then terminated the arbitration agreement, and no further voluntary settlements have been reached.

The company's agreement to recognize that the plant's emissions were damaging the orchards and to compensate the orchardists for the damage under an arbitration arrangement is to be complimented, and future such agreements to be encouraged. Such conduct is strong evidence that the company was attempting to fulfill its societal obligations by accounting for the damage its operations were causing to its neighbors. Though laudable, this conduct does not entirely shield the company from punitive damages liability, for it came about after some eight years of the plant's operation and after the company was faced with numerous lawsuits claiming damages. As the Oregon Supreme Court noted in *Byers v. Santiam Ford, Inc.*, 281 Or. 411, 574 P.2d 1122 (1978):

> In the case here at issue the evidence of contrition and a conciliatory attitude of one of defendant's agents after the complaint was filed has scant relevance respecting the state of mind of other agents of defendant at the time the car was sold to plaintiff. Assuming the evidence established the good faith and good will of defendant's president toward plaintiff, such conduct came as response to the complaint, which prayed for substantial punitive damages. The evidence shows a desire to "buy peace" and minimize the risk of an award of punitive damages and not that defendant dealt in good faith with plaintiff in selling the car. 281 Or. at 417, 574 P.2d at 1125.

Unlike Byers, however, in this case the company's agreement to arbitrate and compensate came during the period for which punitive damages are sought, not entirely after the events giving rise to liability. The *Renken* consent decree was entered after the 1965 and 1966 growing seasons but before the 1967–71 seasons. Therefore, I consider the arbitration agreement relevant to the determination of punitive damages liability in this case.

If the company during the 1965–71 claim period had cooperated fully in ascertaining the harm from the plant's emissions and in effecting some combination of efficient emission control combined with compensation for the remaining harm, I would rule against the plaintiff's request for punitive damages. The company's participation in the arbitration system is certainly indicative of corporate social responsibility but is insufficient to overcome its failure in the other two respects.

IV. AWARD OF PUNITIVE DAMAGES.

I am satisfied by the evidence in this case that an award of punitive damages is appropriate for the earlier portion of the claim period. It is difficult to put a precise date on the watershed of the company's conduct showing a sufficient compliance with societal obligation so as to rule out punitive damages. In this regard, I rely heavily upon the testimony of Barney McPhillips, who may almost be regarded as the father of Oregon's pollution control progress. While his testimony was generalized, and did not contain any particular dates, nonetheless it furnishes more than adequate support for a finding that midway through the

1965–71 claim period a change occurred in both the attitude of the company and its efforts to carry out pollution control measures so as to behave like a good neighbor. One cannot look at a single event alone, since the attitude of society (both private and governmental) was in a state of substantial change. And as society's attitude changed, as was evidenced by the movement toward a more careful attention to the earth around us and the necessity of its preservation, so also did society's laws and regulations, and with that the response of its components—both of the antagonists here, aluminum company and orchardist. I conclude, therefore, that a punitive damage award is available for the claim years 1965 through 1968. If the claim years here were only 1969–71, I would not award punitive damages. By this time—the late 60s and early 70s—on the record in this case, it cannot be said that the company was in sufficient disregard of its societal obligations so as to be liable for punitive damages. And while, of course, the only period of time before me in this case is 1965–71, and the only orchards involved are the ones of this plaintiff, nonetheless it is difficult to see how any claim for punitive damages would succeed as to any period of time in and after about 1969, in view of all of the developments during the 1969–71 period and since that time. Indeed, though of course I need not and do not decide the question, it seems most unlikely that a punitive damage claim for any period of time after 1971 based on the record in this case would even go to a jury.

Because the company did not cooperate in ascertaining the nature, severity and scope of the harm inflicted upon the plaintiff by the plant's emissions or in arranging to prevent this damage or to neutralize it through voluntary compensation arrangements, the company is liable to the plaintiff for an award of punitive damages.

Previous judicial opinions provide little guidance as to the proper amount of such an award. Courts often state that such an award should be sufficient to deter continuation or repetition of the offending conduct. In this case the offending conduct was the company's refusal either to implement economically efficient emission control measures or voluntarily to compensate the plaintiff for the damage caused by the plant's emissions. Thus, punitive damages should be awarded in an amount that will deter this and other companies from attempting to impose a portion of their costs of production upon their neighbors by compelling those damaged by the emissions to resort to the uncertainties of the legal process in order to obtain compensation.

Under the circumstances here, I believe an appropriate and measured award for punitive damages is $200,000 for the claim period here through the year 1968, but none thereafter.

The foregoing constitutes findings of fact and conclusions of law, pursuant to Rule 52, Fed.R.Civ.P.

Notes and Questions

1. Punitive Damages: Property Rule versus Liability Rule? The court quoted the *Harrell* case in which the court stated: "To justify an award of punitive damages, it is not necessary that the act have been done maliciously or with bad motive. Where it has become apparent, as it has here, that compensatory damages alone, while they might compensate the injured party, will not deter the actor from committing similar trespasses in the future, there is ample justification for an award of punitive damages." A liability rule would allow the trespasser to pollute at will so long as the trespasser paid compensation to the injured property owner. Obviously, the court was not happy with that result. Would the court be satisfied with a property rule which required bargaining prior to the pollution? Or, would the court still be concerned that other property owners were not protected?

2. Externalities and Efficiency: The court noted "...we tolerate externalities such as pollution as long as the enterprise remains productive: that is, producing a greater value than the total of its internalized and externalized costs of production." Does this perspective require compensation of the injured party? Recall the discussion of Kaldor-Hicks and Pareto Efficiency in Chapter II. Under Kaldor-Hicks Efficiency, all that is necessary is for the polluter to be able to compensate. Pareto Efficiency requires compensation.

3. Class Actions and Incentives: Do you agree with the court's analysis of class actions? Are there any entrepreneurs who have the incentive to solve the free rider problem? If so, does the court's logic justify the imposition of punitive damages when a business fails to meet its "societal obligation not to obstruct legal procedures designed to provide compensation to persons harmed by externalized costs of production"?

4. Bargaining and the Coase Theorem: Does the creation of societal obligations and the possibility of punitive damages increase or decrease the likelihood of Coasian bargaining? Has the court merely increased the bargaining position of landowners? Or, has it increased the transaction costs of a negotiated solution?

2. Positive Externalities

Positive externalities exist when the social benefits of engaging in an activity are greater than the private benefits to the individual or individuals engaging in the activity. Classic examples of positive externalities include inoculation against contagious disease and the pollination of fruit trees by a beekeeper's bees. For example, in the case of inoculation against contagious disease, when Hank purchases and takes a vaccination against polio, he receives the private benefit of reduced risk of contracting polio and the other members of society receive spillover benefits in that it is less likely that they will contract polio from Hank or anyone else. The nature of the positive externality is illustrated further by recognition that if everyone except Hank were inoculated, then there would be no need for Hank to be inoculated.

Positive externalities, by definition, occur when the marginal social benefit is greater than the marginal private benefit of the activity. In general, the presence of positive externalities means that the activity producing the positive externality is being engaged in at a rate below the social optimum—where marginal social benefit equals marginal social cost. For example, individuals in a market economy make decisions based on comparisons of their marginal private benefits and marginal private costs. The market failure associated with positive externalities is that individuals' decisions are based on private rather than social benefit. Production decisions are based on private costs and benefits, and production will be below the optimum level.

Figure VI-3

Equilibrium and Inefficiency with a Positive Externality

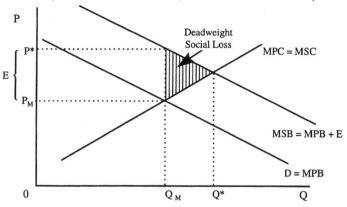

The market failure of positive externalities is shown in Figure VI-3. Marginal private benefits (MPB) are less than marginal social benefits (MSB). The positive externality (E) is the difference between the marginal private benefits and the marginal social benefits, so that E = MSB – MPB. Marginal private costs (MPC) equal marginal social costs (MSC), which means negative externalities are not present. The private market solution is at Q_M, where MPB = MPC. The optimal level of production is at Q^*, where MSC = MSB. Thus, the market failure is illustrated by the suboptimal level of production, $Q^* – Q_M$. For units of output between Q^* and Q_M, the marginal benefit to society is greater than the marginal cost to society, but those transactions do not occur in the private market. The deadweight social loss as a result of the positive externality is indicated by the shaded area.

In some instances, individuals have incentives to capture, or *internalize*, the positive externalities created by their activities. For example, a beekeeper benefits the owner of an apple orchard when the beekeeper's bees increase the pollination of the apple trees which increases the trees' productivity. One way to internalize this externality is for the beekeeper to purchase the orchard — or, for the owner of the orchard to keep bees. Suppose a beekeeper and the owner of the apple orchard have adjoining land. The beekeeper's bees fly into the orchard and pollinate the apple blossoms making the orchard more productive. If the beekeeper were to reap the consequences of the increased value of the orchard, the yield on his investment in bees would rise and he would raise more bees. But, under these circumstances, his bees' social services are provided free. Government intervention is not always called for to deal with this positive externality, however. Individuals might settle matters privately because the cost of intervening might be prohibitive. To enhance the bees' contribution to the orchard's productivity, the orchard owner could contract with the beekeeper to supply more bees. Alternatively, the orchard owner could raise his own bees. As long as the beekeeper's marginal costs of raising additional bees are less than the value the bees contribute to the orchard owner, it will be possible for both parties to reach an agreement that will leave each better off. Such private contracting effectively eliminates the apple/bee externality and makes public intervention unnecessary.

A more dramatic example of the internalization of positive externalities is the development of Disney World in central Florida. The Disney Corporation knew that the building of Disney World would greatly increase the value of the land surrounding the actual site of Disney World. Instead of simply giving this benefit to the surrounding landowners, Disney secretly purchased much more land than was needed for its own development before announcing its development plans to the public. The result of this was that Disney captured a large portion—but clearly not all—of the positive externalities associated with its development.

In other instances, individuals may not have the incentive or ability to capture the positive externalities associated with their activities. This, of course, is the definition of a market failure. In order to solve the market failure, government intervention may be necessary in order to get producers to produce the optimal level of output. The possible forms of government intervention are discussed below.

C. Dealing with Externalities

The world is full of trivial externalities, in the sense that the situation is not worth anybody's effort to do anything about it. Your neighbors messy yard may disturb your sense of propriety, you may be willing to pay her $50 a year to clean up the mess but her price to clean it up is $600 a year. The messy yard is a nuisance, but not enough of a nuisance to cause sufficient demand to get the yard cleaned up. On principle, the best thing to do with an irrelevant externality is to leave it alone because it costs more than it is worth to correct the problem. A relevant externality creates sufficient demand on the part of those affected by it to change the situation. Suppose that your neighbor is willing to clean up her messy yard for $10, and you are willing to pay as much as $50. In this case, you can make an effective offer to correct the externality and reach a deal with your neighbor. With relevant externalities, it is worthwhile to correct the situation because the benefits of correction exceed the cost.

When market incentives and private contractual arrangements result in output that is greater than or less than the social optimum, the externality is said to have created a market failure. In an economy with an ideal government interested in promoting the general welfare through increased economic efficiency, the government would attempt to correct the market failure attributable to externalities by promoting the production of goods that create positive externalities and discouraging the production of goods that create negative externalities. Of course, not all externalities are worthy of government intervention. The key issue in deciding whether the government should intervene to correct an externality is whether the externality is irrelevant or relevant. Externalities are termed irrelevant when the externality generates insufficient demand by the affected party to change the situation.

Economic theory suggests that the correction of relevant externalities can be approached in a number of different ways. In general, these can be categorized as defining property rights and allowing bargaining, taxing negative externalities or subsidizing positive externalities, or establishing regulatory controls.

1. The Assignment and Enforcement of Property Rights

The existence of externalities is not, by itself, justification for government intervention to correct the externality. In some instances, private contractual arrangements can make public intervention unnecessary. This was illustrated for positive externalities in the bee example where it was possible for the orchard owner to contract with the beekeeper for an increase in the number of bees. Externality problems generally persist because of the presence of some element of common ownership. The beekeepers and the apple growers ownership rights are clearly established and are easily transferable. In such a situation, it will be in the interests of both parties to conclude an agreement that places resources in their most highly valued uses. In the case of a polluting factory, does the factory have the right to use the air as it pleases or do the people in the surrounding community have the right to clean air? Air use rights are indefinite and nontransferable. It is generally impossible for people to buy and sell rights to use the air. In this case, there is no reason to suspect that the pursuit of individual interests will promote the use of air in the most highly valued manner. Since nonownership is a source of market failure, the creation of ownership is a means of correcting market failure. The establishment of ownership rights is a potential means of eliminating problems associated with externalities.

a. Bargaining and the Coase Theorem

If property rights are well defined and if transaction costs are low, negative externalities can be internalized through bargaining and contracting. Assume that Ken owns all of the land surrounding a polluting factory and that he does not own any rights to have clean air (indeed, no one owns those rights). This means, in effect, that the factory has the right to pollute the air. Assume that the pollution is very localized and affects only Ken's property. Since all of the external costs of the pollution are borne by Ken, it is reasonable to assume that he is in a position to bargain with the factory about the amount of pollution emitted by the factory. For example, if the pollution reduces the value of Ken's land by $1,000, then Ken would be willing to pay up to $1,000 to reduce the pollution. If the factory can reduce the pollution at a cost less than $1,000, say $800, then the factory will benefit from contracting with Ken for the reduction in pollution emissions. The contract price will be somewhere between $1,000 and $800. If the factory cannot reduce the pollution at Ken's price, then it will continue to pollute. Note, however, that the imposition of the negative externality in the latter case is not free: the factory forfeits a potential payment of up to $1,000 when it decides to pollute. In economic terms, Ken's willingness to pay represents an opportunity cost to the factory.

An interesting and important insight about the contractual solution to externalities is that the solution is not altered even if Ken has a legally enforceable property right to smoke-free air. Once again, if the pollution can be abated at a cost of less than $1,000, then the factory will not pollute. If pollution abatement will cost more than $1,000, then the factory will offer Ken enough money to induce Ken to agree to allow the factory to emit the smoke (at least $1,000). With this new set of property rights, the opportunity cost to Ken of breathing clean air is whatever the factory is willing to pay to pollute.

As discussed in Chapter I, the insight that the same property rights assignment will emerge regardless of the initial assignment of ownership rights, when the costs of negotiation are nonexistent or trivial, is referred to as the **Coase Theorem.** Moreover, Coase pointed out that the same degree of pollution will occur even if the neighbors have the legal right to stop the firm from emitting any pollution rather than the firm having the legal right to pollute as much as it wants. In this case, the firm can pay the neighbors for the right to pollute. Regardless of whether the firm or the neighbors have the initial right, the gains from trade are exhausted when the marginal benefit to the firm of polluting are equal to the marginal cost that is imposed on the neighbors.

Prah v. Maretti

Supreme Court of Wisconsin
108 Wis. 2d 223; 321 N.W.2d 182 (1982)

Abrahamson, Justice.

This appeal from a judgment of the circuit court for Waukesha county, Max Raskin, circuit judge, was certified to this court by the court of appeals, sec. (Rule) 809.61, Stats. 1979–80, as presenting an issue of first impression, namely, whether an owner of a solar-heated residence states a claim upon which relief can be granted when he asserts that his neighbor's proposed construction of a residence (which conforms to existing deed restrictions and local ordinances) interferes with his access to an unobstructed path for sunlight across the neighbor's property. This case thus involves a conflict between one landowner (Glenn Prah, the plaintiff) interested in unobstructed access to sunlight across adjoining property as a natural source of energy and an adjoining landowner (Richard D. Maretti, the defendant) interested in the development of his land.

The circuit court concluded that the plaintiff presented no claim upon which relief could be granted and granted summary judgment for the defendant. We reverse the judgment of the circuit court and remand the cause to the circuit court for further proceedings.

I.

According to the complaint, the plaintiff is the owner of a residence which was constructed during the years 1978–1979. The complaint alleges that the residence has a solar system which includes collectors on the roof to supply energy for heat and hot water and that after the plaintiff built his solar-heated house, the defendant purchased the lot adjacent to and immediately to the south of the plaintiff's lot and commenced planning construction of a home. The complaint further states that when the plaintiff learned of defendant's plans to build the house he advised the defendant that if the house were built at the proposed location, defendant's house would substantially and adversely affect the integrity of plaintiff's solar system and could cause plaintiff other damage. Nevertheless, the defendant began construction. The complaint further alleges that the plaintiff is entitled to "unrestricted use of the sun and its solar power" and demands judgment for injunctive relief and damages.

After filing his complaint, the plaintiff moved for a temporary injunction to restrain and enjoin construction by the defendant. In ruling on that motion the circuit court heard testimony, received affidavits and viewed the site.

The record made on the motion reveals the following additional facts: Plaintiff's home was the first residence built in the subdivision, and although plaintiff did not build his house in the center of the lot it was built in accordance with applicable restrictions. Plaintiff advised defendant that if the defendant's home were built at the proposed site it would cause a shadowing effect on the solar collectors which would reduce the efficiency of the system and possibly damage the system. To avoid these adverse effects, plaintiff requested defendant to locate his home an additional several feet away from the plaintiff's lot line, the exact number being disputed. Plaintiff and defendant failed to reach an agreement on the location of defendant's home before defendant started construction. The Architectural Control Committee of the subdivision and the Planning Commission of the City of Muskego approved the defendant's plans for his home, including its location on the lot. After such approval, the defendant apparently changed the grade of the property without prior notice to the Architectural Control Committee. The problem with defendant's proposed construction, as far as the plaintiff's interests are concerned, arises from a combination of the grade and the distance of defendant's home from the defendant's lot line.

The circuit court denied plaintiff's motion for injunctive relief, declared it would entertain a motion for summary judgment and thereafter entered judgment in favor of the defendant.

*   *   *

The plaintiff presents three legal theories to support his claim that the defendant's continued construction of a home justifies granting him relief: (1) the construction constitutes a common law private nuisance; (2) the construction is prohibited by sec. 844.01, Stats. 1979–80; and (3) the construction interferes with the solar easement plaintiff acquired under the doctrine of prior appropriation.[4]

As to the claim of private nuisance the circuit court concluded that the law of private nuisance requires the court to make "a comparative evaluation of the conflicting interests and to weigh the gravity of the harm to the plaintiff against the utility of the defendant's conduct." The circuit court concluded: "A comparative evaluation of the conflicting interests, keeping in mind the omissions and commissions of both Prah and Maretti, indicates that defendant's conduct does not cause the gravity of the harm which the plaintiff himself may well have avoided by proper planning." The circuit court also concluded that sec. 844.01 does not apply to a home constructed in accordance with deed and municipal ordinance requirements. Further, the circuit court rejected the prior appropriation doctrine as "an intrusion of judicial egoism over legislative passivity."

---

4. Under the doctrine of prior appropriation the first user to appropriate the resource has the right of continued use to the exclusion of others.

The doctrine of prior appropriation has been used by several western states to allocate water, *Paug Vik v. Wards Cove*, 633 P.2d 1015 (Alaska 1981), and by the New Mexico legislature to allocate solar access, secs. 47-3-1 to 47-3-5, N.M. Stats. 1978. See also Note, *The Allocation of Sunlight: Solar Rights and the Prior Appropriation Doctrine*, 47 Colo. L. Rev. 421 (1976).

We consider first whether the complaint states a claim for relief based on common law private nuisance. This state has long recognized that an owner of land does not have an absolute or unlimited right to use the land in a way which injures the rights of others. The rights of neighboring landowners are relative; the uses by one must not unreasonably impair the uses or enjoyment of the other.[5] VI-A *American Law of Property* sec. 28.22, pp. 64–65 (1954). When one landowner's use of his or her property unreasonably interferes with another's enjoyment of his or her property, that use is said to be a private nuisance. *Hoene v. Milwaukee*, 17 Wis. 2d 209, 214, 116 N.W.2d 112 (1962).

The private nuisance doctrine has traditionally been employed in this state to balance the conflicting rights of landowners, and this court has recently adopted the analysis of private nuisance set forth in the Restatement (Second) of Torts. The Restatement defines private nuisance as "a nontrespassory invasion of another's interest in the private use and enjoyment of land." Restatement (Second) of Torts sec. 821D (1977). The phrase "interest in the private use and enjoyment of land" as used in sec. 821D is broadly defined to include any disturbance of the enjoyment of property. The comment in the Restatement describes the landowner's interest protected by private nuisance law as follows:

> "The phrase 'interest in the use and enjoyment of land' is used in this Restatement in a broad sense. It comprehends not only the interests that a person may have in the actual present use of land for residential, agricultural, commercial, industrial and other purposes, but also his interests in having the present use value of the land unimpaired by changes in its physical condition. Thus the destruction of trees on vacant land is as much an invasion of the owner's interest in its use and enjoyment as is the destruction of crops or flowers that he is growing on the land for his present use. 'Interest in use and enjoyment' also comprehends the pleasure, comfort and enjoyment that a person normally derives from the occupancy of land. Freedom from discomfort and annoyance while using land is often as important to a person as freedom from physical interruption with his use or freedom from detrimental change in the physical

---

5. In *Abdella v. Smith*, 34 Wis. 2d 393, 399, 149 N.W.2d 537 (1967), this court quoted with approval Dean Prosser's description of the judicial balancing of the reciprocal rights and privileges of neighbors in the use of their land:

"Most of the litigation as to private nuisance has dealt with the conflicting interests of landowners and the question of the reasonableness of the defendant's conduct: The defendant's privilege of making a reasonable use of his own property for his own benefit and conducting his affairs in his own way is no less important than the plaintiff's right to use and enjoy his premises. The two are correlative and interdependent, and neither is entitled to prevail entirely, at the expense of the other. Some balance must be struck between the two. The plaintiff must be expected to endure some inconvenience rather than curtail the defendant's freedom of action, and the defendant must so use his own property that he causes no unreasonable harm to the plaintiff. The law of private nuisance is very largely a series of adjustments to limit the reciprocal rights and privileges of both. In every case the court must make a comparative evaluation of the conflicting interests according to objective legal standards, and the gravity of the harm to the plaintiff must be weighed against the utility of the defendant's conduct." Prosser, Law of Torts, sec. 89, p. 596 (2d ed.1971) (Citations omitted).

condition of the land itself." Restatement (Second) of Torts, Sec. 821D, Comment b, p. 101 (1977).

Although the defendant's obstruction of the plaintiff's access to sunlight appears to fall within the Restatement's broad concept of a private nuisance as a nontrespassory invasion of another's interest in the private use and enjoyment of land, the defendant asserts that he has a right to develop his property in compliance with statutes, ordinances and private covenants without regard to the effect of such development upon the plaintiff's access to sunlight. In essence, the defendant is asking this court to hold that the private nuisance doctrine is not applicable in the instant case and that his right to develop his land is a right which is per se superior to his neighbor's interest in access to sunlight. This position is expressed in the maxim "cujus est solum, ejus est usque ad coelum et ad infernos," that is, the owner of land owns up to the sky and down to the center of the earth. The rights of the surface owner are, however, not unlimited.

The defendant is not completely correct in asserting that the common law did not protect a landowner's access to sunlight across adjoining property. At English common law a landowner could acquire a right to receive sunlight across adjoining land by both express agreement and under the judge-made doctrine of "ancient lights." Under the doctrine of ancient lights if the landowner had received sunlight across adjoining property for a specified period of time, the landowner was entitled to continue to receive unobstructed access to sunlight across the adjoining property. Under the doctrine the landowner acquired a negative prescriptive easement and could prevent the adjoining landowner from obstructing access to light.

Although American courts have not been as receptive to protecting a landowner's access to sunlight as the English courts, American courts have afforded some protection to a landowner's interest in access to sunlight. American courts honor express easements to sunlight. American courts initially enforced the English common law doctrine of ancient lights, but later every state which considered the doctrine repudiated it as inconsistent with the needs of a developing country. Indeed, for just that reason this court concluded that an easement to light and air over adjacent property could not be created or acquired by prescription and has been unwilling to recognize such an easement by implication.

Many jurisdictions in this country have protected a landowner from malicious obstruction of access to light (the spite fence cases) under the common law private nuisance doctrine. If an activity is motivated by malice it lacks utility and the harm it causes others outweighs any social values. This court was reluctant to protect a landowner's interest in sunlight even against a spite fence, only to be overruled by the legislature. Shortly after this court upheld a landowner's right to erect a useless and unsightly sixteen-foot spite fence four feet from his neighbor's windows, *Metzger v. Hochrain*, 107 N.W. 267, 83 N.W. 308 (1900), the legislature enacted a law specifically defining a spite fence as an actionable private nuisance. Thus a landowner's interest in sunlight has been protected in this country by common law private nuisance law at least in the narrow context of the modern American rule invalidating spite fences.

This court's reluctance in the nineteenth and early part of the twentieth century to provide broader protection for a landowner's access to sunlight was premised on three policy considerations. First, the right of landowners to use their property as they wished, as long as they did not cause physical damage to a neighbor, was jealously guarded.

Second, sunlight was valued only for aesthetic enjoyment or as illumination. Since artificial light could be used for illumination, loss of sunlight was at most a personal annoyance which was given little, if any, weight by society.

Third, society had a significant interest in not restricting or impeding land development. *Dillman v. Hoffman*, 38 Wis. 559, 574 (1875). This court repeatedly emphasized that in the growth period of the nineteenth and early twentieth centuries change is to be expected and is essential to property and that recognition of a right to sunlight would hinder property development. The court expressed this concept as follows:

> "As the city grows, large grounds appurtenant to residences must be cut up to supply more residences.... The cistern, the outhouse, the cesspool, and the private drain must disappear in deference to the public waterworks and sewer; the terrace and the garden, to the need for more complete occupancy.... Strict limitation [on the recognition of easements of light and air over adjacent premises is] in accord with the popular conception upon which real estate has been and is daily being conveyed in Wisconsin and to be essential to easy and rapid development at least of our municipalities." *Miller v. Hoeschler*, supra, 126 Wis. at 268, 270; quoted with approval in *Depner, supra*, 202 Wis. at 409.

Considering these three policies, this court concluded that in the absence of an express agreement granting access to sunlight, a landowner's obstruction of another's access to sunlight was not actionable. *Miller v. Hoeschler, supra*, 126 Wis. at 271; *Depner v. United States National Bank, supra*, 202 Wis. at 410. These three policies are no longer fully accepted or applicable. They reflect factual circumstances and social priorities that are now obsolete.

First, society has increasingly regulated the use of land by the landowner for the general welfare. *Euclid v. Ambler Realty Co.*, 272 U.S. 365 (1926); *Just v. Marinette*, 56 Wis. 2d 7, 201 N.W.2d 761 (1972).

Second, access to sunlight has taken on a new significance in recent years. In this case the plaintiff seeks to protect access to sunlight, not for aesthetic reasons or as a source of illumination but as a source of energy. Access to sunlight as an energy source is of significance both to the landowner who invests in solar collectors and to a society which has an interest in developing alternative sources of energy.[11]

Third, the policy of favoring unhindered private development in an expanding economy is no longer in harmony with the realities of our society. *State v.*

---

11. State and federal governments are encouraging the use of the sun as a significant source of energy. In this state the legislature has granted tax benefits to encourage the utilization of solar energy. See Ch. 349, 350, Laws of 1979. See also Ch. 354, Laws of 1981 (eff. May 7, 1982) enabling legislation providing for local ordinances guaranteeing access to sunlight.

The federal government has also recognized the importance of solar energy and currently encourages its utilization by means of tax benefits, direct subsidies and government loans for solar projects. Energy Tax Act of 1978, Nov. 9, 1978, P.L. 95-618, 92 Stat. 3174, relevant portion codified at 26 U.S.C.A. sec. 44© (1982 Supp.); Energy Security Act, June 30, 1980, P.L. 96-294, 94 Stat. 611, relevant portion codified at 12 U.S.C.A. sec. 3610 (1980); Small Business Energy Loan Act, July 4, 1978, P.L. 95-315, 92 Stat. 377, relevant portion codified within 15 U.S.C.A. secs. 631, 633, 636, and 639 (1982 Supp.); National Energy Conservation Policy

Deetz, 66 Wis. 2d 1, 224 N.W.2d 407 (1974). The need for easy and rapid development is not as great today as it once was, while our perception of the value of sunlight as a source of energy has increased significantly.

Courts should not implement obsolete policies that have lost their vigor over the course of the years. The law of private nuisance is better suited to resolve landowners' disputes about property development in the 1980's than is a rigid rule which does not recognize a landowner's interest in access to sunlight. As we said in *Ballstadt* v. *Pagel,* 202 Wis. 484, 489, 232 N.W. 862 (1930), "What is regarded in law as constituting a nuisance in modern times would no doubt have been tolerated without question in former times." We read *State* v. *Deetz,* 66 Wis. 2d 1, 224 N.W.2d 407 (1974), as an endorsement of the application of common law nuisance to situations involving the conflicting interests of landowners and as rejecting *per se* exclusions to the nuisance law reasonable use doctrine.

*   *   *

We recognized in Deetz that common law rules adapt to changing social values and conditions.[12]

*   *   *

Yet the defendant would have us ignore the flexible private nuisance law as a means of resolving the dispute between the landowners in this case and would have us adopt an approach, already abandoned in Deetz, of favoring the unrestricted development of land and of applying a rigid and inflexible rule protecting his right to build on his land and disregarding any interest of the plaintiff in the use and enjoyment of his land. This we refuse to do.[13]

Act, Nov. 9, 1978, P.L. 95-619, 92 Stat. 3206, relevant portion codified at 42 U.S.C.A. secs. 1451, 1703-45 (1982 Supp.); Energy Conservation and Production Act, Aug. 14, 1976, P.L. 94-385, 90 Stat. 1125, relevant portion codified at 42 U.S.C.A. sec. 6881 (1977).

12. This court has recognized "that the common law is susceptible of growth and adaptation to new circumstances and situations, and that courts have power to declare and effectuate what is the present rule in respect of a given subject without regard to the old rule.... The common law is not immutable, but flexible, and upon its own principles adapts itself to varying conditions." *Dimick* v. *Schiedt,* 293 U.S. 474, 487 (1935), quoted with approval in *Schwanke* v. *Garlt,* 219 Wis. 367, 371, 263 N.W. 176 (1935).

In *Bielski* v. *Schulze,* 16 Wis. 2d 1, 11, 114 N.W.2d 105 (1962), this court said: "Inherent in the common law is a dynamic principle which allows it to grow and to tailor itself to meet changing needs within the doctrine of stare decisis, which, if correctly understood, was not static and did not forever prevent the courts from reversing themselves or from applying principles of common law to new situations as the need arose. If this were not so, we must succumb to a rule that a judge should let others 'long dead and unaware of the problems of the age in which he lives, do his thinking for him.' Mr. Justice Douglas, Stare Decisis, 49 Columbia Law Review (1949). 735, 736."

"The genius of the common law is its ability to adapt itself to the changing needs of society." *Moran* v. *Quality Aluminum Casting Co.,* 34 Wis. 2d 542, 551, 150 N.W.2d 137 (1967). See also *State* v. *Esser,* 16 Wis. 2d 567, 581, 115 N.W.2d 505 (1962).

13. Defendant's position that a landowner's interest in access to sunlight across adjoining land is not "legally enforceable" and is therefore excluded per se from private nuisance law was adopted in *Fontainebleau Hotel Corp.* v. *Forty-five Twenty-five, Inc.,* 114 So. 2d 257 (Fla. Ct. App. 1959), *cert. den* 117 So. 2d 842 (Fla. 1960). The Florida district court of appeals permitted construction of a building which cast a shadow on a neighboring hotel's swimming pool. The court asserted that nuisance law protects only those interests "which [are] recognized and protected by law," and that there is no legally recognized or protected right to access to sunlight. A property owner does not, said the Florida court, in the absence

Private nuisance law, the law traditionally used to adjudicate conflicts between private landowners, has the flexibility to protect both a landowner's right of access to sunlight and another landowner's right to develop land. Private nuisance law is better suited to regulate access to sunlight in modern society and is more in harmony with legislative policy and the prior decisions of this court than is an inflexible doctrine of non-recognition of any interest in access to sunlight across adjoining land.[14]

We therefore hold that private nuisance law, that is, the reasonable use doctrine as set forth in the Restatement, is applicable to the instant case. Recognition of a nuisance claim for unreasonable obstruction of access to sunlight will not prevent land development or unduly hinder the use of adjoining land. It will promote the reasonable use and enjoyment of land in a manner suitable to the 1980's. That obstruction of access to light might be found to constitute a nuisance in certain circumstances does not mean that it will be or must be found to constitute a nuisance under all circumstances. The result in each case depends on whether the conduct complained of is unreasonable.

Accordingly we hold that the plaintiff in this case has stated a claim under which relief can be granted. Nonetheless we do not determine whether the plaintiff in this case is entitled to relief. In order to be entitled to relief the plaintiff must prove the elements required to establish actionable nuisance, and the conduct of the defendant herein must be judged by the reasonable use doctrine.

*   *   *

Because the plaintiff has stated a claim of common law private nuisance upon which relief can be granted, the judgment of the circuit court must be reversed. We need not, and do not, reach the question of whether the complaint states a claim under sec. 844.01, Stats. 1979–80, or under the doctrine of prior appropriation. *Attoe v. Madison Professional Policemen's Assoc.*, 79 Wis. 2d 199, 205, 255 N.W.2d 489 (1977).

For the reasons set forth, we reverse the judgment of the circuit court dismissing the complaint and remand the matter to circuit court for further proceedings not inconsistent with this opinion.

*   *   *

---

of a contract or statute, acquire a presumptive or implied right to the free flow of light and air across adjoining land. The Florida court then concluded that a lawful structure which causes injury to another by cutting off light and air—whether or not erected partly for spite—does not give rise to a cause of action for damages or for an injunction. See also *People ex rel Hoogasian v. Sears, Roebuck & Co.*, 52 Ill 2d 301, 287 N.E.2d 677 (1972).

We do not find the reasoning of Fontainebleau persuasive. The court leaped from rejecting an easement by prescription (the doctrine of ancient lights) and an easement by implication to the conclusion that there is no right to protection from obstruction of access to sunlight. The court's statement that a landowner has no right to light should be the conclusion, not its initial premise. The court did not explain why an owner's interest in unobstructed light should not be protected or in what manner an owner's interest in unobstructed sunlight differs from an owner's interest in being free from obtrusive noises or smells or differs from an owner's interest in unobstructed use of water. The recognition of a per se exception to private nuisance law may invite unreasonable behavior.

14. For a discussion of nuisance law, see Ellickson, *Alternatives to Zoning: Covenants, Nuisance Rules, and Fines as Land Use Controls*, 40 U. Chi. L. Rev. 681 (1973); Comment, *Nuisance as a Modern Mode of Land Use Control*, 46 Wash. L. Rev. 47 (1970).

William G. Callow, J. (dissenting).

*   *   *

The majority arrives at its conclusion that the common law private nuisance doctrine is applicable by analogizing this situation with the spite fence cases which protect a landowner from malicious obstruction of access to light. *Supra*, at 233–235. *See Piccirilli v. Groccia*, 114 R.I. 36, 39, 327 A.2d 834, 837, (1974) (plaintiff must prove allegedly objectionable fence was erected *solely* for the avowed purpose of damaging the abutting neighbor and not for the advantage of the person who constructed the fence); *Schorck v. Epperson*, 74 Wyo. 286, 287–88, 287 P.2d 467 (1955) (doctrine of private nuisance founded on maxim that no one should have a legal right to make a malicious use of his property for no benefit to himself but merely to injure another). *Accord Daniel v. Birmingham Dental Mfg. Co.*, 207 Ala. 659, 661, 93 S. 652 (1922); *Green v. Schick*, 194 Okla. 491, 492, 153 P.2d 821 (1944). *See also Comment, Obstruction of Sunlight as a Private Nuisance*, 65 Calif. L. Rev. 94, 99–102 (1977) ("the ironclad rule has been that the obstruction of a neighbor's light and air is not a nuisance if it serves *any* useful purpose"). Id. at 101 (emphasis in original). Courts have likewise refused to limit interference with television reception and other broadcast signals. *The People ex rel. Hoogasian v. Sears, Roebuck and Co.*, 52 Ill. 2d 301, 305, 287 N.E.2d 677 (1972), cert. denied, 409 U.S. 1001. Clearly, the spite fence cases, as their name implies, require malice which is not claimed in this case.

The majority then concludes that this court's past reluctance to extend protection to a landowner's access to sunlight beyond the spite fence cases is based on obsolete policies which have lost their vigor over the course of the years. *Supra*, at 237. The three obsolete policies cited by the majority are: (1) Right of landowners to use their property as they desire as long as no physical damage is done to a neighbor; (2) In the past, sunlight was valued only for aesthetic value, not a source of energy; and (3) Society has a significant interest in not impeding land development. *Supra*, at 235. See Comment, Obstruction of Sunlight as a Private Nuisance, supra at 105–12. The majority has failed to convince me that these policies are obsolete.

It is a fundamental principle of law that a "landowner owns at least as much of the space above the ground as he can occupy or use in connection with the land." As stated in the frequently cited and followed case of *Fontainebleau Hotel Corp. v. Forty-Five Twenty-Five, Inc.*, 114 So. 2d 357 (Fla. Dist. Ct. App. 1959), cert. denied, 117 So. 2d 842 (Fla. 1960):

> "There being, then, no legal right to the free flow of light and air from the adjoining land, it is universally held that where a structure serves a useful and beneficial purpose, it does not give rise to a cause of action, either for damages or for an injunction under the maxim *sic utere tuo ut alienum non laedas*, even though it causes injury to another by cutting off the light and air and interfering with the view that would otherwise be available over adjoining land in its natural state, regardless of the fact that the structure may have been erected partly for spite." *Id.* at 359.

See Venuto v. Owens-Corning Fiberglas Corp., 22 Cal. App. 3d 116, 127, 99 Cal. Rptr. 350, 357 (1971). I firmly believe that a landowner's right to use his property within the limits of ordinances, statutes, and restrictions of record where such use is necessary to serve his legitimate needs is a fundamental precept of a free society which this court should strive to uphold.

*　*　*

I know of no cases repudiating policies favoring the right of a landowner to use his property as he lawfully desires or which declare such policies are "no longer fully accepted or applicable" in this context. *Supra*, at 236.[2] The right of a property owner to lawful enjoyment of his property should be vigorously protected, particularly in those cases where the adjacent property owner could have insulated himself from the alleged problem by acquiring the land as defense to the potential problem or by provident use of his own property.

*　*　*

Regarding the third policy the majority apparently believes is obsolete (that society has a significant interest in not restricting land development), it cites *State v. Deetz*, 66 Wis. 2d 1, 224 N.W.2d 407 (1974). I concede the law may be tending to recognize the value of aesthetics over increased volume development and that an individual may not use his land in such a way as to harm the *public*. The instant case, however, deals with a private benefit. I note that this court in *Deetz* stated: "The reasonable use rule retains . . . a policy of favoring land improvement and development." *Id*. at 20. *See also id*. at 15. *Accord Moritz v. Buglewicz*, 187 Neb. 819, 194 N.W.2d 215 (1972). I find it significant that community planners are dealing with this country's continued population growth and building revitalization where "[t]he number of households is expected to reach almost 100 million by the end of the decade; that would be 34 percent higher than the number in 1970." F. Strom, *1981 Zoning and Planning Law Handbook*, sec. 22.02[3], 396 (1981). It is clear that community planners are acutely aware of the present housing shortages, particularly among those two groups with limited financial resources, the young and the elderly. Id. While the majority's policy arguments may be directed to a cause of action for public nuisance, we are presented with a private nuisance case which I believe is distinguishable in this regard.[3]

I would submit that any policy decisions in this area are best left for the legislature. "What is 'desirable' or 'advisable' or 'ought to be' is a question of policy, not a question of fact. What is 'necessary' or what is 'in the best interest' is not a fact and its determination by the judiciary is an exercise of legislative power when each in-

---

2. Perhaps one reason courts have been hesitant to recognize a cause of action for solar blockage is that such a suit would normally only occur between two abutting landowners, and it is hoped that neighbors will compromise and reach agreement between themselves. This has, undoubtedly, been done in a large percentage of cases. To now recognize a cause of action for solar blockage may thwart a policy of compromise between neighbors. *See* Williams, *Solar Access and Property Rights: A Maverick Analysis*, 11 Conn. L. Rev. 430, 441–42 (1979). *See also* S. Kraemer, *Solar Law*, 138 (1978) ("[a] deterring factor to the use of private nuisance to assure access to direct sunlight is the resultant litigation between neighbors").

3. I am amused at the majority's contention that what constitutes a nuisance today would have been accepted without question in earlier times. *Supra* 237. This calls to mind the fact that, in early days of travel by horses, the first automobiles were considered nuisances. Later, when automobile travel became developed, the horse became the nuisance. Ellickson, *Alternatives to Zoning: Covenants, Nuisance Rules, and Fines as Land Use Controls*, 40 U. Chi. L. Rev. 681, 731 (1973). This makes me wonder if we are examining the proper nuisance in the case before us. In other words, could it be said that the solar energy user is creating the nuisance when others must conform their homes to accommodate his use? I note that solar panel glare may temporarily blind automobile drivers, reflect into adjacent buildings causing excessive heat, and otherwise irritate neighbors. Certainly in these instances the solar heating system constitutes the nuisance.

volves political considerations." *In re City of Beloit*, 37 Wis. 2d 637, 644, 155 N.W.2d 633 (1968). I would concur with these observations of the trial judge: "While temptation lingers for the court to declare by judicial fiat what is right and what should be done, under the facts in this case, such action under our form of constitutional government where the three branches each have their defined jurisdiction and power, would be an intrusion of judicial egoism over legislative passivity."

The legislature has recently acted in this area. Chapter 354, Laws of 1981 (effective May 7, 1982), was enacted to provide the underlying legislation enabling local governments to enact ordinances establishing procedures for guaranteeing access to sunlight. This court's intrusion into an area where legislative action is being taken is unwarranted, and it may undermine a legislative scheme for orderly development not yet fully operational.

*   *   *

In order for a nuisance to be actionable in the instant case, the defendant's conduct must be "intentional and unreasonable." It is impossible for me to accept the majority's conclusion that Mr. Maretti, in lawfully seeking to construct his home, may be intentionally and unreasonably interfering with the plaintiff's access to sunlight. In addressing the "unreasonableness" component of the actor's conduct, it is important to note that "[t]here is liability for a nuisance only to those to whom it causes significant harm, of a kind that would be suffered by a normal person in the community or by property in normal condition and used for a normal purpose." Restatement (Second) of *Torts* sec. 821F (1979). The comments to the Restatement further reveal that "[if] normal persons in that locality would not be substantially annoyed or disturbed by the situation, then the invasion is not a significant one, even though the idiosyncrasies of the particular plaintiff may make it unendurable to him."

I conclude that plaintiff's solar heating system is an unusually sensitive use. In other words, the defendant's proposed construction of his home, under ordinary circumstances, would not interfere with the use and enjoyment of the usual person's property. *See* W. Prosser, *supra*, sec. 87 at 578–79. "The plaintiff cannot, by devoting his own land to an unusually sensitive use, such as a drive-in motion picture theater easily affected by light, make a nuisance out of conduct of the adjoining defendant which would otherwise be harmless." *Id.* at 579 (footnote omitted).

*   *   *

I further believe that the majority's conclusion that a cause of action exists in this case thwarts the very foundation of property law. Property law encompasses a system of filing and notice in a place for public records to provide prospective purchasers with any limitations on their use of the property. Such a notice is not alleged by the plaintiff. Only as a result of the majority's decision did Mr. Maretti discover that a legitimate action exists which would require him to defend the design and location of his home against a nuisance suit, notwithstanding the fact that he located and began to build his house within the applicable building, municipal, and deed restrictions.

*   *   *

...I do not believe that an adjacent lot owner should be obliged to experience the substantial economic loss resulting from the lot being rendered unbuildable by the contour of the land as it relates to the location and design of the adjoining home using solar collectors.[8]

I am troubled by the majority's apparent retrospective application of its decision. I note that the court in *Deetz* saw the wisdom and fairness in rendering a prospective decision. 66 Wis. 2d at 24. Surely, a decision such as this should be accorded prospective status. Creating the cause of action after the fact results in such unfair surprise and hardship to property owners such as Maretti.

Because I do not believe that the facts of the present case give rise to a cause of action for private nuisance, I dissent.

Notes and Questions

1. Opportunity Costs, Bargaining, and the Coase Theorem: Whenever you have a choice, there is a cost. Review subsection B.5 "Externalities, Property Rights, and the Coase Theorem" in Chapter I. Pay particular attention to the graphical analysis as well as the *Notes and Questions* after *Fontainebleau.*

2. A Benchmark for Analysis of Internalization of Externalities: The Coase Theorem provides a benchmark for analyzing externality problems. It shows what would have happened in a world of zero bargaining and transactions costs. Many real world externality problems can be analyzed with the Coase Theorem. The Coase Theorem implies that the market is more important than the law under some circumstances. Every conflict does not require a judicial or regulatory solution. There are, however, numerous caveats to this analysis. The major caveats to this analysis are discussed in Chapter I and the remainder of this Chapter.

3. Technological Changes and the Evolution of Property Rights: Private property rights can provide a powerful way to internalize externalities. However, costs of acquiring and enforcing property rights in some resources may be high. For example, it is harder to find and enforce property rights in the air because the wind blows and the air moves. How could anyone know whose air it is, whose air is whose? This drawback makes private property rights nearly impossible in some cases while technology provides a solution to the problem in other cases. For example, when grazing lands in the American West became crowded in the mid-nineteenth century, people found it difficult to keep their cattle separate and it became hard to enforce property rights in cattle. Fences might have helped, but wood to make fences was too expensive. The solution emerged from two new ideas, branding cattle and barbed wire fencing, which was cheaper than wood.

4. Of Nintendo and Free Agents: To further illustrate the power of the Coase Theorem, consider the following example from Steven M. Crafton, *Quantitative Methods for Lawyers* (1991). Assume the creation of a new sports league, the National Nintendo League. Each player is required to sign a contract, with his or her respective team, containing a "reserve clause" which forbids the player from selling his services to other teams in the league. Thus, if the Los Angeles "Zeldas"

---

8. Mr. Prah could have avoided this litigation by building his own home in the center of his lot instead of only ten feet from the Maretti lot line and/or by purchasing the adjoining lot for his own protection. Mr. Maretti has already moved the proposed location of his home over an additional ten feet to accommodate Mr. Prah's solar collector, and he testified that moving the home any further would interfere with his view of the lake on which the property faces.

wanted a player presently on the Washington "Mario Brothers," the "Zeldas" would have to purchase the player's contract directly from the "Mario Brothers." In other words, L.A. could not contract directly ("tamper") with the player. The owners argue that the "reserve clause" is necessary because abolition (or weakening) of the clause would allow the wealthier teams to buy up all the top Nintendo players. Does the Coase Theorem shed any light on this argument? Assume we have a player, Matthew, who currently is with the Washington team. Assume, for simplicity, that he is not paid a salary. He provides (marginal) revenue to the team of $1,000,000 per year. That is, his presence increases Washington's net revenue by $1,000,000. The L.A. team estimates that his expected worth to the "Zeldas" is $950,000. What will happen under the reserve clause? Since Washington values Matthew more than L.A., there will be no trade and Matthew will stay in Washington. Now consider the alternative institutional arrangement (legal rule)—free agency—which allows Matthew to bargain directly with any team in the league. Washington would pay Matthew up to $1,000,000. L.A. would offer only $950,000. Why? Thus, if Matthew is only interested in maximizing his salary income, he will remain in Washington. Different rule, same result.

5. Transaction Costs: In addition to the distributional considerations involved in selecting a particular legal rule, the transaction costs—that is, the costs of negotiating and enforcing agreements—of allocating property rights in response to particular legal rules can play an important role in evaluating whether a particular legal rule is efficient. This is the topic of the following subsection.

b. Transaction Costs

In many instances involving negative externalities, the private solutions to externalities envisioned by Coase are of little practical importance because transaction costs make it impossible to reach agreement among all affected parties. In the pollution example, it would be impossible to negotiate a private agreement if thousands of property owners lived within the geographic area affected by the smoke. Coase clearly recognized that transaction costs were an important part of his analysis. High transaction costs could prevent exchanges from taking place, thus making judicial and regulatory solutions more likely. The importance of transaction costs is illustrated by the following hypothetical.

Assume that smoke from a factory causes $75 damage to the laundry hung outdoors by 5 nearby residents. If no corrective action is taken, the damages (the negative externalities) imposed on the neighbors equals $375 ($75 × 5). There are several ways to solve this externality. One possible solution is for a smoke screen to be installed at the factory. This would cost $150, or $30 per resident. Another alternative is that electric dryers could be purchased for $50 each by the residents. Or each resident could move, let's say at $100, for a total cost of $500. Or it could be assumed that it would cost the factory $500 for it to move. The efficient solution in terms of cost minimization is the smoke screen, because it only costs $150.

The residents are mad about the smoke. What happens? The first step in this analysis is to determine the entitlement. Who has the right to what and why? This is usually a political decision. The second question then is to determine the rule to protect the entitlement, either a property rule or a liability rule. There are four possible combinations of entitlements and rules:

Rule #1— the factory has the right to pollute. Under this property rule, the factory could sell its right to pollute.

Rule #2— the factory has the right to pollute, but residents have the right to clean air and are entitled to damages. This is called a liability rule, because the residents do not have to consent to the factory's decision to impose costs on them. Under this liability rule, their rights are limited to the receipt of compensation in the form of damages.

Rule #3— residents are entitled to an injunction forbidding pollution. Under this property rule in favor of the residents, the residents may get the injunction or they can sell the right to impose the injunction.

Rule #4— residents are entitled to an injunction, but must pay compensatory damages to the factory (e.g., if the residents force the factory to move). This is a liability rule where damages are imposed on the factory.

The impact of alternate rules can be analyzed by comparison of the results under two conditions—zero transaction costs and positive transaction costs. The efficient solution in Table VI-1 is indicated by the asterisk (*). With zero transac-

Table VI-1. Impact of Transaction Costs on Allocation of Property Rights

(A) Zero Transaction Costs	(B) Positive Transaction Costs
Rule 1—Factory has right to pollute. (Property Rule)	
Residents have 4 choices:	
1) be injured for $375	1) $375
*2) buy smokescreen for $150	2) $150 + $300 (TC) = $450
3) buy dryers for $250	3) $250 *
4) move $500	4) $500
Rule 2—Factory has right to pollute, but residents have right to clean air and are entitled to damages. (Liability Rule)	
Factory has 4 choices:	
1) pay damages of $375	1) $375
*2) install smokescreen for $150	2) $150 *
3) buy dryers for $250	3) $250
4) shut down $500	4) $500
Rule 3—Residents are entitled to an injunction forbidding pollution (Property Rule)	
Factory has 4 choices:	
1) pay damages of $375	1) $375
*2) install smokescreen for $150	2) $150 *
3) buy dryers for $250	3) $250
4) shut down $500	4) $500
Rule 4—Residents are entitled to an injunction, but must pay compensatory damages to the factory. (Liability Rule for Damages imposed on the factory).	
Residents have 5 choices:	
1) be injured for $375	1) $375
*2) buy smokescreen for $150	2) $150 + $300 (TC) = $450
3) buy dryers for $250	3) $250 *
4) move $500	4) $500
5) get injunction & pay $500	5) $500 + $300 (TC) = $800

tion costs, the smokescreen is installed for $150 under all four rules as indicated in column A. This is the efficient solution. The addition of positive transaction costs impacts the allocation. Assume it costs each resident $60 to get together to negotiate with the factory or to agree on collective action. In column B, we see that the outcome changes under the different rules due to the transaction costs. Rules 2 and 3 still result in the factory installing the smokescreen. The factory does not need to engage in any collective decision making with itself. Rules 1 and 4 have different outcomes because the transaction costs make the buying of dryers more attractive relative to the collective action and negotiation associated with people agreeing to pay for the smokescreen and then having the factory install it. Thus, the Coase Theorem suggests that when transaction costs are high, it is important for property rights to be allocated to the party who values them most highly.

Boomer v. Atlantic Cement Co., Inc.
Court of Appeals of New York
26 N.Y.2d 219; 257 N.E.2d 870 (1970)

Bergan, J.

Defendant operates a large cement plant near Albany. These are actions for injunction and damages by neighboring land owners alleging injury to property from dirt, smoke and vibration emanating from the plant. A nuisance has been found after trial, temporary damages have been allowed; but an injunction has been denied.

The public concern with air pollution arising from many sources in industry and in transportation is currently accorded ever wider recognition accompanied by a growing sense of responsibility in State and Federal Governments to control it. Cement plants are obvious sources of air pollution in the neighborhoods where they operate.

But there is now before the court private litigation in which individual property owners have sought specific relief from a single plant operation. The threshold question raised by the division of view on this appeal is whether the court should resolve the litigation between the parties now before it as equitably as seems possible; or whether, seeking promotion of the general public welfare, it should channel private litigation into broad public objectives.

A court performs its essential function when it decides the rights of parties before it. Its decision of private controversies may sometimes greatly affect public issues. Large questions of law are often resolved by the manner in which private litigation is decided. But this is normally an incident to the court's main function to settle controversy. It is a rare exercise of judicial power to use a decision in private litigation as a purposeful mechanism to achieve direct public objectives greatly beyond the rights and interests before the court.

Effective control of air pollution is a problem presently far from solution even with the full public and financial powers of government. In large measure adequate technical procedures are yet to be developed and some that appear possible may be economically impracticable.

It seems apparent that the amelioration of air pollution will depend on technical research in great depth; on a carefully balanced consideration of the economic impact of close regulation; and of the actual effect on public health. It is likely to require massive public expenditure and to demand more than any local community can accomplish and to depend on regional and interstate controls.

A court should not try to do this on its own as a by-product of private litigation and it seems manifest that the judicial establishment is neither equipped in the limited nature of any judgment it can pronounce nor prepared to lay down and implement an effective policy for the elimination of air pollution. This is an area beyond the circumference of one private lawsuit. It is a direct responsibility for government and should not thus be undertaken as an incident to solving a dispute between property owners and a single cement plant—one of many—in the Hudson River valley.

The cement making operations of defendant have been found by the court at Special Term to have damaged the nearby properties of plaintiffs in these two actions. That court, as it has been noted, accordingly found defendant maintained a nuisance and this has been affirmed at the Appellate Division. The total damage to plaintiffs' properties is, however, relatively small in comparison with the value of defendant's operation and with the consequences of the injunction which plaintiffs seek.

The ground for the denial of injunction, notwithstanding the finding both that there is a nuisance and that plaintiffs have been damaged substantially, is the large disparity in economic consequences of the nuisance and of the injunction. This theory cannot, however, be sustained without overruling a doctrine which has been consistently reaffirmed in several leading cases in this court and which has never been disavowed here, namely that where a nuisance has been found and where there has been any substantial damage shown by the party complaining an injunction will be granted.

The rule in New York has been that such a nuisance will be enjoined although marked disparity be shown in economic consequence between the effect of the injunction and the effect of the nuisance.

The problem of disparity in economic consequence was sharply in focus in Whalen v. Union Bag & Paper Co. (208 N.Y. 1). A pulp mill entailing an investment of more than a million dollars polluted a stream in which plaintiff, who owned a farm, was "a lower riparian owner." The economic loss to plaintiff from this pollution was small. This court, reversing the Appellate Division, reinstated the injunction granted by the Special Term against the argument of the mill owner that in view of "the slight advantage to plaintiff and the great loss that will be inflicted on defendant" an injunction should not be granted (p. 2). "Such a balancing of injuries cannot be justified by the circumstances of this case," Judge Werner noted (p. 4). He continued: "Although the damage to the plaintiff may be slight as compared with the defendant's expense of abating the condition, that is not a good reason for refusing an injunction" (p. 5).

Thus the unconditional injunction granted at Special Term was reinstated. The rule laid down in that case, then, is that whenever the damage resulting from a nuisance is found not "unsubstantial," viz., $100 a year, injunction would follow. This states a rule that had been followed in this court with marked consistency (McCarty v. Natural Carbonic Gas Co., 189 N.Y. 40; Strobel v. Kerr Salt Co., 164 N.Y. 303; Campbell v. Seaman, 63 N.Y. 568).

There are cases where injunction has been denied. McCann v. Chasm Power Co. (211 N.Y. 301) is one of them. There, however, the damage shown by plaintiffs was not only unsubstantial, it was non-existent. Plaintiffs owned a rocky bank of the stream in which defendant had raised the level of the water. This had no economic or other adverse consequence to plaintiffs, and thus injunctive relief was denied. Similar is the basis for denial of injunction in Forstmann v. Joray Holding Co. (244 N.Y. 22) where no benefit to plaintiffs could be seen from the injunction sought (p. 32). Thus if, within Whalen v. Union Bag & Paper Co. *supra* which authoritatively states the rule in New York, the damage to plaintiffs in these present cases from defendant's cement plant is "not unsubstantial," an injunction should follow.

Although the court at Special Term and the Appellate Division held that injunction should be denied, it was found that plaintiffs had been damaged in various specific amounts up to the time of the trial and damages to the respective plaintiffs were awarded for those amounts. The effect of this was, injunction having been denied, plaintiffs could maintain successive actions at law for damages thereafter as further damage was incurred.

The court at Special Term also found the amount of permanent damage attributable to each plaintiff, for the guidance of the parties in the event both sides stipulated to the payment and acceptance of such permanent damage as a settlement of all the controversies among the parties. The total of permanent damages to all plaintiffs thus found was $185,000. This basis of adjustment has not resulted in any stipulation by the parties.

This result at Special Term and at the Appellate Division is a departure from a rule that has become settled; but to follow the rule literally in these cases would be to close down the plant at once. This court is fully agreed to avoid that immediately drastic remedy; the difference in view is how best to avoid it.*

One alternative is to grant the injunction but postpone its effect to a specified future date to give opportunity for technical advances to permit defendant to eliminate the nuisance; another is to grant the injunction conditioned on the payment of permanent damages to plaintiffs which would compensate them for the total economic loss to their property present and future caused by defendant's operations. For reasons which will be developed the court chooses the latter alternative.

If the injunction were to be granted unless within a short period—e.g., 18 months—the nuisance be abated by improved methods, there would be no assurance that any significant technical improvement would occur.

The parties could settle this private litigation at any time if defendant paid enough money and the imminent threat of closing the plant would build up the pressure on defendant. If there were no improved techniques found, there would inevitably be applications to the court at Special Term for extensions of time to perform on showing of good faith efforts to find such techniques.

---

* Respondent's investment in the plant is in excess of $45,000,000. There are over 300 people employed there.

Moreover, techniques to eliminate dust and other annoying by-products of cement making are unlikely to be developed by any research the defendant can undertake within any short period, but will depend on the total resources of the cement industry Nationwide and throughout the world. The problem is universal wherever cement is made.

For obvious reasons the rate of the research is beyond control of defendant. If at the end of 18 months the whole industry has not found a technical solution a court would be hard put to close down this one cement plant if due regard be given to equitable principles.

On the other hand, to grant the injunction unless defendant pays plaintiffs such permanent damages as may be fixed by the court seems to do justice between the contending parties. All of the attributions of economic loss to the properties on which plaintiffs' complaints are based will have been redressed.

The nuisance complained of by these plaintiffs may have other public or private consequences, but these particular parties are the only ones who have sought remedies and the judgment proposed will fully redress them. The limitation of relief granted is a limitation only within the four corners of these actions and does not foreclose public health or other public agencies from seeking proper relief in a proper court.

It seems reasonable to think that the risk of being required to pay permanent damages to injured property owners by cement plant owners would itself be a reasonable effective spur to research for improved techniques to minimize nuisance.

The power of the court to condition on equitable grounds the continuance of an injunction on the payment of permanent damages seems undoubted. (See, e.g., the alternatives considered in McCarty v. Natural Carbonic Gas Co., *supra*, as well as Strobel v. Kerr Salt Co., *supra*.)

The damage base here suggested is consistent with the general rule in those nuisance cases where damages are allowed. "Where a nuisance is of such a permanent and unabatable character that a single recovery can be had, including the whole damage past and future resulting therefrom, there can be but one recovery" (66 C.J.S., Nuisances, § 140, p. 947). It has been said that permanent damages are allowed where the loss recoverable would obviously be small as compared with the cost of removal of the nuisance (Kentucky-Ohio Gas Co. v. Bowling, 264 Ky. 470, 477).

The present cases and the remedy here proposed are in a number of other respects rather similar to Northern Indiana Public Serv. Co. v. Vesey (210 Ind. 338) decided by the Supreme Court of Indiana. The gases, odors, ammonia and smoke from the Northern Indiana company's gas plant damaged the nearby Vesey greenhouse operation. An injunction and damages were sought, but an injunction was denied and the relief granted was limited to permanent damages "present, past, and future" (p. 371).

Denial of injunction was grounded on a public interest in the operation of the gas plant and on the court's conclusion "that less injury would be occasioned by requiring the appellant [Public Service] to pay the appellee [Vesey] all damages suffered by it...than by enjoining the operation of the gas plant; and that the maintenance and operation of the gas plant should not be en-joined" (p. 349).

The Indiana Supreme Court opinion continued: "When the trial court refused injunctive relief to the appellee upon the ground of public interest in the continuance of the gas plant, it properly retained jurisdiction of the case and awarded full compensation to the appellee. This is upon the general equitable principle that equity will give full relief in one action and prevent a multiplicity of suits" (pp. 353–354).

It was held that in this type of continuing and recurrent nuisance permanent damages were appropriate. See, also, City of Amarillo v. Ware (120 Tex. 456) where recurring overflows from a system of storm sewers were treated as the kind of nuisance for which permanent depreciation of value of affected property would be recoverable.

There is some parallel to the conditioning of an injunction on the payment of permanent damages in the noted "elevated railway cases" (Pappenheim v. Metropolitan El. Ry. Co., 128 N.Y. 436, and others which followed). Decisions in these cases were based on the finding that the railways created a nuisance as to adjacent property owners, but in lieu of enjoining their operation, the court allowed permanent damages.

Judge Finch, reviewing these cases in Ferguson v. Village of Hamburg (272 N.Y. 234, 239–240), said: "The courts decided that the plaintiffs had a valuable right which was being impaired, but did not grant an absolute injunction or require the railway companies to resort to separate condemnation proceedings. Instead they held that a court of equity could ascertain the damages and grant an injunction which was not to be effective unless the defendant failed to pay the amount fixed as damages for the past and permanent injury inflicted." (See, also, Lynch v. Metropolitan El. Ry. Co., 129 N.Y. 274; Van Allen v. New York El. R. R. Co., 144 N.Y. 174; Cox v. City of New York, 265 N.Y. 411, and similarly, Westphal v. City of New York, 177 N.Y. 140.)

Thus it seems fair to both sides to grant permanent damages to plaintiffs which will terminate this private litigation. The theory of damage is the "servitude on land" of plaintiffs imposed by defendant's nuisance. (See United Sates v. Causby, 328 U.S. 256, 261, 262, 267, where the term "servitude" addressed to the land was used by Justice Douglas relating to the effect of airplane noise on property near an airport.)

The judgment, by allowance of permanent damages imposing a servitude on land, which is the basis of the actions, would preclude future recovery by plaintiffs or their grantees (see Northern Indiana Public Serv. Co. v. Vesey, *supra*, p. 351).

This should be placed beyond debate by a provision of the judgment that the payment by defendant and the acceptance by plaintiffs of permanent damages found by the court shall be in compensation for a servitude on the land.

Although the Trial Term has found permanent damages as a possible basis of settlement of the litigation, on remission the court should be entirely free to reexamine this subject. It may again find the permanent damage already found; or make new findings.

The orders should be reversed, without costs, and the cases remitted to Supreme Court, Albany County to grant an injunction which shall be vacated upon payment by defendant of such amounts of permanent damage to the respective plaintiffs as shall for this purpose be determined by the court.

Jasen, J. (dissenting)

I agree with the majority that a reversal is required here, but I do not subscribe to the newly enunciated doctrine of assessment of permanent damages, in lieu of an injunction, where substantial property rights have been impaired by the creation of a nuisance.

It has long been the rule in this State, as the majority acknowledges, that a nuisance which results in substantial continuing damage to neighbors must be enjoined. (Whalen v. Union Bag & Paper Co., 208 N.Y. 1; Campbell v. Seaman, 63 N.Y. 568; see, also, Kennedy v. Moog Servocontrols, 21 N Y 2d 966.) To now change the rule to permit the cement company to continue polluting the air indefinitely upon the payment of permanent damages is, in my opinion, compounding the magnitude of a very serious problem in our State and Nation today.

In recognition of this problem, the Legislature of this State has enacted the Air Pollution Control Act (Public Health Law, §§ 1264–1299-m) declaring that it is the State policy to require the use of all available and reasonable methods to prevent and control air pollution (Public Health Law, § 1265).

The harmful nature and widespread occurrence of air pollution have been extensively documented. Congressional hearings have revealed that air pollution causes substantial property damage, as well as being a contributing factor to a rising incidence of lung cancer, emphysema, bronchitis and asthma.

The specific problem faced here is known as particulate contamination because of the fine dust particles emanating from defendant's cement plant. The particular type of nuisance is not new, having appeared in many cases for at least the past 60 years. (See Hulbert v. California Portland Cement Co., 161 Cal. 239 [1911].) It is interesting to note that cement production has recently been identified as a significant source of particulate contamination in the Hudson Valley. This type of pollution, wherein very small particles escape and stay in the atmosphere, has been denominated as the type of air pollution which produces the greatest hazard to human health. We have thus a nuisance which not only is damaging to the plaintiffs, but also is decidedly harmful to the general public.

I see grave dangers in overruling our long-established rule of granting an injunction where a nuisance results in substantial continuing damage. In permitting the injunction to become inoperative upon the payment of permanent damages, the majority is, in effect, licensing a continuing wrong. It is the same as saying to the cement company, you may continue to do harm to your neighbors so long as you pay a fee for it. Furthermore, once such permanent damages are assessed and paid, the incentive to alleviate the wrong would be eliminated, thereby continuing air pollution of an area without abatement.

It is true that some courts have sanctioned the remedy here proposed by the majority in a number of cases, but none of the authorities relied upon by the majority are analogous to the situation before us. In those cases, the courts, in denying an injunction and awarding money damages, grounded their decision on a showing that the use to which the property was intended to be put was primarily for the public benefit. Here, on the other hand, it is clearly established that the cement company is creating a continuing air pollution nuisance primarily for its own private interest with no public benefit.

This kind of inverse condemnation (Ferguson v. Village of Hamburg, 272 N.Y. 234 may not be invoked by a private person or corporation for private gain or advantage. Inverse condemnation should only be permitted when the public is primarily served in the taking or impairment of property. (Matter of New York City Housing Auth. v. Muller, 270 N.Y. 333, 343; Pocantico Water Works Co. v. Bird, 130 N.Y. 249, 258.) The promotion of the interests of the polluting cement company has, in my opinion, no public use or benefit.

Nor is it constitutionally permissible to impose servitude on land, without consent of the owner, by payment of permanent damages where the continuing impairment of the land is for a private use. (See Fifth Ave. Coach Lines v. City of New York, 11 N.Y. 2d 342, 347; Walker v. City of Hutchinson, 352 U.S. 112.) This is made clear by the State Constitution (art. I, § 7, subd. [a]) which provides that "[p]rivate property shall not be taken for *public use* without just compensation" (emphasis added). It is, of course, significant that the section makes no mention of taking for a private use.

In sum, then, by constitutional mandate as well as by judicial pronouncement, the permanent impairment of private property for private purposes is not authorized in the absence of clearly demonstrated public benefit and use.

I would enjoin the defendant cement company from continuing the discharge of dust particles upon its neighbors' properties unless, within 18 months, the cement company abated this nuisance.

It is not my intention to cause the removal of the cement plant from the Albany area, but to recognize the urgency of the problem stemming from this stationary source of air pollution, and to allow the company a specified period of time to develop a means to alleviate this nuisance.

I am aware that the trial court found that the most modern dust control devices available have been installed in defendant's plant, but, I submit, this does not mean that *better* and more effective dust control devices could not be developed within the time allowed to abate the pollution.

Moreover, I believe it is incumbent upon the defendant to develop such devices, since the cement company, at the time the plant commenced production (1962), was well aware of the plaintiffs' presence in the area, as well as the probable consequences of its contemplated operation. Yet, it still chose to build and operate the plant at this site.

In a day when there is a growing concern for clean air, highly developed industry should not expect acquiescence by the courts, but should, instead, plan its operations to eliminate contamination of our air and damage to its neighbors.

Accordingly, the orders of the Appellate Division, insofar as they denied the injunction, should be reversed, and the actions remitted to Supreme Court, Albany County to grant an injunction to take effect 18 months hence, unless the nuisance is abated by improved techniques prior to said date.

Notes and Questions

1. The Assignment of Property Rights: Who has the entitlement? How was it protected? Which "rule" (from the example preceding the case) is adopted by the court? Is the rule efficient? In what sense? What is the relevance of the firm's investment? What is meant by permanent damages?

2. Bargaining and the Coase Theorem: Did high transaction costs prevent bargaining to resolve the incompatible uses of property? Or, was the absence of clearly defined property rights the reason for the lawsuit?

3. The Normative Coase Theorem: The preceding analysis leads to the development of what is referred to as the Normative Coase Theorem. If efficiency is the goal, the preferred legal rule is the rule that minimizes the effects of transactions costs. Thus, we should assign the right initially to the party who would end up with it if transactions costs were equal to zero. When an externality has arisen, the court should choose between the liability rule and the property rule on the basis of the parties' ability to cooperate in resolving the dispute. When transactions costs are low, the preferred remedy is the awarding of an injunction against the defendant's interference with the plaintiff's property. This property rule forces bargaining. Where transactions costs are high, the preferred remedy is a liability rule with compensatory damages. When these standards are applied in practice, the preferred remedy depends in large part on how many parties must participate in the settlement. The larger the number of parties, the more preferable is the liability rule with damages. In general, a property rule works best for private wrongs, a liability rule better for public wrongs. In many instances the public wrongs are dealt with through land use planning, environmental regulations or public nuisance laws.

4. Trivial Externalities: Generally, when transaction costs are high, government intervention to correct the market failure associated with negative externalities may be justified on efficiency grounds. In this regard, however, it is important to recognize that the combination of small externalities and nontrivial costs of government intervention suggests that many externalities are not worth correcting. For example, the playing of loud music at a public park may impose external costs on people who went to the park to enjoy its peace and quiet, but the costs of governmental intervention to silence the portable stereos—BOOM BOXES—might be much greater than the benefits to the other parties.

Spur Industries, Inc. v. Del E. Webb Development Co.

Supreme Court of Arizona, En Banc.
108 Ariz. 178; 494 P.2d 700 (1972)

Cameron, J.

From a judgment permanently enjoining the defendant, Spur Industries, Inc., from operating a cattle feedlot near the plaintiff Del E. Webb Development Company's Sun City, Spur appeals. Webb cross-appeals. Although numerous issues are raised, we feel that it is necessary to answer only two questions. They are:

1. Where the operation of a business, such as a cattle feedlot is lawful in the first instance, but becomes a nuisance by reason of a nearby residential area, may the feedlot operation be enjoined in an action brought by the developer of the residential area?

2. Assuming that the nuisance may be enjoined, may the developer of a completely new town or urban area in a previously agricultural area be required to

indemnify the operator of the feedlot who must move or cease operation because of the presence of the residential area created by the developer?

The facts necessary for a determination of this matter on appeal are as follows. The area in question is located in Maricopa County, Arizona, some 14 to 15 miles west of the urban area of Phoenix, on the Phoenix-Wickenburg Highway, also known as Grand Avenue. About two miles south of Grand Avenue is Olive Avenue which runs east and west. 111th Avenue runs north and south as does the Agua Fria River immediately to the west....

Farming started in this area about 1911. In 1929, with the completion of the Carl Pleasant Dam, gravity flow water became available to the property located to the west of the Agua Fria River, though land to the east remained dependent upon well water for irrigation. By 1950, the only urban areas in the vicinity were the agriculturally related communities of Peoria, El Mirage, and Surprise located along Grand Avenue. Along 111th Avenue, approximately one mile south of Grand Avenue and 1 1/2 miles north of Olive Avenue, the community of Youngtown was commenced in 1954. Youngtown is a retirement community appealing primarily to senior citizens.

In 1956, Spur's predecessors in interest, H. Marion Welborn and the Northside Hay Mill and Trading Company, developed feed-lots, about 1/2 mile south of Olive Avenue, in an area between the confluence of the usually dry Agua Fria and New Rivers. The area is well suited for cattle feeding and in 1959, there were 25 cattle feeding pens or dairy operations within a 7 mile radius of the location developed by Spur's predecessors. In April and May of 1959, the Northside Hay Mill was feeding between 6,000 and 7,000 head of cattle and Welborn approximately 1,500 head on a combined area of 35 acres.

In May of 1959, Del Webb began to plan the development of an urban area to be known as Sun City. For this purpose, the Marinette and the Santa Fe Ranches, some 20,000 acres of farmland, were purchased for $15,000,000 or $750.00 per acre. This price was considerably less than the price of land located near the urban area of Phoenix, and along with the success of Youngtown was a factor influencing the decision to purchase the property in question.

By September 1959, Del Webb had started construction of a golf course south of Grand Avenue and Spur's predecessors had started to level ground for more feedlot area. In 1960, Spur purchased the property in question and began a rebuilding and expansion program extending both to the north and south of the original facilities. By 1962, Spur's expansion program was completed and had expanded from approximately 35 acres to 114 acres.

Accompanied by an extensive advertising campaign, homes were first offered by Del Webb in January 1960 and the first unit to be completed was south of Grand Avenue and approximately 2½ miles north of Spur. By 2 May 1960, there were 450 to 500 houses completed or under construction. At this time, Del Webb did not consider odors from the Spur feed pens a problem and Del Webb continued to develop in a southerly direction, until sales resistance became so great that the parcels were difficult if not impossible to sell. Thomas E. Breen, Vice President and General Manager of the housing division of Del Webb, testified at deposition as follows:

"Q: Did you ever have any discussions with Tony Cole at or about the time the sales office was opened south of Peoria concerning the problem in sales as the development came closer towards the feed lots?

"A: Not at the time that that facility was opened. That was subsequent to that.

"Q: All right, what is it that you recall about conversations with Cole on that subject?

"A: Well, when the feed lot problem became a bigger problem, which, really, to the best of my recollection, commenced to become a serious problem in 1963, and there was some talk about not developing that area because of sales resistance, and to my recollection we shifted—we had planned at that time to the eastern portion of the property, and it was a consideration.

"Q: Was any specific suggestion made by Mr. Cole as to the line of demarcation that should be drawn or anything of that type exactly where the development should cease?

"A: I don't recall anything specific as far as the definite line would be, other than, you know, that it would be advisable to stay out of the southwestern portion there because of sales resistance.

"Q: And to the best of your recollection, this was in about 1963?

"A: That would be my recollection, yes.

    *   *   *

"Q: As you recall it, what was the reason that the suggestion was not adopted to stop developing towards the southwest of the development?

"A: Well, as far as I know, that decision was made subsequent to that time.

"Q: Right. But I mean at that time?

"A: Well, at that time what I am really referring to is more of a long-range planning than immediate planning, and I think it was the case of just trying to figure out how far you could go with it before you really ran into a lot of sales resistance and found a necessity to shift the direction.

"Q: So the plan was to go as far as you could until the resistance got to the point where you couldn't go any further?

"A: I would say that is reasonable, yes."

By December 1967, Del Webb's property had extended south to Olive Avenue and Spur was within 500 feet of Olive Avenue to the north. Del Webb filed its original complaint alleging that in excess of 1,300 lots in the southwest portion were unfit for development for sale as residential lots because of the operation of the Spur feedlot.

Del Webb's suit complained that the Spur feeding operation was a public nuisance because of the flies and the odor which were drifting or being blown by the prevailing south to north wind over the southern portion of Sun City. At the time of the suit, Spur was feeding between 20,000 and 30,000 head of cattle, and the facts amply support the finding of the trial court that the feed pens had become a nuisance to the people who resided in the southern part of Del Webb's development. The testimony indicated that cattle in a commercial feedlot will produce 35 to 40 pounds of wet manure per day, per head, or over a million pounds of wet manure per day for 30,000 head of cattle, and that despite the admittedly good feedlot management and good housekeeping practices by Spur, the resulting odor and flies produced an annoying if not unhealthy situation as far as the senior citizens of southern Sun City were concerned. There is no doubt that some of the citizens of Sun City were unable to enjoy the outdoor living which Del Webb had advertised and that Del Webb was faced with sales resistance from prospective purchasers as well as strong and persistent complaints from the people who had purchased homes in that area.

Trial was commenced before the court with an advisory jury. The advisory jury was later discharged and the trial was continued before the court alone. Findings of fact and conclusions of law were requested and given. The case was vigorously contested, including special actions in this court on some of the matters. In one of the special actions before this court, Spur agreed to, and did, shut down its operation without prejudice to a determination of the matter on appeal. On appeal the many questions raised were extensively briefed.

It is noted, however, that neither the citizens of Sun City nor Youngtown are represented in this lawsuit and the suit is solely between Del E. Webb Development Company and Spur Industries, Inc.

MAY SPUR BE ENJOINED?

The difference between a private nuisance and a public nuisance is generally one of degree. A private nuisance is one affecting a single individual or a definite small number of persons in the enjoyment of private rights not common to the public, while a public nuisance is one affecting the rights enjoyed by citizens as a city or neighborhood. City of Phoenix v. Johnson, 51 Ariz. part of the public. To constitute a public nuisance, the nuisance must affect a considerable number of people or an entire community or neighborhood. City of Phoenix v. Johnson, 51 Ariz. 115, 75 P.2d 30 (1938).

Where the injury is slight, the remedy for minor inconveniences lies in an action for damages rather than in one for an injunction. Kubby v. Hammond, 68 Ariz. 17, 198 P.2d 134 (1948). Moreover, some courts have held, in the "balancing of conveniences" cases, that damages may be the sole remedy. See Boomer v. Atlantic Cement Co., 26 N.Y.2d 219, 309 N.Y.S.2d 312, 257 N.E.2d 870, 40 A.L.R.3d 590 (1970), and annotation comments, 40 A.L.R.3d 601.

Thus, it would appear from the admittedly incomplete record as developed in the trial court, that, at most, residents of Youngtown would be entitled to damages rather than injunctive relief.

We have no difficulty, however, in agreeing with the conclusion of the trial court that Spur's operation was an enjoinable public nuisance as far as the people in the southern portion of Del Webb's Sun City were concerned.

§ 36-601, subsec. A reads as follows: "§ 36-601. Public nuisances dangerous to public health.

"A. The following conditions are specifically declared public nuisances dangerous to the public health:"

"1. Any condition or place in populous areas which constitutes a breeding place for flies, rodents, mosquitoes and other insects which are capable of carrying and transmitting disease-causing organisms to any person or persons."

By this statute, before an otherwise lawful (and necessary) business may be declared a public nuisance, there must be a "populous" area in which people are injured:

> "...[It] hardly admits a doubt that, in determining the question as to whether a lawful occupation is so conducted as to constitute a nuisance as a matter of fact, the locality and surroundings are of the first importance. (citations omitted) A business which is not per se a public nuisance may become such by being carried on at a place where the health, comfort, or convenience of a populous neighborhood is affected.... What might amount to a serious nuisance in one locality by reason of the density of the population, or character of the neighborhood affected, may in another place and under different surroundings be deemed proper and unobjectionable...." MacDonald v. Perry, 32 Ariz. 39, 49–50, 255 P. 494, 497 (1927).

It is clear that as to the citizens of Sun City, the operation of Spur's feedlot was both a public and a private nuisance. They could have successfully maintained an action to abate the nuisance. Del Webb, having shown a special injury in the loss of sales, had a standing to bring suit to enjoin the nuisance. Engle v. Clark, 53 Ariz. 472, 90 P.2d 994 (1939); City of Phoenix v. Johnson, supra. The judgment of the trial court permanently enjoining the operation of the feedlot is affirmed.

MUST DEL WEBB INDEMNIFY SPUR?

A suit to enjoin a nuisance sounds in equity and the courts have long recognized a special responsibility to the public when acting as a court of equity:

§ 104. Where public interest is involved.

"Courts of equity may, and frequently do, go much further both to give and withhold relief in furtherance of the public interest than they are accustomed to go when only private interests are involved. Accordingly, the granting or withholding of relief may properly be dependent upon considerations of public interest..." 27 Am.Jur.2d, Equity, page 626.

In addition to protecting the public interest, however, courts of equity are concerned with protecting the operator of a lawfully, albeit noxious, business from the result of a knowing and willful encroachment by others near his business.

In the so-called "coming to the nuisance" cases, the courts have held that the residential landowner may not have relief if he knowingly came into a neighborhood reserved for industrial or agricultural endeavors and has been damaged thereby:

> Plaintiffs chose to live in an area uncontrolled by zoning laws or restrictive covenants and remote from urban development. In such an area plaintiffs cannot complain that legitimate agricultural pursuits are being carried on in the vicinity, nor can plaintiffs, having chosen to build in an agricultural area, complain that the agricultural pursuits carried on in the area depreciate the value of their homes. The area being primarily agricultural, any opinion reflecting the value of such property must take this factor into account. The standards affecting the value of residence property in an urban setting, subject to zoning controls and controlled planning techniques, cannot be the standards by which agricultural properties are judged.

"People employed in a city who build their homes in suburban areas of the county beyond the limits of a city and zoning regulations do so for a reason. Some do so to avoid the high taxation rate imposed by cities, or to avoid special assessments for street, sewer and water projects. They usually build on improved or hard surface highways, which have been built either at state or county expense and thereby avoid special assessments for these improvements. It may be that they desire to get away from the congestion of traffic, smoke, noise, foul air and the many other annoyances of city life. But with all these advantages in going beyond the area which is zoned and restricted to protect them in their homes, they must be prepared to take the disadvantages." Dill v. Excel Packing Company, 183 Kan. 513, 525, 526, 331 P.2d 539, 548, 549 (1958). See also East St. Johns Shingle Co. v. City of Portland, 195 Or. 505, 246 P.2d 554, 560–562 (1952).

And: "...a party cannot justly call upon the law to make that place suitable for his residence which was not so when he selected it..." Gilbert v. Showerman, 23 Mich. 448, 455, 2 Brown 158 (1871).

Were Webb the only party injured, we would feel justified in holding that the doctrine of "coming to the nuisance" would have been a bar to the relief asked by Webb, and, on the other hand, had Spur located the feedlot near the outskirts of a city and had the city grown toward the feedlot, Spur would have to suffer the cost of abating the nuisance as to those people locating within the growth pattern of the expanding city:

"The case affords, perhaps, an example where a business established at a place remote from population is gradually surrounded and becomes part of a populous center, so that a business which formerly was not an interference with the rights of others has become so by the encroachment of the population...." City of Ft. Smith v. Western Hide & Fur Co., 153 Ark. 99, 103, 239 S.W. 724, 726 (1922).

We agree, however, with the Massachusetts court that:

"The law of nuisance affords no rigid rule to be applied in all instances. It is elastic. It undertakes to require only that which is fair and reasonable under all the circumstances. In a commonwealth like this, which depends for its material prosperity so largely on the continued growth and enlargement of manufacturing of diverse varieties, 'extreme rights' cannot be enforced..." Stevens v. Rockport Granite Co., 216 Mass. 486, 488, 104 N.E. 371, 373 (1914).

There was no indication in the instant case at the time Spur and its predecessors located in western Maricopa County that a new city would spring up, full-blown, alongside the feeding operation and that the developer of that city would ask the court to order Spur to move because of the new city. Spur is required to move not because of any wrongdoing on the part of Spur, but because of a proper and legitimate regard of the courts for the rights and interests of the public.

Del Webb, on the other hand, is entitled to the relief prayed for (a permanent injunction), not because Webb is blameless, but because of the damage to the people who have been encouraged to purchase homes in Sun City. It does not equitably or legally follow, however, that Webb, being entitled to the injunction, is then free of any liability to Spur if Webb has in fact been the cause of the damage Spur has sustained. It does not seem harsh to require a developer, who has taken advantage of the lesser land values in a rural area as well as the availability of large tracts of land on which to build and develop a new town or city in the area, to indemnify those who are forced to leave as a result.

Having brought people to the nuisance to the foreseeable detriment of Spur, Webb must indemnify Spur for a reasonable amount of the cost of moving or shutting down. It should be noted that this relief to Spur is limited to a case wherein a developer has, with foreseeability, brought into a previously agricultural or industrial area the population which makes necessary the granting of an injunction against a lawful business and for which the business has no adequate relief.

It is therefore the decision of this court that the matter be remanded to the trial court for a hearing upon the damages sustained by the defendant Spur as a reasonable and direct result of the granting of the permanent injunction. Since the result of the appeal may appear novel and both sides have obtained a measure of relief, it is ordered that each side will bear its own costs.

Affirmed in part, reversed in part, and remanded for further proceedings consistent with this opinion.

Notes and Questions

1. The Assignment of Property Rights: Who has the entitlement? How was it protected? Which "rule" (from the example preceding the *Boomer* case) is adopted by the court? Is the rule efficient? In what sense?

2. Reciprocal Causation: Who "caused" the injury?

3. Bargaining and the Coase Theorem: Did high transaction costs prevent bargaining to resolve the incompatible uses of property? Or, was the absence of clearly defined property rights the reason for the lawsuit?

2. Corrective Taxes and Subsidies

One government strategy for dealing with externalities is to encourage decision makers to internalize the externalities by taxing the production of negative externality goods and subsidizing the production of positive externality goods. When the government taxes firms that produce negative externality goods, the goal is to set the per unit tax so that the producer's marginal private costs of production plus the tax equals the marginal social cost of production.

The impact of an excise tax on the sale of a product that involves negative externalities is shown in Figure VI-4. The tax is assumed to be paid by the producer, so it is treated as an addition to the marginal private costs of production (MPC). That is, the optimal tax should be equal to the difference between the MPC and MSC, so that MPC + T = MSC. The competitive firm would equate MSC (MPC + T = MSC=P) to price and the externality would be internalized

Figure VI-4

Tax on Pollution

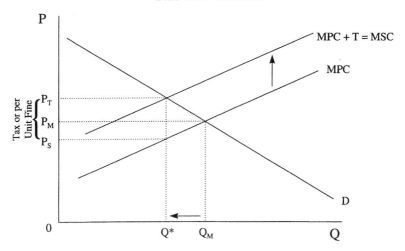

in the firm's output decision. That is, the firm will produce the output where MSC = P, which is the correct output from society's point of view. The tax causes the market to clear at Q*, the optimal level of production. The new market price is at P_T, which indicates that the market price did not increase by the full amount of the tax. That is, the burden of the tax is shared by both the producers who receive a lower after-tax price ($P_S = P_T - T$) and consumers who pay P_T instead of P_M. Prior to the imposition of the corrective tax, consumers as well as producers benefitted from the producers' ability to shift some costs to third parties.

Taxation is a form of indirect regulation. Thus, taxing a firm that pollutes forces the firm to act as if it were taking all social costs of its activities into account, thereby resulting in an optimum level of output. Again, as we saw with the Coase Theorem, the socially optimal level of pollution is not zero. At some point, clean air costs more than it is worth.

The government can impose the correct tax in Figure VI-4 only if it has sufficient information to calculate the marginal cost to other people, so that it can set the appropriate level of the tax and then adjust the tax rate when the marginal cost to other people changes. Such information is necessarily subjective (since some people are more sensitive to some externalities than others) and, consequently, is revealed through the political process.

Similarly, a **subsidy** is a government cash grant or tax break to producers of certain goods. Examples of goods subsidized because they produce positive externalities include vaccinations and schools. The optimal subsidy is equal to the size of the positive externality—the difference between the marginal private benefits of consuming the good and the marginal social benefits of consuming the good. Instead of paying the subsidy to the consumers, which would increase the marginal private benefit of consumption, a subsidy is typically paid to the producers.

Figure VI-5   Positive Externality and per Unit Subsidy

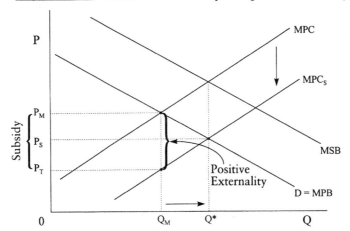

The impact of a per unit subsidy is illustrated in Figure VI-5. The subsidy reduces the marginal private cost of production from MPC to MPC_S. As a result, the market output increases to Q^*, where MPC_S = MPB. The price falls to P_S, indicating that the producers pass on some of the subsidy to consumers.

3.   Government Regulation

Another government strategy for dealing with externalities is direct regulation of the behavior of firms. An example of this type of response to the market failure is local land-use zoning laws which prohibit, say, the opening of a 24-hour convenience store in certain residential areas. Another example is the current federal regulation of industrial pollution. For example, the primary federal response to pollution has been to place limits on the amount that firms can legally discharge.

The efficiency goal of the government regulation is to require industry output to be the economically efficient level at the quantity where the marginal private cost equals marginal social costs. In the 1970s, the federal government sought to control pollution through direct regulation of polluters. Environmental regulation generally consists of detailed rules about the technology that firms must adopt to control pollution. Firms in identified industries must install special pollution control equipment as a condition of being able to stay in the industry. This is a practical way to control pollution. Each firm must clean up its emissions in the prescribed manner. Note that direct regulation does not allow firms to choose the most efficient means of staying below the allowable level of pollution, nor are firms allowed to choose to pollute (and pay compensatory damages) or not pollute or to select among different types of pollution control technology. They must follow the detailed rules laid down by the government.

The experience of over twenty years of intensive federal regulation of environmental risks has demonstrated the severe drawbacks of centralized environmental policy. The "command and control" regulatory strategy that dominates environmental policy has proven to be inadequate: it has not set intelligent priorities, has squandered resources devoted to environmental quality, has discouraged environmentally superior technologies, and has imposed unnecessary penalties on innovation and investment:

> Our current environmental regulatory system was an understandable response to a perceived need for immediate controls to prevent a pollution crisis. But the system has grown to the point where it amounts to nothing less than a massive effort at Soviet-style central planning of the economy to achieve environmental goals. It strangles investment and innovation. It encourages costly and divisive litigation and delay. It unduly limits private initiative and choice. The centralized command system is simply unacceptable as a long-term environmental protection strategy for a large and diverse nation committed to the market and decentralized ordering.

Richard B. Stewart, *Controlling Environmental Risks Through Economic Incentives*, 13 Colum. J. Envtl. L. 153, 154 (1988).

a. Direct Regulation v. Corrective Taxes

Regulation can be effective from an efficiency perspective, however, only if the government also has reliable up-to-date information about the economically efficient quantity and it can impose that quantity on firms in an efficient manner. Taxes can provide better incentives than regulations. For example, suppose that the government wants to limit the total amount of pollution from an industry. If it does so through regulation, a firm that learns a new method to reduce pollution may have no incentive to adopt that method. However, if the government limits pollution by taxing it, the firm may be able to reduce its taxes and raise its profits by adopting the new method. Also, taxes can provide firms with more effective incentives to use new lower cost methods of reducing pollution than regulations can provide. Taxes have a second benefit over regulations to internalize externalities. They generate revenue for the government, allowing reductions in other taxes. If the government were to receive $100 billion from taxes on pollution, it could reduce income taxes by that amount, lowering the deadweight social losses from both the income taxes and pollution.

b. Selling Rights to Pollute

A straightforward alternative to corrective taxes and direct regulation is to establish a market for externality rights, such as the right to pollute. In this approach, the government sets an allowable level of pollution and sells the right to pollute. In theory, this market works like any other market. Those who value the pollution rights must, however, buy and hold them. Firms will make decisions about whether it is less costly to install pollution control equipment or to buy pollution rights. Government does not tell industry how to clean up the air. Instead, it sets the allowable level of pollution and lets firms decide how to control their pollution. This market-like approach to pollution control has the virtue of insuring that the acceptable level of pollution is reached at the lowest possible cost.

In fact, the 1990 Amendments to the Clean Air Act allowed the federal government to start experimenting with a program of marketable emission permits for smoke stack emissions of public utilities. Under this program, utilities are allowed to trade pollution rights. Environmental policy analysts argued that the new market for pollution rights would give utilities the incentives to lower the cost of their pollution control efforts. The early results on this are encouraging, as suggested by the following newspaper report:

> (CHICAGO) The price of permits for coal-fired utility plants to pollute the air is expected to dip to its lowest level yet when the Chicago Board of Trade announces on Tuesday the results of the annual auction it runs for the Environmental Protection Agency.
>
> The price decline is likely to lead to new questions about how badly Congress overestimated the financial burdens of cleaning the air and whether utilities should now be required to make deeper cuts in their emissions of sulfur dioxide. That pollution is thought to be the major source of acid rain that kills trees and fish in the Northeast.
>
> "The cost of preventing pollution has fallen by half in just two years," said Daniel Jaffe, executive director of the National Healthy Air License Exchange, a Cleveland-based environmental group that buys permits in the auction to keep them out of the hands of utilities. Each permit allows the release of one ton of sulfur dioxide.
>
> Although the Board of Trade will not finish tabulating the bids until Monday, Mr. Jaffe's group has been told that bids of $70 a permit that it submitted would be filled. His group's bids used more than $20,000 raised by schoolchildren in Glens Falls, N.Y. Traders say the average successful bid for the permits, technically known as allowances, could be as low as $66 this year, half the $132 of a year ago.
>
> This year's auction, the fourth, will be the biggest so far, with 150,000 permits available for immediate use, triple last year's number. The E.P.A. will also sell 25,000 allowances usable in 2002 and 100,000 for 2003.
>
> The Board of Trade said today that the number of bids, many of them for thousands of permits, was up 60 percent from the 150 bids received last year. Traders say the sharp increase may signal a new maturity in the market.
>
> The Board of Trade expects to fill many bids below the current spot market price of $70 to $75. But if the lowest price that clears all the remaining permits off the table is only a few dollars less than the spot price, enough bidders could be caught short to create buying pressure in the spot market.
>
> "It could bounce back to $100 fairly quickly," said Carlton Bartels, director of Cantor Fitzgerald Environmental Brokerage Services in New York, citing the price that prevailed in over-the-counter trading as recently as December.
>
> The auction and the over-the-counter trading are outgrowths of the Clean Air Act of 1990, which mandated reductions in the overall levels of sulfur dioxide emitted by utilities, starting in 1995. It set up a market system to give the industry a way of reaching the goals as inexpensively as possible.

The market in pollution permits encourages utilities to switch to cleaner coal and to install air pollution control equipment or make operating changes to reduce pollution.

The utilities can sell allowances they do not need to other utilities that might find it cheaper to buy the permits rather than take action to cut pollution. Such utilities might, for example, be far from sources of low-sulfur coal or have older plants not well suited to renovation.

When the Clean Air Act passed in 1990, the allowances were expected to trade for $300 to $750 each. Utility executives said then that meeting the air-quality requirements would cost their industry as much as $5 billion. Restrictions under the act were imposed on the worst polluters starting last year, but industrywide limits will not take effect until the year 2000.

What Congress did not anticipate in 1990 was that railroad deregulation would drastically cut the cost of shipping low-sulfur coal from the huge Powder River Basin deposits in Wyoming. The price of scrubbers, which grab pollutants out of smokestacks, has also fallen by 50 percent. And utilities have learned to be more efficient about blending different coals to cut pollution.

As the cost of reducing pollution fell, utilities accelerated their compliance programs, taking millions of tons of pollution out of the air sooner than expected. Indeed, the utilities put twice the required number of power plants into the program at the start in 1995, so that the utilities could get more of the pollution allowances issued directly by the E.P.A.

Some utilities have stockpiled enough allowances to defer spending hundreds of millions of dollars they would otherwise have had to spend to upgrade power plants before the tougher emissions limits take effect four years from now.

With pollution control costing less, the average price of an allowance at the Board of Trade auction has fallen from $159 in 1994 to the $132 of last year and to this year's projected result below $70. Between auctions, the over-the-counter price has steadily drifted downward as well.

"So far, procrastination has saved buyers money," Mr. Carlton said. The auction has become a headache for market makers like Mr. Carlton's firm. In the months preceding the auction, speculators sell short— that is, sell borrowed allowances—confident that in the flood of allowances released by the auction they will be able to buy back at prices below those in the spot market.

"The auction just inserts volatility," Mr. Carlton said. "It's a classic example of the Government harming a marketplace by trying to help it along."

But environmental organizations like Mr. Jaffe's group disagree. They see the opportunity to buy allowances as an important education tool and a practical if small way to reduce pollution. "The auction is a real democratizing feature," said Mr. Jaffe, whose group hopes to retire as many as 600 allowances this year.

BARNABY J. FEDER, Lower Bids Seen At Sale of Rights To Pollute Air, The New York Times March 23, 1996 (Section 1; Page 35; Column 5), Copyright 1996 The New York Times Company.

Difficulties can arise in such a permit marketing scheme, however. Indeed, under either a pollution tax, direct regulation, or a pollution permit market, someone must determine the optimal level of pollution. The relevant knowledge in this case is economic rather than technical. The government's interest is not in describing the damage done by varying degrees of air pollution, rather it is in determining the values individuals and our society attach to the different degrees of damage. Such knowledge is not easy to come by. Moreover, both the tax scheme and a pollution rights scheme, in a manner very similar to direct regulation, must be monitored and enforced by government. With such actions, tax evasion and pollution without permit will be serious problems.

D. Market Failures and Government Failures

In Chapter II, public choice economics was introduced as a theory of government failure. Political institutions often prevent economic regulations from achieving their theoretical goals. Accordingly, it is naive to expect imperfect markets to be replaced by perfect government regulations and perfect government regulators. In the following excerpt, Professor Terry Anderson challenges much of the conventional wisdom about governmental efforts to correct externalities.

The New Resource Economics: Old Ideas and New Applications
Terry L. Anderson
AMERICAN JOURNAL OF AGRICULTURAL ECONOMICS, Vol. 64, No. 5, December 1982

*   *   *

In this paper I will first argue why the existing way of thinking would benefit from reform. Following this I will integrate property rights, public choice, and Austrian economics with the standard neoclassical paradigm thereby identifying the salient components of NRE. Finally, evidence will be presented to support why NRE is gaining support.

Old Resource Economics (ORE)
Until recently the vast majority of the writing in natural resource economics has been confined to the neoclassical paradigm. The central elements of this paradigm are (a) marginal analysis, (b) information and uncertainty, (c) interest theory.

The marginal revolution in the late 1800s formed the watershed between classical and neoclassical economics. From Jevons to Samuelson, we have learned that economic decisions involve a comparison of marginal benefits with marginal costs. Until sufficient action has been taken to equate the two, optimization cannot be attained. Once this principle is mastered, it becomes clear that many incremental adjustments are possible and that neither demand nor supply are perfectly inelastic. Barnett and Morse drove this point home by demonstrating that substitution holds the key to mitigating the impacts of resource scarcity.

In recognizing that these incremental adjustments take place in a world with uncertainty and imperfect information, neoclassical economists have extended the model to incorporate these problems. The extension has basically taken two courses. First, following marginal analysis, the economics of information suggests that there is an optimal amount of search put into collecting information. In this sense, information is produced like any other input. Since any given decision maker will not have an infinite amount of free information available, actual equilibrium results will differ from those derived from textbook models. The second course has been to consider how expectations are formed and how risk preferences affect decisions. Again, the emphasis has been on marginal analysis with equilibrium depending on the formation of rational expectation.

Since most decisions involve some degree of allocation over time, the time preference of individuals and the time productivity of resources are crucial for determining intertemporal allocation. The work in the 1930s by Fisher and Hotelling led economists to be skeptical of notions such as maximum sustained yield and to realize that natural resources, like other assets, will have prices related to the discount rate. The specific application of intertemporal choice to natural resources has dramatically changed how economists look at exhaustible and renewable resources.

The tools of ORE are those of scientific resource managers who hold that the marginal concepts provide an ideal way for formulating the multiple use problem. In this formulation, the optimal production mix in a management plan is the one where the values of various uses are equated at the margin. Since the managers using the concepts are not motivated by profit or by self-interest, it is hoped that they will apply economic theory and quantitative method in impartial and efficient ways to accomplish the goals of their respective agencies. The scientific managers propose agendas that "insist on real decentralization and real decision-authority,... rely on administration, not legislation,...[and] let professionals manage" * * * Since "politicizing land management and land managers...will lead to less professionalism and poor land management," scientific managers argue that they should be insulated from the political process. * * * Like the economist, the scientific manager armed with economic tools is supposed to be "always analytical....Always, the economist's reasoning, his *analytical* framework..., his data, and his conclusions are exposed forthrightly to the examination and criticism of others. In these ways, *scientific objectivity* is actively sought. Polemics, pamphleteering and outright advocacy are left to others, or to the economist in his nonprofessional role as a citizen and a human being." * * * But, * * * the resource manager cannot escape being an advocate and therefore cannot remain scientifically objective.

When managers do not act with objectivity, ORE economists have proposed perfecting bureaucracy. * * *

In summary, ORE generally has taught us that market failure is pervasive in natural resource allocation and that cost/benefit analysis applied by scientific, objective managers can improve on the failures. Building on marginal analysis, the neoclassical paradigm has lent itself well to mathematical modeling and statistical estimation, and many believe that the rigorous mathematical/statistical approach to economics allows shadow prices to be derived and used in lieu of actual market processes. Furthermore, government agencies, such as the Forest Service and Bureau of Land Management (BLM) are enamored with building models that generate sophisticated mathematical and statistical results designed to improve resource management. The assumption is that, given sufficient data and large enough computers, it is possible to produce wise (efficient?) management plans. * * *

Toward a New Resource Economics Paradigm

In contrast to ORE, NRE focuses attention on information and incentives which result from market and nonmarket institutions. Fisher captures the essence of NRE: "We have already abandoned the assumption of a complete set of competitive markets, leading to all the difficulties discussed earlier. But, if we now similarly abandon the notion of a perfect planner, it is not clear, in my judgment, that the government will do any better. Apart from the question of the planner's motivation to behave in the way assumed in our models, to allocate resources efficiently, there is the question of the ability to do so" (p. 54).

Because ORE pays little or no attention to institutions which structure and provide information and incentives, resource economists often seem surprised and puzzled at the fact that neoclassical policy implications are not more widely adopted in the policy arena. Such concepts are useful in the private sector because private decision makers have information in the form of market prices and incentives to act on that information. In the public sector neither of these conditions hold. The "products" which are being generated from public lands for the most part are zero priced. Given the lack of markets, the public lands manager is forced to make marginal comparisons without the benefit of information contained in prices. This lack of economic information forces the public land manager into trading off in terms of political currencies, and this currency, at best, provides distorted measures of value.

The second problem for public resource management is that the incentive structure in the public sector is quite different from that in the private sector. In the private sector individuals in the decision process are residual claimants. * * * This means that someone receives the residual which is left after all costs have been paid. The owner/residual claimant has an incentive to discover good information and use that information to improve efficiency which in turn enhances the residual claim. In the public sector, however, there is no residual claimant. The rewards for public land managers are not dependent on maximizing the net value of joint production. While there is not total agreement in the economics literature about what is maximized by bureaucrats, it is agreed that efficiency is not the main goal of decision makers. If the public resource manager were to follow the tenets of joint production theory, it would have to be because they were honest, sincere folks interested in the public interest and not because of self-interest.

Because information and incentives have not been emphasized in the ORE, the standard neoclassical paradigm can be improved on by incorporating elements of property rights, public choice, and Austrian economics. While this NRE paradigm is by no means complete, it is being extended to bring more reality to natural resource economics. What follows is a brief synthesis of that emerging way of thinking.

The starting point for the new paradigm is the individual — especially the entrepreneur. Following marginal analysis, entrepreneurs search for situations where marginal benefits and actions exceed marginal costs. Their responsiveness to opportunities moves resources to higher valued alternatives and improved efficiency and thus moves the system closer to equilibrium. The question is whether the opportunities they discover and the actions they take will increase the size of the pie for society.

If entrepreneurs face the full opportunity costs of their actions, they will take only those actions that produce positive net benefits for themselves and for society. The entrepreneur who discovers a higher valued use for timber, for example, stands to gain. If allocation to that higher use requires the entrepreneur to bear the opportunity costs of current use, the reallocation will only take place if the net difference is positive. Responsibility for opportunity costs is the key.

The property rights structure will determine who is responsible for which opportunity costs. If these rules are to govern market allocation of natural resources, property rights must be well-defined, enforced, and transferable. When property rights are well-defined, individuals have a clear idea of what actions they can take regarding resources. This is necessary for market trades, which depend on interested parties knowing what is being traded.

Enforcement will determine how likely it is that an owner can enjoy the benefits of his ownership. Since rights cannot be perfectly enforced, ownership will always be probabilistic; but when the probability of capturing benefits from a use is low, it is less likely that the owner will devote the resource to that use. For example, if a water owner decides to leave water in the stream to improve fish habitat but is unable to exclude fishermen who do not pay for using the stream, he will have less incentive to provide water for that use. In this sense, enforcement is the ability to exclude other users. As long as exclusion is possible, resource owners can capture the benefits from the various uses of their resources.

If the owner is to be fully aware of the opportunity costs of his actions, property rights must be transferable. When the owner is not allowed to transfer his resource to another use, he will not consider the full opportunity costs of the other use. If the other use has a higher value, that value will be ignored, and inefficiency will result. Various land use regulations restrict the transfer of ownership rights, and laws forbidding the use of water in coal slurry pipeline tell the water owner that he must ignore the value of water in this use. Even if water used for a coal slurry is more valuable than for irrigation, the owner cannot capture the higher value. Again, well-defined, enforced, and transferable property rights must be included in the rules of the game if entrepreneurial efforts are to enlarge the size of the pie.

At this point, it is important to emphasize that all decisions are made under uncertainty and that mistakes will be made. When an entrepreneur moves a resource from one use to another, he does so with the expectation that the new use has a higher value. This expectation depends on the entrepreneur's subjective evaluation of the world. The basic economic problem, therefore, becomes one of utilizing "knowledge which is not given to anyone in totality." * * * As Hayek points out, the refinements in the neoclassical model have tended to divert attention from this problem and focused attention on the possibility of planning. When we realize that knowledge is dispersed and cannot be condensed into a single variable for planning purposes and that entrepreneurs are making decisions based on their "best guess" about the future, we must recognize that decisions may not be efficient *ex post*.

The second thing to remember about uncertainty is that there is an optimal amount of search. To the extent that entrepreneurs can gather information to reduce uncertainty, they will do so to the point where the expected additional benefits from the search activity are equal to the expected additional costs. Of course, given varying preferences, what may be the optimal amount of search for one entrepreneur may be different for another, so it will be easy for outsiders to argue that better decisions could result if more information were collected. But optimal search tells us that perfect information is not the norm to which we should compare the real world.

In this context, it is useful to consider market systems as information systems. By consistently seeking out the margins within which they can improve their welfare, purposive actors search for substitutes for scarce resources and attempt to move resources to more highly valued uses. In this context the ultimate resource becomes the creative potential of self-interested individuals. When increased relative scarcity is translated into increased potential profits, the creative energies of entrepreneurs are unleashed.

With well-defined, enforced, and transferable property rights, the entrepreneur is part of a pie-enlarging process; but what if private property rights do not exist and there is a gap between authority and responsibility? To answer this question, remember that the entrepreneur is continually searching for unforeseen opportunities that will generate rents for himself. An efficient property rights system insures that the entrepreneurial process will create rents, thus producing the only free lunch available to society. But the entrepreneur is not concerned with whether he is creating a free lunch or dining at someone else's expense. Imagine that the entrepreneur faces two opportunities for success: one in which rents can be created only through improved allocation of privately owned resources and one in which rents are derived from exploiting a common pool resource or from transfers available from government.

First, consider the economics of a common pool resource. Traditional natural resource literature has made us keenly aware of the inefficiency associated with the "tragedy of the commons." * * * Exploiting the common pool resource will benefit the individual, but it will be a negative-sum game for society.

The second opportunity for entrepreneurs to participate in a negative-sum game is for them to engage in rent seeking. Simply put, rent seeking includes efforts to use the coercive power of the government to increase personal wealth for some at the expense of others. For example, when a group of producers succeeds in getting the state to license all producers and, thereby, restricts entry, monopoly rents will be earned. Since these rents come at the expense of the consumer, they represent a redistribution of wealth. Hence, both producers and consumers will invest entrepreneurial talents and other resources in efforts to prevent or obtain the transfer. The "taking issue" in land-use planning is an excellent example of this process. Zoning restrictions in many cases represent a redistribution of rights. Similarly, when the Department of Interior decides whether public lands will be used for timber, grazing, recreation, or wildlife, they are affecting the distribution of benefits to consumers. It is not surprising that interest groups employ valuable resources trying to influence these decisions. When the entrepreneur discovers unforeseen opportunities to use government to increase his wealth, rent creation—a positive-sum game—is replaced with rent seeking—a negative-sum game.

While such entrepreneurial efforts explain the demand for rent-seeking, the activities of politicians and bureaucrats explain the supply. Just as entrepreneurs in the marketplace recognize and fill demands for goods and services, politicians and bureaucrats discover previously unforeseen opportunities to meet the demands of various constituencies. In both cases, niches are being filled, but the constraints on each are very different. For the successful entrepreneur in the marketplace, new goods and services can only be provided if the benefits from those goods and services exceed the opportunity costs of the resources used in production. Private property rights provide a reality check on the entrepreneur.

In the political system, however, the politician or bureaucrat who provides goods and services to interest groups does not have to pay the opportunity cost of expended resources. Property rights to resources that are "owned" by the government are only informally defined and can be disputed at every legislative session. For example, the Forest Service "owns" vast amounts of timberland, and rights to use these lands are informally held by the groups who derive benefits from them. Since these rights are informal, if timber interests, for example, want an increase in the allowable cut, they can attempt to convince bureaucrats to take rights away from recreation and environmental groups. If the bureaucrat does so, he might be concerned with alienating the losing groups, but he does not have to face the full opportunity costs.

Each bureaucrat, in seeking to maximize budgetary discretion, realizes that he has access to the common pool treasury of the government. * * * He asks the question, "What is the gain to my organization (and, hence, to me) of capturing more from the treasury?" The bureaucrat, the agency, and the constituency enjoy the benefits of an increased budget, while the costs are spread among all other bureaucracies in terms of lost opportunities. In order to increase his agency's capture, each bureaucrat must find ways to increase the magnitude and scope of agency activity. As a result, they pursue programs that concentrate benefits while dispersing costs, thereby building up a constituency for increased agency activities.

Since opportunity costs are not internalized in the political allocation process, there is no direct reality check on whether a given situation can be improved on. Therefore, it is possible for enterprising politicians and bureaucrats to pursue inefficient policies; witness the water project pork barrel. The economies of public choice has taught us to view public sector activities as we might any others. Politicians and bureaucrats have objectives that they are trying to maximize, such as votes, budgets, power, prestige, and discretion. While it is not clear which goal may be dominant, it is clear that public servants generally are not trying to maximize efficiency. As they pursue these goals through collective action, the cost functions they face differ from those where voluntary consent is required. Collective action essentially allows those who bear the costs to be separated from those who receive the benefits.

Building on the premise that actors in the political system are as likely as those in the private sector to be motivated by self-interest, the public choice paradigm has taught us to think in terms of rational voter ignorance, special interest effects, and shortsightedness effects from politicians. Hence, the information and incentive structures are as likely to generate governmental failure as they are to generated market failure. Not only does inefficiency result, but entrepreneurial talents are expended by interest groups trying to influence political decisions and by politicians and bureaucrats trying to supply political benefits. Without the reality check inherent in the private property system, the potential for negative-sum games is real.

The Value of NRE

Applications of the NRE paradigm are only beginning to emerge, but those applications raise two important questions. First, how pervasive is market failure in the natural resource area? Second, has collective action actually improved on market allocation, however imperfect market processes may be? A few brief examples of answers to these questions are all that space permits.

ORE has focused on market failure due to open access, public goods, and externalities; NRE, on the other hand, has recognized the potential for private contracting to correct market failure. The property rights literature has improved our understanding of the evolution of property rights and contracts. * * * By considering the wide range of contract options available in the market, we have been forced to reexamine bees pollinating apple blossoms as an example of an externality...and lighthouses as an example of a public good...Furthermore, it has been shown that well-established private rights to Great Lakes timber resulted in efficient markets rather than the "rape and run" tactics alleged by conservationists....

NRE is also focusing on market responses to environmental quality. Baden and Stroup brought to our attention the Audubon Society's Rainy Wildlife Sanctuary, where natural gas has been extracted since the 1960s with no significant diminution of environmental quality. As a residual claimant, the National Audubon Society has an incentive to cooperate with oil companies and vice versa. In that particular case, coordination and cooperation have been substituted for the challenge and conflict inherent in the public planning process. As the value of wildlife has risen along with other amenities, private efforts to improve management have been undertaken. Groups such as the Nature Conservancy and Trout Unlimited have increase their efforts to improve wildlife habitat. The International Paper Company recognizes that proper management of game can increase the income potential of timberlands. With land holdings of seven million acres, it is not surprising that IP is investing in this possibility. It should be noted that all of these examples commonly fall under the ORE category of market failure.

NRE is also documenting the existence of government failure. A book entitled *Bureaucracy vs. Environment* (Baden and Stroup 1981) documents energy policies that promote such programs as synfuels production, legislation that promotes overgrazing of BLM land, timber production that has negative value, and rest-rotation grazing and chaining practices that destroy the environment on federal grazing land. Higgs has shown how fishery management has led to technical regress and salmon harvests that have negative net social value.

The Future of NRE

In this paper I have attempted to draw together the essential ingredients of neoclassical, property rights, public choice, and Austrian economics to construct a new, systematic approach to natural resource economics. When old paradigms no longer adequately explain the world, it is necessary to seek alternatives. The marginal conditions derived from complex ORE models have little value for policy decisions because they have implicitly assumed that knowledge is given and that it will be used by dispassionate, highly organized, professional technicians who care primarily about efficiency. While such models may explain what an efficient world should look like, they tell us very little about why we have failed to attain the "bliss point." While NRE may be nothing more than new applications of old ideas, it does offer an alternative view of the world. It sets a new agenda for research from which testable hypotheses must be generated and evidence to test the hypotheses must be mustered.

It should be emphasized that NRE, like ORE, recognizes the possibility of market failure. The existence of market failure, however, does not necessarily call for a nonmarket alternative. * * * [T]he relevant comparison is between imperfect market solutions and imperfect bureaucratic solutions. Good NRE gives the kind of rigorous theoretical and empirical attention to government failure that ORE has given to market failure; this compares real-world alternatives rather than unattainable ideals.

In terms of Randall's groupings quoted at the beginning of this paper, NRE lies on the free-market side of the middle; but the new resource economists are not necessarily zealots. Perhaps the users of NRE present the paradigm with ardor and enthusiasm partially based on faith in inductive and deductive reasoning. This faith, however, is derived from what is seen as a preponderance of evidence supporting the efficiency of the market processes. If the NRE is to flourish, it must be subjected to systematic testing.

Notes and Questions

1. Externalities and Residual Claims: Externalities exist because of poorly defined property rights, high transaction costs, or some combination of the two. The NRE structure is based on incentives and information. In this regard, government ownership of natural resources looks a lot like poorly defined property rights—everyone owns the national forests, so no one owns them. Moreover, because the government managers are not residual claimants, they do not have the incentive to maximize the value of the forest. Absent some objective way to measure their performance, government policies are particularly susceptible to political meddling.

2. Property Rights and Non-Profits: Anderson points to National Audubon Society's Rainy Wildlife Sanctuary as an example of where private ownership has resulted in a better balancing of environmental and commercial interests. Should non-profit organizations be trusted with protecting the public interest? Who owns the non-profits? What individuals are the residual claimants?

Chapter VII

Economics of Information

Information is necessary to the proper functioning of any market. Information, however, is scarce and costly to obtain. Individuals invest in information gathering up to the point where the expected marginal benefits of collecting additional information equal the marginal costs of collecting additional information. This suggests that, in many instances, individuals will act without complete information; that is, rational individuals will act when uncertain about the results of their action. The positive costs of information means that individuals gamble on their decision making.

In most cases, either the costs of collecting information or the costs of acting without complete information are trivial. This is especially true for frequently purchased products, such as individual food products in the grocery store. On the other hand, the technical characteristics of many goods and services make it very difficult (that is, costly) for purchasers to gather the amount of information necessary to make satisfactory choices. For example, most purchasers do not possess the technical expertise to evaluate the quality of automobiles, washing machines, televisions, doctors, lawyers, and so forth. Because mistakes in the purchasing of such goods and services can be very expensive, consumers gather information from numerous sources, including sales staff, *Consumer Reports*, as well as friends and relatives. Moreover, sellers attempt to convey information to consumers by developing reputations for providing the level of quality that the consumer desires.

This chapter considers how market participants function when confronted with scarce and costly information. Section A considers the public good characteristics of information. Section B deals with bargaining and information in the context of the contract law doctrines of mistake and impossibility. Section C presents an overview of market responses to asymmetric information. Section D considers consumer search costs and the economics of advertising. Section E introduces agent-principal contracting and the economics of monitoring performance. Section F presents game theory as an explanation for much of economic behavior.

A. Information as a Public Good

Information is scarce and costly to produce. Once produced, however, it is difficult to exclude others from using the information. Information has the public good characteristic of nonexcludability. Because it is difficult for producers of information to prevent others from appropriating the value of the information, there is a concern that a public-good type of market failure could lead to an underproduction of socially-beneficial information. One widely-used solution to this concern is the legal creation of a right of excludability through intellectual property law—copyright, patent, trademark, and the common law of trade secrets.

International News Service v. Associated Press
Supreme Court of the United States
248 U.S. 215 (1918)

PITNEY, J.

The parties are competitors in the gathering and distribution of news and its publication for profit in newspapers throughout the United States. The Associated Press, which was complainant in the District Court, is a co-operative organization, incorporated under the Membership Corporations Law of the state of New York, its members being individuals who are either proprietors or representatives of about 950 daily newspapers published in all parts of the United States... Complainant gathers in all parts of the world, by means of various instrumentalities of its own, by exchange with its members, and by other appropriate means, news and intelligence of current and recent events of interest to newspaper readers and distributes it daily to its members for publication in their newspapers. The cost of the service, amounting approximately to $3,500,000 per annum, is assessed upon the members and becomes a part of their costs of operation, to be recouped, presumably with profit, through the publication of their several newspapers. Under complainant's by-laws each member agrees upon assuming membership that news received through complainant's service is received exclusively for publication in a particular newspaper, language, and place specified in the certificate of membership, that no other use of it shall be permitted, and that no member shall furnish or permit any one in his employ or connected with his newspaper to furnish any of complainant's news in advance of publication to any person not a member. And each member is required to gather the local news of his district and supply it to the Associated Press and to no one else.

Defendant is a corporation organized under the laws of the state of New Jersey, whose business is the gathering and selling of news to its customers and clients, consisting of newspapers published throughout the United States, under contracts by which they pay certain amounts at stated times for defendant's service. It has widespread news-gathering agencies; the cost of its operations amounts, it is said, to more than $2,000,000 per annum; and it serves about 400 newspapers located in the various cities of the United States and abroad, a few of which are represented, also, in the membership of the Associated Press.

The parties are in the keenest competition between themselves in the distribution of news throughout the United States; and so, as a rule, are the newspapers that they serve, in their several districts.

Complainant in its bill, defendant in its answer, have set forth in almost identical terms the rather obvious circumstances and conditions under which their business is conducted. The value of the service, and of the news furnished, depends upon the promptness of transmission, as well as upon the accuracy and impartiality of the news; it being essential that the news be transmitted to members or subscribers as early or earlier than similar information can be furnished to competing newspapers by other news services, and that the news furnished by each agency shall not be furnished to newspapers which do not contribute to the expense of gathering it. And further, to quote from the answer: "Prompt knowledge and publication of worldwide news is essential to the conduct of a modern newspaper, and by reason of the enormous expense incident to the gathering and distribution of such news, the only practical way in which a proprietor of a newspaper can obtain the same is, either through co-operation with a considerable number of other newspaper proprietors in the work of collecting and distributing such news, and the equitable division with them of the expenses thereof, or by the purchase of such news from some existing agency engaged in that business."

The bill was filed to restrain the pirating of complainant's news by defendant in three ways: First, by bribing employees of newspapers published by complainant's members to furnish Associated Press news to defendant before publication, for transmission by telegraph and telephone to defendant's clients for publication by them; second, by inducing Associated Press members to violate its by-laws and permit defendant to obtain news before publication; and, third, by copying news from bulletin boards and from early editions of complainant's newspapers and selling this, either bodily or after rewriting it, to defendant's customers.

*   *   *

The only matter that has been argued before us is whether defendant may lawfully be restrained from appropriating news taken from bulletins issued by complainant or any of its members, or from newspapers published by them, for the purpose of selling it to defendant's clients. Complainant asserts that defendant's admitted course of conduct in this regard both violates complainant's property right in the news and constitutes unfair competition in business. And notwithstanding the case has proceeded only to the stage of a preliminary injunction, we have deemed it proper to consider the underlying questions, since they go to the very merits of the action and are presented upon facts that are not in dispute. As presented in argument, these questions are: 1. Whether there is any property in news; 2. Whether, if there be property in news collected for the purpose of being published, it survives the instant of its publication in the first newspaper to which it is communicated by the news-gatherer; and 3. whether defendant's admitted course of conduct in appropriating for commercial use matter taken from bulletins or early editions of Associated Press publications constitutes unfair competition in trade.

*   *   *

In considering the general question of property in news matter, it is necessary to recognize its dual character, distinguishing between the substance of the information and the particular form or collocation of words in which the writer has communicated it.

No doubt news articles often possess a literary quality, and are the subject of literary property at the common law; nor do we question that such an article, as a literary production, is the subject of copyright by the terms of the act as it now stands....

But the news element—the information respecting current events contained in the literary production—is not the creation of the writer, but is a report of matters that ordinarily are *publici juris*; it is the history of the day. It is not to be supposed that the framers of the Constitution, when they empowered Congress "to promote the progress of science and useful arts, by securing for limited times to authors and inventors the exclusive right to their respective writings and discoveries" (Const. art. 1, § 8, par. 8), intended to confer upon one who might happen to be the first to report a historic event the exclusive right for any period to spread the knowledge of it.

We need spend no time, however, upon the general question of property in news matter at common law, or the application of the copyright act, since it seems to us the case must turn upon the question of unfair competition in business. * * *

Obviously, the question of what is unfair competition in business must be determined with particular reference to the character and circumstances of the business. The question here is not so much the rights of either party as against the public but their rights as between themselves. See *Morison v. Moat*, 9 Hare, 241, 258. And, although we may and do assume that neither party has any remaining property interest as against the public in uncopyrighted news matter after the moment of its first publication, it by no means follows that there is no remaining property interest in it as between themselves. For, to both of them alike, news matter, however little susceptible of ownership or dominion in the absolute sense, is stock in trade, to be gathered at the cost of enterprise, organization, skill, labor, and money, and to be distributed and sold to those who will pay money for it, as for any other merchandise. Regarding the news, therefore, as but the material out of which both parties are seeking to make profits at the same time and in the same field, we hardly can fail to recognize that for this purpose, and as between them, it must be regarded as quasi property, irrespective of the rights of either as against the public.

*   *   *

The question, whether one who has gathered general information or news at pains and expense for the purpose of subsequent publication through the press has such an interest in its publication as may be protected from interference, has been raised many times, although never, perhaps, in the precise form in which it is now presented.

*   *   *

Not only do the acquisition and transmission of news require elaborate organization and a large expenditure of money, skill, and effort; not only has it an exchange value to the gatherer, dependent chiefly upon its novelty and freshness, the regularity of the service, its reputed reliability and thoroughness, and its adaptability to the public needs; but also, as is evident, the news has an exchange value to one who can misappropriate it.

The peculiar features of the case arise from the fact that, while novelty and freshness form so important an element in the success of the business, the very processes of distribution and publication necessarily occupy a good deal of time. Complainant's service, as well as defendant's, is a daily service to daily newspapers; most of the foreign news reaches this country at the Atlantic seaboard, principally at the city of New York, and because of this, and of time differentials due to the earth's rotation, the distribution of news matter throughout the country is principally from east to west; and, since in speed the telegraph and telephone easily outstrip the rotation of the earth, it is a simple matter for defendant to take complainant's news from bulletins or early editions of complainant's members in the eastern cities and at the mere cost of telegraphic transmission cause it to be published in western papers issued at least as early as those served by complainant. Besides this, and irrespective of time differentials, irregularities in telegraphic transmission on different lines, and the normal consumption of time in printing and distributing the newspaper, result in permitting pirated news to be placed in the hands of defendant's readers sometimes simultaneously with the service of competing Associated Press papers, occasionally even earlier.

Defendant insists that when, with the sanction and approval of complainant, and as the result of the use of its news for the very purpose for which it is distributed, a portion of complainant's members communicate it to the general public by posting it upon bulletin boards so that all may read, or by issuing it to newspapers and distributing it indiscriminately, complainant no longer has the right to control the use to be made of it; that when it thus reaches the light of day it becomes the common possession of all to whom it is accessible; and that any purchaser of a newspaper has the right to communicate the intelligence which it contains to anybody and for any purpose, even for the purpose of selling it for profit to newspapers published for profit in competition with complainant's members.

The fault in the reasoning lies in applying as a test the right of the complainant as against the public, instead of considering the rights of complainant and defendant, competitors in business, as between themselves. The right of the purchaser of a single newspaper to spread knowledge of its contents gratuitously, for any legitimate purpose not unreasonably interfering with complainant's right to make merchandise of it, may be admitted; but to transmit that news for commercial use, in competition with complainant—which is what defendant has done and seeks to justify—is a very different matter. In doing this defendant, by its very act, admits that it is taking material that has been acquired by complainant as the result of organization and the expenditure of labor, skill, and money, and which is salable by complainant for money, and that defendant in appropriating it and selling it as its own is endeavoring to reap where it has not sown, and by disposing of it to newspapers that are competitors of complainant's members is appropriating to itself the harvest of those who have sown. Stripped of all disguises, the process amounts to an unauthorized interference with the normal operation of complainant's legitimate business precisely at the point where the profit is to be reaped, in order to divert a material portion of the profit from those who have earned it to those who have not; with special advantage to defendant in the competition because of the fact that it is not burdened with any part of the expense of gathering the news. The transaction speaks for itself and a court of equity ought not to hesitate long in characterizing it as unfair competition in business.

The underlying principle is much the same as that which lies at the base of the equitable theory of consideration in the law of trusts—that he who has fairly paid the price should have the beneficial use of the property. Pom. Eq. Jur. § 981. It is no answer to say that complainant spends its money for that which is too fugitive or evanescent to be the subject of property. That might, and for the purposes of the discussion we are assuming that it would furnish an answer in a common-law controversy. But in a court of equity, where the question is one of unfair competition, if that which complainant has acquired fairly at substantial cost may be sold fairly at substantial profit, a competitor who is misappropriating it for the purpose of disposing of it to his own profit and to the disadvantage of complainant cannot be heard to say that it is too fugitive or evanescent to be regarded as property. It has all the attributes of property necessary for determining that a misappropriation of it by a competitor is unfair competition because [it is] contrary to good conscience.

The contention that the news is abandoned to the public for all purposes when published in the first newspaper is untenable. Abandonment is a question of intent, and the entire organization of the Associated Press negatives such a purpose. The cost of the service would be prohibited if the reward were to be so limited. No single newspaper, no small group of newspapers, could sustain the expenditure. Indeed, it is one of the most obvious results of defendant's theory that, by permitting indiscriminate publication by anybody and everybody for purposes of profit in competition with the news-gatherer, it would render publication profitless, or so little profitable as in effect to cut off the service by rendering the cost prohibitive in comparison with the return. The practical needs and requirements of the business are reflected in complainant's by-laws which have been referred to. Their effect is that publication by each member must be deemed not by any means an abandonment of the news to the world for any and all purposes, but a publication for limited purposes; for the benefit of the readers of the bulletin or the newspaper as such; not for the purpose of making merchandise of it as news, with the result of depriving complainant's other members of their reasonable opportunity to obtain just returns for their expenditures.

*   *   *

There is some criticism of the injunction that was directed by the District Court upon the going down of the mandate from the Circuit Court of Appeals. In brief, it restrains any taking or gainfully using of the complainant's news, either bodily or in substance from bulletins issued by the complainant or any of its members, or from editions of their newspapers, *"until its commercial value as news to the complainant and all of its members has passed away."* The part complained of is...indefinite, [yet] it is no more so than the criticism. Perhaps it would be better that the terms of the injunction be made specific, and so framed as to confine the restraint to an extent consistent with the reasonable protection of complainant's newspapers, each in its own area and for a specified time after its publication, against the competitive use of pirated news by defendant's customers. But the case presents practical difficulties; and we have not the materials, either in the way of a definite suggestion of amendment, or in the way of proofs, upon which to frame a specific injunction; hence, while not expressing approval of the form adopted by the District Court, we decline to modify it at this preliminary stage of the case, and will leave that court to deal with the matter upon appropriate application made to it for the purpose.

The decree of the Circuit court of Appeals will be Affirmed.

Mr. Justice HOLMES:

When an uncopyrighted combination of words is published there is no general right to forbid other people repeating them—in other words there is no property in the combination or in the thoughts or facts that the words express. Property, a creation of law, does not arise from value, although exchangeable—a matter of fact. Many exchangeable values may be destroyed intentionally without compensation. Property depends upon exclusion by law from interference, and a person is not excluded from using any combination of words merely because some one has used it before, even if it took labor and genius to make it. If a given person is to be prohibited from making the use of words that his neighbors are free to make some other ground must be found. One such ground is vaguely expressed in the phrase unfair trade. This means that the words are repeated by a competitor in business in such a way as to convey a misrepresentation that materially injures the person who first used them, by appropriating credit of some kind which the first user has earned. The ordinary case is a representation by device, appearance, or other indirection that the defendant's goods come from the plaintiff. But the only reason why it is actionable to make such a representation is that it tends to give the defendant an advantage in his competition with the plaintiff and that it is thought undesirable that an advantage should be gained in that way. Apart from that the defendant may use such unpatented devices and uncopyrighted combinations of words as he likes. The ordinary case, I say, is palming off the defendant's product as the plaintiff's but the same evil may follow from the opposite falsehood—from saying whether in words or by implication that the plaintiff's product is the defendant's, and that, it seems to me, is what has happened here.

Fresh news is got only by enterprise and expense. To produce such news as it is produced by the defendant represents by implication that it has been acquired by the defendant's enterprise and at its expense. When it comes from one of the great news collecting agencies like the Associated Press, the source generally is indicated, plainly importing that credit; and that such a representation is implied may be inferred with some confidence from the unwillingness of the defendant to give the credit and tell the truth. If the plaintiff produces the news at the same time that the defendant does, the defendant's presentation impliedly denies to the plaintiff the credit of collecting the facts and assumes that credit to the defendant. If the plaintiff is later in Western cities it naturally will be supposed to have obtained its information from the defendant. The falsehood is a little more subtle, the injury, a little more indirect, than in ordinary cases of unfair trade, but I think that the principle that condemns the one condemns the other. It is a question of how strong an infusion of fraud is necessary to turn a flavor into a poison. The [sic] does seems to me strong enough here to need a remedy from the law. But as, in my view, the only ground of complaint that can be recognized without legislation is the implied misstatement, it can be corrected by stating the truth; and a suitable acknowledgment of the source is all that the plaintiff can require. I think that within the limits recognized by the decision of the Court the defendant should be enjoined from publishing news obtained from the Associated Press for hours after publication by the plaintiff unless it gives express credit to the Associated Press; the number of hours and the form of acknowledgment to be settled by the District Court.

Mr. Justice McKENNA concurs in this opinion.

Mr. Justice BRANDEIS dissenting.

*   *   *

No question of statutory copyright is involved. The sole question for our consideration is this: Was the International News Service properly enjoined from using, or causing to be used gainfully, news of which it acquired knowledge by lawful means (namely, by reading publicly posted bulletins or papers purchased by it in the open market) merely because the news had been originally gathered by the Associated Press and continued to be of value to some of its members, or because it did not reveal the source from which it was acquired?

*   *   *

News is a report of recent occurrences. The business of the news agency is to gather systematically knowledge of such occurrences of interest and to distribute reports thereof. The Associated Press contended that knowledge so acquired is property, because it costs money and labor to produce and because it has value for which those who have it not are ready to pay; that it remains property and is entitled to protection as long as it has commercial value as news; and that to protect it effectively, the defendant must be enjoined from making, or causing to be made, any gainful use of it while it retains such value. An essential element of individual property is the legal right to exclude others from enjoying it. If the property is private, the right of exclusion may be absolute; if the property is affected with a public interest, the right of exclusion is qualified. But the fact that a product of the mind has cost its producer money and labor, and has a value for which others are willing to pay, is not sufficient to ensure to it this legal attribute of property. The general rule of law is, that the noblest of human productions—knowledge, truths ascertained, conceptions, and ideas—became, after voluntary communication to others, free as the air to common use. Upon these incorporeal productions the attribute of property is continued after such communication only in certain classes of cases where public policy has seemed to demand it. These exceptions are confined to productions which, in some degree, involve creation, invention, or discovery. But by no means all such are endowed with this attribute of property. The creations which are recognized as property by the common law are literary, dramatic, musical, and other artistic creations; and these have also protection under the copyright statutes. The inventions and discoveries upon which this attribute of property is conferred only by statute, are the few comprised within the patent law. There are also many other cases in which courts interfere to prevent curtailment of plaintiff's enjoyment of incorporeal productions; and in which the right to relief is often called a property right, but is such only in a special sense. In those cases, the plaintiff has no absolute right to the protection of his production; he has merely the qualified right to be protected as against the defendant's acts, because of the special relation in which the latter stands or the wrongful method or means employed in acquiring the knowledge or the manner in which it is used. Protection of this character is afforded where the suit is based upon breach of contract or of trust or upon unfair competition.

The knowledge for which protection is sought in the case at bar is not of a kind upon which the law has heretofore conferred the attributes of property; nor is the manner of its acquisition or use nor the purpose to which it is applied, such as has heretofore been recognized as entitling a plaintiff to relief.

*   *   *

…Plaintiff further contended that defendant's practice constitutes unfair competition, because there is "appropriation without cost to itself of values created by" the plaintiff; and it is upon this ground that the decision of this court appears to be based. To appropriate and use for profit, knowledge and ideas produced by other men, without making compensation or even acknowledgment, may be inconsistent with a finer sense of propriety; but, with the exceptions indicated above, the law has heretofore sanctioned the practice. Thus it was held that one may ordinarily make and sell anything in any form, may copy with exactness that which another has produced, or may otherwise use his ideas without his consent and without the payment of compensation, and yet not inflict a legal injury; and that ordinarily one is at perfect liberty to find out, if he can by lawful means, trade secrets of another, however valuable, and then use the knowledge so acquired gainfully, although it cost the original owner much in effort and in money to collect or produce.

*   *   *

It is also suggested that the fact that defendant does not refer to the Associated Press as the source of the news may furnish a basis for the relief. But the defendant and its subscribers, unlike members of the Associated Press, were under no contractual obligation to disclose the source of the news; and there is no rule of law requiring acknowledgment to be made where uncopyrighted matter is reproduced....

*   *   *

...The great development of agencies now furnishing country-wide distribution of news, the vastness of our territory, and improvements in the means of transmitting intelligence, have made it possible for a news agency or newspapers to obtain, without paying compensation, the fruit of another's efforts and to use news so obtained gainfully in competition with the original collector. The injustice of such action is obvious. But to give relief against it would involve more than the application of existing rules of law to new facts. It would require the making of a new rule in analogy to existing ones....

The rule for which the plaintiff contends would effect an important extension of property rights and a corresponding curtailment of the free use of knowledge and of ideas; and the facts of this case admonish us of the danger involved in recognizing such a property right in news, without imposing upon news-gatherers corresponding obligations....

*   *   *

A legislature, urged to enact a law by which one news agency or newspaper may prevent appropriation of the fruits of its labors by another, would consider such facts and possibilities and others which appropriate inquiry might disclose. Legislators might conclude that it was impossible to put an end to the obvious injustice involved in such appropriation of news, without opening the door to other evils, greater than that sought to be remedied....

Or legislators dealing with the subject might conclude, that the right to news values should be protected to the extent of permitting recovery of damages for any unauthorized use, but that protection by injunction should be denied, just as courts of equity ordinarily refuse (perhaps in the interest of free speech) to restrain actionable libels, and for other reasons decline to protect by injunction mere political rights; and as Congress has prohibited courts from enjoining the illegal assessment or collection of federal taxes. If a Legislature concluded to recognize property in published news to the extent of permitting recovery at law, it might, with a view to making the remedy more certain and adequate, provide a fixed measure of damages, as in the case of copyright infringement.

Or again, a legislature might conclude that it was unwise to recognize even so limited a property right in published news as that above indicated; but that a news agency should, on some conditions, be given full protection of its business;

and to that end a remedy by injunction as well as one for damages should be granted, where news collected by it is gainfully used without permission. If a legislature concluded (as at least one court has held, *New York & Chicago Grain & Stock Exchange v. Board of Trade*, 127 Ill. 153, that under certain circumstances news-gathering is a business affected with a public interest; it might declare that, in such cases, news should be protected against appropriation, only if the gatherer assumed the obligation of supplying it at reasonable rates and without discrimination, to all papers which applied therefor. If legislators reached that conclusion, they would probably go further, and prescribe the conditions under which and the extent to which the protection should be afforded; and they might also provide the administrative machinery necessary for insuring to the public, the press, and the news agencies, full enjoyment of the rights so conferred.

Courts are ill-equipped to make the investigations which should precede a determination of the limitations which should be set upon any property right in news or of the circumstances under which news gathered by a private agency should be deemed affected with a public interest. Courts would be powerless to prescribe the detailed regulations essential to full enjoyment of the rights conferred or to introduce the machinery required for enforcement of such regulations. Considerations such as these should lead us to decline to establish a new rule of law in the effort to redress a newly disclosed wrong, although the propriety of some remedy appears to be clear.

Notes and Questions

1. Public Good Characteristics of Information: Recall from Chapter VI that a public good is nonrivalrous in consumption and nonexcludable. Does the information gathered by the Associated Press satisfy these criteria? Justice Brandeis characterized the gathered information, once it has been disseminated, as "free as the air to common use." Certainly, newspaper readers are nonrivalrous in consumption, but it appears that pirating of the information is rivalrous because it reduces the ability of Associated Press to earn a return on its investment in news gathering. The issue in the case is, of course, whether or not it is excludable.

2. Static v. Dynamic Benefits of Property Rights: Once a news story has been reported, failure to recognize a property interest in that particular story does not impact the behavior that has already occurred. However, the dynamic effect of not enforcing a property right is to reduce the news organizations' incentives to set up news gathering networks in the first instance. As a consequence, less news will be reported. The trade-off is between the optimal incentives to gather the information versus the optimal incentives to use the information once it has been gathered. Justice Brandeis opines that the Court is actually creating new rules on value and property rights rather than expressing old values of law. The Court is stretching past doctrine to reach their goal of economic incentives through the protection of intellectual property. Has the Court adopted a forward-looking *ex ante* perspective?

3. The Optimal Amount of Protection for Intellectual Property Rights: In a recent dissenting opinion, Judge Alex Kozinski suggested that there could be too much protection for intellectual property rights:

> Saddam Hussein wants to keep advertisers from using his picture in unflattering contexts. Clint Eastwood doesn't want tabloids to write

about him. Rudolf Valentino's heirs want to control his film biography. The Girl Scouts don't want their image soiled by association with certain activities. George Lucas wants to keep Strategic Defense Initiative fans from calling it "Star Wars." PepsiCo doesn't want singers to use the word "Pepsi" in their songs. Guy Lombardo wants an exclusive property right to ads that show big bands playing on New Year's Eve. Uri Geller thinks he should be paid for ads showing psychics bending metal through telekinesis. Paul Prudhomme, that household name, thinks the same about ads featuring corpulent bearded chefs. And scads of copyright holders see purple when their creations are made fun of.

Something very dangerous is going on here. Private property, including intellectual property, is essential to our way of life. It provides an incentive for investment and innovation; it stimulates the flourishing of our culture; it protects the moral entitlements of people to the fruits of their labors. But reducing too much to private property can be bad medicine. Private land, for instance, is far more useful if separated from other private land by public streets, roads and highways. Public parks, utility rights-of-way and sewers reduce the amount of land in private hands, but vastly enhance the value of the property that remains.

So too it is with intellectual property. Overprotecting intellectual property is as harmful as underprotecting it. Creativity is impossible without a rich public domain. Nothing today, likely nothing since we tamed fire, is genuinely new: Culture, like science and technology, grows by accretion, each new creator building on the works of those who came before. Overprotection stifles the very creative forces it's supposed to nurture.

*   *   *

...Intellectual property rights aren't free: They're imposed at the expense of future creators and of the public at large. Where would we be if Charles Lindbergh had an exclusive right in the concept of a heroic solo aviator? If Arthur Conan Doyle had gotten a copyright in the idea of the detective story, or Albert Einstein had patented the theory of relativity? If every author and celebrity had been given the right to keep people from mocking them or their work? Surely this would have made the world poorer, not richer, culturally as well as economically.

This is why intellectual property law is full of careful balances between what's set aside for the owner and what's left in the public domain for the rest of us: The relatively short life of patents; the longer, but finite, life of copyrights; copyright's idea-expression dichotomy; the fair use doctrine; the prohibition on copyrighting facts; the compulsory license of television broadcasts and musical compositions; federal preemption of overbroad state intellectual property laws; the nominative use doctrine in trademark law; the right to make soundalike recordings. All of these diminish an intellectual property owner's rights. All let the public use something created by someone else. But all are necessary to maintain a free environment in which creative genius can flourish.

White v. Samsung Electronics America, Inc., 989 F.2d 1512 (1993) (Kozinski, Circuit Judge, dissenting). Are the dissenting opinions in INS engaged in the same type of trade-off analysis?

4. Value as Property: Justice Holmes states that property does not arise from value, yet he acknowledges that International News Service (INS) had damaged Associated Press (AP) because of the unfair advantage INS gained competitively. Holmes implies that if INS had cited AP for their stories then everything would be fine. However, would the court reach the same verdict if all INS had to do was cite AP, or would INS still have to pay AP for the right to use the stories? The majority implies that value creates property rights.

B. Bargaining, Information, and the Contract Law Doctrines of Mistake and Impossibility

Because information is intangible, it is often difficult (that is, costly) or impossible to determine whether an individual knows something or doesn't. This fact, of course, makes bargaining and negotiation sessions difficult and interesting. It also makes for some interesting litigation because two important defenses to contract formation turn on the basic question of who knew (or should have known) what. Mistake (mutual or unilateral) and impossibility are the defenses under which a court will excuse a promisor from performance. One way to distinguish mistake and impossibility cases is that mistake deals with the materialization of an endogenous risk (such as the parties' realization that the subject of the contract is of different make or model of automobile than they had thought) and impossibility deals with performance made burdensome by an exogenous event (such as a dramatic, unprecedented increase in prices caused by some unpredictable event beyond the control of the contracting parties). As with any potential excuse from performance, one must be careful to make sure that an opportunistic promisor does not use the excuse to take advantage of changed circumstances—usually the result of new information or dramatic changes in market conditions.

1. Mistake

A precondition for mutually beneficial exchange is that the parties understand and agree on what is being exchanged. Obviously, if one or both of the parties were mistaken about the facts of the contract, the terms of their agreement are in doubt. If Andy agrees to sell Sarah a tract of land believed to be 10 acres, but they learn that the tract is only 7 acres, then the terms of the contract have not been agreed upon and the contract is voidable.

Wilkin v. 1st Source Bank

Court of Appeals of Indiana, Third District
548 N.E.2d 170 (1990)

HOFFMAN, J.

Respondents-appellants Terrence G. Wilkin and Antoinette H. Wilkin (the Wilkins) appeal from the judgment of the St. Joseph Probate Court in favor of petitioner-appellee 1st Source Bank (Bank). The Bank, as personal representative of the estate of Olga Mestrovic, had filed a petition to determine title to eight drawings and a plaster sculpture owned by Olga Mestrovic at the time of her death but in the possession of the Wilkins at the time the petition was filed. The probate court determined that the drawings and sculpture were the property of the estate, and the court ordered the Wilkins to return the items to the Bank.

At the request of the Bank, the probate court entered findings of fact and conclusions of law. Neither party disputes the validity of the findings of fact. Accordingly, this Court will accept the findings as true. *Dept. of Environmental Manag. v. Amax* (1988), Ind.App., 529 N.E.2d 1209, 1211. The findings of fact may be summarized as follows.

Olga Mestrovic died on August 31, 1984. Her last will and testament was admitted to probate on September 6, 1984, and the Bank was appointed personal representative of the estate.

At the time of her death, Olga Mestrovic was the owner of a large number of works of art created by her husband, Ivan Mestrovic, an internationally-known sculptor and artist.[1] By the terms of Olga's will, all the works of art created by her husband and not specifically devised were to be sold and the proceeds distributed to members of the Mestrovic family.

Also included in the estate of Olga Mestrovic was certain real property. In March of 1985, the Bank entered into an agreement to sell the real estate to the Wilkins. The agreement of purchase and sale made no mention of any works of art, although it did provide for the sale of such personal property as the stove, refrigerator, dishwasher, drapes, curtains, sconces and French doors in the attic.

Immediately after closing on the real estate, the Wilkins complained that the premises were left in a cluttered condition and would require substantial cleaning effort. The Bank, through its trust officer, proposed two options: the Bank could

---

1. Ivan Mestrovic lived from 1883 to 1962. A Yugoslavian sculptor, Mestrovic became internationally known and spent his final working years in the United States. He taught at Syracuse University and at the University of Notre Dame. Much of his instruction as well as his own creative work involved religious themes.

Mestrovic is represented in the United States in the Brooklyn Museum, Art institute of Chicago, Colgate University, Syracuse University, Syracuse Museum of Fine Arts and University of Notre Dame; in England, in the Leeds Art Gallery, Birmingham Museum of Art, Victoria and Albert Museum and Tate Gallery; and in various collections in Canada, Spain, Belgium and Italy. A great number of churches in various parts of the world own his works. *See* McGraw-Hill Dictionary of Art Vol. 4, p. 53 (1969); Phaidon (Press) Encyclopedia of Art and Artists, p. 440 (1978).

retain a rubbish removal service to clean the property or the Wilkins could clean the premises and keep any items of personal property they wanted. The Wilkins opted to clean the property themselves. At the time arrangements were made concerning the cluttered condition of the real property, neither the Bank nor the Wilkins suspected that any works of art remained on the premises.

During their clean-up efforts, the Wilkins found eight drawings apparently created by Ivan Mestrovic. They also found a plaster sculpture of the figure of Christ with three small children. The Wilkins claimed ownership of the works of art, based upon their agreement with the Bank that if they cleaned the real property then they could keep such personal property as they desired.

The probate court ruled that there was no agreement for the purchase, sale or other disposition of the eight drawings and plaster sculpture. According to the lower court, there was no meeting of the minds, because neither party knew of the existence of the works of art.

On appeal, the Wilkins contend that the court's conclusions of law were erroneous. When the error charged is the trial court's application of the law, then this Court must correctly apply the law to the trial court's findings of fact. See *Indiana Industries, Inc. v. Wedge Products* (1982), Ind.App., 430 N.E.2d 419, 422.

Mutual assent is a prerequisite to the creation of a contract. *Board of School Com'rs of City of Indianapolis v. Bender* (1904), 36 Ind.App. 164, 172, 72 N.E. 154, 157. Where both parties share a common assumption about a vital fact upon which they based their bargain, and that assumption is false, the transaction may be avoided if because of the mistake a quite different exchange of values occurs from the exchange of values contemplated by the parties. J. Calamari & J. Perillo, The Law of Contracts § 9-26 (1987). There is no contract, because the minds of the parties have in fact never met.

The necessity of mutual assent, or "meeting of the minds," is illustrated in the classic case of *Sherwood v. Walker* (1887), 66 Mich. 568, 33 N.W. 919. The owners of a blooded cow indicated to the purchaser that the cow was barren. The purchaser also appeared to believe that the cow was barren. Consequently, a bargain was made to sell at a price per pound at which the cow would have brought approximately $80.00. Before delivery, it was discovered that the cow was with calf and that she was, therefore, worth from $750.00 to $1,000.00. The court ruled that the transaction was voidable:

> "The mistake was not of the mere quality of the animal, but went to the very nature of the thing. A barren cow is substantially a different creature than a breeding one. There is as much difference between them.... as there is between an ox and a cow...." *Id.* at 577, 33 N.W. at 923.

Like the parties in *Sherwood*, the parties in the instant case shared a common presupposition as to the existence of certain facts which proved false. The Bank and the Wilkins considered the real estate which the Wilkins had purchased to be cluttered with items of personal property variously characterized as "junk," "stuff" or "trash". Neither party suspected that works of art created by Ivan Mestrovic remained on the premises.

As in *Sherwood*, one party experienced an unexpected, unbargained-for gain while the other party experienced an unexpected, unbargained-for loss. Because the Bank and the Wilkins did not know that the eight drawings and the plaster sculpture were included in the items of personalty that cluttered the real property, the discovery of those works of art by the Wilkins was unexpected. The resultant gain to the Wilkins and loss to the Bank were not contemplated by the parties when the Bank agreed that the Wilkins could clean the premises and keep such personal property as they wished.

The following commentary on *Sherwood* is equally applicable to the case at bar:

> "Here the buyer sought to retain a gain that was produced, not by a subsequent change in circumstances, nor by the favorable resolution of known uncertainties when the contract was made, but by the presence of facts quite different from those on which the parties based their bargain."

Palmer, Mistake and Unjust Enrichment 16–17 (1962), *quoted in* J. Calamari & J. Perillo, The Law of Contracts § 9-26 (1987). The probate court properly concluded that there was no agreement for the purchase, sale or other disposition of the eight drawings and plaster sculpture, because there was no meeting of the minds.

The judgment of the St. Joseph Probate Court is affirmed.

Notes and Questions

1. Mistake or Ex Ante Risk Allocation?: The defense of mistake applies to situations where there was a genuine misunderstanding of the facts at the time the contract was made, not where some contingency occurred after the contract was made. That is, the fundamental issue is not risk allocation, but rather whether the parties actually agreed. Subsequent legal research on the facts of *Sherwood v. Walker* has revealed that, at the time of contract, both parties recognized that there was some probability that Rose 2d was not barren. If this is correct, didn't the contract terms then reflect the probability that Rose 2d could become pregnant? That is, didn't the parties agree to shift the risk? If so, then why should Walker get to keep the gain that resulted from the occurrence of the highly unlikely contingency? Moreover, since Walker was in a better position to calculate the probability of the contingency occurring, doesn't the decision in the case represent an unwarranted windfall for Walker?

2. Mistake, Fraud, Disclosure, and Regulation: The producer or seller typically has an informational advantage over the buyer. A market-oriented response to concerns that sellers will use their informational advantage to abuse purchasers is that the market will eventually punish a seller for such indiscretions. While generally effective, in some instances the process of market adjustment is inadequate. Such a situation is typically attributable to the amount of harm that may accompany the first occurrence of fraud, deception, or accident due to unsafe design. For example, an individual who has been permanently maimed by an unsafe product takes little pleasure in knowing that the market will adjust to the company's marketing of unsafe products. Thus, the market adjustment process is supplemented by common law rules and statutory regulations. For example, government intervention is often justified when informational asymmetries are such that consumers, investors, and workers are exposed to risks of which they are unaware. Government intervention can take the form of disclosure regulation (e.g., federal securities regulation) or direct regulation of acceptable risks (e.g., the Occupational Health and Safety Administration's workplace regulations or the Food and Drug Administration's drug approval process). Market adjustments to different types of risk are discussed in Chapter IX, "Risk."

2. Discharge by Impossibility

There are four basic situations that will generally qualify for discharge of contractual obligations due to impossibility: *(1) Impossibility and Personal Services Contracts.* The first type of impossibility would occur when an actress contracts to play the leading role in a movie, but becomes ill and dies before production of the movie starts; *(2) Impossibility and Destruction of Specific Subject Matter.* The second type of discharge for objective impossibility—destruction of the specific subject matter of the contract—can be illustrated by a lease of a building that is destroyed by fire. If the possibility of a fire is not contemplated by the contracting parties, then it cannot be said that the risk of fire has been allocated by the contract. Discharge for this type of impossibility of performance, however, is not appropriate where the parties include a clause specifying the obligations of the parties in the event of fire; *(3) Impossibility and Change in Public Policy.* A subsequent change of law declaring the subject of the contract to be illegal will release the parties from their obligations under the contract. An example of this type of discharge would be a contract for the sale of asbestos where the sale of asbestos is declared illegal before the execution of the contract; *(4) The Doctrine of Commercial Impracticability.* The doctrine of commercial impracticability—which is the modern version of the doctrine of impossibility—is the result of a growing trend to allow parties to discharge contracts when the performance that was originally contemplated turns out to be more difficult or more expensive than originally anticipated. This development does not appear to be justified when at least one party to the contract is aware, or at least should be aware, of the possibility that performance may be more difficult than expected.

Canadian Industrial Alcohol Co. v. Dunbar Molasses Co.
Court of Appeals of New York
179 N.E. 383 (1932)

CARDOZO, Ch. J.

A buyer sues a seller for breach of an executory contract of purchase and sale.

The subject-matter of the contract was "approximately 1,500,000 wine gallons Refined Blackstrap [molasses] of the usual run from the National Sugar Refinery, Yonkers, N.Y., to test around 60% sugars."

The order was given and accepted December 27, 1927, but shipments of the molasses were to begin after April 1, 1928, and were to be spread out during the warm weather.

After April 1, 1928, the defendant made delivery from time to time of 344,083 gallons. Upon its failure to deliver more, the plaintiff brought this action for the recovery of damages. The defendant takes the ground that, by an implied term of the contract, the duty to deliver was conditioned upon the production by the National Sugar Refinery at Yonkers of molasses sufficient in quantity to fill the plaintiff's order. The fact is that the output of the refinery, while the contract was in force, was 485,848 gallons, much less than its capacity, of which amount 344,083 gallons were allotted to the defendant and shipped to the defendant's customer. The argument for the defendant is that its own duty to deliver was proportionate to the refinery's willingness to supply, and that the duty was discharged when the output was reduced.

The contract, read in the light of the circumstances existing at its making, or more accurately in the light of any such circumstances apparent from this record, does not keep the defendant's duty within boundaries so narrow. We may assume, in the defendant's favor, that there would have been a discharge of its duty to deliver if the refinery had been destroyed (Stewart v. Stone, 127 N.Y. 500; Dexter v. Norton, 47 N.Y. 62; Nitro Powder Co. v. Agency of C.C. & F. Co., 233 N.Y. 294, 297), or if the output had been curtailed by the failure of the sugar crop (Pearson v. McKinney, 160 Cal. 649; Howell v. Coupland, 1 Q.B.D. 258; 3 Williston on Contracts, §1949) or by the ravages of war (Matter of Badische Co., [1921] 2 Ch. 331; Horlock v. Beal, [1916] 1 A.C. 486) or conceivably in some circumstances by unavoidable strikes (American Union Line v. Oriental Navigation Corp., 239 N.Y. 207, 219; Normandie Shirt Co. v. Eagle, Inc., 238 N.Y. 218, 229; Delaware, L. & W. Co. v. Bowns, 58 N.Y. 573; and cf. Blackstock v. New York & Erie R.R. Co., 20 N.Y. 48; also 2 Williston on Contracts, §1099, pp. 2045, 2046). We may even assume that a like result would have followed if the plaintiff had bargained not merely for a quantity of molasses to be supplied from a particular refinery, but for molasses to be supplied in accordance with a particular contract between the defendant and the refiner, and if thereafter such contract had been broken without fault on the defendant's part. The inquiry is merely this, whether the continuance of a special group of circumstances appears from the terms of the contract, interpreted in the setting of the occasion, to have been a tacit or implied presupposition in the minds of the contracting parties, conditioning their belief in a continued obligation....

Accepting that test, we ask ourselves the question what special group of circumstances does the defendant lay before us as one of the presuppositions immanent in its bargain with the plaintiff? The defendant asks us to assume that a manufacturer, having made a contract with a middleman for a stock of molasses to be procured from a particular refinery would expect the contract to lapse whenever the refiner chose to diminish his production, and this in the face of the middleman's omission to do anything to charge the refiner with a duty to continue. Business could not be transacted with security or smoothness if a presumption so unreasonable were at the root of its engagements. There is nothing to show that the defendant would have been unable by a timely contract with the refinery to have assured itself of a supply sufficient for its needs. There is nothing to show that the plaintiff in giving the order for the molasses, was informed by the defendant that such a contract had not been made, or that performance would be contingent upon obtaining one thereafter. If the plaintiff had been so informed, it would very likely have preferred to deal with the refinery directly, instead of dealing with a middleman. The defendant does not even show that it tried to get a contract from the refinery during the months that intervened between the acceptance of the plaintiff's order and the time when shipments were begun. It has wholly failed to relieve itself of the imputation of contributory fault (3 Williston on Contracts, § 1959). So far as the record shows, it put its faith in the mere chance that the output of the refinery would be the same from year to year, and finding its faith vain, it tells us that its customer must have expected to take a chance as great. We see no reason for importing into the bargain this aleatory element. The defendant is in no better position than a factor who undertakes in his own name to sell for future delivery a special mill. The duty will be discharged if the mill is destroyed before delivery is due. The duty will subsist if the output is reduced because times turn out to be hard and labor charges high....

The judgment should be affirmed with costs.

Notes and Questions

1. Subjective Impossibility: In determining whether the parties to a contract are discharged from their duties, the courts distinguish between objective impossibility ("It can't be done") and subjective impossibility ("I can't do it"). Examples of subjective impossibility are failure to deliver on time because of a shortage of trucks and failure to pay on time because accounts receivable have not been paid. Normally, subjective impossibility will not relieve a party of duties under the contract, and the party will be liable for damages for the breach. In terms of the allocation of risk of subjective impossibility, the nonperforming party clearly accepts the risk that it will be unable to perform. Moreover, this legal rule appears to promote efficiency because it places liability on the party who is in the best position to control whether or not performance is possible. For example, if breaching parties were relieved from liability under all cases of subjective impossibility, then the incentive to perform contracts under difficult circumstances would be lessened (with a corresponding reduction in the value of contracts).

2. Comparative Advantage and Risk Allocation: The court seems to explicitly adopt the view that the party with the informational advantage about the risk should be held liable. In general, the courts should encourage the parties best able to calculate a risk to bear that risk in the absence of a specific contract term. This risk allocation perspective is reflected in other cases. For example, in *Transatlantic Financing Corporation v. United States*, 363 F.2d 312 (D.C.Cir. 1966), a case involving the closing of the Suez Canal, the court determined that the closing did not discharge a carrier from its obligation to deliver wheat to a port in Iran. The court determined that the closing of the canal was foreseeable, and this is crucial in commercial impracticability cases. It is assumed that risks that are foreseeable are taken into account when agreeing on the price of the contract at the time of negotiations. Thus, the doctrine only applies: 1) when the burden of complying is extreme; *and,* more importantly, 2) when the additional burden was not recognizable when the contract was formed. Thus, the cases usually turn on the fact question of whether the risks were recognized — or whether they should have been recognized — by at least one of the parties.

3. Uniform Commercial Code and Commercial Impracticability: The doctrine of commercial impracticability exists at common law, but is liberalized under U.C.C. § 2-615, titled "Excuse by Failure of Presupposed Conditions." This section applies when, for one reason or another, the conditions fail under which both parties assumed a contract would be performed, and it becomes impossible or impracticable to perform the contract as contemplated. *Eastern Air Lines v. Gulf Oil Corporation*, 415 F.Supp. 429 (S.D. Fla., 1975), *infra* Chapter IX, "Risk," is a good example of a commercial impracticability case under the U.C.C. There the court scrutinized the relationship of the contracting parties, including their relatively ability to anticipate the contingency that occurred, and found that the case involved risk allocation instead of impracticability.

C. Asymmetric Information and Market Responses

As mentioned above, consumers frequently do not know how quality varies across brands of products or services. There is asymmetric information: one party (usually the seller) to a transaction knows a material fact (the quality of the good or service) that the other party (usually the buyer) does not know. At first glance, the phenomenon of asymmetric information appears to present sellers with the opportunity to exploit buyers. However, further analysis reveals that asymmetric information can be a major problem for the seller.

1. The Market for "Lemons"

The used car market is a nice vehicle (pun intended) for illustrating this point. Assume that Cindy wants to sell her 1994 Ford Mustang GT. Cindy has perfect information about the quality of her car — she is the original owner of the car; she has been a careful, non-abusive driver; she has followed all routine maintenance procedures; the car has not required any major repairs; in sum, she knows that the car is in great condition. However, it is well known that (1) some Mustang GTs have had serious problems requiring numerous major repairs; and (2) many owners of Mustang GTs drive them hard and fast. Unfortunately for both Cindy and the potential buyers of 1994 Ford Mustang GTs, it is very difficult for potential buyers to distinguish between Cindy's "cream puff" and the "lemons" lurking in the market. At best, potential buyers know the probability of getting a good car.

If buyers cannot distinguish between good and bad used cars, all used 1994 Mustang GTs sell for the same price (assuming they have the same mileage). As a result, bad cars are overvalued and good cars are undervalued. But this is not the end of the analysis. Because Cindy knows that she has a good car, she is not going to sell it at a market price that undervalues her car. Moreover, the owners of bad cars are encouraged to sell their cars because the market overvalues bad cars. This phenomenon is referred to as **adverse selection**: the only sellers who select to participate in the market are the ones who benefit from the asymmetric information. As more bad cars are offered for sale and fewer good cars are offered, the market price is forced downward to reflect the increasing probability that any given buyer will end up with a lemon. The bad cars drive out the good cars, and there is no market for good used cars. The lemons sour the market.

Obviously, the "lemons market" phenomenon has the potential to destroy markets whenever there is asymmetric information. Both sellers and buyers, who see potential mutually-beneficial exchanges frustrated, have incentives to solve the lemons problem. Cindy, for example, could show her maintenance records (and even her driving record) to potential buyers. However, many buyers will remain suspicious of the quality of her information. Used car dealers attempt to solve the lemons problem by offering warranties on "certified pre-owned cars." Numerous alternative mechanisms for solving problems associated with asymmetric information are discussed in this section.

2. Adverse Selection and Insurance Contracts

The "lemons market" phenomenon poses a particularly challenging problem in insurance markets because the parties wishing to purchase insurance often know much more about their particular circumstances than it is possible for the insurers to know. For example, individuals who apply for health insurance know their own health record and may be able to conceal important information from insurers. The asymmetric information can lead to adverse selection in the insurance pool, as high risk individuals find insurance to be a good deal for them but low risk individuals decide to forego insurance coverage. As more high risk individuals purchase insurance, higher payouts by insurance companies will force them to raise rates which, in turn, makes the insurance less attractive to low risk individuals. Insurance companies, of course, are well aware of this potential and devote a great deal of effort to avoid adverse selection. For example, life insurance companies and health insurance companies attempt to control the riskiness of their insurance pools by requiring applicants to answer detailed questions on the application form and to undergo medical examinations.

Waxse v. Reserve Life Insurance Company
Supreme Court of Kansas
809 P.2d 533 (1991)

Herd, J.

This is an action on a medical insurance contract. The estate of Maurice Behnke, deceased, asserts Reserve Life Insurance Company (Reserve Life) breached its contract to provide major medical insurance when it refused to pay benefits under the contract for medical expenses incurred by Behnke. In defense, Reserve Life argues it properly rescinded the coverage and contract due to material misrepresentations by Behnke on the application for insurance concerning his health history. Both parties filed motions for summary judgment. The district court determined Behnke made a fraudulent misrepresentation on the application for insurance and granted Reserve Life's motion for summary judgment. We reverse.

We review the facts in the light most favorable to Behnke. On June 12, 1987, Behnke underwent a blood test at Life Lab, a private laboratory facility. Prior to taking the test, Behnke believed he might test positive for the Human Immunodeficiency Virus (HIV) because of his prior hepatitis and multiple sexual partners. In July 1987, Life Lab informed Behnke that he had tested positive for the presence of HIV antibodies. The letter from Life Lab also recommended a complete medical evaluation by Behnke's personal physician. A physician did not administer the blood test at Life Lab nor inform Behnke of the test results or its meaning. However, Behnke was informed by Life Lab that testing positive for HIV antibodies did not mean that he currently had Acquired Immune Deficiency Syndrome (AIDS) or AIDS-Related Complex (ARC).

HIV is a virus which is spread by unsafe sexual contact, by needle sharing, or through blood or its components. The HIV virus may cause AIDS, a disease of the human immune system that leaves the body vulnerable to diseases which it can normally repel. AIDS is a disease of the immune system; it is not a blood disorder. A diagnosis of AIDS depends on the presence of opportunistic diseases which invade on the loss of immunity. The presence of these diseases plus a positive test for HIV antibodies makes possible a diagnosis of AIDS. A positive HIV test indicates that an individual may have been infected with the virus, but does not mean the individual is certain to develop AIDS.

On September 11, 1987, Behnke completed an application for major medical and life insurance with AmWay Group Major Medical & Life Insurance — Reserve Life Insurance Company. He understood that any coverage extended was based upon truthfulness of the application information and that any information discovered untruthful was grounds for rescission.

No question on the application specifically asked whether the applicant had undergone HIV antibody testing for AIDS or any other questions concerning AIDS.

Question 5(c) of the application asked whether the applicant had been treated for or had any indication of specific disorders, including any blood disorders. Behnke answered negatively.

Question 7 asked, "Do you know of any other impairment now existing in the health or physical condition of any proposed insured?" Behnke responded. "No," on the theory his health was not impaired even though he had received a positive HIV test. At the time of filing the application, Behnke felt well.

Question 8 asked, "Has any proposed insured been examined or treated by a doctor during the past three years for anything other than the conditions listed above?" Behnke responded "Yes" and explained in Paragraph 9 he had suffered minor sore throats, colds, etc.

Behnke did not indicate he had tested HIV positive because he found none of the questions were applicable. However, Behnke realized Question 8 was propounded to determine if the applicant had any pre-existing condition. Behnke also determined that Question 8 did not require revelation of the HIV test because it inquired about examinations conducted by doctors and the blood test he had undergone was not administered by a doctor.

At the time Behnke submitted the application to Reserve Life, he had health insurance coverage with Blue Cross-Blue Shield through his former employer, Mid America Directs. Behnke sought the Reserve Life Insurance contract for several reasons. First, as an independent contractor rather than an employee of Mid America Directs, he was required to reimburse the company on a monthly basis. Secondly, Behnke believed the Blue Cross-Blue Shield premiums were soon going to increase. Finally, Behnke believed Mid America Directs might change insurance carriers. Under Reserve Life's insurance policy, Behnke's premium decreased from $72 a month to $47 a month.

At the time of his application with Reserve Life, Behnke had no signs of any illness and was not convinced in his own mind that he was HIV positive. Behnke was skeptical of the HIV test result because he had undergone a pre-employment physical exam for Eastern Airlines in 1987 and was offered a job, thereby indicating to him his health condition was satisfactory.

Behnke received a validation of coverage under the Reserve Life policy with an effective date of October 1, 1987. Early in 1988 Behnke developed arthritis but waited until April of that year to inform his physicians about the prior HIV-positive test. In July 1988, Behnke was hospitalized at Research Medical Center and diagnosed with having AIDS. Behnke's medical records at Research Medical Center indicated he had tested positive for HIV antibodies nearly a year earlier.

Upon receipt of the Research Medical Center records, a claims examiner for AmWay Distributors of Reserve Life requested information from Behnke concerning the date and place of testing referred to in the records. In response, Behnke informed the claims examiner about his pre-employment physical examination for Eastern Airlines, but he did not provide any information pertaining to the June 1987 blood test at Life Lab.

Based upon the information provided in the Research Medical Center records concerning the pre-application positive HIV test, Reserve Life rescinded its contract of insurance with Behnke and refunded previously paid premiums.

The district court determined that as a matter of law Reserve Life was entitled to summary judgment based upon fraudulent misrepresentation by Behnke in the insurance application.

As a result of Behnke's death during the pendency of the appeal, the administrator of his estate was substituted as a party. On appeal, the estate contends summary judgment was erroneous because Reserve Life failed to establish an essential element of fraud. Specifically, the estate asserts Reserve Life has not shown that Behnke made a false answer on the insurance application with an intent to deceive.

The issue we address is whether the evidence supports the district court's determination that there was a material and fraudulent misrepresentation by Behnke sufficient to support Reserve Life's rescission of the contract.

The existence of fraud is normally a question of fact. Therefore, upon appeal, our standard of review is limited to determining whether the district court's findings of fact are supported by substantial competent evidence and whether the findings are sufficient to support the district court's conclusions of law.

The elements necessary to establish actionable fraud are well established. Fraudulent misrepresentation in an action to rescind an insurance contract includes an untrue statement of fact, known to be untrue by the party making it, made with the intent to deceive or recklessly made with disregard for the truth, where another party justifiably relies on the statement and acts to his injury and detriment. Fraud is never presumed and must be shown by clear and convincing evidence. In addition, the falsity of a material application statement does not bar recovery under the policy unless the false statement actually contributes to the contingency or event on which the policy becomes due and payable.

The estate first argues Behnke did not make an untrue statement on the application. It urges that Question 8 of the application inquires about any prior examination or treatment *by a doctor* and is not concerned with any other type of medically related examinations or treatments. Thus, the estate contends, since a doctor was not present during the Life Lab blood testing, Behnke did not make a false statement in answering the question negatively.

For support, Behnke relies upon *Galloway v. Insurance Co.*, 112 Kan. 720, 212 Pac. 887 (1923). In *Galloway*, an application for life insurance asked for the dates and complaints of the applicant which were attended to by a physician. The plaintiff failed to list an osteopath who had diagnosed plaintiff with a retroflexed uterus, the ultimate cause of plaintiff's death. This court determined the insurer was not entitled to rescind the contract for fraudulent misrepresentation because the question literally asked for only the dates and complaints, and the plaintiff's understanding of "physician" as a general practitioner, although erroneous, was not inconsistent with good faith. 112 Kan. at 723–24. See also *Day v. National Reserve Life Ins. Co.*, 144 Kan. 619, 624–25, 62 P.2d 925 (1936) (negative response to inquiry concerning intestinal disease was not false because plaintiff believed symptoms were chronic constipation); *Jackson v. National Life and Acc. Ins. Co.*, 150 Kan. 86, 90, 90 P.2d 1097 (1939) (plaintiff's failure to list treatment by chiropractor in response to inquiry concerning treatments by a physician held not fraudulent).

We find the estate's argument valid. Behnke answered the questionnaire honestly. No inquiry was made as to AIDS or HIV. Admittedly, Behnke could have gone farther in his disclosure, but to do so he would have had to act as a volunteer about a matter which he did not consider an impairment of his health. It was the insurance company's responsibility to ask the questions to which it wanted answers. This it did not do.

The next issue we address is whether there was substantial competent evidence to support a finding that Behnke intended to deceive or recklessly disregarded the truth in omitting information of the HIV-positive test from the insurance application. The estate argues the district court failed to apply the requisite subjective standard to determine whether fraudulent intent was established. It also contends the district court finding of fraud was erroneous because, although the application may have contained a false answer, it was unintentionally false and, therefore, did not constitute fraud.

A representation made innocently and in good faith does not constitute fraud. Thus, an answer which denied the existence of any stomach disease on a life insurance application was not considered fraudulent even though the applicant had consulted physicians concerning a digestive disturbance because the applicant had enjoyed good health and had answered the questions in good faith. In *Scott v. National Reserve Life Ins. Co.*, 143 Kan. 678, however, an applicant falsely denied on the insurance application that he previously had been turned down by life insurance companies. The *Scott* court determined the plaintiff's false answer was material and his concealment of a material fact indicated a lack of good faith. Thus, the court upheld the insurer's rescission of the contract.

In the case at hand, we believe Behnke omitted the information of a positive HIV test in good faith. It was not inquired about, and we find no evidence of fraud.

The judgment of the trial court is reversed. Summary judgment is granted to the appellant.

Notes and Questions

1. Regulation by the Court. Isn't the court saying that whenever there is a discrepancy between the insurance company and the consumer, the consumer gets the benefit of the doubt if he/she acted in good faith? If so, isn't the court simply regulating the market? Companies will increase premiums on all consumers to pay for those consumers who "slip through the cracks." Thus, we all pay for this ability to receive the benefit of the doubt.

2. Economics of Insurance: Chapter 9, "Risk", includes a detailed discussion of the economics of insurance.

3. Adverse Selection. The selection of people who purchase insurance is not a normal, random sample of the population, but rather includes some people with private information about their personal situations that makes it likely they will receive a higher than average level of benefit under the insurance policy. For example, high risk patients (e.g., cancer-prone, drug users, etc.) apply to insurance companies while young healthy persons do not. Insurance deals with this adverse selection problem in a variety of ways. The most obvious is to require the disclosure of information on the long application forms with boiler-plate provisions to try and keep out risky patients. Insurance companies set limits on pre-existing conditions, through either limited coverage or higher premiums for the additional risk.

3. Reputational Bonds and Other Market Mechanisms for Disclosing Information About Quality

Consumers are understandably concerned about the quality of the products and services that they purchase in the market. This concern is a problem for the sellers of high-quality products and services because some consumers are not going to pay for quality unless they are assured that they will receive it. Sellers respond to this problem by offering warranties, guarantees, and follow-up services. Sellers also invest in developing a reputation for high quality products and services. A reputation is an important asset of a seller—but, it is also very fragile in the sense that it can be quickly destroyed by the seller failing to live up to the expectations generated by the reputation. Imagine the damage done to Sears' reputation when, in 1992, the state of California brought charges alleging that Sears Auto Centers were overcharging customers an average of $230 for unneeded and undone repairs. Because the reputational asset can be destroyed by the firm's own behavior, the reputational asset is very similar to a performance bond. Thus, a forfeitable reputational bond assures consumers that they will get what they bargained for. This is just one of many examples of how firms attempt to solve information problems in the market.

The Role of Market Forces in Assuring Contractual Performance
Benjamin Klein & Keith Leffler
89 Journal of Political Economy 615 (1981)

I. Introduction

An implicit assumption of the economic paradigm of market exchange is the presence of a government to define property rights and enforce contracts. An important element of the legal-philosophical tradition upon which the economic model is built is that without some third-party enforcer to sanction stealing and reneging, market exchange would be impossible. But economists also have long considered "reputations" and brand names to be private devices which provide incentives that assure contract performance in the absence of any third-party enforcer. This private-contract enforcement mechanism relies upon the value to the firm of repeat sales to satisfied customers as a means of preventing nonperformance....

This paper examines the nongovernmental repeat-purchase contract-enforcement mechanism. To isolate this force, we assume throughout our analysis that contracts are not enforceable by the government or any other third party. Transactors are assumed to rely solely on the threat of termination of the business relationship for enforcement of contractual promises.[3] This assumption is most realistic for contractual terms concerning difficult-to-measure product characteristics such as the "taste" of a hamburger. However, even when the aspects of a contract are less complicated...and performance more easily measurable by a third party such as a judge, specification, litigation, and other contract-enforcement costs may be substantial. Therefore, explicit guarantees to replace or repair defective goods (warranties) are not costless ways to assure contract performance. Market arrangements, such as the value of lost repeat purchases, which motivate transactors to honor their promises may be the cheapest method of guaranteeing the guarantee.

...[O]ur approach is general in the sense that the value of future exchanges can motivate fulfillment of all types of contractual promises,...

In Section II, the conditions are outlined under which firms will either honor their commitments to supply a high level of quality or choose to supply a quality

---

3. This assumption is consistent with the pioneering work of Macaulay (1963), where reliance on formal contracts and the threat of explicit legal sanctions was found to be an extremely rare element of interfirm relationships. Macaulay provides some sketchy evidence that business firms prevent nonfulfillment of contracts by the use of effective nonlegal sanctions consisting primarily of the loss of future business. This "relational" nature of contracts has been recently emphasized by Macneil (1974), and also by Goldberg (1976) and Williamson (1979).

lower than promised. In order to emphasize the ability of markets to guarantee quality in the absence of any government enforcement mechanism, a simple model is presented which assumes that consumers costlessly communicate among one another. Therefore, if a firm cheats and supplies to any individual a quality of product less than contracted for, all consumers in the market learn this and all future sales are lost. A major result of our analysis is that even such perfect inter-consumer communication conditions are not sufficient to assure high quality supply. Cheating will be prevented and high quality products will be supplied only if firms are earning a continual stream of rental income that will be lost if low quality output is deceptively produced. The present discounted value of this rental stream must be greater than the one-time wealth increase obtained from low quality production.

This condition for the "notorious firm" repeat-purchase mechanism to assure high quality supply is not generally fulfilled by the usual free-entry, perfectly competitive equilibrium conditions of price equal to marginal and average cost. It becomes necessary to distinguish between production costs that are "sunk" firm-specific assets and those production costs that are salvageable (i.e., recoverable) in uses outside the firm. Our analysis implies that firms will not cheat on promises to sell high quality output only if [the] price is sufficiently above salvageable production costs. [That is, the price of the product must be sufficiently high to assure profits above those that can be recovered by liquidating the assets to assure high quality.] While the perfectly competitive price may imply such a margin above salvageable costs, this will not necessarily be the case. The fundamental theoretical result of this paper is that market prices above the competitive price and the presence of nonsalvageable capital are means of enforcing quality promises.

In Section III our theoretical model (of quality-guaranteeing price premiums above salvageable costs) is extended to examine how the capital value of these price-premium payments can be dissipated in a free-entry equilibrium. The quality-guaranteeing nature of nonsalvageable, firm-specific capital investments is developed. Alternative techniques of minimizing the cost to consumers of obtaining a high quality product are investigated. We also explore market responses to consumer uncertainty about quality-assuring premium levels. Advertising and other production and distribution investments in "conspicuous" assets are examined as competitive responses to simultaneous quality and production-cost uncertainties. Finally, a summary of the analysis and some concluding remarks are presented in Section IV.

II. Price Premiums and Quality Assurance

　　　　*　　*　　*

Intuitively, the quality-assuring price treats the potential value of not producing minimum quality as an explicit opportunity cost to the firm of higher quality production. Hence the quality-assuring price must not only compensate the firm for the increased average production costs incurred when quality above that detectable prior to purchase is produced, but must also yield a normal rate of return on the foregone gains from exploiting consumer ignorance. This price "premium" stream can be thought of as "protection money" paid by consumers to induce high quality contract performance. Although the present discounted value of this stream equals the value of the short-run gain the firm can obtain by cheating, consumers are not indifferent between paying the "premium" over time or permitting the firm to cheat. The price "premium" is a payment for high quality [rather than spending time and energy determining quality before purchase]. The relevant consumer choice is between demanding minimum quality output at a perfectly competitive (costless information) price or paying a competitive price "premium," which is both necessary and sufficient, for higher quality output.

There is a possibility that the required quality-guaranteeing price premium may exceed the increased consumer surplus of purchasing higher quality rather than the minimum quality product. If consumers can easily substitute increased quantity of the low quality product for increased quality, then the value of guaranteed high quality will be relatively low. Therefore, although a quality-guaranteeing price exists, a higher than minimum quality product may not be produced. For those goods where the substitution possibilities between quality and quantity are lower (e.g., drugs), consumer demand for confidence will be relatively high and the high quality guarantee worth the price premium. We assume throughout that we are dealing with products where some demand exists for the high quality good in the range of prices considered.

III. Competitive Market Equilibrium: Firm-specific Capital Investments

Our analysis has focused on the case where costless information (perfectly competitive) prices do not imply sufficient firm-specific rents to motivate high quality production. A price premium was therefore necessary to induce high quality supply...

A. Brand Name Capital Investments

Competition to dissipate the economic profits being earned by existing firms must therefore occur in nonprice dimensions.... The competition involves *firm-specific capital* expenditures. This firm-specific capital competition motivates firms to purchase assets with (nonsalvageable) costs equal to the capital value of the premium rental stream earned when high quality is supplied at the quality-assuring price.... Such firm-specific capital costs could, for example, take the form of sunk investments in the design of a firm logo or an expensive sign promoting the firm's name. Expenditures on these highly firm-specific assets are then said to represent brand name (or selling) capital investments.

*   *   *

If the firm decides to cheat it will experience a capital loss equal to its anticipated future profit stream.... That is, the market value of the competitive firm's brand name capital is equal to the value of total specific or "sunk" selling costs made by the firm which, in turn, equals the present value of the anticipated premium stream from high quality output....

What assures high quality supply is the capital loss...of future business if low quality is produced. Since the imputed value of the firm's brand name capital is determined by the firm's expected quasi rents on future sales, this capital loss from supplying quality lower than promised is represented by the depreciation of this firm-specific asset. [As direct profits are gained from lower quality goods they are offset by indirect losses in the form of lost reputation.] The expenditures on brand name capital assets are therefore similar to collateral that the firm loses if it supplies output of less than anticipated quality and in equilibrium the premium stream provides only a normal rate of return on this collateral asset.

* * *

C. Consumer Cost Uncertainty: A Role for Advertising

The discussion to this point has assumed complete consumer knowledge of firms' costs of producing alternative quality outputs and knowledge of the extent to which any capital production costs or brand name capital selling costs are salvageable. This knowledge is necessary and sufficient to accurately calculate both the quality-guaranteeing premium and price. However, consumers are generally uncertain about cost conditions and therefore do not know the minimum quality-guaranteeing price with perfect accuracy. In fact, consumers cannot even make perfect anticipated quality rankings across firms on the basis of price. That one firm has a higher price than another may indicate a larger price premium or, alternatively, more inefficient production. In this section, we examine how the more realistic assumption of consumer cost uncertainty influences market responses to prepurchase quality uncertainty.

We have shown that increases in the price premium over average recoverable cost generally increase the relative returns from production of promised (high) quality rather than deceptive minimum (low) quality. The existence of a high price premium also makes expenditures on brand name capital investments economically feasible. The magnitude of brand name capital investments in turn indicates the magnitude of the price premium. When a consumer is uncertain about the cost of producing a particular high quality level of output and therefore the required quality-assuring premium, information about the actual level of the price premium will provide information about the probability of receiving high quality. If consumers are risk averse, this uncertainty about receiving anticipated high or deceptively low quality output will increase the premium that will be paid. The premium will include both a (presumably unbiased) estimate of the quality-assuring premium and an extra payment to reduce the risk of being deceived.

* * * Implicit information about the sufficiency of price as a guarantee can be supplied by "conspicuous" specific asset expenditures. Luxurious storefronts and ornate displays or signs may be supplied by a firm even if yielding no direct consumer service flows. Such firm-specific assets inform consumers of the magnitude of sunk capital costs...and hence the opportunity cost to the firm if it cheats. Both the informational services and the direct utility producing services of assets are now relevant considerations for a firm in deciding upon the most valuable form the brand name capital investment should take.

The value of information about the magnitude of a firm's specific or "sunk" capital cost, and therefore the magnitude of the price premium, is one return from advertising. Indeed, the role of premiums as quality guarantors provides foundation for Nelson's (1974) argument that advertising, by definition, supplies valuable information to consumers—namely, information that the firm is advertising. A sufficient investment in advertising implies that a firm will not engage in short-run quality deception since the advertising indicates a nonsalvageable cost gap between price and production costs[. T]hat is, the existence of a price premium. This argument essentially reverses Nelson's logic. It is not that it pays a firm with a "best buy" to advertise more, but rather that advertising implies the supply of "best buys," or more correctly, the supply of promised high quality products. Advertising does not directly "signal" the presence of a "best buy," but "signals" the presence of firm-specific selling costs and therefore the magnitude of the price premium. We would therefore expect, ceteris paribus, a positive correlation not between advertising intensity and "best buys," as Nelson claims, but between advertising intensity and the extent of quality that is costly to determine prepurchase.

Conspicuous sunk costs such as advertising are, like all sunk costs, irrelevant in determining future firm behavior regarding output quality. However, consumers know that such sunk costs can be profitable only if the future quasi rents are large. In particular,...a price premium on future sales sufficient to prevent cheating is estimated to exist....

Our theory also suggests why endorsements by celebrities and other seemingly "noninformative" advertising such as elaborate (obviously costly to produce) commercials, sponsorships of telethons, athletic events, and charities are valuable to consumers. In addition to drawing attention to the product, such advertising indicates the presence of a large sunk "selling" cost and the existence of a price premium. And because the crucial variable is the consumers' estimate of the stock of advertising capital (and not the flow), it also explains why firms advertise that they have advertised in the past (e.g., "as seen on 'The Tonight Show'"). Rather than serving a direct certifying function (e.g., as recommended by *Good Housekeeping* magazine), information about past advertising informs consumers about the magnitude of the total brand name capital investment.

Firms may also provide valuable information by publicizing the large fees paid to celebrities for commercials. Information about large endorsement fees would be closely guarded if the purpose were to simulate an "unsolicited endorsement" of the product's particular quality characteristics rather than to indicate the existence of a price premium. Viewed in this context, it is obviously unnecessary for the celebrity to actually use the particular brand advertised. This is contrary to a recent FTC ruling (see Federal Trade Commission 1980).

This analysis of advertising implies that consumers necessarily receive something when they pay a higher price for an advertised brand. An expensive name brand aspirin, for example, is likely to be better than unadvertised aspirin because it is expensive. The advertising of the name brand product indicates the presence of a current and future price premium. This premium on future sales is the firm's brand name capital which will be lost if the firm supplies lower than anticipated quality. Therefore, firms selling more highly advertised, higher priced products will necessarily take more precautions in production.[4]

We have emphasized the informational value of advertising as a sunk cost. Other marketing activities can serve a similar informational role in indicating the presence of a price premium. For example, free samples, in addition to letting

---

4. The greater is the cost to consumers of obtaining deceptively low quality, the greater will be the demand for quality assurance. The very low market share of "generic" children's aspirin (1 percent) vis-à-vis generic's share of the regular aspirin market (7 percent) is consistent with this implication (see IMS America, Ltd. 1978). Many individuals who claim "all aspirin is alike" apparently pay the extra price for their children where the costs of lower quality are greater and therefore quality assurance is considered more important.

consumers try the product, provide information regarding future premiums and therefore anticipated quality. Such free or low-price samples thus provide information not solely to those consumers that receive the samples but also to anyone aware of the existence and magnitude of the free or low-price sample program. More generally, the supply by a firm of quality greater than anticipated and paid for by consumers is a similar type of brand name capital investment by the firm. By forgoing revenue, the firm provides information to consumers that it has made a nonsalvageable investment of a particular magnitude and that a particular future premium stream is anticipated to cover the initial sunk alternative cost.

*   *   *

IV. Conclusion

* * * We have analyzed the generally unrecognized importance of increased market prices and nonsalvageable capital as possible methods of making quality promises credible. We obviously do not want to claim that consumers "know" this theory in the sense that they can verbalize it but only that they behave in such a way as if they recognize the forces at work. They may, for example, know from past experience that when a particular type of investment is present such as advertising they are much less likely to be deceived. Therefore, survivorship of crude decision rules over time may produce consumer behavior very similar to what would be predicted by this model without the existence of explicit "knowledge" of the forces we have examined.

Our analysis implies that consumers can successfully use price as an indicator of quality. We are not referring to the phenomenon of an ignorant consumer free riding on the information contained in the market price paid by other more informed buyers but rather to the fact that consumer knowledge of a gap between firm price and salvageable costs, that is, the knowledge of the existence of a price premium, supplies quality assurance....

*   *   *

We do not wish to suggest that use of implicit (price premium-specific investment) contracts is always the cheapest way to assure quality supply. When quality characteristics can be specified cheaply and measured by a third party, and hence contract enforcement costs are anticipated to be low, explicit contractual solutions with governmentally enforced penalties (including warranties) may be a less costly solution. When explicit contract costs are high and the extent of short-run profit from deceptively low quality supply and hence the quality-assuring price premium is also high, governmental specification and enforcement of minimum quality standards may be an alternative method of reducing the costs of assuring the supply of high quality products.

*   *   *

...More generally, however, all market transactions, including those "within" the firm such as employer-employee agreements, consist of a combination of the two basic forms of contractual arrangements. Some elements of performance will be specified and enforced by third-party sanctions and other elements enforced without invoking the power of some outside party to the transaction but merely by the threat of termination of the transactional relationship.

*   *   *

Notes and Questions

1. A Price Premium for Being a Hostage: The Klein-Leffler analysis claims that price premiums are quality guaranteeing because the present value of the price premiums is a return on a firm-specific, non-salvageable investment. If the firm does not produce the promised quality, it will lose the price premium and go out of business. The firm-specific investment will be lost. The firm effectively holds itself hostage by promising to "fall on the sword" if it does not perform as promised. Consumers are convinced of the value of the guarantee. Try to come up with examples of these types of investments. You might want to start by looking at law firms.

2. Reputation as a Bonding Mechanism: Individuals or businesses invest in developing their reputation for good-faith performance, high-quality workmanship, etc. These investments take time and cost money, and they are very valuable assets. If a business develops a good reputation, it can purchase supplies on more favorable terms and charge higher prices to customers. However, if the business then starts acting in an manner inconsistent with the reputation, the business reputation is forfeited. In other words, the reputation is a forfeitable performance bond—if the business fails to perform as promised, it is penalized in the market. The potential penalty not only gives firms the incentive to perform, it also saves transaction costs by allowing contracting parties to rely on less formal contractual arrangements in dealing with the reputable firm.

3. Advertising as "Collateral": Klein and Leffler state that a celebrity does not have to use the product to show the existence of a price premium. If that is the case, do companies need celebrities at all or will other large public expenditures also show their dedication to high quality?

4. Organizational Economics: Chapter 10, "Organizational Economics," applies many of the concepts introduced by Klein and Leffler to the organization of economic activity within firms and between firms.

D. Search Costs and the Economics of Advertising

In the perfect competition model, firms are price takers. If one firm raises its price above the equilibrium price, it loses all of its customers. In most markets, however, buyers have limited information. When a store raises its price, many buyers may not realize that the product is cheaper elsewhere, so the store may lose only some of its customers. Similarly, when a store reduces its price, many people may continue to buy from higher-priced competitors because the consumers have not learned about the price cut. Firms face downward-sloping demand curves when buyers have limited information about prices.

A buyer with limited information may search for the best price. This search for a lower price or better products has costs (of time, travel, phone calls, and so forth). Search costs are the time and money costs of obtaining information about prices and products. The optimal amount of search occurs when the expected marginal benefit of searching (the expected benefit of trying one more store) equals its expected marginal cost. Because of search costs, it is perfectly rational for people to pay a high price when they are reasonably sure that a lower price is available. In most instances, people do not know which stores charge high prices. They must learn from experience and from other sources, such as talking with friends about the expected benefits of searching and paying attention to advertising.

Advertising is defined as any communication that businesses offer customers in an effort to increase demand for their products. No subject in the economics of market structure—industrial-organization economics—has been debated as intensively as advertising. Some economists consider advertising to be wasteful or "self-canceling," while others consider it to be evidence of the presence of vigorous competition.

One of the primary sources of debate among economists has been over the information content of advertising. Critics of advertising argue that most ads are tasteless, wasteful assaults on consumers' senses and that it creates illusory differences between products that are actually very close substitutes for one another. In this view, advertising is not productive because it merely allocates demand among competing firms producing goods that are fundamentally alike.

On the other hand, defenders of advertising argue that it offers real information about products and their characteristics (including their prices). The provision of such information lowers the consumers' cost of searching for goods, and permits consumers to make a rational choice among competing goods. Moreover, the Klein-Leffler excerpt in the preceding section argues that the very fact that a firm is advertising (that is, investing in a firm-specific non-salvageable asset) conveys important information to consumers.

Bates v. State Bar of Arizona
Supreme Court of the United States
433 U.S. 350 (1977)

[Read case and Notes and Questions from Chapter V]

Regardless of one's position on the value of nonfraudulent information, almost all economists would accept the proposition that false advertising is socially wasteful. In fact, all of the questionable criticisms of nonfraudulent advertising are valid criticisms of false advertising. False advertising is not only socially wasteful, but it also harms consumers by inducing them to purchase goods and services that they might otherwise not purchase. Moreover, it harms competing producers who lose potential customers to the fraudulent advertiser.

Morales v. Trans World Airlines, Inc.
Supreme Court of the United States
504 U.S. 374 (1992)

Justice SCALIA.

The issue in this case is whether the Airline Deregulation Act of 1978, 49 U.S.C. App. § 1301 *et seq.*, preempts the States from prohibiting allegedly deceptive airline fare advertisements through enforcement of their general consumer protection statutes.

I

Prior to 1978, the Federal Aviation Act of 1958 (FAA), 72 Stat. 731, as amended, 49 U.S.C. App. § 1301 *et seq.*, gave the Civil Aeronautics Board (CAB) authority to regulate interstate air fares and to take administrative action against certain deceptive trade practices. It did not, however, expressly pre-empt state regulation, and contained a "saving clause" providing that "[n]othing…in this chapter shall in any way abridge or alter the remedies now existing at common law or by statute, but the provisions of this chapter are in addition to such remedies." 49 U.S.C. App. § 1506. As a result, the States were able to regulate intrastate air fares (including those offered by interstate air carriers) and to enforce their own laws against deceptive trade practices.

In 1978, however, Congress, determining that "maximum reliance on competitive market forces" would best further "efficiency, innovation, and low prices" as well as "variety [and] quality…of air transportation services," enacted the Airline Deregulation Act (ADA). 49 U.S.C. App. §§ 1302 (a)(4), 1302 (a)(9). To ensure that the States would not undo federal deregulation with regulation of their own, the ADA included a pre-emption provision, prohibiting the States from enforcing any law "relating to rates, routes, or services" of any air carrier. § 1305 (a)(1). The ADA retained the CAB's previous enforcement authority regarding deceptive trade practices (which was transferred to the Department of Transportation (DOT) when the CAB was abolished in 1985), and it also did not repeal or alter the saving clause in the prior law.

In 1987, the National Association of Attorneys General (NAAG), an organization whose membership includes the attorneys general of all 50 States, various Territories, and the District of Columbia, adopted Air Travel Industry Enforcement Guidelines[5] containing detailed standards governing the content and format of airline advertising, the awarding of premiums to regular customers (so-called "frequent flyers"), and the payment of compensation to passengers who voluntarily yield their seats on overbooked flights. These guidelines do not purport to "create any new laws or regulations" applying to the airline industry; rather, they claim to "explain in detail how existing state laws apply to air fare advertising and frequent flyer programs." NAAG Guidelines, Introduction (1988).

[The DOT and Federal Trade Commission objected to enforcement of the NAAG Guidelines. Nonetheless the attorneys general threatened enforcement. The airlines then filed an action seeking a declaratory judgment that the guidelines were preempted. The district court found for the airlines and issued a permanent injunction against enforcement of the guidelines. The Court of Appeals affirmed.]

III

We now turn to the question whether enforcement of the NAAG guidelines on fare advertising through a State's general consumer protection laws is pre-

---

5. The court reproduced the NAAG Guidelines as an appendix to its opinion. That appendix is omitted here.

empted by the ADA. As we have often observed, '[p]re-emption may be either express or implied, and compelled whether Congress' command is explicitly contained in its structure and purpose." *FMC Corp. v. Holliday*, 498 U.S. 52, 56–57 (1990) (internal quotation marks omitted); *Shaw v. Delta Air Lines, Inc.*, 463 U.S. 85, 95 (1983). The question, at bottom, is one of statutory intent, and we accordingly "begin with the language employed by Congress and the assumption that the ordinary meaning of that language accurately expresses the legislative purpose." *Holliday, supra,* at 57; *Park 'N Fly, Inc. v. Dollar Park and Fly, Inc.*, 469 U.S. 189, 194 (1985).

A

Section 1305(a)(1) expressly preempts the States from "enact[ing] or enforc[ing] any law, rule regulation, standard, or other provision having the force and effect of law relating to rate, routes, or services of any air carrier..." For purposes of the present case, the key phrase, obviously, is "relating to." The ordinary meaning of these words is a broad one — "to stand in some relation; to have bearing or concern; to pertain; refer; to bring into association with or connection with," Black's Law Dictionary 1158 (5th ed. 1979) — and the words thus express a broad preemptive purpose.

*   *   *

[The Court held that (1) a general savings clause preserving "remedies now existing at common law or by statute" does not undermine a specific preemption provision, (2) the preemption provision applies not only to statutes directed specifically in the airline industry but also general regulatory statutes, and (3) that preemption applies even if the state regulation is consistent with federal regulation].

B

It is hardly surprising that petitioner rests most of his case on such strained reading of § 1305(a)(1), rather than contesting whether the NAAG guidelines really "relat[e] to" fares. They quite obviously do. Taking them *seriatim:* Section 2.1, governing print advertisements of fares, requires "clear and conspicuous disclosure" [defined as the lesser of one-third the size of the largest typeface in the ad or ten-point type] of restrictions such as "limited time availability, limitations on refund or exchange rights, time-of-day or day-of-week restrictions, length-of-stay requirements, advance-purchase and round-trip-purchase requirements, variations in fares from or to different airports in the same metropolitan area, limitations on breaks or changes in itinerary, limits on fare availability" and "[a]ny other material restriction on the fare." Section 2.2 imposes similar, though somewhat less onerous, restrictions on broadcast advertisements of fares; and § 3 requires billboard fare ads to state clearly and conspicuously "Substantial restrictions apply" if there are any material restrictions on the fares' availability. The guidelines further mandate that an advertised fare be available in sufficient quantities to "meet reasonably foreseeable demand" on every flight on every day in every market in which the fare is advertised; if the fare will not be available on this basis, the ad must contain a "clear and conspicuous statement on the extent of unavailability." § 2.4. Section 2.5 requires that the advertised fare include all taxes and surcharges; round-trip fares, under § 2.6, must be disclosed at least as prominently as the one-way fare when the fare is only available on round trips; and §2.7 prohibits use of the words "'sale,' 'discount,' [or] 'reduced'" unless the advertised fare is available for only a limited time and is "substantially below the usual price for the same fare with the same restrictions."

One cannot avoid the conclusion that these aspects of the guidelines "relate to" airline rates. In its terms, every one of the guidelines enumerated above bears a "reference to" air fares.... And, collectively, the guidelines establish binding requirements as to how tickets may be marketed if they are to be sold at given prices. Under Texas law, many violations of these requirements would give consumers a cause of action (for at least actual damages, see Tex. Bus. & Com. Code Ann. § 17.50 (1987 and Supp. 1991–1992)) for an airline's failure to provide a particular advertised fare—effectively creating an enforceable right to that fare when the advertisement fails to include the mandated explanations and disclaimers. This case therefore appears to us much like *Pilot Life*, in which we held that a common-law tort and contract action seeking damages for the failure of an employee benefit plan to pay benefits "relate[d] to" employee benefit plans and was preempted by ERISA, 481 U.S., at 43–44, 47–48.

In any event, beyond the guidelines' express reference to fares, it is clear as an economic matter that state restrictions on fare advertising have the forbidden significant effect upon fares. Advertising "serves to inform the public of the... prices of products and services, and thus performs an indispensable role in the allocation of resources." *Bates v. State Bar of Arizona*, 433 U.S. 350, 346 (1977). Restrictions on advertising "serv[e] to increase the difficulty of discovering the lowest cost seller...and [reduce] the incentive to price competitively." *Id.*, at 377. Accordingly, "where consumers have the benefit of price advertising, retail prices often are dramatically lower than they would be without advertising." *Ibid.* As Judge Easterbrook succinctly put it, compelling or restricting "[p]rice advertising surely 'relates to' price." *Illinois Corporate Travel v. American Airlines, Inc.*, 889 F.2d. 751, 754 (CA7 1989), cert. denied, 495 U.S. 919 (1990).

Although the State insists that it is not compelling or restricting advertising, but is instead merely preventing the market distortion caused by "false" advertising, in fact the dynamics of the air transportation industry cause the guidelines to curtail the airlines' ability to communicate fares to their customers. The expenses involved in operating an airline flight are almost entirely fixed costs; they increase very little with each additional passenger. The market for these flights is divided between consumers whose volume of purchases is relatively insensitive to price (primarily business travelers) and consumers whose demand is very price sensitive indeed (primarily pleasure travelers.) Accordingly, airlines try to sell as many seats per flight by selling seats at much lower prices to the second group (since almost all the costs are fixed even a passenger paying far below average cost is preferable to an empty seat). In order for this marketing process to work, and for it ultimately to redound to the benefit of price-conscious travelers, the airlines must be able to place substantial restrictions on the availability of the lower priced seats (so as to sell as many seats as possible at the higher rate), and must be able to advertise the lower fares. The guidelines severely burden their ability to do both at the same time: The sections requiring "clear and conspicuous disclosure" of each restriction make it impossible to take out small or short ads, as does (to a lesser extent) the provision requiring itemization of both the one-way and round-trip fares. Since taxes and surcharges vary from State to

State, the requirement that advertised fares include those charges forces the airlines to create different ads in each market. The section restricting the use of "sale," "discount," or "reduced" effectively prevents the airlines from using those terms to call attention to the fares normally offered to price-conscious travelers. As the FTC observed, "[r]equiring too much information in advertisements can have the paradoxical effect of stifling the information that customers receive." Letter from FTC to Christopher Ames, Deputy Attorney General of California, March 11, 1988, App. to Brief for Respondent Airlines 23a. Further, § 2.4, by allowing fares to be advertised only if sufficient seats are available to meet demand or if the extent of unavailability is disclosed, may make it impossible to use this marketing process at all. All in all, the obligations imposed by the guidelines would have a significant impact upon the airlines' ability to market their product, and hence a significant impact upon the fares they charge.

In concluding that the NAAG fare advertising guidelines are preempted, we do not, as Texas contends, set out on a road that leads to pre-emption of state laws against gambling and prostitution as applied to airlines. Nor need we address whether state regulation of the no price aspects of fare advertising (for example, state laws preventing obscene depictions) would similarly "relat[e] to" rates; the connection would obviously be far more tenuous. To adapt to this case our language in *Shaw*, "[s]ome state actions may affect [airline fares] in too tenuous, remote, or peripheral a manner" to have preemptive effect. 463 U.S., at 100, n. 21. In this case, as in *Shaw*, "[t]he present litigation plainly does not present a borderline question, and we express no views about where it would be appropriate to draw the line." *Ibid.* Finally, we note that our decision does not give the airlines *carte blanche* to lie to and deceive consumers; the DOT retains the power to prohibit advertisements which in its opinion do not further competitive pricing, see 49 U.S.C. App. § 1381.

*   *   *

We hold that the fare advertising provisions of the NAAG guidelines are preempted by the ADA, and affirm the judgment of the Court of Appeals insofar as it awarded injunctive and declaratory relief with respect to those provisions. Insofar as that judgment awarded injunctive relief directed at other matters, it is reversed and the injunction vacated.

It is so ordered

Justice SOUTER took no part in the consideration or decision of this case.

*   *   *

Justice STEVENS, with whom THE CHIEF JUSTICE and Justice BLACKMUN join, dissenting.

*   *   *

IV

Even if I were to agree with the Court that state regulation of deceptive advertising could "relat[e] to rates" within the meaning of § 105(a) if it had a "significant impact" upon rates, ... I would still dissent. The airlines' theoretical arguments have not persuaded me that the NAAG guidelines will have a significant impact upon the price of airline tickets. The airlines' argument (which the Court adopts, . . .) is essentially that (1) airlines must engage in price discrimination in order to compete and operate efficiently; (2) a modest amount of misleading price advertising may facilitate that practice; (3) thus compliance with the NAAG guidelines might increase the cost of price advertising or reduce the sales generated by the advertisements; (4) as the costs increase and revenues decrease, the airlines might purchase less price advertising; and (5) a reduction in price advertising might cause a reduction in price competition, which, in turn, might result in higher airline rates. This argument is not supported by any legislative or judicial findings.

Even on the assumption that the Court's economic reasoning is sound and restrictions on price advertising could affect rates in this manner, the airlines have not sustained their burden of proving that compliance with the NAAG guidelines would have a "significant" effect on their ability to market their product and, therefore, on their rates. Surely Congress could not have intended to pre-empt every state and local law and regulation that similarly increases the airlines' costs of doing business and, consequently, has a similar "significant impact" upon their rates.

For these reasons, I respectfully dissent.

Notes and Questions

1. Punishment or Efficient Policing?: The court is allowing both regulation of airline advertising and private lawsuits to occur in the same setting. What rationale is the court employing by allowing this "double whammy?" Are the courts trying to penalize airlines twice for their advertising violations or are the courts making the policing of the market more efficient by allowing these private lawsuits?

2. The Distribution of Prices: Some buyers know more about prices than others. Tourists, for example, have less information than local residents about which stores charge high prices. Moreover, it may be costly for tourists to acquire that information. For that reason, tourists are more likely to buy products at high-priced stores. When some customers have better information than others, a distribution of prices can exist even in very competitive markets. Informed consumers go to low-priced stores. Some uninformed consumers go to the low-priced stores by chance, but others buy from high-priced stores because they don't know that other stores offer lower prices.

3. Better Information Reduces Prices: As consumers get better information about prices, they pay lower average prices. With better information, more buyers go to low-priced stores and fewer to high-priced stores, which gives high-priced stores incentives to reduce their prices. Better information can reduce prices even if all consumers are not equally informed because the information improves their guesses about which stores charge lower prices.

4. Consumer Sovereignty and "Tunas with Good Taste" versus "Tuna that Tastes Good": In response to the critics' claim that advertising is tasteless, defenders of advertising argue that the critics are merely trying to substitute their own subjective judgments for consumer sovereignty. In essence, the critics do not have faith in the intelligence of the average consumer, and the defenders do.

5. Search Costs versus Advertising Costs: Evaluate the following statement: "If it were not cheaper for sellers to provide the information in lieu of having consumers search for it, some sellers would cease to advertise and would lower their prices by more than the cost to consumers of getting the information. Non-advertising sellers could then drive out of the market those sellers who continued to advertise. This, of course, has not happened."

6. Price Discrimination and Airline Ticket Prices: Review the discussion of price discrimination in Chapter V, Section D, *infra*. How well does the airline ticket market satisfy the criteria for successful price discrimination?

E. Monitoring Contractual Performance: Agent-Principal Contracting

Specialization and comparative advantage mean that individuals often find it desirable to hire someone to engage in activities on their behalf. In the jargon of the law-and-economics literature, a **principal** hires an **agent** to do something on his or her behalf. People hire a general contractor to build their house, a real estate agent to sell their house, and a stock broker to buy and sell stocks for them. Shareholders hire managers (officers and directors) to run their corporations. Citizens elect legislators to represent their interests. Professors hire publishing companies to publish their books, and so forth.

These principal-agent contracts are usually executory in the sense that performance takes place some period of time after the agency relationship is created. In order to make sure that the agent does what he has agreed to do, the principal must monitor the agent's performance. This monitoring is costly for at least three reasons. First, information costs—information is scarce and costly to obtain. Second, opportunity costs—the principal must spend some time monitoring the agent. Third, specialized knowledge—the principal often does not know enough about the specialized task undertaken by the agent to determine whether the agent is in fact doing what he promised to do. **Agency costs**, which are the costs associated with the agent's ability to not act in the principal's best interest, include the costs to the principal of the agent not acting as promised plus the costs incurred by the principal to prevent the agent from deviating from the promised action. Like all economic decisions, the principal has the incentive to monitor their agent's behavior up to the point where the marginal costs of additional monitoring is equal to the expected marginal benefit from making the agent behave according to their agreement. The existence of positive monitoring costs means that the principal will make a rational decision to not attempt to monitor all of the agent's actions.

Positive monitoring costs also means that the agent knows that there is a range of activity in which the agent can shirk—not perform as promised—with little concern about repercussions. Moreover, this incentive to shirk is often exacerbated by the existence of more immediate incentive conflicts between the best interests of the principal and the best interests of the agent. **Agent-principal conflicts** arise when the agent's incentives are not aligned with the principal's interests. Specifically, when the agent acting on behalf of the principal bears costs that

Figure VII-1

Agent-Principal Conflict

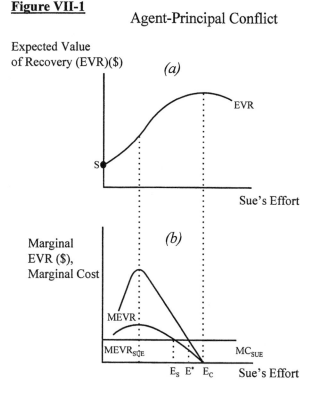

the principal does not bear, or when the agent receives benefits that the principal does not receive, the divergence between costs and benefits is likely to drive a wedge between what is best for the agent and what is best for the principal.

Attorney-client relationships are fraught with potential agent-principal conflicts. Consider the situation of a personal injury lawyer working under a contingency fee. Assume that the client, Charles, has retained the lawyer, Sue, to represent him in a case involving the alleged wrongful death of his wife. Sue is to receive 33.33% of any amount recovered through settlement, trial, or appeal. Sue is an experienced litigator, and she has determined that their chances for success depend on the amount of time and effort that Sue (and her team of associates, clerks, and paralegals) devotes to the case. Defendant's insurance company is pushing for a negotiated settlement prior to trial. The settlement offer is tempting for Sue because one-third of the proposed offer is a guaranteed fee for the firm—it is the proverbial "bird in the hand"—while a potentially larger recovery is speculative and will require much more work by her team. Nevertheless, Sue believes that the additional effort by her team will increase both the dollar amount of potential settlement offers and the potential amount awarded after the trial. On the other hand, Sue's continued prosecution of the case involves considerable opportunity cost—her practice is booming and continued work on Charles' case takes her away from other profitable opportunities. Charles is interested only in maximizing his Expected Value of Recovery.

The potential agent-principal conflict can be demonstrated diagrammatically. In Figure VII-1 (a), Expected Value of Recovery (EVR) is shown on the vertical axis and Sue's effort (a proxy for the effort of her litigation team) on the horizontal axis. The EVR curve begins at level S because the settlement amount (S) can be recovered without any additional effort. The EVR curve then increases at an increasing rate, but eventually increases at an decreasing rate as the law of diminishing marginal returns sets in, and ultimately begins to decline at E_C. Charles would prefer, and probably expects, Sue to use effort level E_C. However, Sue's incentives are different because she must bear the marginal costs of additional effort by her team. In order to demonstrate this, we need to transform the EVR curve (which depicts *total* EVR) into a marginal curve, MEVR, which is shown in Figure VII-1 (b).

Now, consider Sue's decision. Assume, for convenience, that Sue's team has constant marginal costs, MC_S, in Figure VII-1 (b). On the margin, Sue expects to recover one-third of Charles' MEVR. In Figure VII-1 (b), this is shown as $MEVR_S$. Sue will continue devoting effort to this case up to the effort level where her marginal expected value of recovery, $MEVR_S$, is equal to her marginal cost, MC_S. Note that the level of effort that maximizes Sue's EVR is E_S.

The agent-principal conflict is clear. Charles wants Sue to work up to E_C and Sue wants to work up to E_S. Sue's marginal cost drives a wedge between what is best for her principal and what is best for her team.

At one level of analysis, principal agent conflicts are simply contracting problems. Informed parties can recognize the potential for conflict and write detailed contracts that specify the precise terms of the principal agent relationship. For example, Charles could include a clause that requires Sue to act as if her marginal costs were zero. Alternatively, Charles and Sue could negotiate a cost sharing arrangement—say, one-third MC paid by Sue and two-thirds paid by Charles—that gets them to E*, where the combined MEVR equals their combined MC. However, negotiating, writing, and enforcing those contracts is a costly endeavor. Consider the difficulty of writing a contract that allocates the law firm's costs. Because of those transaction costs, not all agency costs will be addressed in the contract.

At another level of analysis, suggested by Klein & Leffler's analysis, agent-principal conflicts are resolved because the anticipated shirking affects the contract price and, thus, agents have incentives to take steps that convince principals that they will not shirk. Agents who develop a reputation for "going the extra yard" for their principals will be more highly valued in the market.

Heinzman v. Fine, Fine, Legum & Fine
Supreme Court of Virginia
234 S.E. 2d 282 (1977)

POFF, J.

We consider whether, when an attorney employed under a contingent fee contract is discharged without just cause and the client employs another attorney who effects a settlement, the discharged attorney is entitled to the contractual fee or to a fee based upon *quantum meruit* for services rendered prior to discharge. The fee in issue was awarded to Fine, Fine, Legum & Fine, Attorneys at Law (hereinafter, Legum), in orders approving settlement of a claim for damages for personal injuries growing out of an automobile accident. These orders were entered in a suit filed by attorney Augustus Anninos for Doyle J. Heinzman against James N. Mouser.

The facts were stipulated. On January 14, 1975, two days after the accident, Heinzman signed a "power of attorney" engaging Legum to represent him and promising to pay a fee of "1/3 of the gross amount recovered" by way of "compromise", "trial", or "appeal". After advising Mouser's insurer that he represented Heinzman, Legum wrote letters to the Norfolk Police Department, DePaul Hospital, and Dr. James H. Phillips requesting reports. On January 29, 1975, Legum settled the property damage claim, deducted a fee of one-third of the gross amount recovered, and remitted the balance to Heinzman. At that time, the question of Heinzman's residual disability had not been determined, and "the (personal injury) case was not in a posture" to be settled. Thereafter, Legum talked by telephone with Dr. Phillips, held conferences with Heinzman, and forwarded a medical report to Mouser's insurer. Other than that, he did "no work at all on the case" and conducted "no investigation or research."

Heinzman approached Legum on March 5, 1975 and asked him to lend him money for living expenses. Explaining that such a loan would violate professional ethics, Legum refused. Heinzman thereupon discharged Legum, demanded his file, and employed Anninos on a contingent fee basis. The next day, Anninos wrote to Legum asking for an itemized account of the work he had done and the amount of the fee he expected. Legum replied that "it is our position that we are entitled to one-third gross of any recovery and that it is not necessary to give you an approximate (sic) of any time that I have spent on the matter."

Anninos filed suit for Heinzman against Mouser, "worked the case from 'A to Z' ", and on the day before trial was scheduled, settled the personal injury claim for $10,000.00. Before entry of an order approving the settlement, Legum filed a motion asking the trial court to award him a fee of one-third of the settlement funds. Following a hearing and argument on the motion, the trial court addressed a letter opinion to counsel holding that "Mr. Legum is entitled to recover his one-third contractual fee out of the settlement funds." By orders entered December 19, 1975 and January 15, 1976, the trial court approved the settlement and awarded Legum an attorney's fee of $3,333.33.

The precise issue we address is a matter of first impression in this Court. Among cases decided elsewhere, the facts and statutes were so disparate that we cannot confidently identify a majority rule or define a developing trend. We must, in any event, determine the rule in Virginia as applied to the facts and circumstances in the case before us.

In support of the trial court's award of the contractual fee, Legum relies, in part, upon Code § 54-69 (Repl. Vol. 1974) which provides:

> ["An attorney shall be entitled, as a fee, to the amount which the clerk is authorized to tax in the bill of costs, in any suit, or for any service as such attorney. But any contract made with an attorney for higher compensation shall be valid and he may recover such sum as he contracts for with the party for whom the service is rendered; and, if there be no such contract, he may recover from such party what his services are reasonably worth."]

Legum cites *Yates and Ayres v. Robertson & Berkeley*, 80 Va. 475 (1885), where this Court construed an 1840 amendment[1] to section 15, chapter 76, Code of 1819, a statutory ancestor of Code § 54-69. Noting that the statute had formerly limited lawyers to fees taxed as costs, we concluded that the amendment had removed the limitation.

> "The policy of the law as to the lawyers, appears to be entirely changed, and they are left free to conduct their business transactions with their fellowmen upon the same basis as other citizens; they and those dealing with them to be mutually bound by their contracts, express or implied." *Id.*, 80 Va. at 479.

That language must be interpreted in context with the circumstances reflected in an instruction granted in *Yates* and approved on appeal. The instruction told the jury that if they believed that the clients

> "employed the (attorneys) to represent them...and it was understood between the parties that (the attorneys) should receive compensation for such services, though the amount of compensation was not fixed; and that (the attorneys)...performed the service...then (the attorneys) are entitled to recover what such services were reasonably worth...." *Id.*, 80 Va. at 478.

Code § 54-69 deals with both express contracts and implied contracts. With respect to implied contracts and in accord with *Yates* where the contract was implied and the attorneys' services had been fully performed, the statute authorizes an attorney to recover "what his services are reasonably worth." With respect to express contracts, the statute provides that an attorney "may recover such sum as he contracts for" but clearly contemplates that he may do so only when "the service is rendered." Contrary to Legum's position, neither *Yates* nor the statute authorizes an attorney to recover the contractual fee where, as here, the services engaged in the contract have not been fully performed.

Legum also relies upon Code § 54-70 (Repl. Vol. 1974) which provides:

> "Any person having or claiming a right of action sounding in tort, or for liquidated or unliquidated damages on contract, may contract with any attorney at law to prosecute the same, and such attorney shall have a lien upon such cause of action as security for his fees for any services rendered in relation to the cause of action or claim. And when any such contract shall be made, and written notice of the claim of such lien shall be given to the opposite party, his attorney or agent, any settlement or adjustment of such cause of action shall be void against the lien so created, except as proof of liability on such cause of action. Nothing in this section shall affect the existing law in respect to champertous contracts."

Legum interprets this statute to mean that, once an attorney and his client have negotiated a contract, the attorney becomes entitled to claim a lien coextensive with the contractual fee. But the statute is not so broad. Rather, it measures the lien by the "fees for any services rendered in relation to the cause of action or claim", *i.e.*, compensation for the quantity and quality of the work performed.

---

1. As codified, that amendment provided in part that "any contract made with an attorney...shall be valid, and may be enforced in like manner with any other contract." Section 11, chapter 164, Code of 1849.

Aside from the statutes, Legum argues that a contract for legal services is the same as any other contract and is governed by the same rules concerning breach and the measure of damages.

We agree that, absent overreaching on the part of an attorney[2], contracts for legal services are valid and when those services have been performed as contemplated in the contract, the attorney is entitled to the fee fixed in the contract and to the lien granted by the statute. The question remains whether, as Legum contends, an attorney employed under a contingent fee contract and discharged without just cause[3] is entitled to recover from the proceeds of a later settlement the full amount of the contractual fee.

Courts which make no distinction between contracts for legal services and other contracts answer this question in the affirmative. The decisions rest upon various rationales: courts cannot convert bilateral contracts into unilateral contracts and relieve one of the parties of the burden of his bargain, *Friedman v. Mindlin*, 91 Misc. 473, 155 N.Y.S. 295 (1915); a client "who has wrongfully broken a contract should not be permitted to reap advantage from his own wrong", *Dolph v. Speckart*, 94 Or. 550, 564, 186 P. 32, 35 (1920); when the client wrongfully frustrates performance, the attorney is entitled to the presumption that he would have fully performed, *McElhinney v. Kline*, 6 Mo.App. 94 (1878).

We reject such rationales, for we believe the premise upon which they rest is wrong. Contracts for legal services are not the same as other contracts.

> "(I)t is a misconception to attempt to force an agreement between an attorney and his client into the conventional modes of commercial contracts. While such a contract may have similar attributes, the agreement is, essentially, in a classification peculiar to itself. Such an agreement is permeated with the paramount relationship of attorney and client which necessarily affects the rights and duties of each." *Krippner v. Matz*, 205 Minn. 497, 506, 287 N.W. 19, 24 (1939).

Seldom does a client stand on an equal footing with an attorney in the bargaining process. Necessarily, the layman must rely upon the knowledge, experience, skill, and good faith of the professional. Only the attorney can make an informed judgment as to the merit of the client's legal rights and obligations, the prospects of success or failure, and the value of the time and talent which he must invest in the undertaking. Once fairly negotiated, the contract creates a relationship unique in the law. The attorney-client relationship is founded upon trust and confidence, and when the foundation fails, the relationship may be, indeed should be, terminated.

Termination of the contract of employment is addressed by Virginia Code of Professional Responsibility, Rule 6:II:DR 2-110. A lawyer is permitted to withdraw upon specified conditions. He is required to withdraw when "discharged by his client." No condition is imposed upon the client's right to discharge his lawyer.

---

2. Virginia Code of Professional Responsibility provides that "(a) lawyer shall not enter into an agreement for, charge, or collect an illegal or clearly excessive fee." Rule 6:II:DR 2-106(A).

3. "(A) lawyer shall not advance or guarantee financial assistance to his client". Rule 6:II:DR 5-103(B). Legum quite properly refused Heinzman's request for a loan, and so far as the stipulated facts disclose, his discharge was entirely without just cause.

Legum does not dispute the fact that a client has an absolute right to discharge his attorney. He contends, however, that when the discharge is without just cause, the act constitutes a breach of contract and that the measure of damages is the fee fixed in the contract. We agree with the courts that hold otherwise.

> "That the client may at any time for any reason or without any reason discharge his attorney is a firmly-established rule.... (T)he attorney may recover the reasonable value of the services which he has rendered but he cannot recover for damages for the breach of contract. The discharge of the attorney by his client does not constitute a breach of the contract, because it is a term of such contract, implied from the peculiar relationship which the contract calls into existence, that the client may terminate the contract at any time with or without cause." *Martin v. Camp*, 219 N.Y. 170, 174, 114 N.E. 46, 48 (1916).

Overruling its prior decisions, the court in *Fracasse v. Brent*, 6 Cal.3d 784, 789–90, 100 Cal.Rptr. 385, 388–89, 494 P.2d 9, 12–13 (1972), applied the same rule and explained the reasons for the rule:

> "The right to discharge is of little value if the client must risk paying the full contract price for services not rendered upon a determination by a court that the discharge was without legal cause. The client may frequently be forced to choose between continuing the employment of an attorney in whom he has lost faith, or risking the payment of double contingent fees equal to the greater portion of any amount eventually recovered.... Unless a rule is adopted allowing an attorney as full compensation the reasonable value of services rendered to the time of discharge, clients will often feel required to continue in their service attorneys in whose integrity, judgment or capacity they have lost confidence."

We share the conclusion that *quantum meruit* is the most functional and equitable measure of recovery. The law does not favor recoveries premised upon conjecture. In awarding the contractual fee, the trial court presupposed that Legum, had he not been discharged, would have achieved a recovery exactly equivalent to that achieved by Anninos. But this is entirely speculative. Legum might have effected a greater settlement or won a larger verdict; considering the vagaries of trial, he might have recovered nothing.

Having in mind the special nature of a contract for legal services, we hold that when, as here, an attorney employed under a contingent fee contract is discharged without just cause and the client employs another attorney who effects a recovery, the discharged attorney is entitled to a fee based upon *quantum meruit*[4] for services rendered prior to discharge and, as security for such fee, to the lien granted by Code § 54-70.

Insofar as the judgment awards Legum a contractual fee, the judgment will be reversed and the case will be remanded with instructions to award Legum a fee based upon *quantum meruit* for services rendered prior to discharge.

---

4. As applied in this context, a quantum meruit determination looks to "the reasonable value of the services rendered, not in benefit to the client, but, in themselves". *County of Campbell v. Howard*, 133 Va. 19, 51, 112 S.E. 876, 885 (1922)....

Reversed and remanded.

Notes and Questions

1. Opportunistic Discharge: The phenomenon of opportunistic behavior, or opportunism, occurs when one party to a contract recognizes that the other party has made contract-specific investments in reliance of the contractual agreement and then engages in post-contractual, pre-performance manipulation of contract terms. Such behavior is rational if it is not possible for the victim to retaliate economically against the opportunist. The opportunist then performs the contract in a manner contrary to the victim's understanding of the terms, but not necessarily contrary to the written or explicit terms of the contract, in order to transfer wealth from the victim. In other words, under certain circumstances, an *ex ante* mutually beneficial contract may be transformed into an ex post unilaterally beneficial contract through the unbridled self-interested opportunistic behavior of a contracting party. Prior to his discharge, Legum had made a client-specific investment that had little, if any, value if Legum were not allowed to continue working on the case. What could Heinzman expect to gain by attempting to extort some of the client-specific investment from Legum? If Legum had no recourse against termination, could Legum be vulnerable to an opportunistic modification of the contract terms to, say, a ten percent fee instead of one-third? Does *quantum meruit* provide adequate protection for Legum? Does the fact that Legum, the agent, is the party who must be concerned about his reputation in the market make him more or less vulnerable to opportunistic termination?

2. Fiduciary Duties and Codes of Professional Conduct: Transaction costs make it difficult to write a fully-specified contract. The gaps in contracts are sometimes filled by fiduciary duties and other codes of professional conduct. Real estate agents, stock brokers, attorneys, and many other professionals are supposed to be constrained by guidelines that solve the agency problem. For example, a lawyer "zealously asserts the client's position under the rules of the adversary system." Model Rules of Professional Conduct, prmbl. (1983). Such professional standards should be good for the profession because, to the extent they lessen principals' concerns about agent loyalty, they increase the demand for the services provided by the profession.

F. Game Theory

Many economic decisions must be made in an atmosphere of imperfect information where one decision maker knows that the actions of other decision makers will impact the outcome of his or her decision. This interdependence requires decision makers to develop a strategy for dealing with the imperfect information. Game theory is the area of economics that has developed to deal with mutual interdependence and imperfect information. Recent developments in game theory have provided many insights for the economic analysis of law.

Game theory analyzes the behavior of "players" in conflict situations governed by rules. As one might expect, the expected outcome—or **dominant strat-**

egy—of the games is determined by the stakes under alternative rules. The relevance of this area of economics to law is obvious, as law is often concerned with conflict within a set of rules. Game theory helps predict how the strategies of players change and how the expected outcomes vary as the players are faced with alternative rules.

The most basic model of game theory is the Prisoner's Dilemma. The Prisoner's Dilemma is best introduced through a hypothetical story. Adam and Baker work together in the accounting office of a major New York bank. They are best friends. One day an auditor shows up and, upon a thorough audit of the bank's accounts, determines that $1 million has been embezzled. Upon further investigation, all available circumstantial evidence indicates that only Adam or Baker could have committed the crime. However, there is no evidence—such as conspicuous consumption of automobiles, vacations and so forth—to indicate which one committed the crime. In fact, the police suspect that they were in it together. Remember—they are (were?) best friends. Both Adam and Baker are charged with embezzlement. The police are confident that they can convict both defendants on the available evidence, but securing a confession of a conspiracy from one of the defendants would save the police a lot of time and effort. Both Adam and Baker claim to be innocent.

Immediately following their arrests, Adam and Baker are held in separate cells in the City Jail. They are totally shut off from one another—communication of any type is impossible. The City Prosecutor, who does not want to go through a long trial, makes the following offer to Adam: (I) If you refuse to testify, and if Baker continues to maintain his silence, you will be convicted of criminally negligent bookkeeping (a new crime created in the wake of the 1980s savings and loan debacle) and sentenced to 3 years in prison; (II) If you agree to testify against Baker, and if Baker continues to maintain his silence, then the charges against you will be dropped; (III) If you refuse to testify, and if Baker testifies against you, then you will go to jail for 15 years; (IV) If both you and Baker testify against each other, then you will both go to jail for 10 years. Finally, the City Prosecutor says that his assistant is making the exact same offer to Baker.

The Prisoner's Dilemma is evident when Adam's choices are presented in matrix form. The payoff to Adam under alternative strategies are represented in Figure VII-2 (a). Cells I–IV indicate the rules of the game as set forth by the City Prosecutor. Baker's behavior, which is totally exogenous (beyond Adam's control), is represented by the column on the left side of the matrix. Adam's strategy is represented by the row at the top of the matrix. The four cells represent the four possible outcomes of Adam's dilemma. In the formal language of game theory, the four cells are referred to as the "choice space" or "opportunity set." Consideration of the matrix reveals that the testify strategy **dominates** the silence strategy. No matter what strategy Baker chooses, Adam is better off having chosen to testify. But this is not the end of the story.

At the same time that the City Prosecutor is making his pitch to Adam, his assistant is making the exact same offer to Baker. Baker's opportunity set is presented in Figure VII-2 (b). Clearly, the testify strategy also dominates for Baker—it always results in the lowest jail sentence.

The Prisoner's Dilemma is revealed when the symmetrical payoff functions are combined in a single matrix. In Figure VII-2 (c), the payoffs to Adam are indicated by the left-hand numbers in each cell. The payoffs to Baker are indicated

<u>Figure VII-2</u>
Prisoner's Dilemma
Figure (a) -- Adam's Payoff

	Adam Stays Quiet	Adam Talks
Baker Stays Quiet	I -3	II 0
Baker Talks	III -15	IV -10

Figure (b) -- Baker's Payoff

	Adam Stays Quiet	Adam Talks
Baker Stays Quiet	I -3	II -15
Baker Talks	III 0	IV -10

Figure (c) -- Combined Payoffs (Adam, Baker)

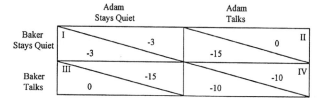

by the right-hand numbers. Since the prosecutors' rules make it individually rational for each party to adopt the testify strategy, the **solution** to this game is predicted to be Cell IV. In economic models, such a predictable solution is referred to as an equilibrium. The true nature of the Prisoner's Dilemma is revealed by the observation that Cell IV contains the largest total number of years in prison. Adam and Baker would both be better off if they could make an enforceable contract under which both agree to remain silent. Cell I appears very attractive relative to ending up in cell IV.

Page v. United States
United States Court of Appeals for the Seventh Circuit
884 F.2d 300 (1989)

Easterbrook, J.

Students of strategy and bargaining cut their teeth on the game of Prisoners' Dilemma. Two prisoners, unable to confer with one another, must decide whether to take the prosecutor's offer: confess, inculpate the other, and serve a year in jail, or keep silent and serve five years. If the prisoners could make a (binding) bargain with each other, they would keep silent and both would go free. But they can't communicate, and each fears that the other will talk. So both confess. Studying Prisoners' Dilemma has led to many insights about strategic interactions. See Thomas C. Schelling, *The Strategy of Conflict* 53–80, 119–61 (1960; 1980 rev.); Robert Axelrod, *The Evolution of Cooperation* (1984). Eldon Page did not have the leisure to study the game before he had to play it.

Page and Maurice Falls were charged with armed bank robbery. On the day set for Page's trial, the prosecutor appeared with Falls in tow. Falls had signed an agreement promising, in exchange for a lower sentence, to plead guilty and testify against Page. After the judge accepted Falls' plea, Page caved in and pleaded guilty too. Back in jail, Falls and Page were able at last to coordinate. Each presently asked leave to withdraw his plea. Too late, the judge said. Both were sentenced and appealed. We affirmed in an unpublished order.

Page tried again, filing a petition under 28 U.S.C. § 2255 and arguing that trial counsel rendered ineffective assistance in letting him plead guilty. This was brought up short by the fact that Page had not argued on his original appeal that trial counsel was constitutionally inadequate. Because Page had fresh counsel for the appeal, the omission forfeits the point unless Page could establish "cause" for and "prejudice" from the neglect. *United States v. Kovic*, 830 F.2d 680, 684 (7th Cir. 1987). See *Wainwright v. Sykes*, 433 U.S. 72 (1977). Ineffective assistance of counsel is "cause," *Murray v. Carrier*, 477 U.S. 478, 488 (1986), so Page maintains that his appellate counsel was ineffective in failing to challenge the effectiveness of trial counsel. See *Evitts v. Lucey*, 469 U.S. 387 (1985). Page also points to other aspects of appellate counsel's performance that he finds deficient. Fearing infinite regress, the district judge brushed aside all questions concerning appellate counsel and went straight to the foundation of the claim, holding that Page's trial counsel had supplied effective assistance and denying the petition for relief.

The first question facing us on Page's appeal is whether ineffective assistance of counsel may be raised at all, and if so in which court. The United States Attorney insists that the attack on appellate counsel comes too late. It, too, was surrendered because not raised on appeal. Such an argument is better suited to the works of Ionesco and Beckett than to the Federal Reporter. How could appellate counsel attack his own competence? Although this is not logically impossible (counsel could say, for example, that although he knew he ought to challenge trial counsel he had not had the time to prepare a brief on the subject), it is so implausible that we cannot demand it of counsel. Few of us have insight into our shortcomings; fewer still have the nerve to flaunt our own failings. Just as trial counsel need not attack his competence during trial, appellate counsel need not protest his inadequacies. That may be left to the next step in the process without fear of forfeiture.

"Where" is slightly more difficult than "whether." Two courts of appeals have held that the defendant's exclusive recourse is a motion asking the court of appeals to recall its mandate on the ground of counsel's inadequacy. *Feldman v. Henman*, 815 F.2d 1318, 1321–22 (9th Cir. 1987); *United States v. Winterhalder*, 724 F.2d 109, 111 (10th Cir. 1983). They reason that because district judges must obey the mandate of the court of appeals, and may not issue orders compelling appellate courts to do anything (such as hear the appeal anew, a common remedy for deficient appellate counsel), the claim must come to the court of appeals in the first instance. Other courts of appeals have allowed defendants to start in the district courts. E.g., *Mack v. Smith*, 659 F.2d 23, 25–26 (5th Cir. 1981); *United States v. DeFalco*, 644 F.2d 132, 137 (3d Cir. 1979). We join this latter group.

Section 2255 authorizes collateral attacks on criminal judgments. It also specifies the forum: "the court which imposed the [contested] sentence." That statutory designation prevails even though relief may call for revision of a judgment that has been affirmed by the court of appeals. Review of existing judgments simply defines a "collateral" attack. If the court of appeals has actually considered and rejected a claim of ineffective assistance of counsel on appeal, that decision binds the district court unless there has been an intervening change of law. *United States v. Mazak*, 789 F.2d 580 (7th Cir. 1986). But if the issue has never been presented on appeal, it is open in the district court as any other question would be under § 2255.

Relief does not require the district court to issue orders to the court of appeals. District courts may grant relief. Ineffective assistance may justify vacating and reentering the judgment of conviction, allowing a fresh appeal. It may also justify a new trial on occasion. Counsel is ineffective only if performance below the norms of the profession causes prejudice. *Strickland v. Washington*, 466 U.S. 668, 687 (1984). Prejudice means a "reasonable probability that, but for counsel's unprofessional errors, the result of the [appeal] would have been different," *id.* at 694. Showing a "reasonable probability" but not certainty supports a new judgment and a new appeal (so that we may decide whether the outcome *actually* would have been different). If the showing goes further and establishes to the district court's satisfaction that reversal would have been a sure thing, this must mean that the district judge has become convinced that there was a fatal error in the trial. *That* error — which may be reached once the ineffective assistance clears away the bar of *Wainwright v. Sykes* — requires a new trial or other remedy adequate to rectify the wrong. So whether the remedy turns out to be a new appeal or a new trial, the district judge need not issue an order binding on this court. No rule of law forbids district courts to entertain proceedings that call into question the adequacy of counsel's performance on appeal. See *Standard Oil Co. v. United States*, 429 U.S. 17 (1976), holding that district courts do not need leave of appellate courts to entertain motions under Fed. R. Civ. P. 60(b) alleging fraud on the court. Because district courts are the best forums to conduct any inquiries into counsel's strategic decisions that may prove necessary, we conclude that Page properly filed this petition in the district court rather than our court.

Having got this far, however, Page is stymied. For appellate counsel need not raise all possible claims of error. *Jones v. Barnes*, 463 U.S. 745 (1983). One of the principal functions of appellate counsel is winnowing the potential claims so that the court may focus on those with the best prospects. Defendants need dedicated, skillful appellate counsel, not routineers who present every non-frivolous claim. (Recall the saw: "He needed a lawyer, and all he had was a member of the bar.") Page has not argued that his appellate counsel failed to advocate his cause skillfully on the initial appeal. He has argued, instead, that counsel left out an issue he deems meritorious. The district court responded by deciding that trial counsel had furnished effective assistance, as if the claim of ineffective appellate counsel were equivalent to proof.

The threshold question is not whether trial counsel was inadequate but whether trial counsel was so *obviously* inadequate that appellate counsel had to present that question to render adequate assistance. Counsel could be constitutionally deficient in omitting a dead-bang winner even while zealously pressing other strong (but unsuccessful) claims. Page falls well short of making such a showing, however. Counsel advised Page to get the best deal he could after Falls turned against him. Page is not the first and will not be the last to feel the sting of Prisoners' Dilemma, and the Constitution does not demand that counsel escape a predicament that game theorists consider inescapable in one-shot performances. The district judge found that Page's lawyer prepared conscientiously for trial, made appropriate motions, and would have gone forward had Page stood on his former plea of innocence. Page insists that trial counsel lied when informing him that Falls would testify against him; as the district court observed, this is what Falls had promised to do in the written plea agreement. We need not agree with the district court's conclusion that trial counsel was adequate to see that appellate counsel could have made a reasoned decision to pursue other arguments instead. Page's remaining claims—that appellate counsel did not consult "meaningfully" with him in preparing the appeal, that counsel's briefs were vague, that counsel did not file a petition for rehearing after losing—are insufficient to call into question the adequacy of the representation. See Morris v. Slappy, 461 U.S. 1, 13–14 (1983).

AFFIRMED.

Notes and Questions

1. Rational Self-Interest: Given the rules of the Prisoner's Dilemma game, neither party would make a different choice even if they could talk before they made their plea. In their meeting, they could say that they would cooperate with each other and not confess, however, a rational self-interested person would nonetheless confess. Also, even if each person *knew* what the other would do, they would still choose to confess on each other. Many students find it difficult to understand why individuals like Adam and Baker are *always* better off by confessing. The most common mistake is inadvertently to change the rules of the game. For instance, many people use sanctions (like the mafia) to change outcomes or they use personal feelings to change the game. Many people say that they would rather cooperate and feel "good" about themselves. However, subject to the caveat in the next note, it is always better to confess against the other person than spend a few extra years in prison.

2. Solving the Prisoner's Dilemma: It has been suggested that one of the reasons the Mafia—or organized crime, in general—has been successful is that the threat of **sanctions** (that is, execution) for testifying against another member has enabled them to avoid Cell IV. What happens in this scenario is that the mafia changes the payoffs of the game. A few more years in prison is preferable to a lesser sentence where you are killed. The federal witness protection program is intended to counteract the threat of revenge.

3. The Prosecutor's Incentives: The rules of the game determine the outcome, and the prosecutor makes the rules. A final point about the nature of game theory is revealed by a consideration of the prosecutor's strategy in the earlier story. Suppose the prosecutor is paid on the basis of how many years of prison sentences he produces per year. Alternatively, suppose the prosecutor is paid on the basis of the number of years times the number of individuals convicted. What is the prosecutor's optimal strategy under either set of rules?

4. Game Theory and the Law: Game theory has many applications to the economic analysis of law. Obviously, as suggested by the basic Prisoner's Dilemma model, it raises questions about the procedural rules that apply to codefendants being represented by the same lawyer. Other applicable areas, include cartel theory and antitrust law, bankruptcy and voidable preferential transfers, bank runs and deposit insurance, constitutional economics and social choice theory, apparently coercive contract terms, and the regulation of two-tier tender offers.

5. Advertising Wars: The prisoner's dilemma model helps explain behavior observed in the business world. Promotions by large fast-food chains are a prime example. McDonalds and Burger King participate in these promotions which raise production costs (prizes, promotional fees, etc.) to try and steal away the competitor's customers. As shown by Figure VII-3, McDonalds would be better off to have the promotion, because no matter what Burger King does, McDonalds realizes more profits (and Burger King has less profits). Of course, Burger King applies the same logic and both franchises offer promotional contests. The dilemma for Burger King and McDonalds is that their joint profits could be maximized if they could coordinate and stay in cell I. Unfortunately for the firms, they are not allowed to communicate about these contests because it would probably be a violation of the antitrust laws. The best action for each firm acting alone is cell IV.

6. One-Shot versus Multiple Series Games: One of the major arguments against the Prisoner's Dilemma game is that it is only played one time. That is, if the actors could play multiple times they would realize the dilemma of the game and move from box IV to box I. These tacit collusive solutions—outcomes without specific, formal agreement—exist where, over an indefinite period of time, firms recognize their own interests will be served when they cooperate and maxi-

Figure VII-3

McDonalds and Burger King Promotional Prisoner's Dilemma

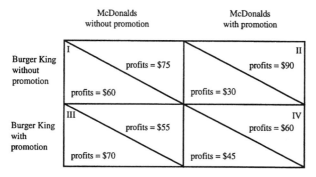

mize both firms' profits. However, in a multiple series game, where there is definite ending point, there is a major incentive to cheat on the last round. That is, each firm cooperates until the last round, then they cheat. However, since each firm knows the other will cheat in the last round they cheat in the round before, and this logic works itself forward until the first round of the game. This is known as backward induction.

Chapter VIII

Labor Markets

The study of labor markets begins with the familiar supply-and-demand model. On the demand side of the labor market are employers whose decisions about the hiring of labor are influenced by conditions in product and capital markets. On the supply side of the labor market are workers and potential workers whose decisions about where and whether to work must take into account alternative uses of their time.

In this chapter, the basic economic model of labor markets is presented. Section A is an overview of the interaction of labor market supply and demand, with applications to the minimum wage, payroll taxes, fringe benefits, and employment at will. Section B provides a more detailed look at employers' behavior, including the demand for labor, investments in employees, and discrimination. Section C considers employees' behavior, including human capital investments and occupational choices. Section D examines the economic role of unions and the collective bargaining process.

A. Supply and Demand Analysis: An Overview

The basic supply-and-demand model for labor is depicted in Figure VIII-1. Employers' demand for workers is downward sloping (due to productivity reasons discussed in Section B). Employees' supply of labor is upward sloping because higher wages attract more workers into the market. The interaction of supply and demand yields a market wage rate, W_M, where Q_M workers are employed. W_M is the market clearing price.

This model provides insights about many aspects of labor markets. Prior to a more detailed analysis of the underpinnings of the market supply and demand curves, an appreciation of the usefulness of this model is illustrated by consideration of the minimum wage, payroll taxes, fringe benefits, and employment at will.

1. The Minimum Wage

The minimum wage is a government-imposed price control that makes it illegal for employers to pay workers less than the minimum wage and makes it illegal

Figure VIII-1

Labor Market

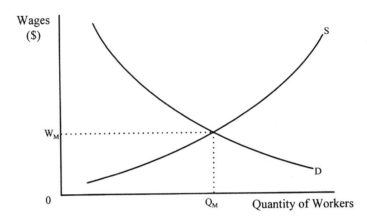

for employees to work for less than the minimum wage. Thus, the minimum wage restricts the freedom and market opportunities of both employers and employees.

In order to be effective, the minimum wage must be above the market wage. The market impact of the minimum wage is illustrated in Figure VIII-2. The market hourly wage, $4.00, is below the minimum wage, $5.65. At $4.00 per hour, the market would clear at Q_M. At $5.65 per hour, the quantity of workers who are willing and able to work increases to Q_S. However, at the minimum wage, employers decrease to Q_D the number of workers they are willing to hire. Thus, the quantity demanded, Q_D, is less than the quantity supplied, Q_S. The minimum wage—a price floor—prevents the market wage from adjusting downward and the market does not clear.

The minimum wage causes unemployment because some workers who want to work are unable to find jobs. Unemployment—a surplus or excess

Figure VIII-2

Employment and the Minimum Wage

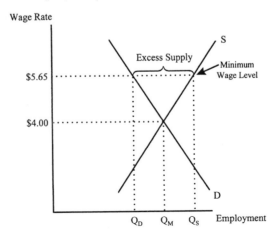

supply of workers—is illustrated by the difference between Q_S and Q_D in Figure VIII-2. The minimum wage increases the earnings of workers who are able to find jobs at the higher wage, but it results in some workers losing their jobs and other workers being disappointed when they can't find work at the above market wage. The number of jobs lost is illustrated by the distance from Q_D to Q_M. The number of disappointed job seekers is illustrated by Q_M to Q_S. The number of workers who receive the higher wage is O to Q_D. However, the workers who receive the higher wage are not necessarily the same workers, O to Q_M, who were working at W_M because some of those workers might be displaced by the new entrants (Q_M to Q_S). Moreover, the excess supply created by the minimum wage gives the employer relatively more discretion in choosing between job applicants. If all workers are equally productive, employers can indulge their personal preferences for women, men, blacks, whites, heavy, slim, political beliefs, age, and so forth, without incurring any costs in terms of lost productivity.

In the absence of governmental restrictions, markets for labor services would clear at the market determined wage for workers of similar skill and qualifications. The market wages of the great majority of workers in the United States are well above the legal minimum wage. Workers that have the skill and qualifications to compete in those markets are not protected by the minimum wage because they can command wages higher than the minimum. In effect, they are protected by the rivalry between employers competing for their services.

On the other hand, the market demand for some workers' services, especially those with little skill, training, or experience, is so weak that the market would normally clear at a wage below the legal minimum. Teenagers, who are typically inexperienced and low-skilled, may not be attractive employees at the minimum wage. In fact, considerable empirical evidence indicates that the adverse employment effects of the minimum wage are often borne most heavily by teenagers.

The adverse employment consequences of the minimum wage do not, by themselves, dictate an absolute condemnation of the minimum wage. This is because the employees who manage to keep their jobs earn more money. Somewhat surprisingly, very little research has addressed the question of whether minimum wage legislation is reaching its intended goal of reducing the incidence of poverty. The few studies that have considered this issue have found that minimum wage legislation has only a minor effect on the aggregate distribution of income. This finding is not surprising because not all low wage workers are members of low income families. Many low wage workers, especially teenagers, are second earners in middle or upper income families. Put another way, minimum wage legislation directly affects low wage workers not necessarily low income families. *See* Ronald Mincy, Raising the Minimum Wage: Effects on Family Poverty, *Monthly Labor Review*, 113(7) July 1990, 18–25. Minimum wage legislation, however, does appear to have a larger effect on the income distribution of black Americans, because black low wage workers are more likely to be members of low income families than are white low wage workers.

2. Payroll Taxes

In the United States, several social insurance programs are financed by payroll taxes. Employers, and in some cases, employees, make mandatory contribu-

Figure VIII-3

Impact of Payroll Taxes on Market Wages

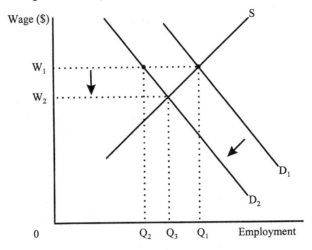

tions to the taxable social insurance trust fund of a fraction of the employee's salary. For example, the Social Security program is financed by a payroll tax paid by both employers and employees. In most states, unemployment insurance and workers compensation insurance programs are financed solely by payroll tax payments made by employers. However, supply-and-demand analysis reveals that the burden of payroll taxes is shared by the employers and employees even though the tax is paid to the government by the employer.

Assume that the employer must pay a payroll tax equal to 10% of total payments to employees. The tax increases the employers' cost of hiring workers. As a result, the demand for workers decreases. In Figure VIII-3, this decrease in demand is illustrated by a shift from D_1 to D_2. At W_1, employers are willing to hire only Q_2 workers instead of the Q_1 they were willing to hire in the absence of the payroll tax. A new equilibrium wage, W_2, emerges after the market adjusts to the change in demand. At this point, the employment level has fallen from Q_1 to Q_3. Thus, employees bear part of the burden of payroll tax in the form of lower wage rates and lower employment levels. The lesson is clear. The party legally liable for the contribution, the employer, is not necessarily the one who bears the full burden of the actual cost.

In general, the extent to which the labor supply curve is sensitive to wages — its elasticity — the proportion of the employer payroll tax that gets shifted to employees' wages. The less responsive labor supply is to changes in wages, the fewer the number of employees who withdraw from the market, and the higher the proportion of the tax that gets shifted to workers in the form of a wage decrease.

3. Fringe Benefits

The preceding supply-and-demand analysis has limited employee compensation to money wages. In order to complete the analysis, it is necessary to recognize that employee compensation often includes a non-wage component called fringe benefits. Fringe benefits include health-care insurance, dental insurance, life insurance, disability income insurance, pension benefits, paid vacation and personal leave, education benefits, on-the-job-training, low-cost on-the-premises child-care services, and so forth. Fringe benefits are an important component of employee compensation.

Fringe benefits are provided by employers to attract and retain good employees who, on the margin, prefer additional fringe benefits to money wages. In making employment decisions, the employer considers the total cost of the compensation package. Typically, employers spend an additional one-third of their payroll on fringe benefits. Employers recognize that different employees have different preferences and thus make different trade-offs between wages and fringe benefits. For example, employees who do not have children do not receive any benefit from on-the-premises child care centers. Similarly, an employee whose spouse's employer provides health-care insurance receives little benefit from health-care insurance provided by his or her own employer. As a consequence, some employers provide their employees with the opportunity to choose from a menu of available benefits within a budget provided by the employer. These "cafeteria" plans allow employers to lower total compensation costs by assuring that the fringe benefits actually benefit those employees who opt for them.

The United States Congress is very adept at spending other people's money. One perennial example of this are the proposals to mandate that employers provide their employees with certain forms of nonwage employee benefits. For example, concern that many low wage workers are not covered by health insurance has led to proposals that all employers be required to provide their employees with at least a minimal level of insurance coverage. Similarly, concern for the welfare of children has led to proposals that employers be required to provide their employees with unpaid parental leave so that they can care for newborn or ill children without the fear of losing their jobs. While the benefit to employees of each proposal for mandated benefits seems clear, each also imposes a cost on employers that unfortunately might ultimately fall on these same employees. In the case of mandated health insurance, the cost to employers is in providing coverage for currently uncovered primarily low wage workers. One study suggested that a recently mandated insurance plan would increase employers' cost for low wage workers by 15–20%. In the case of parental leave, the employers' costs would include any loss of output suffered when workers are on leave and the cost of hiring and training temporary replacements. As with payroll taxes, these costs to employers may be partially or completely passed on to workers in the form of lower wages.

4. Market Wages and Comparable Worth

It has been argued that Title VII of the Civil Rights Act of 1964 should be interpreted to prohibit sexually discriminatory male and female pay differences even when the work performed is *not* substantially equal. This concept is often referred to as "equal pay for comparable worth." Equal pay for comparable worth is based on the dubious principle that employees should be compensated according to perceptions as to the relative value in terms of training, skill, effort and responsibility that are involved in performing different jobs. In economic terms, comparable worth concentrates on the supply side of the market while ignoring the demand for different types of jobs. In practice, comparable worth means that jobs must be identified and rated according to the degree of skill, training, effort, and responsibility required. The typical comparable worth proposal envisions some type of bureaucratic rating body. Jobs assigned the same rating (that is, the same "worth") would be compared to see if they are paid comparable wages. If the wages are not comparable, then the jobs would be examined to determine whether the jobs are predominately occupied by males or females. In instances where equally rated jobs exhibited different wages and an imbalance in the number of male versus female employees, the comparable worth provision would require that the wages of the lower paying job be increased to that of the higher paying comparable job.

American Federation of State, County, and Municipal Employees, (AFSCME) v. State of Washington
United States Court of Appeals, Ninth Circuit
770 F.2d 1401 (1985)

KENNEDY, Circuit Judge:

In this class action affecting approximately 15,500 of its employees, the State of Washington was sued in the United States District Court for the Western District of Washington. The class comprises state employees who have worked or do work in job categories that are or have been at least seventy percent female. The action was commenced for the class members by two unions, the American Federation of State, County, and Municipal Employees (AFSCME) and the Washington Federation of State Employees (WFSE). In all of the proceedings to date and in the opinion that follows, the plaintiffs are referred to as AFSCME. The district court found the State discriminated on the basis of sex in violation of Title VII of the Civil Rights Act of 1964, 42 U.S.C. § 2000e-2(a) (1982), by compensating employees in jobs where females predominate at lower rates than employees in jobs where males predominate, if these jobs, though dissimilar, were identified by certain studies to be of comparable worth. The State appeals. We conclude a violation of Title VII was not established here, and we reverse.

The State of Washington has required salaries of state employees to reflect prevailing market rates. See Wash.Rev.Code Ann. § 28B.16.100(16) (1983) (effective March 29, 1979); State Civil Service Law, ch. 1, § 16, 1961 Wash.Laws 7, 17. Throughout the period in question, comprehensive biennial salary surveys were conducted to assess prevailing market rates. The surveys involved approximately 2,700 employers in the public and private sectors. The results were reported to state personnel boards, which conducted hearings before employee representatives and agencies and made salary recommendations to the State Budget Director. The Director submitted a proposed budget to the Governor, who in turn presented it to the state legislature. Salaries were fixed by enactment of the budget.

In 1974 the State commissioned a study by management consultant Norman Willis to determine whether a wage disparity existed between employees in jobs held predominantly by women and jobs held predominantly by men. The study examined sixty-two classifications in which at least seventy percent of the employees were women, and fifty-nine job classifications in which at least seventy percent of the employees were men. It found a wage disparity of about twenty percent, to the disadvantage of employees in jobs held mostly by women, for jobs considered of comparable worth. Comparable worth was calculated by evaluating jobs under four criteria: knowledge and skills, mental demands, accountability, and working conditions. A maximum number of points was allotted to each category: 280 for knowledge and skills, 140 for mental demands, 160 for accountability, and 20 for working conditions. Every job was assigned a numerical value under each of the four criteria. The State of Washington conducted similar studies in 1976 and 1980, and in 1983 the State enacted legislation providing for a compensation scheme based on comparable worth. The scheme is to take effect over a ten-year period. Act of June 15, 1983, ch. 75, 1983 Wash.Laws 1st Ex.Sess. 2071.

AFSCME filed charges with the Equal Employment Opportunity Commission (EEOC) in 1981, alleging the State's compensation system violated Title VII's prohibition against sex discrimination in employment. The EEOC having taken no action, the United States Department of Justice issued notices of right to sue, expressing no opinion on the merits of the claims. In 1982 AFSCME brought this action in the district court, seeking immediate implementation of a system of compensation based on comparable worth. The district court ruled in favor of AFSCME and ordered injunctive relief and back pay. Its findings of fact, conclusions of law, and opinion are reported. American Federation of State, County, and Municipal Employees v. Washington, 578 F.Supp. 846 (W.D.Wash. 1983) (AFSCME I).

AFSCME alleges sex-based wage discrimination throughout the state system, but its explanation and proof of the violation is, in essence, Washington's failure as early as 1979 to adopt and implement at once a comparable worth compensation program. The trial court adopted this theory as well. AFSCME I, 578 F.Supp. at 865–71. The comparable worth theory, as developed in the case before us, postulates that sex-based wage discrimination exists if employees in job classifications occupied primarily by women are paid less than employees in job classifications filled primarily by men, if the jobs are of equal value to the employer, though otherwise dissimilar. See, e.g., Jacobs, Comparable Worth, Case & Com., March–April 1985, at 12; Bellak, Comparable Worth: A Practitioner's View, in 1 Comparable Worth: Issue for the 80's, at 75 (United States Commission on Civil Rights, June 6–7, 1984); Northrup, Comparable Worth and Realistic Wage Setting, in 1 Comparable Worth: Issue for the 80's, at 93 (United States Commission on Civil Rights, June 6–7, 1984), see also American Nurses' Association v. Illinois, 606 F.Supp. 1313, 1315 (N.D.Ill.1985) (mem.). We must determine whether comparable worth, as presented in this case, affords AFSCME a basis for recovery under Title VII.

Section 703(a) of Title VII states in pertinent part:

> It shall be an unlawful employment practice for an employer —
>
> (1)...to discriminate against any individual with respect to his compensation, terms, conditions, or privileges of employment, because of such individual's...sex...or
>
> (2) to limit, segregate, or classify his employees or applicants for employment in any way which would deprive or tend to deprive any individual of employment opportunities...because of such individual's...sex....

42 U.S.C. § 2000e-2(a) (1982) (emphasis added).

The Bennett Amendment to Title VII, designed to relate Title VII to the Equal Pay Act[1], see County of Washington v. Gunther, 452 U.S. 161, 173–76, 101 S.Ct. 2242, 2249–51, 68 L.Ed.2d 751 (1981), and eliminate any potential inconsistencies between the two statutes, provides:

> It shall not be an unlawful employment practice under this subchapter for any employer to differentiate upon the basis of sex in determining the amount of the wages or compensation paid or to be paid to employees of such employer if such differentiation is authorized by the provisions of section 206(d) of title 29.

42 U.S.C. § 2000e-2(h) (1982). It is evident from the legislative history of the Equal Pay Act that Congress, after explicit consideration, rejected proposals that would have prohibited lower wages for comparable work, as contrasted with equal work. The legislative history of the Civil Rights Act of 1964 and the Bennett Amendment, however, is inconclusive regarding the intended coverage of Title VII's prohibition against sex discrimination, and contains no explicit discussion of compensation for either comparable or equal work. The Supreme Court in *Gunther*, stressing the broad remedial purposes of Title VII, construed the Bennett Amendment to incorporate into Title VII the four affirmative defenses of the Equal Pay Act, but not to limit discrimination suits involving pay to the cause of action provided in the Equal Pay Act. 452 U.S. at 168–71, 101 S.Ct. at 2247–49. The Court noted, however, that the case before it did not involve the concept of comparable worth, id. at 166, 101 S.Ct. at 2246, and declined to define "the precise contours of lawsuits challenging sex discrimination in compensation under Title VII." Id. at 181, 101 S.Ct. at 2254.

In the instant case, the district court found a violation of Title VII, premised upon both the disparate impact and the disparate treatment theories of discrimination. Under the disparate impact theory, discrimination may be established by showing that a facially neutral employment practice, not justified by business necessity, has a disproportionately adverse impact upon members of a group protected under Title VII. Proof of an employer's intent to discriminate in adopting a particular practice is not required in a disparate impact case. The theory is based in part on the rationale that where a practice is specific and focused we can address whether it is a pretext for discrimination in light of the employer's explanation for the practice. Under the disparate treatment theory, in contrast, an employer's intent or motive in adopting a challenged policy is an essential element of liability for a violation of Title VII. It is insufficient for a plaintiff alleging discrimination under the disparate treatment theory to show the employer was merely aware of the adverse consequences the policy would have on a protected group. The plaintiff must show the employer chose the particular policy because of its effect on members of a protected class. *Id.* We consider each theory of liability in turn. Though there are both questions of fact and law in the district court's opinion, the result we reach is

---

1. The Equal Pay Act provides in relevant part:
No employer ... shall discriminate ... between employees on the basis of sex by paying wages to employees in such establishment at a rate less than the rate at which he pays wages to employees of the opposite sex in such establishment for equal work on jobs the performance of which requires equal skill, effort, and responsibility, and which are performed under similar working conditions, except where such payment is made pursuant to (i) a seniority system; (ii) a merit system; (iii) a system which measures earnings by quantity or quality of production; or (iv) a differential based on any factor other than sex.
29 U.S.C. § 206(d)(1) (1982).

the same under either the clearly erroneous or the de novo standard of review. See Spaulding, 740 F.2d at 699. We begin by reviewing the district court's judgment in favor of AFSCME under the disparate impact theory.

The trial court erred in ruling that liability was established under a disparate impact analysis. The precedents do not permit the case to proceed upon that premise. AFSCME's disparate impact argument is based on the contention that the State of Washington's practice of taking prevailing market rates into account in setting wages has an adverse impact on women, who, historically, have received lower wages than men in the labor market. Disparate impact analysis is confined to cases that challenge a specific, clearly delineated employment practice applied at a single point in the job selection process. The instant case does not involve an employment practice that yields to disparate impact analysis. As we noted in an earlier case, the decision to base compensation on the competitive market, rather than on a theory of comparable worth, involves the assessment of a number of complex factors not easily ascertainable, an assessment too multifaceted to be appropriate for disparate impact analysis. In the case before us, the compensation system in question resulted from surveys, agency hearings, administrative recommendations, budget proposals, executive actions, and legislative enactments. A compensation system that is responsive to supply and demand and other market forces is not the type of specific, clearly delineated employment policy contemplated by [leading precedents]; such a compensation system, the result of a complex of market forces, does not constitute a single practice that suffices to support a claim under disparate impact theory. Under these principles and precedents, we must reverse the district court's determination of liability under the disparate impact theory of discrimination.

We consider next the allegations of disparate treatment. Under the disparate treatment theory, AFSCME was required to prove a prima facie case of sex discrimination by a preponderance of the evidence. As previously noted, liability for disparate treatment hinges upon proof of discriminatory intent. In an appropriate case, the necessary discriminatory animus may be inferred from circumstantial evidence. Our review of the record, however, indicates failure by AFSCME to establish the requisite element of intent by either circumstantial or direct evidence.

AFSCME contends discriminatory motive may be inferred from the Willis study, which finds the State's practice of setting salaries in reliance on market rates creates a sex-based wage disparity for jobs deemed of comparable worth. AFSCME argues from the study that the market reflects a historical pattern of lower wages to employees in positions staffed predominantly by women; and it contends the State of Washington perpetuates that disparity, in violation of Title VII, by using market rates in the compensation system. The inference of discriminatory motive which AFSCME seeks to draw from the State's participation in the market system fails, as the State did not create the market disparity and has not been shown to have been motivated by impermissible sex-based considerations in setting salaries.

The requirement of intent is linked at least in part to culpability. That concept would be undermined if we were to hold that payment of wages according to prevailing rates in the public and private sectors is an act that, in itself, supports the inference of a purpose to discriminate. Neither law nor logic deems the free market system a suspect enterprise. Economic reality is that the value of a particular job to an employer is but one factor influencing the rate of compensation for that job. Other considerations may include the availability of workers willing to do the job and the effectiveness of collective bargaining in a particular industry...[E]mployers may be constrained by market forces to set salaries under prevailing wage rates for different job classifications. We find nothing in the language of Title VII or its legislative history to indicate Congress intended to abrogate fundamental economic principles such as the laws of supply and demand or to prevent employers from competing in the labor market.

While the Washington legislature may have the discretion to enact a comparable worth plan if it chooses to do so, Title VII does not obligate it to eliminate an economic inequality that it did not create. Title VII was enacted to ensure equal opportunity in employment to covered individuals, and the State of Washington is not charged here with barring access to particular job classifications on the basis of sex.

We have recognized that in certain cases an inference of intent may be drawn from statistical evidence. We have admonished, however, that statistics must be relied on with caution. Though the comparability of wage rates in dissimilar jobs may be relevant to a determination of discriminatory animus, job evaluation studies and comparable worth statistics alone are insufficient to establish the requisite inference of discriminatory motive critical to the disparate treatment theory. The weight to be accorded such statistics is determined by the existence of independent corroborative evidence of discrimination. We conclude the independent evidence of discrimination presented by AFSCME is insufficient to support an inference of the requisite discriminatory motive under the disparate treatment theory.

AFSCME offered proof of isolated incidents of sex segregation as evidence of a history of sex-based wage discrimination. The evidence...consists of "help wanted" advertisements restricting various jobs to members of a particular sex. These advertisements were often placed in separate "help wanted—male" and "help wanted—female" columns in state newspapers between 1960 and 1973, though most were discontinued when Title VII became applicable to the states in 1972. At trial, AFSCME called expert witnesses to testify that a causal relationship exists between sex segregation practices and sex-based wage discrimination, and that the effects of sex segregation practices may persist even after the practices are discontinued. However, none of the individually named plaintiffs in the action ever testified regarding specific incidents of discrimination. The isolated incidents alleged by AFSCME are insufficient to corroborate the results of the Willis study and do not justify an inference of discriminatory motive by the State in the setting of salaries for its system as a whole. Given the scope of the alleged intentional act, and given the attempt to show the core principle of the State's market-based compensation system was adopted or maintained with a discriminatory purpose, more is required to support the finding of liability than these isolated acts, which had only an indirect relation to the compensation principle itself.

We also reject AFSCME's contention that, having commissioned the Willis study, the State of Washington was committed to implement a new system of compensation based on comparable worth as defined by the study. Whether comparable worth is a feasible approach to employee compensation is a matter of debate. Assuming, however, that like other job evaluation studies it may be useful as a diagnostic tool, we reject a rule that would penalize rather than commend employers for their effort and innovation in undertaking such a study. The results of comparable worth studies will vary depending on the number and types of factors measured and the maximum number of points allotted to each factor.

A study that indicates a particular wage structure might be more equitable should not categorically bind the employer who commissioned it. The employer should also be able to take into account market conditions, bargaining demands, and the possibility that another study will yield different results.

We hold there was a failure to establish a violation of Title VII under the disparate treatment theory of discrimination, and reverse the district court on this aspect of the case as well. The State of Washington's initial reliance on a free market system in which employees in male-dominated jobs are compensated at a higher rate than employees in dissimilar female-dominated jobs is not in and of itself a violation of Title VII, notwithstanding that the Willis study deemed the positions of comparable worth. Absent a showing of discriminatory motive, which has not been made here, the law does not permit the federal courts to interfere in the market-based system for the compensation of Washington's employees.

* * *

Notes and Questions

1. Policy Analysis: The policy underlying comparable worth is to increase the salaries of jobs that have traditionally been dominated by females. For example, it is conceivable that truck drivers and secretaries would receive equal ratings (that is, be rated to have comparable worth) and thus secretaries' wages would be raised to equal truck drivers' wages. At the outset, it should be noted that the market has already performed a rating of jobs through the interaction of supply and demand. Interferences with one aspect of markets often have repercussions in other areas. It is useful to consider a simple two-sector labor market model. In Figure VIII-4, panel (a) represents a labor market dominated by males, truck driving, and panel (b) represents a labor market dominated by females, secretaries. Although the jobs are rated as comparable, the market wage for truck drivers, W_T, is greater than the market wage for secretaries, W_S. Equal pay for comparable worth requires that the wage for secretaries be increased to W_T. At W_T, the quantity supplied of secretaries increases and the quantity demanded of secretaries decreases—that is, there is a surplus of secretaries. Are truck drivers becoming secretaries? Are more women attracted to the traditional female-domi-

Figure VIII-4

Equal Pay for Comparable Worth

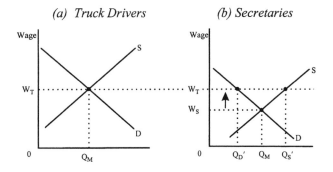

nated occupation? Does this price floor help the intended beneficiaries? Perhaps the wage difference is due to the market compensating a skill that is in shorter supply, or is offsetting a negative job perception, rather than making arbitrary distinctions based on discrimination.

2. Barriers to Entry: Assume that women are discriminated against and denied entry into a male-dominated occupation. Women prevented from entering that occupation then are forced into female-dominated occupations. The increased supply of women in female-dominated occupations depresses wages. The proper solution, however, is not to raise the wages of female-dominated occupations while ignoring the barriers to entry. Such a remedy would merely combat one inefficiency in the economy (barriers to entry) by creating a second inefficiency (a minimum wage in female dominated occupations). Moreover, the remedy would be paid by the employers in the female-dominated industry who have not discriminated against women. But this is the perverse incentive created by comparable worth.

3. Some Repercussions: By implementing comparable worth, some repercussions must follow. When wages in jobs dominated by women are artificially raised, the number of jobs will shrink, as employers seek to substitute other, and now cheaper, inputs (e.g. word processors for typists), and as customers substitute other products for those made by firms whose wage bills and prices have risen because of comparable worth. At the same time, men will start competing more for those jobs, enticed by the higher wages. As a result, employment for women may decline in those jobs. These displaced female workers may displace others in predominately male jobs, maybe even truck drivers. However, their personal utility will be lower since they could currently have those jobs, but choose not to. Another repercussion is that women, by receiving higher wages, will not invest as much in their human capital. Human capital is discussed in section C(1), *infra.* Thus, comparable worth may not have much of an affect on occupational sex segregation.

4. Treating the Symptoms, Not the Underlying Problem: Much of the preceding economic analysis suggests that the economic status of women cannot be improved without altering the basic market conditions. In this view, lower wages for women are the symptom of significant underlying structural conditions. Efforts like comparable worth that concentrate on supply conditions and wages are doomed to failure because the most likely cause for the differential treatment for women is employers' demand. Equality of treatment will not be achieved until men and women are equal in the employers' eyes. Artificial wage structures will not solve the issue. In fact, the analysis of equal pay for equal work suggests that women leaders should advocate hiring quotas for women in order to combat the adverse employment effects of equal pay provisions. As discussed in Section B, however, such affirmative action programs create an entirely new set of incentives that may have an adverse impact on women in the labor market.

B. Employers' Behavior

Employers are purchasers in the labor market. They must determine how much labor to hire, how much to invest in hiring and training employees, how to deal with workforce diversity, and how to terminate employees.

1. The Demand for Labor

The demand for labor, or any factor of production, is a **derived demand**. The demand for the factors of production is derived from the demand for the products that the factors produce. Thus, the demand for labor is directly related to the demand for goods and services that the labor is used to produce. If the demand for lawyers increases, then the derived demand for law professors increases. If the demand for law and order increases, the derived demand for police officers increases. Derived demand also obeys the law of demand. All things being equal, if the price of an input increases, then less of it will be used by firms.

Firms combine various factors of production, mainly capital and labor, to produce goods or services that are sold in a product market. Their total output, and the way in which they combined labor and capital, depend on product demand, the amount of labor and capital they can acquire at given prices, and the choice of technologies available to them. Study of the demand for labor focuses on finding out how the number of workers employed by a firm, or set of firms, is affected by changes in one or more of these three forces. To simplify the discussion, it is assumed that all other forces, except for the one being studied, are held constant.

A fundamental question is how the number of employees demanded varies when wages change. Suppose that the wages facing a certain industry vary over a long period of time, but the technology available, the conditions under which the capital is supplied, and the relationship between product prices and product demand are unchanged. An increase in the wage rate impacts the quantity of labor demanded in two ways. First, higher wages imply higher costs and usually higher product prices. Because consumers respond to higher prices by buying less, employers tend to reduce their level of output. Lower output levels, of course, imply lower employment levels, other things being equal. This decline of employment is called a **scale effect**—the effect on desired employment of a smaller scale of production. Second, as wages increase, assuming the price of capital does not change, at least initially, employers have incentives to cut costs by adopting a technology that relies more on capital and less on labor. Thus, if wages rise, desired employment falls because of the shift towards a more capital-intensive mode of production. This second effect is called a **substitution effect**, because as wages rise, capital is substituted for labor in the production process.

These two insights yield a demand curve for labor. It shows how the desired level of employment (measured in either labor hours or number of employees) varies with changes in the price of labor when the other forces affecting demand are held constant. These other forces are the product demand schedule, the conditions under which capital can be obtained, and the set of technologies available. If wages change and these other factors do not, one can determine the change in quantity demanded by moving either up or down along the demand curve.

The interaction of supply and demand for labor results in an equilibrium wage. Once this wage is established, the individual buyers of labor are price takers. Since the equilibrium wage is established, the point of interest becomes the quantity of labor that an individual firm chooses to hire. Assume that the firm has many inputs, one of which is labor. Also, let the quantities of all inputs except labor be fixed. Labor, in other words, is the only variable input in the short run. So, in order to produce more output, the firm must hire more labor. Suppose the firm in this instance is a lawyer who must decide whether to hire a paralegal to help with legal research. Hiring the paralegal will increase output which is sold to clients to obtain revenue. At the same time, hiring a paralegal will increase the cost of production because the paralegal must be paid. The lawyer makes a profit maximizing decision at the margin. If hiring the paralegal increases total revenue more than it increases total cost, then hiring the paralegal will increase profits. The lawyer will always hire a paralegal if doing so increases profits—that is, if the marginal revenue is greater than the marginal cost. Suppose the lawyer is thinking about hiring a second paralegal. The same decision process is repeated. If the marginal revenue is greater than the marginal cost of the second paralegal, then he or she will be hired. This process continues with every prospective paralegal.

Recall from Chapter V that the law of diminishing marginal returns states that as more and more of a variable input is added to a production process in which there is a fixed input the marginal product of the variable input eventually declines. Here, the focus is on the role of workers as a variable input. As more paralegals are hired, the extra output of each paralegal eventually falls. Since each additional paralegal adds less and less to total output, the additional revenue that each paralegal produces eventually falls below the additional cost of hiring. At some point, the lawyer will stop hiring additional paralegals. In short, the profit maximizing lawyer should hire all paralegals that add more to revenue than to costs, but stop hiring at the point when the addition to revenue is just equal to the addition to cost.

The example of the lawyer's decision to hire paralegals can also be expressed in equation form with economic terminology. The extra output that each additional unit of labor adds to total output is called the **marginal product of labor**, MP_L.

$$MP_L = \Delta TP / \Delta L$$

Where ΔTP is the change in total product and ΔL is the one unit increase in labor. Adding more of the variable input to other fixed inputs will eventually lead to a decrease in the marginal product of the variable input in the short run. Table VIII-I shows a marginal product of labor schedule and summarizes the hypothetical choices available to the lawyer. The first column shows the number of paralegals. The second column shows the marginal product of the paralegal, the amount by which total output increases as one more unit of labor is added to the production process. The first paralegal adds 14 units of output, the second adds 12 units of output, and so forth. MP_L decreases as the amount of labor increases, according to the law of diminishing marginal returns.

Table VIII-1

Number of Paralegals	Marginal Product of labor MP_L	Revenue $MR_C = P$	Marginal Revenue Product $MRP_L = MR_C \times MP_L$	Marginal Factor Cost $MFC_L = $ Wage
1	14	$2	$28	$7
2	12	2	24	7
3	10	2	20	7
4	8	2	12	7
5	6	2	12	7
6	4	2	8	7
7	2	2	4	7
8	0	2	0	7

When the extra legal services produced by each additional paralegal is sold, the resulting increase of total revenue is called the **marginal revenue product of labor**, MRP_L.

$$MRP_L = \Delta TR / \Delta L$$

Where ΔTR is the change in total revenue and ΔL is the change in the amount of the labor hired. Another method of expressing MRP_L is

$$MRP_L = MR_C \times MP_L$$

Where MR_C is the marginal revenue under competitive conditions (that is, MR_C is the increase in total revenue resulting from selling one more unit of output) and MP_L is the marginal product of labor. For the firm that sells its product in a perfectly-competitive market, marginal revenue is equal to the price of the product. Thus, the marginal revenue product is simply the price of the final product times the marginal product of each unit of labor. As shown in Table VIII-1, the marginal revenue product of the firm's first unit of labor is found by multiplying the marginal product by the price of the product. Marginal revenue product, MRP_L, declines as more paralegals are hired because MP_L declines.

Regardless of the economic shorthand used, the profit maximizing firm will continue adding units of labor as long as the additional revenues that labor produces are greater than the additional costs of labor. The firm will stop hiring when the additional revenues are less than the additional costs of hiring. The extra cost of hiring one more unit of labor is called the **marginal factor cost of labor** (MFC_L).

$$MFC_L = \Delta TC / \Delta L$$

Where ΔTC is the change in total cost and ΔL is the one unit change in labor. Under competitive conditions, the firm may purchase all of the labor it wants at the prevailing wage rate. Each additional paralegal in Table VIII-1 has a marginal factor cost equal to the wage rate ($MFC_L = W$).

The profit maximizing lawyer will hire additional paralegals to the point where $MRP_L = MFC_L$ — or, in the alternative, $MRP_L = W$. The numbers in Table VIII-1 indicate that if the lawyer should hire 6 paralegals. Each unit of labor from the first to the sixth adds more to the revenue than to cost. Hiring 6 units the lawyer adds as much as possible to profit. However, the seventh paralegal adds more to cost than to revenue and, therefore, will not be hired.

This process is derived from the manner in which the competitive firm determines its profit maximizing output. The firm follows the same process to equate its marginal cost to marginal revenue in hiring inputs as it does in selling its product. In fact, when the firm hires the profit maximizing quantity of labor, that amount of labor produces the profit maximizing level of output. The numbers used in Table VIII-1 are presented in graphical form in Figure VIII-5. The MP_L curve is drawn by plotting the points from columns 1 and 2. The demand curve for the lawyers services as shown in panel (b) where price equals $2.00. The MRP_L is shown in panel (c). The competitive wage is $7.00, stated as MFC_L. The profit maximizing quantity of labor is the point where the MFC_L curve crosses the MRP_L curve. At this point, the marginal revenue product of labor equals the marginal factor cost of labor.

Obviously, firms employ many inputs other than labor. The profit maximizing rule for the level of employment is the same for each resource. Marginal pro-

Figure VIII-5

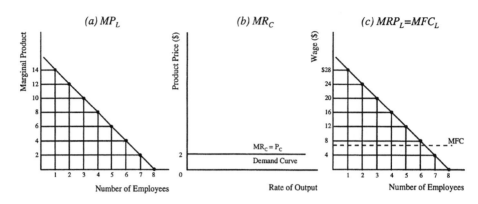

The Profit Maximizing Quantity of Labor

ductivity theory gives insight into the purchasing behavior of firms. In the short run, when labor is the only variable input, the firm is willing to purchase or hire additional units up to the point where $MRP_L = W$. Thus, MRP_L traces the relation between the price of labor, the wage rate, and the amount of labor a firm is willing to purchase. In other words, the marginal revenue product curve is also the firm's short run demand curve for labor. Figure VIII-6 illustrates this. At wage rate, W_0, the firm chooses Q_0 units of labor. At a higher wage, such as W_1, less labor is hired. For each wage, the firm adjusts the level of employment to maintain the equation $MRP_L = W$.

The demand for labor changes when the factors that are normally held constant are changed. For example, suppose the demand for the product of a particular industry increases so that, at any price, more of the goods or services in

Figure VIII-6

Firm's Demand for Labor

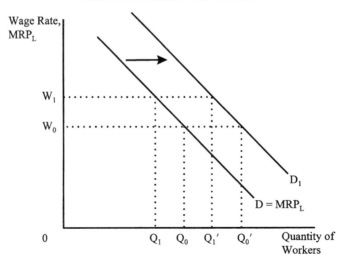

question can be sold. If the technology and the conditions in which capital and labor are made available to industry do not change, then output levels will rise as firms in the industry seek to maximize profits. This scale, or output effect, would increase the demand for labor at any given wage rate. As long as the relative prices of capital and labor remained unchanged, there is no substitution effect. As a result, the entire demand curve shifts to the right. This rightward shift from D to D_1 in Figure VIII-6 indicates that at every possible wage rate, the number of workers demanded has increased.

Consider what would happen if the product demand schedule, technology, and labor supply conditions remain the same, but the supply of capital changes so that the price of capital falls to fifty percent of its prior level. The effect on labor demanded by the change in price of another input can be divided into two parts—the scale and substitution effects. First, when capital prices decline, the cost of producing tends to decline. Lower producer costs stimulate increases in production which tends to raise the level of desired employment at any given wage. The scale effect of a fall in capital rates thus tends to increase the demand for labor at each wage level. The second effect of a fall in capital prices is a substitution effect, whereby firms adopt more capital intensive technologies in response to cheaper capital. Such firms would substitute capital for labor and use less labor to produce a given amount of output than before. With less labor being desired at each wage rate, the labor demand curve tends to shift to the left. The fall in capital prices thus generates two opposite effects on the demand for labor. The scale effect will push the labor demand curve rightward, while the substitution effect will push it to the left. Either effect could dominate; thus economic theory does not yield a clear-cut prediction regarding how a fall in capital prices will effect the demand for labor. A rise is capital prices would generate the same overall ambiguity of effect on the demand for labor.

The hypothesized changes due to changes in product demand and changes in capital prices tend to shift the demand curve for labor. It is important to distinguish between a shift in a demand curve and a movement along the curve. A labor demand curve graphically shows the labor desired as a function of the wage rate. When the wage changes and other forces are held constant, one moves along the curve. However, when one of the other forces changes, the labor demand curve shifts. Unlike wages, these forces are not directly shown when the demand curve for labor is drawn. Thus, when they change, a different relationship between wages and desired employment prevails and this shows up as a shift of the demand curve. If more labor is desired at any given wage rate, then the curve has shifted to the right. If less labor is demanded, then demand curve has shifted left.

The demand for labor can be analyzed on three levels: (1) to analyze the demand for labor by a particular firm, one would examine how an increase in the wage of, say, a paralegal, would affect his employment by a particular law firm; (2) to analyze the effect of this wage increase on the employment of paralegals in the entire law firm industry, one would use an industry demand curve; (3) finally, to see how the wage increase would affect the entire labor market for paralegals in all industries in which they are used, one would use a market demand curve. For example, paralegals are also used in government agencies such as the Securities Exchange Commission. Firm, industry, and market labor demand curves vary in shape, to some extent because scale and substitution effects have different strengths at each level. However, it is important to remember that the scale and substitution effects on wage changes work in the same direction at each level so that firm, industry, and market demand curves all slope downward. One can also distinguish between long run and short run labor demand curves. Over very short periods of time, employers find it difficult to substitute capital for labor, or vice versa. The customers may not alter their product demand very much in response to a price increase. It takes time to fully adjust consumption and production pay. Over long periods of time, of course, responses to changes in wages and other factors affecting the demand for labor are larger and more complete.

A typical objection that is sometimes raised to the theory of labor demand introduced here is that the theory assumes a degree of sophistication on the part of real world employers that is just not there. It is hard to imagine an employer uttering the words "marginal revenue product of labor." Employers, it is argued, are both unfamiliar with the textbook rules of profit maximization and unable in many situations accurately to measure or value the output of individual units of labor. The typical reply to this objection is that whether employers can verbalize the profit maximizing conditions, or whether they can explicitly measure the marginal revenue product of labor, they must at least intuit them to survive in a competitive market. This is true because competition weeds out employers who are not good at generating profits in much the same manner as competition weeds out pinball players who do not understand the intricacies of how speed, angles, and spin affect the motion of bodies through space. Yet it would be surprising if the best pinball players in America could verbalize Newton's laws of motion. The point is that employers can know concepts without being able to verbalize them. Those who are not good at maximizing profits will not last very long in competitive markets. Conversely, those who survive, whether they can verbalize the general concepts or not, know how to maximize profits.

2. Employer Investments

Employers attempt to maximize profits by selecting the optimal combination of inputs. The selection and development of employees is an extremely important part of most firms' decision making. Since people vary in their skills and working habits, it often behooves firms to invest time and resources in selecting the right individuals at the lowest possible cost as well as to invest in training some individuals once they have been hired.

a. Hiring

Firms often incur significant costs in selecting employees. Since firms often bear the cost of hiring and training workers, they prefer to obtain a work force of a given quality at the least possible cost. Similarly, they prefer to hire workers who are fast learners, because those workers can be trained at less cost. Unfortunately, it may prove expensive for firms to investigate extensively the background of every possible individual who applies for a job in order to ascertain his or her skill level and ability to undertake training. One way to reduce these search costs is to rely on credentials or signals in a hiring process, rather than intensely investigating the qualities of individual applicants. For example, if, on average, college graduates are more productive than high school graduates, an employer might specify that a college degree is a requirement for the job. Rather than interviewing and testing all applicants to try to ascertain the productivity of each, the firm may simply select its new employees from the pool of applicants who meet the educational standard. Similarly, if employees believe that married men are less likely to quit their jobs than single men, or that 25 year olds are less likely to quit than teenagers, then they may want to give preferential treatment to married men and 25 year olds over single men and teenagers in the hiring process.

Such forms of statistical discrimination, meaning judging individuals by group characteristics, have obvious costs. On the one hand, for example, some high school graduates may be fully qualified to work for a firm that insists on college graduates. Excluding them from the pool of potential applicants imposes costs on them, in the sense that they do not get the job. It also imposes costs on the employer if other qualified applicants cannot be readily found. On the other hand, there may be some unproductive workers among the group of college graduates, and the employer who hires them may well suffer losses while they are employed. However, if the reduction in hiring costs that arises when signals such as educational credentials, marital status, or age are used is large, then it may prove profitable for an employer to use them even if an occasional unsatisfactory worker sneaks through. In other words, the total costs of hiring, training, and employing workers may well be lower for some firms when hiring standards are used than when such firms rely on more intensive investigations of applicant characteristics. Firms also use employment agencies to help them identify and hire employees.

Consultants & Designers, Inc. v. Butler Service Group, Inc.
United States Court of Appeals, Eleventh Circuit
720 F.2d 1553 (1983)

TJOFLAT, Circuit Judge:

In these consolidated appeals we must decide whether a restrictive covenant in a contract of employment is enforceable under state law...

I.

A.

Butler Service Group, Inc. (Butler), and Consultants and Designers, Inc. (C & D), are two of a large number of firms in the technical service industry. This industry may be viewed as a variant of the employment agency industry. Firms in this industry serve as middlemen and providers of information in the market for highly skilled, relatively mobile technically trained workers in fields such as engineering, designing, drafting, and data processing. These workers are generally referred to as "job shoppers." A technical service firm (TSF) recruits job shoppers from a national and in some cases an international market.

The job shoppers are recruited to service the needs of client firms. The client is likely to have a need for short-term, highly skilled technical workers that it cannot satisfy from its local area. Though the employment offered to job shoppers is temporary, it may last for several years. The TSF specializes in bringing together firms seeking these kinds of workers with individuals seeking this sort of work.

Job shoppers, though they work on the client's premises and under its supervision, are paid by the TSF and are in that sense employees of the TSF. The TSF earns its income by charging the client firm a price per employee per pay period which exceeds what it must in turn pay the employee. Unlike a traditional employment agency the TSF receives no finder's fee from either the job shopper or the client firm for the initial placement of the employee with the client. Because of the diminished job security and the lack of other employee benefits, client firms, in order to attract job shoppers, must be willing to pay the job shopper approximately thirty percent more than they pay their direct employees performing the same task.

TSFs generally structure their relationships with job shoppers and client firms through contract. In serving as an intermediary in the market between job shoppers and client firms, TSFs must not only compete with one another, but face competition from employment agencies and from disintermediation, i.e., firms and workers searching for and contracting with one another directly without a TSF acting as an intermediary.

B.

In the early 1970's, the Tennessee Valley Authority (TVA) embarked on a program calling for the design and construction of several nuclear power plants. By 1979, TVA had thirteen of these plants under construction in the states of Tennessee and Alabama, and its nuclear program was the largest in the United States. To complete its program and to augment its permanent staff, TVA turned to TSFs to supply contract personnel for the design and construction of its nuclear power plants.

In 1976, Butler obtained a contract to supply technical employees to TVA. The contract between Butler and TVA provided that TVA would pay Butler an hourly wage to be received by each employee, plus a markup. These payments were "[d]eemed to cover all wages and salaries; all general, administrative, and overhead expenses; any and all other direct or indirect costs or expenses, including Workmen's Compensation, Federal and State Unemployment Insurance and FICA, and profit." The contract provided that during its term neither TVA nor Butler would hire the other's employees. The contract contained no restriction on TVA's solicitation or hiring of job shoppers after the expiration of the contract. The contract was terminable by either party on seven days' notice. The contract was extended a number of times. The final extension commenced in April 1979, and continued the agreement until May 3, 1980.

The relationship between Butler and its job shoppers was similarly constrained and conditioned by contract. Butler's contract with its job shoppers working at TVA contained the following clause:

> Employees shall not accept employment directly or indirectly by client for a period of ninety (90) days following the completion of assignments to said client and/or assignment to the work of said client performed, on employer's premises out in the field without the written consent of employer.

In 1979, TVA requested a number of TSFs, including Butler and C & D, to submit proposals for contracts to supply employees to TVA upon the expiration of Butler's contract in May 1980. In March 1980, TVA decided to award the new contracts to C & D and H.L. Yoh Co., and advised Butler that its contract with TVA would end on May 3, 1980. After receiving notice that its contract would be terminated, Butler, in April 1980, notified each employee assigned to TVA that its contract with TVA was being terminated and that it would enforce its restrictive covenant and would attempt to find a new job for every employee who was interested. Butler gave C & D, Yoh, and CDI Corporation notice of its restrictive covenant and of its intent to enforce the covenant. Butler offered to enter into a "bridge or extended contract" with TVA during which C & D and Yoh would replace the Butler employees on an individual basis as they could. Butler also offered to the successor TSFs to negotiate a waiver of its claimed rights under the restrictive covenant.

Having learned that C & D had begun soliciting Butler's TVA employees, and that both C & D and Yoh intended to staff positions under their TVA contracts by employing Butler employees at TVA, Butler sued C & D and Yoh in the United States District Court for the Southern District of New York. Butler sought damages for tortious interference with its contracts with its employees and an injunction to prevent C & D and Yoh from attempting to hire away Butler's job shoppers at TVA. Butler applied for an ex parte temporary restraining order, which was issued on May 6, 1980.

After the restraining order was entered, TVA accepted Butler's offer of a bridge contract of ninety days duration terminable on seven days' notice. This contract was intended to keep Butler and its job shoppers in place for a period of time during which C & D and Yoh would gradually replace Butler's job shoppers with their own. On May 22, 1980, the district court, having been informed of the bridge contract, concluded that Butler's claim for injunctive relief was moot and therefore dissolved the temporary restraining order.

On June 9, 1980, C & D and several former Butler job shoppers (referred to collectively as C & D) brought an antitrust action in the Northern District of Alabama seeking injunctive relief and damages under the theory that Butler's attempted enforcement of its restrictive employment covenant violated sections 1 & 2 of the Sherman Act. On June 11, 1980, C & D amended its answer in the New York case to include a counterclaim alleging tortious interference by Butler with C & D's contract with TVA, abuse of process, malicious prosecution and unjust enrichment. C & D, joined by Yoh, moved the New York court to transfer the case to the Northern District of Alabama, and on August 29, 1980, the court granted the motion. See 28 U.S.C. § 1404(a) (1976).

On February 10, 1981, the court below consolidated the New York and Alabama cases, and set the cases for trial on the limited question of the validity and enforceability of Butler's restrictive employment covenant under state law and section 1 of the Sherman Act. A bench trial was held in July and on November 3, 1981, the court handed down a memorandum opinion, in which it found that the covenant was unenforceable under state law, but that neither the covenant nor its attempted enforcement violated section 1 of the Sherman Act.

The court entered a partial final judgment, in conformance with its opinion, under Fed.R.Civ.P. 54(b). The court also denied Butler's motion for summary judgment on C & D's claim under section 2 of the Sherman Act and certified its ruling for appeal under 28 U.S.C. § 1292(b) (1976). All parties appealed.

II.

Three related issues are raised for our review in this appeal. Each of these issues revolves around the restrictive covenant in the contract between Butler and the job shoppers it hired and employed at the TVA's work sites. The first is whether this restrictive covenant is enforceable under state law. The second is whether it constitutes a "contract...in restraint of trade" under section 1 of the Sherman Act. The third is whether, given the factual record already established and our analysis of those facts, Butler is entitled to summary judgment on C & D's claim under section 2 of the Sherman Act that Butler "monopolize[d], attempt[ed] to monopolize, or conspire[d]...to monopolize" the relevant part of the technical service industry.

A.

The parties agreed at the trial that the validity and enforceability of Butler's restrictive covenant was to be governed as to the Alabama employees by the stricter of Alabama and New Jersey law, and as to the Tennessee employees by the stricter of Tennessee or New Jersey law. We concur in the finding of the court below that there is no significant difference in the law of the three states. The district court correctly stated that:

> Notwithstanding the vastness and variety of cases, the touchstone of this analysis has not varied since the grandfather case of Mitchell v. Reynolds cited as 1 P.Wms. 181, 24 Eng.Rep. 347 (O.B.1711).... Lord Macclesfield applied a "reasonableness" or balancing test which has survived, with many enlightening applications, to this day. We thus sail into that cherished legal haven, "Is it reasonable under the circumstances?"

In judging reasonableness, the district court looked both to the Restatement (2d) of Contracts, § 188, and to the appropriate case law. The Restatement fleshes out the legal standard a bit. It states that the covenant "[i]s unreasonably in restraint of trade if (a) the restraint is greater than is needed to protect promisee's legitimate interest, or (b) the promisee's need is outweighed by the hardship to the promisor and the likely injury to the public." As the district court correctly noted, "[p]recedents are of less than usual value because the question of reasonableness must be decided on an ad hoc basis. There is no inflexible formula. Allright Auto Parks, Inc. v. Barry, 409 S.W.2d 361 (1966)."

It is clear that the district court was correct in its finding that the time and area restraints are not unreasonable. The covenant is limited to a period of ninety days and to the specific client worksite at which Butler placed the individual employee. It would be difficult to conceive of a more limited post-employment covenant. Nonetheless, the covenant cannot pass muster if it fails to meet the reasonableness standard enunciated in the Restatement.

In evaluating the reasonableness of any covenant not to compete, it is essential that we determine in what business the promisee is engaged. We cannot otherwise determine whether the employer is attempting to prevent ordinary competition, something which "[t]he employer has no legitimate interest" in preventing, Whitmyer Bros. v. Doyle, 274 A.2d 577, 581 (1971), or whether he has some legitimate protectible interest.

While in a technical sense the relationship between Butler and its job shoppers was employer-employee, this characterization of the relationship does more to obscure the relevant issues than to enlighten them. It is more revealing to recognize Butler's role as that of the much maligned but time-honored middleman. Butler served as an intermediary in the market for highly-skilled, technically-trained workers. There were individuals seeking such employment and firms seeking to employ them. In a pristine world in which information is costless, there would be no need for the essential service that Butler performs. The client firms and the prospective employees would each know what the other has to offer and could negotiate a contract instantaneously and costlessly. That, however, is not the nature of the world in which we live. Butler and C & D, and the fifteen other firms that applied for the contract with TVA, as well as a myriad of other firms in the technical service and related industries, exist and flourish because information is a costly and valuable commodity.

Whatever ancillary services Butler supplied to TVA, it was as a provider of information that Butler performed its essential function. Butler's role was to gather, distill, and provide to TVA information on available and suitable people for TVA's positions and simultaneously to provide to prospective job shoppers information about TVA and the positions it was offering. Thus, in this sense, Butler was serving as a form of an employment agency. In the market for the information in which Butler dealt, it had to compete with: (1) all other technical service firms; (2) conventional employment agencies; and (3) disintermediation by firms and workers. Disintermediation is the actualization of the ever-present cry to eliminate the middleman, i.e., direct solicitation, negotiation and contracting between the firm and the worker. Eliminating the middleman is at first blush a facile and attractive alternative. However, middlemen exist because they provide a useful and highly-valued service. If Butler's covenant with its job shoppers is to have any justification, that justification must be to protect Butler's role as a middleman in the market for information between job shoppers and client firms.

Once (1) a job shopper has been informed about a client and vice versa; (2) the job shopper has expressed a desire to work for the client and vice versa; and (3) the employment has commenced and each is satisfied with the other, the primary mission of the technical service firm is complete. At that point, barring some form of contractual constraint, the client firm and the job shopper could sever their relationships with the TSF and consummate a relationship with one another. The job shoppers and client firms could thereby opportunistically appropriate the work product of the TSF without paying it the full value of its services. If the TSF is to receive a reward for the services of the job shopper proportional to the latter's contribution to the client firm, the TSF must find some contractual means to protect its future income stream from the ravages of opportunistic disintermediation.

The covenant between Butler and TVA not to hire one another's employees and the restrictive covenants in Butler's contracts with its job shoppers were clearly crafted to prevent such disintermediation. But for these contractual constraints the job shoppers and the TVA could get the benefit of Butler's services without paying the full price of those services. The application of Butler's restrictive covenant after the termination of its contract with TVA was designed to protect against TVA terminating Butler and then hiring either directly, or indirectly through another technical service firm, the Butler job shoppers. TVA had the power and the right to terminate Butler, but not to abrogate Butler's property interest in its job shoppers. Butler's rights under its employment contracts need not have been enforced. They could have been sold. Regardless of whether Butler would have struck a deal with the job shoppers, TVA, or the successor TSF, Butler was nonetheless protected by the covenant from opportunistic termination of the relationship by TVA. Therefore we conclude that Butler had a legitimate interest in protecting from opportunistic appropriation its investment in acquiring the information necessary to carry on its business, and that the covenant was reasonably well crafted to carry out that task. This satisfies the first prong of the Restatement's reasonableness test.

As to the second prong, whether either the job shoppers who are held to this covenant, or third parties, including the public at large, are sufficiently adversely affected by the covenant to render it unenforceable, the answer must be no. The TVA and all the parties to this action, with the exception of Butler, would gain if the restrictive covenant is held to be unenforceable. If the covenant is enforced, Butler has a property interest in the ninety days of employment of its ex-job shoppers at TVA. TVA, the job shoppers, and C & D could each gain by the extinguishment of this property right. In that sense, Butler's loss must be someone else's gain, and Butler's gain is someone's loss. Such a pecuniary loss to C & D, the TVA, or the job shoppers cannot serve to invalidate an otherwise valid covenant. The value of this loss has already been compensated for presumably in the consideration for the contracts negotiated between Butler and the TVA, Butler and its job shoppers, and C & D and the TVA.

The essence of the inquiry under the second prong of the Restatement should be directed at the effect of the covenant on the general public. The proper posture from which this inquiry is to be undertaken is not after the termination of Butler by TVA (ex post), but rather before the formation of the contracts between Butler, on the one hand, and its job shoppers and TVA on the other (ex ante). In precisely the same spirit that it was in TVA's and the job shoppers' interest to eliminate Butler after Butler had performed its services, and before it had received all the income from those services, so too it was in the public's interest at that time that the covenant not be enforced. The public suffers a loss as a result of the enforcement of the covenant. The loss is not, however, that the nuclear power plant at which the job shoppers were employed will suffer any delay in completion. Rather, the loss to the public, if any, will come in the form of higher electric rates. The covenant grants a property right to Butler which would doubtless have been negotiated away, resulting in a wealth transfer from one or more of the other concerned parties to Butler. The cost of purchasing this waiver might ultimately have been passed on to TVA consumers.

In applying the second prong of the Restatement test, and assessing the effect of this restrictive covenant on the public at large, we must focus on its effect at the time the contract was formed. The question before us is whether on balance the public gained or lost as a result of Butler's ability to secure itself from opportunistic behavior on the part of its client TVA and its job shoppers working there. There is some optimal investment for society in the resources required to find and place technical workers at places such as TVA. The goal of the legal system in this regard is to provide a framework and structure out of which the incentives to the individual firms making the decisions will correspond to those required to achieve the optimal investment for society. If the firms in the industry can receive the benefits of investment without paying the costs they will tend to overinvest. On the other hand if they pay the costs but cannot be assured of receiving the benefits they will tend to underinvest.

The protection that Butler believed it acquired as a result of this restrictive covenant permitted Butler to invest at a level closer to the optimum in the assets required to find personnel for TVA. By protecting the future stream of income that Butler would receive from its job shoppers, Butler was induced to invest more in searching for job shoppers than it otherwise would. Thus the public at large can be expected to gain from the enforcement of this and similar restrictive covenants to the extent that these covenants encourage optimal investment. The covenants therefore survive the second prong of the test provided by the Restatement supra.

Our conclusion is not that the enforcement of this restrictive covenant is the only or even the best way for Butler to protect its legitimate interest in the future employment of its job shoppers. Nor does our conclusion that it is reasonable under the circumstances imply that it is in Butler's ultimate self-interest to employ this covenant. Such a determination would be beyond the intellectual power of this or any other court. Ultimately it is the market which will be the final arbiter of the efficiency, or lack thereof, of this covenant. If Butler should persist in offering this covenant and its competitors do not, the market will have the opportunity to choose between them. What we are dealing with are contracts made between and among consenting adults and corporations. Presumably they will act in such a way as to maximize their individual welfare, and it would be presumptuous and harmful if we were to substitute our ex-post judgment for their ex-ante choice. Therefore we hold that the restrictive covenant in the contracts between Butler and its job shoppers at TVA is enforceable under state law. We reverse the district court's contrary holding and remand for further proceedings consistent with this opinion.

*   *   *

Notes and Questions

1. Restrictive Covenants and the Middleman: A restrictive covenant is a contract between an employer and employee that restricts the employee from competing against the employer for a certain amount of time after termination. As the court points out, this allowed Butler to invest in the resources necessary to find jobs for its job-shoppers. Butler is a middleman whose service is to help the market function by matching buyers and sellers of services. The restrictive covenant allows Butler to earn a profit on the investment of time and resources in getting the buyers and sellers together. Butler is compensated by, in effect, marking up the job-shoppers' salary. The mark-up is a tempting target for both TVA and the job shoppers because it should be possible for them to agree on a new contract with a salary between the salary paid by Butler to the job seekers and the fees recieved by Butler from TVA. Butler is vulnerable because its investment in finding workers jobs at TVA is both firm-specific to TVA as well as specific to each employee. The restrictive covenant protects Butler from opportunistic behavior by either the ultimate employer or the job-shoppers. From this viewpoint, the restrictive covenant is necessary for Butler to stay in business. Is enforcement of the restrictive covenant beneficial to the job shoppers? Is it beneficial to the employers?

2. Wages: How does a restrictive covenant affect wages? Does it allow for higher wages — or does it depress wages?

b. Training

It is useful to conceptually distinguish between two types of training: **General training** increases an individual's productivity to many employers equally, and **specific training** increases an individual's productivity only to the firm in which he or she is currently employed. General training might include teaching an applicant basic reading skills, or teaching an aspiring paralegal how to conduct legal research. Specific training might include teaching a secretary how to use a law firm's unique filing system. Employees, in the absence of some type of contractual restraint, will tend to bear the costs of general training because the employees are generally free to take it with them to another employer. Often times, employees bear these general training costs in the form of lower wages during a training period or an apprenticeship. Lower salaries for judicial clerks, and entry level associates in law firms can be explained from this perspective. On the other hand, the employer is expected to pay for specific training, since the employer will receive higher productivity from the employee from that training, yet the employee will be unable to receive any benefits in the form of higher wages from that training by moving to another job. One major implication of the provision of specific training is that firms who invest in specific training are reluctant to lay off workers in whom they have invested. Another implication of the distinction between general and specific theory has to do with the effects of the minimum wage on training. Since firms will offer general training only if the employees fully pay for it, the employees must receive an initial period wage that is below actual marginal productivity by an amount equal to the direct costs of training. If the minimum wage is set so that receiving such a low wage is precluded, the employers will not offer them training. They may be willing to hire workers if the minimum wage is not above the marginal productivity. However, any training would have to take place off the job.

3.   Discrimination

Managers, like many other people, have prejudices that are reflected, consciously or unconsciously, in hiring decisions. When one group controls the hiring for most jobs, their prejudices can, and often do, affect their hiring decisions. Whether prejudices should be allowed to affect the hiring decision is a normative question decided through the political process. Virtually every level of government in the U.S. has passed laws making it illegal for employers to discrimination on the basis of race, religion, sex, age, disability, or national origin. Economists cannot provide answers to the normative question of whether society should allow discrimination. Economists can, however, provide insights into how discrimination, and society's attempts to eliminate it, affect the economy.

Discrimination is a fact of life. Some people, for whatever reason, do not like members of other groups of people. Historically, members of majority groups (e.g., white males) have discriminated against minorities and women. If people with those preferences are in positions that control hiring decisions, then the market demand for minorities and women will be below the market demand for members of the decision making group. As illustrated in Figure VIII-7, the demand for minorities is to the left of the demand for whites. The result is lower wages (W_M) and fewer job opportunities (Q_M) for minorities. Conceptually, there

<u>Figure VIII-7</u>

Impact of Direct Wage Discrimination

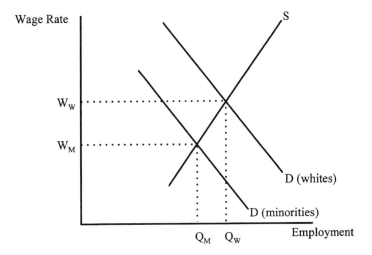

is a dual labor market—one for whites and one for minorities. Whites, or the favored groups, are preferred, but the lower wage for minorities makes it expensive for employers to discriminate by substituting expensive white workers for equally productive (yet less expensive) minority workers. In other words, discrimination can be expensive to employers.

Implicit in the preceding analysis is the assumption that white and minority workers are equally productive—that is, there is no economic justification for the employer's distinction between workers. The following case deals with compensation differences when there is an economic justification for the distinction.

Los Angeles Department of Water and Power v. Manhart

Supreme Court of the United States
98 S.Ct. 1370 (1978)

Mr. Justice STEVENS delivered the opinion of the Court.

As a class, women live longer than men. For this reason, the Los Angeles Department of Water and Power required its female employees to make larger contributions to its pension fund than its male employees. We granted certiorari to decide whether this practice discriminated against individual female employees because of their sex in violation of § 703(a)(1) of the Civil Rights Act of 1964, as amended.[2]

---

2. The section provides:
"It shall be an unlawful employment practice for an employer—
"(1) to fail or refuse to hire or to discharge any individual, or otherwise to discriminate against any individual with respect to his compensation, terms, conditions, or

For many years the Department has administered retirement, disability, and death-benefit programs for its employees. Upon retirement each employee is eligible for a monthly retirement benefit computed as a fraction of his or her salary multiplied by years of service. The monthly benefits for men and women of the same age, seniority, and salary are equal. Benefits are funded entirely by contributions from the employees and the Department, augmented by the income earned on those contributions. No private insurance company is involved in the administration or payment of benefits.

Based on a study of mortality tables and its own experience, the Department determined that its 2,000 female employees, on the average, will live a few years longer than its 10,000 male employees. The cost of a pension for the average retired female is greater than for the average male retiree because more monthly payments must be made to the average woman. The Department therefore required female employees to make monthly contributions to the fund which were 14.84% higher than the contributions required of comparable male employees. Because employee contributions were withheld from paychecks a female employee took home less pay than a male employee earning the same salary.

Since the effective date of the Equal Employment Opportunity Act of 1972, the Department has been an employer within the meaning of Title VII of the Civil Rights Act of 1964. See 42 U.S.C. § 2000e (1970 ed., Supp. V). In 1973, respondents brought this suit in the United States District Court for the Central District of California on behalf of a class of women employed or formerly employed by the Department. They prayed for an injunction and restitution of excess contributions.

*   *   *

The Department and various amici curiae contend that: (1) the differential in take-home pay between men and women was not discrimination within the meaning of § 703(a)(1) because it was offset by a difference in the value of the pension benefits provided to the two classes of employees; (2) the differential was based on a factor "other than sex" within the meaning of the Equal Pay Act of 1963 and was therefore protected by the so-called Bennett Amendment...

I

There are both real and fictional differences between women and men. It is true that the average man is taller than the average woman; it is not true that the average woman driver is more accident prone than the average man. Before the Civil Rights Act of 1964 was enacted, an employer could fashion his personnel policies on the basis of assumptions about the differences between men and women, whether or not the assumptions were valid.

It is now well recognized that employment decisions cannot be predicated on mere "stereotyped" impressions about the characteristics of males or females. Myths and purely habitual assumptions about a woman's inability to perform

---

privileges of employment, because of such individual's race, color, religion, sex, or national origin...." 78 Stat. 255, 42 U.S.C. § 2000e-2(a)(1).

certain kinds of work are no longer acceptable reasons for refusing to employ qualified individuals, or for paying them less. This case does not, however, involve a fictional difference between men and women. It involves a generalization that the parties accept as unquestionably true: Women, as a class, do live longer than men. The Department treated its women employees differently from its men employees because the two classes are in fact different. It is equally true, however, that all individuals in the respective classes do not share the characteristic that differentiates the average class representatives. Many women do not live as long as the average man and many men outlive the average woman. The question, therefore, is whether the existence or nonexistence of "discrimination" is to be determined by comparison of class characteristics or individual characteristics. A "stereotyped" answer to that question may not be the same as the answer that the language and purpose of the statute command.

The statute makes it unlawful "to discriminate against any individual with respect to his compensation, terms, conditions, or privileges of employment, because of such individual's race, color, religion, sex, or national origin." 42 U.S.C. § 2000e-2(a)(1). The statute's focus on the individual is unambiguous. It precludes treatment of individuals as simply components of a racial, religious, sexual, or national class. If height is required for a job, a tall woman may not be refused employment merely because, on the average, women are too short. Even a true generalization about the class is an insufficient reason for disqualifying an individual to whom the generalization does not apply.

That proposition is of critical importance in this case because there is no assurance that any individual woman working for the Department will actually fit the generalization on which the Department's policy is based. Many of those individuals will not live as long as the average man. While they were working, those individuals received smaller paychecks because of their sex, but they will receive no compensating advantage when they retire.

It is true, of course, that while contributions are being collected from the employees, the Department cannot know which individuals will predecease the average woman. Therefore, unless women as a class are assessed an extra charge, they will be subsidized, to some extent, by the class of male employees. It follows, according to the Department, that fairness to its class of male employees justifies the extra assessment against all of its female employees.

But the question of fairness to various classes affected by the statute is essentially a matter of policy for the legislature to address. Congress has decided that classifications based on sex, like those based on national origin or race, are unlawful. Actuarial studies could unquestionably identify differences in life expectancy based on race or national origin, as well as sex. But a statute that was designed to make race irrelevant in the employment market...could not reasonably be construed to permit a take-home-pay differential based on a racial classification.

Even if the statutory language were less clear, the basic policy of the statute requires that we focus on fairness to individuals rather than fairness to classes. Practices that classify employees in terms of religion, race, or sex tend to preserve traditional assumptions about groups rather than thoughtful scrutiny of individuals. The generalization involved in this case illustrates the point. Separate mortality tables are easily interpreted as reflecting innate differences between the sexes; but a significant part of the longevity differential may be explained by the social fact that men are heavier smokers than women.

Finally, there is no reason to believe that Congress intended a special definition of discrimination in the context of employee group insurance coverage. It is true that insurance is concerned with events that are individually unpredictable, but that is characteristic of many employment decisions. Individual risks, like individual performance, may not be predicted by resort to classifications proscribed by Title VII. Indeed, the fact that this case involves a group insurance program highlights a basic flaw in the Department's fairness argument. For when insurance risks are grouped, the better risks always subsidize the poorer risks. Healthy persons subsidize medical benefits for the less healthy; unmarried workers subsidize the pensions of married workers; persons who eat, drink, or smoke to excess may subsidize pension benefits for persons whose habits are more temperate. Treating different classes of risks as though they were the same for purposes of group insurance is a common practice that has never been considered inherently unfair. To insure the flabby and the fit as though they were equivalent risks may be more common than treating men and women alike; but nothing more than habit makes one "subsidy" seem less fair than the other.

An employment practice that requires 2,000 individuals to contribute more money into a fund than 10,000 other employees simply because each of them is a woman, rather than a man, is in direct conflict with both the language and the policy of the Act. Such a practice does not pass the simple test of whether the evidence shows "treatment of a person in a manner which but for that person's sex would be different." It constitutes discrimination and is unlawful unless exempted by the Equal Pay Act of 1963 or some other affirmative justification.

II

Shortly before the enactment of Title VII in 1964, Senator Bennett proposed an amendment providing that a compensation differential based on sex would not be unlawful if it was authorized by the Equal Pay Act, which had been passed a year earlier. The Equal Pay Act requires employers to pay members of both sexes the same wages for equivalent work, except when the differential is pursuant to one of four specified exceptions. The Department contends that the fourth exception applies here. That exception authorizes a "differential based on any other factor other than sex."

The Department argues that the different contributions exacted from men and women were based on the factor of longevity rather than sex. It is plain, however, that any individual's life expectancy is based on a number of factors, of which sex is only one. The record contains no evidence that any factor other than the employee's sex was taken into account in calculating the 14.84% differential between the respective contributions by men and women. We agree with Judge Duniway's observation that one cannot "say that an actuarial distinction based entirely on sex is 'based on any other factor other than sex.' Sex is exactly what it is based on." 553 F.2d 581, 588 (1976).

We are also unpersuaded by the Department's reliance on a colloquy between Senator Randolph and Senator Humphrey during the debate on the Civil Rights Act of 1964. Commenting on the Bennett Amendment, Senator Humphrey expressed his understanding that it would allow many differences in the treatment of men and women under industrial benefit plans, including earlier retirement options for women. Though he did not address differences in employee contributions based on sex, Senator Humphrey apparently assumed that the 1964 Act would have little, if any, impact on existing pension plans. His statement cannot, however, fairly be made the sole guide to interpreting the Equal Pay Act, which had been adopted a year earlier; and it is the 1963 statute, with its exceptions, on which the Department ultimately relies. We conclude that Senator Humphrey's isolated comment on the Senate floor cannot change the effect of the plain language of the statute itself.

*   *   *

Mr. CHIEF JUSTICE BURGER, with whom Mr. Justice REHNQUIST joins, concurring in part and dissenting in part.

I join Part IV of the Court's opinion; as to Parts I, II, and III, I dissent.

Gender-based actuarial tables have been in use since at least 1843, and their statistical validity has been repeatedly verified. The vast life insurance, annuity, and pension plan industry is based on these tables. As the Court recognizes, ante, at 1375, it is a fact that "women, as a class, do live longer than men." It is equally true that employers cannot know in advance when individual members of the classes will die. Ante, at 1375. Yet, if they are to operate economically workable group pension programs, it is only rational to permit them to rely on statistically sound and proved disparities in longevity between men and women. Indeed, it seems to me irrational to assume Congress intended to outlaw use of the fact that, for whatever reasons or combination of reasons, women as a class outlive men.

The Court's conclusion that the language of the civil rights statute is clear, admitting of no advertence to the legislative history, such as there was, is not soundly based. An effect upon pension plans so revolutionary and discriminatory—this time favorable to women at the expense of men—should not be read into the statute without either a clear statement of that intent in the statute, or some reliable indication in the legislative history that this was Congress' purpose. The Court's casual dismissal of Senator Humphrey's apparent assumption that the "Act would have little, if any, impact on existing pension plans," ante, at 1378, is to dismiss a significant manifestation of what impact on industrial benefit plans was contemplated. It is reasonably clear there was no intention to abrogate an employer's right, in this narrow and limited context, to treat women differently from men in the face of historical reliance on mortality experience statistics. Cf. ante, at 1378 n. 25.

The reality of differences in human mortality is what mortality experience tables reflect. The difference is the added longevity of women. All the reasons why women statistically outlive men are not clear. But categorizing people on the basis of sex, the one acknowledged immutable difference between men and women, is to take into account all of the unknown reasons, whether biologically or culturally based, or both, which give women a significantly greater life expectancy than men. It is therefore true as the Court says, "that any individual's life expectancy is based on a number of factors, of which sex is only one." Ante, at 1377. But it is not true that by seizing upon the only constant, "measurable" factor, no others were taken into account. All other factors, whether known but variable—or unknown—are the elements which automatically account for the actuarial disparity. And all are accounted for when the constant factor is used as a basis for determining the costs and benefits of a group pension plan.

Here, of course, petitioners are discriminating in take-home pay between men and women. The practice of petitioners, however, falls squarely under the exemption provided by the Equal Pay Act of 1963, 29 U.S.C. § 206(d), incorporated into Title VII by the so-called Bennett Amendment, 78 Stat. 257, now 42 U.S.C. § 2000e-2(h). That exemption tells us that an employer may not discriminate between employees on the basis of sex by paying one sex lesser compensation that the other "except where such payment is made pursuant to . . . a differential based on any other factor other than sex. . . ." The "other factor other than sex" is longevity; sex is the umbrella-constant under which all of the elements leading to differences in longevity are grouped and assimilated, and the only objective feature upon which an employer—or anyone else, including insurance companies—may reliably base a cost differential for the "risk" being insured.

This is in no sense a failure to treat women as "individuals" in violation of the statute, as the Court holds. It is to treat them as individually as it is possible to do in the face of the unknowable length of each individual life. Individually, every woman has the same statistical possibility of outliving men. This is the essence of basing decisions on reliable statistics when individual determinations are infeasible or, as here, impossible.

Of course, women cannot be disqualified from, for example, heavy labor just because the generality of women are thought not as strong as men—a proposition which perhaps may sometime be statistically demonstrable, but will remain individually refutable. When, however, it is impossible to tailor a program such as a pension plan to the individual, nothing should prevent application of reliable statistical facts to the individual, for whom the facts cannot be disproved until long after planning, funding, and operating the program have been undertaken.

I find it anomalous, if not contradictory, that the Court's opinion tells us, in effect, ante, at 1380, and n. 33, that the holding is not really a barrier to responding to the complaints of men employees, as a group. The Court states that employers may give their employees precisely the same dollar amount and require them to secure their own annuities directly from an insurer, who, of course, is under no compulsion to ignore 135 years of accumulated, recorded longevity experience.

*   *   *

Notes and Questions

1. Ex Ante Bonus: Women, as a class, live longer than men. With the defined benefit plan that the Los Angeles Water Department had, women, as a class, received more pension benefits than men. Is this a sufficient reason to require women to receive an equal wage? Isn't this really a bonus for women? Essentially, it raises the costs to the employer of hiring (or promoting) women. Thus, the Los Angeles Water Department has an incentive not to hire (or promote) women. Did the Supreme Court envision this response?

2. *Individualism:* The statute stresses regarding everyone as an individual instead of part of a group. From the employers perspective, *ex ante*, how do you know which individual will be close to the statistical median? Is it in the employer's interest to create a pension plan that selects people on a defined set of very strict criteria that achieves the same goal? For example, the pension contracts could be based on factors such as weight, height, hair length, etc., to select women. The general response has been to move from defined benefit plans to defined contribution plans. These plans allow a individual to place a certain portion of their wages into a pension plan. Generally, the employer matches a percentage of whatever the employee puts in. Would this solution be better for the employer? How about the employee? Does it eliminate the perverse incentive of not hiring (or promoting) women?

3. *What About the Market?:* Why not let the market govern the types of situations discussed in *Manhart*? If a company went to the open market to purchase an annuity for each of its employees, differences in such costs could be passed on to individual employees. Insurance companies make distinctions between males and females for the purpose of determining premiums. Why shouldn't employers be allowed to do the same? That is, this ruling seems to force companies to use a third party to administer their pension plan, thereby raising the costs of the plan. This hurts all employees. Does the Court consider this? If not, how might the Court respond?

4. *Different Types of Discrimination:* There are differences in economic productivity between some groups. In this regard, it is helpful to distinguish three types of discrimination: (1) discrimination based on individual characteristics that affect job performance; (2) discrimination based on correctly perceived statistical characteristics of the group; and (3) discrimination based on individual characteristics that don't affect job performance. An example of the first type is that restaurants might discriminate against applicants with sourpuss personalities, or banks might try to hire young loan officers because the bank's clients like to borrow from younger rather than older employees. An example of the second type of discrimination is that a firm may correctly perceive that young people in general have a lower probability of staying on a job than do older people, and therefore discriminate against younger people. An example of the third type of discrimination is a firm might not hire people over 50 because the supervisor doesn't like working with older people, even though older people may be just as productive as, or even more productive than, younger people. This third type of discrimination should be the easiest to eliminate because it doesn't have an economic motivation. In fact, discrimination based on individual characteristics that don't affect job performance is costly to a firm, and market forces will work toward eliminating it. Discrimination of the first two types is based on characteristics that do affect job performance, either directly or statistically and thus, the discrimination will be harder to eliminate. In some cases, not discriminating can be costly to the firm, so political forces that eliminate sources of discrimination will be working against market forces. Whenever discrimination saves the employer money, it has an economic incentive to attempt to avoid the anti-discrimination laws. Where does the discrimination in *Manhart* fit into this economic classification of types of discrimination?

5. *Discrimination and Disabilities:* Judge Richard Posner recognized the distinctions between types of discrimination in his discussion of the types of discrimination covered by the Americans with Disabilities Act:

In 1990, Congress passed the Americans with Disabilities Act. The stated purpose is "to provide a clear and comprehensive national mandate for the elimination of discrimination against individuals with disabilities," said by Congress to be 43 million in number and growing. "Disability" is broadly defined. It includes not only "a physical or mental impairment that substantially limits one or more of the major life activities of [the disabled] individual," but also the state of "being regarded as having such an impairment." The latter definition, although at first glance peculiar, actually makes a better fit with the elaborate preamble to the Act, in which people who have physical or mental impairments are compared to victims of racial and other invidious discrimination. Many such impairments are not in fact disabling but are believed to be so, and the people having them may be denied employment or otherwise shunned as a consequence. Such people, objectively capable of performing as well as the unimpaired, are analogous to capable workers discriminated against because of their skin color or some other vocationally irrelevant characteristic.

The more problematic case is that of an individual who has a vocationally relevant disability—an impairment such as blindness or paralysis that limits a major human capability, such as seeing or walking. In the common case in which such an impairment interferes with the individual's ability to perform up to the standards of the workplace, or increases the cost of employing him, hiring and firing decisions based on the impairment are not "discriminatory" in a sense closely analogous to employment discrimination on racial grounds. The draftsmen of the Act knew this. But they were unwilling to confine the concept of disability discrimination to cases in which the disability is irrelevant to the performance of the disabled person's job. Instead, they defined "discrimination" to include an employer's "not making reasonable accommodations to the known physical or mental limitations of an otherwise qualified individual with a disability who is an applicant or employee, unless...[the employer] can demonstrate that the accommodation would impose an undue hardship on the operation of the...[employer's] business."

Vande Zande v. State of Wisconsin Department of Administration, 44 F.3rd 538 (7th Cir. 1995).

6. Emotion, Discrimination, and Policy Analysis: Issues relating to employment discrimination and unequal pay elicit emotional responses from many people. This is to be expected because the federal laws affect the livelihood of almost all Americans. In many instances, the emotional responses have hindered sound policy analysis. The economic analysis presented in this section attempts to rise above the emotional aspects of employment discrimination law and address both the economic presumptions underlying the laws and the economic impact of the laws.

From Equal Opportunity to "Affirmative Action"
Thomas Sowell, *Civil Rights: Rhetoric or Reality?* (1984)

The very meaning of the phrase "civil rights" has changed greatly since the *Brown* decision in 1954, or since the Civil Rights Act of 1964. Initially, civil rights meant, quite simply, that all individuals should be treated the same under the law, regardless of their race, religion, sex or other such social categories. For blacks, especially, this would have represented a dramatic improvement in those states where law and public policy mandated racially separate institutions and highly discriminatory treatment.

Many Americans who supported the initial thrust of civil rights, as represented by the *Brown v. Board of Education* decision and the Civil Rights Act of 1964, later felt betrayed as the original concept of equal individual *opportunity* evolved toward the concept of equal group *results*. The idea that statistical differences in results were weighty presumptive evidence of discriminatory processes was not initially an explicit part of civil rights law. But neither was it merely an inexplicable perversion, as many critics seem to think, for it followed logically from the civil rights *vision*.

If the causes of intergroup differences can be dichotomized into discrimination and innate ability, then nonracists and non-sexists must expect equal results from nondiscrimination. Conversely, the persistence of highly disparate results must indicate that discrimination continues to be pervasive among recalcitrant employers, culturally biased tests, hypocritical educational institutions, etc. The early leaders and supporters of the civil rights movement did not advocate such corollaries, and many explicitly repudiated them, especially during the congressional debates that preceded passage of the Civil Rights Act of 1964. But the corollaries were implicit in the vision—and in the long run that proved to be more decisive than the positions taken by the original leaders in the cause of civil rights. In the face of crying injustices, many Americans accepted a vision that promised to further a noble cause, without quibbling over its assumptions or verbal formulations. But visions have a momentum of their own, and those who accept their assumptions have entailed their corollaries, however surprised they may be when these corollaries emerge historically.

FROM RIGHTS TO QUOTAS

"Equal opportunity" laws and policies require that individuals be judged on their qualifications as individuals, *without regard* to race, sex, age, etc. "Affirmative action" requires that they be judged *with regard* to such group membership, receiving preferential or compensatory treatment in some cases to achieve a more proportional "representation" in various institutions and occupations.

The conflict between equal opportunity and affirmative action developed almost imperceptibly at first, though it later became a heated issue, repeatedly debated by the time the Civil Rights Act of 1964 was being considered by Congress. The term "affirmative action" was first used in a racial discrimination context in President John F. Kennedy's Executive Order No. 10, 925 in 1961. But, as initially presented, affirmative action referred to various activities, such as monitoring insubordinate decision makers to ensure the fairness of their hiring and promotion decisions, and spreading information about employment or other opportunities so as to encourage previously excluded groups to apply—after which the actual selection could be made *without regard* to group membership. Thus, it was both meaningful and consistent for President Kennedy's Executive Order to say that federal contractors should "take affirmative action to ensure that the applicants are employed, and that employees are treated during employment, without regard to their race, creed, color, or national origin."

Tendencies toward shifting the emphasis from equality of prospective opportunity toward statistical parity of retrospective results were already observed, at both state the federal levels, by the time that the Civil Rights Act of 1964 was under consideration in Congress. Senator Hubert Humphrey, while guiding this bill through the Senate, assured his colleagues that it "does not require an employer to achieve any kind of racial balance in his work force by giving preferential treatment to any individual or group." He pointed out that subsection 703(j) under Title VII of the Civil Rights Act "is added to state this point expressly." That subsection declared that nothing in Title VII required an employer "to grant preferential treatment to any individual or group on account of any imbalance which may exist" with respect to the numbers of employees in such groups "in comparison with the total number or percentage of persons of such race, color, religion, sex, or national original in any community, State, section or other area."

Virtually all the issues involved in the later controversies over affirmative action, in the specifically numerical sense, were raised in the legislative debates preceding passage of the Civil Rights Act. Under subsection 706(g) of that Act, an employer was held liable only for his own "intentional" discrimination, not for societal patterns reflected in his work force. According to Senator Humphrey, the "express requirement of intent is designed to make it wholly clear that inadvertent or accidental discriminations will not violate the Title or result in the entry of court orders." Vague claims of differential institutional policy impact— "institutional racism"—were not to be countenanced. For example, tests with differential impact on different groups were considered by Humphrey to be "legal unless used for the purpose of discrimination." There was no burden of proof placed upon employers to "validate" such tests.

In general there was to be no burden of proof on employers; rather the Equal Employment Opportunity Commission (EEOC) created by the Act "must prove by a preponderance" that an adverse decision was based on race (or, presumably, other forbidden categories), according to Senator Joseph Cark, another leading advocate of the Civil Rights Act. Senator Clark also declared that the Civil Rights Act "will not require an employer to change existing seniority lists," even though such lists might have differential impact on blacks as the last hired and first fired. Still another supporter, Senator Harrison Williams, declared that an employer with an all-white work force could continue to hire "only the best qualified persons even if they were all white."

In short, Congress declared itself in favor of equal opportunity and opposed to affirmative action. So has the American public. Opinion polls show a majority of blacks opposed to preferential treatment, as is an even larger majority of women. Federal administrative agencies and the courts led the change from the prospective concept of individual equal opportunity to the retrospective concept of parity of group "representation" (or "correction" of "imbalances").

The key development in this process was the creation of the Office of Federal Contract Compliance in the U.S. Department of Labor by President Lyndon Johnson's Executive Order No. 11,246 in 1965. In May 1968, this office issued guidelines containing the fateful expression "goals and timetables" and "representation." But as yet these were still not quotas, for 1968 guidelines spoke of "goals and timetables for the prompt achievement of full and equal employment opportunity." By 1970, however, new guidelines referred to "results-oriented procedures," which hinted more strongly at what was to come. In December 1971, the decisive guidelines were issued, which made it clear that "goals and timetables" were meant to "increase materially the utilization" of minorities and women, with "under-utilization" being spelled out as "having fewer minorities or women in a particular job classification than would reasonably be expected by their availability..." Employers were required to confess to "deficiencies in the utilization" of minorities and women whenever this statistical parity could not be found in all job classifications, as a first step toward correcting this situation. The burden of proof—and remedy—was on the employer. "Affirmative action" was now decisively transformed into a numerical concept, whether called "goals" or "quotas."

Though lacking in either legislative authorization or public support for numerical group preferences, administrative agencies of government were able to enforce such policies with the support of the federal courts in general and the U.S. Supreme Court in particular. In the landmark *Weber* case the Supreme Court simply rejected "a literal interpretation" of the words of the Civil Rights Act. Instead, it sought the "spirit" of the Act, its "primary concern" with the economic problems of blacks. According to Justice William Brennan, writing the majority opinion, these words do not bar "temporary, voluntary, affirmative action measures undertaken to eliminate manifest racial imbalance in traditionally segregated job categories." This performance received the sarcastic tribute of Justice Rehnquist that it was "*a tour de force* reminiscent not of jurists such as Hale, Holmes, and Hughes but of escape artists such as Houdini." Rehnquist's dissent inundated the Supreme Court with the legislative history of the Act, and Congress' repeated and emphatic rejection of the whole approach of correcting imbalances or compensating for the past. The spirit of the Act was as contrary to the decision as was the letter.

EQUALITY OF RIGHTS AND RESULTS

Those who carry the civil rights vision to its ultimate conclusion see no great difference between promoting equality of opportunity and equality of results. If there are not equal results among groups presumed to have equal genetic potential, then some inequality of opportunity must have intervened somewhere, and the question of precisely where is less important than the remedy of restoring the less fortunate to their just position. The fatal flaw in this kind of thinking is that there are many reasons, besides genes and discrimination, why groups differ in their economic performances and rewards. Groups differ by large amounts demographically, culturally, and geographically—and all of these differences have profound effects on incomes and occupations.

Age differences are quite large. Blacks are a decade younger than the Japanese. Jews are a quarter of a century older than Puerto Ricans. Polish Americans are twice as old as American Indians. These represent major differences in the quantity of work experience, in an economy where income differences between age brackets are even greater than black-white income differences. Even if the various racial and ethnic groups were identical in every other respect, their age differences alone would prevent their being equally represented in occupations requiring experience or higher education. Their very different age distributions likewise prevent their being equally represented in colleges, jails, homes for the elderly, the armed forces, sports and numerous other institutions and activities that tend to have more people from one age bracket than from another.

Cultural differences add to the age differences. As noted in Chapter 1, half of all Mexican American wives were married in their teens, while only 10 percent of Japanese American wives married that young. Such very different patterns imply not only different values but also very different future opportunities. Those who marry and begin having children earlier face more restricted options for future education and less geographic mobility for seeking their best career opportunities. Even among those young people who go on to colleges and universities, their opportunities to prepare themselves for the better paid professions are severely limited by their previous educational choices and performances, as well as by their selections of fields of study in the colleges and universities. All of these things vary enormously from one group to another.

For example, mathematics preparation and performance differ greatly from one ethnic group to another and between men and women. A study of high school students in northern California showed that four-fifths of Asian youngsters were enrolled in the sequence of mathematics courses that culminate in calculus, while only one-fifth of black youngsters were enrolled in such courses. Moreover, even among those who began this sequence in geometry, the percentage that persisted all the way through to calculus was several times higher among the Asian students. Sex differences in mathematics preparation are comparably large. Among both black and white freshman at the University of Maryland, the men had four years of mathematics in high school more than twice as often as the women.

Mathematics is of decisive importance for many more professions than that of mathematician. Whole ranges of fields of study and work are off-limits to those without the necessary mathematical foundation. Physicists, chemists, statisticians, and engineers are only some of the more obvious occupations. In some colleges, one cannot even be an undergraduate economics major without having had calculus, and to go on to graduate school and become a professional economist requires much more mathematics, as well as statistical analysis. Even if fields where mathematics is not an absolute prerequisite, its presence or absence makes a major difference in one's ability to rise in the profession. Mathematics is becoming an important factor in the social sciences and is even beginning to invade some of the humanities. To be mathematically illiterate is to carry an increasing burden into an increasing number of occupations. Even the ability to pass a civil service examination for most clerical jobs is helped or hindered by one's facility in mathematics.

It is hardly surprising that test scores reflect these group differences in mathematics preparation. Nationwide results on the Scholastic Aptitude Test (SAT) for college applicants show Asians and whites consistently scoring higher on the quantitative test than Hispanics or blacks, and men scoring higher than women. Nor are these differences merely the result of socioeconomic "disadvantage" caused by "society." Black, Mexican American, and American Indian youngsters from families with incomes of $50,000 and up score lower than Asians from families whose incomes are just $6,000 and under. Moreover, Asians as a group score higher than whites as a group on the quantitative proportion of the SAT and the Japanese in Japan specialize in mathematics, science and engineering to a far greater extent than do American students in the United States. Cultural differences are real, and cannot be talked away by using pejorative terms such as "stereotypes" or "racism."

The racial, ethnic, and sex differences in mathematics that begin in high school (or earlier) continue on through to the Ph.D. level, affecting career choices and economic rewards. Hispanic Ph.D.'s outnumber Asian Ph.D.'s in the United States by three-to-one in history, but the Asians outnumber the Hispanics by ten-to-one in chemistry. More than half of all Asian Ph.D.'s are in mathematics, science or engineering, and more than half the Asians who teach college teach in those fields. By contrast, more than half of all black doctorates are in the field of education, a notoriously undemanding and less remunerative field. So are half the doctorates received by American Indians, not one of whom received a Ph.D. in either mathematics or physics in 1980. Female Ph.D.'s are in quantitatively-based fields only half as frequently as male Ph.D.'s.

Important as mathematics is in itself, it is also a symptom of broader and deeper disparities in educational choices and performances in general. Those groups with smaller quantities of education tend also to have lower qualities of education, and these disparities follow them all the way through their educational careers and into the job market. The children of lower income racial and ethnic groups typically score lower on tests all through school and attend lower quality colleges when they go to college at all, as well as majoring in the easier courses in fields with the least economic promise. How much of this is due to the home environment and how much to the deficiencies of the public schools in their neighborhoods is a large question that cannot be answered here. But what is clear is that what is called the "same" education, measured in years of schooling, is not even remotely the same in reality.

The civil rights vision relies heavily on statistical "disparities" in income and employment between members of different groups to support its sweeping claims of rampant discrimination. The U.S. Civil Rights Commission, for example, considers itself to be "controlling for those factors" when it examines people of the same age with the same number of years of schooling—resolutely ignoring the substance of that schooling.

Age and education do not begin to exhaust the differences between groups. They are simply more readily quantifiable than some other differences. The geographic distributions of groups also vary greatly, with Mexican Americans being concentrated in the southwest, Puerto Ricans in the northeast, half of blacks in the South, and most Asians in California and Hawaii. Differences in income between the states are also larger than black-white income differences, so that these distributional differences affect national income differences. A number of past studies, for example, have shown black and Puerto Rican incomes to be very similar nationally, but blacks generally earn higher incomes than Puerto Ricans in New York and other places where Puerto Ricans are concentrated. Their incomes nationally have shown up in these studies as similar, because there are very few Puerto Ricans living in low-income southern states.

One of the most important causes of differences in income and employment is the way people work—some diligently, carefully, persistently, cooperatively, and without requiring much supervision or warnings about absenteeism, tardiness, or drinking, and others requiring much such concern over such matters. Not only are such things inherently difficult to quantify; any suggestion that such differences even exist is sure to bring forth a storm of condemnation. In short, the civil rights vision has been hermetically sealed off from any such evidence. Both historical and contemporary observations on intergroup differences in work habits, discipline, reliability, sobriety, cleanliness, or cooperative attitude—anywhere in the world—are automatically dismissed as evidence only of the bias or bigotry of the observers. "Stereotypes" is the magic word that makes thinking about such things unnecessary. Yet despite this closed circle of reasoning that surrounds the civil rights vision, there is some evidence that cannot be disposed of in that way.

Self-employed farmers, for example, do not depend for their rewards on the biases of employers or the stereotypes of observers. Yet self-employed farmers of different ethnicity have fared very differently on the same land, even in earlier pre-mechanization times, when the principal input was the farmer's own labor. German farmers, for example, had more prosperous farms than other farmers in colonial America—and were more prosperous than Irish farmers in eighteenth-century Ireland, as well as more prosperous than Brazilian farmers in Brazil, Mexican farmers in Mexico, Russian farmers in Russia, and Chilean farmers in Chile. We may ignore the forbidden testimony from all these countries as to how hard the German farmers worked, how frugally they lived, or how sober they were. Still, the results speak for themselves.

That Jews earn far higher incomes than Hispanics in the United States might be taken as evidence that anti-Hispanic bias is stronger than anti-Semitism—if one followed the logic of civil rights vision. But this explanation is considerably weakened by the greater prosperity of Jews than Hispanics *in Hispanic countries* throughout Latin America. Again, even if one dismisses out of hand all the observers who see great differences in the way these two groups work, study, or save, major tangible differences in economic performance remain that cannot be explained in terms of the civil rights vision.

One of the commonly used indices of intergroup economic differences is family income. Yet families are of different sizes from group to group, reflecting differences in the incidence of broken homes. Female headed households are several times more common among blacks than among whites, and in both groups these are the lowest income families. Moreover, the proportion of people working differs greatly from group to group. More than three-fifths of all Japans American families have multiple income earners while only about a third of Puerto Rican families do. Nor is this a purely socioeconomic phenomenon, as distinguished from a cultural phenomenon. Blacks have similar incomes to Puerto Ricans, but the proportion of black families with a woman working is nearly three times that among Puerto Ricans.

None of this disproves the existence of discrimination, nor is that its purpose. What is at issue is whether statistical differences mean discrimination, or whether there are innumerable demographic, cultural, and geographic differences that make this crucial automatic interference highly questionable.

EFFECTS VERSUS HOPES

Thus far, we have not even considered the actual effects of the incentives and constraints created by affirmative action policies—as distinguished from the rationales, hopes or claims made for these policies. Because these policies are invoked on behalf of the most disadvantaged groups, and the most disadvantaged classes within these groups, it is especially important to scrutinize the factual record of what has happened to the economic position of such people under both equal opportunity and affirmative policies.

Before crediting either political policy with economic gains, it is worth considering what trends were already under way before they were instituted. Much has been made of the number of blacks in high-level occupations before and after the Civil Rights Act of 1964. What has been almost totally ignored is the historical *trend* of black representation in such occupations before the Act was passed. In the period from 1954 to 1964, for example, the number of blacks in professional, technical, and similar high-level positions more than doubled. In other kinds of occupations, the advance of blacks was even greater during the 1940s— when there was little or no civil rights policy—than during the 1950s when the civil rights revolution was in its heyday.

The rise in the number of blacks in professional and technical occupations in the two years from 1964 to 1966 (after the Civil Rights Act) was in fact *less* than in the one year from 1961 to 1962 (before the Civil Rights Act). If one takes into account the growing black population by looking at percentages instead of absolute numbers, it becomes even clearer that the Civil Rights Act of 1964 represented no acceleration in trends that had been going on for many years. The percentage of employed blacks who were professional and technical workers rose less in the five years following the Civil Rights Act of 1964 than in the five years preceding it. The percentage of employed blacks who were managers and administrators was the same in 1967 as in 1964—and in 1960. Nor did the institution of "goals and timetables" at the end of 1971 mark any acceleration in the long trend of rising black representation in these occupations. True, there was an appreciable increase in the percentage of blacks in professional and technical fields from 1971 to 1972, but almost entirely offset by a reduction in the percentage of blacks who were managers and administrators.

The history of Asians and Hispanics likewise shows long-term upward trends that began years before the Civil Rights Act of 1964 and were not noticeably accelerated by the Act or by later "affirmative action" policies. The income of Mexican Americans rose relative to that of non-Hispanic whites between 1959 and 1969 (after the Civil Rights Acts), but no more so than from 1949 to 1959 (before the Act). Chinese and Japanese Americans overtook other Americans in income by 1959—five years before the Civil Rights Act.

Ignoring trends already in progress for years makes before-and-after comparisons completely misleading. Yet that is precisely the approach of supporters of the civil rights vision, who proceed as if "before" was a static situation. Yet the notion that the Civil Rights Act and "affirmative action" have had a dramatic impact on the economic progress of minorities has become part of the folklore of the land, established primarily through repetition and vehemence, rather than evidence.

The evidence of the *political* impact of civil rights changes in the 1960s is far more clear-cut. The number of black elected officials, especially in the South, increased many-fold in a relatively few years, including blacks elected to public office in some places for the first time since the Reconstruction era after the Civil War. Perhaps even more important, white elected officials in the South had to change both their policies and their rhetoric to accommodate the new political reality that blacks could vote.

What is truly surprising—and relatively ignored—is the economic impact of affirmative action on the disadvantaged, for whom it is most insistently invoked. The relative position of disadvantaged individuals within the groups singled out for preferential treatment has generally *declined* under affirmative action. This is particularly clear in data for individuals, as distinguished from families.

Family income data have too many pitfalls to be taken at face value. There are, for example, significant variations in what constitutes a family, both from time to time and from group to group. But since many people insist on using such data, these statistics cannot be passed over in silence. In 1969, *before* the federal imposition of numerical "goals and timetables," Puerto Rican family income was 63 percent of the national average. By 1977, it was down to 50 percent. In 1969, Mexican American family income was 76 percent of the national average. By 1977 it was down to 73 percent. Black family income fell from 62 percent of the national average to 60 percent over the same span.

There are many complex facts behind these numbers. The point here is simply that they do not support the civil rights vision. A finer breakdown of the data for blacks shows the most disadvantaged families—the female-headed, with no husband present—to be not only the poorest and with the slowest increase in money income during the 1970s (a decline in *real* income) but also with money incomes increasing even more slowly than among white, female-headed families. By contrast, black husband-wife families had money incomes that were rising faster than that of their white counterparts. It is part of a more general pattern of the most disadvantaged falling farther behind during the affirmative action era, while the already advantaged forged ahead.

Individual data tell the same story, even more clearly. Those blacks with less education and less job experience—the truly disadvantaged—have been falling farther and farther behind their white counterparts under affirmative action, during the very same years when blacks with more education and more job experience have been advancing economically, both absolutely and relative to their white counterparts. First, the disadvantaged: Black male high school dropouts with less than six years of work experience earned 79 percent of the income of white male high school dropouts with less than six years of work experience in 1967 (before affirmative action quotas), and this *fell* to 69 percent by 1978 (after affirmative action quotas). Over these very same years, the income of black males who had completed college and had more than six years of work experience *rose* from 75 percent of the income of their white counterparts to 98 percent. Some economic trends can be explained in terms of general conditions in the economy, but such diametrically opposite trends during the very same span of years obviously cannot.

There is additional evidence that the advantaged have benefited under affirmative action while the disadvantaged have fallen behind. Black faculty members with numerous publications and Ph.D.'s from top-rated institutions earned more than white faculty members with the same high qualifications, but black faculty members who lacked a doctorate or publications earned less than whites with the same low qualifications. The pattern of diametrically opposite trends in economic well-being among advantaged and disadvantaged blacks is also shown by the general internal distribution of income among blacks. The top fifth of blacks have absorbed a growing proportion of all income received by blacks, while each of the bottom three fifths has received declining shares. Black college-educated couples with husband and wife working had by 1980 achieved incomes higher than white couples of the same description. Meanwhile, at the other end of the spectrum, the black female-headed household was receiving only 62 percent of the income of white, female-headed households—down from 70 percent in 1970.

*   *   *

BY THE NUMBERS

Averages versus Variance

One of the remarkable aspects of affirmative action is that, while numbers— and *assumptions* about numbers—abound, proponents of the program are almost never challenged to produce positive numerical evidence for its effectiveness or to support their statistical presuppositions. The mere fact that some group is *x* percent of the population but only *y* percent of the employees is taken as weighty presumption of employer discrimination. There are serious statistical problems with this approach, quite aside from substantial group differences in age, education, and cultural values.

Even in a random world of identical things, to say that it happens a certain way *on the average* is not to say that it happens that way *every time*. But affirmative action deals with averages almost as if there were no variance. If Hispanics are 8 percent of the carpenters in a given town, it does not follow that *every* employer of carpenters in that town would have 8 percent Hispanics if there were no discrimination. Even if carpenters were assigned to employers by drawing lots (or by some other random process), there would be *variance* in the proportion of Hispanic carpenters from one employer to another. To convict those employers with fewer Hispanics of discrimination in hiring would be to make statistical variance a federal offense.

To illustrate the point, we can consider some process where racial, sexual, or ideological factors do not enter, such as the flipping of the coin. There is no reason to expect a persistent preponderance of heads over tails (or vice versa) on the *average*, but there is also no reason to expect half heads and half tails every time we flip a coin a few times. That is, *variance* will exist.

To illustrate the effect of statistical variance, a coin was flipped ten times and then this experiment was repeated ten times. Here are the results:

Heads	3	4	3	4	6	7	2	4	5	3
Tails	7	6	7	6	4	3	8	6	5	7

At one extreme, there were seven heads and three tails, and at the other extreme eight tails and two heads. Statistics not only have averages, they have variance.

Translate this into employment decisions. Imagine that you are the employer who ends up with eight employees from one group and two from another, even though both groups are the same size and no different in qualifications, and even though you have been unbiased in selecting. Try explaining to EEOC and the courts that you ended up with four times as many employees from one group by random chance! You may be convicted of discrimination, even if you have only been guilty of statistical variance.

Of course some employers are biased, just as some coins are biased because of the way their weight is distributed on the design. This particular coin might have been biased; over all, it came up heads 41 percent of the time and tails 59 percent. But even if the coin was biased towards tails, it still came up heads seven times out of ten in one set of flips. If an employer were similarly biased in *favor* of a particular group, he could still be convicted of discrimination *against* that very group, if they ended up with less than half the "representation" of some other group.

No one needs to assume that this particular coin was unbiased or even that the results were accurately reported. Anyone can collect ten people and have them flip a coin ten times, to see the statistical variance for himself. Frivolous as this might seem, the results have deadly serious implications for the way people are convicted of violating federal laws, regulations, and guidelines. It might be especially instructive if this little experiment were performed by editorial writers for publications that fervently support affirmative action, or by clerks of the Supreme Court.

Even when conclusions are based only on differences statisticians call "statistically significant," this by no means eliminates the basic problem. What is statistically significant depends upon the probability that such a result would have happened by random chance. A common litmus test used by statisticians is whether the event would occur more than 5 times out of a hundred by random chance. Applying this common test of statistical significance to affirmative action means that even in the most extreme case imaginable—zero discrimination and zero difference among racial, ethnic, and other groups—the EEOC could still run 10,000 employers' records through a computer and come up with about 500 "discriminators."

The illustration chosen is in fact too favorable to the proponents of affirmative action, because it shows the probability of incorrectly calling an employer a discriminator when there is only *one* group in question that might be discriminated against. Affirmative action has a number of groups whose statistical pattern can lead to charges of discrimination. To escape a false charge of discrimination, an employer must avoid being in the fatal 5 percent for *all* the groups in question simultaneously. That becomes progressively harder when there are more groups.

While there is a 95 percent chance for a non-discriminatory employer to escape when there is only one group, this falls to 86 percent when there are three separate groups and to 73 percent when there are six. That is, even in a world of zero discrimination and zero differences among groups, more than one-fourth of all employers would be called "discriminators" by this common test of statistical significance, when there are six separate groups in question.

What this means is that the courts have sanctioned a procedure which insures that large-scale statistical "discrimination" will exist forever, regardless of what the actual facts may be. They have made statistical variance a federal offense.

Shopping for Discrimination

Often the very same raw data point to different levels of aggregation. For example, statistics have shown that black faculty members earn less than white faculty members, but as these data are broken down by field of specialization, by number of publications, by possession (or non-possession) of a Ph.D. and by the ranking of the institution that issued it, then the black-white income difference not only shrinks but disappears, and in some fields reverses—with black faculty earning more than white faculty with the same characteristics. For those who accept statistics as proof of discrimination, how much discrimination there is, and in what direction, depends upon how finely these data are broken down.

There is no "objective" or "scientific" way to decide at what level of aggregation to stop breaking the data down into finer categories. Nor have the laws or the courts specified in advance what will and what will not be the accepted way to break down the statistics. Any individual or organization contemplating a lawsuit against an employer can arrange that employer's statistics in any number of possible ways and then go shopping among the possibilities for the one that will present the employment pattern in the worst light. This is a very effective strategy in a society in which groups differ enormously in their characteristics and choices, while the prevailing vision makes deviations from a random distribution evidence against the employer.

A discrimination case can depend entirely on what level of statistical breakdown the judge accepts, for different groups will be represented—or "under-represented"—differently according to how precisely occupations and qualifications are defined. While there were more black than Asian American "social scientists" receiving a Ph.D. in 1980, when social scientists were broken down further, there were nearly three times as many Asian as black *economists*. While male recipients of Ph.D.'s in the social sciences outnumbered female recipients of Ph.D.'s by slightly less than two-to-one in 1980, men outnumbered women by more than four-to-one among doctorates in economics and by ten-to-one among doctorates in econometrics. What is the employer hiring: social scientists, economists or econometricians? He may in fact be looking for an econometrician specializing in international trade—and there may be no statistics available on that. Nor can anyone infer the proportion of women or minority members available in that specialty from their distribution in broader categories, for the distribution changes at every level of aggregation.

The same principle applies in other fields as well. A computer manufacturer who is looking for an engineer is not looking for the same kind of engineer as a company that builds bridges. Nor is there the slightest reason to expect all groups to be distributed the same in these sub-specialties as they are among engineers in general. Even within a narrow occupational range such as mathematical specialists, blacks outnumber Asian Americans in gross numbers but Asian Americans outnumber blacks more than two-to-one among statisticians.

When comparing any employer's work force with the available labor pool to determine "under-representation," everything depends on how that labor pool is defined—at what level of aggregation. Those who wish to argue for discrimination generally prefer broad, loose, heterogeneous categories. The concept of a "qualified" worker aids that approach. When the barely qualified is treated as being the same as the most highly skilled and experienced, it is the same as staying at a very general level of aggregation. Anything that creates or widens the disparity between what the job requires and how the categories are defined increases the potential for statistical "discrimination."

An employer may be guilty or innocent according to what level of statistical aggregation a judge accepts, after the plaintiffs have shopped around among the many possibilities. But that is only part of the problem. A more fundamental problem is that *the burden of proof is on the accused* to prove his innocence, once suspicious numbers have been found. Shopping around for suspicious numbers is by no means difficult, especially for a federal agency, given statistical variance, multiple groups, multiple occupations, and wide-ranging differences in the characteristics and choices of the groups themselves.

Statistical aggregation is a major factor not only in courts of law but also in the court of public opinion. Many statistics from a very general level of aggregation are repeatedly presented in the media as demonstrating pervasive discrimination. The finer breakdowns are more likely to appear in specialized scholarly journals, read by a relative handful of people. Yet these finer breakdowns of statistics often tell a drastically different story, not only for black-white differences and male-female differences but for other groups as well.

For example, American Indian males earn significantly less than white males, and Asian males earn significantly more. Yet, as one holds a wide range of variables constant, these income differences shrink to the vanishing point. Asian Americans, for example, are distributed geographically in a very different pattern from whites. Asians are concentrated in higher income states, in more urban areas, and have more education. When all of this is held constant, their income advantage vanishes. By the same token, when various demographical and cultural variables—notably proficiency in the English language—are held constant, the income disadvantages of Hispanic and American Indian males also disappear.

It can hardly be expected that discrimination lawsuits and discrimination as a political issue will be correspondingly reduced any time soon. The methods by which it is measured in the courts and in politics insures that it will be a continuing source of controversy.

Poverty and huge intergroup differences in income are serious matters, whether or not discrimination is the cause—and whether or not affirmative action is the cure. Yet any attempt to deal with these very real disadvantages must first cut through the fog generated by a vision more powerful than its evidence—and, in fact, a vision shaping what courts will accept as evidence.

Notes and Questions

1 . Equal Pay for Equal Work: The Equal Pay Act of 1963 applies to discrimination based on sex that results in unequal pay for equal work. Equal work is defined as work on jobs the performance of which requires equal effort, skill, and responsibility, where the jobs are performed under similar working conditions. The act allows for pay differentials among employees of the opposite sex when the differential is based on a seniority system, merit system, system which determines wages by the quantity or quality of production, or where the wage differential is based on any fact other than sex. The Equal Pay Act is a governmental effort to change the status quo of employment practices. It is important, however, to first recognize that an initial understanding of the status quo will facilitate an economic analysis of the applicable federal laws. For example, it is possible to generate a long list of explanations for why women are typically paid less than men in similar occupations. Only one of the explanations is that employers are sexist. Other explanations look to the employment histories of women relative to men and find that women's careers tend to be interrupted much more often than men's. One obvious explanation for the interruptions is that women leave work to have children and raise a family. From the employer's perspective, such interruptions tend to lower productivity and raise costs, thus making women less desirable employees relative to men. Thus, the employer's decision to pay lower wages to women may be based on the economics of the situation, not necessarily on sexist preferences. Although valid (i.e., non-discriminatory) productivity reasons may explain why the market wages for women are often less than the market wages for men in similar jobs, assume (for analytical convenience) that the difference in wages is due exclusively to employers' sexist preferences. If men and women are equal in terms of productivity, and women can be hired at a lower wage, then it is costly for employers to hire men instead of women. When employers are required to pay women the same as men, women are no longer a bargain, relative to men. This has several adverse effects on women, as illustrated in Figure VIII-8. Figure VIII-8 is a two-sector market where otherwise equally productive women are paid less, W_W, than men, W_M, because of employers' sexist preferences. The equal pay requirement raises the women's wage to W_M in panel b. As a result of the higher wage, more women enter the job market and employers simultaneously hire less women. The resulting surplus of women at the higher wage allows employers to pick and choose among qualified women applicants using discriminatory criteria other than sex (for example, age, appearance, race, etc.). Of course, the women who manage to keep their jobs or get hired at the higher wage are made better off. But, as the graphical analysis clearly indicates, the increased well-being of some is purchased at the expense of others. The individuals most likely to need assistance in the job market are the ones most likely to be displaced. Moreover, a policy designed to decrease discrimination has actually made discrimination more likely to occur. Most observers would agree that such results are perverse. On the other hand, if women generally are paid lower wages for reasons solely due to differences in productivity, a higher wage rate will result in more women entering the job market and employers hiring fewer women. This again results in a surplus of women workers (however, employers are not discriminating on the basis of sex, but on the basis of productivity). The most productive women will be hired (or keep

Figure VIII-8

Equal Pay for Equal Work

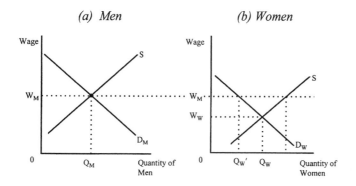

(a) Men   (b) Women

their jobs) and are better off. Those who cannot justify the higher wages on productivity grounds will lose their jobs (or not be hired). Thus, it appears the result (surplus of women workers) is the same regardless of whether lower wages for women is due to sexism or for productivity reasons.

2. Institutional Discrimination. Another type of discrimination is institutional demand-based discrimination in which the structure of the job makes it difficult or impossible for certain groups of individuals to succeed. Consider the policies of colleges and universities. To succeed as a professor, university administrator, or other professional in the academic market, one must devote an enormous amount of effort during one's twenties and thirties, while these years are precisely the years when given genetics and culture, many women have major family responsibilities that make it difficult to succeed in the academic market. Thus, one can argue that women face institutional demand-based discrimination in universities. Academic institutions could change their job settings by increasing the number of positions at universities that are designed for high-level part-time work, thus making it easier for women to advance. Of course, one might also argue that it is the supply side institutions where the discrimination occurs, because in relationships, women get more child rearing responsibilities than men. For instance, when parents have a sick child, someone must stay home and in the majority of relationships, the woman, not the man, stays home and jeopardizes her advancement. In general, it is important to recognize that discrimination can be deeply embedded in institutions and that the lack of direct discriminatory actions does not necessarily mean that discrimination does not exist.

4. Employment At Will

Traditionally, employment contracts in the United States are negotiated between individual employers and employees. Third parties, such as governments or unions, were not involved in these contractual relationships. The growth of an industrialized economy and the welfare state have altered these traditional individualistic values. These alterations, especially striking in the areas of unionization and employment discrimination, are also evident in even the simplest employment relationships. Although many areas of the employment relation have become inundated with federal and state regulations, the duration of the contract between the parties has, until recently, avoided alteration by either the judicial decree or legislation. That is, the employment contract is typically governed by contract law.

The freedom of contract philosophy underlying the common law of contracts applies to employment contracts. With respect to the duration of a contract, the *laissez-faire* approach means that the common law will enforce any contract length that is reasonable. Moreover, the Thirteenth Amendment of the Constitution prohibits involuntary servitude and thus prevents the enforcement by employers of contracts that amount to slavery. This effectively means that employees are always free to quit a job. The other side of this approach is that contracts that fail to specify a duration for the relationship are deemed to be at the will of either party. That is, employees are free to quit at anytime; and employers are free to fire at anytime. It does not matter whether the employer's motives in the firing are justified or not. This is the essence of the employment-at-will doctrine.

Kumpf v. Steinhaus

United States Court of Appeals for the Seventh Circuit
779 F.2d 1323 (1985)

EASTERBROOK, Circuit Judge.

From 1973 until August 1983 William A. Kumpf was the president and chief executive officer of Lincoln National Sales Corp. of Wisconsin (Lincoln Wisconsin). He owned 20% of Lincoln Wisconsin's stock. Lincoln National Sales Corp. (Lincoln Sales) owned the other 80% of the stock, and two of the three members of Lincoln Wisconsin's board of directors were employees of Lincoln Sales. Lincoln Sales is in turn a subsidiary of Lincoln National Life Insurance Co. (Lincoln Life). Lincoln Sales is the marketing arm of Lincoln Life; Lincoln Wisconsin was the Wisconsin agency of Lincoln Sales.

In April 1981 Orin A. Steinhaus became an executive vice-president of Lincoln Life, leaving a post as head of Lincoln's sales agency in Columbus, Ohio. The president of Lincoln Life gave Steinhaus and other employees the task of revising the firm's sales structure, which was losing money. Lincoln Life closed 25 sales agencies and decided to consolidate others. In August 1983 Steinhaus decided to consolidate five midwestern sales agencies into a single agency. (Doubtless other officers of Lincoln Life concurred in these decisions, but for simplicity we write as if Steinhaus made all decisions himself.) He instructed Lincoln Sales's directors on the board of Lincoln Wisconsin to approve a merger of Lincoln Wisconsin into Lincoln Chicago Corp. (Lincoln Chicago); Lincoln Wisconsin's board approved the merger by a vote of two to one, over Kumpf's dissent. Lincoln Wisconsin disappeared, and so did Kumpf's job. This litigation is the residue.

The district court dismissed most of Kumpf's claims for relief but sent to the jury a claim that Steinhaus and the Lincoln corporations tortiously interfered with the employment contract between Kumpf and Lincoln Wisconsin. Kumpf was an employee at will, but even at-will employment is contractual and therefore potentially the basis of a tort action. Mendelson v. Blatz Brewing Co., 9 Wis. 2d 487, 101 N.W.2d 805 (1960). Kumpf was fired by Lincoln Wisconsin, and Lincoln Wisconsin cannot "interfere" with its own employment relations. But because Lincoln Sales owned only 80% of Lincoln Wisconsin's stock, Kumpf argued that other participants in the Lincoln family of firms could not intervene.

The defendants maintain that their interference with Kumpf's contract was privileged because it took place in the course of business. Kumpf replied that it was not privileged because it was done with an improper motive. After the reorganization, Steinhaus became president of Lincoln Chicago. In the insurance business the head of an agency receives a percentage of the agency's revenue. Income that used to go to Kumpf now went to Steinhaus, and the reorganization increased Steinhaus's total income. Kumpf argued that Steinhaus engineered the reorganization to advance his personal interests, and that this defeats the claim of privilege.

Kumpf asked the judge to instruct the jury that if the defendants' acts were "based—even in part—upon personal considerations, malice or ill will" then their acts were not privileged. Kumpf later proposed an instruction that would make privilege turn on "predominant" motivation. The district court, however, told the jury that "if you find that the actions of the defendants were motivated solely by a desire for revenge, ill will or malice, or in the case of the defendant Orin Steinhaus, solely by personal considerations, then you may find their actions improper." The jury returned a verdict for the defendants, and Kumpf attacks the "sole motive" instruction.

The Supreme Court of Wisconsin has dealt twice with related questions of privilege, and its position on whether mixed proper and improper motives defeat the privilege is unclear. Mendelson, the first case, quoted with apparent favor from a federal decision adopting the rule that any legitimate motive will support the privilege. 101 N.W.2d at 808, quoting from Tye v. Finkelstein, 160 F. Supp. 666, 668 (D. Mass. 1958). But it also described, with apparently equal favor, an earlier decision said to establish that "malice is supplied when the act of procuring the discharge is done with an improper motive." The most recent case says that it is sufficient "to allege that the act of procuring a breach of contract was done with an improper motive." Lorenz v. Dreske, 62 Wis. 2d 273, 287, 214 N.W.2d 753 (1974). Kumpf has asked us to certify to the Supreme Court of Wisconsin the question whether mixed proper and improper motives undercut the privilege. If we thought the case turned on this, certification would be an attractive route. But the case does not turn on this.

Malice, ill will, and the like mean, in Wisconsin, an intent to act without justification. So the initial question is whether Kumpf has identified an unsupportable consideration that led to his dismissal. The only one Kumpf presses on us is Steinhaus's self-interest (Kumpf calls it "greed"). The defendants asked the district court to dismiss the case at the close of Kumpf's evidence on the ground that Steinhaus's financial motivations were proper, and therefore the acts were privileged. The district judge allowed the jury to render a decision. When denying Kumpf's motion for a new trial, however, the judge remarked that "even had the predominant instruction been granted, . . . the jury would have had no other alternative than to find for the defendant." This is a ground on which we may affirm the judgment, see, and we think the defendants have a compelling argument.

The basis of the privilege in question is the economic relations among the Lincoln family of corporations. The managers of the firm at the apex of the structure have an obligation to manage the whole structure in the interests of investors. Kumpf and Lincoln Wisconsin knew that when they started—when Kumpf took the risks associated with owning 20% of the stock, and holding one of three seats on the board, in a subsidiary of Lincoln Life. The superior managers in such a structure try to serve the interests of investors and other participants as a whole, and these interest will not always be congruent with the interests of managers of subsidiaries. Corporate reorganizations may reduce the costs of operation and put the structure in the hands of better managers, though this may be costly to existing managers.

If Kumpf had directly challenged the wisdom of a business decision of the managers of Lincoln Life, he would have been rebuffed with a reference to the business judgment doctrine—a rule of law that insulates business decisions from most forms of review. Courts recognize that managers have both better information and better incentives than they. The press of market forces—managers at Lincoln Life must continually attract new employees and capital, which they cannot do if they exploit existing participants or perform poorly—will more effectively serve the interests of all participants than will an error-prone judicial process. See Joy v. North, 692 F.2d 880, 885–87 (2d Cir. 1982), cert. denied, 460 U.S. 1051 (1983); Daniel R. Fischel, The Business Judgment Rule and the Trans-Union Case, 40 Bus. Law. 1437, 1439–43 (1985).

The privilege to manage corporate affairs is reinforced by the rationale of employment at will. Kumpf had no tenure of office. The lack of job security gave him a keen motive to do well. Security of position may diminish that incentive. See Richard A. Epstein, In Defense of the Contract at Will, 51 U. Chi. L. Rev. 947 (1984). Employment at will, like the business judgment doctrine, also keeps debates about business matters out of the hands of courts. People who enter a contract without a fixed term know there is some prospect that their business partners may try to take advantage of them or simply make a blunder in deciding whether to continue the relationship. Yet people's concern for their reputation and their ability to make other advantageous contracts in the future leads them to try to avoid both mistakes and opportunistic conduct. Contracting parties may sensibly decide that it is better to tolerate the risk of error—to leave correction to private arrangements—than to create a contractual right to stay in office in the absence of a "good" reason. The reason for a business decision may be hard to prove, and the costs of proof plus the risk of mistaken findings of breach may reduce the productivity of the employment relation.

Many people have concluded otherwise; contracts terminable only for cause are common. But in Wisconsin, courts enforce whichever solution the parties select. A contract at will may be terminated for any reason (including bad faith) or no reason, without judicial review; the only exception is a termination that violates "a fundamental and well-defined public policy as evidenced by existing law." ... Greed—the motive Kumpf attributes to Steinhaus—does not violate a "fundamental and well-defined public policy" of Wisconsin. Greed is the foundation of much economic activity, and Adam Smith told us that each person's pursuit of his own interests drives the economic system to produce more and better goods and services for all. "It is not from the benevolence of the butcher, the brewer, or the baker, that we expect our dinner, but from their regard to their own interest. We address ourselves, not to their humanity but to their self-love, and never talk to them of our own necessities but of their advantages." The Wealth of Nations 14 (1776; Modern Library ed.).

The reasons that led Wisconsin to hold in Brockmeyer that it is "unnecessary and unwarranted for the courts to become arbiters of any termination that may have a tinge of bad faith attached" (335 N.W.2d at 838) also establish that greed is not the sort of prohibited motive that will support Kumpf's tort action. In Mendelson the court stated that majority shareholders possess a privilege "to take whatever action they deem advisable to further the interests of the corporation." 101 N.W.2d at 808. The court then quoted with approval from a text stating that a person enjoys no privilege "if his object is to put pressure upon the plaintiff and coerce him into complying with the defendant's wishes in some collateral matter."

If Steinhaus got rid of Kumpf because Kumpf would not marry Steinhaus's daughter, that would have been pressure in a "collateral matter." It is quite another thing to say that a jury must determine whether Steinhaus installed himself as head of Lincoln Chicago "predominantly" because he thought that would be good for Lincoln Life or "predominantly" because Steinhaus would enjoy the extra income. The decision to consolidate agencies and change managers is not "collateral" to the business of Lincoln Life, and the rationale of the business judgment rule interdicts any attempt to look behind the decision to determine whether Steinhaus is an astute manager.

Often corporations choose to align the interests of investors and managers by giving the managers a share of the firm's revenue or profits. Commissions, the ownership of stock or options, and bonuses all make managers and investors do well or poorly together. Lincoln Life chose to give managers a financial stake in each agency's revenues. Steinhaus was privileged to act with that incentive in mind. Suppose a major auto manufacturer decides to pay its chief executive officer $1 per year plus a percentage of the firm's profit. The officer then closes an unprofitable subsidiary (owned 80% by the firm), discharging its employees. Under Kumpf's theory any of the employees would be entitled to recover from the executive if the jury should estimate that in the executive's mind making money for himself predominated over making money for the firm. Yet since the two are the same thing, that would be a bootless investigation, and one with great potential to stifle the executive's vigorous pursuit of the firm's best interests. We do not think this is the law in Wisconsin or anywhere else.

Kumpf presents one last argument. He asked the judge to charge the jury that it should consider "recognized ethical codes or standards for a particular area of business activity" and "concepts of fair play" in deciding whether the defendants' acts were privileged. This "business ethics" instruction, Kumpf contends, would have allowed the jury to supplement the rules of tort and contract with "'the rules of the game'" in business. Although language of this sort appears in the Restatement (Second) of Torts § 767 comment j at p. 37 (1979), it was not designed to be given to a jury. It would leave the jury at sea, free to impose a brand of ethics for which people may not have bargained. No case in Wisconsin has required an instruction even remotely like this one....

The "rules of the game" are important in deciding what sorts of acts are privileged. If Lincoln Life had assured Kumpf that his agency would not be obliterated without his being given an opportunity to take a new job within the firm, that might cast a different light on his claim for interference with contract. But Kumpf does not say that he received such assurance or that any other understood "rule" has been breached. He therefore had to be content with the rules reflected in the definition of privileged acts.

The contention that businesses should be more considerate of their officers should be addressed to the businesses and to legislatures. Some firms will develop reputations for kind treatment of executives, some will be ruthless. Some will seek to treat executives well but find that the exigencies of competition frustrate their plans. The rule of this game is that Kumpf was an employee at will and had no right to stay on if his board wanted him gone. His board was dominated by people who answered to Lincoln Sales, which answered to Lincoln Life. Kumpf did not bargain for legal rights against Lincoln Life, and the judge properly declined to allow the jury to convert moral and ethical claims into legal duties.

AFFIRMED.

Notes and Questions

1. Employer's Reputation. In many instances, employers are prevented from abusing the discretion of the employment-at-will doctrine because market forces constrain arbitrary behavior. Consider the following proposition. An employer who develops a reputation for unjustly firing her employees will have a difficult time attracting good employees. Employees who take the risk of working for such an employer are usually being compensated in the form of higher wages. This proposition may not be immediately obvious. The initial reaction is that such an employer would be unlikely to offer higher wages to her employees. Those employees who have their choice of where they want to work will not choose to work for this employer; instead, they will work for other employers who are not as prone to fire employees without cause. This will leave our "firing" employer with a choice of employees who are unable to find jobs with other employers at a comparable wage. Accordingly, the lower quality employees are paid higher wages to work in the job where they have a greater likelihood of being fired. Thus, our hypothetical employer pays higher wages not out of choice, but through the natural selection process from the available pool of employees choosing where they want to work. Of course, this analysis does not apply to all employment situations, but it does serve to point out that businesses do not exercise their right to fire at will lightly.

2. Employees' Incentives: Just as the market creates a barrier to an employer firing employees at will, the market consequences of employment-at-will limits the ability of employees quitting at will. A worker whose employment record indicates that the individual cannot hold a job will have a difficult time finding employment. That is, exercising your right to quit is not free. In summary, the free contracting philosophy underlying the employment-at-will doctrine does not mean that labor markets are characterized by random behavior or very short-term contracts.

3. Decline of Employment at Will: In recent years, state courts have been moving away from a "strict" application of the employment-at-will doctrine. Recent opinions have limited the "at will" doctrine through an extension of contract law doctrine and an implied "good faith" contract term that prevents termination without cause. This approach limits the discharge of employees for malicious purposes such as resisting sexual advances or to avoid paying an employee commissions earned, but not vested. Other cases alter the doctrine on the grounds that the employee's firing violated some "public policy," such as discharge for serving jury duty or filing a complaint with a regulatory agency. Almost one-half of the states have modified the doctrine in some manner. The typical justification for judicial or statutory modification of the employment-at-will doctrine is that society has become more complex and thus complex legal rules are necessary to deal with complicated interdependencies. Such a conclusion, however, does not necessarily follow. For example, it seems just as plausible that simple rules are more appropriate for dealing with complex fact patterns. In general, the more complicated the facts and the more "sophisticated" the legal rule, then the less likely that contracting parties will understand the legal consequences of their actions and the less likely that the bargain will encompass all foreseeable consequences. The abandonment of a simple rule like the employment-at-will doctrine is as likely to frustrate peoples' expectations as it is to facilitate their realization.

C. Employees' Behavior:
The Supply of Labor

An individual's decision to enter the job market reflects his or her tradeoff of the benefits of work against the opportunity costs of work. Costs of work include opportunity costs and direct costs. The opportunity costs of work might include foregone leisure or educational opportunities, time away from young children, or lost welfare payments. Direct costs include commuting expenses, additional clothes, child care expenses, etc. Individuals choose to work when their personal evaluation determines that the benefits are greater than the costs.

Once the decision to work has been made, the employee must decide how much work to engage in. Conceptually, at higher wages, individuals are willing to supply more labor. The market supply of labor is obtained by horizontally summing the supply curves of individual workers. As the wage rate rises, a larger quantity of labor is supplied. Supply of labor to any particular occupation thus follows the familiar law of supply.

1. Human Capital Investments

Much of the supply and demand analysis of labor markets emphasizes the effects of current wages, employee benefits, and psychic income on worker decisions. Many labor supply choices, however, require substantial initial investment on the part of the worker. These investments, by definition, entail an initial cost that one hopes to recover over some period of time. Thus, for many labor supply decisions, current wages and working conditions are not the only decision variables. Understanding these decisions requires developing a framework that incorporates investment behavior.

Workers undertake three major kinds of labor market investments: education and training, migration, and search for new jobs. All three investments involve an initial cost, and all three are made in the hope and expectation that the investment will pay off well into the future. To emphasize the essential similarity of these investments to other kinds of investments, economists refer to them as investments in **human capital**. The knowledge and skills a worker has, which come from education and training, including the training that experience yields, generate a stock of productive capital. However, the value of this amount of productive capital is derived from how much these skills can earn in the labor market. Job search and migration are activities that increase the value of one's human capital by increasing the price or wage received from a given stock of skills. Expected returns on human capital investments are a higher level of earnings, greater job satisfaction over one's lifetime, and a greater appreciation of leisure activities and interests.

Generally speaking, human capital investment expenditures can be divided into three categories: (1) out-of-pocket, or direct expenses, including tuition and books, moving expenses and gasoline (education, migration, and job search, respectively); (2) foregone earnings are another source of cost because during the investment period it is usually impossible to work, at least not full time; and (3) psychic losses are incurred because education is difficult, because job search is tedious and nerve-racking, and because migration means saying goodbye to old friends.

Gaining human capital requires an investment period, such as three years in law school. This investment involves a large opportunity cost. A law student loses the next best alternative when attending law school. For many law students, the lost opportunity is the income they would have earned if they had been working in a job commensurate with their college education. Figure VIII-9 portrays a simplified version of two alternative lifetime income streams for an individual. After graduating from college at age 22, individuals have a choice—they may enter the labor market immediately and earn Earnings Stream A from that time until retirement at age 65. This income stream should rise through the years as the individual acquires job related skills. On the other hand, some individuals may decide to go to law school. From age 22 to 25, they do not earn steady full-time income. The opportunity cost of going to law school—that is, the income that individuals forego by choosing not to work—is represented by the shaded area above the horizontal axis between ages 22 and 25. In addition, they must pay the direct costs of college, tuition, books, and so on. The shaded area below the horizontal axis, between ages 22 and 25, represents the direct costs of law school, conceptually a negative income. The total costs of going to law school is the sum of both the opportunity cost and the direct costs of college. After graduation, these individuals enter the labor market at Earnings Stream B. The shaded area between the earnings streams indicates the gross benefits

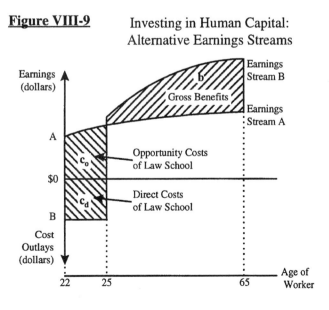

Figure VIII-9   Investing in Human Capital:
Alternative Earnings Streams

of their human capital investment—their starting pay at age 25, after completing law school, is higher than it would have been had they not gone to law school. Yet, in order for the human capital investment to make financial sense, Earnings Stream B must offset the three years of negative income. If the deciding factor is money, then the individual determines the relative values of the two income streams and chooses the higher one. One method of doing so is to compare areas c_o and c_d, the investment period, with area b. Areas c_o and c_d represents the total cost of going to law school, the direct cost plus the lost income. Area b represents the benefits of going to law school. It is the income earned with a law degree. If area b is greater than areas c_o and c_d, then it pays to go to college. Of course, the values of c_o, c_d and b must be discounted to present value as is the case for any investment.

O'Brien v. O'Brien
Court of Appeals of New York
498 N.Y.S.2d 743 (1985)

SIMONS, Judge.

In this divorce action, the parties' only asset of any consequence is the husband's newly acquired license to practice medicine. The principal issue presented is whether that license, acquired during their marriage, is marital property subject to equitable distribution under Domestic Relations Law § 236(B)(5). Supreme Court held that it was and accordingly made a distributive award in defendant's favor. It also granted defendant maintenance arrears, expert witness fees and attorneys' fees. On appeal to the Appellate Division, a majority of that court held that plaintiff's medical license is not marital property and that defendant was not entitled to an award for the expert witness fees. It modified the judgment and remitted the case to Supreme Court for further proceedings, specifically for a determination of maintenance and a rehabilitative award. The matter is before us by leave of the Appellate Division.

We now hold that plaintiff's medical license constitutes "marital property" within the meaning of Domestic Relations Law § 236(B)(1)(c) and that it is therefore subject to equitable distribution pursuant to subdivision 5 of that part. That being so, the Appellate Division erred in denying a fee, as a matter of law, to defendant's expert witness who evaluated the license.

I

Plaintiff and defendant married on April 3, 1971. At the time both were employed as teachers at the same private school. Defendant had a bachelor's degree and a temporary teaching certificate but required 18 months of postgraduate classes at an approximate cost of $3,000, excluding living expenses, to obtain permanent certification in New York. She claimed, and the trial court found, that she had relinquished the opportunity to obtain permanent certification while plaintiff pursued his education. At the time of the marriage, plaintiff had completed only three and one-half years of college but shortly afterward he returned to school at night to earn his bachelor's degree and to complete sufficient premedical courses to enter medical school. In September 1973 the parties moved to Guadalajara, Mexico, where plaintiff became a full-time medical student. While he pursued his studies defendant held several teaching and tutorial positions and contributed her earnings to their joint expenses. The parties returned to New York in December 1976 so that plaintiff could complete the last two semesters of medical school and internship training here. After they returned, defendant resumed her former teaching position and she remained in it at the time this action was commenced. Plaintiff was licensed to practice medicine in October 1980. He commenced this action for divorce two months later. At the time of trial, he was a resident in general surgery.

During the marriage both parties contributed to paying the living and educational expenses and they received additional help from both of their families. They disagreed on the amounts of their respective contributions but it is undisputed that in addition to performing household work and managing the family finances defendant was gainfully employed throughout the marriage, that she contributed all of her earnings to their living and educational expenses and that her financial contributions exceeded those of plaintiff. The trial court found that she had contributed 76% of the parties' income exclusive of a $10,000 student loan obtained by defendant. Finding that plaintiff's medical degree and license are marital property, the court received evidence of its value and ordered a distributive award to defendant.

Defendant presented expert testimony that the present value of plaintiff's medical license was $472,000. Her expert testified that he arrived at this figure by comparing the average income of a college graduate and that of a general surgeon between 1985, when plaintiff's residency would end, and 2012, when he would reach age 65. After considering Federal income taxes, an inflation rate of 10% and a real interest rate of 3% he capitalized the difference in average earnings and reduced the amount to present value. He also gave his opinion that the present value of defendant's contribution to plaintiff's medical education was $103,390. Plaintiff offered no expert testimony on the subject.

The court, after considering the life-style that plaintiff would enjoy from the enhanced earning potential his medical license would bring and defendant's contributions and efforts toward attainment of it, made a distributive award to her of $188,800, representing 40% of the value of the license, and ordered it paid in 11 annual installments of various amounts beginning November 1, 1982 and ending November 1, 1992. The court also directed plaintiff to maintain a life insurance policy on his life for defendant's benefit for the unpaid balance of the award and it ordered plaintiff to pay defendant's counsel fees of $7,000 and her expert witness fee of $1,000. It did not award defendant maintenance.

*   *   *

II

The Equitable Distribution Law contemplates only two classes of property: marital property and separate property (Domestic Relations Law § 236[B][1] [c], [d]). The former, which is subject to equitable distribution, is defined broadly as "all property acquired by either or both spouses during the marriage and before the execution of a separation agreement or the commencement of a matrimonial action, regardless of the form in which title is held " (Domestic Relations Law § 236[B][1][c] [emphasis added]; see § 236[B][5] [b], [c]). Plaintiff does not contend that his license is excluded from distribution because it is separate property; rather, he claims that it is not property at all but represents a personal attainment in acquiring knowledge. He rests his argument on decisions in similar cases from other jurisdictions and on his view that a license does not satisfy common-law concepts of property. Neither contention is controlling because decisions in other States rely principally on their own statutes, and the legislative history underlying them, and because the New York Legislature deliberately went beyond traditional property concepts when it formulated the Equitable Distribution Law. Instead, our statute recognizes that spouses have an equitable claim to things of value arising out of the marital relationship and classifies them as subject to distribution by focusing on the marital status of the parties at the time of acquisition. Those things acquired during marriage and subject to distribution have been classified as "marital property" although, as one commentator has observed, they hardly fall within the traditional property concepts because there is no common-law property interest remotely resembling marital property. "It is a statutory creature, is of no meaning whatsoever during the normal course of a marriage and arises full-grown, like Athena, upon the signing of a separation agreement or the commencement of a matrimonial action. [Thus] [i]t is hardly surprising, and not at all relevant, that traditional common law property concepts do not fit in parsing the meaning of 'marital property' " (Florescue, "Market Value", Professional Licenses and Marital Property: A Dilemma in Search of a Horn, 1982 N.Y.St.Bar Assn.Fam.L.Rev. 13 [Dec.]). Having classified the "property" subject to distribution, the Legislature did not attempt to go further and define it but left it to the courts to determine what interests come within the terms of section 236(B)(1)(c).

     *   *   *

Section 236 provides that in making an equitable distribution of marital property, "the court shall consider: * * * (6) any equitable claim to, interest in, or direct or indirect contribution made to the acquisition of such marital property by the party not having title, including joint efforts or expenditures and contributions and services as a spouse, parent, wage earner and homemaker, and to the career or career potential of the other party [and] * * * (9) the impossibility or difficulty of evaluating any component asset or any interest in a business, corporation or profession " (Domestic Relations Law § 236[B][5][d][6], [9] [emphasis added]). Where equitable distribution of marital property is appropriate but "the distribution of an interest in a business, corporation or profession would be contrary to law" the court shall make a distributive award in lieu of an actual distribution of the property (Domestic Relations Law § 236[B][5][e]). The words mean exactly what they say: that an interest in a profession or professional career potentially is marital property which may be represented by direct or indirect contributions of the non-title-holding spouse, including financial contributions and nonfinancial contributions made by caring for the home and family.

The history which preceded enactment of the statute confirms this interpretation. Reform of section 236 was advocated because experience had proven that application of the traditional common-law title theory of property had caused inequities upon dissolution of a marriage. The Legislature replaced the existing system with equitable distribution of marital property, an entirely new theory which considered all the circumstances of the case and of the respective parties to the marriage. Equitable distribution was based on the premise that a marriage is, among other things, an economic partnership to which both parties contribute as spouse, parent, wage earner or homemaker. Consistent with this purpose, and implicit in the statutory scheme as a whole, is the view that upon dissolution of the marriage there should be a winding up of the parties' economic affairs and a severance of their economic ties by an equitable distribution of the marital assets. Thus, the concept of alimony, which often served as a means of lifetime support and dependence for one spouse upon the other long after the marriage was over, was replaced with the concept of maintenance which seeks to allow "the recipient spouse an opportunity to achieve [economic] independence"

The determination that a professional license is marital property is also consistent with the conceptual base upon which the statute rests. As this case demonstrates, few undertakings during a marriage better qualify as the type of joint effort that the statute's economic partnership theory is intended to address than contributions toward one spouse's acquisition of a professional license. Working spouses are often required to contribute substantial income as wage earners, sacrifice their own educational or career goals and opportunities for child rearing, perform the bulk of household duties and responsibilities and forego the acquisition of marital assets that could have been accumulated if the professional spouse had been employed rather than occupied with the study and training necessary to acquire a professional license. In this case, nearly all of the parties' nine-year marriage was devoted to the acquisition of plaintiff's medical license and defendant played a major role in that project. She worked continuously during the marriage and contributed all of her earnings to their joint effort, she sacrificed her own educational and career opportunities, and she traveled with plaintiff to Mexico for three and one-half years while he attended medical school there. The Legislature has decided, by its explicit reference in the statute to the contributions of one spouse to the other's profession or career (see, Domestic Relations Law § 236[B][5][d][6], [9]; [e]), that these contributions represent investments in the economic partnership of the marriage and that the product of the parties' joint efforts, the professional license, should be considered marital property.

The majority at the Appellate Division held that the cited statutory provisions do not refer to the license held by a professional who has yet to establish a practice but only to a going professional practice (see, e.g., Arvantides v. Arvantides, 64 N.Y.2d 1033, 489 N.Y.S.2d 58, 478 N.E.2d 199; Litman v. Litman, 61 N.Y.2d 918, 474 N.Y.S.2d 718, 463 N.E.2d 34). There is no reason in law or logic to restrict the plain language of the statute to existing practices, however, for it is of little consequence in making an award of marital property, except for the purpose of evaluation, whether the professional spouse has already established a practice or whether he or she has yet to do so. An established practice merely represents the exercise of the privileges conferred upon the professional spouse by the license and the income flowing from that practice represents the receipt of the enhanced earning capacity that licensure allows. That being so, it would be unfair not to consider the license a marital asset.

Plaintiff's principal argument, adopted by the majority below, is that a professional license is not marital property because it does not fit within the traditional view of property as something which has an exchange value on the open market and is capable of sale, assignment or transfer. The position does not withstand analysis for at least two reasons. First, as we have observed, it ignores the fact that whether a professional license constitutes marital property is to be judged by the language of the statute which created this new species of property previously unknown at common law or under prior statutes. Thus, whether the license fits within traditional property concepts is of no consequence. Second, it is an overstatement to assert that a professional license could not be considered property even outside the context of section 236(B). A professional license is a valuable property right, reflected in the money, effort and lost opportunity for employment expended in its acquisition, and also in the enhanced earning capacity it affords its holder, which may not be revoked without due process of law. That a professional license has no market value is irrelevant. Obviously, a license may not be alienated as may other property and for that reason the working spouse's interest in it is limited. The Legislature has recognized that limitation, however, and has provided for an award in lieu of its actual distribution (see, Domestic Relations Law § 236[B][5][e]).

      *   *   *

...Limiting a working spouse to a maintenance award, either general or rehabilitative, not only is contrary to the economic partnership concept underlying the statute but also retains the uncertain and inequitable economic ties of dependence that the Legislature sought to extinguish by equitable distribution. Maintenance is subject to termination upon the recipient's remarriage and a working spouse may never receive adequate consideration for his or her contribution and may even be penalized for the decision to remarry if that is the only method of compensating the contribution. As one court said so well, "[t]he function of equitable distribution is to recognize that when a marriage ends, each of the spouses, based on the totality of the contributions made to it, has a stake in and right to a share of the marital assets accumulated while it endured, not because that share is needed, but because those assets represent the capital product of what was essentially a partnership entity." The Legislature stated its intention to eliminate such inequities by providing that a supporting spouse's "direct or indirect contribution" be recognized, considered and rewarded.

Turning to the question of valuation, it has been suggested that even if a professional license is considered marital property, the working spouse is entitled only to reimbursement of his or her direct financial contributions...Such a result is completely at odds with the statute's requirement that the court give full consideration to both direct and indirect contributions "made to the acquisition of such marital property by the party not having title, including joint efforts or expenditures and contributions and services as a spouse, parent, wage earner and homemaker" (Domestic Relations Law 236[B][5][d][6] [emphasis added]). If the license is marital property, then the working spouse is entitled to an equitable portion of it, not a return of funds advanced. Its value is the enhanced earning capacity it affords the holder and although fixing the present value of that enhanced earning capacity may present problems, the problems are not insurmountable. Certainly they are no more difficult than computing tort damages for wrongful death or diminished earning capacity resulting from injury and they differ only in degree from the problems presented when valuing a professional practice for purposes of a distributive award, something the courts have not hesitated to do. The trial court retains the flexibility and discretion to structure the distributive award equitably, taking into consideration factors such as the working spouse's need for immediate payment, the licensed spouse's current ability to pay and the income tax consequences of prolonging the period of payment and, once it has received evidence of the present value of the license and the working spouse's contributions toward its acquisition and considered the remaining factors mandated by the statute (see, Domestic Relations Law § 236[B][5][d]

[1]–[10]), it may then make an appropriate distribution of the marital property including a distributive award for the professional license if such an award is warranted. When other marital assets are of sufficient value to provide for the supporting spouse's equitable portion of the marital property, including his or her contributions to the acquisition of the professional license, however, the court retains the discretion to distribute these other marital assets or to make a distributive award in lieu of an actual distribution of the value of the professional spouse's license.

*   *   *

MEYER, Judge (concurring).

I concur in Judge Simons' opinion but write separately to point up for consideration by the Legislature the potential for unfairness involved in distributive awards based upon a license of a professional still in training.

An equity court normally has power to "change its decrees where there has been a change of circumstances." The implication of Domestic Relations Law § 236(B)(9)(b), which deals with modification of an order or decree as to maintenance or child support, is, however, that a distributive award pursuant to section 236(B)(5)(e), once made, is not subject to change. Yet a professional in training who is not finally committed to a career choice when the distributive award is made may be locked into a particular kind of practice simply because the monetary obligations imposed by the distributive award made on the basis of the trial judge's conclusion (prophecy may be a better word) as to what the career choice will be leaves him or her no alternative.

The present case points up the problem. A medical license is but a step toward the practice ultimately engaged in by its holder, which follows after internship, residency and, for particular specialties, board certification. Here it is undisputed that plaintiff was in a residency for general surgery at the time of the trial, but had the previous year done a residency in internal medicine. Defendant's expert based his opinion on the difference between the average income of a general surgeon and that of a college graduate of plaintiff's age and life expectancy, which the trial judge utilized, impliedly finding that plaintiff would engage in a surgical practice despite plaintiff's testimony that he was dissatisfied with the general surgery program he was in and was attempting to return to the internal medicine training he had been in the previous year. The trial judge had the right, of course, to discredit that testimony, but the point is that equitable distribution was not intended to permit a judge to make a career decision for a licensed spouse still in training. Yet the degree of speculation involved in the award made is emphasized by the testimony of the expert on which it was based. Asked whether his assumptions and calculations were in any way speculative, he replied: "Yes. They're speculative to the extent of, will Dr. O'Brien practice medicine? Will Dr. O'Brien earn more or less than the average surgeon earns? Will Dr. O'Brien live to age sixty-five? Will Dr. O'Brien have a heart attack or will he be injured in an automobile accident? Will he be disabled? I mean, there is a degree of speculation. That speculative aspect is no more to be taken into account, cannot be taken into account, and it's a question, again, Mr. Emanuelli, not for the expert but for the courts to decide. It's not my function nor could it be."

The equitable distribution provisions of the Domestic Relations Law were intended to provide flexibility so that equity could be done. But if the assumption as to career choice on which a distributive award payable over a number of years is based turns out not to be the fact (as, for example, should a general surgery trainee accidentally lose the use of his hand), it should be possible for the court to revise the distributive award to conform to the fact. And there will be no unfairness in so doing if either spouse can seek reconsideration, for the licensed spouse is more likely to seek reconsideration based on real, rather than imagined, cause if he or she knows that the nonlicensed spouse can seek not only reinstatement of the original award, but counsel fees in addition, should the purported circumstance on which a change is made turn out to have been feigned or to be illusory.

    *   *   *

Notes and Questions

1. The License as Marital Property: The O'Brien court decides that the husband's medical license is marital property subject to a distributive award. Is this consistent with the discussion of property rights as developed throughout this casebook? If so, is there a solution to the marital assets problem that is consistent with the Coase Theorem? Why does the court consider an award to Mrs. O'Brien equal to the dollar amount of her contributions during the marriage to be an inadequate form of compensation? Is such a conclusion consistent with economic theory? How does the *O'Brien* decision impact the incentives of married couples to invest in human capital? Couples considering marriage? Couples considering divorce? Are these "side-effects" justifiable on-balance? The concurring opinion expressing concern that decisions such as the one made in *O'Brien* may in effect force Dr. O'Brien to practice a particular type of medicine for the sole purpose of being able to pay the award to Mrs. O'Brien. Is this a justifiable concern? How does it balance with the need for judicial efficiency?

2. Valuing the Homemaker's Services: The services performed by homemakers are not sold in the market place, but this does not imply they are not valuable. For purposes of settling claims involving the wrongful death of a homemaker and often in cases in which property must be divided upon divorce, it is important to place a value on homemakers services. Three approaches can be taken in evaluating these services. One method is to estimate what the homemaker would have been able to earn if she or he had worked for pay—the opportunity cost approach. Of course, many married women do not work for pay at all, which implies that they value the services they provide at home at more than their potential market earnings. Using the foregone wage to estimate the value of their services, thus, results in an underestimate. An estimate of the value of the typical homemaker's services using this approach comes to about $10,630 per year in 1992 after taxes and work related expenses. The second method is to measure how much a homemaker's services would cost if they were to be purchased in the market place—the market prices approach. Thus, the market cost of child care, cleaning, cooking and other services are aggregated to form an overall estimate. The results of one careful study using this approach implied that the market value of services performed by a full time homemaker in a two adult family with two children under age six was $18,780 in 1992 dollars. The problem with this method is that in cases in which market services are available but not purchased, the household must believe that such services are not worth their cost. For these households, the value assigned by the market prices approach overstates the value of the homemakers services. A third method is to treat homemakers as self-employed individuals who either increase hours at home if their marginal household productivity exceeds their market wage, or to reduce hours at home if wage exceeds marginal household product (MHP)—the self-employment approach. If MHP exceeds W, even when hours for work for pay are zero, the homemaker works full time at home. If W exceeds MHP, even when working full time for pay, the person works full time outside the home. If the person is at home part of the time, and also works part time for pay, theory suggests that marginal household productivity, MHP, and W must be equal. Thus for those homemakers that work for pay part of the time, it can be inferred that the value of their marginal productivity at home is equal to their net market wage. Using this wage as an estimate of their marginal household productivity, it is possible to estimate a production function for their value of household services. Applying this production function to full time homemakers, it has been estimated that the typical homemaker working exclusively in the home produces services worth, in 1992 terms, $24,530 to the family. Full time married homemakers with children under age six were estimated to provide services worth $32,630 in 1992. See generally, Carmel Ullman Chiswick, The Value of a Housewife's Time, *Journal of Human Resources,* 16, Summer 1982, 113–425.

3. Severance Pay: An important economic function of alimony is to provide the spouse who remains at home with a form of severance pay or unemployment benefits. Where one of the marriage partners specializes in household production, any market skills that they may have developed prior to the decision to stay at home depreciate. As a result, the stay-at-home spouse loses prime employment possibilities should the present marriage dissolve. The next best alternative at this point may be to remarry and form a new household. Although some other kind of work could always be found in the marketplace, the skilled household producer forced to work as a waitress or file clerk is like the lawyer who, unable to find a legal job, becomes a process server. Thus, alimony pays the stay-at-home spouse unemployment rather than force them to find inefficient work in the marketplace.

a. The Cobweb Model: Earnings Differences and the Demand for Education

The demand for education is influenced by the differences in earnings made possible by an educational investment in human capital. However, the returns to education are themselves affected by the number of people who attend school. To obtain an overall picture of how enrollments and returns are interrelated, it is necessary to return briefly to our simple model of the labor market.

Figure VIII-10 shows the labor market demand for, and supply of, law school graduates. The reason the supply curve for law school graduates slopes upward is that expected wages need to increases to attract applicants with progressively higher opportunity costs. If the earnings of law school graduates were to rise, more individuals would want to attend law school. If they were to rise still more, even more students would enroll in law school. If the demand for law school graduates were to shift outward, more graduates would be demanded at

Figure VIII-10

The Labor Market for Lawyers

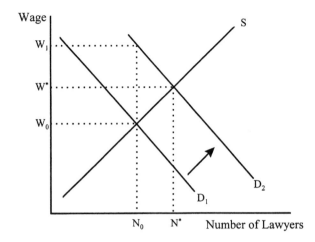

any given wage, as illustrated by a shift in the demand curve from D_1 to D_2. Because it takes time to produce law school graduates, the number of lawyers available in the short run does not shift dramatically from N_0. As a result, the wages of law school graduates would rise from W_0 to W_1. This increase in wages of law school graduates would serve as an incentive for more people to attend law school and the number of law school graduates would rise. This increase in quantity supplied will drive down wages to W^*.

The adjustment of law school enrollments to changes in the returns to education is not always smooth or rapid. The problem is that if lawyers' wages were to go up suddenly in 1997, the supply of law school graduates would not be affected for three years, owing to the time that it takes to complete school and be admitted to the bar. Likewise, if lawyers' wages fall, many students enrolled in law school would understandably be reluctant to leave the field immediately. They have already invested a lot of time and effort, and they prefer to take their chances in law, rather than devote more time and money to learning a new field. The inability to respond immediately to changed market conditions can cause boom and bust cycles in the market for highly technical workers such as lawyers and engineers. Suppose the market for lawyers is in equilibrium, where the wage is W_0 and the number of lawyers is N_0, as shown in Figure VIII-11. Now assume that the demand curve for lawyers shifts from D_0 to D_1. Initially, this increase in the demand for lawyers does not induce the supply of lawyers to increase beyond N_0, because it takes a long time to become a lawyer once one has decided to do so. Thus, while the increased demand for lawyers causes more people to decide to enter the field, the number available for employment at the moment is still N_0. These N_0 lawyers, therefore, can currently obtain a wage of W_1. In effect, there is a vertical supply curve at N_0 for a few years, until the supply of law school graduates increases.

Now, W_1, the current lawyers wage, is above W^*, the new long run equilibrium wage, caused by the intersection of D_1 and S_1. Market participants, how-

Figure VIII-11
The Labor Market for Lawyers:
A Cobweb Model

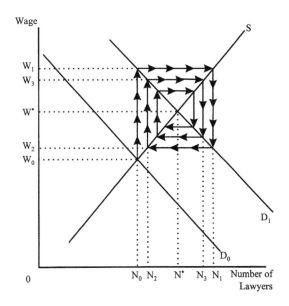

ever, are unaware of W*, observing only W_1. If people assume that W_1 is the new equilibrium wage, N_1 number of people will enter the legal profession. When these N_1 graduate, there will be a surplus of lawyers. Remember that W_1 is above long run equilibrium. With the number of lawyers now temporarily fixed at N_1, the wage falls to W_2. This causes students and workers to shift out of law, but that effect will not be fully felt for a few years. In the meantime, note that W_2 is below long run equilibrium, still at W*. Thus, when supply does adjust, it will adjust "too much" — all the way to N_2.

Then, there will be another shortage of lawyers, because after supply adjusts to N_2, quantity demanded (N_1) exceeds quantity supplied (N_2) at a wage W_2. This causes wages to rise to W_3, and the cycle repeats itself. Over time, the swings become smaller and, eventually, equilibrium is reached. Because the adjustment path in Figure VIII-11 looks somewhat like a cobweb, the adjustment process described above is sometimes called a Cobweb Model. Critical to cobweb models is the assumption that workers form myopic expectations about the future behavior of wages. In the preceding example, they first assume that W_1 will prevail in the future, and ignore the possibility that the occupational choice decisions of others will, in three years, drive the wage below W_1. Just how workers and other economic actors, such as investors and taxpayers, form expectations about future wages or price levels is very important to the understanding of many key issues affecting the labor market. The simplest and most naive way to predict future wage levels is to assume that what is observed today will occur in the future. This naive assumption underlies the cobweb model. A more sophisticated way to form predictions about the future is with an adaptive expectations approach. Adaptive expectations form by setting future expected wages equal to a weighted average of current and past wages. While more weight may be given to the current than past wages in forecasting future wage levels, changes in those levels, prior to the current period, are not ignored. Thus, it is likely that wage expectations formed adaptively do not alternatively overshoot and undershoot the equilibrium wage as much as those formed using the naive approach. If adaptive expectations, however, also lead workers to first over predict, and then under predict the equilibrium wage, cobweb-like behavior of wages and labor supply will still be observed, although the fluctuations will be of a smaller magnitude if the predictions are closer to the mark than if they are made naively.

Clearly, how people form expectations is an important and unsettled issue. In the case of lawyers, doctors, and engineers, periodic fluctuations that characterize the cobweb model have been found. Whether these fluctuations are the result of naive expectations or not, the lesson to be learned from cobweb models should not be lost on government policy makers. When government policy makers attempt to take an active role in dealing with labor shortages and surpluses, they must be aware that because supply adjustments are slow in highly technical markets, wages in those markets tend to over adjust. In other words, to the extent possible, governmental predictions and market interventions should be based on rational expectations. For example, at the initial stages of a shortage, when wages are rising towards W_1, the government should be pointing out that W_1 is likely to be above the long run equilibrium. Instead, if it attempts to meet the current shortage by subsidizing people already in that field, it will be encouraging an even greater surplus later on. The moral of the story is that a complete knowledge of how markets work is necessary before one can be sure that government intervention will do more good than harm.

2. Occupational Choice and Compensating Wage Differentials

One of the major functions of the labor market is to provide the signals and the mechanisms by which workers seeking to maximize their utility can be matched to employers trying to maximize profits. Matching is a formidable task because workers have varying skills and preferences and because employers offer jobs that differ in skill content and working environment. The process of finding the worker-employer pairings that are best for each is truly one of trial and error, and whether the process is woefully deficient or reasonably satisfactory is a question implicitly underlying this analysis. The assumption that workers are attempting to maximize utility implies that they are interested in both the pecuniary and nonpecuniary aspect of their jobs. On the one hand, high compensation levels in an occupation, holding job tasks constant, attracts more workers to that occupation. Different occupations have different tasks and workers have different preferences concerning these duties. At a given level of pay, only a certain numbers of workers will be interested in a particular occupation. If the level of pay rises, others will become attracted to it. On the other hand, it is clear that pay is not all that matters. Occupational tasks and how workers' preferences mesh with those tasks are critical elements in the matching process.

If all jobs were exactly alike and located in the same place, an individual's decision about where to seek work would be relatively simple. He or she would attempt to obtain a job where the compensation was highest. Any difference in compensation would cause workers to seek work with the highest paying employers and avoid applying for work with the low paying ones. The high paying employers, having an abundance of applicants, might decide they were paying more than they had to in order to fill vacancies. The low paying employers would have to raise their wage offers in order to compete for workers. Ultimately, if the market worked without hindrance, the compensation paid to all employees would equalize.

However, all jobs are not the same. Some jobs require much more education or training than others, some jobs are in clean modern offices, while others are in noisy, dusty and dangerous factories. Some permit the employee discretion over the hours or pace of work, while others allow less flexibility. Some employers offer more generous employee benefit packages than others, and different places of employment involve different commuting distances and neighborhood environments. The desire of workers to avoid unpleasantness or risk should force employers offering unpleasant or risky jobs to pay higher wages than they would otherwise have to pay. In other words, in order to attract a work force, these employers will have to pay higher wages to their workers—called a compensating wage differential—than firms that offer pleasant and safe jobs to comparable workers. This compensating wage differential serves two related socially desirable goals. First, it serves a social need by giving people an incentive to voluntarily do dirty, dangerous or unpleasant work. Likewise, the existence of a compensating wage differential imposes a financial penalty on employers who have unfavorable working conditions. Second, at an individual level, it serves as a reward to workers who accept unpleasant jobs by paying them more than comparable workers in more pleasant jobs.

Any society has a number of jobs that are unavoidably nasty or would be very costly to make safe and pleasant. Coal mining, deep sea diving, police work, and garbage collection are examples. There are essentially two ways to recruit the necessary labor for such jobs. One is to compel people to do these jobs. The military draft is the most obvious American example of forced labor. The second way is to induce people to do the jobs voluntarily. Most modern societies rely mainly on incentives or compensating wage differentials to recruit labor to do unpleasant jobs voluntarily. Workers who mine coal, bolt steel beams together 50 stories off the ground, or agree to work at night do so because compared to alternative jobs for which they could qualify, these jobs pay better. Night work, for example, could be stressful because it disrupts normal patterns of sleep and patterns of family interactions. However, employers often find it efficient to keep their plants and machines in operation around the clock. Results indicate that manufacturing production employees that work at night are paid about three percent more than they would have received if they worked during the day.

Compensating wage differentials also serve as individual rewards by paying those who accept bad or arduous working conditions more than they would otherwise receive. Analogously, those who opt for more pleasant conditions have to buy them by accepting lower pay. For example, if a person makes $8.00 an hour with firm X, he or she is giving up the $8.50 per hour with the less pleasant conditions in firm Y. The better conditions are being bought in a very real sense for $0.50 per hour. Professors who claim that they are underpaid because they could earn more money in the private business sector are mischaracterizing the reality of their job situation. In effect, they are giving up that pay in order to consume the many perquisites that go along with being a university professor. Thus, compensating wage differentials become the prices at which good working conditions can be purchased or bad ones sold to workers. Contrary to what is commonly asserted, a monetary value can be attached to events or conditions with effects that are primarily psychological in nature. Compensating wage differentials provide the key to the valuation of these nonpecuniary aspects of employment.

The predicted outcome of this theory of job choice is not that employees working under bad conditions receive more than those working under good conditions. The prediction is that holding worker characteristics constant, employees working under poor conditions receive higher wages than those working under more pleasant conditions. The characteristics that must be held constant include all the other things that influence wages: skill level, age, race, gender, union status, region of the country, and so forth. The basic point is that observed wage differences across occupations may reflect differences in nonmonetary aspects of employment. There are many reasons for wage differences other than those caused by human capital investments. In addition to the observation that wages will vary directly with the disagreeableness of the job, several more reasons for wage differences have been identified: the more seasonable or irregular the job, the higher the pay will be; jobs that require trustworthiness will carry a higher wage; jobs with greater risk to health will have higher pay; jobs that carry the possibility of tremendous success will have a lower wage; jobs will vary by region.

3. Occupational Licensing

The public interest explanation for occupational licensing is that protection of consumers from unlicensed competitors may be justified in order to allow a profession to upgrade the quality of services offered for sale in the marketplace. This upgrading is thought to occur from the imposition of higher educational standards on potential practitioners who wish to offer their services for sale. It is argued that licensing is the most effective way to protect the public from low quality professional services.

An alternative, interest-group explanation is that professional associations seek licensing to restrict entry into the profession, thereby decreasing competition and increasing earnings. Indeed, regulation may not be necessary to achieve the public interest goals because advertising and other market mechanisms — such as developing a reputation as an "honest lawyer" — could provide information to consumers about the quality of unlicensed professionals. Moreover, the existence of the licensing requirement might give consumers a false sense of protection when, in fact, the licensing is designed to restrict entry, not control quality.

States license many professions — from morticians and barbers to doctors and lawyers. In addition, professional associations impose state-approved restrictions on entry and conduct. Failure to conform to these requirements can result in legal action being instituted to stop an individual from engaging in the unauthorized practice.

In Re: Hansen

Supreme Court of Minnesota
275 N.W.2d 790 (1978)

KELLY, Justice.

This case comes before the court pursuant to petitioner's request for review of a decision by the State Board of Law Examiners (Board) that petitioner would not be allowed to sit for the Minnesota State Bar examination because he had not graduated from an approved law school as required by Rule II(4)[3] of the Supreme Court Rules for Admission to the Bar. We affirm.

Petitioner, originally a Minnesota resident, is a 1977 graduate of Western State University College of Law (Western State), San Diego, California. Although not admitted to the University of Minnesota Law School, petitioner had the opportunity to attend a number of the 166 law schools accredited by the American Bar Association (ABA). After one month at Marquette University Law School, petitioner decided to transfer to Western State Law School. Western State has never applied to the ABA for accreditation. It has been accredited both by the California Committee of Bar Examiners and by the Western Association of Schools and Colleges.

Prior to leaving Marquette petitioner had a conference with the Dean who advised him to remain at Marquette, partly because of its ABA-approved status. Nevertheless, petitioner decided to leave Marquette and enroll at Western State.

In the fall of 1976, when petitioner was a senior student at Western State, he applied to the Board for permission to sit for the July, 1977, bar examination. The Board denied his application because he was not a graduate of an approved law school. According to the Rules for Admission to the Bar, an approved law school is one "that is provisionally or fully approved by the Section of Legal Education for Admissions to the Bar of the American Bar Association."

Thereafter, petitioner requested and was granted a formal hearing before the Board, pursuant to Rule X, Rules for Admission to the Bar. On March 11, 1977, after a full hearing, at which petitioner waived his right to appear, the Board

---

3. Rule II delineates the general requirements for applicants who wish to sit for the bar examination. It reads as follows:

"No person shall be admitted to practice law who has not established to the satisfaction of the State Board of Law Examiners:

"(1) That he is at least 18 years of age;

"(2) That he is a person of good moral character; *

"(3) That he is a resident of this state; or maintains an office in this state; or has designated the Clerk of the Supreme Court as his agent for the service of process for all purposes;

"(4) That he has graduated from an approved law school;**

"(5) That he has passed a written examination.

"* Character traits that are relevant to a determination of good moral character must have a rational connection with the applicant's present fitness or capacity to practice law, and accordingly must relate to the State's legitimate interest in protecting prospective clients and the system of justice.

"**An approved law school is a law school that is provisionally or fully approved by the Section of Legal Education and Admissions to the Bar of the American Bar Association."

found that he did not satisfy the requirements of Rule II(4) and therefore again denied him permission to sit for the bar examination.

On May 11, 1977, petitioner sought a hearing before this court which was denied on June 7, 1977. His request for a reconsideration of his petition, filed on August 22, 1977, was granted. During this interim period petitioner wrote and passed the California Bar Examination and was admitted to practice in California in January, 1978.

This case presents the following issues for decision:

(1) Whether Rule II(4) of the Supreme Court rules for Admission to the Bar is constitutional; and,

(2) Whether, granting its constitutionality, the requirement of graduating from an ABA-accredited law school should be waived in this case.

1. Petitioner and Western State, as amicus curiae, suggest that Minnesota's rule requiring proof of graduation from an ABA-approved law school as a prerequisite to sitting for the bar examination is unconstitutional under both the due process and the equal protection clauses of the Fourteenth Amendment to the United States Constitution. We disagree. As long as the requirements established by state supreme courts to regulate the practice of law are reasonable ones, they comply with applicable constitutional principles.

All United States Supreme Court decisions concerning state regulation of the practice of law recognize that a state has a substantial interest in the qualifications of those it admits to the legal profession. As the Supreme Court noted recently in Goldfarb v. Virginia State Bar, 421 U.S. 773 (1975):

> "* * * (T)he States have a compelling interest in the practice of professions within their boundaries, and * * * as part of their power to protect the public health, safety, and other valid interests they have broad power to establish standards for licensing practitioners * * * . The interest of the States in regulating lawyers is especially great since lawyers are essential to the primary governmental function of administering justice, and have historically been 'officers of the courts.'"

Nevertheless, the Court has also recognized that "(t)he practice of law is not a matter of grace, but of right for one who is qualified by his learning and his moral character." Baird v. State Board of Arizona, 401 U.S. 1, 8, (1971). Thus, while "(a) state can require high standards of qualifications, such as good moral character or proficiency in its law, before it admits an applicant to the bar, * * * any qualification must have a rational connection with the applicant's fitness or capacity to practice law." Schware v. Board of Bar Examiners, 353 U.S. 232, 239.

The test that emerges from these cases is that, despite the strong interest of the applicant in being able to practice law, the state can regulate admission as long as such regulation is reasonably related to its interest in a competent bar. A procedure is reasonable as long as it is not arbitrary and capricious. Only if the complainant is a member of a suspect class or if the procedure at issue violates a fundamental right must the state demonstrate a compelling state interest for its system of regulation to pass constitutional muster.

The procedure being challenged in this case is Minnesota's requirement that an applicant wishing to take the bar examination demonstrate, among other things, that he graduated from a law school which is provisionally or fully accredited by the American Bar Association. Rule II(4), Supreme Court Rules for Admission to the Bar. Although there have been numerous challenges over the years to educational requirements similar to those of Rule II, both state and federal courts have consistently found such requirements to be constitutional.

In all the decisions upholding a state's educational requirements as a valid prerequisite to admission to the bar, courts have required only that there be a rational reason for the imposition of the requirement. As the court stated in Application of Schatz, 80 Wash.2d 604:

> "The policy of the board sets forth a condition precedent to take the bar examination in this state and it applies to all general applicants who are not otherwise qualified under the Admission to Practice Rules. It is correlative and explicit with the ultimate purpose of all regulations for the admission of attorneys to assure the courts the assistance of advocates of ability, learning, and sound character and to protect the public from incompetent and dishonest practitioners."

A similar theme is . . . :

> "* * * (T)he public interest in seeing that all members of the bar have an adequate education is a valid basis for an 'accredited schools' test, which insures that each applicant uniformly has performed the minimum required study. * * *

> "Moreover, it has been well established that educational standards such as those contained in the Alaska bar rule have a rational connection with an applicant's fitness to practice law. * * * By this means the state may be assured that attorneys have had suitable training by qualified instructors so that as lawyers they will be capable of adequately representing members of the public. The exchange of ideas between classmates and teachers, the legal knowledge, and the sense of ethics acquired through meeting requirements for graduation from an accredited law school are all reasonably related to the state's interest in seeing that those who hold themselves out to the public as attorneys at law, and thus as officers of the court, are properly qualified."

It is also rational for a state supreme court to conclude that the ABA is best equipped to perform the function of accrediting law schools. The Florida Supreme Court explained its reasons for requiring graduation from an ABA-accredited law school:

> "We were persuaded to follow the American Bar Association standards relating to accreditation of law schools because we sought to provide an objective method of determining the quality of the educational environment of prospective attorneys. This was deemed especially necessary because of the rapid growth in the number of educational institutions awarding law degrees. We wished to be certain that each of these many law schools provided applicants with a quality legal education, but we were unequipped to make such a determination ourselves because of financial limitations and the press of judicial business.

> "* * * (W)e share the view of educators that growth in numbers and size must not be allowed to detract from the quality of a student's education. Accordingly, we continue to require that applicants for admis-

sion to the Florida Bar Examination be graduates of accredited law schools."

A similar rationale compelled the three-judge federal court in Rossiter (Supra p. 12) to uphold Colorado's reliance on ABA accreditation:

> "No consideration is more critical in evaluating the qualifications of an applicant for admission to the bar than the quality and caliber of his legal education. A good lawyer must possess a complete and workable legal education; developed through exposure to many branches of law, contacts and communication with competent and professional instructors, experience in legal research and writing, interaction with other students, and access to current and complete research materials. Clearly, these demands compel the establishment and maintenance of standards and systems for the evaluation of institutions which propose to equip new attorneys to join the legal profession. It is also patently obvious that judicial bodies are singularly ill-equipped to bring to bear the resources and expertise necessary to conduct a case-by-case evaluation of United States and foreign law schools. For this reason, it is fortuitous that the American Bar Association, since early in this century, has undertaken to evaluate the law schools which train America's lawyers."

Prior to 1977 the ABA, as a matter of policy, refused even to consider accrediting proprietary law schools. Its opposition stemmed from its belief that the establishment of an educational institution for profit would have to affect negatively the caliber of the education provided to the students. When the goal of a law school is to make money, the reasoning went, the administration will skimp on services, and the students will necessarily suffer. More recently, however, persons within the ABA have challenged this assumption. In response to this pressure the ABA established a committee to study whether the organization should accredit proprietary law schools. The Committee to Study the Accreditation of Proprietary Law Schools recommended, however, that before the Association decided to modify the accreditation process, it should be sure of the incorrectness of its assumption that a school's proprietary status is a shorthand measure of other educational deficiencies. Thus, the Committee recommended that it should permit proprietary law schools to apply for provisional accreditation. If they are able to meet the other ABA requirements, the Association will permanently repeal the standard relating to nonproprietary status.

Petitioner also argues that he received a superior education at Western State and claims that it was much better than what was offered at Marquette, an ABA-accredited institution. In spite of the changes in the ABA rules, he contends that the proscription against proprietary law schools is completely unrelated to a school's potential for educational excellence. However, Western State did not exhaust its remedies by applying for accreditation and testing that proscription before the ABA and subsequently in this court. Petitioner's argument might have carried some weight a few years ago, but has been seriously undermined by recent events.

In order to implement this new position toward proprietary law schools the Council of the Section of Legal Education and Admissions to the Bar resolved on February 12, 1977, that it was willing to grant variances to any proprietary law school that believed it could demonstrate substantial compliance with all other standards for accreditation. On June 18, 1977, it resolved to accept applications for provisional approval from proprietary law schools until June 30, 1979. Despite this waiver, Western State has never applied for provisional accreditation although it was invited to apply on two occasions. Thus, the ABA has not had the opportunity to determine whether it is in substantial compliance with the remaining standards.

Petitioner argues that if Western State were not a proprietary school it would certainly have been accredited, or, alternatively, that it is an excellent school whose excellence goes unrecognized by the ABA because of its proprietary nature. Western State contends that the fact of its accreditation by the California Committee of Bar Examiners and by the Western Association of Schools and Colleges either entitles it automatically to accreditation by the ABA or should cause this court to waive the requirement of ABA accreditation for graduates of Western State. But, as the ABA responds, we have nothing but the bare assertions of petitioner and his law school that Western State offers a quality education and is in substantial compliance with all relevant factors that go into the quality education formula. Because Western State has refused to apply for provisional accreditation, despite ABA requests that it do so, no ABA personnel have visited its campuses to evaluate its programs. Thus, we have no way of knowing whether Western State could have substantially complied with the other ABA requirements for accreditation.

Had the ABA turned down the application of Western State, petitioner could have then approached us with his argument that the ABA standards are arbitrary and capricious. Under existing circumstances, however, there is no record on which we can determine the validity of petitioner's claim.

Clearly, it is reasonable for Minnesota to require proof that an applicant's legal education was of a high quality as a general prerequisite to admission to the bar. Similarly, it is neither arbitrary nor capricious for us to measure the quality of legal education with the same standards as those utilized by the ABA. This is particularly true as we would permit a review by this court if Western State were denied approval after applying. We then could judicially determine the validity of the ABA standards as applied to Western State. Western State has failed to exhaust its remedies by not applying for approval and then if turned down, seeking a review in this court. Thus, petitioner's argument that Rule II(4) is an unconstitutional violation of the due process clause of the Fourteenth Amendment has no merit.

Likewise, we find no violation of the equal protection clause. Under traditional equal protection analysis classifications will be upheld as long as they are reasonably related to some legitimate governmental purpose. We have already established that the distinction between graduates of accredited and nonaccredited law schools is reasonably related to ensuring a competent bar. Thus, Rule II(4) does not operate to deny petitioner the equal protection of the laws. In an attempt to force us to apply a stricter standard of review than the rational-basis test, petitioner contends that he has some sort of right to practice law in his home state. There is, of course, no merit either to this argument or to his position that Rule II(4) interferes with his fundamental right to travel. See, Moore v. Supreme Court of South Carolina, 447 F.Supp. 527 (D.S.C.1977). Our rules do not require residency as an office in this state or appointment of our clerk of court as an agent for service will suffice.

Petitioner also argues that our adoption of Rule II(4) constitutes an unlawful delegation of power from the court to the ABA, a private organization. Petitioner misconstrues the relationship, however. We have not delegated our authority to the ABA but, instead, have simply made a rational decision to follow the standards of educational excellence it has developed. Furthermore, Western State could always petition this court for a review of any adverse decision by the ABA. We have neither the time nor the expertise to investigate individually the special training of an applicant or the program offered by specific law schools, and any attempt by us to do so would be inefficient and chaotic. Thus, it does not offend the constitution for us to decide to utilize instead standards developed by a nongovernmental body with expertise in the area of legal education. See, Rossiter v. Law Committee of the State Board of Law Examiners, Civil Action No. C-4767 (D.Colo.1975); Rosenthal v. State Bar Examining Committee, 116 Conn. 409, 165 A. 211 (1935); LaBossiere v. Florida Board of Bar Examiners, 279 So.2d 288 (Fla.1973); Henington v. State Board of Bar Examiners, 60 N.M. 393, 291 P.2d 1108 (1956); Application of Schatz, 80 Wash.2d 604, 497 P.2d 153 (1972). Deciding otherwise would violently interfere with our constitutionally mandated duty to hear and decide cases.

2. Petitioner and Western State both argue that whether or not the court decides that Rule II(4) is unconstitutional, petitioner still deserves to have the requirement waived. Four grounds are advanced to support such a waiver. Petitioner takes the position that because he believes that he is qualified by education and intellect to write the Minnesota bar examination, we should give him the opportunity to prove his qualifications to the court. He advances as a related argument that his passage of the California bar examination, which he describes as the most difficult examination in the country, demonstrates that he possesses the very qualities ABA accreditation is supposed to measure. Thus, we should waive Rule II(4) in his case. He also argues that extenuating circumstances require us to waive the rule. Finally, it is claimed that since other accrediting organizations, like the California Committee of Bar Examiners and the Western Association of Schools and Colleges, are as competent to accredit law schools as the ABA, we should waive Rule II(4) for graduates of law schools accredited by them. Each of these arguments has fatal flaws.

Petitioner fails to realize that once Rule II(4) is labeled as a reasonable attempt to measure the totality of one's law school experience rather than as an irrebuttable presumption, no compelling reason to waive the requirement can be found. Furthermore, it would be impossible for petitioner to amass and present to the court sufficient information about the operation of Western State to permit us to make a reasoned decision on the quality of the education he received there.

Rule II(4) represents our determination that many different experiences help to create a law school education that is likely to provide a potential attorney with the skills necessary to make him an effective member of his profession. Rule II(4) does not, however, contain a complete list of exactly what those experiences are. If pressed, it would be extremely difficult for members of this court to decide which factors are absolutely necessary to the creation of a well-rounded attorney and which are not. By adopting Rule II(4), we have chosen to leave these difficult questions to the accrediting body in whom we have confidence. We also leave to the ABA the task of monitoring institutions to ensure that the standards are maintained even after accreditation is conferred. For these reasons permitting applicants from nonaccredited institutions to appear before either us or the Board, our agent, in order to attempt to demonstrate the educational validity of their law school experiences would serve no useful purpose. It makes much more sense for us to utilize the specialized services of our chosen accrediting agency, the ABA. See, LaBossiere v. Florida Board of Bar Examiners, 279 So.2d 288 (Fla.1973).

The second basis for petitioner's claim to a waiver is the fact that he has passed the California bar examination and been admitted to practice law in the State of California. The mere passage of a bar examination in another state, however, does not necessitate a waiver of the educational rule of the state in which petitioner now seeks to practice. In re Stephenson, 511 P.2d 136 (Alaska 1973); In re Lorring, 75 Nev. 330, 340 P.2d 589 (1959). We do not believe that passage of a bar examination is necessarily an equivalent measure of the characteristics of legal education which are important in the accrediting decision.

The only extenuating circumstance that petitioner presents is the inconvenience to him of practicing law away from his family. Yet, because he knew that his transfer to Western State could create this hardship, he cannot be heard to complain to us at this time. See, Application of Saunders, 295 F.Supp. 263 (D.V.I.1969).

Finally, we reject the contention that we should accept the decision of some other accrediting organization that Western State offers its students a quality education. The Western Association of Schools and Colleges is a general regional accrediting organization. According to the ABA, Western State is the only law school that it has accredited. Thus, we do not believe that its expertise is comparable to that of the ABA which specializes in evaluating legal education. Western State is also accredited by the California Committee of Bar Examiners, but we refuse to treat California's decision to accredit Western State as equivalent to our decision to approve only ABA-approved law schools because of the dissimilarity in the way California and Minnesota appear to control admission to the legal profession. California contains many law schools, only some of which are accredited either by the ABA or by the California Committee of Bar Examiners. Even if one is not a graduate of a law school accredited either by California or by the ABA, however, it is still possible to take the California bar examination. Thus, California appears to utilize its examination as the major form of control over admissions to the bar. The situation in Minnesota is completely different. We use a two-pronged test graduation from an accredited law school plus passage of the bar examination to determine whether an attorney should be admitted to practice. Unlike California, we rely primarily on the educational process, and we use the bar examination only to weed out the small number who are unfit to practice law despite their exposure to educational environments of high quality. Given the different functions served by the bar examinations in California and Minnesota, it would be irrational for us to defer to California's decision regarding the quality of the education offered at Western State. We agree with the position taken by the Washington Supreme Court, in response to an argument similar to petitioner's, that "(a) stat is not required to subordinate its laws and policies concerning peculiarly domestic affairs and matters involving local sovereignty to the law and policies of other states." Application of Schatz, 80 Wash.2d 604, 610, 497 P.2d 153, 157 (1972).

Were petitioner able to demonstrate that Minnesota's rules regarding graduation from an ABA-accredited law school came as a complete surprise to him, there might be some support for the argument that principles of fairness require us seriously to consider waiving Rule II(4). Nothing forced petitioner to attend a nonaccredited law school, however. He chose to transfer from an ABA-approved school to a nonaccredited one far away from his home state knowing that this move would pose problems for him if he later wanted to return to Minnesota to practice law. Thus, equity requires no waiver here. Were we to grant the waiver as requested, we would have to consider similar requests by students from other nonaccredited law schools with chaotic results. Each and every case would have to be decided on its own merits. Undoubtedly claims would be made as in this case that the applicants had a quality education but without any foundation for such claims by experts chosen by this court to pass on that issue.

Affirmed.

YETKA, Justice (dissenting).

*   *   *

I regret to see Minnesota refuse applicant's petition because there is much to be said for a rule that would allow Any applicant who has passed the bar examination of Any other state and has been admitted to practice in that state to take the bar examination of any other state in the union. Why these barriers? What state or states do we fear are so lenient in their admission standards that we will not permit their lawyers to even take our examination? If our examination is tough enough to screen out the unqualified applicants, we need not have concern for anyone who wishes to take it. And if it is not tough enough to do so, there is little reason for the existence of the bar examination at all.

What precedent do we fear will be set by allowing petitioner to take the examination? I disagree that we would be holding that every applicant from every law school would have the right to take our examination. Our waiving the rule in this case would mean simply that we are holding that an applicant who graduated from a law school approved by the California Committee of Bar Examiners, by the Western Association of Schools and Colleges, and who successfully passed the California Bar Examination, and who is a Minnesota native can take our bar examination the holding would stand for no more.

*   *   *

Notes and Questions

1. Public Interest Restriction on Entry?: Many state bar associations require that applicants graduate from an ABA accredited law school. Thus, lawyers must be accepted and graduate from an acceptable law school and pass the bar exam. The Court in *Hansen* advances several justifications for such requirements. Are these public interest arguments valid? Are they consistent with economic theory? Is the market capable of protecting the consumers of legal services or is some form of intervention necessary? If intervention is necessary, what does economic theory suggest regarding the nature of such regulation? What are the impacts of professional licensing requirements on incentives to invest in human capital?

2. The Deadweight Loss of Licensing: The licensing system used by the legal profession can be considered a barrier to entry that restricts the supply of lawyers relative to what would be forthcoming in an unrestricted market. This barrier raises the prices that lawyers can charge and society is forced to pay more for legal services than would be the case under unrestricted entry. Because of the higher prices, some legal services that would have been sought in the absence of licensing are not purchased. Like any other monopoly or cartel restriction of output, the licensing of the legal profession results in a deadweight loss. See Chapter V. Which members of society are harmed the most by professional licensing? Does the legal profession take other steps to alleviate such disparate impacts?

3. *Antitrust and Occupational Licensing:* Occupational licensing, because of its potentially anticompetitive side effects, may be subject to legal constraints under the antitrust laws. The courts tend to grant immunity from the antitrust laws to occupational self-regulation involving members of a "learned profession," but only if the licensing does not involve price fixing. In *Goldfarb v. Virginia State Bar*, 421 U.S. 773 (1975), which is excerpted in Chapter V, the Supreme Court held that a fee schedule adopted by a county bar association and adhered to by virtually all members was a violation of the antitrust laws. Thus, while it is permissible to regulate quality of service, it is impermissible to regulate the price of the service.

D. Labor Unions and Collective Bargaining

The preceding section on the employment contract examined the relationship between an employee and an employer. Although government regulations limit the flexibility of some of the terms of that contractual relation, the predominant aspect of those labor contracts was the interaction of *individual* employees with an employer. In this section, the emphasis changes dramatically as the role of unions in representing *groups* of individual employees is examined.

The primary appeal of unions to the U.S. worker is economic. Workers organize a union in order to get higher wages, better benefits, and improvements in other conditions of employment. Economists point out, however, that such improvements are not free to the employer, workers as a group, or society in general..

Economic welfare is maximized when resources are allocated to their highest valued uses through the operation of unconstrained competitive forces. Unions interfere with the allocative role of the market by generating wages above the competitive level. To the economist, unions are legalized cartels attempting to monopolize labor markets in much the same manner that business firms attempt to monopolize a product market. Monopolies, or monopoly behavior by cartels, misallocate resources relative to the way that they would be allocated in a competitive market. The economic analysis of unions is similar.

Unions increase wages above market wages by either (a) restricting entry of non-union workers into union controlled jobs and allowing the market to clear at a higher price or (b) negotiating higher wages with employers. These two

Figure VIII-12

Supply Restrictions, Bargaining Power, and Wage Rates

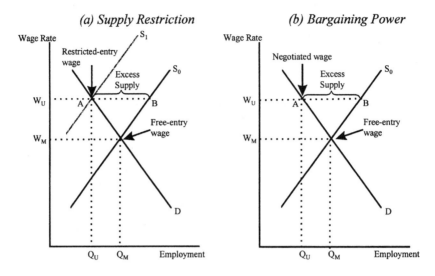

(a) Supply Restriction   *(b) Bargaining Power*

strategies are demonstrated in panels (a) and (b), respectively, of Figure VIII-12. Both panels reflect an initial market clearing wage of W_M. In panel (a), the supply restriction, in effect, shifts the supply curve back to the left and the market clears at W_U. In panel (b), the negotiated wage of W_U results in an excess supply of workers willing and able to work. The union allocates the limited number of jobs, Q_U, among its members. The supply restriction strategy is discussed in the following case.

Connell Construction Company, Inc. v. Plumbers and Steamfitters Local Union No. 100

United States Court of Appeals, Fifth Circuit
483 F.2d 1154 (1973)

LEWIS R. MORGAN, Circuit Judge:

This action is brought by Connell, a general contractor, against Plumbers Local 100, alleging that a contract with that union which Connell entered under pressure from the union violates the antitrust laws. After trial, the District Court for the Northern District of Texas held for the defendant union, finding that Congress had, in amendments to the National Labor Relations Act, expressly recognized the validity of contracts such as the one in issue as a legitimate union tool in the construction industry. Connell appeals from that judgment.

I

Connell is a general contractor engaged in the construction industry in Texas. Connell was first contacted by the union and asked to enter a contract with the union whereby Connell agreed not to do any business with any plumbing and mechanical firm unless such firm was a party "to an executed, current collective bargaining agreement" with the union. This initial missive from the union indicated that if Connell did not sign with 10 days, the union would undertake to place pickets at various construction sites where Connell was the general contractor. When Connell failed to sign this proposed contract, the union placed a single picket at The Bruton Venture Project in Dallas, Texas, on which Connell was the general contractor.

Upon the commencement of this picketing about 150 employees (both of Connell and its various subcontractors) left the site of this project, effectively halting construction. In January of 1971, Connell instituted this action in a Texas state court alleging a violation of the Texas antitrust laws. The Texas court granted a temporary injunction against the picketing. The union then removed the case to federal court and, after the district court refused to remand the case back to state court, Connell entered, under protest, an agreement not to do any business with subcontractors who did not have a current collective bargaining agreement with the union. It is this agreement, substantially what the union sought through its picketing, that Connell alleges to be an antitrust violation.

Connell did not have any employees of its own who were members of the appellee union at the time of the demand to contract and the picketing. In fact, Connell has never at any time material to this case had any of its own employees who belonged to this union. The subcontractor who was being used by Connell at The Bruton Venture Project did, in fact, at that time have a current collective bargaining contract with the union.

It is undisputed that Connell itself is in the practice of virtually always contracting out the mechanical work on its construction jobs. It appears that this subcontracting is generally done on the basis of bids from various mechanical subcontractors. Connell has in the past given these jobs to both unionized and nonunionized subcontractors on approximately an equal basis.

II

It becomes readily apparent that while this case is framed in the terms of antitrust, its origins and implications are most intimately connected with and extremely important to the delicate balance of labor-management power in the construction industry and national labor policy pertaining thereto. This is in a sense a labor problem and must be analyzed in light of national labor policy as set forth by Congress. The antitrust aspects of the case are bottomed on the claim that the union is undertaking to restrict competition by forcing this general contractor through contract with the union to give all its work to unionized subcontractors. It is such a contract which Connell claims restricts trade and violates the antitrust laws.

III

*   *   *

IV

The first question which we face in this case is whether or not this action can be maintained under federal antitrust statutes. After careful consideration, we find that it cannot be. Labor unions enjoy no blanket exemptions from the antitrust laws. See United Mine Workers v. Pennington, 381 U.S. 657 (1941). They do, however, have a somewhat special status in the realm of antitrust. The test, as it has come down in various Supreme Court opinions, seems to turn on the union's combination with non-labor groups to create a monopoly among various conspiratory interests. In other words, the purposes sought by the conspiracy must have goals which go beyond legitimate union aims and result in an anticompetitive situation.

* * *

...In United States v. Hutcheson, 312 U.S. 219 (1941), Justice Frankfurter addressed the question of the use of conventional peaceful activities by a union against an employer in a dispute with a rival union as an antitrust violation. In the underlying dispute, the union was having difficulty with the employer over assignment of certain contested work. To achieve its ends, the union engaged in primary and secondary activities. The strike activities were directed against the employer's product as well as the employer and the contractors who were doing the disputed work.

In a well-reasoned opinion, Mr. Justice Frankfurter reviewed the history of labor unions and the antitrust laws in both the courts and Congress. In an oft-quoted passage he states:

> So long as a union acts in its self-interest and does not combine with non-labor groups, the licit and the illicit under section 20 are not to be distinguished by any judgment regarding the wisdom or unwisdom, the rightness or wrongness, the selfishness or unselfishness of the end of which the particular union activities are the means. There is nothing remotely within the terms of section 20 that differentiates between trade union conduct directed against an employer because of a controversy arising in the relation between employer and employees, as such, and conduct similarly directed but ultimately due to a internecine struggle between two unions seeking the favor of the same employer. 312 U.S. at 232, 61 S.Ct. at 466.

The Court went on to find the conduct involved was expressly protected by section 20 of the Clayton Act. Finally, the Court stated that Norris-LaGuardia was intended by Congress to reestablish the broad labor union exemption which it thought it had written in section 20 of the Clayton Act but which had been frustrated by the courts in cases such as Duplex. Id. 254 U.S. at 236, 41 S.Ct. 172.

As might be expected, cases subsequent to Hutcheson have explored and refined the exception therein that whenever a union conspired with a non-labor group in restraint of trade, the broad exemption of labor unions from the antitrust laws was not applicable. In Allen Bradley v. I. B. E. W. Local 3, 325 U.S. 797, 65 S.Ct. 1533, 89 L.Ed. 1939 (1945), the Supreme Court applied the Hutcheson exception to find a union guilty of antitrust violation. The evidence established that the electrical union became partners with electrical manufacturers and independent contractors in the City of New York to create a monopoly for all three. It obtained various closed shop agreements from contractors and manufacturers which by cross-obligations required the contractors to buy equipment only from manufacturers having a current bargaining agreement with the local and, in turn, obligated those manufacturers with regard to sales in the Metropolitan New York area to sell only to independent contractors having current agreements with the local. Over time, these individual agreements expanded into an area-wide, industry-wide undertaking with the contractors, manufacturers and union jointly participating to fix prices and control recalcitrant members.

The resulting monopoly brought great success to the contractors, manufacturers and the union.

Noting that the agreement here would clearly be an antitrust violation without the presence of the union, Mr. Justice Black went on to frame the question before the Court quite precisely:

> Our problem in this case is therefore a very narrow one — do labor unions violate the Sherman Act when, in order to further their own interest as wage earners, they aid and abet businessmen to do the precise things which that Act prohibits?

Following a review of the legislative and judicial history of labor unions and antitrust, the Court directly addressed the problem of reconciling two declared congressional policies — preservation of a competitive business economy and the rights of labor to organize to better its condition.

The ultimate resolution of these competing policies was stated quite clearly:

> ...we think Congress never intended that unions could, consistently with the Sherman Act, aid non-labor groups to create business monopolies and to control the marketing of goods and services. 325 U.S. at 808, 65 S. Ct. at 1539.

In further commentary the Court made expressly clear that the antitrust exemption was lost only because of the obvious violation by the business interest:

> The primary objection of all the Anti-trust legislation has been to preserve business competition and to proscribe business monopoly. It would be a surprising thing if Congress, in order to prevent a misapplication of that legislation to labor unions, had bestowed upon such unions complete and unreviewable authority to aid business groups to frustrate its primary objective. For if business groups, by combining with labor unions, can fix prices and divide up markets, it was little more than a futile gesture for Congress to prohibit price fixing by business groups themselves. Id. at 809–810, 65 S.Ct. at 1540.

*   *   *

The complaint of Connell in this case contains no allegation of this union's participation in a scheme or conspiracy with a non-labor group to create a monopoly for that non-labor group. In fact, Connell bases its claim on the ground that this contract simply restricts the way in which it is free to carry out its business. It is Connell itself which is alleging serious injury from the agreement despite the fact that it is indeed the sole non-labor party to the agreement. There is no allegation of any conspiracy between the union and unionized subcontractors nor does the proof allude to any such conspiracy.

*   *   *

In American Federation of Musicians v. Carroll, 391 U.S. 99 (1968), the Court was presented with a situation in which several orchestra leaders sued the musicians' union alleging that union restrictions on their ability as independent contractors to deal with third parties seeking their services violated the antitrust laws.

The Supreme Court, in an opinion by Mr. Justice Brennan, held that due to the community of interests and possible inter-competition between the band leaders and union members, the setting of uniform prices by the union and the agreement thereto by the orchestra leaders did not violate the antitrust laws. The question of possible conspiracy with a non-labor group was found not relevant as the Court held that the orchestra leaders were themselves a labor group for the purposes of the Norris-LaGuardia Act. The Court then turned to the question of legitimate union interest with regard to the union's price setting. Pointing out that the crucial determinant was the impact which the price setting had on the union's membership, the majority found the activity protected. The Court indicated that such an agreement was necessary to protect the wages and other legitimate concerns of the union members because undercutting by the independent contractor-orchestra leaders generally led to a "skimping" on the amounts paid the member musicians.

Justice White, joined by Justice Black, dissented in an opinion stressing that the benefit to the union members was to be weighed against the anticompetitive impact of the agreement when evaluating the scope of a legitimate union interest. He felt that the elimination of price competition was too great despite the union's legitimate interest in not having orchestra leaders undercut wages to musicians. It is obvious that one of his major concerns was that, by dictating the price to be charged, the union here eliminated all normal competitive devices available to the independent contractor-orchestra leaders, including those competitive advantages not directly based on wages paid and work standards of union members. In short, the union practice of setting a minimum price floor eliminated from certain leaders the right to use competitive devices to cut the price lower even though such reductions in prices could conceivably have been obtained without corresponding reductions in wages or working conditions of union members.

We now must evaluate the "legitimate union interest" test as it applied to what the plumbers' union was seeking from Connell in this case. At the outset, we note that elimination of that part of competition based on differences in wages and other labor standards has long been recognized the primary objective of any national labor organization. See Apex Hosiery v. Leader, 310 U.S. 469. Such a conclusion, of course, flows from the very nature and history of the organized labor movement. All labor unions tend to limit competition to the extent that they raise wages and labor standards forcing employers to either raise prices to cover the costs of increased standards or to use other competitive devices which are not directly tied to wages or conditions of work. All labor unions have a legitimate interest in the elimination of that component of competition which is based on differences in labor standards.

Is the union in this case seeking an agreement involving a legitimate union interest? We feel it clearly is....

The plumbers' union is simply seeking to eliminate competition based on differences in labor standards and wages. Even if the construction unions involved herein were to obtain contracts from every general contractor and subcontractor in the area, so long as there were no allegations of conspiracy to prohibit new entries or to otherwise create a monopoly for the signatory non-labor interests, the antitrust exemption cannot be lost because of the legitimate union interest underlying this agreement. In this regard it is extremely important to realize that the legitimate union interest requirement does not have to be considered until such time as the conspiracy allegations, if any, have been found to be unavailable as a grounds for removing the exemption. Thus, most of the evils which can result from such market closing schemes as were found in Allen Bradley can simply be covered under the conspiracy rubric. Even legitimate union interest cannot serve to exempt a union from antitrust sanctions when in securing that legitimate goal the union agrees to a market allocation or other conspiracy to create an unfair business advantage for the non-labor parties. That is the clear teaching of Allen Bradley and Pennington but, as noted, that is not the situation which Connell presents at this point in time.

The central reason that the union wants the agreement sought in this case is that it will be helpful in organizing other subcontractors. The direct relation of this type agreement to that goal is clear. These agreements tend to eliminate any edge that a nonunionized subcontractor has in bidding on a job when that competitive edge rests solely or primarily on the fact that he pays less wages or grants lower working standards than a unionized subcontractor. Thus, the achievement of a contract such as the one here with Connell gives the union a strong weapon in its quest to unionize other subcontractors.

It is clear in this case that the union is trying to get around an inherent situation which has long been recognized as making the construction industry unique in the field of labor relations. The core of this problem stems from the fact that work in the construction industry is ambulatory in nature and that there is a decided lack of continuity between the various parties—owner, general contractor, subcontractor, and employees-who are related to an individual project. The owner, of course, is basically the money source for the job which, by its nature, is obviously intended to be completed in a limited duration of time. The general contractor, with or without employees of his own, is the one who is actually in charge of getting the job done. As a general rule, the general contractor hires subcontractors, usually on the basis of competitive bids, who actually perform that construction which his own employees do not do. These subcontractors are independent businessmen and their relationship to the general contractor is limited to the duration of the job on which they are the successful bidder. The subcontractors have their own employees and in most instances the subcontractors are the immediate employers with whom the union has to deal.

Thus, the union is faced with a fairly difficult problem because of the impact that the isolated general contractor has on the labor relations of the independent subcontractors. A permanent relationship with the subcontractor does not in any way ensure the union of a permanency of available work and thus differs from manufacturing where there is far more continuity between the parties dealing with the union and the ones in control.

It can be readily seen that construction unions have a direct interest in seeing that general contractors hire subs using union labor...

* * *

What this all comes down to is the realization that antitrust is not the proper method of handling this problem as it is presented in the complaint.

VII

At this point is seems necessary to consider how the element of legitimate union interest is affected by the form in which the challenged agreement is obtained. In short, does it matter for purposes of the antitrust laws in a case where no conspiracy to monopolize is alleged that the agreement entered into or the method that agreement was achieved may possibly be an unfair labor practice? We think not.

*   *   *

The above analysis amply illustrates that for antitrust purposes the term "legitimate union interest" is not controlled by whether or not the goal sought or the methods used in attempting to reach that goal violate the ground rules for labor relations set forth in the NLRA. If and when those ground rules are violated, punishment must come through the procedures and in the manner specified by Congress in the labor laws. Absent a viable conspiracy allegation, a union retains its exemption from antitrust attack so long as the terms of the agreement it seeks are designed to benefit its members in the hours, conditions, and other immediately relevant concerns of the working man.

The union here is seeking a weapon in its battle to eliminate competition based on differences in wage and labor standards. It might be argued here that this agreement with Connell goes further because it restricts agreements to unionized subcontractors, not just to those who pay union wage scale. However, this would be true in all cases of union activity because the primary way to eliminate these differences is through unionization of all the employees in a particular industry. Furthermore, unionization of all the employees in an industry has itself always been recognized as a proper goal of labor organizations.

It has long been established that labor unions have a clear right to approach and, in some ways, "persuade" consumers and other third parties from using or dealing in non-union-made goods, despite the fact that these actions restrict full and free competition....

*   *   *

Therefore, we are convinced that the complaint before the district court in this case was insufficient to avoid application of the union's exemption from general antitrust attack.

*   *   *

Notes and Questions

1. "Displaced" Workers: Employers respond to the higher wages associated with unionization by reducing the number of employees. Of course, the workers that keep their jobs experience an increase in wealth, but this is of little value to the displaced employees. Moreover, the workers that keep their jobs tend to be the highest skilled workers, so unions increase the wages of higher skilled workers at the expense of lower skilled workers. This disparity is magnified even further when it is realized that the "displaced" workers from the union jobs increase the supply of workers in nonunion jobs, which drives down nonunion wages. This effect is illustrated in Figure VIII-13, which shows a two-sector, union and non-union, labor market where the workers are substitutes for each other. In the absence of the union wage, the market wage, W_M would prevail and Q_M employees would have jobs in each sector. The union wage, W_U, would attract more workers, Q_S in panel (a), but employers would reduce their quantity demanded to Q_U. The displaced workers are represented by the reduced employment in the union sector from Q_M to Q_U. The displaced workers are added to the supply curve in the non-union sector, resulting in a shift to the right of the supply curve. The influx of displaced workers forces the non-union wage down to W_{N-U}. Does the union exemption discussed in *Connell* address such concerns? In light of this

Figure VIII-13

Two Sector Model With "Displaced" Workers

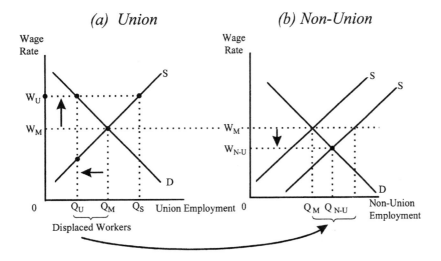

economic analysis, should Congress revamp its policy towards labor unions? Can you articulate a justification for the trade-offs involved in the current policy towards labor unions as articulated in *Connell*?

2. The American Federation Dissent: The *Connell* court discusses the dissenting Supreme Court opinion in *American Federation of Musicians* authored by Justice White. Justices White and Black suggest that the benefit to union members from the antitrust exemption be balanced against the overall anticompetitive impact of the labor agreement. Given the state of congressional policy as discussed in *Connell*, is the balancing approach suggested by Justices White and Black more in line with sound economic reasoning? Why does the *Connell* court dismiss this approach?

3. Labor Economics, Industrial Relations, and the Role of Unions: There has been widespread disagreement over the role of unions in a capitalistic economy since small trade unions were first organized in the eighteenth century. In this century, economists have debated the merits of unionization. Until recently, economists were split in their evaluations, with some stressing the positive effects of unions and others focusing on the adverse effects of unions on productivity. In recent years, the economics profession appears to have become united in its condemnation of unions. Other academics, particularly in the field known as industrial relations, continue to defend unions on the basis of their positive impacts on productivity.

4. The Industrial Relations View of Unions: In contrast to the economic view of unions, the industrial relations view of unions portrays unions as productive organizations that not only protect the interests of their members but also represent the political interest of all workers. *See* Richard B. Freeman & James L. Medoff, "The Two Faces of Unionism," 57 The Public Interest 69–93 (Fall, 1979). Industrial relations specialists point to several impacts of unionization that may actually lead to greater productivity and enhance economic efficiency. The general theme of their assertions is that unions promote industrial harmony, which in turn increases productivity. By providing for means through which disputes may be resolved, unions reduce the number of firings and employees who quit. This resulting reduction in turnover reduces the costs of hiring and training new employees. With less disruptions in the daily operations, productivity is maintained. Conflict among workers is reduced through specified seniority programs that tie wages and benefits to length of service. Employees are thus encouraged to devote their energies to performing their jobs through cooperation, since competition among workers is senseless in a seniority system. However, it is also well recognized that seniority programs may adversely affect productivity by promoting employees to positions for which they are not qualified. Unionism is also alleged to raise efficiency by increasing the awareness of employees that their wages may be tied to the profitability of the employer. Employees often have an informational advantage over employers in daily operations of the company, and because of this they often have good ideas about how to improve productivity. It is alleged that union employees have a greater incentive to pass on such ideas to management than do nonunion employees. However, it must be pointed out that many nonunion employers implement incentives programs designed to tap their employees' knowledge and expertise. The major economic criticism of these allegedly productive attributes of unionization may be summed up in the following question: If unions are so efficient and productive, why do profit maximizing employers invariably oppose unionization? In fact, it would appear that employers would have a comparative advantage at helping unions organize as employers can act as the agent who overcomes the free-riding problem that often plagues union organizing efforts.

5. The Distribution of Income and Higher Union Wages: In addition to the "displaced worker" effect discussed prior to *Connell,* unions can also cause wage differentials between workers of comparable skills. This will result if the pool of skilled workers is sufficiently large to fill all union jobs with workers left over. In general, extreme inequities of pay among workers of the same skill (horizontal inequities) and among workers of differing skills (vertical inequities) may be counterproductive. Given these observations, labor economists have wondered whether unions really have the best interests of their fellow workers at heart. In direct contrast to the economist's view of union impact on the distribution of income, the industrial relations view suggests that the unions must attempt to reduce inequality in order to have the support of the majority of its members. This political argument is misleading in two respects. First, majority support can always be gained by transferring wealth from 49 percent of the workers to the 51 percent covered by the union contract. Second, and most importantly, it compares wages within a union, rather than between different unions or between the union and nonunion sector. The economic analysis is based on union versus nonunion wages. Any examples that illustrate union efforts at equality of wages by appealing to union policies without comparing them to nonunion practices is misleading. For example, union seniority provisions and standard wage rates may increase equality within the union, but is says nothing about the impact of the above market union wage on the nonunion labor markets.

6. Unions and Discrimination: A major economic criticism of unions was that they lower the cost to employers of discriminating against minorities, thus, in effect, encouraging discrimination. It is axiomatic that when unions raise wages above competitive rates, the number of workers willing and able to perform the job increase while the number of jobs available decrease. These changes in the quantity demanded (jobs available) and the quantity supplied (workers available) result in a surplus of workers. This surplus puts both unions and employers in stronger positions with respect to their ability to discriminate against workers (fellow workers, in the case of unions) on whatever basis they see fit, including race, sex, national origin, and religion. The shortage of jobs (another way of saying "surplus of workers") must be rationed in some manner, and it is very easy (that is, inexpensive) for union leaders and employers to indulge their preferences for discrimination in rationing jobs. The history of unionization in the United States indicates that unions often have been as guilty of discrimination in their membership practices as have employers in their hiring practices. Supporters of unions counter this analysis with several observations—two of which are based on empirical studies. First, unionization reduces discrimination within firms by having wages determined by standard rate and seniority promotion policies. Of course, this does not relate to the discrimination argument, which is based on discrimination in hiring. A second observation tends to refute the discrimination in hiring argument: a larger percentage of black workers are organized than are white workers. Third, although organized white workers tend to be paid more than organized black workers, the divergence is smaller than the divergence in wages between unorganized whites and unorganized blacks. On the basis of this evidence, union supporters conclude that unions increase the status of black workers.

7. *Political Activity of Unions:* Union political activity is often controversial (as is corporate political activity). Unions may exert political clout in several ways. See generally Chapter 14, "Labor in National and State Politics," in Derek C. Bok and John T. Dunlop, Labor and the American Community (1970). Unions can lobby, endorse candidates, contribute money to campaigns, and have their members become active in political campaigns by engaging in voter registration drives, handing out campaign literature before and on election day, addressing envelopes, providing rides to the polls for sympathetic voters, etc. Traditionally, the sheer number of members in unions have dictated that they engage in the more labor-intensive types of campaigning. Moreover, lobbying is utilized extensively by almost all unions. Unions representing over one-half of the union members have lobbying offices in Washington, D.C., while not a single Fortune 100 corporation is headquartered there. It is clear that union political activity is largely motivated by economic considerations affecting the union. Union political activity, in addition to being concerned with the unionization of workers, is also concerned with maintaining the demand for goods and services produced by unionized employers because such goods and services typically cost more due to higher wages. Consider the following statement:

> Much of the political activism of unions can be understood as attempts to protect or increase the demand of union labor. Examples are the union label ("Always look to the union label..."), tariffs and quotas on foreign goods competing with union-made products (Japanese cars), law requiring "Made in Korea" labels, building codes that require installation of union-supplied material or labor, reduced class sizes to expand the demand for school teachers, federal subsidies to unionized industries

like the merchant marine or mass transit, or opposition to contracting out work to outside bidders. Other political measures promoted by unions—restrictions on foreign immigration, compulsory apprenticeship requirements, child labor laws, minimum wage rates, and occupational licensing—restrict trade by hampering the ability of other suppliers to serve the market, so that union labor is relatively more attractive.

Morgan O. Reynolds, The History and Economics of Labor Unions 9 (1985). Unions often claim to represent the political interests of not only all workers, including minorities, but also the interests of all disadvantaged and lower income persons. In this regard, unions were a vital part of the liberal political coalition that engineered the adoption of much of the welfare state legislation. The good intentions of advocates of those types of programs is not to be disputed here, but there is overwhelming evidence that many of those programs have not worked and indeed may have been counterproductive. Theoretical and empirical evidence has demonstrated that programs like affirmative action, equal pay for equal work, social security, and the minimum wage all create incentives that may end up injuring the (stated) intended beneficiaries. Either union politics that lead to such results must be changed by the unions, or the unions' motives in supporting such policies must be examined more carefully. In general, economic analysis suggests that union political activities benefit the union at the expense of other workers.

8. Capital and Labor: In a competitive market, firms respond to prices and wages to find the optimal, or most efficient, mix of capital and labor in their production processes. When unions raise wages, the firm's optimal mix of capital and labor shifts in favor of employing more capital. That is, at higher wages the firm will substitute capital for labor because of the higher price of labor. The inefficiency of this adjustment results because the additional capital must be released from some other presumably higher valued use in the free market and the released workers go to other areas of the economy. The market prior to higher union wages had already indicated the efficient means of production in its mix of capital and labor. The allocative inefficiency is that the firm uses more capital and less labor than the efficient allocation in the market. Unions may also cause inefficiencies by imposing work rules that decrease productivity and lower society's output through strikes and other disruptive practices.

Chapter IX

Risk

Life, by its very nature, is risky. Most people do not like risk, yet reducing risk is expensive. Therefore, individuals, businesses, and governments must make trade-offs between the costs of living in a risky world and the costs of reducing that risk. Everyone through their behavior indicates that they are willing to take on certain risks in their lives. The fact that people ride in automobiles, as opposed to riding in tanks or armored vehicles which are much safer, indicates that individuals make trade-offs between the cost and comfort of an automobile and a safer mode of travel. In general, individuals engage in risk avoidance activities up to the point where the marginal benefit of the reduced risk is equal to the marginal cost of reducing the risk. The fact that people do not spend the resources to make their life risk free suggests that life itself is not priceless.

This chapter covers several ways that individuals and society attempt to deal with risk. After a review of the economics of uncertainty and risk in Section A, the next two sections consider essentially private, market-based ways of dealing with risk. Section B covers the demand for and supply of insurance. Section C is an overview of the manner in which market prices for products, services, and jobs adjust to reflect the associated risk. Section D analyzes how tort law deals with accidents and injuries that result from a non-contractual, non-negotiated relationship. Section E presents an overview and critique of federal risk regulation.

A. Economics of Uncertainty and Risk

Individuals and firms must make decisions when they are not certain of the outcome. However, they often have some idea of the range of possible outcomes. This section explains how the size of the range of possible outcomes has an impact on decision making. The first subsection introduces some basic concepts from probability theory which are then used to calculate some descriptive statistics—expected value and variance—regarding the range of possible outcomes for a decision. The next subsection describes the assumption that individuals are risk averse and explores some implications of that assumption.

1. Basic Probability Theory

Some theoretical economic models—for example, the perfect competition model in Chapter V—rely on the assumption that individuals have perfect information regarding the outcome of any particular decision. Such decisions have **certain outcomes**. A more realistic assumption is that individuals contemplate a variety of potential outcomes and assign relative likelihoods to their actual occurrence. In such cases, the decisions have **uncertain outcomes**. When decision makers have information regarding possible outcomes and their relative likelihoods, the tools of probability theory can be used to analyze economic decisions.

A **probability** is a number between 0 and 1, inclusive, that expresses the likelihood that some specific event will occur. Some probabilities can be estimated through a process of experimentation. For example, we would expect that the probability of getting "tails" as a result of flipping a fair coin is .5 (which is equal to ½ or 50%). When probabilities can be established in this fashion, they are **objective probabilities**. In other cases, probabilities are estimated on the basis of a subjective "best guess" or one's prior experiences. When a particular individual's opinion enters the estimation, she is using a **subjective probability**.

It will often be useful to identify situations in which two probabilistic events are independent of each other. Events are **independent** when the probabilistic outcome of one decision does not affect the probabilistic outcome of a second decision. For example, while driving through Missouri on a cross-country road trip, Jerry decides to purchase a state lottery ticket. This decision over the use of funds has an uncertain outcome to which probabilities can be assigned. After purchasing the Missouri state lottery ticket, Jerry continues his trip across the country. While in Kansas, Jerry decides to purchase a lottery ticket for the state lottery of Kansas. However, by purchasing a lottery ticket in Kansas, Jerry has not changed the probability that he will win the lottery in Missouri. Thus, the probabilities for winning either lottery are independent of each other. Note that this is different than estimating the probability that Jerry would win both lotteries. The probability of two independent events both occurring is simply the product of the probabilities. Thus, if Jerry had a 25% chance of winning the Missouri lottery and a 25% chance of winning the Kansas lottery, then his chance of winning both lotteries would be 25% × 25% = 6.25%

For purposes of analysis, assume that outcomes and probabilities are both **complete** and **mutually exclusive**. Completeness suggests that while the decision maker does not know the specific outcome of any decision, she is aware of all potential outcomes. Mutual exclusivity indicates that the result of a particular decision will be x or y, not x and y. These two assumptions allow the use of the notion of an expected value in analyzing uncertain decisions.

2. Expected Value and Variance

Given a set of objective or subjective probabilities and all possible outcomes, the expected outcome of an uncertain decision can be calculated. The **expected value** of an uncertain decision is the product of outcomes and their probabilities summed across all possible outcomes:

$$E(x) = P_1(x_1) + P_2(x_2) + \ldots + P_n(x_n)$$

where $E(x)$ is the expected value of x, P_i is the probability of any outcome I, and x_i is the actual value of outcome I. Each P_i must be between 0 and 1, inclusive; and the sum of all P_is must equal 1.

Consider the following example. Suppose that you are representing a widower in a wrongful death suit. The case has just gone to the jury, and the defendants offer to settle for $1,000,000. In deciding whether to accept this offer, you must consider the amount of damages you expect to collect by waiting to hear from the jury. Based upon your experience as an attorney and the willingness of the defendant to settle at this point in the litigation, you feel quite confident that the plaintiff will be awarded a substantial judgment. Moreover, because the trial is complete, your costs in terms of time and resources are the same whether you settle or wait for the jury. You feel that there is a 30% chance that the jury will award $750,000, a 50% chance that the jury will award $1,000,000, and a 20% chance that the jury will award $2,000,000. Thus, the expected value of the jury award is:

$$E(x) = .30(750,000) + .50(1,000,000) + .20(2,000,000) = \$1,125,000$$

By your calculation, the expected result of the jury award exceeds the settlement offer by $125,000—at a 33% contingency fee this is $41,250 towards your income. In other words, based upon your experience, you believe that the jury award will probably be greater than the settlement offer. Is there any question about what to do?

The decision about whether or not to accept the settlement offer, could be guided by the following simple decision rule: When faced with uncertain outcomes, choose that decision with the highest expected value. However, there is reason to believe that such a decision rule would not comport with the way in which people actually make decisions. While the expected jury award is $1,125,000, there is a 30% chance that the award will be $750,000—$250,000 less than the settlement offer. Are you willing to advise your client to take this risk? Moreover, are there any professional responsibility implications for advising your client to take this risk? On the other hand, there is a 20% chance that the jury will award $2,000,000 which exceeds the settlement value by $1,000,000. There is the possibility of doubling your client's money by taking the risk.

The analysis in the preceding paragraph suggests that there might be some level of variability in the results which would discourage some individuals from choosing the option with the highest expected value. Greater variability implies that there is less certainty regarding the potential outcome, and thus more risk involved in the decision. To the extent that individuals are concerned about the riskiness of decisions, they are interested in some measure of the variability of outcomes for any particular decision.

Variability or risk is quantified by a measure of the average dispersion of actual results around the expected value known as the **variance**. Variance is equal to the weighted average of squared deviations from the expected value:

$$\sigma^2 = P_1(x_1 - E(x))^2 + P_2(x_2 - E(x))^2 + \ldots + P_n(x_n - E(x))^2$$

where σ^2 is the variance, P_i the probability of the outcome I, x_i is the actual result for outcome I, and $E(x)$ is the expected value as calculated above. Thus, for the jury award contemplated earlier, the variance is:

$$\sigma^2 = .30(750,000-1,125,000)^2 + .50(1,000,000-1,125,000)^2$$
$$+ .20(2,000,000-1,125,000)^2$$

$$= 203,125,000,000$$

Because of the squared terms in the variance calculation, the answer is not in the same units as the inputs—in this case dollars. As a result, it is sometimes difficult to interpret the meaning of the variance calculation. This difficulty can be resolved by using standard deviation. **Standard deviation** is also a measure of the dispersion around expected values and it is measured in the same units as the original inputs. Standard deviation is simply the square root of the variance. For the jury award example, the standard deviation of possible awards is:

$$\sigma = \$450,694$$

The decision as to whether or not a dispersion or variability of $450,694 is too risky is a matter of individual preference. The key to analyzing decisions under uncertainty is to recognize the fundamental economic tradeoff involved in these decisions. Specifically, how willing is a particular individual to sacrifice some amount of expected value for a reduction in risk? Ultimately, the decision regarding whether to take the certain settlement or the uncertain jury award depends upon the decision maker's subjective attitude toward risk.

3. Expected Utility and Risk Preference

Most people do not like risk and thus might be willing to sacrifice some amount of expected money value for a reduction in risk. People tend to prefer certain outcomes to uncertain outcomes even if the expected value of the uncertain outcome is greater than that of the certain outcome. In other words, sometimes individuals get more utility from reducing risk than maximizing expected money outcomes. When faced with uncertainty, individuals attempt to maximize expected utility, not expected value.

Figure IX-1 presents a utility function for a hypothetical individual. Money value is marked along the horizontal axis and utility on the vertical—for this ex-

<u>**Figure IX-1**</u>   Utility Curve Exhibiting Diminishing Marginal Utility of Money Value

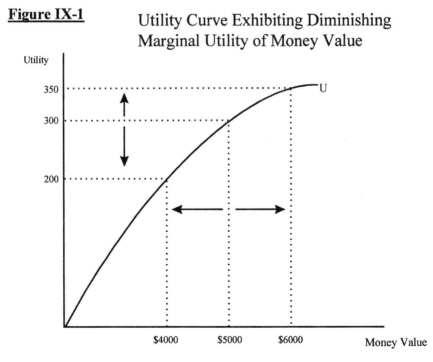

ample, utility is a function of money value. Notice that the utility function, U, increases at a decreasing rate. This suggests that an individual with this type of utility function exhibits **diminishing marginal utility of money value.**

Consider an individual who starts off with $5,000. Such an individual has a utility of 300 utils—where utils are an imaginary measurement of utility. If this individual's money holdings were increased by $1,000, her utility would increase to 350 utils—an increase of 50 utils. On the other hand, if $1,000 were taken away from this individual, her utility would decline to 200 utils—a loss of 100 utils. Thus, this individual's utility is affected more by losses than by gains. In other words, while the gain of $1,000 would increase utility, the loss of $1,000 would decrease utility by a larger amount. This suggests that the individual would be averse to some risk involving a potential gain or loss of $1,000. We can conclude from this analysis that an individual who exhibits diminishing marginal utility of money is **risk averse.**

Figure IX-2 presents the dynamics of decision making under uncertainty for the risk averse individual. The uncertain decision faced by this individual has an expected value of $10,000. However, there is a 50% chance that the payoff from this uncertain decision will be $15,000 and a 50% chance of a $5,000 payoff. The utility curve indicates how this individual regards uncertain decisions. Notice that a certain $15,000 payoff provides the individual with utility corresponding to level A. A certain $5,000 payoff provides utility that corresponds to level B. Furthermore, the utility from a certain $10,000 payoff provides utility up to level C. However, the uncertain decision does not provide $10,000 with certainty. In fact, although $10,000 is the expected value, it will not occur. When the expected value is some combination of $5,000 and $15,000, the expected

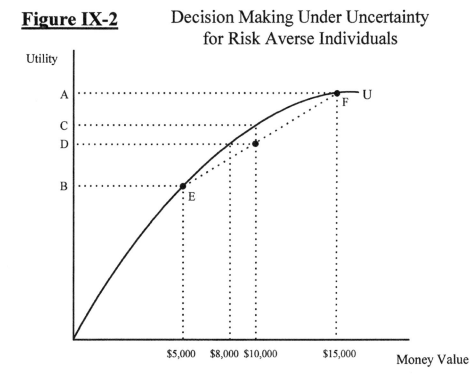

Figure IX-2 Decision Making Under Uncertainty for Risk Averse Individuals

utility from the payoff can be determined by using the dotted line segment from E to F. The expected utility associated with an expected value of $10,000 corresponds to level D—found by moving directly to the left from the dotted line segment until intersecting with the utility curve. The expected utility from an expected value of $10,000—level D—is less than the utility associated with a certain $10,000 payoff—level C. In general, greater concavity in the utility function—the more marginal utility of money value diminishes—suggests that individuals are more risk averse and less willing to accept uncertain outcomes.

Figure IX-2 also demonstrates another important fact regarding risk averse individuals. Notice that a certain $8,000 payoff provides the same utility as the expected uncertain $10,000 payoff. This is consistent with the earlier observation that risk averse individuals might be willing to sacrifice some amount of money value for reduced risk. Furthermore, it suggests that a risk averse individual might be willing to sacrifice an amount equal to $2,000 ($10,000 – $8,000) to avoid having to take the uncertain outcome. In effect, the person is paid $2,000 in expected value in order to be induced to take on the riskier venture. This $2,000 payment is known as a **risk premium**. This topic will be addressed in greater detail in the section on insurance.

Risk aversion describes the preferences revealed by much of the normal behavior observed everyday. Yet, this does not mean that all individuals are risk averse. Some individuals are **risk neutral**—they appear to be indifferent toward risk. Moreover, some individuals seem to actively seek risky situations. Such individuals are known as **risk seekers**. Both risk neutral and risk seeking behavior can be incorporated into the expected utility analysis developed in this chapter.

Figure IX-3 presents expected utility analysis for the risk neutral individual. Notice that the utility curve increases at a constant rate. This suggests that an in-

Figure IX-3   Risk Neutral

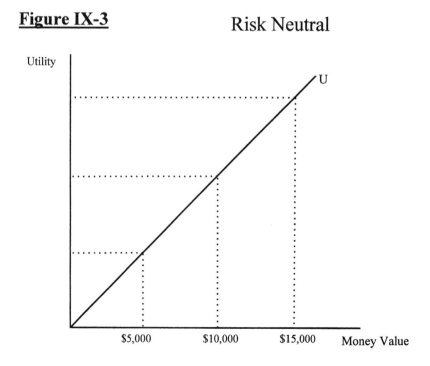

<u>Figure IX-4</u>   Risk Seeker

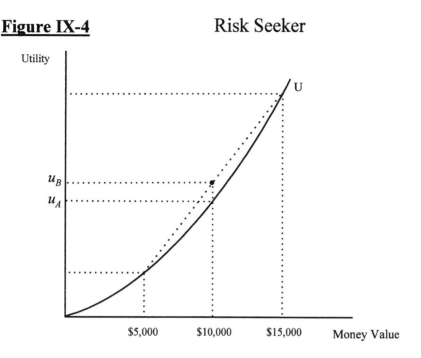

crease in money holdings would have the same marginal effect on utility as an equal loss in money holdings. Consider the relationship between the utility for a certain payoff of $10,000 and an uncertain expected payout of $10,000. The straight utility function indicates that the utility of the certain outcome is the same as the utility for the uncertain outcome. Risk neutral individuals are indifferent between certain and uncertain outcomes—their decisions are guided only by expected value. To these individuals, there is no difference between a $1 million bet and a $1 bet so long as the expected value is the same. When risk neutral individuals maximize their expected value, they are also maximizing their expected utility.

Figure IX-4 presents the expected utility analysis for a risk-seeking individual. Notice that the utility curve increases at an increasing rate. This suggests that an increase in money holdings would have a greater marginal effect on utility than would an equal loss in money holdings. Consider the relationship between the utility for a certain payoff of $10,000 and an uncertain expected payout of $10,000. Because of the upward sloping nature of the utility function, the utility of the certain outcome (u_A) is less than the utility for the uncertain outcome (u_B). Risk seekers prefer uncertain outcomes to certain outcomes.

B. Insurance

The general assumption in economics is that people are risk averse concerning gambles that affect a significant proportion of their wealth. One of the important behavioral implications of this is that individuals are willing to sacrifice certain amounts of money in order to avoid larger uncertain losses. A clear example of this is the decision to purchase insurance, whether it is health insurance, automobile insurance, disability insurance, homeowners insurance, where people who purchase insurance in effect give up a certain relatively small sum of money in order to avoid an uncertain, yet potentially larger, downside. This section considers the demand and supply of insurance as well as some of the problems that must be confronted by insurance providers.

1. Demand for Insurance

The demand for insurance is derived from individuals' risk preferences. Perhaps the best way to see this is to consider an everyday example. Suppose an individual owns a home that is worth $100,000. If there is a one percent chance that the home will be destroyed by fire in the next year, the expected loss from the fire is $1,000. If an individual does not purchase insurance, one of two things will happen: the house will survive the year unscathed and there will be no loss; or, the house will be destroyed by fire and there will be a $100,000 loss. Thus, the expected loss for the year is $1,000, although the individual will never be exactly $1,000 dollars worse off. The individual will either loose nothing or be $100,000 worse off. Intuitively, the variance across possible outcomes is wide. A risk averse individual might be willing to pay, let's say, up to $2,000 for insurance to guarantee that the house is replaced in the event that it is destroyed. The individual's position for the year then is $98,000—$100,000 minus the $2,000 insurance premium—with certainty as opposed to an uncertain $99,000—$100,000 minus the expected loss of $1,000. As a result of purchasing insurance, there is only one possible outcome—$98,000—and the variance of possible outcomes is zero. In this case, insurance reduces the financial risk to zero.

2. Supply of Insurance

Insurance companies are in a much different situation than the individual homeowner. Insurance companies are in the business of pooling the risk of a large number of homeowners. A statistical phenomenon known as the "law of large numbers" allows insurance companies to pool the risks of a large number of homeowners, take the statistical likelihood of homes being destroyed, and convert it into estimates that approach certainty. For example, if all homes have a one percent chance of being destroyed by fire in the next year, and an insurance company has written policies for 1,000 homes, the expected number of homes to burn in any year is one percent times 1,000. Thus, you would expect 10 homes to burn with, say, an average loss of $100,000. Therefore, the insurance company would expect to payout $1,000,000 per year for 10 houses burning down. Due to the law of large numbers, the variance of the insurance company's estimates approaches certainty as more homes are added to the risk pool. Moreover, there is no risk aversion in their calculations. They deal purely with the monetary calculations.

However, each individual homeowner is still faced with the large potential variance in the results between losing $0 or $100,000. The expected claim per policy for the insurance company is $1,000—that is, the $1,000,000 the insurer expects to payout divided by the 1,000 homes insured. Earlier, it was assumed that homeowners are willing to pay up to $2,000 per insurance policy. This wedge between the price the consumer is willing to pay and the cost to the insurance company of providing the product creates an opportunity for an insurance market to emerge.

Insurance companies also have administrative costs associated with the selling and pricing of policies, servicing policy holders, and adjusting claims. Successful insurance companies must price their policies so they cover their expected losses and their administrative costs. Moreover, insurance companies who do a better job of investing their cash reserves (before they have to pay out the claims owed to policyholders) receive a larger return and are able to offer lower prices. To the extent that the insurance market is competitive, prices are pushed below the $2,000 per policy that consumers are willing to pay towards a price that reflects the cost of operating in the industry.

Controlling the cost of operation is an important challenge for all insurance companies. Every insurer must deal with two basic problems—adverse selection and moral hazard—which were introduced in Chapter VII.

a. Adverse Selection

Adverse selection is a precontractual problem in the sense that it comes from the phenomenon that the potential insured party knows much more about their own risk than does the potential insurer. As a result of this asymmetric information, people who are risky (that is, pose a greater than average risk) are more likely to attempt to purchase insurance than are people who have a below average risk. This adverse selection can lead to the lemons market phenomenon which was discussed in Chapter VII.

Insurance companies attempt to deal with adverse selection by providing exclusions for coverage dealing with preexisting conditions, looking for various statistical phenomenon that are likely to result in higher claims from various groups, checking out applicants' backgrounds, and a variety of other devices that are designed to avoid ending up with a lemon's pool. Sometimes risky insureds might be allowed into the pool but will have to pay higher rates. Typical examples of ways to deal with this type of adverse selection include charging higher homeowners insurance rates for people who smoke, higher health insurance rates for people who smoke, higher automobile insurance rates for males under age 25, and so forth.

Read

Waxse v. Reserve Life Insurance Company
Supreme Court of Kansas
248 Kan. 582; 809 P.2d 533 (1991)

and accompanying *Notes and Questions*
Supra Chapter VII

b. Moral Hazard

Moral hazard is the name of the problem that arises when the behavior of the insured changes after the purchase of the insurance so that the probability of loss or size of loss increases. Moral hazard is a post-contractual problem concerned with insured parties changing their behavior once they have become insured. This can range from individuals deciding to take up skydiving shortly after they purchase a life insurance policy to individuals exercising less care with respect to preventing their car or their personal property from being stolen when they have insurance.

Insurance companies must recognize these moral hazard incentives and develop methods to deal with them. Insurance companies deal with the moral hazard problem by a combination of deductibles which must be paid by the insured party prior to any payment by the insurer and copayments which are payments of which a proportion are borne by insured as payments are paid by the insurer. Most people are familiar with this practice involving their health care insurance policy.

Atwater Creamery Company v. Western National Mutual Insurance Company
Supreme Court of Minnesota
366 N.W.2d 271 (1985)

WAHL, Justice.

Atwater Creamery Company (Atwater) sought a declaratory judgment against its insurer, Western National Mutual Insurance Company (Western), seeking coverage for losses sustained during a burglary of the creamery's storage building. Atwater joined Strehlow Insurance Agency and Charles Strehlow (Strehlow), its agent, as defendants, seeking damages in the alternative due to Strehlow's alleged negligence and misrepresentation. The Kandiyohi County District Court granted a directed verdict for Strehlow because Atwater failed to establish an insurance agent's standard of care by expert testimony. The trial court then dismissed the jury for lack of disputed issues of fact and ordered judgment in favor of the insurer, concluding that the burglary insurance policy in effect defined burglary so as to exclude coverage of this burglary. We affirm the directed verdict for Strehlow but reverse as to the policy coverage.

Atwater does business as a creamery and as a supplier of farm chemicals in Atwater, Minnesota. It was insured during the time in question against burglary, up to a ceiling of $20,000, by Western under Mercantile Open Stock Burglary Policy SC10-1010-12, which contained an "evidence of forcible entry" requirement in its definition of burglary. The creamery had recovered small amounts under this policy for two separate burglaries prior to the events in this case.

Atwater built a separate facility, called the Soil Center, a few blocks away from its main plant in 1975 for the purpose of storing and selling chemicals. The Soil Center is a large rectangular building with two regular doors along the north side and two large, sliding doors, one each on the east and west sides. There are no other entrances or exits to or from the building itself. One of the doors on the north side leads into the office in the northwest corner of the building. It is secured by a regular dead bolt lock, opened with a key. There is no access into the main portion of the building from the office. Persons entering the main area must use the other door on the north side which is secured by a padlock after hours. The large sliding doors on the east and west are secured by large hasps on each side of each door which are held tight by turnbuckles that must be loosened before the doors can be opened.

Inside the main area of the building, along the north wall, is a large storage bin with three separate doors, each of which is secured by a padlock. Between the storage bin and the office is an "alleyway," entered through the large sliding doors, which runs east and west the length of the building. Trucks are stored in the alleyway when not in use.

Sometime between 9:30 p.m., Saturday, April 9, and 6 a.m., Monday, April 11, 1977, one or more persons made unauthorized entry into the building, took chemicals worth $15,587.40, apparently loading them on the truck that had been parked inside and driving away after loosening the turnbuckles on the east door and closing it. The truck was later found parked near the town dump, with the key still in the ignition.

Larry Poe, the plant manager at the Soil Center, had left at 9:30 p.m. on Saturday, after making sure everything was properly secured. On Monday morning, the north side doors were locked securely, but two of the three doors to the storage bin were ajar. Their padlocks were gone and never found. The turnbuckles had been loosened on the east sliding door so that it could be easily opened or closed.

An investigation by the local police, the Kandiyohi County Sheriff's Department, and the Minnesota Bureau of Criminal Investigation determined that no Atwater Creamery employees, past or present, were involved in the burglary. Suspicion settled on persons wholly unconnected with the creamery or even with the local area, but no one has been apprehended or charged with the crime.

Atwater filed a claim with Western under the burglary policy. Western denied coverage because there were no visible marks of physical damage to the exterior at the point of entrance or to the interior at the point of exit, as required by the definition of burglary in the policy. The creamery then brought suit against Western for the $15,587.40 loss, $7,500 in other directly related business losses and costs, disbursements and reasonable attorney fees.

Charles H. Strehlow, the owner of the Strehlow Insurance Agency in Willmar, Minnesota, and Western's agent, testified that he is certain he mentioned the evidence-of-forcible-entry requirement to Poe and members of the Atwater Board of Directors but was unable to say when the discussion occurred. Poe and the board members examined do not remember any such discussion. None of the board members had read the policy, which is kept in the safe at the main plant, and Poe had not read it in its entirety. He stated that he started to read it but gave up because he could not understand it.

The issues on appeal are:

*   *   *

2. whether the reasonable expectations of the insured as to coverage govern to defeat the literal language of the policy;

*   *   *

2. APPLICATION OF THE POLICY DEFINITION OF BURGLARY.

The definition of burglary in this policy is one used generally in burglary insurance. Courts have construed it in different ways.[1] It has been held ambiguous and construed in favor of coverage in the absence of visible marks of forceable entry or exit. *United States Fidelity & Guaranty Co. v. Woodward*, 118 Ga.App. 591, 164 S.E.2d 878 (1968). We reject this analysis because we view the definition in the policy as clear and precise. It is not ambiguous.

In determining the intent of the parties to the insurance contract, courts have looked to the purpose of the visible-marks-of-forcible-entry requirement. These purposes are two: to protect insurance companies from fraud by way of "inside jobs" and to encourage insureds to reasonably secure the premises. See 5 Appleman § 3176 at 517. As long as the theft involved clearly neither an inside job nor the result of a lack of secured premises, some courts have simply held that the definition does not apply. Limberis v. Aetna Casualty & Surety Co., 263 A.2d 83 (Me.1970); Kretschmer's House of Appliances, Inc. v. United States Fidelity & Guaranty Co., 410 S.W.2d 617 (Ky.1966).

In the instant case, there is no dispute as to whether Atwater is attempting to defraud Western or whether the Soil Center was properly secured. The trial court found that the premises were secured before the robbery and that the law enforcement investigators had determined that it was not an "inside job." To enforce the burglary definition literally against the creamery will in no way effectuate either purpose behind the restrictive definition. We are uncomfortable, however, with this analysis given the right of an insurer to limit the risk against which it will indemnify insureds.

At least three state courts have held that the definition merely provides for one form of evidence which may be used to prove a burglary and that, consequently, other evidence of a burglary will suffice to provide coverage. Ferguson v. Phoenix Assurance Co. of New York, 189 Kan. 459, 370 P.2d 379 (1962); National Surety Co. v. Silberberg Bros., 176 S.W. 97 (Tex.Civ.App.1915); Rosenthal v. American Bonding Co. of Baltimore, 124 N.Y.S. 905 (N.Y.Sup.Ct.1910). The Nebraska Supreme Court recently rejected this argument in Cochran v. MFA Mutual Insurance Co., 201 Neb. 631, 271 N.W.2d 331 (1978). The Cochran court held that the definition is not a rule of evidence but is a limit on liability, is unambiguous and is applied literally to the facts of the case at hand. We, too, reject this view of the definition as merely a form of evidence. The policy attempts to comprehensively define burglaries that are covered by it. In essence, this approach ignores the policy definition altogether and substitutes the court's or the statute's definition of burglary. This we decline to do, either via the conformity clause or by calling the policy definition merely one form of evidence of a burglary.

Some courts and commentators have recognized that the burglary definition at issue in this case constitutes a rather hidden exclusion from coverage. Exclusions in insurance contracts are read narrowly against the insurer. Running through the

---

1. See 5 Appleman, Insurance Law and Practice § 3176, "External and Visible Marks in Burglary Losses," 516 (1970, Supp.1983).

many court opinions refusing to literally enforce this burglary definition is the concept that the definition is surprisingly restrictive, that no one purchasing something called burglary insurance would expect coverage to exclude skilled burglaries that leave no visible marks of forcible entry or exit. Professor Robert E. Keeton, in analyzing these and other insurance cases where the results often do not follow from the rules stated, found there to be two general principles underlying many decisions. These principles are the reasonable expectations of the insured and the unconscionability of the clause itself or as applied to the facts of a specific case. Keeton, Insurance Law Rights at Variance with Policy Provisions, 83 Harv.L.Rev. 961 (1970). Keeton's article and subsequent book, Basic Text on Insurance Law, (1971), have had significant impact on the construction of insurance contracts.

The doctrine of protecting the reasonable expectations of the insured is closely related to the doctrine of contracts of adhesion. Where there is unequal bargaining power between the parties so that one party controls all of the terms and offers the contract on a take-it-or-leave-it basis, the contract will be strictly construed against the party who drafted it. Most courts recognize the great disparity in bargaining power between insurance companies and those who seek insurance. Further, they recognize that, in the majority of cases, a lay person lacks the necessary skills to read and understand insurance policies, which are typically long, set out in very small type and written from a legalistic or insurance expert's perspective. Finally, courts recognize that people purchase insurance relying on others, the agent or company, to provide a policy that meets their needs. The result of the lack of insurance expertise on the part of insureds and the recognized marketing techniques of insurance companies is that "[t]he objectively reasonable expectations of applicants and intended beneficiaries regarding the terms of insurance contracts will be honored even though painstaking study of the policy provisions would have negated those expectations." Keeton, 83 Harv.L.Rev. at 967.

The traditional approach to construction of insurance contracts is to require some kind of ambiguity in the policy before applying the doctrine of reasonable expectations. Several courts, however, have adopted Keeton's view that ambiguity ought not be a condition precedent to the application of the reasonable-expectations doctrine.

As of 1980, approximately ten states had adopted the newer rule of reasonable expectations regardless of ambiguity. Davenport Peters Co. v. Royal Globe Insurance Co., 490 F.Supp. 286, 291 (D.Mass.1980). Other states, such as Missouri and North Dakota, have joined the ten since then.[2] Most courts recognize that insureds seldom see the policy until the premium is paid, and even if they try

---

2. Some of the major cases adopting the doctrine are: Gray v. Zurich Ins. Co., 65 Cal.2d 263, 54 Cal.Rptr. 104, 107, 419 P.2d 168, 171 (1966); Smith v. Westland Life Ins. Co., 15 Cal.3d 111, 123 Cal.Rptr. 649, 539 P.2d 433 (1975); Corgatelli v. Globe Life & Acc. Ins. Co., 96 Idaho 616, 533 P.2d 737 (1975) (overruled, see text); C & J Fertilizer, Inc. v. Allied Mutual Ins. Co., 227 N.W.2d 169 (Iowa 1975); Collister v. Nationwide Life Ins. Co., 479 Pa. 579, 388 A.2d 1346 (1978). Missouri has recently adopted it in Estrin Construction Co. v. Aetna Casualty & Surety Co., 612 S.W.2d 413 (Mo.App.1981); and North Dakota, in Mills v. Agrichemical Aviation, Inc., 250 N.W.2d 663 (N.D.1977), showed its similarity to North Dakota's doctrine of contract of adhesion, which was followed in that case. Two of the original ten have overruled earlier cases and have reverted to the traditional rule. Hallowell v. State Farm Mutual Automobile Insurance Co., 443 A.2d 925 (Del.1982),

to read it, they do not comprehend it. Few courts require insureds to have minutely examined the policy before relying on the terms they expect it to have and for which they have paid.

The burglary definition is a classic example of a policy provision that should be, and has been, interpreted according to the reasonable expectations of the insured. C & J Fertilizer, Inc. v. Allied Mutual Insurance Co., 227 N.W.2d 169 (Iowa 1975). C & J Fertilizer involved a burglary definition almost exactly like the one in the instant case as well as a burglary very similar to the Atwater burglary. The court applied the reasonable-expectations-regardless-of-ambiguity doctrine, noting that "[t]he most plaintiff might have reasonably anticipated was a policy requirement of visual evidence (abundant here) indicating the burglary was an 'outside' not an 'inside' job. The exclusion in issue, masking as a definition, makes insurer's obligation to pay turn on the skill of the burglar, not on the event the parties bargained for: a bona fide third party burglary resulting in loss of plaintiff's chemicals and equipment." Id. at 177. The burglary in C & J Fertilizer left no visible marks on the exterior of the building, but an interior door was damaged. In the instant case, the facts are very similar except that there was no damage to the interior doors; their padlocks were simply gone. In C & J Fertilizer, the police concluded that an "outside" burglary had occurred. The same is true here.

Atwater had a burglary policy with Western for more than 30 years. The creamery relied on Charles Strehlow to procure for it insurance suitable for its needs. There is some factual dispute as to whether Strehlow ever told Poe about the "exclusion," as Strehlow called it. Even if he had said that there was a visible-marks-of-forcible-entry requirement, Poe could reasonably have thought that it meant that there must be clear evidence of a burglary. There are, of course, fidelity bonds which cover employee theft. The creamery had such a policy covering director and manager theft. The fidelity company, however, does not undertake to insure against the risk of third-party burglaries. A business that requests and purchases burglary insurance reasonably is seeking coverage for loss from third-party burglaries whether a break-in is accomplished by an inept burglar or by a highly skilled burglar. Two other burglaries had occurred at the Soil Center, for which Atwater had received insurance proceeds under the policy. Poe and the board of the creamery could reasonably have expected the burglary policy to cover this burglary where the police, as well as the trial court, found that it was an "outside job."

The reasonable-expectations doctrine gives the court a standard by which to construe insurance contracts without having to rely on arbitrary rules which do not reflect real-life situations and without having to bend and stretch those rules to do justice in individual cases. As Professor Keeton points out, ambiguity in the language of the contract is not irrelevant under this standard but becomes a factor in determining the reasonable expectations of the insured, along with such factors as whether the insured was told of important, but obscure, conditions or exclusions and whether the particular provision in the contract at issue is an item known by the public generally. The doctrine does not automatically remove from

---

and Casey v. Highlands Insurance Co., 600 P.2d 1387 (Idaho 1979). Both courts saw the new rule as relieving the insured of any responsibility for reading the policy.

the insured a responsibility to read the policy. It does, however, recognize that in certain instances, such as where major exclusions are hidden in the definitions section, the insured should be held only to reasonable knowledge of the literal terms and conditions. The insured may show what actual expectations he or she had, but the factfinder should determine whether those expectations were reasonable under the circumstances.

We have used the reasonable-expectations-of-the-insured analysis to provide coverage where the actual language interpreted as the insurance company intended would have proscribed coverage. Canadian Universal Insurance Co. v. Fire Watch, Inc., 258 N.W.2d 570 (Minn.1977). Western correctly points out that the issue there concerned a special endorsement issued subsequent to the policy which reduced coverage without notice to the insured. While the issue is somewhat different in the instant case, it is not so different that the general concept is made inapplicable.

In our view, the reasonable-expectations doctrine does not automatically mandate either pro-insurer or pro-insured results. It does place a burden on insurance companies to communicate coverage and exclusions of policies accurately and clearly. It does require that expectations of coverage by the insured be reasonable under the circumstances. Neither of those requirements seems overly burdensome. Properly used, the doctrine will result in coverage in some cases and in no coverage in others.

We hold that where the technical definition of burglary in a burglary insurance policy is, in effect, an exclusion from coverage, it will not be interpreted so as to defeat the reasonable expectations of the purchaser of the policy. Under the facts and circumstances of this case, Atwater reasonably expected that its burglary insurance policy with Western would cover the burglary that occurred. Our holding requires reversal as to policy coverage.

Notes and Questions

1. Why the Physical Damage Requirement?: There are two stated reasons for the physical damage requirement. First, insurance companies are trying to protect themselves from "inside jobs" by giving insured employers incentives to monitor their employees' fidelity. Clearly, the employers are in a better position to assess the risk of employee infidelity. Second, the requirement gives the insured company the incentive to invest in security precautions up to the point that any burglar must leave some physical trace of entry. Thus, the insurance company, by providing this "loophole" helps to align the insured's incentives to invest in the company's security.

2. Dealing with Moral Hazard: Insurance companies recognize the presence of moral hazard incentives and attempt to develop methods to deal with them. Clearly, Western's physical damage requirement attempts to address such issues. Given the outcome in *Atwater*, how might Western now go about protecting itself from moral hazard incentives? The court suggests that insurance companies now have a burden to communicate coverage and exclusions accurately and clearly. How would an insurance company prove that it communicated coverage and exclusions accurately and clearly? Would the insurance company face further incentive problems in collecting such evidence? One possibility is to have the insured place her initials on the contract next to exclusions which are explained by the insurer. Would such a practice help insurers to avoid the reasonable-expectations doctrine? Wouldn't the difficulty of obtaining proof of accurate and clear communication result in higher premiums, therefore, excluding some from insurance altogether?

3. Getting What You Paid For: The general policy of construing exclusions narrowly makes it more difficult for insurance companies to protect against moral hazard incentives. In effect, such a policy expands the insurers' risk exposure. Atwater paid premiums that were related to Western's expected risk exposure. Who bears the cost when Western is forced to pay on a risk not contemplated by the insurance contract? Did Atwater get more than it paid for? Economic efficiency would seem to suggest that the least cost avoider of risk should bear the cost? Does the court's result achieve this end?

c. Insurer's Duty to Settle

The insurance market, like any other voluntary market, is founded on mutually beneficial exchange. The claim's payment process, as indicated by the prior cases in this section, can often result in conflicts between the insured and the insurer. Potential conflicts arise when a plaintiff is attempting to negotiate a settlement with an insured defendant and the defendant's insurance company. Consider the incentives faced by the insured and insurer in the following case.

Mowry v. Badger State Mutual Casualty Company
Supreme Court of Wisconsin
129 Wis. 2d 496; 385 N.W.2d 171 (1986)

OPINION BY: CECI, J.

This is a review of the circuit court's decision and judgment against Badger State Mutual Casualty Company (Badger State) in the amount of $159,000. In a decision filed on May 23, 1984, the circuit court for Waukesha county, Robert T. McGraw, circuit judge, held that Badger State breached its contract and committed bad faith in refusing to defend its insured and in refusing to settle the third-party claim of victim Bradley Mowry within the liability limits of an insurance policy. We reverse the judgment of the circuit court.

*   *   *

The issue is whether the circuit court erred in holding that Badger State breached its contract with its insured and committed the tort of bad faith in refusing to defend its insured and in refusing to negotiate a settlement within policy limits when Badger State had sought a separate trial on the issue of coverage, under sec. 803.04(2)(b). We address whether an insurer who receives and loses a separate trial on the issue of coverage and then immediately offers the policy limits under an insurance contract may be held liable for damages adjudged against its insured which exceed the liability limits of the insurance policy. We determine that, under the facts of this case, Badger State should not be held responsible for the excess judgment entered against its insured. The trial court erred in holding that Badger State breached its contractual duty to defend and that it committed bad faith in refusing to settle Mowry's claim within its insured's policy limits.

The historical facts of this case are undisputed. On May 3, 1975, Bradley Mowry, then age 19, was injured in an automobile accident and suffered serious bodily injury, including the amputation of part of one foot. He was a passenger in an automobile driven by Steven McCarthy. The vehicle left a roadway and collided with a bridge abutment. McCarthy's parents were insured by Badger State and had policy limits of $15,000 for damages to any one person and medical coverage up to $1,000.

Upon being notified of the accident, Badger State began to investigate the circumstances surrounding the accident. The claims manager for Badger State, John Graeber, concluded after reading the police report and interviewing all of the automobile's occupants that the case was one of probable liability on McCarthy's part. He also determined that the case would probably involve damages to Mowry in excess of the $16,000 policy limits.

Badger State's investigations indicated to it, however, that a question of policy coverage existed. The question revolved around the ownership of the vehicle which McCarthy was driving at the time of the accident. The insurer believed that it was unclear whether McCarthy or his parents were the true owners of the automobile involved in the accident. Its investigation disclosed that the car was titled in McCarthy's mother's name, but that McCarthy had paid for the car with his own money, did not need permission to drive the car, and had told several people at the scene of the accident that he owned the vehicle and that it was uninsured. Given these circumstances, Graeber concluded that the issue of ownership was debatable and that a serious question of coverage had arisen.

In March, 1976, ten months after the accident, Mowry filed suit against McCarthy, McCarthy's parents, Badger State, and an insurance agent. * * *... Mowry's counsel and other parties present agreed to a bifurcated trial in which a determination on coverage would precede any trial on the issue of liability. In relating the events of the pretrial conference to Badger State, Attorney Frauen wrote, "Everyone seemed to feel that if the coverage issue were resolved, the rest of the case would not have to be tried." Mowry's counsel reiterated Mowry's offer of settlement on September 26, 1977, but Badger State again refused to accept it.

A subsequent stipulation and order set April 4, 1979, as the commencement date for the trial on the issue of coverage; the issues of liability and damages were to be held in abeyance until the resolution of the coverage issue. On March 12, 1979, approximately three weeks before the coverage trial, Mowry once more demanded that Badger State pay the limits of McCarthy's liability insurance policy plus $ 1,000 under the medical payments coverage; he set a March 23, 1979, deadline for its acceptance. Badger State's counsel, in correspondence to Mowry's counsel, stated that he felt the settlement demand was contrary to the stipulation and order separating the coverage issue from the liability and damages issues: "The court has in fact bifurcated the trial...to resolve the coverage dispute before proceeding with the plaintiff's case." Mowry's counsel responded that he believed that stipulating to a bifurcation of issues "should not in any way be construed as barring plaintiff from attempting to negotiate settlement of his entire claim."

Badger State refused Mowry's March 12 settlement offer. On April 4, 1979, the coverage issue was tried before a jury. The jury returned a verdict the next day which found that McCarthy's parents owned the vehicle in question at the time of the accident. Coverage was thereby afforded Steven McCarthy under the policy.

On April 6, 1979, Badger State offered the limits on its liability policy and medical payments coverage. On January 10, 1980, Badger State's counsel informed McCarthy that it would assume McCarthy's defense in the action. Following negotiations between counsel for Mowry and Badger State, the parties entered into a stipulation of judgment in October, 1980, thereby rendering a trial on the liability and damages issues unnecessary. The judgment was in favor of Mowry and against Badger State for $ 16,000 and against Steven McCarthy for $175,000. The stipulation further called for McCarthy to assign to Mowry any and all causes of action which McCarthy might have against Badger State, in satisfaction of Mowry's judgment against McCarthy. Following that stipulation and entry of judgment, Mowry, suing under McCarthy's assignment of rights, brought the present action against Badger State for bad faith and breach of contract.

The circuit court, in holding that Badger State breached its contract in refusing to defend and that it committed bad faith in refusing to negotiate a settlement, was indignant that an insurer would delay settlement negotiations until the coverage issue has been judicially determined, particularly when liability and excess damages are undisputed. The court felt that Badger State's posture of not negotiating a settlement until the determination of the coverage issue placed all the risk of an excess judgment on the insured. It found that an insurance company who refuses to defend and refuses to negotiate may not protect itself from a claim for damages in excess of policy limits by tendering the policy limits only upon losing the coverage issue of a bifurcated trial. Citing *Luke v. American Family Mut. Ins. Co.*, 476 F.2d 1015 (8th Cir. 1973), Judge McGraw stated that the proper rule should be " 'when an offer of settlement within the policy limits has been made and ignored, a good faith refusal to defend is not a valid defense to a claim in excess of the policy limits....' " *Luke*, 476 F.2d at 1021. The court then awarded Mowry damages in the amount of $159,000, representing the stipulated amount of liquidated damages for which Badger State would be liable in any action brought by Mowry as assignee against Badger State.

Badger State appealed. The court of appeals, in its certification memorandum, framed the issue to be whether an insurance carrier "should be held liable for damages in excess of its policy coverage where its belief that there was no coverage led it to reject" an earlier offer of settlement within the policy limits. The court noted that this particular scenario presents an unaddressed area of insurance law in this state.

The parties assert the same arguments here as they did below. Mowry states that, in refusing to negotiate a settlement and in refusing to defend McCarthy, Badger State breached contractual and fiduciary duties it owed to McCarthy. Badger State argues that it committed no bad faith in pursuing a fairly debatable coverage question within the framework of a bifurcated trial. In effect, it argues that any duty to negotiate a settlement is suspended when a bifurcated trial has been granted on a threshold issue of coverage. If it breached its contractual duty to defend, Badger State believes that damages should be limited to the liability limits of the policy. Because we hold that Badger State did not act in bad faith, nor did it breach its contractual duties owed to McCarthy, we do not reach the matter of calculation of damages.

We note the competing interests on each side of this case. When an insurer is certain of its insured's liability for an accident and where damages to the victim exceed policy limits, the insurer would normally be responsible for indemnifying its insured to the extent of its policy limits. The insurer, however, experiences a conflict of interests whenever an offer of settlement within policy limits is received where a legitimate question of coverage under the policy also exists. See, Keeton, *Liability Insurance and Responsibility for Settlement*, 67 Harv. L. Rev. 1136 (1954). See also, *Hilker v. Western Automobile Ins. Co.*, 204 Wis. 1, 14, 235 N.W. 413 (1931) (on rehearing). The insurer will be reluctant to settle within policy limits if there is a likelihood that coverage does not exist. On the other hand, an insurer's failure to settle a victim's claim within policy limits may subject an insured to a judgment in excess of his policy limits. This case presents a good example of these conflicting interests.

BAD FAITH CLAIM

An insurer owes a general duty to its insured to settle or compromise a claim made against the insured. Hilker, 204 Wis. at 13. This duty does not arise out of an express contractual provision; rather, it is implied from the terms of the contract which give the insurer the absolute control of the defense of the action against the insured. Id. at 13–14.

The insurer has the right to exercise its own judgment in determining whether a claim should be settled or contested. But "exercise of this right should be accompanied by considerations of good faith." Id. at 14. In order to be made in good faith, a decision not to settle a claim must be based on a thorough evaluation of the underlying circumstances of the claim and on informed interaction with the insured. This gives rise to several obligations on the part of the insurer. First, the insurer must exercise reasonable diligence in ascertaining facts upon which a good-faith decision to settle or not settle must be based. Second, where a likelihood of liability in excess of policy limits exists, the insurer must so inform the insured so that the insured might properly protect himself. Id. at 15–16. Third, the insurer must keep the insured timely abreast of any settlement offers received from the victim and of the progress of settlement negotiations. *Baker v. Northwestern Nat. Casualty Co.*, 22 Wis. 2d 77, 83, 125 N.W.2d 370 (1963).

These three obligations arise as a result of the insurer's general duty owed to its insured to settle a claim. The duty to settle, in turn, emanates from the contractual terms giving the insurer the absolute control of the defense of the victim's action against the insured. Because the insured has given up something of value to the insurer—namely, the right to defend and settle a claim—the insurer has been said to be in the position of a fiduciary with respect to an insured's interest in settlement of a claim. *See, Alt v. American Family Mut. Ins. Co.*, 71 Wis. 2d 340, 348, 237 N.W.2d 706 (1976). Whenever a question of policy coverage exists, however, an insurer's duty to settle under the contract is in doubt. Its duty to settle is dependent upon whether the policy extends coverage for the circumstances underlying the harm sustained. Mowry argues that the insurer's mistaken decision about the nonexistence of coverage should render Badger State liable for the excess judgment entered against the insured. He does not assert that Badger State breached any of the three traditional obligations arising out of the general duty to settle. Rather, he asserts that Badger State acted in bad faith in deciding to disclaim coverage where it was convinced that no real issue as to liability or damages existed. Moreover, he argues that Badger State's liability for damages caused by its refusal to settle an excess liability claim is not excused by a good-faith failure to defend.

To support his argument, Mowry cites cases from other jurisdictions which ostensibly are on point. In *Luke*, 476 F.2d 1015, the court held that an insurer who denied coverage to its insured because the insurer doubted that coverage existed under the contract was liable to the insured's assignees for the entire excess judgment for the breach of its duty to settle. Like the instant case, the insurer in *Luke* believed that an issue as to automobile ownership had arisen. The insurer denied coverage on that basis. It also received several offers of settlement within policy limits. However, the offers were ignored. In addition, the insurance company refused to consider a declaratory action concerning the coverage issue. Despite this conduct, the lower court held that the insurer exercised good faith in refusing to provide coverage. Id. at 1018–20.

The Eighth Circuit Court of Appeals found that the insurer refused to settle and refused to defend and, therefore, had breached its contract with the insured. Good faith, the court found, is irrelevant to a breach of contract action. "When an insurer refuses to defend and, additionally, refuses to accept a reasonable settlement within the policy limits, the company's liability for damages may be measured as well by its rejection of the offer to settle and may thus exceed the policy limits." Id. at 1020.

We do not find *Luke* to be persuasive in the present situation. First, in this case there was no breach of contract for failure to defend (for reasons which will be discussed below) as there was in Luke. Good faith, although of no importance in breach of contract actions, is a consideration in actions claiming a breach of the duty to settle, which arises out of fiduciary principles. Alt, 71 Wis. 2d at 348. *Johnson v. American Family Mut. Ins. Co.*, 93 Wis. 2d 633, 646, 287 N.W.2d 729 (1980). Second, the insurer in *Luke* refused the plaintiff's offer to hold the suits in abeyance in order to give the insurer an opportunity to file a declaratory judgment suit. Here, Badger State sought out an agreement based on a statutory provision whereby the coverage issue could be judicially determined prior to any liability and damages issues. It did not simply ignore the victim's claim, as the insurer in *Luke* apparently did.

Mowry also cites *Comunale v. Traders & General Ins. Co.*, 50 Cal. 2d 654, 328 P.2d 198 (1958). Comunale involves another "refusal to defend" case. The insurer, believing that the insurance contract did not provide coverage for the victim's injury, refused to defend its insured. The trial proceeded to judgment against the insured, which included an award to the victim in excess of the insured's policy limits. Under assignment, the victim sued the insurer. The Supreme Court of California stated,

> "When there is great risk of a recovery beyond the policy limits so that the most reasonable manner of disposing of the claim is a settlement which can be made within those limits, a consideration in good faith

of the insured's interest requires the insurer to settle the claim. Its unwarranted refusal to do so constitutes a breach of the implied covenant of good faith and fair dealing." 50 Cal. 2d at 659, 328 P.2d at 201.

That court then held the insurer liable for the excess judgment entered against the insured, representing the insured's damages for breach of the duty to settle.

The *Comunale rule*, in effect, renders an insurer strictly liable for any decision not to settle within policy limits, whether or not made in good faith, when a subsequent judgment against the insured exceeds policy limits:

> " 'An insurer who denies coverage does so at its own risk, and, although its position may not have been entirely groundless, if the denial is found to be wrongful it is liable for the full amount which will compensate the insured for all the detriment caused by the insurer's breach of the express and implied obligations of the contract. 50 Cal. 2d at 660, 328 P.2d at 202.' " *Johansen v. California State Auto. Assn. Inter-Ins. Bureau*, 15 Cal. 3d 9, 15, 538 P.2d 744, 123 Cal. Rptr. 288 (1975).

In *Johansen*, the California court further explained the upshot of its strict liability approach:

> "[T]he only permissible consideration in evaluating the reasonableness of the settlement offer becomes whether, in light of the victim's injuries and the probable liability of the insured, the ultimate judgment is likely to exceed the amount of the settlement offer. Such factors as the limits imposed by the policy, a desire to reduce the amount of future settlements, or a belief that the policy does not provide coverage, should not affect a decision as to whether the settlement offer in question is a reasonable one." 15 Cal. 3d at 16, 538 P.2d at 748–49.

Although we acknowledge the apparent goal of the California approach—to protect the insured from liability for an excess judgment by placing the risk of an erroneous decision not to settle on an insurer—we decline to accept that strict approach for this jurisdiction. Such a policy is unduly oppressive on insurance companies and would force them to settle claims where coverage may be dubious. The California approach is particularly unseemly in a jurisdiction such as our own, where an insurer may seek judicial determination of coverage issues prior to litigating liability and damages issues. See, sec. 803.04(2)(b), Stats. The California approach is unrealistic if only to the extent that an insurer's belief that an insurance policy does or does not provide coverage must necessarily "affect a decision as to whether the settlement offer in question is a reasonable one." *Johansen*, 15 Cal. 3d at 16, 538 P.2d at 749.

We have held that an insurer has a right to exercise its own judgment in deciding whether to settle or contest a claim, within parameters of good faith considerations. *Hilker*, 204 Wis. at 14. An insurer need not accept every offer of settlement within policy limits under sanction of liability for an excess judgment against its insured. See, *Johnson*, 93 Wis. 2d at 645–46. The *Hilker* and *Johnson* cases did not involve an issue of coverage as a basis for denial of settlement offers. Whether an insurer who rejects an offer to settle within policy limits because of a coverage question shall be liable for some measure of damages upon a determination of coverage depends upon whether the insurer acted in bad faith in determining that a coverage question existed. The tort of bad faith is "the knowing failure to exercise an honest and informed judgment." *Anderson v. Continental Ins. Co.*, 85 Wis. 2d 675, 692, 271 N.W.2d 368 (1978). To hold that Badger State breached its duty to settle requires a finding that it committed the tort of bad faith.[3] Badger State asks this court to adopt the standard set forth in Anderson.

Bad faith in deciding to litigate rather than settle a claim involves more than a mere finding of negligence on the part of the insurer. *Warren v. American Family Mut. Ins. Co.*, 122 Wis. 2d 381, 385, 361 N.W.2d 724 (Ct. App. 1984). Where there is no bad faith, an insured (or an insured's assignee) may not "surcharge an overage against his insurance company merely because of" any possible negligence on the insurer's part in deciding to litigate rather than to settle. *Baker v. Northwestern Nat. Casualty Co.*, 26 Wis. 2d 306, 314–15, 132 N.W.2d 493 (1965).

In *Anderson*, a first-party claim case, this court held that an insurance company may challenge claims which are fairly debatable. 85 Wis. 2d at 693. We said,

> "To show a claim for bad faith, a plaintiff must show the absence of a reasonable basis for denying benefits of the policy and the defendant's knowledge or reckless disregard of the lack of a reasonable basis for denying the claim." Id. at 691.

An insurer will have committed the tort of bad faith only when it has denied a claim without a reasonable basis for doing so, that is, when the claim is not fairly debatable.

This court has held that in third-party claim situations, it is not bad faith for an insurer to refuse to settle a victim's claim "under the bona fide belief that the insurer might defeat the action...." *Johnson*, 93 Wis. 2d at 646. See also, *Maroney v. Allstate Ins. Co.*, 12 Wis. 2d 197, 200–01, 107 N.W.2d 261 (1961). Although the "bona fide belief" language applies to a third party's action against the insured, we similarly hold that it is not bad faith for an insurer to refuse to settle an insured's claim within the policy limits when the question of policy coverage is fairly debatable and when the grounds for the refusal, if determined in the insurer's favor, would wholly defeat the indemnity responsibility of the insurer to its insured.

We hold that the circuit court erred in finding in this case that Badger State committed bad faith by refusing to settle and negotiate a settlement within policy limits. A finding of bad faith must not be measured solely against a backdrop that coverage was ultimately found to exist under the policy. Bad faith should be found in this case only if there was no fairly debatable coverage question. However, the circuit court, sitting without a jury, did not use this standard to reach its bad faith conclusion. The court concluded that Badger State's posture of waiting to defend the action and to negotiate a settlement until the coverage issue was determined itself constituted bad faith. Because the circuit court did not rely on

---

3. We reiterate that Mowry does not assert that Badger State failed to meet any of the obligations arising out of the duty to settle. See, Baker, 22 Wis. 2d at 82–83. An insurer must exercise reasonable diligence in the undertaking of these obligations. *Hilker*, 204 Wis. at 15.

appropriate and applicable law in making its bad faith determination, its holding is an abuse of discretion and, as such, is erroneous. See, *Hartung v. Hartung*, 102 Wis. 2d 58, 66, 306 N.W.2d 16 (1981).

The upshot of the trial court's holding would be to require the insurer to accept an offer within policy limits even where a fairly debatable coverage question exists. We have, however, rejected the California approach, which would make an insurer strictly liable for an offer of settlement within policy limits.

Although this court might otherwise remand a matter to the circuit court for further consideration where the appropriate law has not been applied, we choose to decide the bad faith issue as a matter of law.

Bad faith is a determination to be made by the trier of fact. *Baker*, 26 Wis. 2d at 315. Like negligence, whether certain conduct constitutes bad faith raises a mixed question of fact and law. See, *Millonig v. Bakken*, 112 Wis. 2d 445, 450, 334 N.W.2d 80 (1983). First a question is raised with respect to what the party allegedly in bad faith did or failed to do. The second inquiry is whether a reasonable insurer would have denied policy coverage under the facts and circumstances of the particular case. See, *Anderson*, 85 Wis. 2d at 692. In instances in which such a matter is tried to a jury, and when the facts are undisputed and the evidence permits only one reasonable inference or conclusion, then the issue of bad faith is to be decided by the court as a matter of law, rather than by the fact finder as a question of fact. See, *Millonig*, 112 Wis. 2d at 450–51. In this case the issue of bad faith was tried to the court, not to a jury. With respect to the court's findings in such an instance,

> "[w]hen the principal facts in a case are undisputed and the controversy centers on what has been called ultimate conclusions of fact, or conclusions of law, this court has indicated it will not be bound by the findings of the trial court." *Chicago, Milwaukee, St. Paul & Pacific R.R. Co. v. Milwaukee*, 47 Wis. 2d 88, 96, 176 N.W.2d 580 (1970).

Here, because the principal facts underlying the bad faith claim are undisputed and because there is only one reasonable inference, we may review the matter of bad faith as a question of law without deference to the trial court or court of appeals.

Badger State's grounds for refusing the settlement offers within policy limits were that it did not believe that the car involved in the accident was owned by its insureds, McCarthy's parents. Badger State, therefore, concluded that the policy did not extend coverage to McCarthy through his parents. Mowry disputes Badger State's conclusion that the coverage question was fairly debatable. He notes that whether a matter is fairly debatable "implicates the question whether the facts necessary to evaluate the claim are properly investigated and developed or recklessly ignored and disregarded." *Anderson*, 85 Wis. 2d at 691. He asserts in his brief that Badger State recklessly ignored the fact that the automobile in question was registered in the name of Mildred McCarthy (who is one of the policy's two named insureds and Steven McCarthy's mother), that McCarthy's father contributed to the purchase price of the car, and that Mildred had driven the car as well as Steven, among other relevant facts.

Badger State responds that McCarthy did not need parental permission to operate the car, that McCarthy said at the accident site that the car was uninsured, and that McCarthy's father told McCarthy to obtain insurance on the car. In addition, Mowry's counsel conceded during the underlying bad faith trial before Judge McGraw that evidence existed which presented a jury issue on coverage. Mowry's counsel stated:

> "I'm willing to stipulate as I have always been that there was a jury issue on the question of coverage[,] period. As attempting to cloak it in the terms of the wise men to the west as being fairly debatable and so on, I object to, but your Honor, there is no question but what there was evidence which presented a jury issue on coverage."

Significantly, the original trial court bifurcated the liability and damages issues from the coverage issue and ordered that the issues of liability and damages be held in abeyance until the determination of the coverage issue. The court of appeals in its certification memorandum stated that the evidence for and against coverage "was at least somewhat balanced."

We hold that Badger State did not act in bad faith in initially denying coverage to McCarthy. The record establishes a reasonable basis for Badger State's denial of coverage. Although the vehicle was registered in Mildred McCarthy's name, other items within the record suggest Steven McCarthy's ownership of the vehicle. Eugene McCarthy, Steven's father, stated that Steven paid for the car with money from Steven's own checking account, but that Eugene also "gave him some money." McCarthy apparently had approached his father about the idea of "buy[ing] the car" from a third party. Steven, according to the elder McCarthy, paid $150 for the car, but Mildred McCarthy's name appeared on the title. McCarthy never had to ask his father or mother for permission to use the car. Eugene McCarthy suggested that his son obtain insurance on the vehicle. In a statement made to a Badger State representative, McCarthy claimed that his mother owned the car on the date of the accident but that he had paid for it. One of the vehicle's occupants on the date of the accident stated that McCarthy said at the accident scene that he owned the car and that it was uninsured.

Although the record itself does not conclusively establish that the vehicle in question was covered under the elder McCarthy's insurance policy (that task was undertaken and resolved by the jury in the coverage trial), the record sufficiently establishes that Badger State was presented with a fairly debatable coverage issue. There is no absence of a reasonable basis for Badger State's denial of coverage. The record gives no indication that Badger State failed to properly investigate the claim, or that important facts were recklessly ignored and disregarded. Badger State did not commit bad faith in failing to settle Mowry's claim within policy limits even though McCarthy's liability for the accident was probable and damages were concededly in excess of policy limits. The question of coverage under the policy was fairly debatable.

Badger State could have protected both its interests and its insured's interests by settling under a reservation of rights agreement, Mowry and the circuit court assert. The record reflects that Badger State's counsel and its claims manager considered such an option, but ultimately decided to pursue the bifurcation procedure. A reservation of rights agreement would result in a settlement of the injured's claims, while preserving the insurer's right to litigate the coverage issue. The insured benefits from this procedure because it is protected from excess judgment. Badger State argues, however, that the reservation of rights procedure will rarely result in the insurer's recouping the payments it made to the victim from the insured where coverage is found not to exist under the policy, because the insured may be judgment-proof.

An insurer is always at liberty to seek a reservation of its rights in settling a claim. But Badger State's failure to seek such a reservation in this case does not, by itself, constitute bad faith. Badger State merely sought a statutory mechanism to bifurcate the coverage issue from the liability and damages issues. To require an insurer to enter into a reservation of rights agreement in addition to proceeding within a separation framework would run contrary to the bifurcation allowed by sec. 803.04(2)(b), Stats. Even though Badger State's determination that coverage did not exist was wrong, its mistake does not mean that it acted in bad faith in refusing to settle if the issue of coverage was fairly debatable. Although the mere ordering of a separate trial on the coverage issue is not conclusive that the coverage issue was fairly debatable, we cannot conclude that failure to enter into a reservation of rights agreement when a bifurcated trial has been granted is bad faith. We note that none of the cases cited by Mowry (e.g., *Luke, Comunale,* and *Johansen*) dealt with situations where the insurer sought and was granted a statutory separation procedure similar to sec. 803.04(2)(b).

Mowry argues that it is inherently unfair for McCarthy to be liable for a judgment in excess of policy limits when the judgment could have been wholly avoided had Badger State settled within policy limits when it had the opportunity to do so. But to require an insurer to settle any claim within policy limits where the insured's liability and the victim's damages in excess of policy limits are relatively certain, without consideration as to whether coverage exists, may result in extortionate lawsuits against the insurer. See, *Anderson,* 85 Wis. 2d at 693. Section 803.04(2)(b), Stats., provides some measure of protection against pressure settlement situations in which an insurer might find itself. We cannot penalize an insurer merely for utilizing such a mechanism. The bad faith standard, moreover, strikes an acceptable balance between the insurer's and insured's competing interests concerning settlement offers within policy limits where liability and damages in excess of policy limits are apparent.

＊　＊　＊

When the insured's liability for an accident is undisputed and damage clearly exceeds policy limits and yet the insurer seeks a separate trial on a coverage issue, the insurer and insured may still interact to avoid an excess judgment against the insured. For example, Mowry's counsel extended several settlement offers to Badger State after a stipulation had been reached and after a separation order had been granted. Although Badger State's acceptance of any of Mowry's offers would have been contrary to its decision to litigate the coverage issue — to be sure, a requirement that Badger State accept any such offers under penalty of bad faith would emasculate any benefit of the statutory separation procedure — Badger State still had the obligation to inform its insured of settlement offers and negotiations. Once an insurer has rejected an offer, the insured should then have the opportunity to settle for the proffered amount. In this case, McCarthy may have wished to accept Mowry's $16,000 offer, thereby limiting his liability for Mowry's damages. If the coverage trial results in a finding of coverage, then the insurer would assume responsibility for its insured's indemnification. If coverage does not exist, then the insured will at least have limited its liability in what was concededly an excess liability case, rather than exposing itself to extensive liability. The victim should be willing to extend the same offer to the insured which it would extend to the insurer; if the victim is unwilling, the insurer and the insured might reasonably conclude that the offer was frivolous. An insurer may ignore a frivolous offer. *Baker*, 26 Wis. 2d at 313.

Because the trial court held that Badger State committed bad faith in refusing to negotiate or settle a claim within its policy limits and did not apply the fairly debatable standard to the coverage question, the trial court erred as a matter of law. We hold that when a coverage issue is fairly debatable, an insurer will not have acted in bad faith in refusing to settle within policy limits, even when the insured's liability for the incident is undisputed and when the victim's damages appear to exceed policy limits. Because no determination was made that the coverage issue was fairly debatable, the circuit court abused its discretion in holding that Badger State acted in bad faith and in holding it liable for McCarthy's excess judgment.

*   *   *

Notes and Questions

1. Specifying the Conflict of Interest: Mowry presents a clear conflict of interest between the insured and the insurer. The parties face a situation in which the insured's liability is near certain and there is a high probability that damages will be in excess of insurance coverage. Thus, the insured has a strong incentive to take any settlement offer that is within the coverage limits. However, to the extent that there is an issue regarding coverage, the insurer's incentives deviate from those of the insured. Specifically, if the insurer pays the settlement and later wins on the coverage issue, the chance of recovering the amount paid in settlement from the insured is remote. Therefore, the insurer prefers to decide the coverage issue first. In short, the issue in *Mowry* is who bears the risk that, by refusing settlement, damages in excess of the policy limits are awarded. Do the concept of freedom of contract and application of the Coase Theorem have any implications for your analysis of this conflict of interest?

2. Strict Liability Duty to Settle: Under a strict liability rule, the insurer always bears the risk of an excess judgment. Insurers could exercise reservation rights, but the value of such rights are diminished by the low probability of *ex post* collection. The court observes that such a rule provides an incentive for "extortionate" law suits. How is this so? Moreover, notice that a strict liability rule constrains the ability of an insurer to negotiate a settlement. In other words, the victim can offer to settle at the maximum required under the policy with a large degree of confidence that the offer will be accepted. Why is this so? How does a strict liability rule impact the cost of providing insurance? From a public policy perspective, why should cost matter?

3. Good Faith Duty to Settle: Under a good faith rule, the insurer can shift the risk of an excess judgment on to the insured. Does this prevent "extortionate" lawsuits and provide a greater degree of flexibility in negotiating settlements? Does a good faith rule place the risk of an excess judgment on the party who *ex ante* was the least cost avoider? How does a good faith rule impact the cost of providing insurance? From a public policy perspective is this a better result than under a strict liability rule?

3. Self-Insurance

Rather than purchasing insurance, some individuals decide to bear the risk themselves. That is, they self insure. Self insurance creates incentives to do a number of different things. First, individuals can invest resources to minimize the probability of an uncertain event occurring. Examples of this would be an individual clearing the brush away from the area surrounding their house to minimize the likelihood that their house will be burnt down in the event of a brush fire. Second, self-insurance also creates incentives to invest in security precautions to minimize the monetary loss in the event the contingency actually occurs. Thus, individuals could install a sprinkler system, fire alarms, smoke detectors with telephone links to the local fire station to minimize the monetary loss in the event that their dwelling catches on fire. Third, self-insurance gives individuals the incentive to set aside reserve funds to cover possible losses. Many large companies self insure their employees' health insurance. The companies often hire a third-party administrator to administer the self insurance process within the company in order to save on transactions costs and to take advantage of the administrator's expertise.

C. Risk and Market Prices

Markets help individuals and firms deal with uncertainty and risk by adjusting and discounting the market price to reflect the risk. This is clearly seen in the case of financial products where riskier stocks receive a higher return than less risky stocks. Similarly, unsafe products or services are often sold at a discount. For example, many people (perhaps mistakenly) believe that some of the discount airlines are not as safe as the major airlines and, thus, they are not willing to fly on the discount airlines even though the price is lower. One way to characterize the market adjustment process here is that the rates have to be lower on the low fare airlines in order to get people to take on the perceived increased risk associated with flying on those airplanes. In general, the market demand curve shifts back to the left as consumers react adversely to labeling of a product as "unsafe." The result is that unsafe products (that is, products that are perceived to be riskier than other products) sell at a price discount relative to the price of safer products.

1. Financial Products

Financial products offer perhaps the clearest evidence of market adjustment to risk. In general, investors must be compensated for greater risks with the expectation of higher returns. Consider two alternative investments, A and B. Both A and B have the same expected annual return for each of the next ten years. Thus, A and B have the same net present value. However, A offers a risk-free rate of return and B has considerable variance in the possible cash flow in each year. In order to induce investors to purchase asset B, it must be sold at a discount relative to A. By forcing the purchase price of B down, the return on that investment increases. Therefore, the market forces a higher return for the riskier investment.

The Rights of Creditors of Affiliated Corporations
Richard A. Posner
43 U. Chi. L. Rev. 499, 501–03 (1976).

Mr. A Smith wants to borrow $1 million to invest in a mining venture together with $2 million of his own money. He wants the loan for only a year since by the end of the year it will be apparent whether the venture has succeeded; if it has, he would then want to obtain longer-term financing. Since Smith is a man of means, if he gives his personal note to the lender the latter would regard a one-year loan of $1 million as riskless and would offer Smith the riskless short-term interest rate, say six percent. But Smith is reluctant to stake more than $2 million on the outcome of the mining venture. He proposes to the lender a different arrangement, whereby the lender will agree to look for repayment of the loan exclusively to the assets of the mining venture, if any exist, a year hence. Under this arrangement, Smith will be able to limit his liability to his investment in the venture.

The lender estimates that there is an 80 percent probability that the venture will be sufficiently successful to enable repayment of the loan and interest on the due date, and a 20 percent probability that the venture will fail so badly that there will be insufficient assets to repay even a part of the loan. On these assumptions[6] the solution to the lender's problem is purely mechanical; he must calculate the amount, payable at the end of a year, that when multiplied by 80 percent (the probability that payment will in fact be made) will equal $1,060,000, the repayment he would have received at the end of the year had he made the riskless loan. That amount is $1,325,000.[7] Accordingly, the lender will charge Smith 32.5 percent interest for the loan if Smith's obligation to repay is limited to the assets of the venture. At this rate of interest the lender is indifferent as between the riskless and the risky loan.

This example illustrates the fundamental point that the interest rate on a loan is payment not only for renting capital but also for the risk that the borrower will fail to return it. It may be wondered why the borrower might want to shift a part of the risk of business failure to the lender, given that he must compensate him for bearing added risk. There are two reasons why the lender might be the superior risk bearer. First, the lender may be in a better position than the borrower to appraise the risk. Compare the positions of the individual shareholder in a publicly held corporation and the banks that lend the corporation its working capital. It may be easier and hence cheaper for the bank to appraise the risk of a default and the resulting liability than it would be for the shareholder, who may know little or nothing about the business in which he has invested. Second, the borrower may be risk averse and the lender less so (or risk neutral, or even risk preferring).[8] Thus, unlimited liability would discour-

    6. Plus the additional assumption that the lender is "risk neutral." This term is explained in note 8 infra.

    7. Calculated by solving .8x = $106 for x.

    8. An individual is risk averse if he prefers the certain equivalent of an expected value to the expectation—the certainty of receiving $1 to a 10 percent chance of receiving $10. A risk preferrer would have the opposite preference, and a risk-neutral individual would be indifferent. A corporation is less likely to be risk averse than an individual because the shareholders of the corporation can offset any risks incurred by that corporation by holding a diversified portfolio of securities. Moreover, a large lender can eliminate or greatly reduce the

age investment in business ventures by individuals who wanted to make small, passive investments in such ventures. It would also discourage even substantial entrepreneurial investments by risk-averse individuals—and most individuals are risk averse.

A borrower could in principle negotiate with the lender for an express limited-liability provision. The more usual course, however, is to incorporate and have the corporation borrow the money. The basic principal of corporation law is that the shareholders of a corporation are not personally liable for the corporation's debts unless they agree to assume such liability. Corporate borrowing therefore automatically limits the borrower's liability to his investment in the corporation. The fact that the law permits Smith to limit his liability by conducting his mining venture in the corporate form does not imply, however, that the law is somehow tilted against creditors or enables venturers to externalize the risks of business failure.... Although incorporation permits Smith to shift a part of the risk of failure to the lender, there is no externality; the lender is fully compensated by the higher interest rate that the corporation must pay by virtue of enjoying limited liability. Moreover, the lender is free to insist as a condition of making the loan that Smith guarantee the debts of the corporation personally or that he consent to including in the loan agreement other provisions that will limit the lender's risk—though any reduction in the risk will reduce the interest rate the lender can charge since a portion of that rate is, as we have seen, compensation to the lender for agreeing to bear a part of the risk of the venture.

There is an instructive parallel here to a fundamental principle of bankruptcy law: the discharge of the bankrupt from his debts. This principle, which was originally developed for the protection of business rather than individual bankrupts, enables the venturer to limit his risk of loss to his current assets; he is not forced to hazard his entire earning capacity on the venture. Incorporation performs the same function of encouraging investment by enabling the risk averse to limit their risk of loss to their investment.

Far from externalizing the risks of business ventures, the principle of limited liability in corporation law facilitates a form of transaction advantageous to both investors and creditors; in its absence the supply of investment and the demand for credit might be much smaller than they are....

2. Products and Services: Risk Allocation and Contract Law

Prices for products and services adjust to reflect the risk associated with the transaction. In essence, freedom of contract allows parties to allocate risk according to which party is willing to accept the risk in light of the price adjustment. This subsection considers three areas where risk is allocated by contract.

---

risk of loss on a particular loan by holding a diversified portfolio of loans. On both counts it seems likely that individual investors would often be more averse to bearing unlimited personal liability for the failure of an enterprise in which they had invested than lenders would be to bearing the risk of that failure to the extent of their loan to the enterprise.

a. Assumption of Risk

Individuals often engage in activities that involve the risk of injury. The doctrine of assumption of the risk is a defense to an action in negligence which prohibits recovery due to injuries that an individual receives when he voluntarily exposes himself to a known and appreciated danger. Four elements are required to establish an assumption of the risk defense. First, the plaintiff must have knowledge of facts which constitute a dangerous condition. Second, plaintiff must know that the condition is dangerous. Third, plaintiff must appreciate the nature or extent of the danger. Fourth, plaintiff must voluntarily expose himself to the danger. Although in some cases, an assumption of the risk is expressly provided for in a written contract, the aforementioned elements make it clear that an implied of assumption of the risk is comparable to an implied contractual agreement.

Suppose, for example, that two electric drills available in a hardware store are priced at $20 and $50. It is explicitly stated on the package of the lower priced drill that it is not safe for use in drilling through concrete. A purchaser of the lower priced drill who plans to drill through concrete does so because the added protection of the more expensive drill is not worth the added cost. Thus, the purchaser assumes the risk of injury that may occur when drilling through concrete. Under contract law and tort law, the purchaser may not be able to recover damages from the manufacturer because voluntarily bearing the risk of injury often serves as a bar to recovery. However, a person can only assume known and appreciated risks. An example often given is that a spectator at a baseball game assumes a certain amount of risk that he or she will be injured if hit by a baseball. A spectator probably assumes the risk of being hit by a baseball in areas that are not protected by screens because most can appreciate the risk they are taking. However, spectators do not assume the risk that a ball will penetrate a protective screen and cause them harm since it is difficult to assess the risk of such an event.

Ordway v. Superior Court of Orange County

California Court of Appeals, Fourth District, Division 3
243 Cal.Rptr. 536 (1988)

CROSBY, Associate Justice.

Does reasonable implied assumption of risk remain a viable defense after the adoption of comparative fault? We hold it does.

I

Judy Casella, a veteran jockey who had ridden in 500 professional horse races without incident, was thrown from her mount and further injured when the equine fell and rolled over her during a quarterhorse race at Los Alamitos Race Course on January 3, 1983. The tragic chain of events began when Over Shadow, owned by petitioner Homer Ordway, tangled with another steed, Speedy Ball, who then stumbled in front of Casella's horse. The California Horse Racing Board determined the jockey riding Over Shadow violated a board rule by "crossing over without sufficient clearance, causing interference," and he was suspended for five racing days. Alleging "negligence, carelessness and unlawful conduct," Casella sued the riders, trainers, and owners of Over Shadow and Speedy Ball.

* * *

The initial question presented in this petition is whether the doctrine of reasonable implied assumption of risk survives in the era of comparative fault...

Courts and legal scholars have traditionally recognized three forms of assumption of risk. Express assumption of risk is exactly what the term describes: Where "the potential plaintiff agrees not to expect the potential defendant to act carefully, thus eliminating the potential defendant's duty of care, and acknowledging the possibility of negligent wrongdoing," the potential plaintiff has expressly assumed the risk of injury....

Reasonable implied assumption of risk is the inferred agreement to relieve a potential defendant of a duty of care based on the potential plaintiff's reasonable conduct in encountering a known danger. A second variety of implied assumption of risk is labeled unreasonable....

The relationship between the concepts of implied assumption of risk and contributory negligence has been the source of some confusion. The two doctrines are quite separate in one sense, but overlap in another. More than thirty years ago, our Supreme Court explained the basic differences between them as follows: "The defenses of assumption of risk and contributory negligence are based on different theories. Contributory negligence arises from a [plaintiff's] lack of due care. The defense of assumption of risk, on the other hand, will negative liability regardless of the fact that plaintiff may have acted with due care. [Citation.] It is available when there has been a voluntary acceptance of a risk and such acceptance, whether express or implied, has been made with knowledge and appreciation of the risk." Prescott v. Ralphs Grocery Co. (1954) 42 Cal.2d 158, 161–162, 265 P.2d 904...

* * *

In Segoviano v. Housing Authority (1983) 143 Cal.App.3d 162, 191 Cal.Rptr. 578, a player was injured during an amateur flag football game when an opponent, in violation of the rules, pushed him out of bounds. Ruling on an in limine motion, the trial court precluded the defendant, the institutional sponsor of the game, from relying on assumption of risk to defeat the plaintiff's claim. The plaintiff prevailed, but the jury discounted his award by 30 percent under comparative fault instructions.

Rejecting the notion "that a plaintiff who has reasonably assumed a risk may not recover damages because that form of assumption of risk negates defendant's duty of care to the plaintiff" (id., at p. 168, 191 Cal.Rptr. 578), Segoviano held only express assumption of risk remained a viable defense after Li. The appellate panel conceded Li explicitly merged only unreasonable assumption of risk into the concept of contributory negligence; but it concluded that where "the plaintiff's conduct [is] entirely reasonable under all of the circumstances, we find no basis in reason or equity for barring his recovery. Elimination of [reasonable implied assumption of risk] as a separate defense avoids punishing reasonable conduct." (Id., at p. 170, 191 Cal.Rptr. 578.) Accordingly, the court not only reversed the judgment but also held the plaintiff's recovery could not be reduced under comparative fault principles because his implied assumption of the risk of injury in a flag football game was reasonable and, as a matter of law, provided no basis for apportionment of the damages.

Having studied the problem anew, we remain unpersuaded by Segoviano's holding. In our view, that opinion turned the law on its head. If plaintiff reasonably consented to participate in a touch football game, how could defendant's sponsorship of the contest be any less reasonable? Plaintiff and defendant had an equal opportunity to anticipate the over-exuberance of one of the participants and the potential for injury. There is no principled basis upon which any responsibility should be assigned to the defendant under those circumstances. The defendant merely provided plaintiff with the chance to play; he was the one who chose to risk an injury. There is also a strong policy basis for absolving the defendant in such circumstances: encouragement of persons and entities to provide opportunities to engage in sports and recreational activities without fear of suits by the participating beneficiaries.

The correct analysis is this: The doctrine of reasonable implied assumption of risk is only another way of stating that the defendant's duty of care has been reduced in proportion to the hazards attendant to the event. Where no duty of care is owed with respect to a particular mishap, there can be no breach; consequently, as a matter of law, a personal injury plaintiff who has voluntarily—and reasonably—assumed the risk cannot prevail. Or stated another way, the individual who knowingly and voluntarily assumes a risk, whether for recreational enjoyment, economic reward, or some similar purpose, is deemed to have agreed to reduce the defendant's duty of care.

The Segoviano court may have been misled because the distinction between the "reasonable" and "unreasonable" plaintiff is superficially anomalous: The former's civil action is barred while the latter's is allowed to go to judgment, reduced only in proportion to fault. But the explanation has nothing to do with rewarding or punishing a plaintiff, as Segoviano suggests. Rather, it is found in the expectation of the defendant. He or she is permitted to ignore reasonably assumed risks and is not required to take extraordinary precautions with respect to them. The defendant must, however, anticipate that some risks will be unreasonably undertaken, and a failure to guard against those may result in liability.

For example, borrowing from an old legal saw, "[Because a] drunken man is as much entitled to a safe street, as a sober one, and much more in need of it" (Robinson v. Pioche (1855) 5 Cal. 460, 461), sidewalks should be constructed with safety in mind. If they are negligently built, inebriety will not bar a pedestrian's lawsuit for injury, although it may reduce his recovery.

Those who have taken a remunerative or recreational risk with a conscious awareness of all it entails, however, are on their own. A circus need not provide a net for an aerialist who does not want one. The owner of a dangerous piece of property, Niagara Falls for example, will have a complete defense to an action by a Hollywood stuntperson who, encased in a barrel, elects to enter the river above the falls. But the garden-variety inattentive member of the public who passes through a gate negligently left open, in the misguided belief that the water above the falls is safe for swimming, will only suffer a proportionate reduction in damages. A defendant must, under appropriate circumstances, anticipate the fool (which is merely another way of describing the careless and negligent). (Bigbee v. Pac. Tel. & Tel. Co. (1983) 34 Cal.3d 49, 192 Cal.Rptr. 857, 665 P.2d 947.)

The conduct of the stuntperson is "reasonable" in the eyes of the law, but not that of the negligent bather. Concededly, it does sound strange to decree that unreasonable plaintiffs may recover and reasonable ones may not; but the problem is not of law but semantics. If the "reasonable-unreasonable" labels were simply changed to "knowing and intelligent" versus "negligent or careless," the concepts would be more easily understood.

*   *   *

...[T]he doctrine of reasonable implied assumption of risk remains viable and, where applicable, provides a complete defense to a cause of action for personal injuries. This is so because the doctrine of reasonable implied assumption of risk, unlike its unreasonable sibling, involves a reduction of a defendant's duty of care. And if a defendant owes no duty, or a lesser one, his negligence provides a much narrower opening for a plaintiff's recovery of damages.

III

Having concluded that the doctrine of reasonable implied assumption of risk is alive and well, we discuss in this section its preclusive impact on Casella's lawsuit, specifically whether her action could be maintained on a theory of recklessness....

Historically, the doctrine of assumption of risk has provided a defense only to actions for negligence. It has little or no application in the case of intentional or reckless conduct. The reason is this: While a potential plaintiff who engages in dangerous activity is "held to have consented to the injury-causing events which are known, apparent or reasonably foreseeable consequences of the participation...participants do not consent to acts [by others] which are reckless or intentional." (Turcotte v. Fell, supra, 68 N.Y.2d at p. 439, 510 N.Y.S.2d 49, 502 N.E.2d 964.) While the line between negligent and intentional conduct is frequently obscured in sports injury litigation, we are satisfied it was not crossed here.

First, Casella's complaint alleged only that her injuries were caused by "the negligent, careless and unlawful manner in which the Defendants...rode,... owned and trained the horses, Over Shadow and Speedy Ball." She never used the words "reckless" or "intentional"; and neither expression would accurately characterize the defendant jockeys' conduct, as she herself described it. Her declaration in opposition to Ordway's motion for summary judgment explained, "[Over Shadow's jockey] severely guided his horse inside and in doing so crossed over and in front of other horses without looking to see whether he could safely do so. His horse crossed in front of Speedy Ball [whose jockey] did not take evasive action and the horses' legs tangled resulting in Speedy Ball tripping and falling onto the track...directly [in front of my mount]." (Emphasis added.) Casella's own assessment of the accident presents a classic case of negligence, i.e., a failure to exercise due care. But by participating in the horse race, she relieved others of any duty to conform their conduct to a standard that would exempt her from the risks inherent in a sport where large and swift animals bearing human cargo are locked in close proximity under great stress and excitement.

Casella seeks to avoid the negligence hurdle by equating suspension of one of the defendant jockeys for violation of California Horse Racing Board Rule No. 1699 (the equine equivalent of an unsafe lane change) with intentional conduct.

We are not persuaded. Mens rea plays no part in the board rule. The penalty is levied when an infraction occurs; no evidence was presented to the trial court which suggested a jockey is suspended only where the conduct is determined to have been intentional.

Casella's allegations are legally indistinguishable from those found insufficient in Turcotte v. Fell, supra, 68 N.Y.2d 432, 510 N.Y.S.2d 49, 502 N.E.2d 964. There, a jockey was injured in an accident very similar to Casella's. He sued his fellow competitor, who had been sanctioned for violating New York's foul riding rule, and the owner of the horse he rode. The trial court dismissed the complaint because there were "no allegations of [the defendant jockey's] wanton, reckless, or intentional conduct." (Id., at p. 436, 510 N.Y.S.2d 49, 502 N.E.2d 964.) The high court of New York unanimously affirmed the dismissal, noting the plaintiff's failure to allege intentional conduct by the defendant rider was fatal to his cause of action: "As the [foul riding] rule recognizes, bumping and jostling are normal incidents of the sport. They are not...flagrant infractions unrelated to the normal method of playing the game and done without any competitive purpose. Plaintiff does not claim that [the other jockey] intentionally or recklessly bumped him, he claims only that as a result of carelessness, [the defendant] failed to control his mount....[A] professional clearly understands the usual incidents of competition resulting from carelessness, particularly those which result from the customarily accepted method of playing the sport, and accepts them. They are within the known, apparent and foreseeable dangers of the sport and not actionable...." (Id., at p. 441, 510 N.Y.S.2d 49, 502 N.E.2d 964, emphasis added.)

Casella's allegations also stand in sharp contrast to the facts...Tomjanovich v. California Sports, Inc. (S.D.Tex., Oct. 10, 1979, No. 78-243). In Tomjanovich, a professional basketball player was severely injured when an opposing player deliberately struck a vicious blow to his face. Tomjanovich sued in federal district court in Texas, and the law of California was applied. The verdict in his favor was in excess of $2 million. The matter settled pending appeal.

A verdict for Tomjanovich was clearly proper. He did assume the risk of being hit in the face by a flying elbow in the course of defending against an opponent's jump shot, suffering a painful insult to his instep by a size-16 foot descending with a rebound, or even being knocked to the court by the sheer momentum of a seven-footer driving home a slam dunk. But the scope of his consent did not extend to an intentional blow considerably beyond the expected risks inherent in basketball. Intentional fouls are part of that game. But where the intent is to injure and the force used is far greater than necessary to accomplish a legitimate objective within the scope of play, a defendant may not prevail on an assumption of risk defense.

*   *   *

Despite Casella's disingenuous assertion that "I did not consider at the time of this race that I was participating in a dangerous activity," professional riders must realize that accidents are always possible and not uncommon. The degree of the risk anticipated varies, of course, from sport to sport. In prize fighting bodily harm is to be expected, but pugilists do not consent to be stabbed or shot in the ring. At the other extreme, in bridge or table tennis bodily harm is not contemplated at all. The correct rule is this: If the defendant's actions, even those which might cause incidental physical damage in some sports, are within the ordinary expectations of the participants—such as blocking in football, checking in hockey, knock-out punches in boxing, and aggressive riding in horse racing— no cause of action can succeed based on a resulting injury. It is of no moment that the participants may be penalized for these actions by the officials. Routine rule violations, such as clipping in football, low blows in boxing, and fouls in horse races are common occurrences and within the parameters of the athletes' expectations.

Here defendant jockeys were attempting to win a horse race. There has never been any suggestion that they, much less the owners of their horses, were motivated by a desire to injure plaintiff. Defendants' conduct, while perhaps negligent, was within the range to be anticipated by the other riders, or should have been. As a professional rider, Casella reasonably assumed the risk of her tragic injury. As with other persons who reasonably assume similar risks, her remedy was to purchase insurance from her athletic income beforehand, not to pursue a lawsuit against her counterparts in the sport afterward. The action, accordingly, is barred as a matter of law. Defendants are entitled to summary judgment....

Notes and Questions

1. Risk Preferences and Assumption of Risk: In general, it is costly for a defendant to satisfy a duty of care owed to a plaintiff. Often, the costs of providing the level of care indicated by tort are passed on to consumers in the form of higher prices, entrance fees, rates, etc. However, some consumers might be willing to release the potential tortfeasor from its duty in order to obtain a lower price. In economic terms, some members of society are risk-seekers. The assumption of risk doctrine allows risk seekers to contract to bear a risk when they have a comparative advantage in risk bearing. That is, the assumption of risk doctrine facilitates voluntary, mutually beneficial exchange.

2. Least Cost Avoiders and Assumption of Risk: Economic efficiency is enhanced if risk is reduced in the least costly manner. In the absence of the assumption of risk doctrine, defendants bear the cost of reducing risk regardless of whether they have a comparative advantage in doing so. In some instances, the party to whom a duty is owed may be able to insure against the occurrence of particular risks more cheaply than the defendant. Such parties would find it in their economic self-interest to relieve the defendant of its duty of care by express agreement.

3. Intentional and Reckless Conduct: The court observes that traditionally assumption of risk has not provided a defense to intentional or reckless conduct. Is the court's rationale for this consistent with economic reasoning?

b. The Bargaining Principle and Least-Cost Risk Avoider

Contract law is a system of rules for enforcing promises. It demonstrates the extent to which our society allows people to make promises or commitments that are legally binding, and the legal consequences of failure by one party to perform as promised. Transaction costs, primarily negotiation and enforcement costs, increase the costs of exchange and thus decrease the number of mutually beneficial exchanges. Contract law reduces transaction costs by imposing external rules that create rights and duties in the parties to the exchange and provides remedies in the event the duties are breached. Instantaneous exchanges, such as the purchase of a Diet Coke from a street vendor, occur without any assistance from contract law. Thus, contract law is most important in situations where the negotiations are not immediately followed by simultaneous performances on both sides of the transaction.

Of course, voluntary, mutually beneficial exchanges take place in the absence of contract law. Continued dealing with the same parties reduces negotiation costs and also increases the likelihood that a contract will be performed in good faith. One may seek to reduce transaction costs by limiting his trading partners to only those who have a reputation for honesty and fair dealing. In a sense, therefore, the market controls dishonest and unfair behavior by reducing the demand for the goods and services provided by dishonest and unfair traders. That is, market adjustments act as an enforcement mechanism.

Contract law reduces transaction costs in a number of ways. First, contract law enforces contract terms by imposing costs—typically in the form of courts ordering the payment of damages—on parties who breach their promises. For example, contract law enforces agreed upon allocations of risk after the occurrence of a contingency that may make performance appear unattractive to one of the parties. Second, the common law of contracts provides a stock of standard form, off-the-rack, contractual provisions that specify the basic details and fill gaps in negotiated contracts. Unless contradicted by the explicit terms of a contract, the common law rules are an implied part of all contracts. This reduces transaction costs by allowing contracting parties to form enforceable contracts without having to specify every standard of performance and without having to negotiate the allocation of risk associated with every conceivable contingency. All executory contracts face the risk of disruption due to totally unanticipated contingencies—circumstances with which the contract cannot deal because the contracting parties don't know what might occur—and contract law provides the basic rules to deal with various contingencies. Third, contract law discourages careless behavior in contracting by penalizing behavior which induces other parties to act in reliance on the first party's actions or representations. In effect, this saves transaction costs by allowing contracting parties to rely on the other party's actions without having to worry about what information the other party really means to convey.

Contract law produces the greatest reduction in transaction costs if the off-the-rack contract rules supplied by contract law mimic the agreements for which most contracting parties would bargain if negotiation costs were zero. For example, if every contracting party would agree that payment should be in U.S. dollars, it is clear that negotiation costs can be reduced by making such a term an implicit part of every contract. This **bargaining principle** provides an analytical framework for analyzing the rules of contract law, as well as other substantive areas of law such as corporation law and bankruptcy.

In applying the bargaining principle, two observations should be kept in mind. First, freedom of contract is an overriding philosophy of contract law—it is almost always possible for the contracting parties to contract around the off-the-rack rules when the contracting parties decide that it is in their interest to do so. Conceptually, if the benefits of altering the standard form rules are greater than the transaction costs of contracting, then the parties are made better off through modification of the standard contract rules. The philosophy of freedom of contract also explains why the common law of contracts is likely to be efficient—in the sense that it comes close to satisfying the bargaining principle. Inefficient contract rules will not be used—contracting parties will contract around them until the courts recognize that the old default rules should be abandoned because of disuse.

Second, although it is not clear what terms most bargaining parties would negotiate in the absence of negotiation costs, some general principles can be derived from assumptions about economic behavior and mutually beneficial exchange. Most economic actors are risk averse—they are willing to pay (or accept a lower price) in order to increase certainty. Moreover, because negotiating parties wish to maximize the total gain from the exchange, they would allocate risk to the lowest-cost risk avoider (i.e., the party with the comparative advantage at avoiding or bearing risk) if transaction costs were zero. This analysis has implications for how courts should interpret contracts when an unforeseeable contingency occurs—courts should allocate risk according to how the contracting parties would have allocated the risk themselves if they had known of the risk at the time of contracting. This determination requires analysis of the relative risk-bearing abilities of the contracting parties. In general, the party with the comparative advantage at bearing a particular risk—the so-called least-cost risk avoider—will be forced to bear the risk.

c. The Allocation of Risk

The *ex ante* expected mutually beneficial aspects of the contract may change as a result of the occurrence of some unforeseen contingency prior to the execution of the contract, so that *ex post* the contract appears to be one-sided to the extent that the performance of the contract is not mutually beneficial. The fact that contract law almost always requires the performance of such contracts suggests that the law implicitly recognizes the importance of risk allocation through contract.

Eastern Air Lines v. Gulf Oil Corporation
United States District Court
415 F.Supp. 429 (1975)

D.J. JAMES LAWRENCE KING.

Eastern Air Lines, Inc., hereafter Eastern, and Gulf Oil Corporation, hereafter Gulf, have enjoyed a mutually advantageous business relationship involving the sale and purchase of aviation fuel for several decades.

This controversy involves the threatened disruption of that historic relationship and the attempt, by Eastern, to enforce the most recent contract between the parties. On March 8, 1974, the correspondence and telex communications between the corporate entities culminated in a demand by Gulf that Eastern must meet its demand for a price increase or Gulf would shut off Eastern's supply of jet fuel within fifteen days.

Eastern responded by filing its complaint with this court, alleging that Gulf had breached its contract and requesting preliminary and permanent mandatory injunctions requiring Gulf to perform the contract in accordance with its terms. By agreement of the parties, a preliminary injunction preserving the status quo was entered on March 20, 1974, requiring Gulf to perform its contract and directing Eastern to pay in accordance with the contract terms, pending final disposition of the case.

Gulf answered Eastern's complaint, alleging that the contract was not a binding requirements contract, was void for want of mutuality, and, furthermore, was "commercially impracticable" within the meaning of Uniform Commercial Code § 2-615; Fla. Stat. §§ 672.614 and 672.615.

The extraordinarily able advocacy by the experienced lawyers for both parties produced testimony at the trial from internationally respected experts who described in depth economic events that have, in recent months, profoundly affected the lives of every American.

[After determining that the requirements contract was enforceable and that Eastern had not breached it, the court addressed the § 2-615 issue.]

In short, for U.C.C. § 2-615 to apply there must be a failure of a pre-supposed condition, which was an underlying assumption of the contract, which failure was unforeseeable, and the risk of which was not specifically allocated to the complaining party. The burden of proving each element of claimed commercial impracticability is on the party claiming excuse. Ocean Air Tradeways, Inc. v. Arkay Realty Corp., 480 F.2d 1112, 1117 (9th Cir. 1973).

The modern U.C.C. § 2-615 doctrine of commercial impracticability has its roots in the common law doctrine of frustration or impossibility and finds its most recognized illustrations in the so-called "Suez Cases", arising out of the various closings of the Suez Canal and the consequent increases in shipping costs around the Cape of Good Hope. Those cases offered little encouragement to those who would wield the sword of commercial impracticability. As a leading British case arising out of the 1957 Suez closure declared, the unforeseen cost increase that would excuse performance "must be more than merely onerous or expensive. It must be positively unjust to hold the parties bound." Ocean Tramp Tankers v. V/O Sovfracht (The Eugenia), 2 Q.B. 226, 239 (1964)....

Other recent American cases similarly strictly construe the doctrine of commercial impracticability. For example, one case found no U.C.C. defense, even though costs had doubled over the contract price, the court stating, "It may have been unprofitable for defendant to have supplied the pickers, but the evidence does not establish that it was impossible. A mere showing of unprofitability, without more, will not excuse the performance of a contract." Schafer v. Sunset Packing Co., 256 Or. 539, 474 P.2d 529, 530 (1970).

Recently, the Seventh Circuit has stated: "The fact that performance has become economically burdensome or unattractive is not sufficient for performance to be excused." We will not allow a party to a contract to escape a bad bargain merely because it is burdensome." "[The] buyer has a right to rely on the party to the contract to supply him with goods regardless of what happens to the market price. That is the purpose for which such contracts are made," Neal-Cooper Grain Co. v. Texas Gulf Sulfur Co., 508 F.2d 283, 293, 294 (7th Cir. 1974)....

[The court held that Gulf had not satisfied the conditions for excused performance.]

But even if Gulf had established great hardship under U.C.C. § 2-615, which it has not, Gulf would not prevail because the events associated with the so-called energy crises were reasonably foreseeable at the time the contract was executed. If a contingency is foreseeable, it and its consequences are taken outside the scope of U.C.C. § 2-615, because the party disadvantaged by fruition of the contingency might have protected himself in his contract, Ellwood v. Nutex Oil Co., 148 S.W.2d 862 (Tex.Civ.App.1941).

The foreseeability point is illustrated by Foster v. Atlantic Refining Co., 329 F.2d 485, 489 (5th Cir. 1964). There an oil company sought release from a gas royalty contract because the royalty provisions of the contract did not contain an escalation clause, with the result that the oil company came to receive a far smaller share of the royalties than it would then have been able to obtain on the market. Citing *Ellwood* with approval, the Fifth Circuit answered the oil company's argument as follows:

> "(One) who unconditionally obligates himself to do a thing possible of performance, must be held to perform it (citing cases); and though performance, subsequent to the contract, may become difficult or even impossible, (this) does not relieve the promisor, and particularly where he might have foreseen the difficulty and impossibility (citing cases)."

The record is replete with evidence as to the volatility of the Middle East situation, the arbitrary power of host governments to control the foreign oil market, and repeated interruptions and interference with the normal commercial trade in crude oil. Even without the extensive evidence present in the record, the court would be justified in taking judicial notice of the fact that oil has been used as a political weapon with increasing success by the oil-producing nations for many years, and Gulf was well aware of and assumed the risk that the OPEC nations would do exactly what they have done.

IV. REMEDY

Having found and concluded that the contract is a valid one, should be enforced, and that no defenses have been established against it, there remains for consideration the proper remedy.

...Gulf presently supplies Eastern with 100,000,000 gallons of fuel annually or 10 percent of Eastern's total requirements. If Gulf ceases to supply this fuel, the result will be chaos and irreparable damage.

...It has previously been found and concluded that Eastern is entitled to Gulf's fuel at the prices agreed upon in the contract. In the circumstances, a decree of specific performance becomes the ordinary and natural relief rather than the extraordinary one. The parties are before the court, the issues are squarely framed, they have been clearly resolved in Eastern's favor, and it would be a vain, useless and potentially harmful exercise to declare that Eastern has a valid contract, but leave the parties to their own devices. Accordingly, the preliminary injunction heretofore entered is made a permanent injunction and the order of this court herein. * * *

Notes and Questions

1. Ex Ante and Ex Post Fairness: Reciprocal benefit is the basis of contractual interaction. Each party agrees to the contract terms in anticipation of benefiting from the other's performance. The fairness of contract terms can be evaluated from two perspectives. *Ex ante* evaluates the terms at the time of agreement *before* unknown or unanticipated contingencies occur. Contracts are presumed to be mutually beneficial *ex ante*. *Ex ante* fairness reflects this mutually beneficial aspect of contractual exchange—if both parties agreed to and understood the terms, then it is fair. *Ex post* fairness means evaluating the contract after the agreement and after the occurrence of contingencies. Some of the most interesting problems in contract law deal with the question of when courts should not enforce contract terms agreed to *ex ante* because of the occurrence of events *ex post*. Recognition of the important roles of contract law in enforcing contract terms and allocating risk *ex ante* makes obvious the potential problems of *ex post* judicial reconstruction of contracts. Moreover, the fairness or unfairness of particular contract terms should not be judged in isolation, but should be evaluated in light of all aspects of the bargaining process.

2. Least-Cost Risk Avoider: As a starting point for the analysis of the efficiency of contractual risk allocation, it must be recognized that some parties in the economy possess a comparative advantage at minimizing the costs associated with risk. Such parties are referred to as the "least-cost avoider of risk." Good examples of such people are grain dealers, who buy and sell contracts for the future delivery of grain. In essence, grain dealers minimize risk by engaging in numerous buy and sell contracts so that an unexpected fluctuation—either up or down—in the market price of grain is not disastrous to them. Moreover, the grain dealers specialize in understanding the grain market and are able to hedge their risks on the basis of their specialized information. On the other hand, the individual farmer does not have the expertise to engage in the pooling of risks on his or her own, but may lock into a guaranteed price long before the market price at harvest is determined. The farmer clearly benefits from not exposing his or her entire income stream to a last minute fluctuation in the market price of grain. Another way of stating this point is that the grain dealer has a diversified portfolio while the individual farm has a non-diversified portfolio. The grain dealer sells insurance (i.e., lower risk) to the risk-averse farmer. Understanding and appreciation of the risk allocation role of contracts leads to richer analyses of various doctrines of contract law. In general, legal rules that enforce contracts when the risk is borne by the least-cost avoider of risk are efficient legal rules.

3. Cost Minimization and Least-Cost Risk Avoider: At the time of contracting, the parties have a mutual interest in reducing the costs associated with the contract as much as possible. If the parties consider the potential risks that might thwart performance or make performance impractical, they would place the risk on the party best able to deal with it—that is, the party with the comparative advantage in foreseeing or taking appropriate precautions to reduce the costs of the risk, or buying insurance. In general, in the absence of a specific agreement, contract law imposes the risk on the party that seems to have the comparative advantage in bearing risk. Indeed, this is how similarly situated parties would be expected to allocate risks if required to bargain explicitly in advance. By assigning risks of nonperformance to the party who can best control the performance, contract law encourages parties to consider risk when negotiating a contract.

3. Compensating Wage Differentials and Market Levels of Safety

The theory of compensating wage differentials which was introduced in Chapter VIII can provide many insights into the manner in which risk and perceptions of risk are dealt with in the market place. In order to isolate the impact of risk of injury on the job, it is necessary to assume that the compensating wage differentials for every other dimension of the job have already been established. In order to obtain a complete understanding of the job selection process and the outcomes of that process, it is necessary, as always, to consider both the employer and the employee sides of a market.

Life is full of trade-offs. Workers are often willing to trade the risk of injury against the receipt of higher wages. The worker who is offered a job for $10.00 per hour in a business firm in which four percent of the work force is injured each year would achieve a certain level of utility from that job. If the risk of injury increased to five percent holding other job characteristics constant, the job would have to pay a higher wage to produce the same level of utility. In this regard, compensating wage differentials provide an *ex ante,* before the fact, compensation related to injury risk. People, of course, differ in their aversion to the risk of being injured. Those who are very sensitive to risk require large wage increases for any increase in risk, while those who are less sensitive require smaller wage increases to hold utility constant.

Workers can also be compensated to keep utility constant by *ex post,* or after the injury, payments for damages. Workers compensation insurance provides for *ex post* payments, but these payments are typically incomplete. There is no way to compensate a worker for his or her own death, and workers compensation does not cover the psychic costs of disfigurement due to permanent impairment. Moreover, the lost income associated with temporary impairments is not completely replaced by workers compensation because not all injury related losses are completely compensated *ex post.* Compensating wage differentials must exist *ex ante* for worker utility to be held constant in the face of increased risk.

Employers are faced with a wage risk trade-off of their own. In general, competitive forces on the employers' side of the market tend to cause low risk to be associated with low wages and high risk to be associated with higher wages, holding other things constant. This conclusion follows from three assumptions. First, it is presumably costly to reduce the risk of injury facing employees. Safety equipment must be placed on machines, production time must be sacrificed for training sessions, protective clothing and other safety gear must be furnished to workers and so forth. Second, competitive pressures force many firms to operate at zero profits, that is, at a point at which all costs are covered and the rate of return on capital is about what it is for similar investments. Third, all of the job characteristics are already determined. The consequence of these assumptions is that if a firm undertakes a program to reduce risk of injury, it must reduce wages to remain competitive. The major point is that if a firm spends more on safety, then it must spend less on other things if it is to remain competitive. Alternatively, this analysis could focus on the trade-off between safety and other working conditions because it is likely that such trade-offs exist. However, this analysis focuses on wage trade-offs because wages are easy to measure and form the largest component of compensation.

From the employer's perspective, there are diminishing marginal returns to safety expenditures. The first expenditure of the firm to reduce risk will have a relatively high return because the firm will clearly choose to attack the most obvious and cheaply eliminated hazard. Thus, at first, the risk and accompanying cost reductions are relatively large and the firm need not reduce wages very much to keep profits constant. At some point, additional expenditures by the firm to reduce risk have diminishing returns because all of the easy ways to solve safety problems have been used. Thus, expanding the safety effort beyond this point results in large wage reductions because further increases in safety are very costly. Furthermore, employers differ in the ease with which they can reduce hazards. In firms where injuries are costly to reduce, large wage reductions are required to keep profits constant in the face of a safety program.

The market matches employers and employees based on, among other things, their wage-risk preference trade-offs. Of course, not all firms are the same, and those with a comparative advantage at risk reduction have a comparative advantage at attracting relatively more risk averse workers. Similarly, not all workers are the same, and those who are relatively less risk averse will be attracted to firms that are forced to pay a risk premium because of their comparative disadvantage in reducing risk.

The market determination of workplace safety is illustrated in Figure IX-5. The range of possible safety levels, from zero safety to no risk, is shown on the

Figure IX-5

Market Determination of Workplace Safety

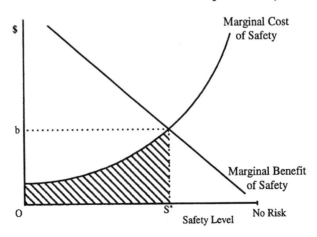

horizontal axis. The marginal costs to the employer of providing additional units of safety increase as the workplace becomes safer. The marginal benefits to workers of "consuming" additional units of workplace safety decline as the level of risk approaches zero. The price that workers are willing to pay for increased safety by accepting a lower wage declines as risk declines. Employers respond to workers' preferences for safety by providing additional units of safety up to the level where the marginal benefit is equal to the marginal cost. In Figure IX-5, the market determined level of workplace safety is S*. Note that this level is below the no-risk level of safety. At S*, the employer spends the shaded area on workplace safety. Additional expenditures beyond S* are not incurred because it costs the employer more to provide the additional safety than the employees are willing to pay by accepting lower wages.

4. Information, Risk, and Price Adjustments

In order for the market to adjust to reflect risky products or risky jobs, it is necessary for the buyers in the market place to have information regarding the risk they are undertaking. If the risk is not readily observable and is not known to other people in the market place, it is very difficult for the market price to reflect that risk. In some instances, the manufacturers of the product may be aware of a risk of which they have not informed consumers. Certainly, many product liability cases have involved allegations of this type of situation. This type of asymmetric information is often solved through regulations requiring warning labels to be placed on various products to alert consumers of the risks they are undertaking. The federal government uses a combination of disclosure regulation and explicit risk reduction regulation to deal with various kinds of risk. In general, many financial and other economic risks are covered by disclosure regulation, while many health and safety risks are covered by direct regulation.

D. Tort Law

The law of torts provides a set of legal rules that allows parties injured as the result of the actions of others to collect damages under certain well-defined circumstances. Bearing the costs of injurious acts provides an incentive to potentially liable parties to alter their behavior to reduce the risk of injury. For instance, many state courts have held grocery store owners liable to customers mugged in unlit parking lots. Impliedly, courts are saying that it is cheaper for stores to light their parking lots to prevent muggings than for customers to hire security guards or provide some other form of personal security. Several often-stated economic goals of tort law are reviewed in this section.

1. Behavior Modification and Minimizing the Costs of Accidents

The economic analysis of tort law begins with the assumption that alternative tort liability rules affect the behavior of individuals and firms in predictable ways. The problem addressed by alternative tort liability rules is how to induce both the potential tortfeasor and the potential victim to exercise an appropriate level of care. One way to characterize economic analysis of tort law is that it is primarily concerned with the prevention of accidents. However, within this view, it is clear that not all accidents are worth preventing. Thus, the economic perspective on tort law has concentrated on developing rules that minimize the total costs associated with accidents, where the total cost is defined as the sum of the cost of prevention and the actual cost of the accidents that occur. When the expected costs of an accident are greater than the cost of accident avoidance, then an efficient legal rule would be one that imposes liability on the party who could have avoided the accident at the lowest possible cost.

The behavior modification goal of tort law is most evident in the comparison of incentives to invest in accident avoidance activities under alternative liability rules. The starting point is an analysis of the duties owed by a reasonable person under a negligence liability standard. Four elements are traditionally required in a cause of action for negligence: (1) a duty to protect the plaintiff against unreasonable risks, (2) a failure to perform the duty, (3) actual loss or damage to the plaintiff, and (4) a reasonably close connection between defendant's conduct and the plaintiff's injury. All four of the elements are important since a cause of action usually fails if any one of the elements is lacking. However, the second element has received a great deal of attention due to Judge Learned Hand's famous economic formulation of the reasonable person standard.

United States v. Carroll Towing Co.
Circuit Court of Appeals, Second Circuit
159 F.2d 169 (1947)

L. HAND, Circuit Judge.

These appeals concern the sinking of the barge, 'Anna C,' on January 4, 1944, off Pier 51, North River. The Conners Marine Co., Inc., was the owner of the barge, which the Pennsylvania Railroad Company had chartered; the Grace Line, Inc., was the charterer of the tug, 'Carroll,' of which the Carroll Towing Co., Inc., was the owner. The decree in the limitation proceeding held the Carroll Company liable to the United States for the loss of the barge's cargo of flour, and to the Pennsylvania Railroad Company, for expenses in salvaging the cargo and barge; and it held the Carroll Company also liable to the Conners Company for one half the damage to the barge; these liabilities being all subject to limitation. The decree in the libel suit held the Grace Line primarily liable for the other half of the damage to the barge, and for any part of the first half, not recovered against the Carroll Company because of limitation of liability; it also held the Pennsylvania Railroad secondarily liable for the same amount that the Grace Line was liable. The Carroll Company and the Pennsylvania Railroad Company have filed assignments of error.

The facts, as the judge found them, were as follows. On June 20, 1943, the Conners Company chartered the barge, 'Anna C.' to the Pennsylvania Railroad Company at a stated hire per diem, by a charter of the kind usual in the Harbor, which included the services of a bargee, apparently limited to the hours 8 A.M. to 4 P.M. On January 2, 1944, the barge, which had lifted the cargo of flour, was made fast off the end of Pier 58 on the Manhattan side of the North River, whence she was later shifted to Pier 52. At some time not disclosed, five other barges were moored outside her, extending into the river; her lines to the pier were not then strengthened. At the end of the next pier north (called the Public Pier), lay four barges; and a line had been made fast from the outermost of these to the fourth barge of the tier hanging to Pier 52. The purpose of this line is not entirely apparent, and in any event it obstructed entrance into the slip between the two piers of barges. The Grace Line, which had chartered the tug, 'Carroll,' sent her down to the locus in quo to 'drill' out one of the barges which lay at the end of the Public Pier; and in order to do so it was necessary to throw off the line between the two tiers. On board the 'Carroll' at the time were not only her master, but a 'harbormaster' employed by the Grace Line. Before throwing off the line between the two tiers, the 'Carroll' nosed up against the outer barge of the tier lying off Pier 52, ran a line from her own stem to the middle bit of that barge, and kept working her engines 'slow ahead' against the ebb tide which was making at that time. The captain of the 'Carroll' put a deckhand and the 'harbormaster' on the barges, told them to throw off the line which barred the entrance to the slip; but, before doing so, to make sure that the tier on Pier 52 was safely moored, as there was a strong northerly wind blowing down the river. The 'harbormaster' and the deckhand went aboard the barges and readjusted all the fasts to their satisfaction, including those from the 'Anna C.' to the pier.

After doing so, they threw off the line between the two tiers and again boarded the 'Carroll,' which backed away from the outside barge, preparatory to 'drilling' out the barge she was after in the tier off the Public Pier. She had only got about seventy-five feet away when the tier off Pier 52 broke adrift because the fasts from the 'Anna C,' either rendered, or carried away. The tide and wind carried down the six barges, still holding together, until the 'Anna C' fetched up against a tanker, lying on the north side of the pier below—Pier 51—whose propeller broke a hole in her at or near her bottom. Shortly thereafter: i.e., at about 2:15 P.M., she careened, dumped her cargo of flour and sank. The tug, 'Grace,' owned by the Grace Line, and the 'Carroll,' came to the help of the flotilla after it broke loose; and, as both had syphon pumps on board, they could have kept the 'Anna C' afloat, had they learned of her condition; but the bargee had left her on the evening before, and nobody was on board to observe that she was leaking. The Grace Line wishes to exonerate itself from all liability because the 'harbormaster' was not authorized to pass on the sufficiency of the fasts of the 'Anna C' which held the tier to Pier 52; the Carroll Company wishes to charge the Grace Line with the entire liability because the 'harbormaster' was given an over-all authority. Both wish to charge the 'Anna C' with a share of all her damages, or at least with so much as resulted from her sinking. The Pennsylvania Railroad Company also wishes to hold the barge liable. The Conners Company wishes the decrees to be affirmed.

*　　*　　*

We cannot...excuse the Conners Company for the bargee's failure to care for the barge, and we think that this prevents full recovery. First as to the facts.

As we have said, the deckhand and the 'harbormaster' jointly undertook to pass upon the 'Anna C's' fasts to the pier; and even though we assume that the bargee was responsible for his fasts after the other barges were added outside, there is not the slightest ground for saying that the deckhand and the 'harbormaster' would have paid any attention to any protest which he might have made, had he been there. We do not therefore attribute it as in any degree a fault of the 'Anna C' that the flotilla broke adrift. Hence she may recover in full against the Carroll Company and the Grace Line for any injury she suffered from the contact with the tanker's propeller, which we shall speak of as the 'collision damages.' On the other hand, if the bargee had been on board, and had done his duty to his employer, he would have gone below at once, examined the injury, and called for help from the 'Carroll' and the Grace Line tug. Moreover, it is clear that these tugs could have kept the barge afloat, until they had safely beached her, and saved her cargo. This would have avoided what we shall call the 'sinking damages.' Thus, if it was a failure in the Conner Company's proper care of its own barge, for the bargee to be absent, the company can recover only one third of the 'sinking' damages from the Carroll Company and one third from the Grace Line. For this reason the question arises whether a barge owner is slack in the care of his barge if the bargee is absent.

As to the consequences of a bargee's absence from his barge there have been a number of decisions; and we cannot agree that it is never ground for liability even to other vessels who may be injured....

...[T]here is no general rule to determine when the absence of a bargee or other attendant will make the owner of the barge liable for injuries to other vessels if she breaks away from her moorings. However, in any cases where he would be so liable for injuries to others obviously he must reduce his damages proportionately, if the injury is to his own barge. It becomes apparent why there can be no such general rule, when we consider the grounds for such a liability. Since there are occasions when every vessel will break from her moorings, and since, if she does, she becomes a menace to those about her; the owner's duty, as in other similar situations, to provide against resulting injuries is a function of three variables: (1) The probability that she will break away; (2) the gravity of the resulting injury, if she does; (3) the burden of adequate precautions. Possibly it serves to bring this notion into relief to state it in algebraic terms: if the probability be called P; the injury, L; and the burden, B; liability depends upon whether B is less than L multiplied by P: i.e., whether B less than PL. Applied to the situation at bar, the likelihood that a barge will break from her fasts and the damage she will do, vary with the place and time; for example, if a storm threatens, the danger is greater; so it is, if she is in a crowded harbor where moored barges are constantly being shifted about. On the other hand, the barge must not be the bargee's prison, even though he lives aboard; he must go ashore at times. We need not say whether, even in such crowded waters as New York Harbor a bargee must be aboard at night at all; it may be that the custom is otherwise, as Ward, J., supposed in 'The Kathryn B. Guinan,' supra; and that, if so, the situation is one where custom should control. We leave that question open; but we hold that it is not in all cases a sufficient answer to a bargee's absence without excuse, during working hours, that he has properly made fast his barge to a pier, when he leaves her. In the case at bar the bargee left at five o'clock in the afternoon of January 3rd, and the flotilla broke away at about two o'clock in the afternoon of the following day, twenty-one hours afterwards. The bargee had been away all the time, and we hold that his fabricated story was affirmative evidence that he had no excuse for his absence. At the locus in quo—especially during the short January days and in the full tide of war activity—barges were being constantly 'drilled' in and out. Certainly it was not beyond reasonable expectation that, with the inevitable haste and bustle, the work might not be done with adequate care. In such circumstances we hold—and it is all that we do hold—that it was a fair requirement that the Conners Company should have a bargee aboard (unless he had some excuse for his absence), during the working hours of daylight.

*   *   *

Notes and Questions

1. The Hand Formula: Judge Hand's Negligence Formula is an economic test that involves the tradeoffs between the costs of avoiding the injury and the expected costs of the injury. Under the famous BPL formulation, B is equal to the burden of avoiding the accident, P is the probability or likelihood that conduct will injure others, and L is the seriousness of injury. P × L is the expected cost of an injury if no avoidance costs are incurred. If B < PL, then the reasonable person would have incurred the avoidance cost. If they didn't incur this cost, then they should be held negligent. If B > PL, then the reasonable person would not have incurred the cost to avoid the accident and, thus, would not be held liable for negligence if the injury occurred. What assumptions regarding risk preferences does the Hand Formula make?

2. Ex ante Analysis: Because the economic model is based on behavior modification and liability rules are supposed to be a guide to behavior, the BPL test should be applied to conditions existing before the accident—at the time the potential tortfeasor was making the decision about how much to invest in accident avoidance. Thus, *ex ante,* the BPL formulation provides a guideline for avoiding negligence through investment in accident avoidance. Obviously, the type of activity will dictate the degree of care that is required. Under the Hand Formula, a dangerous activity which has a high probability of causing very serious injuries to many people would require great expenditures in order to avoid a judgment of negligence. On the other hand, if the activity is "safe"—that is, the probability of an accident is very small and the expected injuries are small—then the expenditures required to avoid a judgment of negligence would be small. Under the Hand Formula, it is not negligence if an injury occurs for which the expenditure to prevent the injury exceeds the *expected* benefits derived from the expenditures. All injuries from flying baseballs can be prevented only at a great cost, whereas the likelihood of injury in certain areas of the stands may be quite low and the severity of injury small. Failure to protect against the risk of a fan being hit by a baseball behind home plate where the risk of injury is great may be negligence, whereas failure to protect fans in the right field stands may not.

3. Full Information and No Liability Standard: Assume that market participants have full information regarding the burden of accident avoidance and expected accident costs. Furthermore, suppose that there is no liability standard. Under this scenario, what level of care would potential tortfeasors exercise? In the absence of a liability rule, what conditions would cause the potential tortfeasor to deviate from this level of care?

4. *Least Cost Avoider of Accidents:* The behavioral modification or deterrence view of tort law generates a public policy prescription based on economic efficiency. If the goal of tort law is to minimize the total cost of accidents, then the "least cost avoider" should be held liable. Of course, this broad public policy prescription raises important questions related to who was the least cost avoider. Alternative liability rules, such as negligence, contributory negligence, comparative negligence and strict liability, can be viewed as placing the risk on parties who are the least cost risk avoiders under different circumstances. In practice, the identification of the "least-cost avoider" is not always obvious. According to Professor Guido Calabresi, one of the leading commentators on tort law, a number of guidelines can be used to identify the party who should bear the loss of accident. According to Professor Calabresi, that party should be the party who can: (1) better evaluate the risk involved; (2) better evaluate the accident-proneness of potential parties on the other side; (3) cause prices to reflect this knowledge; (4) insure most cheaply against liability; and/or (5) more likely avoid having the loss shifted in a way that reduces the incentive to avoid the loss. G. Calabresi, "Faults, Accidents, and the Wonderful World of Blum and Kalven," 75 Yale Law Journal 216 (1965). Can you determine from Calabresi's criteria what he views as the purpose (or purposes) of tort law?

5. *Marginal Analysis.* Recall from Chapter I that our basic decision rule for individuals, firms, or government regulators is that it is optimal to engage in an activity up to the point where the marginal benefit equals the marginal cost. In this regard, a more precise statement of the Hand Formula should be based on marginal costs and marginal benefits from investing in care. This can be illustrated diagrammatically as shown in Figure IX-6. The horizontal axis indicates units of care in terms of risk avoidance activity. The B starts low at low units of care and rises rapidly taking on an upward sloping shape because it is assumed that cost of reducing accidents or reducing the damages associated with accidents goes up as the likelihood of accidents or the cost of accidents is reduced—that is, on the margin, the cost of further reductions in risk increase as the units of care increase. The PL curve is downward sloping based on the notion that as more units of care are incurred, either P will be reducing because of a lower probability of accidents or L will be reducing in the sense that the damage that will be caused when more units of care are invested is likely to be less. B can be thought of as a marginal cost curve which increases with the number of units of care. The PL curve is a marginal benefit curve which suggests that the marginal benefit of additional units of care declines as more and more units of care are used. The marginal benefit and marginal cost of investing in care are equal at C* units of care. That is the efficient standard of care. Any additional investments in care mean that the marginal cost is greater than the marginal benefit. Fewer investments in care indicate that the reduced marginal benefit from reducing care is greater than the marginal costs that are saved from reducing the care. Under this marginal formulation of the Hand formula, an individual should be held negligent if they failed to invest C* units of care. That is, to the left of C*, B < PL and they should be held liable under the Hand negligence standard. Firms or individuals who invest more than C* are operating in the range where B > PL, and they should not be held liable under this negligence standard. Thus, the negligence

Figure IX-6

The Hand Formula

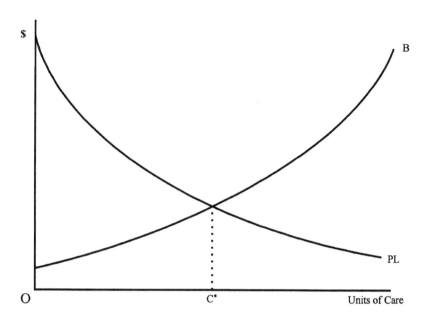

standard of care is expected to induce the efficient amount of accident avoidance expenditures.

6. Absolute Liability and Deterrence Effects: An important insight derived from this model of accident avoidance is that if the liability rule is changed from one of negligence to what amounts to absolute liability (defined as the tortfeasor pays even if not at fault) then the injurer will invest the same amount in accident avoidance as under the negligence rule. This is because up until the C* level of care the expected cost to the injurer associated with accidents is greater than the expected cost of risk avoidance (B). Because of those expectations, the benefit of avoiding accidents is greater than the cost of accidents up to the level C*. Beyond that level, the cost of avoiding accidents is greater than the expected payout to injured parties. Thus, the injurer will decide to not make investments beyond C* even though the injurer realizes that he or she will have to pay damages in the event an accident occurs. Thus, rather than focusing on deterrence and behavior modification, the absolute or strict liability standard appears to some extent to be driven by distributional considerations.

7. Defenses to Negligence: Because the economic perspective on tort law concentrates on minimizing the total costs associated with accidents, the Hand Formula should also be applied to the behavior of potential victims. The defenses to negligence rely in part on a similar analysis of the cost of avoiding the injury and the expected loss from the injury. A potential defendant did not exercise reasonable care if the injury could have been avoided at a cost that is lower than the expected cost of the injury. There would be a certain "unfairness" (economic inefficiency) if this analysis applied only to the defendant. The appropriate inquiry must also consider the possibilities available to the plaintiff to avoid the injury. Could the plaintiff have avoided the injury at a lower cost than the defendant? If so, was the plaintiff acting as a reasonable prudent person would act under similar circumstances? Alternatively, suppose that both parties can avoid (or prevent) the injury at an equally low cost, but that the plaintiff is a gambler in the sense that he or she would rather pocket the cost of avoiding the accident and take the chances of being injured. Would it be efficient to allow such a person to pocket the money and then sue if injured?

8. Defenses to Negligence: Contributory and Comparative Negligence: Contributory and comparative negligence are important when the plaintiff, as well as the defendant, is at least partially responsible for his or her injury. The defense of **contributory negligence** is the failure of the plaintiff—the injured party—to exercise reasonable care which contributes to the injury. Traditionally, contributory negligence would completely bar recovery for injuries. The result has been the adoption by most states of the doctrine of **comparative negligence** which allows a proration of the damages resulting from the combined negligence of the parties. If a plaintiff's injuries amount to $100,000 and they are 40% the result of plaintiff's negligence and 60% the result of defendant's negligence, then the plaintiff's recovery would be limited to only $60,000. Some states provide that if plaintiff's negligence is greater than 50%, then recovery is barred. The economic justification for the contributory negligence defense is that it provides an incentive for the plaintiff to take care when it is efficient for the plaintiff or both parties to avoid the loss. The concern is that a simple negligence standard creates a moral hazard in that those at risk do not have the incentive to take self-protective or loss-avoidance measures. The absolute defense of contributory negligence controls moral hazard by the plaintiff, but may lead to a similar problem with the defendant's behavior:

> The question of whether contributory or comparative negligence should be adopted in this state is riddled with economic considerations. Judge Learned Hand formulated an algebraic equation to determine negligence: The defendant is liable if the loss (injury) caused by the accident multiplied by the probability of its occurrence is greater than the cost of avoiding the accident. United States v. Carroll Towing Co., 159 F.2d 169 (2d Cir. 1947). The economically efficient solution, therefore, is to require the smaller cost to be incurred if it will prevent the larger accident cost. R. Posner, Economic Analysis of Law (2d ed. 1977), at 122–25.
>
> In application to contributory negligence, if the plaintiff can prevent a $1000 accident at a cost of $50 and the defendant's avoidance cost is $100, the economically efficient solution is to refuse the plaintiff any recovery for failure to avoid the total loss at the lesser cost. If the defendant is liable in all instances without regard to the precautionary measures the plaintiff could have taken, there is no economic incentive for the plaintiff to avert the accident. Posner, supra.
>
> On the other hand, if the defendant is able to avoid the $1000 loss at a cost of $50 and the plaintiff's cost is $100, the defense of contributory negligence (assuming it is applicable) still mandates that the plaintiff cannot recover at all. In essence, therefore, this defense sanctions the least economically efficient solution because it provides no incentive for the defendant to spend the lesser avoidance cost cognizant that, if the plain-

tiff contributed even a little bit, the defendant will incur no liability (expense) at all.

The doctrine of comparative negligence where the plaintiff's damages are diminished by the percentage of his own negligence that contributed to the accident is not the panacea either. This doctrine tacitly advocates that more than the economically efficient amount of precautionary measures be taken. Using the same figures immediately above, if the defendant would be two-thirds liable and the plaintiff one-third liable, incurring $666.67 and $333.33 of the $1000 loss respectively, then both parties would opt for the lesser avoidance cost at an aggregate prevention cost of $150. This results in economic inefficiency because either amount alone would have been sufficient to avoid the total loss.

Conversely, neither party may decide to opt for the lesser avoidance cost in reliance upon the fact that the other party has an economic incentive to take precautionary measures. This results in compensating a total loss of $1000 that could have been avoided at the lesser amount of $50 or $100, individually, or at a collective amount of $150. Even though the combined expense of $150 is over precautionary, economically speaking, it is at least more economically efficient than incurring the total or partial accident expense. Posner, supra.

This economic analysis becomes more intricate as we approach an examination of the respective forms of comparative negligence. I feel that we do this area of the law and the public a great disservice by failing to recognize, work through and resolve the economic issues endemic to this dilemma.

Golden v. McCurry, 392 So.2d 815 (1980), (Justice Faulkner, dissent). Many argue that comparative negligence controls moral hazard in a more equitable manner. What do you think?

9. *Negligence versus Strict Liability, and Activity Levels.* Professor Steven Shavell has added some additional elements to the basic BPL model of negligence liability:

> By definition, under the negligence rule all that an injurer needs to do to avoid the possibility of liability is to make sure to exercise due care if he engages in his activity. Consequently, he will not be motivated to consider the effect on accident losses of his choice of whether to engage in his activity or, more generally, of the level at which to engage in his activity; he will choose his level of activity in accordance only with the personal benefits so derived. But surely any increase in his level of activity will typically raise expected accident losses (holding constant the level of care). Thus he will be led to choose too high a level of activity; the negligence rule is not "efficient."
>
> Consider by way of illustration the problem of pedestrian-automobile accidents (and, ... let us imagine the behavior of pedestrians to be fixed). Suppose that drivers of automobiles find it in their interest to adhere to the standard of due care but that the possibility of accidents is not thereby eliminated. Then, in deciding how much to drive, they will contemplate only the enjoyment they get from doing so. Because (as

they exercise due care) they will not be liable for harms suffered by pedestrians, drivers will not take into account that going more miles will mean a higher expected number of accidents. Hence, they will do too much driving; an individual will, for example, decide to go for a drive on a mere whim despite the imposition of a positive expected cost to pedestrians.

However, under a rule of strict liability, the situation is different. Because an injurer must pay for losses whenever he is involved in an accident, he will be induced to consider the effect on accident losses of both his level of care and his activity level. His decisions will therefore be efficient. Because drivers will be liable for losses sustained by pedestrians, they will decide not only to exercise due care in driving, but also to drive only when the utility gained from it outweighs expected liability payments to pedestrians.

S. Shavell, *Strict Liability versus Negligence*, 9 Journal of Legal Studies 1, 2–3 (1980). In effect, a strict liability standard forces the manufacturer to be an insurer of unavoidable risks. Thus, according to Shavell, a strict liability standard forces the manufacturer to contemplate the level of unavoidable risk which results from his activity. Why, even in this case, is the manufacturer assumed to be the least cost avoider? Does Shavell's "externality argument" simply obscure the issue of economic efficiency?

10. Behavior Modification and Compensation: The pure behavioral modification perspective on tort law suggests that compensation of the accident victim is irrelevant. The important point is that the potential tortfeasor expects to have pay damages if held liable and, thus, responds to the incentives created by the liability rule. Damages can be paid to anyone—the victim, the state, the University of Kansas Law and Organizational Economics Center—because it is assumed that the potential recipient of the damages does not affect the potential tortfeasor's incentives. After all, distributional considerations are routinely ignored when the tortfeasor is not liable in the sense that the victim isn't compensated for the injury suffered. This is not to suggest, however, that deterrence should be the exclusive goal of tort law.

2. Loss Spreading and Insurance

Another economic approach to tort law is to consider it as a form of insurance. Recall that risk averse individuals buy insurance to reduce the downside risk associated with many of life's activities. In the absence of tort liability, tort victims would be forced to bear large losses. Tort rules can be used to compensate unlucky victims. According to this view, the party who is in the best position to spread the loss of the injury should be held liable. With respect to injuries resulting from products, for example, it is argued that the manufacturer is often in the best position to cover the costs of compensation because a portion of the expected accident costs is reflected in the price of the product. All consumers, not just the unlucky few who happen to be injured by the product, bear some of the costs. In effect, all purchasers of a product would pay a slightly higher price which, in effect, buys them an insurance policy for compensation in the event of injury while using the product.

Greenman v. Yuba Power Products, Inc.
Supreme Court of California
59 Cal. 2d 57; 377 P.2d 897 (1963)

OPINION BY: TRAYNOR

Plaintiff brought this action for damages against the retailer and the manufacturer of a Shopsmith, a combination power tool that could be used as a saw, drill, and wood lathe. He saw a Shopsmith demonstrated by the retailer and studied a brochure prepared by the manufacturer. He decided he wanted a Shopsmith for his home workshop, and his wife bought and gave him one for Christmas in 1955. In 1957 he bought the necessary attachments to use the Shopsmith as a lathe for turning a large piece of wood he wished to make into a chalice. After he had worked on the piece of wood several times without difficulty, it suddenly flew out of the machine and struck him on the forehead, inflicting serious injuries. About 10½ months later, he gave the retailer and the manufacturer written notice of claimed breaches of warranties and filed a complaint against them alleging such breaches and negligence.

After a trial before a jury, the court ruled that there was no evidence that the retailer was negligent or had breached any express warranty and that the manufacturer was not liable for the breach of any implied warranty. Accordingly, it submitted to the jury only the cause of action alleging breach of implied warranties against the retailer and the causes of action alleging negligence and breach of express warranties against the manufacturer. The jury returned a verdict for the retailer against plaintiff and for plaintiff against the manufacturer in the amount of $ 65,000. The trial court denied the manufacturer's motion for a new trial and entered judgment on the verdict. The manufacturer and plaintiff appeal. Plaintiff seeks a reversal of the part of the judgment in favor of the retailer, however, only in the event that the part of the judgment against the manufacturer is reversed.

Plaintiff introduced substantial evidence that his injuries were caused by defective design and construction of the Shopsmith. His expert witnesses testified that inadequate set screws were used to hold parts of the machine together so that normal vibration caused the tailstock of the lathe to move away from the piece of wood being turned permitting it to fly out of the lathe. They also testified that there were other more positive ways of fastening the parts of the machine together, the use of which would have prevented the accident. The jury could therefore reasonably have concluded that the manufacturer negligently constructed the Shopsmith. The jury could also reasonably have concluded that statements in the manufacturer's brochure were untrue, that they constituted express warranties, and that plaintiff's injuries were caused by their breach.

The manufacturer contends, however, that plaintiff did not give it notice of breach of warranty within a reasonable time and that therefore his cause of action for breach of warranty is barred by section 1769 of the Civil Code. Since it cannot be determined whether the verdict against it was based on the negligence or warranty cause of action or both, the manufacturer concludes that the error in presenting the warranty cause of action to the jury was prejudicial.

Section 1769 of the Civil Code provides: "In the absence of express or implied agreement of the parties, acceptance of the goods by the buyer shall not discharge the seller from liability in damages or other legal remedy for breach of any promise or warranty in the contract to sell or the sale. But, if, after acceptance of the goods, the buyer fails to give notice to the seller of the breach of any promise or warranty within a reasonable time after the buyer knows, or ought to know of such breach, the seller shall not be liable therefor."

Like other provisions of the Uniform Sales Act (Civ. Code, §§ 1721–1800), section 1769 deals with the rights of the parties to a contract of sale or a sale. It does not provide that notice must be given of the breach of a warranty that arises independently of a contract of sale between the parties. Such warranties are not imposed by the sales act, but are the product of common-law decisions that have recognized them in a variety of situations. It is true that in many of these situations the court has invoked the sales act definitions of warranties (Civ. Code, §§ 1732, 1735) in defining the defendant's liability, but it has done so, not because the statutes so required, but because they provided appropriate standards for the court to adopt under the circumstances presented.

The notice requirement of section 1769, however, is not an appropriate one for the court to adopt in actions by injured consumers against manufacturers with whom they have not dealt. "As between the immediate parties to the sale [the notice requirement] is a sound commercial rule, designed to protect the seller against unduly delayed claims for damages. As applied to personal injuries, and notice to a remote seller, it becomes a booby-trap for the unwary. The injured consumer is seldom 'steeped in the business practice which justifies the rule,' [James, Product Liability, 34 Texas L. Rev. 44, 192, 197] and at least until he has had legal advice it will not occur to him to give notice to one with whom he has had no dealings." (Prosser, Strict Liability to the Consumer, 69 Yale L. J. 1099, 1130, footnotes omitted.)... We conclude, therefore, that even if plaintiff did not give timely notice of breach of warranty to the manufacturer, his cause of action based on the representations contained in the brochure was not barred.

Moreover, to impose strict liability on the manufacturer under the circumstances of this case, it was not necessary for plaintiff to establish an express warranty as defined in section 1732 of the Civil Code. A manufacturer is strictly liable in tort when an article he places on the market, knowing that it is to be used without inspection for defects, proves to have a defect that causes injury to a human being. Recognized first in the case of unwholesome food products, such liability has now been extended to a variety of other products that create as great or greater hazards if defective.

Although in these cases strict liability has usually been based on the theory of an express or implied warranty running from the manufacturer to the plaintiff, the abandonment of the requirement of a contract between them, the recognition that the liability is not assumed by agreement but imposed by law, and the refusal to permit the manufacturer to define the scope of its own responsibility for defective products make clear that the liability is not one governed by the law of contract warranties but by the law of strict liability in tort. Accordingly, rules defining and governing warranties that were developed to meet the needs of commercial transactions cannot properly be invoked to govern the manufacturer's liability to those injured by its defective products unless those rules also serve the purposes for which such liability is imposed.

We need not recanvass the reasons for imposing strict liability on the manufacturer. They have been fully articulated in the cases cited above. The purpose of such liability is to insure that the costs of injuries resulting from defective products are borne by the manufacturers that put such products on the market rather than by the injured persons who are powerless to protect themselves. Sales warranties serve this purpose fitfully at best. In the present case, for example, plaintiff was able to plead and prove an express warranty only because he read and relied on the representations of the Shopsmith's ruggedness contained in the manufacturer's brochure. Implicit in the machine's presence on the market, however, was a representation that it would safely do the jobs for which it was built. Under these circumstances, it should not be controlling whether plaintiff selected the machine because of the statements in the brochure, or because of the machine's own appearance of excellence that belied the defect lurking beneath the surface, or because he merely assumed that it would safely do the jobs it was built to do. It should not be controlling whether the details of the sales from manufacturer to retailer and from retailer to plaintiff's wife were such that one or more of the implied warranties of the sales act arose. "The remedies of injured consumers ought not to be made to depend upon the intricacies of the law of sales." (Ketterer v. Armour & Co., 200 F. 322, 323; Klein v. Duchess Sandwich Co., Ltd., 14 Cal.2d 272, 282 [93 P.2d 799].) To establish the manufacturer's liability it was sufficient that plaintiff proved that he was injured while using the Shopsmith in a way it was intended to be used as a result of a defect in design and manufacture of which plaintiff was not aware that made the Shopsmith unsafe for its intended use.

*   *   *

The judgment is affirmed.

Notes and Questions

1. Overlap of Deterrence and Loss Spreading Goals: It is often argued that the manufacturer's superior ability to spread the loss can be consistent with the goal of minimizing the costs of accidents, as Justice Traynor wrote in Escola v. Coca Cola Bottling Co, 159 P.2d 436 (1944):

> ...I believe the manufacturer's negligence should no longer be singled out as the basis of a plaintiff's right to recover in [products liability] cases...In my opinion it should now be recognized that a manufacturer incurs an absolute liability when an article that he has placed on the market, knowing that it is to be used without inspection, proves to have a defect that causes injury to human beings....Even if there is no negligence, however, public policy demands that responsibility be fixed wherever it will most effectively reduce the hazards to life and health inherent in defective products that reach the market. It is evident that the manufacturer can anticipate some hazards and guard against the recurrence of others, as the public cannot. Those who suffer injury from defective products are unprepared to meet its consequences. The cost of an injury and the loss of time or health may be an overwhelming misfortune to the person injured, and a needless one, for the risk of injury can be insured

by the manufacturer and distributed among the public as a cost of doing business. It is to the public interest to discourage the marketing of products having defects that are a menace to the public. If such products nevertheless find their way into the market it is to the public interest to place the responsibility for whatever injury they may cause upon the manufacturer, who, even if he is not negligent in the manufacture of the product, is responsible for its reaching the market. However intermittently such injuries may occur and however haphazardly they may strike, the risk of their occurrence is a constant risk and a general one. Against such a risk there should be general and constant protection and the manufacturer is best situated to afford such protection.

Id. at 453 (concurring). This view, in effect, turns a manufacturer into an insurer. Justice Traynor appears to be assuming that manufacturers can insure against nonnegligent risk more cheaply than consumers. Is there any justification for this assumption?

2. *The Limits of Risk Aversion and Loss Spreading:* Although loss spreading is a widely accepted goal of tort law, some judges do recognize that there must be limits to how many injuries can be compensated under such a theory. In *Shepard v. Superior Court*, 76 Cal. App.3d 16 (1977), a dissenting judge argued against allowing recovery for plaintiffs' alleged physical injuries resulting from the emotional shock of watching their daughter being killed in an automobile accident:

*   *   *

...To start with, it is noted that the avowed purpose of imposing strict liability upon the manufacturer is twofold: (1) loss-distribution or risk-spreading and (2) injury-reduction by enhanced safety. The first rationale, risk-spreading, holds the manufacturer liable for injuries resulting from the use of his product because he is in the best position to distribute the loss either by insurance or by increasing the price of his product. As stated in *Greenman v. Yuba Power Products, Inc.*, the purpose of strict tort liability is to insure that the costs of injuries resulting from defective products are borne by the manufacturers who put such products on the market rather than by the injured persons who are powerless to protect themselves. Echoing the same idea, the court in *Vandermark v. Ford Motor Co.* (1964) 61 Cal.2d 256, 262–263, 37 Cal.Rptr. 896, 391 P.2d 168; reemphasized that strict liability on the manufacturer affords protection to the injured person and works no injustice because the manufacturers can protect themselves through obtaining insurance and dispersing the cost through the prices of the products. The second rationale, the theory of injury reduction, holds the manufacturer liable because he is in the best position to discover and correct the dangerous aspects of his products before any injury occurs. Again, the manufacturer may pass on to the consumer the increased product costs by incorporating them in the purchase price of the merchandise.

Although since its inception the courts have generally tended to broaden the scope of products liability, there are few cases, if any, which have embarked on a thorough and delicate analysis to explore whether the above stated policy goals are indeed promoted by the ever-expanding scope of enterprise liability. It is time for such an examination.

The basic facts of economy teach us that the fashionable trend of a wholesale extension of strict liability proves to be counterproductive in many instances by hampering and arresting, rather than promoting, the policy objectives underpinning the doctrine. Thus, it requires no special economic expertise to realize that the double demand posed by the law, i.e., to make the product absolutely safe on the one hand, and to spread the cost of the ever increasing insurance premiums together with the expense of safety measures to the consumer on the other, becomes increasingly difficult, if not entirely impossible, to meet. It is well to remember that economic forces do not work in a vacuum, but rather in a strict and realistic economic environment where prices of merchandise are greatly influenced (if not entirely determined) by economic rivalry and competition. Under these circumstances, the fundamental assumption of spreading the risk of the enterprise to the consumers at large cannot be attained and materialized. While some portion of the ever growing safety and insurance cost may pass directly to the consumer by way of a higher dollar price, the remainder will take the form of decreased quality not affecting safety and decreased profits. The decreased profits affect the manufacturers first (among them mainly the large segment of small businessmen with limited or marginal capital who have to shoulder the strict enterprise liability side by side with the huge corporations), then society as a whole. The motion and realistic operation of economic forces have been graphically described by one observer as follows: "*Decreased profits, however, do not stop with the manufacturer.* He distributes them to the shareholders of his corporation, just as he distributes increased prices to the consumers of his product. Moreover, decreased profits do not stop with the shareholders. *Rather, in more or less attenuated form, they pass on to other, broader classes.* The major distribution of decreased profits occurs when shareholders switch their investment to other, more profitable enterprises. When this happens, the liability-bearing manufacturer's enterprise loses its ability to attract investment capital resulting in decreased industrial activity. *This decreased activity results in losses to several categories. First, the consumer will feel the loss because the manufacturer's ability to produce a better, safer product will diminish. Second, reduced industrial activity will affect labor. Severely diminished profits may force the manufacturer out of business. Even less drastic reductions, however, could reduce the number of new jobs. Finally, reduced economic activity will affect the entire society, in a more or less attenuated form, through lower tax revenues, lower wages, and lower profits for distribution.*" (Alden D. Holford, The Limits of Strict Liability for Product Design and Manufacture (1973) 52 Tex.L.Rev. 81, 87, emphasis added.)

Paying heed to economic realities rather than our own fancy, the courts as a matter of judicial policy must stop the further extension of the strict liability of entrepreneurs, at least to areas where, as here, the determination of damages is speculative and conjectural rather than real and definable. In doing so, we are in line with established law which holds that the manufacturer is not an insurer of the product and that the strict liability of entrepreneurs may not be equated with absolute, limitless liability. As has been emphasized time and time again, in determining the parameters of enterprise liability we must draw a proper balance between the need for adequate recovery and the survival of viable enterprises. The guiding principles to achieve these goals are judicial temperance, evenhandedness and, first and foremost, fairness to all.

* * *

... it is to be noted that despite the ever expanding scope of the manufacturer's strict liability, the feudalistic notion that the tortfeasor must be held liable simply because he caused an injury regardless of fault or the existence of a duty to the injured person has been effectively resisted by the California courts which in two notable instances have exonerated the manufacturer from responsibility. One, in spite of arduous arguments to the contrary, the Supreme Court refused to extend the strict liability doctrine to, and denied recovery for, economic loss alone (Seely v. White Motor Co., supra, 63 Cal.2d 9, 45 Cal.Rptr. 17, 403 P.2d 145). Two, the California courts likewise consistently hold that the theory of strict liability does not obtain to services either. As we put it in Shepard v. Alexian Brothers Hosp., supra, 33 Cal.App.3d 606, 614, 109 Cal.Rptr. 132, 136, "those who sell their services for the guidance of others in their economic, financial and personal affairs are burdened only with a duty of reasonable performance under the circumstances and cannot be made liable in the absence of negligence or intentional misconduct." These latter examples but further underline that the strict liability of the manufacturer must have reasonable limits and that such liability by no means may be made equivalent to an unlimited or absolute responsibility.

Id. at 26–31. This opinion clearly recognizes the presence of opportunity costs to a loss spreading theory of strict liability. Should courts consider such costs in their application of liability rules? Does Justice Traynor consider such costs in *Greenman*?

The Current Insurance Crisis and Modern Tort Law
George Priest
96 Yale Law Journal 1521 (1987)

This paper is an effort to understand the source of the crisis in insurance that has recently disrupted product and service markets in the United States. From press accounts, the crisis seemed to peak in the early months of 1986, when reports became common of extraordinary changes in commercial casualty insurance markets. Insurers had increased premiums drastically for an unusual set of products, such as vaccines, general aircraft, and sports equipment, and for an equally diverse set of services, such as obstetrics, ski lifts, and commercial trucking. In still other cases—intrauterine devices, wine tasting, and day care,—insurers had refused to offer coverage at any premium, forcing these products and services to be withdrawn from the market.

This paper argues that the characteristic of contemporary tort law most crucial to understanding the current crisis is the judicial compulsion of greater and greater levels of provider third-party insurance for victims. The progressive shift to third-party corporate insurance coverage, since its beginnings in the mid-1960's, has systematically undermined insurance markets.

*   *   *

This explanation of the crisis uncovers what I believe to be a tragic paradox of our modern civil liability regime. The expansion of liability since the mid-1960's has been chiefly motivated by the concern of our courts to provide insurance to victims who have suffered personal injury. The most fundamental of the conceptual foundations of our modern law is that the expansion of tort liability will lead to the provision of insurance along with the sale of the product or service itself, with a portion of the insurance premium passed along in the product or service price. Expanded tort liability, thus, is a method of providing insurance to individuals, especially the poor, who have not purchased or cannot purchase insurance themselves. This insurance rationale suffuses our modern civil law, and must be acknowledged as one of the great humanitarian expressions of our time.

The paradox exposed by my theory is that the expansion of tort liability has had exactly the opposite effect. The insurance crisis demonstrates graphically that continued expansion of tort liability on insurance grounds leads to a reduction in total insurance coverage available to the society, rather than to an increase. The theory also shows that the parties most drastically affected by expanded liability and by the current insurance crisis are the low-income and poor, exactly the parties that courts had hoped most to aid.

*   *   *

II. MODERN TORT LAW AND ITS ECONOMIC EFFECTS

Since the early 1960's, courts have steadily expanded tort liability for injuries suffered in the context of product and service use. These changes in the law result from the acceptance of a coherent and powerful theory that justifies the use of tort law to compensate injured parties, a theory its founders called "enterprise liability." According to the theory, expanded provider liability serves three important functions: to establish incentives for injury prevention; to provide insurance for injuries that cannot be prevented; and to modulate levels of activity by internalizing costs, including injury costs.

The second feature of the theory—the importance of providing insurance for unpreventable losses—is most crucial for understanding our current insurance crisis. According to enterprise liability theory, expanded legal liability does more than achieve optimal control of accident and activity rates. Expanded tort liability improves social welfare, in addition, because it provides a form of compensation insurance to consumers. A provider, especially a corporate provider, is in a substantially better position than a consumer to obtain insurance for product- or service-related losses, because a provider can either self-insure or can enter one insurance contract covering all consumers—in comparison to the thousands of insurance contracts the set of consumers would need—and can easily pass the proportionate insurance premium along in the product or service price. Most importantly, to tie insurance to the sale of the product or service will provide insurance coverage to consumers who might not otherwise obtain first-party coverage, in particular the poor or low-income among the consuming population.

The insurance rationale was central to the first judicial adoption of enterprise liability theory, by the California Supreme Court in Greenman v. Yuba Power Products, in 1963. The approach was rapidly extended across the various state jurisdictions, first in the products liability field and, later, in other areas of tort law. Briefly, however, enterprise liability theory has justified both restrictions in available legal defenses and expansion of substantive liability standards.

As examples, since the mid-1960's, courts have invoked the insurance rationale to limit the defenses of contributory negligence, assumption of risk, and consumer product misuse; to eliminate defenses related to the status of the victim (as in actions brought by licensees and trespassers against property owners); and to restrict the effectiveness of statutes of limitation. At the same time, the theory has supported the affirmative extension of liability through the adoption of standards of strict liability, retrospective liability, and unreasonably dangerous per se, relaxation of causation requirements, and, more generally, through the near-universal acceptance of comparative negligence, which permits a jury to render judgments against defendants even if they are responsible only in some small proportion for a plaintiff's injury.

These legal changes have particularly affected insurers because courts have simultaneously expanded the scope of the insurance contract. Again, under the influence of enterprise liability theory, courts have adopted the maximization of insurance coverage as the principal interpretive objective in insurance contract disputes. Thus, courts have interpreted policy coverage provisions broadly and policy exclusions narrowly to achieve the compensation goal.

As a result of these doctrinal developments, both the range of defendants against whom a plaintiff might collect a judgment and the range of plaintiffs to whom a corporate defendant might ultimately be liable, have expanded. Courts have also expanded the range of losses for which compensation might be sought, chiefly by allowing increased recovery of emotional and other non-economic losses.

Understanding the insurance crisis requires that the economic effects of expanded liability be analyzed precisely. Putting aside administrative costs, a legal rule or agency regulation can have two principal economic effects: (1) it can influence investments in loss prevention to affect the accident rate; and (2) it can influence the provision of insurance for losses not prevented. These two effects, prevention and insurance, are the only important economic consequences of any legal or regulatory policy. It is irrelevant which goals a court, a regulatory agency, or society is trying to achieve. It is unimportant if the motivation for a legal policy is some moral imperative, some vague or specific sense of justice, or personal or pecuniary advantage. The only important economic effects that any legal policy can have are effects on levels of investments in prevention of losses and of insurance for losses not prevented.

It is well accepted that the optimal level of accident prevention will be attained if incentives are created for both the provider and consumer to make additional safety investments up to the point at which the marginal costs of such investments equal their marginal benefits. Regardless of context, the accident prevention question is whether it was cost-effective for the provider or for the consumer to have made greater investments to prevent the loss. If the finder of fact determines that neither party could have prevented the loss in a cost-effective manner, then the resolution of the dispute in favor of the plaintiff or the defendant serves only to determine which party is to be the insurer for the loss, that is, where the loss should lie, given that the loss could not have been efficiently pre-vented.

Some courts and agencies appear to believe that increasing the obligation of providers to compensate victims will always increase these providers' investments in safety. Where damage measures are compensatory, however, there is a very definite ceiling to the accident prevention investments that any provider will make.[92] Providers will make investments to reduce the accident rate only to the extent that such investments are cost-effective—that is, that the marginal costs of preventive investments are less than the marginal gain in expected accident cost reduction. Beyond that point, it is less costly to pay damage claims or judg-ments than to prevent accidents from occurring. Thus, extending liability beyond that point will not affect the level of safety investments.

There are insurance implications, however, of every liability decision. If a lia-bility standard were set only to require cost-effective preventive investments by a provider, some losses would still occur.[93] Victims would bear these losses, and thus would bear the obligation to obtain insurance for them through some first-party insurance mechanism. In contrast, if a provider were held liable for losses which the provider could not cost-effectively have prevented, the provider would bear the obligation to provide insurance. Either through self-insurance or some form of third-party insurance, the provider insures victims for losses that cannot efficiently be prevented.

The economic effects of steadily increasing provider liability thus are quite simple in structure. A liability rule can compel providers of products and services to make investments that reduce the accident rate up to the level of optimal (cost-effective) investments.[94] After providers have invested optimally in preven-tion, however, any further assignment of liability affects only the provision of in-surance. More extensive provider liability will generate more extensive provider insurance and nothing more.

The expansion of liability under modern tort law has obviously increased the provision of provider insurance. Any standard beyond a bare cost-benefit test (often identified with negligence)[95] will provide an insurance effect. Courts, of course, have extended liability far beyond the simple cost-benefit standard. Thus, modern tort law compels a very substantial level of provider insurance.

More precisely, modern tort law has broadly shifted the insurance obligation from first-party insurance to third-party or self-insurance by providers. Even a bare-bones cost-benefit standard has insurance consequences: Such a standard cre-ates an obligation of potential victims to obtain market insurance or to self-insure

---

92. Awards in excess of compensatory damages, such as punitive damages, can in the-ory lead to either an increase or a reduction in aggregate safety levels. See Priest, Punitive Damages and Enterprise Liability, 56 S. CAL. L. REV. 123, 128–32 (1982);

93. Injurers and victims are likely to make errors in choosing optimal forms of accident prevention and some accidents are not worth preventing.

94. Again, this analysis puts aside considerations of greater than compensatory dam-ages. See supra note 92.

95. See Posner, A Theory of Negligence, 1 J. LEGAL STUD. 29 (1972). I am very skep-tical that the negligence standard, as it is applied by courts and juries, closely resembles an economically efficient cost-benefit standard.

for unpreventable losses. Modern tort law has shifted that obligation to providers, requiring providers either to obtain third-party market insurance or to self-insure for the losses suffered by consumers of their products or services. The expansion of tort liability since the mid-1960's has expanded the range of contexts in which provider insurance must be offered. Courts understand this point perfectly. Much of the modern extension of tort liability has been expressly justified by the salutary insurance consequences that are supposed to result. Thus it is a paradox that the modern regime somehow has led to the reduction of insurance availability.

*   *   *

III. HOW INSURANCE OPERATES

*   *   *

Tort law, of course, provides insurance through a third-party mechanism: the insurer pays money to the victim through the medium of the product or service provider who purchases the insurance policy. Although third-party institutional arrangements are somewhat more complex than first-party arrangements, the determinants of the insurance function are the same.

In third-party insurance, there are two sets of risk pools. Consumers of products or services comprise one set of risk pools. To consumers, the insurance policy and the premium are tied to the sale of the product. It is advantageous to define risk pools narrowly for consumers in third-party contexts for exactly the same reasons that it is advantageous to define risk pools narrowly in typical first-party insurance contexts. Defining consumer risk pools narrowly increases product sales, because the premium added to the price of the product more closely approximates the consumer's expected loss.

Manufacturers, for example, will attempt to segregate consumers into risk pools by product design and by advertising and marketing techniques. A chain-saw manufacturer, for example, may design one model appropriate for industrial use and a second model appropriate for occasional gathering of firewood. Of course, such design differences may also be related to different consumer preferences for product features—in this example, features related to safety. But the point is that, if the demand for chain saw injury insurance coverage differs between the professional and the weekender, both consumers and the manufacturer will gain if the manufacturer can design products that differentiate the two markets. In this example, market differentiation would reduce one very broad risk pool into two more narrow risk pools. Narrowing the pools allows the manufacturer to charge different insurance premiums to the two markets and to increase product sales.

Similarly, the accident insurance premium added to the price of an airline ticket from the United States to Europe will be greater on, say, the Concorde than on low-budget or charter lines.[125] The risk of an accident among the vari-

---

125. I ignore here the effects of the Geneva and proposed Montreal Conventions limiting damages for international (but not United States originating) air travel. 47 Stat. 2021 (1929). These Conventions reduce differences in risk pools by limiting damages owed by the airlines to victims of air crashes.

ous airlines may be the same, but the accident payout risks brought into the pool by passengers on the Concorde are likely to be much greater than the risks brought by charter passengers, if only because of their greater expected future income. The third-party insurance premium must be adjusted in response. In this respect, the qualitative differences between the Concorde and the charters in terms of accident insurance are no different than qualitative differences in meals, time of transit, or other amenities. Indeed, much of the attraction of the charters derives exactly from the ability of these firms to narrow the pool of consumers of their product. Those passengers who travel on low-fare flights are those who prefer or are willing to tolerate lower levels of amenities in return for a lower ticket price.

The second set of risk pools within third-party insurance contexts includes the service and product providers themselves. Providers of products and services purchase market insurance for the same purposes as any first-party insured: to equalize monetary returns over time in the face of some probabilistic chance of loss. Providers will choose market insurance if its costs are lower than the costs of alternatives.[126]

The costs a provider faces by deciding not to purchase insurance depend upon diversification within the provider firm or the provider's ability to diversify risk by other means.[127] As suggested above, marketing different models of a product is a form of diversification, if the risks of loss attending sales of the respective models are uncorrelated. Of course, organization in the conglomerate form or investing retained earnings in diversified assets are other ways in which providers can self-insure.[128]

Insurance companies, however, can (and do) compete for the custom of providers by trying to define narrow risk pools that make market insurance more attractive than self-insurance alternatives. Insurers attempt to aggregate within a pool a set of providers whose risks are uncorrelated, and will set individual premiums for the firms according to the risk each brings to the pool. The insurer's diversification of risk, again, can be achieved either by aggregating a very disparate pool, by holding other assets whose riskiness is uncorrelated, or by reinsuring—hiring another insurer to provide meta-diversification.

These simple insurance principles seem very general, but they provide an explanation for the insurance crisis we are currently observing. The next Section attempts to apply these principles to the changes in tort law discussed in Section II, in order to predict the effects of modern law on insurance availability.

---

126. The most common and best-known alternative to market insurance is self-insurance—the maintenance of reserves adequate to meet expected losses and the threat of bankruptcy if these reserves prove too low. See infra notes 190–93 and accompanying text. Self-insurance has been popularly called "going bare." A recently popular alternative to market insurance, that is something of a hybrid of going bare and buying standard insurance, is insuring through industry mutuals. See infra text accompanying notes 227–42.

127. The purchase of market insurance by a firm, thus, is likely to involve more complicated questions of corporate finance. See Mayers & Smith, On the Corporate Demand for Insurance, 55 J. BUS. 281 (1982); see also infra text accompanying note 164.

128. For a discussion of the corporate demand for insurance, see infra text accompanying notes 159–64.

IV. HOW CONTEMPORARY TORT LAW AFFECTS
INSURANCE MARKETS

...the expansion of corporate liability has progressively undermined the insurance function by increasing the variance (coefficient of variation) of existing insurance risk pools. As described in the preceding Section, increasing the variance of a risk pool endangers the pool because it increases the likelihood that the pool will unravel as low-risk members drop out, either by self-insuring or by ceasing to engage in the potentially injury-related activity. This Section shows these effects in both consumer and provider risk pools. Thus, it shows that contemporary tort law has restricted rather than expanded insurance availability. The parties that have been most adversely affected are the low-income and poor who, in terms of tort recoveries, are the low-risk members of the consuming population.

...If there has been no increase in the accident rate and if the largest majority of tort law claimants already possess first-party insurance, then the expansion of corporate legal liability has chiefly shifted coverage from (private and government) first-party sources to corporate defendant third-party sources. The question, then, is why the shift from first- to third-party insurance sources has led to a breakdown in insurance markets?

I believe that there are very clear insurance reasons why the shift towards third-party coverage has undermined the commercial casualty insurance industry, generating the crisis. In comparison to first-party insurance, third-party tort law insurance provides coverage in excessive amounts, in a manner that substantially restricts risk segregation, and at costs that far exceed the costs of first-party insurance. For both consumer and provider risk pools, these differences will increase the correlation of risks within existing pools and, as a consequence, increase the extent of adverse selection, leading to the breakdown of the pools.

A. *Why Consumer Risk Pools Have Unraveled*

Provider tort law insurance coverage differs substantially from first-party insurance coverage. One of the objectives of the tort system is to create incentives for appropriate investments in preventing injury. To obtain optimal incentives for injury prevention, a party that has violated a legal standard must pay full losses to the victim, including both pecuniary and non-pecuniary losses.

The award of both pecuniary and non-pecuniary losses, however, is inappropriate for providing optimal insurance for unpreventable losses. The effort to extend insurance coverage through modern tort law represents a confusion of incentive objectives with insurance objectives. Third-party insurance payments administered through the tort system differ from first-party insurance payments in two ways. First, as described in Section III, no first-party insurance market provides coverage of non-pecuniary losses. Non-pecuniary losses do not affect the marginal value of wealth across states of the world. In addition, moral hazard and adverse selection problems make coverage of these losses exceedingly costly. Losses representing pain and suffering or other emotional effects of an injury, therefore, are never insured in first-party markets because it is not worthwhile for consumers to pay the premiums necessary to support coverage of them.

Secondly, deductibles and co-insurance are features of every first-party insurance contract. Third-party insurance through the tort system, in contrast, never incorporates deductibles or co-insurance to control victim moral hazard. Yet victim moral hazard is as serious a problem in a third-party context as in a first-party context. Preferences for extra visits to a doctor, prolonged hospitalization, or more advanced forms of medical treatment do not diminish because the source of the injury is a third-party defendant.

These two differences mean that, for the same injury, first-party insurance coverage—which corresponds to what consumers are willing to purchase—is substantially different in magnitude than the third-party insurance coverage provided through tort law.

    *   *   *

All first-party medical plans incorporate detailed limitations on the nature of available care and on the extent of specific forms of care. Blue Cross-Blue Shield plans, for example, limit coverage to semi-private room accommodations, limit coverage of hospitalization or of skilled nursing facility care to 120 days, and exclude coverage altogether of services such as "custodial care designed to assist an individual in meeting activities of daily life." Of course all consumers would prefer more coverage to less, but these limitations—though they force consumers sometimes to make difficult decisions about medical treatment—represent the best accommodation with the insurance premiums consumers are willing to pay. Because of moral hazard, additional medical services would require increases in insurance premiums beyond their value to consumers.

In contrast, under third-party insurance provided through tort law, there is little reason for the beneficiary of the insurance—the tort plaintiff—to engage in difficult decisions about appropriate levels of medical treatment. Both because of the specific policy care limitations and because every first-party insurance claimant must pay a not-insubstantial portion of medical costs, he or she must consider very carefully which medical procedures will be most effective as well as whether, and the extent to which, extended care is needed. The tort plaintiff, on the other hand, loses nothing by requesting (or asserting as essential) all available advanced methods of medical treatment regardless of cost.

The shift from first-party to third-party insurance sources, thus, will prompt greater expenditures for advanced medical care, as well as more extended and elaborate hospitalization and subsequent care. For example, holding severity of injury constant, the frequency of claims for twenty-four hour nursing care is likely to be substantially higher under third-party tort law insurance than under first-party insurance.[149]

    *   *   *

Some might regard the additional level of insurance coverage provided by tort law to be beneficial to consumers because it affords them greater compensation for the injuries they suffer. But this view misunderstands the consumer inter-

---

149. There is some confirmation from studies of damage awards that have found the largest increases in medical damage claims in recent years in cases that involve more severe injuries, cases in which this moral hazard component is greatest. M. PETERSON, supra note 140, at 23–27

est in insurance. Of course, after an injury has been suffered, the victim would prefer a greater to a lesser award. But the ex ante interest of the victim is an award tied to the victim's pecuniary losses, not an award greater than these losses. Where the victim is the product or service purchaser, the victim must pay for the insurance in advance. To compel insurance greater than the amount demanded by the purchaser reduces, rather than increases, his or her welfare. To illustrate: if my $100,000 home burns down, I of course would be happier if my insurer gave me $234,000 rather than the $100,000 of coverage I purchased. But, I would object strongly if I were compelled in advance of the fire to purchase $234,000 coverage since I could replace the home in its entirety for an amount in the range of $100,000. A similar concern for optimal insurance extends to contexts involving pure third-party injuries—for example, when bystanders are harmed by the product or service use of others. In modern society, all of us are at once product and service purchasers and bystanders of products and services used by others. Again, in terms solely of insurance, each of us ex ante prefers that the optimal level of insurance be provided by tort law, the level that optimizes insurance coverage subject to insurance costs.

The provision of insurance coverage through tort law in amounts greater than consumers would willingly purchase has additional effects that implicate the recent crisis. An increase of 64% to 134% in the level of insurance coverage under tort law will not operate as a scalar, but will increase consumer risk pool variance and will lead to the unraveling of consumer risk pools.

The increase in the level of insurance coverage from the shift to the third-party tort mechanism is not likely to be uniform over all cases. The empirical observation that pain and suffering awards constitute 47% of total damages is an average figure. Pain and suffering and other non-pecuniary amounts comprise a much higher proportion of large damage judgments. For this reason, risk pool variance is likely to be greater under third-party tort insurance than under first-party insurance.

More importantly, segregating risks into narrow risk pools is substantially more difficult in third-party than in first-party insurance contexts. First-party insurers, by using insurance applications, can distinguish insureds by age, income, occupation, the level of coverage desired, and other personal characteristics related to levels of risk brought to the insurance pool. Moreover, the administration of first-party insurance allows the insurer to distinguish insureds by past loss experience. The collection of these data allows a first-party insurer to define risk pools of very narrow scope, increasing the likelihood that low-risk individuals will find insurance attractive. Narrow risk differentiation maximizes the availability of insurance.

Very little information about individual risks, however, is available to third-party insurers. A product manufacturer, for example, may design and market a product with reference to characteristics of discrete sets of average consumers. But the manufacturer must sell the product on equivalent terms to all who wish to buy it, and cannot distinguish among consumers with respect to the insurance policy provided in the product price.

Some products, of course, will attract relatively homogeneous sets of consumers. A very wide range of products, however, are accessible to and are purchased by consumers of different income levels. Studies of consumers of individual products show that, for virtually all products, the income levels and personal characteristics of consumers of the product differ widely.

The difficulty of segregating risk pools in third-party contexts means that third-party tort insurance pools are likely to be substantially broader than first-party pools even without the effects, described above, of levels of coverage. Compare, for example, the risks of non-preventable injuries from auto use. The first-party insurer can create separate driver pools for teenagers and other age groups; it can segregate insureds by levels of driving, total mileage, distance from home to office, and car type; and it can rate the policies by accident experience and by moving violations within previous time periods. It can allow the insured to choose whether to purchase medical expense and disability coverage in the auto policy or to rely on separate medical and disability policy coverage set according to the deductible the insured prefers and according to the insured's income level. Each of these techniques helps keep premiums low for the low-risk drivers of the consuming population—those who drive little, are very skilled or careful, or generate small claims because of low expected income losses.

In contrast, the auto manufacturer—that must buy third-party liability insurance for all those injured in its cars and pass on the premiums in vehicle prices—can implement none of these distinctions. Some auto models may be more or less attractive to commuters, to teenagers, or to the very wealthy, but, except for these crude distinctions, the auto manufacturer must provide insurance to all who buy the model, high-risk and low-risk alike. Consequently, the variance in the insurance pool is vastly greater in the third-party context, and the premium is commensurately higher—even if the same level of coverage is offered. Of course, given the greater amount of coverage provided under a third-party policy, the variance and the premium are higher yet.

One of the most seriously deleterious effects of lumping consumers into undifferentiated third-party risk pools is glaringly inconsistent with the judicial objective of aiding the poor. That is the regressive redistributional effect of third-party insurance. The largest items of damages in most third-party personal injury contexts, especially those involving permanent disability, are lost income and pain and suffering, which are highly correlated with individuals' expected future income streams. As a consequence, these damage elements constitute the largest component of the third-party insurance premium tied to the sale of any product or service.

The third-party premium is set with reference to average expected loss. Thus, the high correlation of total awards with income means that premiums reflect the average income of the population of consumers. The implication of charging each consumer a premium related to average income is that consumers with high incomes are charged a premium lower than their expected loss, and consumers with low incomes are charged a premium higher than their expected loss. Third-party insurance thus requires low-income consumers to subsidize high-income consumers.

Moreover, third-party insurance requires low-income individuals to subsidize both pecuniary and non-pecuniary losses of high-income individuals. Compare the insurance premium that a low-income consumer would pay in a first-party auto, product, or disability policy to the premium tied to the product or service in a third-party provider policy that includes coverage to the high-income consumer. The auto or product manufacturer cannot charge the low-income consumer a lower price based on the lower dollar risk the consumer brings to the risk pool. The first-party casualty or disability carrier can do so, and thus can increase the availability of insurance.

As a consequence, the disadvantages of third-party insurance coverage are substantial. Courts justified third-party insurance coverage based on how easy it seemed to be for manufacturers or service providers to aggregate risks by adding an insurance premium to the price of the product or service. Whatever comparative advantage providers enjoy in risk aggregation, however, is overwhelmed by the disadvantages of excessive coverage, the inability to segregate risks in third-party contexts, and regressive distributive effects.

How do the differences between first-party and third-party tort insurance mechanisms affect the behavior of consumers? The shift towards greater corporate-provided tort law insurance will lead low-risk consumers to reduce consumption of products whose prices incorporate high tort insurance premiums. For low-risk consumers, especially low-income consumers, the tort law insurance premium tied to the product or service price may be much greater than the benefit the insurance provides. As a consequence, though the effect may be subtle, these consumers will drop out of the market.

*   *   *

Notes and Questions

1. The Enterprise Liability Paradox: Enterprise liability is motivated by a desire to provide insurance to victims of non-negligent accidents. At its base, the theory supposes that expanded tort liability will lead to the provision of insurance along with the sale of the product or service itself. Manufacturing and service providers will pass on as much of the liability insurance premium through price as is possible, given demand elasticity. According to the theory, the poor are especially benefitted by expanded liability because they could not otherwise afford to purchase insurance for such loses. Professor Priest suggests that the impact of this ever expanding liability has had a paradoxical effect. That is, enterprise liability theory has lead to a reduction in the total insurance coverage available to society, rather than an increase. Particularly harmed by enterprise liability under Priest's analysis are the poor. Do you find Professor Priest's analysis persuasive? If so, what type of action should be taken to correct this judicially imposed problem?

2. Variance in Risk Pools: At the heart of Professor Priest's analysis is the fact that enterprise liability has lead to an increase in risk pool variance. In general, an individual is willing to purchase insurance if the premium paid reflects the expected damages. When insurers are able to segregate risk pools it allows them to take full advantage of the law of large numbers—the insurer can begin to predict with certainty the total losses which any risk pool will incur. In other words, segregating risk pools and taking advantage of the law of large numbers allows the insurer to substantially reduce the variance of expected losses. This reduced variance allows insurers to set premiums at a level that reflects the expected damages of risk pool members. Anything that would cause variance to increase results in the premium charged being less reflective of some risk pool members expected damages. For high risk members of the pool this is a subsidy.

Low risk members find that the premium is too high in comparison to expected damages. Therefore, low risk members drop out of the risk pool. Within this line of reasoning, Professor Priest identifies two factors which have contributed to the current insurance crisis. First, are damages for non-pecuniary losses and the corresponding adverse selection and moral hazard problems associated with such damages. Second, are the greater difficulties in risk pool segregation due to the third party context. Can you think of other factors that contribute to risk pool variance? Does enterprise liability have any impacts that reduce risk pool variance? Are there any mitigating factors that justify a continuation of enterprise liability theory?

3. Ending the Vicious Circle: Following the reasoning of Professor Priest's analysis leads one into a vicious circle. As low risk insureds drop out of the risk pool, premiums increase. The increased premiums cause further drop outs and so on. How does this vicious circle resolve itself? Professor Priest provides examples of several services that were forced out of the market due to enterprise liability theory. Is this result acceptable; justifiable? What do such results portend for the future of American business?

4. Ultrahazardous Activities, Personal Injury, and Risk Spreading: Is the argument for imposition of enterprise liability more powerful when applied to ultrahazardous activities? In *Richman v. Charter Arms Corporation*, 571 F.Supp. 192 (1983), a murder victim's mother brought a wrongful death action against a manufacturer of a handgun used in the killing seeking to recover on strict liability theories of unreasonably dangerous product and ultrahazardous activity. In refusing to grant summary judgment for the manufacturer on the ultrahazardous activity claim, the court said:

> The defendant maintains that, if liability is imposed in this case, no company that markets handguns for sale to the general public will be able in the future to obtain insurance. The result, according to the defendant, will be catastrophic for handgun manufacturers: all such companies will be forced either to alter their marketing practices radically or to go out of business. This argument has a ring of plausibility to it. At the same time, however, it is highly speculative.
>
> *   *   *
>
> Perhaps the most significant fact the defendant ignores is that increased insurance costs can be passed on to consumers in the form of higher prices for handguns. The people who benefit most from marketing practices like the defendant's are handgun manufacturers and handgun purchasers. Innocent victims rarely, if ever, are beneficiaries. Consequently, it hardly seems unfair to require manufacturers and purchasers, rather than innocent victims, to pay for the risks those practices entail. Furthermore, economic efficiency seems to require the same result. In an important article on ultrahazardous activities and risk allocation, Professor Clarence Morris makes just this point. Morris, "Hazardous Enterprises and Risk Bearing Capacity," 61 Yale L.J. 1172 (1952). In his view, "the avowed goal of the absolute liability approach is allocation of loss to the party better equipped to pass it on to the public: the superior risk bearer." Id. at 1176. Professor Morris discusses a variety of examples to show that the defendant is not always the superior risk bearer in an ultrahazardous

activity case. Here is what he says, however, about bodily injury and risk-bearing capacity:

> The financial burden of disabling personal injury overwhelms most people. While many can bear the cost of minor injury, prolonged infirmity and extended medical expense often exceed the financial competence of common men. Unless [common man] happens to be rich or covered by one of the more generous workman's compensations plans, he will probably bear the risk less easily than Enterpriser. The preponderant likelihood is that Enterpriser is the better risk bearer of the two. Id. at 1177.

Another prominent legal scholar, Wex Malone, in an article on Louisiana tort law, says much the same thing:

> If, as would seem proper, the inescapable accident cost of a given hazardous activity ought to be so allocated by law that this cost can ultimately be passed on in dilution as a charge upon the numerous consumers or users of the goods or services produced by the activity, then it would seem that the enterprise—the individual or corporation that conducts the activity—is the appropriate unit that should initially shoulder the cost burden; for the enterpriser is in the best position to convert the anticipated accident charge into an item of capital cost, to insure against it, and to transfer the resulting premium cost into the price structure of the goods or services the activity produces. Furthermore, it is only the enterpriser who is in a position to adopt or to devise those precautionary measures that may serve in the future to minimize the chance of a recurrence of the tragedy.

Malone, "The Work of the Louisiana Appellate Courts for the 1969–70 Term—Torts," 31 La.L.Rev. 231, 241 (1971). Thus, both fairness and economic efficiency suggest that the community would be better off if the defendant's marketing practices were classified as ultrahazardous.

Id. at 202–204. How does this analysis square with that of Professor Priest?

5. Other Goals of Tort Law: Appeasement: Appeasement as a goal of tort law means that the purpose of the law is to limit the negative impact of the infliction of injury to the event of the injury itself. Tort law provides a way to right the wrong without the injured party retaliating through some destructive means. That is, the victim's vengeance is bought off by imposing tort liability on the wrongdoer. The victim is appeased in two ways: receipt of compensation and knowledge of the fact that the transgressor is punished by being required to pay.

6. Other Goals of Tort Law: Justice and Liability: The law of torts is sometimes viewed as the expression of a moral principle—one who by his fault has caused damage to another ought to make compensation as a matter of justice. There are two views in support of this position—and either variant is simply a different way of saying the same thing. First, the principle of ethical retribution places emphasis upon the fact that the payment of compensation is harmful to the offender, and that justice requires that the offender suffer the harm. Second, the principle of ethical compensation looks at the same situation form the point of view of the victim. It emphasizes the fact that the payment of compensation is a benefit to the victim of the wrong, and declares that justice requires that the victim should receive this compensation. Regardless of the perspective one chooses, the policy implications are the same.

3. Allocative Efficiency

The risk of injury associated with products or services is sometimes characterized as an externality imposed on third parties. In this view, tort law increases allocative efficiency by forcing the internalization of externalities. However, to the extent the risk of injury is known by the injured party, the market price should reflect the risk so that there is no externality. Nevertheless, under some circumstances, there might be questions about the ability of the market price to reflect the risk.

Doe v. Miles Laboratories, Inc.
United States District Court, D. Maryland
675 F.Supp. 1466 (1987)

RAMSEY, District Judge.

A plague inflicts society and this Court is called upon to adjudicate the extent to which the effects will be visited upon its victims. The facts are tragic. In the autumn of 1983, plaintiff Jane Doe, who a week previous had given birth, sought emergency medical treatment for vaginal bleeding. During the course of treatment, the attending physician ordered the administration of 500 units of "Konyne," a blood-coagulation-factor concentrate produced by Cutter Laboratories, a division of Miles. Treatment appeared successful and plaintiff eventually was discharged.

Over the course of the months to follow, plaintiff suffered from a succession of ailments, ultimately being diagnosed as infected by the HTLV-III virus, and as having Acquired Immuno-Deficiency Syndrome-Related Complex (ARC), a predecessor of AIDS. On July 6, 1986, plaintiffs Jane and John Doe filed suit, alleging claims for strict liability in tort, for breach of warranties, and for loss of consortium. Later plaintiffs amended the complaint to include negligence counts, and for punitive damages. Defendant Miles, following other procedural actions, filed this motion for summary judgment on plaintiffs' counts for breach of warranties, for strict liability in tort, and for strict liability in tort—failure to warn; and further seeks summary judgment on the counts for loss of consortium and punitive damages to the extent they are derivative of the first three.

*   *   *

Products Liability Law

Defective products cause accidents that result in both economic losses and injuries either to persons or property. Allowing victims to recover for such losses was long a controversial issue. Indeed, the common law has followed a confusing and torturous path in perceiving and remedying the situation.

*   *   *

Once liability in negligence became established, the concept of strict products liability gained favor as an alternative theory of recovery for injuries from defec-

tive products. It is commonly stated that there are three reasons for holding manufacturers and dealers strictly liable for personal or property injury caused by defective products. First, innocent victims should not be forced to bear the costs of
accidents, which still occurs far too often, for even a negligence action may impose an evidentiary burden impossible to meet. Second, that strict liability promotes accident prevention, for the manufacturers are in a better position to ascertain and control the risks associated with their products. Third, that
manufacturers are in a better position than victims to bear the costs, for they can
distribute the losses across the many who purchase the product, whereas an individual victim, unless he or she is exceptionally well-to-do or heavily insured, will
be driven into bankruptcy or into social welfare programs. Prosser, supra p. 4,
§ 98 at 692–93.

Implicit in the above justification for strict products liability, though perhaps
not clearly articulated, is a fourth argument, namely that strict products liability
can promote the efficient allocation of resources. Society has chosen to allow
market forces to set the price for goods and thus to determine their availability
and distribution. In some respects the market is very efficient. The price purchasers pay invariably reflects direct costs such as raw products, capital investment, labor, plus a reasonable rate of return. However, in other respects the market is not efficient. Prices often do not reflect indirect costs. These hidden costs
can include the effects of pollution or the expenses of accidents, and are what
economists refer to as "externalities."

When the price of an item does not reflect both its direct costs and its externalities, the price will be lower than its actual cost. This lower price will stimulate an inefficient allocation of resources, for persons will be encouraged to buy more of the
product than they might if they were paying its true price. Society thus may increase
the consumption of the very goods that create pollution, and thus have indirect
cleanup costs, or that are defective, and thus have indirect accident costs. Strict
products liability shifts the cost back to manufacturers, who will then reprice the
goods to reflect their actual costs. Strict products liability therefore affords society a
mechanism for a rational allocation of resources.[3] Absent it, the costs of externalities
are thrust upon victims or upon society through its governmental welfare programs.
In essence, without it there is a subsidy given to the polluting or defective produc

*   *   *

These conceptual difficulties are evident in Greenman v. Yuba Power Products, Inc., 59 Cal.2d 57, 27 Cal.Rptr. 697, 377 P.2d 897 (1963), which inaugu-
rated strict products liability in tort as an alternative theory of recovery. . . .

*   *   *

Whatever the theory of recovery, whether negligence or strict liability, it is
now clear that the test in products liability is the same. A plaintiff must show 1)

---

3. The argument is often made that strict products liability has the potential to bankrupt manufacturers. Such an argument misses the salutory economic role strict products liability plays. Understood properly, it can be seen that strict liability promotes a rational market place. Society cannot make rational decisions concerning the allocation of resources
unless the price reflects the true costs. When the price rises greatly, reflecting the fact the
product produces either substantial direct costs or creates widespread externalities, it is rational to discourage or even abandon consumption of that product. Strict products liability
thus allows the marketplace to make better informed decisions.

the existence of a defect; 2) the attribution of the defect to the seller; and 3) a causal relation between the defect and the injury. Jensen v. American Motors, 50 Md.App. 226, 234, 437 A.2d 242, 247 (1981).

*   *   *

STRICT LIABILITY IN TORT

Defendant argues... for an exemption from strict liability in tort for blood or blood products....

*   *   *

Do policy considerations warrant exempting blood and blood products from strict products liability in tort? Defendant argues that the "unavoidably unsafe products" exemption provided to § 402A by Comment k applies to it. Comment k reads:

> There are some products which, in the present state of human knowledge, are quite incapable of being made safe for their intended and ordinary use. These are especially common in the field of drugs. An example is the vaccine for the Pasteur treatment of rabies, which not uncommonly leads to very serious and even permanently injurious consequences when it is injected. Since the disease itself invariably results in a dreadful death, both the marketing and the use of the vaccine are fully justified, notwithstanding the unavoidably high degree of risk which they involve. Such a product, properly prepared and accompanied by proper directions and warnings, is not defective, nor is it unreasonably dangerous. The same is true of many other vaccines, drugs and the like, many of which for that very reason cannot legally be sold except to physicians, or under the prescription of a physician. It is also true, in particular, of many new or experimental drugs as to which, because of lack of time and opportunity for sufficient medical experience, there can be no assurance of safety, or perhaps even of purity of ingredients, but such experience as there is justifies the marketing and use of the drug notwithstanding a medically recognizable risk. The seller of such products, again with the qualification that they are properly prepared and marketed, and proper warning is given where the situation calls for it, is not to be held to strict liability for unfortunate consequences attending to their use, merely because he has undertaken to supply the public with an apparently useful and desirable product, attended with a known but apparently reasonable danger.

Maryland courts have never expressly adopted Comment k. Several decisions in this federal district court, though, have relied on Comment k, holding that Maryland courts would adopt it if an appropriate case were before them. Weinberger v. Bristol-Myers Co., 652 F.Supp. 187, 191 (D.Md.1986); see Werner v. Upjohn Company, Inc., 628 F.2d 848, 858 (4th Cir.1980). Those cases, however, involved prescription medications and did not address whether blood, especially blood infected with disease, fell within Comment k 's exemption.

This Court is not prepared to find that HTLV-III carrying blood presents a "reasonable danger" as Comment k requires. It is estimated that up to 95% of severe hemophiliacs test positive for exposure to the HTLV-III virus. Ray v. School District of Desoto County, 666 F.Supp. 1524, 1527 (M.D.Fla.1987).

The nearly complete exposure by the group most in need of coagulant-factors and the inevitably fatal nature of the disease for those who actually develop it are stark facts. The fact the virus was indetectible prior to 1985 is not a mitigating factor. The best view is to consider blood containing indetectible diseases to be a defective product and therefore that strict liability is applicable. 2 L. Frumer & M. Friedman, Products Liability, § 3.03[4][f][I] at 3-572 (1987). See Rostocki v. Southwest Florida Blood Bank, 276 So.2d 475 (Fla.1973); DeBattista v. Argonaut-Southwest Ins. Co., 403 So.2d 26 (La.1981); Reilly v. King Co. Cent. Blood Bank, Inc., 6 Wash.App. 172, 492 P.2d 246 (1971).

It is argued that providers of blood and blood products are promoting the general welfare by making possible improved health. It is argued that it is a fundamental social policy of the State of Maryland to promote the supply of blood and blood products. And it is argued that to allow strict products liability, which given the wide exposure to AIDS due to transfusions could create potentially substantial liability, would so raise costs of production that the supply of blood could be choked off.

The arguments are unpersuasive....Those who choose to operate in the economic marketplace play by the rules applicable to all.

The arguments in favor of strict products liability apply as persuasively to blood and blood products as they do to any other product. First, there is no reason why victims of defective blood should bear the costs where victims of other defective products do not. Second, strict liability would provide the incentive to promote all possible accident prevention, for it is a rational business decision to keep costs down. Third, the producers are in a better position to spread the costs than are individual consumers. Finally, it makes for a more efficient allocation of social resources when the price of a transfusion of blood or blood products reflects its true costs.

Entrepreneurs by their nature are risk taking individuals. To the extent they need an incentive to engage in socially beneficial activities, the law already provides it in the form of a corporate shield on personal liability. To do as defendant argues, and exempt blood from strict liability would be to subsidize the product by forcing either victims or government through its social welfare programs to bear accident costs. In the absence of a clear expression on the part of the legislature of an intent to subsidize a particular product, it is not this Court's role to create the subsidy indirectly by carving out a Judge made exemption to strict products liability.

Accordingly, the Court will deny defendant's motion for summary judgment on plaintiffs' claim for strict products liability.

*   *   *

Notes and Questions

1. Strict Liability and Externalities: Markets characterized by zero transaction costs, perfect information, and risk neutral participants are able to obtain the optimal level of accident prevention even in the absence of any liability standard. If information regarding risk is not perfectly communicated, then there is an economic justification for a strict liability standard. In general, however, a strict liability standard does not result in a greater level of accident prevention relative to a negligence standard. Thus, strict liability serves only to allocate responsibility for insuring against non-negligent accidents. Certainly, the presence of non-negligent accidents represents a cost that society would like to avoid. Economic efficiency suggests that such costs be borne by the party who can most cost effectively insure against non-negligent accidents. The court clearly assumes that Miles Laboratories can most cost effectively insure against such risks. Is there any justification for this conclusion? If someone other than Miles could provide the most cost effective insurance, is it fair to say that such defendants receive a "subsidy" from the victims or government?

2. *Externalities, Property Rights, and Coase Theorem:* In general, externalities arise because of poorly defined or unenforceable property rights. What property rights were in question in *Miles Laboratories*? Did the supposed externalities arise because of poorly defined property rights, an inability to enforce such rights, or some other reason? What implications does the Coase Theorem have for this problem? Does strict liability allow the Coase Theorem to operate? Do you agree with the court's belief that its interpretation of strict liability supports a rational market place? In a sense, doesn't the court's externality approach really just obscure much of the efficiency analysis of alternative liability rules?

4. Tort Damages and Incentives

Losing tort defendants are generally subject to the rule that they must make their victims whole, by paying sufficient damages to put plaintiffs in the same positions as before the tortious act. The potential of being ordered to pay damages provides an economic incentive that alters the behavior of potential tortfeasors. Damages affect the PL portion of the Learned Hand formula, thereby shifting C* and the optimal amount of prevention.

a. Compensatory Damages

Most of the damages awarded in individual tort cases are intended to make the plaintiff whole again, at least financially. Such **compensatory damages** usually consist of three major types of loss. They are (1) past and future medical expenses, (2) past and future economic loss, and (3) past and future pain and suffering.

Read

O'Shea v. Riverway Towing Co.
U.S. Court of Appeals, Seventh Circuit
677 F.2d 1194 (1982)

and accompanying **Notes and Questions**
Supra Chapter IV

b. Punitive Damages

Courts also award punitive damages in some cases. **Punitive damages** are awards designed to punish individual defendants and to deter potential tortfeasors. The typical cases in which punitive damages would be awarded are intentional torts and negligence cases where the defendant's conduct fell to a level of "gross negligence" or "willful and wanton" disregard for the plaintiff's safety.

Sturm, Ruger & Co., Inc. v. Day
Supreme Court of Alaska
594 P.2d 38 (1979)

CONNOR, Justice.

This is a products liability case.

Appellee Michael James Day bought a .41 magnum single action revolver on June 1, 1972. The gun had been manufactured two years before by appellant Sturm, Ruger and Company, in August of 1970, but was purchased new by Day.

On July 30, 1972, Day was sitting in the cab of his small pickup truck with two young friends when he decided to unload his gun. As he was unloading the revolver, the gun slipped out of his hands. When he grabbed for the gun it fired, the bullet striking his leg and causing serious injuries.

Day filed suit against Sturm, Ruger and Company. His second amended complaint was based on a theory of strict tort liability, and included a claim for punitive damages....

The jury returned a verdict for the plaintiff, finding specifically that the revolver was designed defectively and that it had a manufacturing defect as well. The jury awarded $137,750.00 in compensatory damages and $2,895,000.00 in punitive damages to the plaintiff.

* * *

III

PUNITIVE DAMAGES

Sturm, Ruger...contends that punitive damages should not be awarded as a matter of public policy. In addition, Sturm, Ruger argues that punitive damages have no place in the "fault-free" context of strict products liability.

* * *

We also reject the argument that punitive damages have no place in a strict liability case, although we do agree with appellant that punitive damages ought not be awarded in every products liability case. Where, however, as in the instant case, plaintiff is able to plead and prove that the manufacturer knew that its product was defectively designed and that injuries and deaths had resulted from the design defect, but continued to market the product in reckless disregard of the public's safety, punitive damages may be awarded.

Punitive damages are designed not only to punish the wrongdoer, but also to deter him and others like him from similar wrongdoing in the future. Restatement (Second) of Torts, § 908(1) (Tent. Draft No. 19, 1973). We believe that as a matter of public policy, punitive damages can serve several useful functions in the products liability area. For example, the threat of punitive damages serves a deterrence function in cases in which a product may cause numerous minor injuries for which potential plaintiffs might decline to sue, or in cases in which it would be cheaper for the manufacturer to pay compensatory damages to those who did present claims then it would be to remedy the product's defect. In addition, if punitive damages could not be awarded in the products liability context, a reckless manufacturer might gain an unfair advantage over its more socially responsible competitors. On balance, we find the arguments advanced by appellant in favor of its position to be outweighed by the sound public policy considerations supporting the imposition of punitive damages in appropriate cases. We therefore decline to jettison the doctrine of punitive damages in this area of the law.

We turn next to Sturm, Ruger's claim that there was insufficient evidence to sustain the jury's award of punitive damages. The evidence presented at trial indicated that top officials at Sturm, Ruger knew that the safety and loading notches of their single action revolver presented a danger of accidental discharge because of the propensity of the engaging middle parts to fail or break. The evidence also reflects knowledge on the part of Sturm, Ruger management that serious injuries had resulted from this deficiency, coupled with procrastination in changing the basic design, at an increased cost of $1.93 per gun. Because we find that fair-minded jurors in the exercise of reasonable judgment could differ as to whether Sturm, Ruger's actions amounted to reckless indifference to the rights of others, and conscious action in deliberate disregard of them, thereby evidencing a state of mind which could justify the imposition of punitive damages, we will not upset the jury's conclusions that punitive damages were warranted.

* * *

Appellant's final contention regarding punitive damages is that the amount awarded was excessive....

One means of determining if an award of punitive damages is excessive is to compare it with the amount of actual damages. Professor McCormick observes:

> "The punitive damages given, it is said, must bear some reasonable proportion to the actual damages. As a rough working scale, this is better than nothing." (footnotes omitted)

McCormick, Law of Damages, Sec. 85, 298 (1935). Exemplary damages may exceed the actual damages, however, and no definite ratio between them is prescribed. Taylor v. Williamson, 197 Iowa 88, 196 N.W. 713 (1924). Other important factors which bear on the question include "the magnitude and flagrancy of the offense, the importance of the policy violated, and the wealth of the defendant." Zhadan v. Downtown L. A. Motors, 66 Cal.App.3d 481, 136 Cal.Rptr. 132, 143 (1976).

In his comprehensive law review article, Punitive Damages in Products Liability Litigation, 74 Mich.L.Rev. 1258 (1976), Professor Owen argues cogently that while punitive damages should be awarded in appropriate cases, the awards should be subjected to greater scrutiny than in many cases in the past. Indeed, he finds a recent trend toward tightened judicial control over punitive damages. Id. at 1321. Moreover, judicial scrutiny over the awards provides a partial justification for allowing such awards in the first place. The specter of bankruptcy and excessive punishment can be in part dispelled to the extent that trial and appellate courts exercise their powers of review.

The compensatory damages awarded to Michael Day and against Sturm, Ruger amounted to $137,750, exclusive of costs, prejudgment interest, and attorney's fees. The punitive damage award of $2,895,000 appears to be so out of proportion to the amount of actual damages as to suggest that the jury's award was the result of passion or prejudice. The jurors apparently responded to an invitation to punish Sturm, Ruger for all wrongs committed against all purchasers and users of its products, rather than for the wrong done to this particular plaintiff. Under the circumstances, it was a mistake and an abuse of discretion for the trial judge not to have reduced the punitive damages or to have ordered a new trial.

After a careful review of the evidence and all of the factors which should bear upon this determination, it is our opinion that if punitive damages are awarded at a second trial, on essentially the same evidence as that presented in the first trial, they should not exceed $250,000. That amount is quite sufficient to achieve the deterrent purposes to be served, without at the same time inflicting a penalty disproportionate to the defendant's wrong.

Of course, at any new trial the court should permit the jury to make the initial determination of punitive damages. If essentially the same evidence as that presented at the first trial is presented at the second trial, and if the jury's award exceeds $250,000, the court should then exercise its power to grant remittitur in accordance with this opinion.

In summary, we reverse the award of compensatory damages, and remand for a new trial as to both compensatory and punitive damages....

*   *   *

BURKE, Justice, dissenting in part.

...The trial court instructed the jury that it could return a verdict for punitive damages for injuries caused by a design defect only upon a finding "that (Sturm, Ruger) acted with reckless indifference towards the safety of its customers, or that its acts...were maliciously or wantonly done." The jury concluded that Sturm, Ruger's conduct came within that instruction, and the record certainly supports such a conclusion. As to the amount of the award, the formula that the jury apparently used suggests to me that its verdict was the result of careful deliberation and a keen sense of justice, rather than impermissible passion and prejudice.

The evidence showed that Sturm, Ruger manufactured over 1,501,000 revolvers of the type causing Day's injury. Sturm, Ruger's profit from the manufacture and sale of those firearms alone was enormous, totaling many millions of dollars. At trial, William Ruger, the president and founder of Sturm, Ruger, testified that redesign of the revolver to cure the defect cost approximately $199,000 and that the increased manufacturing cost per revolver was $1.93. The figure agreed upon by the jury as an appropriate award for punitive damages equaled the amount of the increased manufacturing cost per item multiplied by the approximate number of revolvers sold: $1.93 × 1,500,000 = $2,895,000. Thus, the amount of the award is roughly equal to the profit directly attributable to Sturm, Ruger's callous disregard for the safety of its customers. Such being the case, I think there is no merit to the contention that the figure was the result of improper passion or prejudice. Certainly, the amount of the punitive damage award far exceeded Day's actual damages. However, given the purpose of punitive damages, the award was not excessive.

Notes and Questions

1. Aren't They Designed to Punish?: Punitive damages are designed to punish the firm that commits a malicious tort. However, as Professor McCormick states, the punitive damages should "bear some reasonable proportion to the actual damages." Why? Doesn't this view of punitive damages skew the entire purpose behind them. That is, punitive damages are designed to punish the tortious firm rather than have *anything* to do with the victim. In essence, this view of the application of punitive damages gives potential tortfeasors the incentive to act grossly negligent or malicious as long as the damages caused by the defective product are lower than the profit earned from the sale of the product. Is a better view the one taken by the jury? They essentially strip the firm of all profit created by this unsafe design. Is this the correct approach? What are problems with this application of punitive damages?

2. Tort Reform, Caps on Punitive Damages, and Insurance: The tort reform movement has championed several reforms in recent years. Some type of cap on punitive damages is almost always part of legislative reform packages. Is a cap on punitive damages a "silver bullet" to solve problems with product liability and tort litigation? Professor George Priest suggests that punitive damages are just part of the problem and, thus, caps on punitive damages cannot solve the problem:

> * * * The most significant changes in the law are (1) monetary caps on non-economic damages, (2) caps or other limitations on punitive damages, (3) abrogation of joint and several liability, (4) elimination of the collateral source rule, and (5) amendments to substantive liability standards for specific activities such as municipal operations, dramshops, or non-profit organizations. If the source of the crisis is the shift from first- to third-party tort law insurance sources, how effective will these reforms be?
>
> The various tort reform statutes have been supported by a coalition of business and insurance interests, chiefly on the simple ground that modern tort liability is excessive and unfair. Observers have not generally appreciated, however, that each of these reform provisions will affect insurance markets in a similar way: they reduce the variance in insurance risk pools. Obviously, caps on non-economic and punitive damages reduce the range of potential liability outcomes. Similarly, abrogation of the doctrine of joint and several liability in favor of strict comparative fault reduces the risk that any one of a group of joint defendants will ultimately be required to satisfy the entire judgment. Deducting first-party insurance benefits from tort judgments will also reduce risk pool variance. More generally, of course, altering liability standards to make recovery more difficult for plaintiffs will diminish expected liability. To the extent that variance in risk pools is reduced, third-party tort law insurance becomes more supportable.
>
> These reforms, while helpful, constitute only partial contributions toward solution of the problems caused by modern tort law. The provision of insurance through tort law has undermined insurance markets. In my view,

these markets will not be fully restored until these insurance issues are dealt with more systematically. The insurance function must be excised from tort law altogether. None of the recent statutory reforms achieves that effect.

A cap on non-economic damages, for example, does shift tort damage awards to more closely resemble levels of insurance purchased in first-party markets. In first-party markets, however, no one purchases any coverage of non-economic losses. Thus, even if non-economic damages in tort law are capped at $450,000 or $250,000, tort law continues to provide a very substantial level of excess insurance coverage.

Similarly, limitations on punitive damages may reduce risk pool variance to some extent. In my view, however, it is appropriate not only to restrain, but to prohibit, punitive damage awards in product liability and other tort contexts. Punitive damage awards can be justified only where there is some likelihood (1) that normal damage measures cannot measure loss accurately — such as in defamation cases; (2) where there is substantial difficulty in detecting the existence of the injury — such as in fraud or, perhaps, some antitrust actions; or (3) where other incentives are needed to stimulate litigation. For cases in which manufacturers or other providers have deliberately misrepresented product safety or effectiveness * * * punitive damages should be awarded on grounds of the fraudulent behavior itself, not on grounds of the defective character of the product. There is no further need to award punitive damages in typical products and service liability contexts. In this respect, a legislative maximum on punitive damage awards or limitations on the conditions under which punitive awards may be made, constitutes only a partial solution.

The source of the insurability crisis is not the level of damages alone. Rather, the diffuse and indiscriminate expansion of substantive tort liability has led to the unraveling of insurance markets in an increasing number of contexts. This unraveling can be arrested only if substantive standards of liability are redefined to focus exclusively on the accident reduction goal. In my view, modern tort law provides inadequate controls on the accident rate and simultaneously creates a tort law insurance regime that disrupts insurance markets and harms the poor. The objectives of tort law reform are uncontroversial: to reduce the accident rate and to provide a more coherent and comprehensive regime of compensation insurance. These objectives cannot be achieved by tinkering with damage measures and by limited changes in liability standards for particularly sympathetic sets of defendants, such as govermental entities, dramshops or non-profit organizations. Instead, modern tort law must be reformed systematically: by a complete redefinition of liability standards to better achieve accident reduction and insurance.

George Priest, The Current Insurance Crisis and Modern Tort Law, 96 Yale Law Journal 1521, 1587–1590 (1987).

3. Crimes and Torts: Crimes and torts are very similar. Both are wrongs. However, a crime is a wrong against society, and a tort is a wrong against a private party. The fundamental economic consequences of criminal law and tort law are the same — deterrence of activities considered to be wrong. Crimes are punished through fines or imprisonment; torts punish tortfeasors by requiring them to compensate injured plaintiffs through an award of money damages. Less fundamental, but important nonetheless, is the role of the law of torts in defining the rights and duties of society's interacting parties, which allocates the risks of particular types of losses. As a general rule, the risk of loss is borne by the least cost avoider of the loss. What this means is that the party who can more efficiently avoid the loss is the one who will bear the cost of the loss if one occurs.

4. Intentional Torts, Unintentional Torts, and Statistics. An intentional tort involves a deliberate action that results in an injury. For example, a company commits an intentional tort when it knowingly makes false statements about the quality of a competitor's products. A negligent tort is an unintentional tort that arises from the failure to use reasonable care toward one to whom a duty is owed, which results in injury. Unintentional torts occur in a variety of business settings—ranging from slip-and-fall accidents in a showroom to defectively designed products. For many types of business behavior, distinguishing between intentional and unintentional torts is not obvious. For example, a hand tool manufacturer that sells millions of power saws per year knows for a statistical fact—because of the large numbers involved—that a certain number of consumers per year will be injured by the saws. Such injuries, however, are typically analyzed as unintentional torts— the manufacturer did not intend to injure any particular individual. The distinction, therefore, appears to be based in part on whether the wrongdoer knows the identity of the injured party prior to the occurrence of the tort.

5. Economic Competition and Intentional Torts. An intentional tort is based on the intentional invasion of a protected interest. It is not necessary that the wrongdoer intend to cause harm, merely that an injury flows from the intentional act. The interest harmed must be a legally protected interest. Thus, normal (or "fair") economic competition between firms in the same industry does not result in an intentional tort if one firm's market share increases at the expense of the other firms' market share.

c. Collateral Source Rule

The collateral source rule applies to situations where the victim receives compensation for his damages from a source independent of the tortfeasor. Under this rule, the payments received from the independent source are not deducted from the award the victim would otherwise receive from the tortfeasor. As a result of this rule, the tortfeasor is not able benefit from the victims foresight in purchasing insurance. From an economic perspective, the collateral source rule raises two primary issues. First, what impact does the collateral source rule have on deterrence? Second, does the collateral source rule allow the victim a double recovery?

Helfend v. Southern California Rapid Transit District
Supreme Court of California
465 P.2d 61 (1970)

TOBRINER, Acting Chief Justice

* * *

1. The facts.

Shortly before noon on July 19, 1965, plaintiff drove his car in central Los Angeles east on Third Street approaching Grandview. At this point Third Street has six lanes, four for traffic and one parking lane on each side of the thoroughfare. While traveling in the second lane from the curb, plaintiff observed an automobile driven by Glen A. Raney, Jr., stopping in his lane and preparing to back into a parking space. Plaintiff put out his left arm to signal the traffic behind him that he intended to stop; he then brought his vehicle to a halt so that the other driver could park.

At about this time Kenneth A. Mitchell, a bus driver for the Southern California Rapid Transit District, pulled out of a bus stop at the curb of Third Street and headed in the same direction as plaintiff. Approaching plaintiff's and Raney's cars which were stopped in the second lane from the curb, Mitchell pulled out into the lane closest to the center of the street in order to pass. The right rear of the bus sideswiped plaintiff's vehicle, knocking off the rearview mirror and crushing plaintiff's arm, which had been hanging down at the side of his car in the stopping signal position.

...Plaintiff acquired some permanent discomfort but no permanent disability from the injuries sustained in the accident. At the time of the injury plaintiff was 67 years of age and had a life expectancy of about 11 years. He owned the Jewel Homes Investment Company which possessed and maintained small rental properties. Prior to the accident plaintiff had performed much of the minor maintenance on his properties including some painting and minor plumbing. For the six-month healing period he hired a man to do all the work he had formerly performed and at the time of the trial still employed him for such work as he himself could not undertake.

Plaintiff filed a tort action against the Southern California Rapid Transit District, a public entity, and Mitchell, an employee of the transit district. At trial plaintiff claimed slightly more than $2,700 in special damages, including $921 in doctor's bills, a $336.99 hospital bill, and about $45 for medicines. Defendant requested permission to show that about 80 percent of the plaintiff's hospital bill had been paid by plaintiff's Blue Cross insurance carrier and that some of his other medical expenses may have been paid by other insurance....

After the jury verdict in favor of plaintiff in the sum of $16,300, defendants appealed, raising only two contentions: (1) The trial court committed prejudicial error in refusing to allow the introduction of evidence to the effect that a portion of the plaintiff's medical bills had been paid from a collateral source. (2) The trial court erred in denying defendant the opportunity to determine if plaintiff had been compensated from more than one collateral source for damages sustained in the accident.

We must decide whether the collateral source rule applies to tort actions involving public entities and public employees in which the plaintiff has received benefits from his medical insurance coverage.

2. The collateral source rule.

The Supreme Court of California has long adhered to the doctrine that if an injured party receives some compensation for his injuries from a source wholly independent of the tortfeasor, such payment should not be deducted from the damages which the plaintiff would otherwise collect from the tortfeasor. As recently as August 1968 we unanimously reaffirmed our adherence to this doctrine, which is known as the 'collateral source rule.'

Although the collateral source rule remains generally accepted in the United States, nevertheless many other jurisdictions have restricted or repealed it. In this country most commentators have criticized the rule and called for its early demise....

The collateral source rule as applied here embodies the venerable concept that a person who has invested years of insurance premiums to assure his medical care should receive the benefits of his thrift. The tortfeasor should not garner the benefits of his victim's providence.

The collateral source rule expresses a policy judgment in favor of encouraging citizens to purchase and maintain insurance for personal injuries and for other eventualities. Courts consider insurance a form of investment, the benefits of which become payable without respect to any other possible source of funds. If we were to permit a tortfeasor to mitigate damages with payments from plaintiff's insurance, plaintiff would be in a position inferior to that of having bought no insurance, because his payment of premiums would have earned no benefit. Defendant should not be able to avoid payment of full compensation for the injury inflicted merely because the victim has had the foresight to provide himself with insurance.

Some commentators object that the above approach to the collateral source rule provides plaintiff with a 'double recovery,' rewards him for the injury, and defeats the principle that damages should compensate the victim but not punish the tortfeasor. We agree with Professor Fleming's observation, however, that 'double recovery is justified only in the face of some exceptional, supervening reason, as in the case of accident or life insurance, where it is felt unjust that the tortfeasor should take advantage of the thrift and prescience of the victim in having paid the premiums.' (Fleming, Introduction to the Law of Torts (1967) p. 131.) As we point out, *infra*, recovery in a wrongful death action is not defeated by the payment of the benefit on a life insurance policy.

Furthermore, insurance policies increasingly provide for either subrogation or refund or benefits upon a tort recovery, and such refund is indeed called for in the present case. (See Fleming, The Collateral Source Rule and Loss Allocation in Tort Law, supra, 54 Cal.L.Rev. 1478, 1479.) Hence, the plaintiff receives no double recovery; the collateral source rule simply serves as a means of by-passing the antiquated doctrine of non-assignment of tortious actions and permits a proper transfer of risk from the plaintiff's insurer to the tortfeasor by way of the victim's tort recovery. The double shift from the tortfeasor to the victim and then from the victim to his insurance carrier can normally occur with little cost in that the insurance carrier is often intimately involved in the initial litigation and quite automatically receives its part of the tort settlement or verdict.

Even in case in which the contract or the law precludes subrogation or refund of benefits, or in situations in which the collateral source waives such subrogation or refund, the rule performs entirely necessary functions in the computation of damages. For example, the cost of medical care often provides both attorneys and juries in tort cases with an important measure for assessing the plaintiff's general damages. (Cf., e.g., Rose v. Melody Lane (1952) 39 Cal.2d 481, 489, 247 P.2d 335.) To permit the defendant to tell the jury that the plaintiff has been recompensed by a collateral source for his medical costs might irretrievably upset the complex, delicate, and somewhat indefinable calculations which result in the normal jury verdict.

We also note that generally the jury is not informed that plaintiff's attorney will receive a large portion of the plaintiff's recovery in contingent fees or that personal injury damages are not taxable to the plaintiff and are normally deductible by the defendant. Hence, the plaintiff rarely actually receives full compensation for his injuries as computed by the jury. The collateral source rule partially serves to compensate for the attorney's share and does not actually render 'double recovery' for the plaintiff. Indeed, many jurisdictions that have abolished or limited the collateral source rule have also established a means for assessing the plaintiff's costs for counsel directly against the defendant rather than imposing the contingent fee system. In sum, the plaintiff's recovery for his medical expenses from both the tortfeasor and his medical insurance program will not usually give him 'double recovery,' but partially provides a somewhat closer approximation to full compensation for his injuries.

If we consider the collateral source rule as applied here in the context of the entire American approach to the law of torts and damages, we find that the rule presently performs a number of legitimate and even indispensable functions. Without a thorough revolution in the American approach to torts and the consequent damages, the rule at least with respect to medical insurance benefits has become so integrated within our present system that its precipitous judicial nullification would work hardship. In this case the collateral source rule lies between two systems for the compensation of accident victims: the traditional tort recovery based on fault and the increasingly prevalent coverage based on non-fault insurance. Neither system possesses such universality of coverage or completeness of compensation that we can easily dispense with the collateral source rule's approach to meshing the two systems. (Cf., e.g., Bilyeu v. State Employees' Retirement System (1962) 58 Cal.2d 618, 629, 25 Cal.Rptr. 562, 375 P.2d 442 (concurring opn. of Peters, J.).) The reforms which many academicians propose cannot easily be achieved through piecemeal common law development; the proposed changes, if desirable, would be more effectively accomplished through legislative reform. In any case, we cannot believe that the judicial repeal of the collateral source rule, as applied in the present case, would be the place to begin the needed changes.

* * *

Notes and Questions

1. *The Collateral Source Rule and Deterrence:* From a deterrence perspective, the collateral source rule reaches the right conclusion. Consider a defendant's incentives if allowed to set up the plaintiff's insurance coverage as a defense to his own responsibility in damages. Suppose that the expected harm from the accident equals $500 and that this harm can be avoided by the defendant at a cost of $400. The defendant's failure to incur these costs results in a finding of negligence under the Hand Formula. However, if the plaintiff's receipt of $500 from the insurance company relieves the defendant of his damages, he no longer has an incentive to avoid this liability. Thus, potential tortfeasors tend to under-

invest in accident prevention in the absence of the collateral source rule. Does this analysis require the potential tortfeasors to know whether their potential victims have purchased insurance?

2. Insurance Rates, Accident Avoidance Costs, and the Collateral Source Rule: Some potential tortfeasors may make investments in accident avoidance because of concern that accidents will cause their insurance rates to increase even if the collateral source rule did not preclude payment of the claim. How does this point affect the analysis in note 1?

3. Insurance Markets, Risk Pools, and the Collateral Source Rule: Abolition of the collateral source rule could improve the functioning of insurance markets because, as suggested by Professor Priest: "Deducting first-party insurance benefits from tort judgments will also reduce risk pool variance." Evaluate this argument.

4. The Collateral Source Rule and Double Recovery: The collateral source rule is not a free lunch for insured victims because insurance rates will adjust to reflect whether the insurance company must cover the victim's expenses. The premiums that an insured pays are a reflection of the rights that the coverage purchases. Consider two different insurance contracts. First, an insurance company could offer a contract that obligated it to pay damages upon the injury of the insured as a result of a third parties negligence without providing the insurer with rights to sue the negligent third party. In short, under this contract, the insurer is stuck with the loss. However, the insurer will charge the insured a higher premium for this contract. Second, consider a contract that contains a term that assigns the legal rights of the insured to the insurer once the insured has been paid under the policy. Under this contract, the insurer has greater protection against bearing the loss and as a result will charge the insured a smaller premium. From this analysis, it is easy to see that when a victim is able to recover from both the insurance company and the defendant, the victim has paid for this, so called, "double recovery" through higher insurance premiums. Therefore, it does not represent a windfall to the victim. However, are all insured parties better off with or without the collateral source rule?

E. Risk Regulation

The earlier discussion of compensating wage differentials demonstrated that the market determined level of workplace safety is below a no-risk level of safety. At some point, workers, consumers, and investors voluntarily accept risk. However, in an increasing number of situations, politicians and government regulators have decided that the risk associated with particular products, services, or activities is unacceptably high and thus should be subjected to regulation. A large portion of the federal regulatory structure deals with health and safety regulation. Examples of agencies responsible for such regulation include the Occupational Safety and Health Administration (OSHA), the Environmental Protection Agency (EPA), Consumer Product Safety Commission (CPSC), and the National Highway Traffic Safety Administration (NHTSA). Over the last thirty years, government risk regulation has become a big business. The purpose of this section is to provide an economic perspective on risk regulation.

1. Cost-Benefit Analysis

Many regulators and the legislative mandates from which they operate contemplate risk-free levels of safety. However, because risk reduction is costly and involves trade-offs, risk-free standards are not feasible. The practical impact of regulators pursuing risk-free standards is that cost considerations are often ignored. Rational economic decision making requires that government risk regulations be subjected to some type of cost-benefit analysis. In considering additional levels of risk reduction, the relevant economic analysis occurs at the margin. The marginal cost of reducing the risk associated with various activities increases as greater amounts of risk are eliminated. Conversely, the marginal benefits of reduced risk decline as greater amounts of risk are eliminated. The optimal risk level occurs at the point where the marginal benefits of risk reduction equal the marginal costs. Beyond this point, risk reduction can occur only if allocative efficiency is sacrificed.

UAW v. Occupational Safety & Health Administration
United States Court of Appeals, District of Columbia Circuit
938 F.2d 1310 (1991)

STEPHEN F. WILLIAMS, Circuit Judge:

Representatives of labor and industry challenge a regulation of the Occupational Safety and Health Administration,[1] "Control of Hazardous Energy Sources (Lockout/Tagout)". 54 Fed.Reg. 36,644 (1989). The regulation deals not with the effects of such subtle phenomena as electrical energy fields but with those of ordinary industrial equipment that may suddenly move and cut or crush or otherwise injure a worker.[2] "Lockout" and "tagout" are two procedures designed to reduce these injuries. Lockout is the placement of a lock on an "energy isolating device", such as a circuit breaker, so that equipment cannot start up until the lock is removed. See 29 CFR § 1910.147(b) (1990). Tagout is the similar placement of a plastic tag to alert employees that the tagged equipment "may not be operated" until the tag is removed. See id. Although OSHA had previously issued specific standards governing especially dangerous equipment,[3] the present rule extends lockout/tagout to virtually all equipment in almost all industries. See 29 CFR § 1910.147(a)(1)(ii) (1990). It generally requires employers to use lockout procedures during servicing and maintenance, unless the employer can show that tagout will provide the same level of safety.

---

1. OSHA is the administrative agency within the Department of Labor that is responsible for promulgating and enforcing standards under the Occupational Safety and Health Act. We here use the terms "Secretary" (of the Department of Labor) and "OSHA" interchangeably.

2. As the agency put it more formally, the rule "addresses practices and procedures that are necessary to disable machinery or equipment and to prevent the release of potentially hazardous energy while maintenance and servicing activities are being performed." 54 Fed.Reg. at 36,644.

3. See, e.g., 29 CFR § 1910.263(k)(12)(I) (1990) (bakery equipment); id. § 1910.265 (c)(12)(v) (sawmills); id. § 1910.262(c)(1) (textile machines); id. § 1910.218(h)(2) (forging machines); id. § 1910.261(b)(4) (paper mill equipment); id. § 1910.217(b)(8)(I) (mechanical power presses); id. § 1910.213(a)(10) (woodworking machinery); id. § 1910.181(f)(2)(c) (derricks); id. § 1910.179(g)(5)(I) (overhead & gantry cranes).

* * *

...the claim of the National Association of Manufacturers that Congress has given so little guidance for rules issued under § 6(b) but not covered by § 6(b)(5) that as to such rules the Act invalidly delegates legislative authority. Although we reject that claim, we find that the interpretation offered by the Secretary is, in light of nondelegation principles, so broad as to be unreasonable. We note, however, the existence of at least one interpretation that is reasonable and consistent with the nondelegation doctrine.

* * *

...the NAM's claim of an excessive delegation of legislative power. The only evident source of constraints remaining is § 3(8). It defines an "occupational safety and health standard" as a standard which requires conditions, or the adoption or use of one or more practices, means, methods, operations, or processes, reasonably necessary or appropriate to provide safe or healthful employment and places of employment." Though the language is exceedingly vague, the Benzene plurality found it the source of a threshold requirement of "significant risk", without which OSHA was not to act under § 6(b) at all. It justified this narrowing construction with the argument (among others) that otherwise "the statute would make such a 'sweeping delegation of legislative power' that it might be unconstitutional under the Court's reasoning in A.L.A. Schechter Poultry Corp. v. United States, 295 U.S. 495 (1935)....

The *Benzene* construction was, of course, a manifestation of the Court's current general practice of applying the nondelegation doctrine mainly in the form of "giving narrow constructions to statutory delegations that might otherwise be thought to be unconstitutional." Mistretta v. United States, 488 U.S. 361, 373 n. 7 (1989).... In effect we require a clear statement by Congress that it intended to test the constitutional waters.

We thus turn to possible constructions.

A

One can imagine broader constructions than the one proposed by OSHA, but not easily. * * *

It is true that price and wage controls blanketing the entire economy have been sustained under quite vague legislative directions. But in view of the inevitable tensions in such controls between such purposes as price stabilization on the one hand and the need for adjustments on ground of changes in cost and other market conditions on the other, compare Stephen G. Breyer & Richard B. Stewart, Administrative Law and Regulatory Policy 86–90 (1985), an insistence on greater clarity from Congress would deny it any power to impose price controls at all. Not so here. Congress can readily articulate some principle by which the beneficent health and safety effects of workplace regulation are to be traded off against the adverse welfare effects. "Policy direction is all that was ever required, and policy direction is what is lacking in much contemporary legislation." John Hart Ely, Democracy and Distrust 133 (1980). OSHA's reading of the Act finds no such direction.

We note that OSHA's claimed discretion is procedurally confined. The agency sets "standards", which would normally apply across an industry, or to a category of machines, or to some other reasonably broad category. Thus, even under its view OSHA would normally not be free to single out the Jones Company for standards embodying strict feasibility while letting the Smith Company off on ones reflecting some different principle. But even the use of general standards leaves opportunities for dangerous favoritism. The cost of compliance with a standard will vary among firms in an industry, so the power to vary the stringency of the standard is the power to decide which firms will live and which will die. At the simplest level, for example, compliance may involve economies of scale, so that a tough standard will erase small, marginal firms and leave the field to a small group of larger ones. Compare Ann P. Bartel & Lacy Glenn Thomas, "Direct and Indirect Effects of Regulation: A New Look at OSHA's Impact", 28 J.L. & Econ. 1, 23–25 (1985).

OSHA's proposed analysis would give the executive branch untrammelled power to dictate the vitality and even survival of whatever segments of American business it might choose. Although in Benzene the Court focused perhaps more on the severity of the power claimed by OSHA than on its variability, the plurality's point is apt here: "In the absence of a clear mandate in the Act, it is unreasonable to assume that Congress intended to give the Secretary the unprecedented power over American industry that would result from the Government's view...." 448 U.S. at 645, 100 S.Ct. at 2865. At least if reasonable alternative readings can be found, OSHA's must be rejected as unreasonable.

B

The NAM argues (as a fallback to its nondelegation claim) that Congress's use of "reasonably necessary or appropriate" in § 3(8) contemplates "cost-benefit" analysis. See NAM Brief at 24–25. Under this interpretation, in imposing standards under § 6(b) but outside the realm of toxics, OSHA may adopt a safety standard if its benefits outweigh its costs, and not otherwise.

Cost-benefit analysis is certainly consistent with the language of § 3(8). "Reasonableness" has long been associated with the balancing of costs and benefits. The "reasonable" person of tort fame is one who takes a precaution if the gravity of the injuries averted, adjusted for their probability, exceeds the precaution's burden. United States v. Carroll Towing Co., 159 F.2d 169, 173 (2d Cir.1947).

And while the legislative history is almost blank on the subject, it suggests concern with market failures, see, e.g., S.Rep. No. 1282, supra, at 4, reprinted in Leg. Hist. at 144, and properly conducted cost-benefit analysis should yield a solution approximating that of a market undistorted by market failures.[8] Application of cost-benefit analysis to safety standards also gives effect to Congress's distinction between slow-acting hazards and others, with its "particular concern for health hazards of 'unprecedented complexity' that had resulted from chemicals

---

8. Indeed, the Regulatory Impact Analysis of the Lockout/Tagout rule assessed it precisely on that basis, identifying worker lack of information and immobility as the relevant sources of market failure, see I J.A. at II-2-6. Compare generally W. Kip Viscusi, Risk by Choice (1983), and especially id. at 44 (finding the safety incentives created by observed job-risk premiums nearly 3000 times stronger than those created by OSHA fines), and id. at 77 (finding systemic preference for jobs whose risks are not readily understood). As OSHA never adopted the Regulatory Impact Analysis as its own reasoning, we cannot treat the rule as an application of cost-benefit analysis; accordingly we do not review the Regulatory Impact Analysis to determine whether it would satisfy that standard.

whose toxic effects 'are only now being discovered.' " Benzene, 448 U.S. at 692, 100 S.Ct. at 2889 (Marshall, J., dissenting).

Moreover, courts have often taken the word "reasonable" in a statute to require that burdens be justified by the resulting benefits. For example, in Consolidated Rail Corp. v. ICC, 646 F.2d 642 (D.C.Cir.1981), this court reviewed an Interstate Commerce Commission adjudication of some shippers' claims that a rate based on the expense of certain safety precautions was not "reasonable", as required by the controlling statute, because the precautions themselves were excessive and therefore unreasonable. We read the statutory criterion as requiring cost-benefit analysis for such costs, which we defined with considerable care:

> The safety measures for which expenditures are made must be reasonable ones, which means first, that they produce an expected safety benefit commensurate to their cost; and second, that when compared with other possible safety measures, they represent an economical means of achieving the expected safety benefit.

Id. at 648.

Similarly, where Congress authorized the Consumer Product Safety Commission to regulate hazards that create "an unreasonable risk" of consumer injury, we understood it to invoke the balancing test of negligence law and to authorize regulation only where the severity of the injury (adjusted for likelihood) offset the harm that the regulation would impose on manufacturers and consumers. Forester v. Consumer Product Safety Commission, 559 F.2d 774, 789 (D.C.Cir.1977); see also Aqua Slide 'N' Dive Corp. v. Consumer Product Safety Commission, 569 F.2d 831, 839 (5th Cir.1978) (same).

In fact, the Ninth Circuit has found cost-benefit analysis a reasonable reading of § 3(8) itself, as applied to standards under § 6(a), where (as here) § 3(8) supplies Congress's sole guide. Donovan v. Castle & Cooke Foods, 692 F.2d 641, 647–49 (9th Cir.1982).[9]

The union argues that prior cases preclude a cost-benefit interpretation here. They do not. The Supreme Court has expressly reserved the question. In Cotton Dust, upholding the Secretary's understanding that the "feasib[ility]" criterion of § 6(b)(5) was not a cost-benefit standard, the Court observed that "[w]hen Congress has intended that an agency engage in cost-benefit analysis, it has clearly indicated such intent on the face of the statute." 452 U.S. at 510, 101 S.Ct. at 2491. But it cited approvingly Forester and Aqua Slide 'N' Dive (which find "unreasonable risk" to incorporate cost-benefit balancing), id. at 510–11 n. 30, 101 S.Ct. at 2491 n. 30, and went on explicitly to leave open the question of § 3(8)'s meaning apart from toxics regulation: "This is not to say that § 3(8) might not require the balancing of costs and benefits for standards promulgated under provisions other than § 6(b)(5) of the Act." Id. at 513 n. 32, 101 S.Ct. at 2493 n. 32.

---

9. In so far as the Castle & Cooke court upheld the action of the Occupational Safety and Health Review Commission on the basis of deference to its view of the statute over that of the Secretary, it may have been marginally undermined by Martin v. OSHRC, 499 U.S. 144, 111 S.Ct. 1171, 113 L.Ed.2d 117 (1991), which requires deference to the Secretary's interpretation of her own regulations. As a holding that cost-benefit is a reasonable reading of § 3(8), however, Castle & Cooke is unimpaired.

Nor is the union's citation of our decision in Building & Construction Trades apt. The cited passage merely restates the holding of Cotton Dust, saying that the Court "made clear that, in light of the feasibility language in § 6(b)(5) [i.e., for standards governed by § 6(b)(5)], 'reasonably necessary' in § 3(8) did not require cost-benefit analysis." 838 F.2d at 1269. Building & Construction Trades did not address the meaning of § 3(8) in contexts unaffected by § 6(b)(5). The same is true of our decision in the cotton dust litigation. American Federation of Labor v. Marshall, 617 F.2d 636, 662–63 (D.C.Cir.1979) (when OSHA is regulating toxics, "no additional constraint is imposed by [§ 3(8)]"), vacated in part on other grounds, Cotton Dust, 452 U.S. 490, 101 S.Ct. 2478, 69 L.Ed.2d 185 (1981).

We briefly note the Fifth Circuit's reading of § 3(8), parts of which appear to agree with our own. It has stated that § 3(8) requires "a specie [sic] of cost-benefit justification." National Grain & Feed Ass'n v. OSHA, 866 F.2d 717, 733 (5th Cir.1989). At first glance, National Grain appears to contemplate an insistence that costs not outweigh benefits, see, e.g., Asbestos Information Ass'n v. OSHA, 727 F.2d 415, 423 (5th Cir.1984), which accords with our understanding of cost-benefit analysis.

But the Fifth Circuit approach seemingly advocates consideration of costs exclusively in terms of impact on the regulated firms (as opposed to workers and consumers). Thus the court said in Asbestos Information Ass'n, "The protection afforded to workers should outweigh the economic consequences to the regulated industry." Id. (emphasis added). Evidently explicating that thought, it seemed to approve the idea that where "the cost of compliance is less than one cent per dollar [of industry sales]", and the danger is "grave", the agency has met its burden. Id. at 424. The court never explains the exclusive focus on firms. In an industry providing a good for which there are no close substitutes (i.e., facing an inelastic demand curve), firms would be scarcely affected at all: their reactions would be some combination of avoiding the costs by substituting equipment for labor, passing the costs back to labor in the form of reduced cash wages, and passing them forward to their consumers in the form of higher prices. We do not understand why one should call an analysis "cost-benefit" if it disregards costs borne by workers and consumers. The exclusion seems especially odd for application of a worker-protection statute; consumers are, after all, mostly workers.

As there appear to be many confusions about cost-benefit analysis, it may be important to make clear what we are not saying when we identify it as a reasonable interpretation of § 3(8) as applied outside the § 6(b)(5) realm. Cost-benefit analysis requires identifying values for lost years of human life and for suffering and other losses from non-fatal injuries. Nothing we say here should be taken as confining the discretion of OSHA to choose among reasonable evaluation methods. While critics of cost-benefit analysis argue that any such valuation is impossible, that is so only in the sense that pin-point figures are necessarily arbitrary, so that the decisionmaker is effectively limited to considering some range of values. In fact, we make implicit life and safety valuations each day when we decide, for example, whether to travel by train or car, the former being more costly (at least if several family members are traveling together) but safer per passenger-mile. Where government makes decisions for others, it may reasonably be expected to make the trade-offs somewhat more explicitly than individuals choosing for themselves. The difficulty of securing agreement even on a range of values hardly justifies making decisions on the basis of a pretense that resources are not scarce. In any event, OSHA has an existing obligation under Executive Order No. 12,291, 46 Fed.Reg. 13,193 (1981), to complete a cost-benefit analysis for each major rulemaking, so use of such a standard not only is doable in the qualified sense of which we have spoken but can be done without additional regulatory resources.

Thus, cost-benefit analysis entails only a systematic weighing of pros and cons, or what Benjamin Franklin referred to as a "moral or prudential algebra". Writing to a friend who was perplexed by a difficult decision, he explained his own approach:

> When those difficult cases occur, they are difficult, chiefly because while we have them under consideration, all the reasons pro and con are not present to the mind at the same time.... To get over this, my way is to divide half a sheet of paper by a line into two columns; writing over the one Pro, and over the other Con. Then, during three or four days consideration, I put down under the different heads short hints of the different motives, that at different times occur to me, for or against the measure. When I have thus got them all together in one view, I endeavor to estimate their respective weights.... And, though the weight of reasons cannot be taken with the precision of algebraic quantities, yet when each is thus considered, separately and comparatively, and the whole lies before me, I think I can judge better, and am less liable to make a rash step, and in fact I have found great advantage from this kind of equation, in what may be called moral or prudential algebra.

Reprinted in Edward M. Gramlich, Benefit-Cost Analysis of Government Programs 1–2 (1981).

As we accept the NAM's contention that § 3(8)'s "reasonably necessary or appropriate" criterion can reasonably be read as requiring cost-benefit analysis, we must reject its nondelegation claim.

We hold only that cost-benefit is a permissible interpretation of § 3(8). Given the ambiguity inherent in that section, there may be other interpretations that conform to nondelegation principles. Accordingly we remand to OSHA, noting that its treatment of some of the parties' other claims, discussed below, will likely turn on its decision. We note, however, that Executive Order No. 12,291 may bear on OSHA's authority to promulgate a safety standard whose benefits fail to outweigh its costs. Section 2 of that order provides:

> In promulgating new regulations... all agencies, to the extent permitted by law, shall adhere to the following requirements...
>
> (b) Regulatory action shall not be undertaken unless the potential benefits to society for the regulation outweigh the potential costs to society;
>
> (c) Regulatory objectives shall be chosen to maximize the net benefits to society....

46 Fed.Reg. 13,193 (1981) (emphasis added).

*   *   *

Accordingly, in light of the NAM's nondelegation claim we reject OSHA's view that under § 3(8) it may impose any restriction it chooses so long as it is "feasible", but we also reject the NAM's nondelegation claim in light of our view that § 3(8) may reasonably be read as providing for cost-benefit analysis.

* * *

V

We have noted above various bases for remand, notably the need for OSHA to address "significant risk" in terms of whatever substantive meaning it lawfully assigns to § 3(8), and particularly to explain its decision to impose lockout/tagout even where the risk appears to be diminutive or zero. That leaves the issue of whether we should vacate the rule pending a remand, a point the parties have not briefed. Although OSHA's reasoning on many issues is extremely obscure, partly because of its failure to identify any intelligible principle that could control its discretion under § 3(8), the likelihood that correction of these defects will alter the ultimate rule is most unclear. See International Union, UMW v. FMSHA, 920 F.2d 960, 967 (D.C.Cir.1990); International Union, UMW v. FMSHA, 928 F.2d 1200, 1203–04 (D.C.Cir.1991). There appear to be segments of the standard (notably its application to some of the high-impact industries) that may well have genuine life-saving effects and are highly likely to survive re-examination. Vacating the rule would interrupt the continued flow of those advantages if employers responded to vacation of the rule by eliminating the safety practices. Of course, many high-impact employers would have no choice but to continue lockout procedures as their industries are already subject to other OSHA lockout standards. Moreover, as many of those standards were promulgated as "national consensus standards", it seems likely that some employers would continue lockout even in the absence of a government command.

On the other hand, industries that ultimately may prove exempt will in the meantime have to incur substantial costs for little or no safety gain. Further, turning the rule off and then on, as it were, will not in itself impose substantial costs, compare International Union, UMW, 920 F.2d at 967, as firms can simply halt their installation of locks and their training programs if they think that the costs of lockout are not justified by any resulting increases in safety.

* * *

Accordingly, we remand the case to OSHA for further consideration in light of this opinion.

So ordered.

STEPHEN F. WILLIAMS, Circuit Judge, concurring:

I write separately to address the UAW's apparent assumption that application of the significant risk/feasibility analysis associated with § 6(b)(5) is necessarily more protective of health and safety than a cost-benefit criterion. This is not self-evidently true.

First, if OSHA applies cost-benefit analysis, then more risks seem likely to qualify as "significant" within the meaning of Benzene; many risks that may seem insignificant if their discovery triggers regulatory burdens limited only by feasibility, as under § 6(b)(5), may be significant if the consequence is cost-justified corrective measures. Cf. Cass R. Sunstein, After the Rights Revolution 196

(1990) (explaining Benzene 's significant risk requirement as an artificial device for handling the unlimited character of the regulatory burden).

Second, even where the application of cost-benefit analysis would result in less stringent regulation, the reduced stringency is not necessarily adverse to health or safety. More regulation means some combination of reduced value of firms, higher product prices, fewer jobs in the regulated industry, and lower cash wages. All the latter three stretch workers' budgets tighter (as does the first to the extent that the firms' stock is held in workers' pension trusts). And larger incomes enable people to lead safer lives. One study finds a 1 percent increase in income associated with a mortality reduction of about 0.05 percent. Jack Hadley & Anthony Osei, "Does Income Affect Mortality?", 20 Medical Care 901, 913 (September 1982). Another suggests that each $7.5 million of costs generated by regulation may, under certain assumptions, induce one fatality. Ralph L. Keeney, "Mortality Risks Induced by Economic Expenditures", 10 Risk Analysis 147, 155 (1990) (relying on E.M. Kitagawa & P.M. Hauser, Differential Mortality in the United States of America: A Study of Socioeconomic Epidemiology (1973)). Larger incomes can produce health by enlarging a person's access to better diet, preventive medical care, safer cars, greater leisure, etc. See Aaron Wildavsky, Searching for Safety 59–71 (1988).

Of course, other causal relations may be at work too. Healthier people may be able to earn higher income, and characteristics and advantages that facilitate high earnings (e.g., work ethic, education) may also lead to better health. Compare C.P. Wen, et al., "Anatomy of the Healthy Worker Effect: A Critical Review", 25 J. of Occupation Medicine 283 (1983). Nonetheless, higher income can secure better health, and there is no basis for a casual assumption that more stringent regulation will always save lives.

It follows that while officials involved in health or safety regulation may naturally be hesitant to set any kind of numerical value on human life,[1] undue squeamishness may be deadly. Incremental safety regulation reduces incomes and thus may exact a cost in human lives. For example, if analysis showed that "an individual life was lost for every $12 million taken from individuals [as a result of the regulation], this would be a guide to a reasonable value tradeoff for many programs designed to save lives." Keeney, "Mortality Risks Induced by Economic Expenditures", 10 Risk Analysis at 158. Such a figure could serve as a ceiling for value-of-life calculated by other means, since regulation causing greater expenditures per life expected to be saved would, everything else being equal, result in a net loss of life.

Notes and Questions

1. MARGINAL Cost-MARGINAL Benefit Analysis: Cost-benefit analysis, when performed properly, should be an analysis of marginal costs and marginal

---

1. Preference-based techniques are a commonly used approach, but are subject to such pitfalls as wealth bias, age bias and inconsistency. See, e.g., Lewis A. Kornhauser, "The Value of Life", 38 Clev.St.L.Rev. 209 (1990). For example, if estimates of the benefit of reducing risks are based on the affected workers' willingness to pay for risk reduction, low-paid workers will receive less protection than better paid ones. See id. at 221. There are, however, solutions. The wealth bias problem, for example, could be avoided by estimating the willingness to pay of persons of median or mean wealth. See id. at 221–22.

benefits. Refer back to the example of arsenic regulation in Chapter I where the average cost per life saved was well below the marginal cost per life saved. If policy decisions were guided by the average cost per life saved (which was substantially below standard value of life measurements used in risk management) an economically inefficient level of regulation would result.

2. Risk Assessment and Risk Management: When analyzing cases that involve cost-benefit analysis, it is helpful to set the framework for the analysis by considering the areas of risk assessment and risk management. These important parts of the regulatory system are described by Judge (now Associate Justice) Stephen Breyer in his influential book, *Breaking the Vicious Cycle: Toward Effective Risk Regulation*:

> ..you must have some idea of how the regulatory system works. The system has two basic parts, a technical part, called "risk assessment," designed to measure the risk associated with the substance, and a more policy-oriented part, called "risk management," which decides what to do about it.
>
> Risk assessment can itself be divided into four activities: (a) *Identifying the potential* hazard, say benzene in respect to cancer: Is it benzene in any context, or just benzene used in industry, or undiluted benzene, or certain solutions of benzene in certain places? (b) *Drawing a dose/response curve:* How does the risk of harm vary with the person's exposure to that substance? The question is critically important, for, as Paracelsus pointed out over four hundred years ago, "the dose alone determines the poison." Drinking a bottle of pure iodine is deadly; placing a drop of diluted iodine on a cut is helpful. Regulators will try to use statistical studies of, say, cancer in humans (epidemiological studies), or experiments with high substance-doses given to animals, to estimate the potential effects of human exposure to low substance-doses over varying periods of time. *(c) Estimating the amount of human exposure:* How many persons in a particular workforce, or in a particular region, or in the public generally, will be exposed to different doses of the substance, and for how long? Suppose exposure to a solution of five parts per million every day for twenty years will be likely to cause five extra deaths per year per million persons. Exposing the entire population may mean 1,250 extra deaths; exposing a hundred thousand persons may mean one extra death every two years. And even in the latter case, if only two persons are exposed to the substance, so that each runs a 50 percent risk of death, there may be a regulatory problem. (d) *Categorizing the result:* Is the substance, in fact, a carcinogen? A strong carcinogen or a weak carcinogen? Based upon the dose/response and exposure findings, how should the risk assessment describe (or categorize) the hazard? In carrying out these activities, particularly in making dose/response and exposure estimates, regulators often find that they simply lack critically important scientific or empirical data: they do not know how many Americans inhale how much benzene at gasoline stations; they do not know the extent to which the biology of a rat or mouse resembles, or differs from, that of a human being. In such instances, they will often make a "default assumption"—a formalized guess—designed to fill the gap and to permit the regulator to continue the analysis.

Risk management determines what the regulator should do about the risks that the assessment reveals. Ideally, the risk manager will consider what will be likely in fact to occur should he choose each of several regulatory potions. On the one hand, to what extent will the regulation actually diminish the specific risk at issue? On the other hand, to what extent will regulation itself produce *different* risks? (Will childproof aspirin bottle tops save children, or will they lead many parents, unable to open the top easily, simply to leave the top off? Will saccharin users, denied saccharin, switch to sugar, gain weight, and die of heart attacks?) To what extent will the regulation deprive users of benefits the substance now brings? To what extent will it impose added costs? The manager also must consider practical problems, such as the difficulty of enforcing a regulation or the political reaction that its promulgation might bring. Ultimately, in light of the identified risks, the risks associated with alternatives, the effect on benefits, the costs, and the practicalities, the risk managing regulator will reach a decision.

Stephen G. Breyer, *Breaking the Vicious Cycle: Toward Effective Risk Regulation* (1993), pp. 9–10.

3. Cost-Benefit Analysis, Compensating Wage Differentials, and Voluntary Risk Taking: A safety or health standard is socially desirable only if the value workers place on risk reduction is commensurate with the cost of complying with the standard. The value workers place on risk reduction can be estimated, in theory at least, from knowledge of compensating wage differentials. However, even if compensating wage differentials were accurately calculated from observations in a market characterized by both widespread information and choice, there are still objections to their use in assessing the benefits of OSHA standards. First, compensating wage differentials reflect the preferences of only those directly involved in the employer/employee contract. It is frequently argued that members of society who are not directly affected by the risk reduction program might be willing to pay something for the benefits that accrue to those who are directly affected. Presumably, this willingness to pay is strongest for family members, relatives and close friends and weakest for strangers. However, even strangers would have some interest in reducing injury and disease if they were to be taxed in order to subsidize the medical treatment of those who are injured or become ill. Thus, it is argued the benefits of OSHA standards extend beyond the direct beneficiaries to other external parties whose willingness to pay should also be counted. The second argument against using only the apparent willingness of workers to pay for risk reduction as a measure of its benefit is that workers may not really know what's best for themselves in the long run. Society frequently prohibits, or at least tries to prohibit, people from indulging in activities that are dangerous to their welfare. Laws against the use of narcotics and gambling are two examples. Some argue that OSHA standards limiting exposure to dangerous substances or situations fall under the category of preventing workers from doing harm to themselves by being lured into dangerous work. Therefore, it is argued, to ask how much they value risk reduction is irrelevant. The conflict between those who claim that workers know what is best for themselves and those who claim they do not, can only be resolved on philosophical grounds.

4. Worker Safety, Compensating Wage Differentials, and the Best Interests of Workers: In 1970, Congress passed the Occupational Safety and Health Act which directed the US Department of Labor to issue and enforce safety and health standards for all private employers. The stated goal of the act was to ensure the "highest degree of health and safety protection for the employee." Despite the ideal that employees should face the minimum possible risk in the work place, implementing this ideal as social policy is not necessarily in the best interest of workers. Some workers are more willing than others to perform risky jobs, and they are usually rewarded with a compensating wage differential. When the government mandates the reduction of risk in a market where workers are compensated for the risk they take, it penalizes workers who are not terribly sensitive to risk and appreciate the higher wages associated with higher risk. The critical issue, of course, is whether workers have the knowledge and choice necessary to generate compensating wage differentials. Many people believe that workers are uninformed, unable to comprehend different risk levels or immobile and thus that most do not choose risky jobs voluntarily. If this belief were true, government regulations could make workers better off. Indeed, while the evidence of a positive realtionship between wage and risk of death should challenge the notion that information and mobility are generally insufficient to create compensating differentials, there are specific areas in which problems obviously exist. For example, the introduction each year of new workplace chemicals whose effects on humans may be unknown for two or more decades, owing to long gestation of most cancers and lung diseases, clearly presents substantial information problems to affected labor market participants. To say that worker utility can be increased by government regulation does not then imply that it will be increased. The outcome depends on how well the unregulated market functions and how careful the government is in setting its standards for risk reduction.

5. OSHA's Feasibility Standard: OSHA proposes the use of a feasibility test in setting regulatory standards. Regulatory stringency under such a test can be characterized as requiring only that technology-based standards be affordable (i.e. capable of being done). Clearly then, a feasibility test does not contemplate a balancing of the marginal costs and marginal benefits. Rather, under a feasibility standard, OSHA simply looks for a "kink" in the marginal cost curve. That is, at what point does it become prohibitively costly to raise the standard. Such a kink may of course occur past the point at which marginal benefits equal marginal costs. What justification can OSHA offer for a feasibility test? Does Judge Williams concurring opinion adequately dismiss such arguments? The Supreme Court's Cotton Dust opinion allows OSHA to use a feasibility standard in the regulation of toxics. What justification allows the feasibility standard to exist in the case of workplace toxics?

6. The Impact of Risk Regulation: Questions regarding the effectiveness of the current regulatory system don't stop after applying a cost-benefit test to stringency levels. In order to justify the existence of regulatory agencies, the regulations should have the desired impact on market behavior:

> Firms will choose to make the necessary investments in health and safety if the OSHA enforcement policy in conjunction with market incentives for safety makes it in the firm's financial self-interest to do so. More specifically, a firm will comply with an OSHA regulation if

Expected cost of compliance	$<$	Probability inspection	$\times$	Expected no. of violations per inspection	$\times$	Average penalty per violation

As discussed, the three links in establishing these incentives—inspections, violations, and penalties—are all relatively weak. A firm has less than one chance in 200 of being inspected in any given year. If inspected, it expects to be found guilty of less than two violations of the standards, and for each violation the average penalty is under $60. Overall, the financial cost per worker is just over fifty cents. A useful comparison is that market forces through compensating differentials in combination with workers' compensation premiums imposed costs in excess of $800 per worker for the same period. Quite simply, OSHA's enforcement effort is too modest to create truly effective financial incentives for safety.

W. Kip Viscusi, John M. Vernon, and Joseph E. Harrington, Jr., *Economics of Regulation and Antitrust*, (Cambridge, MA: The MIT Press, 1996), p. 816. Based on this information what justification is there for the continued existence of OSHA? Does it appear that the market has a comparative advantage in allocating the types of risk that OSHA is attempting to regulate? It appears that in regard to both stringency and enforcement, regulatory agencies like OSHA have ignored the reality of the market.

7. Wealthier is Healthier: Judge Stephen Williams, in his concurring opinion, cautions that the costs of health and safety regulations might actually result in more lives lost than saved. This counter-intuitive result flows from the empirical evidence that shows strong correlations between average national income levels and measures of national health, such as life expectancy and infant mortality. Wealthier is Healthier. Moreover, regulations—even those that are supposed to reduce risk—that do not pass a cost-benefit analysis can reduce wealth and, thus, reduce health. Jobs are lost and wealth is destroyed when regulations force businesses to make inefficient expenditures. Similarly, new product innovation is suppressed whenever government too strictly regulates the development, distribution, and use of products with life-saving potential. Risk experts Richard J. Zeckhauser and W. Kip Viscusi argue that "overreaction to very small risks impedes the kind of technological progress that has historically brought dramatic improvements in both health and material well-being." Richard J. Zeckhauser and W. Kip Viscusi, "Risk Within Reason," Science, Vol. 248 (May, 1990), p. 559. Does the court give adequate attention to such facts? What incentives would drive OSHA to ignore such facts?

8. Cost-Benefit Analysis and Discounting: In some cases, the benefits that may result from regulatory efforts are not realized until many years into the future. For example, environmental regulations often contemplate current expenditures for delayed benefits. In order to determine the relevant costs and benefits of such regulations, regulators must discount future benefits and costs to present values. On numerous occasions, EPA has argued that future benefits should not be discounted. By not discounting, the benefits of EPA regulations appear to be much larger.

9. Marginal Analysis and Heterogeneity: Use of marginal analysis suggests something about the manner in which regulatory standards should be applied across different industries or firms. Consider the case of a regulation that would be applied across several different industries. According to the regulator, the marginal benefit per unit of safety is the same across all industries. However, it is unlikely that firms in each of these different industries face the same marginal cost curves. Therefore, across industries, the level of safety at which marginal benefits equal marginal costs will be different. Suppose that the regulating agency chooses a level of safety where the marginal benefits equal the marginal costs of what the agency considers to be a representative firm. If a single standard is imposed regardless of industry, then the regulating agency losses the opportunity for further risk reduction. If a firm has lower marginal costs than contemplated by the regulation, then it would be efficient for this firm to be required to have a higher safety standard. Thus, a single standard misses inexpensive opportunities to reduce risk. On the other hand, if a firm has higher marginal costs than supposed by the regulation, then the single standard will result in economic inefficiency. This results in lower incomes and therefore sacrificed safety. By using marginal analysis, regulatory agencies would be able to maximize the risk reducing benefits of their regulations across industries and across firms.

2. Measuring Risk: All Risks are Relative

Absolute levels of risk provide very little relevant information in the absence of some relative comparison. For example, suppose that living five years at the boundary of a nuclear power plant site increased one's annual death risk by one chance in one million. Should you be concerned? Should there be additional regulation? Now consider the fact that risk of traveling six minutes by canoe will also increase your annual death risk one chance in one million. Both of these risks have the same impact on annual death rates. However, many individuals might be outraged if tax dollars were being spent to eliminate the risk of being killed during a six minute canoe trip. By considering a risk that sounds intimidating relative to risks that individuals freely undertake daily, it becomes much easier to achieve a conceptual understanding of risk measures. Gaining a conceptual measure of risk is important because regulatory agencies often attempt to regulate risks that are very small relative to the types of risks that individuals expose themselves to in their everyday lives. Furthermore, gaining an appreciation for the relative impacts of different risk reduction proposals helps in analyzing the efficacy of regulatory performance.

Corrosion Proof Fittings v. Environmental Protection Agency
United States Court of Appeals, Fifth Circuit
947 F.2d 1201 (1991)

JERRY E. SMITH, Circuit Judge:

The Environmental Protection Agency (EPA) issued a final rule under section 6 of the Toxic Substances Control Act (TSCA) to prohibit the future manufacture, importation, processing, and distribution of asbestos in almost all products. Petitioners claim that the EPA's rulemaking procedure was flawed and that the rule was not promulgated on the basis of substantial evidence.... Because the EPA failed to muster substantial evidence to support its rule, we remand this matter to the EPA for further consideration in light of this opinion.

I.
Facts and Procedural History.

Asbestos is a naturally occurring fibrous material that resists fire and most solvents. Its major uses include heat-resistant insulators, cements, building materials, fireproof gloves and clothing, and motor vehicle brake linings. Asbestos is a toxic material, and occupational exposure to asbestos dust can result in mesothelioma, asbestosis, and lung cancer.

The EPA began these proceedings in 1979, when it issued an Advanced Notice of Proposed Rulemaking announcing its intent to explore the use of TSCA "to reduce the risk to human health posed by exposure to asbestos." See 54 Fed.Reg. 29,460 (1989). While these proceedings were pending, other agencies continued their regulation of asbestos uses, in particular the Occupational Safety and Health Administration (OSHA), which in 1983 and 1984 involved itself with lowering standards for workplace asbestos exposure.

An EPA-appointed panel reviewed over one hundred studies of asbestos and conducted several public meetings. Based upon its studies and the public comments, the EPA concluded that asbestos is a potential carcinogen at all levels of exposure, regardless of the type of asbestos or the size of the fiber. The EPA concluded in 1986 that exposure to asbestos "poses an unreasonable risk to human health" and thus proposed at least four regulatory options for prohibiting or restricting the use of asbestos, including a mixed ban and phase-out of asbestos over ten years; a two-stage ban of asbestos, depending upon product usage; a three-stage ban on all asbestos products leading to a total ban in ten years; and labeling of all products containing asbestos.

Over the next two years, the EPA updated its data, received further comments, and allowed cross-examination on the updated documents. In 1989, the EPA issued a final rule prohibiting the manufacture, importation, processing, and distribution in commerce of most asbestos-containing products. Finding that asbestos constituted an unreasonable risk to health and the environment, the EPA promulgated a staged ban of most commercial uses of asbestos. The EPA estimates that this rule will save either 202 or 148 lives, depending upon whether the benefits are discounted, at a cost of approximately $450–800 million, depending upon the price of substitutes.

*   *   *

III.
Rulemaking Defects.

The petitioners allege that the EPA's rulemaking procedure was flawed. Specifically, the petitioners contend that the EPA erred by not cross-examining petitioner's witnesses, by not assembling a panel of experts on asbestos disease risks, by designating a hearing officer, rather than an administrative law judge (ALJ), to preside at the hearings on the rule, and by not swearing in witnesses who testified. Petitioners also complain that the EPA did not allow cross-examination of some of its witnesses and did not notify anyone until after the hearings were over that it intended to use "analogous exposure" estimates and a substitute pricing assumption to support its rule. Most of these contentions lack merit and are part of the petitioners' "protest everything" approach, but we address specifically the two EPA actions of most concern to us, the failure of the EPA to afford cross-examination of its own witnesses and its failure to provide notice of the analogous exposure estimates.

*   *   *

...The EPA failed to give notice to the public, before the conclusion of the hearings, that it intended to use "analogous exposure" data to calculate the expected benefits of certain product bans. In general, the EPA should give notice as to its intended methodology while the public still has an opportunity to analyze, comment, and influence the proceedings. The EPA's use of the analogous exposure estimates, apart from their merits, thus should have been subjected to public scrutiny before the record was closed. While it is true that "[t]he public need not have an opportunity to comment on every bit of information influencing an agency's decision," Texas v. Lyng, 868 F.2d 795, 799 (5th Cir.1989), this cannot be used as a defense to the late adoption of the analogous exposure estimates, as they are used to support a substantial part of the regulation finally promulgated by the EPA.[10]

*   *   *

In short, the EPA should not hold critical analysis in reserve and then use it to justify its regulation despite the lack of public comment on the validity of its basis. Failure to seek public comment on such an important part of the EPA's analysis deprived its rule of the substantial evidence required to survive judicial scrutiny...

*   *   *

B.
The EPA's Burden Under TSCA

*   *   *

We conclude that the EPA has presented insufficient evidence to justify its asbestos ban. We base this conclusion upon two grounds: the failure of the EPA to consider all necessary evidence and its failure to give adequate weight to statutory language requiring it to promulgate the least burdensome, reasonable regulation required to protect the environment adequately. Because the EPA failed to address these concerns, and because the EPA is required to articulate a "reasoned" basis for its rules, we are compelled to return the regulation to the agency for reconsideration.

1.
Least Burdensome and Reasonable.

TSCA requires that the EPA use the least burdensome regulation to achieve its goal of minimum reasonable risk. This statutory requirement can create problems in evaluating just what is a "reasonable risk." Congress's rejection of a no-risk policy, however, also means that in certain cases, the least burdensome yet still adequate solution may entail somewhat more risk than would other, known regulations that are far more burdensome on the industry and the economy. The

---

10. According to the EPA, if the analogous exposure estimates were not included, the benefits of the rule would decrease from 168 to 120 deaths avoided, discounted at 3%. 54 Fed.Reg. at 29,469, 29,485. The analogous exposure estimates, adopted after hearings were concluded, thus increase the purported benefits of the rule by more than one-third.

very language of TSCA requires that the EPA, once it has determined what an acceptable level of non-zero risk is, choose the least burdensome method of reaching that level.

In this case, the EPA banned, for all practical purposes, all present and future uses of asbestos—a position the petitioners characterize as the "death penalty alternative," as this is the most burdensome of all possible alternatives listed as open to the EPA under TSCA. TSCA not only provides the EPA with a list of alternative actions, but also provides those alternatives in order of how burdensome they are. The regulations thus provide for EPA regulation ranging from labeling the least toxic chemicals to limiting the total amount of chemicals an industry may use. Total bans head the list as the most burdensome regulatory option.

By choosing the harshest remedy given to it under TSCA, the EPA assigned to itself the toughest burden in satisfying TSCA's requirement that its alternative be the least burdensome of all those offered to it. Since, both by definition and by the terms of TSCA, the complete ban of manufacturing is the most burdensome alternative—for even stringent regulation at least allows a manufacturer the chance to invest and meet the new, higher standard—the EPA's regulation cannot stand if there is any other regulation that would achieve an acceptable level of risk as mandated by TSCA.

We reserve until a later part of the opinion a product-by-product review of the regulation. Before reaching this analysis, however, we lay down the inquiry that the EPA should undertake whenever it seeks total ban of a product.

The EPA considered, and rejected, such options as labeling asbestos products, thereby warning users and workers involved in the manufacture of asbestos-containing products of the chemical's dangers, and stricter workplace rules. EPA also rejected controlled use of asbestos in the workplace and deferral to other government agencies charged with worker and consumer exposure to industrial and product hazards, such as OSHA, the CPSC, and the MSHA. The EPA determined that deferral to these other agencies was inappropriate because no one other authority could address all the risks posed "throughout the life cycle" by asbestos, and any action by one or more of the other agencies still would leave an unacceptable residual risk.[16]

Much of the EPA's analysis is correct, and the EPA's basic decision to use TSCA as a comprehensive statute designed to fight a multi-industry problem was a proper one that we uphold today on review. What concerns us, however, is the manner in which the EPA conducted some of its analysis. TSCA requires the EPA to consider, along with the effects of toxic substances on human health and the environment, "the benefits of such substance[s] or mixture[s] for various uses and the availability of substitutes for such uses," as well as "the reasonably ascertainable economic consequences of the rule, after consideration for the effect on the national economy, small business, technological innovation, the environment, and public health."

---

16. EPA argues that OSHA can only deal with workplace exposures to asbestos and that the CPSC and MSHA cannot take up the slack, as the CPSC can impose safety standards for asbestos products based only upon the risk to consumers, and MSHA can protect against exposure only in the mining and milling process. These agencies leave unaddressed dangers posed by asbestos exposure through product repair, installation, wear and tear, and the like.

The EPA presented two comparisons in the record: a world with no further regulation under TSCA, and a world in which no manufacture of asbestos takes place. The EPA rejected calculating how many lives a less burdensome regulation would save, and at what cost. Furthermore the EPA, when calculating the benefits of its ban, explicitly refused to compare it to an improved workplace in which currently available control technology is utilized. See 54 Fed.Reg. at 29,474. This decision artificially inflated the purported benefits of the rule by using a baseline comparison substantially lower than what currently available technology could yield.

Under TSCA, the EPA was required to evaluate, rather than ignore, less burdensome regulatory alternatives. TSCA imposes a least-to-most-burdensome hierarchy. In order to impose a regulation at the top of the hierarchy—a total ban of asbestos—the EPA must show not only that its proposed action reduces the risk of the product to an adequate level, but also that the actions Congress identified as less burdensome also would not do the job. The failure of the EPA to do this constitutes a failure to meet its burden of showing that its actions not only reduce the risk but do so in the Congressionally-mandated least burdensome fashion.

Thus it was not enough for the EPA to show, as it did in this case, that banning some asbestos products might reduce the harm that could occur from the use of these products. If that were the standard, it would be no standard at all, for few indeed are the products that are so safe that a complete ban of them would not make the world still safer.

This comparison of two static worlds is insufficient to satisfy the dictates of TSCA. While the EPA may have shown that a world with a complete ban of asbestos might be preferable to one in which there is only the current amount of regulation, the EPA has failed to show that there is not some intermediate state of regulation that would be superior to both the currently-regulated and the completely-banned world. Without showing that asbestos regulation would be ineffective, the EPA cannot discharge its TSCA burden of showing that its regulation is the least burdensome available to it.

Upon an initial showing of product danger, the proper course for the EPA to follow is to consider each regulatory option, beginning with the least burdensome, and the costs and benefits of regulation under each option. The EPA cannot simply skip several rungs, as it did in this case, for in doing so, it may skip a less-burdensome alternative mandated by TSCA. Here, although the EPA mentions the problems posed by intermediate levels of regulation, it takes no steps to calculate the costs and benefits of these intermediate levels. See 54 Fed.Reg. at 29,462, 29,474. Without doing this it is impossible, both for the EPA and for this court on review, to know that none of these alternatives was less burdensome than the ban in fact chosen by the agency.

The EPA's offhand rejection of these intermediate regulatory steps is "not the stuff of which substantial evidence is made." Aqua Slide, 569 F.2d at 843. While it is true that the EPA considered five different ban options, these differed solely with respect to their effective dates. The EPA did not calculate the risk levels for intermediate levels of regulation, as it believed that there was no asbestos exposure level for which the risk of injury or death was zero. Reducing risk to zero, however, was not the task that Congress set for the EPA in enacting TSCA. The EPA thus has failed "cogently [to] explain why it has exercised its discretion in a given manner," Chemical Mfrs. Ass'n, 899 F.2d at 349, by failing to explore in more than a cursory way the less burdensome alternatives to a total ban.

2.
The EPA's Calculations.

Furthermore, we are concerned about some of the methodology employed by the EPA in making various of the calculations that it did perform. In order to aid the EPA's reconsideration of this and other cases, we present our concerns here.

First, we note that there was some dispute in the record regarding the appropriateness of discounting the perceived benefits of the EPA's rule. In choosing between the calculated costs and benefits, the EPA presented variations in which it discounted only the costs, and counter-variations in which it discounted both the costs and the benefits, measured in both monetary and human injury terms. As between these two variations, we choose to evaluate the EPA's work using its discounted benefits calculations.

Although various commentators dispute whether it ever is appropriate to discount benefits when they are measured in human lives, we note that it would skew the results to discount only costs without according similar treatment to the benefits side of the equation. Adopting the position of the commentators who advocate not discounting benefits would force the EPA similarly not to calculate costs in present discounted real terms, making comparisons difficult. Furthermore, in evaluating situations in which different options incur costs at varying time intervals, the EPA would not be able to take into account that soon-to-be-incurred costs are more harmful than postponable costs. Because the EPA must discount costs to perform its evaluations properly, the EPA also should discount benefits to preserve an apples-to-apples comparison, even if this entails discounting benefits of a non-monetary nature. See What Price Posterity?, The Economist, March 23, 1991, at 73 (explaining use of discount rates for non-monetary goods).

When the EPA does discount costs or benefits, however, it cannot choose an unreasonable time upon which to base its discount calculation. Instead of using the time of injury as the appropriate time from which to discount, as one might expect, the EPA instead used the time of exposure.

The difficulties inherent in the EPA's approach can be illustrated by an example. Suppose two workers will be exposed to asbestos in 1995, with worker X subjected to a tiny amount of asbestos that will have no adverse health effects, and worker Y exposed to massive amounts of asbestos that quickly will lead to an asbestos-related disease. Under the EPA's approach, which takes into account only the time of exposure rather than the time at which any injury manifests itself, both examples would be treated the same. The EPA's approach implicitly assumes that the day on which the risk of injury occurs is the same day the injury actually occurs.[18] Such an approach might be proper when the exposure and injury are one and the same, such as when a person is exposed to an immediately fatal poison, but is inappropriate for discounting toxins in

---

18. Recently, in a different context, we observed the important distinction between present and future injury. See Willett v. Baxter Int'l, Inc., 929 F.2d 1094, 1099–1100 & n. 20 (5th Cir.1991).

which exposure often is followed by a substantial lag time before manifestation of injuries.[19]

Of more concern to us is the failure of the EPA to compute the costs and benefits of its proposed rule past the year 2000, and its double-counting of the costs of asbestos use. In performing its calculus, the EPA only included the number of lives saved over the next thirteen years, and counted any additional lives saved as simply "unquantified benefits." 54 Fed.Reg. at 29,486. The EPA and intervenors now seek to use these unquantified lives saved to justify calculations as to which the benefits seem far outweighed by the astronomical costs. For example, the EPA plans to save about three lives with its ban of asbestos pipe, at a cost of $128–227 million (i.e., approximately $43–76 million per life saved). Although the EPA admits that the price tag is high, it claims that the lives saved past the year 2000 justify the price. See generally id. at 29,473 (explaining use of unquantified benefits).

Such calculations not only lessen the value of the EPA's cost analysis, but also make any meaningful judicial review impossible. While TSCA contemplates a useful place for unquantified benefits beyond the EPA's calculation, unquantified benefits never were intended as a trump card allowing the EPA to justify any cost calculus, no matter how high.

The concept of unquantified benefits, rather, is intended to allow the EPA to provide a rightful place for any remaining benefits that are impossible to quantify after the EPA's best attempt, but which still are of some concern. But the allowance for unquantified costs is not intended to allow the EPA to perform its calculations over an arbitrarily short period so as to preserve a large unquantified portion.

*   *   *

Under the EPA's calculations, a twenty-year-old worker entering employment today still would be at risk from workplace dangers for more than thirty years after the EPA's analysis period had ended. The true benefits of regulating asbestos under such calculations remain unknown. The EPA cannot choose to leave these benefits high and then use the high unknown benefits as a major factor justifying EPA action.

We also note that the EPA appears to place too great a reliance upon the concept of population exposure. While a high population exposure certainly is a factor that the EPA must consider in making its calculations, the agency cannot count such problems more than once. For example, in the case of asbestos brake products, the EPA used factors such as risk and exposure to calculate the probable harm of the brakes, and then used, as an additional reason to ban the products, the fact that the exposure levels were high. Considering that calculations of the probable harm level, when reduced to basics, simply are a calculation of pop-

---

19. We also note that the EPA chose to use a real discount rate of 3%. Because historically the real rate of interest has tended to vary between 2% and 4%, this figure was not inaccurate. The EPA also did not err by calculating that the price of substitute goods is likely to decline at a rate of 1% per year, resulting from economies of scale and increasing manufacturing prowess. Because the EPA properly limited the scope of these declines in its models so that the cost of substitutes would not decline so far as to make the price of the substitutes less than the cost of the asbestos they were forced to replace, this was not an unreasonable real rate of price decline to adopt.

ulation risk multiplied by population exposure, the EPA's redundant use of population exposure to justify its actions cannot stand.

3.
Reasonable Basis.

*   *   *

Most problematical to us is the EPA's ban of products for which no substitutes presently are available. In these cases, the EPA bears a tough burden indeed to show that under TSCA a ban is the least burdensome alternative, as TSCA explicitly instructs the EPA to consider "the benefits of such substance or mixture for various uses and the availability of substitutes for such uses." Id. § 2605(c)(1)(C). These words are particularly appropriate where the EPA actually has decided to ban a product, rather than simply restrict its use, for it is in these cases that the lack of an adequate substitute is most troubling under TSCA.

As the EPA itself states, "[w]hen no information is available for a product indicating that cost-effective substitutes exist, the estimated cost of a product ban is very high." 54 Fed.Reg. at 29,468. Because of this, the EPA did not ban certain uses of asbestos, such as its use in rocket engines and battery separators. The EPA, however, in several other instances, ignores its own arguments and attempts to justify its ban by stating that the ban itself will cause the development of low-cost, adequate substitute products.

As a general matter, we agree with the EPA that a product ban can lead to great innovation, and it is true that an agency under TSCA, as under other regulatory statutes, "is empowered to issue safety standards which require improvements in existing technology or which require the development of new technology." Chrysler Corp. v. Department of Transp., 472 F.2d 659, 673 (6th Cir.1972). As even the EPA acknowledges, however, when no adequate substitutes currently exist, the EPA cannot fail to consider this lack when formulating its own guidelines. Under TSCA, therefore, the EPA must present a stronger case to justify the ban, as opposed to regulation, of products with no substitutes.

*   *   *

This presents two problems. First, TSCA instructs the EPA to consider the relative merits of its ban, as compared to the economic effects of its actions. The EPA cannot make this calculation if it fails to consider the effects that alternate substitutes will pose after a ban.

Second, the EPA cannot say with any assurance that its regulation will increase workplace safety when it refuses to evaluate the harm that will result from the increased use of substitute products. While the EPA may be correct in its conclusion that the alternate materials pose less risk than asbestos, we cannot say with any more assurance than that flowing from an educated guess that this conclusion is true.

Considering that many of the substitutes that the EPA itself concedes will be used in the place of asbestos have known carcinogenic effects, the EPA not only cannot assure this court that it has taken the least burdensome alternative, but cannot even prove that its regulations will increase workplace safety. Eager to douse the dangers of asbestos, the agency inadvertently actually may increase the risk of injury Americans face. The EPA's explicit failure to consider the toxicity of likely substitutes thus deprives its order of a reasonable basis. Cf. American Petroleum Inst. v. OSHA, 581 F.2d 493, 504 (5th Cir.1978) (An agency is required to "regulate on the basis of knowledge rather than the unknown.").

*   *   *

In short, a death is a death, whether occasioned by asbestos or by a toxic substitute product, and the EPA's decision not to evaluate the toxicity of known carcinogenic substitutes is not a reasonable action under TSCA. Once an interested party brings forth credible evidence suggesting the toxicity of the probable or only alternatives to a substance, the EPA must consider the comparative toxic costs of each. Its failure to do so in this case thus deprived its regulation of a reasonable basis, at least in regard to those products as to which petitioners introduced credible evidence of the dangers of the likely substitutes.

4.
Unreasonable Risk of Injury.

The final requirement the EPA must satisfy before engaging in any TSCA rulemaking is that it only take steps designed to prevent "unreasonable" risks. In evaluating what is "unreasonable," the EPA is required to consider the costs of any proposed actions and to "carry out this chapter in a reasonable and prudent manner [after considering] the environmental, economic, and social impact of any action." 15 U.S.C. § 2601(c).

As the District of Columbia Circuit stated when evaluating similar language governing the Federal Hazardous Substances Act, "[t]he requirement that the risk be 'unreasonable' necessarily involves a balancing test like that familiar in tort law: The regulation may issue if the severity of the injury that may result from the product, factored by the likelihood of the injury, offsets the harm the regulation itself imposes upon manufacturers and consumers." Forester v. CPSC, 559 F.2d 774, 789 (D.C.Cir.1977). We have quoted this language approvingly when evaluating other statutes using similar language. See, e.g., Aqua Slide, 569 F.2d at 839.

That the EPA must balance the costs of its regulations against their benefits further is reinforced by the requirement that it seek the least burdensome regulation. While Congress did not dictate that the EPA engage in an exhaustive, full-scale cost-benefit analysis, it did require the EPA to consider both sides of the regulatory equation, and it rejected the notion that the EPA should pursue the reduction of workplace risk at any cost. See American Textile Mfrs. Inst., 452 U.S. at 510 n. 30, 101 S.Ct. at 2491 n. 30 ("unreasonable risk" statutes require "a generalized balancing of costs and benefits" (citing Aqua Slide, 569 F.2d at 839)). Thus, "Congress also plainly intended the EPA to consider the economic impact of any actions taken by it under...TSCA." Chemical Mfrs. Ass'n, 899 F.2d at 348.

Even taking all of the EPA's figures as true, and evaluating them in the light most favorable to the agency's decision (non-discounted benefits, discounted costs, analogous exposure estimates included), the agency's analysis results in figures as high as $74 million per life saved. For example, the EPA states that its ban of asbestos pipe will save three lives over the next thirteen years, at a cost of

$128–227 million ($43–76 million per life saved), depending upon the price of substitutes; that its ban of asbestos shingles will cost $23–34 million to save 0.32 statistical lives ($72–106 million per life saved); that its ban of asbestos coatings will cost $46–181 million to save 3.33 lives ($14–54 million per life saved); and that its ban of asbestos paper products will save 0.60 lives at a cost of $4–5 million ($7–8 million per life saved). See 54 Fed.Reg. at 29,484–85. Were the analogous exposure estimates not included, the cancer risks from substitutes such as ductile iron pipe factored in, and the benefits of the ban appropriately discounted from the time of the manifestation of an injury rather than the time of exposure, the costs would shift even more sharply against the EPA's position.

While we do not sit as a regulatory agency that must make the difficult decision as to what an appropriate expenditure is to prevent someone from incurring the risk of an asbestos-related death, we do note that the EPA, in its zeal to ban any and all asbestos products, basically ignored the cost side of the TSCA equation. The EPA would have this court believe that Congress, when it enacted its requirement that the EPA consider the economic impacts of its regulations, thought that spending $200–300 million to save approximately seven lives (approximately $30–40 million per life) over thirteen years is reasonable.

As we stated in the OSHA context, until an agency "can provide substantial evidence that the benefits to be achieved by [a regulation] bear a reasonable relationship to the costs imposed by the reduction, it cannot show that the standard is reasonably necessary to provide safe or healthful workplaces." American Petroleum Inst., 581 F.2d at 504. Although the OSHA statute differs in major respects from TSCA, the statute does require substantial evidence to support the EPA's contentions that its regulations both have a reasonable basis and are the least burdensome means to a reasonably safe workplace.

The EPA's willingness to argue that spending $23.7 million to save less than one-third of a life reveals that its economic review of its regulations, as required by TSCA, was meaningless. As the petitioners' brief and our review of EPA caselaw reveals, such high costs are rarely, if ever, used to support a safety regulation. If we were to allow such cavalier treatment of the EPA's duty to consider the economic effects of its decisions, we would have to excise entire sections and phrases from the language of TSCA. Because we are judges, not surgeons, we decline to do so.[23]

*   *   *

---

23. See Environmental Defense Fund, 636 F.2d at 1275 n. 17 ("[W]e must construe the statute 'so that no provision will be inoperative or superfluous'" (quoting Motor & Equip. Mfrs. Ass'n v. EPA, 627 F.2d 1095, 1108 (D.C.Cir.1979), cert. denied, 446 U.S. 952, 100 S.Ct. 2917, 64 L.Ed.2d 808 (1980))); see also Old Colony R.R. v. Commissioner, 284 U.S. 552, 560, 52 S.Ct. 211, 213, 76 L.Ed. 484 (1932) (in interpreting statutory language, "the plain, obvious and rational meaning of a statute is to be preferred to any curious, narrow, hidden sense").

As the petitioners point out, the EPA regularly rejects, as unjustified, regulations that would save more lives at less cost. For example, over the next 13 years, we can expect more than a dozen deaths from ingested toothpicks—a death toll more than twice what the EPA predicts will flow from the quarter-billion-dollar bans of asbestos pipe, shingles, and roof coatings. See L. Budnick, Toothpick-Related Injuries in the United States, 1979 Through 1982, 252 J. Am. Med. Ass'n, Aug. 10, 1984, at 796 (study showing that toothpick-related deaths average approximately one per year).

V.

Substantial Evidence Regarding Least Burdensome, Adequate Regulation

*   *   *

A.

Friction Products

*   *   *

We note that of all the asbestos bans, the EPA did the most impressive job in this area, both in conducting its studies and in supporting its contention that banning asbestos products would save over 102 discounted lives. Id. at 29,48 5. Furthermore, the EPA demonstrates that the population exposure to asbestos in this area is great, while the estimated cost of the measure is low, at least in comparison to the cost-per-life of its other bans. Were the petitioners only questioning the EPA's decision to ban friction products based upon disputing these figures, we would be tempted to uphold the EPA, even in the face of petitioners' arguments that workplace exposure to friction product asbestos could be decreased by as much as ninety percent using stricter workplace controls and in light of studies supporting the conclusion that some forms of asbestos present less danger. Decisions such as these are better left to the agency's expertise.

Such expertise, however, is not a universal talisman affording the EPA unbridled latitude to act as it chooses under TSCA. What we cannot ignore is that the EPA failed to study the effect of non-asbestos brakes on automotive safety, despite credible evidence that non-asbestos brakes could increase significantly the number of highway fatalities, and that the EPA failed to evaluate the toxicity of likely brake substitutes. As we already mentioned, the EPA, in its zeal to ban asbestos, cannot overlook, with only cursory study, credible contentions that substitute products actually might increase fatalities.

The EPA commissioned an American Society of Mechanical Engineers (ASME) study that concluded that while more research was needed, it appeared that many of the proposed substitutes for friction products are not, and will, not soon be available, especially in the replacement brake market, and that the substitutes may or may not assure safety.[25] Despite this credible record evidence, by a study specifically commissioned by the EPA, that substitute products actually might cause more deaths than those asbestos deaths predicted by the EPA, the agency did not evaluate the dangers posed by the substitutes, including cancer deaths from the other fibers used and highway deaths occasioned by less effective, non-asbestos brakes. This failure to examine the likely consequence of the EPA's regulation renders the ban of asbestos friction products unreasonable.

---

25. One of the study's authors, Mr. Anderson, submitted written testimony that the "replacement/substitution of asbestos-based with non-asbestos brake linings will produce grave risks" and that "the expected increase of skid-related highway accidents and resultant traffic deaths would certainly be expected to overshadow any potential health-related benefits of fiber substitution." The ASME report itself concludes only that "[i]f the eventual elimination of all asbestos in friction products is to be accomplished, additional future studies are required." This is an insufficient basis upon which to support the EPA's judgment that non-asbestos brakes are just as safe as asbestos brakes.

This failure would be of little moment, were the relevant market confined to original equipment disk brakes and pads. For these original equipment brakes, it appears that manufacturers already have developed safe substitutes for asbestos, considering that nearly all new vehicles come with non-asbestos disk brakes, with non-asbestos drum brakes apparently soon to follow. See id. at 29,493. The ASME Report concluded that "at the present rate of technological progress, most new passenger cars could be equipped with totally non-asbestos frictional systems by 1991, and most light trucks and heavy trucks with S-cam brakes, by 1992." See id. at 29,494.

Although the petitioners dispute the evidence, we find particularly telling the fact that manufacturers already are producing most vehicles with newly designed, non-asbestos brakes. The ban of asbestos brakes for these uses here appears reasonable and, had the EPA taken the proper steps to consider and reject the less burdensome alternatives, we might find the ban of these products supported by substantial evidence.

With respect to the aftermarket replacement market, however, the EPA's failure to consider the safety ramifications of its decisions is problematic. Original equipment, non-asbestos brakes are designed from the start to work without the superior insulating properties of asbestos. The replacement market brakes, on the other hand, were designed with asbestos, rather than substitutes, in mind. As the EPA itself states, "[c]ommenters generally agreed that it is easier to develop replacement asbestos-free friction materials for use in vehicles that are intentionally designed to use such materials than it is to develop asbestos-free friction materials for use as after-market replacement products in vehicles currently in use that have brake systems designed to use asbestos." Id. Because of these difficulties, the EPA decided to use a stage 3 ban for replacement brakes.

Despite acknowledging the difficulty of retrofitting current asbestos brakes, however, the EPA decided that the problem with non-asbestos brakes was not that they are inferior, but that they are less safe because the government does not regulate them. Based upon this conclusion, the EPA decided that it need not consider the safety of alternative brakes because, after consultation with the National Highway Traffic Safety Administration (NHTSA), the EPA concluded that regulation of non-asbestos brakes soon would be forthcoming. Id.

This determination is insufficient to discharge the EPA's duties under TSCA. The EPA failed to settle whether alternative brakes will be as safe as current brakes, even though, by its own admission, the "EPA also acknowledges that a ban on asbestos in the brake friction product categories may increase the uncertainty about brake performance." Id. at 29,495. The EPA contends that it can rely upon NHTSA to discharge its regulatory burdens, but it ignores the fact that the problem with non-asbestos brakes may be technical, rather than regulatory, in nature.

Future consideration by the NHTSA cannot support a present ban by the EPA when the record contains conflicting and non-conclusive evidence regarding the safety of non-asbestos brake replacement parts. After being presented with credible evidence "that a ban on asbestos use in the aftermarket for brake systems designed for asbestos friction products will compromise the performance of braking systems designed for asbestos brakes," id. at 29,494, the EPA under

TSCA had to consider whether its proposed ban not only was reasonable, but also whether the increased deaths caused by less efficient brakes made the ban of asbestos in the replacement brake market unreasonable.

In short, while it is apparent that non-asbestos brake products either are available or soon will be available on new vehicles, there is no evidence indicating that forcing consumers to replace their asbestos brakes with new non-asbestos brakes as they wear out on their present vehicles will decrease fatalities or that such a ban will produce other benefits that outweigh its costs. Furthermore, many of the EPA's own witnesses conceded on cross-examination that the non-asbestos fibrous substitutes also pose a cancer risk upon inhalation, yet the EPA failed to examine in more than a cursory fashion the toxicity of these alternatives. Under these circumstances, the EPA has failed to support its ban with the substantial evidence needed to provide it with a reasonable basis.

Finally, as we already have noted, the structure of TSCA requires the EPA to consider, and reject, the less burdensome alternatives in the TSCA hierarchy before it can invoke its power to ban a product completely. It may well be true, as the EPA contends, that workplace controls are insufficient measures under TSCA and that only a ban will discharge the EPA's TSCA-imposed duty to seek the safest, reasonable environment. The EPA's failure to consider the regulatory alternatives, however, cannot be substantiated by conclusory statements that regulation would be insufficient. See Texas Indep. Ginners Ass'n v. Marshall, 630 F.2d 398, 411–12 (5th Cir.1980); Aqua Slide, 569 F.2d at 843. We thus conclude that while the EPA may have presented sufficient evidence to underpin the dangers of asbestos brakes, its failure to consider whether the ban is the least burdensome alternative, and its refusal to consider the toxicity and danger of substitute brake products, in regard to both highway and workplace safety, deprived its regulation of the reasonable basis required by TSCA.

B.
Asbestos-Cement Pipe Products.

The EPA's analysis supporting its ban of asbestos-cement (A/C") pipe is more troublesome than its action in regard to friction products. Asbestos pipe primarily is used to convey water in mains, sewage under pressure, and materials in various industrial process lines. Unlike most uses of asbestos, asbestos pipe is valued primarily for its strength and resistance to corrosion, rather than for its heat-resistant qualities. The EPA imposed a stage 3 ban on asbestos pipe. 54 Fed.Reg. at 29,462.

Petitioners question EPA's cost/benefit balancing, noting that by the EPA's own predictions, the ban of asbestos pipe will save only 3–4 discounted lives, at a cost ranging from $128–227 million ($43–76 million per life saved), depending upon the price of substitutes. Id. at 29,484. Furthermore, much of EPA's data regarding this product and others depends upon data received from exposures observed during activities similar to the ones to be regulated—the "analogous exposure" analysis that the EPA adopted subsequent to the public comment period, which thus was not subjected to cross-examination or other critical testing. Finally, the petitioners protest that the EPA acted unreasonably because the most likely substitutes for the asbestos pipe, PVC and ductile iron pipe, also contain known carcinogens.

Once again we are troubled by the EPA's methodology and its evaluation of the substitute products. Many of the objections raised by the asbestos cement pipe producers are general protests about the EPA's studies and other similar complaints. We will not disturb such agency inquiries, as it is not our role to delve into matters better left for agency expertise. We do, however, examine the EPA's methodology in places to determine whether it has presented substantial evidence to support its regulation.

As with friction products, the EPA refused to assess the risks of substitutes to asbestos pipe. Id. at 29,497–98. Unlike non-asbestos brakes, which the EPA contends are safe, the EPA here admits that vinyl chloride, used in PVC, is a human carcinogen that is especially potent during the manufacture of PVC pipe. As for the EPA's defense of the ductile iron pipe substitute, the EPA also acknowledges evidence that it will cause cancer deaths but rejects these deaths as overestimated, even though it can present no more support for this assumption than its own ipse dixit.

The EPA presented several plausible, albeit untested, reasons why PVC and ductile iron pipe might be less of a health risk than asbestos pipe. It did not, however, actually evaluate the health risk flowing from these substitute products, even though the "EPA acknowledges that the individual lifetime cancer risk associated with the production of PVC may be equivalent to that associated with the production of A/C pipe." Id. at 29,497. The agency concedes that "[t]he population cancer risk for the production of ductile iron pipe could be comparable to the population cancer risk for production of A/C pipe." Id.

It was insufficient for the EPA to conclude that while its data showed that "the number of cancer cases associated with production of equivalent amounts of ductile iron pipe and A/C pipe 'may be similar,' the estimate of cancer risk for ductile iron pipe 'is most likely an overestimate,' " see 54 Fed.Reg. at 29,498, unless the agency can present something more concrete than its own speculation to refute these earlier iron pipe cancer studies. Musings and conjecture are "not the stuff of which substantial evidence is made," Aqua Slide, 569 F.2d at 843, and "[u]narticulated reliance on Commission 'experience' may satisfy an 'arbitrary, capricious' standard of review, but it does not add one jot to the record evidence." Id. at 841–42 (citations omitted). "While expert opinion deserves to be heeded, it must be based on more than casual observation and speculation, particularly where a risk of fatal injury is being evaluated." Id. These concerns are of special note where the increased carcinogen risk occasioned by the EPA's proposed substitutes is both credible and known.

This conclusion only is strengthened when we consider the EPA's failure to analyze the health risks of PVC pipe, the most likely substitute for asbestos pipe, which the EPA concedes poses a cancer risk similar to that presented by asbestos pipe. The failure of the EPA to make a record finding on the risks of PVC pipe is particularly inexplicable, as the EPA already is studying increasing the stringency of PVC regulation in separate rulemaking proceedings, an action that one of the very intervenors in the instant case has been urging for years. See NRDC v. EPA, 824 F.2d 1146, 1148–49 (D.C.Cir.1987) (en banc).

The EPA, in these separate proceedings, has estimated the cancer risk from PVC plants to be as high as twenty deaths per year, a death rate that stringent controls might be able to reduce to one per year, see id. at 1149, far in excess of the fractions of a life that the asbestos pipe ban may save each year, by the EPA's own calculations. Considering that the EPA concedes that there is no evidence showing that ingested, as opposed to inhaled, asbestos is a health risk, while the

EPA's own studies show that ingested vinyl chloride is a significant cancer risk that could cause up to 260 cancer deaths over the next thirteen years, see id.; 54 Fed.Reg. at 29,498, the EPA's failure to consider the risks of substitute products in the asbestos pipe area is particularly troublesome. The agency cannot simply choose to note the similar cancer risks of asbestos and iron pipe and then reject the data underpinning the iron and PVC pipe without more than its own conclusory statements.

We also express concern with the EPA's cavalier attitude toward the use of its own data. The asbestos pipe industry argues that the exposure times the EPA used to calculate its figures are much higher than experience would warrant, a contention that the EPA now basically concedes. Rather than recalculate its figures, however, based upon the best data available to it, the EPA merely responds that while the one figure may be too high, it undoubtedly underestimated the exposure levels, because contractors seldom comply with OSHA regulations. In the words of its brief, "[t]hus, EPA concluded that its estimates contain both over- and underestimates, but nevertheless represented a reasonable picture of aggregate exposure."

The EPA is required to support its analysis with substantial evidence under TSCA. When one figure is challenged, it cannot back up its position by changing an unrelated figure to yield the same result. Allowing such behavior would require us only to focus on the final numbers provided by an agency, and to ignore how it arrives at that number. Because a conclusion is no better than the methodology used to reach it, such a result cannot survive the substantial evidence test.

Finally, we once again note that the EPA failed to discharge its TSCA-mandated burden that it consider and reject less burdensome alternatives before it impose a more burdensome alternative such as a complete ban. The EPA instead jumped immediately to the ban provision, without calculating whether a less burdensome alternative might accomplish TSCA's goals. See 54 Fed.Reg. at 29,489. We therefore conclude that the EPA failed to present substantial evidence to support its ban of asbestos pipe.

C.
Gaskets, Roofing, Shingles, and Paper Products.

We here deal with the remaining products affected by the EPA ban. Petitioners challenge the basis for the EPA's finding that beater-add and sheet gaskets, primarily used in automotive parts, should be banned. The agency estimated its ban would save thirty-two lives over a thirteen-year time span, at an overall cost of $207–263 million ($6–8 million per life saved). Id. at 29,484.

We have little to add in this area, beyond our general discussion and comments on other products, apart from a brief highlight of the EPA's use of analogous exposure data to support its gasket ban. For these products, the analogous exposure estimate constituted almost eighty percent of the anticipated total benefits—a proportion so large that the EPA's duty to give interested parties notice that it intended to use analogous exposure estimates was particularly acute.[27]

---

27. The EPA estimates drop from 32.24 discounted lives to 6.68 discounted lives without the analogous exposure data.

Considering some of the EPA's support for its analogous exposure estimates—such as its assumption that none of the same workers who install beater-add and sheet gaskets ever is involved in repairing or disposing of them, and the unexplained discrepancy between its present conclusion that over 50,000 workers are involved in this area and its 1984 estimate that only 768 workers are involved in "gasket removal and installation," see 51 Fed.Reg. 22,612, 22,665 (1986)—the petitioners' complaint that they never were afforded the opportunity to comment publicly upon these figures, or to cross-examine any EPA witnesses regarding them, is particularly telling.

The EPA also banned roof coatings, roof shingles, non-roof coatings, and asbestos paper products. Again, we have little to add beyond our discussions already concluded, especially regarding TSCA's requirement that the EPA always choose the least burdensome alternative, whether it be workplace regulation, labeling, or only a partial ban. We note, however, that in those cases in which a complete ban would save less than one statistical life, such as those affecting asbestos paper products and certain roofing materials, the EPA has a particular need to examine the less burdensome alternatives to a complete ban.

Where appropriate, the EPA should consider our preceding discussion as applicable to their bans of these products. By following the dictates of Chemical Mfrs. Ass'n, 899 F.2d at 359, that the quantities of the regulated chemical entering into the environment be "substantial," and that the human exposure to the chemical also must be "substantial" or "significant," as well as our concerns expressed in this opinion, the EPA should be able to determine the proper procedures to follow on its reconsideration of its rule and present the cogent explanation of its actions as required under Chemical Manufacturers Association.

D.
Ban of Products Not Being Produced in the United States.

Petitioners also contend that the EPA overstepped TSCA's bounds by seeking to ban products that once were, but no longer are, being produced in the United States. We find little merit to this claim, considering that sections 5 and 6 of TSCA allow the EPA to ban a product "that presents or will present " a significant risk. (Emphasis added.)

Although petitioners correctly point out that the value of a product not being produced is not zero, as it may find some future use, and that the EPA here has banned items where the estimated risk is zero, this was not error on the part of the EPA. The numbers appear to favor petitioners only because even products with known high risks temporarily show no risk because they are not part of this country's present stream of commerce. This would soon change if the product returned, which is precisely what the EPA is trying to avoid.

Should some unlikely future use arise for these products, the manufacturers and importers have access to the waiver provision established by the EPA for just these contingencies. Under such circumstances, we will not disturb the agency's decision to ban products that no longer are being produced in or imported into the United States.

Similarly, we also decide that the EPA properly can attempt to promulgate a "clean up" ban under TSCA, providing it takes the proper steps in doing so.

A clean-up ban, like the asbestos ban in this case, seeks to ban all uses of a certain toxic substance, including unknown, future uses of the substance. Although there is some merit to petitioners' argument that the EPA cannot possibly evaluate the costs and benefits of banning unknown, uninvented products, we hold that the nebulousness of these future products, combined with TSCA's language authorizing the EPA to ban products that "will" create a public risk, allows the EPA to ban future uses of asbestos even in products not yet on the market.

E.
Fundamental EPA Choices.

Finally, we note that there are many other issues raised by petitioners, such as the EPA's decision to treat all types of asbestos the same, its conclusion that various lengths of fibers present similar toxic risks, and its decision that asbestos presents similar risks even in different industries. See generally 54 Fed.Reg. at 29,470–71 (detailing differences in potency of chrysotile and other forms of asbestos and toxicity of various fiber lengths). We mention these concerns now only to reject them.

On these, and many similar points, the petitioners merely seek to have us reevaluate the EPA's initial evaluation of the evidence. While we can, and in this opinion do, question the agency's reliance upon flawed methodology and its failure to consider factors and alternatives that TSCA explicitly requires it to consider, we do not sit as a regulatory agency ourselves. Decisions such as the EPA's decision to treat various types of asbestos as presenting similar health risks properly are better left for agency determination and, while the EPA is free to reconsider its data should it so choose when it revisits this area, it also is free to adopt similar reasoning in the future.

VI.
Conclusion.

In summary, of most concern to us is that the EPA has failed to implement the dictates of TSCA and the prior decisions of this and other courts that, before it imposes a ban on a product, it first evaluate and then reject the less burdensome alternatives laid out for it by Congress. While the EPA spent much time and care crafting its asbestos regulation, its explicit failure to consider the alternatives required of it by Congress deprived its final rule of the reasonable basis it needed to survive judicial scrutiny.

Furthermore, the EPA's adoption of the analogous exposure estimates during the final weeks of its rulemaking process, after public comment was concluded, rather than during the ten years during which it was considering the asbestos ban, was unreasonable and deprived the petitioners of the notice that they required in order to present their own evidence on the validity of the estimates and its data bases. By depriving the petitioners of their right to cross-examine EPA witnesses on methodology and data used to support as much as eighty percent of the proposed benefits in some areas, the EPA also violated the dictates of TSCA.

Finally, the EPA failed to provide a reasonable basis for the purported benefits of its proposed rule by refusing to evaluate the toxicity of likely substitute products that will be used to replace asbestos goods. While the EPA does not have the duty under TSCA of affirmatively seeking out and testing all possible substitutes, when an interested party comes forward with credible evidence that the planned substitutes present a significant, or even greater, toxic risk than the substance in question, the agency must make a formal finding on the record that its proposed action still is both reasonable and warranted under TSCA.

We regret that this matter must continue to take up the valuable time of the agency, parties and, undoubtedly, future courts. The requirements of TSCA, however, are plain, and the EPA cannot deviate from them to reach its desired result. We therefore GRANT the petition for review, VACATE the EPA's proposed regulation, and REMAND to the EPA for further proceedings in light of this opinion.[28]

Notes and Questions

1. All Risk is Relative: Much of the court's opinion discusses the relative risk of asbestos alternatives. In many instances, there was evidence that suggested that the risk of substitute products outweighed the risk of asbestos. By ignoring the relative risks of different products, the EPA's rulemaking might have resulted in a net increase in lost lives. Why does the EPA choose to ignore such trade-offs. Why isn't the EPA more concerned with regulating these substitute products?

2. Establishing an Unreasonable Risk: The Toxic Substances Control Act (TSCA) contemplates that "unreasonable" risks will be regulated. In interpreting this statutory language, courts often refer to the reasonableness standard used in tort law. That is, if the severity of injury multiplied by the probability of injury is greater than the costs of regulation, then an unreasonable risk is presumed to exist. Even under an interpretation of the evidence most favorable to the EPA, the court has doubts as to the need for any regulation. Do you agree with the court's conclusion in this regard? The court often gave dollar values for the cost of lives saved under the EPA regulation. What value was the court placing on the expected benefit of a life saved? After considering the numerous methodological and procedural errors made by the EPA is it clear that an unreasonable risk exists? Was the EPA simply sloppy in quantifying the riskiness of asbestos? What other incentives might the EPA face which would cause it to make the type of errors discussed by the court?

3. The Least Burdensome Regulation: Once an unreasonable risk has been identified, TSCA requires that the least burdensome approach to regulation be taken. EPA provides information regarding the benefits and costs of essentially a complete banning of asbestos. The court's primary concern in this regard is that it does not have information as to whether a complete ban or some other level of regulation provides the largest net benefit. In other words, the court interprets TSCA as requiring the most bang for the regulatory buck. Can you explain this

---

28. Pursuant to the Internal Operating Procedures accompanying Fifth Cir.Loc.R. 47, Judge Brown reserves the right to file a separate opinion.

standard in terms of marginal analysis? Is this an appropriate guide by which risk regulation should be approached?

4. Irrationality and Uncertainty: Empirical studies suggest that many individuals have difficulty conceptualizing probabilities. As a result, individuals tend to overestimate the risks of low probability events and underestimate the risks of high probability events. This result has a variety of implications for risk regulation. First, it suggests that even if market participants were supplied with full information, the optimal level of risk might not prevail. However, in the case of small probabilities such results would suggest the presence of over regulation. Second, to the extent that policy makers are responsive to public perceptions of risk, government regulation will not be optimal. Furthermore, studies suggest that individuals tend to overestimate the risks of events which are frequently reported on the news. Thus, even though the chance of being killed in a car wreck is substantially higher than death from AIDS, public perception often places the relative likelihoods of these two risks much closer together.

3. Risk v. Risk

Well intentioned risk regulations often have the unintended consequence of increasing other types of risk. For example, empirical studies indicate that regulations requiring safety belts in cars changed drivers attitudes towards speeding. In short, when safely buckled into their car, many drives felt that it was less risky to speed. The unintended consequence was to increase the risk to pedestrians and motorcyclist of being hit by a car. Thus, the safety belt regulation while potentially saving the lives of those driving cars inadvertently increased the risk to other groups of being killed.

Perhaps the most basic error made by risk regulators in this regard is to forget that risk outcomes are function of both the characteristics of the product or service in question and individual behavior. As a consequence, regulators often ignore the predictable rational economic responses of resourceful individuals. Recall the REMM model from Chapter I. Suppose that government regulators believed that requiring child resistant caps on cleaning products would reduce the risk of child poisoning from 1 in 100,000 children to 1 in 200,000 children per year. Before adopting this regulation, however, the agency should engage in **risk trade-off analysis** (RTA). RTA forces regulators to go through the process of thinking about how reducing one form of risk impacts human behavior and consequently the presence of other types of risk—Risk v. Risk. For example, the child resistant cap regulation proposed above may have an impact on parents' perceptions of the marginal benefits of precautionary measures that they took to avoid child poisonings prior to the adoption of the regulation. For instance, because of the child safety caps, parents might be less diligent about placing cleaning products on high shelves and some children might be poisoned because they had easier access to the cleaning products. Thus, the RTA suggests that some portion of the benefits derived from child safety caps might be offset by a reduction in individual care. The difficulty from the regulators perspective is to quantify these risk trade-offs in order to determine the net risk impact.

Read

Competitive Enterprise Institute v. NHTSA
U.S. Court of Appeals, D.C. Circuit
956 F.2d 321 (1992)

and accompanying **Notes and Questions**
Supra Chapter I

4. Risk Regulation Priorities

Risk reduction is costly. Therefore, every decision to reduce a particular risk entails opportunity costs—the opportunity to reduce some other form of risk. Thus, decisions need to be made regarding which risks will be attacked through regulation. The analysis in preceding subsections suggest several guidelines that should be kept in mind when setting these priorities. First, risk reduction at a point where marginal costs are greater than marginal benefits not only increases risk by reducing the size of the economic pie, but also takes resources away from cost effective risk reduction efforts. Second, risk-tradeoff analysis suggests that regulations with the largest net reduction in risk per dollar spent should be pursued first. In other words, regulations that save lives at lower costs should take priority over those that save lives at high costs. An empirical study by Dr. Tammy Tengs suggests that the current regulatory approach ignores these factors.

> Results indicate that we incur opportunity costs of approximately $31.1 billion, 60,200 premature deaths, or 636,000 years of life lost every year in order to maintain our present pattern of investment in these 185 life-saving interventions. At our current level of resource consumption, we could double the survival benefits of our expenditures. Alternatively, we could retain our present level of risk reduction and, in addition, save billions of dollars.

Tammy O. Tengs, Optimizing Societal Investments in the Prevention of Premature Death, doctoral dissertation, Harvard School of Public Health, June, 1994, p. 2.

In the context of determining the appropriate priorities for risk regulation, it is important to recognize that regulation does not operate within a vacuum. Specifically, both the market and the legal system have an impact on prevailing safety levels. Thus, the prioritization question should not be limited to the cost effectiveness of different regulations, but rather should include the relative cost effectiveness of all sources of risk reduction. For example, empirical evidence on compensating wage differentials suggests that workers are generally capable of identifying on the job safety hazards, such as working with dangerous machinery. On the other hand, workers have a more difficult time identifying health hazards, such as the carcinogenic risk due to on the job toxins. Despite these facts, OSHA has focused it emphasis primarily on regulating safety hazards.

5. Political Economy of Health and Safety Regulation

Cost-benefit analysis suggests that many risk regulations are too strict, yet government regulators continue to promulgate such regulations. Rather than assuming that the regulators are either ignorant, evil, or both, it might be helpful to consider the political incentives of those responsible for the oversight of the regulatory process. In general, risk regulators' incentives push them to adopt regulations that ignore the efficient determination of optimal risk levels. Three specific sources of these perverse incentives should be noted.

First, the literature on the economics of bureaucracy suggests that bureaucrats are motivated to maximize the size of their budget. In this regard, risk regulators have an incentive to increase the size and budget of their agency by using command and control methods of regulation rather than encourage the most efficient means for risk reduction. Often times, regulators attempt to reduce risk by imposing a particular set of technological requirements on an industry. This provides the regulatory agency with a large degree of control over how risk reduction is achieved. The agency needs a larger budget in order to control activity.

Second, both politicians and regulators tend to be risk averse because negative news impacts their personal interest more than positive news. Consider the case of a new drug that is expected to save 1,000 lives within its first year. Unfortunately, 100 individuals are expected to die because of adverse side effects. Politicians and bureaucrats reasonably expect that the 100 killed will be bigger news than the 1,000 saved. When budgets and re-election are a function of political popularity, very few individuals will want to be known as the regulator or politician who allowed a new drug to go on the market that killed 100 people. Understandably, bureaucrats and politicians have an incentive to seek higher than optimal levels of risk reduction in order to maintain their jobs or their political status. Furthermore, to the extent that politicians respond to voter preferences and voters overestimate the risk of low probability events and underestimate the risk of higher probability events, an inefficient level of risk regulation is likely to result.

Finally, risk regulators and politicians often ignore the costs that they impose on others. The cost-benefit analysis of risk regulations clearly indicates that many areas are being regulated too intensively. More intelligent priority setting—that is, reallocation of risk reducing resources from one area to another—seems to be called for. However, it's important to recognize that the cost-benefit analysis compares the private cost of one industry with the benefits to society. If a particular industry is granted regulatory relief, the money saved by that industry is not available to regulators to use more wisely in regulating other industries. The savings belong to the industry. Thus, regulators have little to gain from reducing regulation to the optimal level.

Chapter X

Organizational Economics

Organizational economics studies the various non-market methods that are used to coordinate economic activities. Instead of characterizing the world as millions of instantaneous market transactions, organizational economics focuses on the manner in which the positive transaction costs of using the market impact the organization of economic activity through long-term contracts and firms. Section A provides a general answer to the fundamental question of why firms exist. Section B goes into greater detail about the costs of using markets to coordinate economic activity and the contractual arrangements that have evolved to control transaction costs. Section C introduces the agency theory approach to organizations which identifies some of the incentive problems associated with firm coordination and how contracts ameliorate those problems. Finally, Section D applies the agency perspective to the issue of corporate governance and examines how market forces resolve some of the conflicts between managers and shareholders in large, publicly-held corporations.

A. The Existence of Firms

Up to this point, the economic analysis presented in this casebook has treated the firm as a producing unit. For example, the graphs of competition and monopoly rely on cost curves which are based on technological constraints imposed by the law of diminishing marginal returns. The firm emerges as an economic entity for purely technical reasons, such as economies of scale in production. In this neoclassical view of the firm, both the existence of the firm and the profit maximizing goal of the firm are taken for granted. Although economics professors enjoy drawing the baffling graphs that illustrate this view of the firm, the technological approach leaves unanswered several important and interesting questions. For example, some economic activities are coordinated by the price system and some are administered explicitly within business organizations; which economic functions will firms perform? Some economic activities are carried out in small businesses with one or two employees and some take place within large, far-flung enterprises whose products evolve under common ownership from the raw material stage to retail outlets; what forces (in addition to technology) determine the size and scope of firms? Some economic activities are performed by non-profit enterprises, some by partnerships, some by mutual companies, some by corporations, and so on; what type of organizational form will the firm adopt?

The modern theory of the firm seeks to provide answers to these questions and explain the choice of methods of coordination among specialized individuals in a market economy. There are two basic methods of economic coordination in a market economy—market coordination and firm coordination. Market coordination is the process through which the price system directs production decisions. In theory, all possible gains from specialization could be realized through market coordination in the absence of transaction costs, which include negotiating, contracting, and enforcing costs. Firm coordination is the process through which production decisions are directed through a "firm"—an economic organization that purchases and organizes resources to produce desired goods and services. In essence, the use of the firm to coordinate and direct the flow of resources represents a substitution of hierarchical or bureaucratic decision making in production processes for production organized through discrete market contracts. Management organizes, coordinates, and monitors the production processes within the firm. The market still serves to guide the economic decisions of the firm with respect to what products or services to produce, but the internal decision processes are directed by the managerial organization of the firm.

The seminal contribution in the development of the modern theory of the firm is Nobel Laureate Ronald Coase's 1937 article entitled "The Nature of the Firm" (4 Economica 386 (1937)). Professor Coase was the first to explain that the emergence of the firm as a method of economic coordination was the result of an effort to reduce the transaction costs of market coordination. In a world with zero transactions costs, there would be no need for the organization of economic activities in firms because all activities could be handled through spontaneous market transactions. However, once transactions costs are added, the least costly, or most efficient, form of coordination of certain economic activities may be through the firm. On the other hand, the use of firm coordination also involves costs—generally through the loss of information and control over employees in the hierarchical organizational structure. These internal administrative control costs explain why firms will not grow without limit—that is, why the economy is not managed by one huge firm. In general, a firm will expand to the point where the marginal benefit in the form of reduced transaction costs is just offset by the marginal cost of internal organization. Profit maximizing firms will tend to evolve to the most efficient size—the size that reflects the optimal mix of market coordination and firm coordination.

The fundamental trade-off between the transaction costs of using the market to coordinate economic activities and administrative costs of using firms to coordinate economic activity are illustrated in Figure X-1. The horizontal axis measures the extent of economic activity that is coordinated through the firm—all coordination is through markets at 0% and all is through firms at 100%. The transaction costs of using the price system (CPS) decline as more and more activities are organized through firms. In the extreme, transaction costs of using the market system are zero because all economic coordination occurs within the firm. On the other hand, the costs of administrative command (CAC) increase as more and more activities are coordinated in firms. With these cost curves moving in opposite directions, the optimal degree of firm coordination can be identified by finding the point that minimizes the total of transaction (CPS) and administrative costs (CAC). The optimal mix of firm and market coordination is at A*, which represents the minimum total cost (TC) where TC = CPS + CAC.

The market is used to coordinate economic activity up to the point where the marginal cost of using the price system is equal to the marginal cost of firm orga-

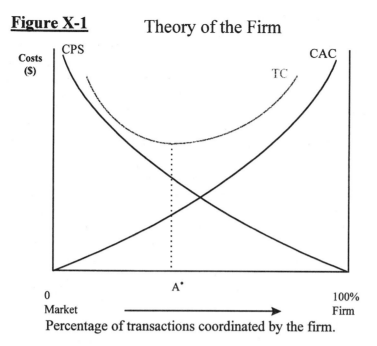

Figure X-1   Theory of the Firm

Percentage of transactions coordinated by the firm.

nization. Note that changes in the parameters that determine the relative positions of CAC and CPS curves will change the value of A*. [One way to think about business schools is that they are in the business of teaching future managers how to find the optimal combination of CPS and CAC, usually by focusing on reducing CAC.] Consider what happens to these curves if advances in auditing techniques improve the ability of an entrepreneur to monitor the production process. The resulting lower CAC should allow the firm to increase in size and scope of production.

Coase's analysis of the firm seems relatively simple today, but it was a big step for economic theory. Economists stopped treating the firm as merely a technological "black box." A great deal of law-and-economics research now focuses on the analysis of the rich and varied set of transactions that constitute the activities of firms—for example, analysis of a firm's decision to use franchising or vertical integration to expand its operations. The next two sections present a more detailed discussion of the sources of transaction and administrative control costs.

B. Transaction Costs in Markets

Transaction costs are the out-of-pocket and opportunity costs of negotiating, drafting, and enforcing contracts. Transaction costs can frustrate potential mutually beneficial market transactions and cause firms to take the transaction away from the market by moving the gains from trade inside the firm. In this section, several types of contractual arrangements that are designed to control transaction costs without complete integration into the firm are examined.

1. Opportunistic Behavior

Opportunistic behavior, or opportunism, has been defined as "self-interest seeking with guile." *See* Oliver Williamson, *Transaction-Cost Economics: The Governance of Contractual Relations*, 22 Journal of Law and Econonmics 233, 234 n. 3 (1979). In more technical terms, opportunism occurs when one party to a transaction recognizes that the other transactor cannot economically retaliate against postcontractual manipulation of the terms of trade, and then engages in such manipulation in order to effect an unexpected transfer of wealth from the other transactor.

Two examples illustrate the basic phenomenon of opportunistic behavior. First, consider a plaintiff's attorney in a private antitrust action. The plaintiff and the attorney have negotiated a contingency contract in which the attorney's fee will equal one-tenth of the total damages award in the case. Suppose the attorney, who has become intimately involved in the case and cannot be replaced on short notice, has presented a very effective case so that prior to final arguments all observers agree that the plaintiff will win the case and recover a substantial treble damages award. However, immediately prior to final arguments, the attorney tells the plaintiff he will intentionally lose the case unless the plaintiff agrees to increase his fee to twenty-five percent. Ignoring for the moment the ethical issues and the legal enforceability of the increase, it seems absolutely clear that the plaintiff must meet the attorney's opportunistic demand or lose the case.

As a second example, suppose individual *A* owns a vacant lot and individual *B* wishes to build a house. *A* could lease the lot to *B* for a short time and *B* could build on the lot, but after the lease expires, *A* will be able to engage in opportunism by raising the rent to reflect the costs to *B* of moving the house to another lot. Instead of submitting himself voluntarily to the possibility of such behavior, *B*, a rational individual, may choose to avoid the exchange altogether. Another solution to this problem would be for *B* to purchase the building lot. Conceptually, this is a form of vertical integration. *See* Klein, Crawford & Alchian, *Vertical Integration, Appropriable Rents, and the Competitive Contracting Process*, 21 Journal of Law and Economics 297, 299 (1978) (emphasizing that vertical integration is a means of economizing on costs and avoiding risks of appropriation of quasi-rents in specialized assets by opportunistic individuals). The costs imposed on one trading party by the opportunistic behavior of the other trading party are important components of transaction costs.

Potential victims of opportunism are protected through several types of activities. Other than avoiding the transaction altogether, five methods of eliminating or reducing the risk of becoming victims should be emphasized: First, it may be possible to avoid the risk of opportunism through vertical integration. In the above examples, the use of an in-house attorney and the purchase of the building lot would avoid the possibility of opportunism. Second, the potential victim may adjust the initial price to deter the occurrence of the opportunism. For example, if the attorney's initial fee in the first example had been twenty instead of ten percent, then the attorney's opportunistic threat would have been less credible because the attorney would have had more to lose had he "thrown" the case. Third, adverse market adjustments may prevent a substantial portion of myopic opportunism. The future value of the attorney's services, for example, will surely diminish as a result of his opportunistic fee manipulation. A lawyer, like a manufacturer, has an economic incentive to establish and maintain a good reputation, a lawyer's "brand name." Fourth, although potential victims may have signed relatively simple contracts, they can rely on implicit contract terms based on legal principles which do not allow for the enforcement of certain types of postcontractual modifications. For example, the attorney's opportunistic distortion may not be enforceable under a pre-existing duty theory. Finally, the parties can agree to and write a complete, fully specified contingent contract and rely on the courts to enforce the agreement. For example, the landowner and the homeowner could specify contractually how the future rent is to be determined upon expiration of the initial lease. These methods will not in all circumstances act as a complete deterrence to opportunism, but they can substantially reduce the risks associated with many transactions.

Two distinct types of opportunistic behavior—appropriation of quasi-rents and free riding—are examined next. This is followed by an analysis of franchising and the manner in which franchise contracts address incentives by both franchisors and franchisees to engage in opportunistic behavior.

a. Firm-Specific Investments and the Appropriation of Quasi-Rents

Transaction failures in procurement and production resulting from opportunistic behavior are most likely to occur when firms become specialized to each other. A major reason firms invest in assets that are specialized to the assets of other firms is to gain the technological advantages of coordinated or joint production processes. The cost savings generated from the improvement in productive efficiency are called "appropriable quasi-rents." These "quasi-rents" represent wealth that is potentially appropriable by an opportunistic party.

One form of opportunism involves the postcontractual manipulation of transfer prices by a supplier and a manufacturer who have become specialized to each other. Consider the example of steel production. The fabrication of steel products requires the shaping of molten steel. Production efficiency is improved by a reduction in the cost of transporting and reheating ingots, if fabrication facilities are located near the point where steel ingots are cast. However, obtaining these technical efficiencies does not require joint ownership of the steel ingots facilities. Technical efficiency requires physical proximity, not joint ownership. Yet ingot casting and fabrication facilities are often commonly owned and vertically integrated, because in the absence of integration, opportunism between separate ingot casting and steel fabrication firms would preclude technical efficiency.

This proposition is easily demonstrated. Imagine that an ingot producer builds an ingot casting plant that is physically integrated with a steel fabricating facility owned by another firm. These separately owned facilities are designed to work together; each is highly specialized to the other. As a result, there are no other ingot facilities that can supply cast steel to the fabricator as cheaply as the caster, and no other fabrication plant that can make steel products from the ingot producer's castings as cheaply as the specialized fabricator. Under these circumstances, opportunistic price manipulation can occur with respect to the transfer price for ingot. If the transfer price of the ingot is greater than the going market price of cold delivered ingot (of comparable quality) plus the costs associated with reheating it, the purchaser can threaten to go to the outside supply source unless the ingot casting plant lowers its price. The price could be forced below the market price plus the cost of reheating, but the ingot caster need not take less than market price of cold ingot. Thus a bargaining range exists that, depending upon circumstances, can leave one of the firms with a much lower than expected rate of return on the investment. More importantly, this uncertainty about the division of the technical cost savings and the rate of return to investment can have an adverse impact on investment behavior.

In the steel example, it was assumed that the ingot and fabrication plants were already built in close physical proximity. The most important transaction failure occurs, however, when the *prospect* of opportunism leads a firm not to become so specialized. Although individuals may agree in advance to split the cost savings, each knows the other may renege *once the plants are built*. Once this occurs, the next best alternative is poor. Thus, each firm becomes subject to opportunistic behavior if it leaves the eventual outcome solely to market-mediated exchange. Opportunistic appropriation of quasi-rents, however, rarely interferes with market-mediated exchange, because firms have developed nonmarket or market-suppressing solutions in response to potential transaction failures. In this regard, the transaction costs that would have led to transaction failures are replaced by the transaction costs of negotiation and search.

Lake River Corporation v. Carborundum Co.

United States Court of Appeals, Seventh Circuit
769 F.2d 1284 (1985)

POSNER, Circuit Judge.

This diversity suit between Lake River Corporation and Carborundum Company requires us to consider questions of Illinois commercial law, and in particular to explore the fuzzy line between penalty clauses and liquidated-damages clauses.

Carborundum manufactures "Ferro Carbo," an abrasive powder used in making steel. To serve its midwestern customers better, Carborundum made a contract with Lake River by which the latter agreed to provide distribution services in its warehouse in Illinois. Lake River would receive Ferro Carbo in bulk from Carborundum, "bag" it, and ship the bagged produce to Carborundum's customers. The Ferro Carbo would remain Carborundum's property until delivered to the customers.

Carborundum insisted that Lake River install a new bagging system to handle the contract. In order to be sure of being able to recover the cost of the new system ($89,000) and make a profit of 20 percent of the contract price, Lake River insisted on the following minimum-quantity guarantee:

> In consideration of the special equipment [i.e., the new bagging system] to be acquired and furnished by LAKE-RIVER for handling the product, CARBORUNDUM shall, during the initial three-year term of this Agreement, ship to LAKE-RIVER for bagging a minimum quantity of [22,500 tons]. If, at the end of the three-year term, this minimum quantity shall not have been shipped, LAKE-RIVER shall invoice CARBORUNDUM at the then prevailing rates for the difference between the quantity bagged and the minimum guaranteed.

If Carborundum had shipped the full minimum quantity that it guaranteed, it would have owed Lake River roughly $533,000 under the contract.

After the contract was signed in 1979, the demand for domestic steel, and with it the demand for Ferro Carbo, plummeted, and Carborundum failed to ship the guaranteed amount. When the contract expired late in 1982, Carborundum had shipped only 12,000 of the 22,500 tons it had guaranteed. Lake River had bagged the 12,000 tons and had billed Carborundum for this bagging, and Carborundum had paid, but by virtue of the formula in the minimum-guarantee clause Carborundum still owed Lake River $241,000 — the contract price of $533,000 if the full amount of Ferro Carbo had been shipped, minus what Carborundum had paid for the bagging of the quantity it had shipped.

When Lake River demanded payment of this amount, Carborundum refused, on the ground that the formula imposed a penalty. At the time, Lake River had in its warehouse 500 tons of bagged Ferro Carbo, having a market value of $269,000, which it refused to release unless Carborundum paid the $241,000 due under the formula. Lake River did offer to sell the bagged product and place the proceeds in escrow until its dispute with Carborundum over the enforceability of the formula was resolved, but Carborundum rejected the offer and trucked in bagged Ferro Carbo from the East to serve its customers in Illinois, at an additional cost of $31,000.

Lake River brought this suit for $241,000, which it claims as liquidated damages. Carborundum counterclaimed for the value of the bagged Ferro Carbo when Lake River impounded it and the additional cost of serving the customers affected by the impounding. The theory of the counterclaim is that the impounding was a conversion, and not as Lake River contends the assertion of a lien. The district judge, after a bench trial, gave judgment for both parties. Carborundum ended up roughly $42,000 to the good: $269,000 + $31,000 – $241,00 – $17,000, the last figure representing prejudgment interest on Lake River's damages. (We have rounded off all dollar figures to the nearest thousand.) Both parties have appealed.

The only issue that is not one of damages is whether Lake River had a valid lien on the bagged Ferro Carbo that it refused to ship to Carborundum's customers — that, indeed, it holds in its warehouse to this day. Although Ferro Carbo does not deteriorate with age, the domestic steel industry remains in the doldrums and the product is worth less than it was in 1982 when Lake River first withheld it. If Lake River did not have a valid lien on the product, then it converted it, and must pay Carborundum the $269,000 that the Ferro Carbo was worth back then.

It might seem that if the minimum-guarantee clause was a penalty clause and hence unenforceable, the lien could not be valid, and therefore that we should discuss the penalty issue first. But this is not correct. If the contractual specification of damages is invalid, Lake River still is entitled to any actual damages caused by Carborundum's breach of contract in failing to deliver the minimum amount of Ferro Carbo called for by the contract. The issue is whether an entitlement to damages, large or small, entitles the victim of the breach to assert a lien on goods that are in its possession though they belong to the other party.

*   *   *

[The court then holds that Lake River's asserted lien was not a lien.]

The hardest issue in the case is whether the formula in the minimum-guarantee clause imposes a penalty for breach of contract or is merely an effort to liquidate damages. Deep as the hostility to penalty clauses runs in the common law, see Loyd, *Penalties and Forfeitures*, 29 Harv. L. Rev. 117 (1915), we still might be inclined to question, if we thought ourselves free to do so, whether a modern court should refuse to enforce a penalty clause where the signator is a substantial corporation, well able to avoid improvident commitments. Penalty clauses provide an earnest of performance. The clause here enhanced Carborundum's credibility in promising to ship the minimum amount guaranteed by showing that it was willing to pay the full contract price even if it failed to ship anything. On the other side it can be pointed out that by raising the cost of a breach of contract to the contract breaker, a penalty clause increases the risk to his other creditors; increases (what is the same thing and more, because bankruptcy imposes "deadweight" social costs) the risk of bankruptcy; and could amplify the business cycle by increasing the number of bankruptcies in bad times, which is when contracts are most likely to be broken. But since little effort is made to prevent businessmen from assuming risks, these reasons are no better than makeweights.

A better argument is that a penalty clause may discourage efficient as well as inefficient breaches of contract. Suppose a breach would cost the promisee $12,000 in actual damages but would yield the promisor $20,000 in additional profits. Then there would be a net social gain from breach. After being fully compensated for his loss the promisee would be no worse off than if the contract had been performed, while the promisor would be better off by $8,000. But now suppose the contract contains a penalty clause under which the promisor if he breaks his promise must pay the promisee $25,000. The promisor will be discouraged from breaking the contract, since $25,000, the penalty, is greater than $20,000, the profits of the breach; and a transaction that would have increased value will be forgone.

On this view, since compensatory damages should be sufficient to deter inefficient breaches (that is, breaches that cost the victim more than the gain to the contract breaker), penal damages could have no effect other than to deter some efficient breaches. But this overlooks the earlier point that the willingness to agree to a penalty clause is a way of making the promisor and his promise credible and may therefore be essential to inducing some value-maximizing contracts to be made. It also overlooks the more important point that the parties (always assuming they are fully competent) will, in deciding whether to include a penalty clause in their contract, weigh the gains against the costs—costs that include the possibility of discouraging an efficient breach somewhere down the road—and will include the clause only if the benefits exceed those costs as well as all other costs.

On this view the refusal to enforce penalty clauses is (at best) paternalistic—and it seems odd that courts should display parental solicitude for large corporations. But however this may be, we must be on guard to avoid importing our own ideas of sound public policy into an area where our proper judicial role is more than usually deferential. The responsibility for making innovations in the common law of Illinois rests with the courts of Illinois, and not with the federal courts in Illinois. And like every other state, Illinois, untroubled by academic skepticism of the wisdom of refusing to enforce penalty clauses against sophisticated promisors, see, e.g., Goetz & Scott, *Liquidated Damages, Penalties and the Just Compensation Principle*, 77 Colum. L. Rev. 554 (1977), continues steadfastly to insist on the distinction between penalties and liquidated damages. To be valid under Illinois law a liquidation of damages must be a reasonable estimate at the time of contracting of the likely damages from breach, and the need for estimation at that time must be shown by reference to the likely difficulty of measuring the actual damages from a breach of contract after the breach occurs. If damages would be easy to determine then, only if the estimate greatly exceeds a reasonable upper estimate of what the damages are likely to be, it is a penalty.

The distinction between a penalty and liquidated damages is not an easy one to draw in practice but we are required to draw it and can give only limited weight to the district court's determination. Whether a provision for damages is a penalty clause or a liquidated-damages clause is a question of law rather than fact, and unlike some courts of appeals we do not treat a determination by a federal district judge on an issue of state law as if it were a finding of fact, and reverse only if persuaded that clear error has occurred, though we give his determination respectful consideration.

Mindful that Illinois courts resolve doubtful cases in favor of classification as a penalty, we conclude that the damage formula in this case is a penalty and not a liquidation of damages, because it is designed always to assure Lake River more than its actual damages. The formula—full contract price minus the amount already invoiced to Carborundum—is invariant to the gravity of the breach. When a contract specifies a single sum in damages for any and all breaches even though it is apparent that all are not of the same gravity, the specification is not a reasonable effort to estimate damages; and when in addition the fixed sum greatly exceeds the actual damages likely to be inflicted by a minor breach, its character as a penalty becomes unmistakable. This case is within the gravitational field of these principles even though the minimum-guarantee clause does not fix a single sum as damages.

Suppose to begin with that the breach occurs the day after Lake River buys its new bagging system for $89,000 and before Carborundum ships any Ferro Carbo. Carborundum would owe Lake River $533,000. Since Lake River would have incurred at that point a total cost of only $89,000, its net gain from the breach would be $444,000. This is more than four times the profit of $107,000 (20 percent of the contract price of $533,000) that Lake River expected to make from the contract if it had been performed: a huge windfall.

Next suppose (as actually happened here) that breach occurs when 55 percent of the Ferro Carbo has been shipped. Lake River would already have received $293,000 from Carborundum. To see what its costs then would have been (as estimated at the time of contracting), first subtract Lake River's anticipated profit on the contract of $107,000 from the total contract price of $533,000. The difference—Lake River's total cost of performance—is $426,000. Of this, $89,000 is the cost of the new bagging system, a fixed cost. The rest ($426,000 − $89,000 = $337,000) presumably consists of variable costs that are roughly proportional to the amount of Ferro Carbo bagged; there is no indication of any other fixed costs. Assume, therefore, that if Lake River bagged 55 percent of the contractually agreed quantity, it incurred in doing so 55 percent of its variable costs, or $185,000. When this is added to the cost of the new bagging system, assumed for the moment to be worthless except in connection with the contract, the total cost of performance to Lake River is $274,000. Hence a breach that occurred after 55 percent of contractual performance was complete would be expected to yield Lake River a modest profit of $19,000 ($293,000 − $274,000).

But now add the "liquidated damages" of $241,000 that Lake River claims, and the result is a total gain from the breach of $260,000, which is almost two and a half times the profit that Lake River expected to gain if there was no breach. And this ignores any use value or salvage value of the new bagging system, which is the property of Lake River—though admittedly it also ignores the time value of money; Lake River paid $89,000 for that system before receiving any revenue from the contract.

To complete the picture, assume that the breach had not occurred till performance was 90 percent complete. Then the "liquidated damages" clause would not be so one-sided, but it would be one-sided. Carborundum would have paid $480,000 for bagging. Against this, Lake River would have incurred its fixed cost of $89,000 plus 90 percent of its variable costs of $337,000 or $303,000. Its total costs would thus be $392,000, and its net profit $88,000. But on top of this it would be entitled to "liquidated damages" of $53,000, for a total profit of $141,000—more than 30 percent more that its expected profit of $107,000 if there was no breach.

The reason for these results is that most of the costs to Lake River of performing the contract are saved if the contract is broken, and this saving is not reflected in the damage formula. As a result, at whatever point in the life of the contract a breach occurs, the damage formula gives Lake River more than its lost profits form the breach—dramatically more if the breach occurs at the beginning of the contract; tapering off at the end, it is true. Still, over the interval between the beginning of Lake River's performance and nearly the end, the clause could be expected to generate profits ranging from 400 percent of the expected contract profits to 130 percent of those profits. And this is on the assumption that the bagging system has no value apart from the contract. If it were worth only $20,000 to Lake River, the range would be 434 percent to 150 percent.

Lake River argues that it would never get as much as the formula suggests, because it would be required to mitigate its damages. This is a dubious argument on several grounds. First, mitigation of damages is a doctrine of the law of court-assessed damages, while the point of a liquidated-damages clause is to substitute party assessment; and that point is blunted, and the certainty that liquidated-damages clauses are designed to give the process of assessing damages impaired, if a defendant can force the plaintiff to take less than the damages specified in the clause, on the ground that the plaintiff could have avoided some of them. It would seem therefore that the clause in this case should be read to eliminate any duty of mitigation, that what Lake River is doing is attempting to rewrite the clause to make it more reasonable, and that since actually the clause is designed to give Lake River the full damages it would incur from breach (and more) even if it made no effort to find a substitute use for the equipment that it brought to perform the contract, this is just one more piece of evidence that it is a penalty clause rather than a liquidated-damages clause.

But in any event mitigation would not mitigate the penal character of this clause. If Carborundum did not ship the guaranteed minimum quantity, the reason was likely to be—the reason was—that the steel industry had fallen on hard times and the demand for Ferro Carbo was therefore down. In these circumstances Lake River would have little prospect of finding a substitute contract that would yield it significant profits to set off against the full contract price, which is the method by which it proposes to take account of mitigation. At argument Lake River suggested that it might at least have been able to sell the new bagging equipment to someone for something, and the figure $40,000 was proposed. If the breach occurred on the first day when performance under the contract was due and Lake River promptly sold the bagging equipment for $40,000, its liquidated damages would fall to $493,000. But by the same token its costs would fall to $49,000. Its profit would still be $444,000, which as we said was more than 400 percent of its expected profit on the contract. The penal component would be unaffected....

...Here, in contrast, it is apparent from the face of the contract that the damages provided for by the "liquidated damages" clause are grossly disproportionate to any probable loss and penalize some breaches much more heavily than others regardless of relative cost.

...

*   *   *

The fact that the damage formula is invalid does not deprive Lake River of a remedy. The parties did not contract explicitly with reference to the measure of damages if the agreed-on damage formula was invalidated, but all this means is that the victim of the breach is entitled to his common law damages. See, e.g., Restatement, Second, Contracts § 356, comment a (1981). In this case that would be the unpaid contract price of $241,000 minus the costs that Lake River saved by not having to complete the contract (the variable costs on the other 45 percent of the Ferro Carbo that it never had to bag). The case must be remanded to the district judge to fix these damages.

Two damages issues remain. The first concerns Carborundum's expenses of delivering bagged Ferro Carbo to its customers to replace that impounded by Lake River. The district judge gave Carborundum the full market value of the bagged Ferro Carbo. Lake River argues that it should not have to pay for Carborundum's expense of selling additional Ferro Carbo—additional in the sense that Carborundum is being given credit for the full retail value of the product that Lake River withheld. To explain, suppose that Carborundum had an order for $1,000 worth of bagged Ferro Carbo, which Lake River was supposed to deliver; and because it refused, Carborundum incurred a transportation cost of $100 to make a substitute shipment of bagged Ferro Carbo to the customer. Carborundum would still get $1,000 from the customer, and if that price covered the transportation cost it would still make a profit. In what sense, therefore, is that cost a separate item of damage, of loss? On all Ferro Carbo (related to this case) sold by Carborundum in the Midwest, Carborundum received the full market price, either from its customers in the case of Ferro Carbo actually delivered to them, or from Lake River in the case of the Ferro Carbo that Lake River refused to deliver. Having received a price designed to cover all expenses of sale, a seller cannot also get an additional damage award for any of those expenses.

If, however, the additional Ferro Carbo that Carborundum delivered to its midwestern customers in substitution for Ferro Carbo previously delivered to, and impounded by, Lake River would have been sold in the East at the same price but lower cost, Carborundum would have had an additional loss, in the form of reduced profits, for which it could recover additional damages. But it made no effort to prove such a loss. Maybe it had no unsatisfied eastern customers, and expanded rather than shifted output to fulfill its midwestern customers' demand. The damages on the counterclaim must be refigured also.

Finally, Lake River argues that Carborundum failed to mitigate its damages by accepting Lake River's offer to deliver the bagged product and place the proceeds in escrow. But a converter is not entitled to retain the proceeds of the conversion even temporarily. Lake River had an opportunity to limit its exposure by selling the bagged product on Carborundum's account and deducting what it claimed was due it on its "lien." Its failure to follow this course reinforces our conclusion that the assertion of the lien was a naked attempt to hold Carborundum hostage to Lake River's view—an erroneous view, as it has turned out—of the enforceability of the damage formula in the contract.

The judgment of the district court is affirmed in part and reversed in part, and the case is returned to that court to redetermine both parties' damages in accordance with the principles in this opinion. The parties may present additional evidence on remand, and shall bear their own costs in this court.

Notes and Questions

1. *Firm-Specific Investment, Forfeitable Reputational Bonds and Penalty Clauses:* Firm specific investment, reputation, brand name, advertising, etc., all play important roles in ensuring contractual performance. Consider the negotiations between Lake River and Carborundum. Carborundum induced Lake River to make a contract-specific investment in the bagging system. (Obviously, the system could be used to bag other products, but its most valuable use to Lake River and, indeed, the reason for the investment was to bag Ferro Carbo.) Apparently, Carborundum did not have any other distributors of Ferro Carbo and, therefore, probably did not have a well-developed reputation for good faith dealing with distributors. In economic terms, Carborundum did not have a forfeitable reputational bond to ensure its performance after Lake River made the investment and, thus, Lake River would not have been willing to make the contract-specific investment unless Carborundum could bond its performance. In this regard, a penalty stipulated damages clause is a substitute for a reputational bond—both carry substantial penalties for nonperformance. Thus, because Carborundum could not bond its performance with a well-developed (yet forfeitable) reputational bond, it convinced Lake River to make the investment by offering a penalty clause. A major difference between the reputational bond and the penalty clause is that the reputational bond penalty is not paid to the promisee and, thus, there is no incentive to induce breach. Does this analysis suggest that penalty clauses such as the one in Lake River should be evaluated in terms of their overall economic context—for example, should the absence of a reputational bond be taken into account?

2. *Unenforceable Penalty Clauses: Efficiency or Paternalism?:* The distinction between enforceable and unenforceable penalty clauses is interesting from a policy perspective. A stipulated damage clause that amounts to a penalty may merely reflect the promisee's very strong desire to have the project finished on schedule. Moreover, it seems unreasonable to suspect that the inclusion of a penalty clause does not impact on other terms in the contract—including the negotiation of the completion date and the total value of the contract. Thus, the re-

fusal of the common law courts to enforce penalty clauses appears to be based on some type of paternalistic notion. On the other hand, it has been suggested that the distinction between penalty clauses and reasonable damage clauses is justified on efficiency grounds because penalty clauses create perverse incentives for the beneficiary of the clauses to induce the breach of the contract in order to collect the penalty. Consider the following analysis:

> An important cost of stipulated damage clauses... results from activities that may induce breach and from activities to prevent breach inducement, both of which waste scarce resources. Consider, for example, a contract to build a bridge with a stipulated damage clause of $500 for each day of delay beyond a specified completion date chosen to correspond with the first day that the purchaser expects to use the bridge. If the clause is carefully drafted, the $500 will closely approximate the expected damage to the purchaser from the actual delay. Suppose, however, that during construction (or, for that matter, even at the time of the initial contract) the cost of delay to the purchaser becomes zero because the bridge could not be used until much later than originally planned. Since the producer's breach would now actually improve the purchaser's position, the purchaser has an incentive to undertake activities to cause delay as long as the additional expected revenues from creating delay ($500 multiplied by the number of days of delay) exceed the additional costs.

> ... [E]ven if all stipulated damage clauses are enforced, the incentive to induce breach would exist only when the potential breach-inducer knows that actual damages will be less than the stipulated amount. This may occur either at the time of initial contracting or, more likely, at some time during performance when circumstances change, affecting the likely amount of damages upon breach. When the incentive for breach inducement is present, a further cost could be incurred since the producer might devote time and resources to detect and prevent possible breach-inducing activities. This may entail additional personnel to acquire information about the purchaser or to monitor activities of the purchaser.

> *Resources spent both on breach-inducing activities and on detecting and preventing breach inducement are wasteful.* They do not produce any real good or service that the contracting parties value, nor do they move resources to production of goods or services whose value is greater than to the contracting parties. Accordingly, the value of *all* resources expended in inducement is wasted and increases the costs of forming, completing, and monitoring the contract. Such expenditures, like those employed to defraud others, are merely necessary inputs in obtaining the benefits from induced breach and, again, like real resources spent to defraud, contribute to overall costs without producing real products. If these costs could be avoided while retaining the desirable outcomes of stipulated damage clauses (and without incurring any new costs), contracting parties as a group, and hence society, would gain.

> Besides incentive, the potential breach-inducer needs opportunity before he will induce breach. Since detected inducement would result in nonenforcement of the clause, thereby removing the incentive to waste resources, breach inducement will present special difficulties only when

the courts are unable to detect it easily. The opportunity to induce breach does arise, however, in situations where inducement is exceedingly costly to detect, particularly where the producer's performance depends at least in part upon the purchaser's cooperation and assistance. For example, a party may intentionally withhold useful information for a critical period of time, yet still comply with the contract. Thus, in our bridge hypothetical, the purchaser may withhold certain information whose existence or source is not known to the producer, such as information about difficult construction conditions. Further, if the contract calls for close cooperation with respect to the building specifications, the purchaser may delay (or become unexpectedly "fussy") in providing assistance necessary to complete construction on time. It may also be possible to supply information or resources that are clearly inferior but within the limits of the contract. Purchasing parties may even provide misleading or erroneous data, such as on the condition of the river bed soil in the bridge case....

Although the policy underlying the distinction has baffled the legal community, for hundreds of years courts have categorized stipulated damage clauses as either liquidated damages or penalties. Finding the previous explanations of this distinction to be unsatisfactory, we have asked whether economic efficiency could justify nonenforcement of stipulated damages in certain situations, and, if so, whether the justification could explain the results, if not the reasoning, of the reported decisions. The answer to both questions supports an economic distinction between liquidated damages and penalties. Through a broad, poorly articulated reasonableness test, the courts appear to have attained efficient results....

Clarkson, Miller, Muris, *Liquidated Damages versus Penalties: Sense or Nonsense?*, 1978 Wis. L. Rev. 351, 368–372. Do the facts in *Lake River* suggest that the breach was induced by Lake River? Judge Posner clearly demonstrates the incentive for Lake River to breach, but did Lake River have the opportunity to induce breach? Given that the court recognized the penal nature of the stipulated damages clause, isn't it reasonable to assume that the contracting parties recognized this as well and took it into account in their initial negotiations over price and other terms?

3. Opportunistic Renegotiation and Appropriable Quasi-Rents: : Exchanges between individuals or firms often require that the parties invest in an asset that is transaction specific. That is, the value of the asset in question is clearly maximized when used for the specific purpose called for in the transaction. These types of assets are highly specialized, meaning that the asset's value in its current use far exceeds its next best alternative. Thus, an attempt to switch specialized assets from one use to another can involve substantial costs to the owner. In a sense, parties who invest in specialized assets are "locked into" the deal and part of the investment can be appropriated by the other contracting party. The notion of "appropriable quasi-rents" has been developed as follows:

Assume an asset is owned by one individual and rented to another individual. The quasi-rent value of the asset is the excess of its value over its salvage value, that is, its value in its next best *use* is another renter. The potentially appropriable specialized portion of the quasi-rent is that portion, if any, in excess of its value to the second highest-valuing *uses*.

Klein, Crawford and Alchian, *Vertical Integration, Appropriable Rents, and the Competitive Contracting Process*, 21 J. Law & Econ. 297 at 298 (1978) (emphasis in original.). When parties are required to bring a specialized asset to the exchange, each has an incentive to take advantage of the other party — the so called **"hold-up" problem.** The buyer can refuse to accept unless the price is reduced and the seller can refuse to deliver unless the price is increased. The buyer will be able to extort a price discount equal to the difference between the agreed upon price and the value of the specialized asset in its next best use. Likewise, the seller can extort a price increase equal to the difference between the agreed upon price and the cost to the buyer of finding a new supplier. This difference — which is the asset owners' quasi-rent — can be opportunistically appropriated. Individuals who bring specialized assets to a transaction desire protection from others' opportunistic behavior. That is, the owners of specialized assets will seek out devices to protect their quasi-rents from being appropriated or "held-up." Klein, Crawford, and Alchian give a numerical example of the determination of the opportunistic post-contractual bargaining range:

> Imagine a printing press owned and operated by party A. Publisher B buys printing services from party A by leasing his press at a contracted rate of $5,500 per day. The amortized fixed cost of the printing press is $4,000 per day and it has a current salvageable value if moved elsewhere of $1,000 (daily rental equivalent). Operating costs are $1,500 and are paid by the printing-press owner, who prints final printed pages for the publisher. Assume also that a second publisher C is willing to offer at most $3,500 for daily services. The current quasi rent on the installed machine is $3,000 ($5,500 − $1,500 − $1,000), the revenue minus operating costs minus salvageable value. However, the daily quasi rent from publisher B relative to use of the machine for publisher C is only $2,000 ($5,500 − $3,500). At $5,500 revenue daily from publisher B the press owner would break even on his investment. If the publisher were then able to cut his offer for the press from $5,500 down to almost $3,500, he would still have the press service available to him. He would be appropriating $2,000 of the quasi rent from the press owner. The $2,000 difference between his prior agreed-to-daily rental of $5,500 and the next best revenue available to the press once the machine is purchased and installed is less than the quasi rent and therefore is potentially appropriable. If no second party were available at the present site, the entire quasi rent would be subject to threat of appropriation by an unscrupulous or opportunistic publisher.

Klein, Crawford & Alchian, *Vertical Integration, Appropriable Rents, and the Competitive Contracting Process*, 21 J. Law & Econ. 297 at 298–99 (1978)

4. Deterrence of Efficient Breaches: The court summarizes one economic view of penalty clauses as follows: "...since compensatory damages should be sufficient to deter inefficient breaches (that is, breaches that cost the victim more than the gain to the contract breaker), penal damages could have no effect other than to deter some efficient breaches." Does the potential forfeiture of a reputational bond deter efficient breaches — that is, does it lead to "inefficient performance?"

b. Free-Riding Behavior: Transaction Failures in Distribution

Manufacturers of some types of goods confront potential transaction failures when they attempt to distribute their output through separately owned distribution networks. The basic problem is that a manufacturer's best interests will not always coincide with the best interests of the distributors and retailers who handle the manufacturer's goods. This conflict of interest presents opportunities for dealers to take opportunistic "free rides" to the detriment of manufacturers.

Whenever the demand for a particular product is positively related to the amount of point-of-sale and post-sale services provided, the possibility of transaction failures caused by free riding is present. An automobile dealership illustrates the provision of these types of services. The typical dealership provides an elaborate showroom, a trained sales force, large amounts of local advertising, a substantial inventory, and a parts department. Of course, these services are costly for dealers to provide. A dealer (dealer X), therefore, would incur these costs only if there was a reasonable expectation of a larger market share and higher profits. The potential for opportunistic behavior will take the form of dealers "free riding" on the service efforts of other dealers. In other words, dealers will not have the incentive to provide the necessary services when they know that the demand for the product has been increased by the service efforts of other dealers of the same brand.

Consider what would happen if another dealer (dealer Y), selling the same brand, but not providing services, opens a dealership across the street from dealer X. As a result, some of the benefits of X's provision of services will flow to Y, and X's expected return on services will not be realized. Since Y does not provide point-of-sale and post-sale services, his lower costs will enable him to charge a lower price for automobiles. The rational consumer will take advantage of X's showroom services and then cross the street and purchase his car from Y. Clearly, Y is taking a "free ride" on X's provision of services.

A transaction failure, an overall degeneration in the provision of services, is caused by this intrabrand free-riding behavior. Since X does not capture the benefits of providing services, he will not provide services. This reduction in the provision of point-of-sale services, a transaction failure, reduces sales and thus reduces the manufacturer's profits. Consumers are also harmed because they are denied access to valuable services for which they would have been willing to pay.

Continental T.V., Inc. v. GTE Sylvania, Inc.
Supreme Court of the United States
433 U.S. 36 (1977)

Read case and "Notes and Questions" in Chapter 5, *supra*.

c. Franchising

Manufacturers, restaurant franchisors, nationwide tax preparation services, and many other providers of goods and services often rely on a system of wholesale distributors and retailers to move their goods and services to consumers. A wide variety of distribution systems are used. Obviously, grocery stores, department stores, and discount stores carry many different competing brands of goods. At the other end of the continuum is the franchisee who represents only one brand, say McDonalds.

Consider the possibilities for opportunism in a successful franchised motel chain. The franchisor's trademark—which is the franchisor's most important asset—signals to consumers a specific standard of quality, service, and rates. Individual franchisees must undertake expenditures if they wish to maintain these attributes. The possibility for opportunistic behavior arises because customers base their decision to stay at franchised motels on their experiences with other motels in the chain. This gives an individual franchisee the incentive to engage in free-riding by shirking on expenditures on quality because he will continue to attract customers who, based on their experience with other motels in the chain, expect to receive, and are willing to pay for, the higher quality. The free-riding franchisee benefits by the full amount of his savings on expenditures and bears only a portion of the costs, which is shared by the franchisor and the other franchisees through the decreased value of the trademark. Consumers, of course, are also injured.

Similarly, the franchisor has opportunities to engage in opportunistic behavior because the franchisee is required to make transaction-specific investments, including payment of an initial franchise fee, which are potentially appropriable by the franchisor. For example, McDonalds' franchisees must make considerable McDonalds' specific investments in the building, equipment, and training. These investments, which are of little value if not used in a McDonalds franchise, make the franchisee vulnerable to extortion by the franchisor. Moreover, franchisors often include a clause allowing for unilateral "at will" termination of the franchise arrangement. The "at will" clause leads to the possibility that the franchisor may engage in opportunistic behavior by terminating a franchisee without cause, thereby appropriating the franchise fee and purchasing back the franchise rights at a distress price. Thus, the typical franchise contract appears to be "unfair" to the franchisees. However, it is important to remember that the franchise relationship is founded on mutually beneficial exchange. With these economic concepts in mind, evaluate the relative economic positions of the contracting parties in the following case.

Corenswet, Inc. v. Amana Refrigeration, Inc.
United States Court of Appeals, Fifth Circuit
594 F.2d 129 (1979)

Wisdom, J.

*   *   *

I.

The primary facts are not disputed. The plaintiff, Corenswet, Inc., is an independent wholesale distributor of appliances, dishware, and similar products. Since 1969 Corenswet has been the exclusive distributor of Amana refrigerators, freezers, room air conditioners, and other merchandise in southern Louisiana. Amana is a Delaware corporation domiciled in Iowa. Under the Amana system, products manufactured by Amana are sold to wholesale distributors such as Corenswet and to Amana's factory wholesale branches. The independent distributors and the factory branches then resell the merchandise to retail dealers who, in turn, sell to the pub-

lic. The first distributorship agreement executed between Amana and Corenswet
was of indefinite duration, but terminable by either party at any time "with or
without cause" on ten days' notice to the other party. According to the record, the
agreement was modified twice, in 1971 and again in July 1975, before the institution of this lawsuit. The 1975 agreement modified the termination provision to
allow termination by either party "at any time for any reason" on ten days' notice.

As is so often the case with franchise and distributorship relationships, the
termination clause in the standard form contract was of little interest or concern
to the parties so long as things were going well between them. At the hearing before the district court, Corenswet introduced testimony that it understood, in the
early 1970's, that the relationship would be a lasting one, a relationship that
would continue so long as Corenswet performed satisfactorily. According to
Corenswet, it developed an organization for wholesale distribution of Amana
merchandise: it hired a manager and salesmen for the line, as well as specially
trained repairmen. Corenswet also expanded its physical plant. In all, Corenswet
contended, it invested over $1.5 million over the period of 1969 to 1976 in de-
veloping the market for Amana products in the southern Louisiana area. The
parties stipulated in district court that the annual sales of Amana products in the
distributorship area increased from $200,000 in 1969 to over $2.5 million in
1976. The number of retail outlets selling Amana products in the area increased
from six in 1969 to seventy-two in 1976. Corenswet, in short, developed an important new market for Amana products. And Amana became as important to
Corenswet as Corenswet became to Amana: sales of Amana products as a percentage of Corenswet's total sales of all products swelled from six percent in
1969 to nearly twenty-six percent in 1976. Over the seven and one-half-year period, Amana representatives repeatedly praised Corenswet for its performance.

At the 1976 mid-year meeting of Amana distributors, however, George Foerstner, Amana's president, informed Corenswet that Amana would soon terminate
its relationship with Corenswet because Corenswet was underfinanced. The parties agree that in early 1976 Corenswet had exceeded its credit limit with Amana,
and that Amana at that time indicated that it might have to take a security interest in Corenswet's Amana inventory. According to a January communication
from Amana, however, the "problem" was viewed by Amana as "a good kind of
problem", reflecting, as it did, the growth of Corenswet's sales and hence purchases of Amana products. It is Corenswet's contention that the problem was not
a serious one. Amana executives, the record reflects, assured Corenswet at the
1976 mid-year meeting that "satisfactory arrangements would be made" and
that, Foerstner's statement notwithstanding, Corenswet would retain its distributorship.

There followed a complicated sequence of negotiations concerning Amana's
security for credit extended. Amana sought a security interest in Corenswet's
Amana inventory, to which Corenswet agreed. Amana asked also that Corenswet
obtain more working capital from its parent corporation, Select Brands, Inc., as
well as a bank letter of credit or line of credit. There is ample evidence in the
record that Corenswet responded adequately to each Amana request, but that
Amana persisted in changing its requirements as quickly as Corenswet could respond to its requests. In September, 1976, Corenswet met in New Orleans with
Amana's representative, George Tolbert. Sam Corenswet, the company's president,
informed Tolbert that Corenswet was ready and able to meet Amana's latest re-

quest: a $500,000 bank letter of credit. Tolbert relayed the information to Foerstner. Within a week Corenswet received a letter, prepared by Tolbert at Foerstner's direction, notifying Corenswet of its decision to terminate the distributorship because Corenswet was "unable to provide us with what we felt to be the minimum guarantees and/or security to sustain a continuing pattern of growth with Amana."

In October 1976, Corenswet filed suit for damages and injunctive relief in state court alleging that Amana had breached the distributorship agreement by terminating it arbitrarily. The reasons given by Amana for the termination, it contended, were pretextual. The state court issued a temporary restraining order barring termination. The TRO was retained in force after Amana removed the case to federal district court.

The district court conducted a three-day hearing on Corenswet's prayer for a preliminary injunction. The court concluded that Amana had indeed acted arbitrarily in deciding to terminate Corenswet. The record reflects that in early 1976, well before the mid-year distributor meeting, Amana began negotiating with another New Orleans concern, George H. Lehleitner & Co., about transferring its area distributorship to Lehleitner. The beginning of Amana's alleged concern over Corenswet's finances corresponded neatly with its Lehleitner negotiations. There was ample evidence in the record, moreover, to support the district court's conclusion that the real factor motivating Foerstner's decision was animosity towards Fred Schoenfeld, the president of Corenswet's parent corporation, Select Brands, Inc. That animosity dated back to 1972, when Schoenfeld's action in protesting to Raytheon Corporation, Amana's parent, aborted Amana's attempt to transfer the distributorship from Corenswet to Corenswet's then Amana sales manager.

The district court ruled that the arbitrary termination was a breach of the distributorship agreement. The court rejected Amana's argument that the termination clause, which permitted either party to terminate the contract "for any reason," permitted termination for any reason be that reason good, bad, or indifferent. Although unwilling to accept Corenswet's position that the term "for any reason" imported a good or just cause limitation, the court ruled that the term means "for some reason, not for no reason... for something that appeals to the reason, to the mind, to the judgment, not for something that is arbitrary, capricious or wanton." In the alternative, the court ruled that the U.C.C.'s "good faith" principle, Iowa Code Ann. § 554.2103, forbids the bad faith termination of exclusive distributorships and found Amana's actions to have been in bad faith. The court issued the preliminary injunction prohibiting Amana from terminating or attempting to terminate the relationship in November 1976.

In late 1977, Corenswet filed a declaratory judgment action in response to Amana's request that Corenswet sign the new standard form distributorship agreement. That civil action was transferred by the district judge to his section of the court. In September of 1977, Amana filed a motion requesting the court to modify or vacate the preliminary injunction to permit Amana to terminate the distributorship. Amana urged that Corenswet's refusal to execute the new distributorship agreement was sufficient cause or reason under the existing agreement and the injunction to justify termination of Corenswet's distributorship. The court denied Amana's motion, but amended the injunction to require Corenswet to execute the agreement within five days or suffer termination of the agreement, and to place restrictions on Amana's rights to refuse to renew the one-year term of the new agreement. The modification of the injunction, entered in November 1977, forbade Amana to refuse to renew the distributorship term "without reason" and enjoined Amana to accord Corenswet equal treatment with Amana's other distributors.

II.

Amana appeals both the entry and the modification of the preliminary injunction. It contests the district court's interpretation of the contract and its view of applicable Iowa law and urges that even "bad faith" or "arbitrary" terminations are permitted by the contract and applicable law. Amana also argues that Corenswet failed to satisfy another requisite for issuance of a preliminary injunction: a showing that it would suffer irreparable harm in the absence of injunctive relief *pendente lite*. It further contends that the district court abused its discretion in issuing a preliminary injunction that requires specific performance of the contract because the injunction has the effect of requiring continuous court supervision of the parties' relationship.

In No. 77-3474 Amana urges that the court erred in failing to rule that Corenswet's post-injunction behavior was good cause for terminating the distributorship. Amana also contends that the court abused its discretion in granting Corenswet an extension of time for executing the agreement and by imposing restrictions on Amana's rights under the new agreement in advance of any conduct on its part giving reason to believe that it would arbitrarily refuse to renew the new agreement at the expiration of its one-year term.

With the exception of the point that the injunction has the effect of forcing these antagonistic parties to maintain their relationship indefinitely and requiring the continuous supervision of the district court, we find little merit in the appellant's attacks on the district court's exercise of its discretion in modifying the injunction. If the district court's view of the contract and the law were correct, we would lack any basis for disturbing the court's modification of the injunction. In general, an appeals court's deference to the trial court's discretion is at its height when litigants challenge that court's administration of its own decrees in equity. Following the entry of the original injunction, the district court, faced with what could justifiably be viewed as an attempt by Amana to circumvent the court's command that it not terminate Corenswet without cause, did Amana a good turn, it seems to us, by permitting Amana, subject to a good cause limitation on its non-renewal rights, to put Corenswet, like all its other distributors, under the new distributorship agreement. Under the court's original ruling Amana had no right to terminate the old contract unilaterally, a contract which was of indefinite duration and terminable, in the district court's view, only for reason. It was no abuse of discretion of the court to accommodate Amana's interest in keeping all of its distributors under a single form of contract in such a way as to preserve Corenswet's rights, as the court viewed them, under the first contract.

Because there was nothing improper in the court's modification of the preliminary injunction (assuming that the injunction was properly issued in the first place) we turn to the issues raised in No. 77-1538.

Amana asserts that the district court erred in construing the contract's termination clause to prohibit unilateral termination of the distributorship except for some "reason" that appeals to the mind. The contractual language "for any reason," it argues, was intended to remove all limitations upon the exercise of the termination power. Because the district court looked to extrinsic evidence in construing the contract its interpretation is, under Iowa law, treated as a factual one. *Allen v. Highway Equip. Co.*, Iowa, 1976, 239 N.W.2d 135, 139. Amana, therefore, has the burden of persuading us that the court's interpretation was clearly erroneous.

In assessing the district court's interpretation of the contract we must look to the appropriate rules of construction found in applicable state law—in this case, as the parties have stipulated, the law of Iowa. Although most distributorship agreements, like franchise agreements, are more than sales contracts, the courts have not hesitated to apply the Uniform Commercial Code to cases involving such agreements. *E.g., Rockwell Engineering Co. v. Automatic Timing & Controls Co.*, 7th Cir. 1977, 559 F.2d 460; *Aaron E. Levine & Co. v. Calkraft Paper Co.*, 1976, E.D. Mich., 429 F. Supp. 1039; *Baker v. Ratzlaff*, 1976, 1 Kan. App. 2d 285, 564 P.2d 153. We therefore look to the constructional rules of the Code, as adopted by Iowa, chapter 554 of the Iowa Code.

The starting point under the Code is the express terms of the agreement. U.C.C. §§ 1-205, 2-208(2); Iowa Code Ann. §§ 554.1205, 554.2208(2). Under the contract, Amana was free to terminate the relationship "at any time and for any reason." The district court did not expressly rely on record evidence concerning the parties' understanding or the common understanding of the term "any reason" in concluding that the term means "something that appeals to the reason, to the mind." In the common understanding, it seems to us, the phrase "for any reason" means "for any reason that the actor deems sufficient." The phrase, that is, is ordinarily used not to limit a power, but to free it from implied limitations of "cause." That this is the intendment of the phrase becomes all the more clear when it is read in conjunction with the immediately preceding phrase "at any time." That phrase plainly frees the termination power from limitations as to timing. The exact parallelism of the two phrases reinforces the interpretation of the "any reason" language as negating any limitations whatsoever. In Webster's *New International Dictionary* (2d Ed. 1939) the first definition of reason is "an expression or statement offered as an explanation of a belief or an assertion or as a justification of an act or procedure." The second of nine definitions given for the word is "a ground or a cause; that in the reality which makes any fact intelligible." *Id.* We consider that this is the usual sense of the word when used in the phrase "for any reason."

The district court's interpretation is understandable in view of Amana's vacilation about the meaning of the contract term. When pressed by the district court to explain Amana's position, one of Amana's attorneys stated: "I think it's Amana's position that 'For any reason' means some reason." He went on to add, however, that he thought the term meant the same thing as "with or without cause." When the judge then commented that he thought the attorney was taking a contradictory position, the attorney explained that "any reason" would include a bad reason. When the judge observed that in his opinion a fictitious reason would be no reason at all, the attorney agreed. Later, another Amana attorney stated that it was Amana's position that it did not need a "good reason" or a "legitimate reason" for terminating the contract. To the court's query whether he then disagreed that Amana needed "some reason" the attorney replied that he did not.

We think that these joustings with the bench over semantics, at the conclusion of the hearing and after the evidence had been received, form too slim a reed to support the court's interpretation of the contract term. Amana never conceded that it needed a justification, in the sense of a reason grounded in Corenswet's conduct, for ending the relationship. Even if it is assumed that Amana needed "some reason" to terminate the contract, that reason is supplied by its evident desire to give the New Orleans distributorship to the Lehleitner company, just as we think that Corenswet would, under the contract, be entitled to terminate the relationship by reason, to take an example, of its wish to handle Kelvinator, rather than Amana, products.

There is no evidence in the record that the parties understood the phrase otherwise. There is testimony that Corenswet officials "understood" that the contract would not be terminated arbitrarily. That, however, is evidence not of Corenswet's understanding of the termination clause as written, but of its expectations about Amana's behavior, that is, its belief that Amana would never use the termination language to Corenswet's detriment. Corenswet has made much of certain testimony given by Amana's president, George Foerstner. Foerstner testified that Amana does "not cancel a distributor without a reason, without a good reason." When asked whether Amana then needed a reason to cancel Corenswet, Foerstner replied: "We needed a reason, yes, but we do not cancel distributors without a reason." This, too, we take not to be evidence of an understanding of the written contractual provision at issue, but as evidence of Amana's usual practice or, at best, of Amana's understanding of how it ought to treat its distributors. The questions posed to Foerstner did not direct his attention to the written contract, much less to the disputed clause. The district court, significantly, did not in its opinion advert to the Foerstner testimony.

We take Corenswet to be arguing that the contractual language must be interpreted in light of Amana's historical treatment of Corenswet and its other distributors. Although Amana's past dealing with Corenswet does not fit the Code categories of sources relevant to contract interpretation usage of trade, course of dealing, and course of performance we may assume that it is a source sufficiently similar to the Code categories to be relevant in construing the contract. Courses of commercial conduct "may not only supplement or qualify express (contract) terms, but in appropriate circumstances may even override express terms." J. White & R. Summers, *Handbook of the Law under the Uniform Commercial Code* § 3-3 at 84 (1972). The Code commands that express contract terms and "an applicable course of dealing or usage of trade shall be construed wherever reasonable as consistent with each other." U.C.C. § 1-205, Iowa Code Ann. § 554.1205; *see also* U.C.C. § 2-208(2), Iowa Code Ann. § 554.2208(2). In this case, however, no reasonable construction can reconcile the contract's express terms with the interpretation Corenswet seeks to glean from the conduct of the parties. The conflict could not be more complete: Amana's past conduct, with regard both to Corenswet and to its other distributors, may have created a reasonable expectation that Amana would not terminate a distributor arbitrarily, yet the contract expressly gives Amana the right to do so. We can find no justification, except in cases of conduct of the sort giving rise to promissory estoppel, for holding that a contractually reserved power, however distasteful, may be lost through nonuse. The express contract term cannot be construed as Corenswet would constitute it, and it therefore controls over any allegedly conflicting usage or course of dealing. U.C.C. §§ 1-205, 2-208(2), Iowa Code Ann. §§ 554.1205, 554.2208(2).

The district court's alternative rationale was that arbitrary termination of a distributorship agreement contravenes the Code's general obligation of good faith dealing. Section 1-203 states: "Every contract or duty within this Act imposes an obligation of good faith in its performance or enforcement." Iowa Code Ann. § 554.1203. The good faith obligation is one of those obligations that section 1-102 of the Code says "may not be disclaimed by agreement." Iowa Code Ann. § 554.1102(3). As courts and scholars have become increasingly aware of the special problems faced by distributors and franchisees, and of the inadequacy of traditional contract and sales law doctrines to the task of protecting the reasonable expectations of distributors and franchisees, commentators have debated the utility of the Code's general good faith obligation as a tool for curbing abuse of the termination power. *See, e.g.,* E. Gellhorn, *Limitations on Contract Termination Rights: Franchise Cancellations,* 1967 Duke L.J. 465; Hewitt, *Good Faith or Unconscionability Franchise Remedies for Termination,* 29 Bus. Law. 227 (1973).

The courts of late have begun to read a good faith limitation into termination clauses of distributorship contracts that permit termination without cause. *E.g., Randolph v. New England Mutual Life Ins. Co.,* 6th Cir. 1975, 526 F.2d 1383 (Ohio law); *De Treville v. Outboard Marine Corp.,* 4th Cir. 1971, 439 F.2d 1099 (South Carolina law); *Tele-Controls, Inc. v. Ford Industries, Inc.,* 7th Cir. 1967, 388 F.2d 48 (Oregon law); *Baker v. Ratzlaff,* 1976, 1 Kan. App. 2d 285, 564 P.2d 153. Of the cited cases, however, only the Baker case relies squarely on the Code. The *Randolph, De Treville,* and *Tele-Controls* cases rested chiefly on state law doctrines that antedated the adoption of the Code.

In similar cases other courts have held that agency or distributorship contracts of indefinite duration are terminable by either party with or without cause. *E.g., Rockwell Engineering Co. v. Automatic Timing & Controls Co.,* 7th Cir. 1977, 559 F.2d 460 (Indiana law); *Aaron E. Levine & Co. v. Calkraft Paper Co.,* 1976, E.D. Mich., 429 F. Supp. 1039 (Michigan law). Those courts have relied on section 2-309(2) of the Code, which states:

> Where the contract provides for successive performances but is indefinite in duration it is valid for a reasonable time but unless otherwise agreed may be terminated at any time by either party.

Iowa Code Ann. § 554.2309(2). The division in the authorities, then, is between those courts that hold that the Code's general good faith obligation overrides the specific rule of section 2-309(2) as applied to distributorship or franchise agreements, and those that give precedence to section 2-309.

The parties have not cited and we have not found Iowa cases on the issue decided under the Uniform Commercial Code. The Iowa case law on this question is pre-Code and follows the common law rule, which is essentially the rule of section 2-309 as applied to distributorship contracts. In *Des Moines Blue Ribbon Distributors, Inc. v. Drewrys Limited, U.S.A., Inc.,* 1964, 256 Iowa 899, 129 N.W.2d 731, the Iowa Supreme Court held that an exclusive distributorship contract of indefinite duration may be terminated without cause only upon reasonable notice. Although the plaintiff in that case did not, so far as appears from the opinion, claim the right not to be terminated without cause, the court's treatment of the issues raised makes it clear that the requirement of reasonable notice was thought by the court to be the only restriction on the manufacturer's right to cancel the agreement.

Because the *Drewrys* case preceded Iowa's adoption of the Uniform Commercial Code, *Erie* does not strictly bind us to that decision. The Code added to Iowa commercial law a statutory good faith obligation. The Iowa law reflected in the *Drewrys* decision has been criticized for treating "what are essentially franchise agreements" as "a series of executory contracts enforceable only if performance has commenced." E. Gellhorn, at 469, n.15. On the other hand, in an area such as this, where considerations of *stare decisis* are of importance, we should hesitate to depart from established case authority absent fair assurance that the state's courts would interpret the Uniform Commercial Code to forbid "bad faith" or "arbitrary" terminations of distributorship contracts. Unlike the federal courts in the *Randolph, De Treville,* and *Tele-Controls* cases, we are not facing the termination issue against the backdrop of existing state law doctrine that forbids arbitrary terminations.

We are not persuaded that the adoption of the Code has effected any change in Iowa law with regard to distributorship terminations. We do not agree with Corenswet that the section 1-203 good faith obligation, like the Code's unconscionability provision, can properly be used to override or strike express contract terms. According to Professor Farnsworth, "(T)he chief utility of the concept of good faith performance has always been as a rationale in a process...of implying contract terms...." Farnsworth, *Good Faith Performance and Commercial Reasonableness under the Uniform Commercial Code,* 30 U. Chi. L. Rev. 666, 672 (1963). He defines the Code's good faith obligation as "an implied term of the contract requiring cooperation on the part of one party to the contract so that another party will not be deprived of his reasonable expectations." Id. at 666. When a contract contains a provision expressly sanctioning termination without cause there is no room for implying a term that bars such a termination. In the face of such a term there can be, at best, an expectation that a party will decline to exercise his rights.

As a tool for policing distributorship terminations, moreover, the good faith test is erratic at best. It has been observed that the good faith approach "is analytically unsound because there is no necessary correlation between bad motives and unfair terminations....The terminated dealer seeks relief against the harsh effects of termination which may be unfairly placed on him, not against the manufacturer's ill will." E. Gellhorn, *supra,* at 521. The better approach, endorsed by Professor Gellhorn, is to test the disputed contract clause for unconscionability under section 2-302 of the Code. The question these cases present is whether public policy forbids enforcement of a contract clause permitting unilateral termination without cause. Since a termination without cause will almost always be characterizable as a "bad faith" termination, focus on the terminating party's state of mind will always result in the invalidation of unrestricted termination clauses. We seriously doubt, however, that public policy frowns on any and all contract clauses permitting termination without cause. Such clauses can have the salutary effect of permitting parties to end a soured relationship without consequent litigation. Indeed when, as here, the power of unilateral termination without cause is granted to both parties, the clause gives the distributor an easy way to cut the knot should he be presented with an opportunity to secure a better distributorship from another manufacturer. What public policy does abhor is economic overreaching, the use of superior bargaining power to secure grossly unfair advantage. That is the precise focus of the Code's unconscionability doctrine; it is not at all the concern of the Code's good faith performance provision. It is the office of the unconscionability concept, and not of the good faith concept, to strike down "unfair" contract terms.

We conclude that, under the better view, the Code does not *ipso facto* bar unilateral arbitrary terminations of distributorship agreements, and that Iowa's adoption of the Code therefore left undisturbed the law reflected in the *Drewrys* decision....

Corenswet's rights with respect to termination extend only to a right to notice. The Amana contract permits termination on ten days' notice. Under the Code, section 2-309(3), and under the *Drewrys* case, however, a distributor is entitled to reasonable notice. Section 2-309(3) of the Code states that "an agreement dispensing with notification is invalid if its operation would be unconscionable." But any claim that Corenswet might have based on inadequate notice would not entitle Corenswet to injunctive relief, for it appears from the *Drewrys* case and from *C. C. Hauff Hardware, Inc. v. Long Mfg. Co.*, 1965, 257 Iowa 1127, 136 N.W.2d 276, that the manufacturer's failure to give proper notice is adequately remediable at law.

The district court's decisions are REVERSED, and the preliminary injunction is VACATED.

Transaction Cost Determinants of "Unfair" Contractual Arrangements
Benjamin Klein
70 American Economic Review 356, 356–62 (1980)

Terms such as "unfair" are foreign to the economic model of voluntary exchange which implies anticipated gains to all transactors. However, much recent statutory, regulatory and antitrust activity has run counter to this economic paradigm of the efficiency properties of "freedom of contract." The growth of "dealer day in court" legislation, FTC franchise regulations, favorable judicial consideration of "unequal bargaining power," and unconscionability arguments, are some examples of the recent legal propensity to "protect" transactors. This is done by declaring unenforceable or illegal particular contractual provisions that, although voluntarily agreed upon in the face of significant competition, appear to be one-sided or unfair. Presentation of the standard abstract economic analysis of the mutual gains from voluntary exchange is unlikely to be an effective counterweight to this recent legal movement without an explicit attempt to provide a positive rationale for the presence of the particular unfair contractual term. This paper considers some transaction costs that might explain the voluntary adoption of contractual provisions such as termination at will and long-term exclusive dealing clauses that have been under legal attack.

I. The "Holdup" Problem
...Given the presence of incomplete contractual arrangements, wealth-maximizing transactors have the ability and often the incentive to renege on the transaction by holding up the other party, in the sense of taking advantage of unspecified or unenforceable elements of the contractual relationship. Such behavior is, by definition, unanticipated and not a long-run equilibrium phenomenon. Oliver

Williamson has identified and discussed this phenomenon of "opportunistic behavior," and my recent paper with Robert Crawford and Armen Alchian attempted to make operational some of the conditions under which this holdup potential is likely to be large. In addition to contract costs, and therefore the incompleteness of the explicit contract, we emphasized the presence of appropriatable quasi-rents due to highly firm-specific investments. After a firm invests in an asset with a low-salvage value and a quasi-rent stream highly dependent upon some other asset, the owner of the other asset has the potential to hold up by appropriating the quasi-rent stream. For example, one would not build a house on land rented for a short term. After the rental agreement expires, the landowner could raise the rental price to reflect the costs of moving the house to another lot....

II. Contractual Solutions

Since the magnitude of the potential holdup may be anticipated, the party to be cheated can merely decrease the initial price he will pay by the amount of the appropriable quasi-rents. For example, if an employer knows that an employee will cheat a certain amount each period, it will be reflected in the employee's wage. Contracts can be usefully thought to refer to anticipated rather than stated performance. Therefore the employee's behavior should not even be considered "cheating." A secretary, for example, may miss work one day a week on average. If secretary time is highly substitutable, the employer can cut the secretary's weekly wage 20 percent, hire 20 percent more secretaries, and be indifferent. The secretary, on the other hand, presumably values the leisure more than the additional income and therefore is better off. Rather than cheating, we have a voluntarily determined, utility-maximizing contractual relationship.

In many cases, however, letting the party cheat and discounting his wage will not be an economical solution because the gain to the cheater and therefore his acceptable compensating wage discount is less than the cost to the firm from the cheating behavior. For example, it is easy to imagine many cases where a shirking manager will impose costs on the firm much greater than his personal gains. Therefore the stockholders cannot be made indifferent to this behavior by cutting his salary and hiring more lazy managers. The general point is that there may not be perfect substitutability between quantity and quality of particular services. Hence, even if one knew that an unspecified element of quality would be reduced by a certain amount in attempting the holdup, an ex ante compensatory discount in the quoted price of the promised high-quality service to the cost of providing the anticipated lower-quality supply would not make the demander of the service indifferent. Individuals would be willing to expend real resources to set up contractual arrangements to prevent such opportunism and assure high-quality supply.

The question then becomes how much of the holdup problem can be avoided by an explicit government-enforced contract, and how much remains to be handled by an implicit self-enforcing contract. This latter type of contract is one where opportunistic behavior is prevented by the threat of termination of the business relationship rather than by the threat of litigation. A transactor will not cheat if the expected present discounted value of quasi-rents he is earning from a relationship is greater than the immediate holdup wealth gain. The capital loss that can be imposed on the potential cheater by the withdrawal of expected future business is then sufficient to deter cheating.

... [O]ne way in which the future-promised rewards necessary to prevent cheating can be arranged is by the payment of a sufficiently high-price "premium." This premium stream can usefully be thought of as "protection money" paid to assure noncheating behavior. The magnitude of this price premium will be related to the potential holdup, this is, to the extent of contractual incompleteness and the degree of specific capital present. In equilibrium, the present discounted value of the price-premium stream will be exactly equal to the appropriable quasi-rents, making the potential cheater indifferent between cheating and not. But the individual paying the premium will be in a preferable position as long as the differential consumer's surplus from high-quality (noncheating) supply is greater that the premium.

One method by which this equilibrium quasi-rent stream can be achieved without the existence of positive firm profits is by having the potential cheater put up a forfeitable-at-will collateral bond equal to the discounted value of the premium stream. Alternatively, the potential cheater may make a highly firm-specific productive investment which will have only a low-salvage value if he cheats and loses future business. The gap between price and salvageable capital costs is analytically equivalent to a premium stream with the nonsalvageable asset analytically equivalent to a forfeitable collateral bond.

III. "Unfair" Contractual Terms

Most actual contractual arrangements consist of a combination of explicit and implicit enforcement mechanisms. Some elements of performance will be specified and enforced by third-party sanctions. The residual elements of performance will be enforced without invoking the power of some outside party to the transaction but merely by the threat of termination of the transactional relationship. The details of any particular contract will consist of forms of these general elements chosen to minimize transaction costs (for example, hiring lawyers to discover contingencies and draft explicit terms, paying quality-assurance premiums, and investing in nonsalvageable "brand name" assets) and may imply the existence of what appear to be unfair contract terms.

Consider, for example, the initial capital requirements and termination provisions common in most franchise contractual arrangements. These apparently one-sided terms may be crucial elements of minimum-cost quality-policing arrangements. Given the difficulty of explicitly specifying and enforcing contractually every element of quality to be supplied by a franchisee, there is an incentive for an individual opportunistic franchisee to cheat the franchisor by supplying a lower quality of product than contracted for. Because the franchisee uses a common trademark, this behavior depreciates the reputation and hence the future profit stream of the franchisor.

The franchisor knows, given his direct policing and monitoring expenditures, the expected profit that a franchisee can obtain by cheating. For example, given the number of inspectors hired, he knows the expected time to detect a cheater. Given the costs of low-quality inputs, he knows the expected extra short-run cheating profit that can be earned. Therefore the franchisor may require an initial lump sum payment from the franchisee equal to this estimated short-run gain from cheating. This is equivalent to a collateral bond forfeitable at the will of the franchisor. The franchisee will earn a normal rate of return on that bond if he does not cheat, but it will be forfeited if he does cheat and is terminated.

In many cases franchisee noncheating rewards may be increased and short-run cheating profits decreased (and therefore franchisor direct policing costs reduced) by...the franchisor...[requiring] franchisees to rent from them short term (rather than own) the land upon which their outlet is located. This lease arrangement creates a situation where termination implies that the franchisor can require the franchisee to move and thereby impose a capital loss on him up to the amount of his initial nonsalvageable investment. Hence a form of collateral to deter franchisee cheating is created.

It is important to recognize that franchise termination, if it is to assure quality compliance on the part of franchisees, must be unfair in the sense that the capital cost imposed on the franchisee that will optimally prevent cheating must be larger than the gain to the franchisee from cheating. Given that less than infinite resources are spent by the franchisor to monitor quality, there is some probability that franchisee cheating will go undetected. Therefore, termination must become equivalent to a criminal-type sanction. Rather than the usually analyzed case of costlessly detected and policed contract breach, where the remedy of making the breaching party pay the cost of the damages of his specific breach makes economic sense, the sanction here must be large enough to make the expected net gain from cheating equal to zero. The transacting parties contractually agree upon a penalty-type sanction for breach as a means of economizing on direct policing costs. Because contract enforcement costs (including litigation costs which generally are not collectable by the innocent party in the United States) are not zero, this analysis provides a rationale against the common-law prohibition of penalty clauses.

The obvious concern with such seemingly unfair contractual arrangements is the possibility that the franchisor may engage in opportunistic behavior by terminating a franchisee without cause, claiming the franchise fee and purchasing the initial franchisee's investment at a distress price. Such behavior may be prevented by the depreciation of the franchisor's brand name and therefore decreased future demand by potential franchisees to join the arrangement. However, this protective mechanism is limited by the relative importance of new franchise sales compared to the continuing franchising operation, that is, by the "maturity" of the franchise chain.

More importantly, what limits reverse cheating by franchisors is the possible increased cost of operating the chain through an employee operation compared to a franchise operation when such cheating is communicated among franchisees. As long as the implicit collateral bond put up by the franchisee is less than the present discounted value of this cost difference, franchisor cheating will be deterred. Although explicit bonds and price premium payments cannot simultaneously be made by both the franchisee and the franchisor, the discounted value of the cost difference has the effect of a collateral bond put up by the franchisor to assure his noncheating behavior. This explains why the franchisor does not increase the initial franchise fee to an arbitrarily high level and correspondingly decrease its direct policing expenditures and the probability of detecting franchisee cheating. While such offsetting changes could continue to optimally deter franchisee cheating and save the real resource cost of direct policing, the profit from and hence the incentive for reverse franchisor cheating would become too great for the arrangement to be stable.

Franchisees voluntarily signing these agreements obviously understand the termination-at-will clause separate from the legal consequences of that term to mean unopportunistic franchisor termination. But this does not imply that the court should judge each termination on these unwritten but understood contract terms and attempt to determine if franchisor cheating has occurred. Franchisees also must recognize that by signing these agreements they are relying on the implicit market-enforcement mechanism outlined above, and not the court, to prevent franchisor cheating. It is costly to use the court to regulate these terminations because elements of performance are difficult to contractually specify and to measure. In addition, litigation is costly and time consuming, during which time the brand name of the franchisor can be depreciated further. If these costs were not large and the court could cheaply and quickly determine when franchisor cheating had occurred, the competitive process regarding the establishment of contract terms would lead transactors to settle on explicit governmentally enforceable contracts rather than rely on this implicit market-enforcement mechanism.

The potential error here is, after recognizing the importance of transaction costs and the incomplete "relational" nature of most real-world contracts, to rely too strongly on the government as a regulator of unspecified terms. While it is important for economic theory to handle significant contract costs and incomplete explicit contractual arrangements, such complexity does not imply a broad role for government. Rather, all that is implied is a role for brand names and the corresponding implicit market-enforcement mechanism I have outlined.

IV. Unequal Bargaining Power

An argument made against contract provisions such as termination-at-will clauses is that they appear to favor one party at the expense of another. Hence it is alleged that the terms of the agreement must have been reached under conditions of "unequal bargaining power" and therefore should be invalid. However, a further implication of the above analysis is that when both parties can cheat, explicit contractual restraints are often placed on the smaller, less well-established party (the franchisee), while an implicit brand-name contract-enforcement mechanism is relied on to prevent cheating by the larger, more well-established party (the franchisor).

If information regarding quality of product supplied by a large firm is communicated among many small buyers who do not all purchase simultaneously, the potential holdup relative to, say, annual sales is reduced substantially compared to the case where each buyer purchased from a separate independent small firm. There are likely to be economies of scale in the supply of a business brand name, because in effect the large firm's total brand-name capital is put on the line with each individual sale. This implies a lower cost of using the implicit contract mechanism, that is, a lower-price premium necessary to assure non-breach, for a large firm compared to a small firm. Therefore one side of the contract will be relatively more incomplete.

For example, in a recent English case using the doctrine of inequality of bargaining power to bar contract enforcement, an individual songwriter signed a long-term (ten-year) exclusive service contract with a music publisher for an agreed royalty percentage. Since it would be extremely costly to write a complete explicit contract for the supply of publishing services (including advertising and other promotion activities, whose effects are felt over time and are difficult to measure), after a songwriter becomes established he has an incentive to take advantage of any initial investment made by a publishing firm and shift to another publisher. Rather than rely on the brand name of the songwriter or require him to make a specific investment which can serve as collateral, the exclusive service contract prevents this cheating from occurring.

The major cost of such explicit long-term contractual arrangements is the rigidity that is created by the necessity of setting a price or a price formula ex ante. In this song publishing case, the royalty formula may turn out ex post to imply too low a price to the songwriter (if, say, his cooperative promotional input is greater than originally anticipated). If the publisher is concerned about his reputation, these royalty terms will be renegotiated, a common occurrence in continuing business relationships.

If an individual songwriter is a small part of a large publisher's total sales, and if the value of an individual songwriter's ability generally depreciates rapidly or does not persist at peak levels so that signing up new songwriters is an important element of a publisher's continuing business, then cheating an individual songwriter or even all songwriters currently under contract by refusing to renegotiate royalty rates will imply a large capital cost to the publisher. When this behavior is communicated to other actual or potential composers, the publisher's reputation will depreciate and future business will be lost. An individual songwriter, on the other hand, does not generally have large, diversified long-term business concerns and therefore cannot be penalized in that way. It is therefore obvious, independent of any appeal to disparity of bargaining power, why the smaller party would be willing to be bound by an explicit long-term contract while the larger party is bound only implicitly and renegotiates terms that turn out ex post to be truly divergent from ex ante, but unspecified, anticipations.

However, the possibility of reverse publisher cheating is real. If, for example, the songwriter unexpectedly becomes such a great success that current sales by this one customer represents a large share of the present discounted value of total publisher sales, the implicit contract enforcement mechanism may not work. Individuals knowingly trade off these costs of explicit and implicit-enforcement mechanisms in settling upon transaction cost-minimizing contract terms. Although it would be too costly in a stochastic world to attempt to set up an arrangement where no cheating occurs, it is naive to think that courts can cheaply intervene to discover and "fix up" the few cases of opportunistic behavior that will occur. In any event, my analysis makes it clear that one cannot merely look at the agreed-upon, seemingly "unfair" terms to determine if opportunism is occurring....

Notes and Questions

1. The Termination Clause: Klein offers several explanations for why it is mutually beneficial for franchisors and franchisees to have termination clauses included in the franchise agreement. Do those explanations apply to the inclusion of the clause in the Amana contract? How about the termination clause in *Continental T.V.* ?

2. Market Protection Against Arbitrary Termination: Franchisors are in the business of selling franchises at the highest price attainable, with the price being determined by the value of the trademark and the franchisor's reputation for dealing fairly with franchisees. A franchisor, in effect, depreciates the value of the trademark when he opportunistically or arbitrarily terminates a franchisee. Managerial talent is limited, competition among franchisors is intense, and the market for franchises offers potential franchisees a large number of opportunities. Even if all franchisors were offering the same expected net cash flow, the best franchisees would not pay as much for franchises from franchisors who have a reputation for mistreating their franchisees.

3. Managerial Discretion, Personal Preferences, and Agency Costs: Was Amana's termination of Corenswet in Amana's best interest or was it a personal vendetta by George Foerstner, the president of Amana? Amana publicly stated that Corenswet was underfinanced and, thus, should not be allowed to continue as a dealer of Amana products. However, behind the scenes, there was strong evidence of a personal fued between the two company presidents. Amana's president desired to terminate Corenswet and replace it with the George H. Lehleitner & Co. Would you expect word of the personal feud to have a negative impact on Amana's ability to attract other dealers? If so, can you determine whether Foerstner was a good agent for Raytheon, Amana's parent?

4. Relative Bargaining Power of Franchisors and Franchisees: Corenswet's Experience: Footnote 12 of the Corenswet opinion offers some insights into the relative bargaining power of franchisees and franchisors:

> Sometime between Corenswet's filing of the lawsuit and the hearing on whether to issue a preliminary injunction the unconscionability issue dropped from the case. The issues for the hearing were narrowed to include only the meaning of the contract and the reasons for Amana's termination of Corenswet. To prevail on a theory of unconscionability Corenswet would have to demonstrate (1) that it had no "meaningful choice" but to deal with Amana and accept the contract as offered, and (2) that the termination clause was "unreasonably favorable" to Amana. Williams v. Walker-Thomas Furniture Co., 1965, 121 U.S. App. D.C. 315, 319, 350 F.2d 445, 449. The record evidence relevant to these questions is scanty. Sam Corenswet testified that Amana in 1969 aggressively sought Corenswet as a distributor and that he only reluctantly decided to commit his company to Amana. Another Corenswet witness, at one point in his testimony, said of the 1975 amended contract that, in view of Corenswet's heavy investment in the Amana line, "we had to take it." The court interrupted that testimony and expressed its view that it was irrelevant to the hearing issues. There was no other evidence regarding the parties' relative bargaining power at the time the relationship began, nor any evidence as to the relative usefulness of the termination clause to the two sides.

Ex ante Corenswet was courted, but after Corenswet made Amana-specific investments Corenswet was vulnerable to opportunistic amendment of the contract. In light of the analysis of the preceding note and the Klein excerpt, one should be hesitant to evaluate individual clauses or individual actions without considering the totality of the circumstances. For example, was the 1975 amendment a substantial change in the contract or was it merely a formal statement of the "off the rack" implied terms?

5. Franchisees as "victims": The Supreme Court, in granting relief to "victims" of the alleged superior bargaining power of franchisors, has exhibited a sympathetic policy to franchisees. Consider, for example the Court's treatment of the Midas Muffler franchise contract. In *Perma Life Mufflers, Inc. v. International Parts Corp.,* a group of franchise dealers operating Midas Muffler shops charged that Midas, its parent International Parts, and two other subsidiaries unlawfully conspired to restrain competition under section 1 of the Sherman Act and section 3 of the Clayton Act. The dealers had accepted contracts to sell Midas mufflers at prices fixed by Midas and not to deal with any of Midas' competitors. In considering these franchise agreements, the Supreme Court noted: "Petitioners (the dealers) apparently accepted many of these restraints solely because their acquiescence was necessary to obtain an otherwise attractive business opportunity." The franchised dealers, who clearly wished to take the benefits of the bargain without the burdens, alleged that Midas and its parent had conspired against them, forcing them to accept the onerous terms of the franchise agreements. The Court apparently viewed the dealers as victims of a superior economic force that had bound them to an unfair and ill-advised bargain. The oppressed dealers, according to the Supreme Court, are entitled to relief under the antitrust laws, which, in effect, allow the federal courts to rewrite their contracts for them. The Supreme Court's willingness to rewrite contracts because of their apparently "unfair" terms reflects the inability of the Court to understand the importance of transaction costs and the relational nature of franchising arrangements. For example, in order to deter franchisee shirking and intrabrand free riding, both of which depreciate the franchisor's brand name, the franchisor insists on a swift and stiff penalty embodied in the termination-at-will clause for cheating franchisees who are caught. The apparent fear of the Supreme Court is that franchisors will not act in "good faith" and will abuse the "unfair" provisions. Although the Court fears that the franchisors may behave opportunistically, the Court ignores the market forces that deter such opportunistic behavior.

6. Opportunism and Wasted Resources: Parties who recognize the possibility of being subjected to opportunistic behavior will invest real resources in attempting to avoid manipulation. On the other hand, parties who recognize the potential to act opportunistically will invest real resources in perpetrating opportunism. These joint expenditures of resources are socially wasteful, in that real resources are not invested for the purpose of creating wealth but solely for the purpose of transferring wealth. Unlike mutually-beneficial exchange, which is a positive sum game, opportunism is a negative sum game. The threat of opportunism, moreover, increases the transaction costs of exchange, which reduces the volume of mutually beneficial exchanges. The net result of this allocation of real resources, for the purpose of opportunistically transferring wealth, is a reduction in the wealth of society and, *a fortiori,* consumer wealth.

7. Other Uncompensated Wealth Transfers and Wasted Resources: Opportunistic behavior wastes resources. One activity that results in an analogous waste of resources is theft. Theft involves more than the transfer of wealth from one party to another; it also involves the investment of time and other resources by thieves in managing the transfer as well as the investment of resources by potential victims in avoidance of the transfer. In the absence of theft, these resources would be invested in other, presumably more productive, uses. *See* Becker, *Crime and Punishment: An Economic Approach,* 76 J. Pol. Econ. 169,

209 (1968) (optimal legislative policies to combat illegal behavior are part of an optimal allocation of resources); Tullock, *The Welfare Costs of Tariffs, Monopolies, and Theft*, 5 Western Econ. J. 224, 231 (1967) ("A successful bank robbery will inspire potential thieves to greater efforts, lead to the installation of improved protective equipment in other banks, and perhaps result in the hiring of additional policemen.").

2. Long-Term, Incomplete, and Relational Contracts

The common law of contracts provides a stock of standard form, off-the-rack contractual provisions that specify the basic details and fill gaps in negotiated contracts. Unless contradicted by the explicit terms of a contract, the common law rules are an implied part of all contracts. This reduces transaction costs by allowing contracting parties to form enforceable contracts without having to specify every standard of performance and without having to negotiate the allocation of risk associated with every conceivable contingency.

All executory contracts face the risk of disruption due to unanticipated or remote contingencies—circumstances the contract cannot deal with because the contracting parties don't know what might occur or circumstances not worth dealing with because there is only a small probability that they will arise—and contract law provides the basic rules to deal with various contingencies. Occasionally, however, the bargaining situation becomes too complicated and otherwise mutually-beneficial transactions fail to occur. In those situations, one alternative is for the parties to integrate into a single entity—the substitution of firm coordination for market coordination.

Another alternative to transaction failure is for the inter-firm activity to be coordinated by relational contract. The nature of a relational contract is found in its contrast with the traditional contingent contract:

> A contract is relational to the extent that the parties are incapable of reducing important terms of the arrangement to well-defined obligations. Such definitive obligations may be impractical because of inability to identify uncertain future conditions or because of inability to characterize complex adaptations adequately even when the contingencies themselves can be identified in advance.

Charles Goetz and Robert Scott, *Principles of Relational Contracts*, 67 Virginia Law Review 1089, 1091 (1981). The goal of relational contract law is the maintenance of the relationship in the face of conflict that would usually result in termination under traditional contract law approaches.

Nanakuli Paving and Rock Co. v. Shell Oil Co.
United States Court of Appeals, Ninth Circuit
664 F.2d 772 (1981)

HOFFMAN

Appellant Nanakuli Paving and Rock Company (Nanakuli) initially filed this breach of contract action against appellee Shell Oil Company (Shell) in Hawaiian

State Court in February, 1976.[1] Nanakuli, the second largest asphaltic paving contractor in Hawaii, had bought all its asphalt requirements from 1963 to 1974 from Shell under two long-term supply contracts; its suit charged Shell with breach of the later 1969 contract.[2] The jury returned a verdict of $220,800 for Nanakuli on its first claim, which is that Shell breached the 1969 contract in January, 1974, by failing to price protect Nanakuli on 7200 tons of asphalt at the time Shell raised the price for asphalt from $44 to $76. Nanakuli's theory is that price-protection, as a usage of the asphaltic paving trade in Hawaii, was incorporated into the 1969 agreement between the parties, as demonstrated by the routine use of price protection by suppliers to that trade, and reinforced by the way in which Shell actually performed the 1969 contract up until 1974. Price protection, appellant claims, required that Shell hold the price on the tonnage Nanakuli had already committed because Nanakuli had incorporated that price into bids put out to or contracts awarded by general contractors and government agencies. The District Judge set aside the verdict and granted Shell's motion for judgment n. o. v., which decision we vacate. We reinstate the jury verdict because we find that, viewing the evidence as a whole, there was substantial evidence to support a finding by reasonable jurors that Shell breached its contract by failing to provide protection for Nanakuli in 1974. We do not believe the evidence in this case was such that, giving Nanakuli the benefit of all inferences fairly supported by the evidence and without weighing the credibility of the witnesses, only one reasonable conclusion could have been reached by the jury.

Nanakuli offers two theories for why Shell's failure to offer price protection in 1974 was a breach of the 1969 contract. First, it argues, all material suppliers to the asphaltic paving trade in Hawaii followed the trade usage of price protection and thus it should be assumed, under the U.C.C., that the parties intended to incorporate price protection into their 1969 agreement. This is so, Nanakuli continues, even though the written contract provided for price to be "Shell's Posted Price at time of delivery," F.O.B. Honolulu. Its proof of a usage that was incorporated into the contract is reinforced by evidence of the commercial context, which under the U.C.C. should form the background for viewing a particular contract. The full agreement must be examined in light of the close, almost symbiotic relations between Shell and Nanakuli on the island of Oahu, whereby the expansion of Shell on the island was intimately connected to the business growth of Nanakuli. The U.C.C. looks to the actual performance of a contract as the best indication of what the parties intended those terms to mean. Nanakuli points out that Shell had price protected it on the two occasions of price increases under the 1969 contract other than the 1974 increase. In 1970 and 1971 Shell extended the old price for four and three months, respectively, after an announced increase. This was done, in the words of Shell's agent in Hawaii, in order to permit Nanakuli's to "chew up" tonnage already committed at Shell's old price.[4]

---

1. Shell removed the suit to United States District Court for the District of Hawaii on March 2 of that year.

2. The parties agree this act is governed by the Uniform Commercial Code, as enacted in Hawaii Rev.Stat. § 490:1-101 *et seq.*

4. Price protection was practiced in the asphaltic paving trade by either extending the old price for a period of time after a new one went into effect or charging the old price for a specified tonnage, which represented work committed at the old price. In addition, several months' advance notice was given of price increases.

We hold that the judge did not abuse his discretion in defining the applicable trade, for purposes of trade usages, as the asphaltic paving trade in Hawaii, rather than the purchase and sale of asphalt alone, given the unusual, not to say unique, circumstances: the smallness of the marketplace on Oahu; the existence of only two suppliers on the island; the long and intimate connection between the two companies on Oahu, including the background of how the development of Shell's asphalt sales on Oahu was inextricably linked to Nanakuli's own expansion on the island; the knowledge of the aggregate business on the part of Shell's Hawaiian representative, Bohner; his awareness of the economics of Nanakuli's bid estimates, which included only two major materials, asphalt and aggregate; his familiarity with realities of the Hawaiian marketplace in which all government agencies refused to include escalation clauses in contract awards and thus pavers would face tremendous losses on price increases if all their material suppliers did not routinely offer them price protection; and Shell's determination to build Nanakuli up to compete for those lucrative government contracts with the largest paver on the island, Hawaiian Bitumuls (H.B.), which was supplied by the only other asphalt company on the islands, Chevron, and which was routinely price protected on materials. We base our holding on the reading of the Code Comments as defining trade more broadly than transaction and as binding parties not only to usages of their particular trade but also to usages of trade in general in a given locality. This latter seems an equitable application of usage evidence where the usage is almost universally practiced in a small market such as was Oahu in the 1960's before Shell signed its 1969 contract with Nanakuli. Additionally, we hold that, under the facts of this case, a jury could reasonably have found that Shell's acts on two occasions to price protect Nanakuli were not ambiguous and therefore indicated Shell's understanding of the terms of the agreement with Nanakuli rather than being a waiver by Shell of those terms.

Lastly we hold that, although the express price terms of Shell's posted price of delivery may seem, at first glance, inconsistent with a trade usage of price protection at time of increases in price, a closer reading shows that the jury could have reasonably construed price protection as consistent with the express term. We reach this holding for several reasons. First, we are persuaded by a careful reading of the U.C.C., one of whose underlying purposes is to promote flexibility in the expansion of commercial practices and which rather drastically overhauls this particular area of the law. The Code would have us look beyond the printed pages of the contract to usages and the entire commercial context of the agreement in order to reach the "true understanding" of the parties. Second, decisions of other courts in similar situations have managed to reconcile such trade usages with seemingly contradictory express terms where the prior course of dealings between the parties, trade usages, and the actual performance of the contract by the parties showed a clear intent by the parties to incorporate those usages into the agreement or to give to the express term the particular meaning provided by those usages, even at times varying the apparent meaning of the express terms. Third, the delineation by thoughtful commentators of the degree of consistency demanded between express terms and usage is that a usage should be allowed to modify the apparent agreement, as seen in the written terms, as long as it does not totally negate it. We believe the usage here falls within the limits set forth by commentators and generally followed in the better reasoned decisions. The manner in which price protection was actually practiced in Hawaii was that it only came into play at times of price increases and only for work committed prior to those increases on non-escalating contracts. Thus, it formed an exception to, rather than a total negation of, the express price term of "Shell's Posted Price at time of delivery." Our decision is reinforced by the overwhelming nature of the evidence that price protection was routinely practiced by all suppliers in the small Oahu market of the asphaltic paving trade and therefore was known to Shell; that it was a realistic necessity to operate in that market and thus vital to Nanakuli's ability to get large government contracts and to Shell's continued business growth on Oahu; and that it therefore constituted an intended part of the agreement, as that term is broadly defined by the Code, between Shell and Nanakuli.

I.

History Of Nanakuli-Shell Relations Before 1973

Nanakuli, a division of Grace Brothers, Ltd., a Hawaiian corporation, is the smaller of the two major paving contractors on the island of Oahu, the larger of the two being Hawaiian Bitumuls (H.B.). Nanakuli first entered the paving business on Oahu in 1948, but it only began to move into the largest Oahu market, Honolulu, in the mid-1950's. Until 1964 or so, Nanakuli only got small paving jobs, such as service stations, driveways, and small subdivision streets; it was not in a position to compete with H.B. for government contracts for major roads, airports, and other large jobs. In the early sixties Nanakuli owner Walter Grace began to negotiate a mutually advantageous arrangement with Shell whereby Shell, which had a small market percentage and no asphalt terminals in Hawaii,[9] would sign a long-term supply contract with Nanakuli that would commit Nanakuli to buy its asphalt requirements from Shell. On the other hand, Nanakuli would be helped to expand its paving business on Oahu through a guaranteed supply and a discount on its asphalt prices. Nanakuli's growth would expand the market for Shell's asphalt on the island, which would justify Shell's capital investment of a half a million dollars on Oahu, to which asphalt would be brought in heated tankers from Shell's refinery in Martinez, California.[10]

...As a symbol of that relationship, Nanakuli painted its trucks "Shell white," placed Shell's logo on those trucks, chose the same orange as used by Shell for its own logo, and put the Shell logo on its stationary.

---

9. Shell and H. B. had previously bought all of their asphalt from Chevron, the marketing division of Standard Oil Company, which at one time owned all or part of H.B. See note 5 supra. Nanakuli needed its own asphalt supply so as not to be dependent on Chevron, whose long-time chief customer was Nanakuli's major competitor.

10. Shell had made a study of the market in Hawaii a year or so before undertaking negotiations with Nanakuli. Its conclusion was that, as things stood, there was not enough volume to justify Shell's shipping asphalt in tankers from the mainland, hence the importance of Shell's efforts to encourage the expansion of Nanakuli on Oahu. Shell built two terminals in Hawaii, both of which were completed in late 1963: one was on Oahu, where it had just signed a seven-year supply contract with Nanakuli, and the other was at Hilo, where it had signed a five-year supply contract with James W. Glover, Ltd.

In 1966 Pacific Cement and Aggregates (P.C. & A.), Nanakuli's landlord at its rented rock quarry at Halawa, was bought by Lone Star Cement Corporation, which later became Lone Star Industries. Lone Star requested that Nanakuli upgrade its plant facilities at the quarry, which Nanakuli estimated would cost between $250,000 to $300,000. Nanakuli, knowing Shell was eager to build up its paving business on Oahu, approached Shell for direct financing of the plant, an idea to which Shell was initially receptive. Lennox [Nanakuli's president] testified that Shell "had a sizeable installation at Iwilei and they didn't think we were selling enough of their product and they wanted us to sell more and that's why we enlarged our plant." Shell management philosophy later changed and it was decided not to finance the plant directly but rather to offer Nanakuli an additional $2 volume discount on all sales over five thousand tons to help finance the plant, according to Bohner. Lennox testified that Shell authorized Nanakuli to tell Lone Star that Shell, with a million-dollar investment in Hawaii, fully supported Nanakuli's plant expansion plans. In 1968 two top Shell asphalt officials came from the mainland to discuss Nanakuli's expansion: Blee from San Francisco and Lewis from New York. Together with Bohner [Shell's Hawaiian representative from 1964–1978] and Nanakuli's Lennox and Smith, they met with officials of Nanakuli's bank to discuss the loan and repayment schedule. The three contracts were finally signed after long negotiations on April 1, 1969. They were to parallel the amortization schedule of the bank loan for the plant: a supply contract, a distributorship contract, and volume discount letter, all three to last until December 31, 1975, at which point each would have the option to cancel on six-months' notice, with a minimum duration of over seven years, April 1, 1969, to July 1, 1976. Such long-term contracts were certainly unusual for Shell and this one was probably unique among Shell's customers, at least by 1974.

Lennox' testimony, which was partially stricken by the court as inadmissible, was that Shell's agreement with Nanakuli in 1969 included a commitment by Shell never to charge Nanakuli more than Chevron charged H.B., in order to carry out the underlying purpose of the agreement to make Nanakuli competitive with H.B. and thus expand its and Shell's respective businesses on Oahu. This testimony was ruled inadmissible as parol evidence. Shell, itself at the end of the trial, read in parts of Smith's earlier deposition in which he made a similar point. Smith's deposition testimony was that, although no written provision was included on price protection, he was led to believe by Shell's Bohner that he would get price protection. "I think there was a thought running between the two parties at that time that something would be done." It was only after the fact, he added, that Bohner told Nanakuli that he had to get permission for price protection from the mainland at the time of price increases; before that, "we had no idea how the pricing was done." Smith's comments on additional terms agreed to were not as probative as those of Lennox, who was president and chief negotiator for Nanakuli of the 1969 contract. Nanakuli's offer of proof by Lennox was that Shell agreed "to sustain that price during those contracts in the same way in which Standard Oil Company (Chevron) sustained its price to the principal paving contractor on the island, Hawaiian Bitumuls, if there was any price increase" and to "not exceed Standard Oil's (Chevron's) posted price for asphalt sold to Hawaiian Bitumuls." It was agreed that Nanakuli would have to submit bids on a fixed-price basis and be price protected to compete with H.B. "We understood that Shell gave us the same protection in our bidding and our purchase of asphalt from them to incorporate in our work," Lennox did testify, adding that by that means Nanakuli could compete with H.B. and Shell would thereby benefit. He said Nanakuli understood the price term to mean that Shell would not increase prices without advance notice and would hold the price on work bid for enough time to allow Nanakuli to use up the tonnage bid at the old price. Smith's testimony backed up that of Lennox: the price was to be "posted price as bid as was understood between the parties," further explaining that it was to be Shell's price at time and place of delivery, except for price increases, at which point the price was time and place of bid for a period of time or a specified tonnage.

Much information relevant to the "commercial context" of the agreement, essential to an understanding of the meaning of the terms, was contained in the testimony of Smith and Lennox. None of it was flatly contradicted by the evasive responses of Bohner to such inquiries. Smith testified that Bohner was in Nanakuli's offices at least weekly, sometimes was involved in the preparation of bids, and knew when a bid had been submitted or a contract awarded, at times attending the awards himself. The amount of time he spent following Nanakuli's progress was understandable; as he explained, in the 1960's and 1970's Nanakuli "was basically...our only customer at this time." Thus Nanakuli felt it had no need to notify Shell in writing of projects awarded; Lennox testified he was only told to do so on one occasion, the award of its first big contract on August 17, 1970. Due to the long shipping time from California, Bohner had to know well in advance Nanakuli's supply needs. Lennox testified that Bohner was "as close to us as any person could be as far as the asphalt supply was concerned. He had to know what we were doing...." Lennox said Bohner was not only aware of Nanakuli's day-to-day progress but knowledgeable about the broader asphaltic paving marketplace in which Nanakuli was competing....

II
Trade Usage Before And After 1969

The key to price protection being so prevalent in 1969 that both parties would intend to incorporate it into their contract is found in one reality of the Oahu asphaltic paving market: the largest paving contracts were let by government agencies and none of the three levels of government-local, state, or federal-allowed escalation clauses for paving materials. If a paver bid at one price and another went into effect before the award was made, the paving company would lose a great deal of money, since it could not pass on increases to any government agency or to most general contractors. Extensive evidence was presented that, as a consequence, aggregate suppliers routinely price protected paving contractors in the 1960's and 1970's, as did the largest asphaltic supplier in Oahu, Chevron. Nanakuli presented documentary evidence of routine price protection by aggregate suppliers as well as two witnesses: Grosjean, Vice-President for Marketing of Ameron H.C. & D., and Nihei, Division Manager of Lone Star Industries for Pacific Cement and Aggregate (P.C. & A.). Both testified that price protection to their knowledge had always been practiced: at H.C. & D. for many years prior to Grosjean's arrival in 1962 and at P.C.&A. routinely since Nihei's arrival in 1960. Such protection consisted of advance notices of increases, coupled with charging the old price for work committed at that price or for enough time to order the tonnage committed. The smallness of the Oahu market led to complete trust among suppliers and pavers. H.C. & D. did not demand that Nanakuli or other pavers issue purchase orders or sign contracts for aggregate before incorporating its aggregate prices into bids. Nanakuli would merely give H.C. & D. a list of projects it had bid at the time H.C. & D. raised its prices, without documentation. "Their word and letter is good enough for us," Grosjean testified. Nihei said P.C. & A. at the time of price increases would get a list of either particular projects bid by a paver or simply total tonnage bid at the old price. "We take either one. We take their word for it." None of the aggregate companies had a contract with Nanakuli expressly stating price protection would be given; Nanakuli's contract with P.C. & A. merely set out that P.C. & A. would not charge Nanakuli more than it charged its other customers.

The evidence about Chevron's practice of price protection came in the form of an affidavit by Bery Jameyson, Chevron's Division Manager-Asphalt in California. He stated that Chevron had routinely price protected H.B. on work bid for many years, the last occasion prior to the signing of the 1969 contracts between Nanakuli and Shell being a price increase put into effect on March 7, 1969, with the understanding that H.B. would be protected on work bid, which amounted to 12,000 tons. In answer to Shell's protest that such evidence was not relevant without the contract itself, Nanakuli introduced the contract into evidence. Much like the contract at issue here, it provided that the price to H.B. would be a given percentage of the price Chevron set for a specified crude oil in California. No mention was made of price protection in the written contract between H.B. and Chevron.

In addition to evidence of trade usages existing in 1969 when the contract at issue was signed, the District Judge let in evidence of the continuation of that trade usage after 1969, over Shell's protest. He stated that, giving a liberal reading to Section 1-205, he felt that later evidence was relevant to show that the expectation of the parties that a given usage would be observed was justified. The basis for incorporating a trade usage into a contract under the U.C.C. is the justifiable expectation of the parties that it will be observed. That later evidence consisted here of more price protection by the aggregate companies on Oahu, as well as continued asphalt price protection. Chevron after 1969 continued price protecting H.B. on Oahu and, on raising prices in 1979, price protected Nanakuli on the island of Molokai, where Nanakuli purchased its asphalt from Chevron. Additionally, Shell price protected Nanakuli in 1977 and 1978 on Oahu.

III
Shell's Course Of Performance Of The 1969 Contract

The Code considers actual performance of a contract as the most relevant evidence of how the parties interpreted the terms of that contract. In 1970 and 1971, the only points at which Shell raised prices between 1969 and 1974, it price protected Nanakuli by holding its old price for four and three months, respectively, after announcing a price increase. In the late summer of 1970, Shell had announced a price increase from $35 to $40 a ton effective September 1, 1970. When Nanakuli protested to Bohner that it should be price protected on work already committed, Blee wrote Bohner an in-house memo that, if Bohner could not "convince" Nanakuli to go along with the price increase on September 1, he should try to "bargain" to get Nanakuli to accept the price raise by at least the first of the year, which was what was finally agreed upon. During that four-month period,

Nanakuli bought 3,300 tons. Shell announced a second increase in October, 1970, from $40 to $42 effective December 31st. Before that increase went into effect, on November 25 Shell increased the raise to $4, making the price $44 as of the first of the year. Shell again agreed to price protect Nanakuli by holding the price at $40, which had been the official price since September 1, for three months from January to March, 1971. Shell did not actually raise prices again until January, 1974, but at several points it believed that increases would be necessary and gave several months' advance notice of those possible increases. Those actions were in accord with Shell's own policy, as professed by Bohner, and that of other asphalt and aggregate suppliers: to give at least several months' advance notice of price increases. On January 14, 1971, Shell wrote its asphalt customers that the maximum 1971 increase would be to $46. On July 9, 1971, another letter promised the price would not go over $50 in 1972. In addition, Bohner volunteered on direct the information that Shell price protected Nanakuli on the only two occasions of price increases after 1974 by giving 6 months' advance notice in 1977 and 3 or 4 months' advance notice in 1978, a practice he described as "in effect carryover pricing," his term for price protection. By its actions, Bohner testified, Shell allowed Nanakuli time to make arrangements to buy up tonnage committed at the old price, that is, to "chew up" tonnage bid or contracted. Shell apparently offered this testimony to impress the jury with its subsequent good faith toward Nanakuli. In fact, it also may have reinforced the impression of the universality of price protection in the asphaltic paving trade on Oahu and, by showing Shell's adherence to that practice on every relevant occasion except 1974, have highlighted for the jury what was the commercially reasonable standard of fair dealing in effect on Oahu in 1974.

IV

Shell-Nanakuli Relations, 1973–74

Two important factors form the backdrop for the 1974 failure by Shell to price protect Nanakuli: the Arab oil embargo and a complete change of command and policy in Shell's asphalt management. The jury was read a page or so from the World Book about the events and effect of the partial oil embargo, which shortened supplies and increased the price of petroleum, of which asphalt is a byproduct. The federal government imposed direct price controls on petroleum, but not on asphalt. Despite the international importance of those events, the jury may have viewed the second factor as of more direct significance to this case. The structural changes at Shell offered a possible explanation for why Shell in 1974 acted out of step with, not only the trade usage and commercially reasonable practices of all suppliers to the asphaltic paving trade on Oahu, but also with its previous agreement with, or at least treatment of, Nanakuli.

Bohner testified to a big organizational change at Shell in 1973 when asphalt sales were moved from the construction sales to the commercial sales department. In addition, by 1973 the top echelon of Shell's asphalt sales had retired. Lewis and Blee, who had negotiated the 1969 contract with Nanakuli, were both gone. n19 Their duties were taken over by three men: Fuller in San Mateo, California, District Manager for Shell Sales, Lawson, and Chippendale, who was Shell's regional asphalt manager in Houston. When the philosophy toward asphalt pricing changed, apparently no one was left who was knowledgeable about the peculiarities of the Hawaiian market or about Shell's long-time relations with Nanakuli or its 1969 agreement, beyond the printed contract.

Shell had begun rethinking its asphalt pricing policies several years before. Swanson, who succeeded Lewis in New York in 1970, wrote an internal memorandum on April 21, 1970, in which he discussed frankly the advantages and disadvantages of price protection of its asphalt buyers. Such a practice assured Shell of captive-volume sales, he wrote. The practice of granting carry-over pricing at times of price increases, however, had the unfortunate side effect of depressing prices in the asphalt market everywhere else, the memorandum concluded. This rethinking apparently led to a November 25, 1970, letter setting out "Shell's New Pricing Policy" at its Honolulu and Hilo terminals. The letter explained the elimination of price protection: "In other words, we will no longer guarantee asphalt prices for the duration of any particular construction projects or for the specific lengths of time. We will, of course, honor any existing prices which have been committed for specific projects for which we have firm contractual commitments." The letter requested a supply contract be signed with Shell within 15 days of the receipt of an award by a customer.

The District Judge based his grant of judgment n. o. v. largely on his belief that, had Nanakuli desired price protection, it should have complied with Shell's request in that 1970 letter, by which we assume he meant Nanakuli should have made a firm contractual commitment with Shell for each project on which its bid was successful within 15 days of award. That conclusion, however, ignores several facts. First, compliance by Nanakuli with the letter's demand that a contract be signed within 15 days of an award would have offered Nanakuli little, if any, protection. Nanakuli still would have been stuck with only charging the government the price incorporated into its bid if Shell raised its price between bid and award. The purpose of price protection was to guarantee the price in effect when a paver made a bid because of the often lengthy time span between bid and award. Second, if price protection was a part of Nanakuli's 1969 agreement with Shell, Shell had no right to terminate unilaterally that protection. Third, the letter was addressed to "Gentlemen" with Nanakuli's name typed in at the top; it was apparently addressed to all Shell's Hawaiian customers. Fourth, Nanakuli officials testified that they did not believe the letter was applicable to its unusual situation of already having a long-term contract with Shell. Smith and Lennox both testified that they did not view the letter as applicable to that supply contract but only to sales it might make to third parties under the distributorship contract. Shell characterized that argument as disingenuous, given Nanakuli's infrequent, if not nonexistent, sales to third parties. Nevertheless, the letter does assume that a Shell customer would need to sign a contract or purchase order setting forth the terms of sale as well as the price for any asphalt they would need to buy after an award. Nanakuli, on the other hand, already had a supply contract with all the terms of sales set forth, a point its two officials made repeatedly at trial. For example, Smith testified he saw no need to notify Shell because Bohner knew of each project and because the supply contract was a firm contractual commitment with Shell. Shell had added in the 1970 letter: "All previous contractual commitments made prior to the date of this letter will, of course, be honored." Smith's reading of this was that Nanakuli's supply contract with Shell was a firm contractual commitment by Shell and that no further contract was needed. "We felt that this letter was unapplicable (sic) to our supply contract, that we already had a contractual commitment with Shell Oil Company which was not to end before 1975." Smith said he did not discuss with Bohner that part of the letter, which also announced the increase in asphalt prices to $44 on January 1, because "(t)here was no need to. The price had been protected before. He knew it. We knew it." There is an additional reason why Nanakuli might have felt that the letter did not apply to its particular situation. The letter announced that Shell would charge "from this date forward...the posted selling price on the date of purchase." This was different from the express term of Nanakuli's contract with Shell, which was the price in effect at time of *delivery*. Either Shell's agreement with Nanakuli embraced price protection, in which case Shell could not unilaterally abrogate Nanakuli's rights by this letter, or, as Shell argues, only the words on the written contract counted, in which case the price to Nanakuli was Shell's price at delivery. In the latter case, Nanakuli could safely ignore any attempt by Shell to change the price to that at purchase. Given Nanakuli's particular agreement, as it understood the agreement to be, the jury could have believed that Nanakuli officials reacted reasonably in believing that parts of the letter dealing with the need to notify Shell of awards won did not apply to Nanakuli.

Nanakuli's strongest argument as to its failure to comply with the letter was that there was no need to notify Shell, as Bohner already knew of each project as it was bid and each award as it was made. Lennox testified, "The Shell Oil representative was in our office frequently and knew what jobs we had successfully bid." At another point Lennox said, "The Shell representative was in the office and was fully aware of what we were doing and what jobs we had gotten. He was familiar and was more or less a partner in this thing; he even attended the bid openings at times. He was fully aware and congratulated us every time we got a nice big job because it was more for Shell." Bohner kept his principals informed of Nanakuli's projects, Lennox said. He added, "(W)e had always been protected and our understanding was that we were protected and it wasn't necessary to keep making notices." Smith in his deposition said that Bohner only told him that he lacked the authority to grant price protection "after the fact." Since he knew nothing about how Shell arrived at its pricing, Smith assumed Bohner could carry out Shell's agreement to price protect Nanakuli each time it was needed without consulting the mainland.

After Shell's December 31, 1973, letter arrived on January 4, 1974, Smith called Bohner, as he had done before at times of price increases, to ask for price protection, this time on 7200 tons. Bohner told Smith that he would have to get in touch with the mainland, but he expected that the response would be negative. Smith wrote several letters in January and February asking for price protection. After getting no satisfaction, he finally flew to California to meet with Lawson, Fuller, and Chippendale. Chippendale, from the Houston office, was acknowledged by the other two to be the only person with authority to grant price protection. All three Shell officials lacked any understanding of Nanakuli and Shell's long, unique relationship or of the asphaltic trade in Oahu. They had never even seen Shell's contracts with Nanakuli before the meeting. When apprised of the three and their seven-year duration, Fuller remarked on the unusual nature of Nanakuli's relations with Shell, at least within his district. Chippendale felt it was probably unique for Shell anywhere. Smith testified that Fuller admitted to knowing nothing, beyond the printed page of Nanakuli's agreement with Shell, of the background negotiation or Shell's past pricing policies toward Nanakuli.

Chippendale could not understand why Nanakuli even had a distributorship contract giving it a $2 commission on sales; he thought Nanakuli had been paid "illegally." No one had ever heard about Shell giving price protection to Nanakuli before. Instead of asking Bohner directly, Chippendale told Fuller to search the files for something on paper. Fuller testified that Shell would not act without *written* proof of Shell's past price protection of Nanakuli. He admitted he was unable to find anything in the files before 1972 because the departments had been reorganized in that year, about which he informed Chippendale. Chippendale accordingly decided to deny Nanakuli any price protection and wrote a draft of a letter for Fuller to send Nanakuli. He wrote a note to Fuller that he should adopt the "least said" approach with Nanakuli and check any letters with the legal department. When asked at trial if he had ever simply asked Bohner about Shell's past pricing practices toward Nanakuli, Fuller answered, "No, I didn't know we had it, other than the standard policy if we had one which we didn't." Chippendale told Smith in the California meeting that, although 7200 tons represented an infinitesimal amount for Shell, it would set a bad precedent for Shell, since price protection was not Shell's "*current* policy." (emphasis supplied). Shell people told him, Smith testified from contemporaneously made notes, that "any past practice was inapplicable at the present time." Smith testified from those same notes that he had left the meeting under the impression that Shell was going out of business in Hawaii.

We conclude that the decision to deny Nanakuli price protection was made by new Houston management without a full understanding of Shell's 1969 agreement with Nanakuli or any knowledge of its past pricing practices toward Nanakuli. If Shell did commit itself in 1969 to price protect Nanakuli, the Shell officials who made the decisions affecting Nanakuli in 1974 knew nothing about that commitment. Nor did they make any effective effort to find out. They acted instead solely in reliance on the 1969 contract's express price term, devoid of the commercial context that the Code says is necessary to an understanding of the meaning of the written word. Whatever the legal enforceability of Nanakuli's right, Nanakuli officials seem to have acted in good faith reliance on its right, as they understood it, to price protection and rightfully felt betrayed by Shell's failure to act with any understanding of its past practices toward Nanakuli.

V
Scope Of Trade Usage

The validity of the jury verdict in this case depends on four legal questions. First, how broad was the trade to whose usages Shell was bound under its 1969 agreement with Nanakuli: did it extend to the Hawaiian asphaltic paving trade or was it limited merely to the purchase and sale of asphalt, which would only include evidence of practices by Shell and Chevron? Second, were the two instances of price protection of Nanakuli by Shell in 1970 and 1971 waivers of the 1969 contract as a matter of law or was the jury entitled to find that they constituted a course of performance of the contract? Third, could the jury have construed an express contract term of Shell's posted price at delivery as reasonably consistent with a trade usage and Shell's course of performance of the 1969 contract of price protection, which consisted of charging the old price at times of price increases, either for a period of time or for specific tonnage committed at a fixed price in non-escalating contracts? Fourth, could the jury have found that good faith obliged Shell to at least give advance notice of a $32 increase in 1974, that is, could they have found that the commercially reasonable standards of fair dealing in the trade in Hawaii in 1974 were to give some form of price protection?

We approach the first issue in this case mindful that an underlying purpose of the U.C.C. as enacted in Hawaii is to allow for liberal interpretation of commercial usages. The Code provides, "This chapter shall be liberally construed and applied to promote its underlying purposes and policies." Haw.Rev.Stat. § 490:1-102(1). Only three purposes are listed, one of which is "(t)o permit the continued expansion of commercial practices through custom, usage and agreement of the parties;...." *Id.* § 490:1-102(2)(b). The drafters of the Code explain:

> This Act is drawn to provide *flexibility* so that, since it is intended to be a semipermanent piece of legislation, it will provide its own machinery for *expansion of commercial practices*. It is intended to make it possible for the law embodied in this Act to be developed by the courts in the light of *unforeseen and new circumstances and practices....*
>
> .... The text of each section should be *read in the light of the purpose and policy* of the rule or principle in question, as also of the Act as a whole, and the application of the language should be *construed narrowly or broadly,* as the case may be, in *conformity with the purposes and policies* involved.
>
> .... (t)he Code seeks to *avoid...interference with evolutionary growth....*
>
> This principle of freedom of contract is subject to specific exceptions found elsewhere in the Act.... (An example being the bar on contractual exclusion of the requirement of good faith, although the parties can set out standards for same.)...In this connection, Section 1-205 incorporating into the agreement prior course of dealing and usages of trade is of particular importance.

Id., Comments 1 & 2 (emphasis supplied). We read that to mean that courts should not stand in the way of new commercial practices and usages by insisting on maintaining the narrow and inflexible old rules of interpretation. We seek the definition of trade usage not only in the express language of the Code but also in its underlying purposes, defining it liberally to fit the facts of the particular commercial context here.[26]

---

26. Shell would have us apply the definition of a merchant in the Code, which is defined as "a person who deals in goods of the kind or otherwise by his occupation holds himself out as having knowledge or skill peculiar to the practices or goods involved in the transaction...." *Id.* § 490:2-104. By that definition, says Shell, it only dealt in or held itself out as knowledgeable about asphalt, not aggregates or even asphaltic paving. Leaving aside the arguable question of whether Shell's Bohner held himself out as knowledgeable about asphaltic paving, see textual discussion supra, the trade usage provisions do not refer to merchants but to "parties." See, e.g. id. 490:1-205(3), (6) & Comments 1, 4, 7 & 9. Probably for that reason Comment 2 to Section 2-104, on which Shell relies, does not list the trade usage provision among those to which one definition or another of "merchant" is applicable. The Comment reads, "The special provisions as to merchants appear only in this Article (on Sales) and they are of three kinds." The first kind are provisions for which "almost every person in business would therefore, be deemed to be a "merchant'...since the practices involved...are non-specialized business practices such as answering mail." The second type includes provisions on warranties of merchantability and entrusting situations, which only apply "to a much smaller group" with "professional status as to particular kinds of goods."

The Code defines usage of trade as "any practice or method of dealing having such regularity of observance in a *place, vocation or trade* as to justify an expectation that it will be observed with respect to the transaction in question." *Id.* § 490:1-205(2) (emphasis supplied). We understand the use of the word "or" to mean that parties can be bound by a usage common to the place they are in business, even if it is not the usage of their particular vocation or trade. That reading is borne out by the repetition of the disjunctive "or" in subsection 3, which provides that usages "in the vocation or trade in which they are engaged or of which they are or should be aware give particular meaning to and supplement or qualify terms of an agreement." *Id.* § 490:1-205(3). The drafters' Comments say that trade usage is to be used to reach the "....commercial meaning of the agreement...." by interpreting the language "as meaning what it may fairly be expected to mean to parties involved in the particular transaction *in a given locality or in a given vocation or trade.*" Id., Comment 4 (emphasis supplied). The inference of the two subsections and the Comment, read together, is that a usage need not necessarily be one practiced by members of the party's own trade or vocation to be binding if it is so commonly practiced in a locality that a party should be aware of it. Subsection 5 also shows the importance of the place where the usage is practiced: "An applicable usage of trade in the place where any part of performance is to occur shall be used in interpreting the agreement as to that part of the performance." The validity of this interpretation is additionally demonstrated by the Comment of the drafters: "Subsection (3), giving the prescribed effect to usages of which the parties "are or should be aware', reinforces the provision of subsection (2) requiring not universality but only the described "regularity of observance' of the practice or method. This subsection also reinforces the point of subsection (2) *that such usages may be either general to trade or particular to a special branch of trade.*" Id., Comment 7 (emphasis supplied). This language indicates that Shell would be bound not only by usages of sellers of asphalt but by more general usages on Oahu, as long as those usages were so regular in their observance that Shell should have been aware of them. This reading of the Code, in our opinion, achieves an equitable result. A party is always held to conduct generally observed by members of his chosen trade because the other party is justified in so assuming unless he indicates otherwise. He is held to more general business practices to the extent of his actual knowledge of those practices or to the degree his ignorance of those practices is not excusable: they were so generally practiced he should have been aware of them.

No U.C.C. cases have been found on this point, but the court's reading of the Code language is similar to that of two of the best-known commentators on the U.C.C.:

Under pre-Code law, a trade usage was not operative against a party who *was not a member of the trade unless he actually knew of it or the other party could reasonably believe he knew of it.*

J. White & R. Summers, *Uniform Commercial Code,* § 12-6 at 371 (1972) (emphasis supplied) (citing 3 A. Corbin, Corbin on Contracts § 557 at 248 (1960)).

The third group includes the special good-faith requirement for merchants, which is Nanakuli's second theory for recovery on its price protection claim. The good faith and other provisions of that group apply to both types of merchants. *See* textual discussion on good-faith requirement for merchants *infra.*

This view has been carried forward by 1-205(3),

> .... (U)sage of the trade is only binding on *members of the trade* involved *or persons who know or should know about it.* Persons who should be aware of the trade usage doubtless *include those who regularly deal with members of the relevant trade,* and also members of a second trade that commonly deals with members of a relevant trade (for example, farmers should know something of seed selling).

White & Summers, *supra,* § 12-6 at 371. Using that analogy, even if Shell did not "regularly deal" with aggregate supplies, it did deal constantly and almost exclusively on Oahu with one asphalt paver. It therefore should have been aware of the usage of Nanakuli and other asphaltic pavers to bid at fixed prices and therefore receive price protection from their materials suppliers due to the refusal by government agencies to accept escalation clauses. Therefore, we do not find the lower court abused its discretion or misread the Code as applied to the peculiar facts of this case in ruling that the applicable trade was the asphaltic paving trade in Hawaii. An asphalt seller should be held to the usages of trade in general as well as those of asphalt sellers and common usages of those to whom they sell. Certainly, under the unusual facts of this case it was not unreasonable for the judge to extend trade usages to include practices of other material suppliers toward Shell's primary and perhaps only customer on Oahu. He did exclude, on Shell's motion *in limine,* evidence of cement suppliers. He only held Shell to routine practices in Hawaii by the suppliers of the two major ingredients of asphaltic paving, that is, asphalt and aggregate. Those usages were only practiced towards two major pavers. It was not unreasonable to expect Shell to be knowledgeable about so small a market. In so ruling, the judge undoubtedly took into account Shell's half-million dollar investment in Oahu strictly because of a long-term commitment by Nanakuli, its actions as partner in promoting Nanakuli's expansion on Oahu, and the fact that its sales on Oahu were almost exclusively to Nanakuli for use in asphaltic paving. The wisdom of the pre-trial ruling was demonstrated by evidence at trial that Shell's agent in Hawaii stayed in close contact with Nanakuli and was knowledgeable about both the asphaltic paving market in general and Nanakuli's bidding procedures and economics in particular.

Shell argued not only that the definition of trade was too broad, but also that the practice itself was not sufficiently regular to reach the level of a usage and that Nanakuli failed to show with enough precision how the usage was carried out in order for a jury to calculate damages. The extent of a usage is ultimately a jury question. The Code provides, "The existence and scope of such a usage are to be proved as facts." Haw.Rev.Stat. § 490:1-205(2).[27] The practice must have "such regularity of observance... as to justify an expectation that it will be observed...." Id. The Comment explains:

> The ancient English tests for "custom" are abandoned in this connection. Therefore, it is not required that a usage of trade be "ancient or immemorial," "universal" or the like.... (Full) recognition is thus available for new usages and for usages currently observed by the great majority of decent dealers, even though dissidents ready to cut corners do not agree.

---

27. Written trade codes, however, are left to the court to interpret. Id.

Id., Comment 5. The Comment's demand that "not universality but only the de-scribed "regularity of observance' " is required reinforces the provision only giv-ing "effect to usages of which the parties "are or should be aware'...." " Id., Comment 7. A "regularly observed" practice of protection, of which Shell "should have been aware," was enough to constitute a usage that Nanakuli had reason to believe was incorporated into the agreement.[28]

Nanakuli went beyond proof of a regular observance. It proved and offered to prove[29] that price protection was probably a universal practice by suppliers to the asphaltic paving trade in 1969.[30] It had been practiced by H.C. & D. since at least 1962, by P.C. & A. since well before 1960, and by Chevron routinely for years, with the last specific instance before the contract being March, 1969, as shown by documentary evidence. The only usage evidence missing was the behavior by Shell, the only other asphalt supplier in Hawaii, prior to 1969. That was because its only major customer was Nanakuli and the judge ruled prior course of dealings be-tween Shell and Nanakuli inadmissible. Shell did not point in rebuttal to one in-stance of failure to price protect by any supplier to an asphalt paver in Hawaii be-fore its own 1974 refusal to price protect Nanakuli. Thus, there clearly was enough proof for a jury to find that the practice of price protection in the asphaltic paving trade existed in Hawaii in 1969 and was regular enough in its observance to rise to the level of a usage that would be binding on Nanakuli and Shell.

Shell next argues that, even if such a usage existed, its outlines were not pre-cise enough to determine whether Shell would have extended the old price for Nanakuli for several months or would have charged the old price on the volume of tonnage committed at that price. The jury awarded Nanakuli damages based on the specific tonnage committed before the price increase of 1974. Shell says the jury could not have ascertained with enough certainty how price protection was carried out to calculate such an award for Nanakuli. The argument is not persuasive. The Code provides, "The remedies provided by this chapter shall be liberally administered to the end that the aggrieved party may be put in as good a position as if the other party had fully performed...." Id. § 490:1-106(1). The Comments list as one of three purposes of this section "to reject any doctrine that damages must be calculable with mathematical accuracy. Compensatory damages are often at best approximate: they have to be proved with whatever definiteness and accuracy the facts permit, but no more." Id., Comment 1. Nanakuli got advance notices of each but the disputed increase by Shell, as well as an extension of several months at the old price in 1970, 1971, 1977, and 1978. Shell protests that in 1970 and 1971 Nanakuli's protected tonnage only

---

28. White and Summers write that Code requirements for proving a usage are "far less stringent" than the old ones for custom. "A usage of trade need not be well known, let alone "universal.' " It only needs to be regular enough that the parties expect it to be observed. White & Summers, supra § 3-3 at 87 (emphasis supplied). "Note particularly (in 1-205 (1) & (2)) that it is not necessary for both parties to be consciously aware of the trade usage. It is enough if the trade usage is such as to "justify an expectation' of its observance." Id. at 84.

29. Nanakuli made an offer of proof, which the judge rejected as not sufficiently rele-vant to the asphaltic paving trade, that cement suppliers routinely price protected pavers for years.

30. All evidence was that trade usage continued to be universally practiced after 1969, even by Shell.

amounted to 3,300 and 1,100 tons, respectively. Chevron's price protection of
H.B. in 1969 however, is also part of the trade usage; H.B.'s protection
amounted to 12,000 tons. The increase in Nanakuli's tonnage by 1974 is explained by its growth since the 1970 and 1971 increases.

In addition, the scope of protection offered by a particular usage is left to
the jury:

> In cases of a well established line of usage varying from the general rules
> of this Act where the precise amount of the variation has not been
> worked out into a single standard, the party relying on the usage is enti-
> tled, in any event, to the minimum variation demonstrated. The whole is
> not to be disregarded because no particular line of detail has been estab-
> lished. In case a dominant pattern (of usage) has been fairly evidenced,
> the party relying on the usage is entitled...to go to the trier of fact on
> the question of whether such dominant pattern has been incorporated
> into the agreement.

Id. § 490:1-205, Comment 9. Summers and White write that a usage, under the
language of 1-205(2), need not be "certain and precise" to fit within the definition
of "any practice or method of dealing." White & Summer, *supra*, § 3-3 at 87. The
manner in which the usage of price protection was carried out was presented with
sufficient precision to allow the jury to calculate damages at $220,800.

VI

Waiver Or Course Of Performance

Course of performance under the Code is the action of the parties in carrying
out the contract at issue, whereas course of dealing consists of relations between
the parties *prior* to signing that contract. Evidence of the latter was excluded by
the District Judge; evidence of the former consisted of Shell's price protection of
Nanakuli in 1970 and 1971. Shell protested that the jury could not have found
that those two instances of price protection amounted to a course of performance of its 1969 contract, relying on two Code comments. First, one instance
does not constitute a course of performance. "A single occasion of conduct does
not fall within the language of this section...." Haw.Rev.Stat. § 490:2-208, Comment 4. Although the Comment rules out one instance, it does not further delineate how many acts are needed to form a course of performance. The prior occasions here were only two, but they constituted the only occasions before 1974
that would call for such conduct. In addition, the language used by a top asphalt
official of Shell in connection with the first price protection of Nanakuli indicated that Shell felt that Nanakuli was entitled to some form of price protection.
On that occasion in 1970 Blee, who had negotiated the contract with Nanakuli
and was familiar with exactly what terms Shell was bound to by that agreement,
wrote of the need to "bargain" with Nanakuli over the extent of price protection
to be given, indicating that some price protection was a legal right of Nanakuli's
under the 1969 agreement.

Shell's second defense is that the Comment expresses a preference for an interpretation of waiver.

> 3. Where it is difficult to determine whether a particular act merely sheds
> light on the meaning of the agreement or represents a waiver of a term of

the agreement, the preference is in favor of "waiver" whenever such construction, plus the application of the provisions on the reinstatement of rights waived..., is needed to preserve the flexible character of commercial contracts and to prevent surprise or other hardship.

Id., Comment 3. The preference for waiver only applies, however, where acts are ambiguous. It was within the province of the jury to determine whether those acts were ambiguous, and if not, whether they constituted waivers or a course of performance of the contract. The jury's interpretation of those acts as a course of performance was bolstered by evidence offered by Shell that it again price protected Nanakuli on the only two occasions of post-1974 price increases, in 1977 and 1978.[31]

VII

Express Terms As Reasonably Consistent With Usage In Course of Performance

Perhaps one of the most fundamental departures of the Code from prior contract law is found in the parol evidence rule and the definition of an agreement between two parties. Under the U.C.C., an agreement goes beyond the written words on a piece of paper. " "Agreement' means the bargain of the parties in fact as found in their language or by implication from other circumstances including course of dealing or usage of trade or course of performance as provided in this chapter (sections 490:1-205 and 490:2-208)." *Id.* § 490:1-201(3). Express terms, then, do not constitute the entire agreement, which must be sought also in evidence of usages, dealings, and performance of the contract itself. The purpose of evidence of usages, which are defined in the previous section, is to help to understand the entire agreement.

> (Usages are) a factor in reaching the commercial meaning of the agreement which the parties have made. The language used is to be interpreted as meaning what it may fairly be expected to mean to parties involved in the particular commercial transaction in a given locality or in a given vocation or trade.... Part of the agreement of the parties...is to be sought for in the usages of trade which furnish the background and give particular meaning to the language used, and are the framework of common understanding controlling any general rules of law which hold only when there is no such understanding.

Id. § 490:1-205, Comment 4. Course of dealings is more important than usages of the trade, being specific usages between the two parties to the contract. "(Course) of dealing controls usage of trade." *Id.* § 490:1-205(4). It "is a sequence of previous conduct between the parties to a particular transaction which is fairly to be regarded as establishing a common basis of understanding for interpreting their expressions and other conduct." *Id.* § 490:1-205(1). Much of the

---

31. Bohner testified on direct for Shell at the 1978 trial that the two later instances of price protection occurred "this" year and "last" year, by which he could have meant 1976 and 1977. Bohner's testimony was that on those later occasions Shell gave Nanakuli six and three or four months' notice of an increase to allow Nanakuli to buy tonnage it had committed at the old price. He defined Shell's actions as "in effect carryover pricing." The jury's finding was reasonable in light of the circumstances of universal price protection by asphalt and aggregate suppliers, as well as by Shell on all price increases except 1974.

evidence of prior dealings between Shell and Nanakuli in negotiating the 1963 contract and in carrying out similar earlier contracts was excluded by the court.[32]

A commercial agreement, then, is broader than the written paper and its meaning is to be determined not just by the language used by them in the written contract but "by their action, read and interpreted in the light of commercial practices and other surrounding circumstances. The measure and background for interpretation are set by the commercial context, which may explain and supplement even the language of a formal or final writing." *Id.*, Comment 1. Performance, usages, and prior dealings are important enough to be admitted always, even for a final and complete agreement; only if they cannot be reasonably reconciled with the express terms of the contract are they not binding on the parties. "The express terms of an agreement and an applicable course of dealing or usage of trade shall be construed wherever reasonable as consistent with each other; but when such construction is unreasonable express terms control both course of dealing and usage of trade and course of dealing controls usage of trade." Id. § 490:1-205(4).

Of these three, then, the most important evidence of the agreement of the parties is their actual performance of the contract. Id. The operative definition of course of performance is as follows: "Where the contract for sale involves repeated occasions for performance by either party with knowledge of the nature of the performance and opportunity for objection to it by the other, any course of performance accepted or acquiesced in without objection shall be relevant to determine the meaning of the agreement." Id. § 490:2-208(1). "Course of dealing... is restricted, literally, to a sequence of conduct between the parties previous to the agreement. However, the provisions of the Act on course of performance make it clear that a sequence of conduct after or under the agreement may have equivalent meaning (Section 2-208)." Id. 490:1-205, Comment 2. The importance of evidence of course of performance is explained: "The parties themselves know best what they have meant by their words of agreement and their action under that agreement is the best indication of what that meaning was. This section thus rounds out the set of factors which determines the meaning of the "agreement'..." Id. § 490:2-208, Comment 1. "Under this section a course of performance is always relevant to determine the meaning of the agreement." Id., Comment 2.[33]

Our study of the Code provisions and Comments, then, form the first basis of our holding that a trade usage to price protect pavers at times of price increases for work committed on nonescalating contracts could reasonably be construed as consistent with an express term of seller's posted price at delivery. Since the agreement of the parties is broader than the express terms and includes usages, which may even add terms to the agreement,[34] and since the commercial background provided

---

32. See footnote 31, supra.

33. Section 2-208, much like 1-205, provides "(t)he express terms of the agreement and any such course of performance, as well as any course of dealing and usage of trade, shall be construed whenever reasonable as consistent with each other; but when such construction is unreasonable, express terms shall control course of performance and course of performance shall control both course of dealing and usage of trade (section 490:1-205)." Id. § 490:2-208(2).

34. "The agreement of the parties includes that part of their bargain found in course of dealing, usage of trade, or course of performance. These sources are relevant not only to the

by those usages is vital to an understanding of the agreement, we follow the Code's mandate to proceed on the assumption that the parties have included those usages unless they cannot reasonably be construed as consistent with the express terms.

Federal courts usually have been lenient in not ruling out consistent additional terms or trade usage for apparent inconsistency with express terms. The leading case on the subject is *Columbia Nitrogen Corp. v. Royster Co.*, 451 F.2d 3 (4th Cir. 1971). Columbia, the buyer, had in the past primarily produced and sold nitrogen to Royster. When Royster opened a new plant that produced more phosphate than it needed, the parties reversed roles and signed a sales contract for Royster to sell excess phosphate to Columbia. The contract terms set out the price that would be charged by Royster and the amount to be sold. It provided for the price to go up if certain events occurred but did not provide for price declines. When the price of nitrogen fell precipitously, Columbia refused to accept the full amount of nitrogen specified in the contract after Royster refused to renegotiate the contract price. The District Judge's exclusion of usage of the trade and course of dealing to explain the express quantity term in the contract was reversed. Columbia had offered to prove that the quantity set out in the contract was a mere projection to be adjusted according to market forces. Ambiguity was not necessary for the admission of evidence of usage and prior dealings.[35] Even though the lengthy contract was the result of long and careful negotiations and apparently covered every contingency, the appellate court ruled that "the test of admissibility is not whether the contract appears on its face to be complete in every detail, but whether the proffered evidence of course of dealing and trade usage reasonably can be construed as consistent with the express terms of the agreement." *Id.* at 9. The express quantity term could be reasonably construed as consistent with a usage that such terms would be mere projections for several reasons:[36] (1) the contract did not expressly state that usage and dealings evidence would be excluded; (2) the contract was silent on the adjustment of price

interpretation of express contract terms, but may themselves constitute contract terms." White & Summers, *supra*, § 3-3 at 84.

35. As discussed earlier, the District Judge here mistakenly equated ambiguity with admissibility. He said, "I think this is a close case. On the face of the contract it would seem to be unambiguous," although acknowledging that liberal commentators on the Code would let in evidence of usage and performance even without ambiguity. He only let in usage evidence because Shell's answer to interrogatory 11 provided some ambiguity, *see* note 16 *supra*, saying "I think if these can be consistently used to explain the apparently unambiguous terms, they should be allowed in." In fact, this court has ruled that ambiguity is not necessary to admit usage evidence. *Board of Trade of San Francisco v. Swiss Credit Bank*, 597 F.2d 146, 148 (9th Cir. 1979).

36. State court cases have interpreted express quantity as mere projections in similar circumstances. E. g., *Campbell v. Hostetter Farms, Inc.*, 251 Pa.Super. 232, 380 A.2d 463, 466–67 (1977). (Express agreement to sell a specified number of bushels of corn, wheat, and soy beans was not, as a matter of law, inconsistent with a usage of the trade that amounts specified in contracts are only estimates of a seller-farmer's farms); *Loeb & Co. v. Martin*, 295 Ala. 262, 327 So.2d 711, 714–15 (Ala. 1976) (It was a jury question whether, in light of trade usage, "all cotton produced on 400 acres" called for all cotton seller produced on 400 acres or for 400 acres of cotton.); *Heggblade-Marguleas-Tenneco, Inc. v. Sunshine Biscuit, Inc.*, 59 Cal.App.3d 948, 131 Cal. Rptr. 183, 188–89 (1976) (Usage in the potato-processing trade that the amount specified in the contract was merely an estimate of buyer's requirements was admissible); *Paymaster Oil Mill Co. v. Mitchell*, 319 So.2d 652, 657–58 (Miss.1975) (Additional term that the seller was not obliged to deliver the full 4000 bushels of soy beans called for in the contract was admissible).

or quantities in a declining market; (3) the minimum tonnage was expressed in the contract as Products Supplied, not Products Purchased; (4) the default clause of the contract did not state a penalty for failure to take delivery; and (5) apparently most important in the court's view, the parties had deviated from similar express terms in earlier contracts in times of declining market. *Id.* at 9–10. As here, the contract's merger clause said that there were no oral agreements. The court explained that its ruling "reflects the reality of the marketplace and avoids the overly legalistic interpretations which the Code seeks to abolish." *Id.* at 10. The Code assigns dealing and usage evidence "unique and important roles" and therefore "overly simplistic and overly legalistic interpretation of a contract should be shunned." *Id.* at 11.

Usage and an oral understanding led to much the same interpretation of a quantity term specifying delivery of 500 tons of stainless-steel solids in *Michael Schiavone & Sons, Inc. v. Securalloy Co.*, 312 F. Supp. 801 (Conn. 1970). In denying summary judgment for plaintiff-buyer, the court ruled that defendant-seller could attempt to prove that the quantity term was modified by an oral understanding, in line with a trade usage, that seller would only supply as many tons as he could, with 500 tons the upper limit. The court reasoned that an additional term with a lesser effect than total contradiction or negation of a contract term can be a consistent term and "(evidence) that the quantity to be supplied by defendant was orally understood to be up to 500 tons cannot be said to be inconsistent with the terms of the written contract which specified the quantity as "500 Gross Ton." Id. at 804.[37]

The Tenth Circuit in *Amerine National Corp. v. Denver Feed Co.*, 493 F.2d 1275 (10th Cir. 1974), found that the warranty that Amerine, the seller, would provide turkeys was not breached by delivery of "H&N" turkeys instead of "Amerine". In light of Amerine's prior dealings and a trade usage that "Amerine" or any trade-name turkey simply meant any turkeys sold by that manufacturer, not a particular kind or breed of turkey, any agreement to provide turkeys did not oblige Amerine to provide only its own strain of turkeys.

The Fifth Circuit, in a carefully reasoned opinion, *Chase Manhattan Bank v. First Marion Bank*, 437 F.2d 1040 (5th Cir. 1971), reversed the lower court's refusal to allow usage and dealing evidence that seemingly contradicted the express

---

37. The Seventh Circuit in dicta has implied that a written contract calling for 36-inch wide steel could be modified by a usage in the steel industry that a 36-inch specification "includes by definition steel which actually measures 37 in width." *Decker Steel Co. v. Exchange National Bank*, 330 F.2d 82, 85 (7th Cir. 1964). That circuit has not been as generous in allowing modification of express terms by course of performance or additional terms. In *V-M Corp. v. Bernard Distributing Co.*, 447 F.2d 864 (7th Cir. 1971), when the manufacturer sued the distributor of electronic equipment for goods delivered, distributor Bernard counter-claimed for breach of warranty. The counterclaim was dismissed because the written contract expressly disclaimed all but an express warranty and limited liability by excluding consequential or special damages, even though the course of performance by V-M had been to accept return of a portion of the goods that were not defective under the express warranty. Where the course of performance cannot be harmonized with the express terms, the court held, the express controls. *Id.* at 867–68. Although the court did not say so, the result might well have been different had usage evidence been presented to reinforce the acts constituting course of performance. In *Luria Brothers & Co. v. Pielet Brothers Scrap Iron & Metal, Inc.*, 600 F.2d 103, 110 (7th Cir. 1979), the court upheld a jury verdict for plaintiff-buyer in a suit for nondelivery, affirming the exclusion of parol evidence of an additional term that seller's obligation to sell scrap metal was conditioned on its ability to obtain the metal from a particular supplier.

term. The standby agreement in *Chase* stated that none of the banks would unilaterally demand that the debtor pay up or sell the collateral stock unless all creditors agreed to the sale. The subordination agreement—signed after the standby agreement, incorporated into it, and by its terms to last a maximum of 18 months—provided that the other creditor banks were subordinated to the extent of $1 a share to Chase because of its further loan to the debtor. The usage of the trade and the course of dealing between the parties, ruled inadmissible by the lower court, were that the parties had not intended to limit the duration of the subordination agreement to 18 months.[38] The appellate court reversed, directing that evidence of usage and dealings be admitted because it "merely delineates a commercial backdrop for intelligent interpretation of the agreement," without "delimit(ing) a particular party's intent, except insofar as it reveals that some ascribed intent might be ludicrous in the commercial world." *Id.* at 1046.[39] The court wrote, "In providing for the admission of such evidence, the Code manifests the law's recognition of the fact that perception is conditioned by environment: unless a judge considers a contract in the proper commercial setting, his view is apt to be distorted or myopic, increasing the probability of error." Id. The court added, "If, in light of banking practices in problem loan situations and Chase's dealings with First Marion, an unsecured loan to the (debtor) would have seemed unreasonable, ambiguities arise within the subordination provision." *Id.* at 1047. Usage and dealings evidence here would "permit analysis of the written agreement in the proper commercial setting. Such evidence might disclose ambiguities within the provisions of the agreement...." *Id.* For a court to use usage evidence to better understand express terms does not mean it is allowing the written instrument to be contradicted; the use of such evidence "simply places the court in the position of the parties when they made the contract, and enables it to appreciate the force of the words they used in reducing it to writing." *Id.* at 1048. "The object of rules of construction generally, and of parol evidence particularly, is to ascertain the intention of the parties." *Id.*[40] It is noteworthy that in Chase, the contradiction was total, not the partial exception Nanakuli argues here.

---

38. Although Section 1-202 did not apply because the contract did not involve the sale of goods, the court looked by analogy to the parol evidence rule in Article 1 of the Code as implicitly restricting the types of evidence that a court could exclude for other types of contracts.

39. Chase had offered proof of a usage "that termination of a subordination agreement prior to extinction of the debt allegedly secured by that agreement, would be commercially unsound. (Thus) no bank or commercial institution would propose or countenance such charity." *Id.* at 1047.

40. More recently the same court has explained that the Code departs from the traditional parol evidence rule, which barred as irrelevant "the subjective intent of one...unless it is shown that that intent was communicated to the other party." *Foxco Industries, Ltd. v. Fabric World, Inc.,* 595 F.2d 976, 984 (5th Cir. 1979). Under the U.C.C., in contrast, the fact that the buyer "did not know of the industry's usage and custom or of the standards in question is of no moment; the parties to a contract such as the one in issue are presumed to have intended the incorporation of trade usage in striking their bargain." Therefore, the buyer's protest that he was not a member of the trade association whose standards were at issue and was unaware of their existence at the time, was not a valid defense. "(The Association's) standards would certainly qualify as trade usage, and thus were admissible, notwithstanding Fabric World's unawareness of them." *Id.* at 985. Accord, Heggblade, *supra,* note 35.

The Fourth Circuit has been similarly liberal in admitting parol evidence to contradict express terms. After its pacesetting decision in *Columbia Nitrogen, supra*, it held in *Brunswick Box Co. v. Coutinho, Caro & Co.*, 617 F.2d 355, 360–61 (4th Cir. 1980), that "the Parol Evidence Rule is not a bar to the introduction of extrinsic evidence as to the intention of the parties in the use of the term "F.A.S. Norfolk, Virginia', in the written agreement," even though "the term, on its face, is unambiguous." The appeals court, therefore, reversed the lower court's exclusion ruling and remanded for trial. The term "F.A.S." is defined by the Code as meaning delivered to the buyer alongside the vessel by the seller, which was also the usage in the port. The plaintiff-seller, however, argued that the dealings between the parties leading to the contract, the actual agreement of the parties, and their course of performance of the contract were that the seller would unload on the dock area. The Code does not bar such evidence "simply because a contract appears on its face to be complete,..." and therefore plaintiff-seller should have been allowed to show that the parties agreed that the seller would unload the material on the dock area rather than alongside the vessel. *Id.* at 359.

The Ninth Circuit's most recent reference to the U.C.C.'s parol evidence rule was in a similar case, *Board of Trade of San Francisco v. Swiss Credit Bank*, 597 F.2d 146 (9th Cir. 1979), in which this court considered the meaning of an express term in a letter of credit requiring presentment of a "full set clean on board bills of lading." When the components for the electronic calculators were sent by air, the bank protested that ocean shipment was required by the trade usage as to the express term. Although the U.C.C.'s definition of bills of lading includes airbills, this court upheld the bank's right to prove a trade usage that in essence contradicted the Code's broad definition of bills of lading by showing that only ocean bills of lading were allowable. The summary judgment for plaintiff was reversed and the case remanded for trial on whether the bank's dishonor of the documentary letter of credit was wrongful. The court cited the California Supreme Court, "The test of admissibility of extrinsic evidence to explain the meaning of a written instrument is not whether it appears to the court to be plain and unambiguous on its face, but whether the proffered evidence is relevant to prove a meaning to which the language of the instrument is reasonably susceptible." *Id.* at 148–49.[41]

* * *

Historically, in an action to determine the parties' contractual rights under an agreement, the court's only inquiry would center around whether the written agreement was a total integration of the parties' intent. If so, absent evi-

---

41. The difference between usage evidence and evidence of additional terms is that the former is always admissible, although not controlling if not reasonably consistent with the express terms, whereas the latter are not even admitted if the court finds the written contract is a complete and exclusive statement of the agreement's terms. Despite the added difficulty, then, of reconciling additional and express terms, courts have admitted additional terms more at variance with the writing than here. For example, in *Pacific Indemnity Co. v. Mc-Dermott Brothers Co.*, 336 F. Supp. 963, 969–70 (M.D.Pa.1971), parol evidence was admissible to show an oral agreement for one party to purchase insurance on the aircraft to cover the other despite the lack of any insurance provision in the sales contract. Similar evidence of an oral agreement was admitted in *Crispin Co. v. Delaware Steel Co.*, 283 F. Supp. 574, 575 (E.D.Pa.1968), to show whether a letter of credit formed a part of a total agreement, along with the sales contract, in which case transportation by charter-party vessel was prohibited and a breach of contract, although not forbidden by the sales contract.

dence of mistake or fraud, the rule barred introduction of *any* extrinsic evidence that varied or altered the terms....However, since the advent of the adoption of the (Code) in practically every state, rigid adherence to the exclusionary effects of the parol evidence rule has seen a relaxation of its application by the courts in many jurisdictions. This has been largely attributed to a combination of the U.C.C.'s intent to facilitate the flow in business and commercial transactions, and the widespread use of standard business forms to evidence the existence of contractual relationships between parties. For example, article 2 of the U.C.C. permits the court to consider a far wider range of extrinsic evidence to discern the intent of the parties than has been permitted under contract law....(W)e think that expansion of the liberal approach toward the receipt of extrinsic evidence, in the face of the proliferation of standard form contracts and commercial paper, gives the courts a wider insight into the real intent of the parties.

J. H. Levie, *Trade Usage and Custom Under the Common Law and the Uniform Commercial Code*, 40 N.Y.U.L.Rev. 1101 (1965), states:

> When trade usage adds new terms to cover matters on which the agreement is silent the court is really making a contract for the parties, even though it says it only consulted trade usage to find the parties' probable intent. There is nothing wrong or even unusual about this practice, which really is no different from reading constructive conditions into a contract. Nevertheless the court does create new obligations, and perhaps that is why the courts often say that usage...must be proved by clear and convincing evidence.

Kirst, Usage of Trade and Course of Dealing: Subversion of the UCC Theory, 1977 Law Forum, 811.

...Here the evidence was overwhelming that all suppliers to the asphaltic paving trade price protected customers under the same types of circumstances. Chevron's contract with H.B. was a similar long-term supply contract between a buyer and seller with very close relations, on a form supplied by the seller, covering sales of asphalt, and setting the price at seller's posted price, with no mention of price protection. The same commentator offers a second guideline:

> Because the stock printed forms cannot always reflect the changing methods of business, members of the trade may do business with a standard clause in the forms that they ignore in practice. If the trade consistently ignores obsolete clauses at variance with actual trade practices, a litigant can maintain that it is reasonable that the courts also ignore the clauses. Similarly, members of a trade may handle a particular subset of commercial transactions in a manner consistent with written terms because the writing cannot provide for all variations or contingencies. Thus, if the trade regards an express term and a trade usage as consistent because the usage is not a complete contradiction but only an occasional but definite exception to a written term, the courts should interpret the contract according to the usage.

Kirst, *supra*, at 824. Levie, *supra*, at 1112, writes, "Astonishing as it will seem to most practicing attorneys, under the Code it will be possible in some cases to use custom to contradict the written agreement....Therefore usage may be used to 'qualify' the agreement, which presumably means to 'cut down' express terms although not to negate them entirely." Here, the express price term was

"Shell's Posted Price at time of delivery." A total negation of that term would be that the buyer was to set the price. It is a less than complete negation of the term that an unstated exception exists at times of price increases, at which times the old price is to be charged, for a certain period or for a specified tonnage, on work already committed at the lower price on nonescalating contracts. Such a usage forms a broad and important exception to the express term, but does not swallow it entirely. Therefore, we hold that, under these particular facts, a reasonable jury could have found that price protection was incorporated into the 1969 agreement between Nanakuli and Shell and that price protection was reasonably consistent with the express term of seller's posted price at delivery.

＊　＊　＊

... [W]e reverse the judgment of the District Court and reinstate the jury verdict for Nanakuli in the amount of $ 220,800, plus interest according to law.

REVERSED AND REMANDED WITH DIRECTIONS TO ENTER FINAL JUDGMENT.

Notes and Questions

1. Interpreting Relational Contracts: Founded in mutually-beneficial exchange, the relational approach abandons the strict reliance on discrete contracts and focuses on the relationship itself. In a sense, the relationship takes on the properties of "a minisociety with a vast array of norms beyond the norms centered on the exchange and its immediate processes." Ian Macneil, *Contracts: Adjustment of Long-Term Economic Relations Under Classical, Neoclassical, and Relational Contract Law*, 72 Northwestern Law Review 854, 887 (1978). The exchange is no longer dominant; that is, the original contractual agreement is no longer considered the only source of adjustment processes when the relationship is in trouble. Instead, "[t]he reference point is the entire relation as it had developed to the time of the change in question (and in many instances as it has developed since the change). This may or may not include an 'original agreement;' and if it does, may or may not result in great deference being given to it." *Id.* at 890. Thus, a relational contract system attempts to save contractual relationships that are in trouble by going beyond the four corners of the orginal contract and look to "the overall context of the whole relation." *Id.* To what extent is the judge in *Nanakuli* adopting a relational perspective?

2. Risk Sharing Under Relational Contracts: A significant advantage of relational contracting is that it not only provides for the sharing of risks but also a possible reduction of risk. This reduction is possible because the long-term nature of relational contracts reduces the incentives of contracting parties to engage in the types of opportunistic behavior that lead to transaction failures in discrete market transactions. What was the nature of the risk sharing in *Nanakuli*? Identify some circumstances where one party could have taken advantage of another but did not.

3. Efficient Breach: If Shell had found a better alternative than Nanakuli, then Shell could have easily breached the contract, paid damages and sold asphalt to a third party. However, was there an efficient breach situation here? Could Shell have done anything to increase the size of the economic pie?

4. *Did Nanakuli Already Pay For the Price Increase?:* In order to make a long term commitment for a specified product and sum, both Nanakuli and Shell must be willing to take a portion of risk with the contract. Nanakuli risked having the market for asphalt collapse or the market price of asphalt plummeting. Shell risked having the price of asphalt increase (as it did here). Both parties seem to have risks that correspond with their more specific knowledge of the industry. However, does this knowledge, *ex ante*, accurately reflect what happened, *ex post*?

5. *Secondary Effects:* If Shell is allowed to raise its prices for all long term contracts, how does this affect other parties? Where will the price increases ultimately fall?

C. Administrative Costs of Firm Coordination

The transaction costs of using markets to coordinate economic activity must be balanced against the administrative costs of firm coordination. The discussion of monopoly in Chapter V identified bureaucratic costs as a primary source of diseconomies of scale that limit the growth of firms. In effect, the administrative (or bureaucratic) costs discussed in this section provide an important explanation for why central planning has not worked either in countries (e.g., the Soviet Union) or in many major corporations (e.g., the relatively recent struggles of General Motors and I.B.M.).

1. The Separation of Ownership and Control

A major intellectual theme in the study of the modern corporation is the "separation of ownership and control" thesis, which was first popularized by Adolf A. Berle and Gardiner C. Means, in 1932 in their famous book *The Modern Corporation and Private Property*. The basic notion is that dispersed owners of the modern corporation do not have the incentive to control corporate management—directors and officers—and that managers often act in their own interests rather than in the stockholders' interests. Over the years, the Berle and Means thesis has provided the basis for many calls for more stringent legal controls on managerial behavior. This area of corporate policy is called "corporate governance," which refers to the manner in which the relations between the parties to the corporate contract are restrained by government regulation or private ordering.

Much of the Berle and Means analysis is based on their belief that shareholders should, but do not, play a major, direct role in monitoring corporate managers. At first glance this seems reasonable because, after all, the voting rules of corporations suggest that corporations are democratic institutions: Shareholders elect directors and have the right to offer recommendations to be voted upon by fellow shareholders through the corporate proxy machinery. Despite these legal rights, however, the reality of the large corporation is far from democratic because shareholders rarely have the incentive to exercise their legal rights. For many individual shareholders, dissatisfaction with the management of the corporation results in the sale of the stock. The so-called "Wall Street Rule" is that "rationally ignorant" shareholders sell their shares rather than become involved in the internal affairs of the corporation. Because of the seeming indifference of shareholders, Berle and Means and their progeny have assumed that directors and managers are free to operate the corporation in a manner that is not necessarily in the shareholders' best interest.

2. Shirking, Free-Riding, and Monitoring

The Berle and Means analysis provided a policy-relevant backdrop to the development of the modern analysis of the firm. Coase's seminal contribution triggered several major contributions. Armen Alchian and Harold Demsetz went beyond identifying circumstances that led to firm coordination and developed a framework for analyzing how the nature of the production process affects the form of organization (e.g., sole proprietorship, partnership, or corporation) and the internal organization of the firm. Alchian & Demsetz, *Production, Information Costs, and Economic Organization*, 62 Am. Econ. Rev. 777 (1972). Alchian and Demsetz argued that centralized direction of the firm would be more efficient than market coordination under those situations where team production makes it impossible for markets to correctly assess the marginal productivity of each member of a team. Alchian and Demsetz addressed the emergence of the firm as a response to the benefits of team production. For some production processes, the least cost method of production requires that individuals work together as a team in order to produce the final product. Whenever a team can produce a product or service at a lower cost, firms will exist. The benefits of team production, however, are not free. The transaction costs associated with team production arise because it is often difficult to monitor the marginal productivity of each individual member of the team and reward him on the basis of his contribution. Of course, the members of the team will realize this, and some will rationally take advantage of the situation by shirking — exerting less than the normal productive effort — because they know that their wages will not fully adjust to reflect their decreased effort. Thus, they asserted that firms developed to allow "managers" to monitor and, therefore, meter the activities of team members. The reward to the firm would be the value resulting from reduced shirking by team members. So long as the increased productive efficiency of team production exceeds the shirking costs (which include the costs of controlling shirking), the firm will expand to replace independent production by individuals.

Alchian and Demsetz's contribution led to the modern agency theory of the firm first elaborated by Michael Jensen and William Meckling. Jensen and Meckling, *Theory of the Firm: Managerial Behavior, Agency Cost, and Ownership Structure*, 3 J. Fin. Econ. 305 (1976). Jensen and Meckling conceived of the corporation as a legal entity that serves as a nexus for a complex set of implicit and explicit contracts among individuals with diverse and often conflicting objectives. It is hypothesized that this **nexus of contracts** model is superior to the perspective that treats the firm as if it were a single "person" with a single well-defined objective by providing richer insights to legal and financial phenomena.

Moreover, the firm (and in this regard its most efficient organizational form, the modern public corporation) can take advantage of efficiencies to the degree that it can foster internal specialization. In the modern business corporation, shareholders specialize in bearing risk while managers develop and utilize special skills in running the corporation. Other contracts will include those with employees, i.e., labor, and suppliers of materials used in the production process. These specialized functions of the firm involve the establishment of a large number of **agency** relationships. Classically, an agency relationship is a contract in which one person, the **principal**, engages another person, the **agent**, to take actions on behalf of the principal which involve the delegation of some decision making authority to the agent. Thus, in the modern agency theory of the firm, the corporation consists of a web of voluntary contracts, some implicit, some explicit, all of which involve to one degree or another an agency relationship.

Jensen and Meckling argued that agency problems will arise from conflicts of interests between and among wealth maximizing individuals where, by necessity, not all contractual duties can be specified. They noted that this conflict gives rise to what are called **agency costs**. Agency costs occur when agents seek to maximize their welfare at the expense of the welfare of their principals. Moreover, because principal-agent contracts are not costlessly written and enforced, agency costs include the costs of structuring, monitoring, and bonding a set of contracts among agents with conflicting interests. In addition, agency costs include the value of any output lost because the cost of full enforcement of contracts exceeds the benefits (the "residual loss"). For example, the provision of accounting information is a form of bonding activity undertaken by managers (agents) to convince shareholders (principals) that they are not acting **opportunistically.**

Oliver Williamson explored the problem of shirking as post-contractual opportunism and has identified contractual arrangements designed to prevent opportunism. Williamson, *Transaction-Cost Economics: The Governance of Contractual Relations*, 22 J. Law & Econ. 233 (1979). Steven Cheung explained why productive individuals would voluntarily submit to the managers' commands within a firm. The key point in understanding this is related to the free rider problem: It is rational for individuals to shirk so long as the other members of the team do not shirk; however, if all of the members of the team shirk, then the wages of all members will decline as each bears a portion of the costs of shirking. Faced with these alternatives, it seems rational for the team members to hire someone to monitor their behavior in order to enhance the productivity of the team. See Cheung, *The Contractual Nature of the Firm*, 143 Journal of Institutional and Theoretical Economics 110, 111 (1987). The monitor is called the manager, but it is not clear who is working for whom within the contractual arrangements. In this perspective, the essence of the firm is "the nexus of contracts restraining the behavior of contractors."

3. The Efficiency of Specialization

The contractual theory of the corporation refutes (or, at least, tempers) the shareholder abuse conclusions of Berle and Means. In the modern corporation, the key contract is between the owners of a modern corporation, i.e., the shareholders, and the managers (agents) hired to run the firm. Under this particular contract, a shareholder invests capital in the corporation in return for a residual claim to the net cashflows that result from differences between inflows of cash and promised payments to the other contractual parties which comprise the firm.

Shareholders bear the residual risk inherent in the ownership of resources *specific* to the corporation and thus will *demand* the right to **control** the organization. In other words, while a corporation is a nexus of contracts among its customers, managers, suppliers of materials, etc., the corporation vests control in the constituency that bears the residual risk of the organization.

Corporate law puts no restrictions on those who can own residual claims and thus makes it possible for other contractual participants to avoid bearing any of the residual risks. Hence, the fact that anyone can own a residual claim allows specialization in risk-bearing by those investors who choose to do so. In addition, unrestricted stock ownership allows the residual risk of the firm to be spread out among many individuals. As discussed in detail in Chapter XI, individuals can reduce the cost of bearing such risks by holding a diversified portfolio of investments. Because the firm only has to pay investors to bear undiversifiable risk, it will be able to raise capital at a lower cost.

In general, the role of the manager in the theory of the firm is to monitor the production process, coordinate team production, and discourage shirking by tying compensation closely to productivity. Of course, this raises the question of who is monitoring the monitors? In an important theoretical contribution, Klein, Crawford, and Alchian focused on the role of residual claimants—the contracting parties with the right to the firm's residual income—and firm-specific investments. Klein, Crawford & Alchian, *Vertical Integration: Appropriable Rents, and the Competitive Contracting Process*, 21 J. Law & Econ. 297 (1978). They suggested that the "monitoring the monitors" problem is often solved by making the owners of the most firm-specific assets the residual claimants. This analysis is most helpful in identifying situations where firms will integrate, and perhaps where firms will have a concentrated ownership structure, but it does not offer much for the organization of the publicly traded corporation. The "monitoring the monitors" issue underlies much of the corporate governance debate in the United States and provides a starting point for the analysis of the contractual theory of the corporation in Section D. The efficiency of this nexus of contracts among individuals who specialize in different functions is attested to by market performance. Since any organizational form can compete for consumers, managers, supplies of capital, etc., those that supply goods to consumers at the lowest prices will succeed. The dominance of the corporate form in large scale organizations indicates that the corporation is a superior form of organization.

4. Shareholder Voting

The Berle and Means thesis is quite simple: managers have gained control of modern corporations and have effectively disenfranchised the owners/voters, i.e., the shareholders. With this control, managers have been able to follow their own agendas to the detriment of shareholders. In other words, managers have been able to maximize their own utility by not maximizing the profits of the corporation. Since management does not generally "own" the corporation, managers receive little or no benefit as a result of an increase in monetary profits that ultimately belongs to the residual claimants, i.e., the common shareholders. Moreover, Berle and Means argued that existing corporate law did not provide sufficient mechanisms for owners to control management. More specifically,

Berle and Means argued that shareholder voting was a sham as there were few contested elections for boards of directors since management controlled the proxy mechanism and was able, in effect, to rig elections. Moreover, as a result of the Berle and Means thesis, political pressures developed (especially during the "New Deal") to increase what is referred to as **corporate democracy**. This is not surprising since the Berle and Means model is a political rather than an economic model of the corporation. One political result of the Berle and Means thesis was sections of federal security laws that increased access by shareholders to the proxy mechanism. Much to the consternation, however, of those who politically adopted the Berle and Means thesis, shareholders showed little interest in these statutory rights.

The Berle and Means critique was based in part on the assumption that shareholders wanted direct control over managers. However, simple economics suggests that shareholders' specialization in bearing the residual risk of the firm does not mean that they have the incentive actively to monitor their agents. In fact, shareholders are characterized as **rationally ignorant** because of the large costs associated with staying informed about the corporation's internal affairs and the very small expected benefits to the individual shareholder of being informed. After bearing the costs of becoming informed, such shareholders are unlikely to be able to influence the corporation's policies and in any event they must share the benefits of intervention if they are successful. Given the divergence of costs and benefits, small shareholders find it rational to **free ride** on other shareholders' monitoring activity:

> Of all those standing in relation to the large corporation, the shareholder is least subject to its power. Through the mechanism of the security markets, his relation to the corporation is rendered highly abstract and formal, quite limited in scope, and readily reducible to monetary terms. The market affords him a way of breaking this relation that is simple and effective. He can sell his stock, and remove himself, qua shareholder, at least from the power of the corporation.

> Shareholder democracy, so-called, is misconceived because the shareholders are not the governed of the corporation whose consent must be sought. If they are, it is only in the most limited sense. Their interests are protected if financial information is made available, fraud and overreaching are prevented, and a market is maintained in which their share may be sold. *A priori*, there is no reason for them to have any voice, direct or representational, in the catalogue of corporate decisions with which this paper began, decisions on prices, wages, and investment. They are no more affected than nonshareholding neighbors by these decisions....they deserve the voiceless position in which the modern development left them.

Chayes, *The Modern Corporation and the Rule of Law,* in The Corporation in Modern Society, 25, 40–41 (E. Mason ed. 1960). If a shareholder does not like what is happening to his or her shares, then that shareholder can exit, i.e., the shareholder can follow what is called the Wall Street Rule. Hence, given the cost and benefits of such ignorance, it is rational for most shareholders to be ignorant of most corporate matters, thus ignoring the "proxy" control mechanism.

Limited liability clearly facilitates this specialization by shareholders because it allows shareholders to be "rationally ignorant" of managerial practices. Because their risk is limited to their initial investment, shareholders do not waste their time trying to monitor managerial behavior. Thus, limited liability allows investors to be passive with respect to the internal affairs of companies and to concentrate on the externally observable traits like profits and rate of return on investment. This analysis, however, does not mean that shareholder voting is not valuable. As Henry Manne explained:

> ... [A]n individual voting share of stock is a package composed of two parts—an underlying investment interest and a vote. The two bear a complex relationship to each other, and to understand this relationship it is necessary first to know why corporate control is a valuable asset. There are four distinct reasons why corporate control is sought. The first of these, of perennial concern in the antitrust field, is the monopoly power one firm may achieve by the elimination or control of a competing firm. Next there is the legitimate advantage that may be derived from cost-saving technological efficiencies or other economies of scale which are unavailable to the single firm. The third reason is the simple desire for salaries and the other perquisites normally associated with control of a corporation. Finally, and most important from the point of view of this paper, there is the substantial gain that may be realized in the price of shares when the company receives improved management.

> With the first three reasons, the price of the vote segment of the share package would tend to rise with the price of the investment portion of the share and for the same underlying reason. However, this relationship is completely reversed in the case of increased capital gains through improved management. As the price of a voting share declines because of any recognizable inefficiency in the management of the company, the possibility of capital gains from improved management increases accordingly. Control will be worth more, and the vote portion of the share package will appreciate at the same time that the price of the share package is declining. The vote therefore becomes valuable largely as a result of the potential for appreciation of the underlying share interest; when the potential gain in shares is lowest the value of the vote will tend towards zero. This may explain why takeovers motivated by a desire for large capital gains are quite rare in regulated industries. The possibility of great improvements in the earnings of a rate-regulated monopoly [is] extremely small; thus little incentive is provided outsiders to compete for control of these companies. In this way, regulation of rates, with its concomitant legalization of monopoly, may have the undesirable side effect of locking-in the incumbent management. By virtue of this "protection" for managers of public utilities, regulation tends to create a true Berle and Means separation of ownership and control.

> In a well-managed company, the value of the vote attributable to potential capital gain approaches zero, and the market price of the package will tend to be identical with that of the investment portion. But the value of the vote portion of the package will also tend to be zero if for any reason a change in control cannot be implemented. Too strict rules against mergers have this effect if alternative take-over techniques are not available. Any move along a continuum away from a completely free market for control tends to cause a decline in the mar-

ket value of the vote. The various proposals for abolishing share voting and for curtailing a free market for control blocks of shares clearly have that effect.

Manne, *Some Theoretical Aspects of Share Voting*, 64 Colum. L. Rev. 1427, 1430–31 (1964). The importance of control transactions is discussed in subsection D.1, "The Market for Corporate Control," *infra*.

5. Agency Costs and Owner/Manager Conflicts

In general, agency theory suggests that unity of ownership and control is not a necessary condition of efficient performance of a firm. This perspective stresses the voluntary, contractual nature of the corporation. A first step in understanding this market-oriented approach is to recognize that it is based in part on the assumption that the shareholders' primary interest is in the maximization of the value of their investments and that the contractual relations among participants in the firm must convince shareholders that managers will not abuse the shareholders' interests. A corporation's managers, which are defined to include its officers and directors, are agents of the shareholders. In this view, the so-called separation of ownership and control in the large corporation is an agency relationship, which exists because the benefits of the relationship exceed the agency costs associated with it. That is, the agency relationship exists because both the principal and the agent share in the benefits of the relationship.

At this point, it is helpful to be more precise in the identification of conflicts between managers and shareholders in the corporate firm.

(1) *Effort*: A primary concern of agency theory and the separation of ownership and control literature is whether entrenched managers have the incentives to maximize their efforts in pursuing the maximum rate of return for shareholders.

(2) *Horizon*: This conflict refers to the issue of how to encourage a manager to act in the shareholders' interests as the manager approaches retirement or prepares to leave the firm for other opportunities.

(3) *Risk Aversion*: Entrenched managers have an incentive to avoid bankruptcy at all costs, but shareholders with diversified portfolios are risk neutral with respect to individual securities in their portfolios. In the absence of corrective governance mechanisms, managers interests will be more closely aligned with those of bondholders than shareholders.

(4) *Under leveraged*: Within a certain range the tax savings from debt and increased leverage can increase a firm's profit, but risk averse managers may not like the increased risk associated with increased leverage and debt service demands although, once again, shareholders could prefer the undertaking of such risk because they specialize in bearing such risks.

(5) *Dividend Payout Problem*: Risk averse managers may prefer to reinvest their firm's profits in the firm rather than distribute them to shareholders even though the shareholders could put them to a more productive use.

This list of conflicts between managers and shareholders is not intended to be exhaustive, but it does serve as a reference for discussing the roles of different corporate governance mechanisms that control corporate agency costs.

Agency theory and transaction costs economics attempt to explain the development of institutional arrangements that convince shareholders voluntarily to allow managers to control their resources. The resources devoted to controlling agency costs are properly identified as agency costs. Thus, agency costs include not only the direct costs associated with agents acting in their own interest at the expense of shareholders, but also the costs of controlling managerial agents through legal or market governance arrangements. Nonetheless, it is crucial to understanding the agency problem to recognize that the parties to the contract will bear the agency costs implicit in the arrangement. Thus, agents have the incentive to attempt to minimize agency costs by writing contracts that provide monitoring and bonding activities to the point where the marginal costs of such activity equals the marginal gain of reducing such costs. According to the contractual theory discussed below, managers select the least cost manner of controlling agency costs. The use of corporate governance mechanisms merely reveals that the costs of monitoring are justified by reducing the costs of an agent's deviation from the behavior that would occur if the agent and principal were one.

D. Corporate Governance and the Contractual Theory of the Corporation

The fundamental insight of the Berle and Means theory—that shareholders should be concerned about delegating control over their financial capital to corporate managers—provides the cornerstone of the contractual theory of the corporation. This section offers a summary of the governance mechanisms and powerful market forces that encourage managers to act in shareholders' interests. Taken together, the identification of these market forces and the understanding of their interaction represent the contractual theory of the corporation. The corporation is based on voluntary contracts, and the realities of the corporate agency relationship dictate that the corporation's managers select the contractual terms that are then offered to potential investors. In order to raise capital at the lowest possible price, managers must offer contract terms—including evidence of the existence of intra-firm incentive structures—that convince investors that agency costs will be minimized.

1. The Market for Corporate Control

If managers control the corporation, then it seems reasonable for shareholders to be concerned that manager-created intra-firm corporate governance devices such as managerial incentive contracts may not always be effective in controlling managerial agency costs. An alternative control mechanism, beyond the direct control of entrenched managers, is found in the stock market. The stock market discipline of managers is manifest in the threat of tender offers, takeovers, or other forms of changes in corporate control whenever entrenched managers adopt strategies and behavior that fail to maximize the value of the corporation's shares. The so-called market for corporate control provides an *external* monitoring mechanism that forces managers to be concerned about their shareholders. Prior to this theoretical development by Henry G. Manne (see Manne, *Mergers and the Market for Corporate Control*, 73 J. Pol. Econ. 110 (1965)), commentators on the modern corporation were at a total loss when it came to explaining how corporate managers could be restrained to act in their shareholders' interests. Because the market for corporate control plays the preeminent role in the other governance mechanisms in the contractual theory of the corporation, it warrants further discussion.

A viable market for corporate control requires freely transferable voting shares so that dissatisfied shareholders can sell their shares rather than attempt to control agency problems through internal control mechanisms. The result of this exit process is that the shares of poorly managed firms trade at a discount below the level that could be attained with better and more loyal managers. This creates the possibility of large capital gains from purchasing shares and replacing incompetent or shirking managers with a new group of more efficient managers.

The identification of firms, trading below their potential value due to management problems, however, is very costly. Prospective bidders monitor the performance of managerial teams by comparing a corporation's potential market value with its value under current management. In this regard, management inefficiency must be understood to include not only the failure to minimize costs and maximize profits through current operations, but also the failure to distribute excess cash flow, the failure to take advantage of acquisitions and restructuring opportunities, and even the failure to communicate to the stock market the health and prospects of the company. If a firm is not performing up to its financial potential under current and expected market conditions, regardless of the reason, then it is an attractive target for a change in corporate control. According to the theory, the acquiring firm purchases the stock of the target company, replaces the inefficient managers with efficient managers, and then reaps a large profit as the stock price rises to reflect the increased earning potential under the more efficient managerial team. The market for corporate control operates through many different forms of control transactions. Of course, the most dramatic is the takeover via a hostile tender offer. In addition, friendly mergers, negotiated tender offers, sales of control by large shareholders, and proxy contests are mechanisms for changing control of corporations and displacing inefficient managers with more efficient managers. In basic terms, the firm's assets are worth more in the hands of the new managers. In many instances, the source of the premium for the replacement of managers is the reduction of agency costs. But a more general view of the role of the market for corporate control is that it is the *threat* of takeover, not the actual occurrence of a takeover, which serves to align managers' interests with shareholders' interests. The following case illustrates some of the issues relevant to tender offers.

Liberty National Insurance v. The Charter Company
United States Court of Appeals for the Eleventh Circuit
734 F.2d 545 (1984)

TJOFLAT, J.

In this securities case, we are called upon to decide whether an issuer can bring suit under sections 10(b), 13(d), and 14(d) and (e) of the Securities and Exchange Act of 1934 (the Exchange Act) to require a shareholder to divest himself of his stock holdings in the issuer. None of these sections expressly authorizes such a suit. We hold that none of these sections impliedly authorizes such a suit. The district court dismissed the issuer's complaint. We affirm.

I.

A.

Between May 4 and December 22, 1981, the Charter Company, and certain of its subsidiaries (Charter), purchased an aggregate of 962,400 shares of the common stock of Liberty National Insurance Holding Company (Liberty), representing approximately 5.1% of Liberty's outstanding common stock. On December 28, 1981, Charter filed a schedule 13D statement with the Securities and Exchange Commission (SEC or Commission) reporting those purchases and other information as required by law. From December 22, 1981, through January 22, 1982, Charter acquired an additional 255,100 shares of Liberty stock, increasing its holdings of outstanding Liberty stock to approximately 6.5%. This additional purchase was the subject of Amendment 1 to Charter's schedule 13D.

On February 1, 1982, Liberty brought this suit against Charter in the district court alleging that Charter had embarked on an unlawful scheme to reap illicit profits by manipulating the market for Liberty stock to bring about an upward displacement in the price, and "attempting to precipitate an auction for control of Liberty" by use of false and misleading schedule 13D statements. Liberty alleged that Charter's conduct violated various provisions of the Exchange Act and of state law and sought an injunctive order requiring Charter to divest itself of all its Liberty shares and in the interim to refrain from exercising its right to vote those shares or otherwise participate as a stockholder in Liberty's affairs. Charter moved to dismiss Liberty's complaint on February 4.

*　　*　　*

Liberty's first claim for relief was based on section 13(d) of the Exchange Act. Liberty alleged that Charter, in carrying out its scheme to acquire a control position, filed false and misleading schedule 13D statements. Section 13(d) of the Exchange Act requires that anyone acquiring more than five percent of any class of equity securities of a company registered with the SEC file with the Commission, any exchanges on which the stock is traded, and the issuing company a schedule 13D statement setting forth, among other things: (a) the background and identity of the purchaser; (b) the source of funds used to purchase the securities; and (c) the purpose of the acquisition and the purchaser's future plans and intentions with respect to the issuer. SEC rule 12(b)20, 17 C.F.R. § 240.12(b)-20 (1983), promulgated under section 13(d), requires periodic updating of schedule 13D statements to reflect changes in the facts previously disclosed. Liberty alleged that Charter's schedule 13D statement, including the amendments thereto, was false and misleading as to the identity of the purchaser, the source of the funds, the purpose of the acquisition and the purchaser's future plans.

Liberty did not allege how the false schedule 13D statement enabled Charter to acquire its shares of Liberty stock; Liberty pled no facts that indicated that Charter's 13D statement was ever communicated to the market or to the Liberty shareholders who sold to Charter.[10] Nor did Liberty allege how it was injured by Charter's 13D statement. Notwithstanding the lack of any allegation of a causal relationship between Charter's schedule 13D statement and Charter's acquisition of Liberty stock, Liberty nevertheless sought the injunctive relief stated above: that Charter be divested of its Liberty shares.

Liberty's second claim for relief was that Charter engaged in a tender offer in violation of sections 14(d) and (e) of the Exchange Act. According to Liberty, Charter solicited and purchased large blocks of Liberty shares at a premium, and this constituted a tender offer. Section 14(d) requires that persons making a tender offer for securities disclose certain prescribed information by filing it with the SEC. This information includes all that is required in a section 13(d) filing. Section 14(e) prohibits fraudulent conduct in connection with a tender offer.

Liberty alleged that Charter failed to file the required information under section 14(d), and that Charter's false and misleading schedule 13D statement amounted to fraudulent conduct under section 14(e). Liberty did not allege how it was injured by this fraudulent conduct. Nor did Liberty allege how it was injured by Charter's failure to comply with section 14(d).[13] Liberty merely alleged that Charter, in seeking a control position in Liberty, had violated sections 14(d) and (e) and that Liberty was therefore entitled to an injunction requiring Charter to divest itself of its holdings in Liberty.

*   *   *

III.

*   *   *

The Williams Act dealt mainly with tender offers. It is clear from the legislative history that the framers of the Williams Act sought to "take extreme care to avoid tipping the balance of regulation either in favor of management or in favor of the person making the takeover bid," and that their goal was to promote "full and fair disclosure for the benefit of investors while at the same time providing the offeror and management equal opportunity to present their case." S.Rep. No. 550 at 3. To give Liberty the relief it asks would defeat this purpose. When an outsider acquires a large amount of stock in a publicly held company this creates at the very least a nascent potential conflict between the outsider and management. To permit the issuer to oust the new stockholder simply because he made a false filing would tip the balance towards management, thereby injuring the existing investors. Moreover, incumbent management could solidify its position by subjecting to suit any outsider who accumulated more than 5%

---

10. Liberty alleged that the false information Charter *disclosed* in its schedule 13D statement was highly favorable to Charter, and thus presumably beneficial to Liberty, and if disclosed to the market would create an increased demand for Liberty stock and a consequent rise in its price; and that Charter's schedule 13D statement *failed to disclose* information highly damaging to Charter, and thus detrimental to Liberty if Charter gained a control position, implying that if the information were communicated to the market, it would cause a sell off of Liberty stock and a consequent fall in its price.

13. Had Charter made a section 14(d) filing, Liberty would have been permitted to file a counterstatement. Liberty did not allege that the deprivation of that opportunity injured it in any way.

of the shares of the company, and thus discourage such accumulations. The threat of this sort of litigation might remove from the field a player whose self-interest is to monitor management, and who is poised to mount a proxy fight or a tender offer.

Ever since Berle & Means' seminal work, *The Modern Corporation and Private Property* (1933), it has been generally recognized that small shareholders in large publicly held companies have an insufficient incentive adequately to monitor the management of the firm. Nevertheless, these shareholders are not bereft of all relief from improper or inefficient management. Large shareholders, or outsiders who may challenge incumbent management, help protect the small shareholders' interest in monitoring—by possibly challenging—incumbent management. The more obstacles that are placed in the path of those who would acquire large holdings, and the more expensive and time consuming the take over process becomes, the less protection for the small shareholder.

The inappropriateness of implying the remedy Liberty seeks is illustrated by an examination of the consequences that remedy would visit on existing shareholders. While section 13(d) is intended to ensure the provision of information to the market through the Commission, the exchanges and management, and it is the investors who are the intended beneficiaries of this legislation, the relief requested by the issuer, here, is at best ambiguous, even in its immediate effect on the shareholders. Requiring that Charter divest itself of Liberty shares, by selling them back to non-parties or on the open market, will depress the price, by increasing the supply of Liberty stock on the market without a corresponding increase in the demand. Removing voting power from Charter will have the effect of removing outside monitoring of management by a shareholder with significant financial interest in policing management. Thus, the divestiture remedy sought by the "issuer" illustrates only too well that the interests of shareholders and management are not likely to be identical with regard to policing schedule 13D filings.

While there is a sense in which management acting through the issuer can efficiently reflect the collective interests of the stockholders, this does not hold true when the interests of the stockholders and management are adverse to one another. When an outsider is perceived as threatening to displace the insiders, management has a clear economic interest in protecting its position, even though this might not be in the economic interest of the firm or its shareholders. The creation of a private right of action on behalf of the firm would allow incumbent management to use corporate resources, rather than their own, to harass and burden aggressive outsiders. Moreover, it would be difficult for the outsider to avoid vexatious litigation by any manner of careful craftsmanship in his filing; all the incumbent management would have to demonstrate to maintain its claim for relief would be that the outsider's schedule 13D statement of his intentions with respect to the issuer was false or misleading. Whether the outsider is unequivocal or equivocates as to his intentions, the issuer could simply allege, as Liberty did in this case, that his true intentions are the opposite. As Judge Friendly pointed out in one of the first cases to construe the Williams Act, "It would be as serious an infringement of these regulations [for the outsider] to overstate the definiteness of [its] plans as to understate them." *Electronic Specialty Co. v. International Controls Corp.*, 409 F.2d 937, 948 (2d Cir.1969).

Measuring the truthfulness of a filing could pose significant problems for a district court as well. The court might find it difficult, even after an extensive evidentiary proceeding, to determine the subjective intentions of the party filing the schedule 13D statement at the time it filed it. And once the court made its determination it might have difficulty withdrawing from the dispute. Having entered a coercive order, enforceable through the court's contempt power, requiring the party to amend its schedule 13D, the court could be faced with still further proceedings. For example, the issuer might find fault with the party's schedule 13D amendment and move the court to issue an order requiring the party to show cause why it should not be held in contempt for filing an inadequate amendment. If the show cause order issued, the court would once again be required to find the party's intent, and the process of an amended filing and a new show cause proceeding might well begin anew.

A final concern to us is the precedential effect a divestiture order in this case would have on the market for securities generally. Parties contemplating the acquisition of large holdings in publicly traded companies would be faced with substantial transaction costs in the form of section 13(d) litigation expenses, including delay, whenever perceived by incumbent management as a threat to their economic welfare. The chilling effect of the remedy Liberty would have us approve could have a deleterious impact on the market for corporate control and the value of securities generally. We therefore agree with the district court that no cause of action under section 13(d) exists for the relief Liberty requests.

IV.

Liberty's second claim for relief, though stated as one claim, actually presents two discrete causes of action, each seeking the same relief: that Charter be required to divest itself of its Liberty holdings and pending such divestiture enjoined from voting any of its shares. Liberty's first cause of action is that Charter made a tender offer without complying with the filing requirements of section 14(d) of the Exchange Act; it neglected to submit an information statement to the SEC. Liberty's second cause of action is that Charter in making the tender offer committed certain fraudulent acts in violation of section 14(e) of the Act; it filed a false schedule 13D statement. Liberty does not inform us how either of these statutory violations injured Liberty or why Congress intended that the relief it seeks be a means of enforcing these two laws.

Section 14(d) requires that persons making a tender offer for securities disclose certain prescribed information by filing it with the Commission and the issuer, and section 14(e) prohibits fraudulent conduct in connection with such a tender offer. Liberty must surmount two hurdles before it can recover under either of these two sections. First, Liberty must demonstrate that an implied right of action exists on behalf of an issuer for the type of injunctive relief sought. Second, Liberty must have alleged sufficient facts to permit a court to infer that Charter conducted a tender offer. We conclude that the right of action Liberty asserts cannot be implied under either section. Accordingly, we need not determine whether Charter made a tender offer.

Sections 14(d) and (e) do not by their language create private rights of action. The existence of and limits on the right to bring a private cause of action are, as we have stated, of judicial origin. The question of whether, and when, an issuer can bring an action under sections 14(d) and (e) is similar to that under section 13(d), in that all of these sections were incorporated into the Exchange Act by the Williams Act and were attempts to protect the same group, investors, and address similar problems. Therefore, our analysis will cover much the same ground we addressed in part III, supra. Nonetheless, there are some facial differences between these sections which must be discussed.

The Supreme Court addressed the existence and limits on private rights of action under sections 14(d) and (e) in *Piper v. Chris-Craft Industries, Inc.*, 430 U.S. 1, 97 S. Ct. 926, 51 L. Ed. 2d 124 (1977). Piper, while not on all fours with the case before us, is nevertheless extremely useful for achieving a proper understanding of implied rights of action under sections 14(d) and (e). Chris-Craft was an unsuccessful tender offeror who sought damages against the management of the company it sought to take over, Piper, Piper's investment adviser, and Bangor Punta Corporation, the successful "white knight"[45] that defeated Chris-Craft in its bid for control of Piper. The Supreme Court held that since the purpose of the Williams Act was to provide protection for shareholders and not for tender offerors, no implied cause of action would lie for a defeated tender offeror.[46]

The Court specifically stated:

> Our holding is a limited one, whether shareholder-offerees, the class protected by § 14(e), have an implied cause of action under § 14(e) is not before us, and we intimate no view on the matter. *Nor is the target corporation's standing to sue in issue in this case.* We hold only that a tender offeror, suing in its capacity as a takeover bidder, does not have standing to sue for damages under § 14(e).

Id. at 42 n. 28 (emphasis added). In view of those words of limitation supplied by the High Court, it would be unseemly to attempt to read a hidden meaning into the Court's holding that was not its voiced intent. With that caution in mind, we must nonetheless make proper use of the reasoning provided by the Court to determine whether the law requires that we find that Congress has implied a cause of action on behalf of issuers under sections 14(d) and (e).

In *Piper*, the Court refined the test it had outlined in *Cort v. Ash*, 422 U.S. 66, 95 S. Ct. 2080, 45 L. Ed. 2d 26 (1975), for determining whether a private remedy is to be found implied in a statute which did not explicitly grant one. *Piper* is fundamentally concerned with legislative intent; which apparently is the focus of the *Cort v. Ash* inquiry. *Touche Ross*, 442 U.S. at 575, 99 S. Ct. at 2489; *Transamerica*, 444 U.S. at 15–16, 100 S. Ct. at 245. As our earlier discussion of

---

45. "White Knight" is a term used to describe a tender offeror friendly to management that attempts to defeat a hostile tender offeror.

46. Though the ostensible purpose of the Williams Act is the protection of investors, a number of commentators have had difficulty in determining what, if any, underlying remedial purpose is actually being served by the Act. *See*, Manne, *Tender Offers and the Free Market*, 2 Merger & Acq. 91 (No. 1, Fall 1966); Manne, *Salute to "Raiders"*, Barron's 1 (Oct. 23, 1967); Manne, *Cash Tender Offers for Shares—A Reply to Chairman Cohen*, 1967 Duke L.J. 231; Jarrell & Bradley, *The Economic Effects of Federal and State Regulation of Cash Tender Offers*, 23 J. of Law and Econ. 371 (1980); *Separate Statement of Frank H. Easterbrook and Gregg A. Jarrell*, S.E.C. advisory committee on Tender Offers: Report of Recommendations p. 70 (July 8, 1983), Federal Sec.Rep. (C.C.H.) special report no. 1028 (July 15, 1983).

section 13(d) makes clear, the purpose of the Williams Act as a whole, and the tender offer provisions in particular, is to provide protection to investors.[47] We must determine, then, by asking the *Cort v. Ash* questions, whether creating a cause of action on behalf of the issuer to seek equitable relief in the form of expelling a tender offeror from the company was the intention of the framers of sections 14(d) and (e).

* * *

V.

* * *

None of Liberty's three claims stated a cause of action. Each claim should have been dismissed with prejudice but was not. Charter has not cross-appealed the court's "without prejudice" disposition, however. Accordingly, for the reasons we have stated the judgment of the district court is

AFFIRMED.

* * *

1. Takeovers, Managers, and the Williams Act: Tender offers are regulated by the Williams Act, which was an amendment to the Securities Exchange Act of 1934. A tender offeror is required to file a Schedule 13D, which in effect mandates complete disclosure of the tender offeror's background, sources of financing, and plans for the corporation if the tender offer is successful. The stated purpose of this regulation, as the court noted from the legislative history, was to establish "an even playing field." However, while that may be the "intent" of the Act, unintended (or, perhaps, intended) consequences of the Williams Act quickly surfaced. Incumbent managers surely benefited from the reduced threat of hostile takeovers.

2. Empirical Evidence: The role of the market for corporate control in the governance of the modern corporation is not based on some mystical or ideological belief in the power of market forces, but rather it is supported by numerous empirical studies. *See* Jensen & Ruback, *The Market for Corporate Con-*

---

47. Though it is shareholders and particularly the shareholders of target corporations who are the intended beneficiaries of the disclosure requirements under section 14(d), there are a number of paradoxes in the reasoning process that undergirds the Williams Act, which make it difficult to see how shareholder interests are served. We will only mention one peculiar anomaly. If the offeror's statement under section 14(d) indicates that its plans for the company should raise the value of the shares considerably, the small shareholder, knowing that his decision to tender or not will have a de minimus effect on the probability of the success of the tender offer, will have an incentive not to tender so as to gain the benefits of the new regime. On the other hand, if the offeror indicates that he will turn over the reigns of the company to incompetents, the shareholder will have a greater incentive to tender, so as not to suffer a loss of value following the change to the new regime. Thus, paradoxically, the more information that is given by the offeror, the less likely that tender offers that would increase value will be successful, and the more likely that those that would decrease value will be successful. Therefore, non-tendering shareholders will be damaged by control moving to, or staying in, those hands less likely to increase the value of the firm. This is a curious result for a piece of legislation that is intended to help shareholders. *See* Cohen, *Tender Offers and Takeover Bids*, 23 Bus.Law 611, 614–615 (1968).

trol: The Scientific Evidence, 11 J. Fin. Econ. 5 (1983); Jarrell, Brickley & Netter, *The Market for Corporate Control: The Evidence Since 1980*, 2 J. Econ. Persp. 49 (1988). *See also* Easterbrook, *Managers' Discretion and Investors' Welfare: Theories and Evidence*, 9 Del. J. Corp. L. 540 (1984). This important insight about the role of the stock market in controlling managerial discretion must be counted as one of the first important steps in the application of economics to corporation law and in the development of the contractual theory of the corporation.

3. Tender Offers and Game Theory: The takeover process under the Williams Act can be viewed as a two by two game. Assume that the tender offeror cannot utilize the technique known as a **takeout merger**. By a takeout merger, we mean once the tender offeror is able to acquire a majority interest in the target firm, the minority shareholders are "taken out" in cash, often at a lower price, and do not receive an equity interest in the new firm. Let us assume that a tender offer at a price of $100 per share is made by Shark, Inc. for the shares of Mom's Apple Pie, Inc. Mom's stock is currently selling for $90 a share. What signal does this tender offer send to shareholders of the target corporation? The value of a corporation will reflect the discounted expected cash flows that can be earned by the shareholders. If Shark offers $100 for the shares, it follows that it must value the corporation at something more than $100 a share. If, based on the Williams Act disclosures, shareholders believe that the offeror can do a better job in operating the corporation and increase the value of the corporation to more than $100 a share, there is an incentive to hold on to their shares, i.e., not tender, since they would expect the value of their shares after the tender offer to be higher than the bid price. In other words, shareholders of the target are tempted to be free riders on the tender offerors' expected ability to increase the value of the firm. However, if enough shareholders attempt to free ride, the bid may be defeated since not enough shares will be tendered. Assume two shareholders, Moe and Joe, are facing the tender offer of $100 for shares currently selling at $90, but who believe that once the takeover is consummated, the market price for the shares will be $110. Figure X-2 presents the payoffs in matrix form. Clearly, each shareholder's strategy *may* lead to a suboptimal result, i.e., neither shareholder tenders. The term "may" is used to reflect the fact that the final outcome will depend on each shareholder's preference for risk. In game theory terminology, there is not a dominant strategy. On the other hand, what if after reading the Williams Act disclosures, the target shareholders believe that the new management would be less efficient than the existing management? The incentive here is also clear: tender your shares. Why? If target shareholders believe the new management would be inferior to the existing management they would expect that the post-acquisition firm's share price would be less than the existing market price and obviously less than the tender bid price. Consider an alternative scenario where the target shareholders believe that the post tender offer value of a corporation would be less than the current value, Moe and Joe would have every incentive to tender their shares and the corporation would end up in inferior hands, shown by Figure X-2(b). Clearly one of the reasons for the development of the takeout merger was to reduce this perverse incentive built into the Williams Act.

4. Managerial Responses to Tender Offers: One of the most heated debates in corporate law during the 1980's involved the question of the proper role of in-

<u>Figure X-2</u>   The Williams Act and Game Theory

**(a) Tender Offer With
Superior Management**

JOE

	Tender	No Tender
Tender	100 for Moe 100 for Joe	100 for Moe 110 for Joe
No Tender	110 for Moe 100 for Joe	90 for Moe 90 for Joe

MOE (left side)

**(b) Tender Offer With
Inferior Management**

JOE

	Tender	No Tender
Tender	100 for Moe 100 for Joe	100 for Moe 80 for Joe
No Tender	80 for Moe 100 for Joe	90 for Moe 90 for Joe

MOE (left side)

cumbent managers of a target corporation when faced with a tender offer for control. The incumbent managers, who are faced with the prospect of losing their jobs if the takeover is successful, may have an incentive to try to defeat the takeover even if it appears to be in the shareholders' best interests. Shareholders are faced with a dilemma in deciding whether managerial defensive tactics are in their best interests. If a firm is a target, the shareholders benefit if the managers' defensive activities result in a higher price as long as their activities do not actually defeat the tender offer. If the defensive tactics defeat the tender offer, shareholders are clearly worse off—the managers have, in effect, denied them the opportunity to sell their shares at a higher price. But all of this reflects an *ex post* analysis of the proper managerial response once a takeover has been initiated; an economic perspective adopts an *ex ante* view of the proper managerial response when the shareholders are not certain that their corporation will become a target.

Changes in the incentives of bidders affect the utility of monitoring by outsiders, and that affects the size of agency costs and in turn the pre-offer price of potential targets' stock. In order to explore the nature of these effects, it would be useful to ask what rational shareholders would do if, *before* a tender offer was in prospect, they could bind the management to resist or acquiesce in any offer.

Consider the effects of two polar rules. Under the first rule, management is passive in the face of tender offers. If there are no competing bidders, the first tender offer will prevail at the lowest premium that will induce the shareholders to surrender their shares. Under the second rule, management uses all available means to resist the offer. This resistance creates an auction, so that no bidder can acquire the target without paying a price almost as high as the shares would be worth under the best practicable management....

Which of these rules maximizes the welfare of [the target's] share-holders? If the question is asked ex post, after a tender offer has been made, then plainly the shareholders would prefer the second rule and the bidding war. But if the shareholders were asked which strategy the managers should pursue ex ante, prior to the offer, they would have substantial reasons to choose acquiescence. It is easy to see why. If the target's shareholders obtain *all* the gains from the transaction, no one has an incentive to make a tender offer, and thus no one will offer a premium for the shares.

See Easterbrook & Fischel, *The Proper Role of a Target's Management in Responding to a Tender Offer*, 94 Harv. L. Rev. 1161, 1177 (1981). This article spurred the debate about managerial response to tender offers. The literature on this debate is too extensive to either summarize or list. In actuality, most firms are never takeover targets (although all are potential targets and thus must respond to the threat of tender offers). The threat effect of a takeover often means that firms will not be attractive targets—the managers are already being forced to act in the shareholders' best interests. Establishing *ex ante* a rule allowing managers to defend against takeover increases the costs of (and reduces the effectiveness of) the market for corporate control as a monitoring mechanism and thus merely increase the problems associated with the separation of ownership and control. That is, raising the defensive tactics provides managers with more room to act in their own interest without being totally concerned about shareholder-welfare. It has been argued that, given a choice, shareholders as a group would be better off *ex ante* under a system that forces all managers to act in the shareholders' best interests at all times as opposed to a system that occasionally results in high stakes takeover battles. This reasoning has led to calls for mandating the role of the market for corporate control in all corporations by legally restricting the ability of managers to defend against takeover bids.

5. Stakeholders: Some commentators, especially those who are concerned about adverse employment effects or harm to some communities, argue that corporate managers should consider more than just shareholders' interests in deciding whether to attempt to defeat a hostile tender offer. In effect, these commentators characterize shareholders as just one of many constituencies, sometimes referred to as stakeholders, of the company. The contractual theory of the corporation suggests that those commentators misunderstand the role of shareholders. Shareholders are not equal to these other constituencies because they bear the residual risk inherent in the ownership of resources *specific* to the corporation and thus will *demand* the right to control the organization. In other words, while a corporation is a nexus of contracts among its customers, managers, suppliers of materials, etc., the corporate contract vests control in the constituency that bears the residual risk of the organization.

6. The Glue: Exclusive reliance on the market for corporate control to solve all of the potential conflicts of interest associated with the separation of ownership and control is neither justified nor necessary. Managerial discretion is constrained by other market and legal mechanisms. For example, in some large corporations, agency costs are reduced by the corporation being owned by shareholders who hold a large percentage of outstanding stock and have the incentive to monitor managerial behavior closely. Nevertheless, the market for corporate control provides a last resort mechanism for correcting excessive managerial discretion and, as a direct consequence, reduces the likelihood that shareholders will be harmed by their agents. The market for corporate control provides the glue that holds together the nexus of contracts.

2. Product Market Competition

Product market competition forces managers to attempt to maximize the profits of the corporation. Failure to maximize profits in competitive markets often means the failure of the firm, which may be as costly for the manager as it is for the shareholders. Because of firm-specific investments in their own human capital and the likelihood of compensation in the form of stock or stock options, managers typically have a larger percentage of their total wealth tied up in the firm they work for relative to the percentage of the typical diversified shareholder's wealth tied up in a particular firm. Thus, managers of firms that do not have market power have a strong incentive to act in the shareholders' interests. Moreover, even if a firm does have market power, the expectation of higher profits will have already been capitalized into the market price of the corporation's shares so that a failure to maximize profits will be reflected in a below-average return on the shareholders' investments, thus making the firm an attractive takeover target.

3. Capital Market Competition and Capital Structure

Most corporations use a mixture of debt and equity financing. In a pathbreaking 1958 article, Franco Modigliani and Merton Miller showed that, under a set of specified assumptions including absence of transaction and information costs, the capital structure of a firm—that is, its debt to equity mix—was irrelevant to the total value of the firm. *See* Modigliani & Miller, *The Cost of Capital, Corporation Finance, and the Theory of Investment*, 48 Am. Econ. Rev. 261 (1958). *See also* Miller, *The Modigliani Miller Propositions After Thirty Years*, 2 J. Econ. Perspectives 99 (1988). This raises the issue of why different capital structures are observed across firms.

The analytical strength of the contractual theory of the corporation is demonstrated by its ability to answer the Modigliani and Miller riddle. In a landmark article, Jensen and Meckling used agency problems and monitoring of managers to identify the relevance of capital structure to the value of a firm. *See* Jensen & Meckling, *Theory of the Firm: Managerial Behavior, Agency Costs, and Ownership Structure*, 3 J. Fin. Econ. 305 (1976). An all-equity structure gives substantial discretion to managers to use corporate assets for their own benefit subject only to the vague proscriptions of fiduciary duties. However, corporation managers have an incentive to minimize their combined costs of debt and equity capital because failure to do so would make them vulnerable to takeover. In order to raise equity capital at the lowest possible cost, a corporation's managers must convince potential shareholders that agency costs will be minimized. Bondholders also must address conflict of interest problems. For example, a debt-heavy structure induces those who hold equity and managers who are responsive to their interests to make highly risky investments that may produce great benefits to the equity holders if they succeed and losses to the debt holders if they fail. Under the

Jensen-Meckling view, different capital structures may be responses to different types of agency costs. There is no one optimal capital structure for all corporations. For more discussion of these financial economics issues, see Chapter XI.

4. Corporate Performance and Executive Compensation

Corporate compensation packages appear to be structured in a manner that solve most of the conflicts between managers and shareholders. Analytically, corporate compensation packages can include three components: (1) unconditional compensation, such as salary and pension and insurance benefits; (2) compensation conditioned on stock market-based performance, such as stock options and bonuses; and (3) compensation conditioned on accounting-based performance, such as profit sharing. Stock market-based performance measures are beyond managers' direct control or manipulation because stock prices reflect all available information, including the discounted value of long-term consequences of short-term actions, regarding the value of a firm. On the other hand, accounting-based performance measures are subject to manipulation by senior executives through, for example, decisions to maximize short-term accounting profitability at the expense of greater long-term (beyond managers' employment terms) profit. Thus, accounting-based performance measure are a potential source of agency costs, and most senior executives' compensation contracts do not include a component based on accounting performance.

Kamin v. American Express Company
Supreme Court of New York, Special Term, New York County
86 Misc. 2d 809; 383 N.Y.S.2d 807 (1976)

Edward J. Greenfield, Judge

In this stockholders' derivative action, the individual defendants, who are the directors of the American Express Company, move for an order dismissing the complaint for failure to state a cause of action pursuant to CPLR 3211 (subd [a], par 7), and alternatively, for summary judgment pursuant to CPLR 3211 (subd [c]).

The complaint is brought derivatively by two minority stockholders of the American Express Company, asking for a declaration that a certain dividend in kind is a waste of corporate assets, directing the defendants not to proceed with the distribution, or, in the alternative, for monetary damages. The motion to dismiss the complaint requires the court to presuppose the truth of the allegations. It is the defendants' contention that, conceding everything in the complaint, no viable cause of action is made out.

After establishing the identity of the parties, the complaint alleges that in 1972 American Express acquired for investment 1,954,418 shares of common stock of Donaldson, Lufken and Jenrette, Inc. (hereafter DLJ), a publicly traded corporation, at a cost of $29,900,000. It is further alleged that the current market value of those shares is approximately $4,000,000. On July 28, 1975, it is alleged, the board of directors of American Express declared a special dividend to all stockholders of record pursuant to which the shares of DLJ would be distributed in kind. Plaintiffs contend further that if American Express were to sell the DLJ shares on the market, it would sustain a capital loss of $25,000,000 which could be offset against taxable capital gains on other investments. Such a sale, they allege, would result in tax savings to the company of approximately $8,000,000, which would not be available in the case of the distribution of DLJ shares to stockholders. It is alleged that on October 8, 1975 and October 16, 1975, plaintiffs demanded that the directors rescind the previously declared dividend in DLJ shares and take steps to preserve the capital loss which would result from selling the shares. This demand was rejected by the board of directors on October 17, 1975.

It is apparent that all the previously-mentioned allegations of the complaint go to the question of the exercise by the board of directors of business judgment in deciding how to deal with the DLJ shares. The crucial allegation which must be scrutinized to determine the legal sufficiency of the complaint is paragraph 19, which alleges: "19. All of the defendant Directors engaged in or acquiesced in or negligently permitted the declaration and payment of the Dividend in violation of the fiduciary duty owed by them to Amex to care for and preserve Amex's assets in the same manner as a man of average prudence would care for his own property."

Plaintiffs never moved for temporary injunctive relief, and did nothing to bar the actual distribution of the DLJ shares. The dividend was in fact paid on October 31, 1975. Accordingly, that portion of the complaint seeking a direction not to distribute the shares is deemed to be moot, and the court will deal only with the request for declaratory judgment or for damages.

Examination of the complaint reveals that there is no claim of fraud or self-dealing, and no contention that there was any bad faith or oppressive conduct. The law is quite clear as to what is necessary to ground a claim for actionable wrongdoing. "In actions by stockholders, which assail the acts of their directors or trustees, courts will not interfere unless the powers have been illegally or unconscientiously executed, or unless it be made to appear that the acts were fraudulent or collusive and destructive of the rights of the stockholders. Mere errors of judgment are not sufficient as grounds for equity interference; for the powers of those entrusted with corporate management are largely discretionary." *Leslie v Lorillard*, 110 NY 519, 532.

More specifically, the question of whether or not a dividend is to be declared or a distribution of some kind should be made is exclusively a matter of business judgment for the board of directors. "Courts will not interfere with such discretion unless it be first made to appear that the directors have acted or are about to act in bad faith and for a dishonest purpose. It is for the directors to say, acting in good faith of course, when and to what extent dividends shall be declared. The statute confers upon the directors this power, and the minority stockholders are not in a position to question this right, so long as the directors are acting in good faith." *Liebman v Auto Strop Co.*, 241 NY 427, 433–434.

Thus, a complaint must be dismissed if all that is presented is a decision to pay dividends rather than pursuing some other course of conduct. A complaint which alleges merely that some course of action other than that pursued by the board of directors would have been more advantageous gives rise to no cognizable cause of action. Courts have more than enough to do in adjudicating legal rights and devising remedies for wrongs. The directors' room rather than the courtroom is the appropriate forum for thrashing out purely business questions which will have an impact on profits, market prices, competitive situations, or tax advantages. As stated by Cardozo, J., when sitting at Special Term, the substitution of someone else's business judgment for that of the directors " 'is no business for any court to follow.' " (*Holmes v Saint Joseph Lead Co.*, 84 Misc 278, 283, quoting from *Gamble v Queens County Water Co.*, 123 NY 91, 99.)

It is not enough to allege, as plaintiffs do here, that the directors made an imprudent decision, which did not capitalize on the possibility of using a potential capital loss to offset capital gains. More than imprudence or mistaken judgment must be shown. "Questions of policy of management, expediency of contracts or action, adequacy of consideration, lawful appropriation of corporate funds to advance corporate interests, are left solely to their honest and unselfish decision, for their powers therein are without limitation and free from restraint, and the exercise of them for the common and general interests of the corporation may not be questioned, although the results show that what they did was unwise or inexpedient." *Pollitz v Wabash R.R. Co.*, 207 NY 113, 124.

Section 720 (subd [a], par [1], cl [A]) of the Business Corporation Law permits an action against directors for "[the] neglect of, or failure to perform, or other violation of his duties in the management and disposition of corporate assets committed to his charge." This does not mean that a director is chargeable with ordinary negligence for having made an improper decision, or having acted imprudently. The "neglect" referred to in the statute is neglect of duties (i.e., malfeasance or nonfeasance) and not misjudgment. To allege that a director "negligently permitted the declaration and payment" of a dividend without alleging fraud, dishonesty or nonfeasance, is to state merely that a decision was taken with which one disagrees.

Nor does this appear to be a case in which a potentially valid cause of action is inartfully stated. The defendants have moved alternatively for summary judgment and have submitted affidavits under CPLR 3211 (subd [c]), and plaintiffs likewise have submitted papers enlarging upon the allegations of the complaint. The affidavits of the defendants and the exhibits annexed thereto demonstrate that the objections raised by the plaintiffs to the proposed dividend action were carefully considered and unanimously rejected by the board at a special meeting called precisely for that purpose at the plaintiffs' request. The minutes of the special meeting indicate that the defendants were fully aware that a sale rather than a distribution of the DLJ shares might result in the realization of a substantial income tax saving. Nevertheless, they concluded that there were countervailing considerations primarily with respect to the adverse effect such a sale, realizing a loss of $25,000,000, would have on the net income figures in the American Express financial statement. Such a reduction of net income would have a serious effect on the market value of the publicly traded American Express stock. This was not a situation in which the defendant directors totally overlooked facts called to their attention. They gave them consideration, and attempted to view the total picture in arriving at their decision. While plaintiffs contend that according to their accounting consultants the loss on the DLJ stock would still have to be charged against current earnings even if the stock were distributed, the defendants' accounting experts assert that the loss would be a charge against earnings only in the event of a sale, whereas in the event of distribution of the stock as a dividend, the proper accounting treatment would be to charge the loss only against surplus. While the chief accountant for the SEC raised some question as to the appropriate accounting treatment of this transaction, there was no basis for any action to be taken by the SEC with respect to the American Express financial statement.

The only hint of self-interest which is raised, not in the complaint but in the papers on the motion, is that 4 of the 20 directors were officers and employees of American Express and members of its executive incentive compensation plan. Hence, it is suggested, by virtue of the action taken earnings may have been overstated and their compensation affected thereby. Such a claim is highly speculative and standing alone can hardly be regarded as sufficient to support an inference of self-dealing. There is no claim or showing that the four company directors dominated and controlled the 16 outside members of the board. Certainly, every action taken by the board has some impact on earnings and may therefore affect the compensation of those whose earnings are keyed to profits. That does not disqualify the inside directors, nor does it put every policy adopted by the board in question. All directors have an obligation, using sound business judgment, to maximize income for the benefit of all persons having a stake in the welfare of the corporate entity. What we have here as revealed both by the complaint and by the affidavits and exhibits, is that a disagreement exists between two minority stockholders and a unanimous board of directors as to the best way to handle a loss already incurred on an investment. The directors are entitled to exercise their honest business judgment on the information before them, and to act within their corporate powers. That they may be mistaken, that other courses of action might have differing consequences, or that their action might benefit some shareholders more than others present no basis for the superimposition of judicial judgment, so long as it appears that the directors have been acting in good faith. The question of to what extent a dividend shall be declared and the manner in which it shall be paid is ordinarily subject only to the qualification that the dividend be paid out of surplus (Business Corporation Law, § 510, subd [b]). The court will not interfere unless a clear case is made out of fraud, oppression, arbitrary action, or breach of trust.

Courts should not shrink from the responsibility of dismissing complaints or granting summary judgment when no legal wrongdoing is set forth. As stated in *Greenbaum v American Metal Climax* (27 AD2d 225, 231–232):

> "It is well known that derivative actions by stockholders generally involve extensive pretrial procedures, including lengthy examinations before trial, and then, finally, prolonged trials; and that they also entail large litigation costs, including the probability of a considerable liability upon the corporation for the defense costs of defendant offices. Such actions are a heavy burden upon the courts and litigants. Consequently, the summary judgment remedy should be fully utilized and given due effect to challenge such an action which appears to be in the nature of a strike suit or otherwise lacks apparent merit[plaintiffs] are bound to bear in mind that matters depending on business judgment are not actionable. (*Cf. Steinberg v Carey*, 285 App Div 1131.) They are required to set forth something more than vague general charges of wrongdoing; their

charges must be supported by factual assertions of specific wrongdoing; conclusory allegations of breaches of fiduciary duty are not enough."

In this case it clearly appears that the plaintiffs have failed as a matter of law to make out an actionable claim. Accordingly, the motion by the defendants for summary judgment and dismissal of the complaint is granted.

Notes and Questions

1. Market Evaluation of American Express's Investment in DLJ: In terms of stock market valuation of the business, American Express made a poor business decision by not taking the substantial capital loss and resulting tax savings. The large accounting loss would have been anticipated by investors who, after all, could observe what had happened to the market value of American Express's investment in DLJ. That is, prior to the board's decision, AMEX's market price already reflected the anticipated losses (and tax savings) from the decline in DLJ stock. See the discussion of efficient capital markets in Chapter XI. By not taking the large capital loss, the expected future cash flows to American Express declined because they now had to pay higher taxes. The stock market price should have fallen in response to this unexpected change.

2. Accounting-Based Compensation. Accounting data can be manipulated by senior managers. In this case, the senior managers wanted to avoid showing an accounting loss from the DLJ investment. Consider how the executives' incentives structures affected this transaction. The four members of the Board of Directors were compensated according to the book value of the firm. The book value is a compilation of all incomes and expenditures, using conventional accounting techniques. However, book value does not always correspond with stock value—in fact, in this case, book value and market value probably moved in opposite directions. But since the compensation of the directors was linked to book value, they could not take the large capital loss without substantially affecting their own salaries. This decision was not in the best interests of shareholders.

The incentive structure was the problem.

3. The Business Judgment Rule. Judicial interpretations of the fiduciary duty of due care protect managers from second-guessing of informed business decisions. See the discussion in this section, *infra*.

4. Typical Compensation Arrangements: Accounting-based profit-sharing arrangements are often used for middle and lower-level employees who are generally not in a position to manipulate accounting data. However, for top-level executives, compensation is usually linked to stock price. The stock market is an external monitor of firm performance and is difficult to fool with accounting shenanigans. With the proper compensation system in place, manipulation does not occur and shareholders are better off.

Managerial salaries and other forms of compensation are often linked to how well the firm is performing. Managers monitor each others' performances and reward achievements with bonuses and salary adjustments as a form of "ex post settling up" that substantially alleviates incentive problems. Also, if managers enjoy especially favorable salaries or other terms of employment, they may be disciplined by the prospect of being fired. Managers' proclivities towards shirking can be reduced even further by the use of stock options and bonus plans which alter a manager's time horizon for her managerial decisions so as to ensure that she acts in accordance with the long-term interests of her principals. As managers approach retirement, defined benefit pension plans under which benefits are linked to the last periods salary resolve some of the horizon problems. Stock options in retirement packages can also serve to alleviate horizon problems. Finally, as illustrated by the next case, "golden parachutes" can be used to allign managers' incentives.

International Insurance Co. v. Johns
United States Court of Appeals, Eleventh Circuit
874 F.2d 1447 (1989)

KING, C.J.

In this appeal we examine golden parachutes[1] and corporate control from an insurance law perspective. A Florida corporation's board of directors adopted golden parachutes for several key executives. After change in corporate control opened the parachutes, a disgruntled shareholder instituted a derivative action, alleging that the parachute payments were corporate waste. The directors settled the action, and sought payment for this compromise under their corporate liability insurance policy. The insurance company denied coverage and filed this declaratory action to justify its refusal to honor the claim. After a three-day trial, the district court found coverage. We now affirm.

FACTS

Southwest Florida Banks, Inc. ("Southwest") was incorporated under the laws of Florida in 1972. From 1972 until 1975, the bank assembled a management group which included the appellees. Under this management, Southwest experienced substantial financial growth and rapid expansion. The consolidated total assets of Southwest grew from $ 226 million in 1972 to $ 1.4 billion in 1982. The net income of the company also increased from $ 1.9 million in 1972 to $ 14.2 million in 1982.[3]

As a result of this growth, Southwest became an attractive takeover target by the end of 1982. The First Boston Corporation ("First Boston"), Southwest's investment banker, informed the management group late in 1982 that the bank easily could be acquired. First Boston told the board that a large amount of Southwest's common stock was held by institutions that were likely to approve a change in management for modest improvements in earnings. First Boston also informed Southwest's management that a recent substantial increase in the number of banking acquisitions had occurred.

---

1. Golden parachutes are essentially termination agreements providing "substantial bonuses and other benefits for managers and certain directors upon a change in control in a company." *Revlon, Inc. v. MacAndrews & Forbes Holdings, Inc.*, 506 A.2d 173, 178 n. 5 (Del. 1986); *see also Schreiber v. Burlington Northern, Inc.*, 472 U.S. 1, 4 n. 2, 105 S. Ct. 2458, 2460 n. 2, 86 L. Ed. 2d 1 (1985).

3. In 1983, however, Southwest's net income declined to $ 12,200,000.

A number of key officers and employees expressed considerable concern about the likelihood and consequences of a merger. Southwest's previous executive bonus system had expired. Southwest's board of directors adopted this plan, linking bonuses to earnings per share, for key executives in 1977. These executives remained with the company during the five years this plan was in operation. Southwest's management believed that if the same executives were to remain in the future, a new compensation system was needed.

On March 21, 1983, Southwest's board of directors established the Performance Incentive Plan ("PIP"). PIP provided for the creation of 400,000 units, each valued at $10.00. Payment of the dollar value of the units would be made to the participants five years after the award of the units, or immediately if a change in the control of Southwest occurred. A specially appointed committee of three directors ("PIP Committee") was to administer PIP by awarding units to the chairman of the board, and recommending to the chairman the other recipients. Only officers and full-time employees of Southwest or its subsidiaries were eligible for PIP payments.

PIP's stated purpose was to induce uniquely important officers and management employees of the company to remain in its employ during the critical next five years. To accomplish this purpose, PIP was to minimize their concerns about the impact a potential acquisition would have on their future employment. Accordingly, PIP offered "additional, but contingent and deferred compensation.

The board adopted PIP by unanimous vote on July 20, 1983, with all fifteen directors voting. Of these fifteen, only three board members were eligible and actual recipients under PIP. The other directors were not eligible because they were not officers or employees of Southwest or its subsidiaries. Although the board believed a merger was probable within the next five years, no particular merger was contemplated when the board voted.

The PIP Committee recommended the following awards: appellees Johns and Sherman were to receive 100,000 units each; appellee McFadden was to receive 50,000 units; appellees Ogletree and Whorton were to be awarded 40,000 units each. Johns, the chairman, made all the recommended awards.

On October 25, 1983, Southwest approved, subject to regulatory and shareholder approvals, a merger of Southwest into Landmark Banking Corporation of Florida ("Landmark"). A key provision of this merger agreement, approved by the board of directors of both Southwest and Landmark, authorized Southwest to enter into a consulting agreement with its former chairman, Johns. The contract provided for a five-year term with annual compensation of $225,000. Both boards intended to accomplish two purposes through this consultation agreement. First, the merged corporation wanted Johns to be available for consultation and to serve as a director when needed. Second, the agreement assured that Johns would not establish any employment relationship with another bank or savings institution without the approval of the merged company. Around April 25, 1984, Southwest and Johns officially entered into the consulting agreement.

In December 1983, Southwest and Landmark mailed a joint proxy statement to their shareholders. The joint proxy statement described the terms of the merger, as well as PIP and the consulting agreement. On January 19, 1984, the shareholders of both Southwest and Landmark voted to approve the merger.

Subsequently, the requisite regulatory approval was obtained. Southwest and Landmark, therefore, merged, and the separate existence of Southwest ended.

On January 10, 1984, Southwest made the monetary awards that the PIP Committee specified. This disbursement of PIP funds gave rise to a lawsuit. A disgruntled Southwest shareholder filed a derivative action in United States District Court contending that PIP and the consulting agreement were a waste of corporate assets. The shareholder sued all of Southwest's directors and the other PIP recipients. On July 12, 1984, Southwest's board convened a special meeting to address the merits of this lawsuit. At the meeting, the board again ratified PIP and the PIP awards, noting that PIP had achieved its purpose of keeping the management group together until the time of the merger.

In February 1985, the parties to the derivative action settled the litigation and the court approved the settlement on April 30, 1985. The settlement provided for the shareholder to dismiss the action in exchange for the return to Landmark of $600,000 awarded under PIP, as well as a reduction in the term of John's consulting agreement from five years to two and one-half years. The directors did not admit liability in the settlement agreement.

The officers and directors, who were sued as defendants in the derivative action, filed a claim against their liability insurance policy seeking to recover this repayment. The policy, issued in December 1982 by International Insurance Company ("International"), covered the directors and officers for all losses (including damages and settlements) resulting from their "wrongful acts" (actual or alleged) committed within the scope of their employment. The policy also contained two key exclusion clauses. The first provision, paragraph 5(c), excluded any loss resulting from any illegal remuneration that the director or officers received without required shareholder approval. The second condition, paragraph 5(b), excluded any loss resulting from any illegal personal gain by the officer or director.

*　*　*

We must review PIP and the consulting agreement under the business judgment rule because both circumstances are found here.[26] A disinterested Southwest board and a majority of Southwest's shareholders approved PIP and the consulting agreement. In addition, the Southwest board's adoption of PIP essentially effectuated the desires of the PIP Committee.

Under the business judgment rule, courts presume that directors have acted properly and in good faith.[27] A court will not call upon a director to account for his action in the absence of a showing of abuse of discretion, fraud, bad faith, or illegality. Essentially, unless the party challenging the board's action can prove

---

26. All parties agrees that both plans should be reviewed under the business judgment rule.

27. In Florida, directors must perform their duties "in good faith, [and] in a manner they reasonably believe to be in the best interest of the corporation, and with such care as an ordinary prudent person in a like position would use under similar circumstances." Fla.Stat. Ann. § 607.111(4). Directors are not liable for actions taken in accord with this statute. Fla. Stat.Ann. § 607.111(6).

one of these four factors, the court will not substitute its judgment for that of the board so long as the action taken was rational.

Because of this great deference, courts do not invalidate executive compensation systems under the business judgment rule unless they constitute corporate waste. Corporate waste exists when the payment is afforded without "adequate" consideration. Under the business judgment rule, adequacy of consideration is left to the sound discretion of the directors, and courts do not invalidate compensation plans so long as the compensation the executive receives bares a reasonable relationship to the services rendered. A compensation plan passes this "reasonable relationship" test if the payment insures that the benefit provided by the services rendered will inure to the corporation.

Necessarily, the reasonable relationship analysis requires a court to conduct three inquiries. First, the court must determine whether the corporation benefited from the services rendered. If the corporation received no benefits in exchange, the payments insured nothing, and the compensation system is corporate waste. Second, a court should examine whether the compensation was so unreasonably disproportionate to the benefits created by the exchange that a reasonable person would think the corporation did not receive a quid pro quo. If no quid pro quo resulted, no true benefit could inure to the corporation, for the payments would constitute corporate gifts, and, therefore, would offset any benefit received in exchange. Finally, a court must conclude that the services rendered triggered the payments.

In conducting these three inquiries for both PIP and the consulting agreement, we note that the parties agreed that International had the burden of proof on this issue in the court below.[31] To prevail, therefore, International must prove that PIP and the consulting agreement were corporate waste. In this respect, International's burden of proof differs from that of the appellees on the issue of whether a loss occurred. The appellees, pursuant to the policy's definition, did not have to prove actual wrongdoing, but only alleged misbehavior.

a. PIP is not corporate waste.

In important respects, PIP is not a typical golden parachute. PIP's payments were not necessarily conditioned upon the change in control clause. The board also designed PIP to provide bonuses to key employees over a five year period. The payments were to be deferred until the fifth year, and paid only if the recipient remained with Southwest. Unlike most golden parachutes, therefore, Southwest was to make the PIP payments irrespective of a change in control.

Southwest's board intended PIP's unique structure to assure that the corporation would receive two primary benefits regardless of an actual change in control. First, Southwest intended to retain its key management employees during a volatile period marked by numerous banking mergers. The board realized that these man-

---

31. Normally, a challenging shareholder has the burden of proving a breach of a fiduciary duty under the business judgment rule. International is not a challenging shareholder. The parties in the district court stipulated that the appellees had the burden of proof on the loss issue and International had the burden of the exclusion issues. Accordingly, International has the burden of proof under the business judgment rule.

agement employees were highly successful in the past, and desired to utilize their skills in the uncertain five year period ahead, when the company may be sold. Second, the board believed PIP's structure would assure Southwest that these employees would continue to act in the corporation's best interest. If faced with a buyout, the board believed PIP assured that these employees could arrange a fair deal. If the company remained independent, the board believed PIP would guarantee that this management group would continue making Southwest a highly profitable venture.

Of utmost importance here is the fact the Southwest actually received these benefits. As the district court noted, the management group remained intact until the merger. Moreover, this management team helped negotiate an acquisition agreement that the shareholders overwhelmingly approved.

These two benefits were, indeed, substantial. Southwest faced serious threats of losing its highly successful management team. Southwest needed a plan that would eliminate this problem so that the phenomenal growth of Southwest could continue. Moreover, the circumstances surrounding the board when it enacted PIP created incentives for the company's key executives to perform less successfully than in the past. Accordingly, Southwest needed a system to assure the management's full devotion. PIP was established to achieve these goals.

The creation of a bonus system to retain key employees is a proper corporate purpose. Generally, these bonus systems assure that key employees will forgo other employment opportunities and remain with the company.

To determine whether a plan assures that an employee will stay with the company we must examine some of the generic factors that influence an executive's choice of employment.[33] As with most professionals, a corporate executive chooses employment for both economic and noneconomic reasons. *See Koenings v. Joseph Schlitz Brewing Co.*, 126 Wis. 2d 349, 377 N.W.2d 593, 601–603 (Wis. 1985). On the economic side, the executive considers salary and vacation pay, *Koenings*, 377 N.W.2d at 601, as well as corporate perks, like medical benefits, company automobile and travel. From the noneconomic perspective, the executive cogitates issues like prestige of the firm, the amount of decision-making authority, degree of professional respect, job security, and career advancement. *Koenings*, 377 N.W.2d at 602–603.

A corporation always desires to have a talented and specialized management. An efficient and profitable management depends upon specialized executives. To become specialized, executives must acquire firm-specific knowledge. To gain this knowledge, executives must expend human capital learning the day to day operations of the firm. Generally, the longer an executive remains with a company the more firm-specific knowledge that executive acquires. Loyal executives, therefore become increasingly specialized as time passes resulting in the corporation's management becoming more efficient.

An executive payment plan incorporating only economic incentives would not suffice to secure specialized executives. These compensation plans ignore the

---

33. The general motivating factors that attract an executive to a firm also provide the basis for the executive's decision to remain with that company. Only the specific incentives within these factors change during the course of employment.

executive's desires for career advancement or job security. Executives would then naturally desire to move to a firm that offered such securities, or one that supplied a better economic package. The employee, therefore, would lose the desire to acquire firm-specific knowledge, for this type of wisdom, by its very nature, is not readily transferable to another company. The end result for the corporation necessarily would be non-specialized executives, and, thus, less efficient management.

If, however, a firm added noneconomic incentives to the compensation package, the executive would be more willing to acquire firm-specific knowledge. Incentives such as career advancement and job security would add a degree of permanency. Executives would look toward the firm as a career and be hesitant to leave for another company. The incentive to become specialized and move up the corporate ladder becomes real. The corporation providing both economic and noneconomic incentives for its executives would acquire and retain specialized employees, and, thus, an efficient and profitable management.

The mere fact of creating such a compensation plan, however, may be insufficient to retain qualified executives. To prevent another company from recruiting a key employee, a corporation must review and update their executive compensation plan. Corporations always look for a successful executive. Corporations, therefore, are willing to "raid" another firm to acquire an executive. The impetus for the raid is usually increased incentives. By offering more money or career incentives, companies hope to lure successful individuals to its door.

To ease the threat of a management raid, a corporation must compensate its successful executives at labor market levels. A bonus system is a convenient manner to achieve this goal, for such a compensation plan often includes both economic and noneconomic incentives. A bonus may be a cash payment, or a stock warrant, or a profit-sharing plan. Accordingly, the bonus system allows the corporation to mix and match economic and noneconomic incentives so the compensation package rapidly adjusts to labor market levels.

When viewed in this light, PIP would have eliminated this threat if Southwest was not taken over. PIP was to provide additional compensation to eight key executives. A disinterested compensation committee considered PIP's economic incentives sufficient to dissipate the departure temptations that these individuals would have faced over the next five years. After considering that Southwest's previous five year bonus system kept the management team in place, PIP most likely would have eliminated the threat of an executive raid.

A corporation facing an imminent takeover has other departure worries. When a corporation that has created both economic and noneconomic incentives for its executives confronts the high probability of a takeover, a separate incentive for the executive to leave arises. With the threat of takeover comes the possibility of displacement from the company. Naturally, threats to both the economic and noneconomic incentives to remain arise. On the economic side, the executive faces the loss of his salary, retirement benefits, vacation pay, and other advantages. *Koenings*, 377 N.W.2d at 601. From the noneconomic perspective, the executive's job security is threatened, as well as career advancement commensurate with seniority and skills, marketability, professional respect, and satisfaction of working at a prestigious company. *Koenings*, 377 N.W.2d at 602–603. The executive believes he can avoid most of the loss in the economic incentives and some of the loss of the noneconomic stimuli by leaving before actual displacement. The executive then will look for another job before a buyout occurs.

The executive's incentive to leave in the takeover context becomes readily apparent through a neoclassical economic analysis. The executive perceives a disequilibrium between the value of his or her services and the expected value of the compensation received in exchange. The executive's compensation is the sum of the economic and noneconomic incentives. The executive's expected value of this compensation is a function of the amount of consideration and the certainty that it will be received. Id. at 916 n. 42. In a company facing a high probability of a buyout, the certainty of the rewards from these compensation incentives becomes less. *Id.* The employee faces a loss of economic compensation and a frustration of the noneconomic benefits. Id. Accordingly, the expected value of the executive's compensation package falls. At the same time, the value of the services the executive performs remains constant. The employee remains performing his or her appointed tasks for the firm. Disequilibrium between the value of services performed and the expected value of the compensation received results. The executive, therefore, has an incentive to increase the expected value of his or her compensation (and, thus, restore equilibrium) by seeking employment elsewhere. *Id.* at 916.

Aside from potentially losing the executive during these unstable times, the corporation faces another problem. As noted above, the threat that causes the executive to contemplate leaving also makes the executive less desirable of gaining firm-specific knowledge. Even if that employee does not leave because a takeover never occurs the acquiring of firm-specific knowledge would be retarded. The executive would take longer to specialize, resulting in less long-term efficiency for management.

Golden parachutes help offset these problems. The golden parachute shifts the risk of displacement from the executive to the corporation. The plan's payment is intended to compensate the executive for most of the economic loss and some of the noneconomic loss associated with forced departure.[34] The executive, therefore, remains at ease. He or she continues to acquire firm-specific knowledge, and the management team remains efficient and profitable.[35]

As a golden parachute, therefore, PIP helped eliminate the short-term departure threat caused by an imminent takeover. PIP provided compensation designed to cover displacement costs in the event of a buyout. A disinterested compensation committee believed the PIP payments would cover all necessary losses that would effect to the economic and noneconomic incentives. The de-

---

34. The payment reflects economic loss, like salary forgone, as well as some of the noneconomic loss, like prestige and marketability. The payments often replace the reduction in prestige and marketability, for large payments, which must be disclosed under the federal securities laws, *see* 15 C.F.R. § 299.402(e) (1986), indicate to the business environment the relative importance of the executive's previous position. Of course, the analysis necessarily applies only to executives not "important" enough to remain in the new organization.

35. The golden parachute also restores the equilibrium in the neoclassical economic model. The golden parachute restores the executive's expected value of the compensation package to the level equaling the value of the services provided.

sign worked, for the management team remained intact until the merger was consummated.

Southwest benefited from PIP in another important respect. In providing further assurances that Southwest executives would act in the corporation's best interests,[36] Southwest necessarily reduced its monitoring costs.[37]

All corporations necessarily incur monitoring costs. Jensen & Meckling, *Theory of The Firm: Managerial Behavior, Agency Costs and Ownership Structure*, 3 J.Fin.Econ. 305, 308 (1976). Because managers generally do not own the corporations they run, their interests may be contrary to the stockholders. Accordingly, management may avoid corporate action because of personal benefit even though the action may be beneficial to the stockholders. *Id.* The corporation, therefore, necessarily incurs monitoring costs—the expenses that arise from management potentially not acting in the best interests of the company.[38] *Id.*

Golden parachutes necessarily reduce these costs. By easing the fears of displacement, the directors would not oppose a takeover just to protect their personal interests. The directors, realizing that the corporation would ease their disassociation losses, could concentrate on a takeover offer from the perspective of fairness and optimality to the corporation. The corporation, therefore, would not incur additional monitoring costs.[39]

---

36. A failure of consideration due to a pre-existing duty is not present in the golden parachute context. The performance of an action one is already legally obligated to do cannot support a promise. *See generally, Henderson v. Kendrick*, 82 Fla. 110, 89 So. 635, 89 So. 635 (Fla. 1921). If a golden parachute was designed to assure performance in accord with fiduciary duties, the plan would fail for lack of consideration. A golden parachute, however, provides additional, bona fide benefits to the corporation. Aside from retaining valuable executives during a volatile time, the golden parachute helps reduce monitoring costs during the takeover threat. *See infra* slip op. p. 2772,. Performance that differs from what was previously due is sufficient consideration to support a separate promise. *Greenfield v. Millman*, 111 So. 2d 480 (Fla. 3d DCA 1959).

37. Corporations desire to minimize monitoring costs, which are termed "agency costs" in neoclassical economics. *See* Jensen & Meckling, *Theory of the Firm*, 3 J.Fin.Econ. 305, 308 (1976).

38. These costs, from a neoclassical economic perspective, would be the actual expenses of supervising and restricting management, as well as opportunity costs presented through each corporate action. In the corporate decision-making context, opportunity costs are the real value associated with the directors adopting the most desirable alternative. To a large extent, these opportunity costs would be lost profits.

39. The golden parachute specifically reduces the opportunity costs aspect of the monitoring costs. In a company without golden parachutes, the directors' interests and those of the company may be diametrically opposed, as in the case of a merger very favorable to the shareholders but that will result in certain director displacement. The directors, after balancing their certain displacement losses with the potential harm arising from a refusal to approve the offer, may lean to protecting their interest and reject the merger. The opportunity cost to the shareholders from this action, that is, the difference in real value to the corporation resulting from the boards' choosing to disapprove rather than approve the merger, is necessarily high. In a company with golden parachutes, the directors' interests will be closer to those of the company. In the case of the favorable merger discussed above, the directors have little concern over displacement, and, therefore, would not risk potential civil liability by disapproving the merger. They would approve the merger, and, therefore, the opportunity cost to the corporation here is minimal.

Neoclassical economic theory reflects these directors' decisions in terms of utility functions. The board makes a decision at a point of indifference between its and the corpora-

This conclusion, however, is not without its critics. The most significant criticism maintains that golden parachutes actually increase monitoring costs. Note, *Golden Parachutes: Untangling the Ripcords*, 39 Stan.L.Rev. 955, 967–8 (1987). This position believes golden parachutes create a risk that management may, in their desire to collect their golden parachute benefits, violate their fiduciary duties. *Id.* at 967. A corporation, therefore, necessarily incurs additional monitoring costs by enacting golden parachutes.

Essentially, this argument considers golden parachutes as insurance for displacement and advocates the problem of moral hazards. The moral hazard of insurance is that one has less incentive to take care because he or she is insured. R. Posner, Economic Analysis of Law, 150 (3d ed.1986). In the golden parachute context, two potential moral hazards are presented: (1) the executive has more incentive to approve a less optimal merger, and, (2) the executive will be rewarded for turning a healthy company into a takeover target. This argument maintains that these moral hazards give rise to the additional monitoring costs. We disagree.

Most likely, a manager would not orchestrate an improvident merger. If he or she did, a violation of a fiduciary duty of care would result, and civil liability would arise. Id. Moreover, the manager's value in the job market would decrease, for the manager's professional reputation in the business community would be blemished.[40] *Id.* In addition, the fact that an "improvident" merger was approved by the shareholders, which is required in Florida, see Fla.Stat.Ann. section 607.221 (West 1977), would seem to indicate that the merger was not actually unwise.

Similarly, a manager would not turn a profitable company into a takeover target. Takeover targets are companies that underachieve, resulting in low shareholder returns. *Id.* at 969 (citing empirical studies). Poor management, at least in part, causes low shareholder returns.[41] *Id.* at 970. An acquirer believes it can improve returns by changing management. *Id.* Management would not intentionally underachieve to increase takeover probability. If a manager did, the executive would have little chance of finding new employment upon discharge. *Id.* The executive's golden parachute, therefore, would have to provide enough returns to offset the financial, social and psychological costs associated with a performance the market recognizes as subpar. *Id.* Whether any board could construct a large enough golden parachute to assure this is doubtful.

---

tion's utilities. Golden parachutes change the directors' utility functions such that a point of indifference of higher utility to the corporation results.

40. An executive's reputation is an economically valuable asset that makes up a significant portion of his or her human capital. *See* Fama, *Agency Problems and The Theory of The Firm*, 88 J.Pol.Econ. 288, 297–98 (1980).

41. Low shareholder returns are primarily caused by less than optimal performance. Poor management, of course, can utilize the limited resources of the firm in an inefficient manner. Optimality, however, should not be judged exclusively from this perspective. A management team could use all the firm's resources in an efficient manner, and low shareholders returns would nonetheless exist. A reason for such a condition would be that the firm was operating in a limited context. In some circumstances, optimality can only be achieved through merger, as where regional companies combine together to operate in a larger geographical market. This type of merger would improve the economies of scale. This situation existed with Southwest. Southwest had a very efficient management team that operated in a regional area. Landmark believed that a merger with Southwest could improve efficiency by increasing economies of scale.

Another criticism maintains that golden parachutes do not reduce monitoring costs.[42] This view advocates that "new" monitoring costs do not arise in a takeover context. This position rests upon the fact that directors always owe a fiduciary duty. The company's monitoring costs must be linked to these duties. Any additional monitoring costs designed to focus upon the directors' fiduciary duties in a takeover situation, therefore, would be superfluous.

A corporation facing a high probability of a buyout, however, incurs additional monitoring costs that are not necessarily linked to the director's fiduciary duties. As noted above, the takeover threat gives the executives an incentive to leave the company. With that incentive comes a desire to avoid acquiring additional firm-specific knowledge. The executive becomes less specialized, and management less efficient. If a takeover never occurs, the executive's continued path toward specialization is retarded. Because a buyout may never occur, a corporation necessarily incurs monitoring costs associated with this hindrance.

The enactment of golden parachutes helps reduce these monitoring costs. The golden parachute decreases the executive's incentive to leave, and, thus, his or her disincentive to become specialized. This lessening in costs is an advantage to the corporation.

PIP provided Southwest with *bona fide* benefits. The plan eliminated the executive's departure threats, and kept the management team in place until the merger. Moreover, PIP kept management operating in Southwest's best interests, and reduced the corporation's monitoring costs.

Even though Southwest benefited from PIP, PIP would still fail if the payments Southwest made in exchange were disproportionately large to offend reasonableness....

*   *   *

In conducting this inquiry, we are very cognizant of the fact that a disinterested PIP committee was empowered to determine both the plan's recipients and award amounts. This committee was an integral part of Southwest. Its members knew of the monumental success Southwest's management enjoyed. The committee could easily determine the precise individuals responsible for Southwest's achievements. The committee was in a unique position to ascertain the precise combination of economic and noneconomic incentives that influenced each of these executives. The committee, therefore, could properly calculate the incentives necessary to keep the key employees in place for both the short and long terms.

We are not in a better position to second guess the committee's determinations. PIP induced these executives to stay with Southwest; therefore, the intended benefits to Southwest were achieved....

*   *   *

CONCLUSION

The district court was correct in its finding that sums paid by officers and directors in settlement of a derivative shareholder's suit for corporate waste was a

---

42. Golden parachutes should not be considered as monitoring costs that arise in a takeover situation. They may be considered monitoring costs of ordinary day-to-day operations of a company. Without them, a corporation faces both the threat of poor performance and executive departure, even if the company is never acquired.

loss within the meaning of the insurance contract, not precluded by any policy exclusion. We, therefore,

AFFIRM.

Notes and Questions

1. Golden Parachutes: One way of aligning managerial interests with shareholder interests is through the so-called **Golden Parachute**. A golden parachute is a compensation package provided to top level management that is triggered if they leave the company subsequent to a takeover. The purpose of the golden parachute is to align the interest of shareholders with management. If the takeover is beneficial to the shareholders, they would want their managers to seek out the best offers available. However, because most of the manager's wealth, i.e., his or her human capital, is invested in the firm, managers will often reject shareholder wealth maximizing takeover offers which may cost them their jobs or accept inferior offers which guarantee their staying with the surviving corporation. Such actions are inconsistent with the agent's duty to maximize shareholder wealth. Therefore, depending on the costs involved, it may be in the shareholder's interest to pay management to accept offers that maximize shareholder wealth rather than offers that maximize management wealth. Some studies have shown that the stock market "believes" that golden parachutes maximize shareholder wealth as their announcement tends to increase the price of the firm stock.

2. What Kind of Golden Parachute?: The golden parachute in *Johns* was constructed so that the directors received large payments without reference to their performance. Does this type of Golden Parachute align incentives correctly? Is it possible for the managers to circumvent the purpose of the Golden Parachute with this structure?

3. Golden Parachutes and the Pre-Existing Duty Rule: At common law, where a party promises to do that which they are already legally obligated to do, no sufficient consideration exists to support the new promise. This is known as the pre-existing duty rule. The executives in *Johns* owed fiduciary duties of loyalty and care to the shareholders of Southwest. Why then did the shareholders need the additional compensation provided by the golden parachutes? What was the court's rationale in this regard? According to the court what served as consideration for the golden parachutes? Do you agree?

4. Southwest's Superior Management?: At several points in the opinion, the court notes that firms can become takeover targets due to managerial underperformance. Southwest was a takeover target, yet the court on several occasions indicates that Southwest had superior management. In fact, according to the court, the purpose of the golden parachutes was to guarantee that this outstanding management team would stay with Southwest. Is there a contradiction here, or are there other reasons why a firm might be a takeover target? As evidence for the conclusion that Southwest had outstanding management, the court appears to rely on an increase in the *absolute* level of assets and net income. Is this evidence adequate to support the conclusion that management was outstanding? What if other banks in the area were able to grow their assets and net income at twice the rate of Southwest? If Southwest's management was poor *relative* to banks in like positions, how then do you justify golden parachutes?

5. Reducing Agency Costs: The conclusion in the *Johns* opinion relies to a large degree on agency costs analysis. Different perspectives on how golden parachutes might impact agency costs were offered in the opinion. Which of these arguments is most persuasive to you? Is the court's analysis consistent with analysis presented in this casebook? What type of evidence does or should the court use to substantiate its agency costs analysis?

5. Markets for Managers

Corporate managers recognize that they can improve the performance of the firm by reducing agency costs. Managers compete with one another to attain the top positions in their companies, and most promotion decisions are made on the basis of an individual's productivity. Shareholders benefit as managers attempt to rise the corporate ladder by improving their productivity and impressing their superiors. Moreover, top-level managers often increase their salaries by jumping to other firms (or at least threatening to do so). Thus, competition for managerial services, both inside and outside the corporation, encourages managers to act in shareholders' best interests.

6. Corporate Hierarchy and the Board of Directors

The board of directors' acquiescence in management's decisions lies at the heart of Berle and Means' attack on the large publicly traded corporation. In this perspective, the board is assumed to reflect the same agency problems as managers. Recent developments in the economics of corporate hierarchy have helped to clarify the board's role as a monitor of managerial decisions. This analysis takes the separation of ownership (residual risk bearing) and control (decision management) analysis one step further and looks at the specialization of functions by agents who control the firm. One branch of this analysis has concentrated on the importance of the structure of the corporate hierarchy to controlling agency costs, while the other has looked at the complementary roles of managers and directors.

The separation of strategic decision making from day-to-day operating decision making was the most important development of the so-called "M-form" revolution. Beginning in the 1920s, the unitary non-divisionalized (U-) form of organization in large firms was gradually replaced by the multi-divisional (M-) form of firm organization. The M-form organization is characterized by a general corporate office and staff that handle long-term entrepreneurial activities of the firm. The existing theoretical and empirical literature suggests that the M-form is more efficient than the U-form for most large enterprises. In particular, the M-form corporation appears to promote an increase in emphasis on strategic management and appears to reduce agency problems. The general office reduces agency costs as it specializes in monitoring the performance of separately staffed, self-contained operating divisions. The success of the general office is then evaluated by externally observable variables — such as stock prices and rate of return.

The role for the board of directors at the top of the M-form firm is to establish an effective decision monitoring structure. The control of the corporation by agents is separated according to function whereby decision management (the initiation and implementation of strategic plans) is entrusted to senior managers and decision control (the ratification and monitoring of the strategy formulation and implementation process) is the domain of the board of directors. That is, the management control functions are delegated to the board by the residual claimants, and the board then delegates most decision management functions and many decision control functions to internal agents, but it retains ultimate control over internal agents—including the right to ratify and monitor major policy initiatives and to hire, fire, and set the compensation of top level decision managers. Agency problems are reduced by tying compensation to these specialized activities. Thus, unlike the Berle and Means's perspective, which views directors as pawns in the managers' hands, the role of directors is important to the control of agency costs and, hence, the long-term survival of the firm.

7. Ownership Structure

Ownership structure often plays an important role in the governance of corporations. In contrast to the convention of viewing the governance role of residual claimants as that of being "rationally ignorant" of the firm's internal affairs and exiting the firm upon dissatisfaction, owners of large blocks of shares may have so much of their wealth tied up in a firm that they cannot afford to ignore the governance of the corporation. Monitoring, or the possibility of monitoring, by large shareholders alters managerial behavior and reduces agency costs. Thus, ownership structure is another of the many corporate governance mechanisms that can be utilized in controlling agency costs. Of course, in many corporations, the ownership structure is so diffuse that shareholders are truly rationally ignorant, making the other governance mechanisms relatively more important.

8. Corporate Law and Fiduciary Duties

Emphasis on the interaction of market forces under the contractual theory of the corporation has led some scholars to argue that markets will lead managers to adopt optimal governance structures and that corporate law is irrelevant. However, market mechanisms may be inadequate to deal with last-period, or one-time, divergences when the agent rationally concludes that the benefits of the one-time use of discretion is worth whatever penalties may be forthcoming in the employment market for the agent's services. In this regard, the corporate law of fiduciary duties serves as a legal constraint on managerial opportunism.

Moreover, because markets do not operate without cost, it appears that corporate law plays a productive role in the contractual theory of the corporation by providing a standard form contract that reduces the transaction and negotiating costs of reaching and adhering to optimal contracts. In fact, some commentators have argued that it is appropriate to view corporation law as a standard form contract. Through the law of fiduciary duties, which proscribes theft and specifies standards of care and loyalty, corporate law substitutes for costly, fully contingent contracts. The directors and the officers occupy a **fiduciary relationship** with the corporation and its shareholders. As fiduciaries, the directors and officers have a duty to act with the highest standard of good faith when acting on behalf of the corporation and its shareholders. The primary enforcement mechanism is to hold directors and officers liable for the losses to the corporation that result from their failure to fulfill their fiduciary duties.

Jordan v. Duff and Phelps, Inc.

United States Court of Appeals, Seventh Circuit
815 F.2d 429 (1987)

EASTERBROOK, Circuit Judge.

Flamm v. Eberstadt, 814 F.2d 1169 (7th Cir.1987), holds that a corporation need not disclose, to investors trading in the stock market, ongoing negotiations for a merger. A public corporation may keep silent until the firms reach agreement in principle on the price and structure of the deal. Things are otherwise for closely held corporations. *Michaels v. Michaels*, 767 F.2d 1185, 1194–97 (7th Cir.1985), holds that a closely held firm must disclose material information to investors from whom it purchases stock, and that a decision to seek another firm with which to merge may be the sort of material information that must be disclosed to the investor selling his shares, even though the firm has not reached agreement in principle on the price and structure of a deal.

The treatment of public and private corporations is different because of the potential effects of disclosure. Often negotiations must be conducted in secrecy to increase their prospects of success. The prospect of disclosure to the public, and therefore to potential rival bidders, may reduce the willingness of some firms to enter negotiations and lead others to cut back on the best price they will offer. Investors are entitled to the benefits of secrecy during the negotiations; a law designed to prevent frauds on investors tolerates silence that yields benefits for investors as a group. *Flamm* also points out that negotiating firms need to know when they must disclose. Uncertainty may lead to premature disclosures that investors would like to avoid. A close corporation may disclose to an investor without alerting the public at large, however, so that disclosure does not injure investors as a whole. Moreover, a rule that the close corporation (or its managers) must disclose in the course of negotiating to purchase stock supplies a timing rule on which the firm may rely. It need disclose the existence of the decision to sell (and the status of negotiations) only to the person whose stock is to be acquired. The face-to-face negotiations allow the investor to elicit the information he requires, while permitting the firm to extract promises of confidentiality that safeguard the negotiations.

This case contains two wrinkles. First, it involves the acquisition of a closely held corporation by a public corporation. Second, the investor in the closely held corporation was an employee, and he was offered shares to cement his loyalty to the firm; yet he quit (and was compelled by a shareholders' agreement to sell his shares) for reasons unrelated to the value of the stock. The parties hotly contest the effects of these facts.

*   *   *

Duff and Phelps, Inc., evaluates the risk and worth of firms and their securities. It sells credit ratings, investment research, and financial consulting services to both the firms under scrutiny and potential investors in them. Jordan started work at Duff & Phelps in May 1977 and was viewed as a successful securities analyst. In 1981 the firm offered Jordan the opportunity to buy some stock. By November 1983 Jordan had purchased 188 of the 20,100 shares outstanding. He was making installment payments on another 62 shares. Forty people other than Jordan held stock in Duff & Phelps.

Jordan purchased his stock at its "book value" (the accounting net worth of Duff & Phelps, divided by the number of shares outstanding). Before selling him any stock, Duff & Phelps required Jordan to sign a "Stock Restriction and Purchase Agreement" (the Agreement). This provided in part:

> Upon the termination of any employment with the Corporation... for any reason, including resignation, discharge, death, disability or retirement, the individual whose employment is terminated or his estate shall sell to the Corporation, and the Corporation shall buy, all Shares of the Corporation then owned by such individual or his estate. The price to be paid for such Shares shall be equal to the adjusted book value (as hereinafter defined) of the Shares on the December 31 which coincides with, or immediately precedes, the date of termination of such individual's employment.

Duff & Phelps enforced this restriction with but a single exception. During 1983 the board of directors of Duff & Phelps adopted a resolution—of which Jordan did not learn until 1984—allowing employees fired by the firm to keep their stock for five years. The resolution followed the discharge of Carol Franchik, with whom Claire Hansen, the (married) chairman of the board, had been having an affair. When Franchik threatened suit, the board allowed her to keep her stock.

While Jordan was accumulating stock, Hansen, the chairman of the board, was exploring the possibility of selling the firm. Between May and August 1983 Hansen and Francis Jeffries, another officer of Duff & Phelps, negotiated with Security Pacific Corp., a bank holding company. The negotiators reached agreement on a merger, in which Duff & Phelps would be valued at $50 million, but a higher official within Security Pacific vetoed the deal on August 11, 1983. As of that date, Duff & Phelps had no irons in the fire.

Jordan, however, was conducting a search of his own—for a new job. Jordan's family lived near Chicago, the headquarters of Duff & Phelps, and Jordan's wife did not get along with Jordan's mother. The strain between the two occasionally left his wife in tears. He asked Duff & Phelps about the possibility of a transfer to the firm's only branch office, in Cleveland, but the firm did not need Jordan's services there. Concluding that it was time to choose between his job and his wife, Jordan chose his wife and started looking for employment far away from Chicago. His search took him to Houston, where Underwood Neuhaus & Co., a broker-dealer in securities, offered him a job at a salary ($110,000 per year) substantially greater than his compensation ($67,000) at Duff & Phelps. Jordan took the offer on the spot during an interview in Houston, but Underwood would have allowed Jordan to withdraw this oral acceptance.

On November 16, 1983, Jordan told Hansen that he was going to resign and accept employment with Underwood. Jordan did not ask Hansen about potential mergers; Hansen did not volunteer anything. Jordan delivered a letter of resignation, which Duff & Phelps accepted the same day. By mutual agreement, Jordan worked the rest of the year for Duff & Phelps even though his loyalties had shifted. He did this so that he could receive the book value of the stock as of December 31, 1983—for under the Agreement a departure in November would have meant valuation as of December 31, 1982. Jordan delivered his certificates on December 30, 1983, and the firm mailed him a check for $23,225, the book value (at $123.54 per share) of the 188 shares of stock. Jordan surrendered, as worthless under the circumstances, the right to buy the remaining 62 shares.

Before Jordan cashed the check, however, he was startled by the announcement on January 10, 1984, of a merger between Duff & Phelps and a subsidiary of Security Pacific. Under the terms of the merger Duff & Phelps would be valued at $50 million. If Jordan had been an employee on January 10, had quickly paid for the other 62 shares, and the merger had closed that day, he would have received $452,000 in cash and the opportunity to obtain as much as $194,000 more in "earn out" (a percentage of Duff & Phelps's profits to be paid to the former investors—an arrangement that keeps the employees' interest in the firm keen and reduces the buyer's risk if profits fall short). Jordan refused to cash the check and demanded his stock back; Duff & Phelps told him to get lost. He filed this suit in March 1984, asking for damages measured by the value his stock would have had under the terms of the acquisition.

       *   *   *

All of this supposes that Duff & Phelps had a duty to disclose anything to Jordan. Most people are free to buy and sell stock on the basis of valuable private knowledge without informing their trading partners. Strangers transact in markets all the time using private information that might be called "material" and, unless one has a duty to disclose, both may keep their counsel. The ability to make profits from the possession of information is the principal spur to create the information, which the parties and the market as a whole may find valuable. The absence of a duty to disclose may not justify a lie about a material fact, but Duff & Phelps did not lie to Jordan. It simply remained silent when Jordan quit and tendered the stock, and it offered the payment required by the Agreement. Duff & Phelps maintains that it was entitled to be silent, as Dirks could trade in silence and tip off his friends, even though it could not have lied in response to the questions Jordan should (in retrospect) have asked but did not.

This argument is unavailing on the facts as we know them. The "duty" in question is the fiduciary duty of corporate law. Close corporations buying their own stock, like knowledgeable insiders of closely held firms buying from outsiders, have a fiduciary duty to disclose material facts. *Kohler* and *Michaels* rest on this duty, as do some of the earliest cases of trading by insiders on material information. The "special facts" doctrine developed by several courts at the turn of the century is based on the principle that insiders in closely held firms may not buy stock from outsiders in person-to-person transactions without informing them of new events that substantially affect the value of the stock....

Because the fiduciary duty is a standby or off-the-rack guess about what parties would agree to if they dickered about the subject explicitly, parties may contract with greater specificity for other arrangements.... The obligation to break silence is itself based on state law, see Dirks, Chiarella, and Barker, and so may be redefined to the extent state law permits. See, e.g., *Toledo Trust Co. v. Nye*, 588 F.2d 202, 206 (6th Cir.1978) (there is no liability under the securities laws for failing to disclose information that has been made irrelevant by contract, in *Nye* a contract allowing someone to purchase shares at a formula price on a date certain). But we need not decide how far contracts can redefine obligations to disclose. Jordan was an employee at will; he signed no contract.

The stock was designed to bind Duff & Phelps's employees loyally to the firm. The buy-sell agreement tied ownership to employment. Understandably Duff & Phelps did not want a viper in its nest, a disgruntled employee remaining only in the hope of appreciation of his stock. So there could have been reason to divorce the employment decision from the value of the stock. Perhaps it would have been rational for each employee to agree with Duff & Phelps to look to salary alone in deciding whether to stay. A contractual agreement that the firm had no duty to disclose would have uncoupled the investment decision from the employment decision, leaving whoever was in the firm on the day of a merger to receive a surprise appreciation. Some might lose by leaving early; some might reap a windfall by buying just before the announcement; all might think it wise to have as little as possible said in the interim.

Yet an explicit agreement to make all employment decisions in ignorance of the value of the stock might not have been in the interests of the firm or its employees. Duff & Phelps was trying to purchase loyalty by offering stock to its principal employees. The package of compensation contained salary and the prospect of appreciation of the stock. Perhaps it paid a lower salary than, say, Underwood Neuhaus & Co., because its package contained a higher component of gain from anticipated appreciation in the stock. It is therefore unwarranted to say that the implicit understanding between Jordan and Duff & Phelps should be treated as if it had such a no-duty clause; we are not confident that this is the clause firms and their employees regularly would prefer. Duff & Phelps has not identified any firm that adopted such a clause explicitly, and the absence of explicit clauses counsels caution in creating implicit exceptions to the general fiduciary duty.

The course of dealing between Jordan and Duff & Phelps suggests that the firm did not demand that employees decide whether to stay or go without regard to the value of the stock. It apparently informed Jordan what the book value was expected to be on December 31, 1983, so that Jordan could decide whether to leave in November (receiving the value as of December 31, 1982) or stay for another six weeks. The firm did not demand that Jordan depart as soon as it learned he had switched loyalties; it allowed employees to time their departures to obtain the maximum advantage from their stock. The Agreement did not ensure that employees disregard the value of the stock when deciding what to do, and neither did the usual practice at Duff & Phelps. So the possibility that a firm could negotiate around the fiduciary duty does not assist Duff & Phelps; it did not obtain such an agreement, express or implied.

The closest Duff & Phelps came is the provision in the Agreement fixing the price of the stock at book value. Yet although the Agreement fixed the price to be paid those who quit, it did not establish the terms on which anyone would leave. Thus cases such as *Toledo Trust and St. Louis Union Trust Co. v. Merrill*

Lynch, Pierce, Fenner & Smith, Inc., 562 F.2d 1040 (8th Cir.1977), do not assist Duff & Phelps. These cases dealt with agreements calling for valuation at a formula price on a fixed date. In *St. Louis Union Trust* the date was the death of the employee, the formula was book value. The court of appeals held that there was no need to pay the employee's estate a different price, just because a few weeks later Merrill Lynch went public at a higher price. The employee presumably did not take the possibility of a merger into account in deciding whether to die, and the formula price made "disclosure" irrelevant. *Toledo Trust*, too, discussed a buyback triggered by death. (The contract allowed a departure from the formula price, but as the court observed, the variance clause "merely stated the truism that parties to a binding contract of sale can mutually agree to sale terms different than those set forth in the contract." 588 F.2d at 206.) Jordan, though, exercised choice about the date on which the formula would be triggered. He could have remained at Duff & Phelps; his decision to depart was affected by his wife's distress, his salary, his working conditions, the enjoyment he received from the job, and the value of his stock. The departure of such an employee is an investment decision as much as it is an employment decision. It is not fanciful to suppose that Mrs. Jordan would have found her mother in law a whole lot more tolerable if she had known that Jordan's stock might shortly be worth 20 times book value.

*   *   *

Our dissenting colleague concludes that all of this is beside the point because Hansen could have said, on receiving Jordan's letter on November 16: "In a few weeks we will pull off a merger that would have made your stock 20 times more valuable. It's a shame you so foolishly resigned. But even if you hadn't resigned, we would have fired you, the better to engross the profits of the merger for ourselves. So long, sucker." This would have been permissible, under our colleague's interpretation, because Jordan was an employee at will and therefore could have been fired at any time, even the day before the merger, for any reason—including the desire to deprive Jordan of a share of the profits. The ability to fire Jordan enabled the firm to "call" his shares, at book value, on whim. On this view, it is foolish to say that Duff & Phelps had a duty to disclose, because disclosure would have been no use to Jordan....Perhaps Duff & Phelps does not want to establish a reputation for shoddy dealing; as our dissenting brother observes, a firm's desire to preserve its reputation is a powerful inducement to treat its contractual partners well. To attribute to a litigant an argument that it will take every possible advantage is to assume that the party wishes to dissipate its reputation, and the assumption is unwarranted.

More than that, a person's status as an employee "at will" does not imply that the employer may discharge him for every reason. Illinois, where Jordan was employed, has placed some limits on the discharge of at-will employees....The silence of the parties may make it necessary to imply other terms—those we are confident the parties would have bargained for if they had signed a written agreement. One term implied in every written contract and therefore, we suppose, every unwritten one, is that neither party will try to take opportunistic advantage of the other. "[T]he fundamental function of contract law (and recognized as such at least since Hobbes's day) is to deter people from behaving opportunistically toward their contracting parties, in order to encourage the optimal timing of economic activity and to make costly self-protective measures unnecessary." Richard A. Posner, Economic Analysis of Law 81 (3d ed. 1986)....

Employment creates occasions for opportunism. A firm may fire an employee the day before his pension vests, or a salesman the day before a large commission becomes payable. Cases of this sort may present difficult questions about the reasons for the decision (was it opportunism, or was it a decline in the employee's performance?). The difficulties of separating opportunistic conduct from honest differences of opinion about an employee's performance on the job may lead firms and their employees to transact on terms that keep such disputes out of court—which employment at will usually does. But no one...doubts that an avowedly opportunistic discharge is a breach of contract, although the employment is at-will....The element of good faith dealing implied in a contract "is not an enforceable legal duty to be nice or to behave decently in a general way." *Zick*, 623 F.Supp. at 929. It is not a version of the Golden Rule, to regard the interests of one's contracting partner the same way you regard your own. An employer may be thoughtless, nasty, and mistaken. Avowedly opportunistic conduct has been treated differently, however.

The stock component in Jordan's package induced him to stick around and work well. Such an inducement is effective only if the employee reaps the rewards of success as well as the penalties of failure. We do not suppose for a second that if Jordan had not resigned on November 16, the firm could have fired him on January 9 with a little note saying: "Dear Mr. Jordan: There will be a lucrative merger tomorrow. You have been a wonderful employee, but in order to keep the proceeds of the merger for ourselves, we are letting you go, effective this instant. Here is the $23,000 for your shares." Had the firm fired Jordan for this stated reason, it would have broken an implied pledge to avoid opportunistic conduct. It may well be that Duff & Phelps could have fired Jordan without the slightest judicial inquiry; it does not follow that an opportunistic discharge would have allowed Duff & Phelps to cash out the stock on the eve of its appreciation. This is the principle underlying *Rao v. Rao*, 718 F.2d 219 (7th Cir.1983), which holds, applying Illinois law, that although an employer may dismiss an at-will employee for the purpose of preventing his becoming a partner, it may not enforce the no-competition clause in the contract even though the contract stated that the clause would become effective if the employee were discharged "for any reason". A short delay would have turned the fired employee into a partner and nullified the restrictive covenant. We concluded that although the discharge was final, the restrictive covenant would not be enforced. So, here, an opportunistic discharge would not necessarily allow Duff & Phelps to buy back the stock. As a result, Jordan's employment at will, the essential ingredient of our colleague's argument that Jordan waived the duty to disclose, does not establish that the firm had no duties concerning the stock.

The timing of the sale and the materiality of the information Duff & Phelps withheld on November 16 are for the jury to determine....

* * *

REVERSED AND REMANDED.

* * *

POSNER, Circuit Judge, dissenting.

A corporate employee at will quit, owning shares that he had agreed to sell back to the corporation at book value. The agreement was explicit that his status as a shareholder conferred no job rights on him. Nevertheless the court holds that the corporation had, as a matter of law, a duty, enforceable by proceedings under Rule 10b-5 of the Securities Exchange Act, to volunteer to the employee information about the corporation's prospects that might have led him to change his mind about quitting, although as an employee at will he had no right to change his mind. I disagree with this holding. The terms of the stockholder agreement show that there was no duty of disclosure, and since there was no duty there was no violation of Rule 10b-5.

*   *   *

...[T]he contingent nature of Jordan's status as a shareholder negates the existence of a right to be informed and hence a duty to disclose. This point is central to my dissent and has now to be explained.

Jordan's deal with Duff and Phelps required him to surrender his stock at book value if he left the company. It didn't matter whether he quit or was fired, retired or died; the agreement is explicit on these matters. My brethren hypothesize "implicit parts of the relations between Duff & Phelps and its employees." But those relations are totally defined by (1) the absence of an employment contract, which made Jordan an employee at will; (2) the shareholder agreement, which has no "implicit parts" that bear on Duff and Phelps' duty to Jordan, and explicitly ties his rights as a shareholder to his status as an employee at will; (3) a provision in the stock purchase agreement between Jordan and Duff and Phelps (signed at the same time as the shareholder agreement) that "nothing herein contained shall confer on the Employee any right to be continued in the employment of the Corporation." There is no occasion to speculate about "the implicit understanding" between Jordan and Duff and Phelps. The parties left nothing to the judicial imagination. The effect of the shareholder and stock purchase agreements (which for simplicity I shall treat as a single "stockholder agreement"), against a background of employment at will, was to strip Jordan of any contractual protection against what happened to him, and indeed against worse that might have happened to him. Duff and Phelps points out that it would not have had to let Jordan withdraw his resignation had he gotten wind of the negotiations with Security Pacific and wanted to withdraw it. On November 14 Hansen could have said to Jordan, "I accept your resignation effective today; we hope to sell Duff and Phelps for $50 million but have no desire to see you participate in the resulting bonanza. You will receive the paltry book value of your shares as of December 31, 1982." The "nothing herein contained" provision in the stockholder agreement shows that this tactic is permitted. Equally, on November 14, at the board meeting before Hansen knew that Jordan wanted to quit, the board could have decided to fire Jordan in order to increase the value of the deal with Security Pacific to the remaining shareholders.

These possibilities eliminate any inference that the stockholder agreement obligated Duff and Phelps to inform Jordan about the company's prospects. Under the agreement, if Duff and Phelps didn't want to give him the benefit of the information all it had to do to escape any possible liability was to give him the information and then fire him....

My brethren correctly observe that, "Because the fiduciary duty is a standby or off-the-rack guess about what parties would agree to if they dickered about the subject explicitly, parties may contract with greater specificity for other arrangements." But, they add, "we need not decide how far contracts can redefine obligations to disclose. Jordan was an employee at will; he signed no contract." It is true that he signed no contract of employment, but he signed a stockholder agreement that defined his rights as a shareholder "with greater specificity." The agreement entitled Duff and Phelps to terminate Jordan as shareholder, subject only to a duty to buy back his shares at book value. The arrangement that resulted (call it "shareholder at will") is incompatible with an inference that Duff and Phelps undertook to keep him abreast of developments affecting the value of the firm.

*   *   *

Was Jordan a fool to have become a shareholder of Duff and Phelps on such disadvantageous terms as I believe he agreed to? (If so, that might be a reason for doubting whether those were the real terms.) He was not. Few business executives in this country have contractual entitlements to earnings, bonuses, or even retention of their jobs. They would rather take their chances on their employer's good will and interest in reputation, and on their own bargaining power and value to the firm, than pay for contract rights that are difficult and costly to enforce. See *Miller v. International Harvester Co.*, 811 F.2d 1150, 1151 (7th Cir.1987); *Tyson v. International Brotherhood of Teamsters, Local 710 Pension Fund*, 811 F.2d 1145, 1147 (7th Cir.1987); *Kumpf v. Steinhaus*, 779 F.2d 1323, 1326 (7th Cir.1985); Epstein, *In Defense of the Contract at Will*, 51 U.Chi.L.Rev. 947 (1984). If Jordan had had greater rights as a shareholder he would have had a lower salary; when he went to work for a new employer in Houston and received no stock rights he got a higher salary.

I go further: Jordan was protected by Duff and Phelps' own self-interest from being exploited. The principal asset of a service company such as Duff and Phelps is good will. It is a product largely of its employees' efforts and skills. If Jordan were a particularly valuable employee, so that the firm would be worth less without him, Hansen, desiring as he did to sell the firm for the highest possible price, would have told him about the prospects for selling the company. If Jordan was not a particularly valuable employee—if his departure would not reduce the value of the firm—there was no reason why he should participate in the profits from the sale of the firm, unless perhaps he had once been a particularly valuable employee but had ceased to be so. That possibility might, but did not, lead him to negotiate for an employment contract, or for stock rights that would outlast his employment. By the type of agreement that he made with Duff and Phelps, Jordan gambled that he was and would continue to be such a good employee that he would be encouraged to stay long enough to profit from the firm's growth. The relationship that the parties created aligned their respective self-interests better than the legal protections that the court devises today.

My brethren are well aware that Duff and Phelps faced market constraints against exploiting its employee shareholders, but seem to believe that this implies that the company also assumed contractual duties. Businessmen, however, are less enthusiastic about contractual duties than lawyers are, see Macauley, *Non-Contractual Relations in Business: A Preliminary Study*, 28 Am. Sociological Rev. 55, 64 (1963), so it is incorrect to infer from the existence of market constraints against exploitation that the parties also imposed a contractual duty against exploitation. Contractual obligation is a source of uncertainty and cost, and is therefore an expensive way of backstopping market forces. That is why employment at will is such a common form of employment relationship. It is strange to infer that firms invariably assume a legal obligation not to do what is not in their self-interest to do, and stranger to suppose—in the face of an explicit disclaimer—that by "allow[ing] employees to time their departures to obtain the maximum advantage from their stock," Duff and Phelps obligated itself to allow them to do this.

Having earlier in its opinion tried to get mileage out of the fact that Jordan "signed no [employment] contract," the majority later tries to get additional mileage from the observation that employment at will is a "contractual relation." This is the kind of legal half-truth that should make us thankful that our opinions are not subject to Rule 10b-5. Employment at will is a voluntary relationship, and thus contractual in the sense in which the word contract is used in the expression "freedom of contract." And the relationship can provide a framework for contracting: if Duff and Phelps had not paid Jordan his agreed-on wage after he had earned it, he could have sued the company for breach of contract. But the only element of employment at will that is relevant to this case is that employment at will is terminable at will, meaning that the employer can fire the employee without worrying about legal sanctions and likewise the employee can quit without worrying about them. Freedom of contract includes freedom not to contract.

*   *   *

The majority's view that "the silence of the parties" is an invitation to judges to "imply other terms—those we [judges] are confident the parties would have bargained for if they had signed a written agreement" is doubly gratuitous. The parties did not want their relationship dragged into court and there made over by judges. And the parties were not silent. The stockholder agreement provides that Jordan's rights under it do not give him any employment tenure.

The inroads that the majority opinion makes on freedom of contract are not justified by its quotation from my academic writings concerning the purpose of contract law (which presupposes an agreement that the parties regard as legally enforceable) or by the possibility that corporations will exploit their junior executives, which may well be the least urgent problem facing our nation. The majority's statement that "one term implied in every written contract and therefore, we suppose, every unwritten one, is that neither party will try to take opportunistic advantage of the other" confuses the underlying rationale of contract law with the actual requirements of that law, and is anyway irrelevant since the parties decided not to subject the relevant parts of their relationship to the law of contracts and not to give Jordan any contractual protections against being fired. There was no "implied pledge to avoid opportunistic conduct" any more than there were "implicit parts of the relations" giving rise to contractual obligations....

And if Duff and Phelps had fired Jordan (or refused to let him withdraw his resignation), this would not necessarily have been opportunistic. One might equally well say (in the spirit of Villada) that by trying to stick around merely to participate in an unexpectedly lucrative sale of Duff and Phelps, Jordan would have been the opportunist. The majority says that "understandably Duff & Phelps did not want a viper in its nest, a disgruntled employee remaining only in the hope of appreciation of his stock." I call that "viper" an opportunist.

*   *   *

Notes and Questions

1. Contract and Incorporation: Although considerable historical and economic evidence indicates that the corporation is founded in private contract, legal recognition of the corporation is gained through the granting of a charter from a state. In essence, the state's corporation law specifies the terms of the contract, including the property rights of the parties to the contract — the shareholders, directors, and officers. Most corporation laws are enabling statutes in the sense that they reflect the philosophy of freedom of contract which has guided corporation law since the first truly modern general incorporation laws were passed in the late nineteenth century. Most, if not all, of the terms can be altered by a specific provision in the articles or bylaws. The state law specifies the terms of the contract in the absence of a specific provision amending the laws. By defining rights, the articles of incorporation perform a function analogous to that of a private constitution. Firms may alter some aspects of the corporation law applicable to them by amending the corporation's articles of incorporation or bylaws to suit their particular needs.

2. Duty of Care, the Business Judgment Rule and Shareholders' Interests: Directors are supposed to direct the management of the corporation's affairs. Failure to do so may result in liability for the resulting losses. A major problem in this area of corporation law, however, is deciding when a director has failed to fulfill the obligations of the position. In general, the courts are hesitant to second-guess managerial decisions that turn out to be mistaken. In most cases, courts give managers the benefit of the doubt and relieve them of liability through application of the **business judgment rule**. The rule protects decisions made by an honest, unbiased judgment, and it also benefits shareholders. A major policy reason in support of the business judgment rule is that holding directors liable in situations where hindsight reveals that they made a mistake would make it difficult to attract top-quality individuals to serve on boards of directors. In recognition of the adverse impact of holding directors and officers liable when they acted in good faith, several states' corporation laws authorize corporations to indemnify (reimburse) directors for liability payments or for expenses incurred in defending against unwarranted suits.

> While it is often stated that corporate directors and officers will be liable for negligence in carrying out their corporate duties, all seem agreed that such a statement is misleading. Whereas an automobile driver who makes a mistake in judgment as to speed or distance injuring a pedestrian will likely be called upon to respond in damages, a corporate officer who makes a mistake in judgment as to economic conditions, consumer tastes or production line efficiency will rarely, if ever, be found liable for damages suffered by the corporation. Whatever the terminology, the fact is that liability is rarely imposed upon corporate directors or officers simply for bad judgment and this reluctance to impose liability for unsuccessful business decisions has been doctrinally labeled the business judgment rule. Although the rule has suffered under academic criticism, it is not without rational basis.
>
> First, shareholders to a very real degree voluntarily undertake the risk of bad business judgment. Investors need not buy stock, for invest-

ment markets offer an array of opportunities less vulnerable to mistakes in judgment by corporate officers. Nor need investors buy stock in particular corporations. In the exercise of what is genuinely a free choice, the quality of a firm's management is often decisive and information is available from professional advisors. Since shareholders can and do select among investments partly on the basis of management, the business judgment rule merely recognizes a certain voluntariness in undertaking the risk of bad business decisions.

Second, courts recognize that after-the-fact litigation is a most imperfect device to evaluate corporate business decisions. The circumstances surrounding a corporate decision are not easily reconstructed in a courtroom years later, since business imperatives often call for quick decisions, inevitably based on less than perfect information. The entrepreneur's function is to encounter risks and to confront uncertainty, and a reasoned decision at the time made may seem a wild hunch viewed years later against a background of perfect knowledge.

Third, because potential profit often corresponds to the potential risk, it is very much in the interest of shareholders that the law not create incentives for overly cautious corporate decisions. Some opportunities offer great profits at the risk of very substantial losses, while the alternatives offer less risk of loss but also less potential profit. Shareholders can reduce the volatility[5] of risk by diversifying their holdings. In the case of the diversified shareholder, the seemingly more risky alternatives may well be the best choice since great losses in some stocks will over time be offset by even greater gains in others.[6] Given mutual funds and similar

---

5. For purposes of this opinion, "volatility" is "the degree of dispersion or variation of possible outcomes." Klein, *Business Organization and Finance* 147 (1980).

6. Consider the choice between two investments in an example adapted from Klein, *Business Organization and Finance* 147–49 (1980):

INVESTMENT A

Estimated Profitability of Outcome	Outcome Profit or Loss	Value
.4	+15	6.0
.4	+ 1	.4
.2	−13	−2.6
1.0		3.8

INVESTMENT B

Estimated Profitability of Outcome	Outcome Profit or Loss	Value
.4	+6	2.4
.4	+2	.8
.2	+1	.2
1.0		3.4

Although A is clearly "worth" more than B, it is riskier because it is more volatile. Diversification lessens the volatility by allowing investors to invest in 20 or 200 A's which will tend to guarantee a total result near the value. Shareholders are thus better off with the varioius firms selecting A over B, although after the fact they will complain in each case of the 2.6 loss. If the courts did not abide by the business judgment rule, they might well penalize the choice of A in each such case and thereby unknowingly injure shareholders generally by creating incentives for management always to choose B.

forms of diversified investment, courts need not bend over backwards to give special protection to shareholders who refuse to reduce the volatility of risk by not diversifying. A rule which penalizes the choice of seemingly riskier alternatives thus may not be in the interest of shareholders generally.

Whatever its merit, however, the business judgment rule extends only as far as the reasons which justify its existence. Thus, it does not apply in cases, *e.g.*, in which the corporate decision lacks a business purpose, *see Singer v. Magnavox*, 380 A.2d 969 (Del.Supr.1977), is tainted by a conflict of interest, *Globe Woolen v. Utica Gas & Electric Co.*, 224 N.Y. 483, 121 N.E. 378 (1918), is so egregious as to amount to a no-win decision, *Litwin v. Allen*, 25 N.Y. S.2d 667 (N.Y.Co.Sup.Ct.1940), or results from an obvious and prolonged failure to exercise oversight or supervision, *McDonnell v. American Leduc Petroleums, Ltd.*, 491 F.2d 380 (2d Cir. 1974); *Atherton v. Anderson*, 99 F.2d 883 (6th Cir. 1938). Other examples may occur.

Joy v. North, 692 F.2d 880, 885–86 (1982).

a. Corporate Federalism

The relationship between shareholders and managers is governed by two sources of law. Federal securities laws, which are primarily concerned with securities transactions, set forth detailed procedures for shareholder votes. Otherwise, state corporation law governs the internal affairs of corporations. Importantly, corporations (or, more correctly, corporations' managers) can incorporate under the laws of any state, regardless of the location of the corporate headquarters. To the extent that there are differences in corporate laws across states, corporate law is one of the governance mechanisms that *can be* selected by the contracting parties to minimize corporate agency costs. States, however, don't always offer laws that appear to be in shareholders' best interests.

Amanda Acquisition Corp. v. Universal Foods Corp.
United States Court of Appeals, Seventh Circuit
877 F.2d 496 (1989)

EASTERBROOK, Circuit Judge.

States have enacted three generations of takeover statutes in the last 20 years. Illinois enacted a first-generation statute, which forbade acquisitions of any firm with substantial assets in Illinois unless a public official approved. We concluded that such a statute injures investors, is preempted by the Williams Act, and is unconstitutional under the dormant Commerce Clause. *MITE Corp. v. Dixon*, 633 F.2d 486 (7th Cir.1980). The Supreme Court affirmed the judgment under the Commerce Clause, *Edgar v. MITE Corp.*, 457 U.S. 624, 643–46 (1982).

Indiana enacted a second-generation statute, applicable only to firms incorporated there and eliminating governmental veto power. Indiana's law provides that the acquiring firm's shares lose their voting power unless the target's directors approve the acquisition or the shareholders not affiliated with either bidder or management authorize restoration of votes. We concluded that this statute, too, is inimical to investors' interests, preempted by the Williams Act, and unconstitutional under the Commerce Clause. *Dynamics Corp. of America v. CTS Corp.*, 794 F.2d 250 (7th Cir.1986). This time the Supreme Court did not agree. It thought the Indiana statute consistent with both Williams Act and Commerce Clause. *CTS Corp. v. Dynamics Corp. of America*, 481 U.S. 69, (1987). Adopting Justice White's view of preemption for the sake of argument the Court found no inconsistency between state and federal law because Indiana allowed the bidder to acquire the shares without hindrance. Such a law makes the shares less attractive, but it does not regulate the process of bidding. As for the Commerce Clause, the Court took Indiana's law to be regulation of internal corporate affairs, potentially beneficial because it would allow investors to avoid the "coercion" of two-tier bids and other tactics.

Wisconsin has a third-generation takeover statute. Enacted after *CTS*, it postpones the kinds of transactions that often follow tender offers (and often are the reason for making the offers in the first place). Unless the target's board agrees to the transaction in advance, the bidder must wait three years after buying the shares to merge with the target or acquire more than 5% of its assets. We must decide whether this is consistent with the Williams Act and Commerce Clause.

I

Amanda Acquisition Corporation is a shell with a single purpose: to acquire Universal Foods Corporation, a diversified firm incorporated in Wisconsin and traded on the New York Stock Exchange. Universal is covered by Wisconsin's anti-takeover law. Amanda is a subsidiary of High Voltage Engineering Corp., a small electronics firm in Massachusetts. Most of High Voltage's equity capital comes from Berisford Capital PLC, a British venture capital firm, and Hyde Park Partners L.P., a partnership affiliated with the principals of Berisford. Chase Manhattan Bank has promised to lend Amanda 50% of the cost of the acquisition, secured by the stock of Universal.

In mid-November 1988 Universal's stock was trading for about $25 per share. On December 1 Amanda commenced a tender offer at $30.50, to be effective if at least 75% of the stock should be tendered.[1] This all-cash, all-shares offer has been increased by stages to $38.00.[2] Amanda's financing is contingent on a prompt merger with Universal if the offer succeeds, so the offer is conditional on a judicial declaration that the law is invalid. (It is also conditional on Universal's redemption of poison pill stock. For reasons that we discuss below, it is unnecessary to discuss the subject in detail.)

No firm incorporated in Wisconsin and having its headquarters, substantial operations, or 10% of its shares or shareholders there may "engage in a business combination with an interested stockholder...for 3 years after the interested

---

1. Wisconsin has, in addition to § 180.726, a statute modeled on Indiana's, providing that an acquiring firm's shares lose their votes, which may be restored under specified circumstances. Wis.Stat. § 180.25(9). That law accounts for the 75% condition, but it is not pertinent to the questions we resolve.

2. Universal contends that an increase after the district court's opinion makes the case moot, or at least requires a remand. It does not. The parties remain locked in combat. Price has no effect on the operation of the Wisconsin law, and as that is the sole issue we shall decide there is no need to remand for further proceedings.

stockholder's stock acquisition date unless the board of directors of the [Wisconsin] corporation has approved, before the interested stockholder's stock acquisition date, that business combination or the purchase of stock", Wis.Stat. § 180.726(2). An "interested stockholder" is one owning 10% of the voting stock, directly or through associates (anyone acting in concert with it), § 180.726(1)(j). A "business combination" is a merger with the bidder or any of its affiliates, sale of more than 5% of the assets to bidder or affiliate, liquidation of the target, or a transaction by which the target guarantees the bidder's or affiliates debts or passes tax benefits to the bidder or affiliate, § 180.726(1)(e). The law, in other words, provides for almost hermetic separation of bidder and target for three years after the bidder obtains 10% of the stock—unless the target's board consented before then. No matter how popular the offer, the ban applies: obtaining 85% (even 100%) of the stock held by non-management shareholders won't allow the bidder to engage in a business combination, as it would under Delaware law. Wisconsin firms cannot opt out of the law, as may corporations subject to almost all other state takeover statutes. In Wisconsin it is management's approval in advance, or wait three years. Even when the time is up, the bidder needs the approval of a majority of the remaining investors, without any provision disqualifying shares still held by the managers who resisted the transaction. The district court found that this statute "effectively eliminates hostile leveraged buyouts". As a practical matter, Wisconsin prohibits any offer contingent on a merger between bidder and target, a condition attached to about 90% of contemporary tender offers.

Amanda filed this suit seeking a declaration that this law is preempted by the Williams Act and inconsistent with the Commerce Clause. It added a pendent claim that the directors' refusal to redeem the poison-pill rights violates their fiduciary duties to Universal's shareholders. The district court declined to issue a preliminary injunction. It concluded that the statute is constitutional and not preempted, and that under Wisconsin law (which the court believed would follow Delaware's) directors are entitled to prevent investors from accepting tender offers of which the directors do not approve.

As a practical matter, the decision denying preliminary relief ends the case. The parties treat their appeals as if taken from the conclusive denial of relief; so shall we. The financial stakes on both sides cancel out, and the question becomes who is right on the merits. CTS, 794 F.2d at 252; see also FTC v. Elders Grain, Inc., 868 F.2d 901, 903–05 (7th Cir.1989). The parties ask us to decide... whether § 180.726 is consistent with the Constitution and federal law.

*   *   *

II

*   *   *

A

If our views of the wisdom of state law mattered, Wisconsin's takeover statute would not survive. Like our colleagues who decided *MITE* and *CTS*, we believe that antitakeover legislation injures shareholders.[5] *MITE*, 633 F.2d at

---

5. Because both the district court and the parties—like the Williams Act—examine tender offers from the perspective of equity investors, we employ the same approach. States

496–98 and 457 U.S. at 643–44, 102 S.Ct. at 2641–42; *CTS*, 794 F.2d at 253–55. Managers frequently realize gains for investors via voluntary combinations (mergers). If gains are to be had, but managers balk, tender offers are investors' way to go over managers' heads. If managers are not maximizing the firm's value — perhaps because they have missed the possibility of a synergistic combination, perhaps because they are clinging to divisions that could be better run in other hands, perhaps because they are just not the best persons for the job — a bidder that believes it can realize more of the firm's value will make investors a higher offer. Investors tender; the bidder gets control and changes things. Michael Bradley, Anand Desai & E. Han Kim, *Synergistic Gains from Corporate Acquisitions and Their Division Between the Stockholders of Target and Acquiring Firms*, 21 J.Fin.Econ. 3 (1988). The prospect of monitoring by would-be bidders, and an occasional bid at a premium, induces managers to run corporations more efficiently and replaces them if they will not.

Premium bids reflect the benefits for investors. The price of a firm's stock represents investors' consensus estimate of the value of the shares under current and anticipated conditions. Stock is worth the present value of anticipated future returns — dividends and other distributions. Tender offers succeed when bidders offer more. Only when the bid exceeds the value of the stock (however investors compute value) will it succeed. A statute that precludes investors from receiving or accepting a premium offer makes them worse off. It makes the economy worse off too, because the higher bid reflects the better use to which the bidder can put the target's assets. (If the bidder can't improve the use of the assets, it injures itself by paying a premium.)

Universal, making an argument common among supporters of anti-takeover laws, contends that its investors do not appreciate the worth of its business plans, that its stock is trading for too little, and that if investors tender reflexively they injure themselves. If only they would wait, Universal submits, they would do better under current management. A variant of the argument has it that although smart investors know that the stock is underpriced, many investors are passive and will tender; even the smart investors then must tender to avoid doing worse on the "back end" of the deal. State laws giving management the power to block an offer enable the managers to protect the investors from themselves.

Both versions of this price-is-wrong argument imply: (a) that the stock of firms defeating offers later appreciates in price, topping the bid, thus revealing the wisdom of waiting till the market wises up; and (b) that investors in firms for

---

could choose to protect "constituencies" other than stockholders. Creditors, managers, and workers invest human rather than financial capital. But the limitation of our inquiry to equity investors does not affect the analysis, because no evidence of which we are aware suggests that bidders confiscate workers' and other participants' investments to any greater degree than do incumbents — who may (and frequently do) close or move plants to follow the prospect of profit. Joseph A. Grundfest, a Commissioner of the SEC, showed in Job Loss and Takeovers, address to University of Toledo College of Law, Mar. 11, 1988, that acquisitions have no logical (or demonstrable) effect on employment. See also Brown & Medoff, The Impact of Firm Acquisitions on Labor, in Corporate Takeovers: Causes and Consequences 9 (A. Auerbach ed. 1988); Roberta Romano, The Future of Hostile Takeovers: Legislation and Public Opinion, 57 U.Cin.L.Rev. 457 (1988); C. Steven Bradford, Protecting Shareholders from Themselves? A Policy and Constitutional Review of a State Takeover Statute, 67 Neb.L.Rev. 459, 529–34 (1988).

which no offer is outstanding gain when they adopt devices so that managers may fend off unwanted offers (or states adopt laws with the same consequence). Efforts to verify these implications have failed. The best available data show that if a firm fends off a bid, its profits decline, and its stock price (adjusted for inflation and market-wide changes) never tops the initial bid, even if it is later acquired by another firm. Gregg A. Jarrell, James A. Brickley & Jeffrey M. Netter, *The Market for Corporate Control: The Empirical Evidence Since 1980*, 2 J.Econ. Perspectives 49, 55 (1988) (collecting studies); John Pound, *The Information Effects of Takeover Bids and Resistance*, 22 J.Fin.Econ. 207 (1988). Stock of firms adopting poison pills falls in price, as does the stock of firms that adopt most kinds of anti-takeover amendments to their articles of incorporation. Jarrell, Brickley & Netter, 2 J.Econ. Perspectives at 58–65 (collecting studies); Michael C. Jensen, *Takeovers: Their Causes and Consequences*, 2 J.Econ. Perspectives 21, 25–28, 41–45 (1988); Michael Ryngaert, *The Effect of Poison Pill Securities on Shareholder Wealth*, 20 J.Fin.Econ. 377 (1988); cf. John Pound, *The Effects of Antitakeover Amendments on Takeover Activity: Some Direct Evidence*, 30 J.L. & Econ. 353 (1987). Studies of laws similar to Wisconsin's produce the same conclusion: share prices of firms incorporated in the state drop when the legislation is enacted. Jonathan M. Karpoff & Paul H. Malatesta, *The Wealth Effects of Second Generation State Takeover Legislation*, University of Washington Graduate School of Business Working Paper (Dec. 22, 1988).

Although a takeover-*proof* firm leaves investors at the mercy of incumbent managers (who may be mistaken about the wisdom of their business plan even when they act in the best of faith), a takeover-*resistant* firm may be able to assist its investors. An auction may run up the price, and delay may be essential to an auction. Auctions transfer money from bidders to targets, and diversified investors would not gain from them (their left pocket loses what the right pocket gains); diversified investors would lose from auctions if the lower returns to bidders discourage future bids. But from targets' perspectives, once a bid is on the table an auction may be the best strategy. The full effects of auctions are hard to unravel, sparking scholarly debate.[6] Devices giving managers some ability to orchestrate investors' responses, in order to avoid panic tenders in response to front-end-loaded offers, also could be beneficial, as the Supreme Court emphasized in *CTS*, 481 U.S. at 92–93, 107 S.Ct. at 1651–52. ("Could be" is an important qualifier; even from a perspective limited to targets' shareholders given a bid on the table, it is important to know whether managers use this power to augment bids or to stifle them, and whether courts can tell the two apart.)

State anti-takeover laws do not serve these ends well, however. Investors who prefer to give managers the discretion to orchestrate responses to bids may do so through "fair-price" clauses in the articles of incorporation and other consensual

---

6. Compare Lucian Arye Bebchuk, *Toward Undistorted Choice and Equal Treatment in Corporate Takeovers*, 98 Harv.L.Rev. 1693 (1985), and Ronald J. Gilson, *Seeking Competitive Bids versus Pure Passivity in Tender Offer Defense*, 35 Stan.L.Rev. 51 (1982), with Alan Schwartz, *Search Theory and the Tender Offer Auction*, 2 J.L., Econ. & Org. 229 (1986), and Sanford J. Grossman & Oliver D. Hart, *Takeover Bids, the Free-Rider Problem and the Theory of the Corporation*, 11 Bell J. Econ. 42 (1980). For the most recent round compare Alan Schwartz, *The Fairness of Tender Offer Prices in Utilitarian Theory*, 17 J. Legal Stud. 165 (1988), with Lucian Arye Bebchuk, *The Sole Owner Standard for Takeover Policy*, id. at 197, with Schwartz, *The Sole Owner Standard Reviewed*, id. at 231.

devices. Other firms may choose different strategies. A law such as Wisconsin's does not add options to firms that would like to give more discretion to their managers; instead it destroys the possibility of divergent choices. Wisconsin's law applies even when the investors prefer to leave their managers under the gun, to allow the market full sway. Karpoff and Malatesta found that state anti-takeover laws have little or no effect on the price of shares if the firm already has poison pills (or related devices) in place, but strongly negative effects on price when firms have no such contractual devices. To put this differently, state laws have bite only when investors, given the choice, would deny managers the power to interfere with tender offers (maybe already *have* denied managers that power). See also Roberta Romano, *The Political Economy of Takeover Statutes*, 73 Va.L.Rev. 111, 128–31 (1987).

B

Skepticism about the wisdom of a state's law does not lead to the conclusion that the law is beyond the state's power, however. We have not been elected custodians of investors' wealth. States need not treat investors' welfare as their summum bonum. Perhaps they choose to protect managers' welfare instead, or believe that the current economic literature reaches an incorrect conclusion and that despite appearances takeovers injure investors in the long run. Unless a federal statute or the Constitution bars the way, Wisconsin's choice must be respected.

Amanda relies on the Williams Act of 1968, incorporated into §§ 13(d), (e) and 14(d)–(f) of the Securities Exchange Act of 1934, 15 U.S.C. §§ 78m(d), (e), 78n(d)–(f). The Williams Act regulates the conduct of tender offers. Amanda believes that Congress created an entitlement for investors to receive the benefit of tender offers, and that because Wisconsin's law makes tender offers unattractive to many potential bidders, it is preempted.

Preemption has not won easy acceptance among the Justices for several reasons. First there is § 28(a) of the '34 Act, 15 U.S.C. § 78bb(a), which provides that "[n]othing in this chapter shall affect the jurisdiction of the securities commission... of any State over any security or any person insofar as it does not conflict with the provisions of this chapter or the rules and regulations thereunder." Although some of the SEC's regulations (particularly the one defining the commencement of an offer) conflict with some state takeover laws, the SEC has not drafted regulations concerning mergers with controlling shareholders, and the Act itself does not address the subject. States have used the leeway afforded by § 28(a) to carry out "merit regulation" of securities — "blue sky" laws that allow securities commissioners to forbid sales altogether, in contrast with the federal regimen emphasizing disclosure. So § 28(a) allows states to stop some transactions federal law would permit, in pursuit of an approach at odds with a system emphasizing disclosure and investors' choice. Then there is the traditional reluctance of federal courts to infer preemption of "state law in areas traditionally regulated by the States", *California v. ARC America Corp.*, 490 U.S. 93, (1989). States have regulated corporate affairs, including mergers and sales of assets, since before the beginning of the nation.

*   *   *

The Williams Act regulates the *process* of tender offers: timing, disclosure, proration if tenders exceed what the bidder is willing to buy, best-price rules. It slows things down, allowing investors to evaluate the offer and management's response. Best-price, proration, and short-tender rules ensure that investors who decide at the end of the offer get the same treatment as those who decide immediately, reducing pressure to leap before looking.[7] After complying with the disclosure and delay requirements, the bidder is free to take the shares. *MITE* held invalid a state law that increased the delay and, by authorizing a regulator to nix the offer, created a distinct possibility that the bidder would be unable to buy the stock (and the holders to sell it) despite compliance with federal law. Illinois tried to regulate the process of tender offers, contradicting in some respects the federal rules. Indiana, by contrast, allowed the tender offer to take its course as the Williams Act specified but "sterilized" the acquired shares until the remaining investors restored their voting rights. Congress said nothing about the voting power of shares acquired in tender offers. Indiana's law reduced the benefits the bidder anticipated from the acquisition but left the process alone. So the Court, although accepting Justice White's views for the purpose of argument, held that Indiana's rules do not conflict with the federal norms.

CTS observed that laws affecting the voting power of acquired shares do not differ in principle from many other rules governing the internal affairs of corporations. Laws requiring staggered or classified boards of directors delay the transfer of control to the bidder; laws requiring supermajority vote for a merger may make a transaction less attractive or impossible. 481 U.S. at 85–86, 107 S.Ct. at 1647–48. Yet these are not preempted by the Williams Act, any more than state laws concerning the *effect* of investors' votes are preempted by the portions of the Exchange Act, 15 U.S.C. § 78n(a)–(c), regulating the process of soliciting proxies. Federal securities laws frequently regulate process while state corporate law regulates substance. Federal proxy rules demand that firms disclose many things, in order to promote informed voting. Yet states may permit or compel a supermajority rule (even a unanimity rule) rendering it all but impossible for a particular side to prevail in the voting. See Robert Charles Clark, *Corporate Law* § 9.1.3 (1986). Are the state laws therefore preempted? How about state laws that allow many firms to organize without traded shares? Universities, hospitals, and other charities have self-perpetuating boards and cannot be acquired by tender offer. Insurance companies may be organized as mutuals, without traded shares; retailers often organize as co-operatives, without traded stock; some decently large companies (large enough to be "reporting companies" under the ' 34 Act) issue stock subject to buy-sell agreements under which the investors cannot sell to strangers without offering stock to the firm at a formula price; Ford Motor Co. issued non-voting stock to outside investors while reserving voting stock for the family, thus preventing outsiders from gaining control (dual-class stock is becoming more common); firms issue and state law enforces poison pills. All of these devices make tender offers unattractive (even impossible) and greatly diminish the power of proxy fights, success in which often depends on buying votes by acquiring the equity to which the vote is attached. See Douglas H. Blair, Devra L. Golbe & James M. Gerard, *Unbundling the Voting Rights and Profit Claims of Common Shares*, 97 J.Pol.

---

7. To reduce is not to eliminate. Investors' options include selling to arbitrageurs in the market. This price fluctuates daily and may drop suddenly if the prospects of the bid's success dim.

Econ. 420 (1989). None of these devices could be thought preempted by the Williams Act or the proxy rules. If they are not preempted, neither is Wis.Stat. § 180.726.

Any bidder complying with federal law is free to acquire shares of Wisconsin firms on schedule. Delay in completing a second-stage merger may make the target less attractive, and thus depress the price offered or even lead to an absence of bids; it does not, however, alter any of the procedures governed by federal regulation. Indeed Wisconsin's law does not depend in any way on how the acquiring firm came by its stock: open-market purchases, private acquisitions of blocs, and acquisitions via tender offers are treated identically. Wisconsin's law is no different in effect from one saying that for the three years after a person acquires 10% of a firm's stock, a unanimous vote is required to merge. Corporate law once had a generally-applicable unanimity rule in major transactions,[8] a rule discarded because giving every investor the power to block every reorganization stopped many desirable changes. (Many investors could use their "hold-up" power to try to engross a larger portion of the gains, creating a complex bargaining problem that often could not be solved.) Wisconsin's more restrained version of unanimity also may block beneficial transactions, but not by tinkering with any of the procedures established in federal law.

Only if the Williams Act gives investors a right to be the beneficiary of offers could Wisconsin's law run afoul of the federal rule. No such entitlement can be mined out of the Williams Act, however. . . . Investors have no right to receive tender offers. More to the point—since Amanda sues as bidder rather than as investor seeking to sell—the Williams Act does not create a right to profit from the business of making tender offers. It is not attractive to put bids on the table for Wisconsin corporations, but because Wisconsin leaves the process alone once a bidder appears, its law may co-exist with the Williams Act.

C

* * *

When state law discriminates against interstate commerce expressly—for example, when Wisconsin closes its border to butter from Minnesota—the negative Commerce Clause steps in. The law before us is not of this type: it is neutral between inter-state and intra-state commerce. . . . Although the scholars whose writings we cited in Part II.A conclude that laws such as Wisconsin's injure investors, Wisconsin is entitled to give a different answer to this empirical question—or to decide that investors' interests should be sacrificed to protect managers' interests or promote the stability of corporate arrangements.

Illinois's law, held invalid in *MITE*, regulated sales of stock elsewhere. Illinois tried to tell a Texas owner of stock in a Delaware corporation that he could not sell to a buyer in California. By contrast, Wisconsin's law, like the Indiana statute sustained by *CTS*, regulates the internal affairs of firms incorporated there. Investors may buy or sell stock as they please. . . .

---

8. See William J. Carney, *Fundamental Corporate Changes, Minority Shareholders, and Business Purposes*, 1980 Am.Bar Found.Res.J. 69, 77–97; Bayless Manning, *The Shareholder's Appraisal Remedy: An Essay for Frank Coker*, 72 Yale L.J. 223, 226–30 (1962), for two descriptions of the rule, both at common law and in the early state corporate codes.

Buyers of stock in Wisconsin firms may exercise full rights as investors, taking immediate control. No interstate transaction is regulated or forbidden. True, Wisconsin's law makes a potential buyer less willing to buy (or depresses the bid), but this is equally true of Indiana's rule. Many other rules of corporate law — supermajority voting requirements, staggered and classified boards, and so on — have similar or greater effects on some persons' willingness to purchase stock.... Every rule of corporate law affects investors who live outside the state of incorporation, yet this has never been thought sufficient to authorize a form of cost-benefit inquiry through the medium of the Commerce Clause.

Wisconsin, like Indiana, is indifferent to the domicile of the bidder. A putative bidder located in Wisconsin enjoys no privilege over a firm located in New York. So too with investors: all are treated identically, regardless of residence. Doubtless most bidders (and investors) are located outside Wisconsin, but unless the law discriminates according to residence this alone does not matter. Every state's regulation of domestic trade (potentially) affects those who live elsewhere but wish to sell their wares within the state. A law making suppliers of drugs absolutely liable for defects will affect the conduct (and wealth) of Eli Lilly & Co., an Indiana firm, and the many other pharmaceutical houses, all located in other states, yet Wisconsin has no less power to set and change tort law than do states with domestic drug manufacturers. "Because nothing in the [Wisconsin] Act imposes a greater burden on out-of-state offerors than it does on similarly situated [Wisconsin] offerors, we reject the contention that the Act discriminates against interstate commerce." *CTS*, 481 U.S. at 88, 107 S.Ct. at 1649. For the same reason, the Court long ago held that state blue sky laws comport with the Commerce Clause. Blue sky laws may bar Texans from selling stock in Wisconsin, but they apply equally to local residents' attempts to sell. That their application blocks a form of commerce altogether does not strip the states of power.

Wisconsin could exceed its powers by subjecting firms to inconsistent regulation. Because § 180.726 applies only to a subset of firms incorporated in Wisconsin, however, there is no possibility of inconsistent regulation. Here, too, the Wisconsin law is materially identical to Indiana's. This leaves only the argument that Wisconsin's law hinders the flow of interstate trade "too much". *CTS* dispatched this concern by declaring it inapplicable to laws that apply only to the internal affairs of firms incorporated in the regulating state. 481 U.S. at 89–94, 107 S.Ct. at 1649–52. States may regulate corporate transactions as they choose without having to demonstrate under an unfocused balancing test that the benefits are "enough" to justify the consequences.

To say that states have the power to enact laws whose costs exceed their benefits is not to say that investors should kiss their wallets goodbye. States compete to offer corporate codes attractive to firms. Managers who want to raise money incorporate their firms in the states that offer the combination of rules investors prefer. Ralph K. Winter, Jr., *State Law, Shareholder Protection, and the Theory of the Corporation,* 6 J. Legal Studies 251 (1977); Fischel, *supra,* 1987 Sup.Ct.Rev. at 74–84. Laws that in the short run injure investors and protect managers will in the longer run make the state less attractive to firms that need to raise new capital. If the law is "protectionist", the protected class is the existing body of managers (and other workers), suppliers, and so on, which bears no necessary relation to state boundaries. States regulating the affairs of domestic corporations cannot in the long run injure anyone but themselves. Professor Fischel makes the point, 1987 Sup.Ct.Rev. at 84:

In the short run, states can enact welfare-decreasing legislation that imposes costs on residents of other states. State anti-takeover statutes...may be paradigm examples of cost-exporting legislation that is enacted in response to lobbying pressure by in-state constituents. [The managers who gain from the law live in-state; the investors who lose may live elsewhere.] In the long run, however, states have no ability to export costs to non-resident investors. When entrepreneurs want to raise capital for a corporate venture, they must decide where to incorporate. The choice of where to incorporate in turn affects the price investors are willing to pay for shares. And because shares of stock have many perfect substitutes which offer the same risk-return combinations, it is impossible for the entrepreneur to pass on the effects of the law to investors....Nor can a state export costs to the founding entrepreneur since corporations can be incorporated anywhere, regardless of the firm's physical location. States that enact laws that are harmful to investors will cause entrepreneurs to incorporate elsewhere.

The long run takes time to arrive, and it is tempting to suppose that courts could contribute to investors' welfare by eliminating laws that impose costs in the short run. See Gregg A. Jarrell, *State Anti-Takeover Laws and the Efficient Allocation of Corporate Control: An Economic Analysis of Edgar v. MITE Corp.*, 2 Sup.Ct.Econ.Rev. 111 (1983). The price of such warfare, however, is a reduction in the power of competition among states. Courts seeking to impose "good" rules on the states diminish the differences among corporate codes and dampen competitive forces. Too, courts may fail in their quest. How do judges know which rules are best? Often only the slow forces of competition reveal that information. Early economic studies may mislead, or judges (not trained as social scientists) may misinterpret the available data or act precipitously. Our Constitution allows the states to act as laboratories; slow migration (or national law on the authority of the Commerce Clause) grinds the failures under. No such process weeds out judicial errors, or decisions that, although astute when rendered, have become anachronistic in light of changes in the economy. Judges must hesitate for these practical reasons—and not only because of limits on their constitutional competence—before trying to "perfect" corporate codes.

> *   *   *

...The Commerce Clause does not demand that states leave bidders a "meaningful opportunity for success"....Investors can turn to firms incorporated in states committed to the dominance of market forces, or they can turn on legislators who enact unwise laws. The Constitution has room for many economic policies. "[A] law can be both economic folly and constitutional." *CTS*, 481 U.S. at 96–97, 107 S.Ct. at 1653–54 (Scalia, J., concurring). Wisconsin's law may well be folly; we are confident that it is constitutional.

AFFIRMED.

Notes and Questions

1. Race for the Bottom: The competition between the states—which is often referred to as the **race for the bottom**—has been criticized because it allegedly lowers the standards of managerial accountability to shareholders. The characterization of the effects of competition is derived from Justice Louis Brandeis' summary of the effects of early jurisdictional competition in the interstate market for charters: "Companies were early formed to provide charters for corporations in states where the cost was lowest and the laws least restrictive. The states joined in advertising their ware. The race was not one of diligence but of laxity." *Liggett Co. v. Lee*, 288 U.S. 517 (1933) (dissenting opinion). In the modern debate on corporate governance, the attack on competition between the states is based on the following syllogism: states gain from chartering corporations; managers prefer fewer restraints on their accountability to shareholders; managers effectively control the selection of the chartering states; therefore, states compete through lowering (to the bottom) the legal fiduciary standards of managerial performance and accountability to shareholders. Assuming, for arguments sake, that the competition does result in a lowering of standards of managerial conduct, the appropriate policy response still depends on how important fiduciary standards are to controlling managerial behavior. Conflicting policy recommendations may be the result of different conceptions of the corporation.

2. *Race for the Top:* Judge Ralph Winter has questioned the logic of the "race to the bottom" analysis:

> (1) If Delaware permits corporate management to profit at the expense of shareholders and other states do not, then earnings of Delaware corporations must be less than earnings of comparable corporations chartered in other states and shares in the Delaware corporations must trade at lower prices. (2) Corporations with lower earnings will be at a disadvantage in raising debt or equity capital. (3) Corporations at a disadvantage in the capital market will be at a disadvantage in the product market and their share price will decline, thereby creating a threat of takeover which may replace management. To avoid this result, corporations must seek out legal systems more attractive to capital. (4) States seeking corporate charters will thus try to provide legal systems which optimize the shareholder-corporation relationship.

Winter, *State Law, Shareholder Protection, and the Theory of the Corporation*, 6 J. Legal Studies, 251, 254 (1977).

Much of the economic literature on the governance of the modern corporation reflects an evolutionary view of the development and use of certain governance mechanisms. This view is clearly reflected in the following statement: "Absent fiat, the form of organization that survives in an activity is the one that delivers the product demanded by customers at the lowest price while covering costs." Fama & Jensen, *Separation of Ownership and Control*, 26 J. Law & Econ. 301, 303 (1983). The modern corporation appears to be passing the test of time.

Chapter XI

Financial Economics

Economics is a field of inquiry which investigates the allocation of scarce resources in the face of unlimited wants and desires. **Financial economics** is a sub-specialty of this inquiry that focuses on the allocation of scarce capital resources. **Capital resources** are those items facilitating the production of output in future periods. For example, rather than using your current paycheck to go to a movie tonight, you might place that income into an account, thus allowing you to purchase a computer sometime in the future. In this example, you are sacrificing current consumption and allocating funds to a use you anticipate will increase your future output. Utility maximization suggests that individuals would be willing to delay current consumption when it is possible to make capital investments, therefore creating future consumption opportunities.

The financial economics subspecialty can be further divided into three narrow lines of inquiry. First, the allocation of capital resources within the boundaries of the firm is studied in the field of **corporate finance**. Second, the allocation of capital resources through external markets, like the New York Stock Exchange, is investigated in the field of **investments**. Third, the role of financial intermediaries, such as the Federal Reserve Bank, is considered in the study of **financial institutions**. In practice, there is a degree of overlap among these three narrower lines of inquiry. For example, corporate stocks and bonds are investment opportunities to individuals as well as an important source of financing for a firm's internal activities.

This chapter presents the basic economic theory and tools used in both corporate finance and investments—the role of financial institutions is beyond the scope of a book focused primarily on microeconomic theory. Section A introduces the concept of leverage and a variety of financial instruments. The efficiency of capital markets is investigated in Section B. Portfolio theory and diversification are discussed in section C. Section D introduces a tool—the Capital Asset Pricing Model—for quantifying risk and return. Finally, Section E discusses a method used for empirical tests of capital market efficiency that is based on the capital asset pricing model.

A. Leverage and Financial Instruments

Due to economies of scale, many profitable capital investment opportunities require sums of money in the tens, hundreds, or even thousands of millions of dollars. However, very few individuals have access to that type of money and, even if they did, they would be unwilling to risk that much of their wealth in a single financial investment. Banks are often unwilling to loan such large amounts for periods greater than five years. Moreover, even if banks were willing to supply such large sums of money, there are legal restrictions prohibiting overly concentrated loan portfolios.

The inability of single entities to finance large scale capital investments or their unwillingness to accept such concentrated risk has given rise to capital markets. **Capital markets** bring together those who desire funds for the purchase of capital goods with groups of individuals who are willing jointly to supply funds and share risks. Convincing individuals to sacrifice current consumption so that others can make capital investments requires that the suppliers of funds receive compensation for the time value of money (opportunity costs) and risk. Thus, those who desire funds for capital resources can either pay interest or share the profits of capital investments with those who supply the funds.

Exchanges of funds in the capital market are supported by contracts that specify the rights and obligations of the users and suppliers of funds. Because of the large sums of money desired, there are numerous suppliers to any given capital investment project. In order to maximize the gains associated with this process, it makes sense for those who desire funds to offer a single set of contract terms to all individuals who are willing to supply funds. The set of identical investment contracts which cover a collection of funds for a particular common enterprise, which is reasonably expected to pay returns, are known as **securities**. Two of the most popular securities are stocks and bonds.

Matching those who need funds with those who are willing to invest is a highly competitive industry. Profit seeking entrepreneurs in the securities industry are constantly finding new ways to match the needs of buyers and sellers of funds. In addition to stocks and bonds, such profit seeking has lead to a wide variety of exotic securities known as derivative instruments. The most common examples of such instruments are futures and options. Many types of derivatives are considered to be commodities rather than securities. Derivative markets often sound quite complex and in fact, the pricing of such instruments can be very difficult. However, the intuition behind these markets is still grounded in basic microeconomic theory. By focusing on the basic economic tools that have been utilized thus far, much of the mystery behind derivative instruments can be clarified.

This section provides an introduction to the wide variety of financial instruments and securities that facilitate trading in capital markets. Specifically, we will consider bonds, stocks, futures, options, and swaps. The Procter & Gamble case, which concludes this subsection, considers the issue of whether a particular financial instrument should be classified as a security, commodity or bilateral contract. Such distinctions are important in terms of identifying the appropriate governing regulation and specifying the nature of the relationship between the parties.

1. Leverage

One of the most important and often underemphasized concepts in finance is leverage. **Leverage** refers to the ability to finance an investment by borrowing from a third party, and thus using only a small amount of one's own funds. Leverage provides many individuals with an opportunity to access investment benefits that would otherwise be precluded. For example, most peoples' homes represent highly leveraged transactions—many mortgages require only a 5% downpayment. In addition, the use of leverage allows individuals to increase investment returns by increasing their risk exposure. Understanding the trade-offs involved in the use of leverage is an important application of the opportunity costs concept. Consider the following example.

Suppose that some asset XYZ is available for sale at a cost of $10,000. One option is to purchase the asset outright with $10,000 in cash. If the value of XYZ increases by 10%, you will have made 10% on your cash investment or $1,000 (10,000 × .10 = $1,000). Likewise, if the value of XYZ falls by 10% you will lose $1,000 and have lost 10% on your cash investment. In this case, the return on your investment is matched 1 to 1 with changes in the value of the underlying asset.

Now suppose that you had the opportunity to buy XYZ by borrowing $8,000 and using $2,000 of your own money. In this case your cash investment represents one fifth of the purchase price—in other words, your investment is leveraged 5 to 1. Thus, the return on the levered investment will be five times that of the unlevered investment. For example, if the value of XYZ increases by 10% you will make $1,000 cash just as in the case of the unlevered investment. However, $1,000 represents a 50% return on your initial $2,000 cash investment (minus, of course, the interest cost of borrowing $8,000). In the alternative, if the value of XYZ were to fall by 10%, you would lose 50% of your $2,000 cash investment. By leveraging the purchase of XYZ, you would lose your entire investment if the value of XYZ declined by 20%.

The returns on each of the financial instruments discussed in this chapter can be levered and in practice often are. However, there are two important limits on the use of leverage. First, some other party has to be willing to make the loan. Thus, your ability to use leverage will be limited by your creditworthiness. As greater amounts of leverage are used and the risk of default increases, so too will the interest rate charged on borrowed funds. In this sense, the market provides a natural limit to the uses of leverage. Second, the amount of leverage allowed in financial instruments purchased on an organized exchange is limited by the governing body of the exchange. Examples of such limits are discussed below.

2. Debt Securities and the Bond Market

Bonds are certificates that evidence a debt drawn against the assets of a corporation or government. Those who issue bonds are contractually bound to pay a set amount of interest and principal at predetermined times. The holder of a bond is a creditor of the issuer and is not considered to have an ownership interest in the assets of the issuer. However, as a creditor, the holder can initiate legal proceedings, including bankruptcy, against an issuer for failing to pay scheduled interest or principal payments. Thus, bonds are a **fixed income security** because they provide a relatively certain stream of funds to investors.

There are virtually an unlimited number of contractual rights or obligations that might accrue to the holders and issuers of a particular bond issue. Such rights and obligations are set forth in a contract known as a **bond indenture**. Two of the most common rights specified in the bond indentures of corporations are callability and convertibility. A **call provision** gives an issuer the right to retire bonds prior to maturity but after a specified call date. When bonds are called, the issuer pays the holder any amount due as principal and typically a small premium. Call provisions are of great value to issuers because it allows them to refinance existing debt if interest rates drop. **Convertible bonds** allow the holder to transform bonds into common stock at a specified price. Convertibility is of value to holders because it allows them to participate in higher returns if the issuer's stock appreciates in value. However, because convertibility is a right and not an obligation, the holder is protected against declines in stock value by refusing to convert. Government bond issues often include call provisions, but they are never convertible because governments cannot issue stock.

A bond indenture also specifies the type of collateral that secures the bond. Corporate bonds which are not secured by specific collateral are known as **debentures**. When the corporation has issued other debt instruments having claims to specific corporate assets, the unsecured bonds are known as **subordinated debentures**. Government issued bonds backed by the full taxing power of the government are known as **general obligation bonds** and are considered to be very secure. However, some bonds issued by governments are backed only by the revenue generating power of the specific project funded by the bonds. Such bonds are known as **revenue bonds** and are only as secure as the revenue generating ability of the sponsored project.

Bonds can be issued either as coupon bonds or pure discount bonds. A **coupon bond** makes a series of regular payments to the holder during the life of the bond. The term coupon bond comes from the physical attributes of the certificate representing such a bond. Coupon bond certificates are issued with detachable slips of paper—the coupons—which are mailed to the issuer in order to redeem the coupon payment. Coupon bonds have both a par value and an coupon rate. **Par value** is the dollar amount printed on the face of the bond at the time it is issued and represents the amount of principal due at maturity. At issuance, coupon bonds are typically sold for an amount equal to their par value. Most bonds carry a par value of $1,000. The **coupon rate** denotes a percentage amount of par value which will be paid to the bond holder at specific time intervals. For example, a 10 year $1,000 par value bond with a 10% coupon rate pays a $100 coupon payment to the holder every year and returns the principal of $1,000 plus a $100 coupon payment in the year of maturity.

A **pure discount bond** is a debt security that makes no coupon payments to its holder. Thus, pure discount bonds are typically referred to as **zero coupon bonds**. Pure discount bonds have both a par value and a discount rate. Unlike coupon bonds which are generally sold at issuance for an amount equal to par value, discount bonds are sold for an amount less than par value. Hence the name pure discount bonds. For example, a 10 year $1,000 par value bond issued when the prevailing interest rate is 10% would sell for approximately $386. This selling price represents the present value of $1,000 received in ten years discounted at 10%. Holders of this pure discount bond would then receive the $1,000 par value at the end of ten years. Thus, the interest earned on a pure discount bonds accrues during the time between issuance and maturity.

Most bonds have a stated **maturity date** at which time the principal payment comes due. The time between issuance and maturity is known as the bonds' **term**. **Short-term bonds** pay all of their interest and principal payments within one year. **Long-term bonds** pay interest and principal for a period greater than ten years. Bonds having a life from two to ten years are known as **intermediate-term bonds**. An exception to the above description are a unique type of coupon bond known as consol bonds. **Consol bonds** never mature or pay back the par value. Rather, consols pay a stream of coupon payments forever. In other words, consol bonds have an infinite term.

In general, bonds with the same credit risks but with various terms to maturity have different interest rates. For example, assume that the United States Government issues bonds that come due in one, two, three, four, and five years. The interest rates on these bonds are 4%, 8%, 9%, 7%, and 6% respectively. Each of these terms and their respective interest rates are plotted in Figure XI-1 with time on the horizontal axis and interest rate on the vertical axis. Recall from Chapter IV that interest rates are selected to reflect the time value of money. Thus, the pattern of interest rates that arise for bonds with the same risks but different terms to maturity provides information regarding the market's perception of how short-term interest rates will fluctuate over time. This pattern is known as the **term structure of interest rates** and the curve connecting the points Figure XI-1 is known as the **yield curve**. The yield curve plotted in Figure XI-1 suggests that short-term interest rates will increase over the next three years and then gradually decline.

Figure XI-1

Term Structure of Interest Rates

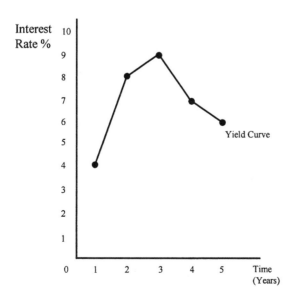

a. Bond Pricing

So far three different types of bonds have been considered: pure discount, coupon, and consol. Estimating a value or price for these different types of bonds can be done by extending the principles of valuation introduced in Chapter IV. The study of bond pricing will begin by examining a pure discount bond or zero coupon bond. As indicated above, a zero coupon bond simply returns the par value upon maturity. Thus, the price of a zero coupon bond is par value discounted to present value.

$$P_z = \text{Par Value} \div (1 + r)^n$$

where P_z is the price of a zero coupon bond, n is the bond's term, and r is the current interest rate for term n. Consider, for example, a three year zero coupon bond with a par value of $1000 and a current market interest rate of 10%. The price for such a bond is:

$$P_z = \$1,000 \div (1 + .10)^3 = \$751.3148$$

Unlike pure discount bonds, coupon bonds make regular payments to the holder until maturity. One method for pricing coupon bonds is to think of them as a series of zero coupon bonds with different maturities. In other words, the coupon paid in period one is treated as a one year zero coupon bond with a par value equal to the coupon payment. This process is then repeated for each coupon payment and the par value paid at maturity. The series of present values are then added together in order to estimate the price of a coupon bond.

$$P_{cpn} = C \div (1 + r) + C \div (1 + r)^2 + \ldots + C \div (1 + r)^n + \text{Par Value} \div (1 + r)^n$$

where P_{cpn} is the price of a coupon bond, C is the coupon payment, n is the bond's term, and r is the current market interest rate for term n. This equation says that the price of a coupon bond is equal to the present value of its coupon payments and the present value of its par value. Consider, for example, a three year coupon bond with a $1,000 par value, 6% coupon rate, and a current market interest rate of 10%. From this information we know that the coupon payments will be $60 ($1,000 x .06 = $60). Thus, the price of this bond is:

$$P_{cpn} = \$60 \div (1 + .10) + \$60 \div (1 + .10)^2 + \$60 \div (1 + .10)^3 + \$1,000 \div (1 + .10)^3$$
$$= \$900.5259$$

From the above calculation, it is easy to see that estimating coupon bond prices can become very tedious if more than just a few years are considered. A more convenient way to value coupon bonds is to think about the coupon payments as an annuity. An **annuity** is a level stream of cash flows paid or collected over a fixed period of time. It can be shown that the present value or price of an annuity is equal to:

$$P_A = C \times [1 - \{1 \div (1 + r)^n\}] \div r$$

By using the annuity formula to estimate the price of a stream of coupon payments, coupon bonds can be priced as:

$$P_{cpn} = \text{Present Value of the Annuity} + \text{Present Value of the Par Value}$$

The annuity method can be used to estimate a price for the three year coupon bond considered in the preceding paragraph. First, the present value of the stream of $60 coupon payments for three years is equal to:

$$PV_A = \$60 \times [1 - \{1 \div (1 + .10)^3\} \div .10 = \$149.2111$$

Second, determine that the present value of the $1,000 par value paid at maturity equals:

$$PV_{Par} = \$1000 \div (1 + .10)^3 = \$751.3148$$

Third, by adding these two numbers together, the present value or price of this coupon bond may be obtained:

$$P_{Cpn} = \$149.2111 + \$751.3148 = \$900.5259$$

Notice that this is the same value obtained when discounting each coupon payment separately. Thus, the annuity method can save a considerable amount of time in pricing coupon bonds.

The third type of bond considered is a consol bond. Consol bonds never mature or pay back the par value. Rather, consols pay a stream of coupon payments forever. In order to determine the price of a consol, use the formula introduced in Chapter IV for valuing perpetuities.

$$P_{cnl} = C \div r$$

where P_{cnl} is the price of a consol bond, C is the coupon payment, and r is the current market interest rate. Thus, for a consol with a $60 coupon and a current market interest rate of 10%, the price is:

$$P_{cnl} = \$60 \div .10 = \$600$$

Throughout the discussion of bond pricing methods, it has been assumed that the stream of future cash flows is received with certainty. However, there are at least two provisions found in bond indentures that introduce uncertainty into the future cash flows of a bond. First, a call provision can eliminate several years of coupon payments and thus, eliminate some future cash flows. Correct pricing of a bond with a call provision requires that a deduction be made relative to an identical bond with no call provision. Second, bonds convertible into common stock introduce the possibility of adding a new stream of cash flows. Therefore, convertible bonds have a premium added to their price relative to an identical bond with no convertibility provision. For both the callability and convertibility provisions, one can use the tools of probability and expected value introduced in Chapter IX to estimate correct prices.

Notwithstanding specific provisions of a bond indenture that might alter the cash flow due a holder, each of the different types of bonds that has been discussed in this chapter provide a relatively stable flow of future payments. For example, barring default, the dollar amount of coupon payments on a coupon bond does not change over time. Likewise, the dollar amount of par value returned at maturity does not change during the course of an investment. However, what might change is the price that any particular investor would be willing to pay some other individual for a given steam of future cash flows.

The basic present value formula demonstrates that the value of a relatively stable cash flow changes depending on the current market rate of interest by which the cash flows are discounted. For example, if the current market rate of interest were to increase, the future cash flows would be discounted by a larger denominator resulting in a reduction in present value. In other words, if interest rates increase, investors will be willing to pay less for a given stream of future cash flows holding all else equal. Alternatively, if market interest rates were to decline, the denominator in the present value formula would decrease resulting in a higher present value. Thus, when interest rates decline, investors are willing to pay more for a given stream of future cash flows holding all else equal. In sum, bond prices are inversely related to the market interest rate.

b. Interest Rate Risk—Duration and Convexity

Analyzing the present value formula suggested that bond prices are inversely related to interest rates. Not surprisingly, investors want information regarding the degree to which bond prices change when interest rates fluctuate. **Interest rate risk** considers the sensitivity of bond prices to a change in market interest rates. In general, a particular bond's interest rate risk is a function of its term, coupon rate, and the level of interest rates at the time rates change. Conceptually, interest rate risk is very similar to the idea of price elasticity introduced in Chapter III. Thus, our measures of interest rate risk will look a lot like elasticity calculations.

Investors have utilized two measures which, when used in combination, can approximate the interest rate risk of bonds. These two measures are known as duration and convexity. Consider a ten year bond whose price for a variety of interest rates is shown graphically in Figure XI-2. Notice that this curve is convex to the origin—that is, it bends inward. This shape assumes that the price impact of changing interest rates diminishes as rates increase. (The validity of this assumption is verified in the last paragraph of this subsection.) In other words, bond prices are more sensitive to interest rate shifts at lower interest rate levels. This curve represents the **value function** for our ten year bond.

As was the case with our elasticity measures, calculation of point estimates for the slope of a value function lead to an understanding of interest rate risk. The formula used to measure the slope of a particular bonds value function is

Figure XI-2

The Value Function

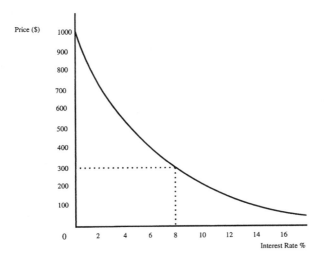

known as dollar duration. **Dollar duration** is calculated as the change in price for a given change in interest rates.

$$DD = -[(P_{+\Delta r} - P_{-\Delta r}) \div (2 \times \Delta r)100]$$

where DD is the dollar duration, $P_{+\Delta r}$ is the price of the bond after a given increase in the current interest rate r, $P_{-\Delta r}$ is the price of the bond after a given decrease in the current interest rate r, and Δr is a given change in the current interest rate r. From this formula, we can see that higher dollar durations are indicative of greater interest rate risk.

One problem with the dollar duration formula is that it measures absolute changes in dollar price. Thus, it is difficult to use the dollar duration measure for a meaningful comparison between bonds of different prices. To remedy this problem, simply alter the numerator in the dollar duration formula to be the percentage change in price. **Modified duration** is calculated as the percentage change in price for a given change in interest rates.

$$MD = -[\{(P_{+\Delta r} - P_{-\Delta r}) \div P_r\} \div (2 \times \Delta r)]$$

where MD is the modified duration, $P_{+\Delta r}$ is the price of the bond after a given increase in the current interest rate r, $P_{-\Delta r}$ is the price of the bond after a given decrease in the current interest rate r, P_r is the bond price at the current interest rate r, and Δr is a given change in the current interest rate r. From this formula, notice that higher modified duration also indicates a greater interest rate risk. However, the modified duration measure allows the comparison of bonds at different price levels.

Duration measures are useful for thinking about interest rate risk. However, duration only tells part of the story. Recall that the slope of a curve at a particular point is given by the slope of a straight line drawn tangent to the curve at that point. Figure XI-3 shows such a tangent for the value function of the ten year bond considered earlier. Notice that the value function is actually higher than the

Figure XI-3

Convexity and Interest Rate Risk

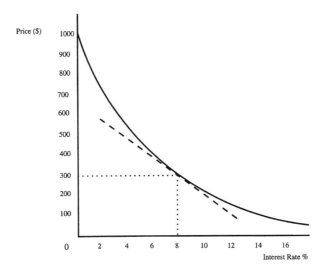

tangent line when interest rates either increase or decrease. This means that when interest rates decrease, the price of a bond grows by more than is indicated by the duration measure alone. Similarly, when interest rates rise, bond prices do not fall by as much as indicated through the duration measures. From Figure XI-3 it can be seen that the error in the duration measure grows larger for greater changes in the interest rate. This error in the duration measure is due to the fact that the value curve is convex and duration is a linear measure. Thus, the more convex a particular bond's value function, the less powerful duration is in estimating interest rate risk.

In order to measure the gain that is not captured by the linear duration formula, investors often use convexity measures. The **dollar gain from convexity** is given by:

$$DC = [\{(P_{+\Delta r} + P_{-\Delta r}) \div 2\} - P_r] \div [(\Delta_r)^2 \times 10,000]$$

where DC is the dollar gain from convexity, P_r is the bond price at the current interest rate r, $P_{+\Delta r}$ is the price of the bond after a given increase in the current interest rate r, and $P_{-\Delta r}$ is the price of the bond after a given decrease in the current interest rate r.

Note, that like dollar duration, the dollar gain from convexity is not very helpful in comparing bonds of different price levels. By making a small alteration to our dollar convexity formula, we find a modified convexity measure that captures percentage rather than absolute changes. **Modified convexity** is given by:

$$MC = 100[(\{(P_{+\Delta r} + P_{-\Delta r}) \div 2\} - P_r) \div P_r] \div [(\Delta_r)^2 \times 10,000]$$

To put the duration and convexity measures to work, use the $1,000 ten year zero coupon bond whose value function was graphed in Figure XI-2. The current market interest rate for this bond is 10%. Three numbers are needed in order to calculate duration and convexity measures. First, determine the price of the bond under the current interest rate. In our example, the zero coupon bond is currently priced at $385.5432 ($1,000 \div (1+.10)^{10}$). Next, calculate the bond's price for a given increase and decrease in interest rates. One-half percent changes are used so that the total interest rate change in the formulas will equal one percent. Thus, if interest rates increased by one-half percent to become 10.5%, the price of this zero coupon bond would be $368.4488 ($1,000 \div (1+.105)^{10}$). Alternatively, if interest rates decreased by one-half percent to 9.5% the price of the zero coupon bond would be $403.5141 ($1,000 \div (1+.095)^{10}$).

Plugging these three numbers into the dollar duration and convexity formulas the following is obtained:

$$DD = - (\$368.4488 - \$403.5141) \div [(2 \times .005) \times 100] = \$35.0653$$

$$DC = [\{(\$368.4488 + \$403.5141) \div 2\} - 385.5432] \div [(.005)^2 \times 10,000] = \$1.753$$

According to these calculations, a one percent increase in the market interest rate causes the dollar value of this bond to decrease by $35.0653 due to duration and increase by $1.75 from convexity. Thus, the total dollar value change from a one percent increase in the interest rate is a decline of $33.3153 (= −$35.0653 + $1.75). If the market interest rate decreased by one percent, the dollar value of our bond would increase by $35.0653 due to duration and by an additional $1.73 from convexity for a total gain of $36.8153.

Plugging our three price numbers into the modified duration and convexity formulas, the following is obtained:

$$MD = -[(\$368.4488 - \$403.5141) \div 385.5432] \div (2 \times .005) = 9.095\%$$

$$MC = 100[(\{(\$368.4488 + \$403.5141) \div 2\} - 385.5432)$$
$$\div 385.5432] \div [(.005)^2 \times 10,000] = .45\%$$

Thus, for a one percent increase in the interest rate, the value of our bond falls by 9.095% due to duration and increases .45% from convexity for a total loss of 8.645%. Alternatively, a one percent decrease in the market interest rate causes the value of the bond to grow by 9.095% due to duration and an additional .45% from convexity for total growth of 9.545%.

An inquisitive individual may began to wonder why an interest rate sensitivity measure is known as duration. Duration seems to imply that some type of time component is involved. Indeed, it can be shown by way of calculus that the modified duration of any zero coupon bond is equal to:

$$MD = n \div (1 + r)$$

where n is the bond's term and r is the market interest rate. In other words, simply divide the number of years until the bond matures by one plus the market interest rate to obtain modified duration. Using the numbers from our example in the preceding paragraphs, it is found:

$$MD = 10 \div (1 + .10) = 9.090$$

This formulation of modified duration can be used to observe an important fact regarding interest rate risk and term to maturity. Namely, that for a given rate of interest, increases in the term to maturity will cause the modified duration of a zero coupon bond to increase. That is, bonds with longer terms to maturity are more sensitive to interest rate shifts, all else equal.

In the preceding examples, the duration of zero coupon bonds was analyzed. Now, the issue of duration for coupon bonds will be explored. Recall the discussion of coupon bonds from the subsection on bond pricing. In that subsection, a coupon bond was treated as a series of zero coupon bonds. The same can be done for purposes of calculating a coupon bond's duration. The first step is to calculate a duration for each component cash flow as though it were an independent zero coupon bond. The second step is to weight each of these component durations by an amount equal to the present value of the individual component cash flow divided by the present value of the sum of component cash flows. The third and final step is to add the weighted component durations together in order to get a measure for the coupon bond's duration.

At the beginning of this subsection, it was stated that bond prices fluctuate in an inverse manner with interest rates but, that the degree of fluctuation is a function of the term to maturity, coupon rate, and level of interest rates at the time interest rates change. The duration concept can help one to see how each of these variables affects bond prices. First, as observed earlier, duration grows as the term to maturity increases. Thus, we know that all else equal, a bond becomes more sensitive to interest rate shifts as it term grows. Second, the effect of coupon payments on interest rate sensitivity can be discovered by considering the formula used to estimate duration for a coupon bond. The effect of a particular coupon payment on a bond's duration is a function of its own duration multiplied by its weight. As the level of coupon payment increases, the weight applied to near term coupon durations grows relative to those applied to far term durations because a greater fraction of the bond's present value is recovered in the near term. When coupon rates are increased, durations with shorter maturities are emphasized in the calculations and the emphasis on shorter maturities means that duration will decline. Thus, a bond becomes more sensitive to interest rates as coupon rates decline, all else equal. Third, an increase in the current interest rate causes the value of future cash flows to decline, and this impact is relatively greater for cash flows further into the future. By way of the same analysis done in regards to coupon rates, the weights of near term components increase relative to those of the long term components. Thus, at higher levels of interest rates, bond prices become less sensitive to any given change in interest rates all else equal.

3. Equity Securities and the Stock Market

Stocks are certificates that evidence an equity or ownership interest in a corporation. As owners of a corporation, stockholders are entitled to share in profits generated by the firm. However, despite ownership status, corporation law provides that in most instances stockholder losses are limited to their initial investment. Thus, stockholders have **limited liability** with respect to debts incurred by the corporation. Stockholders have the right to elect a board of directors, which in turn selects management and oversees the firm's operations. In addition to electing board members, stockholders also vote on important issues affecting the future of the firm. Through the voting process, shareholders ultimately exercise control over the firm. The specific rights of shareholders are set forth in a corporate charter or articles of incorporation.

Stocks are a **variable income security** because they provide an uncertain stream of funds to investors. Stockholders participate in a firm's profits through dividend payments. **Dividend payments** are a distribution of corporate earnings to the firm's shareholders. In most instances, dividends are paid in the form of cash, but they can be paid with additional stock or other property. Dividends are paid at the discretion of the board of directors. Thus, stockholders are not guaranteed to receive dividend payments in any particular period. The decision to pay dividends depends upon a variety of factors including the firm's historical or expected profitability, current cash flows, and plans for internally financed growth.

In general, corporations can issue two types of equity securities—common and preferred stock. At a basic level, the difference between common and preferred shares is a matter of risk and return. **Common stocks** are subordinate to all other claims on the firm's earnings and assets. During any given period, common stockholders must wait until all other parties receive their share of corporate earnings before they receive any dividend payment. Thus, if there is only enough money to pay principal and interest payments on the firm's bonds, then common stockholders receive nothing. Moreover, in the event of bankruptcy, common stockholders receive money only after all other claimants have been fully satisfied. **Preferred stocks** have a superior claim relative to common stocks on the firm's earnings and assets. In other words, dividends on preferred shares are paid before any dividends are paid to common stockholders. Moreover, in the event of bankruptcy, preferred shareholders' claims to corporate assets are superior to claims of common shareholders. However, preferred shareholders are still subordinate to all creditors with regard to both earnings and assets.

Dividends on preferred shares are usually equal to a fixed percentage of the stock's par value. Most preferred shares have a par value of $100. For example, a preferred share with a three percent dividend rate would pay a $3.00 dividend. Preferred shares can require either cumulative or non-cumulative dividends. Most preferred shares provide for cumulative dividends. In the case of **cumulative dividends**, if the board of directors decides not to pay dividends during a particular period, then the dividend due preferred shareholders is carried forward. In most cases, therefore, when the board decides to pay dividends again, preferred shareholders receive current plus past dividends before common shareholders receive any dividends. However, if the firm earns economic profits, preferred shareholders are not able to participate in the profits beyond the stated dividend payment.

For dividends paid on common stocks, the board of directors not only determines the timing but also the dollar amount. Thus, if the firm earns economic profits, common stockholders do have the ability to participate through higher dividend payments. However, dividends on common stock are generally non-cumulative. In the case of **non-cumulative dividends**, if the board of directors decides not to pay dividends in a particular period, the shareholders are simply out of luck—that is, nothing carries forward. It is apparent from the above descriptions, that common stocks bear relatively more risk when compared to preferred stocks. Specifically, the holders of common stock have the greatest chance of receiving nothing from their investment. As compensation for this added risk bearing, common stocks have a higher potential rate of return because the dollar amount of dividends is not limited. Thus, the fundamental difference between common and preferred stock is a matter of risk and return.

An important factor affecting risk and return on stock market investments is the use of leverage. Stock market investors introduce leverage into their investments by **buying on margin**. Buying on margin requires investors to establish a margin account with their broker. The investor is required to maintain some minimum balance in the margin account. That balance can be maintained in cash or other eligible securities. For example, a broker might require that 50% of the price of any stock purchased on that account be maintained as margin. In this case, the investor is able to borrow the other 50% of the purchase price from his broker. Investors must pay interest on the borrowed funds, but interest is not due until the levered stocks are sold. If the value of the stocks purchased on margin declines substantially, there is the possibility that selling the stock won't be able to cover the amount borrowed from the broker. The broker will have a minimum percentage level by which the value of an investment can decline before she takes action. Technically, the minimum percentage can be determined by the broker, but it cannot fall below the level specified by the Federal Reserve Board—currently 75%. When the value of the investment declines by the predetermined percentage, the broker will close out the account and sell the shares unless the investor deposits additional funds in the margin account. This process is known as a **margin call**. When an investor cannot meet the margin call he may be forced to sell the stocks at a loss even though he believes that share prices will rise substantially in the future.

The present value model introduced in Chapter IV is used to determine the value of a given share of stock. The approach to stock valuation is similar to that used for valuing bonds. Specifically, the price of a given stock is equal to the discounted value of all future cash flows accruing to the stockholder. In general, when investors purchase stocks, they expect cash flow from two different sources. First, investors expect to receive dividend payments over the years that the stock is held. Second, investors expect to sell the stock for a higher price than their purchase price. Any reasonable model for estimating stock price ought to incorporate these two investor expectations.

Suppose that after your own analysis of the litigation risk facing Philip Morris, you suspect that the current market price of $40 is too low. In fact, suppose that you were quite certain that the price will be at $65 one year from now. Moreover, after checking with the *Value Line Investment Surveys*, you estimate that the annual dividend payment on Philip Morris next year will be $5.00. Additionally, you decide that based on market returns for the last ten years, a 15% return is satisfactory. You now have all the information you need to generate a present value calculation for the cash flows to be received from a one year investment in Philip Morris. Based on the foregoing information we could calculate the present value of these cash flows as:

$$\text{Present Value} = (D_1 + P_1) \div (1 + r)$$

where D_1 is the estimate for next year's dividend, P_1 is the estimate for next year's price, and r is the appropriate discount rate (i.e., your required return). In this context, present value can be equated with the price (P_0) you would be willing to pay to purchase this share of stock during the current period. So far this model appears to meet the requirements that it account for dividend payments and price appreciation. In the Philip Morris example, two sources of future cash flow exist—a dividend payment of $5.00 and a sales price of $65.00. Furthermore, this amount is discounted at 15% for one year. According to proper estimates, the present value of the cash flows from the Philip Morris investment is:

$$P_0 = (\$65 + \$5) \div (1 + .15) = \$60.87$$

Thus, at a current market price of $40, consider this stock to be a real steal.

The goal in the above calculation was to estimate the current price you would be willing to pay for a share of Philip Morris. To do this, an estimate for the share price in the next year was assumed. The astute observer will notice that the price estimation problem has simply been pushed one year into the future. Estimating the price one year into the future is an extension of the process that was completed for determining the current price. Specifically, the stock's price in one year will be equal to the value of dividends and sales price at the end of year two discounted at the appropriate rate for year two. Formally, we estimate P_1 as:

$$P_1 = (D_2 + P_2) \div (1 + r)$$

where P_1 is the price of the stock in one year, D_2 is the dividend paid on the stock at the end of two years, P_2 is the price of the stock at the end of two years, and r is your required rate of return during year two. To determine the current price, P_0, just substitute the estimate for P_1 from above into the following formula for P_0.

$$P_0 = [D_1 + \{(D_2 + P_2) \div (1 + r)\}] \div (1 + r)$$

By dividing through, this simplifies to:

$$P_0 = [D_1 \div (1 + r)] + [D_2 \div (1 + r)^2] + [P_2 \div (1 + r)^2]$$

This transforms the problem into that of determining the price of the stock at the end of period two. In short, the price that we need to determine can continue to be pushed further into the future. From the study of valuation, it is known that at some point in the future, the present value of the price that is to be determined will be so infinitely close to zero that for practical purposes it can be ignored. Thus, by pushing the price that is supposed to be determined far into the future, our formula for determining current stock price becomes:

$$P_0 = [D_1 \div (1 + r)] + [D_2 \div (1 + r)^2] + [D_3 \div (1 + r)^3] + \ldots + [D_{\tilde{n}} \div (1 + r)^{\tilde{n}}]$$

This formula suggests that the current price of a stock is equal to the present value of all future dividend payments. Moreover, this formula meets the requirement for a reasonable model for estimating stock price. First, it takes into account the stream of all future dividend payments. Second, from the process used to derive this formula, it is clear that price appreciation is imbedded in the model. However, the problem of estimating the stream of future dividends still remains.

The current dividend is the one piece of information that may help to estimate future dividends. In order to make this piece of information useful, however, at least one of two simplifying assumptions must be made. First, it could be assumed that the firm will forever pay the same dividend every year—a **zero growth model**. Second, it could be assumed that the firm will allow dividends to forever grow at a constant rate every year—a **constant growth model**.

First, examine the zero growth model. A zero growth model assumes that the dividend is the same in every period and continues on forever. These assumptions allow the use of the model for valuing perpetuities examined in Chapter IV. In the context of stock prices, this formula becomes:

$$P_0 = D \div r$$

where P_0 is the current market price, D is the assumed constant dividend and r is your required rate of return. Notice also that this model fits very well with the properties of a preferred stock. Recall that preferred stock pays a constant dividend for an infinite period of time. Thus, determining the value of preferred stock is simply a specific application of the zero growth model.

Returning to the study of Philip Morris, what would be the price of a single share if the CEO were to announce that the dividend would remain at $5.00 forever? Utilizing the zero growth model, we find that the current price would be:

$$P_0 = 5 \div .15 = \$33.33$$

Notice that this is less than the amount estimated previously. The reason is that in the prior example price appreciation was assumed, and as the model development exhibits, this is a function of growing dividends. When dividends stay flat, so too do future cash flows. Thus, a lower estimate for current price.

Now consider the constant growth model. In order to utilize this model, determine the rate at which the firm will allow dividends to grow. This growth rate may be identified by looking at historical data. Alternatively the firm's CEO might announce, in a convincing manner, that the firm plans to grow dividends at some particular rate. Thus, next period's dividend is estimated by using the formula:

$$D_1 = D_0 \times (1 + g)$$

where D_1 is the dividend next period, D_0 is the dividend in the current period, and g is the estimated dividend growth rate. By repeating this process, the dividend in period two would be equal to:

$$D_2 = D_1 \times (1 + g)$$

Where D_2 is the dividend in period two. By substituting the estimate for D_1 into the formula for determining D_2 we find:

$$D_2 = [D_0 \times (1 + g)] \times (1 + g)$$

Which simplifies to:

$$= D_0 \times (1 + g)^2$$

The resulting stream of dividends are very similar to those of the perpetuity model, except for the fact that the future cash flow grows at a constant rate. This stream of future cash flows can be characterized as a growing perpetuity. As long as the growth rate is less than the required rate of return, the present value of growing perpetuities are estimated by using the following formula:

$$P_0 = D_1 \div (r - g)$$

where D_1 is the dividend in the next period (i.e., $D_1 = D_0 \times (1 + g)$), r is the required rate of return, and g is the dividend growth rate.

Returning to the analysis of stock in Philip Morris, the constant growth model can be used to calculate a shares' value if the CEO were to announce that the firm would allow dividends to grow at 10%:

$$P_0 = \$5.00 (1 + .10) \div .15 - .10 = \$110$$

In this case, the estimate of current price is higher than that of the original calculation. This is due to the fact that the growth rate assumed in the current example is higher than the implicit growth rate in the higher sales price for the original example. Again, notice that when the expected future cash flows grow, so does the current price for a share of stock.

The constant and zero growth models both provide a method for thinking about current stock prices. However, it is important to emphasize that both of these models make crucial assumptions which may or may not comport with reality. Specifically, absolute zero or constant growth in the dividend rate would be hard to find in practice. To the extent that actual dividend growth deviates from these assumptions, the model should be supplemented with other information. Nevertheless, the fundamental intuition behind our stock price estimation models is always valid—that the current price of any stock is equal to the present value of future cash flows accruing to that stock.

Before discussion of the constant growth model concludes, it is important to note that it can also be used to estimate the required return on investment. By rearranging terms, the constant growth model becomes:

$$(r - g) = D_1 \div P_0$$
$$r = (D_1 \div P_0) + g$$

According to this form of the model, the required return on the investment is equal to the dividend yield ($D_1 \div P_0$) plus growth rate (g). The dividend yield is the expected return on the investment due to next period's dividend payment. Furthermore, because the dividend grows at rate g, it can be concluded that the stock's price also grows at rate g. Thus, the required rate of return equals the amount of return expected from dividend payments plus the amount expected from price appreciation.

Thus far, the analysis of stock valuation has assumed a level of information certainty that rarely exists in the real world. As a matter of fact, stocks have a much larger degree of uncertainty surrounding their valuation than do bonds. Specifically, stocks are generally more difficult to value because of three added uncertainties. First, in the case of common stock, the exact dollar amount of future cash receipts is not known. Second, because dividend payments are made at the discretion of the board of directors, the timing of future receipts of cash are not certain. Third, a series of publicly available interest rates does not exist to derive an appropriate discount factor. In short, each of these uncertainties must be dealt with in a manner similar to that introduced in Chapter IX on Risk.

4. Derivative Instruments

A **derivative instrument** is a financial contract which *derives* value from an underlying commodity, security, interest rate, or currency. There is a wide and growing variety of derivative instruments. The most common types of derivatives are futures, options, and swaps. Derivative instruments provide at least three benefits to their users. First, derivatives provide an additional outlet for investable funds. Second, derivatives facilitate the shifting of risk and return among various parties. Third, derivatives are used in the creation of financially engineered products with risk and return specifications tailor-made for a particular buyer.

Derivatives can be used to further both hedging and speculation strategies. **Hedging strategies** use derivatives in order to avoid undesirable fluctuations in a market price, interest rate, or exchange rate. Hedging is a method for reducing risk exposure by sacrificing some amount of potential return. In this sense, hedging is very much like purchasing an insurance contract. **Speculation strategies** involve the use of derivatives in order to profit from fluctuations in a market price, interest rate, or exchange rate. Speculating is a method for increasing one's risk exposure in the hope of greater returns. It is important to note that the benefits of hedging cannot be achieved without the presence of speculators. In other words, in order for one party to reduce their risk exposure, some other party has to be willing to increase their risk exposure.

Financial engineering refers to the repackaging of financial assets into new instruments in order to customize risk and return. For example, suppose that Merrill Lynch purchased a large block in a government bond series at a recent Treasury auction. Rather than resell the Treasury Bonds as is, Merrill Lynch might separate the rights to the coupon payments from the right to receive the principal payments. The process of breaking up a financial asset is called **stripping**. By stripping the right to receive coupon payments from the Treasury bonds, Merrill Lynch can now issue a new series of securities that make payments like an annuity. Likewise, the strip of principal payments can be repackaged as a new set of securities that behaves like zero coupon bonds. Each of these repackaged securities is a derivative instrument because their value is derived from the original government bonds. In other words, the full faith and credit of the United States Government now backs both the annuities and zero-coupon bonds.

Historical accounts report the use of derivative type agreements from as many as two thousand years ago. Nevertheless, the use of derivatives has expanded greatly since the early 1970s. Along with this growth in usage has come an increase in the number of legal disputes surrounding derivative instruments. Many of the legal issues arising from these disputes present matters of first impression. As a result, the study of derivative instruments currently represents one of the most important intersections between legal and financial theory.

Most derivative instruments are priced by using complex mathematics. Rather than focus on such formulas, this subsection develops the intuition behind the use of futures, options, and swaps. Much of the mystery behind these sometimes complex instruments can be removed by focusing on the economic rationale for their existence. By doing so, the lawyer should be able to identify the relevant issues and ask the appropriate questions when confronted with disputes arising from such transactions.

a. Futures

A **futures contract** is an agreement that requires a party to buy or sell a particular item on a designated future date for a price determined at the time of contracting. Notice that at a minimum, each futures contract contains three important terms. First, each futures contract specifies some quantity of an item to be delivered or received. In general, three types of items are the subjects of futures contracts. **Commodity futures** include such items as wheat, hogs, and orange juice. **Industrial futures** include such items as copper, crude oil, and natural gas. **Financial futures** exist for such items as stock indexes, interest rates, and foreign currency. Second, each contract contains a **futures price** which identifies the price at which the parties have agreed to transact in the future. Futures prices are quoted on a per unit rather than per contract basis. Thus, a quoted futures price must be multiplied by the number of units covered by the contract in order to determine the contract's price. Third, a **settlement date** specifies the day on which the parties have agreed to conduct the transaction.

In order to create liquid markets for futures contracts, the terms of the agreement must be standardized. In other words, at any given time tens of thousand of futures contracts with the same terms might be trading on a given exchange. Organized exchanges facilitate the trading of futures by specifying the terms used in the contracts. For example, the Kansas City Board of Trade (KC) currently facilitates trading in wheat futures. KC has specified that the contracts will be for 5,000 bushels of wheat to be delivered in July. However, before a contract with these terms can be offered by an exchange, it must be approved by the **Commodity Futures Trading Commission** (CFTC)—a federal government agency similar to the SEC which is responsible for the oversight of futures trading. To obtain CFTC approval, KC must demonstrate an economic purpose for the contract.[4]

---

4. Contracts which contemplate a future exchange at a price determined on the day of contracting, but are not standardized or traded on an organized exchange are known as **for-**

The fundamental economic purpose of a futures contract is to allow producers and users of particular items to hedge against undesirable shifts in a market price. Consider, for example, the plight of a sugar cane farmer in Louisiana who will have 112,000 pounds of sugar available for delivery in May. It will end up costing the farmer around 18.50¢ per pound or $20,720 total to make delivery of the sugar. Despite the fact that this farmer has an idea of both the quantity and cost of her output, she is concerned that the market price could be relatively low. If there is a bumper sugar crop internationally, the price per pound of sugar may be driven down to 13.45¢ per pound in which case the farmer will suffer a loss of $5,656 ($20,720–$15,064). Alternatively, insects might devour the crops of a large foreign competitor driving the price up to 22.30¢ per pound providing the farmer with a profit of $4,256 ($24,976–$20,720).

As a risk averse individual, the farmer is willing to sacrifice some of the upside potential in order to avoid possible down side losses. Thus, she calls her **futures commission merchant** (FCM)—a futures broker. The FCM informs the farmer that the Coffee, Sugar and Cocoa Exchange (CSCE) in New York has futures contracts for the delivery of 112,000 pounds of sugar in May which are currently trading for 20.10¢ per pound. By *selling* a sugar futures contract at this price, the farmer could lock in a profit of $1,792 ($22,512–$20,720). In this instance, the availability of a futures contract on sugar helps the farmer to hedge against the risk of declining sugar prices. In other words, futures contracts can be used as a risk management tool.

At the same time that the Louisiana sugar cane farmer is deciding what to do regarding her May delivery, Hershey's Chocolates is planning its May candy bar production runs. Executives at Hershey's decide that they will need 112,000 pounds of sugar in May. By way of a similar reasoning process used above, the executives decide that they would rather *buy* the May sugar contract offered by the Louisiana farmer than face potential losses due to high sugar prices. In other words, buying a futures contract on sugar allows Hershey's to lock in its sugar costs months in advance. Thus, Hershey's purchases a sugar futures contract in order to hedge against increasing sugar prices—again, a form of risk management.

In the preceding example, parties with offsetting interests in May sugar were assumed to exist. However, it is not necessary that both parties to a futures contract be interested in the actual delivery of sugar. For example, there may be an individual who has studied the weather patterns around the world and has decided that there will in fact be a huge drought resulting in the ruin of a large portion of the world's sugar cane crop. In fact, this individual predicts that the prevailing market price for sugar in May will be 28.50¢ per pound. Thus, this individual has an incentive to speculate in the futures market. By purchasing the futures contract offered by the Louisiana sugar cane farmer at 20.10¢ per pound, the speculator expects to clear a profit of $9,408—that is, the speculator would be able to buy 112,000 pounds of sugar at $22,512 and sell it for $31,920. Under an alternative scenario both the seller and buyer of a futures contract could be speculators. In order for this to occur,

---

ward contracts. Trading in forward contracts is therefore generally not as liquid as futures trading. Moreover, forward trading is not regulated by the CFTC. Despite these differences, the economic logic behind futures contracts is applicable to forwards.

all that would be needed is for a difference of opinion to exist as to the whether the market price in May will be higher or lower than the current futures price.

In most instances, the parties to a futures contract do not participate in the actual delivery of the underlying asset. In fact, it is estimated that the physical delivery contemplated under futures contracts occurs less than 2% of the time. In order to realize a profit or loss on futures contracts, a party need only liquidate its position. This is done by purchasing an offsetting position to the same futures contract. For example, suppose that a speculator *buys* a June futures contract on the Chicago Mercantile Exchange (CME) for 62,500 British Pounds at $1.20 per pound. The total cost of this futures contract in June would be $75,000. Assume that subsequent to the speculator's purchase, political developments in the United States cause the price of the dollar to decrease relative to the pound. Thus, June futures contracts on British Pounds are now trading for $1.60 per pound—a total value of $100,000. The speculator decides that this is high enough and decides to liquidate his currency position by *selling* a June futures contract at the prevailing futures price. The speculator now has the right to sell 62,500 pounds at $100,000 and an obligation to buy 62,500 pounds for $75,000. This leaves the speculator with a $25,000 profit ($100,000–$75,000) without ever having to handle British Pounds.

At this point, one may be wondering what happens to the other party to each of these contracts. After two parties are initially matched on the exchange as buyer and seller of a futures contract, their relationship ends. The exchange then inserts itself as the buyer for every sale and the seller for every buy. As a result, investors are free to liquidate their positions at any time without concern for the other party.

Futures markets have a reputation of being reserved for big time players. This reputation is a function of the high levels of leverage that are used in the futures markets. In order to take a position in a futures contract, a party need only deposit some fractional amount of the contact's total money value. This sum of money, or its acceptable equivalent, is used as a guarantee that the party will make good on any losses. The dollar amount of the minimum deposit is set by the exchange where the contract trades, and is known as the **initial margin**. Using the initial margin in a process called marking-to-market, the exchange and its members guarantee the performance of all futures contracts. This process can be best understood by considering the following example.

Assume that currently a futures contract on December Hogs is trading for 67.50¢ per pound on the CME. At 40,000 pounds per contract, this comes to a cost of $27,000. Then assume that the CME has set the margin requirement on hogs contracts at 10% of the contract price. Thus, each party to the contract must deposit $2,700 into a margin account maintained by their FCM. If, on the following day, the price of these contracts closes at 68.10¢ per pound, then the price of the contract is $27,240, up $240. In a process called **marking-to-market**, $240 is added to the *buyer's* account and $240 is deducted from the *seller's* account. Intuitively this makes sense. Consider the case of the buyer. On the first day, the investor purchased the right to buy 40,000 pounds of hogs at 67.50¢ per pound for a total cost of $27,000. On the second day, the price rose to 68.10¢ per pound. At this point, the investor could have sold a futures contract giving him the right to sell 40,000 pounds of hogs for $27,240. His total profit on the hypothetical deal would be $240. In order to guarantee performance of financial obligations, the exchange transfers profits and losses daily based upon the closing market price. On the other hand, if the price closed on the next day at 66.90¢ per pound, the contract is worth $26,760, down $240. Thus, when margin accounts are marked-to-market, $240 is subtracted from the buyer's account and $240 is added to the seller's account. If the deduction from the margin account takes the account balance below the initial margin requirement, the investor must place more money into the account. If the investor fails to do so within 24 hours, the FCM must cover the loss and liquidate the position. However, if as a result of marking-to-market, an investor has an amount of money in the account greater than the initial margin requirement, such excess funds may be withdrawn.

Now, consider the effect of leverage on the transactions in the above example. In the first instance, the contract price rose by $240. This $240 increase occurred on an initial cash outlay of only $2,700. Thus, the one day return on money actually invested by the buyer was approximately 9% despite the fact that the contract price rose less than 1%. In the same manner, if the price had declined by $240, the buyer would have lost 9% of his invested money in a single day. From this it is easy to see that buying on margin can transform moderate swings in the prices of future contracts into big time gains or losses—thus giving futures markets their high flying reputations. However, low margin requirements also allow parties who might not otherwise be able to afford to pay the price for an entire futures contract to insure against risk.

b. Options

An **option** is a contract giving the purchaser the right, but not the obligation, to buy or sell an asset, currency, or futures at a fixed price for a specified period of time. Options can be used both to speculate and to manage risk by hedging. The purchaser's rights are granted by writing an option contract. The seller of an option is also known as its **writer**. As consideration for the rights granted under an option contract, the writer charges the buyer a price known as an **option premium**. The price specified in the option contract at which an underlying asset can be purchased or sold is known as the **exercise price** or **strike price**. Strike prices are quoted on a per unit rather than a per contract basis. Thus, the strike price must be multiplied by the total number of units covered by the contract in order to know the total cost of exercising the option. The date on which the rights granted under the option contract become void is known as the **expiration date**. An option that can be exercised at any point up until the expiration date is known as an **American option**. An option that can be exercised only on the expiration date is known as a **European option**. Like futures, an options position can be traded or closed out by taking an offsetting position. However, unlike futures, the holders of options very often desire to complete the transaction contemplated by the contract.

Call options grant the purchaser the right, but not the obligation, to *buy* a particular asset, currency, or futures at a particular price for a specified period of time. Consider an investor who purchases a call option on the stock of Chrysler Corporation with a $30 strike price and a July expiration date. This contract is referred to as a July 30 call on Chrysler. This option provides its holder with the right to purchase a round lot—a round lot equals 100 shares—of Chrysler stock for $3,000 ($30 × 100). The following example demonstrates that the purchaser of a call option is making a bet that the market price of the underlying asset, currency, or futures will rise above the strike price before the expiration date.

Suppose that the investor considered above purchased a July 30 call on Chrysler when the current market price for the stock was $25. When the exercise price on a call option is greater than the current market price of the underlying asset, the call is said to be **out of the money**. At that point in time, the investor would have no desire to exercise the call because he can purchase the stock for less than $30 on the open market. However, what if over the course of the next two months, the price of Chrysler stock goes to $35? When the exercise price on a call option is less than the current market price of the underlying asset, the call is said to be **in the money**. At that point in time, the investor would be willing to exercise his option because he can purchase the Chrysler stock for $30 from the writer and sell it for $35 on the open market. For the round lot, this would be a profit of $500 minus the option premium. From this example, it is easy to see that the purchaser of a call option is making a bet that the price of the underlying asset will increase to a level greater than the strike price before the expiration date. Likewise, the writer of a call option is making a bet that the price of the underlying asset will remain equal to or stay below the strike price until after the expiration date.

Put options grant the purchaser the right, but not the obligation, to *sell* a particular asset, currency, or futures at a particular price for a specified period of time. Consider an investor who purchases a put option on the stock of America Online with a $50 strike price and a July expiration date. This contract is referred to as a July 50 put on America Online. This option provides its holder with the right to sell a round lot of America Online stock for $5,000 ($50 × 100). The following example demonstrates that the purchaser of a put option is making a bet that the market price of the underlying asset, currency, or futures will fall below the strike price before the expiration date.

Suppose that an investor purchased a July 50 put on America Online when the current market price for stock was $55. When the exercise price on a put option is less than the current market price of the underlying asset, the put is said to be **out of the money**. At that point in time, the investor would have no desire to exercise the put because he can sell the stock for more than $50 on the open market. However, what if over the course of the next two months, the price of America Online Stock falls to $40? When the exercise price on a put option is greater than the current market price of the underlying asset, the put is said to be **in the money**. At that point in time, the investor would be willing to exercise his option because he can purchase America Online stock for $40 on the open market and force the writer to buy it for $50. For the round lot, this would be a profit of $1,000 minus the option premium. From this example, it is easy to see that the purchaser of a put option is making a bet that the price of the underlying asset will fall below the strike price before the expiration date. Likewise, the writer of a put option is making a bet that the price of the underlying asset will remain equal to or stay above the strike price until after the expiration date.

Individuals interested in purchasing stock often find options to be more appealing because options expose the investor to a smaller loss potential. For example, suppose that the option premium for July 30 calls on Chrysler is $5. Thus, when an investor purchases this call his total cash outlay is $500 ($5 × 100). If the current market price of Chrysler suddenly goes to zero, the options will be worthless on expiration and the investor losses the $500 initial investment. If, on the other hand, this investor had simply purchased a round lot of Chrysler stock for its current market price of $25 he would have lost $2,500 during this period. This same type of reasoning can be used for the purchasers of put options. In short, losses to the purchasers of options are always limited to the amount they pay for the option premium.

Consider the position of an investor who writes call options. If an investor writes a July 30 call on Chrysler for a $5 option premium at a time when the stock price was $25 and the price suddenly goes to $50 two things can happens. First, suppose that the writer of the call already owned a round lot of Chrysler stock worth $2,500 on the day that the call was written. When the writer already owns the underlying asset when the call is written, it is said to be a **covered call**. When the market price jumps to $50, the option holder will exercise the call. Thus, the writer will be forced to sell a round lot of stock worth $5,000 for $3,000. However, this $2,000 loss is offset by the price appreciation on the original stock investment and the option premium. Second, suppose that the writer does not own any Chrysler stock when the call is written. When the writer does not own any of the underlying asset when the call is written, it is said to be a **naked call**. Now when the option is exercised, the writer must purchase a round lot for $5,000 ($50 × 100) on the open market and then sell it immediately for $3,000. This results in a $2,000 loss that is offset only by the option premium. Because stock prices can theoretically increase to an infinite amount, the writers of calls take on an unlimited liability.

Now consider the position of an investor who writes puts. Suppose that an investor writes a July 50 put on America Online for a $5 option premium when the stock price was $60 and the stock price suddenly goes to $25. According to the terms of the contract, the writer must purchase the round lot for $5,000. However, the writer can sell the America Online stock for only $2,500 on the open market. Thus, the writer suffers a $2,000 loss—the $2,500 loss on the sale of stock is offset by the $500 collected for the option premium. Because the stock price can only fall to zero, the writer of a put has limited liability equal to the strike price minus the option premium.

In addition to providing an avenue for speculation, options also provide investors with additional tools for hedging. For example, consider an investor who owns a round lot of Exxon common stock. Exxon is currently selling at $60 which means that the round lot is worth $6,000. This is perfect, because the investor needs that money to make a $5,500 down payment on a new condominium in Florida in January. However, the investor fears that the stock market will collapse in the coming months, but is unwilling to sell the stock because of certain year-end tax implications. This investor faces a risk that can be managed by using an option contract. Suppose that the investor buys a January 60 Exxon put for a $5 option premium. By doing this, the investor has guaranteed himself that he will have $5,500 available to him in January. If the stock price stays the same or goes up, the option is worthless, and the stock will be sold for some amount greater than or equal to $6,000. This will leave the investor with at least $5,500 once the cost of the option premium is deducted. If the market tanks and the stock drops to $20, then the investor simply exercises his option. Thus, the investor is able to sell the stock for $60. This leaves the investor with $5,500 (the

$6,000 from the sale of stock minus the $500 option premium.) In short, the owner of stock can insure against a market downturn for the cost of an option premium—much like the purchaser of an insurance contract.

Options can also be combined with futures in a hedging position. Consider a farmer who sells a futures contract obligating him to deliver 5,000 bushels of wheat for $3.50 per bushel. This guarantees the farmer $17,500 (5,000 × $3.50) for his wheat. However, the farmer is annoyed by the opportunity cost of his futures contract. That is, he hates giving up the potential revenue that can be earned if the price of wheat goes up by the delivery date. To hedge against this possibility, the farmer purchases a call option on wheat futures with a $3.50 per bushel exercise price. Thus, if the price of wheat goes up, the farmer's futures option will appreciate in value as well. This price appreciation allows the farmer to participate in the price gains to the extent that they cover the option premium.

c. Swaps

A **swap** is a contract in which a set of counterparties agree to exchange future periodic cash flows. Many swap agreements are used to hedge against interest rate fluctuations and changes in currency exchange rates. In addition to risk management, swaps can be used to further exploit the comparative advantages of different parties. Most swaps contain highly customized terms which prohibit any sort of active trading. However, some swaps, known as plain vanillas, are standardized enough to allow some over-the-counter (OTC) trading. OTC refers to trading that does not occur on an organized exchange. Each swap contract contains a notional value and a set of reference rates. The **notional value** is a money amount by which reference rates are multiplied in order to determine the periodic cash flow transfers. This amount is never actually exchanged. **Reference rates** determine the periodic payments that each counterparty makes. Swaps are characterized by the nature of the periodic payments exchanged. In general, there are four types of swaps: interest rate swaps, interest rate-equity swaps, equity swaps, and currency swaps.

Interest rate swaps require a set of counterparties to exchange cash flows which are determined by applying different interest rates to the same notional value. For example, consider a three year annual interest rate swap formed between parties A and B. The swap has a notional value of $1,000,000. By the terms of the swap, A must pay to B an annual payment based upon an 8% fixed interest rate—that is, A will pay B 8% of $1,000,000 or $80,000 in each of the next three years. However, B must pay to A an annual payment based upon a floating interest rate. B's reference rate is the London interbank offered rate (or LIBOR, which is the rate of interest that large international banks with high quality credit ratings charge each other for loans) on December 31st of each year plus 3%. If at the end of the first year, LIBOR is at 4%, B will pay A $70,000 (.07 × 1,000,000). Thus, when LIBOR is below 5%, B makes money. However, if LIBOR goes above 5%, B will lose money on the swap.

The previous example demonstrates that an interest rate swap can be used by a speculator as a bet on the direction of interest rates. However, many firms will have a business or economic justification for entering into an interest rate swap—in particular, hedging against particular types of risk. For example, assume that C is a bank headquartered in the United States which specializes in making loans for new homes. C is preparing to loan $1,000,000 on a series of new home mortgages at a fixed 7% interest rate. However, C needs to obtain $1,000,000 in financing itself in order to make these new loans. Strong demand for corporate fixed rate debt has driven the interest rate on such notes to 10%. At this level, C would be paying 10% on its borrowed money while receiving 7% on its loans. Clearly C would lose money by borrowing at this rate. C is able to arrange variable rate financing for $1,000,000. The variable rate that C must pay to its creditors is equal to LIBOR plus 1%. With its variable rate financing in hand, C originates $1,000,000 worth of home loans at a fixed 7% rate. Thus, C will receive $70,000 from its borrowers every year during the course of the loans. If LIBOR for a given year is 4%, then C will pay 5% to its creditors for a total cost of $50,000. Under these rates, C will make $20,000. In general, whenever the LIBOR is below 6%, C earns a profit. However, if the LIBOR goes above 6%, C will not have enough money to pay its creditors. C would like to find a way to eliminate its interest rate risk exposure.

Now consider the plight of D, a bank headquartered in Germany. D desires to loan $1,000,000 to European corporations expanding their U.S. operations. D is familiar with the credit risks of these companies and expects the expansions to be highly profitable. However, these corporations cannot obtain financing from American banks because the German corporations represent an unknown credit risk from the perspective of American banks. D wants to finance the German corporate borrowers at a variable rate equal to LIBOR plus 1%. However, D needs to obtain $1,000,000 in financing itself in order to make the loans. D would like to have access to the variable rates offered to American banks, but those creditors are unwilling to lend to an unfamiliar German Bank. The best rate that D can obtain for itself is a 6% fixed rate.

With its fixed rate in hand, D loans $1,000,000 to the German corporations at LIBOR plus 2%. D knows for a fact that it owes its creditors $60,000 every year. If the LIBOR were 6% in a particular year, then D would collect $80,000 from its loans. This would give D a profit of $20,000 in those years. In general, in years when the LIBOR is above 4%, D makes money. If however, the LIBOR drops below 4%, D will lose money. D would like to find a way to eliminate its interest rate risk exposure.

There are two economic problems faced by C and D in this hypothetical example. First, C has a comparative advantage in obtaining the type of financing desired by D. Likewise, D has a comparative advantage in obtaining the type of financing desired by C. Second, each has an interest rate risk exposing them to potential losses. Both C and D would like to find an appropriate risk management tool. Suppose that C and D decide to enter into an interest rate swap. That swap had a notional value of $1,000,000. C pays to D an amount equal to 7% of the notional amount or $70,000. D pays to C an amount equal to the LIBOR plus 2%. By exercising the swap, D is able to lock in a $10,000 profit every year. (D receives $70,000 from A and pays $60,000 to its creditors every year). Likewise, C has a guaranteed profit equal to 1% of the notional value, or $10,000, every year (C receives the LIBOR plus 2% from D and pays the LIBOR plus 1% to its creditors). By employing the swap, the parties specialize in obtaining the cheapest source of financing available to them and mitigate any interest rate risk.

In most cases, it would be very difficult to find counterparties with perfectly offsetting needs as in the previous hypothetical. However, this is generally unnecessary. Large derivatives dealers are often willing to enter into swaps as a counterparty to their clients. The derivatives dealer then enters into a variety of swaps with many different counterparties each of whom transfers a different type of risk to the dealer. By maintaining a portfolio of swaps, the dealer is able to offset much of the risk transferred to it even though no two parties have identically offsetting needs. Any residual risk not eliminated by the portfolio of swaps can be hedged by using other derivative instruments such as futures and options. By maintaining portfolios of swaps in this manner, derivatives dealers have greatly enhanced the potential for trading derivatives.

Interest rate-equity swaps allow one party to exchange a periodic cash flow determined by reference to an interest rate with a party whose payment is determined based upon the return on an equity index. For example, consider an interest rate-equity swap with a $1,000,000 notional value. Party Y makes annual payments to Z at a fixed interest rate of 12% or $120,000 per year. However, Party Z's yearly payment to Y is determined by the annual return on the S&P 500 stock index. Thus, if this index returns 15% in a year, Z pays Y $150,000. On the other hand, if the S&P index returns 10%, then Z only pays Y $100,000. It should be obvious that interest rate-equity swaps can be used by speculators as a bet on stock market performance. However, as was the case with pure interest rate swaps, interest rate-equity swaps are often used by businesses for risk reduction purposes.

Equity swaps provide for the counterparties to exchange periodic payments on the basis of returns from two different stock indexes. For example, consider an equity swap with a $1,000,000 notional value. Party A's payment to party B is determined by reference to the S&P 500 stock index. Thus, if the S&P index returns 13% next year, A will pay B $130,000. Party B's payment to A is determined by reference to the Hang Seng stock market index in Hong Kong. Thus, if the Hang Seng returns 15% next year, B will pay A $150,000. Equity swaps can be used by speculators to bet on the relative performance of different portfolios of stock. Whichever party chooses the better performer will make more money. Again, however, equity swaps provide a risk hedging tool for many businesses.

In our previous examples, all of the parties made payments based upon the same notional currency—$1,000,000. However, in a **currency swap**, the counterparties exchange periodic cash flows in different currencies. For example, consider a currency swap with a $1,000,000 notional value for party C and its equivalent in the United Kingdom of £1,640,300 for party D. Party C agrees to pay D an amount equal to 9% of the $1,000,000 notional value every year or $90,000. D agrees to pay C an amount equal to 6% of the £1,640,300 notional value or £98,418. Thus, the counterparties to a currency swap make or lose money on the basis of how the exchange rate fluctuates over time. Currency swaps play a very important economic role for many companies doing international business by allowing them to hedge their exchange rate risk exposure.

It is easy at this point to see how the complexity of swaps can grow very quickly. By simply combining the attributes of the swaps considered above, very interesting derivative instruments can be created. For example, consider a swap contract that combined a currency swap with an equity swap. Two difficulties arise for purchasers of more complex swaps. First, it becomes more difficult to get a feel for the economic intuition behind when the swap will make or lose money. Second, the pricing of such instruments becomes very complex. Consider the following example. Party Y makes payment to Z in Yen based upon S&P 500 stock index and Z makes payments to Y in US Dollars based upon Japan's Nikkei stock index. For this swap, the annual payments are a function of both currency exchange rates and the performance of different stock portfolios.

In addition to purchasing swaps outright, parties can purchase **swaptions**— an option to exercise a swap at a later date. Swaptions can be very useful to parties who feel that they might need a swap in the future by allowing them to line up the swap at an attractive price without full commitment. Two other devices commonly found in the swaps arena are caps and floors. These devices can be used to set boundaries on the amount that a swap counterparty with a floating rate would pay. **Caps** allow a party who pays according to a floating rate to limit the maximum amount paid during a given period. For example, consider a swap with a periodic payment based upon the LIBOR. The party with this reference rate might pay some amount to its counterparty to have 10% be the maximum rate payable. Thus, on a $1,000,000 notional value contract, the maximum that this party would ever pay is $10,000. **Floors** provide the party who receives payment from a counterparty on a floating rate with a minimum periodic payment. For example, a counterparty who receives an annual payment based on the LIBOR rate might pay some amount to its counterparty to have 3.5% as the minimum reference rate. Thus, on a $1,000,000 notional value contract, the minimum annual payment would be $35,000. When a swap has both a cap and a floor it is said to be **collared**. When the prices paid for the cap and the floor are equal, the swap contains a **costless collar**.

Swaps are on the cutting edge of derivatives development. As a result, disputes involving swap transactions have taken place in largely untested areas of the law. In particular, it is not clear whether swaps are securities, commodities, or simply bilateral contracts. Resolving this definitional problem is important because it dictates the federal agency which will have jurisdiction over these transactions. Furthermore, the nature of the relationship between swap counterparties has not been clearly specified. For example, do swap dealers stand in a fiduciary relation to their clients? *Procter & Gamble v. Bankers Trust* is one of the first attempts to resolve these issues.

Procter & Gamble Co. v. Bankers Trust
United States District Court for the Southern District of Ohio, Western Division
925 F. Supp. 1270 (1996)

John Feikens

I. Introduction

Plaintiff, The Procter & Gamble Company ("P&G"), is a publicly traded Ohio corporation. Defendant, Bankers Trust Company ("BT"), is a wholly-owned subsidiary of Bankers Trust New York Corporation ("BTNY"). BTNY is a state-chartered banking company. BT trades currencies, securities, commodities and derivatives. Defendant BT Securities, also a wholly-owned subsidiary of BTNY, is a registered broker-dealer. The defendants are referred to collectively as "BT" in this opinion.

P&G filed its Complaint for Declaratory Relief and Damages on October 27, 1994, alleging fraud, misrepresentation, breach of fiduciary duty, negligent misrepresentation, and negligence in connection with an interest rate swap transaction it had entered with BT on November 4, 1993. This swap, explained more fully below, was a leveraged derivatives transaction whose value was based on the yield of five-year Treasury notes and the price of thirty-year Treasury bonds ("the 5s/30s swap").

On February 6, 1995, P&G filed its First Amended Complaint for Declaratory Relief and Damages, adding claims related to a second swap, entered into between P&G and BT on February 14, 1994. This second swap was also a leveraged derivatives transaction. Its value was based on the four-year German Deutschemark rate. In its First Amended Complaint, P&G also added Counts alleging violations of the federal Securities Acts of 1933 and 1934, the Commodity Exchange Act,...

BT now moves, under Federal Rule of Civil Procedure ("Fed.R.Civ.P.") 12(b)(6), to dismiss the following Counts of P&G's Second Amended Complaint:

Count VII   Fraudulent Sale of a Security Under Section 17 of the Securities Act of 1933

Count VIII   Violation of Section 10(b) of the Exchange Act of 1934 and Rule 10b-5

*   *   *

Count XII   Willful Deception, Fraud and Cheating in Violation of the Commodity Exchange Act, § 4b

Count XIII   Scheme or Artifice to Defraud in Violation of the Commodity Exchange Act, § 4o

*   *   *

This motion involves questions of first impression whether the swap agreements fall within federal securities or commodities laws...These are questions of law, not questions of fact. "The judiciary is the final authority on issues of statutory construction...." *Chevron U.S.A., Inc. v. Natural Resources Defense Council, Inc.*, 467 U.S. 837 (1984). Mr. Justice Powell stated, in determining Congressional intent, "the task has fallen to the Securities and Exchange Commission (SEC), the body charged with administering the Securities Acts, and ultimately to the federal courts to decide which of the myriad financial transactions in our society come within the coverage of these statutes." *United Housing Foundation, Inc. v. Forman*, 421 U.S. 837 (1975).

I conclude that the 5s/30s and DM swap agreements are not securities as defined by the Securities Acts of 1933 and 1934...; that these swap agreements are exempt from the Commodity Exchange Act; that there is no private right of action available to P&G under the antifraud provisions of that Act;...Therefore, P&G's claims in Counts VII through XV of its Second Amended Complaint are dismissed.

BT also moves for summary judgment on Counts III–V (Negligent Misrepresentation, Breach of Fiduciary Duty, and Negligence). I conclude that as a counterparty to swap agreements, BT owed no fiduciary duty to P&G. P&G's claims of negligent misrepresentation and negligence are redundant, as I have set forth the duties and obligations of the parties under New York law. Therefore, summary judgment is granted as to Counts III–V.

II. Background

Financial engineering, in the last decade, began to take on new forms. A current dominant form is a structure known as a derivatives transaction. It is "a bilateral contract or payments exchange agreement whose value derives...from the value of an underlying asset or underlying reference rate or index." Derivatives transactions may be based on the value of foreign currency, U.S. Treasury bonds, stock indexes, or interest rates. The values of these underlying financial instruments are determined by market forces, such as movements in interest rates. Within the broad panoply of derivatives transactions are numerous innovative financial instruments whose objectives may include a hedge against market risks, management of assets and liabilities, or lowering of funding costs; derivatives may also be used as speculation for profit.

This case involves two interest rate swap agreements. A swap is an agreement between two parties ("counterparties") to exchange cash flows over a period of time. Generally, the purpose of an interest rate swap is to protect a party from interest rate fluctuations. The simplest form of swap, a "plain vanilla" interest-rate swap, involves one counterparty paying a fixed rate of interest, while the other counterparty assumes a floating interest rate based on the amount of the principal of the underlying debt. This is called the "notional" amount of the swap, and this amount does not change hands; only the interest payments are exchanged.

In more complex interest rate swaps, such as those involved in this case, the floating rate may derive its value from any number of different securities, rates or indexes. In each instance, however, the counterparty with the floating rate obligation enters into a transaction whose precise value is unknown and is based upon activities in the market over which the counterparty has no control. How the swap plays out depends on how market factors change.

One leading commentator describes two "visions" of the "explosive growth of the derivatives market." Hu, *Hedging Expectations: "Derivative Reality" and the Law and Finance of the Corporate Objective*, Vol. 73 Texas L. Rev. 985 (1995). One vision, that relied upon by derivatives dealers, is that of perfect hedges found in formal gardens. This vision portrays the order—the respite from an otherwise chaotic universe—made possible by financial science. Corporations are subject to volatile financial and commodities markets. Derivatives, by offering hedges against almost any kind of price risk, allow corporations to operate in a more ordered world.

The other vision is that of "science run amok, a financial Jurassic Park." Using this metaphor, Hu states:

> In the face of relentless competition and capital market disintermediation, banks in search of profits have hired financial scientists to develop new financial products. Often operating in an international wholesale market open only to major corporate and sovereign entities—a loosely regulated paradise hidden from public view—these scientists push the frontier, relying on powerful computers and an array of esoteric models laden with incomprehensible Greek letters. But danger lurks. As financial creatures are invented, introduced, and then evolve and mutate, exotic

risks and uncertainties arise. In its most fevered imagining, not only do the trillions of mutant creatures destroy their creators in the wholesale market, but they escape and wreak havoc in the retail market and in economies worldwide.

Given the potential for a "financial Jurassic Park," the size of the derivatives market[1] and the complexity of these financial instruments, it is not surprising that there is a demand for regulation and legislation. Several bills have been introduced in Congress to regulate derivatives. BT Securities has been investigated by the Securities and Exchange Commission ("SEC") and by the Commodities Futures Trading Commission ("CFTC") regarding a swap transaction with a party other than P&G. Bankers Trust has agreed with the Federal Reserve Bank to a Consent Decree on its leveraged derivatives transactions.

At present, most derivatives transactions fall in "the common-law no-man's land beyond regulations — . . . interest-rate and equity swaps, swaps with embedded options ('swaptions')," and other equally creative financial instruments. Cohen, *The Challenge of Derivatives*, Vol. 63 Fordham L. Rev. at 2013. This is where the two highly specialized swap transactions involved in this case fall.

III. The P&G/BT Swap Agreements

Those swaps transactions are governed by written documents executed by BT and P&G. BT and P&G entered into an Interest Rate and Currency Exchange Agreement on January 20, 1993. This standardized form, drafted by the International Swap Dealers Association, Inc. ("ISDA"), together with a customized Schedule and written Confirmations for each swap, create the rights and duties of parties to derivative transactions. By their terms, the ISDA Master Agreement, the Schedule, and all Confirmations form a single agreement between the parties.

During the fall of 1993, the parties began discussing the terms of an interest rate swap which was to be customized for P&G. After negotiations, the parties agreed to a swap transaction on November 2, 1993, which is referred to as the 5s/30s swap; the written Confirmation is dated November 4, 1993.

In the 5s/30s swap transaction, BT agreed to pay P&G a fixed rate of interest of 5.30% for five years on a notional amount of $200 million. P&G agreed to pay BT a floating interest rate. For the first six months, that floating rate was the prevailing commercial paper ("CP") interest rate minus 75 basis points (0.75%). For the remaining four-and-a-half years, P&G was to make floating interest rate payments of CP minus 75 basis points plus a spread. The spread was to be calculated at the end of the first six months (on May 4, 1994) using the following formula:

$$\text{Spread} = \frac{\left(98.5 \times \dfrac{[5 \text{ year CMT}]}{5.78\%} - 30 \text{ T Price}\right)}{100}$$

In this formula, the "5 year CMT" (Constant Maturity Treasury) represents the yield on the five-year Treasury Note, and the "30 T Price" represents the

---

1. Estimates of the amount of usage of derivatives range from $14 trillion to $35 trillion in face or notional amounts. Cohen, *The Challenge of Derivatives*, Vol. 63 Fordham L. Rev. 1993 (1995).

price of the thirty-year Treasury Bond. The leverage factor in this formula meant that even a small movement up or down in prevailing interest rates results in an incrementally larger change in P&G's position in the swap.

*   *   *

In late January 1994, P&G and BT negotiated a second swap, known as the "DM swap", based on the value of the German Deutschemark. The Confirmation for this swap is dated February 14, 1994. For the first year, BT was to pay P&G a floating interest rate plus 233 basis points. P&G was to pay the same floating rate plus 133 basis points; P&G thus received a 1% premium for the first year, the effective dates being January 16, 1994 through January 16, 1995. On January 16, 1995, P&G was to add a spread to its payments to BT if the four-year DM swap rate ever traded below 4.05% or above 6.01% at any time between January 16, 1994, and January 16, 1995. If the DM swap rate stayed within that band of interest rates, the spread was zero. If the DM swap rate broke that band, the spread would be set on January 16, 1995, using the following formula:

$$\text{Spread} = 10 \times [4 \text{ year DM swap rate} - 4.50\%]$$

The leverage factor in this swap was shown in the formula as ten.

P&G unwound both of these swaps before their spread set dates, as interest rates in both the United States and Germany took a significant turn upward, thus putting P&G in a negative position vis-à-vis its counterparty BT. BT now claims that it is owed over $200 million on the two swaps, while P&G claims the swaps were fraudulently induced and fraudulently executed, and seeks a declaratory verdict that it owes nothing.

IV. Federal Securities Claims (Counts VII and VIII)

In the 1933 Securities Act, Congress defined the term "security" as any note, stock, treasury stock, bond, debenture, evidence of indebtedness, certificate of interest or participation in any profit-sharing agreement, collateral-trust certificate, preorganization certificate or subscription, transferrable share, investment contract, voting-trust certificate, certificate of deposit for a security, fractional undivided interest in oil, gas, or other mineral rights, any put, call, straddle, option, or privilege on any security, certificate of deposit, or group or index of securities (including any interest therein or based on the value thereof), or any put, call, straddle, option, or privilege entered into on a national securities exchange relating to foreign currency, or, in general, any interest or instrument commonly known as a "security", or a certificate of interest or participation in, temporary or interim certificate for, receipt for, guarantee of, or warrant or right to subscribe to or purchase, any of the foregoing.

*   *   *

P&G asserts that the 5s/30s and DM swaps fall within any of the following portions of that definition: 1) investment contracts; 2) notes; 3) evidence of indebtedness; 4) options on securities; and 5) instruments commonly known as securities.

Congress intended a broad interpretation of the securities laws and flexibility to effectuate their remedial purpose of avoiding fraud. *SEC v. Howey*, 328 U.S. 293, 90 L. Ed. 1244, 66 S. Ct. 1100 (1946). The United States Supreme Court has held, however, that Congress did not "intend" the Securities Acts "to provide a broad federal remedy for all fraud." The threshold issue presented by P&G's securities fraud claims is whether a security exists, i.e., whether or not these swaps are among "the myriad financial transactions in our society that come within the coverage of these statutes."

Economic reality is the guide for determining whether these swaps transactions that do not squarely fit within the statutory definition are, nevertheless, securities. * * *

A. Investment Contracts

For purposes of the federal securities laws, an "investment contract" is defined as "a contract, transaction or scheme whereby a person invests his money in a common enterprise." Howey, 328 U.S. at 298–99. Stated differently, the test whether an instrument is an investment contract is whether it entails "an investment in a common venture premised on a reasonable expectation of profits to be derived from the entrepreneurial or managerial efforts of others." The U.S. Court of Appeals for the Sixth Circuit has interpreted the Howey test as a "flexible one 'capable of adaptation or meeting the countless and variable schemes devised by those who seek the use of the money of others on the promise of profits.'"

BT argues that the swaps are not investment contracts because 1) neither P&G nor BT invested any money; rather, they agreed to exchange cash payments at future dates; 2) the swaps did not involve an investment in a "common enterprise," which involves the pooling of funds in a single business venture, and 3) any gains to be derived from the swaps were not "profits," which are defined as "capital appreciation" or "participation in earnings" of a business venture.... BT contends that cash payments to be made arise not from the efforts of others, but from changes in U.S. and German interest rates.

P&G counters that the swaps are investments of money because an investment exists where an investor has committed its assets in such a way that it is subject to a financial loss and that the commitment to make future payments is sufficient to constitute an investment; further, that the swaps meet the "common enterprise" tests because its swaps, when combined with those of other parties, became part of the capital used to support BT's derivatives business. Specifically, P&G argues, BT combines its sales in one hedge book to offset all of its customers' transactions, and unwind prices reflect BT's overall portfolio risk. P&G further contends that its profit motive was its desire to reduce its overall interest costs and that it expected to derive profits from the efforts of BT in structuring and monitoring the swaps.

While the swaps may meet certain elements of the Howey test whether an instrument is an investment contract, what is missing is the element of a "common enterprise." P&G did not pool its money with that of any other company or person in a single business venture. How BT hedged its swaps is not what is at issue—the issue is whether a number of investors joined together in a common venture. Certainly, any counterparties with whom BT contracted cannot be lumped together as a "common enterprise." Furthermore, BT was not managing P&G's money; BT was a counterparty to the swaps, and the value of the swaps depended on market forces, not BT's entrepreneurial efforts. The swaps are not investment contracts.

B. Notes or "Family Resemblance" to Notes

BT asserts that the swaps are not notes because they did not involve the payment or repayment of principal. P&G responds that the counterparties incurred payment obligations that were bilateral notes or the functional equivalent of notes.

As with the test whether an instrument is an investment contract, these swap agreements bear some, but not all, of the earmarks of notes. At the outset, and perhaps most basic, the payments required in the swap agreements did not involve the payment or repayment of principal. * * *

In Reves, the Supreme Court set out a four-part "family resemblance" test for identifying notes that should be deemed securities. Those factors are: 1) the motivations of the buyer and seller in entering into the transaction (investment for profit or to raise capital versus commercial); 2) a sufficiently broad plan of distribution of the instrument (common trading for speculation or investment); 3) the reasonable expectations of the investing public; and 4) whether some factor, such as the existence of another regulatory scheme, significantly reduces the risk of the instrument, thereby rendering application of the securities laws unnecessary.

In explaining the first prong of the "family resemblance" test, the Court in Reves distinguished between the motivations of the parties in entering into the transaction, drawing a line between investment notes as securities and commercial notes as non-securities. The Court said:

> If the seller's purpose is to raise money for the general use of a business enterprise or to finance substantial investments and the buyer is interested primarily in the profit the note is expected to generate, the instrument is likely to be a "security." If the note is exchanged to facilitate the purchase and sale of a minor asset or consumer good, to correct for the seller's cash-flow difficulties, or to advance some other commercial or consumer purpose, on the other hand, the note is less sensibly described as a "security."

There is no "neat and tidy" way to apply this prong of the test, in part because P&G and BT were counterparties, not the typical buyer and seller of an instrument. BT's motive was to generate a fee and commission, while P&G's expressed motive was, in substantial part, to reduce its funding costs. These motives are tipped more toward a commercial than investment purpose. As to P&G, there was also an element of speculation driving its willingness to enter a transaction that was based on its expectations regarding the path that interest rates would take. Thus, this prong of the Reves test, standing alone, is not a sufficient guide to enable one to make the determination whether the 5s/30s and DM swaps were notes within the meaning of the Securities Acts.

The second prong of the Reves test examines the plan of distribution of the instrument "to determine whether it is an instrument in which there is 'common trading for speculation or investment.'" While derivatives transactions in general are an important part of BT's business, and BT advertises its expertise in putting together a variety of derivatives packages, the test is whether the 5s/30s and DM swaps in particular were widely distributed. * * * The 5s/30s and DM swaps were customized for Procter & Gamble; they could not be sold or traded to another counterparty without the agreement of BT. They were not part of any kind of general offering.

Thus, I conclude that the 5s/30s and DM swaps were not widely distributed and do not meet the second prong of the Reves test.

Application of the third Reves factor—the public's reasonable perceptions—does not support a finding that these swap agreements are securities. They were not traded on a national exchange, "the paradigm of a security." Reves, 494 U.S. at 69. I recognize that some media refer to derivatives generally as securities and that some commentators assume that all derivatives are securities. * * * However, what is relevant is the perception of those few who enter into swap agreements, not the public in general. P&G knew full well that its over-the-counter swap agreements with BT were not registered with any regulatory agency. P&G's "perception" that these swap agreements were securities did not surface until after it had filed its original Complaint in this case.

Thus, I conclude that the 5s/30s and DM swaps do not meet the third prong of the Reves test.

The fourth Reves factor is whether another regulatory scheme exists that would control and thus reduce the risk of the instrument, making application of the securities laws unnecessary.

*   *   *

While the 5s/30s and DM swaps may meet this prong of the Reves "family resemblance" test, this is not enough to bring these transactions within the statutory definition of a "note" for purposes of the securities laws.

Balancing all the Reves factors, I conclude that the 5s/30s and DM swaps are not notes for purposes of the Securities Acts.

C. Evidence of Indebtedness

P&G argues that if the swaps are not notes, they are evidence of indebtedness because they contain bilateral promises to pay money and they evidence debts between the parties. * * *

The test whether an instrument is within the category of "evidence of indebtedness" is essentially the same as whether an instrument is a note.

*   *   *

I do not accept P&G's definition of "evidence of indebtedness" in large part because that definition omits an essential element of debt instruments—the payment or repayment of principal. Swap agreements do not involve the payment of principal; the notional amount never changes hands.

D. Options on Securities

An option is the right to buy or sell, for a limited time, a particular good at a specified price.

Five-year notes and thirty-year Treasury bonds are securities; therefore, P&G contends that the 5s/30s swap is an option on securities. It argues that because the 5s/30s swap spread was based on the value of these securities, it falls within the statutory definition: "any put, call, straddle, option or privilege on any security, group or index of securities (including any interest therein or based on the value thereof)." It describes the 5s/30s swap as "a single security which can be decomposed into a plain vanilla swap with an embedded put option. The option is a put on the 30-year bond price with an uncertain strike price that depends on the level of the 5-year yield at the end of six months."

BT contends that the 5s/30s swap is not an option because no one had the right to take possession of the underlying securities....I agree that the 5s/30s swap was not an option on a security; there was no right to take possession of any security.

    *   *   *

Two Orders by the Security and Exchange Commission must be considered. These rulings involve transactions between BT and Gibson Greetings, Inc. in swaps that have some similarities to the 5s/30s swap. In these cases, the SEC ruled that a "Treasury-Linked Swap" between BT and Gibson Greetings, Inc. was a security within the meaning of the federal securities laws. The SEC stated: "While called a swap, the Treasury-Linked Swap was in actuality a cash-settled put option that was written by Gibson and based initially on the 'spread' between the price of the 7.625% 30-year U.S. Treasury bonds maturing on November 15, 2022 and the arithmetic average of the bid and offered yields of the most recently auctioned obligation of a two-year Treasury note."

These SEC Orders were made pursuant to Offers of Settlement made by BT Securities...In both Orders, the SEC acknowledged that its findings were solely for the purpose of effectuating the respondents' Offers of Settlement and that its findings are not binding on any other person or entity named as a defendant or respondent in any other proceeding. They are not binding in this case, in part because of the differences between the transactions; nor do they have collateral estoppel effect. * * *

Even though both the Gibson Greetings, Inc. swap and the P&G 5s/30s swap derived their values from securities (Treasury notes), they were not options. While these swaps included option-like features, there is a missing essential element of an option. These swaps were exchanges of interest payments; they did not give either counterparty the right to exercise an option or to take possession of any security. Neither party could choose whether or not to exercise an option; the stream of interest payments under the swap was mandatory. Consequently, I conclude that the 5s/30s swap is not an option on a security or an option based on the value of a security.

E. Instruments Commonly Known as Securities

Finally, P&G contends that both the 5s/30s and the DM swaps are securities simply because that is how these instruments were offered and how they have become known through a course of dealing. In support of this position, P&G points to the SEC Orders in the Gibson Greetings matter and asserts that BT labels leveraged derivatives as investments, speculative, and options; and that the financial markets and the media characterize derivatives as securities.

The Supreme Court uses the Howey test for both "investment contracts" and the more general category of an "instrument commonly known as a "security." *Landreth Timber Co. v. Landreth*, 471 U.S. 681, 691 n. 5, 85 L. Ed. 2d 692, 105

S. Ct. 2297 (1985); Forman, 421 U.S. at 852 ("We perceive no distinction, for present purposes, between an 'investment contract' and an 'instrument commonly known as a 'security.'" In either case, the basic test for distinguishing the transaction from other commercial dealings is 'whether the scheme involves an investment of money in a common enterprise with profits to come solely from the efforts of others.'" Howey, 328 U.S. at 301").

*   *   *

...In each of these cases, the Court emphasized that when a party seeks to fit financial instruments into the non-specific categories of securities, those instruments must nevertheless comport with the Howey test, which "embodies the essential attributes that run through all of the Court's decisions defining a security. The touchstone is the presence of an investment in a common venture premised on a reasonable expectation of profits to be derived from the entrepreneurial or managerial efforts of others." Forman, 421 U.S. at 852.

*   *   *

In any event, the contracts between P&G and BT do not meet the Howey criteria, particularly because there is no way that they can be construed to be a pooling of funds in a common enterprise. These swap's do not qualify as securities.

It is important to point out that the holdings in this case are narrow; I do not determine that all leveraged derivatives transactions are not securities, or that all swaps are not securities. Some of these derivative instruments, because of their structure, may be securities. I confine my ruling to the 5s/30s and the DM swaps between P&G and BT.

*   *   *

VI. Commodities (Counts XII–XIV)

The Commodity Exchange Act ("CEA") includes in its definition of a commodity "all services, rights, and interests in which contracts for future delivery are presently or in the future dealt in." BT asserts that the swaps are not futures contracts; P&G claims that they are.

Under the CEA, The Commodity Futures Trading Commission has exclusive jurisdiction over "accounts, agreements...and transactions involving contracts of sale of a commodity for future delivery traded or executed on a contract market...or any other board of trade, exchange, or market, and transactions [in standardized contracts for certain commodities]." As of January 19, 1996, the CFTC had "not taken a position on whether swap agreements are futures contracts." This opinion does not decide that issue because the 5s/30s and DM swaps are within the Swaps Exemption to the CEA and because P&G has not stated a claim under § 4b, § 4o, or 17 C.F.R. § 32.9, as discussed below.

A. Swaps Exemption

Even if the 5s/30s and DM swaps are defined as commodities, swap agreements are exempt from all but the antifraud provisions of the CEA under the CFTC Swap Exemption. Title V of the Futures Trading Practices Act of 1992 granted the CFTC the authority to exempt certain swaps transactions from CEA coverage.

In response to this directive, on January 22, 1993, the CFTC clarified its July 1989 safe-harbor policy regarding swap transactions[5] in order to "promote domestic and international market stability, reduce market and liquidity risks in financial markets, including those markets (such as futures exchanges) linked to the swap market, and eliminate a potential source of systemic risk. * * *

To qualify for exemption, a transaction must fit within the CFTC's definition and meet four criteria. The CFTC defines a "swap agreement" as

(I) An agreement (including terms and conditions incorporated by reference therein) which is a rate swap agreement, basis swap, forward rate agreement, commodity swap, interest rate option, forward foreign exchange agreement, rate cap agreement, rate floor agreement, rate collar agreement, currency swap agreement, cross-currency rate swap agreement, currency option, any other similar agreement (including any option to enter into any of the foregoing);

* * *

The 5s/30s and DM swaps fit within this definition.

The four criteria for exemption are: 1) The swap must be entered into solely between "eligible swap participants;" 2) the swap may not be part of a fungible class of agreements standardized as their material economic terms; 3) counterparty creditworthiness is a material consideration of the parties in entering into the swap agreement; and 4) the swap is not entered into and is not traded on or through an exchange market.

The 5s/30s and DM swaps meet these criteria. First, the definition of "eligible swap participants" includes a "bank or trust company (acting on its own behalf or on behalf of another eligible swap participant)" and corporations with total assets exceeding $10,000,000. BT and P&G are within this definition. Second, these swaps are customized and not fungible as they could not be sold to another counterparty without permission. Third, creditworthiness is a consideration of the parties. Fourth, the swaps are private agreements not traded on any exchange.

While exempting qualified swap agreements from CEA requirements such as trading only on an exchange, the CFTC specifically reserved the antifraud provisions in Sections 4b and 4o of the Act.

* * *

B. Violation of Section 4b (Count XII)

Section 4b of the Commodity Exchange Act makes it "unlawful...(2) for any person, in or in connection with any order to make, or the making of, any contract of sale of any commodity for future delivery, made, or to be made, for or on behalf of any other person..." to engage in certain fraudulent conduct.

---

5. The CFTC identified those swap transactions that would not be regulated as futures or commodity options transactions under the CEA to include those that had 1) individually-tailored terms; 2) an absence of exchange-style offset; 3) an absence of a clearing organization or margin system; 4) limited distribution with the transaction undertaken in conjunction with the parties' lines of business, thus precluding public participation; and 5) a prohibition against marketing to the public. Policy Statement Concerning Swap Transactions, 54 Fed. Reg. 30,694 (July 21, 1989).

BT asserts that Count XII, alleging a violation of Section 4b, should be dismissed because BT did not act "for or on behalf of" P&G. Rather, BT "acted solely as a principal, dealing with—not for—P&G on an arm's length basis."

P&G contends that BT's advertisements and representations are promises that BT would use its experience, sophistication and expertise on behalf of its clients to advise them in the complex financial area of leveraged derivatives. P&G relies on Judge Friendly's decision in *Leist v. Simplot*, 638 F.2d 283 (2d Cir. 1980), aff'd sub nom. *Merrill Lynch, Pierce, Fenner & Smith, Inc. v. Curran*, 456 U.S. 353, 72 L. Ed. 2d 182, 102 S. Ct. 1825 (1982). Judge Friendly noted, "None of the cases recognizing an implied right of action under § 4b suggest limitation to the broker-customer relation."...however, the Court in Curran did not create a blanket private right of action under § 4b or delete the requirement that the transaction must be conducted "for or on behalf of" the defrauded party. * * *

I conclude that BT was not acting for or on behalf of P&G as that relationship is generally construed in the customer-broker context. As counterparties, P&G and BT were principals in a bilateral contractual arrangement. This is not to say that BT had no duties to P&G. Those duties are set out in Section VIII. below. However, P&G has no private right of action under § 4b.

C. Violation of Section 40 (Count XIII)

Section 40, 7 U.S.C. § 60, provides:

(1) It shall be unlawful for a commodity trading advisor...by use of the mails or any means or instrumentality of interstate commerce, directly or indirectly—

(A) to employ any device, scheme or artifice to defraud any client or participant or prospective client or participant; or

(B) to engage in any transaction, practice, or course of business which operates as a fraud or deceit upon any client or participant or prospective client or participant.

In Jarrett v. Kassel, the Sixth Circuit applied the holding in Curran to § 4o claims. The court in Jarrett held that, just as there is a private right of action under § 4b for an investor defrauded by his broker, there is an implied private right of action under § 4o against commodity trading advisors and commodity pool operators. The question is whether BT was P&G's commodity trading advisor.

The CEA defines "commodity trading advisor" as: any person who

(I) for compensation or profit, engages in the business of advising others, either directly or through publications, writing, or electronic media, as to the value of or the advisability of trading in—

(I) any contract of sale of a commodity for future delivery made or to be made on or subject to the rules of a contract market;

(II) any commodity option authorized under section 6c of this title; or

(III) any leverage transaction authorized under section 23 of this title; or

(ii) for compensation or profit, and as part of a regular business, issues or promulgates analyses or reports concerning any of the activities referred to in clause (I).

Section (I) of the definition does not apply because the 5s/30s swaps were not traded on any contract market and are not subject to the rules of any contract market under the Swaps Exemption. Section (II) refers to commodity options authorized under section 6c. This provision prohibits all option trading in commodities unless authorized by CFTC rules. Because of the Swaps Exemption, swaps are specifically exempt from CFTC rules. Thus, Section (II) may not be applicable. Section (III) does not apply, because the 5s/30s and DM swaps do not fit within the CFTC's regulations for leverage contracts.

A commodity trading advisor is one who is "in the business of advising others on the value or advisability of trading in the purchase or sale of futures contracts or options" or as an "investment adviser." *F.D.I.C. v. Hildenbrand*, 892 F. Supp. 1317, 1324–35 (D. Colo. 1995). I recognize that representatives from BT Securities had conversations with P&G regarding market conditions, past performance of Treasury notes and bonds, prognostications for the future, and the like. There is also evidence that these representatives gave P&G a sales pitch regarding the potential benefits of their product. These representatives also discussed P&G's view of interest rates. Thus, while BT Securities representatives came close to giving advice,[8] P&G representatives used their own independent knowledge of market conditions in forming their own expectation as to what the market would do in the 5s/30s and DM swaps. That expectation (central to the two swaps) was not based on commodity trading advice. That expectation was clearly P&G's sole decision. Thus, P&G's claims in Count XIII are dismissed.

*　　*　　*

VIII. The Duties and Obligations of the Parties

P&G contends that a fiduciary relationship existed between it and BT. It argues that it agreed to the swap transactions because of a long relationship it had with BT and the trust that it had in BT, plus the assurance that BT would take on the responsibility of monitoring the transactions and that BT would look out for its interests.

P&G points to its trust in BT in that it divulged confidential corporate information to BT. By entering into complex swaps transactions with BT, which represented itself as experts in such transactions, P&G relied on that expertise and BT statements that it would tailor the swaps to fit P&G's needs. Even accepting these contentions as true, these contentions fail. New York case law is clear.

In *Beneficial Commercial Corp. v. Murray Glick Datsun, Inc.*, 601 F. Supp. 770, 772 (S.D. N.Y. 1985) that law is summarized with case citations as follows:

> New York law is clear that a fiduciary relationship exists from the assumption of control and responsibility and is founded upon trust reposed by one party in the integrity and fidelity of another. No fiduciary

---

8. In response to an Offer of Settlement, the CFTC entered an Order against BT Securities on December 22, 1994, with regard to an unspecified OTC derivative transaction with Gibson Greetings, Inc. The CFTC indicated that the facts were sufficient to show that BT Securities had an advisory relationship with Gibson. Apparently, Gibson did not understand the ramifications of the transaction, and BT Securities was aware of that lack of financial sophistication. As with the SEC Consent Order, the CFTC Order provides: "These findings are not binding on any other person or entity named as a defendant or respondent in any other proceeding." Thus, while an indicator that the CFTC viewed BT Securities as a commodity trading advisor as to Gibson, the CFTC's Order is not binding here.

relationship exists...[where] the two parties were acting and contracting at arm's length....

P&G and BT were in a business relationship. They were counterparties. Even though, as I point out hereafter, BT had superior knowledge in the swaps transactions, that does not convert their business relationship into one in which fiduciary duties are imposed. Thus, I grant summary judgment on Count IV in favor of BT.

This does not mean, however, that there are no duties and obligations in their swaps transactions.

Plaintiff alleges that in the negotiation of the two swaps and in their execution, defendants failed to disclose vital information and made material misrepresentations to it. For these reasons plaintiff has refused to make any payments required by the swaps transactions to defendants. Plaintiff requests that a jury verdict should declare that it owes nothing to defendants.... Since plaintiff's Amended Complaint is based on allegations of defendants' fraud and material misrepresentations, I must determine what the duties and obligations of the parties are to each other.

This requires 1) an analysis of the written contracts between the parties,... and 3) the Uniform Commercial Code as well as the Restatement (Second) Contracts, the Code having been made a part of New York statutory law and the principles of the Restatement having been accepted by New York courts.

I note, at the outset, that plaintiff's complaint does not clearly state a cause of action based on breach of contract; plaintiff rather alleges fraudulent conduct and material misrepresentation, and alludes to this as tortious wrong. I recognize that plaintiff can put in its proofs on either basis.

The analysis to be made is necessary to an understanding of the underpinning that gives rise to the duties and obligations of the parties in the swap transactions.

I turn first to the written agreement. The sections in the ISDA Agreement that appear to be relevant to these swap transactions are as follows:

In Section 3.(a)(v), this appears: "Obligations Binding. Its obligations under this Agreement...to which it is a party constitute its legal, valid and binding obligations, enforceable in accordance with their respective terms...."

Section 4., which reads: "Each party agrees with the other that so long as it has or may have any obligation under this Agreement...to which it is a party: (a) It will deliver to the other party: (ii) any other documents specified in Part 3 of the Schedule or any Confirmation."

Section 9.(d), which reads: "Except as provided in this Agreement, the rights, powers, remedies, and privileges provided in this Agreement are cumulative and not exclusive of any rights, powers, remedies, and privileges provided by law."

Under Section 4., each party must furnish specified information and that information must also relate to any documents specified in any Confirmation. Documents that are referred to in the Confirmation (here I allude specifically to the documents that will enable a party to determine the correlation between the price and yields of the five-year Treasury notes and thirty-year Treasury bonds, the sensitivity tables, the spreadsheets regarding volatility, and documents relating to the yield curve) should be provided.

I turn to the statute law of New York. The Uniform Commercial Code, as part of New York statute law, particularly Section 1-203, states: "Every contract or duty written in this Act imposes an obligation of good faith in its performance or enforcement." New York has also adopted the principles in the Restatement (Second) Contracts, § 205, that every contract imposes upon each party a duty of good faith and fair dealing in its performance and enforcement.

New York case law establishes an implied contractual duty to disclose in business negotiations. Such a duty may arise where 1) a party has superior knowledge of certain information; 2) that information is not readily available to the other party; and 3) the first party knows that the second party is acting on the basis of mistaken knowledge....

*   *   *

Thus, I conclude that defendants had a duty to disclose material information to plaintiff both before the parties entered into the swap transactions and in their performance, and also a duty to deal fairly and in good faith during the performance of the swap transactions. I confine these conclusions to the parameters outlined in this opinion.

One final point must be made. No matter how plaintiff proceeds to prove its case, under New York law the burden of proving fraud requires clear and convincing evidence, and not mere preponderance....

*   *   *

It is so ordered.

Notes and Questions

1. Characterizing Swap Transactions: The court in *Procter & Gamble v. Bankers Trust* decides that the swaps before it do not qualify as securities subject to regulation by the Securities and Exchange Commission. For the most part, the analysis consisted of a subjective balancing of a variety of factors. Based upon the forgoing discussion of bonds, stocks, futures, and options is the court's analysis acceptable? Were there other factors which should have been considered? Is there an economic justification for distinguishing swaps from securities? The court also decides that the swaps in this case are exempt from commodities regulations and are thus, outside the reach of the Commodities Futures Trading Commission. Why were the swaps exempted? Are the reasons for exemption consistent with the boundaries of futures regulation discussed above? Is there an economic justification for distinguishing between swaps and commodities? The court claims that its opinion is limited to the specific swaps considered in this case. What characteristics would a swap need to have at a minimum to qualify as either a security or a commodity under the court's analysis? Why is P&G trying to fit its swaps into securities or commodities regulation? Why is P&G concerned with establishing Bankers Trust as a fiduciary? Aren't the contract and tort actions available to P&G adequate? If you were to represent Procter & Gamble in this case on an appeal to the United States Supreme Court, what economic based arguments would you advance?

2. In Re: Gibson Greetings: Like Procter & Gamble, Gibson was also involved in a complex, highly leveraged swaps disaster with Bankers Trust. As was the case with P&G, it is not clear how well Gibson understood the derivative transactions they were undertaking. Both Gibson and P&G have claimed that they relied on Bankers Trust to do what was in their best interest. In particular, both P&G and Gibson claim that they did not understand how their derivatives were valued and that Bankers Trust would not share its mathematical valuation models. Bankers Trust, on the other hand, argues that both P&G and Gibson are sophisticated financial parties who understood the nature of their swap contracts. However, with regard to the Gibson Greetings case, Bankers Trust was caught with smoking gun tapes. In particular, conversations among Bankers Trust employees, which were taped for internal security purposes, revealed that Bankers Trust was routinely lying to Gibson regarding losses on its swap transactions. Moreover, taped conversations revealed that Bankers Trust itself thought of Gibson as a naive party who barely understood its swaps and relied heavily on Bankers Trust's advice. As a result of these taped conversations, settlement with Gibson came quickly and both the SEC and CFTC issued strong reprimands and fines against Bankers Trust.

3. Leveraging Swap Transactions: In practice, financial instruments can be leveraged in a variety of ways in addition to debt. Spreads on swaps provide a simple example of a non-debt based leverage technique. Consider, for example, a swap that contained a spread with an annual payment equal to $200 million minus ¥10 billion. If the current exchange rate is equal to 100 yen to the dollar, then ¥10 billion is equal to $100 million (¥10 billion ÷ 100 = $100 million). Thus, at the current exchange rate, the annual payment would equal $100 million ($200 million − $100 million = $100 million). If the exchange rate fluctuates so that the value of the yen, relative to the dollar, increases by 10% (i.e. 90 yen to the dollar), the payment owed under the swap will change. In the case of a 10% increase in the relative value of the yen, the annual payment will equal $88.89 million ($200,000,000 − $111,110,000 = $88.89 million)—approximately a 10% decline in the value of the annual payment. This swap can be leveraged simply by increasing the absolute value of the numbers used in the spread formula. For example, suppose that the spread equaled $300 million minus ¥20 billion. At the original exchange rate (100 yen to the dollar) the payment under the swap is the same. However, after a 10% increase in the value of the yen, the annual payment under the leveraged swap is $77.77 million ($300,000,000 − $222,222,222 = $77.77 million). In this case, the 10% change in the value of the yen leads to an approximately 20% change in the value of the annual payment. In effect, this swap is now leveraged 2 to 1.

4. The SEC and CFTC: The court dismisses evidence that both the SEC and CFTC have been involved in swaps regulation. In particular, the court acknowledges that both agencies were involved in sanctioning Bankers Trust in the Gibson Greetings affair. The CFTC and the SEC jointly fined Bankers Trust $10 million. Language in the SEC order appeared to indicate that certain over-the-counter swap transactions were now subject to its securities regulation. Additionally, the CFTC's order indicates that Bankers Trust was a commodity trading adviser in regards to Gibson—language which suggests a fiduciary relationship. The court in *Procter & Gamble v. Bankers Trust* dismisses SEC and CFTC involvement as only being necessary to effectuate a settlement. Given the above facts, do you agree with this conclusion? What economic incentives do the regulators at the SEC and CFTC have that encourage them actively to seek to regulate swaps?

B. Capital Market Efficiency

Much of the analysis developed in this casebook has focused on identifying the characteristics of efficient markets. Questions of market efficiency also arise in the context of allocating scarce capital resources. Capital resources are allocated efficiently when they are placed in their highest risk-adjusted return uses. Many financial decision models assume perfect market efficiency. Thus, it is important to investigate and understand the characteristics of a perfectly efficient capital market. The efficient market hypothesis provides the foundation for such analysis.

1. The Efficient Market Hypothesis

The **efficient markets hypothesis** (EMH) states that capital markets instantaneously and fully reflect, in an unbiased manner, all economically relevant information regarding a security's prospective risk and returns. Therefore, EMH predicts that current security prices equal the present value of a firm's expected future cash flows (i.e., purchasing stock is a zero-net present value transaction). This conclusion suggests that there are no opportunities to earn economic profits through buying or selling mispriced securities. In short, the EMH suggests that investors should expect to earn a normal return on capital market investments over the long-run. Capital market efficiency results from intense competition among investors. Such competition is driven by the desire to identify mispriced securities and realize positive economic returns. The dynamic, competitive process works to guarantee that very few such opportunities exist.

Empirical investigation of the EMH has lead to its dissection into three specific sub-hypotheses. In particular, a given capital market might be characterized as weak form, semi-strong form, or strong form efficient. Each of these sub-hypotheses is based upon the nature of the information available to market participants.

A market is considered to be **weak form efficient** if current market prices reflect all *historical* market data. Examples of such data include the history of market prices, returns, and trading volume. The crucial implication of the weak-form hypothesis is that historical information is not useful in formulating a trading strategy that yields above normal economic profits. This result follows because such information is already incorporated into the prevailing market price. **Technical analysis** attempts to use historical market data to develop profitable trading strategies. However, to the extent that markets are weak-form efficient, technical analysis is not useful in developing a long-term trading strategy that results in economic profits. The vast weight of empirical evidence suggests that capital markets are efficient in a weak form context.

A market is considered to be **semi-strong form efficient** if current market prices reflect all *public* information. Examples of public information include annual reports, articles in the *Wall Street Journal*, and reports published by investment advisors. Included in the set of public information is all historical market data. Thus, a market that is semi-strong efficient is weak form efficient by definition. According to semi-strong form efficiency, an individual cannot earn economic profits on the basis of publicly available information. In general, the existing empirical evidence has been relatively supportive of the notion of semi-strong form market efficiency.

Strong form efficiency describes a market in which current prices reflect *all* information both public and private. Accordingly, a market that exhibits strong form efficiency is both weak form and semi-strong form efficient. Strong form efficiency suggests that not even those trading on inside information can earn economic profits. Clearly, the returns earned by insiders and others with access to private information casts doubt on the efficacy of strong form efficiency. However, as the following excerpt describes, there is reason to believe that much private information comes to be reflected in market prices in a relatively efficient manner. The relationship between the EMH sub-hypotheses and the mechanisms driving efficient capital markets are the focus of discussion in the following excerpt.

The Mechanisms of Market Efficiency
Ronald J. Gilson and Reinier H. Kraakman
70 Virginia Law Review 549 (1984)

Of all recent developments in financial economics, the efficient capital market hypothesis ("ECMH") has achieved the widest acceptance by the legal culture. It now commonly informs the academic literature on a variety of topics; it is addressed by major law school casebooks and textbooks on business law; it structures debate over the future of securities regulation both within and without the Securities and Exchange Commission; it has served as the intellectual premise for a major revision of the disclosure system administered by the Commission; and it has even begun to influence judicial decisions and the actual practice of law. In short, the ECMH is now the context in which serious discussion of the regulation of financial markets takes place.

*   *   *

I. PRELIMINARY DEFINITIONS

The language of efficient capital market theory reveals its origins as a vocabulary of empirical description. The common definition of market efficiency, that "prices at any time 'fully reflect' all available information," is really a shorthand for the empirical claim that "available information" does not support profitable trading strategies or arbitrage opportunities. Similarly, Eugene Fama's landmark 1970 review article first proposed the now-familiar division of the ECMH into "weak," "semi-strong," and "strong" forms as a device for classifying empirical tests of price behavior. Weak form tests examined the claim that the histories of securities prices could not yield lucrative trading opportunities.[25] Semi-strong form tests probed the same prediction about categories of publicly available information of obvious interest to investors.[26] Finally, strong form tests examined the

---

25. Numerous weak form tests support the hypothesis that the history of securities prices does not yield exploitable trading opportunities. Generally, these tests take two forms: serial correlation analyses, which establish little or no relationship between changes in securities prices over successive periods, and analyses of "filter rule" trading strategies, which reject the possibility that trading on more complex patterns of price movements of the sort employed by "chartists" can yield abnormal returns.

26. Studies of semi-strong form efficiency are tests of how long market prices require to adjust to price-relevant information that is released to the public. These studies typically ask whether trading activity that follows the release of such information can earn investors abnormally high returns and focus on the security's price history before and after the test pe-

extension of the hypothesis to information that was available only to particular groups of privileged investors.[27] In this usage, the weak, semi-strong, and strong form categories have proved both useful and precise. The hypothesized dearth of arbitrage opportunities, whatever its explanation, clearly grows in strength with each successive genre of test. The more private the information, the more intuitively reasonable the proposition that one might profit by trading on it, and so the stronger the opposing claim that such profitable trading is impossible.

Over time, however, scholars have pressed the weak, semi-strong, and strong form categories beyond their original service as a classification of empirical tests into more general duty as a classification of market responses to particular kinds of information. For example, prices might be said to incorporate efficiently one genre of information that is semi-strong or public, but fail to reflect another that is strong form, or non-public. Indeed, taken a step further, scholars sometime describe markets themselves as weak, semi-strong, or strong form efficient. Without ever being quite explicit, this powerful shorthand implies that different market dynamics are involved in the reflection of different kinds of information into price, and that varying degrees of market efficiency might well be the consequence.

The recognition that different market mechanisms operate on different types of information is central to our analysis of market efficiency. But before we explore this conclusion in greater detail, it is first necessary that we define the key terms of the ECMH, and that we do so conceptually rather than operationally. Four basic concepts are critical. Two of these are encompassed within the operational definition of market efficiency: that prices "fully reflect" all "available" information. The third inheres in the expanded use of the weak, semi-strong, and strong form categories to describe price response to different kinds of information. We need a concept of "relative efficiency" that distinguishes among and ranks the different market dynamics according to how closely they approximate the ideal of ensuring that prices always fully reflect all available information. Finally, we need a working definition of the most basic concept of all, that of "information," in order to specify the processes by which price comes to reflect not only the actual occurrence of events, but also changes in perceptions of the probability of future events.

*　*　*

---

riod. The discovery of abnormal returns indicates trading opportunities and, therefore, possible market inefficiency. The results thus far indicate efficient price responses to a wide variety of publicly released information, ranging from earning reports and dividend announcements to accounting changes, stock splits, press evaluations, and even changes in Federal Reserve Board policy.

27. Unlike weak and semi-strong form tests, which probe for trading opportunities that might arise from particular kinds of information, strong form studies cannot test for analogous opportunities arising from the generation of non-public information because investigators are unlikely to learn about such information (or if they do, they are unlikely to employ it for research purposes). For this reason, strong form tests must probe indirectly for trading opportunities arising from non-public information. Such tests seek to identify investors who are likely to possess non-public information and to determine whether these traders consistently earn net returns higher than the market average. The results have been mixed. Corporate insiders, such as officers, directors and affiliated bankers, systematically outperform the market. So do specialists on the major stock exchanges who possess non-public information about unexecuted investor orders. Mutual funds, however, appear to outperform the market only well enough to cover administrative and trading costs.

II. MECHANISMS OF MARKET EFFICIENCY

Review of the basic vocabulary of efficient market theory reveals a missing link: an account of the mechanisms of market efficiency that its terms foreshadow but do not explicitly detail. Once the "full reflection" of information into price is reformulated as an identity between an existing equilibrium price and a fully informed equilibrium price, the general contours of these mechanisms become clear. They must be trading processes that, with more or less promptness (or "relative efficiency"), force prices to a new, fully informed equilibrium. Moreover, clarifying the meaning of informational "availability" also reveals the chief obstacle to any mechanism that serves to push prices toward a fully informed equilibrium. New information is "available" to the capital market under an extraordinary variety of circumstances, ranging from the extreme of near-universal initial distribution of information—when everyone really does know the information—to the opposite extreme of initial distribution to only a very few traders. A satisfactory account of the mechanisms of market efficiency must describe their operation over this entire continuum of availability, including those circumstances in which the initial distribution is extremely limited to incomplete. Finally, and most important, the insight implicit in the extended application of the weak/semi-strong/strong form categories to information sets and markets suggests how one can explain distinct levels of relative efficiency over the entire continuum of informational availability. We must search for several different mechanisms, each of which can operate over an information set of particular availability to market traders, and each of which can generate its own dynamics of price equilibration.

Fortunately, the most difficult step in this search—the identification of a basic repertoire of mechanisms to explain the incorporation of new information into equilibrium securities prices—has already been taken. Over the past dozen years, financial economists have proposed four general forms of mechanisms, which may be termed "universally informed trading," "professionally informed trading," "derivatively informed trading," and "uninformed trading." In accordance with the economists' rigorous conventions of formal exposition, each of these mechanisms has thus far been modeled in isolation, as if it singlehandedly could explain the dynamics of price equilibration. Yet from the perspective of policy formulation, the precise operation of these mechanisms in vacuo is of less interest than the fact that all four shape the formation of prices in the same securities markets. Moreover, they do so in a fashion that can account for the reflection of information in price over the entire range of informational availability. We shall present these four mechanisms as components of a single complex repertoire of market responses. Our contribution lies not in identifying a new efficiency mechanism, but in specifying how the "fit" among the original four can supply the foundations for an explicit account of price equilibration.

Three features of the relation among the market mechanisms are critical. First, only one of the market mechanisms at a time can ordinarily operate to cause a particular bit of new information to be reflected in price. Second, which mechanism will dominate the dynamics of price change at any time depends on how widely the particular information is distributed in the market. Third, each of the mechanisms operates with a characteristic level of relative efficiency that depends on how widely information must be distributed in order to trigger it.

The wider the initial distribution of information that a mechanism requires, the more rapidly that mechanism operates.

Together, these characteristic interrelationships permit us to array the four market mechanisms on a continuum based on the initial distribution of information among traders, that is, on how many traders learn of the new information. Although all four mechanisms can ultimately lead to efficient equilibrium prices, the dynamics of equilibration will take longer as one moves from wide to narrow distribution mechanisms. Thus, just as the extended use of the weak/semi-strong/strong form categories implies, less "available" information will require more time for "full reflection" in price because its narrower distribution will force a qualitatively more circuitous form of price equilibration. Correlatively, the individual trader who initially learns of new information can capture an increasing portion of its trading value as the initial distribution of the information narrows and the dominant market mechanism shifts accordingly.

A. Universally Informed Trading

The simplest efficiency mechanism that causes prices to behave "as if" all traders knew of information is a market in which all traders are, in fact, costlessly and simultaneously informed. To be sure, universally informed trading in its purest sense results in efficient prices tautologically, and may seem more a statement of a sufficient condition for market efficiency than an active mechanism. But several varieties of price-relevant information at least approximate the ideal of universal dissemination. "Old" information, embedded in securities prices, is one example. Ongoing market activity assures its distribution to all interested traders, and precisely because all know it, we do not expect it to reveal arbitrage opportunities in the form of lucrative screens or trading rules that all alike could exploit. Another example is important news items—from presidential election results, which most citizens learn almost instantaneously, to changes in Federal Reserve Board policy, which are announced after trading hours precisely in order to ensure widespread dissemination. Thus, the universally informed trading mechanism ranges over all "old" price information and much that is new. It lumps together traditional "weak-form" information about price histories with information about current events into a single information set that prices reflect rapidly and with near perfect dynamic efficiency.

B. Professionally Informed Trading

In contrast to news about price and current events, however, much so-called "public" information is not universally disseminated among traders. Many traders are too unsophisticated to make full use of the technical accounting information contained in mandated disclosure reports; much disclosure data is accessible in the first instance only through documents on file with government agencies; and much information about a firm's prospects may be announced initially only to small groups of securities analysts and other market professionals. How, then, do prices come to reflect this semi-public information? The answer, as identified in general terms by Fama and many others, is that rapid price equilibration does not require widespread dissemination of information, but only a minority of knowledgeable traders who control a critical volume of trading activity. From this perspective, the universally informed trading mechanism is actually only a special case of price formation through the activity of traders who are direct re-

cipients of information. Subgroups of informed traders, or even a single knowledgeable trader with sufficient resources, can also cause prices to reflect information by persistent trading at a premium over "uninformed" price levels. The ra-
pidity of such price adjustments depends on the volume of informed trading. And
although a precise account of that process has yet to be offered, it seems plausible that the relative efficiency of price adjustment to new information that proceeds through professionally informed trading declines only gradually as initial
access to the information narrows to a threshold minority of traders, after which
it declines rapidly.

In today's securities markets, the dominant minority of informed traders is
the community of market professionals, such as arbitrageurs, researchers, brokers and portfolio managers, who devote their careers to acquiring information
and honing evaluative skills. The trading volume in most securities that these
professionals control, directly or indirectly, seems sufficient to assure the market's
rapid assimilation into price of most routine information.[69] Of course, the relative efficiency of the assimilation is never perfect. Since informed trading is costly,
market professionals must enjoy some informational advantage that permits
them to earn a commensurate return. But given competitive arbitrage and the
market for analyst services, we would not expect the long-run returns of individual professionals to exceed the market average by very much, especially in exchange markets where professionals dominate trading. This expectation is largely
confirmed by empirical studies of mutual fund returns.

In sum, the professionally informed trading mechanism explains why any information that is accessible to significant portions of the analyst community is
properly called "public," even though it manifestly is not. Such information is
rapidly assimilated into price, with only minimal abnormal returns to its professional recipients. And it is these characteristics, we submit, that largely convey
the meaning of a "semi-strong form" market response.

---

69. As of 1977, institutional trades, presumably directed by market professionals, accounted for 70% of public trading volume on the New York Stock Exchange. M. Blume &
I. Friend, *The Changing Role of the Individual Investor,* 4 (1978). Although individual investors are far more important on the smaller exchanges and in the over-the-counter market,
id. at 5, many of these investors also depend on the informed view of market professionals.
See Advisory Committee Report, *supra* note 3, at 290–91 (brokers are major information
source for individual investors).

Direct estimates of how rapidly prices reflect information after it becomes widely accessible to market professionals are difficult to come by, but one indication may be the market's
response to news of block trades. According to one study, it requires a mere 15 minutes—
too short an interval for post-trade arbitrage—for prices to stabilize after such trades.
Dann, Mayers & Raab, *Trading Rules, Large Blocks and the Speed of Price Adjustment,* 4 J.
Fin. Econ. 3, 18–21 (1977). Evidence that securities with little or no analyst following sell at
a discount indirectly confirms the contribution of market professionals to market efficiency.
"Investors are willing to purchase neglected, 'informationally naked' securities only at a discount relative to what they would pay for comparable...'informationally covered,' securities." Arbel & Strebel, *Pay Attention to Neglected Firms!,* J. Port. Manag., Winter 1983, at
37, 40. There is some evidence that this phenomenon may be due in part to statistical problems with the measurement techniques used. *See,* e.g., Roll, *A Possible Explanation of the
Small Firm Effect,* 36 J. Fin. 879 (1981). But more recent empirical research suggests an
anomaly in return levels that cannot be entirely explained either by methodological deficiencies or by any purely economic factor, such as tax selling or higher transactions costs, suggested thus far. See Schwert, *Size and Stock Returns, and Other Empirical Regularities,* 12 J.
Fin. Econ. 3, 3–4, 7–9 (1983) (surveying literature).

C. Derivatively Informed Trading

Yet not all information is public, even within the narrow confines of the professional analyst community. Corporate insiders and exchange specialists, for example, enjoy easy access to information that would be prohibitively costly for anyone else to obtain, while professional analysts conduct in-depth research that generates occasional informational monopolies. In these and similar instances of monopolistic access, information first enters the market through a very small number of traders whose own resources are not large enough to induce speedy price equilibration. But reflection of this information in price does not depend exclusively on the trading efforts of these insiders. Derivatively informed trading enhances relative efficiency and erodes the insider's advantage by capitalizing on the "informational leakage" associated with trading itself.

Informational leakage can assume many forms. Pure leakage—inadvertent, direct communication of trading information to outsiders—doubtlessly plays a significant role in rendering markets more efficient, even if its effects remain erratic. But beyond such direct disclosure by accident or "theft," two forms of indirect leakage also contribute to market efficiency. These are trade decoding and price decoding.

Trade decoding occurs whenever uninformed traders glean trading information by directly observing the transactions of informed traders. Myron Scholes' classic study of secondary distributions documents a common example of this phenomenon by demonstrating that only some large block sales of stock lead to substantial, permanent declines in share price. The declines are especially pronounced when sellers are officers or other insiders of the issuer; moderate when sellers are investment companies and mutual funds (which act on the advice of research staffs); and barely noticeable when sellers are individuals, bank trust departments, and other traders who may liquidate their holding for reasons other than investment gain. The clear implication is that uninformed traders use the identities of large sellers to deduce whether the latter are likely to possess valuable information, and then proceed to trade accordingly. Moreover, incidental evidence suggests that trade decoding is pervasive well beyond the limited context of block trades. Indeed, the Federal Securities Acts themselves provide prime opportunities for trade decoding by the uninformed by forcing insiders and other informationally-advantaged traders to disclose their activities, if not their motives.[82]

Pervasive though it may be, however, the trade decoding remains limited by a significant constraint: uninformed traders must be able to identify informed traders individually and observe their trading activities directly. By contrast, the second form of indirect leakage, price decoding, does not require uninformed traders to discover the identity of their informed cohorts. It merely requires uninformed traders to observe and interpret anonymous data on price and trading

---

82. *E.g.,* § 13(d) of the Securities Exchange Act of 1934, 15 U.S.C. § 78m(d) (1982) (requiring reporting, within 10 days, of boilerplate information regarding the purchase of any security that gives the owner more than 5 percent of that class of security); § 16(a) of the 1934 Act, 15 U.S.C. § 78p (1982) (requiring directors, officers, and 10% beneficial owners to report purchases and subsequent changes in ownership of issuer's equity securities within 10 days after initial acquisition and 10 days "after the close of each calendar month thereafter").

volume against the backdrop of other information or expectations that these traders possess.

In theory, at least, the logic of price decoding is simple. When trading on inside information is of sufficient volume to cause a change in price, this otherwise inexplicable change may itself signal the presence of new information to the uninformed. Why, after all, would anyone persistently trade against the market unless they possessed such information? But beyond the "weak" learning involved in identifying the presence of new information, uninformed traders may also succeed in decoding the actual content of the information. The trick here, and admittedly it is no mean feat, is the uninformed trader's ability to employ knowledge of the informational constituents of the old price to deduce which possible accretion of new information would successfully explain observed price changes.[85] Yet, probabilistically, such "strong" learning may be less difficult than it at first appears; consider, for example, how frequently increases in price signal the presence of inside information about impending tender offers.

The theory of "weak" learning from prices is standard economic fare, traditionally linked with the contributions of Friedrich Hayek. Attempts to model "strong" learning, however, are comparatively recent and are still in a developmental stage in which they must radically simplify the learning processes of real markets. Nevertheless, they not only provide the best available account of this commonplace market phenomenon, but they also raise a question that cuts to the core of efficient market theory. Why would anyone incur the cost and risk of acquiring restricted-access information, if hair-triggered "decoders" will extract the bulk of its value? The answer must be that prices are not fully informative and, indeed, that the acquisition effort is made precisely because they are not. As Grossman and Stiglitz recently demonstrated, a market in which price decoding was both costless and accurate could not support an efficient equilibrium in which prices fully reflect trading information. Rather, such a market would be doomed to an oscillating dynamic of enlightenment and ignorance. Traders would initially acquire information because, in an inefficient market, they could earn returns on their investment in acquisition. As more traders became initially informed, however, the price system would convey more information to uninformed traders, thereby lowering the returns to informed traders. At the point at which the market became fully efficient, there would be no return to informed traders for having acquired the information, and, as a result, information acquisition would cease. The market would sink into informational inefficiency once more, only to repeat the cycle as soon as some traders again found information acquisition profitable.

Perhaps it is fortunate, then, that fully-effective price decoding remains a theoretical concept rather than a market reality. It is only because uninformed traders cannot infer all information from price—i.e., because prices are

---

85. Thus, unlike screening rules or other attempts to discover trading opportunities in price data alone, price decoding relies principally on the interaction between price changes and independent information about firms. The more widespread this independent information is among traders, of course, the more widely distributed correct deductions from price changes will be, and the less likely it is that price decoding will yield trading profits. But if incipient price changes can only be interpreted by a few traders who have already acquired detailed knowledge about the firm, or if unexpected price changes lead a handful of traders to research the firm, these price changes may well yield trading profits.

"noisy"—that informed traders enjoy a return on their information up to the point at which further trading moves prices beyond the noise threshold. Thus, the reflection of non-public information into price is a two-stage process; it is first triggered by initially informed "inside" trading, but, at a critical threshold, it rapidly accelerates as a result of reactive trades. This much ensures that price reflects each "bit" of decoded information with a moderate degree of relative efficiency—less, to be sure, than a wider initial distribution might provide, but far more than the trades of initially informed investors alone could produce.[93] For the price system as a whole, background noise implies an "equilibrium degree of disequilibrium." Noise levels regulate the numbers of informed traders much like returns on initially informed trading regulate entry into the community of market professionals in the context of professionally informed trading. The number of informed traders, in turn, determines the volume of limited-access information that influences prices at any particular moment, and the end result is perpetual, if constrained, disequilibrium.

In short, derivatively informed trading, whether it operates through trade-or price-decoding, is self-limiting. It guarantees neither full efficiency nor inefficiency, but rather a level of relative efficiency that is jointly determined by the effort required to acquire information and the decoding possibilities that limit its exploitation. Derivatively informed trading thus explains how prices can come to reflect much information that is truly "non-public," even while suggesting the inevitable limits to the process.

D. Uninformed Trading

The three trading mechanisms that we have considered thus far each describe processes by which prices come to reflect particular key trading facts. Such pieces of information have strong and straightforward implications for price....however, information is not limited to hard facts; it also includes soft information, the stuff of forecasts and predictions, that is at least as critical to trading as key trading facts. Both in developing forecasts of future events and in making a master forecast of value, traders employ, in addition to key facts, a wide variety of secondary facts, differing beliefs, and diverse levels of predictive skills.[96] This heterogeneity of information, beliefs, and skills adds additional uncertainty to that

---

93. The concomitant risks of price decoding are, of course, the danger that price change may communicate misinformation, or that it may be incorrectly interpreted. These risks, which inhibit price decoding, are likely to be greater than the analogous misinformation risks associated with pure leakage and trade decoding, if only because the latter are intrinsically richer information channels. Thus, price decoding may typically work in tandem with these other models of derivatively informed trading, even when price signals are wrong.

96. That the fact-forecast dichotomy is in some respects a simplification of the structure of information is apparent from the reference to "key" trading facts. Key facts such as earnings figures, dividend payments, major business decisions, and reports of likely fraud, dominate trader information sets with strong, unproblematic implications for price. Secondary facts, which imply marginal or contingent adjustments in expected value, are among the raw materials of "soft" forecasts; they have compelling significance for trader expectations only in the aggregate. An example of a secondary fact would be evidence of an issuer's product performance in one of many local markets. Finally, certain third party forecasts themselves can assume the status of key trading facts when they reflect secondary facts and judgments that are otherwise unavailable to the market. An example would be an earnings projection by an issuer.

stemming from the inherent indeterminacy of the future. The uncertainty arises from the sheer impossibility of acquiring both the full range of secondary facts and the complete repertoire of skills necessary to frame optimal forecasts. To return to a concept used earlier, a hypothetical fully informed trader would form optimal forecasts as a result of access to the aggregate information, beliefs, and skills of all traders in the market, but individual traders would remain ignorant of this optimal forecast information. Such information is "available" to the market, but it nonetheless lies at the extreme pole of the continuum depicting the initial distribution of information to traders. In extreme contrast to the virtually complete distribution of information that underlies universally informed trading, optimal forecast information is not available to any individual trader. At this juncture, the basic question of market efficiency resurfaces. What is the mechanism by which the market comes to reflect the diverse and imperfect forecasts of individual traders into the aggregate forecast of price, and how well does this mechanism function as measured against the yardstick of optimal forecast data?

The final market efficiency mechanism, uninformed trading, permits prices, in some circumstances, to reflect aggregate — or consensus — forecasts that are more nearly optimal over the long run than those of any individual trader. In this sense, prices can reflect information about which all traders are uninformed.[100] For expository purposes, it is useful first to develop the uninformed trading mechanism in its simplest form, as a pure, "naive" aggregation of information in price that occurs before traders discover the value of price as a forecasting statistic.

If each trader's forecast about the likelihood of a future event is informed in part by secondary facts and evaluations to which only he has access, then an aggregation of all forecasts draws on an information pool much larger than that possessed by any individual trader. Although each trader's own forecasts are skewed by the unique constraints on his or her judgment, other traders will have offsetting constraints. As trading proceeds, the random biases of individual forecasts will cancel one another out, leaving price to reflect a single, best-informed aggregate forecast. Uninformed trading, then, resembles a regression in which the dependent variable is price, the independent variables as the "bits" of information bearing on an unbiased forecast, and the weights attached to each bit are determined by the buy-sell decisions of individual traders. Although individual traders will attach biased weights because each knows only a fraction of the relevant information, the cumulative weights will be unbiased unless trading volume is itself skewed toward the views of one set of uninformed traders. In this respect, unsystematic bias "washes out" over trading in the same way that unsystematic risk "washes out" in a diversified portfolio. Moreover, if any bias persists, it does so because the "errors" of individual traders are perversely correlated, just as unsystematic risks might be in a poorly diversified portfolio.

---

100. Note, however, that uninformed trading never leads to prices that reflect wholly optimal forecast data. Rather, this mechanism can lead to prices that reflect a better approximation, over the long run, of such hypothetical optimal forecasts than can the parallel assessments made by individual traders. For this reason, the uninformed trading mechanism has the lowest relative efficiency of any of the four market mechanisms. As measured against the yardstick of the target information — i.e., optimal forecast data — it can never assure fully informed prices, even though it may reflect consensus forecasts in price much more rapidly than, say, derivatively informed trading will reflect inside information in price.

Robert Verrecchia has modeled the conditions under which the regression-like behavior of uninformed trading aggregates all forecast information available to the market—but not to all individual traders—into a consensus best estimate of value. Of course, real markets at best can only approximate these conditions, but the interesting issue here, as with the other market mechanisms, is the identification of the factors that determine when and how well uninformed trading operates. Verrecchia's model requires traders to make independent assessments of the value of risky securities based on their own facts and forecasts, which in the aggregate form a bounded, unbiased distribution around the hypothetical price that a fully informed trader would assign the security. The first of these conditions, that trader assessments be independent, requires an absence of collusion, "learning," or shared prejudice among traders that would render individual forecasting errors mutually reinforcing.[107] Complete independence, of course, is unlikely in real markets, but so is widespread mutual dependence where it contradicts the independent judgments of many traders. No one ever earned money in the market, after all, by consciously discounting his or her personal knowledge without good reason. The second condition of uninformed trading, that trader assessments be "bounded," merely requires that all such assessments fall in the same ball park. Traders with widely-skewed personal assessments will impede price convergence—reduce the relative efficiency of the uninformed trading mechanism—and may even preclude it entirely in thinly-traded markets. Again, however, market discipline in the form of heavy trading losses will restrain idiosyncratic traders and may even eliminate them through a "Darwinian" process of natural selection.

It is the third condition of uninformed trading, that aggregate trader assessments remain unbiased with respect to the optimal price estimate of a fully informed trader, that may be the most demanding. This condition embraces the preceding two requirements, since either widely-shared forecasting errors or idiosyncratic trading can bias the aggregate-level distribution of trader assessments. But, in addition, the "no-bias" condition carries implications for the acquisition of new key trading facts that can significantly alter individual assessments. Until the market fully incorporates such key information into price, the independent assessments of uninformed traders—traders who do not know of the new information—are inevitably systematically biased. Once any trader acquires a new key fact that renders hitherto uncertain contingencies more (or less) likely, the consensus forecast of uninformed traders, as embodied in existing price, is biased relative to the newly-available information. Moreover, it remains so until the market fully incorporates the new key information into price, through one of the three "informed" trading mechanisms previously described.

This complementary relationship among the market mechanisms can be viewed either from the perspective of uninformed trading or from that of the three informed trading mechanisms. When viewed from the perspective of unin-

---

107. Widespread trade or price decoding would violate the independence condition. One would not expect high volume derivatively informed trading, however, in the absence of new key trading facts. Such facts would, in any event, render aggregate forecasts obsolete. Better examples of assessment bias might be the expectations induced by market "gurus." Note, however, that if traders condition their beliefs on both price and their own independent assessments—i.e., engage in "weak" learning but not price decoding—the independence condition is not violated.

formed trading, the informed market mechanisms are "shortcuts" to the elimination of sudden informational bias in consensus prices. They rely on the speedy transmission of information to traders rather than on the much slower and less certain process of market discipline. By contrast, when uninformed trading is viewed from the perspective of the three informed market mechanisms, it represents an interstitial mechanism that operates between the appearances of new key trading facts. Uninformed trading "fine-tunes" equilibrium price and assures that price registers any gradually developing consensus about future contingencies.

The example of a truly innovative investment contract, such as a radically novel form of bond indenture, further illustrates the complementary nature of the market mechanisms. When an issuer first announces such an innovative security, all traders will be uncertain about its worth. Although the issuer may make good-faith representations about value, most traders will discount these as self-interested puffery. Absent convincing assurances, the initial pricing of the innovative security will be left to the uninformed trading mechanism, which will tend to "undervalue" it relative to the information possessed by the good-faith issuer — but not, of course, relative to the aggregate forecasts of the uninformed traders. Thus, the security's uninformed equilibrium price will be "biased," and relatively inefficient. Efficiency is possible only if the issuer succeeds in making its representations credible, or if an enterprising trader independently acquires the key facts that establish their accuracy. In the first case, subsequent price equilibration would proceed rapidly through the universally informed or professionally informed trading mechanisms; in the second, it would proceed more slowly through derivatively informed trading.

Yet this depiction of the relationship between uninformed and informed trading mechanisms still remains incomplete in one important respect: it ignores the fact that traders themselves are acute observers of market behavior. If prices successfully aggregate all available information, including consensus forecasts and secondary facts, traders will begin to condition their trading activity on price as well as on their individual assessments of value. This conditioning on price adds "learning" to the basic aggregation mechanism of uninformed trading and is precisely the "weak learning" from price that we previously contrasted with the "strong learning" of price decoding. Weak learning in this sense occupies a middle ground between uninformed and derivatively informed trading. Unlike price decoding, which transmits key trading facts, weak learning conveys refracted data about consensus opinion that is already fully impounded in price and has comparatively little potential for revising individual traders' facts and forecasts. In many instances, the simple aggregation process of uninformed trading will obscure the sources of weak or gradual price changes and so preclude any deduction about their meaning other than the obvious one — that a shift has occurred in consensus market expectations. But even where traders are able to associate price and volume signals with shifts in particular aggregate forecasts, such as an altered consensus forecast about future Federal Reserve Board policies, they will only acquire an indication of whether the market disagrees with them, not of why it does. The force of such an indication depends on each trader's level of confidence. Individual estimates of value will move toward existing prices, and individual forecasts toward consensus predictions, in rough proportion to how highly each trader assesses the comparative quality of his or her own collection of information.

The existence of weak learning from price itself indicates that, on average, such learning improves the quality of individual trading decisions. To the extent that it succeeds, it will also have a beneficial "feedback" effect on the core aggregation processes of uninformed trading by decreasing unwarranted dispersion in individual assessments of value. The amount and importance of weak learning that occurs, however, are also constrained by the level of price noise—the same random fluctuation in price that masks the transmission of key trading facts through price decoding. Price noise, then, regardless of its source, establishes the limits on the ultimate efficiency of uninformed trading.[121] On the other hand, the instances in which the market has "guessed" right are an index of the success of uninformed trading. The paradigmatic examples are the many occasions on which publication of Federal Reserve Board policy decisions, fluctuations in money supply, and similar data of interest to investors have resulted in no discernable effect on prices. Not surprisingly, these examples differ from the case of the novel innovative security in that they concern future events about which all traders are likely to possess well-specified, reasonably exact forecasts.

In sum, the formulation of expectations in response to uncertainty will always constitute a major portion of the task of valuing securities. Over much of this domain, the uninformed trading mechanism will bear the burden of reflecting these expectations in price.

E. Summary

The uninformed trading mechanism completes the array of capital market mechanisms that, in our view, constitutes an essential element of efficient market theory. For any initial distribution of information in the market, including an initial distribution to no one in the case of optimal aggregate forecasts, one or more efficiency mechanisms facilitate the eventual "reflection" of information into price.[124] Moreover, the four efficiency mechanisms are complementary; each functions over a characteristic segment of the continuum of initial distributions of information among traders.

*   *   *

Universally informed trading extends over all widely-disseminated information, including the price-history information that underlies weak form tests. Professionally informed trading operates on all publicly available information, but it is particularly active where information is "semi-public"—i.e., initially distributed or useful to only a minority of sophisticated trading professionals. Professionally informed trading thus links the information sets sampled by semi-strong form tests and by those strong form tests, including studies of mutual fund performance, that aggregate returns to sophisticated traders over time. By contrast, derivatively informed trading acts most prominently on key trading facts over

---

121. Stated differently, it limits the extent to which price can converge to a single best estimate that reflects not only key trading facts, but also optimal forecasts of all residual uncertainties affecting a security's value.

124. This is not to say that all information will be fully reflected in price, regardless of its initial distribution or trading import. Some inside information may never trigger a sufficiently powerful price signal to alert uninformed traders. Nor is it likely that uninformed trading will ever fully reflect optimal forecast data in price, no matter how rapidly it operates.

which very small numbers of traders exercise monopolistic access. It dominates the remaining strong form tests that routinely demonstrate substantial market inefficiency, such as those involving corporate insiders and market specialists. Finally, uninformed trading acts on the "soft" information of forecasts and assessments that is not directly sampled by any of the other tests.

The foregoing analysis does more, however, than merely vindicate a familiar classificatory schem. It also renders explicit the intuition behind the expansion of these categories from a classification of tests to a descriptive language of market responses that implicitly distinguishes among levels of relative market efficiency,...The step of focusing explicitly on efficiency mechanisms, we submit, completes the project of giving theoretical content to the operational vocabulary of market efficiency theory—the project that began more than a decade ago with analytical efforts to clarify the basic definition of market efficiency.

          *   *   *

Much work remains to be done in further illuminating the operation of the four market efficiency mechanisms. Not only is the modeling of each mechanism, considered independently, still in its developmental stage, but attempts to model the synergistic interaction of the mechanisms are even more preliminary. Research of the latter type may help explain puzzling discrepancies between the actual response of price to new information and the response that any one of the mechanisms considered alone might lead one to expect. Why, for example, does informed trading appear to operate with little loss in relative efficiency down to a quite narrow initial distribution of information among traders, a critical threshold floor of initially informed traders? One answer might be that a threshold number of traders is required to emit a strong price signal. In this case, derivatively informed trading may "amplify" professionally informed trading by alerting the entire analyst community to the existence of new semi-public information. Similarly, uninformed trading, by reducing price noise levels, may help accelerate price decoding and so contribute to the relative efficiency of derivatively informed trading.

Finally, the cycle is complete when uninformed trading generates prices that reflect high-quality forecasts about future events or facts that are as yet unknown to the market. Such anticipation minimizes the discrepancies between ex ante "uninformed" and ex post "informed" equilibrium price levels and thereby enhances the relative efficiency of all three informed trading mechanisms. However, because uninformed trading works best when large numbers of traders form well-specified assessments about future facts and future events, it will be most efficient when traders are well aware of the importance of such contingencies in advance. That is, uninformed trading works best for "known" uncertainties: those future events that are likely to be widely anticipated before they are known, and widely known when they occur. Such "future facts" are rapidly assimilated into price by the universally informed and professionally informed trading mechanisms.[129] Conversely, when key trading facts that bear on the forecasting of future events

---

129. Uninformed trading works best for "known" uncertainties for two reasons. Many traders will form careful, independent forecasts about these contingencies, thus expanding the information base that is aggregated by price; and, because these contingencies are familiar to the market, trader forecasts will fall within a bounded distribution of expected outcomes, thus increasing the predictive quality of the assessments reflected into price.

are rapidly disseminated, they help minimize the bias of individual trader assessments and thereby enhance the relative efficiency of uninformed trading. Thus, the efficiency mechanisms discriminate jointly as well as separately among information sets. Some types of information, such as Federal Reserve Board announcements and routine disclosure reports, are efficiently reflected in price in two ways: ex ante in the form of accurate anticipation, and ex post in the form of rapid assimilation through the most efficient informed trading mechanisms. Other types of information, of which data about innovation is the best example, may be subject to relatively inefficient assimilation both ex ante and ex post.

The exact nature and magnitude of such interaction among mechanisms, which presumably contributes to total market efficiency across all available information sets, must await future investigation. At this juncture, we must content ourselves with the more limited observation that the four capital market mechanisms function with decreasing relative efficiency. Thus, we expect the breadth of the initial distribution of information among traders to determine the relative efficiency of the market's response.

III. THE INFORMATION MARKET

In the previous section we suggested that the capital market's relative efficiency depends on the initial distribution of information, and that the various capital market mechanisms are not equally effective for all distributions of information. We illustrated these points by arraying both the mechanisms and Fama's original trichotomy of weak, semi-strong and strong form efficiency along a continuum representing the breadth of initial distribution of trading information. Fama's trichotomy, we suggested, was really an approximation of an underlying relationship between how broadly information is initially distributed, and the particular market mechanism—and level of market efficiency—with which it is reflected in price. But while this analysis explains how (and how much) efficiency is achieved given the initial distribution of information among traders, it tells only half the story.

Given the operative capital market mechanisms, the relative efficiency of the market's response to particular information depends on the initial distribution of that information among traders. The question now is, what determines that initial distribution?

To answer that question, the focus of our analysis shifts to the operation of a different market: the market for information. Although the distribution of information determines which capital market mechanism will operate and, therefore, how efficient the capital market will be, it is the information market that determines how information is initially distributed. Analysis of the overall process of market efficiency thus requires careful consideration of the structure of the information market.

A. The Central Role of Information Costs

Since efficiency in the capital market depends on the distribution of information, it is ultimately a function of the cost of information to traders. The lower the cost of particular information, the wider will be its distribution, the more effective will be the capital market mechanism operating to reflect it in prices, and the more efficient will be the market with respect to it. Understanding market efficiency, then, requires detailed analysis of the nature and dynamics of information costs.

Notes and Questions

1. EMH as a Dynamic Competitive Process: Gilson and Kraakman provide substance to the EMH. In particular, they describe how a process of rivalrous competition in capital markets can force different types of information to be reflected in price. Are there other mechanisms of market efficiency that are not accounted for in their model? How does regulation of securities markets impact the mechanisms of market efficiency? Gilson and Kraakman's analysis leads one back to the economics of information. Chapter VII suggested that obtaining new information involves costs. What does this suggest regarding the efficient level of information in capital markets? Describe then the relationship between information and an EMH equilibrium.

2. The Economics of EMH: Jonathan Macey and Geoffrey Miller have identified four factors relevant to an economic analysis of EMH. First, different types of information are incorporated into price at varying speeds. Thus, a particular market may be more efficient with respect to one type of information than another. Second, the characteristics of the market and its participants are relevant to market efficiency. Some markets like the NYSE are organized around a central trading location which substantially reduces transaction costs. Other markets, known as over-the-counter (OTC) markets, are organized by way of telecommunications. OTC markets might involve higher transaction costs and, thus, relatively less market efficiency. Third, the nature of the security type and the difficulties involved in its valuation impact efficiency. Most stocks are easier to value than are options or futures. Fourth, the credibility of information provided by a stock's issuer impacts efficiency. If the market is skeptical of the firm's announcement of the discovery of new gold reserves, it may take a long time for such information to be incorporated in market price. See Jonathan Macey and Geoffrey Miller, "Good Finance, Bad Economics: An Analysis of Fraud-on-the-Market Theory," 42 *Stanford Law Review,* 1059 (April 1990).

3. Dartboard Analysis: The EMH suggests that it is very difficult, but not impossible, to earn an economic return on investments. This has lead some commentators to suggest that stock pickers might do just as well by throwing darts at the financial pages. Such logic implies a sense of randomness to the investment process. Is randomness consistent with EMH, portfolio theory, or CAPM? Regardless, for many years, the *Wall Street Journal* has conducted a contest between market professionals and a portfolio of stocks selected by throwing darts at the financial pages. As of April 1997, the pros lead the series 48–34. However, when compared with market averages, the pros have only a 42–40 lead. *The Wall Street Journal,* Wednesday, April 9, 1997, Section C, p. 1. When one considers the amount of time that professional investors spend in selecting stocks, such statistics clearly indicate the difficulty of beating the market. In other words, it appears rather difficult to obtain information capable of earning positive economic returns—i.e., the market is fairly efficient.

4. How About My Mutual Funds?: Mutual funds represent an ever growing part of the individual investor's portfolio. Mutual funds, however, require investors to sacrifice a portion of the return made on invested money to cover the cost of running the fund. Is it worth it? According to the Vanguard Index Trust Annual Report 1995, over a ten year period more than 70% of all equity mutual funds were out paced by the S&P 500 Index. This, again, further indicates the difficulty of obtaining information capable of earning positive economic returns.

5. Market Timing: Weak form market efficiency suggests that investors cannot systematically earn economic returns by using historical market data. This suggests that for the most part it is futile to attempt to time the market. In other words, firms that are waiting for the market to go up before issuing stock or investors who are waiting for the market to go down before buying stock are wasting their time. In fact, studies indicate that individual investors do better on average by using a process known as dollar-cost averaging. With **dollar-cost averaging**, the individual simply invests the same amount of money every period—for example, monthly. This eliminates the futile timing game and forces the investor to buy more of an investment when prices are low and less when prices are high.

2. Fraud on the Market Theory

Securities and Exchange Commission Rule 10b-5 makes it unlawful, in connection with the purchase or sale of any security, to make untrue statements of material fact or to omit to state a material fact necessary in order to make statements made, in light of circumstances under which they were made, not misleading. Traditionally, plaintiffs in such securities fraud cases have had to prove that they actually relied upon the misstatements or omissions of the defendant in order to recover damages. For example, securities fraud plaintiffs might have been required to prove that they actually heard or read the misstatements or omissions. The Supreme Court in *Basic, Inc. v. Levinson* significantly altered the nature of the reliance requirement by adopting fraud-on-the-market theory, a derivative of the EMH.

Basic, Inc. v. Levinson
Supreme Court of the United States
485 U.S. 224 (1988)

JUSTICE BLACKMUN delivered the opinion of the Court.

This case requires us to apply the materiality requirement of § 10(b) of the Securities Exchange Act of 1934, and the Securities and Exchange Commission's Rule 10b-5, promulgated thereunder, in the content of preliminary corporate merger discussions. We must also determine whether a person who traded a corporation's shares on a securities exchange after the issuance of a materially misleading statement by the corporation may invoke a rebuttable presumption that, in trading, he relied on the integrity of the price set by the market.

I

Prior to December 20, 1978, Basic Incorporated was a publicly traded company primarily engaged in the business of manufacturing chemical refractories for the steel industry. As early as 1965 or 1966, Combustion Engineering, Inc., a company producing mostly alumina-based refractories, expressed some interest in acquiring Basic, but was deterred from pursuing this inclination seriously because of antitrust concerns it then entertained. In 1976, however, regulatory action opened the way to a renewal of Combustion's interest. The "Strategic Plan," dated October 25, 1976, for Combustion's Industrial Products Group included the objective: "Acquire Basic Inc. $30 million." App 337.

Beginning in September 1976, Combustion representatives had meetings and telephone conversations with Basic officers and directors, including petitioners here, concerning the possibility of a merger. During 1977 and 1978, Basic made three public statements denying that it was engaged in merger negotiations.[4] On December 18, 1978, Basic asked the New York Stock Exchange to suspend trading in its shares and issued a release stating that it had been "approached" by another company concerning a merger. On December 19, Basic's board endorsed Combustion's offer of $46 per share for its common stock, and on the following day publicly announced its approval of Combustion's tender offer for all outstanding shares.

Respondents are former Basic shareholders who sold their stock after Basic's first public statement of October 21, 1977, and before the suspension of trading in December 1978. Respondents brought a class action against Basic and its directors, asserting that the defendants issued three false or misleading public statements and thereby were in violation of § 10(b) of the 1934 Act and of Rule 10b-5. Respondents alleged that they were injured by selling Basic shares at artificially depressed prices in a market affected by petitioners' misleading statements and in reliance thereon.

The District Court adopted a presumption of reliance by members of the plaintiff class upon petitioners public statements that enabled the court to conclude that common questions of fact or law predominated over particular questions pertaining to individual plaintiffs. See Fed. Rule Civ. Proc. 23(b)(3). The District Court therefore certified respondents' class. On the merits, however, the District Court granted summary judgment for the defendants. It held that, as a matter of law, any misstatements were immaterial: there were no negotiations ongoing at the time of the first statement, and although negotiations were taking place when the second and third statements were issued, those negotiations were not "destined, with reasonable certainty, to become a merger agreement in principle."

The United States Court of Appeals for the Sixth Circuit affirmed the class certification, but reversed the District Court's summary judgment, and remanded the case. 786 F. 2d 741 (1986). The court reasoned that while petitioners were under no general duty to disclose their discussions with Combustion, any state-

---

4. On October 21, 1977, after heavy trading and a new high in Basic stock, the following news item appeared in the Cleveland Plain Dealer:

"[Basic] President Max Muller said the company knew no reason for the stock's activity and that no negotiations were under way with any company for a merger. He said Flintkote recently denied Wall Street rumors that it would make a tender offer of $25 a share for control of the Cleveland-based maker of refractories for the steel industry."

On September 25, 1978, in reply to an inquiry from the New York Stock Exchange, Basic issued a release concerning increased activity in its stock and stated that

"management is unaware of any present or pending company development that would result in the abnormally heavy trading activity and price fluctuation in company shares that have been experienced in the past few days." Id., at 401.

On November 6, 1978, Basic issued to its shareholders a "Nine Months Report 1978." This Report stated:

"With regard to the stock market activity in the Company's shares we remain unaware of any present or pending developments which would account for the high volume of trading and price fluctuations in recent months."

ment the company voluntarily released could not be "'so incomplete as to mislead.'" *Id.,* at 746, quoting *SEC v. Texas Gulf Sulphur Co.* 401 F. 2d 833, 862 (CA2 1968) (en banc), cert. denied sub nom. *Coats v. SEC,* 394 U. S. 976 (1969). In the Court of Appeals' view, Basic's statements that no negotiations were taking place, and that it knew of no corporate developments to account for the heavy trading activity, were misleading. With respect to materiality, the court rejected the argument that preliminary merger discussions are immaterial as a matter of law, and held that "once a statement is made denying the existence of any discussions, even discussions that might not have been material in absence of the denial are material because they make the statement made untrue." 786 F. 2d, at 749.

The Court of Appeals joined a number of other circuits in accepting the "fraud-on-the-market theory" to create a rebuttable presumption that respondents relied on petitioners' material misrepresentations, noting that without the presumption it would be impractical to certify a class under Fed. Rule Civ. Proc. 23(b)(3).

We granted certiorari to resolve the split among the Courts of Appeals as to the standard of materiality applicable to preliminary merger discussions, and to determine whether the courts below properly applied a presumption of reliance in certifying the class, rather than requiring each class member to show direct reliance on Basic's statements.

*   *   *

III

*   *   *

C

*   *   *

As we clarify today, materiality depends on the significance the reasonable investor would place on the withheld or misrepresented information. The fact-specific inquiry we endorse here is consistent with the approach a number of courts have taken in assessing the materiality of merger negotiations. Because the standard of materiality we have adopted differs from that used by both courts below, we remand the case for reconsideration of the question whether a grant of summary judgment is appropriate on this record.

IV

A

We turn to the question of reliance and the fraud-on-the-market theory. Succinctly put:

> "The fraud on the market theory is based on the hypothesis that, in an open and developed securities market, the price of a company's stock is determined by the available material information regarding the company and its business.... Misleading statements will therefore defraud purchasers of stock even if the purchasers do not directly rely on the misstatements.... The causal connection between the defendants' fraud and the plaintiffs' purchase of stock in such a case is no less significant than in a case of direct reliance on misrepresentations." *Peil v. Speiser,* 806 F. 2d 1154, 1160–1161 (CA3 1986).

Our task, of course, is not to assess the general validity of the theory, but to consider whether it was proper for the courts below to apply a rebuttable presumption of reliance, supported in part by the fraud-on-the-market theory. . . .

This case required resolution of several common questions of law and fact concerning the falsity or misleading nature of the three public statements made by Basic, the presence or absence of scienter, and the materiality of the misrepresentations, if any. In their amended complaint, the named plaintiffs alleged that in reliance on Basic's statements they sold their shares of Basic stock in the depressed market created by petitioners. . . . Requiring proof of individualized reliance from each member of the proposed plaintiff class effectively would have prevented respondents from proceeding with a class action, since individual issues then would have overwhelmed the common ones. The District Court found that the presumption of reliance created by the fraud-on-the-market theory provided "a practical resolution to the problem of balancing the substantive requirement of proof of reliance in securities cases against the procedural requisites of [Fed. Rule Civ. Proc.] 23." The District Court thus concluded that with reference to each public statement and its impact upon the open market for Basic shares, common questions predominated over individual questions, as required by Fed. Rule Civ. Proc. 23(a)(2) and (b)(3).

Petitioners and their *amici* complain that the fraud-on-the-market theory effectively eliminates the requirement that a plaintiff asserting a claim under Rule 10b-5 prove reliance. They note that reliance is and long has been an element of common-law fraud, *see e.g.,* Restatement (Second) of Torts § 525 (1977); Prosser and Keeton on The Law of Torts § 108 (5th ed. 1984), and argue that because the analogous express right of action includes a reliance requirement, so too must an action implied under § 10(b).

We agree that reliance is an element of a Rule 10b-5 cause of action. Reliance provides the requisite causal connection between a defendant's misrepresentation and a plaintiff's injury. There is, however, more than one way to demonstrate the causal connection. Indeed, we previously have dispensed with a requirement of positive proof of reliance, where a duty to disclose material information had been breached, concluding that the necessary nexus between the plaintiffs' injury and the defendant's wrongful conduct had been established. Similarly, we did not require proof that material omissions or misstatements in a proxy statement decisively affected voting, because the proxy solicitation itself, rather than the defect in the solicitation materials, served as an essential link in the transaction.

The modern securities markets, literally involving millions of shares changing hands daily, differ from the face-to-face transactions contemplated by early fraud cases, and our understanding of Rule 10b-5's reliance requirement must encompass these differences.

> "In face-to-face transactions, the inquiry into an investor's reliance upon information is into the subjective pricing of that information by that investor. With the presence of a market, the market is interposed between seller and buyer and, ideally, transmits information to the investor in the processed form of a market price. Thus the market is performing a substantial part of the valuation process performed by the investor in a face-to-face transaction. The market is acting as the unpaid agent of the in-

vestor, informing him that given all the information available to it, the value of the stock is worth the market price." In re LTV Securities Litigation, 88 F. R. D. 134, 143 (ND Tex. 1980).

Accord, e.g., *Peil v. Speiser*, 806 F. 2d, at 1161 ("In an open and developed market, the dissemination of material misrepresentations or withholding of material information typically affects the price of the stock, and purchasers generally rely on the price of the stock as a reflection of its value"); *Blackie v. Barrack*, 524 F. 2d 891, 908 (CA9 1975) ("the same causal nexus can be adequately established indirectly, by proof of materiality coupled with the common sense that a stock purchaser does not ordinarily seek to purchase a loss in the form of artificially inflated stock"), cert. denied, 429 U. S. 816 (1976).

B

Presumptions typically serve to assist courts in managing circumstances in which direct proof, for one reason or another, is rendered difficult. The courts below accepted a presumption, created by the fraud-on-the-market theory and subject to rebuttal by petitioners, that persons who had traded Basic shares had done so in reliance on the integrity of the price set by the market, but because of petitioners' material misrepresentations that price had been fraudulently depressed. Requiring a plaintiff to show a speculative state of facts, i.e., how he would have acted if omitted material information had been disclosed would place an unnecessarily unrealistic evidentiary burden on the Rule 10b-5 plaintiff who has traded on an impersonal market.

Arising out of considerations of fairness, public policy, and probability, as well as judicial economy, presumptions are also useful devices for allocating the burdens of proof between parties. The presumption of reliance employed in this case is consistent with, and, by facilitating Rule 10b-5 litigation, supports, the congressional policy embodied in the 1934 Act. In drafting that Act, Congress expressly relied on the premise that securities markets are affected by information, and enacted legislation to facilitate an investor's reliance on the integrity of those markets:

> "No investor, no speculator, can safely buy and sell securities upon the exchanges without having an intelligent basis for forming his judgment as to the value of the securities he buys or sells. The idea of a free and open public market is built upon the theory that competing judgments of buyers and sellers as to the fair price of a security brings [sic] about a situation where the market price reflects as nearly as possible a just price. Just as artificial manipulation tends to upset the true function of an open market, so the hiding and secreting of important information obstructs the operation of the markets as indices of real value." H. R. Rep. No. 1383, *supra*, at 11.

See *Lipton v. Documation, Inc.*, 734 F. 2d 740, 748 (CA11 1984), cert. denied, 469 U. S. 1132 (1985).[23]

---

23. Contrary to the dissent's suggestion, the incentive for investors to "pay attention" to issuers' disclosures comes from their motivation to make a profit, not their attempt to preserve a cause of action under Rule 10b-5. Facilitating an investor's reliance on the market, consistently with Congress' expectations, hardly calls for "dismantling the federal scheme which mandates disclosure."

The presumption is also supported by common sense and probability. Recent empirical studies have tended to confirm Congress' premise that the market price of shares traded on well-developed markets reflects all publicly available information, and, hence, any material misrepresentations.[24] It has been noted that "it is hard to imagine that there ever is a buyer or seller who does not rely on market integrity. Who would knowingly roll the dice in a crooked crap game?" Indeed, nearly every court that has considered the proposition has concluded that where materially misleading statements have been disseminated into an impersonal, well-developed market for securities, the reliance of individual plaintiffs on the integrity of the market price may be presumed. Commentators generally have applauded the adoption of one variation or another of the fraud-on-the-market theory.[26] An investor who buys or sells stock at the price set by the market does so in reliance on the integrity of that price. Because most publicly available information is reflected in market price, an investor's reliance on any public material misrepresentations, therefore, may be presumed for purposes of a Rule 10b-5 action.

C

The Court of Appeals found that petitioners "made public material misrepresentations and [respondents] sold Basic stock in an impersonal, efficient market. Thus the class, as defined by the district court, has established the threshold facts for proving their loss."[27] The court acknowledged that petitioners may rebut proof of the elements giving rise to the presumption, or show that the misrepresentation in fact did not lead to a distortion of price or that an individual plaintiff traded or would have traded despite his knowing the statement was false.

Any showing that severs the link between the alleged misrepresentation and either the price received (or paid) by the plaintiff, or his decision to trade at a fair market price, will be sufficient to rebut the presumption of reliance. For example, if petitioners could show that the "market makers" were privy to the truth about

---

24. *See* In re LTV Securities Litigation, 88 F. R. D. 134, 144 (ND Tex. 1980) (citing studies); Fischel, *Use of Modern Finance Theory in Securities Fraud Cases Involving Actively Traded Securities*, 38 Bus. Law. 1, 4, n. 9 (1982) (citing literature on efficient-capital-market theory); Dennis, *Materiality and the Efficient Capital Market Model: A Recipe for the Total Mix*, 25 Wm. & Mary L. Rev. 373, 374–381, and n. 1 (1984). We need not determine by adjudication what economists and social scientists have debated through the use of sophisticated statistical analysis and the application of economic theory. For purposes of accepting the presumption of reliance in this case, we need only believe that market professionals generally consider most publicly announced material statements about companies, thereby affecting stock market prices.

26. See, e.g., Black, *Fraud on the Market: A Criticism of Dispensing with Reliance Requirements in Certain Open Market Transactions*, 62 N. C. L. Rev. 435 (1984); Note, *The Fraud-on-the-Market Theory*, 95 Harv. L. Rev. 1143 (1982); Note, *Fraud on the Market: An Emerging Theory of Recovery Under SEC Rule 10b-5*, 50 Geo. Wash. L. Rev. 627 (1982).

27. The Court of Appeals held that in order to invoke the presumption, a plaintiff must allege and prove: (1) that the defendant made public misrepresentations; (2) that the misrepresentations were material; (3) that the shares were traded on an efficient market; (4) that the misrepresentations would induce a reasonable, relying investor to misjudge the value of the shares; and (5) that the plaintiff traded the shares between the time the misrepresentations were made and the time the truth was revealed.

Given today's decision regarding the definition of materiality as to preliminary merger discussions, elements (2) and (4) may collapse into one.

the merger discussions here with Combustion, and thus that the market price would not have been affected by their misrepresentations, the causal connection could be broken: the basis for finding that the fraud had been transmitted through market price would be gone.[28] Similarly, if, despite petitioners' allegedly fraudulent attempt to manipulate market price, news of the merger discussions credibly entered the market and dissipated the effects of the misstatements, those who traded Basic shares after the corrective statements would have no direct or indirect connection with the fraud. Petitioners also could rebut the presumption of reliance as to plaintiffs who would have divested themselves of their Basic shares without relying on the integrity of the market. For example, a plaintiff who believed that Basic's statements were false and that Basic was indeed engaged in merger discussions, and who consequently believed that Basic stock was artificially underpriced, but sold his shares nevertheless because of other unrelated concerns, e.g., potential antitrust problems, or political pressures to divest from shares of certain businesses, could not be said to have relied on the integrity of a price he knew had been manipulated.

V

In summary:

5. It is not inappropriate to apply a presumption of reliance supported by the fraud-on-the-market theory.

6. That presumption, however, is rebuttable.

7. The District Court's certification of the class here was appropriate when made but is subject on remand to such adjustment, if any, as developing circumstances demand.

The judgment of the Court of Appeals is vacated and the case is remanded to that court for further proceedings consistent with this opinion.

It is so ordered.

Notes and Questions

1. Forms of Efficiency in Basic?: Fraud on the market is based upon the notion that all material information regarding a company and its business is reflected in stock prices. While this theory is clearly based upon the EMH, the Court does not endorse any particular form of the EMH. In fact, the Court attempts to side step the issue altogether: "we do not intend conclusively to adopt any particular theory of how quickly and completely publicly available information is reflected in price." Does the *Basic* Court leave future plaintiffs with any indication of whether fraud on the market theory contemplates weak form, semi-strong form, or strong form efficiency? Knowing which form of efficiency the Court was endorsing is a matter of great importance because future plaintiffs must demonstrate that the market for the shares they traded was efficient in order to prove reliance under the fraud-on-the-market theory. Some commenta-

---

28. By accepting this rebuttable presumption, we do not intend conclusively to adopt any particular theory of how quickly and completely publicly available information is reflected in market price. Furthermore, our decision today is not to be interpreted as addressing the proper measure of damages in litigation of this kind.

tors have indicated that the Court adopted the semi-strong form whether it wanted to or not:

> It is clear that the Supreme Court implicitly applied the semi-strong form of the ECMH in *Basic*. Plaintiff shareholders claimed in *Basic* that three misleading public statements about potential merger prospects depressed the value of their stock relative to its "true" value. In holding for the plaintiffs, the Court unambiguously rejected the strong form of the ECMH: If the market were strong-form efficient, *Basic's* share price would have adjusted to reflect *all* relevant information, including the fact that the statements issued by Basic were false. In other words, the strong form of the ECMH and the fraud-on-the-market theory are fundamentally incompatible. Critical to the strong form of the ECMH is the assumption that the stock market cannot be fooled because it always accurately reflects all corporate information relevant to the pricing of a security. Critical to the fraud-on-the-market theory is the assumption that the market can trade at "incorrect" prices due to "artificial" distortions caused by misstatements or omissions.
>
> Similarly, weak-form efficiency and the fraud-on-the-market theory as adopted by the Court are incompatible. The Court's version of the ECMH assumes that "the market price of shares traded on well-developed markets reflects all publicly available information, and, hence, any material misrepresentations." The weak form of the ECMH assumes merely that current share prices fully reflect whatever information is implied by historical share prices. If the market were only weak-form efficient, plaintiffs could not reasonably rely on the market price of a security to reflect all publicly available information about the relevant firm.
>
> Thus, if the market were as efficient as implied by the strong form of ECMH, plaintiffs could never be injured by relying on market prices, because such share prices would accurately reflect both public and nonpublic information. Similarly, if the market were only weak-form efficient, plaintiffs would not be entitled to the presumption of reliance provided by the fraud-on-the-market theory, because the weak form of the ECMH presumes that only historical information is incorporated in a firm's share prices; it does not presume that share prices reflect current public information. Thus, it seems clear that in *Basic* the Court, knowingly or not, embraced the semi-strong form of the ECMH. Several statements in the opinion echo phraseology of the semi-strong form of the ECMH and reinforce this conclusion.

Jonathan Macey and Geoffrey Miller, "Good Finance, Bad Economics: An Analysis of the Fraud-on-the-Market Theory," 42 *Stanford Law Review,* 1059 (April 1990). Do you agree with Macey and Miller? Can you formulate another argument based upon the language in *Basic*? Assuming that the Court has not adopted any particular form, which form should they adopt?

2. Economics of the EMH: Recall the discussion regarding the economics of EMH from above. In that discussion, information, market attributes, security type, and the issuer were identified as variables affecting market efficiency. Does the Court in *Basic* use any of these in its analysis? In fact, doesn't the Court assume that simply because Basic is traded on the NYSE its price must have been efficiently determined? Why is the Court so careless in its economic analysis when adopting a new theory to be used by lower courts?

3. *Economics of Information and the Market for Corporate Control:* The cost of obtaining new and valuable information is an important factor affecting market efficiency. Combustion Engineering invested substantial resources in identifying Basic as a potential merger target. Identification of merger targets is a valuable source of efficiency gains in capital markets. In effect, identifying targets is tantamount to identifying undervalued assets. Information regarding such undervalued assets represents an important source of property rights to the acquiror. When acquirors or their targets must reveal the presence of merger negotiations, competing acquirors are immediately alerted to the presence of an undervalued asset. The difference is that the newly alerted acquirors are able to free ride off the initial acquiror's investment in identifying the target. In a sense, release of this information severely diminishes the acquiror's property rights in information. If *Basic* makes it relatively more likely that potential mergers or takeovers will be revealed before consummation, it seems likely to have an adverse affect on the market for corporate control. (See the discussion of the importance of the market for corporate control in Chapter X.) In particular, potential acquirors will be reluctant to invest in identifying targets if other firms are allowed to free ride off its efforts. One might argue that, regardless of the impact on the market for corporate control, the managers and directors of Basic had a fiduciary duty to maximize shareholder wealth and thus to reveal material information regarding a potential merger when a failure to do so would be misleading under the circumstances. This raises the question of whether it is ever in the shareholders' wealth maximizing interest to have managers and directors withhold information that would have an immediate and positive impact on market price. From an *ex post* perspective its seems clear that a rule favoring release better serves the wealth maximizing interest of shareholders. In *Basic,* for example, the shareholders who sold out before news of the merger sold their shares at lower prices. A rule favoring release might have resulted in wealth gains to these shareholders. Therefore, by allowing recovery for the difference between the pre-announcement selling price and the merger price, the plaintiffs in Basic are better off *ex post*. However, it is important to remember that the fiduciary duties of managers and directors are, in effect, standard, off-the-rack, gap fillers to the corporate contract. Because voluntary mutually beneficial exchange maximizes wealth, it is reasonable to ask what fiduciary duties shareholders would bargain for in a fully specified contingent contract. That is, in order to identify the type of behavior expected from fiduciaries, we must utilize the hypothetical bargaining principle introduced earlier in this casebook. Most investors hold a portfolio of stocks. Because takeovers often result in positive economic returns, most shareholders desire to have as many firms in their portfolio taken over as is possible. Thus, *ex ante*, shareholders would prefer a rule that maximized the chance for takeovers. Therefore, it is reasonable to conclude that shareholders would bargain for a fiduciary duty that sometimes allowed managers to engage in strategic misrepresentations if such behavior improved the probabilities of takeovers. Moreover, shareholders would agree to this rule *ex ante* even though in some instances they might be worse off *ex post* because the expected gains from managers strategic misrepresentations outweigh expected *ex post* losses. What does this analysis suggest regarding the preferences of pro-disclosure shareholders toward securities regulations?

C. Risk, Return and Portfolio Diversification

Capital market history provides two general principles regarding the nature of risk and return. First, on average, there is a reward for bearing risk. Second, risk and potential return have a positive relationship. This potential reward, or return on investment, provides an incentive for individuals to invest money in capital markets. However, most individuals exhibit some degree of risk aversion. Thus, most investors do not take on as much risk as they possibly could even though the potential return for such activity is extremely large. Instead, the goal for many investors is to maximize the return on their investment at some comfortable level of risk or, in the alternative, to minimize risk for some target rate of return. Holding a diversified portfolio of assets is a method for achieving this result.

1. Measuring Risk and Return

The discussion of uncertainty and risk in Chapter IX yielded several measures of risk. Specifically, by calculating an expected value and comparing that result to actual values, we were able to estimate a variance and standard deviation. Variance and standard deviation are used as a measure of the potential dispersion of actual values around the expected value. Moreover, standard deviation measures the potential dispersion in the same units as the expected value. This dispersion around the expected value is used as a proxy for the riskiness of decisions made under uncertainty—greater uncertainty about the expected value increases this dispersion. These same tools are used in financial analysis in order to measure the risk of various financial assets.

The **expected return** on an investment is equal to the weighted average of possible returns.

$$E(R) = w_1(r_1) + w_2(r_2) + \ldots + w_N(r_N)$$

where w_i is the weight or probability of the return and r_i is the estimated return for all values of i. Consider, for example, the possible returns on some stock A in an economy that has three potential states of being. If the economy performs better than average next year, we predict that the return on A will be 26%. If the economy has an average year, the predicted return on A is 18%. If the economy performs below average, the predicted return on A is 16%. Moreover, we estimate that the probabilities of a good, average, or bad year are 30%, 40%, and 30%, respectively. Given the estimated probabilities for returns and states of the economy, the expected return on stock A is:

$$E(R_A) = .30(.26) + .40(.18) + .30(.16) = .198 \text{ or } 19.8\%$$

The **variance of return** on an investment is equal to the weighted average of squared deviations.

$$\sigma^2 = w_1(r_1 - E(R))^2 + w_2(r_2 - E(R))^2 + \ldots + w_N(r_N - E(R))^2$$

where σ^2 is the variance, w_i is the weight or probability of the return, r_i is the estimated return under that state, $E(R)$ is the expected return as calculated above. Thus, for stock A, the variance is:

$$\sigma^2 = .30(.26 - .198)^2 + .40(.18 - .198)^2 + .30(.16 - .198)^2 = .001716$$

Table XI-1

Economy	Probability	Stock A	Stock B	Eqally Weighted Portfolio of A & B
Good	30%	26%	20%	23%
Average	40%	18%	15%	16.5%
Bad	30%	16%	13%	14.5%
Return and Risk				
Expected Return		19.8%	15.9%	17.85%
Standard Deviation		4.14%	2.81%	3.47%

And, as before, the **standard deviation** is simply the square root of the variance. Thus, the standard deviation for returns on stock A is:

$$\sigma = .0414 \text{ or } 4.14\%$$

Consider the risk and return numbers on a second potential investment, stock B. During periods when the economy performs better than average, stock B earns a 20% return. During periods of average performance, stock B earns a 15% return. During a period of below average performance, stock B has a 13% return. As was the case with stock A, the probabilities of a good, average, or bad year are 30%, 40%, and 30% respectively. Given this information, the expected return on stock B is:

$$E(R_B) = .30(.20) + .40(.15) + .30(.13) = .159 \text{ or } 15.9\%$$

The variance and standard deviation for stock B are:

$$\sigma^2 = .30(.20 - .159)^2 + .40(.15 - .159)^2 + .30(.13 - .159)^2 = .000789$$

$$\sigma = .0281 \text{ or } 2.81\%$$

Relative to stock B, the expected return on stock A is 3.9% higher. However, the standard deviation on stock A is 4.14% compared to 2.8% on stock B. This indicates that increased risk must be assumed in order to earn the higher return. The decision to invest in either stock A or stock B will be based on the risk preference of a particular individual. Table XI-1 summarizes the return and risk information for stocks A and B.

Instead of placing all of one's money into a single asset, most individuals invest in a variety of assets. This collection of assets is known as a **portfolio**. **Portfolio theory** is concerned with the manner in which risk and return are affected by the particular assets in a portfolio. By returning to the analysis of stocks A and B, the risk and return relationships of portfolios can be studied. **Portfolio expected return** is the weighted average of the expected returns from each individual asset:

$$E(R_p) = w_A(E(R_A)) + w_B(E(R_B)) + \ldots + w_N(E(R_N))$$

where W_i is the percentage of the total value of the portfolio invested in a particular asset i. For example, consider an investor who places half of his total investment in stock A and the other half in stock B. The expected return on this portfolio would be:

$$E(R_p) = .50(.198) + .50(.159) = .1785 \text{ or } 17.85\%$$

The question of how to measure the riskiness of a portfolio remains. One's first inclination may be to calculate the weighted average variance or standard deviation across the assets in a portfolio. Following such a method, the variance and standard deviation for the portfolio of A and B would be calculated as follows:

Portfolio Variance = .50(.001716) + .50(.000789) = .0012525

Portfolio Standard Deviation = .0354 or 3.54%

Unfortunately, this method will generally not provide the correct answer. Rather, **portfolio variance** is calculated correctly using the following formula:

$$(\sigma_p)^2 = (w_A)^2 \, (\sigma_A)^2 + (w_B)^2 \, (\sigma_B)^2 + 2w_A w_B \rho_{AB} \sigma_A \sigma_B$$

where w_i is the portfolio weight, σ_i is standard deviation, and ρ_{ij} is the correlation coefficient for any two assets i and j. For portfolios with more than two assets, we calculate $(w_i)^2 \, (\sigma_i)^2$ for each asset and $w_i w_j \rho_{ij} \sigma_i \sigma_j$ for each possible combination of two assets and then sum the results. The **portfolio standard deviation** is the square root of the portfolio variance. For the portfolio of A and B, variance and standard deviation are:

$$(\sigma_p)^2 = (.50)^2 \, (.0414)^2 + (.50)^2 \, (.0280)^2 + 2(.50)(.50)(.995)(.0414)(.0281) = .00120512$$

$$\sigma_p = .0347 \text{ or } 3.47\%$$

Notice that portfolio risk (σ_p = 3.47%) is less than the weighted average risk of individual assets (3.54%). Thus, it appears that somehow risk can be reduced by combining assets in a portfolio. The explanation of this result is the focus for the remainder of this section. Simply note for now that the key to this explanation is the, as of yet unexplained, correlation coefficient ρ_{ij}. The relevant return and risk information for our equally weighted portfolio of A and B is summarized in Table XI-1.

2. Systematic and Unsystematic Risk

Risk is a function of uncertainty. Capital market risk is a function of the uncertainty surrounding a particular investment's future cash flows. Uncertainty regarding future cash flows can arise for a number of different reasons. These various sources of uncertainty lead to different types of risk. Such distinctions are important because not all risk-taking is rewarded in the same manner. The **total risk** on an investment is composed of both systematic and unsystematic risk.

Total Risk = Systematic Risk + Unsystematic Risk

The uncertainty surrounding future cash flows that arises from factors specific to a particular firm or small subset of firms is called **unsystematic risk, unique risk,** or **diversifiable risk.** Consider, for example, the uncertainty surrounding future cash flows at the Boeing and Merck Companies. Some of the uncertainty regarding each company's future cash flows stems from events specific to that company. What would happen to the future cash flows of these two companies if Boeing's employees were to go on strike? Clearly, the strike would have a negative impact on Boeing's future cash flows. However, it is unlikely that the Boeing strike will have any appreciable effect on Merck's future cash flows. Similarly, if Merck discovers a new wonder drug in the fight against cancer, one would expect the future cash flows of Merck to increase, while it is doubtful that Boeing's future cash flows would be affected by such an announcement. On the other hand, uncertainty regarding future cash flows may also be due to events that affect all companies. The part of an investment's future cash flows that are uncertain due to factors affecting the market as a whole are known as **systematic** risks, **market risks**, or **nondiversifiable risks.** Consider the effect on Boeing and Merck of a significant decline in economic growth. It is likely that the future cash flows of both of these companies would be adversely affected.

Now, consider an investor who has a portfolio composed of stock in both Boeing and Merck. Moreover, assume that the announcements regarding the Boeing strike and the Merck wonder drug are made on the same day. What would happen to the future cash flows attributable to the investor's portfolio? Maintain the previous assumptions that the strike will cause Boeing's future cash flows to decrease while Merck's discovery will cause its cash flows to increase. Thus, to some extent, by holding some of each of these stocks, our investor has offset the full effect of the announcements. This example illustrates the **principle of diversification**—a portfolio consisting of diversified assets has the potential to eliminate some of the risks associated with investments.

The announcement of a labor strike at Boeing and the discovery of a wonder drug at Merck are unsystematic risks because they are unique to the cash flow potential of those companies. In the preceding example, our investor was able to reduce unsystematic risk through the process of diversification. The occurrence of some type of systematic risk, such as a decline in economic growth, would reduce the future cash flows of both companies to a greater or lesser extent. Thus, the impact on the portfolio's future cash flows is clearly negative. This leads us to an important observation regarding systematic risk and portfolio diversification—systematic risks cannot be eliminated by diversification because a systematic risk affects all investments.

Consider Figure XI-4, displaying the relationship between standard deviation (or risk) and the number of different stocks in a portfolio. Notice that as the number of stocks in the portfolio increase, the riskiness of the portfolio declines. The effects of diversification are most pronounced during the initial addition of assets as indicated by the rather steep initial decline in risk. As more assets are added to the portfolio, it becomes more difficult to eliminate risk. This suggests

<u>Figure XI-4</u>

Eliminating Unsystematic Risk Through Diversification

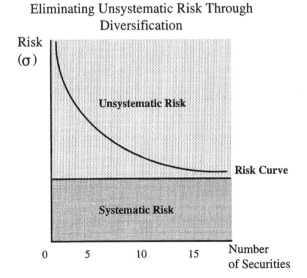

that the ability to eliminate risk through the process of diversification is limited. Specifically, it is limited by the presence of systematic risk.

Given this information, the question of why portfolio risk is generally less than the weighted average risk of each asset in the portfolio can now be addressed. The analysis of the unsystematic risk facing Boeing and Merck demonstrates that the prices of different stocks do not necessarily fluctuate in the same direction or in perfect unison. Statisticians describe this phenomenon by saying that the prices of stocks are not perfectly correlated. This effect is captured by the correlation coefficient (ρ_{ij}) in our portfolio variance equation.

Correlation coefficients measure the degree to which two variables tend to move together. The correlation coefficient between any two assets i and j is estimated by:

$$\rho_{ij} = COV_{ij} \div \sigma_i\sigma_j$$

where ρ_{ij} is the correlation coefficient, COV_{ij} represents the covariance between any two assets i and j, and $\sigma_i\sigma_j$ is the product of standard deviations for i and j. **Covariance** measures the relative dependence or independence for any two variables. Variables with positive covariation tend to move in the same direction; variables with negative covariation tend to move in opposite directions, and covariance of zero indicates that the two variables are independent. Correlation measures the strength of the covariance relationship. Covariance is estimated as the sum across all potential states of the products for the deviations of i and j weighted by the probability of that state of the world.

$$COV_{ij} = w_1[(r_i-E(R_i))(r_j-E(R_j))] + w_2[(r_i-E(R_i))(r_j-E(R_j))] + \ldots + w_N[(r_i-E(R_i))(r_j-E(R_j))]$$

where w_n represents the probability of each potential state n, r_i and r_j are the projected returns on assets i and j for state n, and $E(R_i)$ and $E(R_j)$ are the expected return for assets i and j. For our two stocks A and B, covariance is:

$$COV_{AB} = .30[(.26-.198)(.20-.159)] + .40[(.18-.198)(.15-.159)] + .30[(.16-.198)(.13-.159)] = .001158$$

thus, the correlation coefficient would be:

$$\rho_{AB} = .001158 \div (.0414)(.0281) = .995$$

This is exactly the number we used earlier as the correlation coefficient when we estimated the portfolio variance and standard deviation for a portfolio comprised of stocks A and B.

Correlation coefficients range from +1 to −1. Positive correlation coefficients indicate that two variables move to a greater or lesser extent in the same direction. A coefficient of +1 suggests perfect positive correlation, meaning that the variables move in the same direction in perfect unison. Negative correlation coefficients indicate that two variables move to a greater or lesser extent in opposite directions. A correlation coefficient of −1 demonstrates perfect negative correlation, meaning that the variables move to the same degree but in opposite directions. A correlation coefficient of zero is indicative of no relationship between two variables.

As long as stock prices are not perfectly correlated, portfolio risk will be less than the weighted average risk of the individual assets. Moreover, greater reductions in portfolio risk can be achieved as the correlation coefficient moves from

Figure XI-5

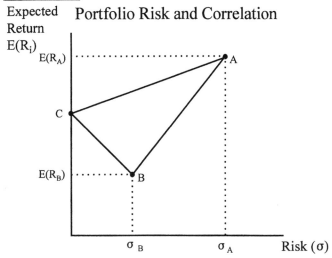

Expected Return $E(R_i)$ — Portfolio Risk and Correlation

+1 to −1. Theoretically, all non-systematic risk could be eliminated in a portfolio with perfect negative correlation. Figure XI-5 demonstrates diagrammatically, the relationship between correlation coefficients and portfolio risk reduction. Risk (σ) is measured along the horizontal axis and expected return is measured along the vertical axis. Earlier calculations found that stock A possessed greater risk and a higher expected return than stock B. Based upon these calculations, a portfolio composed entirely of stock A or B is denoted by points A and B, respectively. If we assume that A and B have perfect positive correlation ($\rho_{AB} = 1$), then both the risk *and* expected return for a portfolio comprised of A and B can be calculated as a simple weighted average. Thus, the line between points A and B would represent the risk and expected return for all possible combinations of a portfolio made up of A and B.

On the other hand, with perfect negative correlation ($\rho_{AB} = -1$), only the expected return on a portfolio of A and B would be a weighted average. The risk for a portfolio of A and B would be less than the weighted average because of a less than perfect positive correlation coefficient. For example, if A and B had perfect negative correlation, the expected risk and return for a portfolio containing 50% A and 50% B would be at point C in Figure XI-5. Point C demonstrates that for some combination of A and B under the assumption of perfect negative correlation, non-systematic risk can be eliminated entirely through diversification. Consider an investor who places 100% of his total investment in stock B. This investor can reduce the riskiness of his portfolio by substituting some of the riskier stock A for B. That is, by moving from B to C, the investor receives a higher expected return while reducing risk. All risk averse investors would choose point C over B because they would not have to pay for the higher return with increased risk. The risk return tradeoff for this investor would begin once he had more than 50% of his portfolio in stock A. This is denoted by movement from C to A. The optimal portfolio along line CA is determined by the individual investor's risk-return preferences.

First Alabama Bank of Montgomery v. Martin

Supreme Court of Alabama

425 So. 2d 415 (1983)

TORBERT, C. J.

This is a class action. The plaintiffs are beneficiaries of approximately 1,250 individual trusts, of which the bank is trustee. As trustee of these individual trusts, the bank invested certain assets comprising the principal of those trusts in participating units of two common trust funds, a bond fund and an equity fund.

After First Alabama purchased and sold certain units and made certain investments that resulted in substantial losses to those funds, the plaintiffs sought a declaration as to the duty of the bank and its liability to account, a declaration that certain investments were imprudent, and affirmative relief requiring the bank to restore to the common trust funds the losses sustained because of the bank's allegedly improper investments.

Prior to the certification of the class, First Alabama took the position that this action would require a full accounting of each of approximately 1,250 individual trusts. The trial court did not agree. After the original appeal to this Court,[1] First Alabama filed a delayed counterclaim, requesting a full accounting of its own acts as the trustee of the individual trusts. The court subsequently struck this counterclaim, without prejudice to First Alabama's right to maintain individual suits for an accounting.

The case then proceeded to trial on the issue of whether the bank was prudent or imprudent in the purchase or sale of thirty specified securities. Over First Alabama's objection, the trial court impaneled an advisory jury pursuant to Rule 39(c), ARCP, to aid the court in its determination of these issues.[2] The testimony was then heard orally by the trial court and the advisory jury. Special interrogatories requiring a "yes" or "no" answer were submitted to the advisory jury and, while it was unable to reach a unanimous verdict, as to the majority of issues it ruled ten to two against First Alabama.

At that time, the trial judge made his own findings of fact and on June 24, 1981, the court entered an order which found that the defendant as trustee of the common bond fund purchased the following debentures: ATICO Mortgage Investors, Barnett Mortgage Trust, Guardian Mortgage Investors, Justice Mortgage Investors, Midland Mortgage Investors, and Security Mortgage Investors. The trial court concluded that the purchase of these securities by the bank as trustee did not measure up to the "prudent man" standard and were, therefore, imprudent. Because it found the purchase of these securities imprudent, the court found it unnecessary to decide whether the sale of these securities also had been

---

1. This case was previously before this Court in an unsuccessful attempt by First Alabama Bank to appeal from the class certification. *First Alabama Bank of Montgomery, N.A. v. Martin,* 381 So. 2d 32 (Ala. 1980).

2. First Alabama had also filed several affirmative defenses dealing with the statute of limitations, laches, estoppel, release, and acquiescence. It was agreed that these issues would not be heard by the advisory jury, so additional evidence was heard on these issues, as well as to the extent of damages suffered by the plaintiffs, after the advisory jury was dismissed.

imprudent. These securities were Real Estate Investment Trusts (REIT's), as described later in this opinion.

In its order, the court also found that the bank as trustee of the common equity fund purchased stock of the following companies as investments for the common equity fund: American Garden Products; Ames Department Stores; Beverage Canners; CNA Financial; Elixir Industries; First Mortgage Investors; Hav-a-Tampa; Kinney Services; Loomis Corporation; Mortgage Associates; Transamerica Corporation; Universal Oil Products; Wynn Oil Co.; Associated Coca-Cola Bottling Company; Cox Broadcasting; Rust Craft Greeting Cards; and Sealed Power. The trial court concluded that the purchase of these securities by the bank as trustee did not measure up to the "prudent man" standard and were, therefore, imprudent. Because it found the purchases of these securities imprudent, the court found it unnecessary to decide whether the sale of these securities also had been imprudent.

The court also found that the bank as trustee of the common equity fund purchased the following securities: Allied Chemicals; Amfac; Blue Bell; Pabst Brewing Company; and Purolator. The court concluded that the bank's purchases of these securities did meet the "prudent man" standard but that their sale did not. The trial court concluded that both the purchase and the sale of Green Giant stock and Syntex stock were prudent. The court based its conclusions upon the test set out in Birmingham Trust National Bank v. Henley, 371 So. 2d 883 (Ala. 1979).

On August 19, 1981, the court ruled against First Alabama on all of its special and affirmative defenses, readopted its class action order of June 24, 1981, and ordered First Alabama to pay $1,226,798.00 into the bond fund and $1,426,354.88 into the equity fund. These sums represented the difference between the purchase and sales prices of the six bond fund securities and twenty-two of the equity fund securities. The bank was further ordered to pay interest on these sums.

At trial, the plaintiffs introduced evidence of a "common trust plan" that had been adopted by First Alabama and approved by the Comptroller of the Currency. Testimony showed that the essential investment purpose of the bond fund was to produce income and that the essential investment purposes of the equity fund were the appreciation of equity and production of income. The plan recognized that the valuation of the investments of the common trust funds would vary periodically and it had specific provisions as to how the funds would be valued quarterly to reflect the market value of investments. The evidence showed that the method of valuation was carefully spelled out in that plan, but that First Alabama did not follow that method.

I.   Evidence as to Imprudence of Investments in the Equity Fund.

In regard to the equity fund, the court found that the purchase of seventeen of the twenty-four designated equity fund securities had been imprudent. As to these seventeen securities, the court found it unnecessary to decide whether their sale was imprudent but did conclude that the sale of five of the remaining seven securities had been imprudent.

Evidence was introduced showing that in 1973 the board of directors of First Alabama reduced to writing what it considered to be minimum standards of safety. Al Byrne, the vice president and senior trust officer of the bank admitted, however, that these standards were followed prior to 1973 as unwritten guidelines and were generally so followed at the time in which the sales and purchases in question were made. These standards were: (1) A rating of B+ or better by the Standard and Poor ratings (S & P) (B+ being an average rating and B being a speculative rating); (2) a minimum of 1,500,000 shares of stock in the hands of the public; and (3) annual sales of at least $100 million. Byrne testified that the bank generally invested in companies with at least ten years' experience in business and a record of increased earnings. He stated that the companies would generally be rated by one of the rating services. First Alabama claimed that the bank's minimum standards were primarily designed for individual trusts, rather than common trust funds, yet Byrne stated that when purchases were made for the two common funds, bank policy required that those minimum standards adopted by the bank be followed. Evidence was also presented showing that deviations were permitted from these standards adopted by the board of directors with the approval of the trust investment committee so as to accomplish its goals.

The plaintiffs offered evidence that these standards had not been followed. For example, Associated Coca-Cola, Cox Broadcasting, Rust Craft Greeting Cards and Sealed Power were rated B+ but failed to meet the Bank's requirement of one hundred million dollars in annual sales. In addition, the following stocks failed to meet the minimum requirement of a B+ rating: American Garden Products; Ames Department Stores; Beverage Canners; CNA Financial; Exixir Industries; First Mortgage Investors; Hav-a-Tampa; Kinney Services; Loomis Corp.; Mortgage Associates; Transamerica Corp.; Universal Oil Products; and Wynn Oil Co.

Dr. Robert Johnston, chairman of the finance faculty of the School of Business of George Mason University and expert witness for the plaintiffs, testified that First Alabama, as trustee, should have invested defensively. According to Johnston, a trustee should first provide for the safety of the principal and then obtain an adequate return. He based his conclusions upon a treatise by Dr. Benjamin Graham, which stated seven criteria for testing the safety of investments. These criteria were (1) a minimum of $100 million in annual sales; (2) a current ratio of at least two to one (current assets should be twice current liabilities); (3) a net working capital to long-term debt ratio of at least one to one (net working capital being current assets less current liabilities and long-term debt meaning obligations that mature in more than one year); (4) earnings stability (positive earnings for the last ten years); (5) a good dividend record; (6) an earnings growth measure of at least one-third per share over a ten-year period, averaging the first three years and the last three years to remove extremes; (7) a moderate price earnings ratio of no more than fifteen to one; and (8) a moderate ratio of price to assets of no more than one and one half to one. Johnston believed that a trustee should not purchase stocks which failed to meet any one of these standards. Applying these standards, Johnston concluded that:

1. The purchase of the Allied Chemicals stock did not meet standards 6 and 7.

2. The purchase of the American Garden Products stock did not meet standards 1, 4, 5, 6, 7, and 8. The trial court concluded that the purchases of these stocks were imprudent.

3. The first purchase of Ames Department Stores stock failed standards 1, 5, 7, and 8. The second purchase of Ames Department Stores stock failed standards 1, 5, and 8. The trial court concluded that the purchases of these stocks were imprudent.

4. The first purchase of Amfac stock failed standard 3. The second purchase of Amfac stock failed standards 3 and 7. The third purchase of Amfac stock failed standards 2 and 3.

5. The purchase of Associated Coca-Cola stock failed standards 1, 2, 3, 5, 7, and 8. The trial court concluded that the purchases of these stocks were imprudent.

6. All four purchases of Beverage Canners stock failed standards 1, 4, 5, 6, 7, and 8. The trial court concluded that the purchases of these stocks were imprudent.

7. The first purchase of Blue Bell stock failed standard 8. The second purchase of Blue Bell stock passed all eight standards.

8. The purchase of CNA Financial stock failed standards 4, 5, and 6. The trial court concluded that the purchases of these stocks were imprudent.

9. Both purchases of Cox Broadcasting stock failed standards 1, 3, 5, 7, and 8. The trial court concluded that the purchases of these stocks were imprudent.

10. All three purchases of Elixir Industries stock failed standards 1, 2, 4, 5, 6, 7, and 8. The trial court concluded that the purchases of these stocks were imprudent.

11. The purchase of First Mortgage Investors stock failed standards 1, 5, 7, and 8. The trial court concluded that the purchases of these stocks were imprudent.

12. Both purchases of Green Giant stock satisfied all eight standards.

13. The purchase of Hav-a-Tampa stock passed all eight standards. The trial court concluded that the purchases of these stocks were imprudent.

14. The Kinney Services securities were convertible preferred securities and should not have been in the equity portfolio. The trial court concluded that the purchases of these stocks were imprudent.

15. Both purchases of Loomis stock failed standards 1, 3, 4, 5, and 6. The trial court concluded that the purchases of these stocks were imprudent.

16. The purchase of the Mortgage Associates stock failed standards 1, 4, 5, 6, 7, and 8. The trial court concluded that the purchases of these stocks were imprudent.

17. The purchase of the Pabst Brewing stock passed all eight standards.

18. The purchase of Purolator stock failed standards 7 and 8.

19. All four purchases of Rust Craft Greeting Cards stock failed standards 1, 2, 7, and 8. The trial court concluded that the purchases of these stocks were imprudent.

20. The purchase of Sealed Power stock failed standards 2, 3, 7, and 8. The trial court concluded that the purchases of these stocks were imprudent.

21. The first purchase of Syntex stock failed standards 7 and 8. The second purchase of Syntex stock failed standard 8.

22. The first purchase of Transamerica stock failed standards 6, 7, and 8 with standards 2 and 3 not being applied. The second and third purchases of Transamerica stock failed standard 6 with standards 2 and 3

not being applied. The trial court concluded that the purchases of these stocks were imprudent.

23. The first purchase of Universal Oil stock failed standards 2, 6, and 7. The second purchase of Universal Oil stock failed standards 2 and 6. The trial court concluded that the purchases of these stocks were imprudent.

24. The Wynn Oil stock failed standards 1, 4, 5, 6, 7, and 8. The trial court concluded that the purchases of these stocks were imprudent.

The bank, however, contested Johnston's opinion by testimony from Walter McConnell, an investment banker from New York, who stated that Graham's book was intended for amateurs and not trustees. Also, Johnston on cross-examination was forced to admit that only five of the thirty stocks in the Dow Jones industrial average would meet these criteria. Johnston did not believe that a trustee could protect the principal against inflation by investing in common stocks. However, he did believe buying stocks in an old established company which paid high dividends is better than investing in a new venture.

Walter McConnell, as an expert witness for the bank, listed various criteria to be applied in testing the soundness of an investment. Among these were the stability of the company, its financial soundness, its debt/equity ratio, the quality of its management, the company's product, and its standing in the industry. He testified that those criteria would not be affected by market cycles or ups and downs in the market. He stated that in his opinion the investments were prudent, though he could not say that his company had recommended the purchase of these stocks while he was an adviser.

McConnell testified that he believed a trustee must take inflation into account in making trust investments. He stated that the most popular approach was to invest in the very best companies, i.e., the best "growth" companies. The idea was that with companies whose earnings and dividends were growing faster than inflation one would be protected against inflation. Another approach, according to McConnell, was not as popular but was still used by some large banks. This approach was to buy stocks in companies that were not well known, i.e., not well recognized and which were selling at much lower prices than the stocks of better known companies. McConnell analyzed the twenty-four stocks at issue and concluded they had a faster growing rate than the general market, and their earnings were also growing faster than the general market, but they were selling at a lower price-earnings ratio. He concluded that First Alabama used a rational investment approach and that the purchases of these twenty-four stocks were prudent. He further testified that S & P ratings were not intended to be used as investment recommendations and that experienced analysts do not use S & P ratings as a guide to sound investments. He further testified that it would be imprudent to buy or sell solely because of the S & P ratings, because one would not be using judgment in his decisions. Evidence was also introduced showing that the S & P ratings were issued with a warning that they should not be used solely as market recommendations.

Eldon Davis, a former trust investment officer of the bank, who was the trust investment officer at the time the investments were made, testified for First Alabama by deposition. He stated that in 1971 and 1972 the stock market was very high. The "Favorite 50" stocks were selling at extremely high prices so he decided to seek out securities that were undervalued in relation to the higher priced ones. He further stated that he did not rely on prospectuses, because the SEC requires a prospectus to be "plastered with a high degree of risk," and "will not let you say anything good about the securities," i.e., will not allow a prospectus to make favorable forecasts or projections. He likewise stated that he saw little difference in stocks rated B, or speculative, and B+, or median, since the rating services "just don't understand the business they are in." It was Davis's opinion that it is best to buy securities in the growth cycle of a company and not after it has matured.

First Alabama also introduced evidence from brokers who had made recommendations as to the stocks in question. Yet, Davis stated that at no time were they recommended as "safe" investments. Evidence was also presented that the recommendations were from brokers who had an interest in inducing the purchase of the stock.

* * *

The principal issues to be determined on the merits of this case are whether the trial court erred (1) in finding that the bank acted imprudently in buying or selling the securities, and finding First Alabama to have breached its trust, (2) in assessing interest as a surcharge for imprudent investments, and (3) in ordering a distribution of money damages to the members of the class without identification of the recipients or calculation of their exact damages.

The standard to be followed in determining whether a trustee has breached his duty to the trust was stated in Birmingham Trust National Bank v. Henley, 371 So. 2d 883 (Ala. 1979):

"The general definition of a trustee's investment duties was first stated by the Supreme Court of Massachusetts in Harvard College v. Amory, 9 Pick, 446, 461, 26 Mass. 446, 461 (1830):

" 'All that can be required of a trustee to invest, is, that he shall conduct himself faithfully and exercise a sound discretion. He is to observe how men of prudence, discretion and intelligence manage their own affairs, not in regard to speculation, but in regard to the permanent disposition of their funds, considering the probable income, as well as the probable safety of the capital to be invested.'

"The Restatement of the Law of Trusts 2d, § 227 (1959), states the rule in the following language:

" 'In making investments of trust funds the trustee is under a duty to the beneficiary'(a) in the absence of provisions in the terms of the trust or of a statute otherwise providing, to make such investments and only such investments as a prudent man would make of his own property having in view the preservation of the estate and the amount and regularity of the income to be derived....' "

"BTNB is liable to the Trust in the Birmingham Realty matter only if it breached some duty to the Trust in refusing to make this investment at the time the decision was made. Was it an investment which a prudent man, managing his own affairs, would have made, based upon information then available? Liability cannot be based on the fact it subsequently developed that the investment would have been a good one. This is but the converse of the rule that a trustee is not liable if he makes an investment in a security which subsequently depreciates in value. III Scott on Trusts, § 204, supra, expresses the rule as follows:

" 'The failure to make a profit which does not result from a breach of trust does not subject the trustee to liability. Thus if by the terms of the trust he is permitted but is not directed to invest in certain securities, he is not liable for failure to make the investment, although the securities subsequently appreciate in value....' "The rule has also been summarized by Headley, Trust Investments, [97] Trusts & Estates 739 (1952), as follows:

" 'The first and all inclusive requirement of the law is that a trustee shall act with complete and undivided loyalty to his trust. Second is that a trustee shall act prudently in the selection and management of investments. The elements of prudence are:

" '(1) Care—a trustee must gather and weigh the facts and base his decisions on them rather than on rumor or guesswork;

" '(2) Skill—a trustee must exercise the skill of the average person as a minimum; and if he has more than average skill he must exercise such skill as he has;

" '(3) Caution—a trustee must not take chances which will imperil the accomplishment of the purposes of the trust.

" '...There must be balance between security of principal and amount and regularity of income; and the governing motive of the trustee must be sound investment for a long period and not speculation for a profit...'

"With specific reference to a trustee's investing in common stocks, this author says:

" '...They represent no promise to return a dollar amount to the investor; their dividends are dependent on earnings and the action of a board of directors; they have always afforded an attractive vehicle for speculation. Nevertheless some of them have demonstrated, over a long period of years, the qualities required for sound permanent investments. Intrinsic values have been maintained and dividends have been adequate and regular. The principal has been reasonably safe for a number of reasons: competent management, sound financing, position in an essential industry, a successful record and an adequate market....' "371 So. 2d at 894–96. Tested by this standard, we cannot say that the trial court committed reversible error in finding that the defendant did not fulfill its duty of caution, to preserve the trust corpus above all else, while striving for a regularity of income.

As to the imprudence of the equity fund, First Alabama contends that since Alabama is a "legal list" state, and since the beneficiaries had given their permission for the bank to invest in items not on the legal list, then the beneficiaries have no complaint for investments that have gone awry. This argument is without merit. As a trustee, First Alabama has a duty to preserve the trust property and make it productive. III Scott on Trusts § 227 (3rd ed. 1967).

First Alabama also contends that the only reason for holding it liable for the losses on the purchase and/or sale of the securities was that the ratings were below B+ on the S & P chart, and that the only reason for holding it liable for the losses on the REIT's was that there was no Moody's or similar rating. First Alabama asserts that to hold it liable here on such evidence would impose a duty upon trustees that would make them absolute insurers against a drop in market price. This, however, is not the case. First Alabama cannot be held liable for its failure to meet its own standards. This is only one factor in the decision. The evidence in this case supports the decision of the trial court that First Alabama failed to fulfill its primary responsibility which was to provide for the safety of the trust's principal. The secondary responsibility was to insure an adequate return.

The difference between speculation and investment is well described by Dr. Headley in Headley, Trust Investments, 97 Trusts & Estates 739 (1952), quoted above in the quotation from Birmingham Trust National Bank v. Henley, 371 So. 2d at 895. As Dr. Headley states, one who buys common stocks with the idea of selling them on the market for higher prices is speculating. One who is making a prudent investment examines the stocks' intrinsic values and purchases them for a long-term investment. Walter McConnell, testifying for the defendant, stated that one approach adopted by trust managers is to pick established stocks and not worry about subsequent turns in the market price. It is obvious that neither Headley's standards, nor those mentioned by McConnell, were consistently used by First Alabama.

Dr. Robert Johnston, an expert witness for the plaintiffs, also testified as to how a trustee should conduct his investments. Dr. Johnson stated that, in his opinion, trustees should invest defensively and protect the principal. He testified that most of the seventeen stocks later found to be imprudent investments would fail to meet his tests. While Walter McConnell, an expert witness for the bank, stated that he believed the purchases to be prudent, he could not say that he, as an investment adviser for a number of trust companies, had ever recommended the purchase of any of the twenty-four stocks at issue.

Finally, the testimony of Eldon Davis, who made the investments at issue, further strengthens the holding of the trial court. As stated above, Mr. Davis testified that he did not look at prospectuses, that he saw little difference between a stock rated B+, or median, and one rated B, or speculative, that he did not think the rating services understood their business, and that he tried to buy undervalued stocks instead of the higher priced, more established ones. All of this evidence, taken together, supports the holding of the trial court that First Alabama was imprudent with regard to purchases made for the equity fund.

We also find no error in the trial court's holding that the sale of the five stocks was imprudent. Even Eldon Davis testified in his deposition that he was against the sale of these stocks and had recommended that they be held. Mr. McConnell, testifying for First Alabama, stated that during the recovery period after the recession the five stocks all had higher recovery rates than the S & P 500. It seems reasonable to state that had these stocks not been sold at the bottom of the market, there would have been no loss. It is true that a trustee will not be held liable under ordinary circumstances for losses due to unforeseen depression or recession of the stock market. Yet, where the course of dealing of the trustee is such that it causes the loss, a trustee will be liable. First Nat. Bank of Birmingham v. Basham, 238 Ala. 500, 191 So. 873 (1939). Here, First Alabama sold these stocks at or near their lowest price levels, against the advice of its own trust officer, and at the time the country was just beginning to recover from the worst recession since the 1930's. We cannot hold as a matter of law that the trial court erred or was plainly and palpably wrong in its conclusion that a reasonable and prudent man would have held these stocks. We therefore affirm the trial court's decision that the sale of the five stocks was imprudent.

It does appear clear from the evidence before the trial court that the investment in six REIT's for the common bond fund was imprudent. The six REIT's were all three years old or less, they were not listed among the top REIT's in the country, and they were among the weakest of the nation's REIT's. They did not meet the standards of Al Byrne, Robert Johnston, and Kenneth Campbell, all experts in the case. Thus, we hold that the trial court committed no error in holding against First Alabama as to the purchase of the six REIT's.

First Alabama also insists that the trial court erred in ordering the bank to pay interest on the lost principal at a rate equal to one-year treasury bill rates. The defendant says that for it to have invested in treasury bills initially would have been improper, and for it now to be forced to calculate interest as if it had invested in this method will also be improper.

The rate and amount of interest is a matter within the sound discretion of the trial court to be determined by the circumstances of each case and should, at a minimum, restore to the beneficiaries the income they otherwise would have received. Pennsylvania Co. v. Wilmington Trust Co., 41 Del. Ch. 153, 189 A. 2d 679 (1963). By using the treasury bill rate, the court set out a readily determinable specific interest rate to be applied in each year. It is our opinion that the trial court did not abuse its discretion here.

Additionally, First Alabama argues that it was improper for the trial court to compound the interest paid on the lost principal on a quarterly basis. First Alabama cites Gordon v. Brunson, 287 Ala. 535, 253 So. 2d 183 (1971), where this Court held that an interest surcharge for breach of trust should be no more than the rate of return that would have been earned had the trustee properly performed his duties and that compound interest would be imposed only where there was an evil or corrupt intent. The defendant states that that case mandates that only simple interest be charged on the judgment. We do not agree.

In Alabama, a court of equity is authorized to mold its decree so as to adjust the equities of the parties and meet the necessities of each situation. Coupounas v. Morad, 380 So. 2d 800 (Ala. 1980); BBC Investment Co. v. Ginsberg, 280 Ala. 148, 190 So. 2d 702 (1966). Where a trustee makes an investment that is improper, it is equitable for the court to put the parties in the position they would have occupied except for the breach of trust. Here, the Bank as trustee of the Common Trust Fund was required to pay income quarterly to the individual trusts. Clearly the Bank as trustee of the individual trusts would have been under a duty to distribute or reinvest the income that should have been received. Since it is clear that such income was not distributed, we hold that the trustee would have been required to reinvest the same. Opinion of the Justices, No. 65, 244 Ala. 456, 13 So. 2d 559 (1943). First Alabama argues that Gordon, supra, mandates that only simple interest is due to the beneficiaries absent a finding of evil or corrupt intent on the part of the trustee. While we agree that a situation where the trustee is guilty of evil or corrupt intent is one situation where interest is compounded, it is clearly not the only one.

We find support for this result from several authorities. Scott indicates, "It has also been held that [the trustee] is liable for compound interest where it was his duty to reinvest interest received by him...." A. W. Scott, Law of Trusts § 207.2 (1967). The Restatement 2d of the Law of Trusts also supports this result:

"If the trustee is under a duty to reinvest interest received by him and accumulate if for the beneficiary, and fails to do so, he is chargeable with compound interest, since if he had not committed a breach of trust he would have received compound interest." Restatement (Second) of Trusts, Comments, § 207 (1959). Since we have held that the trustee would have been required to reinvest the income on the lost principal, it is clear that the trial court's order to compound interest and to make such computations on a quarterly basis is without error.

Finally, the defendant contends that the trial court ordered a distribution of the fund to the class members without identification of the members or of their exact loss. This is not the case. The evidence shows the names of the beneficiaries of the 1,250 trusts, all of which names are on file in First Alabama's computer. The order of the trial court sets out in detail how this calculation and distribution are to take place. Thus, we cannot agree with the defendant that the trial court was in error on this point.

After careful consideration of the many issues presented on appeal, this Court has determined that the trial court did not err in finding for the plaintiffs. We reaffirm the "prudent man rule," which states that a trustee must only exercise sound discretion, conduct himself faithfully, and manage funds entrusted to him as men of prudence, discretion, and intelligence would manage their own affairs, having due regard for the safety of the corpus and probable income. Harvard College v. Armory, 26 Mass. (9 Pick) 446 (1830). See also, Birmingham Trust National Bank v. Henley, 371 So. 2d 883 (Ala. 1979). We conclude that the trial court applied the "prudent man rule." Based upon the foregoing principles and the ore tenus rule, the finding of the trial court are due to be affirmed.

AFFIRMED

Notes and Questions

1. Portfolio Theory and the Duty of a Trustee: In *First Alabama*, the court uses a "prudent man" standard to evaluate the investment decisions of the trustees. The specific language of the "prudent man" standard invoked by the court contemplates an investor who avoids speculation and has concern for the probable income and safety of the investment. In the terminology developed in this chapter, the "prudent man" does not take unnecessary risks and considers the expected return and standard deviation of an investment. Does such a standard contemplate the use of portfolio theory and the principle of diversification? Did the *First Alabama* court utilize portfolio theory in its decision?

2. The Ore Tenus Rule: The court in *First Alabama* uses the *ore tenus* rule as a standard for reviewing the decision of a lower court. Under this rule, the reviewing court will affirm the decision of a lower court unless its findings are plainly and palpably erroneous. Evaluating the risk and return of an individual security from a portfolio will provide only limited information regarding the wisdom of purchasing that security. To investigate the reasonableness of selecting some security to add to a portfolio, the relationship between risk and return on that security *and* the other assets that make up the portfolio must be considered. In order to evaluate portfolio risk, the analyst needs to know something about the correlations of returns for the various assets in a portfolio. Should the failure to consider the risk and return relationship among the various individual securities in a portfolio be grounds for declaring a lower court's decisions plainly erroneous?

3. Investigating the Source of Portfolio Losses: Each of the participating trust funds into which the beneficiaries money had been invested lost over $1 million. Were these losses due primarily to systematic or unsystematic risks? In answering this question, what types of information would you consider to be relevant evidence? Can a trustee fail to be prudent even if all losses are attributable to systematic risk?

4. The Expert Testimony: Both the plaintiffs and defendants in *First Alabama* procure expert testimony as to the prudence of particular investments. Each of these experts enumerated a list of standards by which the prudence of an investment could measured. What types of risk do each of the standards used by the experts measure? Does either expert explain his analysis in terms of portfolio theory? Which expert's standards did you find most relevant in the determination of prudence?

D. Systematic Risk and the Capital Asset Pricing Model

There is a reward for bearing risk. However, there is no reward for unnecessarily bearing risk. Because unsystematic risk can be diversified away, market pricing does not generate a compensating risk premium for bearing such risk. In other words, regardless of the amount of total risk for any particular asset, the reward for holding a risky asset is a function of the systematic component only. Thus, in order to determine the return on an investment, some measure of systematic risk is needed.

1. Systematic Risk and Beta

Beta coefficients measure the systematic risk of an asset relative to the market as a whole. Measurements of the market are made by use of a market portfolio. A **market portfolio** is a portfolio comprised of all assets in the market. For practical applications involving financial analysis, the Standard and Poor's 500 Index is often used as a proxy for a market portfolio. Beta is estimated as the covariance of returns on some asset i with the returns on a market portfolio divided by the variance on the market portfolio. Formally,

$$\beta_i = \rho_{im}\sigma_i\sigma_m \div (\sigma_m)^2$$

where β_i represents the beta coefficient—systematic risk—for some asset i, $\rho_{im}\sigma_i\sigma_m$ represent the covariance of returns between some asset i and a market portfolio, and $(\sigma_m)^2$ denotes variance of returns on the market portfolio. Note that the covariance of returns on a market portfolio with itself is equal to the variance of returns on a market portfolio. Thus, the beta of a market portfolio is equal to the variance on a market portfolio divided by the variance on a market portfolio. That is, the beta on a market portfolio is equal to 1.

The systematic risk of a market portfolio is simply the average of systematic risk across all assets. Thus, the market portfolio with its beta of 1 represents average systematic risk. Thus, an asset with a beta of 2 has twice as much systematic risk as the average asset. On the other hand, an asset with a beta of 0.5 has half as much systematic risk as the average asset. Because the expected return on an asset is a function of systematic risk, it follows that assets with higher betas have greater expected returns.

The notion behind beta coefficients addresses the degree to which an asset's future cash flows are affected by systematic risk. In the previous section, we assumed that the possibility of a decline in economic growth represented systematic risk to both the Boeing and Merck Companies. That is, an announcement of declining economic growth would have a negative impact on the expected future cash flows of both companies. Beta coefficients measure the degree to which such an announcement would affect the future cash flows and, thus, the market value of a particular investment relative to the market as a whole. If the beta for a particular asset is greater than 1, then its market price would decline by more than those of a market portfolio upon the announcement of declining economic growth. The reverse is also true. If the beta for a particular asset is less than 1, then its market price would decline by less than those of a market portfolio upon the announcement of declining economic growth. Variations in the responsiveness to systematic risk among assets explains differences in the required rate of return among investments.

Consider two stocks Y and Z. Y has a standard deviation of 22% and a Beta of .75. Z has a standard deviation of 14% and a beta of 1.50. The total risk on stock Y (σ = 22%) is greater than that of stock Z (σ = 14%). However, the systematic risk of stock Z (β = 1.50) is greater than that of stock Y (β = .75). Thus, even though the total risk of Y is greater, the expected return on Z will be higher because its has more systematic risk. In other words, Y has more unsystematic, diversifiable risk than Z.

Combining assets in a portfolio also affects beta. Specifically, **portfolio beta** is the weighted average of betas in the portfolio:

$$\beta_P = w_A(\beta_A) + w_B(\beta_B)$$

where w_i is the percentage of the total value of the portfolio invested in a particular asset and β_i is the beta for that asset. Thus, for an equally weighted portfolio of stocks Y and Z the portfolio beta is:

$$\beta_P = .50(.75) + .50(1.50) = 1.125$$

This portfolio has greater than average systematic risk (β > 1). Consider the addition of some security X with a beta of 1.75 to this portfolio. If each of the assets continues to be equally represented, the portfolio beta becomes:

$$\beta_P = .33(.75) + .33(1.50) + .33(1.75) = 1.33$$

Thus, by adding an asset with more systematic risk than the portfolio average, the riskiness of the portfolio increases. The reverse is also true. That is, by adding an asset with systematic risk below that of the portfolio average, the riskiness of the portfolio declines. Thus, the risk of a well-diversified portfolio depends on the systematic risk of the assets that compose the portfolio.

2. The Security Market Line

The least risky of all possible investments are U.S. Treasury bills. This follows from the fact that time until maturity is very short and there is no possibility of default. In this sense, the return on a U.S. Treasury bill is unaffected by what occurs in the market. Thus, the beta on a U.S. Treasury bill is 0. Recall that a market portfolio has average systematic risk and, therefore, a beta of 1. Because of differences in the systematic risk of these two potential investments, investors require a different rate of return for each. Specifically, a higher rate of return is required as the systematic risk of an investment grows. In this subsection, the return-to-risk relationship is examined in greater detail.

Investors require that the return on U.S. Treasury bills cover the time value of money—the inflation rate—and provide them with some real return to cover transaction costs and provide a profit. Because the beta on U.S. Treasury bills equals 0, the expected return on such an investment is called the risk-free rate of return—denoted by r_f. Investors in a market portfolio require the same return provided on U.S. Treasury bills—r_f—plus some additional amount for bearing systematic risk. The expected return for bearing average systematic risk is denoted by r_m—the return on a market portfolio. The difference between the return on a market portfolio and the return on U.S. Treasury bills—$(r_m - r_f)$—is called the **market risk premium**. The **risk premium** on any given asset is the difference between the expected return on the asset and the risk-free rate of return, denoted by $r - r_f$. An asset's risk premium describes the return-to-risk component of the return on that asset.

Suppose that an investor is able to invest in U.S. Treasury bills or a market portfolio and borrow money at the risk free rate (r_f). Consider four possible combinations that such an investor might choose. First, if the investor placed all of her investment into a market portfolio, her investment would have a beta of 1 and an expected risk premium equal to $r_m - r_f$. Second, if she decides to place her entire investment into U.S. Treasury bills, her investment would have a beta of 0 and no market risk premium—$r_f - r_f = 0$. Third, suppose that the investor placed half of her investment into a market portfolio and the other half into U.S. Treasury bills. Given these proportions, the beta on the investor's portfolio would be:

$$\beta_p = .50(1) + .50(0) = .50$$

Moreover, the expected risk premium on the investment would be equal to:

$$r - r_f = .50(r_m - r_f) + .50(0) = .50(r_m - r_f)$$

Where $r - r_f$ is the expected risk premium and $r_m - r_f$ is the risk premium on the market portfolio. Fourth, consider what would happen if the investor borrowed enough money at the risk free rate to double her investment and placed it all into a market portfolio. The beta on her investment would equal:

$$\beta_p = 2(1) + -1(0) = 2$$

The expected risk premium on such an investment would equal:

$$r - r_f = 2(r_m - r_f) + -1(0) = 2(r_m - r_f)$$

Figure XI-6 plots each of these four potential investments with expected return on the vertical axis and beta on the horizontal axis. U.S. Treasury bills with a beta of 0 and expected return equal to the risk free return (r_f) are denoted by point A. The market portfolio with a beta of 1 and an expected return equal to the return on the market (r_m) is denoted by point B. The market risk premium is equal to the vertical distance between r_m and r_f. An investment composed of equal amounts of U.S. Treasury bills and a market portfolio had a beta of .5 and a market return of $.5(r_m - r_f)$—that is, its expected return was half way between

Figure XI-6

The Security Market Line

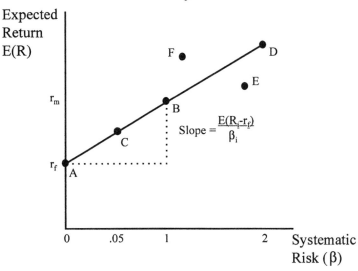

the risk free rate and the market rate. This investment is denoted by point C. The investment with double the investor's personal wealth—made possible by a loan—had a beta of 2 and a expected return equal to $2(r_m - r_f)$. This investment is denoted by point D.

Notice that each of these investments fall on a straight line. This line is known as the security market line. The **security market line** (SML) describes a relationship between beta or systematic risk and expected return on investment. The slope of any line is equal to the "rise" over the "run". For the SML, this means that the slope represents the amount of risk premium for a given amount of systematic risk. That is, it describes a return-to-risk ratio. Formally, the slope of the security market line and the **return-to-risk ratio** on any given asset is $(r - r_f) \div \beta$.

Each of the four possible investments is attainable by all investors. That is, investors can purchase any combination of U.S. Treasury bills and a market portfolio. Because of this, investors will not accept an investment that does not provide at least the same return-to-risk ratio as that provided by the SML. Thus, investments that fall below the SML—say, for example, point E in Figure XI-6—and offer a lower return-to-risk ratio will be sold. In an efficient market, such selling would cause the price of these investments to fall until the return-to-risk ratio is on the SML. Recall that asset price and return move in opposite directions. On the other hand, if an investment offered a greater return-to-risk ratio than investments made up of treasury bills and a market portfolio—such as point F in Figure XI-6—investors would bid the price of these assets up until their return-to-risk ratio fell to the SML. In an efficient market, buying and selling among investors guarantees that the return-to-risk ratio of all investments lies on the SML.

A market portfolio lies on the security market line, with a beta equal to 1 and a risk premium described by $r_m - r_f$. The market portfolio's return-to-risk relationship is equal to the slope of the SML. Thus, the slope of the SML is equal to:

$$\text{Slope of the SML} = (r_m - r_f) \div 1 = (r_m - r_f)$$

Because all assets in an efficient market must have a return-to-risk ratio that lies on the SML, the return-to-risk ratio for any asset can be described by the following relationship:

$$(r - r_f) \div \beta = (r_m - r_f)$$

which is equal to:

$$(r - r_f) = \beta(r_m - r_f)$$

Thus, the risk premium on any given asset in an efficient market is equal to the product of its beta and the market risk premium.

3. The Capital Asset Pricing Model (CAPM)

Throughout this chapter and Chapter IV on valuation, the notion of an expected return or required rate of return has been discussed (and used as a part of many formulas). Despite the extensive use of this variable, little information has been provided on its actual estimation. The **Capital Asset Pricing Model** (CAPM) is a tool used to estimate the expected return or required rate of return on an investment. CAPM can be derived by rearranging terms in the SML equation for estimating risk premiums on investments. Starting with:

$$(r - r_f) = \beta(r_m - r_f)$$

and adding r_f to each side, the CAPM is:

$$r = r_f + \beta(r_m - r_f)$$

In addition to allowing the calculation of specific expected returns, the CAPM also demonstrates that expected return on any given asset is a function of three important concepts. First, expected return accounts for the time value of money r_f. Second, expected return depends on the actual level of the market risk premium $r_m - r_f$. Third, expected return is a function of the actual systematic risk of an asset β.

Cede & Co. v. Technicolor, Inc.
Court Of Chancery Of Delaware, New Castle
1990 Del. Ch. Lexis 259

ALLEN

On January 24, 1983, MacAndrews and Forbes Group Incorporated ("MAF") (acting through a wholly owned subsidiary) completed the second step in its acquisition of Technicolor, Inc., a Delaware corporation. The transaction that occurred that day was a cash-out merger in which the 17.81% of the Technicolor common stock not owned by MAF was converted into a right to receive $23 in cash. The first step in this acquisition had been completed several weeks earlier by December 31, 1982, when MAF closed a public cash tender offer for up to all of the Technicolor common stock at $23.00. Both the merger and the predicate tender offer had been negotiated with and agreed to by the Technicolor board of directors, which was (with two arguable exceptions) free of any pre-existing entanglement or involvement with MAF or its principal stockholder, Ronald O. Perelman.

Pending in this court are two actions that arise out of that second-step merger. Plaintiff in each is Cinerama, Inc., the beneficial owner of some 201,200 shares of Technicolor common stock (4.4% of the outstanding stock). Cinerama elected to dissent from the merger and promptly filed the first of these actions which seeks a judicial appraisal of the fair value of its stock pursuant to Section 262 of the Delaware General Corporation Law.[1] The second action was filed on January 22, 1986. It is directed against individuals who comprised the Technicolor board of directors and against MAF and Mr. Perelman. This second action, in brief, claims that the directors have the burden to establish the entire fairness of the MAF acquisition and that they cannot do so because neither the process they followed nor the $23 price they endorsed was fair to Cinerama as a Technicolor shareholder. Specifically, it alleges that the Technicolor board was negligent in its dealing with Mr. Perelman, acted without proper inquiry or information and in some respects had conflicting interests that allegedly affected its actions. It is also alleged that disclosures made in connection with the tender offer and the merger were inadequate or misleading and that Mr. Perelman had complicity for these alleged lapses and independently violated a duty he owed to the plaintiff at the time of the merger. Finally, it is claimed that the merger was not properly authorized by the board and that that fact was covered up. This second action (the personal liability action) seeks rescissory damages in the amount of $162 per share.

The two cases were consolidated for trial. Evidence was taken from 21 witnesses over the course of 47 extended days of trial. This opinion reflects the decision of the court on the issues raised in the first of these cases, which requires an appraisal of the "fair value" of petitioner's Technicolor stock "exclusive of any element of value arising from accomplishment or expectation of the merger." 8 Del. Code Ann. § 262(h).

The evidence in the appraisal case was structured around the elaborate testimony of dueling experts. Each expert employed a discounted cash flow analysis of Technicolor as of January 24, 1983, but significant methodological and input differences yielded radically different estimates of value. Petitioner's expert was Mr. John Torkelsen, a financial analyst in his own firm, Princeton Venture Research ("PVR"). He opined, for reasons in part described below, that his best estimation of the statutory fair value of Technicolor on a per share basis as of January 24, 1983 was $62.75. Respondent's principle expert was Professor Alfred Rappaport of Northwestern University Graduate Business School who also functions in a consulting firm, Alcar. Professor Rappaport stated his opinion that the statutory fair value of Technicolor on a per share basis as a going concern at the time of the merger was $13.14. The dynamics of litigation no doubt contribute to this distressingly wide difference.

For the reasons set forth below I conclude, attempting to consider all pertinent factors as of the date of the merger, exclusive of elements of value arising from the expectation or accomplishment of the merger, and acting within the confines of the record created by the parties at trial, that the fair value of a share of Technicolor stock for purposes of appraisal was $21.60...

---

1. Cinerama's stock was held in street name through the nominee Cede & Co., which is therefore a nominal but necessary party to the appraisal action.

I.

Ronald Perelman's leveraged acquisition of Technicolor in the two-step transaction agreed upon on October 29, 1982, by the Technicolor board must rank as one of the most successful change of corporate control transactions in a decade that was to become first crowded and later littered with such transactions. MAF's $23 cash price represented a large (more than 100%) premium over the September 1982 market prices of Technicolor's stock. The $105 million stock acquisition cost was funded almost entirely with bank credit and other borrowings. Upon acquiring control of the company Mr. Perelman and his associates, Bruce Slovin and Robert Carlton began to dismember what they saw as a badly conceived melange of businesses. Within one year these entrepreneurs had sold several of those businesses for approximately $55.7 million in cash ($11 per share) and paid about half of the bank debt used to acquire the company. Remarkably, the sale of these businesses did not significantly alter Technicolor's positive cash flow. The remaining businesses (including importantly Technicolor's traditional business of theatrical film processing and a new business of producing videocassette under contract with copyright owners) were apparently thereafter managed with skill and good luck.

As modified during the course of MAF's ownership, Technicolor was later sold in an arm's length transaction to Carlton, PLC in 1988 for some $738 million in cash. In the annals of the effective uses of leverage, the account of MAF's original minimal cash contribution to the acquisition of Technicolor certainly deserves a place.

   *   *   *

C. Technicolor's Stock Price

Technicolor's stock was traded on the New York Stock Exchange. It was widely held. There was no control block, or even any large stockholders...

On June 30, 1978, the end of its 1978 fiscal year, Technicolor's stock was trading on the New York Stock Exchange at $7.75. The following year, Technicolor's consolidated net income grew, climbing from $3.5 million in FY1978 to $7.9 million in FY1979. The company experienced a corresponding increase in its stock price to $10.333 on June 30, 1979. Consolidated net income more than doubled again in FY1980 to more than $17 million. Of that amount, however, about $9 million reflected the value of silver recovered from film processing. (Silver prices — and silver recovery profits — soared during the period because of an attempt by the Hunt Brothers to corner the silver market). Technicolor's stock price rose during that period, reaching $24.667 by June 30, 1980. The benefit from high silver reclamation profits was short-lived, however, as the silver market subsided in 1981.

Despite receiving abnormally high profits from the sale of silver in FY1981, Technicolor's consolidated net income stagnated during that period. As earnings stagnated and silver began to fall, Technicolor's stock, which reached a high of $28.50 on April 7, 1981, began to decline.

On June 4, 1981, Technicolor announced its decision to enter the One Hour Photo business. At the time of the announcement, Technicolor's stock was trading at $22.13. The stock market's reaction to the announcement was negative. By July 7, Technicolor's stock price had fallen to $18.63. The decline continued during the balance of 1981 and in 1982 as the company struggled and experienced a further drop in earnings. On June 30, 1982, the stock closed at $10.37. In September 1982, it reached $8.37 and at the end of that month stood at $11.25.

II. A Preliminary: A Note on Judicial Method In this Appraisal Proceeding

In this case the expert opinions on value cover an astonishing range. Two experts looking at the same historic data and each employing a discounted cash flow valuation technique arrive at best estimates as different as $13.14 per share and $62.75 per share.[2]

In many situations, the discounted cash flow technique is in theory the single best technique to estimate the value of an economic asset. Prior to our Supreme Court's decision in Weinberger v. U.O.P. however, that technique was not typically employed in appraisal cases in this jurisdiction. But with Weinberger's implicit encouragement this technique has become prominent. The DCF model entails three basic components: an estimation of net cash flows that the firm will generate and when, over some period; a terminal or residual value equal to the future value, as of the end of the projection period, of the firm's cash flows beyond the projection period; and finally a cost of capital with which to discount to a present value both the projected net cash flows and the estimated terminal or residual value.

*   *   *

While the basic three-part structure of any two DCF models of the same firm, as of the same date, will be the same, it is probably the case (and is certainly true here) that the details of the analysis may be quite different. That is, not only will assumptions about the future differ, but different methods may be used within the model to generate inputs. This fact has a significant consequence for the way in which this matter is adjudicated. Sub-parts of the DCF models used here are not interchangeable. With certain exceptions, each expert's model is a complex, interwoven whole, no part of which can be removed from that model and substituted into the alternative model.[3]

*   *   *

An appraisal action is a judicial, not an inquisitorial, proceeding. The parties, not the court, establish the record and the court is limited by the record created. The statutory command to determine fair value is a command to do so in a judicial proceeding, with the powers and constraints such a proceeding entails. Accepting that the expert testimony has been so structured as to largely foreclose the court from accepting parts of one DCF model and sections of the other, it follows that the court must decide which of the two principal experts has the greater claim overall to have correctly estimated the intrinsic value of Technicolor stock at the time of the merger. Having decided that question, it will be open to me to critically review the details of that expert's opinion in order to determine if the record will permit, and judicial judgment require, modification of any inputs in that model. What the

---

2. A significant part of this difference is accounted for by the differing discount rates used in the DCF models. If one substitutes the higher discount rate used by respondent's principal expert for the lower rate used by petitioner's expert and makes no other adjustment to either DCF model the difference reduces from $49.61 a share to $20.86...

3. The most notable exceptions are, the cost of capital component and, the long-term debt figure. They are free standing and may be adjusted without affecting other aspects of the model.

record will not permit is either a completely independent judicially created DCF model[4] or a pastiche composed of bits of one model and pieces of the other.

III.

The estimation of the fair value as of January 24, 1983, of Technicolor of Professor Rappaport is, in my considered opinion, a more reasonable estimation of statutory fair value than is the alternative valuation of petitioner's expert. In reaching that judgment I have considered a large number of factors, none of which was itself decisive. Together these factors point overwhelmingly to this conclusion.

*   *   *

C. Discounting With the Cost of Capital

The cost of capital supplies the discount rate to reduce projected future cash flows to present value. The cost of capital is a free-standing, interchangeable component of a DCF model. It also allows room for judicial judgment to a greater extent than the record in this case permits in other areas of the DCF models.

Professor Rappaport used the Capital Asset Pricing Model (CAPM) to estimate Technicolor's costs of capital as of January 24, 1983. That model estimates the cost of company debt (on an after tax basis for a company expected to be able to utilize the tax deductibility of interest payments) by estimating the expected future cost of borrowing; it estimates the future cost of equity through a multi-factor equation and then proportionately weighs and combines the cost of equity and the cost of debt to determine a cost of capital.

The CAPM is used widely (and by all experts in this case) to estimate a firm's cost of equity capital. It does this by attempting to identify a risk-free rate for money and to identify a risk premium that would be demanded for investment in the particular enterprise in issue. In the CAPM model the riskless rate is typically derived from government treasury obligations. For a traded security the market risk premium is derived in two steps. First a market risk premium is calculated. It is the excess of the expected rate of return for a representative stock index (such as the Standard & Poor 500 or all NYSE companies) over the riskless rate. Next

---

4. For good reasons aside from technical competence, one might be disinclined to do so. Simply to accept one experts' view or the other would have a significant institutional or precedential advantage. The DCF model typically can generate a wide range of estimates. In the world of real transactions (capital budgeting decisions for example) the hypothetical, future-oriented, nature of the model is not thought fatal to the DCF technique because those employing it typically have an intense personal interest in having the best estimates and assumptions used as inputs. In the litigation context use of the model does not have that built-in protection. On the contrary, particularly if the court will ultimately reject both parties DCF analysis and do its own, the incentive of the contending parties is to arrive at estimates of value that are at the outer margins of plausibility—that essentially define a bargaining range. If it is understood that the court will or is likely to accept the whole of one witnesses testimony or the other, incentives will be modified. While the incentives of the real world applications of the DCF model will not be replicated, at least the parties will have incentives to make their estimate of value appear most reasonable. This would tend to narrow the range of estimates, which would unquestionably be a benefit to the process.

the individual company's "systematic risk"—that is the nondiversified risk associated with the economy as a whole as it affects this firm—is estimated. This second element of the risk premium is, in the CAPM, represented by a coefficient (beta) that measures the relative volatility of the subject firm's stock price relative to the movement of the market generally. The higher that coefficient (i.e., the higher the beta) the more volatile or risky the stock of the subject company is said to be. Of course, the riskier the investment the higher its costs of capital will be.

The CAPM is widely used in the field of financial analysis as an acceptable technique for estimating the implicit cost of capital of a firm whose securities are regularly traded. It is used in portfolio theory and in capital asset budgeting decisions. See generally R. Brealey & S. Myers, Principles of Corporate Finance (3d ed. 1988) at pp. 47–66 and 173–196; V. Brudney & M. Chirelstein, Corporate Finance (3d ed. 1987) at pp. 75–113. It cannot, of course, determine a uniquely correct cost of equity. Many judgments go into it. The beta coefficient can be measured in a variety of ways; the index rate of return can be determined pursuant to differing definitions, and adjustments can be made, such as the small capitalization premium, discussed below. But the CAPM methodology is certainly one of the principle "techniques or methods...generally considered acceptable [for estimating the cost of equity capital component of a discounted cash flow modeling] in the financial community..." Weinberger v. UOP, Inc. See, e.g., Northern Trust Co. v. C.I.R., 87 T.C. 349, 368 (1986).

In accepting Professor Rappaport's method for estimating Technicolor's costs of capital, I do so mindful of the extent to which it reflects judgments. That the results of the CAPM are in all instances contestable does not mean that as a technique for estimation it is unreliable. It simply means that it may not fairly be regarded as having claims to validity independent of the judgments made in applying it.

With respect to the cost of capital aspect of the discounted cash flow methodology (in distinction to the projection of net cash flows and, in most respects, the terminal value) the record does permit the court to evaluate some of the variables, used in that model chosen as the most reasonable of the two (i.e., Professor Rappaport's) and to adjust the cost of capital accordingly. I do so with respect to two elements of Professor Rappaport's determination of costs of equity for the various Technicolor divisions. These businesses were all (excepting One Hour Photo, Consumer Photo Processing and Standard Manufacturing) assigned a cost of equity of 22.7% and a weighted average cost of capital of 20.4%. The remaining businesses were assigned a cost of equity of 20.4% and a weighted average cost of capital of 17.3%.

In fixing the 22.7% cost of equity for film processing and other businesses Professor Rappaport employed a 1.7 beta which was an estimate published by Merrill Lynch, a reputable source for December 1982. That figure seems intuitively high for a company with relatively stable cash flows. Intuition aside, however, it plainly was affected to some extent by the striking volatility in Technicolor's stock during the period surrounding the announcement of MAF proposal to acquire Technicolor for $23 per share. Technicolor stock rapidly shot up to the $23 level from a range of $9 to $12 in which it traded for all of September and the first week of October. Technicolor stock was thus a great deal more volatile than the market during this period. Applying the same measure of risk— the Merrill Lynch published beta—for September yields a significantly different beta measurement: 1.27. Looking at other evidence with respect to Technicolor betas I conclude that 1.27 is a more reasonable estimate of Technicolor's stock beta for purposes of calculating its cost of capital on January 24, 1983, than 1.7, even though that latter figure represents a December 1982 estimation.

The second particular in which the record permits and my judgment with respect to weight of evidence requires a modification of Mr. Rappaport's cost of capital calculation relates to the so-called small capitalization effect or premium. This refers to an unexplained inability of the capital asset pricing model to replicate with complete accuracy the historic returns of stocks with the same historic betas. The empirical data show that there is a recurring premium paid by small capitalization companies. This phenomena was first noted in 1981 and has been confirmed. The greatest part of the additional return for small cap companies appears to occur in January stock prices. No theory satisfactorily explaining the phenomena has been generally accepted.

Professor Rappaport classifies Technicolor as a small capitalization company and expressed the view that its cost of equity would include a 4% premium over that generated by the CAPM.

The question whether the premium can be justified in this instance is difficult because of the inability of academic financial economists to generate an accepted theory of the phenomena. While Technicolor may qualify as a small cap company, the particulars of its situation are different from many small cap companies. It was an old, not a new company. It existed in a relatively stable industry—motion picture film processing. That industry was an oligopoly and Technicolor was a leader. It had "brand name" identification. Do these distinctive characteristics that Technicolor had in common with many giant capitalization companies, matter at all in terms of the "small cap" anomaly? One cannot say. Yet the impact of a 4% increase in the cost of equity (yielding a 3.44% increase in the cost of capital of the Film Processing & Videocassette divisions) would be material to the value of the company and the appraisal value of a share. In these circumstances, I cannot conclude that it has been persuasively shown that the statutory fair value of Technicolor stock would more likely result from the inclusion of a small capitalization premium than from its exclusion. In this circumstance, I conclude it should not be considered.

Thus, in summary, I find Professor Rappaport's calculation of a cost of capital follows an accepted technique for evaluating the cost of capital; it employs that technique in a reasonable way and, except for the two particulars noted above, in a way that is deserving of adoption by the court. Applying these adjustments they lead to a cost capital of 15.28% for the main part of Technicolor's cash flow and 14.13% for the One Hour Photo related cash flows.

Mr. Torkelsen suggests a range of discount rates from 9.96% (weighted average cost of capital of MAF) to 15% (the average cost of capital for all manufacturing companies). He uses a 12.50% rate (an average of these two) to generate the $62.75 figure which he presents as his best estimation of value. This technique of estimating a discount rate is decidedly less reliable than Professor Rappaport's technique. It is not an acceptable professional technique for estimating Technicolor's cost of capital to look to the cost of capital (CAPM derived) of the acquiring company. Mr. Torkelsen's alternative of the average of all industrial concerns is far too gross a number to use except where no finer determination is feasible, which is not the case here.

D. Corroborative Indicia of Value

(a) Stock Price

The only more or less objective indicia of value is the market for Technicolor shares. Market prices are of course not conclusive of "intrinsic value" but they may have pertinence in attempting to estimate that value.

In Application of Delaware Racing Assoc., 213 A.2d 203, 211 (1965) the Delaware Supreme Court said, with respect to the market value of shares for which an appraisal was sought:

> It is, of course, axiomatic that if there is an established market for shares of a corporation the market value of such shares must be taken into consideration in an appraisal of their intrinsic value. Chicago Corporation v. Munds, 20 Del. Ch. 142, 172 A. 452. And if there is no reliable established market value for the shares a reconstructed market value, if one can be made, must be given consideration. Tri-Continental Corp. v. Battye, supra. It is, of course, equally axiomatic that market value, either actual or constructed, is not the sole element to be taken into consideration in the appraisal of stock.

Market price of a traded security must always be evaluated to ascertain the degree of weight it deserves in an appraisal. In some cases it will deserve very little weight: where, for example, as in a recent case, a control block of stock renders the stock market capitalization an especially poor measure of the corporation's value. See also Bell v. Kirby Lumber Corp., Del. Supr., 413 A.2d 137 (1980) (control block present).

In this instance the market place of Technicolor's stock is one important factor of several indicating that Professor Rappaport's valuation is a more reasonable estimation of statutory fair value than is Mr. Torkelsen's. The stock was traded on the New York Stock Exchange. The market was a relatively active one. The stock price showed trends that appear related to the company's underlying economic performance and prospects. Thus, while we are directed to consider "all relevant factors" and can in no instance rest an appraisal upon a market price alone, those prices are undoubted relevant in this case.

The market price following announcement of the MAF transaction (and certainly following closing of the MAF tender offer) was quite obviously not reflecting a proportionate interest in a going concern but was supported by the prospect of a $23 cash payment at or near the merger date. It was the price unaffected by the merger that has relevance here (that relevance is not affected, as it theoretically could be, by intervening changes in the business of Technicolor, or markets within which it operated, as I conclude that there were no such material changes). That market price was, from June through September floating in a range roughly between $9 and $11 per share. After the first week of October it began to climb. It moved from $11.875 on October 8 to $17.375 on October 27.

I here employ the market price data not as an independent source of valuation but as corroboration of the judgment that Professor Rappaport's valuation is a reasonable estimation of intrinsic value of Technicolor as of January 24, 1983, exclusive of elements of value arising from expectation or accomplishment of the merger, and Mr. Torkelsen's is not.

This market price history, itself, makes implausible but not impossible the correctness of Mr. Torkelsen's opinion that Technicolor had an inherent value of $62.75 on January 24, 1983. The assertion by petitioner that the stock price of Technicolor prior to the announcement of the MAF deal is irrelevant, because of the changes in the company observable by January 24, 1983 due to the "Perelman plan" is rejected for two reasons. First, even if one accepts that petitioner is entitled to a pro rata share of value created by the "Perelman plan" it would not render the earlier stock price irrelevant. The Perelman plan did not radically transform the company in a twinkling. Its immediate financial effect on value was modest.

Secondly, in my opinion, petitioner is entitled to the "going concern" value of Technicolor. This means it is not entitled to share in value created by MAF in the circumstances of this case. Therefore the earlier stock price remains one relevant consideration in valuing "what petitioner was deprived of by the merger."

(b) Corroborative Indicia of Value: The decision of knowledgeable insiders to accept $23...

The Technicolor insiders (especially Mr. Kamerman [Technicolor's CEO]) had substantial ownership interests that were personally important to them. It is safe to say that no one knew more about Technicolor as a going concern than Mr. Kamerman. The allegations that he had a dominating conflicting interest in the transaction are unpersuasive. As will be more fully set forth in the forthcoming opinion in the personal liability case, the contract that was negotiated concerning his employment cannot be seen in context as presenting a real incentive to support the acquisition, if he thought substantially more might be achieved elsewhere.

If petitioner's expert was close to correct in his opinion on value, the opportunity cost involved in the sale of the company was enormous. Yet knowledgeable officers and directors all sold their stock for $23 per share. This fact while itself not conclusive is relevant in concluding that as of January 24, 1983, sophisticated, knowledgeable persons would not have concluded that Technicolor stock had an inherent value of $62.75 (or $48.89 or $91.00, being other numbers that Mr. Torkelsen mentions as fallbacks by using differing capitalization rates).

       *   *   *

For the foregoing reasons, I conclude that Professor Rappaport's model presents a reasonable method to estimate the value of Technicolor on January 24 under either the assumption that the entity he valued is subject to the business plan of the Kamerman management, or that of the Perelman management; that the value of the Kamerman managed company as of January 24, 1983, is the relevant value here; that Professor Rappaport's opinion as to value is far more likely then that of Mr. Torkelsen to correctly estimate the fair value of Technicolor, excluding value arising only from the expectation or accomplishment of the merger, as of the date of the merger; and that that estimate of value as modified by adjustment to the discount rate as indicated above and to the long-term corporate debt figure, is reasonable and is determined as the fair value, as defined in our statute, of a share of Technicolor stock on that day. That value is $20.48 (see Stipulation of August 16, 1990) plus $1.12 adjustment for long-term debt or $21.60 per share.

Notes and Questions

1. Subjectivity in CAPM: The *Technicolor* court notes that despite the quantitative nature of CAPM, subjectivity does enter the estimations. On the basis of their experience, each of the experts in this case made subjective decisions regarding the appropriate proxy for a market portfolio and the selection of beta and a risk free rate of return. However, the court is careful to recognize that despite presence of subjectivity, estimations using the CAPM technique are reliable. In other words, estimations made by CAPM are only as good as the selection of inputs.

2. Selecting the Appropriate Beta: Much of the court's analysis surrounding the estimation of an appropriate cost of capital or discount rate involves the selection of an appropriate beta. In this regard, note that the goal is to estimate the going concern value as of January—that is, the going concern value on the date of the cash-out merger. Moreover, estimations of going concern value were to be "exclusive of any element of value arising from the accomplishment or expectation of the merger." The defendant's expert (Rappaport) used a beta of 1.7 which was published by Merrill Lynch in December. The court rejects this beta and opts for a beta of 1.27 published by Merrill Lynch in September. This rejection is based on the fact that the December beta reflected stock price volatility due to the announcement of the merger. In fact, the merger announcement caused the stock price to rise by over 100%. In light of the court's rationale and the stock price history, was the court's adjustment to beta appropriate?

3. Arbitrage Pricing Theory: CAPM estimates the expected return on a security as a function of a single risk factor—systematic risk. However, some empirical evidence suggests that the expected return on a security is a function of multiple risk factors. **Arbitrage pricing theory** (APT) is a model for estimating expected returns based on multiple risk factors. APT is estimated by:

$$r_i = r_f + \beta_{1i}(E(R)_1 - r_f) + \beta_{2i}(E(R)_2 - r_f) + \ldots + \beta_{Ni}(E(R)_N - r_f)$$

where r_i is the expected return on security I, r_f is the risk free rate of return, $(E(R)_n - r_f)$ is the risk premium on some risk factor n, and β_{ni} is the sensitivity of r_i to risk factor n. In contrast to the CAPM which specifies systematic risk as the only relevant risk factor, APT does not specify what the relevant risk factors for any particular security should be. Thus, the relevant risk factors for different securities may vary. For example, the return on some securities may be sensitive to industrial production. On the other hand, industrial production may have no effect at all on some other set of securities. Moreover, asset return may or may not be related to systematic risk under APT. Use of APT is not nearly as widespread as CAPM. However, it is used on occasion and represents a serious critique of CAPM. Thus, it is important to be familiar with its principles and properties.

4. Return to First Alabama Bank: One of the secondary issues discussed in the *First Alabama* opinion is the appropriate interest rate to apply on the lost principal. Several alternatives are discussed in the opinion, with the selection ultimately based on precedent and equity. An alternative solution to this problem would have been to estimate an appropriate return by using CAPM.

5. The Small Capitalization Adjustment: Rappaport makes an adjustment to the return generated by his CAPM analysis. Specifically, he adds 4% to the required return because he considers Technicolor to be a small capitalization company. Why is the small capitalization factor not captured by CAPM? Based on its own analysis, the court concludes that Technicolor cannot fairly be characterized as a small capitalization company. Thus, it rejects Rappaport's "small cap" premium. Do you agree with the court's decision? If the parties to the suit had a chance to present evidence on this issue, would this question have been resolved in the same manner?

6. Corroborative Indicia of Value: In addition to its own reasoning, the court uses both Technicolor's stock price and the decision of insiders to tender their shares as further evidence in support of Rappaport's testimony. One of the fundamental lessons of economics is the importance of an objectively determined market price. How could the plaintiff's expert have ignored the market price? What assumptions must one make when ignoring a market price? Does the court take appropriate account of the market price? Furthermore, notice that the court's analysis concerning the decision of insiders to tender their shares is inherently based on the assumption that individuals are rational, evaluative maximizers.

E. Event Study Methodology

Event studies are an empirical methodology developed by financial economists to measure the impact of new information on expectations regarding a firm's future cash flows. The theoretical arguments behind the EMH and CAPM provide the foundation for event study methodology. Specifically, event studies take advantage of semi-strong form market efficiency. Semi-strong form efficiency suggests that all public information is immediately reflected in an unbiased manner in market price. Thus, event studies can provide empirical support in answering two fundamental questions. First, measuring how quickly new public information comes to be fully reflected in market price is a test of a market's efficiency relative to EMH predictions. Second, because an unbiased response is assumed, event studies provide a measure for the value of new public information in terms of a firm's expected future cash flow. The following excerpt and notes and questions explore both the methodology and its uses in legal analysis.

The Role of Financial Economics in Securities Fraud Cases: Applications at the Securities and Exchange Commission
2 The Business Lawyer (February 1994) 545
Mark L. Mitchell and Jeffry M. Netter*

INTRODUCTION

Litigants, including the Securities and Exchange Commission (SEC), increasingly have applied modern financial economics in securities fraud cases. One of the most important applications of financial economics for securities law comes from the efficient markets hypothesis. * * * This Article discusses how tech-

---

* Both authors formerly worked at the United States Securities and Exchange Commission. The views expressed here are those of the authors and do not necessarily reflect the views of the Commission.

niques developed by financial economists can be used to establish the materiality of information allegedly used in securities fraud, and to compute profits (or losses avoided) resulting from fraudulent actions. It then shows how the methodology was applied in recent SEC enforcement cases.

* * *

An event study, a technique developed and refined by financial economists, can be very useful in securities fraud cases. An event study relates changes in stock prices to the release of new information. Researchers have applied event studies to all types of events ranging from mergers to regulatory actions. In securities fraud law, event studies are particularly beneficial because they allow the investigator to discern whether information that is used in an allegedly fraudulent action is important to investors and to determine the value of the information. This Article illustrates the application of this event study methodology in SEC enforcement cases. The application, however, can be used easily in private suits as well.

* * *

EVENT STUDY METHODOLOGY

An event study is a statistical technique that estimates the stock price impact of occurrences such as mergers, earnings announcements, and so forth.[85] The basic notion is to disentangle the effects of two types of information on stock prices—information that is specific to the firm under question (e.g., dividend announcement) and information that is likely to affect stock prices marketwide (e.g., change in interest rates). Eugene F. Fama, Lawrence Fisher, Michael Jensen and Richard Roll from the University of Chicago were the first researchers to apply this methodology. Their seminal work examined the stock price reaction to stock splits and subsequently was published by the *International Economic Review* in 1969.[86]

Event study methodology has its foundation in the efficient markets hypothesis. This well-known hypothesis states that security prices reflect all available information. While theoreticians have developed various definitions of this basic statement, for event studies the relevant definition is that stock prices reflect all publicly available information. Numerous event studies in the academic finance, accounting, economics, marketing, and legal literatures incorporated the idea that if stock prices reflect all public information, price changes around public announcements is due generally to the arrival of new information stemming from that announcement. Consistent with the efficient markets hypothesis, studies have shown that stock prices react quickly to the arrival of new information, often within a matter of seconds.[88]

---

85. *See generally* Cynthia Campbell & Charles Wasley, *Measuring Security Price Performance Using Daily NASDAQ Returns,* 33 J. Fin. Econ. 73 (1993); Laurentius Marais & Katherine Schipper, Application and Event Study Methods in Litigation Support (1992); Glenn V. Henderson, Jr., *Problems and Solutions in Conducting Event Studies,* 57 J. Risk & Ins. 282 (1990); Pamela P. Peterson, *Event Studies: A Review of Issues and Methodology,* 28 Q. J. Bus. & Econ 36 (1989); Stephen J. Brown & Jerold B. Warner, *Using Daily Stock Returns: The Case of Event Studies,* 14 J. Fin. Econ. 3 (1985).

86. Eugene F. Fama et al., *The Adjustment of Stock Prices to New Information,* 10 Int'l Econ. Rev. 1 (1969).

88. *See generally* James M. Patell & Mark Wolfson, *The Intraday Speed of Adjustment of Stock Prices to Earnings and Dividend Announcements,* 13 J. Fin. Econ. 223 (1984);

The execution of an event study is quite simple. It involves the identification of an event that causes investors to change their expectations about the value of a firm. The investigator compares a stock price movement contemporaneous with the event to the expected stock price movement if the event had not taken place. There are three basic steps in conducting an event study: (i) define the event window; (ii) calculate abnormal stock price performance around the event; and (iii) test for statistical significance of the abnormal stock price performance.

DEFINING THE EVENT WINDOW

The first step in the event study is selecting an event window. The event window is the period when information about the event becomes available to the stock market and thus may affect the relevant company's stock price. For most publicly-traded corporations, the event is disseminated publicly by newswire sources such as Dow Jones & Company and Reuters. In the case of Dow Jones & Company, the news is distributed via the *Dow Jones Broadtape* immediately after receipt of the news release from the corporation or government agency. For the relatively important news releases, Dow Jones also reports the event in the *Wall Street Journal* on the next business day.

The efficient markets hypothesis is influential in determining the length of the event window. Because the efficient markets hypothesis, supported by considerable empirical evidence, suggests that stock prices react quickly to the release of new information, in many cases the event window will be relatively short, sometimes as short as one trading day. In determining the length of an event window, an important tradeoff exists. The longer the event window, the more likely the window includes the period during which all the new information about the event is released.The tradeoff, however, is that long event windows may include noise and information from other events, making it difficult to isolate the impact of the relevant event.

The extent of the difficulty in defining the event window length varies across events. In those instances where the release of new information is a complete surprise to the market, it is relatively easy to establish the beginning of the event period. Consider an airline crash, for example. Because airline crashes are unanticipated, the first day of the event period is either the day of the crash or the subsequent trading day if the crash occurred after the market close. Even when it is easy to identify the beginning of the event window, it can be difficult to establish the end of the event window. In the airline example, the end of the period would depend on when all of the relevant information regarding the crash was made available to market participants. For some crashes, it may take several days or perhaps even weeks before the market receives all the relevant information; in these cases, a longer event window is more necessary than for a crash in which all information is available within a few hours following the crash. In most cases, however, the bulk of the information is released at the announcement of the event. Because the market processes information rapidly, it is conventional to expand the window only a short period

---

Larry Y. Dann et al., *Trading Rules, Large Blocks, and the Speed of Price Adjustment*, 4 J. Fin. Econ. 3 (1977).

after the announcement. The current academic standard is to extend the event period to the close of trading on the day after the release of the pertinent information.[94]

For those events that are subject to leakage, defining the beginning of the event window can be problematic. Consider the case of a merger in which the target company is rumored to be "in play " prior to the announcement. For such a case, the event window should begin prior to the actual merger announcement, perhaps as long as a week or two. Ideally, the first day of the event window corresponding to a merger would be the date on which investors began trading on news about the upcoming merger, regardless of whether the news was based on rumors, inside information, a Schedule 13D filing, or a public announcement that merger talks were in process. In practice, this date is difficult to define and some degree of judgment is required generally based on price and volume movements prior to the merger announcement.

With respect to securities fraud cases, there is substantial variation in the complexity of determining the length of an event window. In some fraud cases, choosing the appropriate event window is straightforward. An example is an insider trading case where the information used by the investor is revealed subsequently in a single public announcement. On the other hand, in many securities fraud cases the relevant information is revealed slowly over time, while during the same period investors receive other, sometimes unrelated, information about the firm(s) in question. In the latter case, it is relatively difficult to choose an appropriate window. The main advice is to carefully identify the exact dates during which the information in question reached the market, and then restrict the window to a short period if possible, generally two or three days around each release of new information.

CALCULATE ABNORMAL STOCK PRICE PERFORMANCE

The next step in the event study is to examine the stock price performance around the event. The goal is to isolate the effect of the event on the contemporaneous stock price movement. Stated differently, the investigator attempts to determine whether the stock price behavior around the event is abnormal. A large abnormal stock price movement occurring at the same time the market receives news about an event suggests that the event caused the abnormal price movement. Furthermore, the link between the event and the price movement is even stronger if there is no other new information reaching the market at the same time that could affect the stock price.

The simplest way to evaluate abnormal stock price performance is to visually examine the stock price movement around the event and assess whether it appears small or large. Of course, the degree to which the stock price movement is small or large depends not only on the absolute value of the movement but also on the movement relative to historical patterns and to contemporaneous overall market movements.

---

94. This is particularly true when the researcher examines a sample of several occurrences of the same type event such as a merger announcement. For a single event that is generally the norm in a securities fraud case, depending upon market factors, the window often can extend beyond the close of trading the day after the public announcement.

Calculation of Stock Returns

In finance terminology, the change in a stock price over a given period is known as the stock price return. The return is expressed as:

$$R = [(P_1 - P_0) + DIV_1]/P_0$$

where

P_1 = price at end of period

P_0 = price at beginning of period

DIV_1 = dividend paid during period.

Thus, the return is simply the change in the stock price during the period plus any payout of dividends during the period, relative to the stock price at the beginning of the period.[96] This discussion focuses on daily stock price returns, which is the standard time interval used in most event studies, although returns can be calculated over any increment of time such as hours or months. In securities fraud litigation, daily stock price returns are typically the appropriate measure. In some cases, an examination of hourly, weekly, or monthly data may be warranted—in such cases, the methodology as described can be applied similarly.

An example of a major event to examine abnormal stock market performance is the Tylenol poisonings of 1982. On September 30, 1982, Johnson & Johnson, the maker of Tylenol, announced that three people died as the result of ingesting cyanide-laced Tylenol capsules. Four more deaths were reported within the next two days. The Tylenol Poisonings resulted in 125,000 stories in the print media alone—an event unprecedented in American business.

To the extent that investors expected the Tylenol poisonings to reduce future cash flows to the stockholders of Johnson & Johnson, its stock price should have declined in response to the announcement of the poisonings. According to the efficient markets hypothesis, the stock price decline will occur quickly. Correspondingly, the return to Johnson & Johnson revealed the Tylenol poisonings, is:

$$-6.5\% = \{\$46.125 - \$43.125]/\$46.125$$

where \$46.215 and \$43.125 are the closing prices on September 29 and 30, respectively.

Calculation of Standard Deviation

A decline of 6.5% on a given day appears quite large, especially for a blue-chip firm such as Johnson & Johnson. It is necessary to perform statistical tests, however, to determine that the 6.5% decline did not occur by chance. One approach is

---

96. Researchers often express returns in logarithmic form as

r = natural logarithm$\{1 + [(P_1 - P_0) + DIV_1]/P_0\}$

or as

r = natural logarithm$\{[P_1 + DIV_1]/P_0\}$.

The logarithmic return is a continuously compounded return whereas the return described in the text is a simple return. For practical purposes the distinction between these two return measures is relatively minor. One benefit of the logarithmic return method is that in statistical terminology, the transformation makes the distribution of the returns closer to a normal distribution, thus improving the validity of statistical testing. For ease of exposition, the simple return measure is focused upon. Further, it is also the case that the simple return measure provides better estimates for disgorgement purposes.

to compare the return to a series of returns over some prior period. The comparison period typically ranges from 100 to 300 trading days. For the Johnson & Johnson example, the trading days for the one-year period ending on September 29, 1982, the day before the public announcement of the poisonings, are used. There are 253 trading days during this period. Interestingly, for only one day during the prior year did Johnson & Johnson's stock move more in absolute value than on September 30, 1982. That day is August 17, 1982 when Johnson & Johnson's stock price increased 7.19%. It so happens that this large positive return is likely due in part to the overall stock market increase of 4.45% that day. The fact that there is only one return during the prior one-year period that is of the magnitude of the September 30, 1982 decline suggests this decline is significant.

To assess the significance of the −6.50% return on September 30, 1982, a well-known metric variation in statistics is relied on, the standard deviation. This metric measures the dispersion in a variable around its mean value. The standard deviation for stock returns is formally expressed as:

$$s = \frac{\sqrt{\Sigma (r_i - \bar{r})^2}}{N - 1}$$

where $\bar{r}$ is the mean return over the sample period and N is the number of trading days in the sample period. As the formula indicates, the greater the variation around the mean value in the sample, the larger the standard deviation. Suppose for example that all the returns had the same value. In such a case, there would be no dispersion around the mean value and thus the formula would indicate a value of zero. Note that the term $(r_i\bar{r})$ is squared—the rationale is the magnitude of the deviation of returns from the mean value is what matters, not whether a return is above or below the mean. The division by $N - 1$ adjusts for the number of returns in the sample. The intuition behind the $N - 1$ term is straightforward. If this divisor were not included, the calculated standard deviation would increase in magnitude as the number of returns increased. Thus, the numerator keeps track of total deviations while the denominator keeps track of the number of deviations. In this light, the ratio represents an average deviation between an observation and its mean.

The standard deviation of the daily return for Johnson & Johnson stock during the 253 trading days period prior to the Tylenol poisonings is 1.84%. What can be inferred about the impact of the Tylenol poisonings on Johnson & Johnson's stock price when there was a −6.5% return on September 30, 1982 and the historical daily mean return and standard deviation of Johnson & Johnson's stock is known? The most common way to analyze this question is to consider the statistical significance of the daily return.

Testing the Statistical Significance of a Stock Return

Once a researcher identified an event window and calculated the return during that event window, he or she then can determine the statistical significance of the return. The question is whether the absolute value of the return is large enough so that the researcher can indicate with confidence that the return is relatively unusual. The importance of the historical average and standard deviation of the daily returns is highlighted in making the assertion that a given daily return is different from the typical daily return. There is an additional consideration in this analysis—the role of the normal distribution.

Many statistical tests rely on the assumption that the data of interest is normally distributed. The normal distribution is attractive because it is a good description of a wide variety of random variables including stock returns. In the normal distribution, the values of the variable are distributed symmetrically around the mean value and are not concentrated around extreme values. A normal distribution has the familiar bell-shape. Also important is that a variable that is distributed normally can be described by its mean and standard deviation. For example, for a normally distributed random variable, the probability is 68.3% that a randomly selected value will lie within one standard deviation of the mean value. Similarly, the probability is 95.5% that a randomly selected value will lie within two standard deviations of the mean value. Expressed differently, there is only a 4.5% chance that a randomly selected observation will not fall within two standard deviations of the mean value. Finally, very few observations fall outside the boundary of three standard deviations from the mean value—the probability is 99.7% that a randomly selected observation will lie within three standard deviations of the mean value.

While visual displays of stock returns suggest returns tend to follow a bell-shaped distribution, prior statistical research indicates that they are not distributed precisely normally. Even so, researchers have shown that the normal distribution is an appropriate approximation for event study analyses. Throughout the remainder of this Article, it is assumed that stock returns actually adhere to the normal distribution so that appropriate hypothesis tests can be constructed to determine whether stock price movements during event windows are statistically significant.

To calculate probability values, the normal distribution must be transformed into the standard normal distribution. A standard normal distribution has a mean value of zero and a standard deviation of one. One can calculate z-statistics with this standard distribution—the z-statistic is expressed as:

z-statistic = (observed value − mean value) / standard deviation.

Most standard statistics texts include a table of the cumulative standard normal distribution. The table reports for various values of the z-statistic the probability that a z of that value or greater will occur. Thus, a researcher usually will convert an observation drawn form a normal distribution into a z-value in order to assess the significance of that value.

The methodology discussed in the previous paragraph is phrased more formally in terms of hypothesis testing. In general, a test of significance aims to answer the question of whether an observed difference is real or simply occurred by chance. In statistical tests, the researcher usually sets out a null hypothesis which states that an observed difference occurred by chance. If the null hypothesis is rejected because a test statistic (such as a z-statistic) is greater than a specified value, then it is unlikely the difference occurred by chance. This result often is called a finding of statistical significance.

For example, researchers apply decision rules to determine whether a given value is significantly different from the mean value. An often used convention is the five percent rule—values greater than or equal to 1.96 standard deviations form the mean value are considered significantly different from the typical value because there is only a five percent chance that randomly selected value will be 1.96 or more standard deviations from the true mean. Thus, if the calculated z-statistic has an absolute value of 1.96 or greater, the observed value could be considered significant at the five percent level. The decision rule may be more stringent. For example, there is only about a one percent likelihood that a randomly selected value will lie outside 2.58 standard deviations or more from the average value. Thus, if the z-statistic is greater than or equal to 2.58, the observed value can be considered significant. A third commonly used decision rule is ten percent—here, the probability is ten percent that a randomly selected value will lie 1.65 standard deviations or more from the mean value. Generally, researchers use a decision rule based on one percent, five percent, or ten percent significance levels.

Stock returns provide a good example of a test of whether an observation is significantly different from the mean. In the case of daily stock returns, the mean daily return is very close to zero: the mean annual return on the stock market over the past thirty years was roughly twelve percent with a corresponding mean daily return of 0.045%. Because the daily return is so small, it is assumed that it is zero for statistical tests and thus a test of whether a daily stock return if different from the mean is just a test of whether a daily return is different from zero. Therefore, the z-statistic is simply the daily return divided by the standard deviation. If the z-statistic is 1.96 or greater (based on a decision rule of five percent), the results indicate the daily return is significantly different from the mean return.

In an article published in the *Virginia Law Review* in 1991,[105] the authors (with Jonathan R. Macey and Geoffrey P. Miller) provided guidelines as to the magnitudes of daily stock price returns that are statistically different from zero. For the stocks of the largest equity-value New York Stock Exchange (NYSE) listed firms, a stock price movement of 2.86% could be considered significantly different from zero at the five percent level. In contrast, for the smallest equity-value NASDAQ firms, the necessary price movement to be considered significant at the five percent level is 10.02%. Therefore, because stock price volatility varies widely across firms, inferences about the significance of a firm's stock returns are made with respect to a comparison with that stock's own return history.

Statistical tests of significance are useful both in establishing materiality and in calculating disgorgement. A finding that a stock return associated with the release of information is large enough that it is unlikely that the return occurred by chance is strong evidence that the information was important. Therefore, if that information was used allegedly in securities fraud, the finding that the associated stock return is large enough to be statistically significant implies the information is material. Furthermore, a finding of statistical significance for stock returns data used in calculations of disgorgement is an indication that the estimates are accurate.

For example, suppose a firm's stock price increases seven percent on the day that management releases a favorable earnings announcement. Suppose, also, that the prior day an insider of the firm purchased stock based on his or her knowledge of the forthcoming announcement. The insider subsequently is charged with illegal insider trading. A finding that the seven percent return on the earnings announcement day is statistically significant is strong empirical evidence that the news was important. Stated differently, it is unlikely that the seven percent increase in the

---

105. [*See generally* Jonathan R. Macey et al., *Lessons From Financial Economics: Materiality, Reliance, and Extending the Reach of* Basic v. Levinson, 77 Va. L. Rev. 1017, 1020 (1991).]

stock price occurred by chance. Furthermore, in calculating profits for disgorgement based on the stock price increase on the announcement day, if the return is statistically significant, then a more credible argument can be made that the seven percent return represents the value of the defendant's inside information.

Returning to the Johnson & Johnson example, recall that the standard deviation during the year prior to the poisoning was 1.84%. Dividing the return to Johnson & Johnson stock of −6.5% by this standard deviation yields a z-statistic of 3.53. It is highly improbable that a randomly selected return from Johnson & Johnson's return history would yield a value that is more than 3.53 standard deviations away from zero. Thus, one can claim with a high degree of confidence that Johnson & Johnson's stock price decline on September 30, 1982 did not occur by chance and thus the decline is likely due to the public announcement of the Tylenol poisonings. It is preferable, however, to correct for overall market movements before calculating the significance of abnormal returns.

Net of Market Stock Price Performance

When the market receives new information about the future cash flows of a company, the stock price quickly moves to a new value reflecting the new information. Often the information is firm specific in nature—e.g., earnings announcements. In addition, stock prices of individual firms move in conjunction with overall stock market movements that are caused by changes in underlying economy-wide factors. Thus, it is important to account for these marketwide movements, especially during periods when the market is volatile. * * * The basic method for accounting for marketwide factors subtracts the marketwide return from the individual stock's return. This estimate is called the net-of-market return.

Several choices are available as proxies for a marketwide return. Two well known measures are the Dow Jones Industrial Average (DJIA) and the Standard & Poor's 500 Index (S&P 500). The DJIA is limited somewhat as a market index as it contains only thirty stocks and thus large movements in this index often can be driven by changes in just a few stocks. With the S&P 500, this problem is less severe. While the S&P 500 is an acceptable index to proxy for the overall market, this Article uses an even broader measure—an index based on all stocks on the NYSE, American Stock Exchange (ASE), and NASDAQ. This index comes from the Center for Research in Security Prices (CRSP) at the University of Chicago and is one of the more comprehensive indexes available. It should be restated, however, that the S&P 500 is an appropriate proxy as well. Because the correlation between these two indexes is close to one, similar results usually are obtained regardless of the choice of index.

On September 30, 1982 when Johnson & Johnson's stock price dropped 6.5%, the overall market, as proxied by the CRSP Value-weighted NYSE, ASE, and NASDAQ index, dropped as well, declining 0.89%. Thus, the net-of-market to Johnson & Johnson stock was −5.61%. As a result, it can be argued that the overall market decline can account for some of the decline in Johnson & Johnson's stock price that day. Even so, the net-of-market return is still quite large. To put this net-of-market return in perspective, it was calculated for the prior 253 trading days. Over this one-year period, a net-of-market return of this magnitude never occurred. The closest in absolute value took place on March 9, 1982, when Johnson & Johnson's net-of-market return was 5.17%. This evidence provides additional support of the notion that the public announcement of the Tylenol poisonings caused a major revaluation of Johnson & Johnson stock. To test for statistical significance, the standard deviation of Johnson & Johnson's net-of-market return over the prior 253 trading day period is computed—this sample standard deviation is 1.42%.[107] Thus, the net-of-market return of −5.61% is highly statistically significant as it is roughly four standard deviations away from a mean return of zero. Stated differently, the z-statistic is 3.95, which is substantially greater than the z-statistic of 2.58 necessary for significance at the one percent level.

Beta-Adjusted Stock Market Performance

Although net-of-market returns, in many cases, provide an appropriate estimate of the stock price effects of new information, there are instances where computation of market-adjusted returns requires a more refined analysis to account for the fact that not all stocks are affected identically by economy-wide factors. That is, the stock returns of some firms move proportionately more than the market in reaction to economy-wide news; the stock returns for some firms track the overall market very closely; and the stock returns of other firms are relatively insensitive to marketwide patterns. The methodology for this adjustment is the market model and requires an estimation of the relation between the stock returns of the individual firm and the returns of the overall market index during a comparison period (also known as the estimation period) which typically precedes the event window. The performance of the firm's stock during the event window is then compared to the predicted performance during the event window. The predicted performance is based on the firm's stock price relationship with the market over the control period.

The first step is to estimate the market model:

$$R_{it} = \alpha_i + \beta_i R_{mt} + \varepsilon_{it}$$

which assumes that the return to a stock i at time t is a function of the market return, R_{mt}, plus a random error term, ε_{it}, that is uncorrelated with the market return. The market model decomposes the return on a stock into two parts, one part due to factors influencing the market and one part due to variables specifically related to the firm itself. The term β, often referred to as beta, measures the sensitivity of a firm's stock returns to overall market returns. Although on average the returns on stocks vary proportionately with the returns on the market index, the returns on individual stocks typically vary more or less than the returns on a market index.

*   *   *

The market model is estimated with regression analysis. The estimation period for this market model equation typically ranges from 100 to 300 trading days preceding the event under study. That is, the researcher uses the estimates of α and β, and the movement of the market to predict how the stock price of the firm would have changed during the event period if there were no firm-specific

---

107. Note that the net-of-market daily return standard deviation of 1.42% is less than the standard deviation (1.84%) of Johnson & Johnson's actual returns over this period. This difference is attributed to the fact that the actual return incorporates marketwide as well as firm-specific factors, and thus is more volatile than the net-of-market return.

information released during the event period. The difference between the predicted return and the actual return on a given date during the event window is known as the abnormal return. The abnormal return expressed as:

$$AR_{it} = r_{it} - (\hat{\alpha}_i + \hat{\beta}_i R_{mt})$$

measures the impact of the event on stock i at time t.

As an example, apply the market model to the Tylenol case. To calculate the abnormal return to Johnson & Johnson stock on September 30, 1982, first the market model for the 253 prior trading days is estimated. As in the computation of the net-of-market return, the overall stock market is proxied by the CRSP value-weighted index of NYSE, ASE, and NASDAQ stocks. The estimated beta for Johnson & Johnson for the one-year period prior to the crash was 1.29. A beta of 1.29 suggests that Johnson & Johnson's stock typically increased (or decreased) 12.9% when the overall market increased (or decreased) 10%. The intercept or alpha term is virtually zero as it is only 0.0975%.

The abnormal return on September 30, 1982 to Johnson & Johnson stock is

$$-5.46\% = -6.5\% - 0.0975\% - (1.29 \times -0.89\%),$$

where -6.5% is the actual return to Johnson & Johnson stock, 0.0975% is the estimate of alpha from the market model, 1.29 is Johnson & Johnson's beta estimate and -0.89% is the market return on September 30, 1982. Notice the abnormal return of -5.46% is not as negative as the net-of-market return of -5.62%. The net-of-market return approach assumes beta is 1.0, whereas the estimated beta for Johnson & Johnson is 1.29. Thus, more of the decline in Johnson & Johnson's stock price on September 30 is accounted for by market factors when it is adjusted with the estimated beta than when assuming beta is 1.0.[110]

As before, statistical tests are necessary to estimate the confidence that the abnormal return is different from zero. In computing the significance of the abnormal stock price performance using the actual return and the net-of-market return, those returns simply are compared to the standard deviations of the actual and the net-of-market returns over the prior 253 trading days, respectively. In computing the statistical significance of the abnormal returns, however, the significance tests are more complex than in the case of the net-of-market return, yet the intuition is still the same.[111] In this case, the researcher estimates the standard error of forecast[112] for the abnormal return as

$$s_{ar} = [s^2(1 + 1/N_e + (R_{mt} - \overline{R_m})^2 / SCCR_m)]^{1/2}$$

---

110. It should be noted that recent works, *see* Eugene F. Fama & Kenneth R. French, *The Cross-Section of Expected Stock Returns,* 47 J. Finance 427 (1992) and Eugene F. Fama & Kenneth R. French, *Common Risk Factors in the Return on Stocks and Bonds,* 33 J. Fin. Econ. 3 (1993), suggest additional risk factors to the overall market, such as firm size and market/book equity, should be accounted for when calculating abnormal returns. Under certain conditions, in a securities fraud case in which the information is released over a long period of time, the additional factors may alter the calculation of the abnormal returns. In the Johnson & Johnson example and the cases that follow, however, the Fama and French multifactor model does not alter the results.

111. For recent articles that describe statistical tests in event studies, see Ekkehart Boehmer et al., *Event-Study Methodology Under Conditions of Event-Induced Variance,* 30 J. Fin. Econ 253 (1991) and Imre Karafiath & David E. Spencer, *Statistical Inference in Multiperiod Event Studies,* 1 Rev. Quantitative Fin. & Acct. 353 (1991). *See also supra* note 85.

112. *See generally* John Johnston, Econometric Methods (1984).

where s^2 is the estimated residual variance from the regression model for the estimation period, N_e is the number of trading days in the estimation period, $\overline{R}_m$ is the estimation period sample mean of the market return, and $CSSR_m$ is the corrected sum of squares of the market return during the event period. This measure is essentially the standard deviation of Johnson & Johnson's returns during the prior 253 trading days accounting for the relation of the returns with the stock market, plus terms to account for the number of observations in the estimation period and overall market deviations on the event date.[113] The estimated standard error of forecast for September 30, 1992 is 1.42%.

Similar to the prior statistical tests, the abnormal return is compared with the standard error of forecast to determine significance. The abnormal return of –5.46 is nearly four times greater than the standard error—the z-statistic is –3.85. This indicates that even after accounting for beta, Johnson & Johnson's stock price declined significantly on Spetember 30, 1982, when Johnson & Johnson revealed that Tylenol was laced with cyanide.

Cumulative Abnormal Returns

As noted earlier, event windows can extend beyond one trading day. For these cases, the abnormal returns can be cumulated to create the cumulative abnormal return formally expressed as:

$$CAR_T = \prod_{t=1}^{T}(1 + AR_t) - 1$$

where T is the length of the event window.[114] The CAR measures the total impact of the event on the firm. Generally, event studies report both the AR and CAR over the event window. For event windows where the information was released

---

113. The term s^2 (0.0002) is the estimated residual variance from the regression model. The square root of this term of 0.0141 or 1.41% and is simply the standard error of the regression model. Notice that this term is virtually identical to the standard deviation of the net-of-market returns over the estimation period. The major distinction is that the standard error from the regression model is a measure of the variation in Johnson & Johnson's return accounting for a more precise relation with the overall market. The first term in brackets is simply 1. The second term $1/N_e$, accounts for the number of days in the estimation period. The longer the estimation period, the more precisely estimated the market model parameters. This term is generally very small as estimation periods typically range from 100 to 300 days. The third term accounts for large stock market movements on the event date. The larger the absolute value of the overall stock market movement on the event date, the larger this term, and hence the larger the standard error of forecast. Consider for example the market crash of 1987 when the overall stock market fell approximately 20%. An abnormal return of 4% on this day would be less significant than an abnormal return of 4% on a day when the market was flat. In general, the second two terms are very small. For example on September 30, the sum of the three terms in brackets was 1.008, resulting in a stnadard error of forecast of 1.42%.

114. Intuitively, cumulative abnormal returns would appear to be simply the sum of the abnormal returns over the event window (this actually would be the case of logarithmic returns). The problem with a simple summation of the abnormal returns does not yield a holding period return. Note that the product of (1 + AR) over the event period is used rather than simply summing the abnormal returns. To illustrate, consider a price movement from $4 to $5 (AR = 25%) on one day and then back to $4 (AR = 20%) the next day. Summing the abnormal returns would yield a value of 5%, yet the holding period return is zero. Taking the product of (1 + .25) and (1 + –0.20) yields the correct cumulative return of zero.

over several days, the CAR often is emphasized. Analogously, simple returns and net-of-market returns can be cumulated as well.

Again, the Tylenol example illustrates measuring abnormal performance over multiday periods. A ten-day event window is constructed, covering the period from September 30 through October 13, 1982. Table 1 reports cumulative measures of Johnson & Johnson's stock price performance over this ten-day period in Panels A–C respectively.[115] Panel A displays the actual returns performance, Panel B displays the net-of-market returns performance, and Panel C displays the abnormal returns performance.

To illustrate the cumulation technique, consider the actual returns on September 30 and October 1 of –6.51% and 1.74%, respectively. The cumulative return is given by the product of $(1 - 0.0651)$ x $(1 - .017) - 1$. Thus, the two-day cumulative return is –4.88%. This process continues throughout the length of the event window. As of the tenth day of the event window, October 13, the cumulative return to Johnson & Johnson stock is –8.9% over the ten-day window, the z-statistic that corresponds to the cumulative return.[116] With respect to the cumulative return of –8.94% over the ten-day window, the z-statistic is 1.54. As this z-statistic is slightly less than 1.65, the –8.94% cumulative return misses statistical significance at the ten percent level.

The cumulative net-of-market returns in Panel B display strikingly divergent estimates from that of the cumulative return. Here, the cumulative net-of-market return on October 13, 1982 is –18.91%. The reason that the cumulative net-of-market return is considerably more negative than the cumulative return is that there were large overall stock market gains during this two-week period. That is, Johnson & Johnson's stock would have realized even a larger absolute decline in value had the market not increased during this event window. Similar results are revealed in Panel C which shows the cumulative abnormal returns, based on the market model estimates. In this case, the cumulative abnormal return is –22.39% by the tenth day following the public announcement of the Tylenol poisonings. Given that Johnson & Johnson's beta exceeds one, its stock price should have outperformed the market over this event window in the absence of the Tylenol poisonings—this fact accentuates the negative cumulative abnormal performance realized by Johnson & Johnson.

The sharply contrasting differences between the returns to Johnson & Johnson and the market-adjusted returns illustrate an important point that is relevant for securities fraud cases. Occasionally, announcements by corporations occur contemporaneous with large overall stock market movements. These market movements must be accounted for to isolate the stock price impact of the firm's announcement. It is then possible to assess the materiality of the information and the value of the information contained in the announcement for disgorgement purposes.

---

115. *See infra* Table 1.

116. The z-statistics for the cumulative returns simply are computed as the square root of the sum of the variances associated with each of the daily returns over the event window. For example, to compute the z-statistic for the cumulative return of –4.88% over the first two days of the event window, the standard error of the forecast for each of the two days is squared to obtain the variance for each of these two days. The square root of the sum of the two variances is the standard error for a two-day cumulative return. The reason to convert to variances before summing is that mathematically, variances can be summed whereas standard deviations cannot. Note that the variances are cumulated based on logarithmic returns due to better specified distributional properties.

A hypothetical example using Johnson & Johnson facts shows how it may be important to account for market movements in using financial economics in securities fraud cases. Supose an employee of Johnson & Johnson found out at his job on September 30 that there were poisonings. He then either sold stock or bought puts in Johnson & Johnson before the public received any news of the poisonings. In an insider trading case brought against this employee, financial economics could be used to show the information he had was material and to calculate disgorgement. As stated previously, the cumulative abnormal return of –22.39% is much more negative than the cumulative return of –8.94% over the period the news about the poisonings became public. Because the insider's information was about factors that affected Johnson & Johnson's stock price and not the overall market, the cumulative abnormal return is theoretically a better measure of the materiality of the information than the cumulative return. In this case the very large cumulative abnormal return of –22.39% significantly buttresses the claim of materiality.

For the same reason, cumulative abnormal returns are also a theoretically better measure than cumulative returns in calculating profits for disgorgement. Cumulative abnormal returns only measure the impact of firm-specific information, in this case the news about poisonings. In a real sense, the value of the information to the trader is best represented by how the information would have affected the stock price in the absence of any other factors—the cumulative abnormal return. Finally, note that this analysis is even more intuitively appealing if the employee in his trading hedged against overall market movements.

In addition, note the role of statistical tests in this example. The cumulative abnormal return of –22.39% has an associated z-statistic of –4.96. That z-statistic indicates that the cumulative abnormal return is highly significant—at the one percent level. Therefore, it is very unlikely that the negative cumulative abnormal return occurred by chance, which is strong evidence that the information about the Tylenol poisonings led to the negative cumulative abnormal return. The finding of statistical significance is thus strong evidence the information was material and it boosts the credibility of disgorgement estimates based on the cumulative abnormal returns.

* * *

SUMMARY

Modern financial economics is becoming increasingly influential in securities fraud law. The efficient markets hypothesis has provided a framework for the analysis of certain questions and a basis for generating empirical evidence on the value of information in individual cases. * * * Of particular importance is an empirical technique derived from the efficient markets hypothesis—the event study. Event studies are useful to establish, among other things, materiality, and to calculate damages in securities fraud litigation. * * *

There are many areas in securities fraud litigation where empirical techniques from financial economics may be useful. Indeed, event study techniques potentially are much more valuable than described in this Article. Event study analysis is useful at all stages of litigation to both defendants and plaintiffs. The analysis is applicable, not just in SEC insider trading cases, but in all types of securities fraud actions, including private suits. Furthermore, by providing objective, relatively precise measures of the importance of information and of illegal profits or damages, the importance of financial economics in securities fraud litigation will continue to increase.

Stock Price Performance for Johnson & Johnson
Following the 1982 Tylenol Poisonings

Panel A: Actual Returns Performance				Cumulative	
Date	Stock Price	Return	Z-statistic	Return	Z-statistic
Sept. 29	46.125				
Sept. 30	43.125	-6.51	-3.55	-6.51	-3.55
Oct. 1	43.875	1.74	0.95	-4.88	-1.88
Oct. 4	41.250	-5.98	-3.29	-10.57	-3.33
Oct. 5	39.000	-5.46	-2.97	-15.45	-4.21
Oct. 6	41.750	7.05	3.84	-9.49	-2.31
Oct. 7	40.375	-3.29	-1.80	-12.47	-2.77
Oct. 8	42.625	5.57	3.04	-7.59	-1.56
Oct. 11	43.500	2.05	1.12	-5.69	-1.10
Oct. 12	41.500	-4.60	-2.51	-10.01	-1.82
Oct. 13	42.000	1.21	0.66	-8.94	-1.54

Panel B: Net-of-Market Returns Performance				Cumulative	
Date	Stock Price	Net-of-Market Return	Z-statistic	Net-of-Market Return	Z-statistic
Sept. 29	46.125				
Sept. 30	43.125	-5.62	-3.95	-5.62	-3.95
Oct. 1	43.875	0.54	0.38	-5.11	-2.54
Oct. 4	41.250	-5.74	-4.03	-10.56	-4.28
Oct. 5	39.000	-5.88	-4.13	-15.82	-5.56
Oct. 6	41.750	3.96	2.78	-12.48	-3.92
Oct. 7	40.375	-5.45	-3.83	-17.25	-4.95
Oct. 8	42.625	3.77	2.65	-14.13	-3.75
Oct. 11	43.500	-0.36	-0.25	-14.43	-3.58
Oct. 12	41.500	-4.61	-3.24	-18.38	-4.30
Oct. 13	42.000	-0.65	-0.45	-18.91	-4.20

Panel C: Abnormal Returns Performance				Cumulative	
Date	Stock Price	Abnormal Return	Z-statistic	Abnormal Return	Z-statistic
Sept. 29	46.125				
Sept. 30	43.125	-5.46	-3.85	-5.46	-3.85
Oct. 1	43.875	0.10	0.07	-5.37	-2.67
Oct. 4	41.250	-5.76	-4.07	-10.83	-4.40
Oct. 5	39.000	-6.10	-4.31	-16.27	-5.73
Oct. 6	41.750	2.98	2.06	-13.78	-4.32
Oct. 7	40.375	-6.17	-4.31	-19.10	-5.47
Oct. 8	42.625	3.16	2.21	-16.54	-4.38
Oct. 11	43.500	-1.15	-0.80	-17.50	-4.33
Oct. 12	41.500	-4.72	-3.33	-21.39	-5.00
Oct. 13	42.000	-1.28	-0.89	-22.39	-4.96

Note: Returns are expressed in percents. Stock price data is from Center for Research Security Prices (CRSP) at the University of Chicago. Market model estimation period is September 30, 1981 through September 29, 1982. Market proxy is CRSP value-weighted index of NYSE AMEX, and NASDAQ stocks. Beta estimate for Johnson & Johnson is 1.29.

Notes and Questions

1. Event Studies and Securities Fraud: Mitchell and Netter argue that event studies can play an influential role in securities fraud cases. In particular, event studies can be used to establish the materiality of new information and to calculate illegal profits for purposes of disgorgement. The full version of the Mitchell and Netter article provides five examples of situations in which the Securities and Exchange Commission actually used event studies in the enforcement of securities laws. In this regard, the authors suggest that event study methodology should be particularly useful when markets are thin or prices are volatile. Can you explain why? How could event study methodology be used to distinguish between the value of information illegally used by insiders and other firm-specific information released during the same time preriod?

2. Uses for Event Studies in Legal Analysis: Event studies can be used to analyze a variety of legal and regulatory issues. For example, W. Kip Viscusi and Joni Hersch examined the stock market impact of product liability lawsuits and regulatory events involving product risks. The purpose of this study was to investigate whether there are any stock market repercussions to lawsuits arising from product risks and, if so, what factors determine the size of these effects. Viscusi and Hersch found that adverse product liability coverage leads to significant negative effects on firm value, but that such effects vary systematically with the evidence that is transmitted to investors. Of particular interest is the fact that product liability events have a larger impact than do regulatory events associated with product safety. Can you think of an economic reason why this might be the case? See W. Kip Viscusi and Joni Hersch, "The Market Response to Product Safety Litigation," 2 *Journal of Regulatory Economics*, 215 (1990).

3. Identifying the Relevant Event Window: Identifying the relevant event window can often times be the most difficult part of conducting an event study. As Mitchell and Netter observe, some events are a complete surprise to the market, and it is therefore relatively easy to identify the appropriate event window. On the other hand, some information which might impact expectations regarding a firm's future cash flow is released gradually over time. For example, new legislation may impact the future cash flows of particular firms or industries. However, at the time new legislation is introduced at the committee level, there is uncertaintiy regarding whether it will ever become law. Investors will use probabilistic estimates of passage to estimate the impact of the proposed legislation on a firm or industry. Investors may change their estimates over time as the proposed legislation winds its way through the political process. Thus, estimating the economic impact of new legislation introduces a great deal of difficulty in identifying the relevant event window. For an example of an event study applied to legislation and a discussion on the difficulties of identifying the appropriate event window in these cases see Roberta Romano, "Comment: What is the Value of Other Constituency Statutes to Shareholders?," 63(3) *University of Toronto Law Journal*, 533 (Summer 1993).

4. Defining the Appropriate Event: Many event studies attempt to compile a sample of firms in order to test the impact of a particular event on firms in general. For example, one might compile a sample of firms that have been subject to hostile takeover attempts in order to investigate the economic value of the market for corporate control. In general, a larger sample size adds to the validity of statistical results. However, use of samples in event studies requires that care be exercised in identifying the relevant event. Sometimes, two events that appear similar are actually two different economic phenomena. In such cases, including two dissimilar events in a single sample may obscure significant abnormal returns for the event of interest. In the hostile takeover attempt sample, for example, some firms may actually be taken over shortly after the announcement while others succesfully defend against the threat. Including both types of firms in a single sample may quiet the abnormal returns generated by firms that are actually taken over. Using samples requires that one recognize the trade offs between sample size and the danger of including confounding events. Theoretically, any two events can be distinguished on economic grounds. However, some level of subjective judgment must be exercised in isolating a relevant event in order to protect the sample size.

5. Testing a Joint Hypothesis?: The market model used in event studies is very similar to the CAPM introduced in the previous subsection. Event studies attempt to isolate the impact of firm-specific information or unsystematic risk on the value of the firm. In order to isolate unsystematic risk, the analyst must account for the impacts of systematic risk. Use of the CAPM beta, allows the systematic risk associated with market returns to be accounted for. However, as indicated earlier, there is a question as to whether the CAPM beta captures all systematic risk, which has lead to the introduction of multifactor risk models such as APT. Event study methodology attempts to isolate the impact of unsystematic risk in the ε_{it} term of the market model. The market model is able to isolate the systematic risk associated with broad market movements in the term $\beta_i R_{mt}$. Moreover, much of the systematic risk that is not captured by $\beta_i R_{mt}$ flows to the α_i term in the market model. However, to the extent that some small portion of systematic risk seaps into the ε_{it} term, the statistical power of event studies may be diminished. This has lead some to suggest that event studies involve a test of both market efficiency and the CAPM—a joint test hypothesis. Empirical analysis of the joint test hypothesis question has found that event study results are not sensitive to model specifications over relatively short event windows. In fact, even the net-of-market methodology has been found to be highly accurate over such event windows. Over longer event windows, the specificaions of the model become more important. What does this distinction suggest in terms of litigation strategy?

6. Multiple Explanations: Event studies provide evidence that particular pieces of information matter to investors. However, event studies do not explain *why* such information matters. Those who conduct event studies must use caution in stating that their results lead to a particular conclusion. Most event studies provide evidence in *support* of a particular argument. In other words, the meaning behind event study results is almost always subject to multiple interpretations. Thus, even though conducting an event study requires statistical prowess, interpreting event study results requires a strong foundation in economic reasoning. Also note that this observation applies to explaining why an event study fails to find abnormal returns.

7. Testing Relative Market Efficiency: Event studies can provide information regarding how quickly a new piece of information is reflected in market price. However, event studies do not provide information on whether the market is efficient in the sense of fairly and accurately valuing securities—that is, whether the stock of XYZ accurately reflects in an unbiased manner the expected future cash flows of XYZ. In other words, event studies only provide a test of *relative* market efficiency. Likewise, any change in firm value associated with a particular event represents a relative change in value.

Glossary of Economics Concepts

Ability-to-pay principle The equity concept that people with larger incomes (or more consumption or more wealth) should be taxed at a higher rate because their ability to pay is presumably greater. The concept is subjective and fails to reveal how much higher the rate of taxation should e as income increases.

Absolute advantage The ability of a nation or a trading partner to produce a product with fewer resources than some other trading partner.

Absolute liability Liability for an act that causes harm even thought the actor was not at fault.

Accounting profits The sales revenues minus the expenses of a firm over a designated time period, usually one year. Accounting profits typically make allowances for changes in the firm's inventories and depreciation of its assets. No allowance is made, however, for the opportunity cost of the equity capital of the firm's owners, or other implicit costs.

Adverse selection A situation in which two people might trade with each other and one person has relevant information about some aspect of the product's quality that the other person lacks.

Advertising Any communication that firms offer customers in an effort to increase demand for their product.

Agency The relationship that exists between a person identified as a principal and another by virtue of which the latter may make contracts with third persons on behalf of the principal.

Agent One who is authorized by the principal or by operation of law to make contracts with third persons on behalf of the principal.

Allocative efficiency The allocation of resources to the production of goods and services most desired by consumers. The allocation is "balanced" in such a way that reallocation of resources could not benefit anyone without hurting someone else.

Allocative inefficiency The use of an uneconomical combination of resources to produce goods and services, or the use of resources to produces goods that are not intensely desired relative to their opportunity cost.

American option An option that can be exercised on any day during its life.

Annuity A level stream of cash flows for a fixed period of time.

Antitrust law A law that prohibits monopolies and cartels or monopoly-like behaviors.

Antitrust policy The laws and agencies created by legislation in an effort to preserve competition.

Arbitrage Buying a good at a place where its price is low and selling it where its price is higher or the process of simultaneously purchasing in one market and selling in another a security or commodity in order to take advantage of price differences in the different markets.

Arbitrage opportunity A recognized price differential that exceeds the costs of arbitrage.

Arbitrage pricing theory A theory of asset pricing in which the expected return is a function of the asset's sensitivity to one or more underlying economic factors.

Assumption of risk The common-law rule that an employee could not sue the employer for injuries caused by the ordinary risks of employment on the theory that the employee had assumed such risks by undertaking the work. The rule has been abolished in those areas governed by workmen's compensation laws and most employers' liability statues.

Asymmetric-information problem A problem arising when either buyers or sellers have important information about the product that is not possessed by the other side in potential transactions.

At-the-money An option in which the price of the underlying stock or futures equals the exercise price.

Average cost Total cost divided by the quantity produced.

Average fixed cost Fixed cost divided by the number of units produced. It always declines as output increases.

Average product The total product (output) divided by the number of units of the variable input required to produce that output level.

Average revenue Total revenue divided by the quantity produced.

Average tax rate A person's tax payment as a fraction of income

Average total cost Total cost divided by the number of units produced. It is sometimes call per unit cost.

Average variable cost The total variable cost divided by the number of units produced.

Bankruptcy A procedure by which one unable to pay debts may be declared a bankrupt, after which all assets in excess of any exemption claim are surrendered to the court for administration and distribution to creditors, and the debtor is given a discharge that releases from the unpaid balance due on most debts.

Barriers to entry Obstacles that limit the freedom of potential rivals to enter an industry.

Benefit principle The notion that people who receive the benefits of publicly provided goods should pay for their production.

Beta coefficient Amount of systematic risk present in a particular risky asset relative to an average risky asset.

Black market An illegal market.

Broker An agent who receives a commission for handling orders to buy and sell securities or futures contracts.

Call An option in which one investor acquires the right, but not the obligation, to buy an underlying asset from another investor for a specified price during a specified period of time.

Call provision Agreement giving the corporation the option to repurchase a bond at a specified price prior to maturity.

Cap A contract that limits the amount the interest rate on a floating rate loan can increase, either annually or over the life of the loan. A transaction in which a party borrowing at a floating rate pays a fee to another party, which reimburses the borrower in the event that the borrower's interest costs exceed a certain level, thus making the effective interest paid on a floating rate loan have a cap or maximum amount.

Capital Resources that enhance our ability to produce output in the future. Also, the net assets of a corporation.

Capital good An input that a firm can use repeatedly to produce other goods.

Capital market The financial market in which long-term securities such as stocks and long-term bonds are traded.

Capital structure The mixture of debt and equity maintained by a firm.

Capitalism An economic system based on private ownership of productive resources and allocation of goods according to the price signals provided by free markets.

Capitalist economy An economic system in which the means of production are privately owned.

Capital asset pricing model (CAPM) Equation of the security market line showing the relationship between expected return and beta.

Capture view of regulation The view that regulatory agencies originally established to serve the general public interest end up serving the special interests of the industries they were intended to regulate.

Cartel An organization of sellers designed to coordinate supply decisions so that the joint profits of the members will be maximized. A cartel will seek to create a monopoly in the market.

Cartel enforcement An effort by the administrators of a cartel to prevent its members from secretly cutting price below the cartel price.

Caveat emptor Let the buyer beware. This maxim has been nearly abolished by warranty and strict tort liability concepts.

Change in demand A change in the numbers in the demand schedule and a shift in the demand curve. An increase in demand shifts the demand curve to the right; a decrease shifts it to the left.

Change in supply A change in the numbers in the supply schedule and a shift in the supply curve. An increase in supply shifts the supply curve to the right; a decrease shifts it to the left.

Choice The act of selecting among alternatives.

Choices at the margin Decisions made by examining the benefits and costs of small, or one-unit, changes in a particular activity.

Classical economists Economics from Adam Smith to the time of Keynes who focused their analysis on economic efficiency and production. With regard to business instability, they thought market prices and wages would decline during a recession quickly enough to bring the economy back to full employment within a short period of time.

Clearinghouse In the futures market, a facility that oversees transactions on a daily basis. The clearinghouse confirms trades made each day, values each contract in every account at the end of every day and readjusts the cash balance of each trader's margin account accordingly, and insures performance of all of the futures contracts.

Coase theorem Externalities will adjust to the same level when ownership rights are assigned and when the costs of negotiation are nonexistent or trivial, regardless of which party receives the rights.

Collar A combination of a cap and a floor in which the purchaser of the cap also sells a floor or the purchaser of a floor also sells a cap. The sale of the cap or floor reduces the cost of the protection and forgoes gains if interest rates move in that party's favor.

Collective bargaining The process by which the terms of employment are agreed upon through negotiations between the employer or employers within a given industry or industrial area and the union or the bargaining representative of the employees.

Collective decision making The method of organization that relies on public-sector decision making (voting, political bargaining, lobbying, and so on). It can be used to resolve the basic economic problems of an economy.

Collusion Agreement among firms to avoid various competitive practices, particularly price reductions. It may involve either formal agreements or merely tacit recognition that competitive practices will be self-defeating in the long run. Tacit collusion is difficult to detect. The Sherman Act prohibits collusion and conspiracies to restrain interstate trade.

Command economy An authoritarian socialist economy characterized by centralized planning and detailed directives to productive units. Individual enterprises have little discretionary decision-making power.

Commissions Fee paid to the broker for buying and/or selling securities or futures contracts.

Commodities Staple items such as wool, sugar, soybeans, pork, copper, gold, and other agricultural or industrial products that are traded on a commodity exchange.

Commodity Futures Trading Commission The federal agency that regulates the futures markets.

Common-property resource A resource for which rights are held in common by a group of individuals, none of whom has a transferable ownership interest. Access to the resource may be open (unrestricted), or may be controlled politically.

Common resource A resource that belongs to no one or to society as a whole.

Common stock Equity without priority for dividends or in bankruptcy.

Comparative advantage The ability to produce a good at a lower opportunity cost than others can produce it. Relative costs determine comparative advantage.

Compensating wage differentials Wage differences that compensate workers for risk, unpleasant working conditions, and other undesirable nonpecuniary aspects of a job.

Competition The process by which people attempt to acquire scarce good for themselves.

Competition as a dynamic process A term that denotes rivalry or competitiveness between or among parties (for example, producers or input suppliers), each of which seeks to deliver a better deal to buyers when quality, price, and product information are all considered. Competition implies a lack of collusion among sellers.

Competitive labor market A labor market in which the wage rate of a particular type of labor is determined by the forces of supply by a large number of sellers of labor is determined by the forces of supply by a large number of sellers of labor and demand by a large number of buyers of labor.

Complements Products that are usually consumed jointly (for example, coffee and nondairy creamer). An increase in the price of one will cause the demand for the other to fall.

Complement inputs Two inputs for which an increase in the price of one raises demand for the other.

Compound interest Interest earned on both the initial principal and the interest reinvested from prior periods.

Concentrated interest A benefit to a small group of people or firms

Consol A type of perpetuity.

Constant-cost Long-run marginal cost and long-run average cost that do not change with the level of output.

Constant-cost industry An industry for which factor prices and costs of production remain constant as market output is expanded. Thus, the long-run market supply curve is horizontal.

Constant returns to scale Unit costs are constant as the scale of the firm is altered. Neither economies or diseconomies of scale are present.

Consumer surplus The difference between the maximum amount a consumer would be willing to pay for a unit of a good and the payment that is actually made.

Consumption of a good The amount of a good people use for their current benefit (wearing, eating, driving, or watching the good, for example).

Convexity The mathematical relationship between the change in a bond price and the change in its yield that is not explained by its duration. Represents the change in the bond price for a given change in the yield.

Corporation A business firm owned by shareholders who possess ownership rights to the firm's profits, but whose liability is limited to the amount of their investment in the firm.

Correlation A measure of how closely two variables are related.

Cost-benefit analysis The process of finding and comparing the costs and benefits of a regulation, tax, or other policy.

Cost of capital The minimum required return on a new investment.

Cost of debt The return that lenders require on the firm's debt.

Cost of equity The return that equity investors require on their investment in the firm.

Costs The expenses of suing or being sued, recoverable in some actions by the successful party, and in others, subject to allocation by the court. Ordinarily they do not include attorney's fees or compensation for loss of time.

Counterparty Term used for either of two parties who agree to enter into a direct financial contract, such as a swap transaction.

Coupon The stated interest payments made on a bond.

Coupon rate The annual coupon divided by the face value of a bond.

Cournot model A model of oligopoly in which each firm believes that other firms will react to its decisions by changing their prices to keep their levels of output and sales fixed.

Covered call A call option sold (written) for which the seller owns the underlying asset.

Credit risk The risk that a party will default on his or her contract.

Cross-price elasticity of demand (or supply) The percentage change in the quantity demanded (or supplied) of one good when the price of another good rises by 1 percent.

Currency swap A swap that allows a party receiving payments based on one currency to exchange these for payments based on another currency. Currency swaps are thus a way of eliminating (or exploiting) differences between international capital markets.

Damages A sum of money recovered to redress or make amends for the legal wrong or injury done.

Deadweight loss A net loss associated with the forgoing of an economic action. The loss does not lead to an offsetting gain for other participants. It thus reflects economic inefficiency.

Deadweight social loss The amount that people would be willing to pay to eliminate an inefficiency.

Dealer One who buys and sells securities and maintains an inventory of such securities. (Brokers, on the other hand, act as agents and do not necessarily keep their own inventory.)

Debenture Unsecured debt, usually with a maturity of 10 or more years.

Demand schedule A table that shows various possible prices and a person's quantity demanded at each price.

Depreciation The fall in the value of a good over time.

Deregulation A situation in which government ceases to regulate a previously regulated industry in an effort to improve the performance of that industry.

Derivative A financial instrument that derives its value from a more basic financial instrument. For example, an option on a stock (a basic form of derivative) derives its value from the underlying stock. Derivatives can be used to either increase or decrease risk.

Differentiated products A product that buyers consider to be a good, but not perfect, substitute for another.

Diffuse interest A benefit that is spread across many people.

Discount rate The rate used to calculate the present value of future cash flows.

Discounted cash flow (DCF) valuation The process of valuing an investment by discounting its future cash flows.

Discounted present value (of a future amount of money) The money you would need to save and invest now to end up with that specific amount of money in the future.

Disequilibrium A situation in which the quantity demanded and the quantity supplied are not equal at the current price.

Distribution of prices A situation in which some sellers charge higher prices than others.

Diversification A method of decreasing risk by spreading investments among different asset categories, such as stocks and bonds, and different companies in different industries within the stocks and bonds, and different companies in different industries within the stock category.

Dividend Payment made out of a firm's earnings to its owners, either in the form of cash or stock.

Dividend growth model Model that determines the current price of a stock as its dividend next period divided by the discount rate less the dividend growth rate.

Dividend yield A stock's expected cash dividend divided by its current price.

Dumping The selling of a product in a foreign nation at a price lower than the domestic market price.

Durable input An input that a firm buys for future use or one that the firm can use repeatedly.

Duration A measure of the size and timing of a bond's cash flows. It also reflects the weighted average maturity of the bond and indicates the sensitivity of the bond's price to a change in its yield.

Economic costs All of a firm's costs, explicit and implicit.

Economic efficiency Proper allocation of resources from the firm's perspective.

Economic goods Scarce goods.

Economic model A description of logical thinking about an economic issue stated in words, graphs, or mathematics.

Economic profit Total revenue minus total economic costs.

Economic rent The price of an input minus the economy's opportunity cost of using that input.

Economically efficient A situation that cannot be changed so that someone gains unless someone else loses.

Economically efficient method of production The technically efficient method with the lowest cost.

Economically efficient (or Pareto efficient) situation A situation that allows no potentially Pareto-improving change.

Economically inefficient A situation that can be changed so that at least one person gains while no one else loses.

Economically inefficient (or Pareto inefficient) situation A situation that is not economically efficient, so a potentially Pareto-improving change could be made.

Economics The study of how a society uses its limited resources to produce, trade, and consume goods and services; also the study of people's incentives and choices and what happens to coordinate their decisions and activities.

Economic system A means of determining what, how, and for whom goods and services are produced.

Economic wage discrimination A situation in which an employer pays individuals in the same occupation different wages, the wage difference based on race, sex, religion, or national origin rather than productivity differences.

Economic welfare The situation in which products and services are offered to consumers at the minimum long-run average total cost of production.

Economies of scale The relation between long-run average total cost and plant size that suggests that as plant size increases, the average cost of production decreases.

Efficiency wage A wage above equilibrium intended to raise worker productivity.

Efficient capital market Market in which security prices reflect available information.

Efficient markets hypothesis (EMH) The hypothesis that actual capital markets, such as the New York Stock Exchange, are efficient.

Egalitarianism The view that fairness requires equal results.

Elastic demand (or supply) Elasticity with an absolute value greater than 1.

Elasticity of demand (or supply) The percentage change in the quantity demanded (or supplied) divided by the percentage change in price.

Eminent domain The power of a government and certain kinds of corporations to take private property against the objection of the owner, provided the taking is for a public purpose and just compensation is made therefor.

Entrepreneur A person who conceives and acts on a new business idea and takes the risk of its success or failure.

Entry When a firm begins producing and selling a product.

Equilibrium A balance of forces permitting the simultaneous fulfillment of plans by buyers and sellers. A state of balance between conflicting forces, such as supply and demand.

Equilibrium price The price at which quantity supplied equals quantity demanded.

Equilibrium quantity The quantity at which quantity supplied equals quantity demanded.

Equity swap An agreement to swap an equity, for example by exchanging a fixed stream of cashflows for a varying stream of cash flows tied to the performance of a specific stock or stock market index.

European option An option that can be exercised only when it expires.

Evidence Any set of facts that helps to convince people that a positive statement is true or false.

Excess burden of taxation A burden of taxation over and above the burden associated with the transfer of revenues to the government. An excess burden usually reflects losses that occur when beneficial activities are forgone because they are taxed.

Excess capacity The opportunity for a firm to reduce its average cost by raising its output.

Exchanges Associations organized to provide a market place for purchasers and sellers of securities. Examples include the New York Stock Exchange, New York Commodities Exchange, and the Chicago Board of Trade.

Exchange rate The price of one country's currency expressed in terms of another country's currency.

Exclusive contract An agreement between manufacturer and retailer that prohibits the retailer from carrying the product lines of firms that are rivals of the manufacturer. Such contracts are illegal under the Clayton Act when they "lessen competition."

Excess demand (shortage) A situation in which the quantity demanded exceeds the quantity supplied.

Excess supply (surplus) A situation in which the quantity supplied exceeds the quantity demanded.

Exercise price The price provided for in an option contract at which the underlying security can be bought (for a call) or sold (for a put) on or before the expiration date of the option. Also referred to as strike price.

Exercising (an option) The actual purchase or sale of the underlying asset of an option; American-style options can be exercised at any time before expiration; European-style options can be exercised only at the time of their expiration.

Exit When a firm stops selling a product.

Expected return Return on a risky asset expected in the future.

Expected value An average of numbers weighted by the probabilities (chances) that they will occur.

Explicit costs Payments by a firm to purchase the services of productive resources.

External benefits Beneficial effects of a group or individual action on the welfare of non-paying secondary parties.

External costs Harmful effects of an individual's or a group's action on the welfare of nonconsenting secondary parties, not accounted for in market prices. Litterbugs, drunk drivers, and polluters, for example, create external costs.

Externalities The side effects, or spillover effects, of an action that influence the well-being of nonconsenting parties. The nonconsenting parties may be either helped (by external benefits) or harmed (by external costs).

Face value The value appearing on the face of a certificate of a fixed-income security (such as a bond, note, or mortgage) that represents the amount due upon maturity of the security.

Fallacy of composition Erroneous view that what is true for the individual (or the part) will also be true for the group (or the whole).

Family People living with others to whom they are related by nature or marriage.

Financial engineering The use of financial instruments, such as derivatives, to obtain the desired mix of risk and return.

Firm An organization that coordinates the activities of workers, managers, owners, lenders, and other participants to produce and sell a good or service.

Fixed costs Costs that do not vary with output. They will be incurred as long as the firm continues in business and the assets have alternative uses.

Fixed input An input whose quantity a firm cannot change in the short run.

Floor A transaction in which a party lending at a floating rate pays a fee to another party, which reimburses the lender in the event that the lender in the event that the lender's interest revenues are below a certain level, thus making the interest received on a floating rate loan have a floor or minimum value.

Foreign currency risk Risk that the value (i.e., exchange rate) of a foreign currency will change adversely in relation to the value of domestic currency. Also called exchange-rate risk.

Forward contract An agreement requiring the delivery of a certain quantity of a currency or other asset by a specified date in the future at a price agreed upon at the time of contracting.

Franchise (a) A privilege or authorization, generally exclusive, to engage in a particular activity within a particular geographic area, as a government franchise to operate a taxi company within a specified city, or a private franchise as the grant by a manufacturer or a right to sell products within a particular territory or for a particular number of years; (b) the right to vote.

Free enterprise Economic freedom to produce and sell or purchase and consume goods without government intervention.

Free entry or exit Entry or exit opportunities with no legal barriers.

Free rider One who receives the benefit of a good without contributing to its costs. Public goods and commodities that generate external benefits offer people the opportunity to become free riders.

Fringe benefits Benefits other than normal money wages that are supplied to employees in exchange for their labor services.

Future value The estimated value at a future date of a present sum of money, based on appropriate interest rates.

Futures commission merchant (FCM) A futures broker

Futures contract An agreement requiring the delivery of a certain quantity of an item by a specified

date in the future at a price agreed upon at the time of contracting. Futures contracts differ from forward contracts in that they are traded on an organized exchange with standardized terms.

Futures market A market in which people buy and sell goods for future delivery

Futures option An option on a futures contract.

Futures price The price of a good for delivery at a future date.

Gains from trade The net benefits to people (as consumers and producers) from trading.

Game theory Analyzes the strategic choices made by competitors in a conflict situation, such as decision made by members of an oligopoly.

Goods All tangible things that satisfy people's wants and desires.

Government failure Failure of government action to meet the criteria of ideal economic efficiency.

Government regulation A limit or restriction on the actions of people or firms, or a required action.

Health and safety regulation Legislation designed to improve the health, safety, and environmental conditions available to workers and/or consumers. The legislation usually mandates production procedures, minimum standards, and/or product characteristics to be met by producers and employers.

Hedging The making of simultaneous contracts to purchase and to sell a particular commodity at a future date with the intention that the loss on one transaction will be offset by the gain on the other.

Historical cost A price paid for something in the past.

Homogeneous product A product of one firm that is identical to the product of every other firm in the industry. Consumers see no difference in units of the product offered by alternative sellers.

Horizontal equity A tax structure under which people with equal incomes pay equal amounts of taxes.

Horizontal merger The combining of the assets of two of more firms engaged in the production of similar products into a single firm.

Household A family or an individual living alone.

Human capital The skills, knowledge, and abilities of people.

Human resources The abilities, skills, and health of human beings that can contribute to the productions of both current and future output. Investment in training and education can increase the supply of human resources.

Imperfect competition A market model in which there is more than one firm but the necessary conditions for a purely competitive solution (homogeneous product, large number of firms, free entry) do not exist.

Implicit costs The opportunity costs associated with a firm's use of resources that it owns. These costs do not involve a direct money payment. Examples include wage income and interest foregone by the owner of a firm who also provides labor services and equity capital to the firm.

Implicit labor contract An informal agreement or understanding about the terms of employment.

Implicit rental price The cost of owning and using a capital good over some period of time.

Import quota A specific quantity (or value) of a good permitted to be imported into a country during a given year.

In the money An option with intrinsic value. A call option is in the money when its exercise price is less than the price of the underlying security. A put option is in the money when its exercise price is greater than the price of the underlying security.

Incentive The expected benefit of a decision minus its opportunity cost.

Income The value of money and goods that a person receives over some time period.

Income effect The part of an increase (decrease) in amount consumed that is the result of the consumer's real income (the consumption possibilities available to the consumer) being expanded (contracted) by a reduction (rise) in the price of a good.

Income elasticity The percent change in the quantity of a product demanded divided by the percent change in consumer income causing the change in quantity demanded. It measures the responsiveness of the demand for a good to a change in income.

Increase in economic efficiency A change that is a potential Pareto improvement.

Increasing cost Long-run marginal cost and long-run average cost that rise with increase in output.

Increasing returns to scale A situation in which average cost of production decreases with higher output.

Increasing-cost industry An industry for which costs of production rise as the industry output is expanded. Thus, the long-run quantity supplied to the market is directly related to price.

Indemnity The right of a person secondarily liable to require that a person primarily liable pay for loss sustained when the secondary party discharges the obligation which the primary party should have discharged; the right of an agent to be paid the amount of any loss or damage sustained without fault because of obedience to the principal's instructions; an undertaking by one person for a consideration to pay another person a sum of money to indemnify that person when a specified loss is incurred.

Indenture Written agreement between the corporation and the lender detailing the terms of the debt issue.

Indifference curve A curve, convex from below, that separates the consumption bundles that are more preferred by an individual from those that are less preferred. The points on the curve represent combinations of goods that are equally preferred by the individual.

Indirect business taxes Taxes that increase the business firm's costs of production and therefore the prices charged to consumers. Examples would be sales, excise, and property taxes.

Inelastic demand (or supply) Elasticity with an absolute value less than 1.

Inferior goods Goods for which the income elasticity is negative. An increase in consumer income causes the demand for such a good to decline.

Inflation A continuing rise in the general level of prices of goods and services. The purchasing power of the monetary unit, such as the dollar, declines when inflation is present.

Inflation premium A component of the money interest rate that reflects compensation to the lender for the expected decrease, due to inflation, in the purchasing power of the principal and interest during the course of the loan. It is determined by the expected rate of future inflation.

Innovation The successful introduction and adoption of a new product or process; the economic application of inventions and marketing techniques.

Interest The price a borrower pays for a loan or a lender receives for saving, measured as a percentage of the amount; the price of not consuming now but waiting to consume in the future.

Interest rate The price of a loan, expressed as a percentage of the loaned amount per year.

Interest rate risk The risk that interest rates will change adversely. For example, the value of a bond decreases when interest rates increase.

Interest rate swaps A swap which allows a party receiving payments based on one measure, such as fixed interest rate, to exchange these for payments based on another measure, such as a variable rate (often called a "floating" rate), or vice-versa.

Intermediate goods Goods purchased for resale or for use in producing another good or service.

Internalizing an externality Changing the private costs or benefits so that they equal social costs or benefits; making people responsible for all the costs to other people of their own actions.

Intertemporal substitution (substitution over time) A change in the current demand or supply of a good caused by a change in its expected future price.

Invention The creation or discovery of a new product or process, often facilitated by the knowledge of engineering and scientific relationships.

Inventories Goods that a firm owns, including raw materials or other inputs, partially finished goods (goods in process), or finished goods that the firm has not yet sold.

Investment The flow of expenditures on durable assets (fixed investment) plus the addition to inventories (inventory investment) during a period. These expenditures enhance our ability to provide consumer benefits in the future. The purchase, construction, or development of capital resources, including both nonhuman capital. Investments increase the supply of capital.

Investment in human capital Expenditures on training, education, skill development, and health designed to increase the productivity of an individual.

Invisible hand principle The tendency of market prices to direct individuals pursuing their own interest into productive activities that also promote the economic well-being of society.

Joint and several contract A contract in which two or more persons are jointly and severally obligated or are jointly and severally entitled to recover.

Labor union A collective organization of employees who bargain as a unit with employers.

Labor turnover The continuing flows of people into and out of the labor force, employment and unemployment, and various jobs.

Laissez-faire A government policy of not interfering with market activities.

Laissez-faire economy A market economy that is allowed to operate according to competitive forces with little or no government intervention.

Law of comparative advantage A principle that states that individuals, firms, regions, or nations can gain by specializing in the production of goods that they produce cheaply (that is, at a low-opportunity-cost) and exchanging those goods for other desired goods for which they are a high-opportunity-cost producer.

Law of demand A principle that states there is an inverse relationship between the price of a good and the amount of its buyers are willing to purchase.

Law of diminishing marginal utility The basic economic principle that as the consumption of a commodity increases, the marginal utility derived from consuming more of the commodity (per unit of time) will eventually decline. Marginal utility may decline even though total utility continues to increase, albeit at a reduced rate.

Law of diminishing returns The postulate that as more and more units of a variable resource are combined with a fixed amount of other resources, employment of additional units of the variable resource will eventually increase output only at a decreasing rate. Once diminishing returns are reached, it will take successively larger amounts of the variable factor to expand output by one unit.

Law of supply A principle that states there is a direct relationship between the price of a good and the amount of it offered for sale.

Legal barriers to entry A legal franchise, license, or patent granted by government that prohibits other firms or individuals from producing particular products or entering particular occupations or industries.

Leverage The ratio of the amount of money represented by an investment to the amount of money actually invested. With a high level of leverage, one experiences large gains or losses as though a much larger amount was invested. Leverage can increase the risk of large losses just as it increases the opportunity for large gains.

Liability Anything that is owed as a debt by a firm and therefore takes away from the net worth of the firm.

Liability rule A legal statement of who is responsible under what conditions for injuries or other harms in a tort.

LIBOR (London interbank offered rate) For banks that deal in Eurodollars, the rate that large international banks with excellent credit ratings charge each other for loans.

License A personal privilege to do some act or series of acts upon the land of another, as the placing of a sign thereon, not amounting to an easement or a right of possession.

Limited liability Loss of contributed capital or investment as maximum liability of investors.

Limited partnership A partnership in which at least one partner has a liability limited to the loss of the capital contribution made to the partnership, and such a partner neither takes part in the management of the partnership nor appears to the public to be a partner.

Liquid asset An asset that can be easily and quickly converted to purchasing power without loss of value.

Liquidated damages A provision stipulating the amount of damages to be paid in event of default or breach of contract.

Logrolling The exchange between politicians of political support on one issue for political support on another.

Long run (in production) A time period long enough to allow the firm to vary all factors of production.

Long-run demand (or supply) curve A curve that shows prices and quantities demanded (or supplied) at each price after buyers (or sellers) have adjusted completely to a price change.

Long-run equilibrium An equilibrium over a time long enough to allow firms to enter or exit the industry; a situation in which entry or exit has adjusted the market until each firm earns zero economic profit.

Loss Deficit of sale revenue relative to the cost of production, once all the resources used have received their opportunity cost. Losses are a penalty imposed on those who use resources in lower, rather than higher, valued used as judged by buyers in the market.

Macroeconomics The branch of economics that focuses on how human behavior affects outcomes in highly aggregated markets, such as the nationwide markets for labor or consumer products.

Mandated benefits Fringe benefits that the government forces employers to include in their total compensation package paid to employees.

Margin The difference in costs or benefits between the existing situation and a proposed change. Also, an investor's cash deposit with a brokerage firm which acts as collateral for leveraged investments. For example, the investor may need to deposit only $1,000 in a margin account as collateral for a contract with a notional value of $10,000.

Margin requirements The minimum amount of cash a brokerage firm requires in a margin account to permit particular investments.

Marginal Term used to describe the effects of a change in the current situation. For example, the marginal cost is the cost of producing an additional unit of a product, given the producer's current facility and production rate.

Marginal analysis Study of the difference in costs and benefits between the status quo and the production or consumption of an additional unit of a specific good or service. This, not the average cost of all goods produced or consumed, is the actual basis for rational economic choices.

Marginal benefit The increase in total benefit from doing something once more.

Marginal costs The extra costs of producing one more unit of output;

the change in total costs divided by the change in output.

Marginal factor cost (MFC)   The cost of employing an additional unit of a resource. When the employer is small relative to the total market, the marginal factor cost in simply the price of the resource. In contrast, under monopsony, marginal factor cost will exceed the price of the resource, since the monopsonist faces an upward-sloping supply curve for the resource because wages must be raised for all workers.

Marginal opportunity costs   The extra costs associated with the production of an additional unit of a product; these costs are the lost amounts of an alternative product.

Marginal private costs   The increase in a firm's total costs resulting from producing one more unit.

Marginal product (MP)   The change in total output that results from the employment of one additional unit of a factor of production — one workday of skilled labor, for example. The increase in the total product resulting from a unit increase in the employment of a variable input. Mathematically, it is the ratio of the change in total product to the change in the quantity of the variable input.

Marginal rate of substitution   The change in the consumption level of one good that is just sufficient to offset a unit change in the consumption of another good without causing a shift to another indifference curve. At any point on an indifference curve, it will be equal to the slope of the curve at that point.

Marginal revenue   The incremental change in total revenue derived from the sale of one additional unit of a product; the change in total revenue divided by the change in amount sold.

Marginal social costs   The increase in total costs to society (the firm plus everyone else) resulting from producing one more unit.

Marginal tax rate (MTR)   Additional tax liability divided by additional income. Thus, if $100 of additional earnings increases one's tax liability by $30, the marginal tax rate would be 30 percent. Since it established the fraction of an additional dollar earned that an individual is permitted to keep, it is an important determinant of the incentive to work.

Marginal utility   The additional utility received by a person from the consumption of an additional unit of a good within a given time period.

Marginal revenue product (MRP)   The change in the total revenue of a firm that results from the employment of one additional unit of a factor of production. The marginal-revenue product of an input is equal to its marginal product multiplied by the marginal revenue (price) of the good or service produced.

Market   An arrangement that brings together buyers and sellers of products and resources; any area in which prices of products or services tend toward equality through the continuous negotiations of buyers and sellers.

Market coordination   The process that directs the flow of resources into the production of desired goods and services through the forces of price mechanism.

Market demand   Demand for a good by all buyers, including the private sector and the government.

Market demand curve   A graph of the market demand schedule.

Market demand schedule   A table of many hypothetical prices of a good and the quantity demanded by all buyers at each price.

Market equilibrium   A situation, described by a combination of price and quantity traded, in which the quantity supplied equals the quantity demanded.

Market failure The failure of the market system to attain hypothetically ideal allocative efficiency. This means that potential gain exists that has not been captured. However, the cost of establishing a mechanism that could potentially capture the gain may exceed the benefits. Therefore, it is not always possible to improve the situation.

Market portfolio The portfolio consisting of all assets in the market.

Market power A situation characterized by barriers to entry of rival firms, giving an established firm control over price and, therefore, profit levels.

Market process The coordination of people's economic activities through voluntary trades.

Market quantity demanded The total amount of a good that all buyers in the economy would buy during a time period if they could buy as much as they wanted at a given price.

Market quantity supplied At a given price, the total amount of a good that all sellers in the economy would sell during a time period if they could sell as much of the good as they wanted.

Market risk premium Slope of the security market line, the difference between the expected return on a market portfolio and the risk-free rate.

Market structure The classification of a market with regard to key characteristics, including the number of sellers, entry barriers into the market, the control of firms over price, and type of products (homogeneous or differentiated in the market.

Market supply curve A curve graphing the market supply schedule.

Market supply schedule A table showing many hypothetical prices of a good and the quantity supplied at each price.

Marking to market The process of recalculating (marking) the value of a contract according to the current market price.

Markup (or profit margin) Price minus average cost.

Maturity Specified date at which the principal amount of a bond is paid.

Maximum legal price (or price ceiling) The highest price at which the government allows people to buy or sell a good.

Mean income Total income divided by the number of people.

Median income The income level at which half of the people have more income and half have less.

Microeconomics The branch of economics that focuses on the behavior of individual decision-making units within an economic system, from individuals to specific households to specific business firms.

Middleman A person who buys and sells, or who arranges trades. A middleman reduces transaction costs, usually for a fee or a markup in price.

Minimum legal price (or price floor) The lowest price at which the government allows people to buy or sell a good.

Minimum wage legislation Legislation requiring that all workers in specified industries be paid at least the stated minimum hourly rate of pay.

Mixed capitalism An economy in which both market forces and government forces determine the allocation of resources.

Money interest rate The interest rate measured in monetary units. It overstates the real cost of borrowing during an inflation period. When inflation is anticipated, an inflationary premium will be incorporated into the nominal value of this rate. The money interest rate is often referred to as the nominal interest rate.

Money market The market for short-term securities.

Money market mutual funds Interest-earning accounts offered by brokerage firms that pool depositors' funds and invest them in highly liquid short-term securities. Since these securities can be quickly converted to cash, depositors are permitted to write checks (which reduce their share holdings) against their accounts.

Money rate of interest The rate of interest in monetary terms that borrowers pay for borrowed funds. During periods when borrowers and lenders expect inflation, the money rate of interest exceeds the real rate of interest.

Monitoring Obtaining information about an agent's actions (perhaps by watching).

Monopolistic competition A situation in which there are a large number of independent sellers, each producing a differentiated product in a market with low barriers to entry. Construction, retail sales, and service stations are good examples of monopolistically competitive industries.

Monopoly A market structure characterized by a (a) single seller of a well-defined product for which there are no good substitutes and (b) high barriers to the entry of other firms into the market for the product.

Monopsony A market in which there is only one buyer. The monopsonist confronts the market supply curve for the resource (or product) bought.

Moral hazard A situation in which a principal cannot observe the actions of an agent who lacks an incentive to act in the best interests of the principal.

Multipart price A price with several components.

Nash equilibrium A situation in which each firm makes its best response, that is maximizes its profit, given the actions of rival firms.

Nationalized firm A firm that the government owns.

Natural monopoly A monopoly that occurs because of a particular relation between industry demand and the firm's average total costs that makes it possible for only one firm to survive in the industry.

Negative correlation A relationship between variables that tend to move in opposite directs (inversely).

Negative externality A cost of producing or consuming a good that is not paid entirely by the sellers or buyers but is imposed on a larger segment of society; a situation in which the social costs of producing or consuming a good are greater than the private costs.

Negative slope The shape of a curve that runs downward and to the right.

Net benefit (or profit) Total benefit minus total cost.

Net present value (NPV) The difference between the present value of an income stream and the present value of an expenditure stream.

Net present value of a durable input The discounted present value of the future value of the input's marginal product minus the discounted present value of its cost.

Neutral tax A tax that does not (1) distort consumer buying patterns or producer production methods or (2) induce individuals to engage in tax-avoidance activities. There will be no excess burden if a tax is neutral.

Nominal (money) wage The wage rate measured in money (such as dollars or yen).

Nominal price The money price of a good.

Nominal return Return on an investment not adjusted for inflation.

Nominal values Values expressed in current dollars.

Nondurable input An input that a firm uses soon after acquiring it and can use only once to produce a product.

Nonexcludable good A good that is prohibitively costly to provide only to people who pay for it while excluding other people from obtaining it.

Nonhuman resources The durable, nonhuman inputs that can be used to produce both current and future output. Machines, buildings, land, and raw materials are examples. Investment can increase the supply of nonhuman resources. Economists often use the term physical capital when referring to nonhuman resources.

Nonpecuniary job characteristics Working conditions, prestige, variety, location, employee freedom and responsibilities, and other nonwage characteristics of a job that influence how employees evaluate the job.

Nonprice competition Any means that individual firms use to attract customers other than price cuts, such as better-quality products or product characteristics designed to match the preferences of specific groups of consumers.

Nonprice rationing A system for choosing who gets how many goods in a shortage.

Nonrival good A good for which the quantity available to other people does not fall when someone consumes it.

Normal (accounting) profit The level of accounting profit required for a zero economic profit.

Normal good A good whose demand increases if income rises.

Normative economics Value judgments about how markets should operate, based on certain moral principles or preferences.

Notional principal The principal amount or face value of a loan or bond. Often used to identify the size of an interest rate or currency swap.

Oligopoly A market situation in which a small number of sellers comprise the entire industry. Oligopoly is competition among the few.

Open-access resource A resource to which access is unrestricted. No one has the right to exclude others from using the resource. Overuse and abuse of such a resource is typical.

Opportunity cost of equity capital The implicit rate of return that must be earned by investors to induce them to continue to supply financial capital to the firm.

Opportunity cost The highest valued alternative that must be sacrificed as a result of choosing among alternatives. The value placed on opportunities forgone in choosing to produce or consume scarce goods.

Optimal contract An agreement that maximizes the principal's profit while providing an incentive for the agent to participate in the agreement.

Optimal taxation A system of tax rates that minimizes the total deadweight social loss from taxes while raising a certain amount of revenue for the government.

Option The right to buy (call) or the right to sell (put) an asset at a specified price within a fixed period of time.

Out of the money An option with no intrinsic value, but which may have some time value. A call option is out of the money when its exercise price is greater than the price of the underlying security. A put option is out of the money when its exercise price is less than the price of the underlying security.

Over-the-counter (OTC) market A market without a centralized exchange where trading is normally done via computers and telephone lines, coordinated through broker-dealers.

Ownership The rights to make decisions about a good, including the use, exclusion, and sale of the good.

Par value The principal amount of a bond that is repaid at the end of the term. Also face value.

Pareto improvement A change that helps at least one person without hurting anyone.

Partnership A business firm owned by two or more individuals who possess ownership rights to the firm's profits and are personally liable for the debts of the firm.

Patent The grant of an exclusive right to use a specific process or produce a specific product for a period of time (17 years in the United States).

Payoff The amount that a players wins or loses in a particular situation in a game.

Percentage change 100 times the change in a number divided by the average (or midpoint) of the original number and the new number.

Perfect competition Competition among price-taking sellers.

Perfect information A condition in which information about prices and products is free to market participants; combined with conditions for pure competition, perfect information leads to perfect competition.

Perfect market A market in which there are enough buyers and sellers to that no single buyer or seller can influence price.

Perfect price discrimination Charging each customer the highest price that a customer is willing to pay.

Perfectly elastic demand (supply) Infinite elasticity illustrated by a demand (or supply) curve that is a horizontal line.

Perfectly inelastic demand (or supply) Elasticity equal to zero, illustrated by a demand (or supply) curve that is a vertical line.

Perpetuity An annuity in which the cash flows continue forever.

Political equilibrium A situation, characterized by peoples' votes and campaign contributions, the positions and strategies of candidates for office, and the decisions and actions of government officials, that shows no tendency for a change unless come underlying condition changes.

Political good Any good (or policy), whether a public good or a private good, supplied through the political process.

Pork-barrel legislation A package of spending projects benefiting local areas at federal expense. The projects typically have costs that exceed benefits, but are intensely desired by the residents of the district getting the benefits without having to pay much of the costs.

Portfolio The collection of all securities (including stocks, bonds, derivatives, etc.) held by an individual or institution.

Portfolio theory An approach to investing that analyzes methods by which, through diversified portfolios, an optimal balance of risk and return can be reached.

Portfolio weight Percentage of a portfolio's total value in a particular asset.

Positive correlation A relationship between variables that tend to rise or fall together.

Positive economics Observations or predictions of the facts of economic life.

Positive externality A benefit of producing or consuming a good that does not accrue to the sellers or buyers but can be realized by a larger segment of society; a situation in which the social benefits of producing or consuming a good are greater than the private benefits.

Positive slope The shape of a curve that runs upward and to the right.

Positive statement A statement of fact, of what is or what would be if something else were to happen; such a statement is either true or false.

Positive-sum game Environment in which everyone can gain at the same time.

Post-hoc fallacy False reasoning that because one event happened before another, the first event must have caused the second event.

Potential Pareto improvement A change that could allow the winners to compensate the losers to make the change a Pareto improvement.

Predatory pricing The practice in which a dominant firm in an industry temporarily reduces price to damage or eliminate weaker rivals, so that prices can be raised above the level of costs at a later time.

Preferred stock Stock with dividend priority over common stock, normally with a fixed dividend rate, sometimes without voting rights.

Present value (PV) The current worth of future income after it is discounted to reflect the fact that revenues in the future are valued less highly than revenues now; the estimated value today of a future sum of money, discounted at an appropriate interest rate.

Price The amount of something that a buyer trades away (pays) per unit of the good he receives.

Price ceiling A legally established maximum price that sellers may charge.

Price control Government intervention in the natural functioning of supply and demand.

Price differential A difference between the prices of identical goods in two different locations.

Price discrimination A practice whereby a seller charges different consumers or groups of consumers different prices for the same product or service. The difference in price is not the result of differences in the costs of supplying the two groups.

Price elasticity of demand The percent change in the quantity of a product demanded divided by the percent change in the price causing the change in quantity. Price elasticity of demand indicates the degree of consumer response to variation in price.

Price floor A legally established minimum price that buyers must pay for a good or resource.

Price rigidity Slow adjustments of prices to changes in costs or demand.

Prices The opportunity costs established in markets for scarce goods, services, and resources.

Price searcher A firm that must choose a price from a range of prices rather than have a single price imposed on it; such a firm has a downward-sloping demand curve for its product.

Price takers Sellers who must take the market price in order to sell their product. Because each price taker's output is small relative to the total market, price takers can sell all of their output at the market price, but are unable to sell any of their output at a price higher than the market price. Thus, they face a horizontal demand curve.

Price taker in an input market A firm that faces a perfectly elastic supply of an input.

Principal One who employs an agent; the person who, with respect to a surety, is primarily liable to the third person or creditor. The capital or face amount of a debt or other obligation upon which interest accrues.

Principal-agent problem The incentive problem arising when the purchaser of services (the principal) lacks full information about the circumstances faced by the seller (the agent) and thus cannot know how well the agent performs the purchased services. The agent may to some extent work toward objectives other than those sought by the principal paying for the service.

Principle of diversification Spreading an investment across a number of assets will eliminate some, but not all, of the risk.

Private benefit The benefit to people who buy and consume a good.

Private cost The cost paid by a firm to produce and sell a good.

Private ownership A property right held by one person or a small group of people.

Private-property rights A set of usage and exchange rights held exclusively by the owner(s) and that can be transferred to others at the owner's discretion.

Privatization Creation of private property rights in a nationalized firm so that it becomes privately owned.

Producer surplus The benefit to a producer from being able to sell goods at the equilibrium price, rather than being unable to sell them at all.

Productivity The average output produced per worker during a specific time period. It is usually measured in terms of output per hour worked.

Profit An excess of sales revenue relative to the cost of production. The cost component includes the opportunity cost of all resources, including those owned by the firm. Therefore, profit accrues only when the value of the good produced is greater than the sum of the values of the individual resources utilized.

Property The rights and interests one has in anything subject to ownership.

Property rights The right to use, control, and obtain the benefits from a good or service.

Proprietorship A business firm owned by an individual who possesses the ownership right to the firm's profits and is personally liable for the firm's debts.

Protective covenant Part of the indenture limiting certain actions that can be taken during the term of the loan, usually to protect the lender's interest.

Public goods Jointly consumed goods. A good that no individual can be excluded from consuming, once it has been provided to another. National defense, poetry, and scientific theories are all public goods.

Public-choice analysis The study of decision making as it affects the formation and operation of collective organizations, such as governments. The discipline bridges the gap between economics and political science. In general, the principles and methodology of economics are applied to political science topics.

Punitive damages Damages in excess of those required to compensate the plaintiff for the wrong done, which are imposed in order to punish the defendant because of the particularly wanton of willful character of wrongdoing.

Pure competition A model of industrial structure characterized by a large number of small firms producing a homogeneous product in a industry (market area) that permits complete freedom of entry and exit.

Pure discount bond A bond, such as a Treasury bill, that pays no coupon but sells for a discount from par value.

Put An option by which one investor acquires the right, but not the obligation, to sell an underlying asset to another investor for a specified price during a specified period of time.

Rational ignorance Voter ignorance resulting from the fact that people perceive their individual votes as unlikely to be decisive. Therefore, they rationally have little incentive to seek the information needed to cast a informed vote.

Rationing An allocation of a limited supply of a good or resource to users who would like to have more of it. Various criteria, including charging a price, can be utilized to allocate the limited supply. When price performs the rationing function, the good or resource is allocated to those willing to give up the most "other things" in order to obtain ownership rights.

Real rate of interest The money rate of interest minus the expected rate of inflation. The real rate of interest indicates the interest premium, in terms of real goods and services, that one must pay for earlier availability.

Real return Return adjusted for the effects of inflation.

Real values Values that have been adjusted for the effects of inflation.

Relative price The price of a product related in terms of other goods that could be purchased rather than in money terms.

Rent seeking The activity of individuals who spend resources in the pursuit of monopoly rights granted by government; the process of spending resources in an effort to obtain an economic transfer.

Repeat-purchase item An item purchased often by the same buyer.

Residual claimant(s) Individuals who personally receive the excess, if any, of revenues over contractual fixed claims (costs).

Resource An input used to produce economic goods. Land, labor, skills, natural resources, and capital are examples.

Resource market A highly aggregate market encompassing all resources (labor, physical capital, land, and entrepreneurship) that contribute to the production of current output. The labor market forms the largest component of this market.

Resource mobility A term that refers to the ease with which factors of production are able to move among alternative uses. Resources that can easily be transferred to a different use or location are said to be highly mobile. In contrast, when a resource has few alternative uses, it is immobile. For example, the skills of a trained rodeo rider would be highly immobile, since they cannot be easily transferred to other lines of work.

Right-to-work laws Laws that prohibit the union shop - the requirement that employees must join a union (after 30 days) as a condition of employment. Each state has the option to adopt (or reject) right-to-work legislation.

Risk premium The excess return required from an investment in a risky asset over a risk-free investment.

Risk-return trade-off The concept in which additional risk must be accepted to increase the expected return.

Scarcity Fundamental concept of economics which indicates a limitation of the amount of resources available to individuals and societies relative to their desires for the products that resources produce.

Scientific thinking Development of theory from basic postulates and the testing of the implications of that theory as to their consistency with events in the real world. Good theories are consistent with and help explain real-world events. Theories that are inconsistent with the real world are invalid and must be rejected.

Secondary effects Economic consequences of an economic change that are not immediately identifiable but are felt only with the passage of time.

Securities and Exchange Commission The federal agency responsible for regulating the securities and options markets.

Security market line (SML) Positively shaped straight line displaying the relationship between expected return and beta.

Selling short Selling shares of a stock that the investor does not own, but which a broker lends to the investor. This will be profitable when the stock price falls, since the investor will then purchase the stock at a price lower than that at which the investor sold it.

Settlement price The official price established by the clearinghouse at the end of each day for use in the daily settlement.

Shareholder A person who owns shares of stock (equity) in a corporation.

Shirking Working at less than a normal rate of productivity, thus reducing output. Shirking is more likely when workers are not monitored, so that the cost of lower output falls on others than themselves.

Short run (in production) A time period so short that firm is unable to vary some of its factors of production. The firm's plant size typically cannot be altered in the short run.

Shortage A condition in which the amount of a good offered by sellers is less than the amount demanded by buyers at the existing price. An increase in price would eliminate the shortage.

Shortsightedness Misallocation of resources that results because public-sector action is biased (1) in favor of proposals yielding clearly defined current benefits in exchange for difficult-to-identify future costs and (2) against proposals with clearly identifiable current costs but yielding less concrete and less obvious future benefits.

Shutdown A temporary halt in the operation of a business in which the firm anticipates a return to operation in the future and therefore does not sell its assets. The firm's variable cost is eliminated for the duration of the shutdown, but its fixed costs continue.

Simple interest Interest earned only on the original principal amount invested.

Social costs The sum of (1) the private costs incurred by a decision maker and (2) any external costs imposed on nonconsenting secondary parties. If there are no external costs, private and social costs will be equal.

Speculation Taking risk, in hope of return, by buying or selling assets in hopes of profiting from market fluctuations. This is the opposite of reducing risk through hedging.

Spot price The current cash price for immediate delivery of goods.

Standard deviation The positive square root of the variance.

Stock An instrument that provides the holder an equity, or ownership, interest in a corporation.

Strict tort liability A product liability theory which imposes liability on the manufacturer, seller, or distributor of goods for harm caused by defective goods.

Strike An action of unionized employees in which they (1) discontinue working for the employer and (2) take steps to prevent other potential workers from offering their services to the employer.

Subsidy A government cash grant to a favored industry.

Substitutes Products that are related such that an increase in the price of one will cause an increase in demand for the other (for example, butter and margarine, Chevrolets and Fords).

Substitution effect That part of an increase (decrease) in amount consumed that is the result of a good being cheaper (more expensive) in relation to other goods because of a reduction (increase) in price.

Sunk costs Costs that have already been incurred as a result of past decisions. They are sometimes referred to as historical costs.

Surplus A condition in which the amount of a good that sellers are willing to offer is greater than the amount that buyers will purchase at the existing price. A decline in price would eliminate the surplus.

Swap An agreement to exchange one set of cashflows for another. Swap agreements are often used to hedge against interest rate changes and fluctuations in foreign exchange rates. A typical example is an agreement to exchange fixed rate interest payments for variable rate interest payments on the same principal amount.

Swap dealer A firm that arranges an interest rate or currency swap between two other parties.

Swaptions An option to enter into a swap agreement.

Systematic risk A risk that influences a large number of assets. Also market risk.

Tariff A tax levied on good imported into a country.

Tax incidence The manner in which the burden of the tax is distributed among economic units (consumers, employees, employers, and so on). The tax burden does not always fall on those who pay the tax.

Tax rate The per unit or percentage rate at which an economic activity is taxed.

Team production A process of production wherein employees work together under the supervision of the owner of the owner's representative.

Technological advancement The introduction of new techniques or methods of production that enable a greater output per unit of input.

Technology The body of skills and technological knowledge available at any given time. The level of technology establishes the relationship between inputs and the maximum output they can generate.

Term structure of interest rates The relationship between interest rates and maturities of zero coupon bonds.

Tie-in sale The requirement imposed by the seller that the buyer of particular goods or equipment also purchase certain other goods from the original property desired.

Tort A private injury or wrong arising from a breach of a duty created by law.

Total cost The costs, both explicit and implicit, of all the resources used by the firm. Total cost includes an imputed normal rate of return for the firm's equity capital.

Total product The total output of a good that is associated with alternative utilization rates of a variable input.

Transaction costs The time, effort, and other resources needed to search out, negotiate, and consummate an exchange.

Uncovered call (naked call) Call options sold (written) for which the seller does not own the underlying asset.

Unlimited liability A legal term that indicates that the owner or owners of a firm are personally responsible for the debts of a firm up to the total value of their wealth.

Unsystematic risk A risk that affects at most a small number of assets. Also unique or asset-specific risks.

User charge A payment that users (consumers) are required to make if they want to receive certain services provided by the government.

Usury The lending of money at greater than the maximum rate of interest allowed by law.

Utility The benefit or satisfaction expected from a choice or course of action.

Variable costs Costs that vary with the rate of output. Examples include wages paid to workers and payments for raw materials.

Variable rate An interest rate that changes along with a specified index (such as LIBOR, U.S. T-bills, etc.).

Variance The average squared difference between the actual return and the average return.

Volatility The extent to which the price of an asset fluctuates. An asset with greater volatility experiences larger price swings. The higher the volatility of a stock, the more expensive are options on that stock.

Welfare loss due to monopoly The lost consumers surplus resulting from the restricted output of a monopoly.

Worker's compensation A system providing payments to workers because they have been injured from a risk arising out of the course of their employment while they were employed at their employment or have contracted an occupational disease in that manner, payment being made without consideration of the negligence or lack of negligence of any party.

Writer A person or institution that sells an option.

Yield curve The relationship between yields on bonds and their maturity.

Yield to maturity (YTM) The rate required in the market on a bond.

Zero coupon bond See Pure discount bond.